The **Rough Guide** to

Scottish Highlands & Islands

written and researched by

Rob Humphreys and Donald Reid

with additional contributions by

Colin Hutchison

NEW YORK • LONDON • DELHI

www.roughguides.com

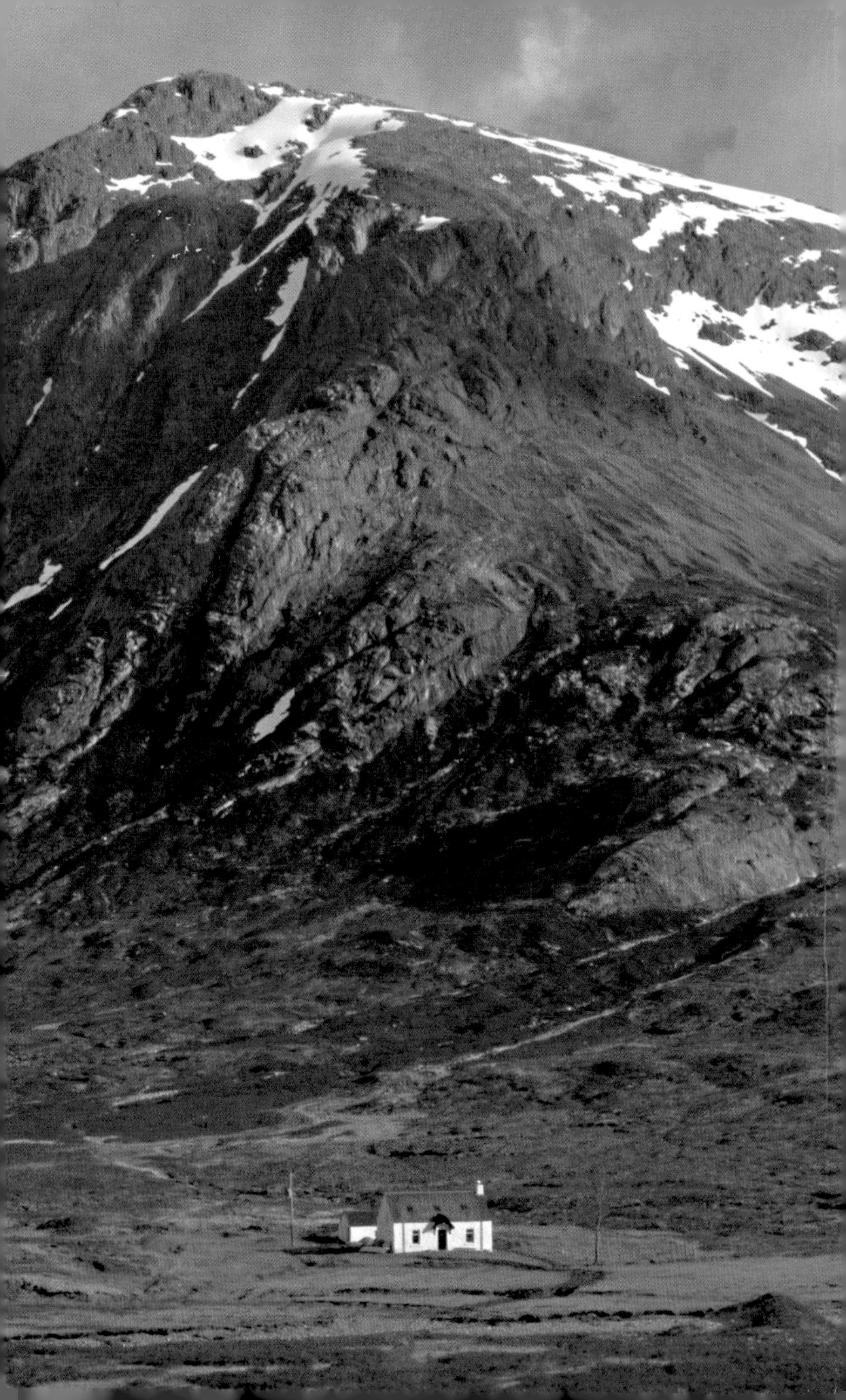

Contents

◀◀ Isle of Mull ◀ Glen Coe

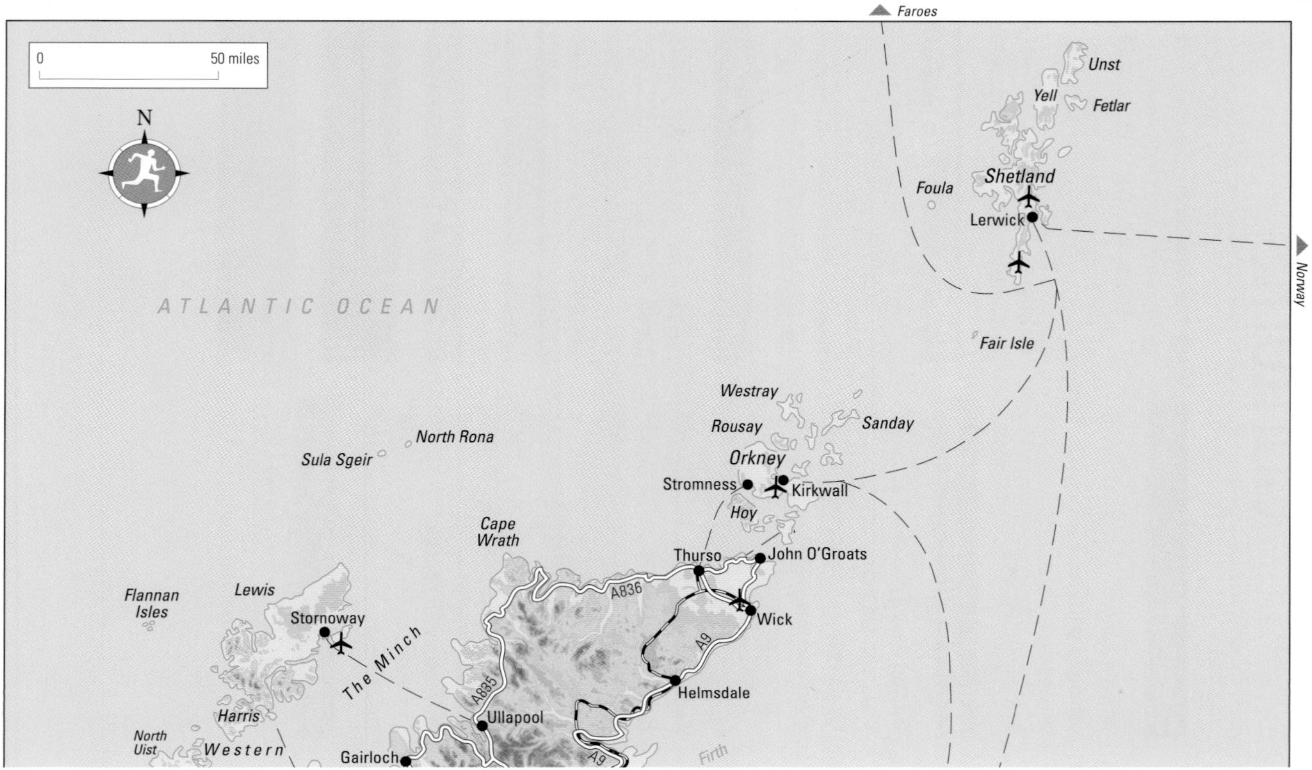

0 50 miles

N

ATLANTIC OCEAN

Faroes

Norway

Unst

Yell

Fetlar

Shetland

Foula

Lerwick

Fair Isle

Westray

Sanday

Rousay

Orkney

Stromness

Kirkwall

Hoy

North Rona

Sula Sgeir

Cape Wrath

Thurso

John O'Groats

A836

Wick

A9

Helmsdale

Flannan Isles

Lewis

Stornoway

The Minch

A835

Ullapool

Harris

North Uist

Western

Gairloch

A9

Firth

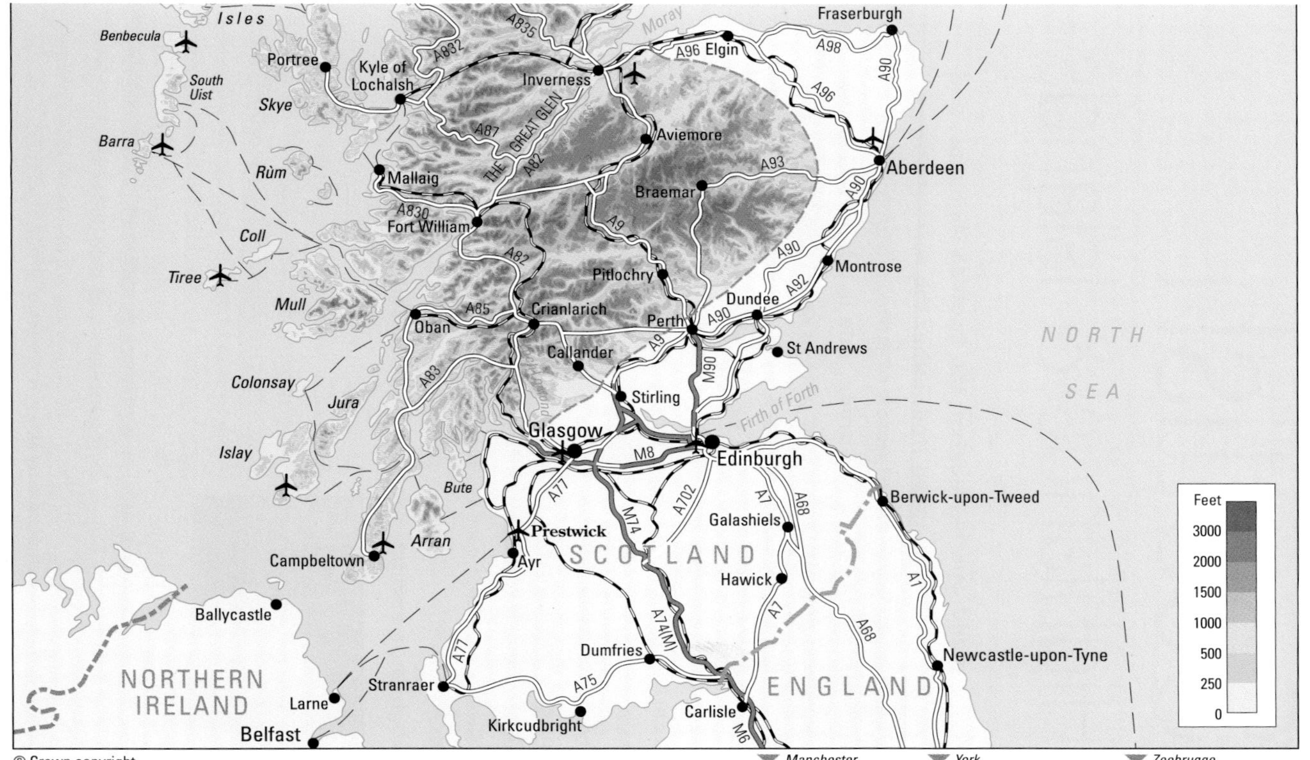
Isles
Benbecula
South Uist
Barra
Portree
Skye
Kyle of Lochalsh
Rùm
Coll
Tiree
Mull
Colonsay
Jura
Islay
Bute
Arran
Campbeltown
Mallaig
Fort William
Oban
Inverness
Moray
Elgin
Fraserburgh
Aviemore
Aberdeen
Braemar
Pitlochry
Montrose
Dundee
Crianlarich
Perth
St Andrews
Callander
Stirling
Firth of Forth
Glasgow
Edinburgh
Prestwick
Ayr
SCOTLAND
Galashiels
Hawick
Berwick-upon-Tweed
Newcastle-upon-Tyne
Dumfries
Carlisle
Stranraer
Kirkcudbright
ENGLAND
NORTH SEA
NORTHERN IRELAND
Ballycastle
Larne
Belfast
THE GREAT GLEN
A832
A835
A87
A82
A830
A85
A83
A9
A96
A98
A90
A93
A92
M90
M8
M74
A77
A702
A7
A68
A1
A74(M)
A75
M6
Feet
3000
2000
1500
1000
500
250
0
Manchester
York
Zeebrugge

Introduction to Scottish Highlands & Islands

Rugged and weather-beaten, the Scottish Highlands and Islands are far removed from either the rural charms or the cosmopolitanism of much of Britain. Stuck out on the northwest fringe of Europe, this is a land where the elements play an important part in everyday life, where the shipping forecast is more than simply a form of sleep therapy. The landscape is raw, shaped over thousands of years by geological shifts, scouring glaciers and the hostile weather systems of the North Atlantic, to create magnificent land- and seascapes. It's a region with a wild, romantic glint in its eye, too, with a regular supply of glorious sunsets that turn the sea lochs gold, and with more deserted beaches than the entire Mediterranean. Sure, the roads can be tortuous, the weather sometimes grim and the midges a pain, but, when the mood is on, the Highlands and Islands rarely fail to seduce.

Despite all its dramatic beauty, it's impossible to travel in the Highlands and Islands without being touched by the fragility of life here. While the Jacobite defeat at Culloden in 1746 was a blow to Scottish pride, it was an unmitigated disaster for the Highlands and Islands, signalling the destruction of the Highland clan system, and ultimately the entire Highland way of life. The Clearances that followed in the nineteenth century more than halved the population, and even today the Highland landscape is littered with the crumbling shells of pre-Clearance crofting communities. Depopulation remains a constant threat, particularly on the islands, and in many cases only the arrival of settlers from outside the region

▲ Eilean Donan Castle

has stemmed the dwindling numbers. The economy, too, struggles, even with government and European Union subsidies. The traditional Highland industries of farming, crofting, fishing and whisky distilling are no longer enough to provide jobs for the younger generation, and have been supplemented by forestry, fish-farming and the oil industry. However, all three of these have a detrimental effect on the environment, whose health is of paramount importance to the region's other important industry – tourism. In the end, it's a tricky juggling act balancing the importance of seizing new opportunities with the will to maintain traditional values.

Tradition and the sense of the past may be vital elements of the Highlands and Islands, but the region is by no means entombed by them. Today visitors come not just to clamber over castles and wrap themselves in tartan nostalgia but to hike up hills or photograph puffins, meditate by standing stones or scuba dive among shipwrecks. You don't have to look too far to find old assumptions being challenged in many aspects of Highland life – these days gourmets steer clear of tearooms serving shortbread to seek out wild venison and west-coast shellfish, landowning lairds are as likely to be Hollywood stars or Formula One racing drivers as titled aristocrats, while even in the remotest corners there are crofters looking after websites as well as shaggy Highland cattle.

Fact file

- Covering over 15,000 square miles, the Highlands and Islands region houses less than 400,000 inhabitants – a population **density** of 25 people per square mile, compared to Scotland's average of 166. The largest centre and only city in the region, **Inverness**, has a population of little more than 66,000.
- The **coastline** of the Highlands and Islands region is nearly 7000 miles long, and Scotland has approximately 790 **islands**, 130 of which are inhabited.
- The highest mountain in the Highlands is **Ben Nevis** (4406 ft), while the bottom of **Loch Morar** is 1017 ft below sea level. The highest point of any island is **Sgurr Alasdair** in the Cuillin on Skye (3258 ft). The highest point on the Shetland and Orkney islands is **Ronas Hill** (a streamlined 1476 ft).
- Almost half of the 130,000 tons of **salmon** farmed annually is exported, mainly to Europe.
- The Highlands and Islands region is represented by fifteen **MSPs** (Members of the Scottish Parliament) in Edinburgh, and seven **MPs** (Members of Parliament) at Westminster.

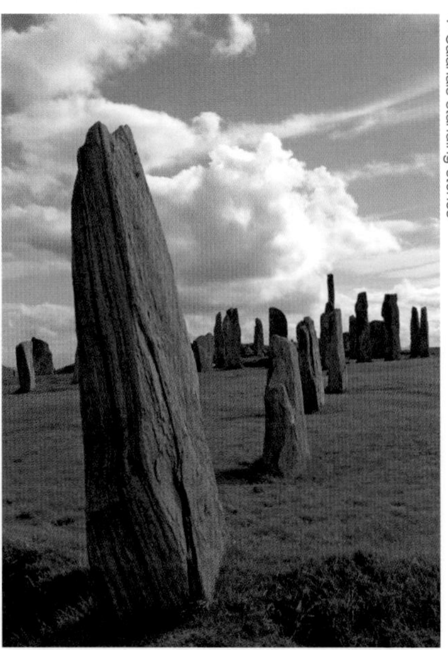

▲ Calanais standing stones

Where to go

There's little to be gained in trying to rush round the Highlands and Islands. Travelling in these parts is time-consuming: distances on land are greater than elsewhere in Britain (and there are no motorways), while getting to the islands means coordinating with ferry or plane timetables and hoping the weather doesn't intervene and spoil your plans. Having said that, the journeys themselves – by spectacular train lines, small aircraft scudding over tiny islands, inter-island ferries or winding, scenic roads – are often memorable.

The most accessible parts of the region are not far at all from Glasgow and Edinburgh: you can be by the banks of Loch Lomond in less than thirty minutes from the former, or use the fast roads and train lines north from the latter to be in Highland Perthshire in a little over an hour. As a result, **Loch Lomond** and the neighbouring hills and wooded glens of the **Trossachs** tend to be busier than other parts of the Highlands, and to escape the day-trippers you need to head further north into **Perthshire** and the **Grampian hills** of Angus and Deeside where the Scottish Highland scenery is at its richest, with colourful woodlands and long glens rising up to distinctive mountain peaks. South of Inverness the mighty **Cairngorm** massif hints at the raw wilderness Scotland can still provide, most memorably in the lonely north and western Highlands. To get to the far north you'll have to cross the **Great Glen**, an ancient geological fissure which cuts right across the country from **Ben Nevis** to **Loch Ness**, a moody stretch of water rather choked with tourists hoping for a glimpse of its monster. Meanwhile, the area with arguably the most memorable scenery of all is the jagged west coast, stretching from **Argyll** all the way north to **Wester Ross** and the looming hills of **Assynt**.

For all the grand splendour of the Highlands, the islands scattered like jigsaw pieces off the west and north coasts are an essential complement. Assorted in

A breath of fresh air

Glance around the Highlands and Islands and you'd be forgiven for assuming that Gore-Tex waterproofs, rather than tartan, were Scotland's national dress. For outdoor enthusiasts the region is a vast adventure playground, a wonderfully rugged and diverse landscape where you can take a bracing walk through an ancient oak forest while a few thousand feet above ice-climbers are practising for the Himalayas. Other hill walkers take to picking off Munros, mountain bikers get muddy in the Trossachs, sailors discover remote anchorages in the Hebrides and skiers hurtle down the Cairngorms. Should you hanker for even more daring thrills, there's white-water rafting on the Tay, Grand Prix conditions for windsurfing in Tiree, the Thurso waves to surf, or paragliding off Ben Nevis. To think some people come to Scotland just to play golf...

▲ Highland cow

size, flavour and accessibility, the long chain of rocky Hebrides which necklace Scotland's Atlantic shoreline include **Mull** and the nearby pilgrimage centre of **Iona**; **Islay** and **Jura**, famous for their wildlife and whisky; **Skye**, the most-visited of the Hebrides, where the snow-tipped Cuillin ridge rises up from the sea; and the **Western Isles**, an elongated archipelago that is the last bastion of Gaelic language and culture. Off the north coast, **Orkney** and **Shetland**, both with a rich Norse heritage, differ not only from each other, but also quite distinctly from mainland Scotland in dialect and culture – far-flung islands buffeted by wind and sea that offer some of the country's wildest scenery, finest bird-watching and best archeological sites.

When to go

The weather is probably the single biggest factor to put you off visiting the Highlands and Islands. It's not so much that the weather's always bad, it's just that it is unpredictable and changeable: in the islands they say you can experience four seasons in one day. Even if the weather's not necessarily good, it's generally interesting, exhilarating, dramatic and certainly photogenic – well suited, in fact, to the landscapes over which it plays such an important role.

The **summer** months of June, July and August are regarded as high season, with local school holidays making July and early August the busiest period.

▲ Gannets

However, the weather at this time is, at best, variable, but the days are generally mild or warm and, most importantly, long, with **daylight** lingering until 9pm or later. In the far north of the mainland and on the Orkney and Shetland islands, darkness hardly falls during midsummer. In August, events such as **Highland Games**, folk festivals or sporting events – most of which take place in the summer months – can tie up accommodation, though normally only in a fairly concentrated local area. The warmer weather does have its drawbacks, however: most significantly, the clouds of **midges**, tiny biting insects which frequently appear around dusk, dawn and in dank conditions, and which can drive even the most committed outdoors type scurrying indoors.

Commonly, **May** and **September** throw up weather every bit as good as, if not better than, the months of high summer. You're less likely to encounter crowds or struggle to find somewhere to stay, and the mild temperatures combined with the changing **colours** of nature mean both are great for outdoor activities, particularly hiking. May is also a good month for

Passing places

Whether marked by a stripy black-and-white pole or a simple white diamond, the first sighting of a passing place is genuine proof that you've escaped the rat race. You can't hurry a passing place: drive too fast and you'll only have to reverse back to the nearest one or dive into a verge. Drivers are forced to acknowledge and even cooperate with one another. Visitors soon get into the swing of it, thanking fellow travellers with a full, cheerful wave, or by raising a finger nonchalantly from the steering wheel. More experienced students of passing place etiquette learn to pull over to allow vehicles to overtake – a gesture that will endear you to the locals more than any amount of vigorous waving.

Ceilidhs

Highlanders have a deserved reputation for knowing how to throw a good party; if you hear rumour of a ceilidh (pronounced "kay-lay") happening nearby, change your plans to make sure you're there. From the Gaelic for "a visit", a ceilidh has its roots in an informal, homespun gathering of music, song, poetry and dancing. These days, often helped along by a dram or two of whisky, they're lively events in the local pub or village hall. The main activity is dancing, to traditional set patterns, with music provided by a fiddler and accordionist. While the whirling reels or jigs appear fiendishly complex, the popular ones aren't hard to pick up and the fun is infectious.

watching nesting **seabirds**; September, however, is stalking season for deer, which can disrupt **access** to the countryside.

The months of **April** and **October** bracket the season for many parts of rural Scotland. A large number of attractions, tourist offices and guesthouses often open for business on Easter weekend in April and shut up shop after the school half-term in mid-October. If places do stay open through the winter, it's normally with reduced opening hours; the October to March period is also the best time to pick up **special offers** at hotels and guesthouses. Note too that in more remote spots public transport will often operate on a reduced winter timetable.

Winter days, from November through to March, occasionally crisp and bright, are more often cold, gloomy and all too brief, although **Hogmanay** and **New Year** has traditionally been a time to visit Scotland for partying and warm hospitality – something which improves as the weather worsens. On a clear night in winter, visitors in the far north of the mainland and the Orkney and Shetland islands might be treated to a celestial display from the **aurora borealis**, while a fall of snow in the Highlands will prompt plenty of activity around the **ski** resorts.

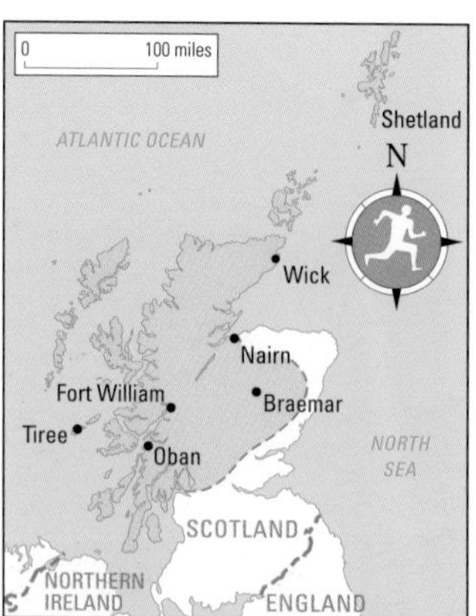

Average temperatures and rainfall

	Jan	Feb	Mar	Apr	May	Jun	Jul	Aug	Sep	Oct	Nov	Dec
Oban												
°C	6	7	9	11	14	16	17	17	15	12	9	7
mm	146	109	83	90	72	87	120	116	141	169	146	172
°F	43	45	48	52	57	61	63	63	59	54	48	45
inches	5.8	4.3	3.3	3.5	2.8	3.4	4.7	4.6	5.6	6.7	5.8	6.8
Tiree												
°C	7	7	8	10	13	15	16	16	15	13	10	8
mm	120	71	77	60	56	66	79	83	123	123	125	123
°F	45	45	47	51	55	59	60	61	58	55	51	47
inches	4.7	2.8	3	2.3	2.2	2.6	3.1	3.2	4.8	4.9	4.8	4.8
Braemar												
°C	4	4	6	9	13	16	17	17	14	11	6	5
mm	93	59	59	51	65	55	58	76	73	87	87	96
°F	39	39	43	48	55	61	63	63	57	52	43	41
inches	3.7	2.3	2.3	2	2.6	2.2	2.3	3	2.9	3.4	3.4	3.8
Nairn												
°C	6	6	9	11	14	17	18	17	16	13	8	7
mm	48	34	33	36	43	46	62	75	50	54	60	52
°F	43	43	47	52	58	62	64	62	61	55	46	45
inches	1.9	1.3	1.3	1.4	1.7	1.8	2.4	3	2	2.1	2.4	2
Fort William												
°C	6	7	9	11	14	17	17	17	15	13	9	7
mm	200	132	152	111	103	124	137	150	199	215	220	238
°F	43	44	47	52	58	62	63	63	60	55	48	45
inches	7.8	5.1	5.9	4.3	4	4.8	5.3	5.9	7.8	8.4	8.6	9.3
Wick												
°C	6	6	7	9	11	14	15	15	14	12	8	7
mm	81	58	55	45	47	49	61	74	68	73	90	82
°F	42	42	45	49	52	58	60	60	57	53	47	45
inches	3.2	2.3	2.1	1.8	1.8	1.9	2.4	2.9	2.7	2.8	3.5	3.2
Shetland												
°C	5	5	6	8	10	13	14	14	13	10	7	6
mm	127	93	93	72	64	64	67	78	113	119	140	147
°F	41	41	42	46	50	55	57	57	55	50	45	42
inches	5	3.7	3.7	2.8	2.5	2.5	2.6	3	4.5	4.7	5.5	5.8

▲ Loch Lomond

30

things not to miss

It's not possible to see everything that the Highlands and Islands have to offer in one trip – and we don't suggest you try. What follows is a selective taste of the area's highlights: great places to visit, popular walks, breathtaking scenery and unforgettable journeys. They're arranged in five colour-coded categories, which you can browse through to find the very best things to see and experience. All entries have a page reference to take you straight into the guide, where you can find out more.

01 **Mousa, Shetland** Page **465** • The mother of all Iron Age brochs, on an island off the coast of Shetland.

02 Hill walking Page **56** • From bumps to bens, taking to the hills is one of the essential activities in the Highlands and Islands.

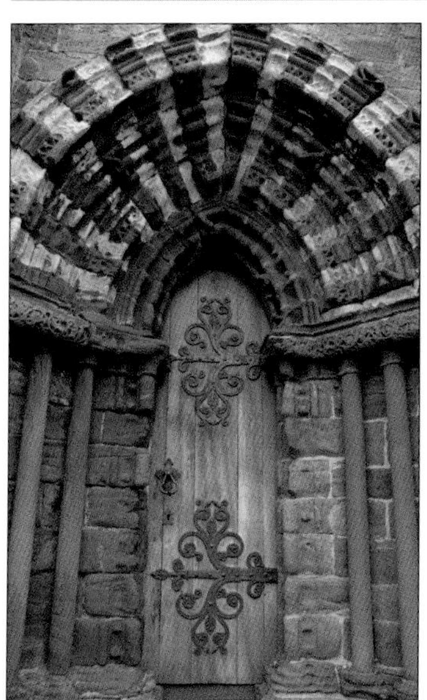

03 St Magnus Cathedral Page **420** • A medieval cathedral in miniature, built by the Vikings using the local red and yellow sandstones.

04 Iona Page **109** • The home of Celtic Christian spirituality, an island of pilgrimage today as in antiquity.

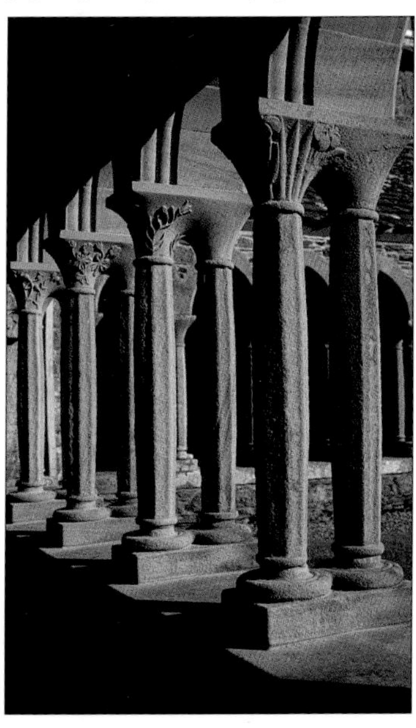

05 Glen Coe Page **235** • Moody, poignant and spectacular glen within easy reach of Fort William.

06 Highland Games Page **54** • An entertaining blend of summer sports day and traditional clan gathering, held in locations across the Highlands.

07 Kinloch Castle, Rùm Page **352** • Stay in the servants' quarters of this Edwardian hideaway or in one of its few remaining four-poster beds.

08 Tobermory Page **99** • Tobermory is the archetypal picturesque fishing village, with colourful houses ranged around a sheltered harbour and backed by steep hills.

09 Gearrannan, Lewis Page **377** • Stay in the thatched blackhouse hostel in this beautifully restored former crofting village.

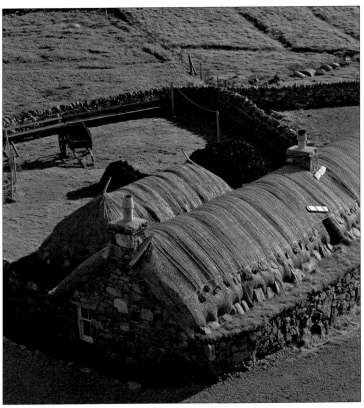

10 Shetland Folk Festival Page **461** • Shetland is the place to experience traditional folk music, and the annual folk festival is the best time to do it.

11 Maes Howe, Orkney Page **412** • Europe's best-preserved Neolithic chambered cairn also contains fine examples of Viking runic inscriptions and drawings.

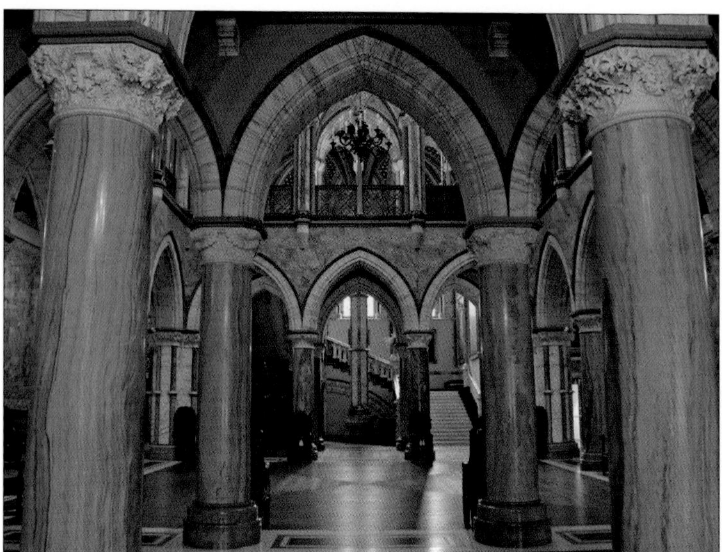

12 **Mount Stuart** Page **85** • Fantastic, over-the-top Scots Baronial pile set amidst lush, wooded grounds on the Isle of Bute.

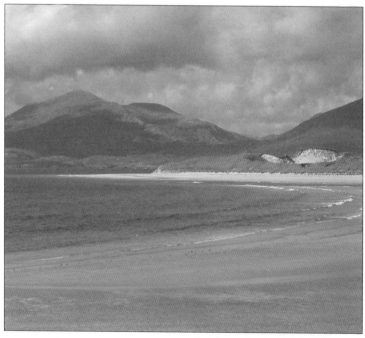

13 **South Harris beaches** Page **384** • Take your pick of deserted golden beaches in South Harris, or further south in the Uists.

14 Calanais, Lewis Page **377** • Prehistoric standing stones that occupy a serene lochside setting in the Western Isles.

15 Pubs Page **48** • Forget the great outdoors and install yourself in one of Scotland's cosy and convivial hostelries.

16 Islay Page **144** • Hebridean island with no fewer than seven whisky distilleries, and wonderfully varied birdlife that includes thousands of wintering geese.

17 **Skye Cuillin** Page **338** • The most spectacular mountain range on the west coast, for viewing or climbing.

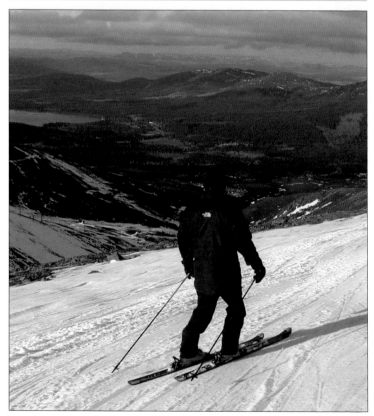

18 **The Cairngorm mountains** Page **204** • Beguilling natural splendour mixed with terrific outdoor activities.

19 Knoydart Page **274** • A brooding peninsula accessible only by boat, and home to mainland Britain's remotest pub.

20 Caledonian forest Page **206** • The few gnarled survivors of the great ancient Highland forests are majestic characters.

21 Eigg Page **355** • Perfect example of a tiny, friendly Hebridean island with a golden beach to lie on, a hill to climb and stunning views across the sea to its neighbour, Rùm.

22 **Flying above Orkney** Page **407** • Take an exhilarating aerial tour of the archipelago in an eight-seater plane.

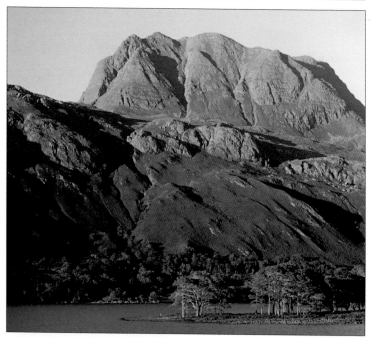

23 **Wester Ross** Page **281** • Where the mountains meet the sea – the sparkling jewel of Highland scenery.

24 **Loch Shiel** Page **270** • Among Scotland's myriad lochs, Shiel stands out for its serene beauty and compelling history.

25 **West Highland Railway** Page **271** • One of the great railway journeys of the world.

26 **Staffa and the Treshnish Isles** Page **105** • View the basalt columns of Staffa's Fingal's Cave from the sea, and then picnic amidst the puffins on the Isle of Lunga.

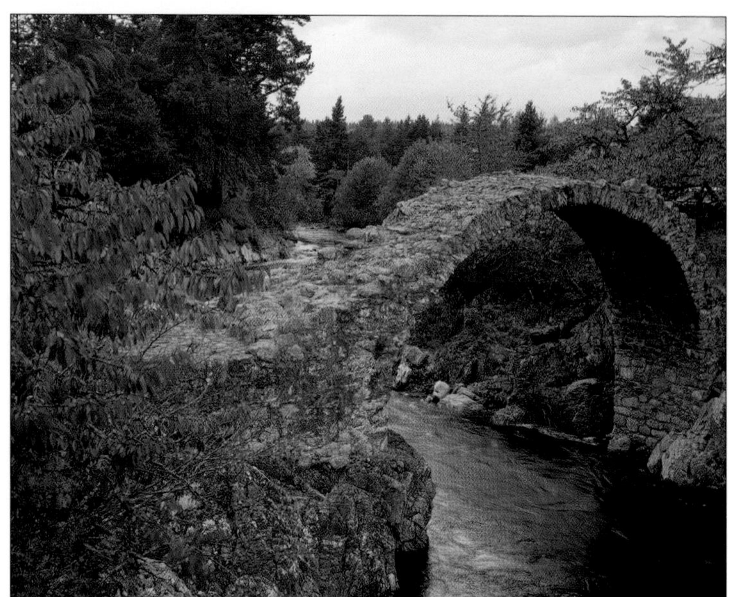

27 Speyside Way Page **214** • A long-distance footpath through Scotland's whisky glens.

28 Whale-watching, Mull Page **106** • Close encounters with a very different type of Highland wildlife.

29 Loch Fyne Oyster Bar Page **78** • Pick up a picnic or enjoy fine dining at Scotland's top smokehouse and seafood outlet, located just outside Inveraray.

30 Jarlshof, Shetland Page **467** • An exceptional archeological site taking in Iron age, Bronze Age, Pictish, Viking and medieval remains.

Basics

Basics

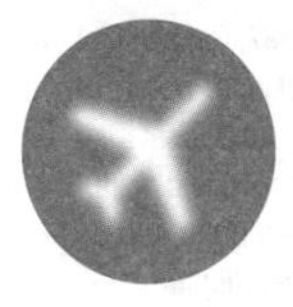

Getting there

There are numerous ways of getting to the Scottish Highlands and Islands but in general, if you're flying, you'll get a much wider choice – and usually lower fares – if you go via England. Although there are a few nonstop flights to Scotland from North America, there are none at all from Australia or New Zealand. Plane is also the cheapest and quickest way to reach Scotland from continental Europe and many parts of Britain. That said, road and rail connections from around Britain are pretty straightforward, and there are direct ferries to Scotland from Ireland, Belgium and Scandinavia.

Scotland has three main **international airports:** Glasgow International, Edinburgh and Aberdeen. Glasgow handles most nonstop scheduled flights from North America; all three have a reasonable spread of European flights. Glasgow Prestwick also has a few scheduled flights to and from Europe, and transatlantic flights via Dublin, but the majority of its custom comes from charter airlines. Note that, although Glasgow International, Edinburgh and Aberdeen are well linked into the **domestic** network, there are no flights from Glasgow Prestwick to anywhere else in Scotland.

Airfares depend primarily on availability, but they also depend on the **season**, with the highest fares charged from mid-June to mid-September and around Christmas and New Year. Fares will ordinarily be cheaper during the rest of the year, which is considered low season, though some airlines also have a "shoulder" season – typically April to mid-June and mid-September to October.

Booking flights online

Loads of people book tickets online nowadays and good deals can often be found through discount or auction sites, as well as through the airlines' own websites.

Ⓦ **www.cheapflights.com** (US); Ⓦ **www.cheapflights.ca** (Canada); Ⓦ **www.cheapflights.com.au** (Australia). All the sites offer flight deals, details of travel agents, and links to other travel sites.

Ⓦ **www.etn.nl/discount.htm** A hub of consolidator and discount agent Web links, maintained by the non-profit European Travel Network.

Ⓦ **www.expedia.com** (US); for Canada Ⓦ **www.expedia.ca**. Discount airfares, all-airline search engine and daily deals.

Ⓦ **www.gaytravel.com** US gay travel agent, offering accommodation, cruises, tours and more.

Ⓦ **www.hotwire.com** Bookings from the US only. Last-minute savings of up to forty percent on regular published fares. Travellers must be at least 18 and there are no refunds, transfers or changes allowed. Log-in required. If you're looking for the cheapest possible scheduled flight, this is probably your best bet.

Ⓦ **www.lastminute.com.au** (Australia only) Good last-minute holiday package and flight-only deals.

Ⓦ **www.priceline.com** Name-your-own-price website that has deals at around forty percent off standard fares.

Ⓦ **www.qixo.com** A comparison search that trawls through other ticket sites – including agencies and airlines – to find the best deals.

Ⓦ **www.skyauction.com** Bookings from the US only. Auctions tickets and travel packages using a "second bid" scheme, just like eBay. You state the maximum you're willing to pay, and the system will bid only as much as it takes to outbid others, up to your stated limit.

Ⓦ **www.travelocity.com** Destination guides, best deals for car rental, accommodation and lodging as well as fares. Provides access to the travel agent system SABRE, the most comprehensive central reservations system in the US.

Ⓦ **www.travelshop.com.au** Australian website offering discounted flights, packages, insurance and online bookings.

Ⓦ **http://travel.yahoo.com** Incorporates some Rough Guides material in its coverage of destination countries and cities across the world, with information about places to eat and sleep.

From North America

If you want to fly nonstop into Scotland **from North America**, there's a limited choice:

Continental from New York to Glasgow and Edinburgh or one of the Canadian budget airlines, Zoom or Air Transat. Most other airlines, and all flights to other Scottish airports, route through London, Manchester, Dublin or Paris.

Figure on six to seven hours' **flight time** nonstop from the east coast to Glasgow, or seven hours to London plus an extra hour and a quarter from London to Glasgow or Edinburgh (not including stopover time). Add three or four hours more for travel from the west coast. Most eastbound flights cross the Atlantic overnight, reaching Britain the next morning; flying back, departure times tend to be morning or afternoon, arriving in the afternoon or evening.

Return **fares** (including taxes) to Glasgow from New York are $400–500 low season, $600–800 high season; from Canada around C$750 low season, C$1000 high season.

Airlines in North America

Aer Lingus ⓣ1-800/IRISH-AIR, ⓦwww.aerlingus.com.
Air Canada ⓣ1-888/247-2262, ⓦwww.aircanada.com.
Air Transat ⓣ1-866/847-1112, ⓦwww.airtransat.ca.
American Airlines ⓣ1-800/433-7300, ⓦwww.aa.com.
bmi ⓣ1-800/788-0555, ⓦwww.flybmi.com.
British Airways ⓣ1-800/AIRWAYS, ⓦwww.ba.com.
Continental ⓣ1-800/231-0856, ⓦwww.continental.com.
Delta ⓣ1-800/241-4141, ⓦwww.delta.com.
United Airlines ⓣ1-800/538-2929, ⓦwww.united.com.
Virgin Atlantic Airways ⓣ1-800/862-8621, ⓦwww.virgin-atlantic.com.
Zoom Airlines ⓣ1-866/359-9666, ⓦwww.flyzoom.com.

Flight agents in North America

Air Brokers International ⓣ1-800/883-3273, ⓦwww.airbrokers.com. Consolidator and specialist in round-the-world tickets.
Airtech ⓣ212/219-7000, ⓦwww.airtech.com. Standby seat broker; also deals in consolidator fares.
Educational Travel Centre ⓣ1-800/747-5551 or 608/256-5551, ⓦwww.edtrav.com. Low-cost fares worldwide, student/youth discount offers, and Eurail passes, car rental and tours.
STA Travel US ⓣ1-800/329-9537, Canada ⓣ1-888/427-5639, ⓦwww.statravel.com. Worldwide specialists in independent travel; also student IDs, travel insurance, car rental, rail passes, and more.
Student Flights ⓣ1-800/255-8000 or 480/951-1177, ⓦwww.isecard.com/studentflights. Student/youth fares, plus student IDs and European rail and bus passes.
TFI Tours International ⓣ1-800/745-8000 or 212/736-1140, ⓦwww.lowestairprice.com. Well-established consolidator with a wide variety of global fares.
Travel CUTS US ⓣ1-800/592-CUTS, Canada ⓣ1-888/246-9762, ⓦwww.travelcuts.com. Popular, long-established student-travel organization, with worldwide offers.
Worldtek Travel ⓣ1-800/243-1723, ⓦwww.worldtek.com. Discount travel agency for worldwide travel.

Tour operators in North America

Abercrombie & Kent ⓣ1-800/554-7016, ⓦwww.abercrombiekent.com. Classy operator with a strong reputation, offering various packages including cruises and rail tours around Scotland.
Adventures Abroad ⓣ1-800/665-3998 or ⓣ604/303-1099, ⓦwww.adventures-abroad.com. Walking and sightseeing tours of Scotland.
Backroads ⓣ1-800/GO-ACTIVE, ⓦwww.backroads.com. Guided walking packages in the Scottish Highlands and Islands.
CIE Tours ⓣ1-800/CIE-TOUR, ⓦwww.cietours.com. Escorted coach tours and self-drive packages.
Golf International Inc ⓣ1-800/833-1389, ⓦwww.golfinternational.com. Scottish golf vacation specialist.
Home at First ⓣ1-800/523-5842, ⓦwww.homeatfirst.com. Flights, cottages, car rental and golf packages.
International Gay Travel Association ⓣ1-800/448-8550, ⓦwww.iglta.org. Trade group with lists of gay-owned or gay-friendly travel agents, accommodation options and other travel-related services.
Jerry Quinlan's Celtic Golf ⓣ1-800/535-6148 or 609/465-0600, ⓦwww.jqcelticgolf.com. Customized golf tours of Scotland.
Mountain Travel Sobek ⓣ1-888/MT-SOBEK, ⓦwww.mtsobek.com. Hiking holidays in the Highlands.
Prestige Tours ⓣ1-800/890-7375, ⓦwww.prestige-tours.com. Fly-drive, all-inclusive coach tours and city breaks.
Rail Europe ⓣ1-877/EUROVAC; ⓦwww.raileurope.com. Rail, air, hotel and car reservations in the UK.

From Australia and New Zealand

Flight time from **Australia** and **New Zealand** to Scotland is at least 22 hours, and can be more depending on routes and transfer times. There's a wide variety of routes, with those touching down in southeast Asia the quickest and cheapest on average. To reach Scotland, you usually have to change planes either in London – the most popular choice – or in another European gateway such as Paris or Amsterdam. One exception to this is if you fly via Dubai, from which Emirates has daily flights direct to Glasgow. Given the length of the journey involved, you might be better off including a night's stopover in your itinerary, and indeed some airlines include one in the price of the flight.

The cheapest direct scheduled flights to London are usually to be found on one of the Asian airlines. Average return **fares** (including taxes) from eastern gateways to London are A$1500–2000 in low season, A$2000–2500 in high season. Fares from Perth or Darwin cost around A$200 less. Return fares from Auckland to London range between NZ$2000 and NZ$3000 depending on the season, route and carrier.

Airlines in Australia and New Zealand

Air New Zealand Australia ⓣ13 24 76, ⓦwww.airnz.com.au; New Zealand ⓣ0800/737 000, ⓦwww.airnz.co.nz.
British Airways Australia ⓣ1300/767 177, New Zealand ⓣ09/966 9777; ⓦwww.ba.com.
Cathay Pacific Australia ⓣ02/9667 3816, New Zealand ⓣ09/275 0847; ⓦwww.cathaypacific.com.
Delta Australia ⓣ02/9251 3211, New Zealand ⓣ09/379 3370; ⓦwww.delta.com.
Emirates Australia ⓣ1300/303 777 or 02/9290 9700, New Zealand ⓣ09/377 6004, ⓦwww.emirates.com.
Garuda Indonesia Australia ⓣ1300/365 330 or 02/9334 9944, New Zealand ⓣ09/366 1862; ⓦwww.garuda-indonesia.com.
KLM Australia ⓣ1300/303 747, New Zealand ⓣ09/302 1792; ⓦwww.klm.com.
Malaysian Airlines Australia ⓣ13 26 27, New Zealand ⓣ0800/777 747 or 649/379 3743; ⓦwww.malaysiaairlines.com.
Qantas Australia ⓣ13 13 13, New Zealand ⓣ09/357 8900 or 0800/808 767; ⓦwww.qantas.com.
Singapore Airlines Australia ⓣ13 10 11 or ⓣ02/9350 0262, New Zealand ⓣ09/379 3209; ⓦwww.singaporeair.com.
Sri Lankan Airlines Australia ⓣ02/9244 2234, New Zealand ⓣ09/308 3353; ⓦwww.srilankan.aero.
Thai Airways Australia ⓣ1300/651 960, New Zealand ⓣ09/377 3886; ⓦwww.thaiairways.com.
Virgin Atlantic Airways Australia ⓣ02/9244 2747, ⓦwww.virgin-atlantic.com.

Flight agents in Australia and New Zealand

Flight Centre Australia ⓣ13 31 33 or 02/9235 3522, ⓦwww.flightcentre.com.au; New Zealand ⓣ0800/243 544 or 09/358 4310, ⓦwww.flightcentre.co.nz.
Holiday Shoppe New Zealand ⓣ0800/808 480, ⓦwww.holidayshoppe.co.nz.
Northern Gateway Australia ⓣ1800/174 800, ⓦwww.northerngateway.com.au.
STA Travel Australia ⓣ1300/733 035 or 02/9212 1255, ⓦwww.statravel.com.au; New Zealand ⓣ0508/782 872 or 09/309 9273, ⓦwww.statravel.co.nz.
Trailfinders Australia ⓣ02/9247 7666 or ⓣ1300/780 212, ⓦwww.trailfinders.com.au.
ⓦwww.travel.com.au Australia ⓣ1300/130 482 or 02/9249 5444; New Zealand ⓣ0800/468 332, ⓦwww.travel.co.nz.

From England and Wales

Crossing the border from England into Scotland is straightforward, with **train** and **bus** services forming part of the British national network. If you add on the time spent getting to and from the airport and checking in, **flying** is no quicker than travelling by train or coach unless you're heading out to the Highlands and Islands. Budget air fares are only really competitive on popular routes such as London to Edinburgh and Glasgow and, again, if you add on the cost of travel to and from the airport (and remember to include airport tax), the savings on the same journey overland are often minimal – and then, of course, there's the environmental impact to consider.

The only airport in the Highlands and Islands that has direct flights from England or Wales is **Inverness**, which has flights from London, Bristol, Birmingham and Manchester. In order to reach the smaller airports in the Highlands and Islands, you'll need to change planes in Glasgow, Edinburgh or Aberdeen (see p.42 for more details of flights within Scotland). The most competitive **air fares** from England and Wales are with the no-frills budget airlines. The leaders in the field are Ryanair, who fly into Glasgow Prestwick, and easyJet, who fly into all the major Scottish airports from London and other regional airports. You can pay as little as £20 for a rock-bottom one-way ticket and £40 for a return (including tax). However, the cheaper tickets need to be booked well in advance and are either non-refundable or only partially refundable, and non-exchangeable. For more reasonable flight times and/or a more flexible, refundable fare from these same budget airlines, you're looking at more like £80 return, a price that British Airways – with a range of flights out of many English airports – can often compete with.

Airlines in Britain

Air Wales ⓣ0870/850 9850, ⓦwww.airwales.com.
British Airways ⓣ0870/850 9850, ⓦwww.ba.com.
bmi ⓣ0870/607 0555, ⓦwww.flybmi.com.
bmibaby ⓣ0870/264 2229, ⓦwww.bmibaby.com.
easyJet ⓣ0871/750 0100, ⓦwww.easyjet.com.
Eastern Airways ⓣ0870/366 9100, ⓦwww.easternairways.com.
Flybe ⓣ0870/889 0908, ⓦwww.flybe.com.
Jet2.com ⓣ0871/226 1737, ⓦwww.jet2.com.
KLM ⓣ0870/507 4074, ⓦwww.klm.com.
Ryanair ⓣ0871/246 0000, ⓦwww.ryanair.com.
ScotAirways ⓣ0870/606 0707, ⓦwww.scotairways.com.

Flight agents in Britain

North South Travel ⓣ01245/608291, ⓦwww.northsouthtravel.co.uk. Friendly, competitive travel agency, offering discounted fares worldwide. Profits are used to support projects in the developing world, especially the promotion of sustainable tourism.
STA Travel ⓣ0870/160 0599, ⓦwww.statravel.co.uk. Worldwide specialists in low-cost flights, overlands and holiday deals. Good discounts for students and under-26s.
Trailfinders ⓣ020/7938 3939, ⓦwww.trailfinders.com. One of the best-informed and most efficient agents for independent travellers.

By train from England and Wales

Glasgow and Edinburgh are both served by frequent **direct train services** from London, and are easily reached from other main English towns and cities, though you may have to change trains en route. The only direct train to the Scottish Highlands and Islands from south of the border is the daytime service to Inverness run by GNER, which departs from London King's Cross and takes eight hours – for more on this, see below.

The alternative method of reaching the Highlands direct is to catch one of the overnight **Caledonian Sleepers**, run by First ScotRail from London Euston (daily except Sat) to Glasgow, Edinburgh, Aberdeen, Inverness and Fort William. A sample return fare to Edinburgh or Glasgow is £89 if booked in advance, with occasional special offers via the Internet. Sleeper cabins contain two beds, so you may have to share (with someone of the same sex) unless you pay a supplement; first-class customers automatically enjoy the luxury of a single-berth cabin. Otherwise, there's the budget option of a relatively comfortable reclining seat, starting at £40 return; while hardly the lap of luxury, this is still a more attractive option than the rather grim overnight bus journey (which is only a few pounds less expensive). You can usually board the train an hour before departure and leave up to an hour after the train arrives.

If you're only going as far as Glasgow or Edinburgh, note that GNER trains depart from **London King's Cross** and run up the east coast via Peterborough, York and Newcastle to Edinburgh, with some going on to Glasgow, Aberdeen or Inverness, while Virgin trains run up the west coast from **London Euston** via Crewe, Preston and Carlisle to Glasgow. Virgin also runs several other long-distance direct services to Scotland that don't originate in London: from **Penzance**, **Plymouth** and **Bournemouth** to Edinburgh or Glasgow via Birmingham and then either the east or the west coast. **Journey times** from London can be as little as 4hr 20min to Edinburgh and 4hr 45min to Glasgow; from Manchester or York, knock off about 2hr; from Bristol add about 2hr; from Penzance, it takes just over 10hr. Beyond Edinburgh or Glasgow, allow another 2hr 30min to reach Aberdeen, or 3hr 30min to Inverness.

Fare structures are fiendishly complex, but if you simply turn up at the station, the cheapest off-peak fare available will be around £85 return; if you book in advance you can get £10–20 off and occasional special offers can bring the price down even further. Return fares from Manchester to Glasgow are around £30 if you book in advance, but more like £50 on the day; from Bristol to Edinburgh, advance returns cost around £70, but over £100 on the day. Various discount **passes** are also available in Britain to nationals and foreign visitors alike, for those under 26, over 60, or travelling with children. For more details, and links to sites where you can book online, visit ⓦwww.nationalrail.co.uk.

Train information

First ScotRail ⓣ0845/755 0033, ⓦwww.firstgroup.com/scotrail.
GNER ⓣ0845/722 5225, ⓦwww.gner.co.uk.
National Rail enquiries ⓣ0845/748 4950, ⓦwww.nationalrail.co.uk.
Virgin ⓣ0845/722 2333, ⓦwww.virgintrains.co.uk.
ⓦ**www.seat61.com** The world's finest train travel website. Amazingly comprehensive, with more detail than you ever wanted to know about train travel in the UK (and worldwide), but full of incredibly useful tips and links.

By road from England and Wales

Inter-town bus services (known as **coaches** throughout Britain) duplicate many train routes, often at half the price or less. The frequency of service is usually comparable to the train, and in some instances the difference in journey time isn't that great; buses are also reasonably comfortable, and on longer routes often have drinks and sandwiches available on board. The main operators are **National Express** (ⓣ0870/580 8080, ⓦwww.nationalexpress.com) and its sister company **Scottish Citylink** (ⓣ0870/550 5050, ⓦwww.citylink.co.uk). Buses run direct from most British cities to Edinburgh and Glasgow, where you'll have to change for Inverness and other destinations in the Highlands and Islands. Typical **fares** from London to Glasgow or Edinburgh (overnight journeys take around 8hr; daytime journeys nearer 10hr) are around £40 return; from Cardiff £50; from Manchester £30. If you book in advance, you can save £10 or so. There are also various discount **passes** available, detailed on the websites.

The two main **driving** routes to Scotland from the south are via the east of England on the A1, or via the west using the M6, A74(M) and M74. The A1, which passes by Peterborough, Doncaster, Newcastle and Berwick-upon-Tweed, gives you the option of branching off onto the A68, which takes the hilly but scenic route over the border at Carter Bar and adds an hour or so to the journey time; the M6 route, which goes around Birmingham, between Manchester and Liverpool and on to Carlisle, offers at least dual-carriageway driving the whole way. Either way, it takes around eight hours to get from London or Cardiff to Edinburgh or Glasgow, barring roadwork delays; two hours less from Birmingham. To reach Aberdeen, add another two hours on the motorway from Edinburgh; to reach Inverness, reckon on slightly longer, depending on the traffic. All other roads in the Highlands and Islands are fairly slow-going, so calculate your journey time using 40mph (65kph) as a very rough indicator of average speed.

From Ireland

Travel **from Ireland** is quickest by plane, with reasonable choice of flights from both Belfast and Dublin. There are also good ferry links with Northern Ireland, so taking the train or driving to Scotland is pretty straightforward.

Flying from **Dublin**, the best airfares are with Ryanair, who fly to Glasgow Prestwick for as little as €20 return, depending on availability. A fully flexible fare with Aer Lingus can cost five or six times that amount, but will allow you to change your ticket or claim a refund. From **Belfast** International, easyJet has return flights to Edinburgh or Glasgow from around £40; British Airways fares from Belfast or **Derry** to Glasgow start from £60 return (including tax).

Airlines in Ireland

Aer Arann Northern Ireland ⓣ0800/587 2324, Republic of Ireland ⓣ0818/210 210, ⓦwww.aerarann.com.
Aer Lingus Northern Ireland ⓣ0845/084 4444, Republic of Ireland ⓣ0818/365 000, ⓦwww.aerlingus.ie.

bmi Northern Ireland ⓣ0870/607 0555, ⓦwww.flybmi.com.
British Airways Northern Ireland ⓣ0870/850 9850, Republic of Ireland ⓣ1800/626 747, ⓦwww.ba.com.
easyJet Northern Ireland ⓣ0871/750 0100, ⓦwww.easyjet.com.
Flybe Northern Ireland ⓣ0870/889 0908, Republic of Ireland ⓣ1890/925 532, ⓦwww.flybe.com.
KLM Northern Ireland ⓣ0870/507 4074, ⓦwww.klmuk.com.
Ryanair Northern Ireland ⓣ0871/246 0000, Republic of Ireland ⓣ0818/303 030, ⓦwww.ryanair.com.

Flight agents in Ireland

ebookers Dublin ⓣ01/488 3507, ⓦwww.ebookers.ie. Low fares on an extensive selection of scheduled flights and package deals.
Joe Walsh Tours Dublin ⓣ01/676 0991, ⓦwww.joewalshtours.ie. Long-established general budget fares and holidays agent.
USIT Belfast ⓣ028/9032 7111, Dublin ⓣ01/602 1600, ⓦwww.usit.ie. Student, youth and independent travel specialists.

By ferry from Ireland

P&O Irish Sea runs several **sea** crossings daily from **Larne** to Cairnryan (takes 1hr 45min by ferry, or 1hr by jetliner) and Troon, just outside Ayr (1hr 50min). Stena Line operates conventional ferries and a high-speed service (HSS) daily from **Belfast** to Stranraer (takes between 1hr 45min and 3hr 15min).

Fares for a small car and driver are pretty complex, and depend on the time, day and month of sailing, on whether you take the fast or slow services, on whether you book in advance and on how long you're staying over in Scotland. Peak period standard returns can cost over £250, though you can save around £50 by booking in advance, and another £50 by travelling off-peak. Passenger-only fares work out at around £50 return.

Ferry companies in Ireland

P&O Irish Sea UK ⓣ0870/242 4777, ⓦwww.poirishsea.com.
Stena Line Northern Ireland ⓣ028/9074 7747, Republic of Ireland ⓣ01/204 7777, ⓦwww.stenaline.co.uk.

By ferry from mainland Europe

Ferries run by Superfast go overnight from **Zeebrugge** in Belgium to Rosyth (daily; 18hr), near Edinburgh. Off-peak return fares start at around €110, plus €165 for a car, and another €50 for a cabin berth. Smyril Line runs summer ferries to Shetland from Norway, **Denmark**, the **Faroe Islands** and **Iceland** (mid-May to early Sept only). The most direct route is from **Bergen** (Norway) to Lerwick (1 weekly; 12hr), with the option of continuing on to Aberdeen (daily; 12hr) on Northlink Ferries. Peak period through-fares from Bergen to Aberdeen cost around 1700kr return per person, or 3000kr with a car.

There's a greater choice of ferry services from Europe to ports in England, the most convenient being those to **Newcastle**, less than an hour's drive south of the Scottish border. DFDS Seaways sails twice weekly to Newcastle from **Kristiansand** in Norway (18hr) and from **Gothenburg** in Sweden (26hr), as well as daily from **IJmuiden** near Amsterdam (16hr). Fjord Line sails three times a week to Newcastle from **Bergen**, **Haugesund** and **Stavanger** (18–25hr). Fares on all routes vary according to the time of year, time and type of crossing, and number travelling – Direct Ferries (ⓣ0871/222 3312, ⓦwww.directferries.ie) has a very useful website that compares all the options.

DFDS Seaways Netherlands ⓣ0255/54 66 66, Norway ⓣ21 62 13 40, Sweden ⓣ031/650 680, UK ⓣ0870/252 0524, ⓦwww.dfdsseaways.com.
Fjord Line Norway ⓣ81 53 35 00, UK ⓣ0870/143 9669, ⓦwww.fjordline.com.
Northlink Ferries UK ⓣ0845/600 0449, ⓦwww.northlinkferries.co.uk.
Smyril Line Norway ⓣ55 59 65 20, UK ⓣ01595/690 845, ⓦwww.smyril-line.com.
Superfast Ferries Belgium 02/226 4060, UK ⓣ0870/234 0870, ⓦwww.superfast.com.

Visas and red tape

Citizens of most European countries can enter the UK with just a passport; EU citizens can stay indefinitely, other Europeans can stay up to three months. US, Canadian, Australian and New Zealand citizens can stay for up to six months, providing they have a return ticket and adequate funds to cover their stay. Citizens of most other countries require a visa, obtainable from the British consular or mission office in the country of application.

For current details about entry and **visa requirements**, consult the UK Foreign and Commonwealth Office's visa website: Ⓦwww.ukvisas.gov.uk. Citizens of EU countries who want to stay in the UK other than as a short-term visitor or tourist can apply for a **residence permit**. Non-EU citizens can apply to extend their visas, though this must be done before the current visa expires. In both cases, you should first contact the **Immigration and Nationality Directorate**, Lunar House, 40 Wellesley Rd, Croydon CR9 2BY Ⓣ0870/606 7766, Ⓦwww.ind.homeoffice.gov.uk. All overseas consulates in the Highlands and Islands are detailed in the listings sections for Kirkwall and Lerwick.

UK embassies abroad

Australia British High Commission, Commonwealth Ave, Yarralumla, Canberra, ACT 2600 Ⓣ02/6270 6666, Ⓦwww.britaus.net.

Canada British High Commission, 80 Elgin St, Ottawa, ON K1P 5K7 Ⓣ613/237-1530, Ⓦwww.britainincanada.org.

Ireland British Embassy, 29 Merrion Rd, Ballsbridge, Dublin 4 Ⓣ01/205 3700, Ⓦwww.britishembassy.ie.

New Zealand British High Commission, 44 Hill St, Thorndon, Wellington Ⓣ04/924 2888, Ⓦwww.britain.org.nz.

USA British Embassy, 3100 Massachusetts Ave NW, Washington DC 20008 Ⓣ202/588-6500, Ⓦwww.britainusa.com.

Customs and tax

Travellers coming into Britain directly **from another EU country** can bring almost as many cigarettes and as much wine or beer into the country as they can carry. The guidance levels are 10 litres of spirits, 90 litres of wine and 110 litres of beer – any more than this and you'll have to provide proof that it's for personal use only. The general guidelines for tobacco are 3200 cigarettes, 400 cigarillos, 200 cigars or 3kg of loose tobacco – note that the limits from some new EU member countries are lower than this. If you're travelling to or from a non-EU country, you can still buy **duty-free goods**, but within the EU, this perk no longer exists. The duty-free allowances are:

Tobacco 200 cigarettes; or 100 cigarillos; or 50 cigars; or 250 grams of loose tobacco.

Alcohol 2 litres of still wine plus 1 litre of drink over 22 percent alcohol; or 2 litres of alcoholic drinks not over 22 percent.

Perfumes 60ml of perfume plus 250ml of toilet water.

Other goods to the value of £145.

If you need any clarification on British import regulations, contact **HM Revenue and Customs** (Ⓣ0845/010 9000 or +4420/8929 0152 for international callers; Ⓦwww.hmrc.gov.uk).

Pets from countries participating in the Pet Travel Scheme (PETS) are allowed into Britain without quarantine, providing their owners follow certain procedures; for more information, phone the helpline Ⓣ0870/241 1710 or check the government website (Ⓦwww.defra.gov.uk).

Most goods in Britain, with the chief exceptions of books and food, are subject to 17.5-percent **Value Added Tax** (VAT), which is included in the marked price of goods – hotel bills are sometimes calculated with the tax added on separately. Visitors from non-EU countries can save a lot of money through the **Retail Export**

Scheme (tax-free shopping), which allows a refund of VAT on goods to be taken out of the country. Note that not all shops participate in this scheme (those doing so will display a sign to this effect), and that you cannot reclaim VAT charged on hotel bills or other services.

Costs, money and banks

Scotland, like the rest of the UK, is a relatively expensive place to visit. Transport, accommodation and restaurant prices are all above average compared with the rest of the EU. The UK has not changed over to the euro, and for the foreseeable future looks unlikely to do so (for more information, visit ⓦwww.euro.gov.uk).

Currency and exchange

The basic unit of currency in the UK is the **pound sterling** (£), divided into 100 pence (p). Coins come in denominations of 1p, 2p, 5p, 10p, 20p, 50p, £1 and £2. Bank of England £5, £10, £20 and £50 banknotes are legal tender in Scotland; in addition the Bank of Scotland (now HBOS), the Royal Bank of Scotland and the Clydesdale Bank issue their own banknotes in all the same denominations, plus a £100 note. All Scottish notes are legal tender throughout the UK, no matter what shopkeepers south of the border might say. In general, few people use £50 or £100 notes, and shopkeepers are likely to treat them with suspicion, since forgeries are widespread. At the time of going to press, £1 was worth around $1.80, €1.50, C$2.10, A$2.35 and NZ$2.60. For the most up-to-date exchange rates, check the useful website ⓦwww.xe.com.

There are **no exchange controls** in Britain, so you can bring in as much cash as you like and change travellers' cheques up to any amount. In every sizeable town, you'll find a branch of at least one of the big Scottish high-street **banks**: Bank of Scotland, Royal Bank of Scotland, Clydesdale and Lloyds TSB Scotland. However, on many islands, and in remoter parts, you may find there is only a **mobile bank** that runs to a timetable (usually available from the local post office). General **banking hours** are Monday to Friday from 9am or 9.30am to 4pm or 5pm, though some branches are open until slightly later on Thursdays. **ATMs** (cash machines) can be few and far between (or simply nonexistent), but supermarkets and some shops and garages offer "cash-back" services.

Carrying money

Credit/debit cards are by far the most convenient way to carry your money. Many hotels, shops and restaurants in Scotland accept the major credit cards, although plastic is less useful in the Highlands and Islands; smaller establishments all over the country, such as B&Bs, will often accept cash only. You can usually withdraw cash on your credit or debit card from **ATMs**; you should contact your bank before you leave, to find out which Scottish banks you can use and how much you'll be charged for the service.

Though a lot more hassle, old-fashioned **travellers' cheques** are still the safest way to carry your money. If the cheques are lost or stolen, the issuing company will expect you to report the loss immediately; most companies claim to replace lost or stolen cheques within 24 hours. Note that in the UK you are unlikely to be able to use your traveller's cheques as cash – you'll always have to cash them first, making them an unreliable source of funds in more remote areas.

Costs

The minimum **expenditure**, if you're cycling or hitching, preparing most of your own food and camping, is in the region of £30 a day, rising to around £40 a day if you're staying at hostels, using some public transport and eating the odd meal out. Couples staying at budget B&Bs, eating at unpretentious restaurants and visiting a fair number of tourist attractions, are looking at around £50 each per day. If you're renting a car, staying in comfortable B&Bs or hotels and eating well, you should reckon on at least £100 a day per person.

Youth and student discounts

Concessionary rates for **senior citizens** (over 60) and **children** (from 5 to 16) apply almost everywhere, from fee-paying attractions to public transport, and typically give around fifty percent discount; you'll need official identification as proof of age. The unemployed and full-time students are often entitled to discounts too, and the under-5s are rarely charged.

Full-time students are eligible for the **International Student ID Card** (ISIC; Ⓦwww.isiccard.com), which entitles you to special air, rail and bus fares and discounts at museums, theatres and other attractions. The **International Youth Travel Card** provides similar benefits for under-26s, while teachers qualify for the **International Teacher Card**. Several other travel organizations and accommodation groups (including the youth hostel organization, IYHF) have their own cards providing various discounts. Specialist travel agencies in your home country (including STA worldwide) can provide more information and application forms.

Service charges and tipping

Some restaurants levy a "discretionary" or "optional" **service charge** of 10 or 12.5 percent. If they've done this, it should be clearly stated on the menu and on the bill. However, you are not obliged to pay the charge, and certainly not if the food or service wasn't what you expected.

Otherwise, although there are no fixed rules for **tipping**, a ten to fifteen percent tip is anticipated by restaurant waiters and expected by taxi drivers. It is not normal to leave tips in pubs, but the bar staff are sometimes offered drinks, which they may accept in the form of money. The only other occasions when you'll be expected to tip are in hairdressers, and in upmarket hotels where porters, bellboys and table waiters rely on being tipped to bump up their often dismal wages.

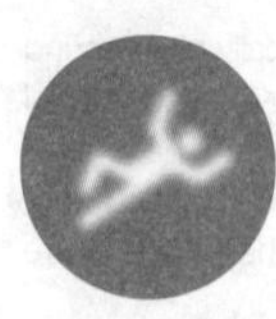

Insurance and health

Visitors are advised to take out an insurance policy before travelling to cover against theft, loss and illness or injury. A typical policy will provide cover for loss of baggage, tickets and – up to a certain limit – cash or travellers' cheques, as well as cancellation or curtailment of your journey. Most exclude so-called dangerous sports unless an extra premium is paid: in Scotland this can mean most water-sports, rock climbing, scuba diving, windsurfing and skiing, though probably not hiking and kayaking.

Medical coverage is strongly advised, though beforehand you should always ascertain whether benefits will be paid as treatment proceeds or only after you return home, and whether there is a 24-hour medical emergency number. When securing **baggage cover**, make sure that the per-article limit will cover your most valuable possession. If you need to make a claim, you should keep receipts for medicines and medical treatment, and in the event you have anything stolen you must obtain an official statement from the police.

Health

No vaccinations are required for entry to the UK. EU citizens are entitled to free medical treatment at National Health Service hospitals on production of an **EHIC** card (which replaces the old E111 form). Australia, New Zealand and several non-EU European countries have reciprocal health-care arrangements with the UK. Citizens of other countries will be charged for all medical services except those administered by Accident and Emergency (A&E) units at National Health Service hospitals. In other words, if you've just been hit by a car, you would not be charged if the injuries simply required stitching and setting in the emergency unit, but would were admission to a hospital ward necessary. Health insurance is therefore extremely advisable for all non-EU nationals.

Pharmacists (known as chemists in Scotland) can dispense only a limited range of drugs without a doctor's prescription. Most are open standard shop hours, though in large towns some may close as late as 10pm; local newspapers carry lists of late-opening pharmacies, or you can contact the local police for current details. **Doctors' (GP's) surgeries** tend to be open from about 9am to noon and then for a couple of hours in the evening; outside surgery hours, you can turn up at the 24-hour casualty (A&E) department of the local **hospital**. In an **emergency**, call an ambulance on ⓣ999 or 112.

Rough Guides travel insurance

In conjunction with Columbus Direct, Rough Guides provides tailor-made travel insurance. Readers can choose from policies that include a low-cost **backpacker** option for long stays; a **short-break** option for city getaways; a typical **holiday package** option; and many others. There are also annual **multi-trip** policies for those who travel regularly, with variable levels of cover available. Different **sports and activities** (trekking, skiing, etc) can be included on most policies, if required. Rough Guides travel insurance can be purchased by residents of 36 countries on our website, ⓦwww.roughguidesinsurance.com, which also has various language options. Alternatively, UK residents can call ⓣ0800/083 9507; US citizens ⓣ1-800/749-4922; and Australians ⓣ1300/669 999. All other nationalities should call ⓣ+44 870/890 2843.

Information, websites and maps

If you want to do a bit of research before arriving in Scotland, as well as visiting the websites listed below, you could also contact VisitBritain – the UK's tourist authority – which has offices worldwide, or the main office of VisitScotland, the Scottish tourist board. Either will send you a wealth of free literature, useful maps, city guides, event calendars and accommodation brochures.

Tourist offices

VisitScotland **tourist offices** (often called Tourist Information Centres or TICs) exist in virtually every major destination in the Scottish Highlands and Islands, though not on some of the smaller, remoter islands, where you'll have to rely on the locals for advice. **Opening hours** are frequently confusing and vary from place to place and month to month; note that many offices close completely in the winter. Frustratingly, phone enquiries are often directed to a central call centre in Livingstone, where the staff have no knowledge of local information other than what appears on their computer screen. Consequently, we've only given telephone numbers in the guide for tourist offices where you can be sure (at the time of going to print) of getting through to that specific office.

As well as being stacked full of souvenirs and other gifts, most TICs have a decent selection of leaflets, displays, maps and books relating to the local area. The staff are usually helpful and will do their best to help with enquiries about accommodation, local public transport, attractions and restaurants, although it is worth being aware that they are reluctant to divulge information about local attractions or accommodation which are not paid-up members of the Tourist Board – and a number of perfectly decent guesthouses and the like choose not to pay the fees. Some offices may make a small charge for a town guide with an accompanying street plan, or an accommodation list, and most will charge a fee of around £3 if they book accommodation for you (see p.44).

British Tourist Authority

Ⓦ **www.visitbritain.com**

Australia Ⓣ 02/9021 4400 or 1300/858 589, Ⓦ www.visitbritain.com/au.
Canada Ⓣ 1-888/847 4885, Ⓦ www.visitbritain.com/ca.
Ireland Ⓣ 01/670 8000, Ⓦ www.visitbritain.com/ie.
New Zealand Ⓣ 0800/700 741, Ⓦ www.visitbritain.com/nz.
USA Ⓣ 1-800/462 2748, Ⓦ www.visitbritain.com/us.

VisitScotland

Ⓦ **www.visitscotland.com**
Information Ⓣ 0845/225 5121. In Scotland: 23 Ravelston Terrace, Edinburgh EH4 3EU. In England: 19 Cockspur St, London SW1Y 5BL.

Regional tourist boards

Aberdeen and Grampian Ⓣ 01224/288828, Ⓦ www.agtb.org.
Angus and Dundee Ⓣ 01382/527527, Ⓦ www.angusanddundee.co.uk.
Argyll, the Isles, Loch Lomond, Stirling and Trossachs Ⓣ 01786/445222, Ⓦ www.visitscottishheartlands.com.
Ayrshire and Arran Ⓦ www.ayrshire-arran.com.
Highlands of Scotland Ⓣ 01997/421160, Ⓦ www.visitscotland.com.
Orkney Ⓣ 01856/872856, Ⓦ www.visitorkney.com.
Perthshire Ⓣ 01738/627958, Ⓦ www.perthshire.co.uk.
Shetland Ⓣ 01595/693434, Ⓦ www.visitshetland.com.
Western Isles Ⓣ 01851/703088, Ⓦ www.visithebrides.com.

Useful websites

Throughout the guide, we've included **websites** for specific accommodation, museums, galleries, transport, entertainment venues and other attractions. If you're looking for more general information about Scotland, or just a different take on things, then the list below is a useful starting point.

Ⓦ **www.aboutscotland.com** Useful for accommodation, easy to use and linked to holiday activities.

Ⓦ **www.ambaile.org.uk** Bilingual online "Gaelic village", which has exhibitions, listings, games, news and language resources on the Highlands and Islands.

Ⓦ **ceolas.org/ceolas.html** A very informative Celtic music site, both historical and contemporary, with lots of music to listen to.

Ⓦ **www.geo.ed.ac.uk/home/scotland/scotland.html** Produced by the Geography Department of Edinburgh University – an introduction to all things Scottish in the way of history, geography and politics. Excellent background information with a myriad of links.

Ⓦ **www.hebrides.com** Beautiful black-and-white photographic journey courtesy of Sam Maynard through the Outer Hebrides (aka the Western Isles).

Ⓦ **www.highlanderweb.co.uk** Styled as a magazine aimed primarily at businesses, but with a mixture of radio, music, products and more.

Ⓦ **www.knowhere.co.uk** A self-styled user's guide to Britain. Up-to-date info, with readers' comments, including best-of and worst-of sections.

Ⓦ **www.rampantscotland.com** Index of links to everything Scottish; well worth going to if you're searching for something specific.

Ⓦ **www.scotland.org.uk** Exhaustive directory of Scottish websites.

Ⓦ **www.scottishislands.org.uk** Website of the SIN (Scottish Islands Network), which puts out a monthly online newsletter on current issues in the islands.

Ⓦ **www.stonepages.com/scotland** An offbeat though perfectly sane and informative website for those hooked on cairns and stone circles.

Ⓦ **www.travelscotland.co.uk** Run in association with the tourist board, this is a lively magazine-format site, full of news, features and reviews.

Ⓦ **www.undiscoveredscotland.co.uk** Great online guide to the country, with everything from features, maps and recipes to lists of boat charters and links to loads of local sites.

Ⓦ **www.wannabethere.com** VisitScotland's adventure holiday website, everything from pony trekking to all-night partying; well worth a look if you need inspiration.

Peculiarly Scottish

Ⓦ **www.hogmanay.net** Where to go and what to sing on Scotland's biggest night out.

Ⓦ **www.met-office.gov.uk** The nation's favourite topic, the weather, discussed in detail with full regional (and shipping) forecasts.

Ⓦ **www.sol.co.uk/d/dickwall/munroes.htm** A comprehensive list of Scotland's Munros (mountains over 3000ft) with pop-up maps to locate them all.

Ⓦ **www.strathspey.org** How to bluff your way in Scottish country dancing (in case you're asked to an obscure cousin's wedding).

Maps

In general, the most comprehensive maps of Scotland are produced by the **Ordnance Survey** or OS (Ⓦwww.ordsvy.gov.uk), renowned for their accuracy and clarity. Unless you prefer to buy just one **road map** of the whole of Scotland, Ordnance Survey's Road series at 1:250,000 covers the Highlands and Islands on two maps. With contours and altitude colouring, these GPS-compatible maps are particularly good for caravan towing or cycling, but carry no tourist information. Alternatively, Estate Publications has a series of maps at various scales, specifically designed to highlight places of interest, recreational facilities, campsites, caravan parks, hostels and the like, but with less accurate information on the topography.

OS's (pink) **Landranger** maps at 1:50,000, or their (orange) **Explorer** series at 1:25,000, provide the best large-scale **topographic** mapping. The full OS range is only available at a few big-city stores, although in any walking district of Scotland you'll find the relevant maps in local shops or tourist offices. If you're planning a walk of more than a couple of hours in duration, or intend to walk in the Scottish hills at all, it is strongly recommended that you carry a relevant map at 1:50,000 or better, and familiarize yourself with how to navigate using it. Scottish hiking specialists Harveys has a series of waterproof walking maps for popular hiking areas. For those determined enough to take part in the traditional Scottish pastime of "Munro-bagging" (climbing mountains and hills over 3000ft, or 914m), Harvey and Collins publish special Munro charts, listing all 284 of them. Sustrans publishes an excellent map at 1:100,000 of the Lochs and Glens Cycle Route from Glasgow across the Highlands to Inverness.

Map websites

Ⓦ **www.multimap.com** Town plans and area maps with scales up to 1:10,000, plus address search, traffic info and more.
Ⓦ **www.streetmap.co.uk** Type in the address or postcode you want and this site will locate it for you in seconds
Ⓦ **www.visitmap.com** The Britain Visitor Atlas has a clickable A–Z of town and city maps.

Map outlets

England and Ireland

Stanfords 12–14 Long Acre, London WC2E 9LP Ⓣ020/7836 1321, Ⓦwww.stanfords.co.uk. Also at 39 Spring Gardens, Manchester Ⓣ0161/831 0250, and 29 Corn St, Bristol Ⓣ0117/929 9966.
National Map Centre Ireland 34 Aungier St, Dublin Ⓣ01/476 0471, Ⓦwww.mapcentre.ie.

USA and Canada

Longitude Books 115 W 30th St #1206, New York, NY 10001 Ⓣ1-800/342-2164, Ⓦwww.longitudebooks.com.
World of Maps 1235 Wellington St, Ottawa, ON, K1Y 3A3 Ⓣ1-800/214-8524 or Ⓣ613/724-6776, Ⓦwww.worldofmaps.com.

Australia and New Zealand

Map World (Australia) 371 Pitt St, Sydney Ⓣ02/9261 3601, Ⓦwww.mapworld.net.au. Also at 900 Hay St, Perth Ⓣ08/9322 5733, Jolimont Centre, Canberra Ⓣ02/6230 4097 and 1981 Logan Road, Brisbane Ⓣ07/3349 6633.
Map World (New Zealand) 173 Gloucester St, Christchurch Ⓣ0800/627 967, Ⓦwww.mapworld.co.nz.

Getting around

There's no getting away from the fact that getting around the Highlands and Islands is a time-consuming business: off the main routes, public transport services are few and far between, particularly in more remote parts of Argyll, the Highland region and the Islands. With careful planning, however, practically everywhere is accessible and you'll have no trouble getting to the main tourist destinations. In most parts of Scotland, especially if you take the scenic back roads, the low level of traffic makes driving wonderfully unstressful.

By train

The **railway** network in the Highlands is skeletal but spectacular, with a number of the lines counted as among the great scenic routes of the world. There are four main lines: the two on the west coast depart Glasgow Queen Street and terminate at Oban and Mallaig (via Fort William); of the two lines from Inverness, one goes to Kyle of Lochalsh and the other to Thurso. Inverness itself has train connections to Glasgow, Edinburgh, Perth and Aberdeen. Fort William and Inverness are not connected directly by train and there are no proper railways on the islands.

First ScotRail runs all the train services in the Highlands. You can buy tickets at stations, from major travel agents, or over the phone and online with a credit card. If the ticket office at the station is closed, you may buy a ticket on board from the inspector using cash or a credit card.

To find out about the numerous discounted national **rail passes**, contact National Rail enquiries. In addition, First ScotRail offers a couple of travel passes worth considering. The most flexible is the **Freedom of Scotland Travelpass**, which gives unlimited train travel within Scotland. It's also valid on all CalMac ferries, Glasgow Underground and on various buses in the remoter regions. Various versions of the pass are available, starting at £92 for four days' travel in an eight-day period, with discounts for national railcard holders. The **Highland Rover** is more limited in scope, allowing unlimited travel on trains within the Highland region, plus the West Highland Line, travel between Aberdeen and Aviemore and a few connecting bus routes; it costs £60 for four out of eight consecutive days.

Much less tempting are the various national rail passes which allow unlimited travel in Scotland, England and Wales. The only one that can be bought in the UK is the **All-Line Rover**, which starts at a whopping £355 for seven consecutive days' travel (with discounts for national rail card holders). **BritRail passes** (Ⓦwww.acprailnet.com/britrail) are only available for purchase before you leave your home country. The pass is available in a wide variety of types, with first- and second-class versions, discounted Youth Passes (second-class only) and Senior Passes (first-class only), and can be purchased as either the BritRail Consecutive Pass, which allows unlimited travel over a certain period (eight days costs US$299); or the BritRail Flexipass, which allows a set number of days' free travel within a two-month period (eight days costs US$385). However, before you consider buying the BritRail Scottish Freedom Pass (US$214 for four days' travel in eight), it's worth checking to see if it wouldn't be cheaper instead to buy the Freedom of Scotland Travelpass when you reach Scotland. Any good travel agent or tour operator can supply up-to-date information, or consult Ⓦwww.raileurope.com (North America), Ⓦwww.railplus.com.au (Australia) or Ⓦwww.railplus.co.nz (New Zealand).

If you've been resident in a European country other than the UK for at least six months, an **InterRail** pass, allowing unlimited train travel within Britain, might be a cost-effective way to travel, if Scotland is part of a longer European trip. For more details, visit Ⓦwww.raileurope.co.uk/inter-rail. Note that **Eurail** passes (Ⓦwww.eurail.com) are not valid in the UK.

On most First ScotRail routes **bicycles** are carried free, but since there are only between two and six bike spaces available, it's essential that you reserve ahead. For details of useful rail contacts see p.31.

By coach and bus

The main centres of the Highlands are served by a few long-distance bus services, known across Britain as **coaches**. Scotland's national operator is **Scottish Citylink** (Ⓣ0870/550 5050, Ⓦwww.citylink.co.uk). On the whole, coaches are cheaper than the equivalent train journey and, as a result, are very popular, so for busy routes and travel at weekends and holidays it's advisable to book ahead, rather than just turn up.

There are various **discount cards** on offer for those with children, those under 26 or over 50 and full-time students: contact Scottish Citylink for more on these. Overseas passport holders can buy a **Brit Xplorer** pass (in 7-, 14- or 28-day versions) in the UK, from National Express travel shops, or at major ports and airports; the seven-day pass costs £79, though you'd have to do a lot of bus travelling to make it pay. Another option is a National Express **Tourist Trail Pass** (Ⓣ0870/580 8080, Ⓦwww.nationalexpress.com), which gives you unlimited travel throughout Britain on National Express and Scottish Citylink coaches.

Local bus services are run by a bewildering array of companies, many of which change routes and timetables frequently. As a general rule, the further away from urban areas you get, the less frequent and more expensive bus services become. On the most remote routes the only service will be the school bus, running at roughly 8.30am and 3.30pm, but only during term times.

Some parts of the Highlands and Islands are only served by the **postbus** network, which operates numerous minibuses carrying mail and three to ten fare-paying passengers. They set off early in the morning, usually around 8am from the main post office, and collect mail (or deliver it) from/to the hinterland. It's a sociable, though often excruciatingly slow, way to travel, and may well be the only means of reaching hidden-away B&Bs and the like. You can get a booklet of routes and timetables from the Royal Mail Customer Service Centre (Ⓣ0845/774 0740, Ⓦwww.royalmail.com/postbus), while details of relevant local services are available at tourist offices.

For comprehensive travel information for buses, as well as trains and ferries, including departure times and timetables, the publicly funded **Traveline Scotland** (Ⓣ0870/608 2608, Ⓦwww.travelinescotland.com) provides a reliable service both online and by phone.

By car

If you want to cover a lot of the Highlands and Islands in a short time, or just want more flexibility, you'll need your own transport. If you're bringing your own car into the UK you should also carry your vehicle registration or ownership document at all times. Furthermore, you must be adequately insured, so be sure to check your existing policy.

In Scotland, as in the rest of the UK, you drive on the left. **Speed limits** are 20–40mph in built-up areas, 70mph on motorways and dual carriageways (freeways), and 60mph on most other roads. As a rule, assume that in any area with street lighting, the limit is 30mph. **Speed cameras** are increasingly used as a deterrent to speeding; if you're caught by one of these, the owner (or renter) of the vehicle will have to pay a fine. In the Highlands and Islands, there are still plenty of **single-track roads** with passing places; in addition to allowing oncoming traffic to pass at these points, you should also let cars behind you overtake. In these remoter regions, the roads are dotted with sheep, which are entirely oblivious to cars, so slow down and edge your way past; should you kill or injure one, it is your duty to inform the local farmer.

The AA (Automobile Association; Ⓦwww.theaa.com, Ⓣ0800/887766), RAC (Royal Automobile Club; Ⓦwww.rac.co.uk, Ⓣ0800/092 2222) and Green Flag (Ⓦwww.greenflag.co.uk, Ⓣ0800/051 0636) all operate **24-hour emergency breakdown** services, as well as other motoring and leisure facilities (including useful online route plans. You may be entitled to free assistance through a reciprocal arrangement with a motoring organization in your home country – check with your own association before setting out. You can make use of these emergency services if you are not a member of the organization, but you will need to join at the roadside and will incur a hefty surcharge too. In remote areas of the Highlands and Islands, you may have a long wait for assistance. Look into their **home-relay** policies, since most standard policies will only get you to the nearest garage, where

Bus tours

If you're backpacking or don't have your own transport, a cheap, flexible and fun way of getting a flavour of Scotland is to join one of the popular **minibus tours** that operate out of Edinburgh and head off into the Highlands. The current leading operator, **Haggis** (Ⓣ0131/557 9393, Ⓦwww.haggisadventures.com), has bright yellow minibuses setting off daily on whistlestop tours of various parts of Scotland lasting between one and six days. In the company of a live-wire guide, the tours aim to show backpackers a mix of classic highlights with a few well-chosen spots off the tourist trail, with an emphasis on keeping the on-board atmosphere lively. A three-day round-trip from Edinburgh starts from £85 (food and accommodation not included).

Several other companies offer similar packages, including **Macbackpackers** (Ⓣ0131/558 9900, Ⓦwww.macbackpackers.com), who run tours linking up their own hostels round the country as well as a jump-on-jump-off service, and **Wild in Scotland** (Ⓣ0131/478 6500, Ⓦwww.wild-in-scotland.com), who take in the Outer Hebrides or Orkney during their tours. The popular **Rabbie's Trail Burners** tours (Ⓣ0131/226 3133, Ⓦwww.rabbies.com) don't aim squarely at the backpacker market and have a rather more mellow approach.

Other tours offering different slants on the Scottish experience are **Heart of Scotland** (Ⓣ0131/558 8855, Ⓦwww.heartofscotlandtours.co.uk), which specialize in one-day tours to the Highlands, Fife or Perthshire, and **Walkabout Scotland** (Ⓣ0131/661 7168, Ⓦwww.walkaboutscotland.com), a company specializing in hill-walking day-trips from Edinburgh.

you can find yourself stranded for days until the part you need is sent from Inverness or Glasgow.

Renting a car

Renting a car in Scotland is expensive and may be cheaper if arranged in advance from home. Over the counter, most firms charge around £25–40 per day, £50 for a weekend or around £140 a week. One exception is the budget car rental firm, easyCar, who offer web fares of under £15 per day, if you book far enough in advance, though there are only one or two small models on offer. Otherwise, small **local agencies** often undercut the major chains, who, with the exception of Arnold Clark, are mostly confined to the big cities – we've highlighted some in the accounts of certain places.

Remember, too that **fuel** in Scotland is expensive – petrol (gasoline) and diesel cost around £1 per litre. **Automatics** are rare at the lower end of the price scale – if you want one, you should book well ahead. Few companies will rent to drivers with less than one year's experience and most will only rent to people between 21 and 75 years of age

Car rental companies

Arnold Clark ⓣ0845/607 4500, ⓦwww.arnoldclarkrental.com.
Avis ⓣ0870/010 0287, ⓦwww.avis.co.uk.
Budget ⓣ0870/153 9170, ⓦwww.budget.co.uk.
easyCar ⓣ0906/333 3333, ⓦwww.easycar.com.
Europcar ⓣ0845/607 5000, ⓦwww.europcar.co.uk.
Hertz ⓣ0870/844 8844, ⓦwww.hertz.co.uk.
Holiday Autos ⓣ0870/400 0099, ⓦwww.holidayautos.co.uk.
National ⓣ0870/536 5365, ⓦwww.nationalcar.co.uk.
Suncars ⓣ0870/500 5566, ⓦwww.suncars.com.
Thrifty ⓣ01494/751600, ⓦwww.thrifty.co.uk.

By ferry

Scotland has over sixty inhabited islands, and nearly fifty of them have scheduled **ferry** links. Most ferries carry cars and vans, and the vast majority can – and should – be booked as far in advance as possible.

Caledonian MacBrayne (abbreviated by most people, and throughout this book, to **CalMac**) has a virtual monopoly on services on the River Clyde and to the Hebrides, sailing to 22 islands and 4 peninsulas. They aren't quick – no catamarans or fast ferries – or cheap, but they do have two types of reduced-fare pass. If you're taking more than one ferry, it's worth asking about the discounted **Island Hopscotch** tickets. If you're going to be taking a lot of ferries, you might be better off with an **Island Rover**, which entitles you to eight or fifteen consecutive days' unlimited ferry travel. It does not, however, guarantee you a place on any ferry, so you still need to book ahead. Prices for the eight-day/fifteen-day pass are £48.50/£71 for passengers and £234/£350 for cars.

Car ferries to Orkney and Shetland from Aberdeen and from Scrabster near Thurso are run by **Northlink Ferries**. **Pentland Ferries** run a car ferry from Gill's Bay, near John O'Groats, to Orkney, and **John O'Groats Ferries** run a summer-only passenger ferry from John O'Groats to Orkney. The various Orkney islands are linked to each other by services run by **Orkney Ferries**; Shetland's inter-island ferries are run in conjunction with the local council, so the local tourist board is your best bet for information. There are also numerous small operators round the Scottish coast that run day-excursion trips; their contact details are given in the relevant chapters of this guide.

Ferry companies

Caledonian MacBrayne ⓣ0870/565 0000, ⓦwww.calmac.co.uk.
John O'Groats Ferries ⓣ01955/611353, ⓦwww.jogferry.co.uk.
Northlink Ferries ⓣ0845/600 0449, ⓦwww.northlinkferries.co.uk.
Orkney Ferries ⓣ01856/872044, ⓦwww.orkneyferries.co.uk.
Pentland Ferries ⓣ01856/831226, ⓦwww.pentlandferries.co.uk.

By plane

Apart from the three major airports of Glasgow, Edinburgh and Aberdeen, Scotland has numerous minor airports, many of them on the islands, some of which are little more than gravel airstrips. Internal **flights** are pretty expensive on the whole – a single fare from Glasgow to Islay will set you back around £80, and there are very few discounted tickets available – but the time saving may make it worthwhile. Another good option is British Airways' **Highland Rover**, which costs just £189, and allows you to take any five flights within seven days; flights to and between Orkney and Shetland are covered, but not inter-island flights within them. Most flights within Scotland are operated by British Airways or Loganair (a BA subsidiary), and the majority should be booked directly through British Airways (Ⓣ0870/850 9850, Ⓦwww.ba.com). For inter-island flights in Shetland (excluding Fair Isle), you need to book direct through Loganair (Ⓣ01595/840246, Ⓦwww.loganair.co.uk). Competition is, however, beginning to emerge, with Highland Airways (Ⓣ0845/450 2245, Ⓦwww.highlandairways.co.uk) currently offering flights from Inverness to Shetland and the Western Isles.

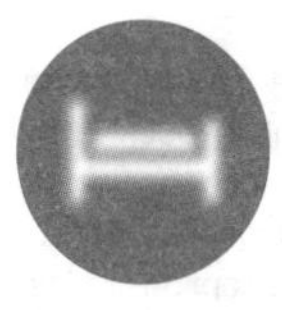

Accommodation

In common with the rest of Britain, accommodation in the Highlands and Islands is expensive. Budget travellers are well catered for with numerous hostels, and those with money to spend will relish the country's middle- and top-range hotels, many of which are converted feudal seats. In the middle ground, however, the standard of many B&Bs, guesthouses and hotels is often disappointing, and it can be hard work finding places with the standards of taste, originality, efficiency and value which you might expect from a country with as well-developed a tourist market as Scotland. Welcoming, comfortable, well-run places do, of course, exist in all parts of the country – but there are just not enough of them to go round.

Hotels, guesthouses and B&Bs

VisitScotland operates a nationwide system for grading **hotels**, **guesthouses** and **B&Bs**, which is updated annually. Although they cover a huge amount of accommodation, not every establishment participates, and you shouldn't assume that a particular B&B is no good simply because it's not on VisitScotland's lists. The tourist board uses **star awards**, from one to five, which are supposed to reflect the quality of welcome, service and hospitality – though you can be sure that anywhere that doesn't have all en-suite rooms, stick a TV in every room, have matching fabrics or provide a trouser press will be marked down. Bear in mind that in the Highlands and Islands many places are only open for the **summer season**, roughly from Easter to October; you'll always find somewhere to stay outside this period, but the choice may be limited.

Hotels come in all shapes and sizes. At the upper end of the market, they can be huge country houses and converted castles offering a very exclusive and opulent experience. Most will have a licensed bar and offer both breakfast and dinner, and often lunch as well. Making a bit of a comeback are **inns** (in other words, pubs), or their modern equivalent, "restaurants with rooms". These will often only have a handful of rooms but their emphasis on creating an all-round convivial atmosphere, as well as serving up top-quality food in a dinner, bed and breakfast package, often makes them worth seeking out.

Guesthouses and **B&Bs** offer the widest and most diverse range of accommodation. VisitScotland uses the term "guesthouse" for a commercial venture that has four or more rooms, at least some of which are en suite, reserving "B&B" for a predominantly private

Accommodation price codes

Throughout this book, accommodation prices have been graded with the **codes** below, corresponding to the cost of the least expensive double room in high season. The bulk of our recommendations fall in categories ❷ to ❺; those in the highest categories are limited to places that are especially attractive. Bear in mind that many of the chain hotels slash their tariffs at the weekend, and that a cheaper establishment may also have a selection of more expensive rooms. Price codes are not given for **campsites**, most of which charge less than £10 per person. Almost all **hostels** and **bunkhouses** charge between £8 and £15 per person per night; the few exceptions to this rule have their prices quoted in the review.

❶ Under £40	❹ £60–69	❼ £110–149
❷ £40–49	❺ £70–89	❽ £150–199
❸ £50–59	❻ £90–109	❾ Over £200

family home that has only a few rooms to let. In reality, however, the different names reflect the pretensions of the owners and the cost of the rooms more than differences in service: in general, guesthouses cost more than B&Bs. Having said that, there's often a great deal of overlap: a small hotel might be indistinguishable in price and quality from an upmarket guesthouse, while a modest guesthouse might be surpassed in terms of service and price by a superbly run B&B. While some guesthouses and B&Bs can seem stuck in a time warp with garish fabrics, mismatching furniture, gawdy trinkets and insipid pictures, others make the most of compensating features such as a great location, an insight into the local way of life, and advice about what's worth seeing in the area. The majority now offer **en-suite** toilets and showers, although often the conviviality of a communal lounge has been sacrificed to the practice of putting intrusive TVs in every room, along with the ubiquitous mini-kettle and basket containing sachets of instant coffee and long-life milk.

At the bottom end of the **price scale** (though not necessarily the quality scale), B&Bs tend to charge £40–50 for a double room, while guesthouse prices can be £70 or more. Hotels, on the other hand, will rarely charge less than £50 a double, with £70 more like the average; an established, award-winning hotel might charge anything between £110 and £150.

Many B&Bs, even the pricier ones, have only a few rooms, so **advance booking** is recommended, especially in the Islands – most places now have a website and/or email. You might also want to book in for dinner, bed and breakfast (not to mention packed lunch), as many islands have limited, or no, eating and drinking options. Most **tourist offices** will help you find accommodation, either by offering you a brochure listing the local options, or by booking a room directly, for which they normally charge a flat fee or a percentage which is then deducted from your first night's bill. If you take advantage of this service, it's worth being clear as to what kind of place you'd prefer, as the tourist office quite often selects for you randomly across the whole range of their membership. The majority of tourist offices also operate a "Book-a-Bed-Ahead" service, whereby you can reserve accommodation in your next port of call for a fee of £3 per booking.

Hostels

There's an ever-increasing number of **hostels** in the Highlands and Islands to cater for travellers – youthful or otherwise – who are unable or unwilling to pay the often exorbitant rates charged by hotels, guesthouses and B&Bs. Many hostels are well equipped, clean and comfortable, sometimes offering doubles and even singles as well as dormitory accommodation. Others concentrate more on keeping the price as low as possible, simply providing a roof over your head and a few basic facilities. Whatever type of hostel you stay in, expect to pay £8–15 per night.

There are eighty or so "official" hostels run by the **Scottish Youth Hostels Association**

(ⓣ0870/155 3255, ⓦwww.syha.org.uk), referred to throughout the guide as "SYHA hostels". While these places often occupy handsome buildings, and have moved a considerable way from the ethic of former days (when you had to perform chores before leaving), many retain an institutionalized air about them. Bunk-bed accommodation in single-sex dormitories, lights out before midnight and no smoking/no alcohol policies are the norm outside the big cities. Breakfast is not normally included in the price, though most hostels have self-catering facilities.

In order to stay in an SYHA hostel, you must be a member of one of the hostelling organizations affiliated to **Hostelling International** (**HI**). If you aren't a member in your home country, you can join at any SYHA hostel for a £6 fee. You can also choose to pay the fee in £1 instalments over your first six nights, meaning that you can avoid the full whack if you end up staying only a couple of nights in hostels. **Advance booking** is recommended, and just about essential at Easter, Christmas and from May to August. You can book by post, phone and sometimes fax, and your bed will be held until 6pm on the day of arrival. If you have a credit card, you can book beds as far as six months in advance via the SYHA website or over the phone.

The Gatliff Hebridean Hostels Trust or **GHHT** (ⓦwww.gatliff.org.uk) is allied to the SYHA that rents out very simple croft accommodation in the Western Isles. Accommodation is basic, and you can't book ahead, but it's unlikely you'll be turned away. Elsewhere in the Highlands and Islands, these places tend to be known as **bothies** or **bunkhouses**, and are usually independently run. In Shetland, camping böds, operated by the **Shetland Amenity Trust** (ⓦwww.camping-bods.co.uk), offer similarly plain accommodation: you need all your usual camping equipment to stay at one (except, of course, a tent). For more details about Gatliff hostels and camping böds, see the relevant chapters in the guide.

Many **independent hostels** now compete with the SYHA hostels. These are usually laid-back places with no membership, fewer rules, mixed dorms and no curfew, housed in buildings ranging from croft houses to converted churches. These are detailed in the annually updated **Independent Hostel Guide** (ⓦwww.independenthostelguide.co.uk). Many of them are also affiliated to the **Independent Backpackers Hostels of Scotland** (ⓦwww.hostel-scotland.co.uk), which has a programme of inspection and lists members in their free "Blue Guide".

Camping and self-catering

One option for campers is to head for one of the hundreds of official **caravan and camping parks** around Scotland, most of which are open from April to October. The most expensive sites, which charge about £10 to pitch a tent, are usually well equipped, with shops, a restaurant, a bar and, occasionally, sports facilities. Most of these, however, are principally aimed at caravans, trailers and motorhomes, and generally don't offer the tranquil atmosphere and independence those travelling with a tent are seeking.

That said, informal sites of the kind **tent campers** relish do exist, and are described throughout this guide, though they are few and far between. Many hostels allow camping, and farmers will usually let folk camp on their land for free or for a nominal sum. Scotland's relaxed trespass law allows you the freedom to **camp wild** in open country, though most outdoor enthusiasts who make use of this emphasize the importance of being discreet and responsible, ensuring that you camp well away from private residences, livestock and cultivated land, and that you remove all signs of your presence when you leave.

The great majority of **caravans** are permanently moored nose-to-tail in the vicinity of some of Scotland's finest scenery; others are positioned singly in back gardens or amidst farmland. Some can be booked for self-catering and, with prices hovering around £100 a week, this can work out as one of the cheapest options if you're travelling with kids in tow.

If you're planning to do a lot of camping at official camping and caravanning sites, it might be worthwhile joining the Camping and Caravanning Club (ⓣ024/7669 4995, ⓦwww.campingandcaravanningclub.co.uk).

Membership costs around £35 and entitles you to pay only a per-person fee, not a pitch fee, at CCC sites. Those coming from abroad can get the same benefits by buying an international camping carnet, available from home motoring organizations or a CCC equivalent.

Self-catering

A **self-catering** cottage or apartment is a good way to cut down on costs. In most cases, however, and particularly during summer, the minimum period of let is a week, and therefore isn't a valid option if you're aiming to tour round the country. The least you can expect to pay in the high season is around £200 per week for a place sleeping four, but something special – such as a well-sited coastal cottage – might cost two or three times that amount. Such is the number and variety of self-catering places on offer that we've mentioned only a few in the guide; the prices given are weekly summer rates, which tend to fall dramatically out of season. A good source of information is VisitScotland's self-catering guide, updated annually and listing over 1200 properties.

Country Holidays ⓣ0870/078 1200, from overseas 01282/846137, ⓦwww.country-holidays.co.uk. Hundreds of reasonably priced properties all over Scotland.

Ecosse Unique ⓣ01835/870779, ⓦwww.uniquescotland.com. Carefully selected cottages across mainland Scotland, plus a few of the Inner Hebrides.

Forest Holidays ⓣ0131/314 6100, ⓦwww.forestholidays.co.uk. Purpose-built cabins sleeping five or six people, in beautiful woodland areas in Strathyre near Callander.

Highland Hideaways ⓣ01631/563901, ⓦwww.highlandhideaways.co.uk. A range of self-catering properties, mainly in Argyll and its islands, which range from a former bank in Oban to a converted boathouse on Loch Awe.

Landmark Trust ⓣ01628/825925, ⓦwww.landmarktrust.org.uk. A very select number of unforgettable, upmarket historical properties in Scotland; first, however, you must buy the brochure (£11, refundable on first booking).

Mackay's Agency ⓣ0870/429 5359, ⓦwww.mackays-self-catering.co.uk. A whole range of properties in every corner of Scotland (except Shetland), from chalets and town apartments to remote stone-built cottages.

National Trust for Scotland ⓣ0131/243 9331, ⓦwww.nts.org.uk. The NTS lets around forty of its converted historic cottages and houses.

Scottish Country Cottages ⓣ0870/078 1100, ⓦwww.scottish-country-cottages.co.uk. Superior cottages with lots of character scattered across the Scottish mainland, plus Skye and Mull.

Scottish Holiday Cottages ⓣ01463/224707, ⓦwww.scottish-holiday-cottages.co.uk. Fifty or so properties mainly in the Highlands and Islands; everything from castles to bothies.

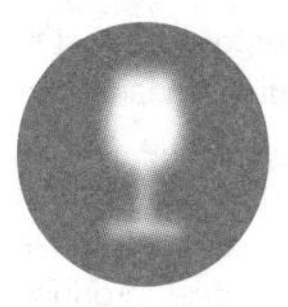

Eating and drinking

The remoteness of some areas in the Highlands and Islands will inevitably restrict your eating and drinking patterns and choices. When you're on the road, it's often a good idea to plan meal locations ahead as you might find serving times restrictive or popular restaurants booked out, particularly in summer. Stocking up on picnic food from a good deli is also worthwhile, particularly as good picnic spots are almost always likely to outnumber good restaurants. However, as we've hinted elsewhere (see the "Scottish food and drink" colour section and "Recipes" in Contexts), the quality of what's available both in restaurants and delis may often exceed visitors' expectations.

Breakfast

In most hotels and B&Bs you'll be offered a **Scottish breakfast**, similar to its English counterpart of sausage, bacon and egg, but typically with the addition of local favourites such as black pudding (blood sausage) and potato scones. Porridge is another likely option, and fish in the form of kippers, smoked haddock or even kedgeree are now part of more imaginative menus. Scotland's staple drink, like England's, is **tea**, made from dubious teabags and drunk strong and with milk, though **coffee** is just as readily available everywhere. However, while designer coffee shops are now a familiar feature in the cities, and decent coffee is available in more and more places across the country, execrable versions of espressos and cappuccinos, as well as instant coffee, are still all too familiar.

Lunches and snacks

The most common lunchtime fare in Scotland remains the **sandwich**, sometimes home-made but increasingly bought from a takeaway. A bowl or cup of hearty **soup** is a typical accompaniment, particularly in the winter months. A **pub lunch** is often an attractive alternative, particularly if you're on the road. Bar menus generally have a standard line-up of filling but unambitious options including soup, filled sandwiches, scampi and chips or steak pie and chips, with vegetarians in particular suffering from a paucity of choice. Having said that, some bar food is very satisfying, with freshly prepared, filling food that equals the à la carte dishes served in the adjacent hotel restaurant. In fact, pubs or hotel bars are among the cheapest options when it comes to eating out – indeed, in the smallest villages these might be your only option.

Restaurants are often, though not always, open at lunchtimes. They tend to be less busy and generally offer a shorter menu compared with their evening service, which can make for a more pleasant and less expensive experience, particularly in the higher-end restaurants.

For morning or afternoon snacks, as well as light lunches, **tearooms** are still at least as common a feature of tourist attractions and villages as latte-serving cafés; it's generally not advisable to go into a tearoom with high expectations, though you may often find decent home-baking.

As for **fast food**, fish and chips is as popular as in England and chip shops, or **chippies**, abound, the best often found in coastal towns within sight of the fishing boats tied up in harbour. Deep-fried battered fish is the standard choice – when served with chips it's known as a "fish supper", even if eaten at lunchtime – though everything from hamburgers to haggis suppers is normally on offer, all deep-fried, of course. Scotland is even credited with inventing the **deep-fried Mars bar** (a caramel-chocolate bar coated in batter and fried in fat) as the definitive badge of a nation with the worst heart-disease statistics in Europe.

Evening meals

If you're travelling in remoter parts of the Highlands and Islands, or planning to stay at a B&B or guesthouse located in the countryside, it's always worth asking for advice about nearby options for your evening meal. Many B&Bs and guesthouses will cook you dinner, but you must book ahead and indicate any dietary requirements, as they're unlikely to be able to offer a great deal of choice.

In general, however, eating out in the evening means heading for a **restaurant**, pub or hotel bar. Standards vary enormously, but Scotland has an ever-increasing number of top-class chefs producing superb dishes with a Scottish slant that certainly rival their English and European counterparts. Small, independent restaurants using good quality local produce and carving out a local reputation are found in many parts of Scotland, not just the big cities, and are well worth seeking out. Less predictable are hotel restaurants, including those which serve non-residents. Some have the budget to employ talented chefs, but in others the food can be very ordinary despite the highfaluting descriptions on the à la carte menu.

There's no doubt that, as with the rest of the UK, eating out in Scotland is expensive. Our restaurant listings include a mix of high-quality and budget establishments. To help give an idea of costs, each place we've reviewed is placed in one of three **price categories**: inexpensive (under £10 per person for a standard two courses, excluding alcohol), moderate (£10–20) or expensive (£20–30). **Wine** in restaurants is marked up strongly, so you'll often pay £15 for a bottle selling for £5 in the shops; house wines generally start around the £10 mark.

Food shopping

When it comes to buying food, most Scots get the majority of their supplies from supermarkets, but the upsurge in interest in sourcing good-quality produce means that you're increasingly likely to come across good delis, farm shops and specialist **food shops** around Scotland. Many of these make a point of stocking local produce alongside imported delicacies, as well as organic fruit and veg, specialist drinks such as locally brewed beer, freshly baked bread and sandwiches and other snacks for take-away. Look out too for **farmers' markets** (Ⓦ www.scottishfarmersmarkets.co.uk), which take place on Saturday and Sunday mornings in town squares or other public spaces; local farmers and small producers from pig farmers to cheese-makers and small smokeries set up stalls to sell their specialist lines.

Scotland is notorious for its sweet tooth, and **cakes and puddings** are taken very seriously. Bakers with extensive displays of iced buns, cakes and cream-filled pastries are a typical feature of any Scottish high street, while home-made shortbread, scones or tablet (a hard, crystalline form of fudge) are considered great treats.

Drinking

As in the rest of Britain, Scottish **pubs**, which originated as travellers' hostelries and coaching inns, are the main social focal points of any community. Pubs in Scotland vary hugely, from old-fashioned inns with open fires and a convivial atmosphere to raucous theme pubs with jukeboxes and satellite TV. Out in the islands, pubs are few and far between, with most drinking taking place in the local hotel bar. In some of the larger towns, by contrast, traditional pubs are being supplemented by modern café-bars.

The national drink is **whisky** (for more on which, see the *Scottish food and drink* colour section), though you might not guess

Meal times

Unfortunately, in many parts of Scotland outside the cities, inflexible and unenlightened **meal times** mean that you have to keep a close eye on your watch if you don't want to miss out on eating. B&Bs and hotels will frequently serve breakfast only until 9am at the latest, lunch is usually over by 2pm, and, despite the long summer evenings, pub and hotel kitchens often stop serving dinner as early as 8pm.

it from the prodigious amount of "alcopops" (bottles of sweet fruit drinks laced with vodka or gin) and ready-made mixers consumed on a Friday and Saturday night. Similarly, Scotland produces some exceptionally good cask-conditioned real ales, yet lager is much more popular. In our listings, we've tended to steer folk towards those pubs that take their beer and whisky seriously, rather than those hell-bent on getting their punters drunk as quickly as possible.

Scotland has very relaxed licensing laws compared with the traditional pattern in England and Wales. Pub **opening hours** are generally 11am to 11pm, but some places stay open later. Whatever time the pub closes, "last orders" will be called by the bar staff about fifteen minutes before closing time to allow a bit of "drinking-up time". In general, you have to be sixteen to enter a pub unaccompanied, though some places are easy about having folk with children in, or have special family rooms and beer gardens where the kids can run free. The legal drinking age is eighteen.

Communications

Communications are pretty modern and reliable in the Highlands and Islands, although out in the more remote parts of the region you'll encounter difficulties: mobile phone coverage may well be patchy, though you'll usually find a payphone within easy walking distance. Internet cafés exist in some towns, and you'll often find computer access available in rural shops, hostels and guesthouses. It's worth keeping in mind that many public libraries offer free Internet access.

Post

Most **post offices** are open Monday to Friday 9am to 5.30pm and Saturday 9am to 12.30 or 1pm. However, in small communities you'll find sub-post offices operating out of a shop, shed, or even a private house. In remote regions, the post office will often keep extremely restricted hours, even if the shop in which the post office counter is located keeps longer hours.

Stamps can be bought at post-office counters, from vending machines outside, or from many newsagents and shops. Domestic UK postage costs 30p first-class, 21p second-class. Airmail letters are 42p to Europe, 47p worldwide, or you can buy a pre-stamped air letter for 42p (from post offices only). Postcard stamps cost 42p to Europe, 47p worldwide. Royal Mail can answer all enquiries (Ⓣ0845/774 0740, Ⓦwww.royalmail.com).

Phones

If you're travelling from overseas and want to use your **mobile phone** in Scotland, it's worth checking before you leave that it's compatible with the UK's GSM (Ⓦwww.gsmworld.com) technology. To save yourself money and hassle, it might be worth simply picking up a "pay-as-you-go" mobile once you've arrived in Britain. All the main UK networks cover Scotland; in general terms Vodaphone has the most reliable signal in the Highlands and Islands, though you'll still find places in among the hills or out on the islands where there's no signal at all. If you're in a rural area and having trouble with reception, simply ask a local where the strongest signals are found nearby.

Most public **payphones** in Scotland are operated by British Telecom, known as BT (Ⓦwww.bt.com) and, in towns, at least, are widespread. Many BT payphones take all

Useful numbers

UK operator ⓣ100
British Telecom directory enquiries ⓣ118 500
Emergency number: ⓣ999 or ⓣ112
International operator ⓣ155
International directory enquiries ⓣ118 505

coins from 10p upwards, with a minimum charge of 30p. Most accept credit and debit cards.

Throughout this guide, every phone number is prefixed by the area code, which is separated from the number by an oblique slash. You don't have to dial the code if you're calling from within the same area, unless you're using a mobile phone. Any number with the prefix ⓣ0800 is toll-free; ⓣ0845 numbers are charged at local rate; ⓣ0870 at long-distance rate; and all ⓣ09 numbers at expensive premium rates. Most numbers beginning ⓣ07 are mobile phones and should be dialled in full.

Phoning home

To the US or Canada ⓣ001 + area code + number.
To Ireland ⓣ00353 + area code without the zero + number.
To Australia ⓣ0061 + area code without the zero + number.
To New Zealand ⓣ0064 + area code without the zero + number.

Telephone charge cards

One of the most convenient ways of phoning home from abroad is with a **telephone charge card**. Using a toll-free UK access code and a PIN number, you can make calls from most hotel, public and private phones that will be charged to your own account. While rates are always cheaper from a residential phone at off-peak rates, that's normally not an option when you're travelling. You may be able to use the card to minimize hotel phone surcharges, but don't depend on it. However, the benefit of calling cards is mainly one of convenience, as rates aren't necessarily cheaper than calling from a public phone while abroad and can't compete with discounted off-peak times many local phone companies offer. But since most major charge cards are free to obtain, it's certainly worth getting one at least for emergencies.

AT&T, MCI, Sprint, Canada Direct and other **North American** long-distance companies all enable their customers to make credit-card calls while overseas. Call your company's customer service line to find out what the toll-free access code is in the UK. Calls made from Scotland will automatically be billed to your home number, although you can also choose to make a collect call via the operator. Elsewhere, charge cards such as Telstra Telecard or Optus Calling Card in **Australia**, and Telecom NZ's Calling Card in **New Zealand**, can be used to make calls abroad, which are charged back to a domestic account or credit card. Apply to Telstra (ⓣ1800/038 000), Optus (ⓣ1300/300 937), or Telecom NZ (ⓣ04/801 9000).

Calling Scotland from abroad

First dial your **international access code** (00 from Ireland and New Zealand; 011 from the US and Canada; 0011 from Australia), followed by **44** for the UK, then the Scottish area code minus its initial zero, then the number.

Email

An easy way to keep in touch while travelling is to sign up for a free web **email** address that can be accessed from anywhere, for example YahooMail (ⓦwww.yahoo.com) or Hotmail (ⓦwww.hotmail.com). Once you've set up an account, you can use these sites to pick up and send mail from any café, library or hotel with Internet access. Internet cafés are most common in the big cities and towns, though a few are now appearing around the Highlands and Islands. That said, the tourist office should be able to tell you of somewhere you can get online for a nominal fee; sometimes the tourist office itself will have an access point, and public libraries often provide cheap or free access. The site ⓦwww.kropla.com gives useful details of how to plug your laptop in when abroad, phone country codes around the world, and information about electrical systems in different countries.

Opening hours, public holidays and admission fees

Traditional shop hours in Scotland are Monday to Saturday 9am to 5.30 or 6pm. Increasingly, you'll find places that stay open on Sundays and large supermarkets typically stay open till 8pm and sometimes as late as 10pm. However, there are still plenty of towns and villages in the Highlands and Islands where you'll find precious little open on a Sunday, with many small towns also retaining an "early closing day" – often Wednesday – when shops close at 1pm.

Many shops and businesses will close on **bank (or public) holidays**, although few tourist-related businesses will observe these, particularly in the summer months. The main holidays include January 1 and 2; the Friday before Easter; the first and last Monday in May; Christmas Day (Dec 25); and Boxing Day (Dec 26); in addition, all Scottish towns and cities have one-day holidays in spring, summer and autumn – dates vary from place to place but normally fall on a Monday.

Admission to museums and monuments

The **tourist season** in the Highlands and Islands runs from Easter to October, and outside this period many indoor attractions are shut, though ruins, parks and gardens are normally accessible year-round. We've given full details of opening hours and adult admission charges in the guide. Note that last entrance can be an hour (or more) before the published closing time.

Many of Scotland's most treasured sights – from castles and country houses to islands, gardens and tracts of protected landscape – come under the control of the privately run **National Trust for Scotland** (Ⓣ0131/243 9300, Ⓦwww.nts.org.uk) or the state-run **Historic Scotland** (Ⓣ0131/668 8800, Ⓦwww.historic-scotland.gov.uk); we've quoted "**NTS**" or "**HS**" respectively for each site reviewed in this guide. Both organizations charge an admission fee for most places, and these can be quite high, especially for the more grandiose NTS estates. If you think you'll be visiting more than half-a-dozen NTS properties, or more than a dozen HS ones, it's worth taking annual membership, which costs £34 (HS) or £35 (NTS), and allows free admission to their properties. In addition, both the NTS and HS offer short-term passes: the **National Trust Discovery Ticket**, which costs from £12 for an adult ticket lasting three days to £42 for a family ticket lasting fourteen days; and the HS's **Explorer Pass**, ranging from £17 for three days to £56 for a family for ten days.

A lot of Scottish stately homes remain in the hands of the landed gentry, who tend to charge around £5–7 for admission to edited highlights of their domain. Many other old buildings, albeit rarely the most momentous structures, are owned by local authorities; admission is often cheap and sometimes free.

The majority of fee-charging attractions in Scotland give 25–50 percent **reductions** for senior citizens, the unemployed, full-time students and children under 16, with under-5s being admitted free almost everywhere. Proof of age will be required in most cases. Family tickets are often available if you're travelling with kids.

A further option, open to non-UK citizens only, is the **Great British Heritage Pass** (Ⓦwww.visitbritain.com/heritagepass), which gives free entry to some 600 sites throughout Britain, including NTS or HS sites and many which are not run by either organization. Costing from £39/US$75 for seven days, it can be purchased online, through most travel agents at home, on arrival at any large UK airport, or from major tourist offices across Britain.

The media

When you're up in the Highlands and Islands it's easy to dismiss the UK's so-called "national media" as London-based and London-biased. Most locals prefer to listen to Scottish radio programmes, read local newspapers, and – albeit to a much lesser extent – watch Scottish TV.

The press

Provincial dailies are more widely read in the Highlands and Islands than anywhere else in Britain. The biggest-selling regional title is Aberdeen's famously parochial *Press and Journal*, which has special editions for each area of the Highlands and Islands. For an insight into local life, there's the staid **weekly** *Oban Times*. More entertaining and more radical is the campaigning weekly *West Highland Free Press*, printed on Skye. All carry articles in Gaelic as well as English. Further north, the lively *Shetland Times* and Orkney's sedate *Orcadian* are essential weekly reads for anyone living in or just visiting those islands.

Given the distances in the Highlands and Islands, you shouldn't always expect to find a daily newspaper arriving with your early morning cup of tea, though unless you're in a particularly remote spot or bad weather is affecting transport links, the papers are normally around by mid-morning. Most easily obtained are **Scottish newspapers.** Principal among these are the two serious dailies – *The Scotsman*, based in Edinburgh, and *The Herald*, published in Glasgow, both of them offering reasonable coverage of the current issues affecting Scotland, along with British and foreign news, sport, arts and lifestyle pages. You should also be able to find a selection of popular tabloids, including Scotland's biggest-selling daily, the down-market *Daily Record*, along with various national titles – from the reactionary *Sun* to the vaguely left-leaning *Daily Mirror* – which appear in specific Scottish editions.

Many **Sunday newspapers** published in London have a Scottish edition, although again Scotland has its own offerings – *Scotland on Sunday*, from the *Scotsman* stable, and the *Sunday Herald*, complementing its eponymous daily. Far more fun and widely read is the anachronistic *Sunday Post*, published by Dundee's mighty D.C. Thomson publishing group. It's a wholesome paper, uniquely Scottish, and has changed little since the 1950s, since which time its two long-running cartoon strips, *Oor Wullie* and *The Broons*, have acquired something of a cult status.

Scottish **monthlies** include the *Scottish Field*, a lowbrow version of England's *Tatler*, and the widely read *Scots Magazine*, an old-fashioned middle-of-the-road publication which promotes family values and lots of good fresh air.

TV and radio

In Scotland there are five main 'terrestrial' **TV channels** (i.e not specifically produced for cable or satellite services): the state-owned BBC1 and BBC2, and the independent commercial channels, ITV1, Channel 4 and Five. The **BBC** continues to maintain its worldwide reputation for in-house quality productions, ranging from expensive costume dramas to intelligent documentaries, split between the avowedly mainstream BBC1 and the more rarefied fare of BBC2. **BBC Scotland** produces news programmes and a regular crop of local-interest lifestyle, current affairs, drama and comedy shows which slot into the schedules of both BBC channels. In northwest Scotland there are also regular programmes broadcast by BBC Gaelic TV. The commercial channel **ITV1** is divided between three regional companies: the populist STV, which is received in most of southern Scotland and parts of the West Highlands; Grampian, based in Aberdeen; and Border, which transmits from Carlisle.

These are complemented by the quirkier **Channel 4**, and eclectic **Five**, which still can't be received in some parts of Scotland. A plethora of satellite and cable channels is also available; the dominant force is Rupert Murdoch's **Sky** organization, which offers, among other channels, blanket sports coverage that plays wall-to-wall in pubs the length of the country.

The **BBC radio** network broadcasts six main channels in Scotland, five of which are national stations originating largely from London: Radio 1 (pop and dance music), Radio 2 (mainstream pop, rock and light music), Radio 3 (classical music), Radio 4 (current affairs, arts and drama) and Radio 5 Live (sports, news and live discussions and phone-ins). Only the award-winning BBC Radio Scotland offers a Scottish perspective on news, politics, arts, music, travel and sport, as well as providing a Gaelic network in the Highlands with local programmes in Shetland and Orkney.

A web of local **commercial radio** stations covers the country, mostly mixing rock and pop music with news bulletins, but a few tiny community-based stations such as Lochbroom FM in Ullapool – famed for its daily midge count – transmit documentaries and discussions on local issues. The most populated areas of Scotland also receive UK-wide commercial stations such as Classic FM, Virgin Radio and TalkSport. With a special DAB **digital radio**, you can get all the main stations crackle-free along with a range of other digital-only ones, most of which can also be picked up on cable or satellite-equipped TVs.

Some Scottish radio stations

BBC Radio Scotland 92–95FM, 810MW Ⓦ www.bbc.co.uk/radioscotland. Nationwide news, sport, music, current affairs and arts.

BBC Radio nan Gaidheal 103.4FM Ⓦ www.bbc.co.uk/scotland/alba. An opt-out from Radio Scotland, with Gaelic-language news, phone-ins and great traditional music shows.

Lochbroom FM 102.2 & 96.8FM Ⓦ www.lochbroomfm.co.uk. One of Britain's smallest radio stations, broadcasting to the northwest coast from Ullapool.

Moray Firth 97.4FM, 1107MW Ⓦ www.mfr.co.uk. Mainstream rock and pop for the youth of the Inverness area.

Nevis Radio 96.6 & 102.3FM Ⓦ www.nevisradio.co.uk. From the slopes of Ben Nevis, all that's happening in Fort William and its surrounds.

SIBC 96.2FM Ⓦ www.sibc.co.uk. Shetland's own independent station.

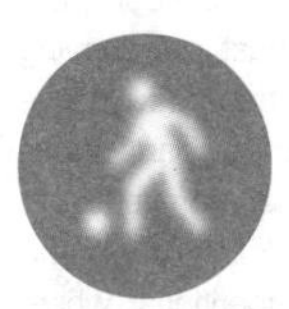

Events and spectator sports

There's a huge range of organized annual events on offer in the Highlands and Islands, reflecting both vibrant contemporary culture and well-marketed heritage. Many tourists will want to home straight in on Highland Games and other tartan-draped theatricals, but it's worth bearing in mind that there's more to Scotland than this: numerous regional celebrations perpetuate ancient customs, and traditional music is still alive and kicking in places such as the Hebrides and the Northern Isles. A few of the smaller, more obscure events, particularly those with a pagan bent, are in no way created for tourists, and indeed do not always welcome the casual visitor; local tourist offices always have full information.

The tourist board publishes a weighty list of all Scottish events twice a year: it's free and you can get it from area tourist offices or direct from their headquarters. Full details are at Ⓦ www.visitscotland.com.

Events calendar

Dec 31 and Jan 1 Hogmanay and Ne'er Day. Traditionally more important to the Scots than Christmas, known for the custom of "first-footing", when groups of revellers troop into neighbours' houses at midnight bearing gifts. More popular these days are huge and highly organized street parties in the larger towns.

Jan 1 Kirkwall Boys' and Men's Ba' Games, Orkney: mass, drunken football game through the streets of the town, with the castle and the harbour the respective goals. As a grand finale the players jump into the harbour.

Last Tues in Jan Up-Helly-Aa, Lerwick, Shetland Ⓦwww.visitshetland.com/uphellyaa. Norse fire festival culminating in the burning of a specially built Viking longship. Visitors will need an invite from one of the locals, or you can buy a ticket for the Town Hall celebrations.

Jan 25 Burns Night. Scots worldwide get stuck into haggis, whisky and vowel-grinding poetry to commemorate Scotland's greatest poet, Robert Burns.

Feb Scottish Curling Championship Ⓦwww.royalcaledoniancurlingclub.org, held in a different (indoor) venue each year.

Early March Braemar Telemark Festival, the biggest ski event in Scotland.

April Shetland Folk Festival (Ⓦwww.shetlandfolkfestival.com). One of the liveliest and most entertaining of Scotland's round of folk festivals.

April 6 Tartan Day. Over-hyped celebration of ancestry by North Americans of Scottish descent on the anniversary of the Declaration of Arbroath in 1320. Ignored by most Scots in Scotland, other than journalists.

Early May Spirit of Speyside Scotch Whisky Festival (Ⓦwww.spiritofspeyside.com), and Isle of Bute Jazz Festival.

Late May Atholl Highlanders Parade at Blair Castle, Perthshire Ⓦwww.blair-castle.co.uk. The annual parade and inspection of Britain's last private army by their colonel-in-chief, the Duke of Atholl, on the eve of their Highland Games.

June Beginning of the Highland Games season across the Highlands, northeast and Argyll. St Magnus Festival, Orkney (Ⓦwww.stmagnusfestival.com) is a classical and folk music, drama, dance and literature festival celebrating the islands.

July Mendelssohn on Mull Festival of classical music. Hebridean Celtic Festival, Stornoway (Ⓦwww.hebceltfest.com).

Late July West Highland Week. A week of yacht racing and shore-based partying which moves en masse from Oban to Tobermory and back again.

Early Sept Ben Nevis Race (for amateurs). Held on the first weekend in the month, running to the top of Scotland's highest mountain and back again. Also Shinty Camanachd Cup Final Ⓦwww.shinty.com. The climax of the season for Scotland's own stick-and-ball game, normally held in one of the main Highland towns.

Late Sept The year's second Spirit of Speyside Whisky Festival (Ⓦwww.spiritofspeyside.com).

Oct The National Mod, held over nine days at a different venue each year. It's a competitive festival and features all aspects of Gaelic performing arts (Ⓦwww.the-mod.co.uk).

Late Oct Glenfiddich Piping Championships. Held at Blair Atholl for the world's top ten solo pipers (Ⓦwww.thepipingcentre.co.uk).

Nov 30 St Andrew's Day. Celebrating Scotland's patron saint.

Highland Games

Despite their name, **Highland Games** are held all over Scotland between May and mid-September, varying in size and the range of events they offer, and although the most famous are at Oban, Cowal and especially Braemar, the smaller events are often more fun. The Games probably originated in the fourteenth century as a means of recruiting the best fighting men for the clan chiefs, and were popularized by Queen Victoria to encourage the traditional dress, music, games and dance of the Highlands; indeed, various royals still attend the Games at Braemar. The most distinctive events are known as the **heavies** – tossing the caber, putting the stone, and tossing the weight over the bar – all of which require prodigious strength and skill. Tossing the caber is the most spectacular, when the athlete must run carrying an entire tree trunk and attempt to heave it end over end in a perfect, elegant throw. Just as important as the sporting events are the **piping** competitions – for individuals and bands – and **dancing** competitions, where you'll see girls as young as three tripping the quick, intricate steps of dances such as the Highland Fling.

Football

While **football** (soccer) is far and away Scotland's most popular spectator sport, its popularity in the Highlands and Islands is a little muted in comparison to the game's following in the Central Belt of the country. The strength of the Highland League (Ⓦwww.highlandfootballleague.com) was, however, recognized in the mid-1990s with the inclusion of Inverness Caledonian Thistle and Ross County in the Scottish Leagues. Inverness Caledonian Thistle have subsequently risen to Scotland's top division, the Scottish Premier League, and as a result the Caledonian Stadium on the shores of the Moray Firth regularly hosts the multi-national stars of Glasgow and Edinburgh's top teams. The **season** begins in early August and ends in mid-May, with most matches taking place on Saturday afternoons at 3pm, and also often on Sunday afternoons and Wednesday evenings. Tickets for Scottish League games are around the £10 mark, but less for Highland League fixtures.

Shinty

Played throughout Scotland but with particular strongholds in the West Highlands and Strathspey, the game of **shinty** (the Gaelic *sinteag* means "leap") arrived from Ireland around 1500 years ago. Until the latter part of the nineteenth century, it was played on an informal basis and teams from neighbouring villages had to come to an agreement about rules before matches could begin. However, in 1893, the **Camanachd Association** – the Gaelic word for shinty is *camanachd* – was set up to formalize the rules, and the first Camanachd Cup Final was held in Inverness in 1896. Today, shinty is still fairly close to its Irish roots in the game of hurling, with each team having twelve players including a goalkeeper, and each goal counting for a point. The game, which bears similarities to an undisciplined version of hockey, isn't for the faint-hearted; it's played at a furious pace, with sticks – called camans or cammocks – flying alarmingly in all directions. Support is enthusiastic and vocal, and if you're in the Highlands during the season, which has recently changed to run from March to October to avoid the perils of midwinter, it's well worth trying to catch a match: check with tourist offices or the local paper to see if there are any local fixtures, or go to ⓦwww.shinty.com.

Curling

The one winter sport which enjoys a strong Scottish identity is **curling** (ⓦwww.royalcaledoniancurlingclub.org), occasionally still played on a frozen outdoor rink, or "pond", though most commonly these days seen in indoor ice rinks. The game, which involves gently sliding smooth-bottomed 18kg discs of granite called "stones" across the ice towards a target circle, is said to have been invented in Scotland, although its earliest representation is in a sixteenth-century Flemish painting. Played by two teams of four, it's a highly tactical and skilful sport, enlivened by team-members using brushes to furiously sweep the ice in front of a moving stone to help it travel further and straighter. The sport received a massive boost in profile when a team from Scotland won gold in the women's event at the 2002 Winter Olympics. If you're interested in seeing curling being played, go along to the ice rink in places such as Perth, Pitlochry or Inverness on a winter evening.

Outdoor pursuits

A large number of visitors to the Highlands and Islands come specifically to enjoy a landscape that, weather conditions apart, is perfect for outdoor pursuits at all levels of fitness and ambition. Recent legislation enacted by the Scottish Parliament has ensured a responsible right of access to hills, mountains, lochs and rivers at a level unrivalled elsewhere in the British Isles. Within striking distance of Glasgow and Edinburgh are two national parks, remote wilderness areas and vast stretches of glens, moorland, and spectacular mountains, which in winter can provide testing climbing and even some skiing. Throughout the country, numerous marked trails range from hour-long ambles to coast-to-coast treks. With thousands of miles of rugged but beautiful coastline Scotland can also be a paradise for the sea-kayaker, sailor and surfer.

Walking and climbing

The whole of the Highlands and Islands offers superb opportunities for **hill walking**, from knobbly island peaks to majestic Highland mountain ranges.

There are several **Long-Distance Footpaths** (LDPs) which take days to walk, though you can, of course, just do a section of them. Well signposted and increasingly well supported, with a range of services from bunkhouses to baggage-carrying services, these are a great way to respond to the challenge of walking in Scotland without taking on the dizzy heights. The best known is the **West Highland Way**, a 95-mile hike from Glasgow to Fort William via Loch Lomond and Glen Coe. Between Fort William and Inverness there's the 73-mile **Great Glen Way**, while the gentler **Speyside Way**, in the northeast, leads for 84 miles from the Cairngorms to the Moray Firth past a number of whisky distilleries. It's even possible to hike over 200 miles from Fort William to Cape Wrath along the "Cape Wrath Trail". The green signposts of the Scottish Rights of Way Society point to these and many other cross-country routes, which include "drove roads", long-established paths through the hills along which clansmen once led their cattle to or from markets held in the larger settlements.

The Highlands provide Scotland's main **climbing** areas, with many challenging peaks as well as great hill walks. There are 284 mountains over 3000ft (914m) in Scotland, known as **Munros** (see p.58) after the man who first classified them: many walkers "collect" or "bag" them, and it's possible to chalk up several in a day. Serious climbers will probably head for **Glen Coe** or **Torridon**, which offer difficult routes in spectacular surroundings. These and some of the other finest Highland areas (Lawers, Kintail, West Affric) are in the ownership of the National Trust for Scotland, while Bla Bheinn on Skye and Ladhar Bheinn (Knoydart) are John Muir Trust (Ⓦwww.jmt.org) properties; both permit year-round access. Elsewhere, the freedom to roam responsibly in wilder parts of the countryside allows extensive walking and climbing, although there may be restricted access during lambing (dogs are particularly unwelcome in April and May) and deerstalking seasons (1 July to 20 October). It's worthwhile picking up the booklet *Hill Phones* published by the Mountaineering Council of Scotland (MCofS), which provides walkers with detailed information for hiking safely during the stalking season.

Numerous short walks (from accessible towns and villages) and several major walks are touched on in this guide. However, you should only use our notes as general outlines, and always in conjunction with a good map. Where possible, we have given details of the best maps to use – in most cases one of the excellent and reliable Ordnance Survey (OS) series (see p.38),

Midges and ticks

Despite being only just over a millimetre long, and enjoying a life span on the wing of just a few weeks, the **midge** (*Culicoides*) – a tiny biting fly prevalent in the Highlands (mainly the west coast) and Islands – is considered to be second only to the weather as the major deterrent to tourism in Scotland. There are more than thirty varieties of midge, though only half of these bite humans. Ninety percent of all midge bites are down to the female *Culicoides impunctatus* or Highland midge (the male does not bite), which has two sets of jaws sporting twenty teeth each; she needs a good meal of blood in order to produce eggs.

These persistent creatures can be a nuisance, but some people also have a violent allergic reaction to midge bites. The easiest way to avoid midges is to visit in the winter, since they only appear between April and October. Midges also favour still, damp, overcast or shady conditions and are at their meanest around sunrise and sunset, when clouds of them can descend on an otherwise idyllic spot. Direct sunlight, heavy rain, noise and smoke discourage them to some degree, though wind is the most effective means of dispersing them. If they appear, cover up exposed skin and get your hands on some kind of **repellent**. Recommendations include Autan, Eureka, Jungle Formula (widely available from pharmacists) and the herbal remedy citronella. An alternative to repellents for protecting your face, especially if you're walking or camping, is a midge net, a little like a bee-keeper's hat; although they appear ridiculous at first, you're unlikely to care as long as they work. The latest deployment in the battle against the midge is a gas-powered machine called a "midge magnet" which sucks up the wee beasties and is supposed to be able to clear up to an acre; each unit costs £300 and upwards, but there's been a healthy take-up by pubs with beer gardens and campsite owners.

If you're anywhere near woodland, there's a possibility you may receive attention from **ticks**, tiny parasites no bigger than a pin head, which bury themselves into your skin. Removing ticks by dabbing them with alcohol, butter or oil is now discouraged; the medically favoured way of extracting them is to pull them out carefully with small tweezers. There is a very slight risk of catching some very nasty diseases, such as encephalitis, from ticks. If flu-like symptoms persist after a tick bite, you should see a doctor immediately.

usually available from local tourist offices, which can also supply other local maps, safety advice and guidebooks/leaflets. Among the many **guidebooks** available for serious walking and climbing, the SMC's series of District Guides offers blow-by-blow accounts of climbs written by professional mountaineers; for other good walking guides see the "Books" section of Contexts (p.526). These, as well as a wide range of maps, are available from most of the good **outdoor stores** scattered around the country (most notably Tiso and Nevisport), which are normally staffed by experienced climbers and walkers, and are a good source of candid advice about the equipment you'll need and favourite hiking areas.

For relatively gentle walking in the company of knowledgeable locals, look out for **guided walks** offered by rangers at many National Trust for Scotland, Forest Enterprise and Scottish Natural Heritage sites. These often focus on local wildlife, and the best can lead to some special sightings, such as a badger's sett or a golden eagle's eyrie.

Useful contacts for walkers

General information

Ⓦ **www.hillphones.info** Daily information for hill walkers about deerstalking activities (July–Oct).

Ⓦ **www.outdooraccess-scotland.com** All you need to know about the Scottish Outdoor Access Code.

Ⓦ **www.walkingwild.com** Smart official site from VisitScotland, with good lists of operators, information

Munro bagging

In recent years hill walking in Scotland has become synonymous with "**Munro-bagging**". Munros are the hills in Scotland over 3000ft in height, defined by a list first drawn up by Sir Hugh Munro in 1891. You "bag" a Munro by walking to the top of it, and once you've bagged all 284 you can call yourself a Munroist and let your chiropodist retire in peace.

Sir Hugh's challenge is an enticing one: 3000ft is high enough to be an impressive ascent but not so high that it's for expert mountaineers only. Nor do you need to aim to do them all – at heart, Munro-bagging is simply about appreciating the great Scottish outdoors. Munros are found across the Highlands and on two of the islands (Mull and Skye), and include many of the more famous and attractive mountains in Scotland.

However, while the Munros by definition include all the highest hills in Scotland, there isn't any quality control, and one of the loudest arguments of critics of the game (known by some as "de-baggers") is that Munro-seekers will plod up a boring pudding of a mountain because it's 3000ft high and ignore one nearby that's much more pleasing but a few feet short of the requisite mark.

Judgement is also required in a few other ways. You do have to be properly equipped, and be aware what you're tackling before you set off – the hills are hazardous in all seasons. But for many the trickiest part of Munro-bagging is getting to grips with the Gaelic pronunciation of some of the hill names. Pronunciation guides are available, but it's often difficult to believe they're not winding you up. However, as it's bad form not to be able to tell the folk in the pub at the end of the day which hills you've just ticked off, beginners are encouraged to stick to peaks such as Ben Vane or Ben More, and resign themselves to the fact that Beinn Fhionnlaidh (pronounced "Byn Yoonly") and Beinn an Dothaidh (pronounced "Byn an Daw-ee") are for the really experienced.

If you want some training, you can set about the **Corbetts** (hills between 2500 and 2999ft) or even the **Donalds** (lowland hills above 2000ft).

on long-distance footpaths and details of deerstalking restrictions and contact phone numbers.

ⓦ **www.walkscotland.com** Comprehensive site with lists of specific walks, mountain routes, news, gear and even a few shaggy dog stories.

Clubs and associations

Mountain Bothies Association ⓦ www.mountainbothies.org.uk. Charity dedicated to maintaining huts and shelters in the Scottish Highlands.

Mountaineering Council of Scotland ⓦ www.mountaineering-scotland.org.uk. The representative body for all mountain activities, with detailed information on access and conservation issues.

Ramblers Association Scotland ⓦ www.ramblers.org.uk/scotland. Campaigning organization with network of local groups and news on events and issues.

Scottish Mountaineering Club ⓦ www.smc.org.uk. The largest mountaineering club in the country. A well-respected organization which publishes a popular series of mountain guidebooks.

Tour operators

Adventure Scotland ⓣ 0870/240 2676, ⓦ www.adventure-scotland.com. Highly experienced operator providing a wide range of courses and one-day adventures, from telemark skiing to climbing, kayaking and biking.

Bespoke Highland Tours ⓣ 01854/612628, ⓦ www.scotland-inverness.co.uk/bht-main.htm. Offers 5–12 day self-led treks with a detailed itinerary along routes such as the Great Glen Way and West Highland Way, organizing baggage transfer and accommodation en route.

Cape Adventure International ⓣ 01971/521006, ⓦ www.capeventure.co.uk. From wonderfully remote northwest location near Kinlochbervie, Cape offers day, weekend and week-long individual and family adventure experiences including wilderness trips, climbing, sea-kayaking and walking.

C-N-Do Scotland ⓣ 01786/445703, ⓦ www.cndoscotland.com. Pride themselves on offering the "best walking holidays in Scotland". Munro-bagging for novices and experts with qualified leaders.

G2 Outdoor ⓣ07946 285612, ⓦwww.g2outdoor.co.uk. Personable, highly qualified adventure specialists offering gorge, hill walking, rock climbing, canoeing and Telemark skiing in the Cairngorms.
Glenmore Lodge ⓣ01479/861256, ⓦwww.glenmorelodge.org.uk. Based within the Cairngorm National Park, and internationally recognized as a leader in outdoor skills and leadership training.
Hebridean Pursuits ⓣ01631/563594, ⓦwww.hebrideanpursuits.com. Established in 1989, offering hill walking, winter and rock climbing in the Hebrides and West Highlands, as well as surf kayaking and sailing trips.
North-West Frontiers ⓣ01854/612628, ⓦwww.nwfrontiers.com. Based in Ullapool, offering guided mountain trips with small groups in the northwest Highlands, Hebrides and even the Shetland Islands. April to Oct.
Rua Reidh Lighthouse Holidays ⓣ01445/771263, ⓦwww.ruareidh.co.uk. From its spectacular northwest location, this company offers guided walks highlighting wildlife; rock climbing courses; and week-long treks into the Torridon hills.
Vertical Descents ⓣ01855/821593, ⓦwww.activities-scotland.com. Ideally located for the Glencoe and Fort William area, activities and courses include canyoning, funyakking (a type of rafting) and climbing.
Walkabout Scotland ⓣ0131/661 7168, ⓦwww.walkaboutscotland.com. A great way to get a taste of hiking in Scotland, from exploring Ben Lomond to the Isle of Arran. Guided day and weekend walking from Edinburgh with all transport included.
Wilderness Scotland ⓣ0131/625 6635, ⓦwww.wildernessscotland.com. Guided, self-guided and customized adventure holidays and trips that focus on exploring the remote and unspoiled parts of Scotland by foot, sea-kayak, yacht and even ski mountaineering.

Winter sports

Skiing and **snowboarding** take place at five different locations in Scotland – Glen Coe, the Nevis Range beside Fort William, Glen Shee, the Lecht and the Cairngorms near Aviemore – but as none of these can offer anything even vaguely approaching an alpine experience it is as well not to come with high expectations. The resorts can go for months on end through the winter with insufficient snow, then see the approach roads suddenly made impassable by a glut of the stuff. That said, when the conditions are good, Scotland's ski resorts have piste and off-piste areas that will challenge even the most accomplished alpine skier or Telemarker.

All the resorts have a combination of chairlifts and tows – Nevis Range boasts a gondola while Cairngorm has a new funicular railway – and equipment can always be rented nearby. Expect to pay up to £25 for a standard day pass at one of the resorts, or £100 for a five-day pass; rental of skis or snowboard comes in at around £16 per day, with reductions for multiday rents. At weekends, in good weather with decent snow, expect the slopes to be packed with trippers from the Central Belt, although midweek usually sees queues dissolving and the experience improving

Staying safe in the hills

Beguiling though the hills of Scotland can seem, you have to be properly prepared before venturing out onto them. Due to rapid weather changes, the mountains are potentially extremely dangerous and should be treated with respect. Every year, in every season, climbers and walkers lose their lives in the Scottish hills.

- Wear sturdy, ankle-supporting footwear and wear or carry with you warm, brightly coloured and waterproof layered clothing, even for what appears to be an easy expedition in apparently settled weather.
- Always carry adequate maps, a compass (which you should know how to use), food, water and a whistle. If it's sunny, make sure you use sun protection.
- Check out a weather forecast before you go. If the weather looks as if it's closing in, get down from the mountain fast.
- Always leave word with someone of your route and what time you expect to return, and remember to contact the person again to let them know that you are back.
- In an emergency, call mountain rescue on ⓣ999.

immeasurably. For a comprehensive rundown of all the resorts, including ticket prices and conditions, visit the Snowsports link at Ⓦwww.scottishsport.co.uk.

Telemark skiing is becoming increasingly popular in Scotland whilst Nordic or cross-country skiing is enjoyed by a minority of winter-sports enthusiasts. The hills around Braemar near Glenshee and the Cairngorms are particularly popular for these pursuits and with reasonable snow-cover can be a great way to free yourself from the crowds on the pistes and explore the Highland wilderness made pristine by the snow. However, the demands on personal fitness and navigational abilities are higher. The best way to get started or to find out about good routes is to contact an outdoor pursuits company that offers Telemark or Nordic rental and instruction; in the Aviemore area try Adventure Scotland (Ⓦwww.adventure-scotland.com, Ⓣ0870/240 2676) or G2 Outdoor Ⓣ07946 285612, Ⓦwww.g2outdoor.co.uk). Also check out the Huntly Nordic and Outdoor Centre in Huntly, Aberdeenshire (Ⓣ01466/794428, Ⓦwww.huntly.net/hnoc). For equipment hire, sales or advice contact Braemar and Cairngorm Mountain Sports (Ⓦ www.braemarmountainsports.com, Ⓣ01339/741242 or 01479/810903).

Pony trekking and horse riding

There are approximately sixty **pony trekking** or **riding centres** across the country, all of them approved by either the Trekking and Riding Society of Scotland (TRSS, Ⓦwww.ridinginscotland.com) or the British Horse Society (BHS, Ⓦwww.bhs.org.uk). As a rule, any centre will offer the option of pony trekking (leisurely ambles on sure-footed Highland ponies), **hacking** (for experienced riders who want to go for a short ride at a fastish pace) and **trail riding** (over longer distances, for riders who feel secure at a canter). In addition, a network of special horse-and-rider B&Bs means you can ride independently on your own horse.

Cycling and mountain biking

Scotland is widely regarded as one of the world's top five mountain bike destinations, with hundreds of miles of off-road, wild terrain that will challenge the most accomplished cyclist. A growing number of dedicated mountain-bike centres such as those in Laggan in Strathspey or on the Black Isle, provide marked trails designed for every level of rider. The types of experience possible in Scotland range from a white-knuckle ride down the World Cup downhill course in Fort William to leisurely rides along the forest trails of the Loch Lomond and Trossachs National Park.

However, despite the popularity of pedal power, **road cyclists** are still treated with notorious neglect by many motorists and by the people who plan the country's traffic systems. Very few of Scotland's towns have proper cycle routes, but if you're hellbent on tackling the congestion, pollution and aggression of city traffic, get a **helmet** and a secure **lock**: cycle theft in Scotland is an organized and highly effective racket. The rural back roads are infinitely more enjoyable, particularly in the gentle landscape of the south and east of the country, where generally amiable gradients and a decent density of pubs and B&Bs make it a perfect area for cycle touring. Out in the countryside, it can be tricky finding spare parts: anything more complex than inner tubes or tyres can be very hard to come by.

Mountain biking is increasingly popular in the Highland walking areas, but riders should always keep to tracks where a right to cycle exists, and pass walkers at considerate speeds. Footpaths, unless otherwise marked, are for pedestrian use only. The Forestry Commission has recently established 1150 miles of excellent off-road routes all over the country, which are detailed in numerous "Cycling in the Forest" leaflets (available from Forest Enterprise offices listed below, and from most tourist offices). Waymarked and graded, these are best attempted on mountain bikes with multi-gears, although many of the gentler routes may be tackled on hybrid and standard road cycles.

A number of **long-distance routes**, including The Great Glen Cycle Way, have been established in Scotland over the last few years using a combination of specially built cycle paths and quieter back roads.

Up-to-date information on these, along with a list of publications detailing specific routes, is available from the cyclists' campaigning group Sustrans (Ⓦwww.sustrans.co.uk), as well as some of the organizations listed on this page.

Transporting your bike by train is a good way of getting to the interesting parts of Scotland without a lot of hard pedalling. Bikes are allowed free on mainline GNER and Virgin Intercity trains, as well as ScotRail trains, but always subject to available space, so you should book the space as far in advance as possible. Bus and coach companies, including National Express and Scottish Citylink, rarely accept cycles unless they are dismantled and boxed; one notable exception is the excellent service operated by Dearman Coaches (Ⓣ01349 883585, Ⓦwww.timdearmancoaches.co.uk) between Inverness and Durness via Ullapool (May–Sept 1 daily Mon–Sat).

Bike rental is available in some towns and many tourist centres though many such outlets still provide only the most basic model of mountain bike which is OK for a brief spin, but not for any serious touring. Expect to pay £10–20 per day; most rental outlets also give good discounts for multi-day rents.

Another option is to shell out on a **cycling holiday package**. These take many forms, but generally include transport of your luggage to each stop, pre-booked accommodation, detailed route instructions, a packed lunch and backup support. Most holiday companies offer some budget packages, with hostel instead of hotel or B&B accommodation, and the cost-cutting option of using your own bike. A week-long tour starts at around £250 per person for hostel accommodation, including bike rental. Britain's biggest cycling organization, the **Cyclists' Touring Club** or CTC, provides lists of tour operators and rental outlets in Scotland, and supplies members with touring and technical advice, as well as insurance. As a general introduction, Visit Scotland's "Cycling in Scotland" brochure is worth getting hold of, with practical advice and suggestions for itineraries around the country. The tourist board's "Cyclists Welcome" scheme gives guesthouses and B&Bs around the country a chance to advertise that they're cyclist-friendly, and able to provide such things as an overnight laundry service, a late meal or a packed lunch.

Useful contacts for cyclists

Cyclists' Touring Club Ⓣ01483/417217, Ⓦwww.ctc.org.uk. Britain's largest cycling organization, and a good source of general advice; their handbook has lists of cyclist-friendly B&Bs and cafés in Scotland. Annual membership £25.

Forest Enterprise Ⓣ0845/367 3787, Ⓦwww.forestry.gov.uk. The best source of information on Scotland's extensive network of forest trails – ideal for mountain biking at all levels of ability.

Full On Adventure Ⓦwww.fullonadventure.co.uk. Among its many offerings, provides fully guided mountain-bike tours of Highland trails.

Nevis Range Ⓣ01397/705825, Ⓦwww.nevisrange.co.uk. The home of Scotland's World Cup downhill and cross-country tracks (May–Oct) outside Fort William with a gondola lift system and bike hire.

North Sea Cycle Route Ⓦwww.northsea-cycle.com. Signposted 6000-km route round seven countries fringing the North Sea, including 1242km in Scotland along the east coast and in Orkney and Shetland.

Scottish Cycle Safaris Ⓣ0131/556 5560, Ⓦwww.cyclescotland.co.uk. Fully organized cycle tours at all levels, from camping to country house hotels, with a good range of bikes available for rent, from tandems to children's bikes.

Scottish Cycling Ⓣ0131/652 0187, Ⓦwww.scuonline.org. Produces an annual handbook and calendar of cycling events (£8) – mainly road, mountain-bike and track races.

Spokes Ⓣ0131/313 2114, Ⓦwww.spokes.org.uk. Active Edinburgh cycle campaign group with plenty of good links and news on events and cycle-friendly developments.

WolfTrax Mountain Bike Centre Ⓣ01528/544786. Based just outside Laggan, this year-round mountain-bike facility has miles of trail for every level of rider and a café to revive weary legs.

Air sports

Scotland has its fair share of fine sunny days, when it's hard to beat scanning majestic mountain peaks, lochs and endless forests from the air. Whether you're a willing novice or an expert **paraglider** or **sky-diver**, there are centres just outside Glasgow, Edinburgh and Perth which will cater to your needs. There are also opportunities to try **ballooning**, **gliding** and **hang-gliding**.

British Gliding Association ⓣ0116/2531051, ⓦwww.gliding.co.uk. Governing body for gliding enthusiasts and schools across the UK with information on where to find many clubs in Scotland.
Flying Fever ⓣ01770/820292, ⓦwww.flyingfever.net. Based on the stunning Isle of Arran, 40 miles southwest of Glasgow. Fully accredited paragliding courses and tandem flights can be enjoyed for as little as £95.
Skydive Strathallan ⓣ01764/662572, ⓦwww.skydivestrathallan.co.uk. Located just outside Auchterarder, this non-commercial school operates year-round. tandem jumps from around £200.

Golf

There are over 400 **golf courses** in Scotland, where the game is less elitist and more accessible than anywhere else in the world. Golf in its present form took shape in the fifteenth century on the dunes of Scotland's east coast, and today you'll find some of the oldest courses in the world on these early coastal sites, known as "links". It's often possible just to turn up and play, though it's sensible to phone ahead; booking is essential for the championship courses.

Public courses are owned by the local council, while private courses belong to a club. You can play on both – occasionally the **private** courses require that you are a member of another club, and the odd one asks for introductions from a member, but these rules are often waived for overseas visitors and all you need to do is pay a one-off fee. The cost of a round will set you back around £10 on a small nine-hole course, and more than £40 for many good quality eighteen-hole courses. In remote areas the courses are sometimes unstaffed; just put the admission fee into the honesty box. Most courses have **resident professionals** who give lessons, and some rent equipment at reasonable rates. Renting a caddie car will add a few pounds to the cost.

Scotland's **championship** courses, which often host the British Open, are renowned for their immaculately kept greens and challenging holes and, though they're favoured by serious players, anybody with a valid handicap certificate can enjoy them. The most famous course in the Highland region is at **Royal Dornoch** in Sutherland (ⓦwww.royaldornoch.com; £72), and, while many of the courses found elsewhere in the Highlands and Islands aren't nearly as well groomed, they often make up for this with spectacular settings and quirky features. ⓦwww.scotlands-golf-courses.com has contacts, scorecards and maps of signature holes for most main courses.

If you're coming to Scotland primarily to play golf, it's worth shelling out for a ticket which gives you access to a number of courses in any one region. There's more information at ⓦwww.scottishgolf.com and ⓦwww.visitscotland.com/golf.

Fishing

Scotland's serrated coastline – with the deep sea lochs of the west, the firths of the east and the myriad offshore islands – encompasses the full gamut of marine habitats, and ranks among the cleanest coasts in Europe. Combine this with an abundance of **salmon**, **sea trout**, **brown trout** and **pike**, acres of open space and easy access, and you have an angler's paradise. Whether you're into game-, coarse- or sea-fishing, you'll be spoilt for choice. The only element in short supply is company; Scotland may offer wonderful fishing, but its unpolluted, open waters don't attract anywhere near the numbers of anglers you'd expect.

No licence is needed to fish in Scotland, although nearly all land is privately owned and its fishing therefore controlled by a landlord/lady or his/her agent. Permission, however, is usually easy to obtain: **permits** can be bought without hassle at local tackle shops, or through fishing clubs in the area – if in doubt, ask at the nearest tourist office. The other thing to bear in mind is that salmon and sea trout have strict **seasons**, which vary between districts but usually stretch from late August to late February. Once again, individual tourist offices will know the precise dates, or you can try to get hold of Visit Scotland's excellent "Fish Scotland" brochure (ⓦwww.visitscotland.com/outdoor). More useful information and contacts can be found at the comprehensive website ⓦwww.fishing-uk-scotland.com.

Sailing, windsurfing and kite-surfing

Like many of the outdoor sports on offer in the Highlands and Islands, the opportunities for **sailing** are outstanding, tainted only by the unreliability of the weather. While you'll find keen sailors all over Scotland, the protected Firth of Clyde sees the most concentrated activity through the year, though in the summer months the scenery, lack of crowds and sheer explorability of the entire west coast are in their element. Yacht racing is popular in the Clyde, while **cruising** is the main focus on the west coast, commonly starting from a number of marinas in the area between Crinan and Oban which usually take in a mix of islands and sheltered sea lochs. Even in summer, however, the full force of North Atlantic weather can be felt, and changeable conditions combined with tricky tides and rocky shores demand good sailing and navigational skills.

Yacht charters are available from various ports, either bareboat or in yachts run by a skipper and crew; contact Sail Scotland (Ⓦwww.sailscotland.co.uk) or the Associated Scottish Yacht Charters (Ⓦwww.asyc.co.uk).

An alternative way to enjoy Scotland under sail is to spend a week at one of the **sailing schools** around the country. These normally offer either dinghy-based tuition from a single onshore centre, or a cruise on a larger boat mixing instruction with exploration. Many sailing schools, as well as small boat rental operations dotted along the coast, will **rent** sailing dinghies by the hour or day, giving you the chance to get out on the water and, in the right circumstances, set off for a nearby island or headland for a picnic. These companies will also often rent **windsurfers**, though the chilly water means you'll always need a wet suit. Scotland's top spot for windsurfing is Tiree, reportedly one of the windiest islands in the UK. An unusually flat island, its stunning white beaches and huge surf have drawn kite-surfers and windsurfers alike for over a decade. For comprehensive details on water-sport options on the island, visit Ⓦwww.tireewindsurfing.com.

Beaches

Scotland is ringed by fine **beaches** and bays, most of them clean and many of them deserted even in high summer – perhaps hardly surprising, given the bracing winds and chilly water which often accompany them. Few people come to Scotland for a beach holiday, but it's worth sampling a beach or two, even if you keep your sweater on. A rash of slightly melancholy seaside towns lie within easy reach of Glasgow, while on the east coast the relatively low cliffs and miles of sandy beaches are ideal for walking. On a hot day, people do swim, though more frequently on the Gulf Stream-washed west coast than the east. Bizarrely enough, given the low temperature of the water, the beaches in the northeast are beginning to figure on surfers' itineraries, attracting enthusiasts from all over Europe (see below). Perhaps the most beautiful beaches of all are to be found on Scotland's islands: endless, isolated stretches that on a sunny day can be paradise.

The Marine Conservation Society (Ⓦwww.goodbeachguide.co.uk) monitors bathing-water quality, and in 2005 recommended fifty beaches in Scotland.

Sea-kayaking and surfing

Despite its chilly waters, Scotland's 6000 miles of coastline teems with marine fauna and flora whilst the sea-borne explorer will delight in finding innumerable skerries, sea-caves and remote white-sand beaches. Scotland may not have the sunshine of Hawaii, but there are dozens of locations where turquoise-blue waters can be found. It's therefore no surprise that the waters of the Outer Hebrides in particular are regarded as world class for **sea-kayaking** and in recent years this activity has witnessed an explosion in popularity. There are a host of operators offering sea-kayaking lessons and expeditions across the country. Canoe Scotland (Ⓦwww.canoescotland.org.uk) can offer useful advice whilst Glenmore Lodge (Ⓦwww.glenmorelodge.org.uk), Canoe Hebrides (Ⓦwww.canoehebrides.com) and Skyak Adventures (Ⓦwww.skyakadventures.com) are highly reputable for either training or tours.

In addition to sea-kayaking, Scotland is fast gaining a reputation as a **surfing** destination, with a good selection of excellent quality breaks. Indeed, there are world-class waves to be found. **Thurso** is the number-one spot on the **north coast**, and boasts one of the finest reef breaks in Europe. In addition, the rest of this coastline – Sango Bay, Torrisdale,

Farr Bay and Armadale, in particular – offers waves comparable to those in Hawaii, Australia and Indonesia. However, Scotland's northern coastline lies on the same latitude as Alaska and Iceland, so the water temperature is very low: even in midsummer it rarely exceeds 15°C, and in winter can drop to as low as 7°C. The one vital accessory, therefore, is a good wet suit (ideally a 5/3mm steamer), wet-suit boots and, outside summer, gloves and a hood, too.

In addition Thurso, the beaches of the **Moray Firth** also offer a good North Sea swell. Of the islands, the west coasts of **Coll**, **Tiree** and **Islay** get great swell from the Atlantic and have good beaches, while the spectacular west coast offers numerous possibilities, in particular one of Britain's most isolated beaches, **Sandwood Bay**. In the Outer Hebrides, the best breaks are along the northern coastline of **Lewis**, near Carloway and Bragar. Many of the best spots are surrounded by stunning scenery, and you'd be unlucky to encounter another surfer for miles. However, this isolation – combined with the cold water and big, powerful waves – means that, in general, much of Scottish surf is best left to **experienced surfers**. If you're a beginner, get local advice before you go in, and be aware of your limitations.

The popularity of surfing in Scotland has led to a spate of **surf shops** opening up, all of which rent or sell equipment, and provide good information about the local breaks and events on the surfing scene (Clan Surf can also organize surfing lessons). Two further sources of information are *Surf UK* by *Rough Guide* author, Wayne "Alf" Alderson (Fernhurst Books; £13.95), with details on over 400 breaks around Britain, and the British Surfing Association (Ⓦwww.britsurf.co.uk).

Surf information, shops and schools

Boardwise 1146 Argyle St, Glasgow Ⓣ0870/750 4423; 4 Lady Lawson St, Edinburgh Ⓣ0870/750 4420. Surf gear, clothes and short-term rental.

Clan Surf 45 Hyndland St, Partick, Glasgow Ⓣ0141/339 6523. Combined surf, skate and snowboard shop. Lessons available.

ESP 5–7 Moss St, Elgin Ⓣ01343/550129. Sales and rental only.

Granite Reef 45 The Green, Aberdeen Ⓣ01224/252752. Sales, hire and lessons.

Thurso Surf Treehouse, Halkirk, Caithness Ⓣ01847/831866 or 0774/836 2397, Ⓦwww.thursosurf.com. Lessons, April–Sept.

Wild Diamond Watersports Isle of Tiree, Ⓣ0771/215 9205, Ⓦwww.tireewindsurfing.com. Instruction and hire for surfing, windsurfing, kite surfing and kayaking.

The best breaks in the Highlands and Islands

***Brimm's Ness** Five miles west of Thurso; p.307. A selection of reef breaks that pick up the smallest of swells.

Machrihanish Bay Mull of Kintyre; p.130. Four miles of beach breaks on one of Scotland's loneliest peninsulas.

Sandwood Bay A day's hike south of Cape Wrath in Sutherland; p.301. Beach breaks on one of the most scenic and remote shorelines in Britain, only accessible on foot.

***Thurso East** Just below the castle; p.307. One of the best right-hand reef breaks in Europe.

***Torrisdale Bay** Bettyhill, on the north coast of the Highlands; p.306. An excellent right-hand river-mouth break.

***Valtos** On the Uig peninsula, Lewis; p.379. A break on one of the Outer Hebrides' most exquisite shell-sand beaches.

**Experienced surfers only*

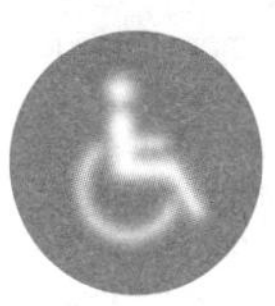

Travellers with specific needs

Travellers with disabilities

Scottish attitudes towards **travellers with disabilities** still lag behind advances towards independence made in North America and Australia. Access to many public buildings has improved recently, with recent legislation ensuring that all new buildings have appropriate facilities. It's worth keeping in mind, however, that installing ramps, lifts, wide doorways and disabled toilets is impossible or inappropriate in many of Scotland's older and historic buildings. Most trains in Scotland have wheelchair lifts and assistance is, in theory, available at all manned stations – for more, go to Ⓦwww.firstscotrail.com and click on "Special needs". Wheelchair users and blind or partially sighted people are automatically given 30–50 percent reductions on train fares, and people with other disabilities are eligible for the **Disabled Persons Railcard** (£14 per year; Ⓦwww.disabledpersons-railcard.co.uk), which gives a third off most tickets. There are no bus discounts for the disabled, and of the major **car-rental** firms only Hertz offers models with hand controls at the same rate as conventional vehicles, and even these are only available in the more expensive categories. It's the same story for **accommodation**, with modified suites for people with disabilities available only at higher-priced establishments and perhaps the odd B&B.

Contacts for travellers with disabilities

UK and Ireland

All Go Here Ⓣ01923/840 463, Ⓦwww.allgohere.com. Provides information on accommodation suitable for disabled travellers throughout the UK, including Northern Ireland.

Capability Scotland Ⓣ0131/313 5510, Ⓦwww.capability-scotland.org.uk. The leading disability organization in Scotland. A well-run, well-connected outfit covering all local disability issues and information.

Equal Adventure Developments Ⓣ01479/861372, Ⓦwww.equaladventure.co.uk. Specialist consultancy focussing on outdoor activities and adventure sports for disabled people. Based at Glenmore Lodge near Aviemore.

Holiday Care Ⓣ0845/124 9971; Ⓦwww.holidaycare.org.uk. Provides free lists of accessible accommodation in the UK. Information on financial help for holidays available.

Irish Wheelchair Association Ⓣ01/818 6400, Ⓦwww.iwa.ie. Useful information provided about travelling abroad with a wheelchair.

RADAR (Royal Association for Disability and Rehabilitation) Ⓣ020/7250 3222, Ⓦwww.radar.org.uk. A good source of advice on holidays and travel in the UK. They produce an annual holiday guide called Holidays in Britain and Ireland for £13 in the UK; £15 to Europe and £18 to other overseas destinations (includes postage), and have a dedicated accommodation website for Britain and Ireland, Ⓦwww.radarsearch.org.

Tripscope Ⓣ0845/758 5641, Ⓦwww.tripscope.org.uk. This registered charity provides a national telephone information service offering free advice on UK and international transport for those with a mobility problem.

North America

Access-Able Ⓦwww.access-able.com. Online resource for travellers with disabilities.

Directions Unlimited 123 Green Lane, Bedford Hills, NY 10507 Ⓣ1-800/533-5343 or 914/241-1700. Travel agency specializing in bookings for people with disabilities.

Mobility International USA 451 Broadway, Eugene, OR 97401 Ⓣ541/343-1284, Ⓦwww.miusa.org. Information and referral services, access guides, tours and exchange programmes. Annual membership $35 (includes quarterly newsletter).

Society for the Advancement of Travelers with Handicaps (SATH) 347 5th Ave, New York, NY 10016 Ⓣ212/447-7284, Ⓦwww.sath.org. Non-profit educational organization that has actively represented travellers with disabilities since 1976.

Wheels Up! Ⓣ1-888/38-WHEELS, Ⓦwww.wheelsup.com. Provides discounted airfare, tour and cruise prices for disabled travellers, also publishes a free monthly newsletter and has a comprehensive website.

Australia and New Zealand

ACROD (Australian Council for Rehabilitation of the Disabled) ⓣ02/6282 4333, ⓦwww.acrod.org.au. Provides lists of travel agencies and tour operators for people with disabilities.

Disabled Persons Assembly ⓣ04/801 9100, ⓦwww.dpa.org.nz. New Zealand resource centre with lists of travel agencies and tour operators for people with disabilities.

Senior travellers

Senior citizens, whether resident in the UK or not, are usually eligible for some kind of discount at sights all over Scotland, so it's always worth asking. Those aged sixty or over might also consider buying a **Senior Railcard** (ⓦwww.senior-railcard.co.uk), which costs £20 and gives a third off standard rail fares. On the coaches, Scottish Citylink have "Senior Special" fares on certain routes. For all sorts of services aimed at the 50-plus age group, including holidays, insurance and even a radio station, contact Saga (ⓣ0800/414525, ⓦwww.saga.co.uk).

Travelling with children

Scottish attitudes to those **travelling with children** can be discouraging, particularly if you've experienced the more indulgent approach of the French or Italians. Restaurateurs would basically prefer it if parents and carers left the kids at home. Inevitably, cafés and bistros are more likely than more formal restaurants to cater for kids by providing high chairs and other facilities. It's in these more relaxed establishments, too, that more enlightened children's menus are starting to appear. Pubs have traditionally had to obtain a special licence to admit children under 16 after a certain time (often 7pm), although these laws are currently being revised. Out in rural areas, particularly in the Islands, attitudes are much more relaxed, and the sight of kids in the hotel lounge bar not so unusual. However, most families with young children opt for self-catering cottages (see p.46) precisely to avoid the hassle of trying to eat out with kids. It's always worth asking about discounted "family tickets" when visiting any attractions or sight. If you're travelling on public transport, it's definitely worthwhile buying a **Family Railcard** (ⓦwww.family-railcard.co.uk), which gives you sixty percent off kids' fares and thirty percent off adult train fares.

Directory

Electricity The current is 240v AC. North American appliances need a transformer and adapter; Australasian appliances need only an adapter.

Gaelic In many areas of the Highlands and Hebrides, road signs are bilingual English–Gaelic. Throughout the guide, where appropriate, we've given the Gaelic translation (in italics and parentheses) the first time any village or island is mentioned, after which the English name is used. The main exception to this rule is in the Western Isles, where signposting is almost exclusively in Gaelic; we've reflected this by giving the Gaelic first and putting the English in parentheses, and thereafter using the Gaelic (except for the islands and ferry ports, which are more familiar in the English form they're given on ferry timetables).

Genealogy Many visitors to Scotland, particularly from North America and Commonwealth countries, have an interest in tracing family connections. Searches can involve days at registrars' offices looking through historical records or speculative wanderings through graveyards. The main official website relating to genealogy in Scotland is ⓦwww.scotlandspeople.gov.uk; you have to register and pay a small fee, but the database is one of the world's largest resources of genealogical information, with a searchable index of Scottish births (1553–1904), marriages (1553–1929) and deaths (1855–1954), as well as census data from 1871 to 1901.

Laundry Coin-operated laundries are found in nearly all large towns in the Highlands and Islands, and are open about twelve hours a day from Monday to Friday, less on weekends. A wash followed by a spin or tumble dry costs about £3; a "service wash" (having your laundry done for you in a few hours) costs about £2 extra. In the remoter regions of Scotland, you'll have to rely on hostel and campsite laundry facilities.

Smoking In 2005 the Scottish Parliament passed legislation that outlaws smoking in all enclosed public spaces. While smoking has been outlawed from just about all public buildings and on public transport for a number of years, in 2006 the ban was extended to all restaurants, bars, pubs and clubs. Breeches of the law will see fines imposed on anyone caught smoking and the proprietors of premises they are in. In effect, smokers are restricted to smoking outdoors or in private homes. Hotel owners may designate certain rooms as smoking bedrooms, but they are not obliged to do this.

Time From late October to late March, Scotland is on Greenwich Mean Time (GMT), which is five hours ahead of US Eastern Standard Time and ten hours behind Australian Eastern Standard Time. Over the summer, clocks go forward an hour for British Summer Time (BST).

Toilets Public loos are found at all train and bus stations and signposted on town high streets; a fee of 10p or 20p is sometimes charged.

Guide

Guide

1

Argyll

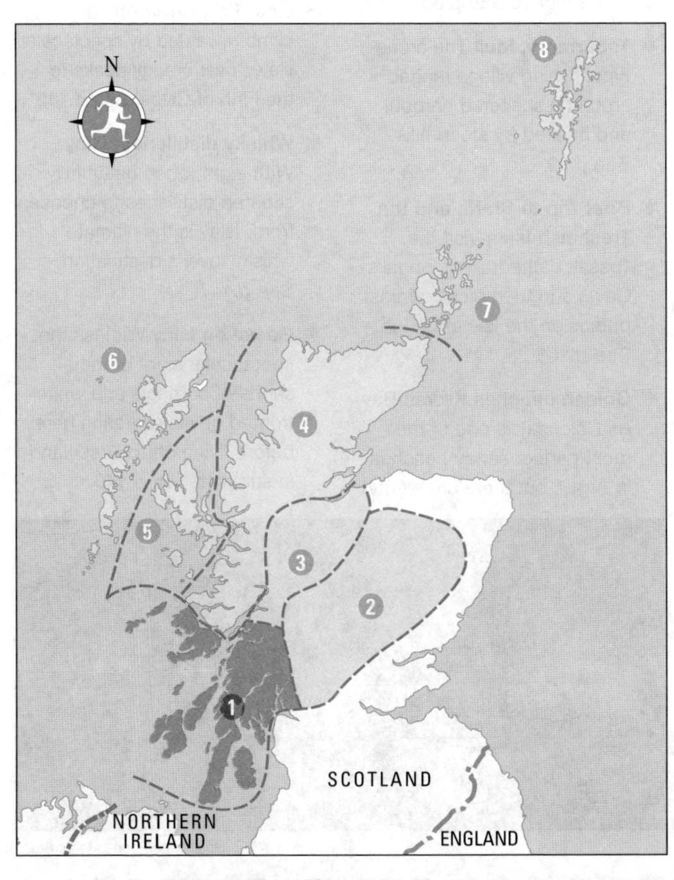

CHAPTER 1 Highlights

* **Loch Fyne Oyster Bar, Cairndow** Dine in or take away at Scotland's finest smokehouse and seafood outlet. See p.78
* **Mount Stuart, Bute** Architecturally overblown mansion set in the most beautiful grounds in the region. See p.85
* **Tobermory, Mull** The archetypal fishing village ranged around a sheltered harbour and backed by steep hills. See p.99
* **Boat trip to Staffa and the Treshnish Isles** Visit the "basalt cathedral" of Fingal's Cave, and then picnic amidst puffins on the Isle of Lunga. See p.105
* **Golden beaches** Kiloran Bay on Colonsay is one of the most perfect sandy beaches in Argyll, but there are plenty more on Islay, Coll and Tiree. See p.119
* **Isle of Gigha** The perfect island escape: sandy beaches, friendly folk and the azaleas of Achamore Gardens – you can even stay at the laird's house. See p.129
* **Goat Fell, Arran** An easy climb rewarded by spectacular views over craggy peaks to the Firth of Clyde. See p.142
* **Whisky distilleries, Islay** With eight, often beautifully situated distilleries to choose from, Islay is the ultimate whisky lover's destination. See p.147
* **Geese on Islay** Witness the spectacular sight of thousands of barnacle and white-fronted geese wintering here before flying off to Greenland in summer. See p.149

△ Horoscope Room, Mount Stuart

1

Argyll

Cut off for centuries from the rest of Scotland by the mountains and sea lochs that characterize the region, **Argyll** remains remote, its scatter of offshore islands forming part of the Inner Hebridean archipelago (the remaining Hebrides are dealt with in Chapters 5 and 6). Geographically as well as culturally, this is a transitional area between Highland and Lowland, boasting a rich variety of scenery, from lush, subtropical gardens warmed by the Gulf Stream to flat and treeless islands on the edge of the Atlantic. It's in the folds and twists of the countryside, the interplay of land and water and the views out to the islands that the strengths and beauties of mainland Argyll lie. The one area of man-made sights you shouldn't miss, however, is the cluster of **Celtic** and **prehistoric sites** near Kilmartin.

Overall, the population is tiny (less than 100,000); even **Oban**, Argyll's chief ferry port, has just eight thousand or so inhabitants, while the prettiest settlement, **Inveraray**, boasts only five hundred. Much of mainland Argyll comprises remote peninsulas separated by a series of long sea lochs. The first peninsula you come to from Glasgow is **Cowal**, cut off from the rest of Argyll by a series of mountains including the Arrochar Alps. Nestling in one of Cowal's sea lochs is the **Isle of Bute**, whose capital, Rothesay, is probably the most appealing of the old Clyde steamer resorts. **Kintyre**, the long finger of land that stretches south towards Ireland, is less visually dramatic than Cowal, though it does provide a stepping stone for several islands including Arran.

Arran, Scotland's most southerly big island – now strictly speaking part of North Ayrshire – is justifiably popular, with spectacular scenery ranging from granite peaks of the north to the Lowland pasture of the south. Of the Hebridean islands covered in this chapter, mountainous **Mull** is the most visited, though it is large enough to absorb the crowds, many of whom are only passing through en route to the tiny isle of **Iona**, a centre of Christian culture since the sixth century, or to **Tobermory**, the island's impossibly picturesque port (aka "Balamory"). **Islay**, best known for its distinctive malt whiskies, is fairly quiet even in the height of summer, as is neighbouring **Jura**, which offers excellent walking opportunities. And, for those seeking further solitude, there's the island of **Colonsay**, with its beautiful golden sands, and the windswept islands of **Tiree** and **Coll**, which also boast great beaches and enjoy more sunny days than anywhere else in Scotland.

The region's name derives from *Aragaidheal*, which translates as "Boundary of the Gaels", the Irish Celts who settled here in the fifth century AD, and whose **kingdom of Dalriada** embraced much of what is now Argyll. Known to the Romans as *Scotti* – hence "Scotland" – it was the Irish Celts who promoted Celtic Christianity, and whose Gaelic language eventually became the national

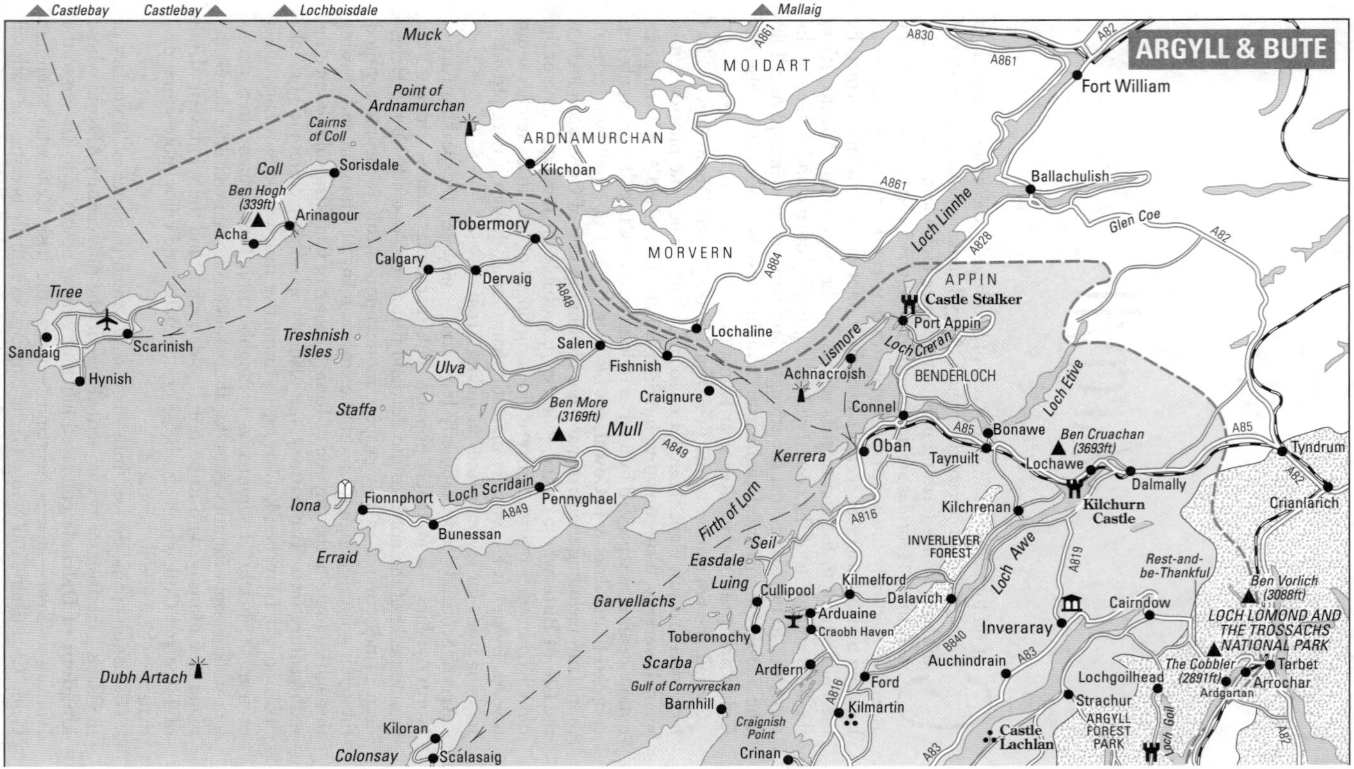

ARGYLL & BUTE

Castlebay
Castlebay
Lochboisdale
Mallaig
Muck
MOIDART
Fort William
Point of Ardnamurchan
Cairns of Coll
ARDNAMURCHAN
Kilchoan
Coll
Sorisdale
Ben Hogh (339ft)
Arinagour
Acha
Ballachulish
Glen Coe
Tobermory
MORVERN
Loch Linnhe
Calgary
Dervaig
APPIN
Castle Stalker
Port Appin
Tiree
Sandaig
Scarinish
Hynish
Treshnish Isles
Lochaline
Lismore
Loch Creran
Salen
Fishnish
Ulva
Achnacroish
BENDERLOCH
Loch Etive
Craignure
Staffa
Ben More (3169ft)
Mull
Connel
Bonawe
Ben Cruachan (3693ft)
Oban
Taynuilt
Lochawe
Tyndrum
Kerrera
Dalmally
Crianlarich
Kilchurn Castle
Iona
Fionnphort
Loch Scridain
Pennyghael
Kilchrenan
Bunessan
Firth of Lorn
Erraid
Seil
Easdale
INVERLIEVER FOREST
Loch Awe
Rest-and-be-Thankful
Luing
Cullipool
Kilmelford
Dalavich
Garvellachs
Arduaine
Craobh Haven
Cairndow
Ben Vorlich (3088ft)
Inveraray
LOCH LOMOND AND THE TROSSACHS NATIONAL PARK
Toberonochy
Scarba
Ardfern
Auchindrain
Lochgoilhead
The Cobbler (2891ft)
Tarbet
Arrochar
Ardgartan
Dubh Artach
Gulf of Corryvreckan
Ford
Strachur
Barnhill
Kilmartin
ARGYLL FOREST PARK
Loch Goil
Kiloran
Craignish Point
Castle Lachlan
Colonsay
Scalasaig
Crinan
A82
A830
A861
A828
A884
A848
A849
A85
A816
A819
B840
A83

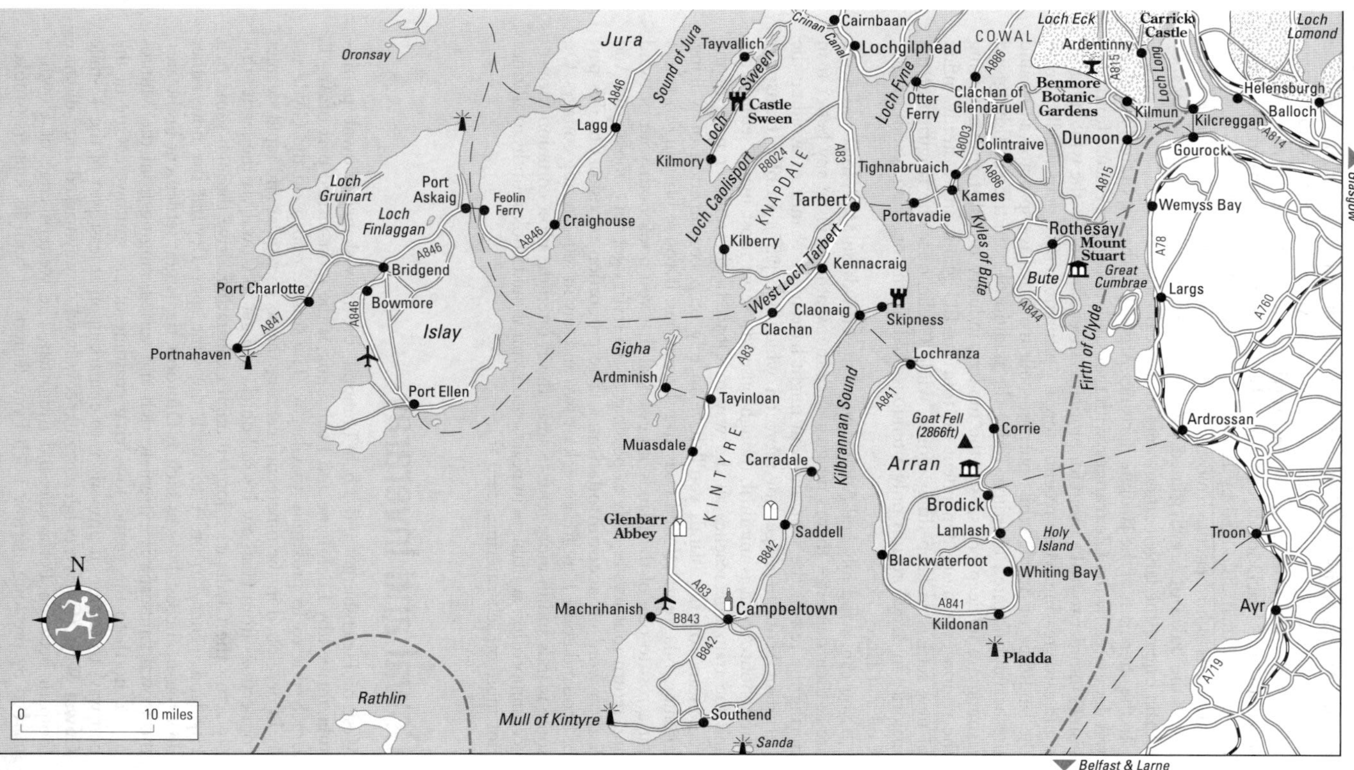
Glasgow
Belfast & Larne
Loch Lomond
Balloch
Helensburgh
Kilcreggan
A814
Carrick Castle
Loch Long
Kilmun
Gourock
Wemyss Bay
A78
Largs
A760
Ardrossan
Troon
Ayr
A719
Loch Eck
Ardentinny
A815
Benmore Botanic Gardens
Dunoon
Rothesay
Mount Stuart
Great Cumbrae
Bute
A844
Firth of Clyde
COWAL
A886
Clachan of Glendaruel
Colintraive
A8003
Tighnabruaich
Kames
Kyles of Bute
Portavadie
Loch Fyne
Otter Ferry
Lochgilphead
Cairnbaan
Crinan Canal
A83
Tarbert
KNAPDALE
B8024
Castle Sween
Loch Sween
Tayvallich
Loch Caolisport
Kilmory
Kilberry
West Loch Tarbert
Kennacraig
Claonaig
Skipness
Clachan
Lochranza
Kilbrannan Sound
Arran
Goat Fell (2866ft)
A841
Corrie
Brodick
Lamlash
Holy Island
Whiting Bay
Blackwaterfoot
Kildonan
Pladda
KINTYRE
Tayinloan
Muasdale
Carradale
Saddell
B842
Glenbarr Abbey
Campbeltown
Machrihanish
B843
Southend
Sanda
Mull of Kintyre
Gigha
Ardminish
Jura
Sound of Jura
A846
Lagg
Craighouse
Feolin Ferry
Port Askaig
Islay
Loch Finlaggan
Loch Gruinart
Bridgend
Bowmore
Port Ellen
Port Charlotte
A847
Portnahaven
Oronsay
Rathlin
N
0
10 miles

tongue. After a period of Norse invasion and settlement, the islands (and the peninsula of Kintyre) fell to the immensely powerful Somerled, who became King of the Hebrides and Lord of Argyll in the twelfth century. Somerled's successors, the MacDonalds, established Islay as their headquarters in the 1200s, but were in turn dislodged by Robert the Bruce. Of Bruce's allies, it was the **Campbells** who benefited most from the MacDonalds' demise and eventually, as the dukes of Argyll, gained control of the entire area – even today, they remain one of the largest landowners in the region.

In the aftermath of the Jacobite uprisings, Argyll, like the rest of the Highlands, was devastated by the **Clearances**, with thousands of crofters evicted from their homes in order to make room for profitable sheep farming – "the white plague" – and cattle rearing. More recently forestry plantations have dramatically altered the landscape of Argyll, while purpose-built marinas have sprouted all around the heavily indented coastline. Today the traditional industries of fishing and farming are in deep crisis, as is the modern industry of fish-farming, leaving the region ever more dependent on tourism, EU grants and a steady influx of new settlers to keep things going, while Gaelic, once the language of the majority in Argyll, retains only a tenuous hold on the outlying islands of Islay, Coll and Tiree.

If you can, avoid July and August, when the crowds on Mull, Iona and Arran are at their densest – there's no guarantee the weather will be any better than during the rest of the year, and you might have more chance of avoiding the persistent Scottish midge (for more on which, see p.57). **Public transport** throughout Argyll is minimal, though buses do serve most major settlements, and the train line reaches all the way to Oban. In the remoter parts of the region and on the islands you'll have to rely on a combination of walking, hitching, bike rental, shared taxis and the postbus. If you're planning to take a car across to one of the islands, it's essential that you book both your outward and return journeys as early as possible, as the ferries get very booked up. And lastly, a word on **accommodation**: a large proportion of visitors to this part of Scotland come here for a week or two and stay in self-catering cottages. On some islands and in more remote areas, this is often the most common form of accommodation available – in peak season, you should book months in advance (for more on self-catering, see p.46).

Cowal and Inveraray

West of Helensburgh and Loch Lomond, the claw-shaped **Cowal peninsula**, formed by Loch Fyne and Loch Long, is the most-visited part of Argyll, largely due to its proximity to Glasgow. The seaside resorts on the Clyde sea lochs developed in the nineteenth century thanks to regular and rapid steamer connections from Glasgow. It's still quicker to get to Cowal via the ferries that ply across the Clyde; it's a long, though exhilarating, drive through some rich Highland scenery in order to reach the same spot. Beyond the now rather down-at-heel coastal towns such as **Dunoon**, the largest settlement in the area, the Cowal landscape is extremely rich and varied, ranging from the Munros of the north to the gentle, low-lying coastline of the southwest. One of the best ways to explore it properly is to embark upon at least part of the 47-mile **Cowal Way** (Ⓦwww.colglen.org.uk/cowalway), a waymarked long-distance footpath between Portavadie and Ardgartan. The western edge of Cowal is marked by the long, narrow Loch Fyne, famous for both its kippers (smoked herring) and, more recently, oysters. The main settlement on the lochside is **Inveraray**, a small but dignified town beside Inveraray Castle, the home of the powerful Dukes of Argyll.

Arrochar to Inveraray

The boundaries of Loch Lomond and the Trossachs National Park extend quite a long way into Cowal, incorporating the **Argyll Forest Park** which stretches west from the village of Arrochar along the shores of Loch Fyne and south as far as Holy Loch. The area has the most grandiose scenery on the peninsula, including the ambitiously named **Arrochar Alps**, whose peaks offer some of the best climbing in Argyll: Ben Ime (3318ft) is the tallest of the range, while Ben Arthur or "The Cobbler" (2891ft), named after the anvil-like rock formation at its summit, is easily the most distinctive. All are for experienced walkers only, although at the other end of the scale there are several gentle forest walks clearly laid out by the Forestry Commission and helpful leaflets are available from tourist offices.

Arrochar and around

Approaching by road from Glasgow, Helensburgh or Loch Lomond, the entry point to Cowal is **ARROCHAR**, at the head of Loch Long. The village itself is ordinary enough, but the setting is dramatic, and it makes a convenient base for exploring the nearby Alps and forests. There's a **train station** a mile or so east, just off the A83 to Tarbet (see p.168), and numerous **hotels** and **B&Bs**; try the very friendly *Lochside Guest House* on the main road (ⓣ01301/702467, ⓦwww.stayatlochlomond.com/lochside; ③), or *Fascadail* (ⓣ01301/702344, ⓦwww.fascadail.com; ③), a guesthouse with a glorious garden situated in the quieter southern part of the village. If you want a bite **to eat**, head for the *Village Inn* (ⓣ01301/702279, ⓦwww.villageinnarrochar.com), which has tables outside overlooking the loch as well as a cosy real-ale bar and en-suite rooms (④).

Two miles west of Arrochar at **ARDGARTAN**, there's a well-maintained lochside Forestry Commission **campsite** (ⓣ01301/702293, ⓦwww.forestholidays.co.uk; April–Oct), and, a little further down the road, in the Ardgartan Visitor Centre is a **tourist office** (daily: July & Aug 10am–6pm; April–June, Sept & Oct 10am–5pm; ⓣ01301/702432), which doubles as a forestry office and has occasional organized walks. There are also waymarked **walks and bike trails** starting from here.

Heading west from Arrochar to Inveraray or the rest of Cowal, you're forced to climb **Glen Croe**, a strategic hill pass whose saddle is called – for obvious

Climbing The Cobbler

The jagged, triple-peaked ridge of Ben Arthur (2891ft) – better known as **The Cobbler** because it is supposed to look like a cobbler bent over his work – is easily the most enticing of the peaks within the Argyll Forest Park. It's surprisingly accessible, with the most popular route starting from the car park at Succoth, halfway between Arrochar and Ardgartan. Skirting the woods, you eventually join the Allt a' Bhalachain, which climbs steeply up to the col between the northern peak (known as The Cobbler's Wife) and The Cobbler itself. Traversing the ridge in order to ascend one or all of the three peaks is a tricky business, and the final scramble should only be attempted by experienced hikers. The total distance of the climb is only five miles, but the return trip will probably take you between five and six hours. For more on safety precautions, see p.59.

reasons – **Rest-and-be-Thankful**. Here the road forks, with the single-track B828 heading down to isolated-feeling **LOCHGOILHEAD**, overlooking Loch Goil. From the village, a road tracks the west side of the loch, petering out after five miles at the picturesque ruins of **Carrick Castle**, a classic tower-house castle built around 1400 and used as a hunting lodge by James IV. Facing this across the water is a hilly peninsula known as **Argyll's Bowling Green** – no ironic nickname, but an English corruption of the Gaelic *Baile na Greine* (Sunny Hamlet).

Cairndow and around

If you'd rather skip Lochgoilhead, continue west towards Inveraray along the A83 via Glen Kinglas to **CAIRNDOW**, at the head of Loch Fyne. Just behind the village, off the main road, you'll find the **Ardkinglas Woodland Garden** (daily during daylight hours; £3; ⓦ www.ardkinglas.com), which contains exotic rhododendrons, azaleas and a superb collection of conifers, some of which rise to over 200ft. The *Cairndow Stagecoach Inn* (ⓣ 01499/600286, ⓦ www.cairndowinn.com; ④), in the village itself, is good for a pint and inexpensive pub food, with views over the loch from some of the (mainly small) bedrooms, but for something a bit special continue a mile or so further along on the A83 to the famous **Loch Fyne Oyster Bar and Shop** (ⓣ 01499/600236, ⓦ www.loch-fyne.com), which sells more oysters than anywhere else in the country, plus lots of other fish and seafood treats. You can easily assemble a gourmet picnic in the shop here or stock up on provisions for the week, and the moderately expensive **restaurant** (daily 9am–9pm) is excellent, though booking is advisable at busy times.

Inveraray

A classic example of an eighteenth-century planned town, **INVERARAY** was built on the site of a ruined fishing village in 1745 by the third Duke of Argyll,

△ Loch Fyne Oyster Bar and Shop

head of the powerful Campbell clan, in order to distance his newly rebuilt castle from the hoi polloi in the town and to establish a commercial and legal centre for the region. Today Inveraray, an absolute set piece of Scottish Georgian architecture, has a truly memorable setting, the brilliant white arches of Front Street reflected in the still waters of Loch Fyne, which separate it from the Cowal peninsula.

The Town

Squeezed onto a promontory some distance from the duke's new castle, there's not much more to Inveraray's New Town than its distinctive **Main Street** (set at a right angle to Front Street), flanked by whitewashed terraces, whose window casements are picked out in black. At the top of the street, the road divides to circumnavigate the town's Neoclassical church, originally built in two parts: the southern half served the Gaelic-speaking community, while the northern half – still in use and worth a peek for its period wood-panelled interior – served those who spoke English.

East of the church is **Inveraray Jail** (daily: April–Oct 9.30am–6pm; Nov–March 10am–5pm; £5.95; Ⓦ www.inverarayjail.co.uk), whose attractive Georgian courthouse and grim prison blocks ceased to function in the 1930s. The jail is now an imaginative and thoroughly enjoyable museum, which graphically recounts prison conditions from medieval times up until the nineteenth century – and even brings it up to date by including a picture of life in Glasgow's Barlinnie Prison. You can also sit in the beautiful semicircular courthouse and listen to a re-enactment of the trial of a farmer accused of fraud.

Moored at the town pier is the **Arctic Penguin** (daily: April–Oct 10am–6pm; Nov–March 10am–5pm; £3.80), a handsome, triple-masted schooner built in Dublin in 1911 – it has some nautical knick-knacks and displays on the maritime history of the Clyde, but is only really worth exploring if you're a naval enthusiast or wet weather inhibits town wanderings. Also based at the pier, an old-time Clyde puffer runs short **boat trips** on the loch.

Inveraray Castle

A ten-minute walk north of the New Town, the neo-Gothic **Inveraray Castle** (June–Sept Mon–Sat 10am–5.45pm, Sun 1–5.45pm; April–May & Oct Mon–Thurs & Sat 10am–1pm & 2–5.45pm, Sun 1–5.45pm; £5.90; Ⓦ www.inveraray-castle.com) remains the family home of the Duke of Argyll. Built in 1745 by the third duke, it was given a touch of the Loire in the nineteenth century with the addition of dormer windows and conical roofs. Inside, the most startling feature is the armoury hall, whose displays of weaponry – supplied to the Campbells by the British government to put down the Jacobites – rise through several storeys; look out for Rob Roy's rather sad-looking sporran and dirk handle (a dirk being a dagger, traditionally worn in Highland dress).

Gracing the extensive **castle grounds** (daily during daylight hours; free) is an attractive Celtic cross from Tiree, and one of three elegant bridges built during the relandscaping of Inveraray (the other two are on the road from Cairndow). Of the walks marked out in the grounds, the most strenuous takes you to the tower atop **Dùn na Cuaiche** (813ft), from where there's a spectacular view over the castle, town and loch.

Practicalities

Inveraray's **tourist office** is on Front Street (April, Sept & Oct Mon–Sat 9am–5pm, Sun noon–5pm; May & June Mon–Sat 9am–5pm, Sun 11am–5pm; July & Aug daily 9am–6pm; Nov–March Mon–Fri 10am–3pm, Sat & Sun

11am–3pm; ⓣ01499/302063), as is the town's chief **hotel**, the historic *Argyll* (ⓣ01499/302466, ⓦwww.the-argyll-hotel.co.uk; ❺), now part of the Best Western group but formerly the *Great Inn*, where Dr Johnson and Boswell once stayed. A cheaper, but equally well-appointed alternative is the Georgian *Fernpoint Inn* (ⓣ01499/302170; ❸), round by the pier, which has a nice pub garden and well-appointed rooms; otherwise, there's the **B&B** *Creag Dhubh* (ⓣ01499/302430, ⓦwww.creagdhubh.com; ❷; March–Nov), set in a large garden overlooking Loch Fyne down the A83 to Lochgilphead. The SYHA **hostel** (ⓣ0870/004 1125, ⓦwww.syha.org.uk; mid-March to Sept) is in a modern building a short distance north on the A819 Dalmally road, while the old Royal Navy base, two miles down the A83 to Lochgilphead, has been converted into the excellent, fully equipped *Argyll Caravan Park* (ⓣ01499/302285, ⓦwww.argyllcaravanpark.com; April–Oct). The **bar** of the central *George Hotel* is the town's liveliest spot, and also serves fine bar **food**; for tea and cakes head for *The Poacher* round by the *Fernpoint Inn*. The best place to sample Loch Fyne's delicious fresh fish and seafood is the superb, moderately priced restaurant of the *Loch Fyne Oyster Bar* (see p.78), six miles northeast back up the A83 towards Glasgow.

Dunoon

The second principal entry point into Cowal from the Glasgow area, though this time by sea, is **DUNOON**, the largest town in Argyll, with 13,000 inhabitants. In the nineteenth century it grew from a mere village to a major Clyde seaside resort and favourite holiday spot for Glaswegians. Nowadays, tourists tend to arrive by ferry from Gourock but while Dunoon is a great position to watch the comings and goings on the Firth of Clyde, it's no longer a thriving place and there's little to tempt you to stay, particularly with attractive countryside beckoning just beyond.

The centre of town is dominated by a grassy lump of rock known as **Castle Hill**, crowned by Castle House, built in the 1820s by a wealthy Glaswegian and the subject of a bitter dispute with the local populace over closure of the common land around his house. The people eventually won, and the grounds remain open to the public to this day, as does the house, which is now home to the **Castle House Museum** (Easter–Oct Mon–Sat 10.30am–4.30pm, Sun 2–4.30pm; £1.50; ⓦwww.castlehousemuseum.org.uk). There's some good hands-on nature stuff for kids, an excellent section on the Clyde steamers as well as details about "Highland Mary", betrothed to Robbie Burns (despite the fact that he already had a pregnant wife), who died of typhus before the pair could see through their plan to elope to the West Indies. A statue of her is in the grounds.

Another more violent scene in local history is commemorated by a memorial on a nearby rock: at least 36 men of the Lamont clan were executed in 1646 by their rivals, the Campbells, who hanged them from "a lively, fresh-growing ash tree". The tree couldn't take the strain, and had to be cut down two years later; tradition has it that blood gushed from the roots when it was felled.

With an hour or so to spare, you could visit the **Cowal Bird Garden** (April–Oct daily 10.30am–6pm; £4), located in woodland one mile northwest along the A885 to Sandbank, or, if the weather's fine, take the **Ardnadam Heritage Trail**, a forty-minute walk located a mile further up the road, which leads to the wonderful Dunan viewpoint looking out to the Firth of Clyde.

Practicalities

Dunoon's **tourist office**, the principal one in Cowal, is located on Alexandra Parade (Mon–Fri 9am–5.30pm, Sat & Sun 10am–5pm; ⓣ01369/703785).

There are two **ferry** crossings across the Clyde from Gourock to Dunoon; the shorter, more frequent service is half-hourly on Western Ferries to Hunter's Quay, a mile north of the town centre; CalMac's boats, though, arrive at the main pier, and have better transport connections if you're on foot.

There's an enormous choice of **B&Bs**, none of them outstanding. You're better off heading out of town or persuading the tourist office to help you, since availability in summer is the biggest problem. Worth considering are the welcoming *Abbot's Brae* half a mile from the pier above West Bay (ⓣ01369/705021, ⓦwww.abbotsbrae.co.uk; ⑤), or the smart *Dhailling Lodge* (ⓣ01369/701253, ⓦwww.dhaillinglodge.com; ④), closer to town on Alexandra Parade. A cheaper and cheery alternative is the traditional *Cot House Hotel* (ⓣ01369/840260, ⓦwww.cothousehotel.com; ②), about ten minutes' drive north at Kilmun. Immediately beside the hotel is a caravan and **campsite** (ⓣ01369/840351; closed Nov & Feb).

Chatters, 58 John St (ⓣ01369/706402; Wed–Sat only; closed Jan & Feb), is Dunoon's best **restaurant**, offering delicious Loch Fyne seafood and Scottish beef. For something a bit less pricey, you could do worse than the simple **café** serving soups, sandwiches and light meals run by the Baptist church right next door to the tourist office; there's also a vast Italian menu at *La Cantina* (ⓣ01369/703595) in Argyll Street. For **bike rental**, head for the Highland Stores on Argyll Street; for **pony trekking**, contact the Velvet Path Riding and Trekking Centre (ⓣ01369/830580) at Inellan, four miles south of town. Dunoon boasts a two-screen **cinema** (a rarity in Argyll) on John Street, but the town's most famous entertainment is the **Cowal Highland Gathering** (ⓦwww.cowalgathering.com), the largest of its kind in the world, held here on the last weekend in August, and culminating in the awesome spectacle of the massed pipes and drums of more than 150 bands marching through the streets.

Holy Loch and Loch Eck

Immediately north of Dunoon lies **Holy Loch**, the former site of a US nuclear submarine base which closed in 1992. On the northern shores of the loch is the elongated settlement of **KILMUN**, where there's a fascinating church with a mausoleum – alas closed to the public – where many a Duke of Argyll is buried, several good stained-glass windows and an organ driven by tap water (the church holds teas and tours in the summer). There's also an **arboretum** at Kilmun, through which the Forestry Commission has laid out several pleasant walks.

Just three miles north of Holy Loch along the A815 is **Loch Eck**, a narrow freshwater loch, squeezed between steeply banked woods which is a favourite spot for trout fishing. At the loch's southern tip are the beautifully laid-out **Benmore Botanic Gardens** (daily: March & Oct 10am–5pm; April–Sept 10am–6pm; £3.50), an offshoot of Edinburgh's Royal Botanic Gardens. Occupying 140 acres of lush hillside, the mild, moist climate of Argyll allows a vast range of unusual plants to grow here, with different sections devoted to rainforest species native to places as exotic as China, Chile and Bhutan. The gardens boast 250 species of rhododendrons and a memorably striking avenue of Great Redwoods, planted in 1863 and now over 150ft high. There's a pleasant, inexpensive **café** by the entrance, open in season, with an imaginative menu. It's easy to combine a visit with one of the local **forest walks**, the most popular being a leisurely stroll up the rocky ravine of **Puck's Glen** (1hr 30min round-trip), which begins from the car park a mile south of the gardens.

Halfway along Loch Eck, the shore-side *Coylet Inn* (ⓣ01369/840426, ⓦwww.coylet-locheck.co.uk; ⑤), a sympathetically renovated coaching inn, makes for a lovely place to eat or **stay**. The family-orientated *Stratheck Country Park* **campsite** at the southern end of Loch Eck (ⓣ01369/840472, ⓦwww.stratheck.co.uk; March–Oct) enjoys a good location, surrounded by wooded slopes, and has caravans for rent – just make sure you've come armed with effective midge repellent.

Southwest Cowal

The mellower landscape of **southwest Cowal**, which stands in complete contrast to the bustle of Dunoon or the Highland grandeur of the Argyll Forest Park, becomes immediate as soon as you head into the area, either over the hill from Dunoon or down the A886 from Glen Kinglas.

There are few more beautiful sights in Argyll than the **Kyles of Bute**, the slivers of water that separate Cowal from the bleak bulk of the Isle of Bute, and constitute some of the best sailing opportunities in Scotland. **COLINTRAIVE**, on the eastern Kyle, marks the narrowest point in the area – barely more than a couple of hundred yards – and is the place from which the small CalMac car ferry departs to Bute. The most popular spot from which to appreciate the Kyles is along the A8003 as it rises dramatically above the sea lochs before descending to the peaceful, lochside village of **TIGHNABRUAICH**, best known for its excellent **sailing school** (ⓣ01700/811717, ⓦwww.tssargyll.co.uk), which offers week-long courses from beginners to advanced. Boat trips, including the *Waverley* paddlesteamer, still call at the pier and the village can be a pleasant place to stay: the impressive *Royal Hotel* (ⓣ01700/811239, ⓦwww.royalhotel.org.uk; ⑥), by the waterside, serves exceptionally good bar meals, and has wonderful views over the Kyles; not quite so grand, but justifiably popular with sailors and walkers, is the *Kames Hotel* (ⓣ01700/811489, ⓦwww.kames-hotel.com; ⑤) in neighbouring **KAMES**. You can get B&B at *Ardeneden Guest House* (ⓣ01700/811354; ③), run by the same people who look after the inexpensive *Burnside Bistro* in the village, while there's camping at *Carry Farm* (ⓣ01700/811717, ⓦwww.carryfarm.co.uk), a few miles south of Kames. If you're driving to Kintyre, Islay or Jura, you can avoid the long haul around Loch Fyne – some seventy miles or so – by using the **ferry** to Tarbert from **Portavadie**, three miles southwest of Kames.

The Kyles can get busy in July and August, but it's possible to escape the crowds by heading for Cowal's deserted west coast, overlooking Loch Fyne. The road meets the loch shore at **OTTER FERRY**, which has a small shingle beach, a wonderful pub and an oyster restaurant, *The Oystercatcher*, with outside tables in good weather. There was once a ferry link to Lochgilphead from here, though the "otter" part is not derived from the furry creature but from the Gaelic *an oitir* (sandbank), which juts out a mile or so into Loch Fyne. If you're continuing north you'll come to the romantic ruin of **Castle Lachlan** – overlooking it, there's another excellent restaurant, *Inver Cottage* (ⓣ01369/860537, ⓦwww.invercottage.co.uk), a contemporary and relaxed place which serves good coffee through the day, light lunches and evening meals based around local produce. For somewhere to stay nearby, try the small roadside B&B, *Balnacarry* (ⓣ01369/860212; ③; March–Oct).

A little way north along the shores of Loch Fyne you'll come across the well-known *Creggans Inn* (ⓣ01369/860279, ⓦwww.creggans-inn.co.uk; ⑥), on the fringes of the village of **STRACHUR**. The inn once belonged to Scottish adventurer and author Sir Fitzroy Maclean, commonly believed to have been used by his friend Ian Fleming as a role model for James Bond. Tucked away in Clachan, a kind of suburb of Strachur, is a church with medieval grave slabs set into its walls and the **Strachur Smiddy** (Easter–Sept Fri–Mon 1–4pm; £1), an old restored blacksmith's which has live shoeing once or twice a year.

Isle of Bute

The island of **Bute** (Ⓦ www.isle-of-bute.com) is in many ways simply an extension of the Cowal peninsula, from which it is separated by the narrow Kyles of Bute. Thanks to its consistently mild climate and its ferry link with Wemyss Bay, Bute has been a popular holiday and convalescence spot for Clydesiders

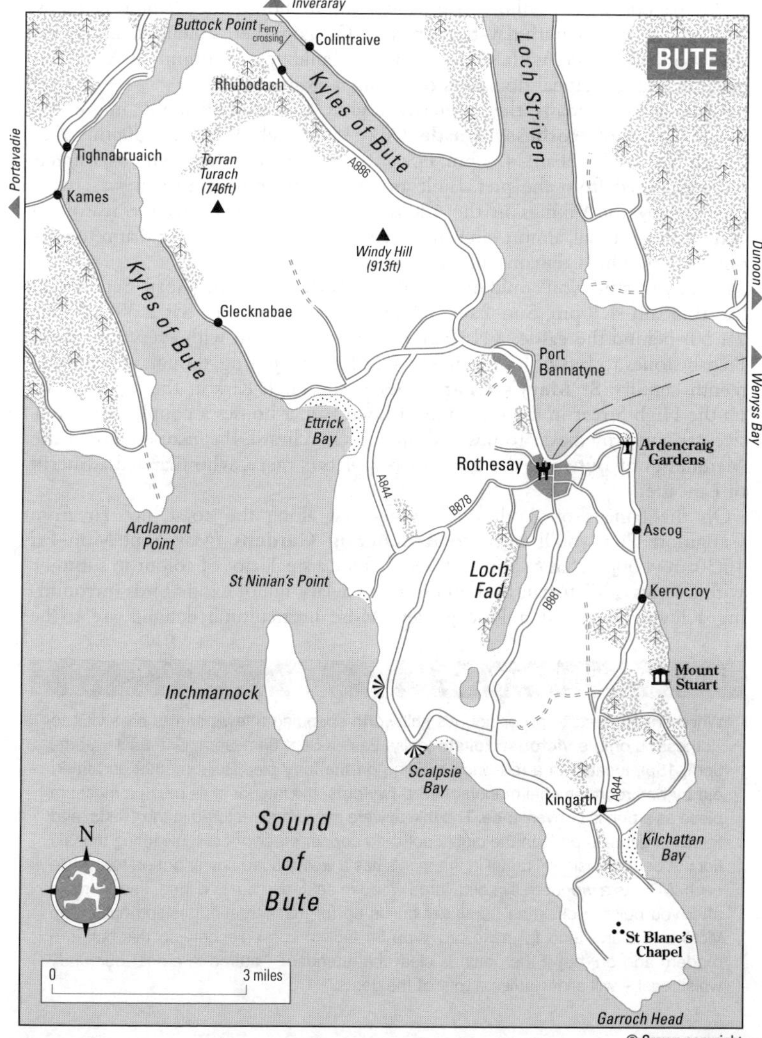

– particularly the elderly – for over a century. Its chief town, **Rothesay**, rivals Dunoon as the major seaside resort on the Clyde, easily surpassing it thanks to some splendidly over-the-top Victorian architecture, excellent accommodation and eating options and the chance to visit **Mount Stuart**, one of Scotland's singular aristocratic piles. Most of Bute's inhabitants live around the two wide bays on the east coast of the island, which resembles one long seaside promenade. Consequently, it's easy enough to escape the crowds by heading for the sparsely populated west coast, which, in any case, has the sandiest beaches.

Rothesay

Bute's only town, **ROTHESAY** is a handsome Victorian resort, set in a wide sweeping bay, backed by green hills, with a classic palm-tree promenade and 1920s pagoda-style pavilion originally built to house the Winter Gardens. Though often busy with day-trippers from Glasgow, there's plenty that's attractive about the place, with some handsome buildings, a prominent Art Deco pavilion and occasional flourishes of wrought-ironwork.

Rothesay also boasts the militarily useless, but architecturally impressive, moated ruins of **Rothesay Castle** (April–Sept daily 9.30am–6.30pm; Oct–March Sat–Wed 9.30am–4.30pm; HS; £3), hidden amid the town's backstreets but signposted from the pier. Built around the twelfth century, it was twice captured by the Vikings in the 1200s; such vulnerability was the reasoning behind the unusual, almost circular, curtain wall, with its four big drum towers, only one of which remains fully intact.

In rainy weather you could hide inside the **Bute Museum** (April–Sept Mon–Sat 10.30am–4.30pm, Sun 2.30–4.30pm; Oct–March Tues–Sat 2.30–4.30pm; £1.50) behind the castle, a classic local history museum with everything from Pictish stones to bits of local shipwrecks. More interesting, though, is the fourteenth-century **St Mary's Chapel**, beside the High Kirk at the top of town up the High Street in the direction of Loch Fad; it houses a couple of impressive canopied medieval tombs and, in the churchyard, the mausoleum of the Marquesses of Bute and the grave of Napoleon's niece, who married a Sheriff of Lancaster.

On the fringes of Rothesay heading east along the coast, not far from Craigmore Pier, you'll come to **Ardencraig Gardens** (May–Sept Mon–Fri 10.30am–4.30pm, Sat & Sun 1–4.30pm; free), a small riot of colour in summer, with a series ofVictorian hothouses and an aviary full of exotic birds surrounding a lovingly tended hillside garden. More horticultural delights are to be

Rothesay's lovely lavvy

Whether you need to go or not, it's still worth spending a few pennies on a visit to Rothesay's ornate **Victorian toilets** (daily: Easter–Sept 8am–9pm; Oct–Easter 9am–5pm; 15p), located in a red-brick building on the ferry pier. Built in 1899 and fitted out by bathroom enamel manufacturers Twyfords, the interior is as much a museum piece as a public convenience. The toilets were saved and restored in the 1990s, and there's a genuine pride in the highly polished copper pipework and gleaming mosaic floor. A central, "island" urinal in the men's has a well-tended flower pot on top, while each WC has a wonderfully solid, large wooden seat, and emits a long, low grumble after you pull the chain as the water builds up for its energetic, gushing flush. The Victorians didn't tend to make provision for ladies' conveniences, so this half is a modern add-on, but if the coast is clear the attendant – attired in a neat burgundy waistcoast – will allow ladies a tour of the gents.

found out along the road to Mount Stuart (see below) at the **Ascog Fernery and Garden** (April to mid-Oct Wed–Sun 10am–5pm; £3), an unusual Victorian fernery that has been lovingly restored and boasts an ancient fern, reputed to be a thousand years old.

Practicalities

Rothesay's **tourist office** (April–June & Sept daily 10am–5pm; July & Aug Mon–Fri 10am–6pm, Sat & Sun 9.30am–5pm; Oct–March Mon–Fri 10am–5pm, Sat & Sun 11am–4pm; ⓣ01700/502151) is in a "Discovery Centre", which occupies the refurbished Winter Gardens alongside the pier, and has some well-presented displays on the life and times of Bute. Staff can also help with **accommodation**, though there's no shortage of B&Bs all along the seafront from Rothesay north to Port Bannatyne. One of the more attractive hotels is *Cannon House* (ⓣ01700/502819, ⓦwww.cannonhousehotel.co.uk; ❹) occupying a Georgian house close to the pier on Battery Place, while the nearby *Commodore* (ⓣ01700/502178, ⓦwww.commodorebute.com; ❷) at no. 12, is a more modest but equally accommodating guesthouse. Alternatively, *The Boat House* (ⓣ01700/502696, ⓦwww.theboathouse-bute.co.uk; ❹) at no. 15 is a stylish "boutique B&B" with classy contemporary furnishings and decor. Further out in Ascog, the B&B at *Ascog Farm* (ⓣ01700/503372; ❷) is exceptionally good value, while *Chandlers Hotel* (ⓣ01700/505577, ⓦwww.visitchandlers.com; ❻) offers a more decadent retreat, with smart modern rooms in an attractive red sandstone villa, and has a good bar and restaurant.

The best **food** option in Rothesay is *The Bistro* in the Winter Gardens, which offers a good-value restaurant menu and a superb view of the bay. If you're prepared to travel a short way, try the highly original and engaging *Port Royal Hotel* in Port Bannatyne, which describes itself as a "Waterfront Russian Tavern" and serves fresh local seafood alongside dishes such as blini, and has a terrific array of real ales. Alternatively, *The Pier at Craigmore* (ⓣ01700/502867), on the coast road out of Rothesay on the way to Mount Stuart, is open through the day for coffee, home-baked cakes and light snacks, and for evening meals in summer. For Rothesay's finest fish and chips, head for the *West End Café* on Gallowgate. The small but stylish café, *Musicker*, just across from the castle has good coffee, and you can also listen to some music and browse through their book selection.

Bute holds its own **Highland Games** on the third weekend in August, an international **folk festival** on the third weekend in July, and a (mainly trad) **jazz festival** over May Bank Holiday (ⓦwww.butejazz.com). There are several golf courses in the area; **pony trekking** at Kingarth Trekking Centre near Kilchattan Bay (ⓣ01700/831673, ⓦwww.kingarthtrekkingcentre.co.uk); and **bike rental** from Rob Cycles (ⓣ01700/500602; April–Sept). An open-topped **tour bus** goes around the southern half of the island (May–Sept 11am, 1pm and 3pm; £6) in about an hour and a half if you want to check out the lay of the land. You can also use this service to get to and from Mount Stuart (£2.50 return).

Mount Stuart

One very good reason for coming to Bute is to visit **Mount Stuart** (May–Sept Sun–Fri 11am–5pm, Sat 10am–1.30pm; tours £7, gardens only £3.50; ⓦwww.mountstuart.com), a fantasy Gothic house set amidst acres of lush woodland gardens overlooking the Firth of Clyde four miles south of Rothesay. Setting for the glamorous wedding in 2003 of Sir Paul McCartney's daughter, Stella,

Mount Stuart is the ancestral home of the seventh Marquess of Bute, also known as Johnny Bute or, in his younger days as a Formula One racing driver, as Johnny Dumfries. The building was created by the marvellously eccentric third Marquess and architect Sir Robert Rowand Anderson after a fire in 1877 had destroyed the family seat. With little regard for expense, the marquess shipped in tons of Italian marble, building a railway line to transport it down the coast and employing craftsmen who had worked with the great William Burges on the marquess's earlier medieval concoctions at Cardiff Castle.

A **bus** runs from Rothesay approximately every forty-five minutes to the gates of Mount Stuart, while the house itself is a pleasant fifteen-minute walk through the gardens from the unexpectedly sleek **visitor centre**, an award-winning piece of contemporary architecture which contains a gallery, shop and excellent **café/restaurant** which serves interesting lunches using produce from the Mount Stuart kitchen garden and other parts of the island; if it's raining it might be worth taking the shuttle service provided.

To see the inside of Mount Stuart itself you'll have to join one of the guided tours that take you around the inside of Mount Stuart house: the showpiece is the columned **Marble Hall**, its vaulted ceiling and stained-glass windows decorated with the signs of the zodiac, reflecting the marquess's taste for mysticism. He was equally fond of animal and plant imagery, hence you'll find birds feeding on berries in the dining-room frieze and monkeys reading (and tearing up) books and scrolls in the library. Look out also for the unusual heraldic plaster ceiling in the drawing room. After all the heavy furnishings, seek aesthetic relief in the **Marble Chapel**, built entirely out of dazzling white Carrara marble, with a magnificent Cosmati floor pattern. Upstairs is less interesting, with the notable exception of the **Horoscope Room**, where you can see a fine astrological ceiling and adjacent observatory.

Although the sumptuous interior of Mount Stuart is not to everyone's taste, it's worth coming here to explore the wonderfully mature **gardens** (daily 10am–6pm), established in the eighteenth century by the third Earl of Bute, who had a hand in London's Kew Gardens. A leaflet outlines various paths criss-crossing the three-hundred acres of mixed woodland, lawn and shoreline; quiet nooks, neat vegetable patches and a solidly built children's adventure playground are all incorporated within the grounds. Before you leave Mount Stuart, take a look at the planned village of **Kerrycroy**, just beyond the main exit, built by the second Marquess in the early nineteenth century for the estate workers. Semi-detached houses – alternately mock-Tudor and whitewashed stone – form a crescent that overlooks a pristine village green and, beyond, the sea.

Around Bute

The Highland–Lowland dividing line passes through the middle of Bute, which is all but sliced in two by the freshwater Loch Fad. As a result, the northern half of the island is hilly, uninhabited and little visited, while the southern half is made up of Lowland-style farmland. The two highest peaks on the island are **Windy Hill** (913ft) and **Torran Turach** (746ft), both in the north; from the latter, there are fine views of the Kyles, but for a gentler overview of the island you can simply walk up to the **viewpoint**, on a hill a few miles east of Rothesay.

Beyond Mount Stuart, six miles south of Rothesay, the east-facing **Kilchattan Bay** has a lovely arc of sand lined by a row of grand Victorian houses. A mile or so inland, **St Blane's Chapel** is a twelfth-century ruin beautifully situated in open countryside amidst the foundations of an earlier Christian settlement established in the sixth century by St Catan, uncle to the local-born St Blane. From the road it's a short uphill walk through farmland; over the brow of a hill you come upon a well-built churchyard wall surrounded by mature trees; the ruined chapel sits amid a rather peculiar two-tier graveyard, the upper area reserved for the men of the parish while the women were consigned to the lower one. Passing the chapel is the route of the thirty-mile **West Island Way**, a waymarked footpath which starts at Kilchattan Bay and stretches the length of the island. It can be done in two long (or three more leisurely) days, though you can of course tackle shorter sections of it. Maps of the Way are available at Rothesay's tourist office.

A good base in the south of the island is the recently renovated *Kingarth Hotel* (Ⓣ01700/831662, Ⓦwww.kingarthhotel.com; ❸), which has a convivial bar serving top-notch pub grub, as well as decent rooms.

Four miles up the west coast is the sandy strand of **Scalpsie Bay,** while, further on, beyond the village of Straad, lies **St Ninian's Point**, where the ruins of a sixth-century chapel overlook another fine sandy strand and the uninhabited island of **Inchmarnock** – to which, according to tradition, alcoholics were banished in the nineteenth century. Bute's finest sandy beach is further north at **Ettrick Bay**, which has a tearoom (April–Oct) and basic camping site at its north end. To get a proper feel for the countryside of rural Bute, you can stay in a remote spot on the west coast at *Glecknabae Farmhouse* (Ⓣ01700/505655, Ⓦwww.isleofbuteholidays.com; ❹), a B&B with a lovely garden and great views over the water.

Oban and around

The solidly Victorian resort of **OBAN** (Ⓦwww.oban.org.uk) enjoys a superb setting – the island of Kerrera to the southwest providing its bay with a natural shelter – distinguished by a bizarre granite amphitheatre, dramatically lit at night, on the hilltop above the town. Despite a population of just 8000, it's by far the largest port in northwest Scotland, the second-largest town in Argyll, and the main departure point for ferries to the Hebrides. If you arrive late, or are catching an early boat, you may have to spend the night here (there's no real need otherwise); if you're staying elsewhere, it's a useful location for wet-weather activities and shopping, and it's a great place to eat fresh seafood, although it does get uncomfortably crowded in the summer.

Oban lies at the centre of the coastal region known as Lorn, named after the Irish Celt Loarn, who, along with his brothers Fergus and Oengus, settled here around 500 AD. Given the number of tourists that pass through or stay in the area, it's hardly surprising that a few out-and-out tourist attractions have developed. The mainland is very picturesque, although its beauty is no secret – to escape the crowds, head off and explore the nearby islands, like **Lismore** or **Kerrera**, just offshore.

Arrival and information

Arriving in Oban **by car** can be a bit of a nightmare in the summer, when traffic chokes the main drag. If you're heading straight for the ferry, make sure you leave an extra hour to allow for sitting in the tailbacks. If you're just coming in to town to look around, use one of the non-central or supermarket car parks. The CalMac **ferry terminal** (Ⓣ01631/566688, Ⓦwww.calmac.co.uk)

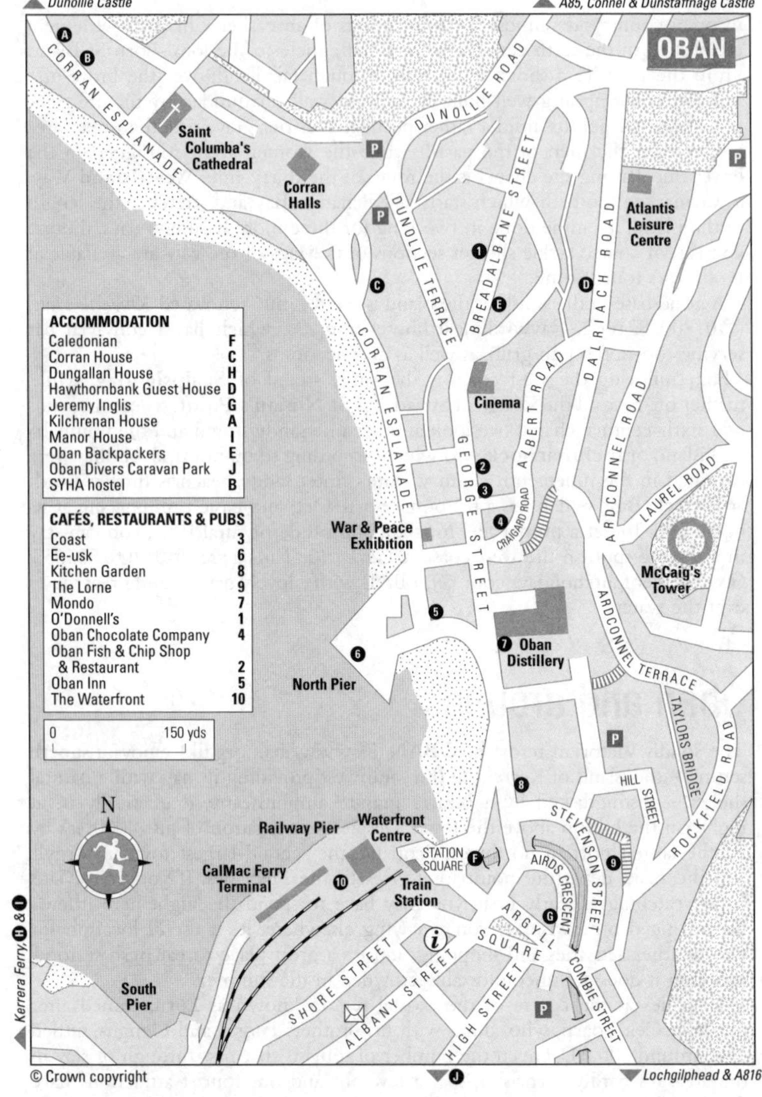

for the islands is on Railway Pier, a stone's throw from the train station, which is itself adjacent to the bus stops on Station Square. The **tourist office** (April Mon–Fri 9am–5pm, Sat & Sun 10am–5pm; May to mid-June Mon–Sat 9am–5.30pm, Sun 10am–5pm; mid- to late June & Sept Mon–Sat 9am–6.30pm, Sun 10am–5pm; July & Aug Mon–Sat 9am–8pm, Sun 9am–7pm; late Sept to Oct Mon–Sat 9am–5.30pm, Sun 10am–4pm; Nov–March Mon–Fri 9.30am–5pm, Sat 10am–4pm, Sun noon–4pm; ⓣ01631/563122) is housed in a converted church on Argyll Square, and has heaps of leaflets and books as well as Internet access.

Accommodation

Oban is positively heaving with **hotels** and **B&Bs**, most of them very reasonably priced and many on or near the quayside. Although it's easy enough to search out a vacancy, in high season it might be wise to pay the fee (£3) charged by the tourist office for finding you a room. It's also worth considering the options a little way out of town, in quieter spots such as Connel and Benderloch (see p.93).

Hotels and B&Bs

Caledonian Hotel Station Square ⓣ0871/222 3415, ⓦwww.go2oban.com. Large old station hotel overlooking the ferry pier, with recently refurbished stylish and contemporary rooms. Economy rooms ❺, luxury "Captains' Rooms" ❼

Corran House Hotel 1 Victoria Crescent ⓣ01631/566040, ⓦwww.corranhouse.co.uk. A good budget option, with a decent en-suite double and family rooms as well as bunk rooms above the popular *Markie Dan*'s pub. ❶

Dungallan House Hotel Gallanach Road ⓣ01631/563799, ⓦwww.dungallanhotel-oban.co.uk. Solid Victorian villa hotel with a dozen rooms set in its own woodland grounds, hidden away on the Gallanach Road, with great views across the Sound of Kerrera. Closed Jan & Feb. ❼

Hawthornbank Guest House Dalriach Road ⓣ01631/562041, ⓦwww.smoothhound.co.uk/hotels/hawthorn.html. Decent traditional guesthouse in the lower back streets of Oban, just across the road from the swimming pool. ❸

Kilchrenan House Corran Esplanade ⓣ01631/562663, ⓦwww.kilchrenanhouse.co.uk. Tasteful, hospitable guesthouse located near the Cathedral, with ten rooms, most of which have sea views, ❹

Manor House Hotel Gallanach Road ⓣ01631/562087, ⓦwww.manorhouseoban.com. Beautiful eighteenth-century manor house, peacefully located on the fringes of town by the shores of the Sound of Kerrera, with a top-notch restaurant attached. ❻

Hostels and campsites

Jeremy Inglis 21 Airds Crescent ⓣ01631/565065. Halfway between a hostel and a B&B, with an eccentric proprietor who also runs *McTavish's Kitchens*. Shared rooms, doubles or family rooms available, plus kitchen facilities; breakfast included.

Oban Backpackers Breadalbane Street ⓣ01631/562107, ⓦwww.scotlands-top-hostels.com. Friendliest, cheapest and most central of Oban hostels, with a pool table, real fire and Internet access. March–Oct & Christmas–New Year.

Oban Divers Caravan Park Glenshellach Road ⓣ01631/562755, ⓦwww.obandivers.co.uk. Pleasant site with lots of camping space situated a mile and a half from Oban up a pretty glen. Open April–Oct.

SYHA hostel Corran Esplanade ⓣ0870/004 1144, ⓦwww.syha.org.uk. Converted Victorian house, with a quieter, modern annexe behind, both a fair trek with a backpack from the ferry terminal along the Corran Esplanade, just beyond the Catholic Cathedral. Two-, three- and four-bed en-suite rooms available.

The Town

Through the summer months, an **open-topped tour bus** offers a basic introduction to the town and surrounds (May–Sept daily 11am & 2pm; £6). Apart from the setting and views, however, the only truly remarkable sight in Oban is the town's landmark, **McCaig's Tower**, a stiff ten-minute climb from the quayside. Built in imitation of Rome's Colosseum, it was the brainchild of a local businessman a century ago, who had the twin aims of alleviating off-season unemployment among the local stonemasons and creating a museum, art gallery and chapel. Originally, the plan was to add a 95-foot central tower, but work never progressed further than the exterior granite walls before McCaig died. In his will, McCaig gave instructions for the lancet windows to be filled with bronze statues of the family, though no such work was ever undertaken. Instead, the folly has been turned into a sort of walled garden which is a popular rendezvous for Oban's youth after dark, but for the rest of the time simply provides a wonderful seaward panorama, particularly at sunset.

Down in the centre of town, you can pass a few hours admiring the boats in the harbour and looking out for scavenging seals in the bay. If the weather's bad, the best option is to sign up for one of the excellent guided tours around **Oban Distillery** (April–Oct Mon–Sat 9.30am–5pm, July–Sept also open until 7.30pm Mon–Fri and Sun noon–5pm; Nov & March Mon–Fri 10am–5pm; Dec & Feb Mon–Fri 12.30–4pm; £5, with £3 redeemable against the cost of a bottle), slap in the centre of town off George Street. The tour ends with a generous dram of Oban's lightly peaty malt. Another refuge is the **War and Peace Exhibition** (Mon–Sat 10am–4pm; free) in the old Oban Times building beside the Art Deco Regent Hotel on the Esplanade; stuffed full of memorabilia and staffed by enthusiasts, it tells the story of the intriguing wartime role of the area around Oban as a flying boat base, mustering point for Atlantic convoys and as a training centre for the D-day landings.

A host of private tour operators can be found around the harbour, on the North, South and Railway piers: their all-inclusive ferry, coach and/or boat **trips and tours** – to Mull, Iona, Staffa, Seal Island and the Treshnish Isles – are worth considering, particularly if you're pushed for time, or have no transport. For a rundown of the best of these trips, see the box on p.100. For a fast and furious alternative which sticks to the local area, Puffin Dive Centre (see below) uses a powerful RIB to head out into the Sound of Mull on the lookout for wildlife on sea and land.

Bike rental is available from Oban Cycles, 29 Lochside St (Ⓣ01631/566996), and **car rental** from Flit on Glencruitten Road (Ⓣ01631/566553, Ⓦwww.selfdrive.me.uk). If you fancy taking the plunge and trying your hand at some **diving**, Puffin Dive Centre is based a mile south of Oban at Port Gallanach (Ⓣ01631/566088, Ⓦwww.puffin.org.uk), though it also has a booking office in town opposite the cinema.

Eating, drinking and nightlife

If you're only here to catch a ferry, you might as well grab a quick langoustine sandwich or dressed fresh crab from John Ogden's excellent **takeaway** seafood shack near the CalMac terminal. Close by, D. Watt's fishmonger is good for smoked fish and fresh seafood. For sit-down snacks, there's a **café** on the mezzanine above the impressive *Kitchen Garden* deli on George Street, while the *Oban Chocolate Company* at 9 Craigard Rd is a friendly little shop and café serving coffee, hot chocolate and lovely hand-made chocolate treats. It was once nearly impossible to get good fresh seafood in Oban, despite the rows of fishing boats at the pier, but things have changed for the better with the arrival of two top fish **restaurants**: on the North Pier the swanky designer *Ee-usk* (Ⓣ01631/565666) serves glistening seafood platters, fresh fish dishes and lighter alternatives such as Thai fish cakes; while in the rather less glamorous setting of the old seamen's mission on the CalMac pier is *The Waterfront* (Ⓣ01631/563110), which has an open kitchen rustling up impressive dishes using scallops, langoustine and the best of the daily catch. *Coast* (Ⓣ01631/569900), a Scottish contemporary bistro, or the cheap, cheerful and more youthful *Mondo*, both on George Street, are alternatives, and, of course, there's always fish and chips from *Oban Fish & Chip Shop & Restaurant*, at 116 George St.

The best **pub** in town is the *Oban Inn* opposite the North Pier, with a classic dark-wood, flagstone-and-brass bar downstairs and lounge bar with stained glass upstairs. The town's nightlife doesn't bear thinking about (though you can read all about it in the *Oban Times*). It's worth noting, however, that Oban is one of the few places in Argyll with a **cinema**, confusingly known as The Highland

Theatre (Ⓣ01631/562444), at the north end of George Street. You should be able to catch some **live music** at the weekend at *O'Donnell's* Irish pub, underneath a restaurant called *The Gathering*, on Breadalbane Street, or in *The Lorne*, a popular bar on Stevenson Street which also serves real ales.

Isle of Kerrera

One of the best places to escape from the crowds that plague Oban is the low-lying island of **Kerrera**, which shelters Oban Bay from the worst of the westerly winds. Measuring just five miles by two, the island is easily explored on foot and often crawling with geology students in the holidays. The island's most prominent landmark is the **Hutcheson's Monument**, best viewed, appropriately enough, from the ferries heading out of Oban, as it commemorates David Hutcheson, one of the Victorian founders of what is now Caledonian MacBrayne. The most appealing vistas, however, are from Kerrera's highest point, **Càrn Breugach** (620ft), over to Mull, the Slate Islands, Lismore, Jura and beyond.

The ferry lands roughly halfway down the east coast, at the north end of **Horseshoe Bay**, where King Alexander II died in 1249. If the weather's fine and you feel like lazing by the sea, head for the island's finest sandy beach, **Slatrach Bay**, on the west coast, one mile northwest of the ferry jetty. Otherwise, there's a very rewarding trail down to **Gylen Castle**, a clifftop ruin enjoying a majestic setting on the south coast, built in 1582 by the MacDougalls and burnt to the ground by the Covenanter General Leslie in 1647. You can head back to the ferry via the Drove Road, where cattle from Mull and other islands were once herded to be swum across the sound to the market in Oban.

The passenger and bicycle **ferry** crosses regularly (roughly every 30min in summer 8.45am–6pm; every 1–2 hours in winter 8.45am–5pm; £3.50 return; Ⓣ01631/563665) through the day from the mainland two miles down the Gallanach road from Oban. In summer, **bus** #431 (departs 10.20am, returns 4.10pm) from Oban Railway Station connects with the ferry. Kerrera has a total population of fewer than thirty – and no shop – so if you're day-tripping make sure you bring enough supplies with you. Alternatively, you can eat home-made, often organic, veggie **snacks** at the *Kerrera Teagarden* (April–Sept Wed–Sun 10.30am–4.30pm), located in a nice spot at Lower Gylen, a 45-minute walk from the ferry. Right beside this is the *Kerrera Bunkhouse* (Ⓣ01631/570223, Ⓦwww.kerrerabunkhouse.co.uk; open all year, but booking advised), a converted eighteenth-century stable building which sleeps seven. For simple **B&B** or self-catering accommodation enquire at *Ardentrive Farm* (Ⓣ01631/570938, Ⓔdavid@ardentrive.fsnet.co.uk; ❶), at the north of the island.

East of Oban

Just beyond the northern satellite suburbs of Oban, on a strategic promontory overlooking the important water crossroads at the mouth of Loch Etive, lie the ruins of **Dunstaffnage Castle** (April–Sept daily 9.30am–6.30pm; Oct–March Mon–Wed, Sat & Sun 9.30am–4.30pm; HS; £2.50). Originally built as a thirteenth-century MacDougall fort, the castle was captured by Robert the Bruce in 1309, and remained in royal hands until it was handed over to the Campbells in 1470. Garrisoned by government forces during the 1745 rebellion, it served as a temporary prison for Flora MacDonald, and was eventually destroyed by fire in 1810.

A couple of miles further up the A85, at **CONNEL**, you can't fail to admire the majestic steel cantilever **Connel Bridge**, built in 1903 to take the old branch railway line across the sea cataract at the mouth of Loch Etive, north to Fort William. The name "Connel" comes from the Gaelic *conghail* (tumultuous flood), which refers to the falls, or rapids, created by tidal streams rushing over a ledge of rock. Known as the Falls of Lora, this is one of the few tidal waterfalls in the country and looks as menacing as it does spectacular. These days the bridge is used by road transport, with the A828 now crossing it to take you on to Benderloch. If you want **to stay** out here in Connel as a more mellow option to Oban, *Ards House* (Ⓣ01631/710255, Ⓦwww.ardshouse.com; ④), a whitewashed Victorian villa by the main road overlooking the water, is a pleasant option, while a good place to admire the kayakers tackling the tidal falls is *Strumhor* guesthouse (Ⓣ01631/710167, Ⓦwww.strumhor.co.uk; ②), whose proprietors run sea kayaking courses from beginners upwards (Ⓦwww.seafreedomkayak.co.uk). There are also rooms at the *Wide-Mouthed Frog* (Ⓣ01631/567005, Ⓦwww.widemouthedfrog.com; ④; mid-Feb to Dec), at Dunstaffnage Marina, a popular hangout for "yotties" which also serves pub grub and has tables outside with views over to the castle. In Connel itself, you can get pub meals and seafood at the *Oyster Inn*, tucked underneath the bridge.

Taynuilt and Loch Etive

TAYNUILT, seven miles east of Connel, at the point where the River Awe flows into the sea at **Loch Etive**, is a small but sprawling village, best known for its iron-smelting works. To reach this industrial heritage site, follow the signpost off the A85 to **Bonawe Iron Furnace** (April–Sept daily 9.30am–6.30pm; HS; £3), which was originally founded by Cumbrian ironworkers in 1753. A whole series of buildings in various states of repair are scattered across the factory site, which employed six hundred people at its height, and eventually closed down in 1876.

From the pier beyond the iron furnace, **boat cruises** (mid-April to Sept Sun–Fri noon & 2pm; £6/2hr, £11/3hr) check out the local seals and explore the otherwise inaccessible reaches of Loch Etive; phone Loch Etive Cruises (Ⓣ01866/822430) for more details. A mile or so east up the A85 from Taynuilt, a sign invites you to visit the tucked-away **Inverawe Fisheries and Smokery** (Easter–Oct & Dec daily 8.30am–5pm, open till 6pm June–Aug; Nov Sat & Sun 8.30am–5pm), where you can buy lots of lovely local food including traditionally smoked fish and mussels, eat the same in their café, check out the exhibition on traditional smoking techniques, learn how to fly-fish, or go for a stroll down to nearby Loch Etive with your picnic.

Loch Awe

Legend has it that **Loch Awe** – at more than 25 miles in length, the longest stretch of fresh water in the country – was created by a witch and inhabited by a monster even more gruesome than the one at Loch Ness. Most travellers only encounter the north end of the loch as they speed along its shores by car or train on the way to Oban. This part of the loch has several tiny islands sporting picturesque ruins. Fifteenth-century **Kilchurn Castle**, strategically situated on a rocky spit – once an island – at the head of the loch and formerly a Campbell stronghold, has been abandoned to the elements since being struck by lightning in the 1760s, and is now one of Argyll's most photogenic lochside ruins. The only way to see the castle properly is to join one of the hour-long steamboat cruises (Ⓣ01838/200440) that set off during summer months from the pier at the small village of **Lochawe**, right by the village's train station (where there's also a small tearoom in a parked railway carriage).

The main attraction on the shores of Loch Awe is, however, rather less picturesque. **Cruachan Power Station** (Easter–Oct daily 9.30am–5pm; Nov–March

Mon–Fri 10am–4pm; £4) is actually constructed inside mighty Ben Cruachan (3693ft), which looms over the head of Loch Awe; it was built in 1965 as part of the hydroelectric network which generates around ten percent of Scotland's electricity. Half-hour guided tours set off every hour from the **visitor centre** by the loch, taking you to a viewing platform above the generating room deep inside the "hollow mountain". The whole experience of visiting an industrial complex hidden within a mountain is very James Bond, and it certainly pulls in the tour coaches, so if you're keen to go, make sure you get there before the queues start to form, particularly in summer.

There aren't many decent **places to stay** around Loch Awe, with the exception of two particularly luxurious hotels on the peaceful northwestern shores, reached by a back road from Taynuilt to the hamlet of Kilchrenan. The *Taychreggan Hotel* (Ⓣ01866/833211, Ⓦwww.taychregganhotel.co.uk; ❼) is an old drovers' inn by the loch now plumped up into an upmarket retreat, while the *Ardanaiseig Hotel* (Ⓣ01866/833333, Ⓦwww.ardanaiseig.com; ❼; closed Jan) is a wonderfully secluded, romantic escape set in a palatial Scottish Baronial pile four miles to the northeast down a dead-end track. Both these hotels have superb, though expensive, restaurants, and the *Ardanaiseig* also has its own glorious **gardens** (daily 9.30am–dusk), home of rare species of azaleas and rhododendrons, worth visiting even if you're not staying here.

North of Oban

On the north side of the Connel Bridge lies the hammerhead peninsula of **Benderloch** (from *beinn eadar da loch*, "hill between two lochs"), which has little to distinguish it other than the fact that it's the location for three of Argyll's most interesting **places to stay**. Standing on its own, right above the beach just west of the village of Benderloch, *Dun Na Mara* (Ⓣ01631/720233, Ⓦwww.dunnamara.com; ❺) is a fine Arts and Crafts-style holiday home where highly stylish contemporary decor is complemented by the warm hospitality (including imaginative breakfasts) of its two young architect owners. A contrast in style can be found on the northern side of the peninsula at **Barcaldine Castle**, an early seventeenth-century Campbell tower house. Bought as a ruin in 1896 and restored, it is now run as a B&B by the current heir, London-born and -bred Roderick, and his wife Caroline. There are no real treasures here, but the castle is fun to explore, with dungeons and hidden staircases and it makes a fairly memorable place to stay (Ⓣ01631/720598, Ⓦwww.freewebs.com/barcaldinecastle; ❺; Oct–March minimum stay 2 nights). If you have an unlimited budget you might like to stay at the area's most exclusive hotel, the *Isle of Eriska*, a luxury, turreted, Scottish Baronial place with a spa, pool and upmarket dining room. It's run by the Buchanan-Smiths on their own 300-acre island off the northern point of Benderloch (Ⓣ01631/720371, Ⓦwww.eriska-hotel.co.uk; ❾).

Since the weather in this part of Scotland can be bad at almost any time of the year, it's as well to know about the **Scottish Sea Life & Marine Sanctuary** (daily: 10am–5pm, open till 6pm July & Aug; £9.50), which is to be found on the A828, along the southern shores of Loch Creran. Here you can see loads of sea creatures at close quarters, touch the (non-)stingrays, do a bit of rockpool dipping, keep a look out for the resident otters and learn how common seal orphan pups are rescued and returned to the wild.

Appin

With the new Creagan Bridge in place – the old wrought-iron railway bridge sadly having been demolished – there's no need to circumnavigate Loch Creran in order to reach the district of **Appin**, best known as the setting for Robert

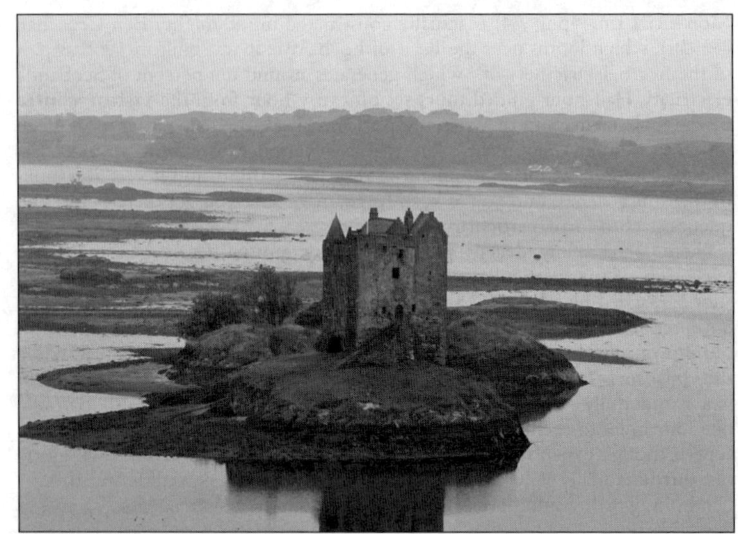

△ Castle Stalker, Appin

Louis Stevenson's *Kidnapped*, a fictionalized account of the "Appin Murder" of 1752, when Colin Campbell was shot in the back, allegedly by one of the disenfranchised Stewart clan.

The name Appin derives from the Gaelic *abthaine*, meaning "lands belonging to the abbey", in this case the one on the island of Lismore (see opposite), which is linked to the peninsula by passenger ferry from **PORT APPIN**, a pretty little fishing village at the westernmost tip of the peninsula. Overlooking a host of tiny little islands dotted around Loch Linnhe, with Lismore and the mountains Morvern and Mull in the background, this is, without doubt, one of Argyll's most picturesque spots. The *Pierhouse Hotel* (Ⓣ01631/730302, Ⓦwww.pierhousehotel.co.uk; ⑤), nicely situated right by the ferry, has a popular bar and an expensive seafood restaurant. If you're wandering around the village, take time to look at the display beside the village hall about the lighthouse on nearby Sgeir Bhuidhe (Yellow Skerry), which one night in 2001 was painted pink with yellow spots by protesters campaigning against its removal.

Framed magnificently as you wind along the single-track road to Port Appin is one of Argyll's most romantic ruined castles, the much-photographed **Castle Stalker**, which occupies a tiny rock island to the north of Port Appin. Built by the Stewarts of Appin in the sixteenth century and gifted to King James IV as a hunting lodge, it inevitably fell into the hands of the Campbells after 1745. The current owners open the castle to the public for very short periods each year, and all visits are by appointment only; ring Ⓣ01631/730354, check Ⓦwww.castlestalker.com or ask at Oban tourist office for opening times. Open all year, however, and offering one of the best outlooks over the castle, the pleasant, modern *Castle Stalker View* **café** (March–Oct daily 9.30am–5.30pm; Nov–Feb Wed–Sun 10am–4pm) is located a little way up the main road north towards Ballachulish. **Bike rental** is available from Port Appin Bikes (Ⓣ01631/730391) and it's worth noting that bicycles travel for free on the passenger ferry to Lismore (see p.96). For other **outdoor pursuits**, head for the Linnhe Marine Water Sports Centre (Ⓣ07721/503981; May–Sept) in Lettershuna (just north of Castle Stalker), which rents out boats of all shapes and sizes, offers sailing and windsurfing lessons, not to mention water-skiing, clay-pigeon shooting and even pony trekking.

Isle of Lismore

Lying in the middle of Loch Linnhe, to the north of Oban, and barely rising above a hillock, the narrow island of **Lismore** (Ⓦwww.isleoflismore.com) offers wonderful gentle walking and cycling opportunities, with unrivalled views, in fine weather, across to the mountains of Morvern, Lochaber and Mull. Legend has it that St Columba and Moluag both fancied the skinny island as a missionary base, but as they raced towards it Moluag cut off his finger and threw it ashore ahead of Columba, claiming the land for himself. Of Moluag's sixth-century foundation nothing remains, but from 1236 until 1507 the island served as the seat of the bishop of Argyll. It was a judicious choice, as Lismore is undoubtedly one of the most fertile of the Inner Hebrides – its name, coined by Moluag himself, derives from the Gaelic *lios mór*, meaning "great garden" – and before the Clearances (see p.505) it supported nearly 1400 inhabitants; the population today is around a tenth of that figure, half of them over 60.

Lismore is about eight miles long and one mile wide, and the ferry from Oban lands at **ACHNACROISH**, roughly halfway along the eastern coastline. To get to grips with the history of the island and its Gaelic culture (and have a cup of tea), follow the signs for the nearby **Comann Eachdraidh Lios Mór**,

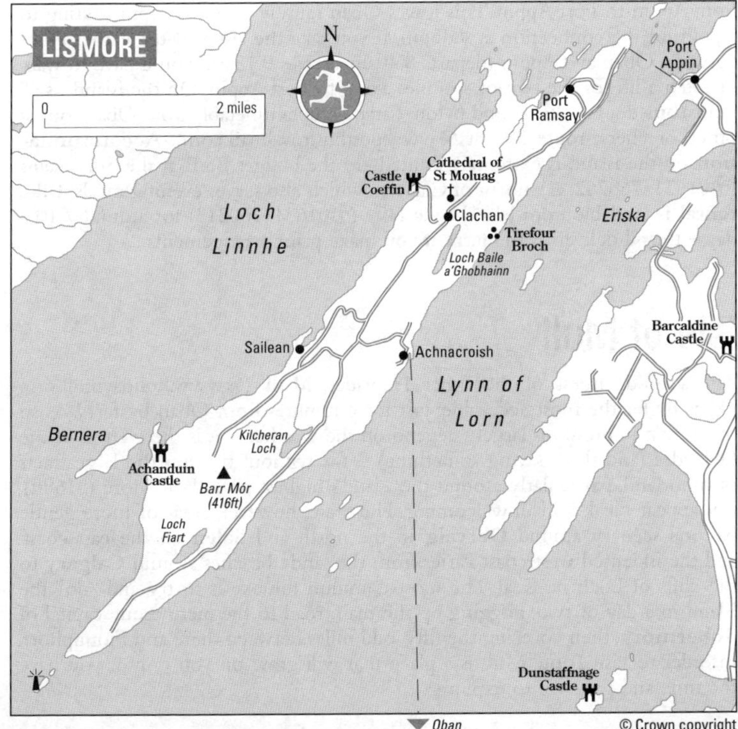

or Lismore Historical Society (May–Sept Mon, Tues, Thurs–Sat 11am–4pm; £2). When you're there, ask if you can pay a visit to a cottar's (landless tenant's) cottage, **Tigh Iseabail Dhaidh**, restored by the Historical Society to the way it would have been in the nineteenth century, with traditionally built stone walls, birch roof timbers and thatched roof. The island post office and shop are along the main road between Achnacroish and **CLACHAN**, a couple of miles northeast, where the diminutive, whitewashed former **Cathedral of St Moluag** stands. All that remains of the fourteenth-century cathedral is the choir, which was reduced in height and converted into the parish church in 1749; inside you can see a few of the original seats for the upper clergy, a stone basin in the south wall, and several medieval doorways. Due east of the church – head north up the road and take the turning signposted on the right – the circular **Tirefour Broch**, over two thousand years old, occupies a commanding position and boasts walls almost 10ft thick in places. West of Clachan are the much more recent ruins of **Castle Coeffin**, a twelfth-century MacDougall fortress once believed to have been haunted by the ghost of Beothail, sister of the Norse prince Caiffen. A few other places worth exploring are **Sailean**, an abandoned quarry village further south along the west coast, with its disused kilns and cottages; the ruins of **Achanduin Castle**, in the southwest, where the bishops are thought to have resided; and Barr Mór (416ft), the island's highest point.

Two **ferries** serve Lismore: a small CalMac car ferry from Oban to Achnacroish (Mon–Sat 2–5 daily; 50min), and a shorter passenger- and bicycle-only crossing from Port Appin to the island's north point (daily every 2hr; 5min). Three buses a day connect Oban to Appin, but only one of these connects with a service from Appin to Port Appin. This leaves Oban railway station at 4pm, getting to Appin for the connection at 4.35pm. If you take the faster of the earlier buses between Oban and Appin (departs 8.40am, arrives 9.15am) you'll have to walk or hitch a lift for the two or so miles along to Port Appin. On the island itself, a **postbus** does a daily round (Mon–Sat; pick up a timetable from Oban tourist office or check route 202 at ⓦwww.postbus.royalmail.com). **Accommodation** on the island is extremely limited: try the budget B&B at the *Schoolhouse* (ⓣ01631/760262; ❷), north of Clachan, which also serves evening meals. **Bike rental** is available from Island Bike Hire (ⓣ01631/760213) for around £10 a day – they'll deliver to the ferry if you make prior arrangements.

Isle of Mull

The second largest of the Inner Hebrides, **Mull** (ⓦwww.holidaymull.org.uk) is by far the most accessible: just forty minutes from Oban by ferry. As so often, first impressions largely depend on the weather – it is the wettest of the Hebrides (and that's saying something) – for without the sun the large tracts of moorland, particularly around the island's highest peak, Ben More (3169ft), can appear bleak and unwelcoming. There are, however, areas of more gentle pastoral scenery around **Dervaig** in the north and **Salen** on the east coast, and the indented west coast varies from the sandy beaches around **Calgary** to the cliffs of Loch na Keal. The most common mistake is to try and "do" the island in a day or two: flogging up the main road to the picturesque capital of **Tobermory**, then covering the fifty-odd miles between there and Fionnphort, in order to visit **Iona**. Mull is a place that will grow on you only if you have the time and patience to explore.

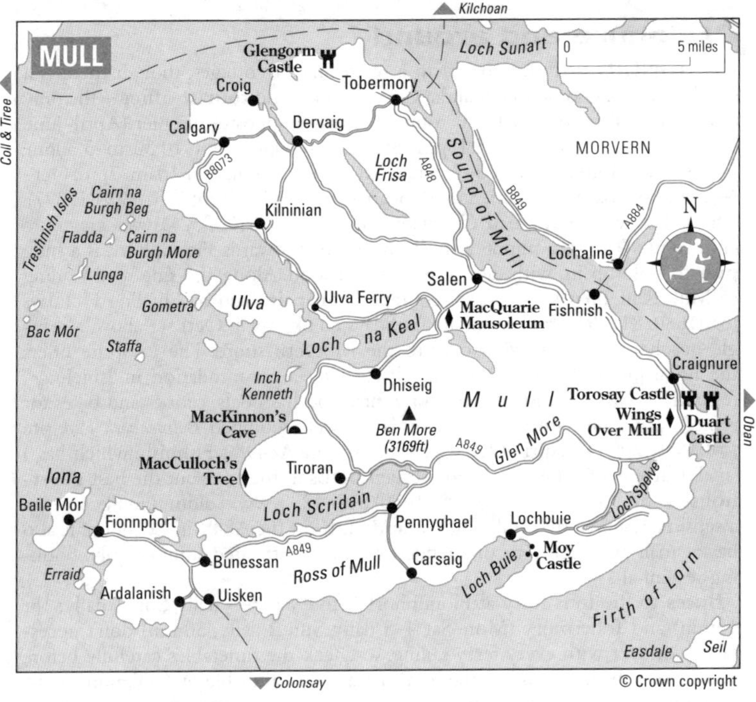

Historically, crofting, whisky distilling and fishing supported the islanders (*Muileachs*), but the population – which peaked at 10,000 – decreased dramatically in the late nineteenth century due to the Clearances and the 1846 potato famine. On Mull, it is a trend that has been reversed, mostly owing to the large influx of settlers from elsewhere in the country, which has brought the current population up to over 2500. One of the main reasons for this resurgence is, of course, tourism – more than half a million visitors come here each year – although, oddly enough, there are very few large hotels or campsites. Mull makes particular efforts to draw visitors to **special events** through the year: these annual events include a wildlife week in May, the Mendelssohn on Mull Festival in July, which commemorates the composer's visit here in 1829, and a rally car event around the island's winding roads in October.

Craignure is the main entry point to Mull, with a frequent daily **car ferry** link to Oban; if you're taking a car over, it's advisable to book ahead for this service. A much smaller and less expensive car ferry crosses daily from Lochaline on the Morvern peninsula (see p.266) to the slipway at Fishnish, six miles northwest of Craignure. Another even smaller car ferry connects Kilchoan on the Ardnamurchan peninsula (see p.268) with Tobermory, 24 miles northwest of Craignure. Both of these two smaller ferries run on a first-come, first-served basis. **Public transport** on Mull is not too bad on the main A849, but there's more or less no service along the west coast (for more information, visit Ⓦwww.mict.co.uk/travel). If you're **driving**, note that the roads are still predominantly single-track, with passing places, which can slow journeys down considerably, particularly during the busier months of summer.

Craignure and around

CRAIGNURE is little more than a scattering of cottages, though there is a small shop, a bar, some toilets and a CalMac ticket and **tourist office** – the only one on the island open all year round – situated opposite the pier (April–June & Sept Mon–Fri 8.30am–5.15pm, Sat 9am–6.30pm, Sun 10.30am–5.30pm; July & Aug Mon–Fri 8.30am–7.30pm, Sat 9am–6.30pm, Sun 10am–7pm; Oct–March Mon–Sat 9am–5pm, Sun 10.30am–noon, 3.30–5pm; ⓣ01680/812377). The old-style, whitewashed *Craignure Inn* (ⓣ01680/812305, ⓦwww.craignure-inn.co.uk; ⑤), just a minute's stroll up the road towards Fionnphort, is a snug **pub** to hole up in, with decent rooms and food. Along the side road leading to Mull Rail, there's also a well-equipped **campsite** run by Shieling Holidays (ⓣ01680/812496, ⓦwww.shielingholidays.co.uk; April–Oct) set above a shingle beach with good views over to the Morvern shore. The campsite offers the usual pitches, plus hostel and self-catering accommodation in "shielings" (essentially large, furnished, hard-top tents), and has boats, canoes and bikes for rent. Another pleasant place to camp is the well-equipped *Balmeanach Park* site (ⓣ01680/300342; April–Oct), five miles up the A849 at Fishnish, which has a small tearoom attached. There are several B&Bs in the area, but the best **guesthouse** is the *Old Mill Cottage* (ⓣ01680/812442, ⓦwww.oldmill.mull.com; ④), a sensitively converted mill, three miles south on the A849 in Lochdon; it also has a small and highly recommended restaurant attached (dinner only; bookings essential).

Buses to the Iona ferry at Fionnphort (Mon–Sat 3–4 daily, Sun 1 daily; 1hr 15min) and Tobermory (Mon–Sat 4–5 daily, Sun 2 daily; 50min) don't necessarily connect with every ferry sailing, so check the timetables carefully before you leave Oban. The other method of transport available at Craignure is the diminutive, narrow-gauge Mull & West Highland Railway, commonly known as **Mull Rail** (Easter to mid-Oct; £4 return; ⓣ01680/812494, ⓦwww.mullrail.co.uk), built in the 1980s and the only working railway in the Scottish islands. The Craignure station is situated beyond the Shieling Holidays campsite, and the line stretches southeast for about a mile and a half to Torosay Castle (see below). If you prefer to take the train one way only, it's a lovely thirty-minute walk along the coast (with the possibility of spotting an otter). The company uses diesel and steam locomotives, so ring ahead if you want to be sure of a steam-driven train.

Torosay and Duart castles

Two castles lie immediately southeast of Craignure. The first, a mile-long walk or short train ride from Craignure, is **Torosay Castle** (April to mid-Oct daily 10.30am–5.30pm; £5.50; ⓦwww.torosay.com), a full-blown Scottish Baronial creation. The house itself is stuffed with memorabilia relating to the present owners, the Guthries, all of it amusingly captioned but of no great importance, with the possible exception of the belongings of the late David Guthrie-James, who made a daring escape from a POW camp in Germany during World War II. Torosay's real highlight, however, is the magnificent **gardens** (daily: summer months 9am–7pm, winter during daylight hours; £4.50) with their avenue of eighteenth-century Venetian statues, Japanese section, and views up Loch Linnhe.

Very different in style is **Duart Castle** (April Sun–Thurs 11am–4pm; May–Oct daily 10.30am–5.30pm; £4.50; ⓦwww.duartcastle.com), a couple of miles east of Torosay, which is perched on a rocky promontory sticking out into the Sound of Mull, making it a striking landmark from the Oban–Craignure ferry.

If you're arriving off the ferry, look out for the Duart Coach, which meets the boats arriving at 10.45am, 12.45pm and 2.45pm (10.15am, 12.15pm and 2.15pm on Sat) for the ten-minute ride to the Castle. Duart was headquarters of the once-powerful MacLean clan from the thirteenth century, but was burnt down by the Campbells and confiscated after the 1745 rebellion. In 1911 the 26th clan chief, Fitzroy MacLean (1835–1936) – not to be confused with the Scottish writer of the same name – managed to buy it back and restore it. Buffeted by winds and weather, the castle is by no means a luxurious country seat: you can peek at the dungeons, climb up to the ramparts, study the family photos, and learn about the world scout movement (the 27th clan chief became Chief Scout in 1959). After your visit, you can enjoy home-made cakes and tea at the castle's friendly tearoom (May–Sept).

Wings Over Mull

A short way past Torosay Castle, a turn-off leads to **Wings over Mull** (mid-Feb to Oct 10.30am–5.30pm; £4.50; Ⓦwww.wingsovermull.com), a conservation centre and sanctuary devoted to birds of prey. While keen bird watchers coming to Mull have an excellent chance of seeing some of Britain's finest birds of prey in the wild, the visitors' centre here, based in a converted steading, has lots of background information about all kinds of owls, hawks, falcons and eagles, as well as details about the work done at the centre to rescue and preserve these species. More memorably, you can take a close look at around forty different birds housed in cages and pens nearby. They're not cooped up all the time, however, with flying displays taking place at noon, 2pm and 4pm each day.

Tobermory

Mull's chief town, **TOBERMORY** (Ⓦwww.tobermory.co.uk), at the northern tip of the islands, is easily the most attractive fishing port on the west coast of Scotland, its clusters of brightly coloured houses and boats sheltering in a bay backed by a steep bluff. Founded in 1788 by the British Society for Encouraging Fisheries, it never really took off as a fishing port and only survived due to the steady influx of crofters evicted from other parts of the island during the Clearances. With a population of more than 800, it is the most important settlement on Mull, and if you're staying any length of time on the island you're bound to want to visit, not least because it has a Womble named after it (or, if you're under 10, because it's the setting for the children's TV show *Balamory*).

Information and accommodation

The **tourist office** (April Mon–Fri 9am–5pm, Sat & Sun noon–5pm; May & June Mon–Fri 9am–5pm, Sat & Sun 11am–5pm; July & Aug Mon–Sat 9am–6pm, Sun 10am–5pm; Sept & Oct Mon–Sat 10am–5pm, Sun noon–5pm; Ⓣ01688/302182) is in the same building as the CalMac ticket office on the pier at the far end of Main Street. If you want to **rent a bike**, head to Archibald Brown, the endearingly old-fashioned ironmongers on Main Street (Ⓣ01688/302020, Ⓦwww.browns-tobermory.co.uk).

The tourist office can book you into a **B&B** for a small fee – not a bad idea in high season, when the places on Main Street tend to get booked up fast, and the rest are a stiff climb from the harbour. The small, friendly SYHA **hostel** is on Main Street (Ⓣ0870/004 1151, Ⓦwww.syha.org.uk; March–Oct) and has Internet and laundry facilities. The nearest **campsite** is *Newdale* (Ⓣ01688/302624, Ⓦwww.tobermory-campsite.co.uk; April–Oct), nicely situated one and a half miles uphill from Tobermory on the B8073 to Dervaig.

Trips and tours by land and sea around Mull, Staffa and Iona

Mull, Staffa and Iona offer such a concentrated range of experiences, from exploring peaceful ruins to seeing killer whales, that it's little surprise that a wide choice of trips and tours is available around the islands. Mull is perhaps second only to Skye when it comes to the number of **coach tours** that clog up the island's single-track roads. Many of these are operated by Bowman's (ⓣ01680/812313, ⓦwww.bowmanstours.co.uk), who offer whistle-stop (if sometimes exhausting) day-tours taking in either Iona and a boat trip to Staffa or Tobermory and a bit of Mull scenery. If you start from Oban, tours begin at around £25; from Craignure, they start at just £20. These trips are organized in conjunction with CalMac (ⓣ01631/562244) and Gordon Grant Marine (see below), both of whom you can use to book. A more intimate way to explore Mull is on a specialized land-based **wildlife tour**, most of which head off in pursuit of the island's three most elusive creatures, the otter, the sea eagle and the golden eagle: try Island Encounter (ⓣ01680/300441, ⓦwww.mullwildlife.co.uk), or Isle of Mull Wildlife Expeditions (ⓣ01688/500121, ⓦwww.torrbuan.com), which both offer a full day's outing, with food, for around £30.

Boat trips, which leave from many different places around Mull, tend to offer a mix of sightseeing and wildlife, with prices ranging from around £15 for a two-hour cruise to £50 for a full day **whale watching**. Sea Life Surveys (ⓣ01688/302916, ⓦwww.whalewatchingscotland.com), which is linked to the research being done by the Hebridean Whale and Dolphin Trust, focuses on seeking out the whales (minke and even killer whales are the most common), porpoises, dolphins and basking sharks that spend time in the waters around the Hebrides. Based in Tobermory, the same outfit also operates Ecocruz, which sticks to coastal waters rather than heading for the open sea, and is particularly good for families. Rather more sedate are the wildlife cruises on the solid gaff-rigged ketch *Solais Na Mara* (ⓦwww.hebrideanadventure.co.uk; book through the CalMac office in Tobermory ⓣ01688/302017), which heads out of Tobermory harbour under sail, weather permitting, for three-hour trips during the day as well as a two-hour sunset cruise. Finally, you can combine a wildlife cruise with a trip to the island of Rum (see p.352) on the dive-charter boat *Silver Swift* (ⓣ01688/302390, ⓦwww.silverswift.co.uk), which goes to the Small Isles on Wednesdays throughout summer (and other days, depending on weather and demand).

Elsewhere on Mull, Turus Mara (ⓣ0800/085 8786, ⓦwww.turusmara.com), based at Ulva Ferry, set out in the direction of Staffa and the Treshnish Isles, where the birdlife, including puffins, is prodigious. They also include Iona in some of their trips. Otherwise, dedicated excursions to Staffa mostly run from Fionnphort and Iona: try Iolaire (ⓣ01681/700358, ⓦwww.staffatrips.f9.co.uk) or Gordon Grant Marine (ⓣ01681/700338, ⓦwww.staffatours.com – trips run twice daily (weather permitting) between April and October and cost around £18, and there's usually a chance to get onto the island to visit Fingal's Cave.

Ach-na-Craiboh Erray Road ⓣ01688/302301, ⓦwww.tobermoryholidays.co.uk. An attractive house at the top of town by the golf course with happily ramshackle grounds and a converted barn containing functional, well-equipped self-catering and B&B apartments. ❸

Baliscate Guest House Salen Road ⓣ01688/302048, ⓦwww.baliscate.co.uk. Good-quality B&B in an imposing whitewashed Victorian guesthouse with a large garden set back from the road to Salen on the edge of Tobermory. ❸

Failte Guest House Main Street ⓣ01688/302495. Prominent guesthouse on the main street with pleasantly furnished en-suite rooms, some of which have views out over the harbour. Open mid-March to Oct. ❹

Glengorm Castle near Tobermory ⓣ01688/302321, ⓦwww.glengormcastle.co.uk. Fairy-tale, rambling Baronial mansion in a superb, secluded setting, five miles northwest of Tobermory, with incredible coastal views, lovely gardens and local walks. Guests get use of the castle's wood-panelled library and lounge; the bedrooms are large and full of splendid features. ❼

Strongarbh House ⓣ01688/302730. Elegant Victorian mansion with three guest rooms, a nice lounge and library, and views down attractive lawns to the Sound of Mull. March–Oct. ❸

Tobermory Hotel Main Street ⓣ01688/302091, ⓦwww.thetobermoryhotel.com. Smallish, fairly smart and comfortable hotel with fifteen rooms situated right on the harbourfront. ❺

The Town

The harbour – known as **Main Street** – is one long parade of multicoloured hotels, guesthouses, restaurants and shops, and you could happily spend an hour or so meandering around: Mull Pottery and the Mull Silver Company are both worth a browse, as is the **Hebridean Whale and Dolphin Trust** (April–Oct daily 10am–4pm; Nov–March Mon–Fri 11am–5pm; free; ⓦwww.hwdt.org), run by a welcoming bunch of enthusiasts. The small office has lots of information on how to identify marine mammals, and on recent sightings. They're very child-friendly, too, and will keep kids amused for an hour or so with computer marine games, word searches and a bit of artwork. Note that you can't book whale-watching trips here – to do this you should contact one of the operators listed in the box on p.100.

Another good wet-weather retreat is the **Mull Museum** (Easter to mid-Oct Mon–Fri 10am–4pm, Sat 10am–1pm; £1), further along Main Street, which packs a great deal of information and artefacts – including a few objects salvaged from the *San Juan* – into one tiny room. Alternatively, there's the minuscule **Tobermory Distillery** (Easter–Oct Mon–Fri 10am–5pm; £2.50) at the south end of the bay, founded in 1795 but closed down three times since then. Today, it's back in business and offers a pretty desultory guided tour, rounded off with a dram.

A stiff climb up Back Brae will bring you to the island's main arts centre, **An Tobar** (Tues–Sat 10am–4pm; June–Aug also Sun 1–4pm; free; ⓦwww.antobar.co.uk), housed in a converted Victorian schoolhouse. The small but attractive centre hosts exhibitions, a variety of live events, and contains a café with comfy sofas set before a real fire. The rest of the upper town is laid out on a classic grid-plan, and merits a stroll, if only for the great views over the bay.

If you've got transport, or are prepared to walk a mile or so uphill out of town, pay a visit to **Sgriob-ruadh Farm** (daily 10am–4pm; free; ⓣ01688/302235,

The Tobermory treasure

The most dramatic event in Tobermory's history was in 1588, when a ship from the **Spanish Armada** sank in mysterious circumstances while having repairs done to its sails and rigging in the town harbour. The story goes that one of the MacLeans of Duart was taken prisoner, but when the ship weighed anchor he made his way to the powder magazine and blew it up. However, several versions of the story exist, and even the identity of the ship has been hotly disputed: for many years it was thought to be the treasure-laden Spanish galleon *Almirante di Florencia*, but it now seems more likely that it was the rather more prosaic troop-carrier *San Juan de Sicilia*. Nevertheless, the possibility of precious sunken booty at the bottom of Tobermory harbour has fired the greed of numerous lairds and kings – in the 1950s, Royal Navy divers were engaged by the Duke of Argyll in a futile hunt for the treasure, and in 1982 another unsuccessful attempt was made. Only the odd ducat and bit of crockery were ever found – what has been raised from the mud is on display in the Mull Museum on Tobermory Main Street.

Ⓦ www.isleofmullcheese.co.uk) on the Glengorm road, where one of Scotland's finest artisan cheeses, the tangy, Cheddar-like "Isle of Mull", is produced. You can usually see some aspect of the cheese-making process going on through viewing windows and if staff are available there's always the chance to find out more about the different types made here, including a tour to the cellars. You can also buy cheese directly from the farm. Four miles further out along the same road are the towers and turrets of **Glengorm Castle** (Ⓦ www.glengormcastle.co.uk), a Scots Baronial pile overlooking the sea which offers accommodation (see p.100) and also has an attractively converted steading, which incorporates a modern café, well-stocked farm shop and art gallery (Easter to mid-Oct daily 10am–5pm; for winter opening, phone Ⓣ 01688/302321). You can walk around their attractive walled garden or take on longer forest and coastal trails.

Eating and drinking

Main Street heaves with **places to eat**, including a highly rated fish and chip van on the old pier which will serve up scallops and chips alongside more traditional fish suppers. The best of the bunch on Main Street is probably *The Water's Edge* in the *Tobermory Hotel*, which makes a good effort to emphasise local produce, particularly seafood, while for something more exotic, *Javier's Restaurant* (Ⓣ 01688/302350) above *MacGochan's* (see below) serves hearty Argentinian/Hispanic cuisine. A good option for imaginatively prepared meals using local produce is the pleasant upstairs café/bistro at the *Mull Pottery* at Ballinsgate, just on the edge of town (Ⓣ 01688/302592), while *Ulva House* (Ⓣ 01688/302044, Ⓦ www.mull-shellfish.co.uk), located above the bay between An Tobar and the prominent *Western Isles Hotel*, is another notch up, serving uncomplicated but very well prepared meals based around a platter of the island's finest seafood. Fine **picnic** fodder, fresh bread and goodies can be found at the excellent Island Bakery, also on the harbourfront.

The lively bar of the *Mishnish Hotel* has been the most popular local **drinking** hole for many years, and features live music at the weekend. Unfortunately, the place lost much of its character (and some of its custom) after a facelift, no doubt prompted by the arrival of *MacGochan's*, a purpose-built, though pleasant enough, pub, which also offers occasional live music, on the opposite side of the harbour near the distillery.

If you want to know what there is in the way of **entertainment** in Tobermory (or anywhere else on Mull), be sure to pick up the free monthly newsletter *Round & About*, and/or buy a copy of *Am Muileach*, the monthly island newspaper. It's worth checking the programme at An Tobar for concerts by touring

Walks around Tobermory

There are a couple of none-too-strenuous **walks** from Tobermory, which will transport you in a matter of minutes into the Scottish countryside. The first is an hour-long coastal walk to the **lighthouse** (a mile to the north of town) and back. The path begins just behind the tourist office, and takes you through mixed woodland, some 50ft above the sea, before descending to the shore. The second, also an hour long, takes you in the opposite direction, starting in the car park by *MacGochans* pub and the distillery and heading southeast around the edge of Tobermory Bay to **Aros Park**, the former grounds of the now-demolished Aros House. The area is currently owned by the Forestry Commission and there are useful signposts along the way. The rhododendrons are spectacular in early summer, as are the park's two impressive waterfalls, especially after a few days' rain.

musicians, while the Mull Theatre (Ⓣ01688/302828, Ⓦwww.mulltheatre.com) uses various venues around the island for its widely acclaimed productions. If you want to watch a film, look out for the *Screen Machine* (Ⓦwww.screenmachine.co.uk; bookings on Ⓣ01463/720890, Ⓦwww.thebooth.co.uk) which often pulls into town: a mobile cinema squeezed into the back of a specially converted articulated lorry, it can seat up to 80 people and shows fairly recent releases.

Dervaig and Calgary

The gently undulating countryside west of Tobermory, beyond the freshwater Mishnish lochs, provides some of the most beguiling scenery on the island. Added to this, the road out west, the B8073, is exceptionally dramatic, with fiendish switchbacks much appreciated during the annual Mull Rally, which takes place each October. Loch Frisa, a long slash in the landscape south of the road, is a well-known nesting place for some of the island's **white-tailed (or sea) eagles**. There's a well-placed hide which has close-up, live CCTV pictures of the nest; if you're here between April and July, when the birds are nesting, guided access to the hide is available through the RSPB (£3; bookings on Ⓣ01688/302038)

The only village of any size on this side of the island is **DERVAIG**, which nestles beside narrow Loch Chumhainn, just eight miles southwest of Tobermory, distinguished by its unusual pencil-shaped church spire and single street of dinky whitewashed cottages and old corrugated-iron shacks. Signposted off the main road a little beyond Dervaig, the **Old Byre Heritage Centre** (Easter–Oct Wed–Sun 10.30am–6.30pm; £3) shows a video on the island's history, and has a gift-festooned tearoom.

Dervaig has a wide choice of **places to stay**. At the upper end of the scale, Victorian *Druimard Country House* (Ⓣ01688/400345, Ⓦwww.druimard.co.uk; ❻), located on the fringe of Dervaig, is a pleasant, comfy place serving good dinners. There's also fine local food served at the *Druimnacroish Hotel* (Ⓣ01688/400274, Ⓦwww.druimnacroish.co.uk; ❺; March–Nov), a lovely country house in a rural setting two miles out on the Salen road. There are several pleasant B&Bs, including the excellent *Cuin Lodge* (Ⓣ01688/400346, Ⓦwww.cuin-lodge.mull.com; ❷), an old shooting lodge overlooking the loch, to the northwest of the village. There's also a **bunkhouse** (Ⓣ01688/400492) right in the centre of the village, with bedding provided and disabled facilities.

The road continues cross-country to **CALGARY**, once a thriving crofting community, now a quiet glen which opens out onto Mull's finest sandy bay, backed by low-lying dunes and machair, with wonderful views over to Coll and Tiree. A few hundred yards back from the beach is a cluster of buildings grouped around the delightful *Calgary Hotel* (Ⓣ01688/400256, Ⓦwww.calgary.co.uk; ❺; March–Nov), one of the island's most pleasant hotels. Also here is the *Carthouse Gallery*, which has an array of top-notch local art as well as a daytime café, the excellent, moderately priced *Dovecote* restaurant, and Calgary Art in Nature, a mile-long walk through mature woodland dotted with sculptures by different artists made from wood, stone, wicker and metal. Down by the beach itself, there's a small but spectacular spot for **camping** rough; the only facilities are the public toilets. For the record: the city of Calgary in Canada does indeed take its name from this little village, though it was not so named by Mull emigrants, but by one Colonel McLeod of the North West Mounted Police, who once holidayed here.

Salen and around

SALEN, on the east coast halfway between Craignure and Tobermory, lies at the narrowest point on Mull. There's not a great deal to the place, though a pair of beached fishing boats and the ivy-covered ruins of Gylen Castle might catch your eye as you pass through. There are, however, several decent places to stay in the vicinity, ranging from the **hostel**-style accommodation of *Arle Lodge* (ⓣ01680/300299, ⓦwww.arlelodge.co.uk; ❷), with twin and family rooms four miles north of Salen on the road to Tobermory, to the pretty, Victorian *Gruline Home Farm* **B&B** (ⓣ01680/300581, ⓦwww.gruline.com; dinner, bed & breakfast ❽), a non-working farmhouse four miles to the southwest near the shores of Loch Na Keal, which serves up extra special dinners (non-residents must reserve). Simpler, less expensive B&B is available next door at *Barn Cottage* (ⓣ01680/300451, ⓦwww.holidaymull.org/barncottage; ❷). Salen itself has a very pleasant place to **eat**, *Mediterranea* (ⓣ01680/300200, ⓦwww.mullonthemed.com; April–Oct; closed Wed), which mixes engaging Scottish hospitality with Sicilian cooking. You can also **rent bikes** here from *On Yer Bike* (ⓣ01680/300501), who have mountain bikes, hybrids and child trailers to rent.

The Isle of Ulva

A chieftain to the Highlands bound
Cries "Boatman, do not tarry!
And I'll give thee a silver pound
To row us o'er the ferry!"
"Now who be ye, would cross Lochgyle
This dark and stormy water?"
"O I'm the chief of Ulva's isle,
And this, Lord Ullin's daughter."

Lord Ullin's Daughter by Thomas Campbell (1777–1844)

Around the time poet laureate Campbell penned this tragic poem, the population of **Ulva** (from the Norse *ulv øy*, or "wolf island") was a staggering 850, sustained by the huge quantities of kelp which were exported for glass and soap production. That was before the market for kelp collapsed and the 1846 potato famine hit, after which the remaining population was brutally evicted. Nowadays barely thirty people live here, and the island is littered with ruined crofts, not to mention a church, designed by Thomas Telford, which would once have seated over three hundred parishioners. It's great walking country, however, with several clearly marked paths crisscrossing the native woodland and the rocky heather moorland interior – and you're almost guaranteed to spot some of the abundant wildlife: at the very least deer, if not buzzards, golden eagles and even sea eagles, with seals and divers offshore. If you like to have a focus for your wanderings, head for the ruined crofting villages and basalt columns similar to those on Staffa along the island's southern coastline; for the island's highest point, Beinn Chreagach (1027ft); or along the north coast to Ulva's tidal neighbour, Gometra, off the west coast.

To **get to Ulva** (ⓦwww.ulva.mull.com), which lies just a hundred yards or so off the west coast of Mull, follow the signs for "Ulva Ferry" west from Salen or south from Calgary – if you've no transport, a postbus can get you there, but you'll have to make your own way back. From **Ulva Ferry**, a small bicycle/passenger-only ferry (£5 return) is available on demand (Mon–Fri 9am–5pm; June–Aug also Sun; at other times by arrangement on ⓣ01688/500226). *The Boathouse*, near the ferry slip on the Ulva side, serves as a licensed **tearoom** selling soup, cakes, snacks, Guinness and Ulva oysters. You can learn more about the history of the island from the **Heritage Centre** exhibition upstairs, and pop into the newly restored thatched smiddy nearby, housing **Sheila's Cottage**, which has been restored to something like its former state when islander Sheila MacFadyen used to live here in the first half of the last century. There's no accommodation, but with permission from the present owners (Ⓣ01688/500264, Ⓔulva@mull.com) you can **camp** rough overnight.

The Isle of Staffa and the Treshnish Isles

Five miles southwest of Ulva, **Staffa** is the most romantic and dramatic of Scotland's many uninhabited islands. On its south side, the perpendicular rockface features an imposing series of black basalt columns, known as the Colonnade, which have been cut by the sea into cathedralesque caverns, most notably **Fingal's Cave**. The Vikings knew about the island – the name derives from their word for "Island of Pillars" – but it wasn't until 1772 that it was "discovered" by the world. Turner painted it, Wordsworth explored it, but Mendelssohn's *Die Fingalshöhle* (the lovely "Hebrides" overture), inspired by the sounds of the sea-wracked caves he heard on a visit here in 1829, did most to popularize the place – after which Queen Victoria gave her blessing, too. Geologists say these polygonal basalt organ pipes were created some sixty million years ago by a massive subterranean explosion. A huge mass of molten basalt burst forth onto land and, as it cooled, solidified into what are, essentially, crystals. Of course, confronted with such artistry, most visitors have found it difficult to believe that their origin is entirely natural – indeed, the various Celtic folk tales, which suggest that the Giant's Causeway in Ireland reached all the way here before being destroyed by rival giants, are certainly more appealing. To **get to Staffa**, you can join one of the many boat trips from Fionnphort, Iona, Ulva Ferry, Dervaig or even Oban (see box on p.100 for full details).

Several operators also offer **boat trips** around the archipelago of uninhabited volcanic islets that make up the **Treshnish Isles** northwest of Staffa. None of the islands is more than a mile or two across, the most distinctive

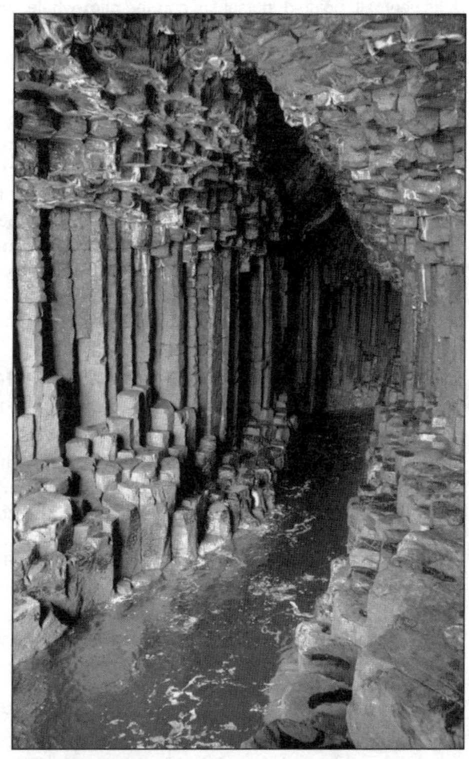

△ Fingal's Cave, Staffa

Whales and dolphins

Watching whales, dolphins and porpoises – collectively known as cetaceans – is a growing tourist industry, and one which, if managed carefully, should eventually make it more lucrative to help preserve these creatures rather than kill them. The Moray Firth (see p.254) is one of the best places in the UK to watch **bottlenose dolphins**, but the waters around the Inner Hebrides have, if anything, a wider variety of cetaceans on offer. Although there are several operators who offer whale-watching boat trips from Oban and Tobermory (see p.100), it is quite possible to catch sight of marine mammals from the shore, or from a ferry. The chief problem is trying to identify what you've seen.

The most common sightings are of **harbour porpoises**, the smallest of the marine mammals, which are about the size of an adult human and have a fairly small dorsal fin. Porpoises are easily confused with dolphins; however, if you see it leap out of the water, then you can be sure it's a dolphin, as porpoises only break the surface with their backs and fins. If you spot a whale, the likelihood is that it's a **minke whale**, which grows to about 30ft in length, making it a mere tiddler in the whale world, but a good four or five times bigger than a porpoise. Minkes are baleen whales, which is to say they have no teeth; instead, they gulp huge quantities of water and sift their food through plates of whalebone. Whales do several things dolphins and porpoises can't do, such as blowing water high into the air, and breaching, which is when they launch themselves out of the water and belly-flop down. The two other whale species regularly seen in Hebridean waters are the **killer whale** or orca, distinguished by its very tall, pointed, dorsal fin, and the **pilot whale**, which is even smaller than the minke, has no white on it, and no throat grooves.

being **Bac Mór**, shaped like a Puritan's hat and popularly dubbed the Dutchman's Cap. Most trips include a stopover on **Lunga**, the largest island, and a nesting place for hundreds of seabirds, in particular guillemots, razorbills (mid-May to July) and puffins (late April to mid-Aug), as well as a breeding ground for common seals (June) and Atlantic greys (early Sept). The two most northerly islands, **Cairn na Burgh More** and **Cairn na Burgh Beag**, have the remains of ruined castles, the first of which served as a lookout post for the Lords of the Isles and was last garrisoned in the Civil War; Cairn na Burgh Beag hasn't been occupied since the 1715 Jacobite uprising.

Ben More and the Ardmeanach peninsula

From the southern shores of Loch na Keal, which almost splits Mull in two, rise the terraced slopes of **Ben More** (3169ft) – literally "big mountain" – a mighty extinct volcano, and the only Munro in the Hebrides outside of Skye. It's most easily climbed from Dhiseig, halfway along the loch's southern shores, though an alternative route is to climb up to the col between Beinn Fhada and A'Chioch, and approach via the mountain's eastern ridge. Further west along the shore the road carves through spectacular overhanging cliffs before heading south past the Gribun rocks which face the tiny island of **Inch Kenneth**, where Unity Mitford lived until her death in 1948. There are great views out to Staffa and the Treshnish Isles as the road leaves the coast behind, climbing over the pass to Loch Scribain, where it eventually joins the equally dramatic Glen More road (A849) from Craignure.

If you're properly equipped for walking, however, you can explore the **Ardmeanach peninsula**, to the west of the road, on foot. On the north coast, a mile or so from the road, is **Mackinnon's Cave** – at 100ft high, one of the largest caves in the Hebrides, and accessible only at low tide. As so often, there's a legend attached to the cave, which tells of an entire party, led by a lone piper, who were once devoured here by evil spirits. On the south coast of the peninsula, it's a longer, rougher six-mile hike from the road to **MacCulloch's Tree**, a forty-foot-high conifer that was engulfed by a lava flow some fifty million years ago and is now embedded in the cliffs at Rubha na h-Uambha. You'll need a good map, sturdy boots and, again, you need to time your arrival with a falling tide. The area is NTS-owned and there is a car park just before *Tiroran House* (Ⓣ01681/705232, Ⓦwww.tiroran.com; ❼), a beautiful secluded **hotel** with six rooms, cosy lounges, good home cooking and a lovely, lush, south-facing garden. They've also got a more affordable room (❺) for hikers tackling nearby Ben More.

The Ross of Mull

Stretching for twenty miles west as far as Iona is Mull's rocky southernmost peninsula, the **Ross of Mull**, which, like much of Scotland, appears blissfully tranquil in good weather, and desolate and bleak in bad climes. Most visitors simply drive through the Ross en route to Iona, but if you have the time it's definitely worth considering exploring, or even staying, in this little-visited part of Mull.

The most scenic spots on the Ross are hidden away on the south coast. If you're approaching the Ross from Craignure, the first of these (to Lochbuie) is signposted even before you've negotiated the splendid Highland pass of Glen More, which brings you to the Ross itself. The road to **LOCHBUIE** skirts Loch Spelve, a sheltered sea loch, followed by the freshwater Loch Uisg, which is fringed by woodland, before emerging, after eight miles, on a fertile plain beside the sea. The bay here is rugged and wide, and overlooked by the handsome peak of Ben Buie (2352ft), to the northwest. Hidden behind a patch of Scots pine are the ivy-strewn ruins of **Moy Castle**, an old MacLean

Unity Mitford on Inch Kenneth

Born in 1914, **Unity Valkyrie Mitford** was the youngest of the Mitford sisters, the daughters of David Mitford, Lord Redesdale. The family became notorious in the 1930s after Unity's older sister, Diana, became involved with (and eventually married) Oswald Mosley, leader of the British Union of Fascists. One of the other daughters, Jessica, was a lifelong Communist, who fought in the Spanish Civil War. Another – Nancy – became a novelist and satirized the family in her first two novels, *The Pursuit of Love* and *Love in a Cold Climate.* However, it was Unity who went on to gain the greatest infamy, due to her close relationship with Hitler, which began after she moved to Germany in 1934. For a while, she became one of Hitler's closest companions, accompanying him on official functions, and even addressing Nazi rallies. On the day that Britain declared war on Germany, Unity attempted to kill herself with a pistol given to her by the Führer, but only succeeded in lodging a bullet in her head. Nine days later she was brought back to Britain, where the press clamoured for her internment. Instead, she was allowed to retire to the island of **Inch Kenneth**, which the family had bought in 1938. She lived there as an invalid, with her mother, Lady Redesdale, eventually dying in a hospital in Oban in 1948. The cause of death was meningitis, brought on by a cerebral abscess caused by the bullet, which was still lodged in her head. Until her death in 1963, Lady Redesdale continued to live for periods on the island, employing a handful of servants and ordering all her groceries from Harrods. Inch Kenneth eventually passed out of Mitford hands in 1966.

stronghold; in the fields to the north is one of the few **stone circles** in the west of Scotland, dating from the second century BC, the highest of its stones about 6ft high. The best accommodation in the vicinity is at *Barrachandroman* (Ⓣ01680/814220, Ⓦwww.barrachandroman.co.uk; ❸), a converted stone barn in Kinlochspelve, overlooking the sea loch. A popular and fairly easy walk is the five-mile hike west along the coastal path to Carsaig (see below).

The main A849 road, single-track (for the most part) and plagued by the large number of coaches that steam down it en route to Iona, hugs the northern coastline of the Ross. The first sign of civilization after Glen More is the small pub, the *Kinloch Hotel*, with an adjoining shop, followed a mile or so later by the tiny settlement of **PENNYGHAEL**, home to the *Pennyghael Hotel* (Ⓣ01681/704288, Ⓦwww.pennyghaelhotel.com; ❼), which has a good restaurant serving local meat and seafood.

A rickety single-track road heads south for four miles from Pennyghael to **CARSAIG**, which enjoys an idyllic setting, looking south out to Colonsay, Islay and Jura. Carsaig is home to the Inniemore School of Painting, but most folk come here either to walk east to Lochbuie (see above), or west under the cliffs, to the **Nuns' Cave**, where nuns from Iona are alleged to have hidden during the Reformation, and then, after four miles or so, at Malcolm's Point, the spectacular **Carsaig Arches**, formed by eroded sea caves, which are linked to basalt cliffs.

Meanwhile, the main road continues for another eleven miles to **BUNESSAN**, the largest village on the peninsula, roughly two-thirds of the way along the Ross. Bunessan has a few useful shops, and a pub and a tearoom, but is otherwise pretty undistinguished.

If the weather's good, it might be worth heading off from Bunessan to the sandy bays of the south coast. There's a car park near the *Ardachy House Hotel* (Ⓣ01681/700505, Ⓦwww.ardachy.co.uk; ❺; March–Oct) – so remote that there's no TV reception – which overlooks the wide expanse of **Ardalanish Bay**, or you can continue to the more sheltered bay of sand and granite outcrops at neighbouring **UISKEN**, a mile to the east. Overlooking the latter is *Uisken Croft* (Ⓣ01681/700307; March–Oct; ❷), a welcoming, modern B&B, a stone's throw from the beach, where you can camp. From Uisken, the Lorn Ferry Service (April to mid-Oct; Ⓣ01951/200320) runs a **passenger-only ferry** to Colonsay (Tues & Sat), though you should phone ahead to check times and book your journey.

The road ends at **FIONNPHORT**, facing Iona, probably the least attractive place to stay on the Ross, though it has a nice sandy bay backed by pink granite rocks to the north of the ferry slipway. Partly to ease congestion on Iona, and to give their neighbours a slice of the tourist pound, Fionnphort was chosen as the site for the **Columba Centre** (Easter–Sept daily 10.30am–1pm & 2–5.30pm; free); inside, a small exhibition outlines Iona's history, tells a little of Columba's life (for more on which, see opposite), and has a few facsimiles of the illuminated manuscripts produced by the island's monks.

If you're in need of a **B&B** in Fionnphort (keeping in mind that it's limited on Iona itself), try the granite *Seaview* (Ⓣ01681/700235, Ⓦwww.seaview-mull.co.uk; ❷), or the whitewashed *Staffa House* (Ⓣ01681/700677, Ⓦwww.staffahouse.co.uk; ❸), both of which are close to the ferry and the local pub, the *Keel Row*, which serves reasonable meals. Just out of Fionnphort (no bad thing), there's also *Achaban House* (Ⓣ01681/700205, Ⓦwww.achabanhouse.co.uk; ❸), an old manse with some character overlooking Loch Pottie. The basic *Fidden Farm* **campsite** (Ⓣ01681/700427; April–Sept), a mile south along the Knockvologan road by Fidden beach, is the nearest to Iona. Fidden beach looks out to the **Isle of Erraid**, where Robert Louis Stevenson is believed to have written *Kidnapped* while staying in one of the island's cottages; *Kidnapped*'s hero, David Balfour, is shipwrecked on the **Torran Rocks**, out to sea to the south of Erraid, beyond which lies the remarkable, stripy **Dubh Artach lighthouse**, built by Stevenson's father in 1862. In the book, Balfour spends a miserable time convinced that he's stranded on Erraid, which can, in fact, be reached across the sands on its eastern side at low tide. The island is now in Dutch ownership, and cared for by the Findhorn Community. **Bikes** for exploring the quiet roads of the Ross can be rented from *Seaview* B&B.

Isle of Iona

Ross: Where is Duncan's body?
Macduff: Carried to Colme-kill,
The sacred storehouse of his predecessors,
And guardian of their bones.

Macbeth (Act II, Scene 4), by William Shakespeare

Less than a mile off the southwest tip of Mull, **IONA** (ⓦwww.isle-of-iona.com) – just three miles long and not much more than a mile wide – has been a place of pilgrimage for several centuries, and a place of Christian worship for more than 1400 years. For it was to this flat Hebridean island that St Columba fled from Ireland in 563 and established a monastery which was responsible for the conversion of more or less all of pagan Scotland as well as much of northern England. This history and the island's splendid isolation have lent it a peculiar religiosity; in the much-quoted words of Dr Johnson, who visited in 1773, "that man is little to be envied . . . whose piety would not grow warmer among the ruins of Iona." Today, however, the island can barely cope with the constant flood of day-trippers, so to appreciate the special atmosphere and to have time to see the whole island, including the often overlooked west coast, you should plan on staying at least one night.

Saint Columba

Legend has it that **St Columba** (Colum Cille), born in Donegal some time around 521, was a direct descendant of the semi-legendary Irish king, Niall of the Nine Hostages. A scholar and soldier priest, who founded numerous monasteries in Ireland, he is thought to have become involved in a bloody dispute with the king when he refused to hand over a copy of *St Jerome's Psalter,* copied illegally from the original owned by St Finian of Moville. This, in turn, provoked the Battle of Cúl Drebene (Cooldrumman) – also known as the **Battle of the Book** – at which Columba's forces won, though with the loss of over 3000 lives. The story goes that, repenting this bloodshed, Columba went into exile with twelve other monks, eventually settling on Iona in 563, allegedly because it was the first island he encountered from which he couldn't see his homeland. The bottom line, however, is that we know very little about Columba, though he undoubtedly became something of a cult figure after his death in 597. He was posthumously credited with miraculous feats such as defeating the Loch Ness monster – it only had to hear his voice and it recoiled in terror – and casting out snakes (and, some say, frogs) from the island. He is also famously alleged to have banned women and cows from Iona, exiling them to Eilean nam Ban (Woman's Island), just north of Fionnphort, for, as he believed, "where there is a cow there is a woman, and where there is a woman there is mischief".

Some history

Whatever the truth about Columba's life (see box, p.109), in the sixth and seventh centuries Iona enjoyed a great deal of autonomy from Rome, establishing a specifically **Celtic Christian** tradition. Missionaries were sent out to the rest of Scotland and parts of England, and Iona quickly became a respected seat of learning and artistry; the monks compiled a vast library of intricately **illuminated manuscripts** – most famously the *Book of Kells* (now on display in Trinity College, Dublin) – while the masons excelled in carving peculiarly intricate crosses. Two factors were instrumental in the demise of the Celtic tradition: a series of Viking raids, the worst of which was the massacre of 68 monks on the sands of Martyrs' Bay in 806; and relentless pressure from the established Church, beginning with the Synod of Whitby in 664, which chose Rome over the Celtic Church, and culminated in its suppression by King David I in 1144.

In 1203, Iona became part of the mainstream church with the establishment of an **Augustinian nunnery** and a **Benedictine monastery** by Reginald, son of Somerled, Lord of the Isles. During the Reformation, the entire complex was ransacked, the contents of the library burnt and all but three of the island's 360 crosses destroyed. Although plans were drawn up at various times to turn the abbey into a Cathedral of the Isles, nothing came of them until in 1899, when the (then) owner, the eighth Duke of Argyll, donated the abbey buildings to the **Church of Scotland**, who restored the abbey church for worship over the course of the next decade. Iona's modern resurgence began in 1938, when **George MacLeod**, a minister from Glasgow, established a group of ministers, students and artisans to begin rebuilding the remainder of the monastic buildings. What began as a mostly male, Gaelic-speaking, strictly Presbyterian community is today a lay, mixed and ecumenical retreat. The entire abbey complex has been successfully restored, and is now looked after by Historic Scotland, while the island, apart from the church land and a few crofts, is in the care of the NTS.

Baile Mór

The passenger ferry from Fionnphort drops you off at the island's main village, **BAILE MÓR** (literally "Large Village"), which is in fact little more than a single terrace of cottages facing the sea. Just inland lie the extensive pink granite ruins of the **Augustinian nunnery**, disused since the Reformation. A beautifully maintained garden now occupies the cloisters, and if nothing else the complex gives you an idea of the state of the present-day abbey before it was restored. Across the road to the north, housed in a manse built, like the nearby parish church, by the ubiquitous Thomas Telford, is the **Iona Heritage Centre** (Easter–Oct Mon–Sat 10.30am–4.30pm; £2), with displays on the social history of the island over the last 200 years, including the Clearances, which nearly halved the island's population of 500 in the mid-nineteenth century. At a bend in the road, just south of the manse and church, stands the fifteenth-century **MacLean's Cross**, a fine late medieval example of the distinctive, flowing, three-leaved foliage of the Iona school.

Iona Abbey

No buildings remain from Columba's time: the present **abbey** (daily: April–Sept 9.30am–6.30pm; Oct–March 9.30am–4.30pm; HS; £3.30) dates from the arrival of the Benedictines in around 1200; it was extensively rebuilt in the fifteenth and sixteenth centuries, and restored virtually wholesale last century. Iona's oldest building, the plain-looking **St Oran's Chapel**, lies south of the

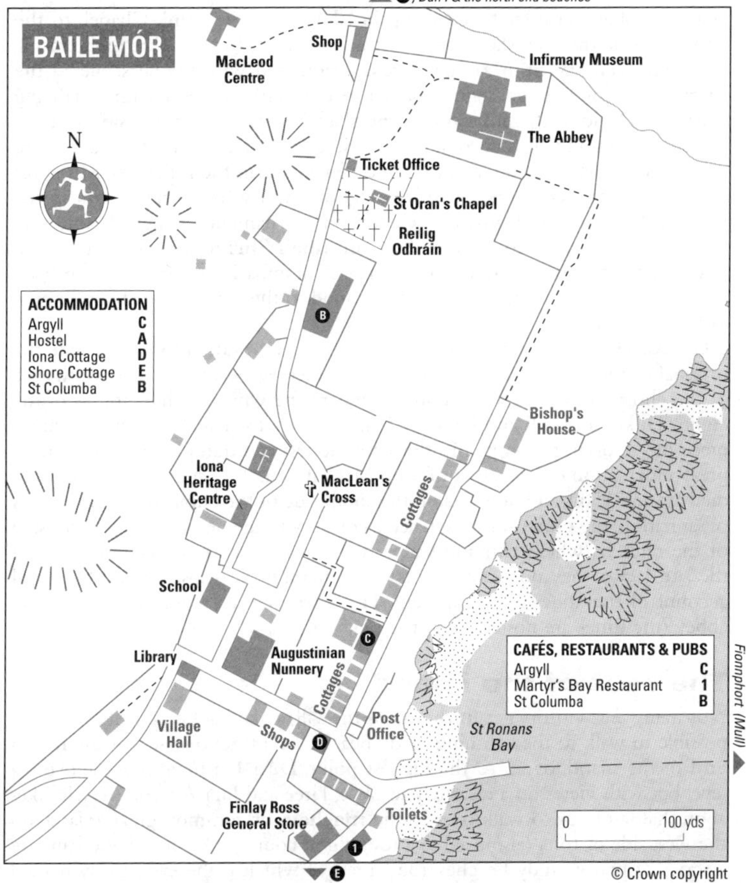

abbey, to your right, and boasts an eleventh-century door. Legend has it that the original chapel could only be completed through human sacrifice. Oran apparently volunteered to be buried alive, and was found to have survived the ordeal when the grave was opened a few days later. Declaring that he had seen hell and it wasn't all bad, he was promptly reinterred for blasphemy.

Oran's Chapel stands at the centre of Iona's sacred burial ground, **Reilig Odhráin** (Oran's Cemetery), which is said to contain the graves of sixty kings of Norway, Ireland, France and Scotland, including Duncan and Macbeth. The best of the early Christian gravestones and medieval effigies which once lay in the Reilig Odhráin have unfortunately been removed to the Infirmary Museum, behind the abbey, and to various other locations within the complex. The graveyard is still used as a cemetery by the island, however, and also contains the grave of the short-lived leader of the Labour Party, **John Smith** (1938–94), who was a frequent visitor to Iona, though he himself was born in the town of Ardrishaig.

Approaching the abbey itself, from the ticket office, you cross an exposed section of the evocative medieval **Street of the Dead**, whose giant pink granite cobbles once stretched from the abbey, past St Oran's Chapel, to the village. Beside the road stands the most impressive of Iona's Celtic high crosses, the eighth-century **St Martin's Cross**, smothered with figural scenes – the Virgin and Child at the centre, Daniel in the lion's den, Abraham sacrificing Isaac and David with musicians in the shaft below. The reverse side features Pictish serpent-and-boss decoration. Standing directly in front of the abbey are the base of St Matthew's Cross (the rest of which is in the Infirmary Museum) and, to the left, a concrete cast of the eighth-century **St John's Cross**, decorated with serpent-and-boss and Celtic spiral ornamental panels. Before you enter the abbey, take a look inside **St Columba's Shrine**, a small steep-roofed chamber to the left of the main entrance. Columba is believed to have been buried either here or under the rocky mound to the west of the abbey, known as Tórr an Aba.

The **Abbey** itself has been simply and sensitively restored to incorporate the original elements. You can spot many of the medieval capitals in the south aisle of the choir and in the south transept, where the white marble effigies of the eighth Duke of Argyll and his wife, Ina, lie in a side-chapel – an incongruous piece of Victorian pomp in an otherwise modest and tranquil place. The finest pre-Reformation effigy is that of John MacKinnon, the last abbot of Iona, who died around 1500, and now lies on the south side of the choir steps. For reasons of sanitation, the **cloisters** were placed, contrary to the norm, on the north side of the church (where running water was available); entirely reconstructed in the late 1950s, they now shelter lots of medieval grave slabs, a useful historical account of the abbey's development. There are free daily guided tours of the abbey (the times are posted up at the ticket office).

The rest of the island

Not many day-visitors get further than the village and abbey, but it's perfectly possible to walk to the stunning sandy beaches and turquoise seas at the **north end** of the island, or up to the highest point, **Dún I**, a mere 328ft above sea level but with views on a clear day to Skye, Tiree and Jura. Alternatively, it takes about half an hour to walk over to the **machair**, or common grazing land, on the west side of Iona (also used as a rough golf course). On the edge of this are a series of pretty sandy beaches, the largest of which is the evocatively named **Camus Cúl an t-Saimh** ("Bay at the Back of the Ocean"), a crescent of pebble and shell-strewn sand with a spouting cave to the south. Those with more time (2–3hr) might hike over to the **south** of the island, where Port a'Churaich ("Bay of the Coracle", also known as St Columba's Bay), the saint's traditional landing place on Iona, is filled with smooth round rocks and multi-coloured pebbles and stones. A short distance to the east is the **disused marble quarry** at Rubha na Carraig Geire, on the southeasternmost point of Iona. Quarried intermittently for several centuries, it was finally closed down in 1914; much of the old equipment is still visible, rusting away by the shore.

Practicalities

There's no **tourist office** on Iona, and as demand far exceeds supply you should organize **accommodation** well in advance. Of the island's two **hotels**, the stone-built *Argyll* (Ⓣ01681/700334, Ⓦwww.argyllhoteliona.co.uk; ⑥), in the village's terrace of cottages overlooking the Sound of Iona, is by far the nicer, although the larger alternative, the *St Columba Hotel* (Ⓣ01681/700304, Ⓦwww.stcolumba-hotel.co.uk; ⑥), has been improving recently. As for **B&Bs**, try *Iona Cottage* (Ⓣ01681/700579, Ⓔck@ionacottage.freeserve.co.uk; ②), which overlooks the jetty or *Shore Cottage* (Ⓣ01681/700744, Ⓦwww.shorecottage.co.uk; Jan–Oct; ❷), a short walk south. **Camping** is not permitted on Iona, but there is a terrific **hostel** (Ⓣ01681/700781, Ⓦwww.ionahostel.co.uk) at the north of the island, where the main room is filled with lovely wooden furniture and huge picture windows look out to the Treshnish Islands. If you want to stay with the **Iona Community** (Ⓣ01681/700404, Ⓦwww.iona.org.uk), either in the abbey itself or the *MacLeod Centre* (popularly known as "The Mac"), you must book well in advance and be prepared to participate fully in the daily activities, prayers and religious services.

Eating options aren't bad: the restaurant at the *Argyll* is notable for its home-grown vegetables and organic produce, though it's worth booking ahead to confirm there's a table; the *St Columba* has more space for lunches and dinners, and the pub grub at the bar adjoining the *Martyr's Bay Restaurant* by the jetty is reasonable too, often serving up locally caught seafood. For something lighter during the day, head for the basic tearoom beside the Heritage Centre (Mon–Fri 11am–3.30pm), which serves home-made soup and tasty cakes.

Visitors are not allowed to bring cars onto the island, but **bikes** can be rented in Fionnphort (see p.109) or from the Finlay Ross general store in the village (Ⓣ01681/700357). There's also a taxi on the island. Some of the Mull-based **boat trips** (see p.100) include Iona and Staffa on their itinerary, while a couple of local operators, Iolaire and Gordon Grant Marine, do the majority of the trips to Staffa. Also based on Iona, Mark Jardine's Alternative Boat Hire (Ⓣ01681/700537, Ⓦwww.boattripsiona.com) takes the lovely wooden gaff-rigged sailing boat *Freya* on short trips to some of the less-visited spots around the Sound of Iona and Erraid.

Coll and Tiree

Coll and **Tiree** are among the most isolated of the Inner Hebrides, and if anything have more in common with the outlying Western Isles than with their closest neighbour, Mull. Each is roughly twelve miles long and three miles wide, both are low-lying, treeless and exceptionally windy, with white sandy beaches and the highest sunshine records in Scotland. Like most of the Hebrides, they were once ruled by Vikings, and didn't pass into Scottish hands until the thirteenth century.

In the 1830s Coll's population peaked at 1440, Tiree's at a staggering 4450, but both were badly affected by the Clearances, which virtually halved their populations in a generation. Coll was fortunate to be in the hands of the enlightened MacLeans, but they were forced to sell in 1856 to the Stewart family, who sold two-thirds of the island to a Dutch millionaire in the 1960s. Tiree was ruthlessly cleared by its owner, the Duke of Argyll, who sent in the marines in 1885 to evict the crofters. After the passing of the Crofters' Act the following year, the island was divided into crofts, though it remains a part of the Duke of Argyll's estate. Both islands have strong Gaelic roots, but the percentage of English-speaking newcomers is rising steadily.

The CalMac **ferry** from Oban calls at Coll (2hr 40min) daily except Thursdays and Fridays, and at Tiree daily (3hr 40min); in winter, the ferry calls at both islands on Tuesdays, Thursdays and Saturdays. On Thursdays – though the day may change – the ferry continues on to Barra in the Western Isles, and calls in at Tiree on the way back, making it possible to visit on a **day-trip from Oban**; a minibus tour of the island is thrown in as part of the package. Tiree also has

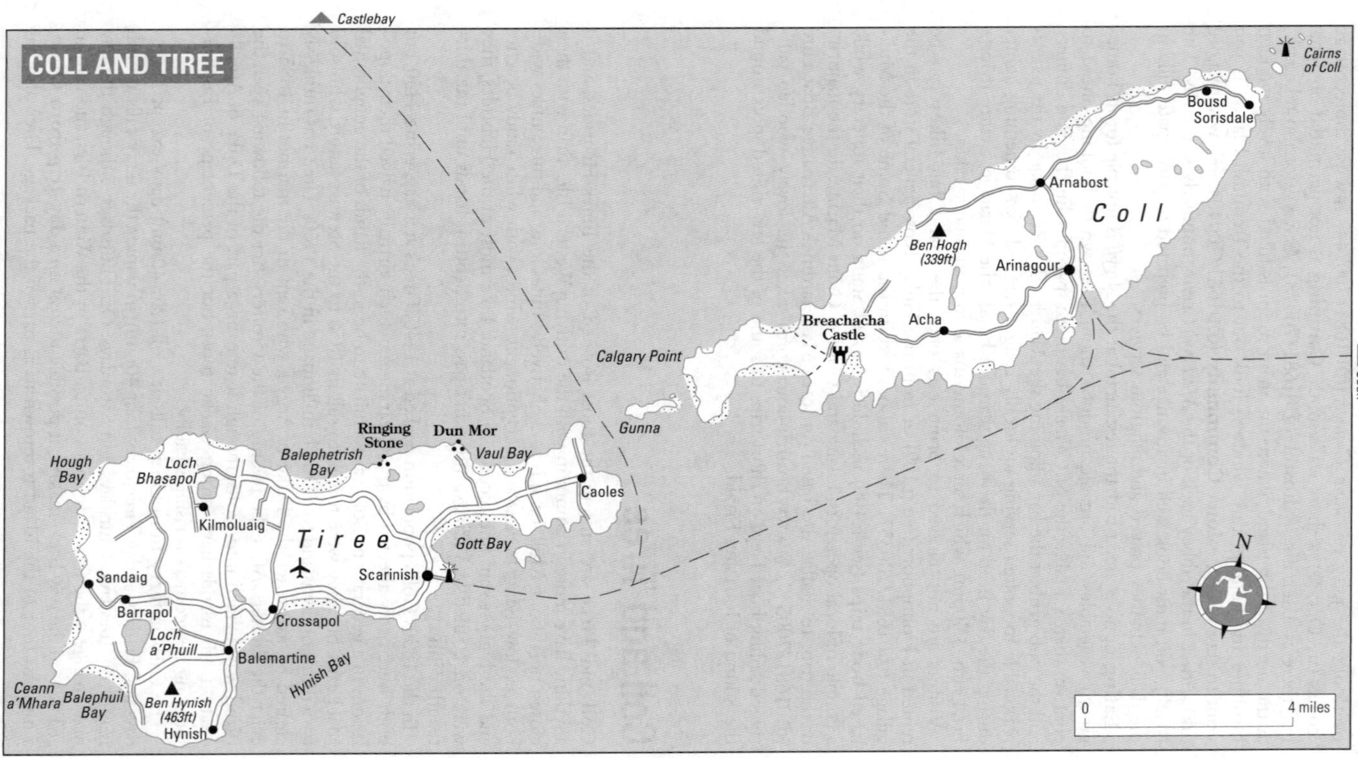
COLL AND TIREE
Castlebay
Cairns of Coll
Bousd
Sorisdale
Arnabost
Coll
Ben Hogh (339ft)
Arinagour
Breachacha Castle
Acha
Calgary Point
Oban
Gunna
Ringing Stone
Dun Mor
Vaul Bay
Hough Bay
Loch Bhasapol
Balephetrish Bay
Caoles
Kilmoluaig
Tiree
Gott Bay
Sandaig
Scarinish
Barrapol
Crossapol
Loch a'Phuill
Balemartine
Hynish Bay
Ceann a'Mhara
Balephuil Bay
Ben Hynish (463ft)
Hynish
N
0
4 miles

an **airport** with daily flights (Mon–Sat) to and from Glasgow. The majority of visitors on both islands stay for at least a week in self-catering accommodation (see p.46), though there are B&Bs and hotels on the islands. Choice is limited, however, so it's as well to book as far in advance as possible (and that goes for the ferry crossing, too).

Isle of Coll

The fish-shaped rocky island of **Coll** (Ⓦwww.isleofcoll.org), with a population of around a hundred, lies less than seven miles off the coast of Mull. The CalMac ferry drops off at Coll's only real village, **ARINAGOUR,** whose whitewashed cottages line the western shore of Loch Eatharna, a popular safe anchorage for boats. Half the island's population lives in the village, and it's here you'll find the island's hotel and pub, post office, churches and a couple of shops; two miles northwest along the Arnabost road, there's even a golf course. The island's petrol pump is also in Arinagour, and is run on a volunteer basis – it's basically open when the ferry arrives.

On the southwest coast there are two edifices, both confusingly known as **Breachacha Castle**, and both built by the MacLeans. The older, at the head of Loch Breachacha, is a fifteenth-century tower house with an additional curtain wall, now used by Project Trust overseas aid volunteers (Ⓦwww.projecttrust.org.uk). The less attractive "new castle", to the northwest, is made up of a central block built around 1750 and two side pavilions added a century later, and is used as holiday cottages. It was here that Dr Johnson and Boswell stayed in 1773 after a storm forced them to take refuge en route to Mull – Johnson considered the place to be "a mere tradesman's box". Much of the area around the castles is now owned by the RSPB, in the hope of protecting the island's precious corncrake population. At Totronald, north of the castles, there is a small RSPB information point, and the warden does guided walks on a Wednesday – if you're here for the birds, visit Ⓦwww.collbirds.co.uk. A vast area of **giant sand dunes** lies to the west of the castles, with two glorious golden sandy bays stretching for over a mile on either side. At the far western end is *Caolas*, where you can get a cup of tea and home-baked goodies – you can also stay here (see below).

For an overview of the whole island, and a fantastic Hebridean panorama, you can follow in Johnson and Boswell's footsteps and take a wander up **Ben Hogh** – at 339ft, Coll's highest point – two miles west of Arinagour, close to the shore. On the summit is a giant boulder known as an "erratic", perilously perched on three small boulders. The island's northwest coast boasts some of the finest sandy beaches in the Hebrides, which take the full brunt of the Atlantic winds. When the Stewart family took over the island in 1856, and raised the rents, the island's population moved wholesale from the more fertile southeast, to this part of the island. However, overcrowding led to widespread emigration; a few of the old crofts in Bousd and Sorisdale, at Coll's northernmost tip, have more recently been restored. From here, there's an impressive view over to the headland, the Small Isles and the Skye Cuillin beyond.

Practicalities

In Arinagour, the small, family-run *Coll Hotel* (Ⓣ01879/230334, Ⓦwww.collhotel.co.uk; ❸) provides excellent **accommodation**. Otherwise, there are a couple of B&Bs to choose from: *Tigh-na-Mara* (Ⓣ01879/230354; ❷), a purpose-built guesthouse near the pier, *Achamore* (Ⓣ01879/230430; ❶), a traditional nineteenth-century farmhouse B&B, just north of Arinagour or, if you really want to get away from it all, book in at *Caolas* (Ⓣ01879/230438, Ⓦwww.caolas.net; full board ❺), a restored farmhouse on the remote western side of the island – phone ahead and your friendly hosts will pick you up and drive you across the sand; you can also stay at their nice, compact bothy (❸) and bikes and boats are available for guests. *Garden House* (Ⓣ01879/230374), down a track on the left before the turn-off for the castles, runs a **campsite** in the shelter of what was formerly a walled garden; wild camping is also possible on Coll – your best bet is to contact the hotel. The *Coll Hotel* doubles as the island's social centre, does excellent **meals** and has a dining-room overflow. Another good eating option is the *First Port of Coll* café, in the old harbour stores overlooking the bay, which offers hot meals all day. For **bike rental**, go to Taigh Solas (Ⓣ01879/230216), opposite the post office.

Isle of Tiree

Tiree (Ⓦwww.isleoftiree.com), as its Gaelic name *tir-iodh* (land of corn) suggests, was once known as the breadbasket of the Inner Hebrides, thanks to its acres of rich machair. Nowadays, crofting and tourism are the main sources of income for the resident population of around 750. One of the most distinctive features of Tiree is its architecture, in particular the large numbers of "pudding" or "spotty" houses, where only the mortar is painted white. In addition, there are numerous "white houses" (*tigh geal*) and traditional "blackhouses" (*tigh dubh*); for more on these, see p.375. Wildlife lovers can also have a field day on Tiree, with lapwings, wheatears, redshank, greylag geese and large, laid-back brown hares in abundance. And, with no shortage of wind, Tiree's sandy beaches attract large numbers of windsurfers for the week-long Tiree Wave Classic (Ⓦwww.tireewaveclassic.com) every October.

The CalMac ferry calls at Gott Bay Pier, now best known for **An Turas** (The Journey), Tiree's award-winning "shelter", an artistic extravaganza, which features two parallel white walls connected via a black felt section to a glass

△ Windsurfing at Tiree

box which punctures a stone dyke and frames a seaview. As a shelter, it's a bit of a non-starter, and as a contemplative space with a good view it is in direct competition with the CalMac waiting room. Just up the road from the pier is the village of **SCARINISH**, home to a post office, some public toilets, a supermarket, the butcher's and the bank, with a petrol pump back at the pier. Also in Scarinish you'll find **An Iodhlann** (June–Sept Tues–Fri noon–5pm; Oct–May Mon–Fri 10.30am–3.30pm; £3) – "haystack" in Gaelic – the island's two-roomed archive, which puts on exhibitions in the summer.

To the east of Scarinish, **Gott Bay** is backed by a two-mile stretch of sand, and just one mile to the north is Vaul Bay, on the north coast, where the well-preserved remains of a dry-stone broch, **Dun Mor** – dating from the first century BC – lie hidden in the rocks to the west of the bay. From here it's another two miles west along the coast to the *Clach a'Choire* or **Ringing Stone**, a huge glacial boulder decorated with mysterious prehistoric markings, which when struck with a stone gives out a metallic sound, thus giving rise to the legend that inside is a crock of gold. The story goes that, should the Ringing Stone ever be broken in two, Tiree will sink beneath the waves. A mile further west you come to the lovely **Balephetrish Bay**, where you can watch waders feeding in the breakers, and look out to sea to Skye and the Western Isles.

The most intriguing sights, however, lie in the bulging western half of the island, where Tiree's two landmark hills rise up. The higher of the two, **Ben Hynish** (463ft), is unfortunately occupied by a "golf-ball" radar station, which tracks incoming transatlantic flights; the views from the top, though, are great. Below Ben Hynish, to the east, is **HYNISH**, with its recently restored **harbour**, designed by Alan Stevenson in the 1830s to transport building materials for the magnificent 140-foot-tall **Skerryvore Lighthouse**, which lies on a sea-swept reef some twelve miles southwest of Tiree. The harbour features an ingenious reservoir to prevent silting and, up on the hill behind, beside the row of light-keepers' houses, a stumpy granite signal tower. The tower, whose signals used to be the only contact the lighthouse keepers had with civilization, now houses a **museum** telling the history of the herculean effort required to erect the lighthouse; weather permitting, you can see the lighthouse from the tower's viewing platform.

On the other side of Ben Hynish, a mile or so across the golden sands of Balephuil Bay, is the spectacular headland of **Ceann a'Mhara** (pronounced "kenavara"). The cliffs here are home to thousands of seabirds, including fulmars, kittiwakes, guillemots, razorbills, shags and cormorants, with gannets and terns feeding offshore; the islands of Barra and South Uist are also visible on the northern horizon. In the scattered west coast settlement of **SANDAIG**, to the north of Ceann a'Mhara, three thatched white houses in a row have been turned into the **Taigh Iain Mhoir** (June–Sept Mon–Fri 2–4pm; free), which gives an insight into how the majority of islanders lived in the nineteenth century.

Practicalities

If you're arriving at the **airport**, about three miles west of Scarinish, you should arrange for your hosts to collect you (most will). Tiree has a Ring'n' Ride **minibus** service (Mon–Sat 7am–6pm, Tues until 10pm; (Ⓣ01879/220419) which will take you anywhere on the island; **bike rental** (Ⓣ01879/220428) or **car rental** (Ⓣ01879/220555) are the other options, not to mention **pony trekking** (Ⓣ01879/220881, Ⓦwww.tireeonhorseback.co.uk).

The island has two **hotels**: the newly refurbished *Scarinish* (Ⓣ01879/220308, Ⓦwww.tireescarinishhotel.com; ④), overlooking the old harbour, and the *Tiree*

Lodge (Ⓣ01879/220368; ❷), a mile or so east of Scarinish along Gott Bay. Other options include the *Kirkapol House* (Ⓣ01879/220729, Ⓦwww.kirkapoltiree.co.uk; ❸), a friendly **B&B** in a tastefully converted kirk beyond the *Tiree Lodge* and *Glebe House* (Ⓣ01879/220758; ❺), the renovated former manse overlooking the pier in Scarinish. Good **hostel** accommodation is available at the *Millhouse* (Ⓣ01879/220435, Ⓦwww.tireemillhouse.co.uk), near Loch Bhasapol, in the northwest of the island, either in bunks or twins (❶). There's no official campsite, but **camping** is allowed with the local crofter's permission.

As for **eating**, the bar meals at both the *Scarnish* and *Tiree Lodge* are good, while unpretentious snacks and meals are available at the pine-clad *Rural Centre* café by the airport. For a map of the island and the daily papers, you need to go to the supermarket at Crossapol.

Isle of Colonsay

Isolated between Mull and Islay, the Isle of **Colonsay** (Ⓦwww.colonsay.org.uk) – eight miles by three at its widest – is nothing like as bleak and windswept as Coll or Tiree. Its craggy, heather-backed hills even support the occasional patch of woodland, plus a bewildering array of plant and birdlife, wild goats and rabbits, and one of the finest quasi-tropical gardens in Scotland. The population is currently around a hundred, down from a pre-Clearance peak of just under

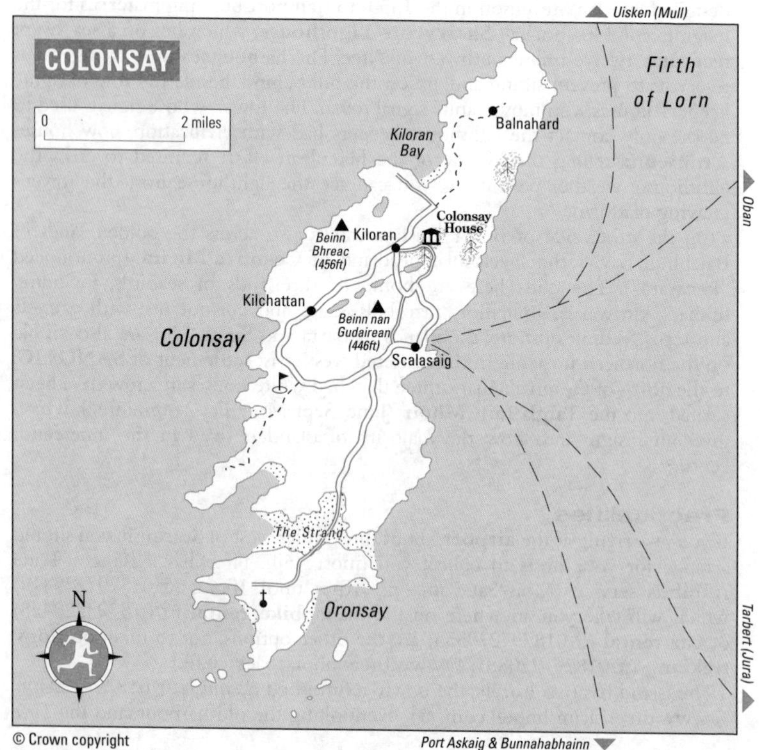

1000. With no camping allowed, only one hotel and infrequent ferry links with the mainland, there's no fear of mass tourism taking over.

The CalMac ferry terminal is at **SCALASAIG**, on the east coast, where there's a post office/shop, a petrol pump, a restaurant and the island's hotel. Right by the pier, the old waiting room now serves as the island's heritage centre and is usually open when the ferry docks. Two miles north of Scalasaig, inland at **KILORAN**, is **Colonsay House**, built in 1722 by Malcolm MacNeil. In 1904, the island and house were bought by Lord Strathcona, who made his fortune building the Canadian Pacific Railway (and whose descendants still own the island). He was also responsible for the house's lovely woodland **gardens** (April–Sept Wed & Fri), which are slowly being restored to their former glory. The outbuildings are now holiday cottages and you're free to wander round the woodland garden to the south, and inspect the strange eighth-century **Riasg Buidhe Cross**, to the east of the house, decorated with an unusually lifelike mug shot (possibly of a monk).

To the north of Colonsay House, where the road ends, you'll find the island's finest sandy beach, the breathtaking **Kiloran Bay**, where the breakers roll in from the Atlantic. There's another unspoilt sandy beach backed by dunes at Balnahard, two miles northeast along a rough track; en route, you might spot wild goats, choughs and even a golden eagle. The island's west coast forms a sharp escarpment, quite at odds with the gentle undulating landscape that characterizes the rest of the island. Due west of Colonsay House around **Beinn Bhreac** (456ft), the cliffs are at their most spectacular, and in their lower reaches provide a home to hundreds of seabirds, among them kittiwakes, cormorants and guillemots in spring and early summer.

Isle of Oronsay

Whilst on Colonsay, most folk take a day out to visit the **Isle of Oronsay** (sometimes written as Oranasay), which lies half a mile to the south and contains the ruins of an Augustinian priory. The two islands are separated by "The Strand", a stretch of tidal mud flats which act as a causeway for two hours either side of low tide (check locally for timings); you can drive over to the island at low tide, though most people park their cars and walk across. Although legends (and etymology) link SS Columba and Oran with both Colonsay and Oronsay, the ruins actually only date back as far as the fourteenth century. You can, nevertheless, still make out the original church and tiny cloisters, abondoned since the Reformation and now roofless. The highlight, though, is the **Oronsay Cross**, a superb example of late medieval artistry from Iona which, along with thirty or so beautifully carved grave slabs, can be found in the restored side chapel. It takes about an hour to walk from the tip of Colonsay across The Strand to the priory (wellington boots are a good option).

Practicalities

CalMac **ferries** call daily except Tuesday and Saturday from Oban (2hr 15min); once a week from Kennacraig via Islay (Wed; 3hr 35min), when a day-trip is possible, giving you around six hours on the island. There's also the passenger/bicycle-only Lorn Ferry Service (April to mid-Oct; ⓣ01951/200320), which runs timetabled services to Uisken on the Ross of Mull (Tues & Sun), Tarbert on Jura (Tues & Fri), and Bunnahabhainn and Port Askaig on Islay (Mon), though you should phone ahead to check times and book your journey. If money's no object, you can also get Seafari (ⓣ01852/300003, ⓦwww.seafari.co.uk), based in Easdale, to take you across in their RIB.

The island's only **hotel**, the *Isle of Colonsay* (Ⓣ01951/200316, Ⓔreception@thecolonsay.com; ❻), is a cosy eighteenth-century inn at heart, within easy walking distance of the pier in Scalasaig; it serves very decent bar snacks and acts as the island's social centre. The best alternative is to stay at the superb *Seaview* **B&B** (Ⓣ01951/200315; ❸; April–Oct), run by the charming Lawson family in Kilchattan on the west coast – it's well worth booking in for dinner, too. Camping is not normally permitted on the island so the budget option is to sleep in the *Keepers' Lodge*, in Kiloran (Ⓣ01951/200312), a very comfortable **hostel** with a real fire. Most people who visit the island, however, stay in **self-catering accommodation**, the majority of which is run by the Colonsay Estate (phone as for hostel), who offer a whole range of cottages. It's also possible to book self-catering places at the aforementioned *Seaview* or, for short or long lets, you can book one of the lodges behind the hotel run by *Isle of Colonsay Lodges* (Ⓣ01951/200320).

An alternative to **eating out** at the hotel bar is *The Pantry*, above the pier in Scalasaig, which offers simple home-cooking as well as teas and cakes (ring ahead if you want to eat in the evening; Ⓣ01951/200325). If you fancy the famous Colonsay oysters or wildflower honey, contact Andrew Abrahams at Pollgorm (Ⓣ01951/200365). All accommodation (and ferry crossings) need to be booked well in advance for the summer; self-catering cottages tend to be booked from Friday to Friday, because of the ferries. A **bus** meets the Wednesday ferry and will take folk around the island, and there's a limited **postbus** service. The hotel, *Seaview* and Archie McConnel (Ⓣ01951/200355) will rent out **bikes**. If you need a map or any books on the Highlands and Islands, go to the very well-stocked **bookshop** next door to the hotel. Incidentally, Colonsay has its own version of Munro-bagging, known as **McPhie-bagging**: a McPhie is defined as any hill over 300ft. There are 22 of them and the aim is to climb them all in the course of one walk.

Mid-Argyll

Mid-Argyll is a vague term which loosely describes the central wedge of land south of Oban and north of Kintyre. **Lochgilphead**, on the shores of Loch Fyne, is the chief town in the area, though it has little to offer beyond its practical use – it has a tourist office, a good supermarket, several banks and is the regional transport hub, though, on the whole, public transport is thin on the ground. The highlights of this gently undulating scenery lie along the sharply indented west coast. Closest to Oban are the melancholy former slate-mining settlements of the Seil, Easdale and Luing, known collectively as the **Slate Islands**. Further south, **Arduaine Gardens** are among Argyll's most celebrated horticultural sights, while the rich Bronze Age and Neolithic remains in the **Kilmartin** valley comprise one of the most important prehistoric sites in Scotland. Just to the south, separating Kilmartin Glen from the **Knapdale** peninsula, is the **Crinan Canal**, a short cut for boats disinclined to round the Mull of Kintyre, which ends in the pint-sized, picturesque port of **Crinan**.

The Slate Islands and the Garvellachs

Just eight miles south of Oban, a road heads off the A816 west to a small group of islands commonly called the **Slate Islands** (Ⓦwww.slate.org.uk), which at their peak in the mid-nineteenth century quarried over nine million slates annually. Today many of the old slate villages are sparsely populated, and an inevitable air of melancholy hangs over them, but their dramatic setting amid crashing waves makes for a rewarding day-trip.

Isle of Seil

The most northerly of the Slate Islands is **Seil**, a lush island, now something of an exclusive enclave. It's separated from the mainland only by the thinnest of sea channels and spanned by the elegant humpback **Clachan Bridge**, built in 1793 and popularly known as the "Bridge over the Atlantic". The pub next door to the bridge is the *Tigh na Truish* (House of the Trousers), where kilt-wearing islanders would change into trousers to conform to the post-1745 ban on Highland dress. The nearby *Willowburn Hotel* (Ⓣ01852/300276, Ⓦwww.willowburn.co.uk; ❼; March–Nov) is the **accommodation** of choice on Seil, a peaceful and very comfortable hotel overlooking Seil Sound, with an excellent restaurant to boot – all rates include dinner, bed and breakfast.

The main village on Seil is **ELLENABEICH**, its neat white terraces of workers' cottages – featured in the film *Ring of Bright Water* – crouching below black cliffs on the westernmost tip of the island. This was once the tiny island of Eilean a'Beithich (hence "Ellenabeich"), separated from the mainland by a slim sea channel until the intensive slate quarrying succeeded in silting it up. Confusingly, the village is often referred to by the same name as the nearby island of Easdale, since they formed an interdependent community based exclusively around the slate industry.

As you enter the village, be sure to take a stroll round the gardens of **An Cala** (April–Oct daily dawn–dusk; £1.50), best visited in early summer for the glorious azaleas and Japanese flowering cherries. In the village itself is the **Scottish Slate Islands Heritage Centre** (April–Oct daily 10.30am–5pm; £2), which is housed in one of the little white cottages. The best feature of the exhibition is the model of the slate quarry as it would have been at the height of its fame in the nineteenth century.

For a good range of snacks, including locally caught **fish and seafood**, pop inside the *Oyster Brewery* (Ⓣ01852/300121, Ⓦwww.oysterbrewery.com) on the way to the ferry, which also brews its own ale. High-adrenaline **boat trips** are offered by Seafari Adventures (Ⓣ01852/300003, Ⓦwww.seafari.co.uk), who are based at the Ellenabeich jetty; the boats are rigid inflatables (RIB) and travel at some speed round the offshore islands and through the Corryvreckan Whirlpool (see p.122).

Isle of Easdale

Easdale (Ⓦwww.easdale.org) remains an island, though the few hundred yards that separate it from Ellanabeich have to be dredged to keep the channel open. On the eve of a great storm on November 23, 1881, Easdale, less than a mile across at any one point, supported an incredible 452 inhabitants. That night, waves engulfed the island and flooded the quarries. The island never really recovered, slate quarrying stopped in 1914, and by the 1960s the population was reduced to single figures.

Recently many of the old workers' cottages have been restored: some as holiday homes, others sold to new families (the present population is now around sixty). One of the cottages houses the interesting **Easdale Folk Museum** (April–Oct daily 10.30am–5.30pm; £2), near the main square, selling a useful historical map of the island, which you can walk round in about half an hour. The council-run **ferry** from Ellenabeich runs on demand (press the buttons in the ferry shed or phone Ⓣ01586/552056), and there's *The Puffer* **bar/restaurant** (Ⓣ01852/300579, Ⓦwww.pufferbar.com; closed Mon, Wed & Sun eves) if you've failed to put together a picnic.

With lots of wonderfully flat stones freely available, Easdale makes the perfect venue for the annual **World Stone Skimming Championships** (ⓦwww.stoneskimming.com), held on the last Sunday of September.

Isle of Luing

To the south of Seil, across the narrow, treacherous Cuan Sound, lies **Luing** (ⓦwww.isleofluing.co.uk) – pronounced "Ling" – a long, thin, fertile island which once supported more than six hundred people, but now has a third of that. During the Clearances, the population was drastically reduced to make way for cattle; Luing is still renowned for its beef and for the chocolate-brown crossbreed named after it. A council-run car **ferry** (Mon–Sat 7.30am–6pm, Sun 11am–6pm; mid-June to Aug also Mon–Sat 6.30–10pm) crosses the Cuan Sound every half-hour or so, though foot passengers can cross later in the evening all year round (Mon–Thurs 7.30am–10pm, Fri & Sat 8am–11.30pm, Sun 11am–6pm). There's a decent **postbus** service on Luing itself (Mon–Sat).

CULLIPOOL, the pretty main village with its post office and general store, lies a mile or so southwest; quarrying ceased here in 1965. Luing's only other village, **TOBERONOCHY**, lies on the more sheltered east coast, three miles southeast of Cullipool; its distinctive white cottages were built by the slate company in 1805. The ruined church contains a memorial to fifteen Latvian seamen who drowned off the nearby abandoned slate island of **Belnahua** during a hurricane in 1936. The only **accommodation** available on the island is self-catering cottages, or one of the static caravans at the tiny *Sunnybrae Caravan Park* (ⓣ01852/314274, ⓦwww.sunnybrae-luing.co.uk; March–Oct), close to the ferry, which also offers **bike rental** (including a tandem).

Scarba and the Garvellachs

Scarba is the largest of the islands around Luing, a brooding 1500-foot hulk of slate, not much more than a couple of miles across, inhospitable and wild – most of the fifty or so inhabitants who once lived here had left by the mid-nineteenth century. To the south, between Scarba and Jura, the raging **Gulf of Corryvreckan** is the site of one of the world's most spectacular whirlpools, thought to be caused by a rocky pinnacle below the sea. It remains calm only for an hour or two at high and low tide; between flood and half-flood tide, accompanied by a southerly or westerly wind, water shoots deafeningly some 20ft up in the air. Inevitably there are numerous legends about the place – known as *coire bhreacain* (speckled cauldron) in Gaelic – concerning *Cailleach* (Hag), the Celtic storm goddess. The best place from which to view it is the northern tip of Jura (see p.153).

The string of uninhabited islands visible west of Luing are known collectively as the **Garvellachs**, after the largest of the group, **Garbh Eileach** (Rough Rock), which was inhabited as recently as fifty years ago. The most northerly, **Dún Chonnuill**, contains the remains of an old fort thought to have belonged to Conal of Dalriada, and **Eileach an Naoimh** (Holy Isle), the most southerly of the group, is where the Celtic missionary Brendan the Navigator founded a community in 542, some twenty years before Columba landed on Iona (see p.109). Nothing survives from Brendan's day, but there are a few ninth-century remains, among them a double-beehive cell and a grave enclosure. One school of thought has it that the island is Hinba, Columba's legendary secret retreat, where he founded a monastery before settling on Iona.

If you're interested in taking a **boat trip** to Scarba, Corryvreckan or the Garvellachs, contact Gemini Cruises (ⓣ01546/830238, ⓦwww.gemini-crinan.co.uk), who operate from Crinan (see p.126), or the high-adrenaline Seafari Adventures (ⓣ01852/300003, ⓦwww.seafari.co.uk), who have a base at Easdale.

Arduaine and Craignish

Probably the finest spot at which to stop and have a picnic on the main road from Oban to Lochgilphead is in **Arduaine Garden** (daily 9.30am–dusk; NTS; £5), which enjoys views over Asknish Bay and out to the islands of Shuna, Luing, Scarba and Jura. Gifted to the National Trust as recently as 1992, the gardens are stupendous, particularly in May and June, and have the feel of an intimate private garden, with pristine lawns, lily-strewn ponds, mature woods and spectacular rhododendrons and azaleas. The gardens' disgruntled former owners, the Wright brothers, still live next door and have an impressive rhododendron display of their own. The best **accommodation** in the area is about three miles back up the road to Oban at *Cnoc na Ceardaich* (Ⓣ01852/200348, Ⓦfreespace.virgin.net/tom.kilmelford; ③; Easter–New Year), an absolutely delightful Victorian former manse, offering B&B in spacious, beautifully decorated rooms, just off the A816.

A couple of miles south, on the far side of Asknish Bay, is the slightly surreal **CRAOBH HAVEN**, a purpose-built holiday village and yacht marina that's reminiscent of a set for a soap opera. However, there is a range of self-catering and B&B **accommodation** close by, in the rambling Baronial pile of *Lunga* (Ⓣ01852/500237, Ⓦwww.lunga.com; ③), run by an eccentric laird. There's also **food** to be had at either the *Lord of the Isles* pub or the *Cabin* bistro café opposite.

There's a fine walk to be had from Craobh Haven along the spine of the **Craignish peninsula** to the southernmost tip some five miles away. Alternatively, you can simply head over to **ARDFERN**, on the sheltered shores of Loch Craignish, a favourite anchorage for visiting yachts. Ardfern is everything Croabh Haven isn't and boasts a real **pub**, the *Galley of Lorne* (Ⓣ01852/500284, Ⓦwww.galleyoflorne.co.uk) with a rather more upmarket restaurant attached. Opposite the pub is *The Crafty Kitchen* (Ⓣ01852/500303; closed Mon), a small popular restaurant (and craftshop) specializing in inexpensive locally sourced and vegetarian food.

Kilmartin Glen

The chief sight on the road from Oban to Lochgilphead is the **Kilmartin Glen**, the most important prehistoric site on the Scottish mainland. The most remarkable relic is the **linear cemetery**, where several cairns are aligned for more than two miles, to the south of the village of Kilmartin. These are thought to represent the successive burials of a ruling family or chieftains, but nobody can be sure. The best view of the cemetery's configuration is from the Bronze Age **Mid-Cairn**, but the Neolithic **South Cairn**, dating from around 3000 BC, is by far the oldest and the most impressive, with its large chambered tomb roofed by giant slabs.

Close to the Mid-Cairn, the two **Temple Wood stone circles** appear to have been the architectural focus of burials in the area from Neolithic times to the Bronze Age. Visible to the south are the impressively cup-marked **Nether Largie standing stones** (no public access), the largest of which looms over 10ft high. **Cup- and ring-marked rocks** are a recurrent feature of prehistoric sites in the Kilmartin Glen and elsewhere in Argyll. There are many theories as to their origin: some see them as Pictish symbols, others as primitive solar calendars. The most extensive markings in the entire country are at **Achnabreck**, off the A816 towards Lochgilphead.

Kilmartin

Situated on high ground to the north of the cairns is the tiny village of **KILMARTIN**, where the old manse adjacent to the village church now

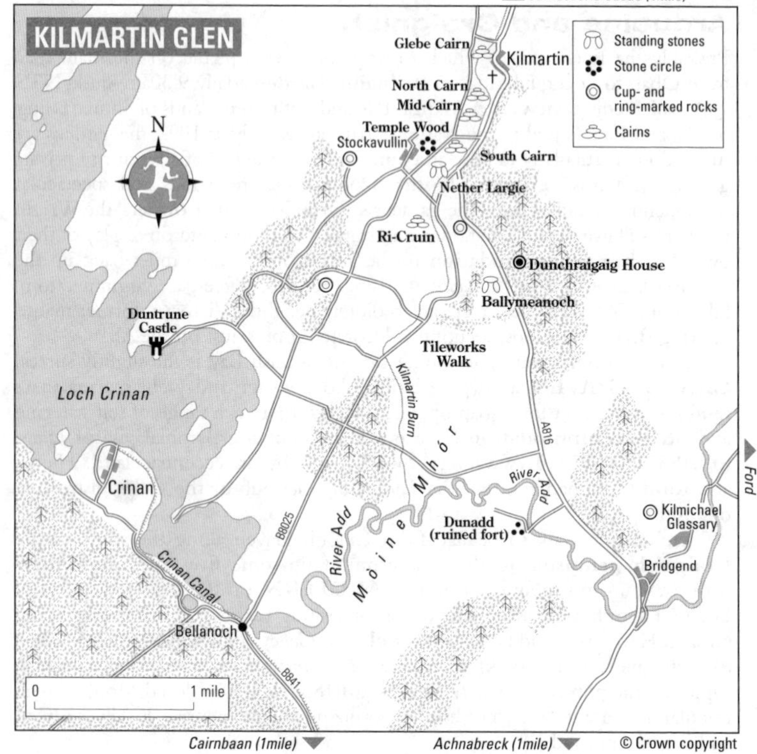

houses a **Museum of Ancient Culture** (daily 10am–5.30pm; £4.50; Ⓦwww.kilmartin.org), which is both enlightening and entertaining. Not only can you learn about the various theories concerning prehistoric crannogs, henges and cairns, but you can practise polishing an axe, examine different types of wood and fur, and listen to a variety of weird and wonderful sounds (check out the Gaelic bird imitations).

Nearby **Kilmartin church** is worth a brief reconnoitre, as it shelters several richly sculptured graves and crosses, while a separate enclosure in the graveyard houses a large collection of medieval grave slabs of the Malcolms of Poltalloch. Kilmartin's own castle is ruined beyond recognition; head instead for the much-less-ruined **Carnasserie Castle**, on a high ridge a mile up the road towards Oban. The castle was built in the 1560s by John Carswell, an influential figure in the Scottish church, who published the first ever book in Gaelic, *Knox's Liturgy*, which contained the doctrines of the Presbyterian faith. Architecturally, the castle is interesting, too, as it represents the transition between fully fortified castles and later mansion houses, and has several original finely carved stone fireplaces, doorways, as well as numerous gun-loops and shot holes.

For something to eat, head for the museum **café**, with home-baked produce on offer, which you can wash it down with heather beer – it's open in the early evening too (Thurs–Sat). The nearest **B&B** is at *Dunchraigaig House* (Ⓣ01546/605209, Ⓔdunchraig@aol.com; ③), a large detached Victorian house situated opposite the Ballymeanoch standing stones.

Mòine Mhór and Dunadd

To the south of Kilmartin, beyond the linear cemetery, lies the raised peat bog of **Mòine Mhór** (Great Moss), now a nature reserve and home to remarkable plant, insect and birdlife. To get a close look at the sphagnum moss and wetlands, head for the **Tileworks Walk**, just off the A816, which includes a short boardwalk over the bog.

Mòine Mhór is best known as home to the Iron Age fort of **Dunadd**, one of Scotland's most important Celtic sites, occupying a distinctive 176-foot-high rocky knoll once surrounded by the sea but currently stranded beside the winding River Add. It was here that Fergus, the first King of Dalriada, established his royal seat, having arrived from Ireland in around 500 AD. Its strategic position, the craggy defences and the view from the top are all impressive, but it's the **stone carvings** (albeit now fibreglass copies) between the twin summits which make Dunadd so remarkable: several lines of inscription in ogham (an ancient alphabet of Irish origin), the faint outline of a boar, a hollowed-out footprint and a small basin. The boar and the inscriptions are probably Pictish, since the fort was clearly occupied long before Fergus got here, but the footprint and basin have been interpreted as being part of the royal coronation rituals of the kings of Dalriada. It is thought that the Stone of Destiny was used at Dunadd before being moved to Scone Palace, then to Westminster Abbey in London, where it languished until it was returned to Edinburgh in 1996.

Lochgilphead

The unlikely administrative centre of Argyll & Bute, **LOCHGILPHEAD** (Ⓦwww.lochgilphead.info), as the name suggests, lies at the head of Loch Gilp, an arm of Loch Fyne. It's a planned town in the same vein as Inveraray, though nothing like as picturesque. If you're staying in the area, however, you're bound to find yourself here at some point, as Lochgilphead has the only bank and supermarket (not to mention swimming pool) for miles. In fine weather, you're best off going for a stroll round **Kilmory Woodland Park**, a couple of miles up the A83 towards Inveraray, with its Iron Age fort, bird hide and lochside views, and take in the gardens laid out in 1830 around Kilmory Castle (now headquarters of the Argyll & Bute District Council). Another fine-weather option is **Castle Riding Centre** (Ⓣ01546/603274, Ⓦwww.brenfield.co.uk), at Brenfield Farm, three miles south, which runs highly enjoyable riding courses lasting from a day to a week, plus trekking and pub rides, and even has golf equipment and **bike rental**.

The **tourist office**, 27 Lochnell St (April–Oct Mon–Sat 10am–5pm, Sun noon–5pm; longer hours in summer; Ⓣ01546/602344), can help find you **accommodation** in the area. If you need a place in Lochgilphead itself, there's *Cairnsmore House* (Ⓣ01546/602885 Ⓦwww.cairnsmorehouse.co.uk; ❸), an attractive Victorian villa with light airy rooms in the quiet backstreet of Manse Brae, or *Allt-na-Craig* (Ⓣ01546/603245, Ⓦwww.allt-na-craig.co.uk; ❺), a very handsome, stylish, detached Victorian guesthouse set back from the road to Ardrishaig. You can also **camp** at the pristinely maintained *Lochgilphead Caravan Park*, a short distance west of town in Bank Park (Ⓣ01546/602003, Ⓦwww.lochgilpheadcaravanpark.co.uk; April–Oct); bike rental is available, too. As for **food**, the best place in town is *Pinto's* (Ⓣ01546/602547; closed Sun), a modern veggie restaurant that offers lunch for a fiver, as well as wraps, soup and sandwiches, and a slightly more expensive set menu in the evening (Thurs–Sat only). *The Smiddy*, on Smithy Lane (closed Sun), does simple café fare – for high-class picnic provisions call in at *Cockles*, a smart deli on the main street that also sells fresh and smoked fish and delicious home-made bread.

Knapdale

Forested **Knapdale** – from the Gaelic *cnap* (hill) and *dall* (field) – forms a buffer zone between the Kintyre peninsula and the rest of Argyll, bounded to the north by the Crinan Canal and to the south by West Loch Tarbert and consisting of three fingers of land, separated by Loch Sween and Loch Caolisport.

Crinan Canal

In 1801 the nine-mile-long **Crinan Canal** opened, linking Loch Fyne, at Ardrishaig south of Lochgilphead, with the Sound of Jura, thus cutting out the long and treacherous journey around the Mull of Kintyre. John Rennie's original design, although an impressive engineering feat, had numerous faults, and by 1816 Thomas Telford was called in to take charge of the renovations. The canal runs parallel to the sea for quite some way before cutting across the bottom of Mòine Mhór and hitting a flight of locks either side of **CAIRNBAAN** (there are fifteen in total); a walk along the towpath is both picturesque and pleasantly unstrenuous. A useful pit stop can be made at the excellent *Cairnbaan Hotel* (ⓣ01546/603668, ⓦwww.cairnbaan.com; ⑥), a really comfortable, eighteenth-century coaching inn overlooking the canal; it also has a decent restaurant and bar meals featuring locally caught seafood – to whip up an appetite you can nip up to the cup- and ring-marked stone behind the hotel.

There are usually one or two yachts passing through the locks, but the most relaxing place from which to view the canal in action is **CRINAN**, the pretty little fishing port at the western end of the canal. Crinan's tiny harbour is, for the moment at least, still home to a small fishing fleet; a quick burst up through Crinan Wood to the hill above the village will give you a bird's-eye view of the sea-lock and its setting. Every room in the *Crinan Hotel* (ⓣ01546/830261, ⓦwww.crinanhotel.com; ⑧) looks across Loch Crinan to the Sound of Jura – one of the most beautiful (and expensive) views in Scotland, especially at sunset, when the myriad islets and the distinctive Paps of Jura are reflected in the waters of the loch. If the *Crinan* is beyond your means, try the secluded **B&B** *Tigh-na-Glaic* (ⓣ01546/830245; ③), perched above the harbour, also with views out to sea, or the superb *Bellanoch House* (ⓣ01546/830149, ⓦwww.bellanochhouse.co.uk; ⑤), a grand, old schoolhouse with stripped pine floors and lots of character, right on the canal, a mile or so before Crinan.

Bar **meals** at the *Crinan* are moderately expensive, but utterly delicious. Down on the lockside there is a cheaper, cheerful **café** called the *Coffee Shop* (Easter–Oct), serving mouthwatering home-made cakes and wonderful clootie dumplings. The **boat trips** organized by Gemini Cruises (ⓣ01546/830238, ⓦwww.gemini-crinan.co.uk), leave from Crinan's other harbour, half a mile further along the coast, though they will pick up from other points along the coast; from here the waymarked three-mile **Crinan Walk** takes you through the nearby Forestry Commission plantation, with excellent views out to sea.

Knapdale Forest and Loch Sween

South of the canal, **Knapdale Forest**, planted in the 1930s, stretches virtually uninterrupted from coast to coast, across hills sprinkled with tiny lochs. The Forestry Commission has set out several lovely **walks**, the easiest of which is the circular, mile-long path which takes you deep into the forest just past **Achanamara** (five miles south of Crinan). The three-mile route around **Loch Coille-Bharr**, which begins from a bend in the B8025, to Tayvallich, is fairly gentle; the other walk, although half a mile shorter, is more strenuous, starting from the B841 (halfway between Crinan and Lochgilphead), which runs along the canal, and ascending the peak of **Dunardry** (702ft). There are also several good cycle routes, from easy to tough, in this area – all clearly waymarked.

Continuing down the western finger of Knapdale you come to the village of **TAYVALLICH** (Ⓦwww.tayvallich.com), with its attractive horseshoe bay, after which the peninsula splits again. The western arm leads eventually to the medieval **Chapel of Keills**, which houses a display of late medieval carved stones, and the remains of a small port where cattle used to be landed from Ireland. There is also a fine view of the **MacCormaig Islands**, the largest of which, Eilean Mór (currently owned by the Scottish National Party), was previously a retreat of the seventh-century St Cormac, but is now a breeding ground for seabirds. The other arm, the **Taynish peninsula**, is a National Nature Reserve and has one of the largest remaining oak forests in Britain, boasting over twenty species of butterfly. If you want to eat or drink round here, then head for the *Tayvallich Inn* (Ⓣ01546/870282), in the village of the same name, for very good local food.

Six miles south of Achanamara, on the eastern shores of **Loch Sween**, is the "Key of Knapdale", the eleventh-century **Castle Sween**, the earliest stone castle in Scotland, but in ruins since 1647. The tranquillity and beauty of the setting is spoilt by the nearby caravan park, an eyesore which makes a visit pretty depressing. You're better off continuing south to the thirteenth-century **Kilmory Chapel**, also ruined but with a new roof protecting the medieval grave slabs and the well-preserved MacMillan's Cross, an eight-foot fifteenth-century Celtic cross showing the Crucifixion on one side and a hunting scene on the other.

The easternmost finger of Knapdale is isolated and fairly impenetrable, but it's worth persevering the fourteen miles of single-track road in order to reach **KILBERRY**, where you can **camp** at the *Port Ban Caravan Park* (Ⓣ01880/770224, Ⓦwww.portban.com; March–Oct), and enjoy the fantastic sunsets and views over Jura, or **stay the night** in comfort and style at the *Kilberry Inn* (Ⓣ01880/770223, Ⓦwww.kilberryinn.com; April–Oct; ⑤); the inn's **food** is also superb (Tues–Sun). There's also a church worth viewing in Kilberry and a small collection of carved medieval grave slabs, while the western shores of West Loch Tarbert are usually replete with birdlife.

Kintyre

But for the mile-long isthmus between West Loch Tarbert and the much smaller East Loch Tarbert, the little-visited peninsula of **KINTYRE** (Ⓦwww.kintyre.org) – from the Gaelic *ceann tire*, "land's end" – would be an island. Indeed, in the eleventh century, when the Scottish king, Malcolm Canmore, allowed Magnus Barefoot, King of Norway, to lay claim to any island he could circumnavigate by boat, Magnus succeeded in dragging his boat across the Tarbert isthmus and added the peninsula to his Hebridean kingdom. During the Wars of the Covenant, the vast majority of the population and property was wiped out by a combination of the 1646 potato blight and the destructive attentions of the Earl of Argyll. Kintyre remained a virtual desert until the earl began his policy of transplanting Gaelic-speaking Lowlanders to the region. They probably felt quite at home here, as the southern third of the peninsula lies on the Lowland side of the Highland Boundary Fault.

There are regular daily **buses** from Glasgow to Campbeltown, via Tarbert and the west coast, and even a skeleton service down the east coast. Bear in mind, though, if you're driving, that the new west coast road is extremely fast, whereas the single-track east coast road takes more than twice as long. There's a **ferry** to Tarbert from Portavadie on the Cowal peninsula, and Campbeltown has an airport, with daily flights from Glasgow, which is only forty miles away by air, compared to over 120 miles by road.

Tarbert

A distinctive rocket-like church steeple heralds the fishing village of **TARBERT** (in Gaelic *an tairbeart*, meaning "isthmus"), sheltering an attractive little bay backed by rugged hills. Tarbert's herring industry was mentioned in the Annals of Ulster as far back as 836 AD, though right now the local fishing industry is down to its lowest level ever. Ironically, it was local Tarbert fishermen, who, in the 1830s, pioneered the method of herring-fishing known as trawling, seining or ring-netting, which eventually wiped out the Loch Fyne herring stocks. Tourism is now an increasingly important source of income, as is the money that flows through the town during the last week in May, when the yacht races of the famous Scottish Series take place, and in the first weekend in July, when traditional boats and a seafood festival hit town.

Tarbert's harbourfront is really quite pretty, and is best appreciated from Robert the Bruce's fourteenth-century **castle** above the town to the south. Only the ivy-strewn ruins of the keep remain, though the view from the overgrown rubble makes the stroll up here worthwhile. There are steps up to the castle and a red-waymarked path from beside the excellent bookshop and gallery on the south side of the harbour. Longer walks are also marked out, including a hike all the way over to Skipness (see p.135). The shortest stroll of all, though, is to the far end of Pier Road, where there's a tiny, but very lovely shell beach.

Tarbert's **tourist office** (April–Oct Mon–Sat 10am–5pm, Sun noon–5pm; longer hours in summer; ⓣ01880/820429) is on the harbour. If you need to **stay**, there's no shortage of B&Bs, though none is outstanding – try *Springside* on Pier Road (ⓣ01880/820413, ⓔmarshall.springside@virgin.net; ❷), which overlooks the harbour. Tarbert's luxury option is *Stonefield Castle Hotel* (ⓣ01880/820836, ⓦwww.innscotland.com; ❽), two miles up the A83 to Lochgilphead, a handsome, grandiose Scots Baronial mansion set in magnificent grounds overlooking Loch Fyne; all bookings are for dinner, bed and breakfast.

The *Ca'Dora* is the caff to head for on the seafront, while *The Anchor* pub, also overlooking the harbour, is a good option for a seafood lunch. The best **food** is to be had courtesy of the French chef at the evening-only *Corner House Bistro* (ⓣ01880/820263), just by the side of the *Corner House* pub, which serves seafood caught by its boat, or at the more expensive, but equally excel-

Ferry connections in and around Tarbert

One reason you might find yourself staying in Tarbert is its proximity to no fewer than four **ferry terminals**. The small CalMac ferry, which connects Kintyre with **Portavadie** on the Cowal peninsula, leaves from Tarbert's Pier Road; the busiest terminal, however, is at **Kennacraig**, five miles south along the A83, which runs daily sailings to Islay and a once-weekly service to Colonsay. From Kennacraig, the B8001 cuts across the peninsula to **Claonaig**, where a summer car ferry (April to mid-Oct) runs to Lochranza on Arran; and finally, south of Kennacraig on the A83, the Gigha ferry departs from **Tayinloan**.

lent *Anchorage* (Ⓣ01880/820881; Oct–March eve only), on the south side of the harbour.

Isle of Gigha

Gigha (Ⓦwww.gigha.org.uk) – pronounced "Geeya", with a hard "g" – is a low-lying, fertile island, just three miles off the west coast of Kintyre, reputedly occupied for 5000 years. The island's Ayrshire cattle produce over a quarter of a million gallons of milk a year, though since the closure of Gigha's creamery in the 1980s, the island's distinctive (occasionally fruit-shaped) cheese has actually been produced on the mainland. Like many of the smaller Hebrides, Gigha was bought and sold numerous times after its original lairds, the MacNeils, sold up, and was finally bought by the 130 or so inhabitants themselves in 2002. The most visible sign of the island's regeneration are the three community-owned wind turbines – Faith, Hope and Charity – at the southern tip of the island, which supply Gigha's electricity needs and feed the surplus into the national grid, thereby generating income.

The ferry from Tayinloan, 23 miles south of Tarbert, deposits you at the island's only village, **ARDMINISH**, where you'll find the post office and shop and the all-denominations island church with some interesting stained-glass windows, including one to Kenneth MacLeod, composer of the well-known ditty *Road to the Isles*. The main attraction on the island is the **Achamore Gardens** (daily 9am–dusk; £4), a mile south of Ardminish. Established by the first postwar owner, Sir James Horlick of hot drink fame, their spectacularly colourful displays of azaleas are best seen in early summer. Achamore House (see p.130) itself is now home to an American who runs a flower essence business (and technically, at least, is the new laird). To the southwest of the gardens, the ruins of the thirteenth-century **St Catan's Chapel** are floored with weathered medieval gravestones; the ogham stone nearby is the only one of its kind in the west of Scotland. The real draw of Gigha, however, apart from the peace and quiet, are the white sandy beaches – including one at Ardminish itself – that dot the coastline.

△ Gigha cheese

Gigha is small – six miles by one mile – and most visitors come here just for the day. However, it's a great place **to stay** too: for simple B&B, try the old *Post Office House* (Ⓣ01583/505251, Ⓦwww.gighastores.co.uk; ❷) or the newly-built *Tighnavinish* (Ⓣ01583/505378, Ⓦwww.gigha.net; ❸), half a mile to the north; if you want to stay in style, head for *Achamore House* (Ⓣ01583/505400, Ⓦwww.achamorehouse.com; ❺), the beautiful house in the midst of Achamore Gardens; if you're interested in **camping**, you should contact the *Gigha Hotel* (Ⓣ01583/505254), the very pleasant social centre of the island just south of the post office. The licensed *Boathouse*, by the pier, is the place to go for delicious **food**, and, occasionally, live music. **Bike rental** is available from the shop (open daily), and there's a nine-hole **golf course**.

The west coast

Kintyre's bleak **west coast** ranks among the most exposed stretches of coastline in Argyll. Atlantic breakers pound the rocky shoreline, while the persistent westerly wind forces the trees against the hillside. However, when the weather's fine and the wind not too fierce, there are numerous deserted sandy beaches to enjoy with great views over to Gigha, Islay, Jura and even Ireland.

There are several **campsites** to choose from along the stretch of coast around **TAYINLOAN**, ranging from the big *Point Sands Caravan Park* (Ⓣ01583/441263; April–Oct), two miles to the north, set back a long way from the main road near a long stretch of sandy beach, to the smaller, more informal *Muasdale Holiday Park*, three miles to the south (Ⓣ01583/421207, Ⓦwww.muasdaleholidays.com; April–Oct), squeezed between the main road and the beach. **Accommodation** along the coast includes the *Balinakill Country House* (Ⓣ01880/740206, Ⓦwww.balinakill.com; ❺), a capacious late-Victorian hotel with lots of period touches, set in its own grounds near Clachan north of Tayinloan; the kitchen produces decent bar food until 7pm, and much more expensive à la carte after that. Another **food** option along the coast is *North Beachmore*, signposted off the A83, just south of Tayinloan, a restaurant boasting panoramic views out to Gigha, Islay and Jura, and serving straightforward snacks, lunches and evening meals (reservations advisable at the weekend; Ⓣ01583/421328).

Two-thirds of the way down the coast you can visit **Glenbarr Abbey** (Easter to mid-Oct daily except Tues 10am–5.30pm; £3; Ⓦwww.highlandconnection.org/clanmacalistercenter.html), an eighteenth-century laird's house filled with tedious memorabilia about the once-powerful MacAlister clan, who now augment their income by giving personal guided tours of their home to the trickle of tourists that pass this way. There are plenty of musty old sofas to lounge around in, a tearoom, and attractive grounds which can provide a brief respite from the Atlantic winds. If you're up for a spot of **horse riding**, get in touch with the nearby Barrglen Equitation Centre, based at Arnicle Farm (Ⓣ01583/421397), two miles inland from Glenbarr Abbey, which offers lessons and longer rides for "the good, the bad and the wobbly". A couple of miles further down the coast, in the tiny settlement of **BELLOCHANTUY**, is the *Argyll Hotel* (Ⓣ01583/421212, Ⓦwww.argyllhotel.co.uk; ❹), a welcoming roadside pub serving bar meals in its conservatory or on outside tables overlooking the sand and sea – you can also camp next door.

Machrihanish

The only major development along the entire west coast is **MACHRIHANISH**, at the southern end of Machrihanish Bay, the longest continuous stretch of sand in Argyll. There are two approaches to the **beach**: from Machrihanish itself, or from Westport, at the north end of the bay, where the A83 swings east towards Campbeltown; either way, the sea here is too dangerous for swimming. Machrihanish itself was once a thriving salt-producing and coal-mining centre – you can still see the miners' cottages at neighbouring Drumlemble – with a light railway link to Campbeltown, but now survives solely on tourism. The main draw, apart from the beach, is the exposed championship **golf links** between the beach and Campbeltown airport on the nearby flat and fertile swath of land known as the Laggan. There's also a tiny **seabird observatory** (Easter–Oct daily; Ⓦwww.machrihanishbirds.org.uk) at Uisaed Point, ten minutes' walk west of the village, though it's best visited in the migration periods, when it provides a welcome shelter for ornithologists trying to spot a rare bird blown off course.

Several of the imposing, detached Victorian town houses overlooking the bay in Machrihanish, such as *Ardell House* (Ⓣ01586/810235; ❸; March–Oct), offer **accommodation**; there's also a large, fully equipped and very exposed **campsite** (Ⓣ01586/810366, Ⓦwww.campkintyre.com; March–Sept) overlooking the golf links, which even has a couple of heated wooden wigwams. In the evening, *The Beachcomber* bar is the liveliest place in Machrihanish.

Campbeltown

CAMPBELTOWN's best feature is its setting, in a deep bay sheltered by Davaar Island and the surrounding hills. With a population of around five thousand, it is also one of the largest towns in Argyll and, if you're staying in the southern half of Kintyre, its shops are by far the best place to stock up on supplies. Originally known as Kinlochkilkerran (*Ceann Loch Cill Chiaran*), the town was renamed in the seventeenth century by the Earl of Argyll – a Campbell – when it became one of the main points for immigration from the Lowlands. As is evident from the architecture, Campbeltown's heyday was the Victorian era, when shipbuilding was going strong, coal was shipped by canal from Drumlemble, there was a light railway connection with Machrihanish, the fishing fleet was vast and Campbeltown Loch was said to be made of whisky. The decline of all its old industries has left the town permanently depressed, and unemployment and underemployment remain persistent problems.

The Town

Nineteenth-century visitors to Campbeltown frequently found the place engulfed in a thick fog of pungent peat smoke from the town's 34 **whisky distilleries**. Today, only Glen Scotia, Springbank and the former Glengyle distillery are left to maintain this regional subgroup of single malt whiskies (see the *Scottish food and drink* colour section for more on whisky), but you can buy a guide to Campbeltown's former distilleries from the tourist office. The deeply traditional, family-owned **Springbank**, off Longrow, is the only distillery in Scotland that does absolutely everything from malting to bottling, on its own premises, and they offer no-nonsense guided tours (Easter–Sept Mon–Thurs by appointment; £3; Ⓣ01586/552085, Ⓦwww.springbankdistillers.com). At the end, you get a voucher to exchange for a miniature at Eaglesome, on Longrow South, whose range of whiskies is awesome.

The town's most ancient sight is the **Campbeltown Cross**, a fourteenth-century blue-green cross with figural scenes and spirals of Celtic knotting, which presides over the main roundabout on the quayside. Until World War II, it used to be rather more impressive in the middle of the main street outside the **Town Hall**, with its distinctive eighteenth-century octagonal clock tower.

Back on the palm-tree-dotted waterfront is the **Wee Pictures**, a dinky little Art Deco cinema on Hall Street, built in 1913 and still going strong (daily except Fri; ⓣ01586/533657, ⓦwww.weepictures.co.uk). Next door is the equally delightful **Campbeltown Museum and Library** (Tues–Sat 10am–1pm & 2–5pm, Tues & Thurs also 5.30–7.30pm; free), built in 1897 in the local sandstone, crowned by a distinctive lantern, and decorated on its harbourside wall with four relief panels depicting each of the town's main industries at the time. Inside, there's a timber-framed ceiling and etched glass partitions to admire, not to mention a rather unusual brass model of the Temple of Solomon (as it might have looked). The museum itself, which you enter through the library, provides a less remarkable rundown on local history: for a more enlightening version, head to the Heritage Centre (described below). The library also hides one new, but little-known sight: the **Linda McCartney Memorial Garden**, which features a slightly ludicrous bronze statue of Linda holding a lamb, commissioned by the ex-Beatle, who spent many happy times with Linda and the kids on the farm he owns near Campbeltown.

It used to be said that Campbeltown had almost as many churches as it did distilleries, and even today the townscape is dominated by its church spires – in particular, the top-heavy crown spire of **Longrow Church**, on the road to Machrihanish. The former Lorne Street Church, known locally as the "Tartan Kirk", partly due to its Gaelic associations and partly due to its stripy bell-cote and pinnacles, has now become the **Campbeltown Heritage Centre** (April–Sept Mon–Sat noon–5pm, Sun 2–5pm; £2). A beautiful wooden skiff from 1906 stands where the main altar once was, and there's plenty on the local whisky industry and St Kieran, the sixth-century "Apostle of Kintyre", who lived in a cave – which you can get to at low tide – not far from Campbeltown. A dedicated ascetic, he would only eat bread mixed with a third sand and a few herbs; he wore chains, had a stone pillow and slept out in the snow – unsurprisingly, at the age of 33, he died of jaundice.

Campbeltown's newest attraction is the **Scottish Owl Centre** (April to early Oct daily except Tues 1.30–4.30pm; £5; ⓦwww.scottishowlcentre.tk), signposted off the B842 to Machrihanish, five minutes' walk out of town. As well as being actively involved in conservation work, the centre has a huge collection of owls spread out in terraced aviaries, ranging from the tiny Scops Owl to the world's largest, the Eurasian Eagle Owl. Try and time your visit with the daily flight display at 2.30pm.

One of the most popular day-trips is to **Davaar Island**, linked to the peninsula at low tide by a mile-long shoal, or *dóirlinn* as it's known in Gaelic. Check the times of the tides from the tourist office before setting out; you have around six hours in which to make the return journey from Kildalloig Point, two miles or so east of town. Davaar is uninhabited and used for grazing (hence no dogs are allowed); its main claim to fame is the cave painting of the Crucifixion executed in secret by local artist Archibald MacKinnon, in 1887, and touched up by him after he'd owned up in 1934; a year later, aged 85, he died. The cave, on the south side of the island, is easy enough to find, but the story is better than the end product, and you're better off walking up to the island's high point (378ft) and enjoying the view.

Practicalities

Campbeltown's **tourist office** is on the Old Quay (April–Oct Mon–Fri 10am–5pm, Sun noon–4pm; Nov–March Mon–Fri 9am–4pm; ⓣ01586/552056), and will happily hand out a free map of the town. The **airport** (ⓣ01586/552571) lies three miles west, towards Machrihanish; there's a bus connection, but you need to phone ahead to book it (Ⓣ01586/552319) – it's part of Campbeltown's **Ring'n'Ride** service, which also operates around the town and to Southend (pick up a bus timetable from the tourist office for more details). As for the **ferry** connection with Ballycastle in Northern Ireland, it should be resumed in the near future.

The best centrally located **accommodation** is the delightful family-run *Ardshiel Hotel*, on Kilkerran Road (Ⓣ01586/552133, Ⓦwww.ardshiel.co.uk; ❺), situated on a lovely leafy square, just a block or so back from the ferry terminal, with a cosy bar, and a more expensive à la carte restaurant. On the north side of the bay, on Low Askomill, is *Craigard House* (Ⓣ01586/554242, Ⓦwww.craigard-house.co.uk; ❻), a former whisky distiller's grandiose sandstone mansion with a hint of the Italian Renaissance. For an inexpensive, central B&B, head for *Westbank Guest House*, on Dell Road (Ⓣ01586/553660; ❷), off the B842 to Southend. Another place worth considering is *Oatfield House* (Ⓣ01586/551551, Ⓦwww.oatfield.org; ❸), a beautifully renovated laird's house set in its own grounds, three miles down the B842 to Southend.

As for **places to eat**, the *Palm Bistro* on the harbourfront serves up standard café fare; the best bar meals are to be found at the aforementioned *Ardshiel Hotel*; while the *Commercial Inn* on Cross Street is a good drinking hole. You can **rent bikes** at The Bike Shop, Longrow (Ⓣ01586/554443). If you're here in the middle of August, be sure to check out the **Mull of Kintyre Music & Arts Festival** (Ⓦwww.mokfest.com), which features some great traditional Irish and Scottish bands.

Southend and the Mull of Kintyre

The bulbous, hilly end of Kintyre, to the south of Campbeltown, features some of the most spectacular scenery on the whole peninsula, mixed with large swaths of Lowland-style farmland. **SOUTHEND** itself, a bleak, blustery spot, comes as something of a disappointment, though it does have a golden sandy beach. Below the cliffs to the west of the beach, a ruined thirteenth-century chapel marks the alleged arrival point of St Columba prior to his trip to Iona, and on a rocky knoll nearby a pair of footprints carved into the rock are known as **Columba's footprints**, though only one is actually of ancient origin. Jutting out into the sea at the east end of the bay is **Dunaverty Rock**, where a force of 300 Royalists was massacred by the Covenanting army of the Earl of Argyll in 1647, despite having surrendered voluntarily. If you're looking for even nicer beaches head further west to Carskey Bay, or Macharioch Bay, three miles east, looking out to distant Ailsa Craig in the Firth of Clyde.

A couple of miles out to sea from Southend lies **Sanda Island**, which contains the remains of St Ninian's chapel, plus two ancient crosses, a holy well, an unusual lighthouse comprised of three sandstone towers and lots of seabirds, including manx shearwater, storm petrels and puffins. The island has its own **pub**, the *Byron Darnton*, named after a 7000-ton vessel wrecked on Sanda in 1946 without any loss of life, as well as a bird observatory and several self-catering cottages; the farmhouse also offers **B&B** (Ⓣ01586/553511, Ⓦwww.sanda-island.co.uk; ❹). Unless you're on a yacht, you'll need to board the *Seren Las* in Campbeltown to reach the island (Ⓣ01586/554667; £20 return) or take a helicopter from Arran (see the website for more details).

Most people venture south of Campbeltown to make a pilgrimage to the **Mull of Kintyre** – the nearest Britain gets to Ireland, whose coastline, just twelve miles away, appears remarkably close on fine days. Although the Mull was made famous by the mawkish number-one hit by sometime local resident **Paul**

McCartney, with the help of the Campbeltown Pipe Band, it's also infamous as the site of the **RAF's worst peacetime accident** when, on June 2, 1994, a Chinook helicopter on its way from Belfast to Inverness crashed, killing all 29 on board. The Ministry of Defence blamed the pilots and, despite the findings of a Scottish enquiry and the opinions of a cross-party select committee, still maintains there were no technical problems with the helicopter. A small memorial can be found on the hillside, not far from the **Gap** (1150ft) – where you must leave your car. There's nothing specifically to see in this godforsaken storm-racked spot, and the road down to the lighthouse, itself 300ft above the ocean waves, is terrifyingly tortuous. It's about a mile from the "Gap" to the lighthouse (and a long haul back up), though there's a strategic viewpoint just ten-minutes' walk from the car park; the principal lightkeeper's cottage, known as *Hector's House*, is now a remote **self-catering** option (phone the NTS; ⓣ0131/243 9331).

Southend still has a **pub**, the *Argyll Arms*: unremarkable except for the fact that it has a post office inside it. The derelict Art Deco Keil Hotel cuts a forlorn figure, set back from the bay, but there are a couple of excellent **B&Bs** in the surrounding area: *Ormsary Farm* (ⓣ01586/830665, ⓔormsaryfarm@tinyworld.co.uk; April–Sept; ❶), a small dairy farm up Glen Breakerie; and the nearby picturesque croft of *Low Cattadale* (ⓣ01586/830205; ❷; March–Nov). **Camping** is possible in the field right by the beach, run by *Machribeg Farm* (ⓣ01586/830249; Easter–Sept). If you're interested in **horse riding**, call the Mull of Kintyre Equestrian Centre at Homeston Farm (ⓣ01586/552437; April–Oct), signposted off the B842 to Southend.

The east coast

The **east coast** of Kintyre is gentler than the west, sheltered from the Atlantic winds and in parts strikingly beautiful, with stunning views across to Arran. However, be warned that there's no bus service between Carradale and Skipness and, if you're driving the thirty or so miles up to Skipness on the slow, winding, single-track B842, you'll need a fair amount of time.

The ruins of **Saddell Abbey**, a Cistercian foundation thought to have been founded by Somerled in 1148, lie ten miles up the coast from Campbeltown, set at the lush, wooded entrance to Saddell Glen. The abbey fell into disrepair in the sixteenth century and, though the remains are not exactly impressive, there's a good collection of medieval grave slabs decorated with full-scale relief figures of knights housed in a new shelter in the grounds. Standing by the privately owned shoreline there's a splendid memorial to the last Campbell laird to live at Saddell Castle, which he built in 1774.

Further north lies the fishing village of **CARRADALE**, the only place of any size on the east coast north of Campbeltown, and "popular with those who like unsophisticated resorts", as one 1930s guide put it. The village itself is rather drab, but the tiny, very pretty harbour with its small fishing fleet, and the wide, sandy beach to the south, make up for it. On the east side of the beach is **Carradale Point**, a wildlife reserve with feral goats and a good example of a **vitrified fort** built more than two thousand years ago on a small tidal island off the headland (best approached from the beach). There are several pleasant walks with good views across to Arran laid out in the woods around Carradale, for which the best starting point is the car park at Port na Storm on the road into the village.

Carradale also has a couple of good wet-weather retreats. First, there's **Network Carradale Heritage Centre** (Easter to mid-Oct Mon–Sat 10.30am–5pm, Sun

12.30–5pm; free), by the aforementioned car park. The displays trace the demise of the local herring fleet and the puffers that used to bring tourists, and the rise of forestry; it's small in scale but informative, and there's good home-baking to be had in the tearoom. A mile or so to the south, in the old laundry of the imposing Scots Baronial Torrisdale Castle, you'll find **Grogport Tannery** (daily 9am–6pm; free), which produces naturally coloured, organically tanned, fully washable sheepskins (gloves and slippers, too); the castle also offers **self-catering** apartments (ⓣ01583/431233, ⓦwww.torrisdalecastle.com).

Accommodation is available at the *Carradale Hotel* (ⓣ01583/431223, ⓦwww.carradalehotel.com; ❸), whose bar is the hub of village social life (and whose food is good), and at *Dunvalanree* (ⓣ01583/431226, ⓦwww.dunvalanree.com; ❹), the big Victorian house overlooking the sheltered little bay of Port Righ, towards Carradale Point – it's beautifully decorated inside and is, in fact, a licensed hotel. There's also the well-equipped *Carradale Bay Caravan Park* **campsite** (ⓣ01583/431665, ⓦwww.carradalebay.com; April–Sept), right by the sandy beach. Carradale boasts a real baker, too – try the treacle scones or cookie pudding (known as bread-and-butter pudding south of the border).

The B842 ends twelve miles north of Carradale at **CLAONAIG**, little more than a slipway for the small summer car ferry to Arran. Beyond here, a dead-end road winds its way along the shore a few miles further north to the tiny village of **SKIPNESS**, where the considerable ruins of the enormous thirteenth-century **Skipness Castle** and a chapel look out across the Kilbrannan Sound to Arran. You can sit outside and admire both, whilst enjoying fresh oysters, delicious queenies (queen scallops), mussels and home-baked cakes from the excellent **seafood cabin** (late May to Sept) at Victorian *Skipness Castle*, which also offers **accommodation** in a family home (ⓣ01880/760207, ⓔsophie@skipness.freeserve.co.uk; ❻). There are several gentle walks laid out in the nearby mixed woodland, up the glen.

Isle of Arran

Shaped like a kidney bean and occupying centre stage in the Firth of Clyde, **Arran** (ⓦwww.visitarran.net) is the most southerly (and therefore the most accessible) of all the Scottish islands. The Highland–Lowland dividing line passes right through its centre – hence the cliché about it being like "Scotland in miniature" – leaving the northern half sparsely populated, spectacularly mountainous and forbidding, while the lush southern half enjoys a much milder climate. The population of around five thousand – many of who are incomers – tend to stick to the southeastern quarter of the island, leaving the west and the north relatively undisturbed.

There are two big crowd-pullers on Arran: **geology** and **golf**. The former has fascinated rock-obsessed students since Sir James Hutton came here in the late eighteenth century to confirm his theories of igneous geology. A hundred years later, Sir Archibald Geikie's investigations were a landmark in the study of Arran's geology, and the island remains a popular destination for university and school field trips. As for golf, Arran boasts seven courses, including three of the eighteen-hole variety at Brodick, Lamlash and Whiting Bay, and a unique twelve-hole course at Shiskine, near Blackwaterfoot; an Arran Golf Pass is available for £80, giving you a round on each course.

Although **tourism** is now by far its most important industry, Arran, at twenty miles in length, is large enough to have a life of its own. While the island's post-1745

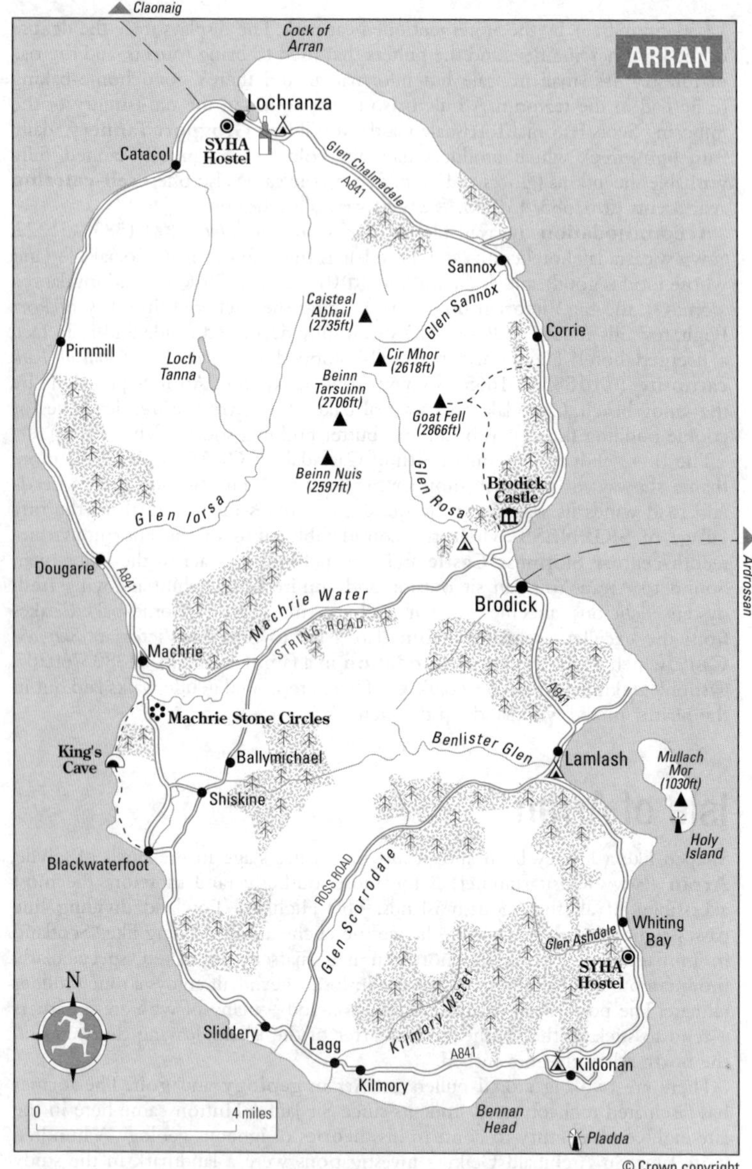

history and the Clearances (set in motion by the local lairds, the dukes of Hamilton) are as depressing as elsewhere in the Highlands, in recent years Arran's population has actually increased, in contrast with more remote islands. Once a county in its own right (along with Bute), Arran was left out of Argyll & Bute in the latest county boundary shake-up, and is coupled instead with mainland North Ayrshire, with which it enjoys year-round transport links, but little else.

Transport on Arran itself is pretty good: daily **buses** circle the island (Brodick tourist office has timetables and an Arran Rural Rover day-ticket costs just £4) and link in with the two **ferry services**: a year-round one from Ardrossan in Ayrshire to **Brodick**; and a smaller ferry from Claonaig on the Kintyre peninsula to **Lochranza** in the north (April–Oct).

Brodick

Although the resort of **BRODICK** (from the Norse *breidr vik*, "broad bay") is a place of only moderate charm, it does at least have a grand setting in a wide, sandy bay set against a backdrop of granite mountains. Its development as a tourist resort was held back for a long time by its elitist owners, the dukes of Hamilton, though nowadays, as the island's capital and main communication hub, Brodick is by far the busiest town on Arran.

Brodick's shops and guesthouses are spread out along the south side of the bay, along with the tourist office and the CalMac pier. However, Brodick's tourist sights, such as they are, are clustered on the west and north side of the bay,

Arran geology

Arran is a top destination for the country's geology students. First, this small island is split in two by the Highland Boundary Fault, and therefore contains a superb variety of rock formations, typical of both the Highlands and the Lowlands. And, second, it is the place where **Sir James Hutton** (1726–97), the "father of modern geology" came in 1787, in order to lay down research for his epic work, *A Theory of the Earth*.

Even if you know very little about geology, it is possible to appreciate some of the island's more obvious features. The most famous location is just beyond **Newton Point**, on the north shore of Loch Ranza, where Allt Beithe stream runs into the sea. Here, two types of rocks by the shore are set virtually at right angles to one another, the older Cambrian schist dipping towards the land, while the younger Devonian sandstone slopes into the sea. This phenomenon became known as **Hutton's unconformity**.

At **Imachar Point**, between Pirnmill and Dougarie, you can view in miniature the geological process known as **folding**, which affected the ancient Cambrian schist around a hundred million years ago, and, on a larger scale, resulted in the formation of mountain ranges such as those of north Arran.

Another classic, more recent geological formation to be seen on Arran is **raised beaches**, formed at the end of the last Ice Age, some fifteen thousand years ago, when the sea level was much higher, and then left high and dry when the sea level dropped. The road that wraps itself around Arran runs along the flat ground that subsequently emerged from the sea. One of the best locations to observe this is at the **King's Cave**, north of Blackwaterfoot (see p.141), where you can see huge sea caves, stranded some distance from today's shoreline.

Down on the south coast, the shoreline below **Kildonan** reveals some superb examples of **dolerite dykes**, formed when molten rock erupted through cracks in the sedimentary sandstone rocks above around sixty million years ago. The molten rock solidified and, being harder, now stands above the surrounding sandstone, forming strange rocky piers jutting out into the sea.

There are numerous other interesting features to look out for, such as **solidified sand dunes** and huge granite boulders, known as **erratics**, on Corrie beach in the northeast of the island, classic **glacial valleys** such as Glen Sannox, and **felsite sills** such as the one at Drumadoon, near Blackwaterfoot, in the southwest. If any of the above whets your appetite, start by getting hold of the geological booklet, *Arran and the Clyde Islands*, produced by Scottish Natural Heritage.

a couple of miles from the ferry terminal. First off, on the road to the castle, there's the **Arran Heritage Museum** (April–Oct daily 10.30am–4.30pm; £2.50; Ⓦwww.arranmuseum.co.uk), housed in a whitewashed eighteenth-century crofter's farm, and containing an old smiddy and a Victorian cottage with box bed and range. In the old stables there are lots of agricultural bits and bobs, plus material on Arran's wartime role, its intriguing geology, and a Neolithic skull found on the island. Other wet-weather options in the **Arran Visitor Centre**, in neighbouring Home Farm, include the Island Cheese Company, where you can see the soft, round crotins of goat's cheese being made and taste Brodick and Glenshant blues; Arran Aromatics where you can watch natural soapmaking, and *Creelers* smokehouse (see opposite) offers succulent seafood. Round the corner in Cladach, right by the castle, you can also visit the **Arran Brewery** (Ⓦwww.arranbrewery.com) and take a guided tour or simply quaff some of their award-winning beers.

Brodick Castle

Even if you're not based in Brodick, it's worth coming here in order to visit **Brodick Castle** (daily: April–Sept 11am–4.30pm; Oct 11am–3.30pm; NTS; £10), former seat of the dukes of Hamilton on a steep bank on the north side of the bay. Just before the entrance, there's a little sandstone jetty where the duke's wine and ice from Canada was landed. It used to serve the village, but the eleventh duke thought the tenants unsightly and had them moved out of sight round the bay. He also closed the barytes mine at Sannox, a vital source of employment for the islanders, on the grounds that it "spoilt the solemn grandeur of the scene".

The bulk of the castle was built in the nineteenth century, giving it a domestic rather than military look, and the **interior** – once you've fought your way past the 87 stags' heads on the stairs – is comfortable but undistinguished. Don't miss the portrait of the eleventh duke's faithful piper, who injured his throat on a grouse bone, was warned never to pipe again, but did so and died. Probably the most atmospheric room is the copper-filled Victorian kitchen, which conjures up a vision of the sweating labour required to feed the folk upstairs.

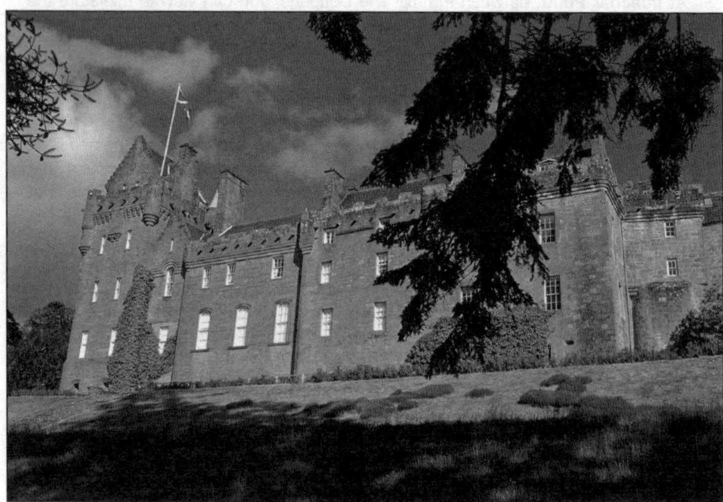

△ Brodick Castle, Arran

Much more attractive, however, are the walled **gardens** (daily 9.30am–dusk; gardens and country park only £5) and extensive grounds, a treasury of exotic plants and trees enjoying the favourable climate (including one of Europe's finest collections of rhododendrons), and commanding a superb view across the bay. There is an adventure playground for kids, but the whole area is a natural playground, with waterfalls, a giant pitcher plant that swallows thousands of midges daily, and a maze of paths. Buried in the grounds there is a bizarre Bavarian-style **summerhouse** lined entirely with pine cones, one of three built by the eleventh duke to make his wife, Princess Marie of Baden, feel at home. For the energetic there is also a **country park** with eleven miles of scenic trails, starting from a small informative, hands-on nature centre. In summer there are guided walks with the rangers, but at any time you can be surprised by red squirrels, nightjars and the abundance of fungi. The excellent castle **tearoom** serves traditional food with a local flavour and is highly recommended.

Practicalities

Brodick's **tourist office** (May–Sept Mon–Thurs & Sat 9am–5pm, Fri 9am–7.30pm, Sun 10am–5pm; Oct–April Mon–Sat 9am–5pm) is by the CalMac pier, and has reams of information on every activity from pony trekking to paragliding. Unless you've got to catch an early-morning ferry, however, there's little reason to stay in Brodick, though there's a decent choice of accommodation should you need to. The best **rooms** close to the ferry terminal are at the excellent *Dunvegan Guest House* (ⓣ01770/302811, ⓔdunveganhouse1@hotmail.com; ④), or *Carrick Lodge* (ⓣ01770/302550; ③; March to mid-Nov), a spacious sandstone manse south of the pier on the Lamlash road. Closer to the castle is the peaceful sandstone farmhouse of *Glencloy* (ⓣ01770/302351, ⓔglencloyfarm@aol.com; ②), which has real fires and a warm welcome. Finally, the luxury option is the tasteful *Kilmichael Country House Hotel* (ⓣ01770/302219, ⓦwww.kilmichael.com; ⑧), originally built in the seventeenth century and still retaining lots of period features; dinner here is very expensive and very formal, but it's one of the best you'll get on the island. The nearest **campsite** is *Glenrosa* (ⓣ01770/302380), a lovely, but very basic, farm site (cold water only and no showers), two miles from town off the B880 to Blackwaterfoot.

For **food**, apart from dinner at the aforementioned *Kilmichael*, the only place that really stands out is the expensive seafood restaurant *Creelers* (ⓣ01770/302797, ⓦwww.creelers.co.uk; Easter–Oct), which has its own smokehouse, by the museum on the road to the castle. The *Brodick Brasserie & Bar*, opposite the post office, does pub food that includes the odd dish of local seafood. Nearer to the ferry terminal, the bar snacks (lunchtime only) at *Mac's Bar* in the *McLaren Hotel* make a cheaper option and there's real ale too. The *Good Food Shop*, on the corner of Auchencrannie Road, bakes fresh wholemeal bread, and has a self-service **laundry** next door. If you want to find out about any other events taking place on Arran, pick up a copy of the island's **weekly newspaper**, the *Arran Banner*.

The south of Arran

The **southern half of Arran** is less spectacular, and less forbidding than the north; it's more heavily forested and the land is more fertile, and for that reason the vast majority of the population lives here. The tourist industry has followed them, though with considerably less justification.

Outdoor activities on Arran

Arran has a highly developed tourist industry, and there are a number of outfits ready and willing to help you enjoy the great outdoors. For **hiking** in the mountains in the northern half of the island, all you need is a good map and the right gear – see p.59 for safety in the hills, while the walks are described in more detail on p.142. The Forestry Commission (Ⓣ01770/302218, Ⓦwww.forestry.gov.uk) has laid out several more gentle **woodland walks** in its various plantations, as well as network of **cycle trails** (Ⓦwww.arranbikeclub.com) on their forestry roads; they also organize various guided forest walks in the summer. **Bike rental** is available from the Boathouse (Ⓣ01770/302868), 300yd from the pier in Brodick. **Horse riding**, from hourly treks in the morning to afternoon hacks for experienced riders, can be sorted out at Cairnhouse Riding Centre in Blackwaterfoot (Ⓣ01770/860466) or North Sannox Pony Trekking Centre (Ⓣ01770/810222). For **boat rental**, contact Lamlash Boat Hire (Ⓣ01770/600998), who are based on the pier in Lamlash. High-adrenalin sports can be organized by Arran Adventure (Ⓣ01770/302244, Ⓦwww.arranadventure.com), who arrange daily power boat trips; the Balmichael Centre, near Blackwaterfoot, offers quad-biking (Ⓣ01770/860526); and for the truly mad, there's the chance to go paragliding with Flying Fever (Ⓣ01770/820292, Ⓦwww.flyingfever.net), based in Kildonan.

Lamlash, Holy Island and Whiting Bay

With its distinctive Edwardian architecture and mild climate, **LAMLASH**, four miles south of Brodick, epitomizes the sedate charm of southeast Arran. Lamlash Bay has in its time sheltered King Haakon's fleet in 1263 before the Battle of Largs and, more recently, served as a naval base in both world wars. The major drawback for the visitor, however, is that its beach is made not of sand but of boulder-strewn mud flats. The monument on the village green marks the spot on which a farewell sermon was given to the eleven families, victims of the Clearances, who, in 1829, sailed from here to Canada.

The best reason for coming to Lamlash is to visit the slug-shaped hump of **Holy Island**, which shelters the bay. The island is owned by a group of Tibetan Buddhists who have established a long-term retreat at the lighthouse on the island's southern tip and built a Peace Centre at the north end of the island. Providing you don't dawdle, it's possible to scramble up to the top of Mullach Mór (1030ft), the island's highest point, and still catch the last ferry back. En route, you might well bump into the island's most numerous residents: feral goats, Eriskay ponies, Soay sheep and rabbits. The Holy Island ferry runs more or less hourly (Ⓣ01770/600998; £8 return), and you can stay at the Peace Centre (Ⓣ01387/373232, Ⓦwww.holyisland.org; full board ④), where they put on a range of courses on yoga, meditation and relaxation throughout the season.

If you want to **stay** in Lamlash, head for the comfortable *Lilybank* (Ⓣ01770/600230, Ⓦwww.smoothhound.co.uk/hotels/lilybank; ③; Easter–Oct), overlooking the bay and offering good home-made food, or the more modern *Shore* (Ⓣ01770/600764, Ⓦwww.arran-shore.co.uk; ④; March–Oct), which does great veggie breakfasts. Another option is the *Aldersyde Bunkhouse* (Ⓣ01770/600959) a basic, purpose-built **hostel** south of the pier behind the *Aldersyde Hotel*. You can also **camp** at the fully equipped *Middleton Camping Park* (Ⓣ01770/600255; April–Oct), just five-minutes' walk south of the centre. The best food options are the **bar meals** at the *Pier Head Tavern*, on the main street, or at the friendly *Drift Inn*, which has tables by the shore. On the subject of eating, it was a Lamlash man, Donald McKelvie, who made Arran potatoes world-famous, breeding in the rich soil of the island Arran Pilot, Arran Chief and Arran Victory, of which Maris Piper is a modern descendant.

An established Clydeside resort for over a century now, **WHITING BAY**, four miles south of Lamlash, is spread out along a very pleasant bay, though it doesn't have quite the distinctive architecture of Lamlash. It's a good base for walking, with the gentle hike up to the **Glenashdale Falls** probably the most popular excursion; the waterfall can be reached via a pretty woodland walk that sets off from beside the SYHA hostel (2hr return). Whiting Bay also has some excellent **places to stay**, including the *Royal Arran* (Ⓣ01770/700286, Ⓦwww.royalarran.co.uk; ❺; March–Oct), and the *Argentine House Hotel*, run (confusingly) by a multilingual Swiss couple (Ⓣ01770/700662, Ⓦwww.argentinearran.co.uk; ❹), both on Shore Road, or *Mingulay* (Ⓣ01770/700346; ❷), a smaller, but equally comfortable B&B on Middle Road. The aforementioned SYHA **hostel** (Ⓣ0870/004 1158; April–Oct) is situated at the southern end of the bay, but was closed for refurbishment at the time of going to press so phone ahead to check. The **food** is very good at the *Burlington Hotel* on Shore Road, and at the nearby *Argentine House Hotel*, though both are expensive. Otherwise, head for *Joshua's*, a café bang on the seafront offering excellent home-made cakes and snacks, along with great views, or the simple bistro fare at the *Pantry* (closed Sun eve) opposite the post office, with views over the bay. For **bike rental**, enquire at the *Coffee Pot* (Ⓣ01770/700382), further south on the seafront.

Kildonan to Lagg

Access to the sea is tricky along the south coast, but worth the effort, as the sandy beaches here are among the island's finest. One place you can get down to the sea is at **KILDONAN**, an attractive small village south of Lamlash, set slightly off the main road, with a good sandy beach, which you share with the local wildlife, and views out to the tiny flat island of Pladda, with its distinctive lighthouse, and, in the distance, the great hump of Ailsa Craig. Kildonan has a nice **campsite** (Ⓣ01770/820320) right by the sea next to the newly refurbished *Kildonan Hotel* (Ⓣ01770/820207, Ⓦwww.kildonanhotel.co.uk; ❺).

KILMORY, four miles west of Kildonan, is the home of the prizewinning **Torrylinn Creamery** (Mon–Thurs 8.30am–2pm, Fri 8.30am–3.30pm; free), which produces a cheddary cheese called Arran Dunlop, and where you can watch the whole process from a viewing window. Next door to Kilmory is the picturesque village of **LAGG**, nestling in a tree-filled hollow by Kilmory Water. The friendly village stores has an excellent **tearoom**; those feeling flush should **stay** at the comfortable *Lagg Inn* (Ⓣ01770/870255, Ⓦwww.lagghotel.com; ❺), an old-fashioned eighteenth-century inn beside the main road, with real fires and good food.

Blackwaterfoot and Machrie

BLACKWATERFOOT, on the western end of the String Road, which bisects the island, is dominated, not to say somewhat spoilt, by the presence of the island's largest hotel, the *Kinloch Hotel*. In every other way, Blackwaterfoot is a beguiling little place, which boasts the only twelve-hole golf course in the world. A gentle two-mile walk north along the coast will bring you to the **King's Cave**, one of several where Robert the Bruce is said to have encountered the famously patient arachnid, while hiding during his final bid to free Scotland in 1306. If you want **to stay**, the late Victorian *Blackwaterfoot Lodge* (Ⓣ01770/860202, Ⓦwww.blackwaterfoot-lodge.co.uk; ❸; Easter–Oct) is a good place to hole up, though there's also a great B&B, *Lochside Guest House*

(Ⓣ01770/860276, Ⓔbannatyne@lineone.net; ❷), just half a mile south along the main road, set beside its very own trout loch.

North of Blackwaterfoot, the wide expanse of **Machrie Moor** boasts a wealth of Bronze Age sites. No fewer than six **stone circles** sit east of the main road and, although many of them barely break the peat's surface, the tallest surviving monolith is over 18ft high. The most striking configuration is at Fingal's Cauldron Seat, with two concentric circles of granite boulders; legend has it that Fingal tied his dog to one of them while cooking at his cauldron. If you're feeling peckish, the Machrie golf course **tearoom** (April to mid-Oct) is a welcome oasis in this sparsely populated area.

The north of Arran

The **north half of Arran** – effectively the Highland part – features wonderful bare granite peaks, the occasional golden eagle and miles of unspoilt scenery, within reach only to those prepared to do some hiking. Arran's most accessible peak is also the island's highest, **Goat Fell** (2866ft) – take your pick from the Gaelic, *goath*, meaning "windy", or the Norse, *geit-fjall*, "goat mountain" – which can be ascended in just three hours from Brodick or from Corrie (return journey 5hr), though it's a strenuous hike (for the usual safety precautions, see p.59).

Corrie and Sannox

Arran's prettiest little seaside village is **CORRIE**, six miles north of Brodick, where a procession of pristine cottages lines the road to Lochranza and wraps itself around an exquisite little harbour and pier. If you want to use Corrie as

Walking in North Arran

Ordnance Survey Explorer no. 361.

The ferociously jagged and barren outline of the mountains of **north Arran** is on a par with that of the Cuillin of Skye. None of the peaks is a Munro, but they are spectacular, nevertheless, partly because they rise up so rapidly from sea level and, in fine weather, offer such wonderful views over sea and land.

One of the most popular walks is the circuit of peaks that surround Glen Rosa. The walk begins with the relatively straightforward ascent of **Goat Fell** (2866ft), which is normally approached from the grounds of Brodick Castle, to the south. From Goat Fell, you can follow a series of rocky ridges that spread out in the shape of an "H". In order to keep to the crest of the ridge, head north to the next peak of **North Goat Fell** (2657ft), and then make the sharp descent to the Saddle, a perfect spot for a rest, before making the ascent of **Cir Mhor** (2618ft), by far the most exhilarating peak in the whole range, and the finest viewpoint of all. The next section of the walk, southwest across the knife's-edge ridge of **A'Chir**, is quite tricky due to the Bad Step, a lethal gap in the ridge, which you can avoid by dropping down slightly on the east side. Beyond A'Chir, the ascent of **Beinn Tarsuinn** (2706ft) and **Beinn Nuis** (2597ft) is relatively simple. A path leads down from the southeast face of Beinn Nuis to Glen Rosa and back to Brodick. If you don't fancy attempting A'Chir, or if the weather closes in, you can simply descend from the Saddle, or from the southwest side of Cir Mhor, to Glen Rosa.

The walk described above covers a total distance of eleven miles, with over 4600ft of climbing, and should take between eight and ten hours to complete. All walks should be approached with care, and the usual **safety precautions** should be observed (see p.59).

a base for hiking, book ahead at the *North High Corrie Croft*, a **bunkhouse** (①01770/302310), ten-minutes' steep climb above the village on a raised beach; it has one large room for group bookings, and an annexe with eight beds. The red sandstone *Corrie Hotel*, at the centre of the village, does bar **meals**, and the tearoom in the *Corrie Golf Club*, confusingly in Sannox, offers good-value food all day in summer.

At **SANNOX**, two miles north, the road leaves the shoreline and climbs steeply, giving breathtaking views over to the scree-strewn slopes around Caisteal Abhail (2735ft). If you make this journey around dusk, be sure to pause in **Glen Chalmadale**, on the other northern side of the pass, to catch a glimpse of the red deer that come down to pasture by the water. Another possibility is to turn off to North Sannox, where you can park and walk along the shore to the **Fallen Rocks**, a major rock-fall of Devonian sandstone.

Lochranza

On fair Lochranza streamed the early day,
Thin wreaths of cottage smoke are upward curl'd
From the lone hamlet, which her inland bay
And circling mountains sever from the world.

The Lord of the Isles by Sir Walter Scott

The ruined castle which occupies the mud flats of the bay, and the brooding north-facing slopes of the mountains which frame it, make for one of the most spectacular settings on the island – yet **LOCHRANZA**, despite being the only place of any size in this sparsely populated area, attracts far fewer visitors than Arran's southern resorts. The castle is worth a brief look inside, but Lochranza's main tourist attraction now is the island's modern whisky **distillery** (mid-March to Oct daily 10am–6pm; Nov & Dec phone ①01770/830264; Ⓦwww.arranwhisky.com; £3.50), a pristine complex distinguished by its pagoda-style roofs at the south end of the village. The tours are entertaining and slick, and end with a free sample of the island's newly emerging single malt.

The finest **accommodation** is to be had at the superb *Apple Lodge* (①01770/830229; ④), the old village manse where you'll get excellent home-cooking, or at the equally welcoming *Lochranza Hotel* (①01770/830223, Ⓦwww.lochranza.co.uk; ②), whose bar is the centre of the local social scene. Lochranza also has a friendly SYHA **hostel** (①0870/004 1140; March–Oct), situated halfway between the distillery and the castle, and a well-equipped **campsite** (①01770/830273, Ⓦwww.arran.net/lochranza; April-Oct), beautifully placed by the golf course on the Brodick road, where deer come to graze in the early evening.

The distillery **café** offers salads, pasta dishes, baguettes and Scottish specialities during the day; in the evening, your only option is **bar meals** at the *Lochranza*. If you're just passing through, you should head for the take-away *Sandwich Station*, situated close to the CalMac terminal.

Catacol and Pirnmill

An alternative to staying or drinking in Lochranza is to continue a mile or so southwest along the coast to **CATACOL**, and stay or drink at the friendly *Catacol Bay Hotel* (①01770/830231, Ⓦwww.catacol.co.uk; ②), which serves basic pub grub (with several veggie options) and real ale. There's a small adjoining **campsite**, seals and shags to view on the nearby shingle, and occasional live music.

Just past the pub there is a row of striking black-and-white cottages, known as the **Twelve Apostles**, built by the eleventh Duke of Hamilton, and intended to house tenants displaced to make way, not for sheep, but for deer (thanks to Queen Victoria's passion for stalking them), though no one could be persuaded to live in them for two years.

From here to the String Road it's very bleak, but ideal for spotting wildlife, on hillside and at sea. The next village of any size is neat-and-tidy **PIRNMILL**, so called because they used to make "pirns" or bobbins for the mills of Paisley here (until they ran out of trees). If you're in need of sustenance, head for the *Lighthouse Café* (Easter–Oct), next to the post office, which does full meals and is renowned for its home-made scones and meringues.

The Isle of Islay

The fertile, largely treeless island of **ISLAY** (pronounced "eye-la") is famous for one thing – single malt **whisky**. The smoky, peaty, pungent quality of Islay whisky is unique, recognizable even to the untutored palate, and all eight of the island's distilleries will happily take visitors on a guided tour, ending with the

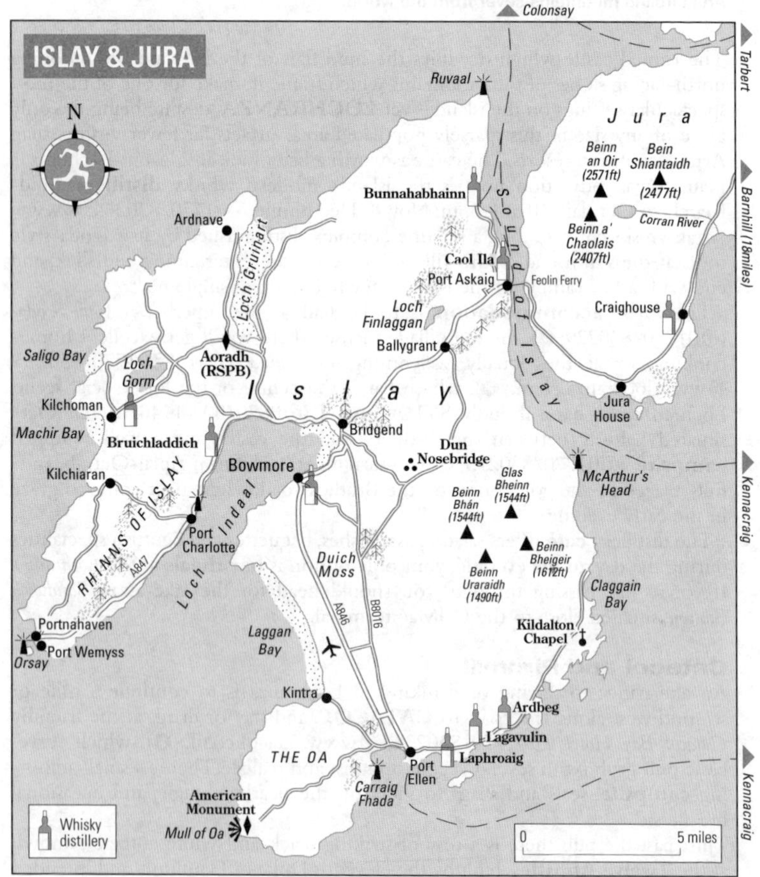

customary complimentary tipple. Yet, despite the fame of its whiskies, Islay still remains relatively undiscovered, especially when compared with Arran, Mull or Skye. Part of the reason may be the expense of the two-hour ferry journey from Kennacraig on Kintyre, or perhaps the relative paucity of luxury hotels or fancy restaurants. If you do make the effort, however, you'll be rewarded with a genuinely friendly welcome from islanders proud of their history, landscape and Gaelic culture.

In medieval times, Islay was the political centre of the Hebrides, with **Finlaggan**, near Port Askaig, the seat of the MacDonalds, Lords of the Isles. The picturesque, whitewashed villages you see on Islay today, however, date from the planned settlements founded by the Campbells in the late eighteenth and early nineteenth centuries. Apart from whisky and solitude, the other great draw is the **birdlife** – there's a real possibility of spotting a golden eagle, or the rare crow-like chough, and no possibility at all of missing the scores of white-fronted and barnacle geese that winter here in their thousands. In late May/early June, the **Feis Ile**, or Islay Festival of Malt and Music (Ⓦwww.feisile.org), takes place, with whisky tasting, piping recitals, folk dancing and other events celebrating the island's Gaelic roots.

Public transport, in the form of buses and postbuses, will get you from one end of the island to the other, but it's as well to know that there is one solitary bus on a Sunday; pick up an island transport guide from the Islay tourist office in **Bowmore**. The **airport**, which lies between Port Ellen and Bowmore, has regular flights to and from Glasgow, and the local bus or postbus will get you to either of the above villages. For a local point of view and news of upcoming events, pick up a copy of the fortnightly *Ileach* or visit their website (Ⓦwww.ileach.co.uk). The island also has its own website Ⓦwww.isle-of-islay.com.

Port Ellen and around

Laid out as a planned village in 1821 by Walter Frederick Campbell, and named after his wife, **PORT ELLEN** is the chief port on Islay, with the island's largest fishing fleet, and main CalMac ferry terminal. The neat whitewashed terraces of Frederick Crescent, which overlook the town's bay of golden sand, are pretty enough, but the strand to the north, up Charlotte Street, is dominated by the modern maltings, on the Bowmore road, whose powerful odours waft across the town. Arriving at Port Ellen by boat, it's impossible to miss the unusual, square-shaped **Carraig Fhada lighthouse**, at the western entrance to the bay, erected in 1832, in memory of Walter Frederick Campbell's aforementioned wife. Just beyond the lighthouse is the prettiest bay on the island's south coast, Traigh Bhán, or the **Singing Sands**, a perfect sandy beach, peppered with jagged rocky extrusions.

The island's main **tourist office** is in Bowmore, and Port Ellen has just an ad hoc office called KOADA, on Frederick Crescent (Mon–Sat 9.30am–12.30pm). If you need a bite to eat, your best bet is actually the *Old Kiln Café* in Ardbeg distillery (see box, p.147), or the mobile *Nippy Chippy* (Fri & Sat only). If you just want **to get online**, however, you can do so at the *Cyber Café* in the MacTaggart community centre, just off Frederick Crescent, and **bike rental** is available at the Playing Fields (Ⓣ01496/302349). There's really not much point in basing yourself in Port Ellen, but if you need **accommodation**, the best place is *Caladh Sona* (Ⓣ01496/302694, Ⓔhamish.scott@lineone.net; ❷; March–Oct), a detached house at 53 Frederick Crescent, followed by the artistic *Carraig Fhada* B&B right by the lighthouse (Ⓣ01496/302114, Ⓔharry.underwood@talk21.com; ❶).

△ Whisky barrels, Islay

Another option is to head out of Port Ellen up the A846 towards the airport, to the excellent *Glenmachrie Farmhouse* (Ⓣ01496/302560, Ⓦwww.glenmachrie.com; ⑤), a whitewashed, family-run guesthouse, which does superb home-cooking, and fantastic breakfasts – the same family now also run the nearby *Glenegedale House Hotel* (Ⓣ01496/302147; ④), opposite the airport building. Alternatively, there's an independent **campsite** at the stone-built *Kintra Farm* B&B (Ⓣ01496/302051, Ⓦwww.kintrafarm.co.uk; ②; April–Sept), three miles northwest of Port Ellen, at the southern tip of Laggan Bay.

Along the coast to Kildalton

From Port Ellen, a dead-end road heads off east along the coastline, passing three distilleries in as many miles. First comes **Laphroaig**, which, as every bottle tells you, is Gaelic for "the beautiful hollow by the broad bay", and, true enough, the whitewashed distillery is indeed in a gorgeous setting by the sea – it even has its own railway for transporting peat to the distillery. Laphroaig also has the stamp of approval from Prince Charles, who famously paid a flying visit to the island in 1994, crashing an airplane of the Queen's Flight in the process. A mile down the road lies **Lagavulin** distillery, beyond which stands **Dunyvaig Castle** (*Dún Naomhaig*), a romantic ruin on a promontory looking out to the tiny isle of Texa. Another mile further on, **Ardbeg** distillery sports the traditional pagoda-style kiln roofs, and has recently been brought back to life by Glenmorangie. In common with all Islay's distilleries, the above three offer guided tours (for more on which, see the box opposite).

Six miles beyond Ardbeg, slightly off the road, the simple thirteenth-century **Kildalton Chapel** boasts a wonderful eighth-century Celtic ringed cross made from the local "bluestone", which is a rich blue-grey. The quality of the scenes matches any to be found on the crosses carved by the monks in Iona: the Virgin and Child are on the east face, with Cain murdering Abel to the left, David fighting the lion on the top, and Abraham sacrificing Isaac on the right; on the west side amidst the serpent-and–boss work are four elephant-like beasts.

The Oa

The most dramatic landscape on Islay is to be found in the nub of land to the southwest of Port Ellen known as **The Oa** (pronounced "O"), a windswept and inhospitable spot, much loved by illicit whisky distillers and smugglers over the centuries. Halfway along the road, a ruined church is visible to the south, testament to the area's once large population dispersed during the Clearances

Islay whisky

Islay has woken up to the fact that its whisky distilleries are a major tourist attraction. Nowadays, each distillery offers guided tours, traditionally ending with a generous dram, and a refund for your entrance fee if you buy a bottle in the shop – be warned, however, that a bottle of single malt is no cheaper at source, so expect to pay £25 and upwards for the privilege. Phone ahead to make sure there's a tour running, as times do change frequently.

Ardbeg ⓣ01496/302244, ⓦwww.ardbeg.com. The ten-year-old Ardbeg is traditionally considered the saltiest, peatiest malt on Islay (and that's saying something). Bought by Glenmorangie in 1997, the distillery has been thoroughly overhauled and restored, yet it still has bags of character inside. The *Old Kiln Café* is excellent (Mon–Fri 10am–4pm; June–Aug daily 10am–5pm). Guided tours regularly 11.30am–2.30pm; £2.

Bowmore ⓣ01496/810671, ⓦwww.morrisonbowmore.com. Bowmore is the most touristy of the Islay distilleries, too much so for some. However, it is by far the most central distillery (with unrivalled disabled access), and also one of the few still doing its own malting and kilning. Guided tours Mon–Fri 10am, 11am, 2pm & 3pm, Sat by appointment; £2.

Bruichladdich ⓣ01496/850190. Bruichladdich was rescued in 2001 by a group of whisky fanatics and is the only independent distillery left on Islay. Regular guided tours take place (Easter–Oct Mon–Fri 10.30am, 11.30am & 2.30pm, Sat 10.30am & 2.30pm; Nov–Easter Mon–Fri 11.30am & 2.30pm, Sat 10.30am; £3).

Bunnahabhain ⓣ01496/840646, ⓦwww.bunnahabhain.com. A visit to Bunnahabhain (pronounced "Bunna-have-in") is really only for whisky obsessives. The road from Port Askaig is windy, the whisky is the least characteristically Islay, and the distillery itself is only in production for a few months each year. Guided tours April–Oct Mon–Fri 10.30am, 12.45pm, 2pm & 3.15pm; free).

Caol Ila ⓣ01496/302760. Caol Ila (pronounced "Cul-eela"), just north of Port Askaig, is a modern distillery, the majority of whose lightly peaty malt goes into blended whiskies. No-frills guided tours are by appointment (April–Oct Mon–Thurs 9.30am, 10.45am & 1.45pm, Fri 9.30am & 10.45am; £3).

Kilchoman ⓣ01496/850011, ⓦwww.kilchomandistillery.com. The first new distillery on the island for over a century, Kilchoman is farm-based and aims to grow the barley, malt, distil, mature and even bottle its whisky on-site. The distillery welcomes visitors (May, June & Sept Mon–Sat 10am–5.30pm; July & Aug daily; Oct–Dec Mon–Fri only) and there are regular guided tours (11am & 3pm; £3).

Lagavulin ⓣ01496/302730. Lagavulin probably is the classic, all-round Islay malt, with lots of smoke and peat. The distillery enjoys a fabulous setting and is extremely busy all year round. Phone ahead for details of the guided tours (Mon–Fri 9.30am, 11.15am & 2.30pm; £3), at the end of which you'll get a taste of the best-selling 16-year-old.

Laphroaig ⓣ01496/302418, ⓦwww.laphroaig.com. Another classic smoky, peaty Islay malt, and another great setting. One bonus at Laphroaig is that you get to see the malting and see and smell the peat kilns. There are regular guided tours (Mon–Fri 10.15am & 2.15pm; free), but phone ahead to book.

– several abandoned villages lie in the north of the peninsula, near **Kintra**. The chief target for most visitors to The Oa, however, is the gargantuan **American Monument**, built in the shape of a lighthouse on the clifftop above the Mull of Oa. It was erected by the American National Red Cross in memory of those who died in two naval disasters that took place in 1918. The first occurred when the troop transporter SS *Tuscania*, carrying over 2000 American army personnel, was torpedoed by a German U-boat seven miles offshore in February 1918. As the lifeboats were being lowered, several ropes broke and threw the occupants into the sea, drowning 266 of those on board. The monument also commemorates those who drowned when the *Otranto* was shipwrecked off Kilchoman (see opposite) in October of the same year. The memorial is inscribed with the unusual sustained metaphor: "On Fame's eternal camping ground, their silent tents are spread, while glory keeps with solemn round, the bivouac of the dead." If you're driving, you can park in a car park, just before Upper Killeyan farm, and follow the duckboards across the soggy peat (now in the hands of the RSPB). En route, look out for choughs, golden eagles and other birds of prey, not to mention feral goats and, down on the shore, basking seals; for a longer walk, follow the coast five miles round to or from Kintra.

Bowmore

At the northern end of the seven-mile-long Laggan Bay, across the monotonous peat bog of Duich Moss, lies **BOWMORE**, Islay's administrative capital, with a population of around 800. It was founded in 1768 to replace the village of Kilarrow, which was deemed by the local laird to be too close to his own residence. It's a striking place, laid out in a grid-plan rather like Inveraray, with the whitewashed terraces of Main Street climbing up the hill in a straight line from the pier on Loch Indaal to the town's crowning landmark, the **Round Church** (Ⓦwww.theroundchurch.org.uk), whose central tower looks uncannily like a lighthouse. Built in the round, so that the devil would have no corners in which to hide, it has a plain, wood-panelled interior, with a lovely tiered balcony and a big central mushroom pillar. A little to the west of Main Street is **Bowmore distillery** (see p.147), the first of the legal Islay distilleries, founded in 1779, and still occupying its original whitewashed buildings by the loch. One of the distillery's former bonded warehouses is now the **MacTaggart Leisure Centre** (closed Mon), whose pool is partially heated by waste heat from the distillery; if you're camping or self-catering, it's as well to know that it has a very useful, minuscule laundry.

Islay's only official **tourist office** is in Bowmore (April–Oct Mon–Sat 10am–5pm; May–Aug also Sun 2–5pm; Nov–March Mon–Fri noon–4pm; Ⓣ01496/810254); it can help you find **accommodation** anywhere on Islay or Jura. Bowmore is central, but not necessarily the best place to stay on the island. If you choose to, however, the *Harbour Inn* (Ⓣ01496/810330, Ⓦwww.harbour-inn.com; ❻), on Main Street, is Bowmore's cosiest and most central pub, or you could stay in one of the town's better B&Bs, such as *Lambeth House* Ⓣ01496/810597; ❷), centrally located on Jamieson Street. Another possibility is the *Bridgend Hotel* (Ⓣ01496/810212; ❻), a couple of miles up the road, positioned by the main road junction, but also close to the island's finest patch of deciduous woodland. **Bike rental** is available from the craft shop beside the post office on Main Street.

At the *Harbour Inn* on Main Street, you can warm yourself by a peat fire in the **pub**, or eat at the inn's outstanding **restaurant**: they make award-winning porridge for breakfast, offer a reasonably priced lunchtime menu, and serve more expensive evening meals. At the other end of the scale, there's an excellent **bakery** on Main Street, and, further up on the same side of the street, *The Cottage* (closed Sun), a cheap and friendly greasy spoon. Somewhat incredibly, there's no permanent fish-and-chip shop in Bowmore, only the mobile *Nippy Chippy* (Thurs only).

Loch Gruinart to Kilchoman

If you're visiting Islay between mid-September and the third week of April, it's impossible to miss the island's staggeringly large wintering population of **Greenland Barnacle** and **Greater White-fronted geese**. During this period, the geese dominate the landscape, feeding incessantly off the rich pasture, strolling by the shores, and flying in formation across the winter skies. In the spring, the geese hang around just long enough to snap up the first shoots of new grass, in order to give themselves enough energy to make the 2000-mile journey to Greenland, where they breed in the summer. Understandably, many local farmers are not exactly very happy about the geese feeding off their land, and some receive compensation for the inconvenience.

You can see the geese just about anywhere on the island – there are an estimated 15,000 white-fronted and 40,000 barnacles here (and rising) – though they are usually at their most concentrated in the fields between Bridgend and Ballygrant. In the evening, they tend to congregate in the tidal mud flats and fields around **Loch Gruinart**, which is an **RSPB nature reserve**. The nearby farm of Aoradh (pronounced "oorig") is run by the RSPB, and one of its outbuildings contains a **visitor centre** (daily 10am–5pm; free), housing an observation point with telescopes and a CCTV link with the mud flats; there's also a hide across the road looking north over the salt flats at the head of the loch. From the hide, you're more likely to see reed buntings, redshank, lapwing, pintail, wigeon, teal and other waterfowl rather than geese.

The road along the western shores of Loch Gruinart to Ardnave is a good place to spot **choughs**, members of the crow family, distinguished by their curved red beaks and matching legs. Halfway along the road, there's a path off to the ruins of **Kilnave Chapel**, whose working graveyard contains a very weathered, eighth-century Celtic cross. The road ends at Ardnave Loch, beyond which lie numerous sand dunes, where seals often sun themselves, and otters sometimes fish offshore. Anyone interested in **birding** or **bushcraft** should get in touch with Islay Birding (Ⓣ01496/850010, Ⓦwww.islaybirding.co.uk), based in Port Charlotte, who organize all sorts of outings and activities. **Accommodation** is available locally at *Coultorsay House* (Ⓣ01496/850298, Ⓔwood.islay@virgin.net; ③), an old farmhouse just beyond Bruichladdich overlooking Loch Indaal.

Without doubt the best **sandy beaches** on Islay are to be found on the isolated northwest coast, in particular, the lovely golden beach of **Machir Bay**, which is backed by great white-sand dunes. The sea here has dangerous undercurrents, however, and is not safe to swim in (the same goes for the much smaller Saligo Bay, to the north). At the nearby settlement of **KILCHOMAN**, set back from Machir Bay, beneath low rocky cliffs, where fulmars nest inland, the church is in a sorry state of disrepair. Its churchyard, however, contains a beautiful fifteenth-century cross, decorated with interlacing on one side and the Crucifixion on the other; at its base there's a wishing stone that should be turned sunwise when wishing. Across a nearby field towards the bay lies the **sailors' cemetery**, containing just 75 graves of the 400 or so who were drowned when the armed merchant cruiser SS *Otranto* collided with another ship in its convoy in a storm in October 1918. The ship was carrying 1000 army personnel (including 665 Americans), the majority of whom made it safely to a ship which came to their aid; of the 400 who had to try and swim ashore, only 16 survived. The sailors' graves lie in three neat rows, from the cook to the captain, who has his own much larger gravestone.

Another poignant memorial stands at **SANAIGMORE**, at the end of a road three miles due west of Loch Gruinart, commemorating 241 Irish emigrants, fleeing the potato famine, drowned when the *Exmouth of Newcastle* was wrecked off the coast in April 1847 – another beautiful sandy beach lies a short walk north of the settlement.

Port Charlotte and the Rhinns of Islay

PORT CHARLOTTE, founded in 1828 by Walter Frederick Campbell and named after his mother, is generally agreed to be Islay's prettiest village. Known as the "Queen of the Rhinns" (derived from the Gaelic word for a promontory), its immaculate whitewashed cottages cluster around a sandy cove overlooking Loch Indaal. On the northern fringe of the village, in a whitewashed former chapel, the imaginative **Museum of Islay Life** (Easter–Oct Mon–Sat 10am–5pm, Sun 2–5pm; Nov–Easter Mon–Sat 10am–4pm; £2) has a children's corner, quizzes, a good library of books about the island, and tantalizing snippets about eighteenth-century illegal whisky distillers. The **Wildlife Information Centre** (Easter–Oct daily except Sat 10am–3pm; July & Aug daily 10am–5pm; £2.50), housed in the former distillery warehouse, is also worth a visit for anyone interested in the island's fauna and flora. As well as an extensive library to browse, there's lots of hands-on stuff for kids: microscopes, a touch table full of natural goodies, a seawater aquarium, a bug world, and owl pellets to examine. Tickets are valid for a week, allowing you to go back and identify things that you've seen on your travels.

Port Charlotte is the perfect place in which to base yourself on Islay. The welcoming *Port Charlotte Hotel* (ⓣ01496/850360, ⓦwww.portcharlottehotel.co.uk; ❻) has the best **accommodation** – the seafood lunches served in the bar are very popular, and there's a good, though expensive restaurant. For B&B, you're actually better off going for the excellent *Octofad Farm* (ⓣ01496/850594, ⓦwww.octofadfarm.com; ❶; April–Oct), a few miles down the road beyond Nerabus, or *Coultorsay House* (ⓣ01496/850298, ⓔwood.islay@virgin.net; ❸), a lovely old farmhouse, halfway between Bruichladdich and Port Charlotte. Port Charlotte itself is also home to Islay's SYHA **hostel** (ⓣ0870/004 1128, ⓦwww.syha.org.uk; April–Sept), housed in an old bonded warehouse next door to the Wildlife Information Centre. The *Croft Kitchen* (ⓣ01496/850230; April-Oct), opposite the museum, serves simple **food**, such as sandwiches and cakes, as well as inexpensive seafood, during the day, and more adventurous, pricier fare in the evenings (except Wed). The **bar** of the *Port Charlotte* is very easy-going, while the local crack (and occasional live music) goes on at the *Lochindaal Inn*, down the road, where you can also tuck into a very good local-bred steak. **Bike rental** is available from a house on Main Street (ⓣ01496/850488), opposite the hotel.

The main coastal road culminates seven miles south of Port Charlotte at **PORTNAHAVEN**, a fishing and crofting community since the early nineteenth century. The familiar whitewashed cottages wrap themselves prettily around the steep banks of a deep bay, where seals bask on the rocks in considerable numbers; in the distance, you can see Portnahaven's twin settlement, **PORT WEMYSS**, a mile south. The communities share a little whitewashed church, located above the bay in Portnahaven, with separate doors for each village. For a drink, head for Portnahaven, which has a tiny **pub**, *an tígh seínnse*, where you can sit outside and enjoy the view in fine weather. A short way out to sea are two islands, the largest of which, Orsay, sports the **Rhinns of Islay Lighthouse**, built by Robert Louis Stevenson's father in 1825; ask around locally if you're keen to visit the island. Also worth a mention, just north of Portnahaven, is the island's ground-breaking wave energy generator, known as the **Limpet** (Ⓦwww.wavegen.co.uk), which harnesses the power of the sea and turns it into electricity.

Finlaggan and Port Askaig

Just beyond Ballygrant, on the road to Port Askaig, a narrow road leads off north to **Loch Finlaggan**, site of a number of prehistoric crannogs (artificial islands) and, for four hundred years from the twelfth century, headquarters of the Lords of the Isles, semi-autonomous rulers over the Hebrides and Kintyre. The site is evocative enough, but there are, in truth, very few remains beyond the foundations. Remarkably, the palace that stood here appears to have been unfortified, a testament perhaps to the prosperity and stability of the islands in those days. Unless you need shelter from the rain, or are desperate to see the head of the commemorative medieval cross found here, you can happily skip the **information centre** (Easter & Oct Tues, Thurs & Sun 2–4pm; May–Sept daily except Sat 2.30–5pm; £2), to the northeast of the loch, and simply head on down to the site itself (access at any time), which is dotted with interpretive panels. Duckboards allow you to walk out across the reed beds of the loch and explore the main crannog, **Eilean Mor**, where several carved gravestones are displayed under cover in the chapel, all of which seem to support the theory that the Lords of the Isles buried their wives and children, while having themselves interred on Iona. Further out into the loch is another smaller crannog, **Eilean na Comhairle,** originally connected to Eilean Mor by a causeway, where the Lords of the Isles are thought to have held meetings of the Council of the Isles.

Islay's other ferry connection with the mainland, and its sole link with Colonsay and Jura, is from **PORT ASKAIG**, a scattering of buildings which tumble down a little cove by the narrowest section of the Sound of Islay or Caol Ila. The only real reason to come here is to catch one of the ferries or go to the hotel bar; if you've time to kill, you can wander round the island's **RNLI lifeboat station** or through the nearby woods of Dunlossit House. Whisky fanatics might want to head half a mile north of Port Askaig to the distilleries of **Caol Ila** and **Bunnahabhain**, a couple of miles further on; both enjoy idyllic settings, overlooking the Sound of Islay, though they are no beauties in themselves (see p.147 for details of their tours).

Easily the most comfortable **place to stay** is the lovely whitewashed *Kilmeny Farmhouse* (Ⓣ01496/840668, Ⓦwww.kilmeny.co.uk; ⑥), southwest of Ballygrant, a place which richly deserves all the superlatives it regularly receives, its rooms furnished with antiques, its dinners (Mon–Fri only) worth the extra £25 a head. The *Ballygrant Inn* is a good **pub** in which to grab a pint, as is the bar of the *Port Askaig Hotel*, which enjoys a wonderful position by the pier at Port Askaig, with views over to the Paps of Jura. For high-adrenalin **boat trips**, contact Islay Sea Safari Ⓣ07768/450000, Ⓦwww.islayseasafari.co.uk), who are based in Port Askaig, and best known for whizzing round the distilleries in a rigid inflatable. It's possible to take a **day-trip to Colonsay** (see p.118) by CalMac ferry on Wednesday. In addition, the passenger-only Lorn Ferry Service (April to mid-Oct; Ⓣ01951/200320) also runs timetabled services from Colonsay to Bunnahabhain and Port Askaig on Islay (Mon), though you should phone ahead to check times and book your journey.

Isle of Jura

Twenty-eight miles long and eight miles wide, the long whale-shaped island of **Jura** is one of the wildest and most mountainous of the Inner Hebrides, its entire west coast uninhabited and inaccessible except to the dedicated walker. The distinctive **Paps of Jura** – so called because of their smooth breast-like shape, though there are in fact three of them – seem to dominate every view off the west coast of Argyll, their glacial rounded tops covered in a light dusting of quartzite scree. The island's name is commonly thought to derive from the Norse *dyr-oe* (deer island) and, appropriately enough, the current deer population of 6000 outnumbers the 180 humans 33 to 1; other wildlife to look out for include mountain hares and eagles. With just one road, which sticks to the more sheltered eastern coast of the island, and only one hotel, a couple of B&Bs and some self-catering cottages, Jura is an ideal place to go for peace and quiet and some great walking.

If you're just coming over for the day from Islay, pop into the **Feolin Research Centre** (daily; free), near the ferry slipway, which has information and displays on the island, and then head off, five miles up the road, to the

Walking the Paps of Jura

Ordnance Survey Explorer map 355

Perhaps the most popular of all the hillwalks on Jura is an ascent of any of the island's famous **Paps of Jura** – Beinn an Oir (2571ft), Beinn a'Chaolais (2407ft) and Beinn Shiantaidh (2477ft) – which cluster together in the south half of the island. It's possible to do a round-trip from Craighouse itself, or from the Feolin Ferry, but the easiest approach is from the three-arched bridge on the island's main road, three miles north of Craighouse. From the bridge, keeping to the north side of the Corran River, you eventually reach Loch an t'Siob. If you only want to climb one Pap, then simply climb up to the saddle between Beinn an Oir and Beinn Shiantaidh and choose which one (Beinn an Oir is probably the most interesting), returning to the bridge the same way. The trip to and from the bridge should take between five and six hours; it's hard going and care needs to be taken, as the scree is unstable.

If you want to try and bag all three Paps, you need to attack Beinn Shiantaidh via its southeast spur, leaving the loch at its easternmost point. This makes for a more difficult ascent, as the scree and large lumps of quartzite are tough going. Descending to the aforementioned saddle, and climbing Beinn an Oir is straightforward enough, but make sure you come off Beinn an Oir via the south spur, before climbing Beinn a'Chaolais, as the western side of Beinn an Oir is dangerously steep. Again, you can return via the loch to the three-arched bridge.

Every year, in the last bank holiday weekend in May, hundreds of masochists take part in a fell race up the Paps, which the winner usually completes in three hours. Given the number of deer on Jura, it's as well to be aware of the **stalking season** (Aug–Oct), during which you should check with the *Jura Hotel* before heading out or phone the walkers' information line (☎01496/300133). At all times of year, you should take all the usual **safety precautions** (see p.59); beware, too, of adders, which are quite numerous on Jura. If you want a guide to help you seek out the wildlife, contact Exploration Jura (☎07899/912116).

George Orwell on Jura

In April 1946, Eric Blair (better known by his pen name of **George Orwell**), intending to give himself "six months' quiet" in which to complete his latest novel, moved to a remote farmhouse called **Barnhill**, at the northern end of Jura, which he had visited for the first time the previous year. He appears to have relished the challenge of living in Barnhill, fishing almost every night, shooting rabbits, laying lobster pots, and even attempting a little farming. Along with his adopted 3-year-old son Richard, and later his sister Avril, he clearly enjoyed his spartan existence. The book Orwell was writing, under the working title *The Last Man in Europe*, was to become *1984* (the title was arrived at by simply reversing the last two digits of the year in which it was finished – 1948). During his time on Jura, however, Orwell was suffering badly from tuberculosis, and eventually he was forced to return to London, where he died in January 1950.

Barnhill, 23 miles north of Craighouse, is as remote today as it was in Orwell's day. The road deteriorates rapidly beyond Lealt, where vehicles must be left, leaving pilgrims a four-mile walk to the house itself. Alternatively, the Richardsons in Kinauachdrachd Farm (Ⓣ07899/912116) can organize a taxi and guided walk, should you so wish. Orwell wrote most of the book in the bedroom (top left window as you look at the house) – at present, there is no public access. If you're keen on making the journey out to Barnhill, you might as well combine it with a trip to the nearby **Gulf of Corryvrechan** (see p.122), which lies between Jura and Scarba, to the north. Orwell nearly drowned in the **whirlpool** during a fishing trip in August 1947, along with his three companions (including Richard): the outboard motor was washed away, and they had to row to a nearby island and wait for several hours before being rescued by a passing fisherman. The best time to see the water whirling is between flood and half-flood tide, with a southerly or westerly wind, and the best place to view it from Jura is Carraig Mhor, seven miles from Lealt.

lovely wooded grounds of **Jura House** (daily 9am–5pm; £2; Ⓦwww.jurahouseandgardens.co.uk), originally built by the Campbells in the early nineteenth century. Pick up a booklet at the entrance to the grounds, and follow the path which takes you down to the sandy shore, a perfect picnic spot in fine weather. Closer to the house itself, there's an idyllic **walled garden**, divided in two by a natural rushing burn that tumbles down in steps. The garden specializes in antipodean plants, which flourish in the frost-free climate; in season, you can buy some of the garden's organic produce or take tea in the tea tent (late May to Aug Mon–Fri 11am–5pm & Sun 11am–4pm).

Anything that happens on Jura happens in the island's only real village, **CRAIGHOUSE**, eight miles up the road from Feolin Ferry. The village enjoys a sheltered setting, overlooking Knapdale on the mainland – so sheltered, in fact, that there are even a few palm trees thriving on the seafront. There's a shop/post office, the island hotel and a tearoom, plus the tiny **Isle of Jura distillery** (Ⓣ01496/820240, Ⓦwww.isleofjura.com), which is very welcoming to visitors and offers guided tours (Easter–Oct Mon–Fri 11am & 2pm; at other times by appointment).

The family-run *Jura Hotel* in Craighouse is the island's one and only **hotel** (Ⓣ01496/820243, Ⓦwww.jurahotel.co.uk; ❺), not much to look at from the outside, but warm and friendly within, and centre of the island's social scene. The hotel does moderately expensive bar meals, and has a shower block and laundry facilities round the back for those who wish to **camp** in the hotel gardens. For **B&B**, look no further than Mrs Boardman at 7 Woodside (Ⓣ01496/820379; ❶; April–Sept).

Very occasionally a **minibus** (☎01496/820314) meets the **car ferry** (☎01496/840681) from Port Askaig – phone ahead to check times. The ferry itself occasionally fails to run if there's a strong northerly or southerly wind, so bring your toothbrush if you're coming for a day-trip. Lorn Ferry Service (April–Sept; ☎01951/200320) also runs a timetabled **passenger/bicycle-only ferry** from Colonsay to Tarbert, half way up the west coast of Jura (Tues & Fri), though you should phone ahead to check times and book your journey. In addition, there's a **water taxi** service to and from Crinan, on the mainland, run by Gemini Cruises (☎01546/830208, Ⓦwww.gemini-crinan.co.uk). For a window on local life, look out for the *Jura Jottings*, the island's "newspaper".

Travel details

Trains

Glasgow (Queen St) to: Arrochar and Tarbert (Mon–Sat 3–4 daily, Sun 1–2 daily; 1hr 15min); Dalmally (Mon–Sat 3–4 daily, Sun 1–2 daily; 2hr 15min); Oban (Mon–Sat 3–4 daily, Sun 1–2 daily; 3hr).

Mainland buses (not postbuses)

Arrochar to: Carrick Castle (Mon–Sat 1–2 daily; 50min); Inveraray (3 daily, Sun 2 daily; 35min); Lochgilphead (3 daily; 1hr 30min); Lochgoilhead (Mon–Sat 1–2 daily; 40min).
Campbeltown to: Carradale (Mon–Sat 4–5 daily, Sun 2 daily; 45min); Machrihanish (Mon–Sat 9 daily, Sun 3 daily; 20–30min); Saddell (Mon–Sat 4–5 daily, Sun 2 daily; 25min); Southend (Mon–Sat 4–5 daily, Sun 2 daily; 23min).
Colintraive to: Dunoon (2 daily; 1hr); Tighnabruaich (Mon–Thurs 1–2 daily; 35min).
Dunoon to: Colintraive (2 daily; 1hr); Inveraray (Mon–Sat 3 daily, Sun 0–3 daily; 1hr 10min); Lochgoilhead (Mon–Sat 3 daily; 1hr).
Glasgow to: Arrochar (3–5 daily; 1hr 10min); Campbeltown (2–3 daily; 4hr 25min); Dalmally (Mon–Sat 4 daily, Sun 2 daily; 2hr 20min); Inveraray (4–6 daily; 1hr 45min); Kennacraig (Mon–Sat 2 daily, Sun 1 daily; 3hr 30min); Lochgilphead (2–3 daily; 2hr 40min); Oban (Mon–Sat 4 daily, Sun 2 daily; 3hr); Tarbert (2–3 daily; 3hr 15min); Taynuilt (Mon–Sat 4 daily, Sun 2 daily; 2hr 45min).
Inveraray to: Dalmally (Mon–Sat 3 daily, Sun 2 daily; 25min); Dunoon (Mon–Sat 3 daily, Sun 0–3 daily; 1hr 10min); Lochgilphead (2–3 daily; 40min); Oban (Mon–Sat 3 daily, Sun 2 daily; 1hr 5min); Tarbert (2–3 daily; 1hr 30min).
Kennacraig to: Claonaig (Mon–Sat 3 daily; 15min); Skipness (Mon–Sat 3 daily; 20min).
Lochgilphead to: Campbeltown (3–5 daily; 1hr 45min); Crinan (Mon–Sat 3–4 daily; 20min); Kilmartin (Mon–Sat 2–5 daily; 15min); Tarbert (5–7 daily; 30min); Tayvallich (3–4 daily; 25min).
Oban to: Appin (Mon–Sat 3 daily, Sun 1 daily; 30min); Benderloch (6 daily; 20min); Kilmartin (Mon–Sat 2–4 daily; 1hr 20min); Lochgilphead (Mon–Sat 2–4 daily; 1hr 30min); Mallaig (daily April–Oct; 2hr 30min).
Tarbert to: Campbeltown (Mon–Sat 4 daily, Sun 2 daily; 1hr 15min); Claonaig (Mon–Sat 3 daily; 30min); Kennacraig (3–6 daily; 15min); Skipness (Mon–Sat 3 daily; 35min); Tayinloan (3–6 daily; 30min).
Tighnabruaich to: Portavadie (Mon–Sat 3–4 daily; 25min); Rothesay (Mon–Thurs 1–2 daily; 1hr).

Island buses

Arran

Brodick to: Blackwaterfoot (Mon–Sat 12 daily, Sun 6 daily; 30min); Corrie (4–6 daily; 20min); Kildonan (3–5 daily; 40min); Lagg (3–5 daily; 50min); Lamlash (Mon–Sat 14–16 daily, Sun 4 daily; 10–15min); Lochranza (Mon–Sat 6 daily, Sun 3 daily; 45min); Pirnmill (4–6 daily; 1hr); Whiting Bay (Mon–Sat 14–16 daily, Sun 4 daily; 25min).

Bute

Rothesay to: Kilchattan Bay (Mon–Sat 4 daily, Sun 3 daily; 30min); Mount Stuart (every 45min; 15min); Rhubodach (Mon–Fri 1–2 daily; 20min).

Colonsay

Scalasaig to: Kilchattan (Mon–Fri 2–4 daily; 30min); Kiloran Bay (Mon–Fri 2–3 daily; 12min); The Strand (Mon–Fri 1 daily; 20min).

Islay

Bowmore to: Port Askaig (Mon–Sat 8–10 daily, Sun 1 daily; 30–40min); Port Charlotte (Mon–Sat 5–6 daily; 25min); Port Ellen (Mon–Sat 9–12 daily,

Sun 1 daily; 20–30min); Portnahaven (Mon–Sat 5–7 daily; 50min).

Mull

Craignure to: Fionnphort (Mon–Sat 3–4 daily, Sun 1 daily; 1hr 10min); Fishnish (3 daily; 10min); Salen (4–6 daily; 20min); Tobermory (4–6 daily; 45min).
Tobermory to: Calgary (Mon–Sat 2 daily; 45min); Dervaig (Mon–Fri 3 daily, Sat 2 daily; 30min); Fishnish (2–4 daily; 40min).

Ferries

Car ferries

Summer timetable only.
To Arran: Ardrossan–Brodick (4–6 daily; 55min); Claonaig–Lochranza (8–9 daily; 30min).
To Bute: Colintraive–Rhubodach (frequently; 5min); Wemyss Bay–Rothesay (every 45min; 30min).
To Coll: Oban–Coll (daily except Thurs; 2hr 40min).
To Colonsay: Kennacraig–Colonsay (Wed 1 daily; 3hr 35min); Oban–Colonsay (1 daily except Tues & Sat; 2hr 15min); Port Askaig–Colonsay (Wed 2 daily; 1hr 15min).
To Dunoon: Gourock–Dunoon (hourly; 20min); McInroy's Point–Hunter's Quay (every 30min; 20min).
To Gigha: Tayinloan–Gigha (hourly; 20min).
To Islay: Colonsay–Port Askaig (Wed 2 daily; 1hr 15min); Kennacraig–Port Askaig (1–3 daily; 2hr); Kennacraig–Port Ellen (1–3 daily; 2hr 10min).
To Jura: Port Askaig–Feolin Ferry (Mon–Sat hourly, Sun 3 daily; 10min).
To Kintyre: Portavadie–Tarbert (hourly; 25min).
To Lismore: Oban–Achnacroish (Mon–Sat 2–5 daily; 50min).
To Luing: Cuan Ferry (Seil)–Luing (every 30min; 5min).
To Mull: Kilchoan–Tobermory (Mon–Sat 7 daily; June–Aug also Sun 5 daily; 35min); Lochaline–Fishnish (Mon–Sat every 50min, Sun hourly; 15min); Oban–Craignure (every 2hr; 45min).
To Tiree: Barra–Tiree (Wed 1 daily; 3hr 5min); Oban–Tiree (1 daily; 3hr 40min).

Passenger-only ferries

Summer timetable only.
To Colonsay: Bunnahabhain (Islay)–Colonsay (Mon; 1hr 45min); Tarbert (Jura)–Colonsay (Tues & Fri; 2hr); Uisken (Mull)–Colonsay (Tues & Sun; 1hr 45min).
To Iona: Fionnphort–Iona (Mon–Sat frequently, Sun hourly; 5min).
To Kerrera: Gallanach–Kerrera (every 30min; 10min).
To Lismore: Port Appin–Lismore (hourly; 5min).

Flights

Glasgow to: Campbeltown (Mon–Fri 2 daily; 40min); Islay (Mon–Fri 2 daily, Sat 1 daily; 40min); Tiree (Mon–Sat 1 daily; 45min).

2

The Central Highlands

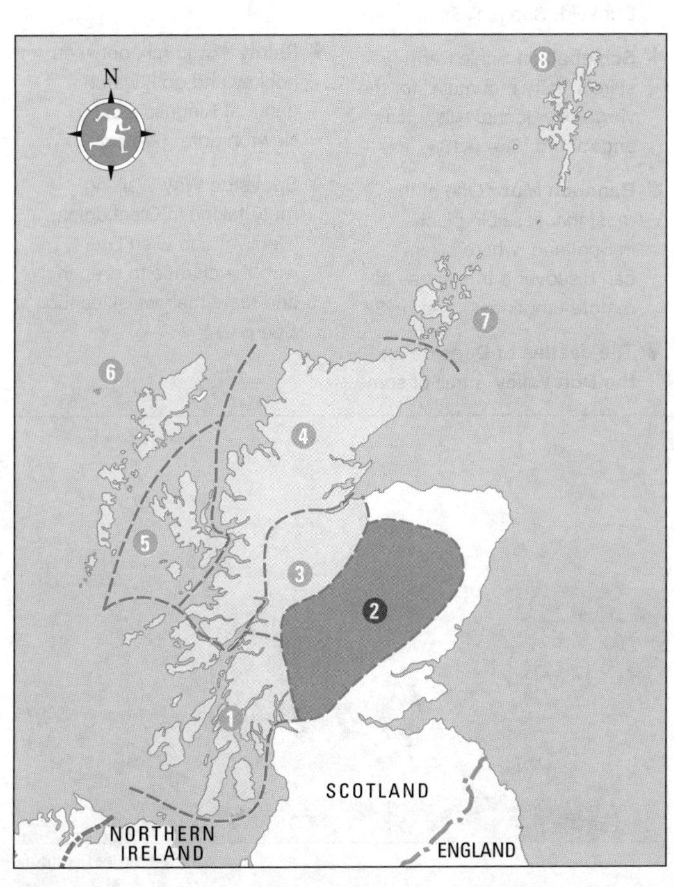

CHAPTER 2

Highlights

* **Mountain biking in the Trossachs** Pocket Highlands with shining lochs, wooded glens and noble peaks, and some superb forest trails. See p.171

* **Folk music** Join in a session at the bar of the *Taybank Hotel* in the dignified town of Dunkeld. See p.178

* **Schiehallion** Scale Perthshire's "fairy mountain" for the views over lochs, hills, glens and moors. See p.186

* **Rannoch Moor** One of the most inaccessible places in Scotland, where hikers can discover a true sense of remote emptiness. See p.186

* **The castles of Deeside and the Don Valley** A trail of some of Scotland's finest castles, from stately piles to moody ruins. See p.195

* **The Cairngorms** Scotland's grandest mountain massif, a place of wild animals, ancient forests, inspiring vistas – and terrific outdoor activities. See p.204

* **Shinty** A wild mix between hockey and golf; watch a game at Kingussie or Newtonmore. See p.213

* **Speyside Way** Walking route taking in Glenfiddich, Glenlivet and Glen Grant, with the chance to drop in and taste their whiskies too. See p.214

△ Walking in the Cairngorms

2

The Central Highlands

The **Central Highlands** lie right in the heart of Scotland, bounded by the country's two major geological fissures, the Highland Fault, which runs along a line drawn approximately from Arran to Aberdeen and marks the southern extent of Scotland's Highlands, and the Great Glen, the string of lochs that run on a similar southwest–northeast axis between Fort William and Inverness. The appeal of the region is undoubtedly its landscape, a concentrated mix of mountain, glen, loch and moorland that responds to each season with a dramatic blend of colour and mood, combined with the outdoor activities the landscape inspires. It's also an area with a rich history stemming in large part from the fact that along the geological divide of north and south is a significant cultural and social shift, and it is no surprise that the region is littered with castles, battlefields and monuments from the centuries of power struggle between the Highlanders and the Sassenachs, whether from lowland Scotland or south of the border.

Northwest of Glasgow, the elongated teardrop of **Loch Lomond** is at the heart of Scotland's first national park. The magnificent scenery around the loch continues east into the fabled mountains and lochs of the **Trossachs**, where hikers and mountain bikers are drawn to explore the forested glens and fugitive Highlanders such as **Rob Roy** once roamed. North of the Trossachs, the massive county of **Perthshire** lies right at the heart of the Central Highlands, with **lochs Tay** and **Rannoch** stacked up across the middle of the region, each surrounded by impressive hills and progressively more countryside.

Further to the east are the **Grampian mountains**: to the south the **Angus glens**, north of Perth and Dundee, are renowned for their prettiness and easy accessibility, while to the north the river valleys of **Deeside** and **Donside** combine the drama of peaks such as **Lochnagar** with the richly wooded glens and dramatic castles which so enchanted Queen Victoria. The northern side of the Grampians are dominated by the dramatic **Cairngorm** massif, the largest area of land over 2500ft in Britain and epicentre of Scotland's second national park. These hills, with their deserved reputation for superb outdoor sports in both summer and winter, are complemented by the atmospheric ancient woodlands of **Strathspey**. A little way downstream is the whisky-producing region of **Speyside**, where various trails lead you to the distilleries, home of some of the world's most famous single malts.

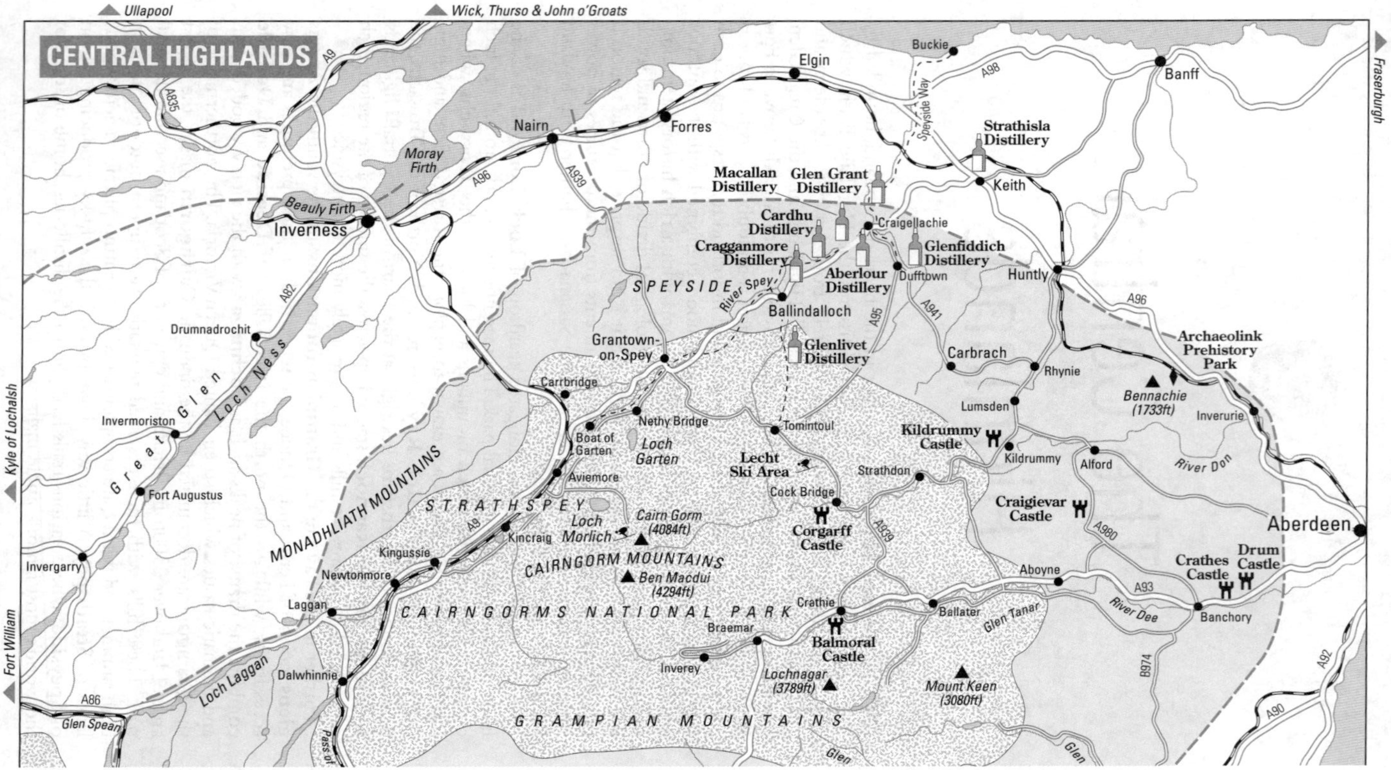

CENTRAL HIGHLANDS

Ullapool
Wick, Thurso & John o'Groats
Fraserburgh
Kyle of Lochalsh
Fort William

Inverness
Beauly Firth
Moray Firth
Nairn
Forres
Elgin
Buckie
Banff
Keith
Huntly
Speyside Way
Strathisla Distillery
Macallan Distillery
Glen Grant Distillery
Cardhu Distillery
Cragganmore Distillery
Craigellachie
Aberlour Distillery
Glenfiddich Distillery
Dufftown
SPEYSIDE
River Spey
Ballindalloch
Glenlivet Distillery
Grantown-on-Spey
Carrbridge
Nethy Bridge
Boat of Garten
Loch Garten
Aviemore
Tomintoul
Lecht Ski Area
Cock Bridge
Corgarff Castle
Strathdon
Carbrach
Rhynie
Lumsden
Kildrummy Castle
Kildrummy
Alford
River Don
Craigievar Castle
Archaeolink Prehistory Park
Bennachie (1733ft)
Inverurie
Aberdeen
Crathes Castle
Drum Castle
Banchory
River Dee
Aboyne
Ballater
Glen Tanar
Crathie
Balmoral Castle
Braemar
Inverey
Lochnagar (3789ft)
Mount Keen (3080ft)
STRATHSPEY
Loch Morlich
Cairn Gorm (4084ft)
CAIRNGORM MOUNTAINS
Ben Macdui (4294ft)
CAIRNGORMS NATIONAL PARK
GRAMPIAN MOUNTAINS
MONADHLIATH MOUNTAINS
Kincraig
Kingussie
Newtonmore
Laggan
Dalwhinnie
Pass of
Loch Laggan
Glen Spean
Glen
Drumnadrochit
Loch Ness
Great Glen
Invermoriston
Fort Augustus
Invergarry
A9
A835
A96
A939
A82
A98
A95
A941
A980
A93
B974
A92
A90
A86

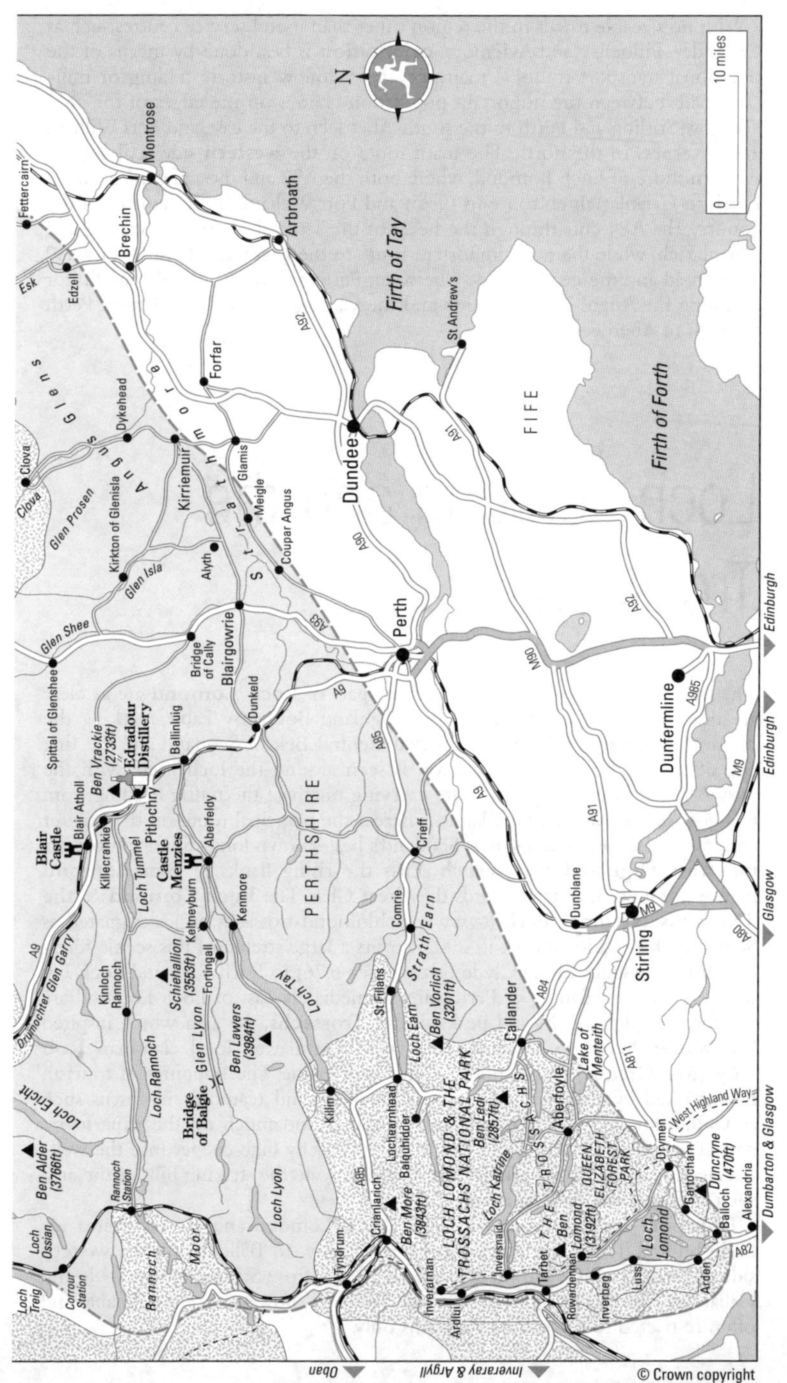

N
0
10 miles
Montrose
Fettercairn
Brechin
Edzell
Esk
Arbroath
Firth of Tay
St Andrew's
Forfar
Dykehead
Glamis
Kirriemuir
Clova
Glen Prosen
Kirkton of Glenisla
Glen Isla
Angus Glens
Strathmore
Meigle
Coupar Angus
Alyth
Dundee
FIFE
Firth of Forth
A92
A91
A90
A93
A9
A85
A84
A811
M90
M9
A985
A80
A82
Perth
Blairgowrie
Bridge of Cally
Glen Shee
Spittal of Glenshee
Dunkeld
Ballinluig
Ben Vrackie (2733ft)
Edradour Distillery
Pitlochry
Blair Castle
Blair Atholl
Killiecrankie
Loch Tummel
Castle Menzies
Aberfeldy
Keltneyburn
Kenmore
Fortingall
Schiehallion (3553ft)
Kinloch Rannoch
Loch Rannoch
Drumochter
Glen Garry
Loch Ericht
Ben Alder (3766ft)
Rannoch Station
Loch Ossian
Corrour Station
Loch Treig
Rannoch Moor
Bridge of Balgie
Glen Lyon
Loch Lyon
Ben Lawers (3984ft)
Loch Tay
Killin
PERTHSHIRE
Crieff
Comrie
Strath Earn
St Fillans
Loch Earn
Ben Vorlich (3201ft)
Lochearnhead
Balquhidder
Callander
Ben Ledi (2857ft)
Lake of Menteith
Aberfoyle
THE TROSSACHS
LOCH LOMOND & THE TROSSACHS NATIONAL PARK
QUEEN ELIZABETH FOREST PARK
Loch Katrine
Ben More (3843ft)
Crianlarich
Tyndrum
Inverarnan
Ardlui
Inversnaid
Tarbet
Ben Lomond (3192ft)
Rowardennan
Inverbeg
Luss
Loch Lomond
Arden
Balloch
Alexandria
Gartocharn
Drymen
Duncryne (470ft)
West Highland Way
Dunblane
Stirling
Dunfermline
Edinburgh
Glasgow
Dumbarton & Glasgow
Inveraray & Argyll
Oban

With no sizeable towns in the region other than useful service centres such as Callander, Pitlochry and Aviemore, **orientation** is best done by means of the traditional transport routes – many of which follow historic trading or military roads between the important population centres on the edges of the area: Glasgow, Stirling and Perth to the south, Aberdeen to the east, and Fort William and Inverness to the north. The main route on the **western** side is along the western shore of Loch Lomond, where both the A82 and the railway line wind north to Crianlarich en route to Oban and Fort William. In the **centre** of the country, the A84 cuts through the heart of the Trossachs between Stirling and Crianlarich, while the most important route to the **eastern** side is the busy A9 trunk road and the nearby railway between Perth and Inverness. Also useful for accessing the Angus glens, Deeside and the Cairngorms is the A93 from Perth through to Aberdeen.

Loch Lomond and the Trossachs

The islands which lie across the southern part of **Loch Lomond** are as clear an indicator as any of the cut of the Highland Boundary Fault, marking the division between the densely populated Central Belt of Scotland and the first rise of the Highlands. The transition is seen around the loch itself, with the busy A82 road on its western shore carrying much of the traffic heading from Glasgow to the western Highlands, whereas the principal route on the quieter and less accessible eastern side is Scotland's best-known long-distance footpath, the **West Highland Way**, which skirts the rising flanks of **Ben Lomond** before heading off north towards the Great Glen. The **Loch Lomond & the Trossachs National Park** (Ⓦwww.lochlomond-trossachs.org), designated as Scotland's first national park in 2002, covers a large stretch of this scenic territory from the lochs of the Clyde Estuary (see p.76) to Loch Earn and Loch Tay, on the southwest fringes of Perthshire. Immediately east of Loch Lomond are the forested glens, lochs and peaks of the **Trossachs**, the area which inspired **Sir Walter Scott** to set down the tales of outlawed local clansman **Rob Roy (MacGregor)** in the novel of the same name. The trappings of tourism first sparked by Scott – evident in twee shops and tearooms in towns such as **Callander** and **Aberfoyle** – don't impinge too much on the experience, particularly if you're ready to explore on foot or by bike deeper into the well-managed **Queen Elizabeth Forest Park**, or scale the striking hills of the area such as **Ben Ledi** or **Ben A'an**.

Transport links to and within the Loch Lomond and Trossachs area are fairly limited. Trains and buses run from Glasgow to Balloch and the western side of Loch Lomond and there are regular buses from Stirling to Aberfoyle and Callander. Services to other parts of the Trossachs, however, are less reliable and often restricted to the summer months only.

Loch Lomond

The largest stretch of fresh water in Britain (23 miles long and up to five miles wide), **Loch Lomond** is the epitome of Scottish scenic splendour, thanks in large part to the ballad which fondly recalls its "bonnie, bonnie banks". The song was said to have been written by a Jacobite prisoner captured by the English, who, sure of his fate, wrote that his spirit would return to Scotland on the low road much faster than his living compatriots on the high road.

Loch Lomond is undoubtedly the centrepiece of the national park, and the most popular gateway into the park is **Balloch**, the town on the southern tip of Loch Lomond; with Glasgow city centre just 19 miles away, both Balloch and the

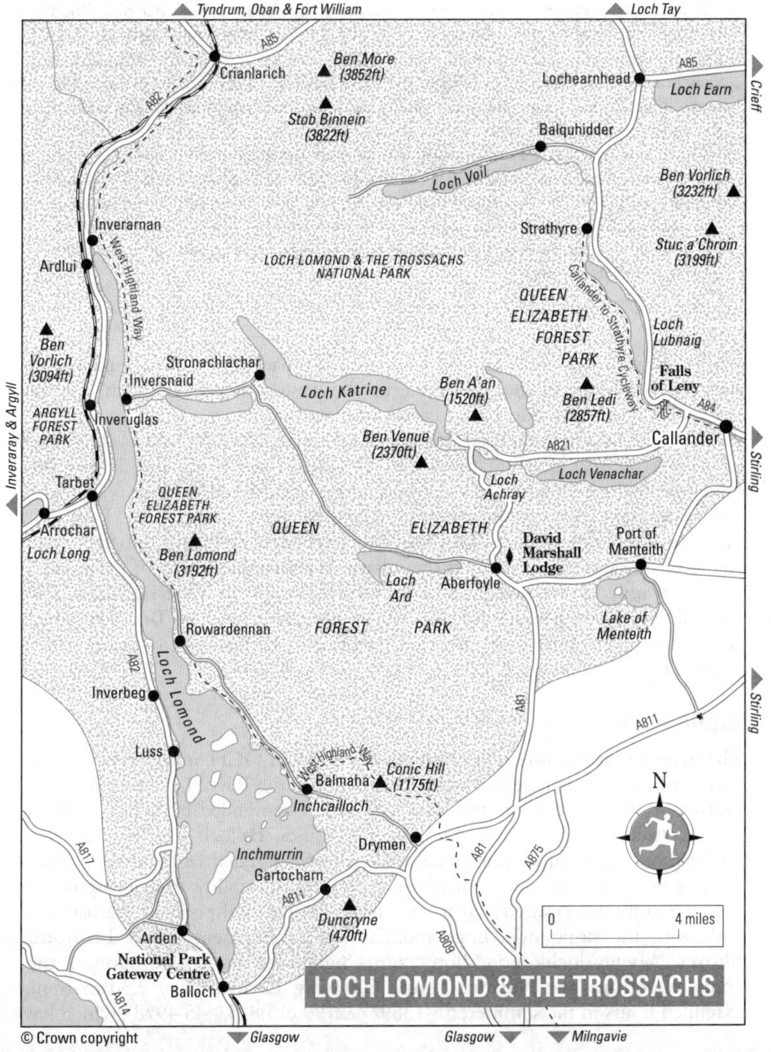

Taking the high road around Loch Lomond

Ordnance Survey Explorer map nos. 347 & 364.

Ben Lomond (3192ft), the most southerly of the "Munros" (see p.58), is one of the most frequently climbed hills in Scotland, its commanding position above Loch Lomond affording amazing views of both the Highlands and Lowlands. You should allow five to six hours for the climb to the summit and back. The most popular route starts in Rowardennan, at the car park just beyond the *Rowardennan Hotel*. It rises through forest and crosses open moors to gain the southern ridge, which leads to the final pyramid. The path zigzags up, then edges the crags of the northeast corrie to reach the summit. You can return the same way or start off westwards, then south, to traverse the subsidiary top of Ptarmigan hill down to the youth hostel in Rowardennan and then along the track back to the start.

If you're looking for an easier climb, but an equally impressive view over Loch Lomond, consider climbing **Conic Hill** (1175ft), further to the south, instead. Start from the large public car park at Balmaha and walk up through the woods. The views open up as soon as you leave the trees behind, so you don't even need to make it all the way to the top. You should allow two to three hours for the walk to the summit and back.

Finally, for an even less strenuous overview of the loch and its islands, climb **Duncryne** (470ft), a small conical hill to the southeast of Gartocharn, on the south side of the loch. The forty-minute walk, which starts from the woods to the south of the village, begins with various cautionary signs erected at the side of the path by the landowner about responsible access, but the route up is undemanding and the view wonderfully rewarding.

southwest side of the loch around **Luss** are often packed with day-trippers and tour coaches. Many of these continue up the western side of the loch, though the fast A82 road isn't ideal for tourists who wish to enjoy a leisurely drive by the lochside. On the loch itself, legislative moves are afoot to control the speed of motorboats that frequent the water on summer weekends and destroy the tranquillity which so impressed Queen Victoria and Sir Walter Scott.

Very different in tone, the eastern side of the loch, abutting the Trossachs, operates at a different pace with wooden ferryboats puttering out to a scattering of tree-covered islands off the village of **Balmaha**. Much of the eastern shore can only be reached by boat or foot, although the West Highland Way long-distance footpath (see p.166) and the distinctive peak of **Ben Lomond** ensure that even these parts are well travelled in comparison to many other areas of the Highlands.

Balloch

The main settlement on Loch Lomond-side is **BALLOCH** at the southwestern corner of the loch, where the water channels into the River Leven for its short journey south to the sea in the Firth of Clyde. Surrounded by housing estates and overstuffed with undistinguished guesthouses, Balloch has few redeeming features, and is little more than a suburb of the much larger factory town of Alexandria, to the south. However, Balloch's accessibility from Glasgow by both car and train ensured that it was chosen as the focal point of the national park with the siting of a huge multifaceted development, **Loch Lomond Shores** (Ⓦwww.lochlomondshores.com). Signposted from miles around, the complex contains the **National Park Gateway Centre** (daily 9.30am–6pm, extended hours in the summer; Ⓣ01389/722199 or 0845/345 4978), which has background on the park, tourist information and a leaflet outlining all transport links within the park, as well as Internet access and a "retail crescent" of shops including a branch of Edinburgh's venerable department store Jenners. Alongside the centre, **Drumkinnon Tower** is a striking, stone-built, cylindrical building which houses a giant-screen auditorium where films about the natural and cultural history of the area are shown; the tower's top-floor lookout post and small café affords excellent views over the loch towards Ben Lomond. At the time of going to press there were plans to transform the lower half of the tower into an aquarium (Ⓣ01389/722406, Ⓦwww.lochlomondaquarium.co.uk).

There are a number of **activities** available, including nature walks, canoe, bike and even pedalo rental with Can You Experience (Ⓣ01389/602576, Ⓦwww.canyouexperience.com), based right beside Drumkinnon Tower, and loch **cruises** (including a 2–3hr trip to Luss) from the nearby slipway with Sweeney's Cruises (Ⓣ01389/752376, Ⓦwww.sweeney.uk.com). Also at the slipway, the partially restored 1950s **paddle steamer** *The Maid of the Loch* is permanently moored at the pier (daily Easter–Oct 11am–4pm; rest of the year weekends only); aboard you can find out about her glory days sailing the loch and have a cup of tea in the onboard café.

For a more edifying aspect to Balloch and the loch, head across the river to the extensive mature grounds of **Balloch Castle Country Park**. In addition to shore-side and sylvan walks, there's a **National Park Centre** (daily: April–June 10am–6pm; July & Aug 10am–6.45pm; Sep–March 10am–5.45pm; Ⓣ01389/722230) in the mock-Gothic castle, which also has information on various aspects of the national park.

Another nearby attraction is the Loch Lomond **Bird of Prey Centre** (Mon–Fri 9am–5pm, Sat & Sun 9am–6pm; £3.50; Ⓣ07751/862416, Ⓦwww.birdsofprey.org.uk), half a mile east of Balloch towards Gartocharn. Here you can eyeball a rare golden eagle, as well as buzzards, hawks and falcons, or for £25 you can take a one-hour "hawk walk", which offers instruction on handling and flying the bird.

Practicalities

Balloch has a direct **train** connection with Glasgow Queen Street. Opposite the train station is a small **tourist office** (daily: May 10am–5pm; June & Sept 10am–5.30pm; July & Aug 9.30am–6pm; closed rest of year; Ⓣ01389/753533) – a larger office can be found at the Loch Lomond Shores Gateway Centre (see opposite). There's really little point in basing yourself in Balloch, although there are one or two more appealing options on the outskirts, including one of Scotland's most impressive SYHA **hostels** (Ⓣ0870/004 1136, Ⓦwww.syha.org.uk; April–Oct); the grand country house with turrets, stained-glass windows and walled gardens lies two miles northwest of Balloch train station, just off the A82; you can either walk there from Balloch, or if you're travelling by bus, ask the driver to drop you off close by. Also on the western side of Balloch, just off the A82 at the Balloch-large roundabout, is *Sheildaig Farm* (Ⓣ01389/752459, Ⓦwww.stayatlochlomond.com; ④), a pleasant **B&B** with a good restaurant. In Gartocharn, a tiny village three miles east of Balloch, the 200-year-old former tollhouse, *Ardoch Cottage* (Ⓣ01389/830452; ③) provides comfortable en-suite accommodation. In Balloch itself there's the year-round *Lomond Woods Holiday Park*, beside Loch Lomond Shores (Ⓣ01389/755000, Ⓦwww.holiday-parks.co.uk), an excellent **campsite**.

The exclusive *Cameron House Hotel* (Ⓣ01389/755565, Ⓦwww.cameronhouse.co.uk; ⑨), just north of Balloch, has three **restaurants**, including the upmarket *Georgian Room*, the *Drawing Room* (for afternoon tea) and the lochside *Marina Restaurant and Bar* which offers Mediterranean-style fare. At Loch Lomond

The West Highland Way

Opened in 1980, the spectacular **West Highland Way** was Scotland's first long-distance footpath, stretching some 95 miles from Milngavie (pronounced "mill-guy"), six miles north of central Glasgow, to Fort William, where it reaches the foot of Ben Nevis, Britain's highest mountain. Today, it is by far the most popular such footpath in Scotland, and while for many the range of scenery, relative ease of walking and nearby facilities make it a classic route, others find it a little too busy in high season, particularly in comparison with the relative isolation which can be found in many other parts of the Highlands.

The route follows a combination of ancient **drove roads**, along which Highlanders herded their cattle and sheep to market in the lowlands, military roads built by troops to control the Jacobite insurgence in the eighteenth century, old coaching roads and disused railway lines. In addition to the stunning scenery, which is increasingly dramatic as the path heads north, walkers may see some of Scotland's rarer **wildlife**, including red deer, feral goats – ancestors of those left behind after the Highland clearances – and, soaring over the highest peaks, golden eagles.

Passing through the lowlands north of Glasgow, the route runs along the eastern shores of Loch Lomond, over the Highland Boundary Fault Line, then round Crianlarich, crossing open heather moorland across the **Rannoch Moor** wilderness area. It passes close to **Glen Coe**, notorious for the massacre of the MacDonald clan, before reaching **Fort William**. Apart from a stretch between Loch Lomond and Bridge of Orchy, when the path is within earshot of the main road, this is wild, remote country: north of Rowardennan on Loch Lomond, the landscape is increasingly exposed, and you should be well prepared for sudden and extreme weather changes.

Though this is emphatically not the most strenuous of Britain's long-distance walks – it passes between lofty mountain peaks, rather than over them – a moderate degree of fitness is required as there are some steep ascents. If you're looking for an added challenge, you could work a climb of Ben Lomond or Ben Nevis into your schedule. You might choose to walk individual sections of the Way (the eight-mile climb from Glen Coe up the Devil's Staircase is particularly spectacular), but to tackle the whole thing you need to set aside at least seven days; avoid a Saturday start from Milngavie and you'll be less likely to be walking with hordes of people, and there'll be less pressure on accommodation. Most walkers tackle the route from south to north, and manage between ten and fourteen miles a day, staying at hotels, B&Bs and bunkhouses en route. Camping is permitted at recognized sites.

Although the path is clearly waymarked, you may want to check one of the many maps or guidebooks published: the **official guide**, published by Mercat Press (£14.99), includes a foldout map as well as descriptions of the route, with detailed cultural, historical, archeological and wildlife information. Further details about the Way, including a comprehensive accommodation list, can be found at Ⓦwww.west-highland-way.co.uk, which also has links to tour companies and transport providers, who can take your luggage from one stopping point to the next.

Shores there are various daytime options, including the viewing gallery café at the top of Drumkinnon Tower. In Balloch, *Balloch House* is popular for **lunches** and snacks, while the *Tullie Inn*, next to the train station, and *The Dog House* are both reliable bets for **pub grub** and a chat with locals.

The eastern shore of Loch Lomond and the islands

The tranquil **eastern shore** is far better for walking and appreciating the loch's natural beauty than the overcrowded western side. The dead-end B837 from Drymen will take you halfway up the east bank, as far as you can get by car or bus (#309 from Balloch and Drymen runs to Balmaha every 2hr), while the West Highland Way sticks close to the shores for the entire length of the loch, beginning at the tiny lochs ide settlement of **BALMAHA**, which stands on the Highland Boundary Fault, the geological fault that separates the Highlands from the Lowlands. If you stand on the viewpoint above the pier, you can see the fault line clearly marked by the series of woody islands that form giant stepping-stones across the loch. Many of the loch's 37 **islands** are privately owned, and rather quaintly an old wooden mail boat still delivers post to four of them. It's possible to join the **mail boat cruise**, which is run by MacFarlane & Son from the jetty at Balmaha (May, June & Sept Mon, Thurs & Sat 11.30am, returns 2pm; July & Aug Mon–Sat 11.30am, returns 2pm; Oct-April Mon & Thurs 10.50am, returns 12.50pm; £8; ⓣ01360/870214; ⓦwww.balmahaboatyard.co.uk). In summer the timetable allows a one-hour stop on Inchmurrin Island, the largest and most southerly of the islands inhabited by just ten permanent residents, and has the ruins of a monastery and castle, and a bar in the *Inchmurrin Hotel* (ⓣ01389/850245). If you're looking for an island to explore, however, a better bet is **Inchailloch**, the closest to Balmaha. Owned by Scottish Natural Heritage, there's a two-mile long nature trail signposted round the island, which was extensively planted with oaks to provide bark for the local tanning industry. Along the way you'll encounter the ruins of a fourteenth-century nunnery and associated burial ground, and there's a picnic and camping site at Port Bawn on the southwestern side of the island, near a pleasant sandy beach. Until the mid-seventeenth century parishioners on the far (western) shore of Loch Lomond used to row across to Inchailloch for Sunday services at the church linked to the nunnery. It's possible to row here yourself using a boat hired from MacFarlane & Son (from £10/hr), or you can make use of their on-demand ferry service (£4 return).

Balmaha gets very busy in summer, not least with day-trippers on the West Highland Way. Beside the large car park is a **National Park Centre** (daily: April–Sept 10am–6pm) where you can find out about local forest walks and occasional wildlife workshops. You can **stay** at the well-run *Oak Tree Inn* (ⓣ01360/870357, ⓦwww.oak-tree-inn.co.uk) set back from the boatyard, in one of their en-suite double rooms (❹) or bunk-bed quads (❸). There's also a convivial pub and all-day **food** served here. A cheaper option is the *Balmaha Bunkhouse Lodge* (ⓣ01360/870084) just across the road. **Camping** is available two miles north, on the lochside at Milarrochy Bay (ⓣ01360/870236; March–Oct), or, a couple of miles or so further up the road, at Cashel, a lovely secluded Forestry Commission campsite (ⓣ01360/870234, ⓦwww.forestholidays.co.uk; mid-March to Oct).

Public transport ends at Balmaha, but another seven miles north through the woods brings you to the end of the road at **ROWARDENNAN**, a scattered settlement which sits below Ben Lomond (see box on p.164). Passenger ferries (Easter–Sept 3 daily, contact *Rowardennan Hotel* to book) cross between Inverbeg and Rowardennan, where **accommodation** is available at the recently refurbished *Rowardennan Hotel* (ⓣ01360/870273, ⓦwww.rowardennanhotel.com; ❺), and, half a mile beyond, at a wonderfully situated SYHA **hostel** (ⓣ0870/004 1148, ⓦwww.syha.org.uk; March–Oct), a classic Scottish stone-built lodge with lawns running down to the shore.

Only walkers can continue further north up the lochside, where the only other settlement is seven miles north at **INVERSNAID**, made famous by a poem of the same name by Gerald Manley Hopkins about a frothing waterfall nearby ("This darksome burn, horseback brown,/His rollrock highroad roaring down . . ."). Though remote, the *Inversnaid Hotel* (☎01877/386223; ④) by the shore is mainly used by coach tours, who arrive via the only road in, the remote B829 from Aberfoyle, though walkers can snap up any free rooms or grab a drink or bite to eat. Up the hill the *Inversnaid Lodge* (☎01877/386254, Ⓦwww.inversnaidphoto.com; ④), once the hunting lodge of the Duke of Montrose, is a photography centre with instruction and workshops from guest tutors; if space allows the centre offers B&B to walkers on the West Highland Way. Situated in an old church on the B829, the *Inversnaid Bunkhouse* (☎01301/702970) with its hot tub and licensed coffeeshop offers a free pick-up service from Inversnaid car park. A **ferry** (£4 one-way/£5 return) crosses to Inveruglas on the western shore but you'll have to phone the *Inversnaid Hotel* to make arrangements. The West Highland Way continues through the Inversnaid RSPB reserve (free access) to the head of the loch, five miles further north.

The western shore of Loch Lomond

Despite the roar of traffic hurtling along the upgraded A82, the **west bank** of Loch Lomond is an undeniably beautiful stretch of water and gives better views of the loch's wooded islands and surrounding peaks than the heavily wooded east side. The exclusive, US-owned **Loch Lomond golf course**, which obscures the view for part of the way, is the venue for the annual Scottish Open.

LUSS, setting for the Scottish TV soap *High Road*, is without doubt the prettiest village in the region, with its prim, identical sandstone and slate cottages garlanded in rambling roses, and its narrow sandy, pebbly strand. However, its charms are no secret, and its streets and beach can become unbearably crowded in summer. If you want to escape the crowds, pop into the parish **church**, which is a haven of peace and has a lovely ceiling made from Scots pine rafters and some fine Victorian stained-glass windows. There's a **National Park Centre** (April–May & Oct daily 10am–5pm; June–Sept daily 10am–6.30pm) adjacent to the massive village car park, which is often choked with coaches, busking bagpipers and souvenir stalls. The cheery *Coach House*, whose owner often sports a spiky blonde haircut and purple kilt, is located just off the main street towards the church, and serves up home-made soup, huge rolls, tea, coffee and cakes.

If you need a place to **stay**, you could do worse than the *Inverbeg Inn* (☎01436/860678, Ⓦwww.inverbeginn.co.uk; ⑦), a few miles further north on the A82, which offers very good **bar food** as well as a few comfortable rooms. A passenger and bicycle **ferry** (Easter–Sept 3 daily; £5) links Inverbeg with Rowardennan on the east bank (see p.167). Seventeen miles north at **TARBET**, the West Highland **train** – the line from Glasgow to Fort William and Mallaig, with a branch line to Oban – reaches the shoreline at the point where the A83 heads off west into Argyll; the A82 continues north along the banks of the loch towards Crianlarich. Tarbet has a small **tourist office** (April–June & Sept–Oct 10am–5pm; July & Aug 10am–6pm; ☎01301/702260), close to which is a small tearoom with great cakes. At the pier near the *Tarbet Hotel* you can hop on an hour-long **loch cruise**, run by Cruise Loch Lomond (daily: March–Oct 8am–5.30pm; Nov–Feb 9am–5pm; from £5; ☎01301/702356). The same operator also offers trips to Inversnaid on the east side.

North of Tarbet, the A82 turns back into the narrow, winding road of old, making for slower but much more interesting driving. There's one more **train station** on Loch Lomond at **ARDLUI**, at the mountain-framed head of the loch, where you can have a pint at the *Ardlui Hotel*, and catch an on-demand

Scottish **food and drink**

Scotland isn't known for its culinary heritage, and the country's poor health records aren't exactly indicative of a healthy relationship with food. Yet Scottish produce – particularly its beef, fish, shellfish and game – can be outstanding, and in whisky the country lays almost complete claim to one of the world's most popular alcoholic drinks. In what is generally termed Modern Scottish cooking, this produce is combined with foreign influences from classic French cooking to Asian fusion to create a cuisine that's more impressive than visitors expect.

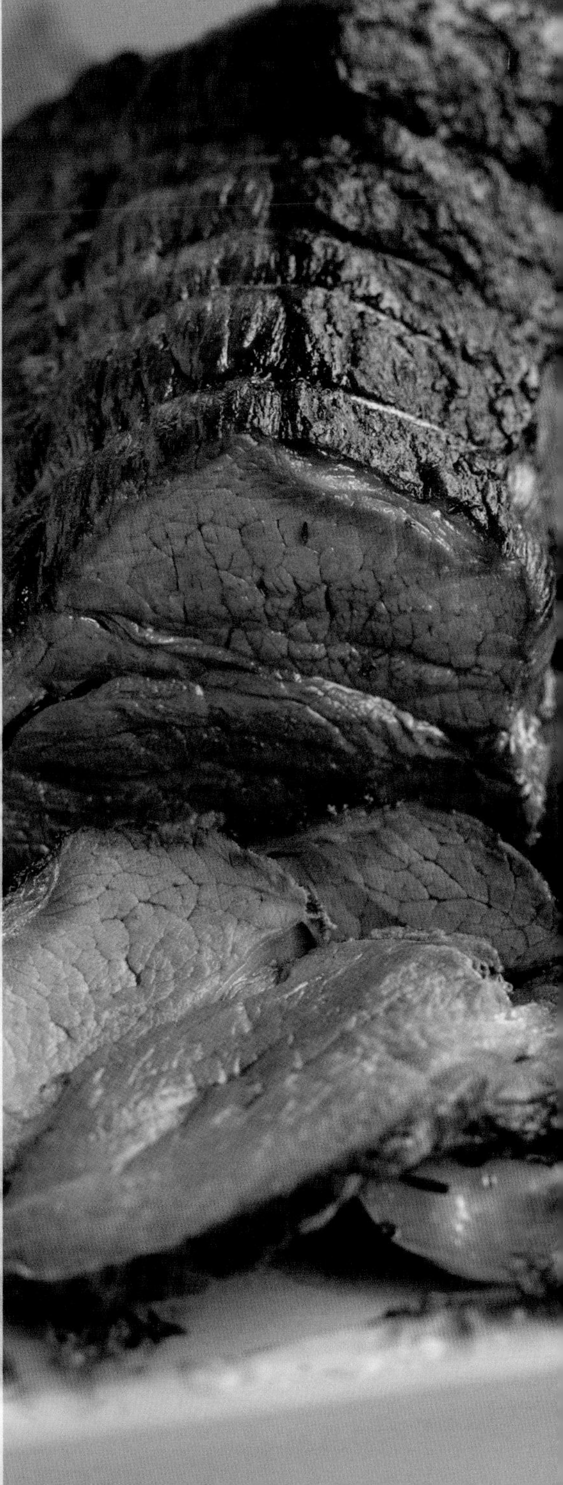

Haggis

Classic dishes

The quintessential Scots dish is **haggis**, a type of rich sausage meat made from spiced liver, offal, oatmeal and onion and cooked inside a bag made from a sheep's stomach. Though more frequently found on tourist-oriented menus than the dining tables of Scots at home, it's surprisingly tasty and satisfying, particularly when eaten with its traditional accompaniments "bashed neeps" (mashed turnips) and "chappit tatties" (mashed potatoes). The humble haggis has become rather trendy in recent years, appearing in swanky restaurants wrapped in filo pastry or drizzled with berry sauce, and a vegetarian version is widely available. Other traditional dishes which you may well encounter include **Scots broth**, a hearty soup made with combinations of lentil, split pea, mutton stock or vegetables and barley. More refined is **Cullen skink**, a rich soup made from smoked haddock, potatoes and cream. **Porridge** is a common offering at breakfast, though the quality is often variable: it's properly made with oatmeal and water and cooked with a pinch of salt, then eaten with a little milk, though some folk like to add honey, fruit or sugar as well. In hotels and guesthouses, breakfast menus may also offer strongly flavoured kippers (hot smoked herring) or more delicate "**Arbroath smokies**" (smoked haddock).

Scotland's **natural larder**

Scottish **fish and shellfish** is the envy of Europe, with a vast array of different types of fish, prawns, lobster, mussels, oysters, crab and scallops found round the extensive Scottish coastline. Elaborate dishes are sometimes concocted using these ingredients, though frankly the best seafood dishes are frequently the simplest. The prevalence of fish farming, now a significant industry in the Highlands and Islands, means that the once-treasured **salmon** is widespread and relatively inexpensive. Both salmon and **trout**, another commonly farmed fish, are frequently smoked and served cold with bread and butter.

Scottish-reared **beef** is often delicious, especially the Aberdeen Angus breed, though Highland cattle is also rated for its depth of flavour. **Venison**, the meat of the red deer, also features large – low in cholesterol and very tasty, it's served roasted or in casseroles, often cooked with juniper and red wine. Other forms of **game** include grouse, which when cooked properly is strong, dark and succulent; pheasant, a lighter meat; and the less commonly served but still tasty pigeon and rabbit.

Loch Fyne shellfish

Beer

Traditional Scottish beer is a thick, dark ale known as **heavy**, served at room temperature in pints or half-pints, with a full head. Quite different in taste from English "bitter", heavy is a more robust, sweeter beer with less of an edge. Scottish beers are graded by the shilling in a system used since the 1870s to indicate the level of potency: the higher the shilling mark (/-), the stronger or "heavier" the beer.

All of Scotland's biggest-name breweries – McEwan's, Tennents, Belhaven and Caledonian – produce a reasonable selection of heavies. However, if you really want to discover Scottish beer, look out for the products of the small **local breweries** of Aviemore, the Black Isle, Arran, Skye, Orkney or Shetland. Look out, too, for Fraoch, mostly available in bottles, a very refreshing, light ale made from heather according to an ancient recipe.

Locally brewed beer

Whisky

Whisky – *uisge beatha*, or the "water of life" in Gaelic – has been produced in Scotland since the fifteenth century, but only really took off in popularity after the 1780 tax on claret made wine too expensive for most people. The taxman soon caught up with whisky distilling, however, and drove the stills underground. Today, many distilleries operate on the site of simple cottages that once distilled the stuff illegally. In 1823, Parliament revised its Excise Laws, in the process legalizing whisky production, and today the drink is Scotland's chief export.

Despite the dominance of the blended whiskies such as Johnnie Walker, Bell's, Teacher's and The Famous Grouse, **single malt whisky** is infinitely superior, and, as a result, a great deal more expensive. Single malts vary enormously depending on the amount of peat used for drying the barley, the water used for mashing, and the type of oak cask used in the maturing process. Malt whisky is best drunk with a splash of water to release its distinctive flavours.

The two most important whisky regions are **Speyside** (see p.214), home of famous varieties such as Glenlivet, Glenfiddich and Macallan, and **Islay** (see p.144), which produces distinctively peaty whiskies such as Laphroaig, Lagavulin and Ardbeg. Many distilleries offer guided tours that range from slick and streamlined to small and friendly. All of them offer visitors a 'wee dram' as a finale, and those distilleries that charge an entrance fee often give a discount if you buy a bottle at the end, though prices are no lower at source than in the shops – between £20 and £30 for the average 70cl bottle.

Making **malt whisky**

Malt whisky is made by soaking barley in **steeps** (water cisterns) for two or three days until it swells; it's then left to germinate as the starch in the barley seed is converted into soluble sugars – a process known as **malting**. The malted barley is then dried in a kiln over an oil- or peat-fired furnace. Only a few distilleries still do their own malting and kilning in the traditional pagoda-style kilns; the rest simply have their malted barley delivered from an industrial maltings. The first process in most distilleries is therefore **milling**, which grinds the malted barley into "grist". Next comes the **mashing**, with the grist infused in hot water in mashtuns, producing a sugary concoction called "wort". After cooling, the wort passes into the washbacks, traditionally made of wood, where it is fermented with yeast for two to three days. The sugar is converted into alcohol, producing a brown foaming liquid known as "wash". **Distillation** now takes place, not once but twice: the wash is steam-heated, and the vapours siphoned off and condensed as a spirit. The spirit is poured into oak casks – second hand bourbon or sherry barrels are typically used to impart flavour and colour – and left to age for a minimum of three years. The average **maturation** period for a single malt whisky, however, is ten years; and the longer it matures, the more expensive it is, because on average two percent evaporates each year. Unlike wine, as soon as the whisky is bottled, maturation ceases.

ferry (9am–8pm; ask at the hotel for further details) to Ardleish on the other side. Also near here is a bistro/bar called *McGregor's Landing* (ⓣ01301/704205, ⓦwww.mcgregorslanding.com; ③), which offers comfortable hotel-style and backpacker accommodation. A couple of miles further north at **Inverarnan**, there's a bridge over the river behind the *Drovers Inn* (ⓣ01301/704234, ⓦwww.droversinn.co.uk; ③), arguably one of the most idiosyncratic **hotels** in Scotland. The bar has a roaring fire, barmen dressed in kilts, weary hill walkers sipping pints and bearded musicians banging out folk songs. Down the creaking corridors, past moth-eaten stuffed animals, are a number of supposedly haunted and resolutely old-fashioned rooms. The owners also run the more modern and plainer *Stagger Inn* directly opposite (ⓣ01301/704274; ③), which provides a rather better ordered but less traditional experience.

Crianlarich and Tyndrum

CRIANLARICH, some eight miles north of the head of Loch Lomond, is an important staging post on various transport routes, including the West Highland Railway which divides here, one branch heading due west towards Oban, the other continuing north over Rannoch Moor to Fort William. The West Highland Way long-distance footpath (see p.166) also trogs past. Otherwise there's little reason to stop here, unless you're keen on tackling some of the steep-sided hills that rise up from the glen.

Five miles further north from here on the A82/A85, the village of **TYNDRUM** owes its existence to a minor (and very short-lived) nineteenth-century gold rush, but today supports little more than a busy service station and several characterless hotels. However, five minutes' walk down a track there's a good campsite and small bunkhouse at *By The Way Hostel and Campsite* (ⓣ01838/400333; ⓦwww.tyndrumbytheway.com), and for a refreshingly different roadside dining experience, it's well worth trying the airy *Real Food Café* (daily until 10pm) on the main road for fresh, fast food that's locally sourced and cooked to order. At Tyndrum the road divides, with the A85 heading west to Oban, and the A82 heading for Fort William via Glen Coe. The railway divides further south at Crianlarich, though the two branches run in parallel to Tyndrum: it's only a short walk from Tyndrum Lower station (on the Oban line) to Tyndrum Upper (on the Fort William line).

The Trossachs

Often described as the Highlands in miniature, the **Trossachs** area boasts a magnificent diversity of scenery, with dramatic peaks and mysterious, forest-covered slopes that live up to all the images ever produced of Scotland's wild land. It is country ripe for stirring tales of brave kilted clansmen, a role fulfilled by Rob Roy Macgregor, the seventeenth-century outlaw whose name seems to attach to every second waterfall, cave and barely discernible path. Strictly speaking, the name "Trossachs", normally translated as either "bristly country" or "crossing place", originally referred only to the wooded glen between **Loch Katrine** and Loch Achray, but today it is usually taken as being the whole area from **Callander** right up to the eastern banks of Loch Lomond, with which it has been grouped as part of Scotland's first national park.

The Trossachs' high tourist profile was largely attributable in the early days to Sir Walter Scott, whose novels *Lady of the Lake* and *Rob Roy* were set in and around the area. According to one contemporaneous account, after Scott's *Lady*

Rob Roy

A member of the outlawed Macgregor clan, **Rob Roy** (meaning "Red Robert" in Gaelic) was born in 1671 in Glengyle, just north of Loch Katrine, and lived for some time as a respectable cattle farmer and trader, supported by the powerful Duke of Montrose. In 1712, finding himself in a tight spot when a cattle deal fell through, Rob Roy absconded with £1000, some of it belonging to the duke. He took to the hills to live as a brigand, his feud with Montrose escalating after the duke repossessed Rob Roy's land and drove his wife from their house. He was present at the Battle of Sheriffmuir during the earlier Jacobite uprising of 1715, ostensibly supporting the Jacobites but probably as an opportunist: the chaos would have made cattle-raiding easier. Eventually captured and sentenced to transportation, Rob Roy was pardoned and returned to **Balquhidder**, northeast of Glengyle, where he remained until his death in 1734.

Rob Roy's status as a local hero in the mould of Robin Hood should be tempered with the fact that he was without doubt a notorious bandit and blackmailer. His life has been much romanticized, from Sir Walter Scott's 1818 novel *Rob Roy* to the 1995 film starring Liam Neeson, although the tale does serve well to dramatize the clash between the doomed clan culture of the Gaelic-speaking Highlanders and the organized feudal culture of lowland Scots, which effectively ended with the defeat of the Jacobites at Culloden in 1746. His **grave** in Balquhidder, a simple affair behind the ruined church, is one of the principal sights on the unofficial Rob Roy trail, though the peaceful graveyard is mercifully underdeveloped and free of the tartan trappings which has seen the Trossachs dubbed "Rob Roy Country".

of the Lake was published in 1810, the number of carriages passing Loch Katrine rose from 50 the previous year to 270. Since then, neither the popularity nor beauty of the region has waned, and in high season the place is jam-packed with coaches full of tourists as well as walkers and mountain-bikers taking advantage of the easily accessed richness of the scenery. Autumn is a better time to come, when the hills are blanketed in rich, rusty colours and the crowds are thinner. In terms of where to stay, **Aberfoyle** has a rather dowdy air while **Callander** feels rather overrun, and you're often better seeking out one of the guesthouses or B&Bs tucked away in secluded corners of the region.

If you don't have your own transport, you could take advantage of the **Trossachs Trundler**, a useful minibus service which loops round Callander, Loch Katrine and Aberfoyle four times a day (10am–4pm) from late May to early Oct; helpfully for walkers, it stops on demand and can also cope with two bikes and wheelchairs. The bus is timed to connect with sailings of the SS *Sir Walter Scott* on Loch Katrine (see p.173), and costs £5 for a day-pass or £12 for two adults and four children (for further details call ⓣ01786/451200).

Aberfoyle and the Lake of Menteith

Each summer the sleepy little town of **ABERFOYLE**, twenty miles west of Stirling, dusts itself down for its annual influx of tourists. Though of little appeal itself, Aberfoyle's position in the heart of the Trossachs is ideal, with **Loch Ard Forest** and **Queen Elizabeth Forest Park** stretching across to Ben Lomond and Loch Lomond to the west, the long curve of Loch Katrine and Ben Venue to the northwest, and Ben Ledi to the northeast.

Don't come here for lively nightlife or entertainment, but for a good, healthy blast of the outdoors. From Aberfoyle you might like to wander north of the village to **Doon Hill**: cross the bridge over the Forth, continue past the cemetery and then follow signs to the **Fairy Knowe** (knoll). A toadstool marker points you through oak and holly trees to the summit of the Knowe where there is a pine tree, said to contain the unquiet spirit of the Reverend Robert Kirk, who studied local fairy lore and published his inquiries in *The Secret Commonwealth* (1691). Legend has it that, as punishment for disclosing supernatural secrets, he was forcibly removed to fairyland where he has languished ever since, although his mortal remains can be found in the nearby graveyard. This short walk should preferably be made at dusk, when it is at its most atmospheric.

Practicalities

Regular **buses** from Stirling pull into the car park on Aberfoyle's Main Street. The **tourist office** next door (daily: April–June, Sept & Oct 10am–5pm; July & Aug 9.30am–6pm; Nov–March Sat & Sun 10am–4pm only) has full details of local accommodation, sights and outdoor activities. The nearby **Scottish Wool Centre** (daily: May–Sept 9.30am–6pm; Oct–April 10am–5pm; free) – a popular stop-off point with tour buses – is a glorified country knitwear shop selling all the usual jumpers and woolly toys as well as featuring daily shows of sheep-shearing and sheep-dog trials (£2.50).

Accommodation options in Aberfoyle itself aren't all that inspiring. Best of the B&Bs is *Creag-Ard House* (ⓣ01877/382297, ⓦwww.creag-ard.co.uk; ❹; Easter–Oct), one mile west of Aberfoyle, where you'll leave in the morning satisfied with a large breakfast including locally sourced haggis. Further west, at the historic and friendly *Altskeith Hotel* (ⓣ01877/387266; ⓦwww.altskeith.com; ❹), there are delightful views over Loch Ard towards Ben Lomond, as well as warm hospitality and delicious evening meals. The **Lake of Menteith**

Hiking and biking in the Trossachs

Despite the steady flow of coach tours taking in the scenic highlights of the area, the Trossachs is ideal for exploring **on foot** or on a **mountain bike**. This is partly because the terrain is slightly more benign than the Highlands proper, but much is due to the excellent management of the **Queen Elizabeth Forest Park**, a huge chunk of the National Park between Loch Lomond and Loch Lubnaig. The main visitor centre for the area, David Marshall Lodge (see p.173), is just outside Aberfoyle, and is well worth a visit if you want to get some orientation on the region and learn about the local trees, geology and wildlife, which includes roe deer and birds of prey.

For **hill walkers**, the prize peak is Ben Lomond (3192ft), best accessed from Rowardennan (see p.167). Other highlights include Ben Venue (2370ft) and Ben A'an (1520ft) on the shores of Loch Katrine, as well as Ben Ledi (2857ft), just northwest of Callander, which all offer relatively straightforward but very rewarding climbs and, on clear days, stunning views. Walkers can also choose from any number of waymarked routes through the forests and along lochsides; pick up a map of these at the visitor centre.

The area is also a popular spot for **mountain biking**, with a number of useful rental shops, a network of forest paths and one of the more impressive stretches of the National Cycle Network cutting through the region from Loch Lomond to Killin. If you don't have your own bike, you can **rent** one from Wheels Cycling Centre (ⓣ01877/331100), next to *Trossachs Backpackers* (see p.175) a mile and a half southwest of Callander, the best rental place in the area, with front or full suspension models available, as well as baby seats and children's cycles. Also well set up is Trossachs Cycles (ⓣ01877/382614), at the *Trossachs Holiday Park* (see p.172) on the A81 two miles south of Aberfoyle, while more centrally located is Mounter Bikes (ⓣ01877/331052) beside the visitor centre in Callander (see p.174).

(see below) is another beautiful place to stay: the *Lake of Menteith Hotel* (Ⓣ01877/385258, Ⓦwww.lake-of-menteith-hotel.com; ⑥) at Port of Menteith has a lovely waterfront setting next to the Victorian Gothic parish church, as well as a classy restaurant.

For **camping**, a couple of miles south of Aberfoyle, off the A81 and on the edge of Queen Elizabeth Forest Park, there's *Cobleland* (Ⓣ01877/382392, Ⓦwww.forestholidays.co.uk; April–Oct), run by the Forestry Commission, which covers five acres of woodland by the River Forth (little more than a stream here). Further south, the excellent family-run *Trossachs Holiday Park* (Ⓣ01877/382614, Ⓦwww.trossachsholidays.co.uk; March–Oct) is twice the size and has **bikes** for rent.

In Aberfoyle, the best of a limited range of **eating** options are the *Forth Inn* on the main street or the *Covenanters Inn* at the large, turreted *Inchrie Castle Hotel*, five minutes' walk from the centre; both serve bar food and smarter restaurant meals.

The Lake of Menteith

About four miles east of Aberfoyle towards Doune, the **Lake of Menteith** is a superb fly-fishing centre and Scotland's only lake (as opposed to loch), so named due to a historic mix-up with the word *laigh*, Scots for "low-lying ground", which applied to the whole area. To rent a **fishing boat** or a rod contact the Lake of Menteith Fisheries (Ⓣ01877/385664; April–Oct).

From the northern shore of the lake, you can take a little ferry (April–Sept daily 9.30am–6.30pm; HS; £4 including ferry) out to the **Island of Inchmahome** in order to explore the lovely ruined Augustine abbey. Founded in 1238, **Inchmahome Priory** is the most beautiful island monastery in Scotland,

△ Lake of Menteith

its remains rising tall and graceful above the trees. The masons employed to build the priory are thought to be those who built Dunblane Cathedral; certainly the western entrance there resembles that at Inchmahome. The nave of the church is roofless, but in the choir are preserved the graves of important families from the surrounding area. Most touching is a late thirteenth-century double effigy depicting Walter, the first Stewart Earl of Menteith, and his Countess Mary who, feet resting on lion-like animals, turn towards each other and embrace.

Also buried here is the adventurer and scholar Robert Bontine Cunninghame Graham, once a pal of Buffalo Bill's in Mexico, an intimate friend of the novelist Joseph Conrad, and first president of the National Party of Scotland. Five-year-old Mary, Queen of Scots was hidden at Inchmahome in 1547 before being taken to France, and there's a formal garden in the west of the island, known as Queen Mary's bower, where legend has it she played. Traces remain of an orchard planted by the monks, but the island is thick now with oak, ash and Spanish chestnut. Visible on a nearby but inaccessible islet is the ruined castle of **Inchtalla**, the home of the earls of Menteith in the sixteenth and seventeenth centuries.

Aberfoyle to Callander

North of Aberfoyle, the A821 road to Loch Katrine winds its way into the Queen Elizabeth Forest, snaking up **Duke's Pass** (so called because it once belonged to the Duke of Montrose). You can walk or drive the short distance to the park's excellent **visitor centre** at David Marshall Lodge (daily: Jan Sat & Sun 10am–4pm; Feb Thurs–Sun 10am–4pm; March–June, Sept & Oct 10am–5pm; July & Aug 10am–6pm; Nov & Dec 10am–4pm; car park £1; ⓣ01877/382258), where you can pick up maps of the walks and cycle routes in the forest, get background information on the flora and fauna of the area (there's a great video relay and plans for a live web-cam to the nests of local peregrine falcons and ospreys), or settle into the café with its splendid views out over the tree tops. Adjacent to the centre, there's an excellent adventure park for kids, and various marked paths wind through the forest, giving glimpses of the lowlands and surrounding hills. The only road in the forest open to cars is the **Achray Forest Drive**, just under two miles further on, which leads through the park and along the western shore of **Loch Drunkie** before rejoining the main road.

Loch Katrine

Heading down the northern side of the Duke's Pass you come first to **Loch Achray**, tucked under Ben A'an. Look out across the loch for the small **Callander Kirk** in a lovely setting alone on a promontory. At the head of the loch a road follows the short distance through to the southern end of **Loch Katrine** at the foot of Ben Venue (2370ft), from where the elegant Victorian passenger **steamer**, the SS *Sir Walter Scott*, has been plying the waters since 1900, chugging up to the wild country of Glengyle. It does two runs from the pier each day, the first departing at 11am and stopping off at Stronachlachar before returning almost two hours later (April–Oct daily; £7.25 return; ⓣ01877/376316); the one-hour afternoon cruise leaves at 1.45pm but doesn't make any stops (April–Oct daily; £6.25). A popular combination is to **rent a bike** from the Katrinewheels (ⓣ01877/376316) hut by the pier, take the steamer up to Stronachlachar, then cycle back by way of the road around the north side of the loch.

From Loch Katrine the A821 heads due east past the tiny village of **Brig o'Turk**, where it's worth looking in on the *Byre Inn*, a tiny pub and restaurant set in an old stone barn with wooden pews and a welcoming open fire. The cosy, wooden-clad *Brig o'Turk Tea-Room* (Easter–Sept 11am–4pm) is also a good place to refresh after a walk or cycle. Carry on along the shores of Loch Venacher to get to Kilmahog, where the road meets the A84 a short distance from Callander.

Callander and around

CALLANDER, on the eastern edge of the Trossachs, sits on the banks of the River Teith at the southern end of the **Pass of Leny**, one of the key routes into the Highlands. Significantly larger than Aberfoyle, eleven miles west, it is a popular summer holiday base and suffers in high season for being right on the main tourist trail from Stirling through to the west Highlands. Callander first came to fame during the "Scottish Enlightenment" of the eighteenth and nineteenth centuries, when the glowing reports of the Trossachs given by Sir Walter Scott and William Wordsworth prompted the first tourists to venture into the wilds by horse-drawn carriage. Development was given a boost when Queen Victoria chose to visit, and then by the arrival of the train line – long since closed – in the 1860s.

Tourists have arrived in throngs ever since, as the plethora of restaurants and tearooms, antique shops, secondhand bookstores and shops selling local woollens and crafts testifies. A typical day in summer sees visitors thronging the pavements and traffic crawling down the long main street; you'd be forgiven the desire to move on swiftly to more tranquil countryside beyond. The chief attraction in town is the **Rob Roy and Trossachs Visitor Centre** in a converted church at Ancaster Square on the main street (daily: March–May & Oct 10am–5pm; June–Sept 10am–6pm; Nov–Feb 11am–4pm; upstairs £3.60. Upstairs a hammed-up audiovisual display offers an entertaining and partisan account of the life and times of Rob Roy and those who have portrayed him in film and fiction.

Practicalities

Callander's **tourist office** is downstairs in the Rob Roy and Trossachs Visitor Centre (same times; ⓣ01877/330342), and can book **accommodation**. Wheels Cycling Centre (ⓣ01877/331100, ⓦwww.scottish-cycling.co.uk), part of *Trossachs Backpackers* (see opposite), offers excellent **bike rental** as well as advice on the best local routes.

Accommodation

Arden House Bracklinn Rd ⓣ01877/330235, ⓦwww.ardenhouse.org.uk. A grand Victorian guesthouse in its own gardens with good views and woodland walks from the back door. Open April–Oct. ⑤

Burnt Inn House Brig o'Turk, ⓣ01877/376212, ⓦwww.burntinnhouse.co.uk. As an alternative to staying in Callander, this historic place offers simpler, farmhouse-style B&B right in the heart of the Trossachs countryside. ③

Callander Meadows 24 Main St ⓣ01877/330181, ⓦwww.callandermeadows.co.uk. Centrally located rooms in an attractive townhouse which boasts three comfortable en-suite rooms and an excellent restaurant. Full board available. ③

The Conservatory Ballachallan ⓣ01877/339190, ⓦwww.ballachallan.co.uk. Three pleasant, well-presented en-suite rooms in an eighteenth-century farmhouse, two miles southeast of town, and a fish restaurant in the conservatory. ④

Roman Camp Country House Hotel Main St ⓣ01877/330003, ⓦwww.roman-camp-hotel.co.uk. The upmarket option in town, a romantic, turreted seventeenth-century hunting lodge situated in twenty-acre gardens on the River Teith. 7

Trossachs Backpackers Invertrossachs Rd ☎01877/331200, www.scottish-hostel.co.uk. A friendly, well equipped and comfortable 32-bed hostel and activity centre with self-catering dorms and family rooms, located a mile southwest of town down a turn-off from the A81 to Port of Menteith. Bike rental available next door. 1

Eating and drinking

Despite Callander's popularity, the town itself has few **restaurants** worth recommending. *Callander Meadows* (see opposite; restaurant closed Tues & Wed) serves up delicious, freshly cooked lunches and dinners. Its "Meadows Wave" option includes every dessert on the menu. *The Conservatory* fish restaurant at Ballachallan (see opposite; closed Mon & Tues), two miles from Callander along the Doune road, serves great Scottish seafood dishes at reasonable prices in a pleasant conservatory dining room. For good **pub food** try the convivial *Lade Inn* in Kilmahog, a mile west of Callander. For unbeatable fresh sandwiches, great coffee and a fine selection of breads, cheeses and other deli items head for *Deli Ecosse* adjacent to the visitor centre.

North of Callander

On each side of Callander, pleasant and untaxing walks wind west for a couple of miles through a wooded gorge to the **Falls of Leny** and north for a mile or so through forest to the **Bracklinn Falls**. Longer walks of varying degrees of exertion thread their way through the surrounding countryside, the most challenging being that to the summit of **Ben Ledi** (2857ft); set off from the public car park at the turn-off marked "Strathyre Forest Cabins".

North of town, you can walk or ride the scenic six-mile Callander to Strathyre (Route 7) Cycleway, which forms part of the network of cycleways between the Highlands and Glasgow. The route is based on the old Caledonian train line to Oban, which closed in 1965, and runs along the western side of Loch Lubnaig. At the head of the loch, the main road runs straight through **STRATHYRE**, though if you're looking for somewhere to stay it's worth turning off to *Creagan House* (☎01877/384638, www.creaganhouse.co.uk; 6), an old farm steading less than half a mile north of Strathyre with cosy rooms and an excellent restaurant, well stocked with fine wines and malt whisky.

Just northwest of here is tiny **BALQUHIDDER**, (#59 bus from Stirling) most famous as the site of the **grave of Rob Roy**, which you'll find in the small yard behind the ruined church. Refreshingly, considering the Rob Roy fever that plagues the region, his grave – marked by a rough stone carved with a sword, cross and a man with a dog – is remarkably underplayed. Small, professional classical **concerts** are held in the atmospheric 150-year-old church on six summer Sundays (late June to early Aug; ☎01877/384265), while the village's tiny wood-panelled library – built by the laird as an alternative distraction to the pub across the road – is now a tearoom (Easter–Oct daily 10am–5pm) serving freshly baked scones to passing cyclists and walkers. Avoid the plethora of Rob Roy-themed **accommodation** in Balquhidder, and drive six miles beyond the village to the award-winning *Monachyle Mhor* hotel (☎01877/384622, www.monachylemhor.com; 6), an eighteenth-century farmhouse with stylish modern rooms and a terrific restaurant (open to non-residents, but book ahead) specializing in locally sourced organic food and with the added bonus of lovely views over the hills surrounding Loch Voil. On the road to the hotel is the unexpected sight of the Dhanakosa Buddhist retreat centre (☎01877/384213 www.dhanakosa.com) – details of weekend or week-long retreats here, with courses ranging from tai chi to hill walking, can be found on their website.

North of Balquhidder the busy A84 slides past Lochearnhead, at the western end of Loch Earn, and Killin, at the western end of Loch Tay, both of which are covered in the Perthshire section (see p.181), before swinging west towards Crianlarich (see p.169) and the west coast.

Perthshire

Genteel **Perthshire** is, in many ways, the epitome of well-groomed rural Scotland. First settled over eight thousand years ago, it was occupied by the Romans and then the Picts before Celtic missionaries established themselves, enjoying the amenable climate, fertile soil and ideal defensive and trading location. North and west of the county town of Perth, there are some magnificent landscapes to be discovered – snow-capped peaks falling away to forested slopes and long, deep lochs – topography which inevitably controls transport routes, influences the weather and tolerates little development. The various mountains, woods and lochs provide terrific walking and watersports, particularly through the **Strath Tay** area, which is dominated by Scotland's longest river, the **Tay**, which flows from **Loch Tay** past the attractive towns of **Dunkeld** and **Aberfeldy**. Further north, the countryside of **Highland Perthshire** becomes more sparsely populated and more spectacular, especially around the towns of **Pitlochry** and **Blair Atholl** and the wild expanses of **Rannoch Moor** to the west.

Transport connections in the region are at their best if you head straight north from Perth, along the main A9 road and train line to Inverness, but buses – albeit often infrequent – also serve the more remote areas. Keep asking at bus stations for details of services, as the further you get from the main villages, the less definitive timetables become.

Out and about in Perthshire

To many, Perthshire is a celebration of the great outdoors, with **activities** ranging from gentle strolls through ancient oak forests to white-knuckle rides down frothing waterfalls. The variety of landscapes and their relative accessibility from the central belt has also led to a significant number of operators basing themselves in the area. Many of these are linked to the tourist board's Activity Line (ⓣ01577/861186, ⓦwww.adventureperthshire.co.uk), which can give advice and contacts for over thirty different outdoor operators who comply with the Adventure Perthshire Operators' Charter. For canyoning, cliff-jumping and an activity called "sphere-ing" which involves tumbling down a hillside inside a giant plastic ball, get in touch with adrenalin junkies Nae Limits (ⓣ01350/727242, ⓦwww.naelimits.co.uk), based in Dunkeld; while for rafting on larger craft through the best rapids on the Tay at Grandtully try Splash (ⓣ01887/829706, ⓦwww.rafting.co.uk) or Freespirits (ⓣ01887/829280, ⓦwww.freespirits-online.co.uk), both based in or near Aberfeldy. Also in Aberfeldy are the National Kayak School (ⓦwww.nationalkayakschool.com) and the rather more sedate Highland Adventure Safaris (ⓣ01887/820071, ⓦwww.highlandadventuresafaris.co.uk), who offer an inspiring introduction to wild Scotland in which you're taken by four-wheel-drive vehicle to search for golden eagle eyries, stags and pine martens.

Strath Tay to Loch Tay

Heading due north from Perth both the railway and main A9 trunk road carry much of the traffic heading into the Highlands, often speeding straight through some of Perthshire's most attractive countryside in its eagerness to get to the bleaker country to the north. Perthshire has been dubbed **Big Tree Country** by the tourist board in recognition of some magnificent woodland in the area, including a number of individual trees which rank among Europe's oldest, tallest and certainly most handsome specimens. Many of these are found around the valley – or "strath" – of the River Tay as it heads towards the sea from attractive **Loch Tay**, set up among the high Breadalbane mountains which include the striking peak of **Ben Lawers**, Perthshire's highest, and the hills which enclose the long, enchanting **Glen Lyon**. Studded around Loch Tay are remains of crannogs, ancient dwellings built on man-made islands, which are brought to life at the **Crannog Centre** beside the village of Kenmore. Not far downriver is the prosperous small town of **Aberfeldy**; from here the Tay drifts southeast between the unspoilt twin villages of **Dunkeld** and **Birnam** before meandering its way past Perth.

Dunkeld and Birnam

DUNKELD, twelve miles north of Perth on the A9, was proclaimed Scotland's ecclesiastical capital by Kenneth MacAlpine in 850. Its position at the southern boundary of the Grampian Mountains made it a favoured meeting place for Highland and Lowland cultures, but in 1689 it was burned to the ground by the Cameronians – fighting for William of Orange – in an effort to flush out troops of the Stuart monarch, James VII. Subsequent rebuilding, however, didn't intrude into the modern era, and as a result the town is one of the area's most pleasant communities, with handsome whitewashed houses, appealing arts and crafts shops and a charming cathedral. The **tourist office** is at The Cross in the town centre (April–June, Sept & Oct Mon–Sat 10am–5pm, Sun 11am–4pm; July & Aug Mon–Sat 9.30am–6.30pm, Sun 10am–5pm; Nov–March Mon, Tues, Fri–Sun 10am–4pm; ⓣ01350/727688).

Dunkeld's partly ruined **cathedral** (daily: May–Sept 9.30am–6.30pm; Oct–April 9.30am–4pm; ⓦwww.dunkeldcathedral.org.uk) is on the northern side of town, in an idyllic setting amid lawns and trees on the east bank of the Tay. Construction began in the early twelfth century and continued throughout the next two hundred years, but the building was more or less ruined at the time of the Reformation. The present structure consists of the fourteenth-century choir and the fifteenth-century nave; the choir, restored in 1600 (and several times since), now serves as the parish church, while the nave remains roofless apart from the clock tower. Inside, note the leper's peep near the pulpit in the north wall, through which lepers could receive the sacrament without coming into contact with the congregation. Also look out for the great effigy of *The Wolf of Badenoch*, Robert II's son, born in 1343. The Wolf acquired his name and notoriety when, after being excommunicated for leaving his wife, he took his revenge by burning the towns of Forres and Elgin and sacking Elgin cathedral. He eventually repented, did public penance for his crimes and was absolved by his brother, Robert III.

Birnam

Dunkeld is linked to its sister community, **BIRNAM**, by Thomas Telford's seven-arched bridge of 1809. This little village has a place in history thanks to

Shakespeare, for it was on Dunsinane Hill, to the southeast of the village, that Macbeth declared: "I will not be afraid of death and bane/Till Birnam Forest come to Dunsinane", only to be told later by a messenger "I look'd toward Birnam, and anon me thought/The Wood began to move . . ."

The **Birnam Oak**, a gnarly old character propped up by crutches which can be seen on the waymarked riverside walk, is inevitably claimed to be a survivor of the infamous mobile forest. Several centuries after Shakespeare, another literary personality, Beatrix Potter, drew inspiration from the area, recalling her childhood holidays here when penning the Peter Rabbit stories. A Potter-themed exhibition and garden, aimed at both children and parents, can be found on the main road in the impressive barrel-fronted **Birnam Institute** (daily 10am–5pm; ⓦwww.birnaminstitute.com), a modern theatre, arts and community centre with a busy programme of events.

Practicalities

Dunkeld is well served by **public transport**: by train between Perth and Inverness, and bus from Perth #23 (Stagecoach) and #957 (Scottish Citylink). There are several large **hotels** in Dunkeld and Birnam, including the *Royal Dunkeld*, Atholl Street (ⓣ01350/727322, ⓦwww.royaldunkeldhotel.co.uk; ❺), which also has cheaper twin rooms in an annexe (❸), and the looming Victorian Gothic *Birnam House Hotel* on Perth Road (ⓣ01350/727462, ⓦwww.birnamhousehotel.co.uk; ❻). Most sumptuous of the lot is the *Dunkeld House Hilton* (ⓣ01350/727771, ⓦwww.hilton.co.uk/dunkeld; ❼ for dinner, B&B), a vast country estate house on the banks of the Tay to the north of town which incorporates a spa, swimming pool and excellent facilities for outdoor pursuits. Much less grand, but full of personality is the central *Taybank Hotel* (ⓣ01350/727340, ⓦwww.taybank.com; ❷), a real beacon for music fans who come for the regular live sessions in the convivial bar. The rooms are simple and inexpensive, and the rate includes a continental breakfast. Local **B&Bs** include the pleasant *Waterbury Guest House* (ⓣ01350/727324, ⓦwww.waterbury-guesthouse.co.uk; ❸) on Murthly Terrace in Birnam, or the more luxurious *The Pend* (ⓣ01350/727586, ⓦwww.thepend.com; ❺) just off the main street in Dunkeld. For **food**, try the decent bar meals at the *Taybank* (the stovies are particularly filling) or the *Tap Inn*, the wee pub beside the *Birnam House Hotel*, which also hosts regular folk and jazz sessions; during the day the *Foyer Café* in the Birnam Institute (see above) serves coffee, cakes and light meals, or you can pick up some delicious snacks and sandwiches at the Robert Menzies deli in Dunkeld.

Around Dunkeld

Dunkeld and Birnam are surrounded by some lovely countryside, both along the banks of the Tay and into the deep forests which seem to close in on the settlement. One of the most rewarding walks is a mile and a half from Birnam to **The Hermitage**, set in a grandly wooded gorge of the plunging River Braan. Here you'll find a pretty eighteenth-century folly, also known as Ossian's Hall, which was once mirrored to reflect the water – the mirrors were smashed by Victorian vandals and the folly was more tamely restored. The hall, appealing yet incongruous in its splendid setting, neatly frames a dramatic waterfall. Nearby you can crane your neck to look up at a Douglas fir which claims the title of tallest tree in Britain – measuring these behemoths isn't easy, but last time the tape was out it managed 212ft.

Two miles east of Dunkeld, the **Loch of the Lowes** is a nature reserve that offers a rare chance to see breeding ospreys and other wildfowl; the visitor centre (April–Sept 10am–5pm; £2; ⓣ01350/727337) has video relay screens and will point you in the direction of the best vantage points. If the surroundings seem appealing enough to warrant lingering a day or two, you could head for the mellow *Wester Caputh Independent Hostel* (ⓣ01738/710449, ⓦwww.westercaputh.co.uk), four miles downstream along the Tay from Dunkeld with small dorms and doubles (❶), a great base with a relaxing and welcoming atmosphere. For details about how to reach Wester Caputh village, phone the hostel direct.

Aberfeldy and around

From Dunkeld the A9 runs north alongside the Tay for eight miles to Ballinluig, a little place marking the turn-off along the A827 to **ABERFELDY**, a generally prosperous settlement of large stone houses and four-wheel-drive vehicles that acts as a service centre for the wider Loch Tay area. The **tourist office** at The Square in the town centre (April–June, Sept & Oct Mon–Sat 9.30am–5pm, Sun 11am–3pm; July & Aug Mon–Sat 9.30am–6.30pm, Sun 10am–4pm; Nov–March Mon–Sat 10am–4pm; ⓣ01887/820276) is good for advice on local accommodation and details of nearby walking trails. If you want to **rent a bike**, head to *Girvans* outdoor store (ⓣ01887/820254), located behind the filling station on your way into town from the east.

Aberfeldy sits at the point where the Urlar Burn – lined by the silver birch trees celebrated by Robert Burns in his poem *The Birks of Aberfeldy* – flows into the River Tay. The Tay is spanned by the humpbacked, four-arch **Wade's Bridge**, built by General Wade in 1733 during his efforts to control the unrest in the Highlands, and one of the general's more impressive pieces of work. Overlooking the bridge from the south end is the **Black Watch Monument**, depicting a pensive, kilted soldier, erected in 1887 to commemorate the first muster of the Highland regiment commissioned to "watch upon the braes" and gathered as a peacekeeping force by Wade in 1740. The regiment, prominent in recent conflicts in Northern Ireland and Iraq, retains close ties with Perthshire, including a regimental museum in Perth.

The main set-piece attraction in town is **Dewar's World of Whisky** at the Aberfeldy Distillery (April–Oct Mon–Sat 10am–6pm, Sun noon–4pm; Nov–March Mon–Sat 10am–4pm; £5; ⓦwww.dewarswow.com), which puts on an impressive show of describing the making of whisky – worthwhile if you haven't been given a similar lowdown at distilleries elsewhere. As with many of the distilleries these days, a connoisseurs' **tour** (£10) is available, giving a more in-depth look around the distillery and a chance to taste (or "nose") the whisky at different stages in its life. The rest of the small town centre is a busy mixture of craft and tourist shops, the most interesting by far being **The Watermill** on Mill Street (Mon–Sat 9am–5pm, Sun noon–5pm, ⓦwww.aberfeldywatermill.com), an inspiring bookshop, art gallery and café located in the town's superbly restored early nineteenth-century mill. Oatmeal was still produced here until a few years ago, and most of the old structure and internal workings have been left in place, lending a certain charm. If you've some time on your hands, it's worth wandering into the most venerable shop in Aberfeldy, Haggarts, located on the corner of Dunkeld Street and Moness Terrace, a classic old-time tweed tailors which sells stout tweed suits and deerstalker hats.

Practicalities

Accommodation in the middle-to-upper price bracket is impressively stylish: in town there's *Guinach House*, by the The Birks (ⓣ01887/820251,

Ⓦwww.guinachhouse.co.uk; ⑥), a tastefully decorated guesthouse in well-tended grounds; while a few miles away is *Farleyer* (Ⓣ01887/820332, Ⓦwww.farleyer.com; ⑥), a smart, contemporary restaurant just beyond Castle Menzies with nine tastefully decorated rooms. For B&B accommodation, try *Balnearn Guest House* (Ⓣ01887/820431, Ⓦwww.balnearnhouse.com; ②), or *Mavisbank*, Taybridge Drive (Ⓣ01887/820223, Ⓔnancynunn@onetel.net; ②; May–Sept), both attractive stone houses in town. There are two **bunk-houses** in the area, both in the settlement of Weem, half a mile from Aberfeldy on the north side of the Tay: *Glassie Farm* (Ⓣ01887/820265, Ⓦwww.thebunkhouse.co.uk) has a lovely location a mile or so up on the hillside above Weem, while *Adventurer's Escape* (Ⓣ01887/820498, Ⓦwww.adventurers-escape.co.uk) occupies an old house and steading right next to the *Weem Hotel* on the road to Castle Menzies. Both are worth contacting if you're interested in trying out the many adventure sports and outdoor pursuits which are available locally.

For something to **eat**, Aberfeldy isn't short on cafés and tearooms; best bet for a good cup of coffee or a bowl of soup at lunchtime is the relaxed café in *The Watermill*, or there are some decent places to buy picnic food, including Farm Fresh deli, 22 Dunkeld Street, and the delicious meats, fish and cheese at Tombuie Smokehouse's stall (March–Sept) beside the main road between town and the distillery. Decent bar meals can be found over Wade's Bridge in Weem at the *Ailean Chraggan Inn*; in town, there's reasonable casual dining at *Kiwi's* on The Square (Ⓣ01887/829229; closed Tue & Wed evenings), or for something more upmarket, *Farleyer Restaurant* (see above) is a couple of miles out of town but well worth considering for both bistro-style and more formal modern Scottish dining.

Castle Menzies and around

One mile west of Aberfeldy, across Wade's Bridge, **Castle Menzies** (April to mid-Oct Mon–Sat 10.30am–5pm, Sun 2–5pm; £3.50; Ⓦwww.menzies.org) is an imposing, Z-shaped, sixteenth-century tower house, which until the middle of the last century was the chief seat of the Clan Menzies (pronounced "Ming-iss"). With the demise of the line, the castle was taken over by the Menzies Clan Society, who since 1971 have been involved in the lengthy process of restoring it. Most of the interior is on view, most of it refreshingly free of fixtures and fittings, displaying an austerity which is much more true to medieval life than many grander, furnished castles elsewhere in the country.

Even if you pass the castle by, it's well worth stopping at **Castle Menzies Farm** next door, where an imaginative modern conversion has turned an old cow byre into the *House of Menzies* (Mon–Sat 10am–5pm, Sun 11am–5pm; Nov–Dec closed Mon; Jan–April closed Mon & Tues, Ⓦwww.houseofmenzies.com), which combines a specialist New World wine shop with a modern café and relatively tasteful gift shop.

A mile or so further along the road by the hamlet with the unfortunate name of **Dull** is Highland Adventure Safaris (Ⓣ01887/820071, Ⓦwww.highlandadventuresafaris.co.uk), where you can join Landrover trips into the heather-clad hills nearby in search of wildlife such as eagles, red deer and grouse. At the lodge you can try your hand at gold and mineral panning (£3), a big hit with kids; there's also a deer park, play area and café.

The road from here carries on either deep into the hills of Glen Lyon (see p.183), or connects north past the striking mountain Schiehallion to Loch Tummel (see p.186).

Loch Tay

Aberfeldy grew up around a crossing point on the River Tay, which leaves it slightly oddly six miles adrift of Loch Tay, a fourteen-mile-long stretch of fresh water which all but hooks together the western and eastern Highlands. Guarding the northern end of the loch is **KENMORE**, where whitewashed estate houses and well-tended gardens cluster around the gate to the extensive grounds of **Taymouth Castle**, built by the Campbells of Glenorchy in the early nineteenth century, and now undergoing extensive renovation to convert it into a top-class hotel and golf resort. The main attraction here is the **Scottish Crannog Centre** (mid-March to Oct daily 10am–5.30pm, Nov Sat & Sun 10am–4pm; £4.75; Ⓦwww.crannog.co.uk), one of the best heritage museums in the country. Crannogs are Iron Age loch dwellings built on stilts over the water, with a gangway to the shore which could be lifted up to defy a hostile intruder, whether animal or human. Following extensive underwater archeological excavations in Loch Tay, the team here has superbly reconstructed a crannog, and visitors can now walk out over the loch to the thatched wooden dwelling, complete with sheepskin rugs, wooden bowls and other evidence of the way life was lived 2500 years ago.

Kenmore is a popular holidaying spot, and as a result there are a number of activity-based operations here. Best of the lot is Croft-na-Caber (Ⓣ01887/830588, Ⓦwww.croftnacaber.com), an impressive **outdoor pursuits** complex situated next door to the Crannog Centre, where you can try various watersports on Loch Tay including water-skiing, fishing, canoeing and sailing. The nicest place to **stay** in town is the pleasant and well-run *Kenmore Hotel*, in the village square (Ⓣ01887/830205, Ⓦwww.kenmorehotel.com; ❻), a descendant of Scotland's oldest inn (established here in 1572); alternatively, *Culdees*, four miles along the

△ Scottish Crannog Centre, Loch Tay

Climbing the Ben Lawers group

Ordnance Survey Explorer map no. 378.

Dominating the northern side of Loch Tay is moody **Ben Lawers** (3984ft), Perthshire's highest mountain; from the top there are incredible views towards both the Atlantic and the North Sea. The ascent – which, despite the well-marked footpath, should not be tackled without all the right equipment (see p.59) – takes around three hours from the NTS **visitor centre** (May–Sept daily 10.30am–5pm; ⓣ01567/820397), which is located at 1300ft and reached by a signposted road off the A827. The centre has an audiovisual show, slides of the mountain flowers – including the rare alpine flora found here – and a nature trail with accompanying descriptive booklet.

The Ben Lawers range offers rich pickings for Munro baggers, with nine hills over 3000ft in close proximity. The whole double-horseshoe-shaped ridge from Meall Greigh in the east to Meall a'Choire Leith in the northwest is too much for one day, though the eastern section from Meall Greigh (3284ft) to Beinn Ghlas (3619ft), taking in Ben Lawers, can be walked in eight to ten hours in good conditions. Standing on its own a little to the east is perhaps the prettiest of the lot, Meall nan Tarmachan ("The Hill of the Ptarmigan"); at 3427ft, a less arduous but rewarding four-hour round-trip from the roadside, a mile or so further on from the visitor centre.

loch's north shore at Fearnan (ⓣ01887/830519, ⓦwww.culdeesbunkhouse.co.uk; ②), has family-friendly bunkhouse and B&B accommodation on a farm which aims to promote permaculture and spiritual values. For something to **eat**, head to *The Courtyard* (ⓣ01887/830763; ⓦwww.taymouthcourtyard.com), an attractive new development beside the Kenmore golf course and caravan site comprising a smart, moderate to expensive restaurant, large bar and well-stocked deli/gift shop.

Killin

The **mountains of Breadalbane** (pronounced "bred–albin", from the Gaelic *braghaid Albin* meaning high country of Scotland) loom over the southern end of Loch Tay. Glens Lochay and Dochart curve north and south respectively from the small town of **KILLIN**, right in the centre of which the River Dochart comes rushing down over the frothy **Falls of Dochart** before disgorging into Loch Tay. A short distance west of Killin the A827 meets the A85, linking the Trossachs (see p.169) with Crianlarich (see p.169), an important waypoint on the roads to Oban, Fort William and the west coast.

There's little to do in Killin itself, but it makes a convenient base for some of the area's best walks. The **tourist office** is located in the ground floor of the old watermill by the falls (March–May & Oct daily 10am–5pm; June & Sept daily 10am–6pm; July & Aug daily 9.30am–6.30pm; ⓣ01567/820254); upstairs is the **Breadalbane Folklore Centre** (same times; £2.50). The centre explores the history and mythology of Breadalbane and holds the thirteen-hundred-year-old "healing stones" of St Fillan, an early Christian missionary who settled in Glen Dochart.

Killin is littered with **B&B**s, including *Fairview House*, halfway along Main Street (ⓣ01567/820667, ⓦwww.fairview-killin.co.uk; ③), a Victorian villa with decent rooms and breakfasts. There's also an SYHA **hostel** (ⓣ0870/004 1131, ⓦwww.syha.org.uk; March–Oct), in a fine old country house just beyond the eastern end of the village, with views out over the loch. The place to grab a bite to **eat** is the *Falls of Dochart Inn*, which is an attractive stone-walled pub right above the famous rapids. If you're interested in **outdoor activities**, make for the helpful and enthusiastic Killin Outdoor Centre and Mountain Shop, on Main Street (Ⓣ01567/820652, Ⓦwww.killinoutdoor.co.uk), which rents out mountain bikes, canoes and tents, sells maps and guidebooks and normally has a local weather forecast chalked up on a blackboard.

Glen Lyon

North of Breadalbane, the mountains tumble down into **Glen Lyon** – at 34 miles long, the longest enclosed glen in Scotland – where, legend has it, the Celtic warrior Fingal built twelve castles. The narrow single track road through the glen starts at **Keltneyburn**, near Kenmore at the northern end of the loch, although a road does struggle over the hills past the Ben Lawers Visitors Centre (see opposite) to **Bridge of Balgie**, halfway down the glen, where the post office has an art gallery and does good tea and scones. Either way, it's a long, winding journey. A few miles on from Keltneyburn, the village of **FORTINGALL** is little more than a handful of pretty thatched cottages, although locals make much of their 5000-year-old yew tree – believed (by them at least) to be the oldest living thing in Europe. The venerable tree can be found in the churchyard, showing its age a little but well looked after, with a timeline nearby listing some of the events the yew has lived through. One of these, bizarrely, is the birth of Pontius Pilate, reputedly the son of a Roman officer stationed near Fortingall in the last years BC. If you're taken by the peace and remoteness of Glen Lyon, you might like to **stay** on a working sheep farm nearby, *Kinnighallen* (Ⓣ01887/830619, Ⓦwww.kinnighallen.co.uk; ❶), a pretty cottage on Duneaves Road not far outside Fortingall.

Highland Perthshire

North of the Tay valley, Perthshire doesn't discard its lush richness immediately, but there are clear indications of the more rugged, barren influences of the Highlands proper. The principal settlements of **Pitlochry** and **Blair Atholl**, both just off the A9, are separated by the narrow gorge of Killiecrankie, a crucial strategic spot in times past for anyone seeking to control movement of cattle or armies from the Highlands to the Lowlands. Though there are reasons to stop in both places, inevitably the greater rewards are to be found further from the main drag, most notably in the winding westward road along the shores of **Loch Tummel** and **Loch Rannoch** past the distinctive peak of **Schiehallion**, which eventually leads to the remote wilderness of **Rannoch Moor**.

Pitlochry

PITLOCHRY has, on the face of it, a lot going for it, not least the backdrop of Ben Vrackie (see box on p.184) and the River Tummel slipping by. It's also undoubtedly a useful place to find somewhere to stay or eat en route to or from the Highlands. However, there's little charm to be found on the main street, filled with crawling traffic and seemingly endless shops selling cut-price woollens, knobbly walking sticks and glass baubles. The town has grown comfortable in its utilitarian, mass-market role and, given its self-appointed role as a "gateway to the Highlands", you'd be perfectly excused if you carried straight on through.

The one attraction with some distinction in the immediate vicinity is the **Edradour Distillery** (March–Oct Mon–Sat 9.30am–6pm, Sun 11.30am–5pm; Nov & Dec Mon–Sat 9.30am–5pm, Sun 11.30am–5pm; Jan & Feb Mon–Sat 10am–4pm, Sun noon–4pm; Ⓦwww.edradour.co.uk), Scotland's smallest, set in an idyllic position tucked into the hills a couple of miles east of Pitlochry on the A924. Although the tour of the distillery itself isn't out of the ordinary, the lack of industralization and the fact that the whole traditional process is done on site and on a small scale gives Edradour more personality than many of its rivals.

It's hard to say the same for Bell's **Blair Athol Distillery**, Perth Road (Easter–Sept Mon–Sat 9.30am–5pm, June–Sept also Sun noon–5pm; Oct Mon–Fri 10am–4pm; Nov–Easter Mon–Fri tours 11am, 1pm & 3pm; £4), at the southern end of the main street (Atholl Road leading to Perth Road) in Pitlochry, where a more modern visitor centre illustrates the process involved in making the Blair Athol Malt, one of the key ingredients of the Bell's blend.

On the western edge of Pitlochry, just across the river, lies Scotland's renowned "Theatre in the Hills", the **Pitlochry Festival Theatre** (Ⓣ01796/484626, Ⓦwww.pitlochry.org.uk). Set up in 1951, the theatre started in a tent on the site of what is now the town curling rink, before moving to the banks of the river in 1981. A variety of productions – mostly mainstream theatre from the resident repertoire company, along with regular music events – are staged in the summer season (May–Oct) and during winter weekends (Nov–April). By day it's worth coming here to wander around **Explorers: the Scottish Plant Hunters' Garden** (daily April–June, Sept & Oct 10am–5pm; July & Aug 10am–7.30pm; £3; tours June–Sept Wed 10.30am & Sun 11.30am & 2.30pm; Ⓦwww.explorersgarden.com), an extended garden and forest area which pays

Walks around Pitlochry

Ordnance Survey Explorer map no. 368

Pitlochry is surrounded by good walking country. The biggest lure has to be **Ben Vrackie** (2733ft), which provides a stunning backdrop for the town and deserves better than a straight up-and-down walk; however, the climb should only be attempted in settled weather conditions, with the right equipment and following the necessary safety precautions (see p.59).

The direct route up the hill follows the course of the Moulin burn past the inn of the same name. Alternatively, a longer but much more rewarding circular route heads north out of Pitlochry, along the edge of attractive Loch Faskally, then up the River Garry to go through the **Pass of Killiecrankie**. This is looked after by the NTS, which has a visitor centre detailing the famous battle here as well as the abundant natural history of the gorge. From the NTS centre walk north up the old A9 and branch off on the small tarred road signposted **Old Faskally**, that twists up under the new A9. The route from here is signposted: continue up the hillside until you finally leave the cultivated land and join a track which zigzags up heathery pasture and then heads across open hillside to reach a saddle by **Loch a'Choire**. Here you join the track from Pitlochry/Moulin that crosses below the dam on the loch and heads directly up the peak. To get back to Pitlochry take the Moulin path back from the loch.

Other worthwhile walks in the area include the trip right round **Loch Faskally**, or you could follow the walk above but turn back from Killiecrankie. A lovely short hill walk from the south end of Pitlochry follows a path through oak forests along the banks of the **Black Spout** burn; when you emerge from the woods it's a few hundred yards further uphill to the lovely Edradour Distillery (see above).

tribute to Scottish botanists and collectors who roamed the world in the eighteenth and nineteenth centuries in search of new plant species. Although many of the trees planted for the opening of the garden in 2003 are a long way from maturity, this is very much a modern rather than traditional garden, with carefully constructed, sinuous trails taking you past some attractive landscapes and features such as an open-air amphitheatre (sometimes used for outdoor performances), sculptures and the David Douglas pavilion, a soaring chamber beautifully constructed from Douglas fir.

A short stroll upstream from the theatre is the **Pitlochry Power Station and Dam**, a massive concrete wall that harnesses the water of the artificial Loch Faskally, just north of the town, for hydroelectric power. The **visitor centre** (April–June & Sept & Oct Mon–Fri 10.30am–5.30pm; July & Aug open daily; £3) offers a pretty thorough run-down on how hydro schemes work, but what draws most attention, apart from the views up the loch, is the **salmon ladder**, a staircase of murky glass boxes through which you might see some nonplussed fish making their way upstream past the dam.

Practicalities

Pitlochry is on the main **train** line to Inverness, and has regular **buses** running from Perth which stop near the train station on Station Road, five minutes' walk up the main street from the **tourist office**, 22 Atholl Rd (July–Sept Mon–Sat 9am–7pm, Sun 9.30am–6pm; April–June & Oct Mon–Sat 9am–6pm, Sun 10am–5pm; Nov–March Mon–Fri 10am–5pm, Sat 10am–4pm; ⓣ01796/472215). The office can sell you a guide to walks in the surrounding area (50p), and also offers an accommodation booking service. For **bike rental**, advice on local cycling routes, as well as general outdoor gear, try Escape Route at 3 Atholl Road (ⓣ01796/473859, ⓦwww.escape-route.biz).

As a well-established holiday town, Pitlochry is packed with grand houses converted into large- and medium-sized **hotels**. The *Moulin Hotel* (ⓣ01796/472196, ⓦwww.moulinhotel.co.uk; ④), at Moulin on the outskirts of Pitlochry along the A924, is a pleasant and popular old travellers' inn with a great bar and its own brewery, while *Craigatin House and Courtyard* (ⓣ01796/472478, ⓦwww.craigatinhouse.co.uk; ④) on the northern section of the main road through town, is an attractive, contemporary **B&B** with large beds, soothing decor and a pleasant garden. Otherwise, try *Ferryman's Cottage*, Port-na-Craig (ⓣ01796/473681, ⓦwww.ferrymanscottage.co.uk; ③), a small, more traditional, but very welcoming B&B in a beautiful position next to the River Tummel and the theatre. Right in the centre *Pitlochry Backpackers Hotel*, 134 Atholl Rd (ⓣ01796/470044, ⓦwww.scotlands-top-hostels.com), is a **hostel** based in a former hotel and offers dorms along with around ten twin and double rooms (①).

Pitlochry is the domain of the tearoom and you have to hunt to find the decent **places to eat**; *The Old Armoury* (ⓣ01796/474281) on a back road between the train station and dam is a civilized restaurant serving expensive taste-of-Scotland-style meals in the evening, with a secluded tea garden which is pleasant for simpler fare during the day. A more moderately priced contemporary bistro can be found in the *Strathgarry Hotel* in the centre of town; the same owners run the *Port-na-craig Inn* which has a beautiful riverside location near the theatre. The best bet for traditional **pub grub** is the *Moulin Inn*, handily placed at the foot of Ben Vrackie. For something a bit smarter altogether, it's worth considering the *Killiecrankie Hotel* (ⓣ01796/473220, ⓦwww.killiecrankiehotel.co.uk; ⑦ B&B, ⑧ dinner, B&B) at Killiecrankie, three miles north of Pitlochry on the old A9, a lovely old manse which serves excellent bar meals and impressive, upmarket Scottish cuisine to both residents and non-residents.

Loch Tummel and Loch Rannoch

West of Pitlochry, the B8019/B846 makes a memorably scenic, if tortuous, traverse of the shores of **Loch Tummel** and then **Loch Rannoch**. These two lochs, celebrated by Harry Lauder in his famous song *The Road to the Isles*, and their adjoining rivers were much changed by the massive hydroelectric schemes built in the 1940s and 50s, yet this is still a spectacular stretch of countryside and one which deserves leisurely exploration. **Queen's View** at the eastern end of Loch Tummel is an obvious vantage point, looking down the loch to the misty peak of **Schiehallion** (3553ft) from the Gaelic meaning "Fairy Mountain", one of the few freestanding hills in Scotland. It's a popular, fairly easy and inspiring mountain to climb, with views on a good day to both sides of Scotland and north to the massed ranks of Highland peaks; the path up starts at Braes of Foss, just off the B846 which links Aberfeldy with Kinloch Rannoch. Expect the climb to the top and back to take around 3–4 hours. At Queen's View, the Forestry Commission's **visitor centre** (April–Oct daily 10am–6pm) interprets the fauna and flora of the area, and also has a tearoom and information on a network of forest walks nearby. A few miles further on, about halfway along Loch Tummel, the cosy *Loch Tummel Inn* (☎01882/634272; ⑤) serves real ale, local venison and salmon and enjoys fine views out across the water and hills.

Beyond Loch Tummel, marking the eastern end of Loch Rannoch, the small community of **KINLOCH RANNOCH** doesn't see a lot of passing trade – fishermen and hill walkers are the most common visitors. Otherwise, the only real destination here is Rannoch Station, a lonely outpost on the Glasgow–Fort William West Highland train line (see p.271), sixteen miles further on. The road goes no further. Here you can contemplate the bleakness of **Rannoch Moor** (see box), a wide expanse of bog, heather and wind-blown pine trees which stretches right across to the imposing entrance to Glen Coe (see box below). A local bus service (#85) from Kinloch Rannoch and a postbus from Pitlochry (#223; departs 8am) provide connections to the railway station.

Rannoch Moor

Rannoch Moor occupies roughly 150 square miles of uninhabited and uninhabitable peat bogs, lochs, heather hillocks, strewn lumps of granite and a few gnarled Caledonian pine, all of it over 1000ft above sea level. Perhaps the most striking thing about the moor is its inaccessibility: one road, between Crianlarich and Glen Coe, skirts its western side, while another struggles west from Pitlochry to reach its eastern edge at Rannoch Station. The only regular form of transport is the West Highland railway, which stops at Rannoch and, a little to the north, Corrour Station, which has no road access at all. There is a simple tearoom in the station building at Rannoch, as well as a pleasant small hotel, the *Moor of Rannoch* (☎01882/633238, ⓦwww.moorofrannoch.co.uk; ⑤), but even these struggle to diminish the feeling of isolation. Corrour, meanwhile, stole an unlikely scene in *Trainspotting* when the four heroes headed here for a taste of the great outdoors; a SYHA hostel is located a mile away on the shores of Loch Ossian (☎0870/004 1139, ⓦwww.syha.org.uk; April–Oct), making the area a great place for hikers seeking somewhere genuinely off the beaten track. From Rannoch Station it's possible to catch the train to Corrour and walk the nine miles back; it's a longer slog west to the *King's House Hotel* (see p.238) at the eastern end of Glen Coe, the dramatic peaks of which poke up above the moor's western horizon. Determined hill walkers will find a clutch of Munros around Corrour, including remote Ben Alder (3765ft), high above the forbidding shores of Loch Ericht.

In Kinloch Rannoch, *Bunrannoch House* (Ⓣ01882/632407, Ⓦwww.bunrannoch.co.uk; ③), a Victorian former shooting lodge, with lovely views, is a good bet for **accommodation** (they also serve evening meals); otherwise, dominating the main square of the village, the huntin', fishin' and shootin' *Dunalastair Hotel* (Ⓣ01882/632218, Ⓦwww.dunalastair.co.uk; ⑥) has lots of rooms and a pricey restaurant. Though uncomplicated, the nearby community-run *Post Taste* tearoom is open every day all year round and is a cheery place for snacks, coffee, takeaway and evening **meals** (not Sun).

North of Pitlochry

Four miles north of Pitlochry, the A9 cuts through the **Pass of Killiecrankie**, a breathtaking wooded gorge which falls away to the River Garry below. This dramatic setting was the site of the **Battle of Killiecrankie** in 1689, when the Jacobites quashed the forces of General Mackay. Legend has it that one soldier of the Crown, fleeing for his life, made a miraculous jump across the 18ft **Soldier's Leap**, an impossibly wide chasm halfway up the gorge. Queen Victoria, visiting here 160 years later, contented herself with recording the beauty of the area in her diary. Exhibits at the slick NTS **visitor centre** (daily: April–Oct 10am–5.30pm; Ⓣ01796/473233; parking £2) recall the battle and examine the gorge in detail. The surroundings here are thick, mature forest, full of interesting plants and creatures – the local ranger often sets off on free **guided walks** which leave from the visitor centre and are well worth joining if you're around at the right time; the centre will let you know what's scheduled when.

Blair Atholl

Three miles north of Killiecrankie, the village of **BLAIR ATHOLL** makes for a much quieter and more idiosyncratic stop than Pitlochry. At the **Atholl Estates Information Centre** (April–Oct daily 9am–4.45pm; Ⓣ01796/481646, Ⓦwww.athollestatesrangerservice.co.uk) you can get details of the extensive network of local walks and bike rides as well as interesting information on surrounding flora and fauna. Right beside this the modest **Atholl Country Life Museum** (May–Sept daily 1.30–5pm, July & Aug opens 10am; £3; Ⓣ01796/481232) offers a homespun and nostalgic look at the history of life in the local glens; in among the old photos and artefacts the star attraction is a stuffed, full-size Highland cow. The grand but reasonably priced *Atholl Arms Hotel* (Ⓣ01796/481205, Ⓦwww.athollarms.co.uk; ④) is the best place in town for a drink or a bar meal; alongside it, in the old petrol station, is a second-hand bookshop called Atholl Browse (a pun on "Atholl Brose", a sickly sweet, whisky-laced dessert). Nearby, you can wander round the **Water Mill** on Ford Road (April–Oct daily 10.30am–5.30pm; £1.50), which dates back to 1613, and witness flour being milled; better still, you can enjoy home-baked scones and light lunches in its pleasant timber-beamed tearoom.

Blair Castle

By far the most important and eye-catching building in these parts, **Blair Castle** (April–Oct daily 9.30am–last admission 4.30pm; Nov–March Tues & Sat only 9.30am–12.30pm; £6.90, grounds only £2.20; Ⓦwww.blair-castle.co.uk) is reached by a driveway leading from the centre of Blair Atholl village. Seat of the Atholl dukedom, this whitewashed, turreted castle, surrounded by parkland and dating from 1269, presents an impressive sight as you approach up the drive. A piper may be playing in front of the castle, one of the Atholl Highlanders, a select group retained by the duke as his private army – a unique privilege afforded to him by Queen Victoria, who stayed here in 1844.

Thirty or so rooms are open for inspection, and display a selection of paintings, antique furniture and plasterwork that is sumptuous in the extreme. Highlights are the soaring **entrance hall**, with every spare inch of wood panelling covered in weapons of some description; the **Tapestry Room**, on the top floor of the original Cumming's Tower, adorned with Brussels tapestries and containing an ostentatious four-poster bed, topped with vases of ostrich feathers which originally came from the first duke's suite at Holyrood Palace in Edinburgh; and the vast **ballroom**, with its timber roof, antlers and mixture of portraits.

As impressive as the castle's interior are its surroundings: Highland cows graze the ancient landscaped grounds and peacocks strut in front of the castle. There is a **riding stable** from where you can take treks, and formal woodland walks take you to various interesting parts of the castle grounds, including the neglected, walled "Hercules" water garden named after the statue which overlooks it, and the towering giant conifers of Diana's Grove. There is also a busy but attractive caravan and **camping** park (ⓣ01796/481263, ⓦwww.blaircastlecaravanpark.co.uk) in the grounds.

Drumochter and Dalwhinnie

A few miles north of Blair Atholl, insistent signs point the way to the House of Bruar, a sprawling emporium of tweeds, waxed jackets and tasty-looking foodstuffs which acts as the final outpost of the Perthshire country set before the A9 sweeps northward over the barren **Pass of Drumochter**, often affected by snowfalls in winter. Beyond this the bleak little village of **Dalwhinnie** has a striking distillery with whitewashed buildings topped by copper pagoda "hats", but little else to draw you in. It lies at the northern end of **Loch Ericht**, around which are some of the most remote high hills in Scotland, including spooky Ben Alder. The scenery all the way is inspiring and desolate, in equal measure. Not far beyond Dalwhinnie you encounter the neighbouring villages of Kingussie and Newtonmore, the start of the Strathspey region (see p.213).

The Grampian Highlands

The high country in the northern part of the county of **Angus**, east of the A9 and north of the Firth of Tay, holds some of the Central Highlands' most pleasant scenery and is relatively free of tourists, most of whom tend to bypass it on their way north. Here the long fingers of the **Angus glens** – heather-covered hills tumbling down to rushing rivers – are overlooked by the southern peaks of the Grampian mountains. Each has its own feel and devotees, **Glen Clova** being, deservedly, one of the most popular, along with **Glen Shee**, which attracts large numbers of people to its ski slopes. Handsome market towns like **Kirriemuir** and **Blairgowrie** are good bases for the area, while the tiny village of **Meigle** at the southern end of Glen Isla has Scotland's finest collection of carved Pictish stones.

North of the Angus glens and west of the city of Aberdeen **Deeside** is a fertile yet ruggedly attractive area made famous by the royal family, who have favoured the estate at **Balmoral** as a summer holiday retreat ever since Queen Victoria fell in love with it back in the 1840s. Hemmed in by imposing mountains, Deeside and the **Don Valley** to the north boast a terrific collection of **castles**, some elegant residences but many the sparse, functional garrisons which were used to guard the routes into the high country of the Cairngorms, often blocked by snow in winter and remote and desolate at any time of year.

The Angus glens

Immediately north of Dundee, the low-lying Sidlaw Hills divide the city from the rich agricultural region of **Strathmore**, whose string of tidy market towns lies on a fertile strip along the southernmost edge of the heather-covered lower slopes of the Grampian Mountains. These towns act as gateways to the **Angus glens** (Ⓦwww.angusglens.co.uk), a series of tranquil valleys penetrated by single-track roads and offering some of the most rugged and majestic landscapes in northeast Scotland. It's a rain-swept, wind-blown, sparsely populated area, whose roads become impassable with the first snows, sometimes as early as October, and where the summers see clouds of ferocious midges. Nevertheless, most of the glens, particularly **Glen Clova**, are well and truly on the tourist circuit, with the rolling hills and dales attracting hikers, bird-watchers and botanists in the summer, grouse shooters and deerhunters in autumn and a growing number of skiers in winter. The most useful road through the glens is the A93, which cuts through **Glen Shee**, linking Blairgowrie to Braemar on Deeside (see p.200). It's pretty dramatic stuff, threading its way over Britain's highest main-road pass, the **Cairnwell Pass** (2199ft).

Public transport in the region is limited: to get up the glens you'll have to rely on the **postbuses** from Blairgowrie (for Glen Shee) and Kirriemuir (for glens Clova and Prosen).

Blairgowrie and Glen Shee

The upper reaches of **Glen Shee**, the most dramatic and best known of the Angus glens, are dominated by its **ski fields**, ranged over four mountains above the Cairnwell mountain pass. During the season (Dec–March), ski lifts and tows give access to gentle beginners' slopes, while experienced skiers can try the more intimidating Tiger run. In summer it's all a bit sad, with lifeless chairlifts and bare, scree-covered slopes, although hang-gliders take advantage of the crosswinds between the mountains and there are some excellent hiking and mountain-biking routes.

To get to Glen Shee from the south you'll pass through the well-heeled little town of **BLAIRGOWRIE**, set among raspberry fields on the glen's southernmost tip and a good place to pick up information and plan your activities. Strictly two communities, Blairgowrie and Rattray, situated on either side of the river Ericht, the town's modest claim to fame is that St Ninian once camped at Wellmeadow, a pleasant grassy triangle in the town centre. If you've time to kill here, wander up the leafy river bank past a series of old mill buildings. Altogether more ambitious is the sixty-four-mile **Cateran Trail**, a long-distance footpath which starts in Blairgowrie then heads off on a long loop into the glens to the north following some of the drove roads used by caterans, or cattle thieves. It's a four- to five-day tramp, though of course it's possible to walk shorter sections of the way. You can get a map and more information from the tourist office, or by going to Ⓦwww.pkct.org/caterantrail.

Blairgowrie **tourist office** (April–June & Sept–Oct Mon–Sat 9.30am–5pm, Sun 11am–3pm; July & Aug Mon–Sat 9.30am–6.30pm, Sun 11am–4pm; Nov–March Mon–Sat 10am–4pm; ⓣ01250/872960, ⓦwww.perthshire.co.uk), on the high side of the Wellmeadow, can help with **accommodation**. A number of Blairgowrie's grand houses offer B&B, among them the attractive *Duncraggan* (ⓣ01250/872082; ❷) on Perth Road and *Heathpark House* (ⓣ01250/870700, ⓦwww.heathparkhouse.com; ❸) on the Coupar Angus Road. **Camping** is available at the year-round *Blairgowrie Holiday Park* on Rattray's Hatton Road (ⓣ01250/876666), walking distance from the Wellmeadow.

Blairgowrie boasts plenty of places to **eat**: *Cargills* by the river on Lower Mill Street (ⓣ01250/876735; closed Tues) is the best bet for a moderately priced formal meal or civilized coffee and cakes; for less elaborate food and takeaways, there's the inexpensive *Dome Restaurant*, just behind the tourist office, which has been run by two local Italian families since the 1920s. For a good local **pub** try the *Ericht Alehouse* on Wellmeadow, which serves real ale and plays real music, or head six miles north of town on the A93 to the welcoming *Bridge of Cally Hotel* (ⓣ01250/886231, ⓦwww.bridgeofcallyhotel.com; ❺) which serves food all day, plus real ale by an open fire. Back in Blairgowrie you can rent **bikes** from Crichton's Cycle Hire, 87 Perth St (ⓣ01250/876100).

Nearly twenty miles north of Blairgowrie, the small settlement of **SPITTAL OF GLENSHEE** (the names derives from the same root as "hospital", indicating a refuge), though ideally situated for skiing, has little to commend it other than the busy *Gulabin Bunkhouse* on the A93, run by Cairnwell Mountain Sports (ⓣ01250/885255, ⓦwww.cairnwellmountainsports.co.uk), which rents out skis and bikes and offers instruction in activities such as kayaking and mountaineering. Tucked away among the hills behind Spittal, *Dalmunzie House* (ⓣ01250/885224, ⓦwww.dalmunzie.com; ❼) is a lovely Highland retreat in the theme of a sporting lodge. From Spittal the road climbs another five miles or so to the ski centre at the crest of the Cairnwell Pass.

Blairgowrie is well linked by hourly **bus** #57 to both Perth and Dundee. To travel up Glen Shee, you'll have to rely on the **postbus**, which leaves town at 7.30am (not Sun) and returns from the Spittal of Glenshee at 12.30pm.

Skiing at Glen Shee

Scotland's **ski resorts** may not amount to much more than gentle training slopes in comparison with those of the Alps or North America, but they make for a fun day out for anyone from beginners to experienced skiers interested in experiencing the conditions. The strongest card of all the resorts is probably their scenic surroundings, and given that **Glen Shee** is both the most extensive and the most accessible of Scotland's ski areas, just over two hours from both Glasgow and Edinburgh, it's as good an introduction as any to the sport in Scotland.

For information, contact Ski Glenshee (ⓣ01339/741320, ⓦwww.ski-glenshee.co.uk), who also offer ski rental and lessons. In addition, lessons, skis and boards are available from Cairnwell Mountain Sports (ⓣ01250/885255, ⓦwww.cairnwellmountainsports.co.uk), at the Spittal of Glenshee. **Ski rental** starts at around £15 a day, while lessons are around £15 per half-day. **Lift passes** cost £22 per day or £88 for a five-day (Mon–Fri) ticket. For the latest snow and **weather conditions**, phone the centre itself or check out the Ski Scotland website (ⓦski.visitscotland.com). Should you be more interested in **cross-country** skiing, there are some good touring areas in the vicinity; contact Cairnwell Mountain Sports (see above) or Braemar Mountain Sports (ⓣ01339/741242, ⓦwww.braemarmountainsports.com) for information and equipment rental.

Meigle and Glen Isla

Fifteen miles northwest of Dundee on the B954 lies the tiny settlement of **MEIGLE**, home to Scotland's most important collection of early Christian and Pictish inscribed stones. Housed in a modest former schoolhouse, the **Meigle Museum** (April–Sept daily 9.30am–6.30pm; HS; £2.20) displays some thirty pieces dating from the seventh to the tenth centuries, all found in and around the nearby churchyard. The majority are either gravestones that would have lain flat, or cross slabs inscribed with the sign of the cross, usually standing. Most impressive is the 7ft-tall great cross slab, said to be the gravestone of Guinevere, wife of King Arthur, carved on one side with a portrayal of Daniel surrounded by lions, a beautifully executed equestrian group, and mythological creatures including a dragon and a centaur. On the other side various beasts are surmounted by the "ring of glory", a wheel containing a cross carved and decorated in high relief. The exact meaning and purpose of the stones and their enigmatic symbols is obscure, as is the reason why so many of them were found at Meigle. The most likely theory suggests that Meigle was once an important ecclesiastical centre which attracted secular burials of prominent Picts.

Glen Isla

Three miles north of Meigle is **Alyth**, near which, legend has it, Guinevere was held captive by Mordred. The sleepy village lies at the south end of **Glen Isla**, which runs parallel to Glen Shee and is linked to it by the A926. Dominated by Mount Blair (2441ft), Glen Isla is a lot less dramatic than its sister glens, and suffers from an excess of angular conifers alongside great bald chunks of hillside waiting to be planted. As you head north along the B954, the River Isla narrows and then plunges some 60ft into a deep gorge to produce the classically pretty waterfall of **Reekie Linn**, or "smoking fall", so called because of the water-mist produced when the fall hits a ledge and bounces a further 20ft into a deep pool known as the Black Dub. Just after this, a side road leads east to the pleasant Loch of Lintrathen, beside which is the *Lochside Lodge* (Ⓣ01575/560340, Ⓦwww.lochsidelodge.com; ❺), a cosy bar set in a converted steading full of old pews and farming implements, with a noted restaurant alongside and bedrooms in the old hay loft. Heading back into the glen proper, you'll come on the tiny hamlet of **KIRKTON OF GLENISLA** ten miles or so up the glen. Here, the cosy *Glenisla Hotel* (Ⓣ01575/582223, Ⓦwww.glenisla-hotel.com; ❸) is great for classy home-made bar food and convivial drinking. There are some relatively easy **hiking** trails in the nearby Glenisla forest, while just before Kirkton, a turn-off on the right-hand side leads northeast up a long bumpy road to the unexpected *Glenmarkie Guesthouse Health Spa and Riding Centre* (Ⓣ01575/582295 Ⓦwww.glenmarkie.co.uk; ❸), which offers both pedicures and pony trekking.

Transport connections into the glen are limited: Alyth is on the main bus routes linking Blairgowrie with Dundee and Kirriemuir, while hourly bus #57 from Dundee to Perth passes through Meigle. Transport up to Kirkton is limited to a postbus which leaves Blairgowrie at 7am (not Sun) and travels via Alyth (confirm on Ⓣ01250/872766).

Kirriemuir and glens Prosen, Clova and Doll

The sandstone town of **KIRRIEMUIR**, known locally as Kirrie, is set on a hill six miles northwest of Forfar on the cusp of glens Clova and Prosen. Despite the influx of hunters up for the "season", it's still a pretty special place, a haphazard confection of narrow closes, twisting wynds and steep braes. The main cluster of streets have all the appeal of an old film set, with their old-fashioned bars, tiled butcher's shop, tartan outlets and haberdasheries somehow managing to avoid being contrived and quaint – although the recent recobbling of the town centre around a twee statue of Peter Pan undermines this somewhat.

Peter Pan's presence is justified, however, since Kirrie was the birthplace of his creator, **J.M. Barrie**. A local handloom-weaver's son, Barrie first came to notice with his series of novels about "Thrums", a village based on his hometown, in particular *A Window in Thrums* and his third novel, *The Little Minister.* The story of Peter Pan, the little boy who never grew up, was penned by Barrie in 1904 – some say as a response to a strange upbringing dominated by the memory of his older brother, who died as a child. **Barrie's birthplace**, a plain little whitewashed cottage at 9 Brechin Rd (April–June & Sept Sat–Wed noon–5pm; July & Aug Mon–Sat 11am–5pm, Sun 1–5pm; NTS; £5, includes entrance to the camera obscura), has been opened up as a visitor attraction, with a series of small rooms decorated as they would have been during Barrie's childhood, as well as displays about his life and works. The wash-house outside – romantically billed as Barrie's first "theatre" – was apparently the model for the house built by the Lost Boys for Wendy in Never-Never Land. Despite being offered a prestigious plot at London's Westminster Abbey, Barrie chose to be buried in Kirrie, and the unassuming family grave can be seen in the town cemetery, a short walk from the **camera obscura** (April–Sept daily noon–5pm depending on weather conditions; NTS; £3.50, or £5 combined ticket with Barrie's birthplace), in the old cricket pavilion above town just off West Hill Road. This unexpected treasure was donated to the town in 1930 by Barrie, and offers splendid views of Strathmore and the glens. Another local son who attracts a handful of rather different pilgrims is **Bon Scott** of the rock band AC/DC, who was born and lived here before emigrating to Australia.

More on Scott, as well as other notable residents of the town, can be found at Kirriemuir's **Gateway to the Glens Museum** (Mon–Wed, Fri & Sat 10am–5pm, Thurs 1–5pm; free), in the old Town House on the main square. The oldest building in Kirrie, it has seen service as a tolbooth, court, jail, post office, police station and chemist; these days you can find two floors of information and exhibits on the town and the Angus Glens, including scale models of Kirrie in 1604, the year the tolbooth was erected, and one of Glen Clova, showing the relief of the hills.

Kirrie's helpful **tourist office** is in Cumberland Close (April–June & Sept Mon–Sat 10am–5pm; July & Aug Mon–Sat 9.30am–5.30pm; ⓣ01575/574097), in the new development behind *Visocchi's* in the main square. **Accommodation** is available at the attractively upgraded *Airlie Arms*, St Malcolm's Wynd (ⓣ01575/572847, ⓦwww.airliearms-hotel.co.uk; ❹), while on the edge of town, and offering a taste of the rolling countryside, is the working *Muirhouses Farm* (ⓣ01575/573128, ⓦwww.muirhousesfarm.co.uk; ❸). *Visocchi's* is great for daytime **snacks** and ice cream, while the *Airlie* and *Hook's Hotel* on Bank Street both serve good food in the evening. Of the **pubs**, *Hook's Hotel* or, opposite the museum, *Three, Bellies Brae*, are the most lively.

Postbuses into glens Clova and Prosen leave from the main post office on Reform Street at 8.30am (not Sun). A second Glen Clova bus leaves at 3.10pm (Mon–Fri), but only goes as far as Clova village before returning to Kirriemuir. The hourly #20 bus runs from Kirriemuir High Street to Forfar and Dundee.

Glen Prosen

Five miles north of Kirrie, the low-key hamlet of **DYKEHEAD** marks the point where **Glen Prosen** and Glen Clova divide. A mile or so up Glen Prosen, you'll find the house where Captain Scott and fellow explorer Doctor Wilson planned their ill-fated trip to Antarctica in 1910–11, with a roadside **stone cairn** commemorating the expedition. From here on, Glen Prosen remains essentially a quiet wooded backwater, with all the wild and rugged splendour of the other glens but without the crowds. To explore the area thoroughly you need to go on foot, but a good road circuit can be made by crossing the river at the tiny village of **GLENPROSEN** and returning to Kirriemuir along the western side of the glen via Pearsie. Alternatively, the reasonably easy four-mile **Minister's Path** (so called because the local minister would walk this way twice every Sunday to conduct services) links Prosen with Clova. It is clearly marked and leaves from near the church in the village.

Glen Clova and Glen Doll

With its stunning cliffs, heather slopes and valley meadows, **Glen Clova** – which in the north becomes **Glen Doll** – is one of the loveliest of the Angus glens. Although it can get unpleasantly congested in peak season, the area is still remote enough to enable you to leave the crowds with little effort. Wildlife is abundant, with deer on the mountains, wild hares and even grouse and the occasional buzzard. The meadow flowers on the valley floor and arctic plants (including great splashes of white and purple saxifrage) on the rocks also make it something of a botanist's paradise.

The B955 from Dykehead and Kirriemuir divides at the Gella bridge over the swift-coursing River South Esk (unofficially, road traffic is encouraged to use the western branch of the road for travel up the glen, and the eastern side going down). Six miles north of Gella, the two branches of the road join up once more at the hamlet of **CLOVA**, little more than the hearty *Glen Clova Hotel* (Ⓣ01575/550350, Ⓦwww.clova.com; ⑤), which also has a refurbished bunkhouse (£11 per night) and a private fishing loch. Meals and real ale are available in the lively *Climbers' Bar* at the side of the hotel. An excellent, if fairly strenuous, four-hour walk from behind the old school at the back of the hotel leads up into the mountains and around the lip of **Loch Brandy**, which legend predicts will one day flood and drown the valley below.

North from Clova village, the road turns into a rabbit-infested lane coursing along the riverside for four miles to the car park, a useful starting point for numerous superb **walks** (see box on p.194). There are, however, no other facilities following the recent closure of both the campsite and SYHA hostel.

△ Mountain-biking in Glen Clova

Walks from Glen Doll

Ordnance Survey Explorer maps nos. 388 & 387.

These walks are some of the main routes across the Grampians from the Angus glens to Deeside, many of which follow well-established old drovers' roads. A number of them cross the royal estate of Balmoral, and Prince Charles's favourite mountain – Lochnagar – can be seen from all angles. The walks all begin from the car park at the end of the tarred road where Glen Clova meets Glen Doll; all routes should always be approached with care, and you should make sure to follow the usual safety precautions.

Capel Mounth to Ballater (15 miles; 7hr). Head across the bridge from the car park turning right after a mile when the track crosses the Cald Burn. Out of the wood, the path zigzags its way up fierce slopes before levelling out on the moorland plateau. Soon descending, the path crosses a scree near the eastern end of Loch Muick. With the loch to your left, walk down along the scree till you reach the River Muick, crossing the bridge to take the quiet track along the river's northern shore to Ballater.

Capel Mounth round-trip (15 miles; 8hr). Follow the above route to Loch Muick, then take the path down to loch level and double back on yourself along the loch's southern shore. When the track crosses the Black Burn, either take the steep left fork or continue along the shore for another mile, heading up the dramatic Streak of Lightning path that follows Corrie Chash. Both paths meet at the ruined stables below Sandy Hillock. Just beyond, take the path to the left, descending rapidly to the waterfall by the bridge at Bachnagairn, where a gentle burn-side track leads the three miles back to Glen Doll car park.

Jock's Road to Braemar (14 miles; 7hr). Take the road north from the car park; after almost a mile, follow the signposted Jock's Road to the right, keeping on the northern bank of the burn. Pass a barn, Davey's Shelter, below Cairn Lunkhard and continue onto a wide ridge towards the path's summit at Crow Craigies (3018ft). From here, the path bumps down over scree slopes to the head of Loch Callater. Go either way round the loch, and follow the Callater Burn at the other end, eventually hitting the main A93 two miles short of Braemar.

Edzell and Glen Esk

Travelling around Angus, you can hardly fail to notice the difference between organic settlements and planned towns built by landowners who forcibly rehoused local people in order to keep them under control, especially after the Jacobite uprisings. One of the better examples of the latter, **EDZELL**, five miles north of Brechin on the B966 (and linked to it by buses #21, #29C and #30), was cleared and rebuilt with Victorian rectitude a mile to the west of its original site in the 1840s. Through the Dalhousie Arch at the entrance to the village the long, wide and ruler-straight main street is lined with prim nineteenth-century buildings, now doing a roaring trade as genteel teashops and antique emporia.

The original village (identifiable from the cemetery and surrounding grassy mounds) lay immediately to the west of the wonderfully explorable red sandstone ruins of **Edzell Castle** (April–Sept daily 9.30am–6.30pm; Oct–March Sun–Wed 9.30am–4.30pm; HS; £3.30), itself a mile west of the planned village. The main part of the old castle is a good example of a comfortable tower house, whose main priority became luxurious living rather than defence, with some intricate decorative corbelling on the roof, a vast fireplace in the first-floor hall and numerous telltale signs of building from different ages. However, it's the **pleasance garden** overlooked by the castle tower that makes a visit to Edzell essential, especially in late spring and early to mid-summer. The garden was built by Sir David Lindsay in 1604, at the height of the optimistic Renaissance, and its refinement and extravagance are evident. The walls contain sculpted images of erudition: the Planetary Deities on the east side, the Liberal Arts (including a decapitated figure of Music) on the south and, under floods of lobelia, the Cardinal Virtues on the west wall. In the centre of the garden, low-cut box hedges spell out the family mottoes and enclose voluminous beds of roses.

Four miles southwest of Edzell, lying either side of the lane to Bridgend which can be reached either by carrying on along the road past the castle or by taking the narrow road at the southern end of Edzell village, are the **Caterthuns**, twin Iron Age hill forts that were probably occupied at different times. The surviving ramparts on the White Caterthun (978ft) – easily reached from the small car park below – are the most impressive, and this is thought to be the later fort, occupied by the Picts in the first few centuries AD. Views from both, over the mountains to the north and the plains and foothills to the south, are stunning.

Just north of Edzell, a fifteen-mile road climbs alongside the River North Esk to form **Glen Esk**, the most easterly of the Angus glens and, like the others, sparsely populated. Ten miles along the Glen, the excellent **Glenesk Folk Museum** (Easter–May Sat & Sun noon–6pm; June to mid-Oct daily noon–6pm; £2; entry arrangements subject to change once refurbishment is completed), brings together records, costumes, photographs, maps and tools from the Angus glens, depicting the often harsh way of life for the inhabitants. The museum is housed in a recently redeveloped shooting lodge known as The Retreat, and is run independently and enthusiastically by the local community. Inside there's also a gift shop and a noted tearoom – due reward for those who have endured the winding glen road. There are some excellent **hiking** routes further up the glen, including one to Queen Victoria's Well in Glen Mark and another up Mount Keen, Scotland's most easterly Munro.

In Edzell, *Alexandra Lodge*, Inveriscandye Road (Ⓣ01356/648266, Ⓦwww.alexandralodge.co.uk; April–Oct; ❸) is a decent **B&B**, while the most attractive of the **hotels** in town, the *Panmure Arms* (Ⓣ01356/648950, Ⓦwww.panmurearmshotel.co.uk; ❺), at the far end of the main street near the turn-off to the castle, has recently been smartened up and offers sizeable rooms and predictable bar meals. Further up the glen, one and a half miles north of the village, you can **camp** at the small, child-friendly *Glenesk Caravan Park* (Ⓣ01356/648565; April–Oct), while at **INVERMARK**, near the head of the Glen and a good jumping-off point for various hiking routes, is *The House of Mark* (Ⓣ01356/670315, Ⓦwww.thehouseofmark.com; ❸), a former manse in a lovely setting, which can arrange evening meals featuring local game and home baking.

Deeside

More commonly known as **Royal Deeside**, the land stretching west from Aberdeen along the River Dee revels in its connections with the royal family, who have regularly holidayed here, at **Balmoral**, since Queen Victoria bought the estate. Eighty thousand Scots turned out to welcome her on her first visit in 1848, but some weren't so charmed: one local journalist remarked that the area was about to be "desolated by cockneys and other horrible reptiles". Today, most locals are fiercely protective of the royal connection.

Many of Victoria's guests weren't as enthusiastic about Deeside as she was: Count von Moltke, then aide-de-camp to Prince Frederick William of Prussia, observed, "It is very astonishing that the Royal Power of England should reside amid this lonesome, desolate, cold mountain scenery", while Tsar Nicholas II whined, "The weather is awful, rain and wind every day and on top of it no luck at all – I haven't killed a stag yet." However, Victoria adored the place, and the woods were said to remind Prince Albert of Thuringia, his homeland.

Deeside is undoubtedly handsome in a fierce, craggy, Scottish way, and the royal presence has helped keep a lid on any unattractive mass development. The villages strung along the A93, the main route through the area, are well heeled and have something of an old-fashioned air. Facilities for visitors hereabouts are first-class, with a number of bunkhouses and hostels, some decent hotels and plenty of castles and grounds to snoop around. It's also an excellent area for **outdoor activities**, with hiking routes into both the Grampian and Cairngorm mountains, and good mountain biking, horse riding and skiing.

Stagecoach Bluebird **bus** #201 from Aberdeen regularly chugs along the A93, serving most of the towns on the way to Braemar.

Drum Castle to Glen Tanar

West of Aberdeen, you'll pass through low-lying land of mixed farming, forestry and suburbs. Easily reached from the main road are the castles of **Drum** and **Crathes**, both interesting fortified houses with pleasant gardens, while the uneventful town of **Banchory** serves as gateway to the heart of Royal Deeside. Further west, **Glen Tanar** is a great example of the area's attractive blend of forest, river and mountain scenery.

Drum Castle and Crathes Castle

Ten miles west of Aberdeen on the A93, **Drum Castle** (daily: April, May & Sept 12.30–5.30pm; June–Aug 10am–5.30pm; grounds 9.30am–sunset all year; NTS; £8, grounds only £3) stands in a clearing in the ancient **woods of Drum**, made up of the splendid pines and oaks that covered this whole area before the shipbuilding industry precipitated mass forest clearance. The castle itself combines a 1619 Jacobean mansion with Victorian extensions and the

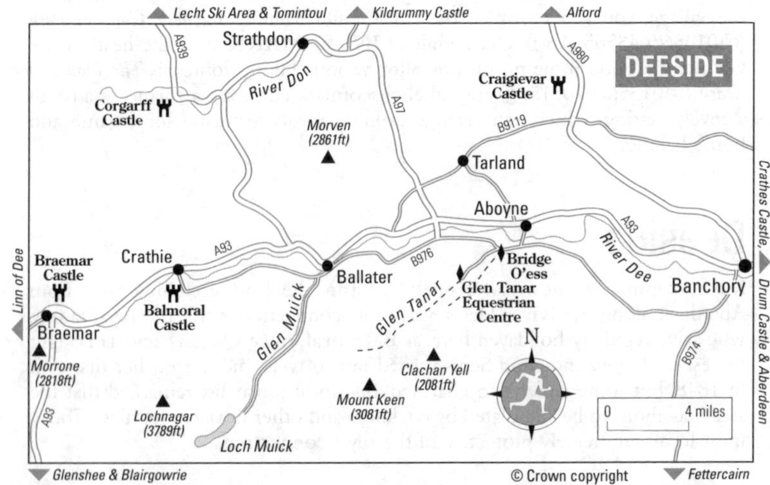

original, huge thirteenth-century keep, which has been restored and reopened. Given by Robert the Bruce to his armour-bearer, William de Irvine, in 1323 for services rendered at Bannockburn, the castle remained in Irvine hands for 24 generations until the NTS took over in 1976. The main part of the house is Victorian in character, with grand, antique-filled rooms and lots of family portraits. The finest room is the library, within the ancient tower; you'll get an even better sense of the medieval atmosphere of the place by climbing up to the upper levels of the Tower, with the battlements offering views out over the forest.

Further along the A93, four miles west of Drum Castle, **Crathes Castle** (daily: April–Sept 10am–5.30pm; Oct 10am–4.30pm; NTS; £10) is a splendid sixteenth-century granite tower house adorned with flourishes such as overhanging turrets, gargoyles and conical roofs. Its thick walls, narrow windows and tiny rooms loaded with heavy old furniture make Crathes rather claustrophobic, but it is still worth visiting for some wonderful painted ceilings, either still in their original form or sensitively restored; the earliest dates from 1602. The grounds include an impressive walled garden complete with yew hedges clipped into various shapes.

By the entrance to Crathes, a cluster of restored stone cottages house various **craft shops** and **galleries** as well as the *Milton* (Ⓣ01330/844566, Ⓦwww.themilton.co.uk; closed Sun & Mon evening), an unexpectedly upmarket **restaurant** serving ambitious, expensive à la carte meals as well as a lighter all-day menu. Beside the cottages, two old railway carriages mark the base camp for a bunch of enthusiasts who are busy rebuilding a stretch of the old Royal Deeside **railway line** – in time they hope to have a small stretch between here and Banchory open for trips.

Banchory

BANCHORY, meaning "fair hollow", is a one-street town which essentially acts as a gateway into rural Deeside. The small local **museum** on Bridge Street, behind High Street (May–Sept Mon–Sat 11am–1pm & 2–4.30pm, plus July & Aug Sun 2–4.30pm; April & Oct Sat 11am–1pm & 2–4.30pm; free), may warrant half an hour or so if you're a fan of local boy James Scott Skinner, renowned fiddler and composer of such tunes as *The Bonnie Lass o'Bon Accord*.

The **tourist office** in the museum (April–June & Sept Mon–Sat 9.30am–1pm & 2–5.30pm; July & Aug Mon–Fri 9.30am–6pm, Sat 9.30am–1pm & 2–6pm, Sun 1–6pm; Oct Mon–Sat 10am–1pm & 2–5pm; Ⓣ01330/822000) can provide information on walking and fishing in the area. There are one or two places **to stay** in town, including the smart *Tor-Na-Coille Hotel* (Ⓣ01330/822242, Ⓦwww.tornacoille.com; ❼), once a retreat for Charlie Chaplin and his family, though there's an understandable temptation to push on into the attractive Deeside countryside. If you do hang around, the *Burnett Arms Hotel*, a friendly former coaching inn at 25 High St (Ⓣ01330/824944, Ⓦwww.burnettarms.co.uk; ❺), has standard rooms but does Banchory's best pub grub, and there are a couple of good delis, including the Dee Larder on Watson Lane, which leads off the main street.

Aboyne and Glen Tanar

Twelve miles west of Banchory on the A93, **ABOYNE** is a typically well-mannered Deeside village at the mouth of **Glen Tanar**, which runs southwest from here for ten miles or so deep into the Grampian hills. The glen, with few steep gradients and some glorious stands of mature Caledonian pine, is ideal for

Exploring Glen Tanar

Ordnance Survey Explorer map no. 395.

Lying to the south of the Deeside town of Aboyne, the easily navigated forest tracks of **Glen Tanar** offer a taste of the changing landscape of the northeastern Highlands, passing through relatively prosperous farmland along the River Dee, through ancient woodland and then to remote grouse moors and bleak hillsides in the heart of the Grampian mountains. Flatter than, and without the vehicle traffic of, Glen Muick to the west, Glen Tanar is a great place to explore on mountain bike, although there is plenty of opportunity for walking and there's also an **equestrian centre** (Ⓣ01339/886448) in the glen, offering one- and two-hour riverside and forest horse trails.

Leave the south Deeside road (B976) at **Bridge o' Ess**, one and a half miles southwest of Aboyne. Here you can enter the forest on the south side of the Water of Tanar, or carry on along a tarred road on the north side for two miles to a car park. Immediately across the river from this is a **ranger information point**, where you can pick up details on the various routes in the glen, as well as some background on the flora and fauna of the area. If you're on **foot**, the best idea is to strike out along the clear forest tracks that follow both sides of the river, connected at various points by attractive stone bridges, allowing for easy round-trips. Most of the time you are surrounded by superb old pine woodland, some of which is naturally seeded remnants of ancient Caledonian forest, with broadleafs in evidence along the river, and wild flowers and fungi when in season. If you're on a **bike**, stick to the track on the north side of the river: not far past the small wooden shelter known as Half Way Hut, you emerge from the forest, with the glen-sides closing in, and **Mount Keen** (3081ft), the most easterly of Scotland's 3000-foot mountains, looming ahead. The end of the glen, at **Shiel of Glentanar**, is eight miles from the car park, from where you can either retrace your path or take to the hills by following the steep track round the back of Clachan Yell. It should take around six hours return, following the main track, or eight hours going via Clachan Yell. The more ambitious can pick up the Mounth road (see p.194) at Shiel of Glentanar, which heads up and over Mount Keen to Invermark at the head of Glen Esk (see p.195).

walking, mountain biking or horse riding; the ranger information point two miles into the glen off the B976 has details of suitable routes, while the Glen Tanar Equestrian Centre (Ⓣ01339/886448) offers one- and two-hour horse rides. Aboyne has some handy retreats for **food** after a day's activity: the excellent *Black Faced Sheep* coffee shop just off the main road serves home-baking and light lunches, while the *Boat Inn* on Charlestown Road, right beside the bridge over the Dee, does good quality pub grub.

Ballater and Balmoral

Ten miles west of Aboyne is the neat and ordered town of **BALLATER**, attractively hemmed in by the river and fir-covered mountains. The town was dragged from obscurity in the nineteenth century when it was discovered that the local waters were useful in curing scrofula, and these days Ballater spring water is back in fashion and on sale around town.

It was in Ballater that Queen Victoria first arrived in Deeside by train from Aberdeen back in 1848; she wouldn't allow a station to be built any closer to Balmoral, eight miles further west. Although the line has long been closed, the town's rather self-important royalism is much in evidence at the restored **train station** in the centre (June–Sept daily 9am–5.45pm; Oct–March daily 10am–4.45pm), where various video presentations and life-sized models relive the comings and goings of generations of royals (though trains have long since stopped running). The local shops, having provided Balmoral with groceries and household basics, also flaunt their connections, with oversized "By Appointment" crests sported above the doorways of most businesses from the butcher to the newsagent.

If you prefer to discover the fresh air and natural beauty that Victoria came to love so much, Ballater is an excellent base for local **walks and outdoor activities**. There are numerous hikes from Loch Muick (pronounced "mick"), nine miles southwest of town, including the Capel Mounth drovers' route over the mountains to Glen Doll (see p.193), and a well-worn but strenuous all-day trek up and around Lochnagar (3789ft), the mountain much painted and written about by the current Prince of Wales. Good-quality **bikes** can be rented from Cabin Fever (Ⓣ01339/754004), beside the station on Station Square, or Cycle Highlands (Ⓣ01339/755864) at 16 Bridge St. Other outdoor equipment, as well as local guidebooks, a full range of OS maps and good advice about heading to the surrounding hills, is available at the friendly Lochnagar Leisure outdoor shop on Station Square (daily 9am–5.30pm).

Practicalities

The **tourist office** is in the renovated train station (daily: July & Aug 9am–6pm; rest of year 10am–5pm; Ⓣ01339/755306). Good-quality **bunkhouse** accommodation is available at the *Schoolhouse*, Anderson Road (Ⓣ01339/756333, Ⓦwww.theschool-house.com), where inexpensive evening meals are served, and there are plenty of reasonable **B&Bs** in town, including non-smoking *Inverdeen House* on Bridge Square (Ⓣ01339/755759, Ⓦwww.inverdeen.com; ❸), which offers a wide choice of breakfasts, most involving local produce and home-baking. Other places to try include the welcoming *Deeside Hotel* (Ⓣ01339/755420, Ⓦwww.deesidehotel.co.uk; ❸), or the small *Green Inn Restaurant*, 9 Victoria Rd (Ⓣ01339/755701, Ⓦwww.green-inn.com; ❹), which has three very comfortable rooms. For **camping**, head for *Anderson Road Caravan Park* (Ⓣ01339/755727; Easter–Oct) down towards the river.

There are numerous **places to eat**, from smart hotel restaurants to bakers and coffee shops: the *Green Inn* is pricey but excellent with its French-influenced menu, while *La Mangiatoia* (Ⓣ01339/755999), on Bridge Square opposite the *Monaltrie Hotel*, is a cheaper and cheerful family pizza/pasta place. The *Station Restaurant*, next door to the tourist office in the Victorian station, serves home-made baking and lunches; a couple of miles east of Ballater on the A93 there's also the *Crannach Coffee Shop and Bakery* (closed Mon), a cultured spot offering good coffees, snacks and light meals, as well as superb cakes and bread from their in-house organic bakery. For **drinking** with locals and the opportunity to sample some real ales, try the back bar (entrance down Golf Street) of the *Prince of Wales*, which faces the main square.

Balmoral Estate and Crathie Church

Originally a sixteenth-century tower house built for the powerful Gordon family, **Balmoral Castle** (April–July daily 10am–5pm; also weekly guided tours Nov & Dec; £6; Ⓣ01339/742534, Ⓦwww.balmoralcastle.com) has been a royal residence since 1852, when it was converted to the Scottish Baronial mansion that stands today. The Royal Family traditionally spend their summer holidays here each August, but despite its fame it can be something of a disappointment even for a dedicated royalist. For the three months when the doors are nudged open, the general riffraff are permitted to view only the ballroom, an exhibition room and the grounds; for the rest of the year it's not even

Deeside and Donside Highland Games

Royal Deeside is the home of the modern **Highland Games**, claiming descent from gatherings organized by eleventh-century Scottish king Malcolm Canmore to help him recruit the strongest and fittest clansmen for his army. The most famous of the local games is undoubtedly the **Braemar Gathering**, held on the first Saturday in September, which can see crowds of 15,000 and usually a royal or two as guest of honour. Vying for celebrity status in recent years has been the **Lonach** gathering in nearby Strathdon (see p.203) on Donside, held the weekend before Braemar, where local laird Billy Connolly dispenses drams of whisky to marching village men and has been known to invite some Hollywood chums along – Steve Martin has appeared dressed in kilt and jacket, while Robin Williams has competed in the punishing hill race. For a true flavour of the spirit of Highland gatherings, however, try to get to one of the events that take place in other local towns and villages at weekends throughout July and August, where locals outnumber tourists and the competitions are guaranteed to be hard-fought and entertaining. Local tourist offices and the tourist board website, Ⓦwww.aberdeen-grampian.com, should be able to tell you what's happening where.

visible to the paparazzi who have been known to snoop around with their long lenses. With so little of the castle on view, it's worth making the most of the grounds and larger estate by following some of the country walks, heading off on a Land Rover safari or joining a two-hour **pony trek** (April–July Mon–Wed & Fri–Sun 10am & 2pm; £30; some riding experience required; call Ⓣ01339/742534 for details).

Opposite the castle's gates on the main road, the otherwise dull granite church of **Crathie**, built in 1895 with the proceeds of a bazaar held at Balmoral, is the royals' local church. A small **tourist office** operates in the car park by the church on the main road (daily: April–June, Sept & Oct 9.30am–5pm; July & Aug 9.30am–5.30pm; Ⓣ01339/742414).

Braemar

Continuing westwards for another few miles, the road rises to 1100ft above sea level in the upper part of Deeside and the village of **BRAEMAR**, situated where three passes meet and overlooked by an unremarkable **castle** (Easter–June & Sept–Oct Mon–Thurs, Sat & Sun 10am–5pm; July & Aug daily; £4). Signs as you enter Braemar boast that it's an "Award-Winning Tourist Village", which just about sums it up, as everything seems to have been prettified to within an inch of its life. That said, it's an invigorating, outdoor kind of place, well patronized by committed hikers, but probably best known for its Highland Games, the annual **Braemar Gathering**, on the first Saturday of September (Ⓦwww.braemargathering.org). Since Queen Victoria's day, successive generations of royals have attended, and the world's most famous Highland Games have become rather an overcrowded, overblown event. You're not guaranteed to get in if you just turn up; the website has details of how to book tickets in advance.

A pleasant diversion from Braemar is to head six miles west to the end of the road and the **Linn of Dee**, where the river plummets savagely through a narrow rock gorge. From here there are countless walks into the surrounding countryside or up into the heart of the Cairngorms (see p.204), including the awesome Lairig Ghru pass which cuts all the way through to Strathspey. There's a very basic SYHA hostel just before the falls at Inverey (Ⓣ0870/004 1126,

Climbing Morrone

Ordnance Survey Explorer map nos. 387 & 404.

Late August and through autumn is the best time to ascend **Morrone** (2818ft; allow 4hr for the return trip), when the mountain is plush with extravagant colours. In winter, it can be a spectacular viewpoint but very exposed. Make your way up Chapel Brae at the west end of Braemar, passing a car park and pond, then Mountain Cottage, and swinging left up through fine birch woods (a nature reserve). Keep right of the fences and house. The track bears right (west), and at a fork take the left branch up to the Deeside Field Club view indicator. Skirt the crags above this to the left, and the path is obvious thereafter. The summit provides a fantastic sweeping view of the Cairngorms. You can descend by the same route, but an easy continuation is to head down by the Mountain Rescue post's access path, which twists along and then down into Glen Clunie. Turn left along the minor road back to Braemar; the walk finishes by heading through the local golf course.

Ⓦwww.syha.org.uk; May–Sept). A postbus runs from Braemar to the Linn of Dee every day except Sunday at 1.20pm.

Practicalities

Braemar's **tourist office** is in the modern building known as the Mews, in the middle of the village on Mar Road (June & Sept daily 9am–5pm; July & Aug daily 9am–6pm; Oct Mon–Sat 9am–5pm, Sun 1–5pm; rest of year Mon–Sat 10.30am–1.30pm & 2–5pm, Sun 1–4pm; Ⓣ01339/741600). **Accommodation** is scarce in Braemar in the lead up to the Games, but at other times there's a wide choice. *Clunie Lodge Guest House*, Clunie Bank Road (Ⓣ01339/741330, Ⓦwww.clunielodge.com; ❷), on the edge of town, is a good **B&B** with lovely views up Clunie Glen, and there's a large SYHA **hostel** at Corrie Feragie, 21 Glenshee Rd (Ⓣ0870/004 1105, Ⓦwww.syha.org.uk; mid-Dec to Oct). Cheery *Rucksacks*, an easy-going bunkhouse well equipped for walkers and backpackers, is just behind the Mews complex (Ⓣ01339/741517), while the *Invercauld Caravan Club Park* (Ⓣ01339/741373), just south of the village off Glenshee Road, has fifteen **camping** pitches – you should phone ahead to reserve one.

For **food**, avoid the large hotels, which tend to be filled with coach parties, and try either *Taste*, a coffee shop and moderately priced contemporary restaurant on the road out to the Linn of Dee, or *The Gathering Place*, a pleasant bistro with reasonably priced meat and game dishes in the heart of the village next door to Braemar Mountain Sports.

Advice on **outdoor activities**, as well as ski, mountain-bike and climbing equipment rental, is available from Braemar Mountain Sports (daily 8.30am–6pm).

The Don Valley

The quiet countryside around the **Don Valley**, once renowned for its illegal whisky distilleries and smugglers, lies at the heart of Aberdeenshire's prosperous agricultural region. From Aberdeen, the River Don winds northwest through **Inverurie**, where it takes a sharp turn west to Alford, then continues past ruined castles through the **Upper Don Valley** and the heather moorlands of the eastern Highlands. This remote and undervisited area is positively littered with ruined castles, Pictish sites, stones and hillforts.

Inverurie is served by the regular Aberdeen to Inverness **train** and various **bus** services up the A96. Stagecoach Bluebird buses #215 and #220 link Aberdeen with Alford, but getting any further by public transport is all but impossible.

Inverurie and around

Some seventeen miles northwest of Aberdeen, the prosperous – if largely unexciting – farming town of **INVERURIE** lies fairly central to the numerous relics and castles in the area. The **tourist office** (Mon–Sat 9am–5pm; July & Aug closes 5.30pm; ⓣ01467/625800) shares space with a bookshop at 18 High St, not far from the station; it's a good place to stop before setting off to find the local sites, many of which are tucked away and confusingly signposted.

Bennachie and Archaeolink

The granite hill **Bennachie**, six miles west of Inverurie, is possibly the site of Mons Graupius, Scotland's first-ever recorded battle, when the Romans defeated the Picts in 84 AD. At 1733ft, this is one of the most prominent tors in the region, with tremendous views, and makes for a stiff two-hour walk. The best route starts from the **Bennachie Centre** (Tues–Sun: April–Oct 10.30am–5pm; Nov–March 9.30am–4pm), a countryside ranger station and interpretation centre located two miles south of **Chapel of Garioch** (pronounced "geery"). A mile immediately west of Chapel of Garioch is one of the most notable Pictish standing stones in the region, the **Maiden Stone**, a ten-foot slab inscribed with marine monsters, an elephant-like beast, and the mirror and comb for which it's named.

A further four miles northwest of Chapel of Garioch on the B9002 at Oyne, the **Archaeolink Prehistory Park** (daily: April–Oct 11am–5pm; Nov–March 11am–4pm; £4.75; ⓦwww.archaeolink.co.uk) gives an insight into the area's Pictish heritage. An ambitious modern attraction, it includes a reconstructed Iron Age farm, a hillside archeological site, and an innovative grass-roofed building containing lively audiovisual displays and hands-on exhibits.

Craigievar Castle

Six miles south of the town of Alford (pronounced "Aa-ford") on the A980, **Craigievar Castle** (NTS; ⓣ01339/883635) is a fantastic pink confection of turrets, gables, balustrades and cupolas bubbling over from its top three storeys. It was built in 1626 by a Baltic trader known as Willy the Merchant, who evidently allowed his whimsy to run riot. The castle's massive popularity, however – it features on everything from shortbread tins to tea towels all over Scotland – has been its undoing, and the sheer number of visitors has caused interior damage which means that the castle will be closed to visitors until Easter 2007 for restoration work. However, you can still visit the well-kept **grounds** (all year 9.30am to sunset; £1).

Lumsden and Rhynie

The A944 heads west from Alford, meeting the A97 just south of the tiny village of **LUMSDEN**, an unexpected hot spot of Scottish sculpture. A contemporary **Sculpture Walk** – heralded by a fabulous skeletal black horse at its southern end – runs parallel to the main road, coming out near the premises of the widely respected **Scottish Sculpture Workshop** (Mon–Fri 9am–5pm, or by arrangement; Ⓦwww.ssw.org.uk), very much an active workshop rather than a gallery, at the northern end of the village.

The village of **RHYNIE**, folded beautifully into the hills three miles further north up the A97, is forever associated with one of the greatest Pictish memorials, the **Rhynie Man**, a remarkable six-foot boulder discovered in 1978, depicting a rare whole figure, clad in a tunic and holding what is thought to be a ceremonial axe. The original is in Woodhill House in Aberdeen, but there's a cast on display at the school in Rhynie, across the road from the church. A further claim to fame for the village is that the bedrock lying deep beneath it, known as **Rhynie Chert**, contains plant and insect fossils up to 400 million years old, making them some of the earth's oldest fossils. A mile or so from the village, along the A941 to Dufftown, a car park gives access to a path up the looming **Tap O'Noth**, Scotland's second-highest Pictish hillfort (1847ft), where substantial remnants of the wall around the lip of the summit show evidence of vitrification (fierce burning), probably to fuse the rocks together.

The Upper Don Valley

Travelling west from Alford, settlements become noticeably more scattered and remote as the countryside takes on a more open, familiarly Highland appearance. Ten miles from Alford stand the impressive ruins of the thirteenth-century **Kildrummy Castle** (April–Sept daily 9.30am–6.30pm; HS; £2.50), where Robert the Bruce sent his wife and children during the Wars of Independence. The castle blacksmith, bribed with as much gold as he could carry, set fire to the place and it fell into English hands. Bruce's immediate family survived, but his brother was executed and the entire garrison hung, drawn and quartered. Meanwhile, the duplicitous blacksmith was rewarded for his help by having molten gold poured down his throat. The sixth Earl of Mar used the castle as the headquarters of the ill-fated Jacobite risings in 1715, but after that, Kildrummy became redundant and it was abandoned as a fortress and residence and fell into ruin. Beside the ruins, the separate **Kildrummy Castle Gardens** (April–Oct daily 10am–5pm; £2.50) are quite a draw, boasting everything from swathes of azaleas in spring to Himalayan poppies in summer. A few miles before you reach the castle, *Frog Marsh Bed & Breakfast* has three tastefully decorated **B&B** rooms (Ⓣ01975/571355, Ⓦwww.frogmarsh.com; ④).

Ten miles further west, the A944 sweeps round into the parish of **STRATHDON**, little more than scattered buildings by the roadside. Four miles north of here, up a rough track leading into Glen Nochty, lies the unexpected **Lost Gallery** (Mon & Wed–Sun 11am–5pm; Ⓦwww.lostgallery.co.uk), which shows work by some of Scotland's leading modern artists in a wonderfully remote and tranquil setting. Heading west again on the A944, you'll come to the walled grounds of Candacraig House, Highland retreat of comedian Billy Connolly. The house is private, but the old laundry on the other side of the main house, *No. 3 Candacraig Square* (Ⓣ01975/651472, Ⓦwww.candacraig.com; ⑤) has been converted into a stylish **B&B** with wooden floors, piles of books and a promise of fresh fish for breakfast. A further eight miles west, just beyond the junction of the Ballater road, lies **Corgarff Castle** (April–Sept daily 9.30am–6.30pm; Oct–March Sat & Sun 9.30am–4.30pm; HS; £3.30), an austere tower house with an unusual star-shaped curtain wall – and an eventful history. Built in 1537, it was turned into a barracks by the Hanoverian government in 1748 in the aftermath of Culloden in order to track down local Jacobite rebels; a century later, English Redcoats were stationed here with the unpopular task of trying to control whisky smuggling. Today the place has been restored to resemble its days as a barracks, with stark rooms and rows of hard, uncomfortable beds – authentic touches which extend to graffiti on the walls and peat smoke permeating the building from a fire on the upper floor. One unexpected bonus here if you're from far-flung parts is the chance to hear the history of the castle in one of the nineteen languages the keeper has recorded it in over the years, ranging from Thai to Icelandic.

Leading to the castle from the south is the old military road, which, unusually, hasn't been covered over by the present road and is fairly clear for about three miles. A mile or so along this from the castle, approached from the main road by the track beside Rowan Tree Cottage, is *Jenny's Bothy* at Dellachuper (ⓣ01975/651449; ⓦwww.upperdonside.org.uk/jenboth), a beautifully remote and simple **bunkhouse**, surrounded by empty scenery and wild animals. You'll have to bring your own supplies if you're coming here, but it's a great base for hiking, cycling or skiing, or just detaching yourself from the madding crowd for a day or two. Another bunkhouse, along with standard **B&B** accommodation, can be found at the *Allargue Arms Hotel* (ⓣ01975/651410; ③), an old wayside inn overlooking Corgarff Castle and a cosy base for skiing, fishing or hiking trips.

The **Lecht Road**, crossing the area of bleak but wonderfully empty high country to the remote mountain village of Tomintoul (see p.220), passes the Lecht ski centre at 2090ft above sea level, but is frequently impassable in winter due to snow.

The Cairngorms and Speyside

Rising high in the heather-clad hills above remote Loch Laggan, forty miles due south of Inverness, the **River Spey**, Scotland's second longest river, drains northeast towards the Moray Firth through one of the Highlands' most spellbinding valleys. Famous for its ancient forests, salmon fishing and ospreys, the area around the upper section of the river, known as **Strathspey**, is dominated by the sculpted **Cairngorms**, Britain's most extensive mountain massif, unique in supporting subarctic tundra on its high plateau. Though the area has been admired and treasured for many years as one of Scotland's prime natural assets, the Cairngorms National Park was declared only in 2004, and even then with grumblings from conservationists about inadequate planning regulations and unnatural boundaries. Outdoor enthusiasts flock to the area to take advantage of the superb hiking, watersports and winter snows, aided by the fact that the area is easily accessible by road and rail from both the Central Belt and Inverness.

A string of villages along the river provide useful bases for setting out into the wilder country, principal among them **Aviemore**, a rather ugly straggle of housing and hotel developments which nevertheless has a lively, youthful feel to it. A little way north, **Grantown-on-Spey** is a more douce foil, with solid Victorian mansions but much less vitality, while smaller settlements such as **Boat of Garten** and **Kincraig** are quieter, well-kept villages popular with those who want to stay close to the natural surroundings.

Downriver, Strathspey gives way to the area known as **Speyside**, famous as the heart of Scotland's **malt whisky** industry. In addition to the Malt Whisky Trail which leads round a number of well-known distilleries in the vicinity of villages such as **Dufftown** and **Craigellachie**, the lesser-known **Speyside Way**, another of Scotland's long-distance footpaths, offers the chance to enjoy the scenery of the region, as well as its whiskies, on foot.

Strathspey

Of Strathspey's scattered settlements, **Aviemore** absorbs the largest number of visitors, particularly in midwinter when it metamorphoses into the UK's busiest ski resort. The village itself isn't up to much, but it's a good first stop for information, to sort out somewhere to stay or to find out about nearby outdoor activities, which are likely to seem very enticing after a glimpse of the stunning mountain scenery provided by the 4000-foot summit plateau of the Cairngorms. The planned Georgian town of **Grantown-on-Spey** makes a good alternative base for summer visitors, but while it has more charm than

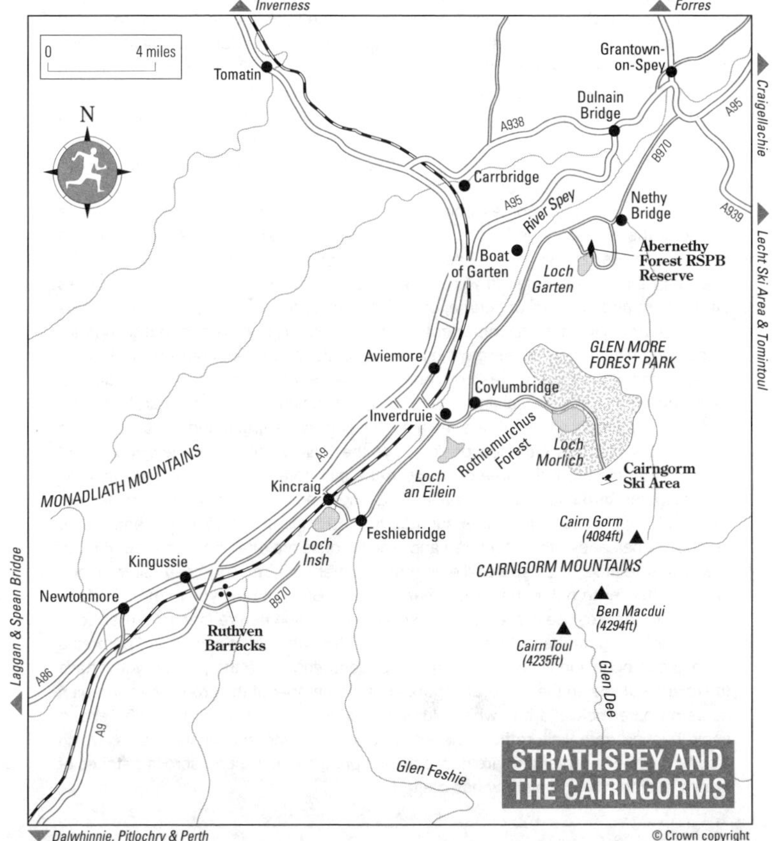

Aviemore, there are fewer facilities. Further upriver, the sedate villages of **Newtonmore** and **Kingussie** are older-established holiday centres, popular more with anglers and grouse hunters than canoeists and climbers, or more recently those seeking to discover *Monarch of the Glen* country, made popular by the TV drama. Rather unusually for Scotland, the area boasts a wide choice of good-quality accommodation, particularly in the budget market, with various easy-going hostels run by and for outdoor enthusiasts.

Aviemore and around

The once-sleepy village of **AVIEMORE** was first developed as a ski and tourism resort in the mid-1960s and, over the years, it fell victim to profiteering developers with scant regard for the needs of the local community. Although a large-scale face-lift has removed some of the architectural eyesores of that era, the settlement remains dominated by a string of soulless shopping centres and

Cairngorms National Park

The **Cairngorms National Park** (@www.cairngorms.co.uk) covers some 1500 square miles and incorporates the **Cairngorms massif**, the largest mountainscape in the UK and the only sizeable plateau in the country over 2500ft. It's the biggest national park in Britain, and while Aviemore and the surrounding area are regarded as the main point of entry, particularly for those planning outdoor activities, it's also possible to access the eastern side of the park from both Deeside and Donside in Aberdeenshire (see p.195). Crossing the range is a significant challenge: by road the only connection is the A939 Tomintoul to Cock Bridge, frequently impassable in winter due to snow, while on foot the only way to avoid the high peaks is to follow the old cattle drovers' route called the **Lairig Ghru**, a very long day's walk between Inverdruie at the edge of Rothiemurchus and the Linn of Dee, near Inverey.

The name Cairngorm comes from the Gaelic *An Carm Gorm*, meaning "the blue hill" after the blueish-tinged stones found in the area, and within the park there are 52 summits over 2953ft, as well as a quarter of Scotland's native woodland, and a quarter of the UK's threatened wildlife species. The conservation of the landscape's unique flora and fauna is, of course, one of the principal reasons national park status was conferred. However, an important role for the park is to incorporate the communities living within it and integrate the array of outdoor activities enjoyed by visitors.

Vegetation in the area ranges from one of the largest tracts of ancient **Caledonian pine and birch forest** remaining in Scotland, at Rothiemurchus, to subarctic tundra on the high plateau, where **alpine flora** such as starry saxifrage and the star-shaped pink flowers of moss campion peek out of the pink granite in the few months of summer that the ground is free of snow. In the pine forests of the river valleys strikingly coloured **birds** such as crested tits, redwings and goldfinches can be observed, along with rarely seen **mammals** such as the red squirrel and pine marten. On the heather slopes above the forest, red and black grouse are often encountered, though their larger relative, the capercaillie, is a much rarer sight, having been reintroduced in 1837 after dying out in the seventeenth century. Birds of prey you're most likely to see are the **osprey**, best seen at the osprey observation centre (see p.211) at Loch Garten or fishing on the lochs around Aviemore, though golden eagles and peregrine falcons can occasionally be seen higher up. Venturing up to the plateau you'll have the chance of seeing the shy **ptarmigan**, another member of the grouse family, which nests on bare rock and has white plumage during winter, or even the dotterel and snow bunting, rare visitors from the Arctic, along with mountain (blue) hares, which also turn white in winter and are best seen in spring as they scurry across patches of brown hillside where the snow has melted.

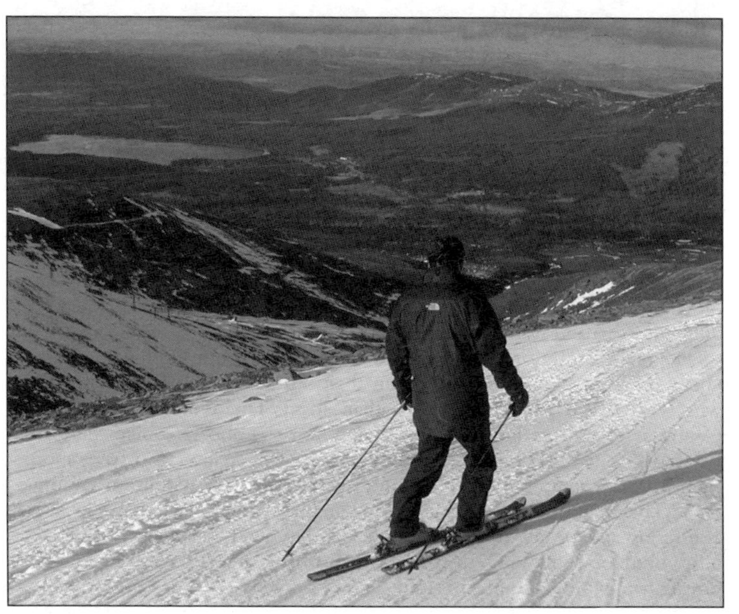

△ Skiing in Aviemore

sprawling housing estates surrounding a Victorian railway station. That said, Aviemore is well-equipped with services and facilities for visitors to the area and is the most convenient base for the Cairngorms, benefits which for most folk far outweigh its lack of aesthetic appeal.

The main attractions of Aviemore are its **outdoor pursuits**, though train enthusiasts are drawn to the restored **Strathspey Steam Railway**, which chugs the short distance between Aviemore and Broomhill, just beyond Boat of Garten village, five times daily through the summer (June–Sept; less regular service at other times; Ⓣ01479/810725, Ⓦwww.strathspeyrailway.co.uk for details). On a slightly more practical level, the most useful local **bus** route is the #31, which runs hourly from Aviemore to the Cairngorm mountain railway via Rothiemurchus and Loch Morlich.

Summer activities

In summer, the main activities around Aviemore are **walking** (see box on p.209) and **watersports**, and there are great opportunities for mountain biking, pony trekking and fly-fishing. Two centres offer sailing, windsurfing and canoeing: the Loch Morlich Watersports Centre (Ⓣ01479/861221, Ⓦwww.lochmorlich.com), five miles or so east of Aviemore on the way to Cairn Gorm mountain, rents equipment and offers tuition in a lovely setting with a sandy beach, while six miles up-valley near Kincraig, the Loch Insh Watersports Centre (see p.212) offers the same facilities in equally beautiful surroundings. It also rents mountain bikes and boats for loch fishing, and gives ski instruction on a short dry slope. If you're looking for something that offers a bit more action, Full On Adventure (Ⓣ07885/835838, Ⓦwww.fullonadventure.com) runs **white-water rafting** trips on the Findhorn river.

Riding and **pony trekking** are on offer up and down the valley: try Alvie Stables near Kincraig (Ⓣ01540/651409 or 07831/495397), or Strathspey Highland Ponies (Ⓣ01479/812345), who set out on hacks and treks from Rothiemurchus Visitor Centre at Inverdruie. **Fishing** is very much part of the local scene; you can fish for trout and salmon on the River Spey, and the Rothiemurchus Estate (Ⓦwww.rothiemurchus.net) has a stocked trout-fishing loch at **Inverdruie**, where success is virtually guaranteed. Instruction and rod rental is available from the centre beside the loch. Fishing permits cost around £5–15 per day to fish a stocked loch and £25 on the Spey itself, and are sold at Speyside Sports (Ⓣ01479/810656) in Aviemore and at Loch Morlich Watersports Centre (see p.207), which also rents rods and tackle. The Aviemore tourist office has a helpful brochure on the complex series of permits required for the different lochs and waters in the Strathspey area.

The area is also great for **mountain biking**, with both Rothiemurchus and Glenmore estates more progressive in their attitude to catering for the sport with waymarked routes and maps than many. The Rothiemurchus Visitor Centre at Inverdruie has route maps, and you can also rent bikes here from Bothy Bikes (Ⓣ01479/810111, Ⓦwww.bothybikes.co.uk), who have another shop in the Aviemore Shopping Centre beside the train station on Grampian Road. They rent out good-quality mountain bikes with front suspension, as well as offering advice and guided bike tours. To buy (and, in some instances, rent) other outdoor equipment, in particular **climbing** and **hill walking** gear, try Cairngorm Mountain Sports in the centre of Aviemore (Ⓣ01479/810903).

Winter activities

Scottish **skiing** on a commercial level first really took off in Aviemore. By continental European and North American standards it's all on a tiny scale, but occasionally snow, sun and lack of crowds coincide and you can have a great day. February and March are usually the best times, but there's a chance of decent snow at any time between mid-November and April. Lots of places – not just in Aviemore itself – sell or rent equipment; for a rundown of ski schools and rental facilities in the area, check out the tourist office's *Ski Scotland* brochure or visit Ⓦski.visitscotland.com.

The **Cairngorm Ski Area**, about eight miles southeast of Aviemore, above Loch Morlich in Glenmore Forest Park, is well served during winter by buses from Aviemore. You can rent skis, boards and other equipment from the Day Lodge at the foot of the ski area (Ⓣ01479/861261, Ⓦwww.cairngormmountain.com), which also has a shop, a bar and restaurant, as well as the base station for the **funicular railway**, the principal means of getting to the top of the ski slopes. Various types of ski pass are available from here – in person, by phone or online. The facilities include a ski school, cafés at three different levels and a separate terrain park for skiers and boarders. If there's lots of snow, the area around **Loch Morlich** and into the **Rothiemurchus Estate** provides enjoyable cross-country skiing through lovely woods, beside rushing burns and even over frozen lochs.

For a crash-course in surviving Scottish winters, you could do worse than try a week at the National Outdoor Training Centre at *Glenmore Lodge* (see p.210) in the heart of the Glenmore Forest Park at the east end of Loch Morlich. This superbly equipped and organized centre offers winter and summer courses in hill walking, mountaineering, alpine ski-mountaineering, avalanche awareness and much besides, including an array of more recreational courses in kayaking, abseiling and the like. To add to the winter scene, there's a herd of reindeer at the **Cairngorm Reindeer Centre** by Loch Morlich (daily 10am–5pm; guided excursions to the main herd 11am, also 2.30pm May–Sept,

£8; ⓣ01479/861228, ⓦwww.reindeer-company.demon.co.uk), while between Loch Morlich and Inverdruie the **Cairngorm Sleddog Adventure Centre** (ⓣ07767/270526, ⓦwww.sled-dogs.co.uk), the UK's only sleddog centre, offers daily tours of the kennels and a small museum (2.30pm; £8), as well as three-hour trips on a wheeled or ski-based sled pulled by ten dogs (Oct–April only; £50 per person) and even a two-day course to learn how to take a team out yourself.

Practicalities

Aviemore's businesslike **tourist office** is in the heart of things at 7 The Parade, Grampian Rd (April–Oct Mon–Sat 9am–5pm, Sun 10am–4pm; Nov–March Mon–Fri 9am–5pm, Sat 10am–4pm). It offers an accommodation booking service and reams of leaflets on local attractions.

There's no shortage of **accommodation** locally. The *Corrour House Hotel* at Inverdruie, two miles southeast of Aviemore (ⓣ01479/810220, ⓦwww.corrourhousehotel.co.uk; ⑤), is secluded and upmarket, while the *Rowan Tree*

Walks around Aviemore

Ordnance Survey Explorer maps nos. 402 & 403 or OS Outdoor Leisure map no. 3.

Walking of all grades is a highlight of the Aviemore area, though before setting out you should heed the usual safety guidelines (see p.59). These are particularly important if you want to climb to the high tops, which include a number of Scotland's loftiest peaks. However, as well as the high mountain trails, there are some lovely and well-signposted **low-level walks** in the area. It takes an hour or so to complete the gentle circular walk around pretty **Loch an Eilean** (with its ruined castle) in the Rothiemurchus Estate, beginning at the end of the back road that turns east off the B970 two miles south of Aviemore. The helpful estate **visitor centres** at the lochside and by the roadside at Inverdruie provide more information on the many woodland trails that crisscross this area. A longer (2–3hr) walk through this estate, famous for its atmospheric native woodland of gnarled Caledonian pines and shimmering birch trees, starts at the near end of **Loch Morlich**. Cross the river by the bridge and follow the dirt road, turning off after about twenty minutes to follow the signs to Aviemore. The path goes through beautiful pine woods and past tumbling burns, and you can branch off to Coylumbridge and Loch an Eilean. Unless you're properly prepared for a 25-mile hike, don't take the track to the **Lairig Ghru**, a famous old cattle drovers' route through a dramatic cleft in the mountain range which eventually brings you out near Braemar on the far side of the Cairngorm range.

Another good shortish (half-day) walk leads along a well-surfaced forestry track from Glenmore Lodge up towards the **Ryvoan Pass**, taking in An Lochan Uaine, known as the "Green Loch" and living up to its name, with amazing colours that range from turquoise to slate grey depending on the weather. The track narrows once past the loch and leads east towards Deeside, so retrace your steps if you don't want a major trek. The **Glenmore Forest Park Visitor Centre** by the roadside at the turn-off to Glenmore Lodge is the starting point for the three-hour round-trip climb of Meall a' Bhuachallie (2654ft), which offers excellent views and is usually accessible year-round. The centre has information on other trails in this section of the forest.

The **Speyside Way** (see p.214), the long-distance footpath which begins on the Moray Firth coast at Buckie and follows the course of the Spey through the heart of whisky country, now extends to Aviemore, with plans for further links down to Kingussie and Newtonmore. A pleasant day-trip involves walking the way from Aviemore to Boat of Garten, on to the RSPB osprey sanctuary at Loch Garten, and then returning on the Strathspey Steam Railway.

Country Hotel (Ⓣ01479/810207, Ⓦwww.rowantreehotel.com; ❺), by Loch Alvie, is a relaxed, comfortable alternative. In Aviemore, *Ravenscraig Guest House* (Ⓣ01479/810278, Ⓦwww.aviemoreonline.com; ❸), on the Grampian Road, has twelve rooms and is welcoming and family-friendly, or *Ardlogie Guest House* (Ⓣ01479/810747, Ⓦwww.ardlogie.co.uk; ❸) on Dalfaber Road is smaller and slightly cheaper. Aviemore's large SYHA **hostel** (Ⓣ0870/004 1104, Ⓦwww.syha.org.uk) is well placed within walking distance of the centre of the village; alternatively, the *Aviemore Bunkhouse* (Ⓣ01479/811181, Ⓦwww.aviemore-bunkhouse.com) is a large, modern place beside the Old Bridge Inn on Dalfaber Road, again within walking distance from the station. Towards the Cairngorms, there's another SYHA hostel at Loch Morlich (Christmas–Oct; Ⓣ0870/004 1137), as well as excellent accommodation in twin rooms (with shared facilities) at *Glenmore Lodge* (Ⓣ01479/861256, Ⓦwww.glenmorelodge.org.uk; ❷) – full use of their superb facilities, which include a pool, weights room and indoor climbing wall is included. There's no shortage of **campsites** either: two of the best are *Rothiemurchus Caravan Park*, among the tall pine trees at Coylumbridge on the way to Loch Morlich (Ⓣ01479/812800, Ⓦwww.rothiemurchus.net), and the Forestry Enterprise site (Ⓣ01479/861271) beside the banks of Loch Morlich.

All along Aviemore's main drag are bistros, hotels and takeaways serving fairly predictable, run-of-the-mill **food**. One exception is the *Mountain Café* (Ⓣ01479/812473), above Cairngorm Mountain Sports, which serves an all-day menu of wholesome snacks and freshly prepared meals, often using local produce. Another good discovery is *The Einich* (Ⓣ01479/812334), tucked away at the Rothiemurchus Visitor Centre at Inverdruie, which is open for lunch every day and moderately priced evening meals Wednesday to Saturday. Alternatively, *The Old Bridge Inn* on the east side of the railway on Dalfaber Road, dishes up decent pub grub and real ales in a mellow, cosy setting, while *Café Mambo*, in Aviemore Shopping Centre on Grampian Road, matches its bright, funky decor with a cheerful burger'n'chips-style menu.

Cairn Gorm mountain

From Aviemore, a road leads past Rothiemurchus and Loch Morlich and winds its way up into the Cairngorms, reaching the Coire Cas car park at a height of 2150ft. Here there's the base station for the ski area and the departure point for the **Cairn Gorm Mountain Railway** (daily 10am–5.15pm; last train up 4.30pm; trains run every 15min; £8.50; Ⓦwww.cairngormmountain.com), a two-car funicular system that runs to the top of the ski area. A highly controversial, £15 million scheme which was bitterly opposed by conservationists objecting to the man-made scar it creates in such a beautiful environment, the railway whisks skiers in winter, and tourists at any time of year, along a mile and a half of track to the top station at an altitude of 3600ft, not far from the summit of Cairn Gorm mountain. The top station incorporates an exhibition/interpretation area and a café/restaurant from which spectacular views can be had on clear days, though you should note that there is no access beyond the confines of the top station and its open-air viewing terrace unless you're embarking on winter skiing; anyone wanting to walk on the subarctic Cairngorm plateau will have to trudge up from the car park at the bottom. In winter the funicular starts earlier in the day if skiing is possible.

At the base station there's a **ranger office** (daily: April–Oct 9am–5pm; Nov–March 8.30am–4.30pm) where you can find out about various trails heading out from the base station. If you're aiming to head to the summits, check here for the latest weather report. The simplest of the walks is around a **Mountain**

Garden Trail, which features shrubs and trees native to the Cairngorms. The *Ptarmigan* **restaurant** at the top station offers self-service meals through the day and, in summer (July–Sept), more formal "sunset dining" on Friday and Saturday evenings, as well as a ceilidh on Thursday evening (July & Aug only). Pre-booking is required for both (Ⓣ01479/861336).

Carrbridge

Worth considering as an alternative to Aviemore – particularly as a skiing base – **CARRBRIDGE** is a pleasant, quiet village about seven miles north. Look out for the spindly Bridge of Carr at the northern end of the village, built in 1717 and still making a graceful stone arch over the River Dulnain. The main attraction in the village is the **Landmark Forest Heritage Park** (daily: April to mid-July 10am–6pm; mid-July to Aug 10am–7pm; Sept–March 10am–5pm; £8.95 Ⓦwww.landmark-centre.co.uk), which combines interactive exhibitions with forest walks, nature trails, a maze and fun rides; it's more tastefully done than some similar places and an excellent place for children to let off steam. For local **accommodation**, both *Carrmoor Guest House*, Carr Road (Ⓣ01479/841244, Ⓦwww.carrmoorguesthouse.co.uk; ❷), and the friendly *Cairn Hotel*, Main Road (Ⓣ01479/841212, Ⓦwww.cairnhotel.co.uk; ❷), are central to the village, while *Feith Mhor Lodge* (Ⓣ01479/841621, Ⓦwww.feithmhor.co.uk; ❸) is an attractive B&B just a mile southwest along Station Road with terrific views. The cosy, basic *Carrbridge Bunkhouse* (Ⓣ01479/841250, Ⓦwww.carrbridge-bunkhouse.co.uk), a timber-lined cabin with its own sauna, is a good base for walkers half a mile or so north of the village on the Inverness road.

Loch Garten and around

The **Abernethy Forest RSPB Reserve** on the shore of **LOCH GARTEN**, seven miles northeast of Aviemore and eight miles south of Grantown-on-Spey, is famous as the nesting site of one of Britain's rarest birds. A little over fifty years ago, the **osprey**, known in North America as the fish hawk, had completely disappeared from the British Isles. Then, in 1954, a single pair of these exquisite white-and-brown raptors mysteriously reappeared and built a nest in a tree half a mile or so from the loch. Although efforts were made to keep the exact location secret, one year's eggs fell victim to a gang of thieves, and thereafter the area became the centre of an effective high-security operation. Now the birds are well established not only here but elsewhere, and there are believed to be up to 150 pairs nesting across the Highlands. The best time to visit is between April and August, when the ospreys return from West Africa to nest and the RSPB opens an **observation centre** (daily 10am–6pm; £3.50; Ⓣ01479/821409), complete with powerful telescopes and CCTV monitoring of the nest. This is the place to come to get a glimpse of osprey chicks in their nest; you'll be luckier to see the birds perform their trademark swoop over water to pluck a fish out with their talons, though nearby Loch Garten, as well as Loch Morlich and Loch Insh, are good places to stake out in the hope of a sighting, while one of the best spots is the Rothiemurchus trout loch at Inverdruie. The reserve is also home to several other species of rare birds and animals, including the Scottish crossbill, capercaillie, whooper swan and red squirrel; once-weekly **guided walks** leave from the observation centre (Wed 9.30am), while during the spring lekking season (April to mid-May) when male capercaillie gather and joust with each other, the centre opens very early in the morning for "Caperwatch" (daily 5.30–8am; £3) so that you can see the activity both live and on CCTV.

Loch Garten is about a mile and a half west of **BOAT OF GARTEN** village: from the village, cross the Spey then take the Grantown road, and the reserve is signposted to the right. An attractive wee place, Boat of Garten has a number of good **accommodation** options: *Fraoch Lodge*, 15 Deshar Rd (Ⓣ01479/831331, Ⓦwww.scotmountain.co.uk; ❶), is an excellent hostel with four twin rooms and a family room that sleeps four, and provides high-quality home-cooked meals along with good facilities such as a purpose-built drying room. It is enthusiastically run by experienced mountaineers, who also offer guided walking holidays and instruction in mountain skills. Alternatively, the *Old Ferryman's House* (Ⓣ01479/831370; ❷), just across the Spey, is a wonderfully homely, hospitable B&B, with no TVs, lots of books and delicious evening meals and breakfasts.

Kincraig

At **KINCRAIG**, six miles southwest of Aviemore on the B9152 towards Kingussie, there are a couple of unusual encounters with animals which offer a memorable diversion if you're not setting off on outdoor pursuits. While the style of the **Highland Wildlife Park** (daily: June–Aug 10am–7pm; April, May, Sept & Oct closes 6pm; Nov–March closes 4pm; last entry 2hr before closing; in snowy conditions call in advance; £8.50; Ⓣ01540/651270, Ⓦwww.highlandwildlifepark.org), with its various captive animals, may not appeal to everyone, it is accredited to the Royal Zoological Society of Scotland and offers a chance to see exotic foreigners such as wolves and bison, as well as many rarely seen natives, including pine martens, capercaillie, wildcat and eagles. Nearby, the engrossing **Working Sheepdogs** demonstrations at Leault Farm (May–Oct Sun–Fri noon & 4pm; Nov–April call Ⓣ01540/651310 to arrange a visit; £4) afford the rare opportunity to see a champion shepherd herd a flock of sheep with up to eight dogs, using whistles and other commands. The fascinating hour-long display also includes a chance to see traditional hand-shearing, duck-herding and displays on how collie pups are trained. Meanwhile, the Loch Insh Watersports Centre (Ⓣ01540/651272, Ⓦwww.lochinsh.com) runs a **Wildlife Passenger Boat safari** around Loch Insh and into Inchmarsh RSPB reserve (four trips daily April–Oct; £8).

There are some good low-price **accommodation** options nearby. The Loch Insh Watersports Centre (see p.207) has basic but practical en-suite B&B and self-catering chalets (❷) as well as a decent waterfront café/restaurant (daily: Feb–Oct 10am–10pm; Nov–Jan 10am–6pm). At the remote *Glen Feshie Hostel* at Balachroick (Ⓣ01540/651323), three miles from Loch Insh down beautiful Glen Feshie, the all-in price includes bed linen and as much porridge as you like for breakfast.

Grantown-on-Spey

Buses run from Aviemore and Inverness to the small town of **GRANTOWN-ON-SPEY** (Ⓦwww.grantownonspey.com), about fifteen miles northeast of Aviemore, a relaxing alternative base for exploring the Strathspey area. Life is concentrated around the central square, with its attractive Georgian architecture, including a small **museum** and resource centre on Burnfield Avenue (March–Dec Mon–Sat 10am–4pm; £2; Ⓦwww.grantownmuseum.co.uk), which tells the story of the town; it also offers **Internet access**. The **tourist office** is on the High Street (March–Oct Mon–Sat 9am–5pm, Sun 10am–4pm). Local **bike rental** is provided by Bike Hire Scotland (Ⓣ07739/901396), who will deliver smart mountain bikes, along with maps, helmets and rucksacks, to your accommodation.

As with much of Speyside, there's a decent choice of **accommodation**. For B&B, *Parkburn Guest House* (Ⓣ01479/873116, Ⓦwww.parkburnguesthouse.co.uk; ❸) on the High Street is welcoming, while if you're after something more upmarket head for the large seventeenth-century *Garth Hotel*, at the north end of the square (Ⓣ01479/872836, Ⓦwww.garthhotel.com; ⑤) or the smart *Auchendean Lodge Hotel* (Ⓣ01479/851347, Ⓦwww.auchendean.com; ⑥; April–Oct), three miles southeast of Grantown near Dulnain Bridge, best known for its gourmet meals. In the budget range, there's a bunkhouse at *Ardenbeg Outdoor Centre* (Ⓣ01479/872824, Ⓦwww.ardenbeg.co.uk), on Grant Road, parallel to the High Street, which also serves as a base for courses in hill walking, climbing, canoeing and skiing, while a mile or two south of town at Nethy Bridge, between Grantown and Boat of Garten, is the tiny, eight-bed *Lazy Duck Hostel* (Ⓣ01479/821642, Ⓦwww.lazyduck.co.uk), a peaceful and comfortable retreat with great moorland walking on its doorstep.

To **eat out** in grand style, head for the *Auchendean Lodge Hotel* (see above) near Dulnain Bridge, where the highly rated meals sometimes include locally collected mushrooms. Within Grantown itself, the new *Glass House* restaurant on Grant Road (Ⓣ01479/872980) serves excellent, moderate to expensive contemporary Scottish food in a relaxed conservatory dining room. *Tyree House Hotel* on the square is the place to go for bar food or a **drink**.

Newtonmore and Kingussie

Twelve miles southwest of Aviemore, close neighbours **NEWTONMORE** and **KINGUSSIE** (pronounced "king-*yoos*-ee") are pleasant villages at the head of the Strathspey Valley separated by a couple of miles of farmland. However, on the **shinty** field their peaceful coexistence is forgotten and the two become bitter rivals; in recent years Kingussie has been the dominant force in the game, a fierce, home-grown relative of hockey (see p.55; Ⓦwww.shinty.com). The chief attraction is the excellent **Highland Folk Museum** (Ⓣ01540/661307, Ⓦwww.highlandfolk.com), split between complementary sites in the two towns. The Kingussie section (April–Sept Mon–Sat 9.30am–5pm; Oct Mon–Fri 9.30am–4pm; rest of the year by appointment; guided tours on the hour; £2.50) contains an absorbing collection of artefacts typical of traditional Highland ways of life, as well as a farming museum, an old smokehouse, a mill, a Hebridean blackhouse, and a traditional herb and flower garden; most days in summer there's a demonstration of various traditional crafts. The larger outdoor site at Newtonmore (April to end Aug daily 10.30am–5.30pm; Sept daily 11am–4.30pm; Oct Mon–Fri 11am–4.30pm; £5, or £6 for both sites), tries to create more of a living history museum, with an old vintage bus offering a jump-on/jump-off tour round reconstructions of a working croft, a water-powered sawmill, a church where recitals on traditional Highland instruments are given and a small village of blackhouses constructed using only authentic tools and materials.

Kingussie is also notable for the ruins of **Ruthven Barracks** (free access), standing east across the river on a hillock. The best-preserved garrison built to pacify the Highlands after the 1715 rebellion, it makes for great exploring by day and is impressively floodlit at night. Taken by the Jacobites in 1744, Ruthven was blown up in the wake of Culloden to prevent it from falling into enemy hands. It was also the place from where clan leader Lord George Murray dispatched his acrimonious letter to Bonnie Prince Charlie, holding him personally responsible for the string of blunders that had precipitated their defeat.

In Kingussie, the best place for local **tourist information** is the Highland Folk Museum (see above). The Wildcat Centre in Newtonmore (varied hours, though generally Mon–Fri 9.30am–12.30pm & 2.15–5.15pm, Sat 9.30am–12.30pm; Oct–March mornings only; ⓣ01540/673131) also offers local information and details of some well-organized walking trails in the area. Bike rental is available at Service Sports on the High Street in Kingussie (ⓣ01540/661228).

One of the most appealing places **to stay** on the whole of Speyside is the relaxed but stylish *The Cross* restaurant with rooms (ⓣ01540/661166, ⓦwww.thecross.co.uk; ⑦) located in a converted tweed mill on the banks of the River Gynack. The best **B&B** accommodation is on the outskirts of the village: the *Auld Poor House* (ⓣ01540/661558, ⓦwww.yates128.freeserve.co.uk; ②), on the road to Kincraig, is a comfortable place with a resident qualified masseuse, while *Ruthven Steadings* (ⓣ01540/662328, ⓦwww.ruthvensteadings.co.uk; ②) has two spacious rooms and is just along the road from the striking ruined barracks. The best of a number of local **hostels** are in Newtonmore: the *Newtonmore Independent Hostel* (ⓣ01540/673360, ⓦwww.highlandhostel.co.uk) is a welcoming and well-equipped place, while the *Strathspey Mountain Hostel* (ⓣ01540/673694, ⓦwww.newtonmore.com/strathspey), just up the road, is also of a high standard and welcomes families and groups.

The most ambitious **food** in the area is served at *The Cross* (see above; restaurant closed Sun & Mon), where the meals, though expensive, make imaginative use of local ingredients and there's a vast wine list. Cheaper food is available at several cafés and pubs in both towns – *Gilly's Kitchen* on the main street in Kingussie is open during the day for simple but good homemade soup, panini, and home-baking, while the *Silverfjord Hotel* by the train station at Kingussie is a good spot for a bar snack or meal.

Speyside

Strictly speaking, the term **Speyside** refers to the entire region surrounding the Spey river, but to most people the name is synonymous with the **whisky triangle**, stretching from just north of Craigellachie, down towards Tomintoul in the south and east to Huntly. Indeed, there are more whisky distilleries

The Speyside Way

The **Speyside Way**, with its beguiling blend of mountain, river, wildlife and whisky, is fast establishing itself as an appealing and less-taxing alternative to the popular West Highland and Southern Upland long-distance footpaths. Starting at **Buckie** on the Moray Firth coast, it follows the fast-flowing River Spey from its mouth at Spey Bay south to **Aviemore** (see p.206), with branches linking it to **Dufftown**, Scotland's malt whisky capital, and **Tomintoul** on the remote edge of the Cairngorm mountains. Some 65-miles long without taking on the branch routes, the whole thing is a five- to seven-day expedition, but its proximity to main roads and small villages means that it is excellent for shorter walks or even bicycle trips, especially in the heart of **distillery** country between Craigellachie and Glenlivet: Glenfiddich, Glenlivet, Macallan and Cardhu distilleries, as well as the Speyside Cooperage, lie directly on or a short distance off the route. Other highlights include the chance to encounter an array of **wildlife**, from dolphins at Spey Bay to ospreys at Loch Garten, as well as the restored **railway** trips on offer at Dufftown and Aviemore. The path uses disused railway lines for much of its length, and there are simple campsites and good B&Bs at strategic points along the route. For more details contact the Speyside Way Visitor Centre at Aberlour (ⓣ01340/881266, ⓦwww.speysideway.org).

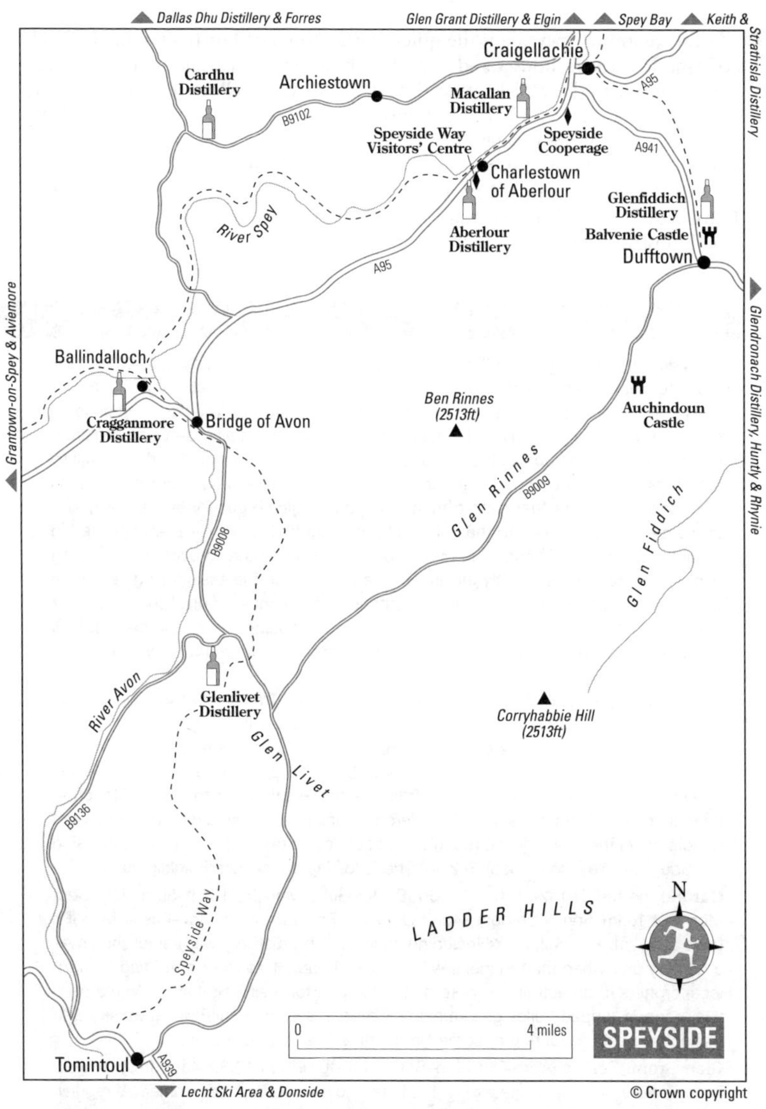

and famous brands concentrated in this small area (including Glenfiddich and Glenlivet) than in any other part of the country. Running through the heart of the region is the River Spey, whose clean, clear, fast-running waters not only play such a vital part in the whisky industry, but are also home to thousands of salmon, making it one of Scotland's finest angling locations. Obviously fertile, the tranquil glens of the area have none of the ruggedness of other parts of the Highlands, and as such its charms are subtle rather than dramatic, with tourism blending into a local economy kept healthy by whisky and farming, rather than dominating it.

At the centre of Speyside is the quiet market town of **Dufftown**, full of solid, stone-built workers' houses and dotted with no fewer than nine whisky distilleries. Along with the well-kept nearby villages of **Craigellachie** and **Aberlour**, it makes the best base for a tour of whisky country, whether on the official Malt Whisky Trail or more independent explorations. Fewer visitors take the chance to discover the more remote glens, such as **Glenlivet**, which push higher up towards the Cairngorm massif, nestled into which is Britain's highest village, **Tomintoul**, situated on the edge of both whisky country and a large expanse of wild uplands.

Touring malt whisky country

Speyside is the heart of Scotland's **whisky** industry, with over fifty distilleries testimony to a unique combination of clear, clean water, benign climate and gentle upland terrain. Yet for all the advertising-influenced visions of timeless traditions and unspoilt glens, it's worth keeping in mind that in these parts whisky is a hard-edged, multimillion-pound business dominated by huge corporations, and to many working distilleries visitors are an afterthought, if not a downright nuisance. It sometimes comes as a surprise to visitors that a lot of distilleries are unglamorous industrial units, and by no means all are open to the public. Having said that, there are plenty located in attractive historic buildings which now go to some lengths to provide an engaging experience for visitors. Mostly this involves a tour around the essential stages in the whisky-making process, though for real enthusiasts a number of distilleries now offer pricier connoisseur tours with a tutored tasting (or **nosing**, as it's properly called) and in-depth studies of the distiller's art. Note that some tours have restrictions on children.

There are eight distilleries on the official **Malt Whisky Trail** (ⓦwww.maltwhiskytrail.com), a clearly signposted seventy-mile meander around the region. Unless you're seriously interested in whisky, it's best to just pick out a couple that appeal. All offer a guided tour (some are free, others charge but then give you a voucher which is redeemable against a bottle of whisky from the distillery shop), with a tasting to round it off; if you're driving you'll often be offered a miniature to take away with you. Most people travel the route by car, though you could cycle parts of it, or even walk using the Speyside Way (see box on p.214). The following are selected highlights:

Cardhu, on the B9102 at Knockando (Easter–June Mon–Fri 10am–5pm; July–Sept Mon–Sat 10am–5pm, Sun noon–4pm; Oct Mon–Fri 11am–4pm; Nov–Easter Mon–Fri tours at 11am, 1pm & 2pm; £4 including voucher). This distillery was established over a century ago when the founder's wife was nice enough to raise a red flag to warn local crofters if the authorities were on the lookout for their illegal stills. With attractive, pagoda-topped buildings in a nice location, it sells rich, full-bodied whisky with distinctive peaty flavours that comes in an attractive bulbous bottle.

Glen Grant, Rothes (April–Oct Mon–Sat 10am–4pm, Sun 12.30–4pm; free). A well-known, floral whisky aggressively marketed to the younger customer. A regular, well-informed tour, but the highlight here is the attractive Victorian gardens, a mix of well-tended lawns and mixed, mature trees which include a tumbling waterfall and a hidden whisky safe.

Glenfiddich, on the A941 just north of Dufftown (April to mid-Oct Mon–Sat 9.30am–4.30pm, Sun noon–4.30pm; rest of year Mon–Fri 9.30am–4.30pm; free). The biggest and slickest of all the Speyside distilleries, despite the fact that it's still owned by the same Grant family who founded it in 1887, this was the first distillery to offer regular tours to visitors. It's a light, sweet whisky packaged in triangular-shaped bottles – unusually, the bottling is still done on the premises and is part of the tour (which is offered in various languages). A Connoisseurs' Tour is available (£12), as well as an

Transport connections are poor through the area, with irregular buses connecting the main villages, and almost no service at all to remoter parts such as Glenlivet and Tomintoul. The only mainline railway stops in the area are at Keith, twelve miles northeast of Dufftown, and Huntly.

Dufftown

The cheery community of **DUFFTOWN**, founded in 1817 by James Duff, the fourth Earl of Fife, proudly proclaims itself "Malt Whisky Capital of the World" for the reason that it produces more of the stuff than any other town in Britain.

even more specialized tour of the linked Balvenie distillery (£20). Glenfiddich also has its own café-bar and an artists-in-residence programme each summer.

Glenlivet, on the B9008 to Tomintoul (April–Oct Mon–Sat 10am–4pm, Sun 12.30–4pm; free). A famous name in a lonely hillside setting. This was the first licensed distillery in the Highlands, following the 1823 Act of Parliament which aimed to reduce illicit distilling and smuggling. The Glenlivet twelve-year-old malt is a floral, fragrant medium-bodied whisky. A stretch of the Speyside Way passes through the distillery grounds.

Strathisla, Keith (April–Oct Mon–Sat 10am–4pm, Sun 12.30–4pm; £5). A small, old-fashioned distillery claiming to be Scotland's oldest (1786); it's certainly one of the most attractive, with classic pagoda-shaped buildings and the River Isla rushing by. Inside there are some impressive and interesting bits of equipment such as an old-fashioned mashtun and brass-bound spirit safes. The malt itself has a rich almost fruity taste and is pretty rare, but is used as the heart of the better known Chivas Regal blend. You can arrive here on board one of the restored trains of the Keith & Dufftown Railway (see p.218).

In addition, the **Speyside Cooperage** at Craigellachie (see p.219) is part of the official trail, and while there's no whisky made here, a visit offers a fascinating glimpse of a highly skilled and vital part of the industry.

There are also a number of other distilleries, not on the official trail, that you can visit:

Aberlour, on the outskirts of the village (April–Oct Mon–Sat 10.30am & 2pm, Sun 11.30am & 3pm; £7.50; booking essential ☎01340/881249). The twice-daily tours are also quite specialized, with a tutored nosing and the chance to buy and fill your own bottle of cask-strength single malt.

Cragganmore, at Ballindalloch (tours July–Sept Mon–Fri 2.30pm; booking essential ☎01479/874700; £4), also offers a personalized, exclusive tour by appointment which includes a tasting.

Macallan, near Craigellachie (April–Oct Mon–Sat 9.30am–5pm, Nov–March Mon–Fri 11am–3pm; ☎01340/872280) can only take ten people on its tours, and therefore doesn't get the coaches pulling in. Three different tours leave from their small, modern visitor centre: the half-hour "Macallan experience" (free), a one-hour, in-depth "Spirit of Macallan" tour (£8), and the "Macallan Precious Whisky Tour" (£15) which includes a tutored nosing of four different Macallan whiskies. Bookings are essential for both the latter two tours, and all tours can be restricted during the "silent season" when whisky isn't distilled, which generally lasts from early July to mid-Aug.

Glendronach, eight miles northeast of Huntly (Mon–Fri tours 10am & 2pm, shop 9am–4pm; free). An isolated distillery that makes much of its malt's place at the heart of the well-known Teacher's blend, as well as the fact that, uniquely, the stills are heated in the traditional method by coal fires.

A more telling statistic, perhaps, is that as a result Dufftown also raises more capital for the exchequer per head of population than anywhere else in the country. There are nine distilleries around Dufftown (not all of them still working), as well as a cooperage and a coppersmith, and an extended stroll around the outskirts of the town gives a good idea of the density of whisky distilling going on, with glimpses of giant warehouses filled with barrels of the stuff and whiffs of fermenting barley or peat smoke lingering on the breeze.

There isn't a great deal to do in the town, but it's a useful starting point for orienting yourself towards the whisky trail. The small, volunteer-run **Whisky Museum** at 24 Fife St (Mon–Fri 1–4pm, Sat & Sun variable hours; free) has a slightly disorganized collection of illicit distilling equipment, books and old photographs. On the edge of town along the A941 is the town's largest working distillery, **Glenfiddich** (see box on p.216), as well as the old Dufftown train station, which has been restored by enthusiasts in recent years and is now the departure point for the **Keith & Dufftown Railway** (April–Sept 3 trips daily Sat & Sun, June–Aug also runs Fri; 40min; ⓣ01340/821181, ⓦwww.keith-dufftown.org.uk for journey times), which uses various restored diesel locomotives to chug through whisky country to Keith, home of the Strathisla distillery (see box on p.217). Beside the platform at Dufftown a permanent buffet car serves coffee, tea, soup and home-baked cakes. Behind Glenfiddich distillery, the ruin of the thirteenth-century **Balvenie Castle** (April–Sept daily 9.30am–6.30pm; HS; £2.50) sits on a mound overlooking vast piles of whisky barrels. The castle was a Stewart stronghold, which was abandoned after the 1745 uprising, when it was last used as a government garrison. There are more atmospheric remains to be seen if you're approaching Dufftown from the south along the A941; look out for the gaunt hilltop ruins of **Auchindoun Castle** about three miles before you reach town. Although you can't go inside, it's enjoyable to wander along the track from the main road to this three-storey keep encircled by Pictish earthworks.

Practicalities

Dufftown's four main streets converge on its main square, scene of a lively annual party on Hogmanay, when free drams are handed out to revellers. The official **tourist office** is located inside the handsome clock tower at the centre of the square (April–June, Sept & Oct Mon–Sat 10am–1pm & 2–5pm, Sun 11am–3pm; July & Aug Mon–Sat 10am–6pm, Sun 11am–3pm; ⓣ01340/820501), though an informal information and accommodation booking service has developed at The Whisky Shop (ⓣ01340/821097) across the road. You'll certainly need to look no further than this for a vast array of whiskies and beers produced not just on Speyside but all over Scotland; nosings and other special events are organized regularly here, most notably the twice-yearly **Spirit of Speyside Whisky Festival** (ⓦwww.spiritofspeyside.com), which draws whisky experts and enthusiasts to the area late April and late September.

There's a handful of places to stay in Dufftown itself, although you may choose to look elsewhere on Speyside where you will feel a bit closer to the attractive countryside. The only **hostel** accommodation nearby is the small self-catering *Swan Bunkhouse* (ⓣ01542/810334), located at Drummuir, three miles northeast of Dufftown; unfortunately there's no public transport this far. In town, *Morven*, on the main square (ⓣ01340/820507, ⓦwww.dufftown.co.uk/morven.htm; ❶), offers simple, cheap **B&B**, while *Tannochbrae*, 22 Fife St (ⓣ01340/820541, ⓦwww.tannochbrae.co.uk; ❸) is a pleasant, enthusiastically run place with a small restaurant, *Scott's*, on the ground floor. You can also rent **bikes** from here.

The smartest of Dufftown's **restaurants** are the expensive *La Faisanderie*, on the corner of The Square and Balvenie Street (ⓣ01340/821273; closed Tues), which serves local produce such as trout and game in a French style and puts on a special whisky-tasting dinner on Fridays; and *Taste of Speyside*, 10 Balvenie St (ⓣ01340/820860), just off The Square, which is moderately priced and manages to be even more Scottish in its presentation. Less pricey are *Scott's*, on Fife Street, or one of the two fish and chip shops in town. Whisky isn't in short supply in the local pubs and hotels, but for the largest collection in the area you have to head to the *Grouse Inn* at Cabrach, tucked away among the hills ten miles out along the A941 to Rhynie.

Craigellachie

Four miles north of Dufftown, the small settlement of **CRAIGELLACHIE** (pronounced "Craig-*ell*-ach-ee") sits above the confluence of the sparkling waters of the Fiddich and the Spey. From the village, you can look down on a beautiful iron bridge over the Spey built by Thomas Telford in 1815. The local distillery isn't open to the public, though Glen Grant with its attractive gardens is only a few miles up the road at Rothes, and, for an unusual alternative to a distillery tour, the **Speyside Cooperage** (Mon–Fri 9.30am–4pm; £3.10) is well worth a visit. After a short exhibition explaining the ancient and skilled art of cooperage, you're shown onto a balcony overlooking the large workshop where the oak casks for whisky are made and repaired by fast-working, highly skilled coopers.

For somewhere **to stay** in the village there's an extremely welcoming and tasteful B&B attached to the *Green Hall Gallery* on Victoria Street (ⓣ01340/871010, ⓦwww.aboutscotland.com/greenhall; ❸); just along the road, the grand *Craigellachie Hotel* (ⓣ01340/881204, ⓦwww.craigellachie.com; ❼) is the epitome of sumptuous, "tartan-draped" Scottish hospitality, with classy cuisine and a bar lined with whisky bottles. In 2003 the hotel was the unlikely setting for peace talks about the disputed region of Nagorno Karabagh in the Caucasus. In Archiestown, a few miles west of Craigellachie, the pleasant, traditional *Archiestown Hotel* (ⓣ01340/810218, ⓦwww.archiestownhotel.co.uk; ❻) caters for fishermen and outdoor types, and serves good evening **meals**. For more down-to-earth pub grub you're better off heading to the busy *Highlander Inn* (ⓣ01340/881446, ⓦwww.whiskyinn.com; ❺) on Victoria Street in Craigellachie, which serves decent meals, has frequent **folk music sessions** in its bar, and five guestrooms. The tiny *Fiddichside Inn*, on the A95 just outside Craigellachie, is a wonderfully original and convivial **pub** with a garden by the river; quite unfazed by the demands of fashion, it has been in the hands of just two landladies (mother and daughter) for the last seventy years or so.

Aberlour

Two miles southwest from Craigellachie is **ABERLOUR**, officially "Charlestown of Aberlour". Founded in 1812 by Charles Grant, its long main street, neat, flower-filled central square and well-trimmed lawns running down to the Spey have all the markings of a planned village. Though you can visit the distillery here, it's another local produce, **shortbread**, which is exported in greater quantity around the world, mostly in tartan tins adorned with kilted warriors. A local baker, **Joseph Walker**, set up shop here at the start of the twentieth century, quickly gaining a reputation for the product which seems to epitomize the Scottish sweet tooth. A small shop on the High Street, though not the original branch, has a suitably old-fashioned facade, and sells a range of shortbread, oatcakes and other bakery; if you're really keen, you can join the coach loads who visit the factory shop on the outskirts of the village.

Aberlour is right on the Speyside Way (see box on p.214), and the **visitor centre** occupies half of the old train station, just back from the main square (May–Oct daily 10am–5pm; Nov–April open when ranger in office; ⓣ01340/881266, ⓦwww.speysideway.org). The centre has detailed information boards about natural history and other aspects of the way, a relief map of the entire route and films about the area; you can also buy maps of the route and pick up accommodation and transport information as well as the latest weather forecast. While the **campsite** here, *Aberlour Gardens Caravan Park* (ⓣ01340/871586, ⓦwww.aberlourgardens.co.uk; March–Dec), is the best in the area, it's a walk of a mile and a half from either Aberlour or Craigellachie. Alternatively, there's simple and inexpensive **B&B** at *Knockside* (ⓣ01340/881561, ⓦwww.speyside.moray.org/Aberlour/knockside.html; ❶), a mile southeast of the town with nice views. The best place to **eat and drink** is the *Mash Tun*, in the heart of Aberlour near the Spey, a pleasant, traditional pub which serves up good bar meals, real ales and all the local whiskies. To stock up for an encounter with the great outdoors, Walker's is the place for bakery, but you'll also find a range of lovely deli produce at the Spey Larder, right by the village square.

Glenlivet

Beyond Aberlour, the Spey and the main road both head generally southwest to Ballindalloch and, a dozen miles beyond that, Grantown-on-Spey, at the head of the Strathspey region (see p.212). South from Ballindalloch are the quieter, remote glens of the Avon (pronounced "A'an") and Livet rivers. The distillery at **GLENLIVET**, founded in 1824 by George Smith, is one of the most famous on Speyside, and certainly enjoys one of the more attractive settings. You can **stay** in George Smith's former house, right beside the distillery: *Minmore House* (ⓣ01807/590378, ⓦwww.minmorehousehotel.com; ❼), has a lovely country house feel with antique furniture and a wood-panelled bar. The owner is a chef and the **meals**, available to non-residents if they book ahead, are superb.

Tomintoul

South of Glenlivet, deep into the foothills of the Cairngorms, **TOMINTOUL** (pronounced "*tom*-in-towel") is, at 1150ft, the highest village in the Scottish Highlands, and is the northern gateway to the **Lecht** ski area (see box opposite). Tomintoul owes its existence to the post-1745 landowners' panic when, as in other parts of the north, isolated inhabitants were forcibly moved to new, planned villages, where a firm eye could be kept on everybody. Its long, thin layout is reminiscent of a Wild West frontier town; Queen Victoria, passing through, wrote that it was "the most tumble-down, poor-looking place I ever saw". A spur of the Speyside Way connects Ballindalloch through Glenlivet to Tomintoul, and there are plenty of other terrific walking opportunities in the area, as well as some great routes for mountain biking. Information and useful maps about the extensive Glenlivet Crown Estate (ⓦwww.crownestate.co.uk/glenlivet), its wildlife (including reindeer) and numerous paths and bike trails are available from the tourist office or the estate's **ranger's office** at the far end of the long main street (open when staff present; ⓣ01807/580283). Land Rover and walking safaris are offered locally by Glenlivet Wildlife (ⓣ01807/590241, ⓦwww.glenlivet-wildlife.co.uk), including trips out to see black grouse, birds of prey and roe deer.

Skiing and go-karting at the Lecht

The Lecht is the most remote of Scotland's ski areas, but it works hard to make itself appealing with a range of winter and summer activities. While its twenty runs include some gentle beginners' slopes, there's little really challenging for experienced skiers other than a Snowboard Fun Park, with specially built jumps and ramps. Snow-making equipment helps extend the snow season beyond January and February, while there are also various summer activities, including quad bikes and "Devalkarts", go-karts with balloon tyres imported from the Alps which you can use to speed down the slopes from the top of the chairlift. Day passes (summer and winter) start at around £20; ski and boot rental costs £14 a day from the ski school at the base station. For **information** on skiing and road conditions here, call the base station on Ⓣ01975/651440 or check Ⓦwww.lecht.co.uk or Ⓦski.visitscotland.com.

In the central square, the **tourist office** (April–June, Sept & Oct Mon–Sat 9.30am–1pm & 2–5pm; July & Aug Mon–Sat 9am–6pm, Sun 1–5pm; Ⓣ01807/580285) also acts as the local **museum** (same times; free), with mock-ups of an old farm kitchen and a smithy. It is possible to **camp** beside the Glenlivet Estate ranger's office, though there are no facilities. There's a recently renovated SYHA **hostel** situated in the old schoolhouse on Main Street (Ⓣ0870/004 1152; mid-March to Sept). Of the **B&Bs**, try *Findron Farmhouse*, a working farm half a mile south of town on the Braemar road (Ⓣ01807/580382, Ⓦwww.findronfarmhouse.co.uk; ❶), while the *Glenavon* (Ⓣ01807/580218, Ⓦwww.glenavon-hotel.co.uk; ❸) is the most convivial of the **hotels** gathered around the main square. For something to eat, head to the *Clockhouse* **restaurant** (Ⓣ01807/580378), also on the square. The Whisky Castle shop at 6 Main St not only stocks something like four hundred different types of whisky, but also operates as a coffee shop and rents out **bikes** (Ⓣ01807/580213).

Travel details

Trains

Aberdeen to: Dundee (every 30min; 1hr 15min); Edinburgh (1–2 hourly; 2hr 35min); Elgin (Mon–Sat 10 daily, 5 on Sun; 1hr 30min); Glasgow (hourly; 2hr 35min); Inverurie (Mon–Sat 10 daily, 5 on Sun; 20min); London (5 daily direct; 7hr); Nairn (Mon–Sat 10 daily, 5 on Sun; 2hr).
Aviemore to: Cairngorm ski area (hourly; 30min); Edinburgh (Mon–Sat 6 daily, 3 on Sun; 2hr 30min); Glasgow (3 daily, 2 on Sun; 2hr 30min); Inverness (Mon–Sat 9 daily, 3 on Sun; 1hr).
Balloch to: Glasgow (every 30min; 40min).
Crianlarich to: Fort William (4 Mon–Sat, 2 Sun; 1hr 50min); Glasgow Queen Street (3–4 Mon–Sat, 2 Sun; 1hr 50min); Oban (6 Mon–Sat, 3 Sun; 1hr 10min).
Dundee to: Aberdeen (every 30min; 1hr 15min); Edinburgh (1–2 hourly; 1hr 15min); Glasgow (hourly; 1hr 15min).
Kingussie to: Edinburgh (Mon–Sat 4 daily, 3 on Sun; 2hr 30min); Glasgow (2 daily; 2hr 30min); Inverness (Mon–Sat 6 daily, 3 on Sun; 1hr).
Perth to: Aberdeen (hourly; 1hr 40min); Blair Atholl (3–7 daily; 40min); Dundee (hourly; 25min); Dunkeld (3–7 daily; 20min); Edinburgh (9 daily; 1hr 25min); Glasgow Queen Street (hourly; 1hr 5min); Inverness (4–9 daily; 2hr); Pitlochry (4–9 daily; 30min); Stirling (hourly; 30min).
Rannoch to: Corrour (2–4 daily; 12min); Fort William (2–4 daily; 1hr); Glasgow Queen Street (2–4 daily; 2hr 45min); London Euston (sleeper service; Sun–Fri daily; 11hr).
Stirling to: Aberdeen (hourly; 2hr 15min); Dundee (hourly; 1hr); Edinburgh (hourly; 1hr); Falkirk Grahamston (hourly; 30min); Glasgow Queen Street (hourly; 30min); Inverness (3–5 daily; 2hr 30min); Perth (hourly; 30min).

Buses

Aberdeen to: Ballater (hourly; 1hr 45min); Banchory (every 30min; 55min); Braemar (hourly; 2hr 10min); Crathie for Balmoral (hourly; 1hr 55min); Dundee (hourly; 2hr); Elgin (hourly; 2hr 35min); Forres (hourly; 2hr 35min); Inverurie (hourly; 45min).
Aberfeldy to: Pitlochry (3 daily; 30min); Killin (5 daily; 1hr).
Aberfoyle to: Callander (June–Sept 4 Thurs–Tues; 25min); Port of Menteith (June–Sept 4 Thurs–Tues; 10min).
Aviemore to: Edinburgh (5 daily; 2hr 30min–3hr 30min); Glasgow (7 daily; 3hr 30min); Grantown-on-Spey (Mon–Sat 6–8 daily; 40min); Inverness (hourly; 45min).
Balloch to: Balmaha (every 2hr; 25min); Luss (8–9 daily; 15min).
Callander to Loch Katrine (June–Sept 4 daily; 55min).
Dufftown to: Aberlour (Mon–Sat hourly; 15min); Elgin (Mon–Sat hourly; 50min).
Dundee to: Aberdeen (hourly; 2hr); Arbroath (hourly; 50min); Blairgowrie (hourly; 1hr); Kirriemuir (hourly; 1hr 10min); Meigle (hourly; 40min).
Kingussie/Newtonmore to: Edinburgh (5 daily direct; 2hr 30min–3hr 30min); Inverness (8 daily; 1hr).
Kinloch Rannoch to: Pitlochry (4 daily; 1hr); Rannoch Station (3 daily; 40min).
Luss to Tarbet (Mon–Sat 4 daily; 10min).
Perth to: Aberfeldy (10 daily; 1hr 15min); Dundee (hourly; 45min); Dunkeld (hourly; 30min); Edinburgh (hourly; 1hr 20min); Glasgow (hourly; 1hr 35min); Gleneagles (hourly; 25min); Inverness (hourly; 2hr 45min); Oban (2 daily; 3hr); Pitlochry (hourly; 45min); Stirling (hourly; 50min).
Stirling to: Aberfoyle (4 daily; 45min); Callander (hourly; 45min); Dollar (6 daily; 35min); Doune (hourly; 25min); Dunblane (hourly; 25min); Dundee (hourly; 1hr 30min); Edinburgh (hourly; 1hr 10min); Falkirk (every 40min; 30min); Glasgow (hourly; 50min); Inverness (every 2hr; 3hr 20min); Killin (3–4 daily; 1hr 30min); Perth (hourly; 40min); St Andrews (3 daily; 2hr).

Flights

Aberdeen to: Belfast (Mon–Fri 1 daily; 1hr 15min); Birmingham (Mon–Fri 2 daily, Sat & Sun 1 daily; 1hr 30min); Dublin (1 daily; 1hr 5min); Glasgow (1 daily; 45min); Kirkwall, Orkney (2 daily; 55min); London Gatwick (4 daily; 1hr 30min); London Heathrow (5–7 daily; 1hr 30min); London Luton (2 daily; 1hr 30min); Manchester (Mon–Fri 6 daily, Sat & Sun 2 daily; 1hr 20min); Newcastle (Mon–Fri 4 daily, 2 on Sun; 1hr); Sumburgh, Shetland (Mon–Fri 3 daily, Sat & Sun 2 daily; 1hr).
Dundee to: London City (Mon–Fri 4 daily, 1 on Sat, 3 on Sun; 1hr 25min).

3

The Great Glen

CHAPTER 3

Highlights

* **Commando Memorial** An exposed but dramatic place to take in sweeping views over Scotland's highest ben (Nevis) and its longest glen (the Great Glen). See p.234
* **Glen Coe** Spectacular, moody, poignant and full of history – a glorious place for hiking or simple admiration. See p.235
* **Fishing on Loch Ness** Chances of seeing the famous monster Nessie aren't high, but tales of "the one that got away" are bound to be unusual. See p.239
* **Glen Affric** Some of Scotland's best hidden scenery, with ancient Caledonian forests and gushing rivers. See p.244
* **Culloden battlefield** Tramp the heather moor of Bonnie Prince Charlie's last stand in 1746. See p.253
* **Dolphins of the Moray Firth** Europe's most northerly school of bottle-nosed dolphins, seen from the shore or on a boat trip. See p.254

△ Dolphin-spotting around the Moray Firth

3

The Great Glen

The **Great Glen**, a major geological fault line cutting diagonally across the Highlands from Fort William to Inverness, is the defining geographic feature of the north of Scotland. A huge rift valley was formed when the northwestern and southeastern sides of the fault slid in opposite directions for more than sixty miles, while the present landscape was shaped by glaciers that retreated only around 8000 BC. The glen is impressive more for its sheer scale than its beauty, but the imposing barrier of loch and mountain means that no one can travel into the northern Highlands without passing through it. With the two major service centres of the Highlands at either end it makes an obvious and rewarding route between the west and east coasts.

Of the Great Glen's four elongated lochs, the most famous is **Loch Ness**, home to the mythical monster; lochs **Oich**, **Lochy** and **Linnhe** (the last of these a sea loch) are less renowned though no less attractive. All four are linked by the Caledonian Canal. The southwestern end of the Great Glen is dominated by **Fort**

The Great Glen Way and cycle path

The seventy-mile cleft of the Great Glen is the most obvious – and by far the flattest – way of traversing northern Scotland from coast to coast. The **Great Glen Way** long-distance footpath (Ⓦwww.greatglenway.com) is a relatively undemanding five- to six-day hike that uses a combination of canal towpath and forest- and hill-tracks between Fort William and Inverness. Accommodation is readily available all the way along the route in campsites, hostels, bunkhouses and B&Bs, though in high season it's worth booking ahead and if you know you're going to arrive late somewhere it's worth checking that you can still get a meal where you're staying or somewhere nearby. The maps you'll need to do the whole thing are Ordnance Survey Landranger maps 41, 34 and 26. Alternatively, *The Great Glen Way and Cycle Route* published by Footprint (£4.50) concisely maps out the route. There are various guidebooks describing the route, including *The Great Glen Way* published by Rucksack Readers (£10.99). A **cycle path** also traverses the Glen, offering a tranquil alternative to the hazardous A82. The path, which shares some of its route with the footpath but also utilizes stretches of minor roads, is well signposted and can be managed in one long day or two easier days. Bikes can be rented at Fort William, Benavie, Fort Augustus, Drumnadrochit and Inverness, from where you can tackle shorter sections. The Forestry Commission publishes *Cycling in the Forest, The Great Glen*, a handy booklet that highlights the various sections of the route (Ⓣ01320/366322 or 01397/702184, Ⓦwww.forestry.gov.uk).

The suggested **direction** for following both routes is from west to east – the direction of the prevailing southwesterly wind.

William, the second-largest town in the Highland region – a useful base, with plenty of places to stay and eat. At the heart of the Lochaber area, Fort William is an excellent hub for accessing a host of outdoor activities. While the town itself is not one of the more charming places you'll encounter in Scotland, the surrounding countryside is a blend of rugged mountain terrain and tranquil sea loch. Dominating the scene to the south is **Ben Nevis**, Britain's highest peak, best approached from scenic Glen Nevis. The most famous glen of all, **Glen Coe**, lies on the main A82 road half an hour's drive south of Fort William, the two separated by the

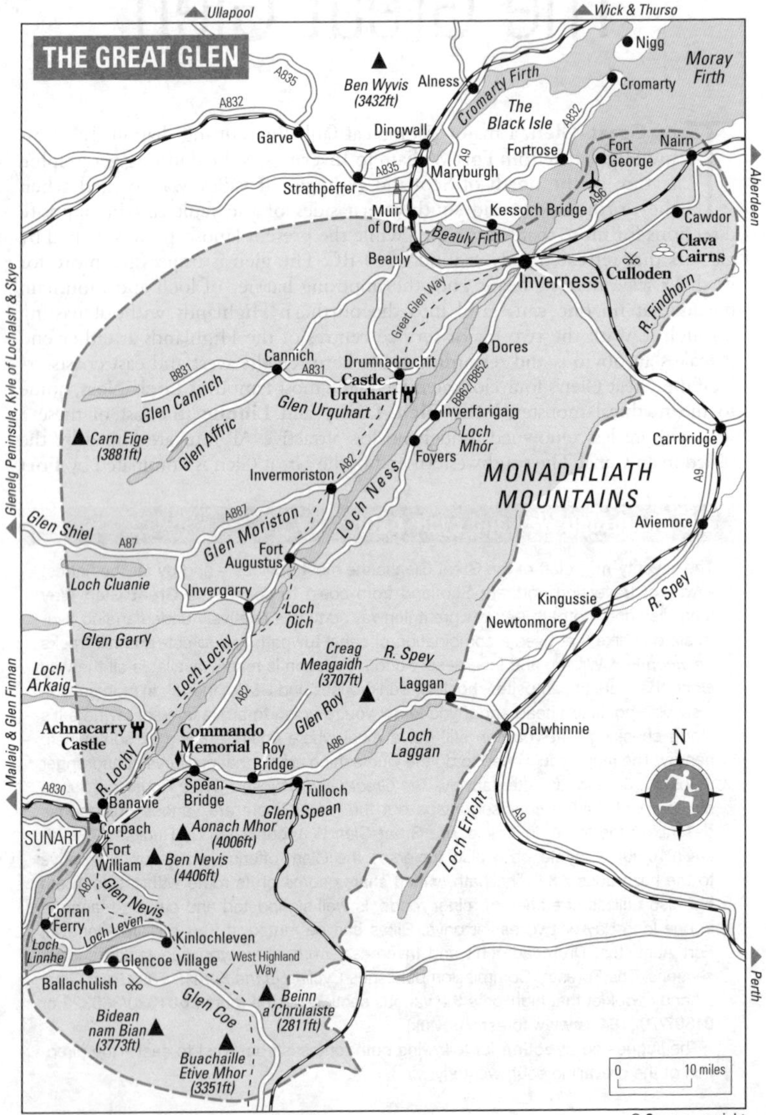

coastal inlet of **Loch Leven**. Nowadays the whole area is unashamedly given over to tourism, and Fort William is swamped by bus tours throughout the summer, but, as ever in the Highlands, within a thirty-minute drive you can be totally alone.

At the northeastern end of the Great Glen is the capital of the Highlands, **Inverness**, a pleasant, unhurried town with a couple of worthwhile sights, but used most often as a springboard to remoter areas further north. Inevitably, most transport links to the northern Highlands, including Ullapool, Thurso and the Orkney and Shetland islands, pass through Inverness.

The area has a turbulent and bloody **history**. Founded in 1655 and named in honour of William III, Fort William was successfully held by government troops during both of the Jacobite risings; the country to the southwest is inextricably associated with Bonnie Prince Charlie's flight after Culloden. Glen Coe is another historic site with a violent past, renowned as much for the infamous massacre of 1692 as for its magnificent scenery.

Transport

The main **A82** road runs the length of the Great Glen, although relatively high traffic levels mean that it's not a fast or particularly easy route to drive. The area is reasonably well served by **buses**, with several daily services between Inverness and Fort William, and a couple of extra buses covering the section between Fort William and Invergarry during school terms. However, the traditional and most rewarding way to travel through the Glen itself is by **boat**. A flotilla of kayaks, small yachts and pleasure vessels take advantage of the canal and its old wooden locks during the summer. Alternatively, an excellent **cycle path** traverses the Glen, as well as a long-distance footpath, the seventy-three mile **Great Glen Way**, which takes five to six days to walk in full (see box p.225).

Fort William

With its stunning position on Loch Linnhe, tucked in below the snow-streaked bulk of Ben Nevis, **FORT WILLIAM** (known by the many walkers and climbers that come here as "Fort Bill"), should be a gem. Sadly, the same lack of taste that nearly saw the town renamed "Abernevis" in the 1950s is evident in the ribbon bungalow development and ill-advised dual carriageway – complete with grubby pedestrian underpass – which have wrecked the waterfront. The main street and the little squares off it are more appealing, though occupied by some decidedly tacky tourist gift shops. Ultimately, however, Fort William is an important regional centre, with useful facilities including a cinema, swimming pool and a large supermarket.

Arrival, information and accommodation

Next to each other at the north end of the High Street are the **bus station** (with services from Inverness) and the **train station** (a stop on the scenic West Highland Railway direct from Glasgow; see p.271). The busy **tourist office** is on Cameron Square, just off High Street (April–May & Sept Mon–Sat 9am–5pm, Sun 10am–4pm; June–Aug Mon–Sat 9am–6pm, Sun 10am–4pm; Oct Mon–Fri 10am–5pm, Sat 10am–4pm; Sun 10am–2pm; Nov–March Mon–Fri 10am–5pm, Sat 10am–4pm; Ⓣ01397/703781, Ⓦwww.visithighlands.com). You'll find a host of outdoor-activity specialists in town. High-spec **mountain bikes** are available for rent at Off Beat Bikes (Ⓣ01397/704008) at 117 High St; they know the best routes, issue free maps and also have a branch open at the Nevis Range gondola base station

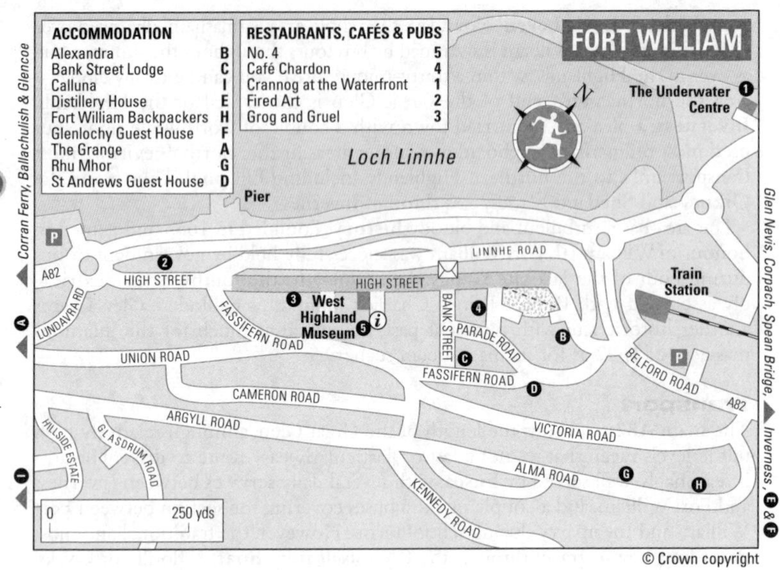

(ⓣ01397/705825; June–Sept) – a location boasting forest rides and which hosts a World Cup downhill mountain-bike event in September each year. The Underwater Centre (ⓣ01397/703786, ⓦwww.theunderwatercentre.co.uk), at the water's edge beyond the train station and Morrison's supermarket, runs PADI courses and offers guided dives; and local **mountain guides** include Alan Kimber of *Calluna* (see opposite) and The **Snowgoose Mountain Centre** (ⓣ01397/772467, ⓦwww.highland-mountain-guides.co.uk), set beside the *Smiddy Bunkhouse and Blacksmith's Hostel* (see p.230), which offers instruction, rental and residential courses including hill walking, mountaineering and canoeing.

Fort William's plentiful **accommodation** ranges from large luxury hotels to budget hostels and bunkhouses. Numerous B&Bs are also scattered across the town, many of them in the suburb of Corpach on the other side of Loch Linnhe, three miles along the Mallaig road (served by regular buses), where you'll also find a couple of good hostels.

In-town accommodation

Hotels and B&Bs

Alexandra Hotel The Parade ⓣ01397/702241, ⓦwww.strathmorehotels.com. Established hotel in the town centre, with well-appointed rooms and a restaurant. 6

Distillery House North Rd ⓣ01397/700103, ⓦwww.visit-fortwilliam.co.uk/distillery-house. Very comfortable, well-equipped upper-range guest house situated ten minutes' walk north of the town centre near the Glen Nevis turn-off . 5

Glenlochy Guest House Nevis Bridge, opposite the Distillery House ⓣ01397/702909, ⓦwww.glenlochy.co.uk. Comfortable, 12-bed B&B in peaceful surroundings. Non-smoking. 4

The Grange Grange Rd ⓣ01397/705516, ⓦwww.thegrange-scotland.co.uk. Top-grade accommodation in a striking old stone house, with four luxurious en-suite doubles and a spacious garden. Vegetarian breakfasts on request. Non-smoking. April–Oct. 6

Rhu Mhor Alma Rd ⓣ01397/702213, ⓦwww.rhumhor.co.uk. Congenial and characterful B&B, ten minutes' walk from the town centre, offering good breakfasts; vegetarians and vegans are catered for by arrangement. 2

Fort William and Glen Coe outdoor activities

As the self-proclaimed "Outdoors Capital of the UK", in and around Fort William and Glen Coe you'll find a high concentration of **outdoor activity** specialists who can help you make the most of the area's spectacular array of lochs, rivers and mountains. Most of the places and people listed below offer guiding, instruction and equipment rental, and they're all good sources of advice about their particular speciality. Other good places to go for **information** and advice are outdoor equipment stores – in Fort William the best is Nevisport, at the train station end of High Street – or backpackers and bunkhouses, many of which are run by outdoor enthusiasts. Nevisport, as well as local bookshops and tourist information offices, also keep a good selection of **guidebooks** outlining local walks.

Climbing For rock climbing or winter mountaineering – a popular sport that ensures that the climbing community is active in this area throughout the year – contact any of the mountain guides listed below under "Walking" or visit Ice-Factor, the world's largest indoor ice-climbing wall, in Kinlochleven (see p.239).

Diving There are some excellent wrecks and kelp forests off the west coast. The Underwater Centre (see opposite) can advise further on any aspect of diving.

Fishing For fly-fishing tuition and guiding, contact Jimmy Couts (see p.234) at Roy Bridge.

Horse riding Turlundy Farm Trout Fishery and Riding Centre, three miles north of Fort William on the A82, caters for experienced riders.

Mountain biking Contact Off Beat Bikes (see p.227) in Fort William, Nevis Range (see below) or check out Ⓦwww.ridefortwilliam.co.uk, or for a guide see Ⓦwww.nofussevents.co.uk.

Skiing Skiing opportunities are available at the Nevis Range Ski Centre (see p.233) and the Glen Coe Ski Centre (see p.237).

Walking Some of the best routes include the Great Glen Way (see p.225), walks in Glen Nevis and on Ben Nevis (see p.231), the Commando Trail (see p.235) and walks in Glen Coe (see p.236). If you're interested in tackling the more difficult peaks, traverses such as the Aonach Eagach ridge in Glen Coe, or want to improve your mountain skills including navigation, it's a good idea to hire a mountain guide, normally for around £100 a day. Contact *Calluna* (see below), Snowgoose Mountain Centre (see opposite), or Glencoe Mountain Sport (see p.237).

Watersports For kayaking, contact Snowgoose Mountain Centre (see opposite); for its derivative, fun-yakking (using inflatable two-man rafts-cum-kayaks), on local rivers, get in touch with Vertical Descents (see p.238).

St Andrews Guest House Fassifern Rd Ⓣ01397/703038, Ⓦwww.standrewsguesthouse.co.uk. Comfortable and extremely central B&B in an attractive converted granite choir school featuring various inscriptions and stained-glass windows. ❷

Hostels and campsites

Bank Street Lodge Bank Street Ⓣ01397/700070. A 43-bed centrally located lodge hostel that's handy for transport and local amenities.

Calluna Heathcroft Ⓣ01397/700451, Ⓦwww.fortwilliamholiday.co.uk. Well-run self-catering and hostel accommodation configured for individual, family and group stays. Free pick-up from town available. Owner is one of the area's top mountain guides, so there's plenty of outdoor advice available.

Fort William Backpackers Alma Rd Ⓣ01397/700711, Ⓦwww.scotlands-top-hostels.com. A busy 38-bed, rambling, archetypal backpacker hostel five minutes' walk up the hill from town, with great views and large communal areas.

Out of town

Hotels and B&Bs

Achintee Farm Guest House Glen Nevis Ⓣ01397/702240, Ⓦwww.achinteefarm.com. Friendly B&B with adjoining hostel located right by the Ben Nevis Inn at start of the Ben Nevis footpath. ❹

Glenloy Lodge B&B A former hunting lodge, six miles north of town on B8004 north of Banavie ⓣ01397/712700. Comfortable, friendly and secluded with views to Ben Nevis. Excellent breakfast. Pine martens occasionally visit. ❺

Inverlochy Castle Two miles north of town on the A82 ⓣ01397/702177, ⓦwww.inverlochycastlehotel.co.uk. A grand country-house hotel set in wooded parkland; exceptional levels of service and outstanding, Michelin-star food – but all at a price. ❾

Rhiw Goch Overlooking Neptune's Staircase with great views to Ben Nevis, this Banavie-based B&B is comfortable and welcoming. Great breakfasts. ⓣ01397/772373, ⓦwww2.prestel.co.uk/rhiwgoch. ❸

Hostels and campsites

Ben Nevis Bunkhouse Achintee Farm, Glen Nevis ⓣ01397/702240, ⓦwww.achinteefarm.com. A more civilized option than the nearby SYHA place, with hot showers and self-catering kitchen adjoining a smart B&B (see p.229). Located just over the river from the Ben Nevis Visitor Centre – reach it by following the Ben Nevis path across the river or by taking Achintee Rd along the north side of the River Nevis from Claggan.

Ben Nevis Inn Achintee, Glen Nevis ⓣ01397/701227. A basic and cosy 20-bed bunkhouse housed within the rustic and lively pub just north of the Achintee Farm Guest House.

Farr Cottage Lodge On the main A830 in Corpach ⓣ01397/772315, ⓦwww.farrcottage.co.uk. Well-equipped, lively hostel with range of dorms and double/twin rooms (❶). Offers a multitude of outdoor activities whilst evening entertainment includes whisky tastings.

Glen Nevis Caravan and Camping Park Two miles up the Glen Nevis road ⓣ01397/702191, ⓦwww.glennevisholidays.co.uk. Well equipped including disabled facilities, hot showers, a shop and restaurant.

Glen Nevis SYHA hostel Two and a half miles up the Glen Nevis road opposite start of path to summit ⓣ0870/004 1120, ⓦwww.syha.org.uk. Though far from town, an excellent base for walkers in a friendly hostel. Very busy in summer.

Smiddy Bunkhouse & Blacksmith's Backpacker Lodge Station Rd ⓣ01397/772467, ⓦwww.highland-mountain-guides.co.uk. A cosy fourteen-bed hostel and simpler 12-bed bunkhouse right next to Corpach train station at the entrance to the Caledonian Canal. Part of the Snowgoose Mountain Centre, offering year-round mountaineering, kayaking and other outdoor activities.

The Town

Fort William's downfall started in the nineteenth century, when the original fort, which gave the town its name, was demolished to make way for the train line. Today, the town is a sprawl of dual carriageways, and there's little to detain you except the splendid and idiosyncratic **West Highland Museum**, on Cameron Square, just off the High Street (June–Sept Mon–Sat 10am–5pm; July & Aug also Sun 2–5pm; Oct–May Mon–Sat 10am–4pm; £3). Its collections cover virtually every aspect of Highland life and the presentation is traditional, but very well done, making a refreshing change from state-of-the-art heritage centres. There's a secret portrait of Bonnie Prince Charlie, the long Spanish rifle used in the famous Appin Murder and even a 550kg slab of aluminium, the stuff that's processed locally into silver foil.

Excursions from town include the 84-mile round-trip to Mallaig (see p.273) on the West Highland Railway Line aboard the **Jacobite Steam Train** (end May to mid-Oct Mon–Fri; mid-July to end Aug also Sun; depart Fort William 10.20am, return 4pm, £26; bookings ⓣ01463/239026, ⓦwww.steamtrain.info). Heading along the shore of Loch Eil to the west coast via historic Glenfinnan (see p.270), the journey takes in some of the region's most spectacular scenery, though these days it's as popular for its role as the locomotive used in the *Harry Potter* films. Several **cruises** also leave from the town pier every day, offering the chance to spot the marine life of Loch Linnhe, which includes seals and seabirds. Try Seal Island Cruises (March–Oct; £7.50; ⓣ01397/700714, ⓦwww.crannog.net) or Seaventures, who offer exhilarating fast boat trips (March–Nov; 1–6hrs from £10; ⓣ01397/701687).

Eating and drinking

Fort William has a reasonable range of places **to eat**. The pick of the bunch is the moderately priced *Crannog at the Waterfront* (☎01397/705589) located next to the Underwater Centre beyond the train station. Attentive staff offer the freshest of seafood, including oysters and langoustines, whilst you drink real ale or wine overlooking the loch. *No. 4*, adjacent to the tourist office, also offers moderately priced Scottish-based dishes including seafood and game. On the High Street, the *Grog and Gruel* is the place to go for Scottish real ales, entertainment and some traditional pub grub. There are also a number of places out of town well worth seeking out for good food: the *Old Pines* near Spean Bridge (see p.233; closed Mon) is superb, while *An Crann* (☎01397/773114; closed Sun), just outside Banavie (Highland Country **bus** #40) on the B8004, offers tasty Scottish dishes in a delightful, cosy setting. The *Ben Nevis Inn* (see opposite) up Glen Nevis is also popular for pub grub. Your best chance of a decent coffee in town is at *Fired Art*, a "paint-your-own-pottery" studio with its own café at 147 High St. A good place for **picnic food** as well as a snack is the *Café Chardon*, up a lane off High Street; they do excellent baguettes, croissants and pastries to eat in or take away.

Around Fort William

Any disappointment you harbour about the dispiriting flavour of Fort William itself should be offset against the wealth of scenery and activities in its immediate vicinity. Most obvious – on a clear day, at least – is **Ben Nevis**, the most popular, though hardly the most rewarding, of Scotland's high peaks, the path up which leaves from **Glen Nevis**, itself a starting point for excellent walks of various lengths and elevations. The mountain abutting Ben Nevis is **Aonach Mhor**, home of Scotland's most modern ski resort and in summer a honey-pot for downhill mountain-bike enthusiasts. Some of the best views of these peaks can be had from **Corpach**, a small village opposite Fort William which marks the start of the **Caledonian Canal.**

The main road travelling up the Great Glen from Fort William towards Inverness is the A82, ten miles along which is the small settlement of **Spean Bridge**, a good waypoint for getting to various remote and attractive walking areas, notably glens **Spean** and **Roy**, found along the A86 trunk road, which links across the central highlands to the A9 and the Speyside region (see p.214).

Glen Nevis

A ten-minute drive south of Fort William, **GLEN NEVIS** is indisputably among the Highlands' most impressive glens: a classic U-shaped glacial valley hemmed in by steep bracken-covered slopes and swaths of blue-grey scree. Herds of shaggy Highland cattle graze the valley floor, where a sparkling river gushes through glades of trees. With the forbidding mass of Ben Nevis rising steeply to the north, it's not surprising this valley has been chosen as the location for scenes in several films, such as *Rob Roy* and *Braveheart*. Apart from its natural beauty, Glen Nevis is also the starting point for the ascent of Britain's highest peak, Ben Nevis, and you can rent **mountain equipment** and **mountain bikes** at the trailhead. The best map is *Harvey's Ben Nevis Walkers Map and Guide*, available from the tourist office and most local bookshops and outdoor stores. Highland Country **bus** #42 runs from the bus station, beside

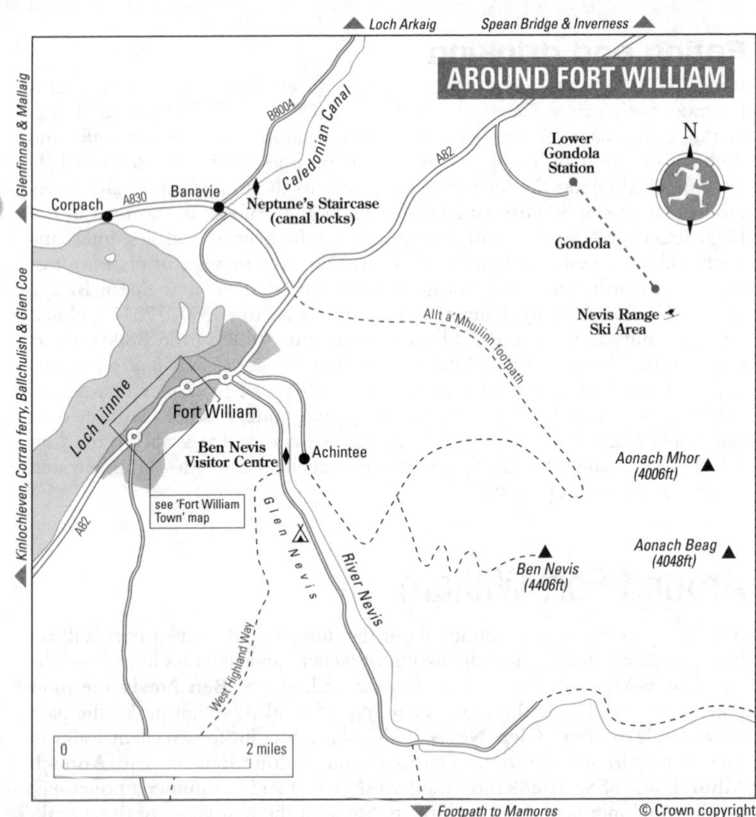

the supermarket and the train station, Fort William (every 1hr 20min), as far as the SYHA hostel, two and a half miles up the Glen Nevis road; some buses carry on another two and a half miles up the glen to the car park by the Lower Falls (late May to Oct only; 10min bus ride beyond the hostel).

A great **low-level walk** (six miles round-trip) runs from the end of the road at the top of Glen Nevis. The good but very rocky path leads through a dramatic gorge with impressive falls and rapids, then opens out into a secret hanging valley, carpeted with wild flowers, with a high waterfall at the far end. It's a pretty place for a picnic and if you're really energetic you can walk the full twelve miles on over Rannoch Moor to **Corrour Station** (see p.186), where you can pick up one of three daily trains to take you back to Fort William.

Of all the walks in and around Glen Nevis, the **ascent of Ben Nevis** (4406ft), Britain's highest summit, inevitably attracts the most attention. Despite the fact that it's quite a slog up to the summit, and that it is by no means the most attractive mountain in Scotland, in high summer the trail is teeming with hikers, whatever the weather. However, this doesn't mean the mountain should be treated casually. It can snow round the summit any day of the year and more people perish here annually than on Everest, so take the necessary precautions (see p.59); in winter, of course, the mountain should be left to the experts. The most obvious **route** to the summit, a Victorian pony path up the whaleback

The Nevis Range

Seven miles northeast of Fort William by the A82, on the slopes of **Aonach Mhor**, one of the high mountains abutting Ben Nevis, the **Nevis Range** (Ⓣ01397/705825, Ⓦwww.nevis-range.co.uk) is, in winter, Scotland's highest ski area. All year round, however, Highland County bus #42 runs from Fort William five times a day (Mon–Sat; 3 on Sun) to the base station of the country's only **gondola** system (10am–5pm; July & Aug daily 9.30am–6pm, closed mid-Nov to mid-Dec for maintenance; £8 return). The one-and-a-half mile gondola trip (15min), rising 2000ft, gives an easy approach to some high-level walking as well as spectacular views from the terrace of the self-service restaurant at the top station. From the top of the gondola station, you can experience Britain's only World Cup standard **downhill mountain bike course** (mid-May to mid-Sept 11am–3pm; £10 includes gondola one-way), a hair-raising 3km route. It's not for the faint-hearted. There's also 25 miles of waymarked off-road bike routes, known as the Witch's Trails, on the mountainside and in the Leanachan Forest, ranging from gentle paths to cross-country scrambles. Off Beat Bikes (Ⓣ01397/704008, Ⓦwww.offbeatbikes.co.uk) rent general mountain bikes as well as full-suspension bikes for the downhill course from their shops in Fort William and at the gondola base station (mid-May to mid-Sept).

south side of the mountain, built to service the observatory that once stood on the top, starts from the helpful Ben Nevis visitor centre (daily Easter to mid-May & Oct 9am–5pm; mid-May to end Sept 9am–6pm; a mile and a half southeast of Fort William along the Glen Nevis road (bus #42 from An Aird in Fort William). Return via the main route or, if the weather is settled and you're confident enough, make a side trip from the wide saddle into the **Allt a'Mhuilinn glen** for spectacular views of the great cliffs on Ben Nevis's north face. Allow a full day for the climb (8hr).

Neptune's Staircase and Corpach

At the suburb of **BANAVIE**, three miles north of the centre of Fort William along the A830 to Mallaig, the Caledonian Canal climbs 64ft in less than half a mile via a punishing but picturesque series of eight locks known as **Neptune's Staircase**. There are stunning views from here of Ben Nevis and its neighbours, and it's a popular point from which to walk or cycle along the canal towpath. Bikes (£12.50 per day) and Canadian canoes (£25 per day) can be rented from *Rhiw Goch* B&B (see p.230) a half-mile up the B8004 in Banavie. If you do choose to cycle along the Caledonian Canal, look out for *The Eagle Inn* at Laggan Locks at the head of Loch Lochy, where fresh seafood and real ale are on offer aboard a cosy 1926 Dutch barge (Ⓣ07789/858567; Easter–Oct).

Back on the A830 and a mile west of Banavie is the suburb of **CORPACH**, the point where the canal enters from Loch Linnhe. The site of a mothballed paper mill, the main event here is the **Treasures of the Earth** exhibition (daily: July–Sept 9.30am–7pm; all other times 10am–5pm, closed Jan; £3.50) a useful rainy-day option for families, which has a dazzling array of rocks, crystals, gemstones and fossils.

Spean Bridge and Glen Spean

Ten miles northeast of Fort William, the village of **SPEAN BRIDGE** marks the junction of the A82 with the A86 from Dalwhinnie (see p.188) and

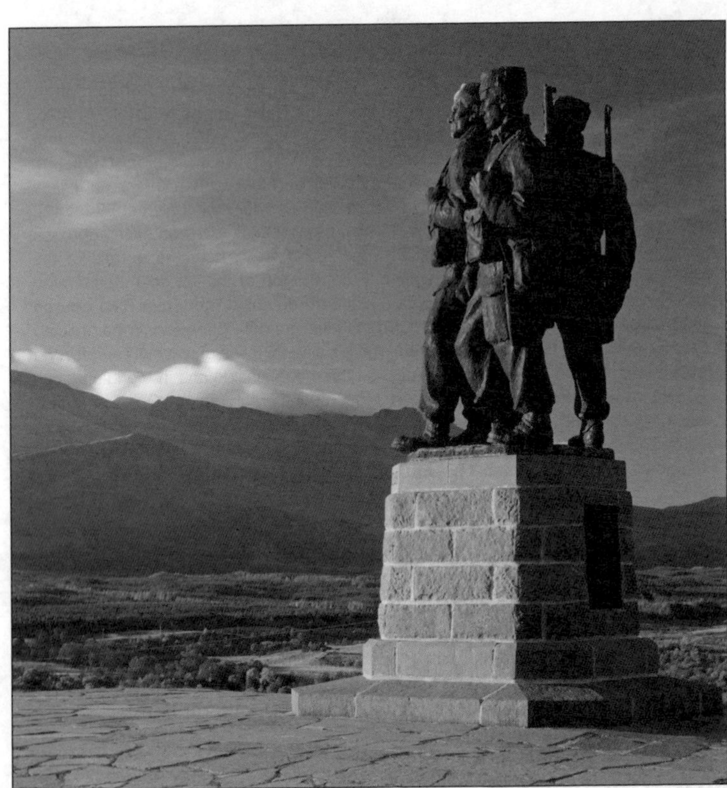

△ World War II Commando Memorial

Kingussie (see p.213). If you're here, it's well worth heading a mile out of the village on the A82 towards Inverness to the **Commando Memorial**, a group of bronze soldiers commemorating the men who trained in the area during World War II. The statue looks out on an awesome sweep of moor and mountain that takes in Lochaber and the Ben Nevis massif. A few hundred yards from the memorial, on the minor B8004 which heads towards **Gairlochy**, is the welcoming and upmarket *Old Pines Hotel and Restaurant* (Ⓣ01397/712324, Ⓦwww.oldpines.co.uk; half-board ⑧, B&B ⑥).

At **ROY BRIDGE**, three miles east of Spean Bridge, a minor road turns off up **Glen Roy**. A couple of miles along the glen, you'll see the so-called "parallel roads": not roads at all, but ancient beaches at various levels along the valley sides which mark the shorelines of a loch confined here by a glacial dam in the last Ice Age. Back on the A86, two miles east of Roy Bridge, *Aite Cruinnichidh* (Ⓣ01397/712315, Ⓦwww.highland-hostel.co.uk) is a comfortable **bunkhouse** in a beautiful setting, with good facilities (including a sauna) and local advice for walkers and cyclists. The nearby Roy Bridge Store is good for provisions while Jimmy Couts (Ⓣ01397/712812, Ⓦwww.fishing-scotland.co.uk) is the man to call for **fly-fishing** tuition and excursions.

Five miles further east, the railway line and road part company at **TULLOCH**, where trains swing south to pass Loch Treig and cross Rannoch Moor (see

The Commando Trail

From 1942 until the end of World War II, the Lochaber district around the southern part of the Great Glen was used as a training area by the elite **commando** units of the British army. A striking **memorial** depicting a group of bronze soldiers, sculpted in 1952 by Scott Sutherland, stands overlooking an awesome sweep of moor and mountain beside the A82 just to the north of Spean Bridge. Nearby, in a room inside the *Spean Bridge Hotel* (Ⓣ01397/712250; ④) the proudly assembled **Commando Exhibition** (April–Oct daily 9.15am–4.45pm; free) has impressive displays of photos, medals and memorabilia.

The soldiers' base was at **Achnacarry Castle**, hereditary seat of the Clan Cameron, around which there's an interesting five-mile **walk** retracing many of the places used by them during their training. To get here, follow the minor B8004 beside the memorial, which branches down to Gairlochy, by the canalside at Loch Lochy's southern tip, then follow the signs for the small **Clan Cameron museum** (Easter to mid-Oct daily 1.30–5.30pm; July & Aug opens at 11am; Ⓦwww.clan-cameron.org; £3), located in the old post office near the castle still occupied by Lady Cameron. The museum tells the clan history, including its involvement in the 1745 rebellion, plus memorabilia relating to the commandos' residency. You can park your car here and walk to the eastern end of **Loch Arkaig**, one of Scotland's most ruggedly wild and remote stretches of water, then walk down the tree-lined **Mile Dorcha**, or Dark Mile. Around here there are various caves and small bothies used by **Bonnie Prince Charlie** when he was on the run after Culloden, dodging government troops, putting trust in only a few loyal companions, and desperately hoping for the arrival of a French ship to carry him to safety. The road leads to the shores of **Loch Lochy**, where the commandos would practise opposed landings, often using live ammunition to keep them on their toes. After a mile by the loch-side, turn right back along the road which leads to the Clan Cameron museum. A **leaflet** giving a fuller description of the trail and the commandos' activities can be obtained from tourist information offices in the area.

p.186). The station building at Tulloch is now a friendly **hostel**, *Station Lodge* (Ⓣ01397/732333, Ⓦwww.stationlodge.co.uk), popular with climbers and walkers. The Caledonian sleeper train from London stops right at the door. Further east, the A86 runs alongside the artificial **Loch Laggan** with the picturesque Ardverikie Castle on its southern shore. In Laggan itself, beyond the far end of the loch, there's the newly opened Laggan Wolftrax mountain-bike centre (Ⓣ01528/544786), boasting a café and nine miles of track to suit all abilities. Two miles east and after turning onto the A889, *The Pottery Bunkhouse* and coffee shop provides convenient, comfortable accommodation (Ⓣ01528/544231, Ⓦwww.potterybunkhouse.co.uk). The whole Strathmashie Forest area including **Creag Meagaidh National Nature Reserve** is great for walkers.

Glen Coe and around

Despite its enduring fame and popularity, **Glen Coe**, half an hour's drive south of Fort William on the main A82 road to Glasgow, can still fairly claim to be one of Scotland's most inspiring places. Arriving from the south across the desolate reaches of Rannoch Moor, the start of the glen, with **Buachaille Etive Mhor** to the south and **Beinn a'Chrùlaiste** to the north, is little short of forbidding. By the heart of the glen, with the three huge rock buttresses known as the **Three Sisters** on one side and the Anoach Eagach ridge on the other combining to close up the sky, it's little wonder that most visitors feel compelled to stop simply to take it all in. Added to the heady mix is the infamous **massacre** of 1692, nadir of the longstanding enmity between the clans MacDonald and Campbell. At its western end, Glen Coe meets Loch Leven: the main road goes west and over the bridge at Ballachulish en route to Fort William, while at the eastern end of the loch is the slowly reviving settlement of **Kinlochleven**, best known now as the site of the world's largest indoor ice-climbing centre and as a waypoint on the **West Highland Way** long-distance footpath (see p.166).

Walks around Glen Coe

Ordnance Survey Explorer map no. 384.

Flanked by sheer-sided Munros, Glen Coe offers some of the Highlands' most challenging **hiking** routes, with long steep ascents over rough trails and notoriously unpredictable weather conditions that claim lives every year. The walks outlined below number among the glen's less ambitious routes, but still require a map. It's essential that you take the proper precautions (see p.59), and stick to the paths, both for your own safety and the sake of the soil, which has become badly eroded in places. For a broader selection of walks, get hold of the Ordnance Survey *Pathfinder Guide: Fort William and Glen Coe Walks*.

A good introduction to the splendours of Glen Coe is the half-day hike over the **Devil's Staircase**, which follows part of the old military road that once ran between Fort William and Stirling. The trail, part of the West Highland Way and a good option for families and less experienced hikers, starts at the village of **Kinlochleven** and is marked by thistle signs, which lead uphill to the 1804ft pass and down the other side into Glen Coe. The Devil's Staircase was named by four hundred soldiers who endured severe hardship to build it in the seventeenth century, but in fine, settled weather the trail is safe and affords stunning views of Loch Eilde and Buachaille Etive Mhor.

Set right in the heart of the glen, the half-day **Allt Coire Gabhail** hike starts at the car park opposite the distinctive Three Sisters massif on the main A82. From the road, drop down to the floor of the glen and cross the River Coe via the wooden bridge, where the path heads straight up the Allt Coire Gabhail for a couple of miles to a false summit directly ahead – actually the rim of the so-called "Lost Valley" which the Clan MacDonald used to flee to and hide their cattle in when attacked. Once in the valley, there are superb views of Bidean nan Bian, Gearr Aonach and Beinn Fhada, which improve as you continue on to its head, another twenty- to thirty-minute walk. Unless you're well equipped and experienced, turn around at this point, as the trail climbs to some of the glen's high ridges and peaks.

Undoubtedly one of the finest walks in the Glen Coe area not entailing the ascent of a Munro is the **Buachaille Etive Beag** circuit, which follows the textbook glacial valleys of Lairig Eilde and Lairig Gartain, ascending 1968ft in only nine miles of rough trail. Park near the waterfall at **The Study** – the gorge part of the A82 through Glen Coe – and walk up the road until you see a sign pointing south to "Loch Etiveside". The path angles up from here to the top of the pass, a rise of 787ft from the road. From here, follow the burn until you can pick up the trail heading up the eastern side of Stob Dubh (the "black peat"), which leads to the col of the Lairig Gartain, and onwards to the top of the pass. Drop down the other side to the main road, where the roughly parallel route of the old military road offers a gentler and safer return to the Study with superb views of the Three Sisters – finer than those ever seen by drivers.

Glen Coe

Breathtakingly beautiful **Glen Coe** (literally "Valley of Weeping"), sixteen miles south of Fort William on the A82, is justifiably the best known of Highland glens: a spectacular mountain valley between velvety-green conical peaks, their tops often wreathed in cloud, their flanks streaked by cascades of rock and scree. In 1692 it was the site of a notorious massacre, in which the MacDonalds were victims of a longstanding government desire to suppress the clans. Fed up with what they regarded as unacceptable lawlessness, and a groundswell of Jacobitism and Catholicism, the government offered a general pardon to all those who signed an oath of allegiance to William III by January 1, 1692. When clan chief **Alastair MacDonald** missed the deadline, a plot was hatched to make an example of "that damnable sept", and **Campbell of Glenlyon** was ordered to billet his soldiers in the homes of the MacDonalds, who for ten days entertained them with traditional Highland hospitality. In the early morning of February 13, the soldiers turned on their hosts, slaying between 38 and 45 and causing more than 300 to flee in a blizzard, some to die of exposure.

Beyond the small village of **GLENCOE** at the western end of the glen, the glen itself (a property of the National Trust for Scotland since the 1930s) is virtually uninhabited, and provides outstanding climbing and walking. The NTS **visitor centre** (March daily 10am–4pm; April–Aug daily 9.30am–5.30pm, Sept & Oct daily 10am–5pm, Nov–Feb Fri–Mon 10am–4pm; NTS; £5), one mile south of the village, is an interesting eco-friendly building where you'll find a good exhibition with a balanced account of the massacre alongside some entertaining material on rock- and hill-climbing down the years. There's also a cabin area providing information on the local weather and wildlife and after sampling the cakes in the café, there's often the chance to join informative ranger-led **guided walks** (Easter & June–Sept) that leave from the centre. Meanwhile, in Glencoe village, you can pay a visit to the delightful heather-roofed Glencoe Folk Museum (May–Sept 10am–5.30pm, closed Sun; £2). Artefacts within the refurbished 1720 croft include a chair that reputedly once belonged to Bonnie Prince Charlie.

At the eastern end of Glen Coe beyond the demanding Buachaille Etive Mhor, the landscape opens out onto the vast Rannoch Moor. From the **Glen Coe Mountain Resort** (Ⓣ01855/851226, Ⓦwww.glencoemountain.com) a chairlift mainly used by skiers in winter (daily year-round, except Nov; £6) climbs 2400ft to Meall a Bhuiridh, giving spectacular views over Rannoch Moor and to Ben Nevis. At the base station, there's a simple but pleasant café.

Practicalities

To get to the heart of Glen Coe from Fort William by **public transport** the best option is to hop on the Glasgow-bound Scottish Citylink coach service (4 daily). The Highland County bus #44 from Fort William to Kinlochleven also stops at least three times a day at Glencoe village.

There's a good selection of **accommodation** in Glen Coe and the surrounding area. Basic options include an SYHA **hostel** (Ⓣ0870/004 1122, Ⓦwww.syha.org.uk) on a back road halfway between Glencoe village and the *Clachaig Inn*; the year-round *Red Squirrel* **campsite** (Ⓣ01855/811256) nearby; and a grassier NTS campsite (Ⓣ01855/811397; April–Oct) on the main road. Glencoe village has a few comfortable **B&Bs**, such as the secluded and friendly *Scorry Breac* (Ⓣ01855/811354, Ⓦwww.scorrybreac.co.uk; ❷), while the best-known **hotel** in the area is the lively *Clachaig Inn* (Ⓣ01855/811252, Ⓦwww.clachaig.com; ❺), a great place to swap stories with fellow climbers and to reward your exertions with cask-conditioned ales and heaped platefuls of food; it's three miles south of Glencoe village on the minor road off the A82. Over ten miles south of here through the glen and before heading into the empty wilds of Rannoch Moor, it's worth stopping for a pint at the atmospheric *Climber's Bar* within the historic though slightly run-down *King's House Hotel* (ⓣ01855/851259; ⓦwww.kingy.com; ④). Further south still at Bridge of Orchy station is the cosy *West Highland Way Sleeper Hostel* (ⓣ01838/400548, ⓦwww.westhighlandwaysleeper.co.uk). Outdoor activity operators in Glencoe include **walking** and climbing specialists Glencoe Guides and Gear (ⓣ01855/811402, ⓦwww.ice-factor.co.uk), while Vertical Descents (ⓣ01855/821593, ⓦwww.verticaldescents.com) offers a type of white-water kayaking called "fun-yakking" (£35 for a half-day) and adrenalin-pumping canyoning trips (from £35) that can include scaling 100ft waterfalls.

Ballachulish and Onich

One mile west of Glencoe village, **BALLACHULISH** was, from 1693 to 1955, a major centre for the quarrying of roofing slates, shipping out 26 million of them at the height of production in the mid-nineteenth century. There's a short, well-maintained all-ability footpath leading from directly opposite Ballachulish tourist office into the now disused slate quarry – a few information boards tell the history of the quarry, which, like many former industrial sites, has an eerie stillness to it. Ballachulish has two parts – the main village on the south of the loch and North Ballachulish on the other side of the road bridge which spans the mouth of Loch Leven. Beyond North Ballachulish on the road to Fort William is the roadside settlement of **ONICH**, a mile or so on from which is **CORRAN**, where a car ferry crosses the narrowest point of Loch Linnhe, providing access to the Morvern and Ardnamurchan peninsulas (see p.266).

Ballachulish's **tourist office** is on Albert Road, sharing space with a coffee and gift shop (daily 9am–5pm, May to end Aug until 6pm; ⓣ01855/811866). From here you can organize somewhere to stay locally using a freephone line. For a cheap bed, head to the welcoming *Inchree Hostel* (ⓣ01855/821287, ⓦwww.inchreecentre.co.uk) at Onich, where accommodation is available in a bunkhouse or chalets and there's a decent real-ale pub and bistro called *The Four Seasons*. In Ballachulish village, *Fern Villa* (ⓣ01855/811393, ⓦwww.fernvilla.com; ②) is a welcoming **B&B**, while *Cuildorag House* (ⓣ01855/821529, ⓦwww.cuildoraghouse.com; ②) in Onich is a particularly pleasant vegetarian and vegan B&B, renowned for its great breakfasts. **Hotels** include the *Ballachulish* (ⓣ01855/821582, ⓦwww.freedomglen.co.uk; ⑧) just below the southern end of the bridge, a grand but welcoming old place where residents have use of the pool and leisure centre at the nearby *Isles of Glencoe Hotel*: in the grounds you'll find Lochaber Watersports (ⓣ01855/821391, ⓦwww.lochaberwatersports.co.uk), where you can rent a small sailing dinghy, rowing boat or canoe.

Kinlochleven

At the easternmost end of Loch Leven, at the foot of the spectacular mountains known as the Mamores, the settlement of **KINLOCHLEVEN** is steadily reviving its fortunes after many years as a tourism backwater best known as the site of a huge, unsightly aluminium smelter built in 1904. The tale of the area's industrial past is told in **The Aluminium Story** (April–Sept Mon–Fri 10am–1pm & 2–5pm, Oct–March closed Fri afternoon; free), a small series of displays in the same building as the town library and tourist information. The disused smelter is now the home of an innovative new indoor mountaineering centre called **The Ice Factor** (Ⓦwww.ice-factor.co.uk). Built at a cost of over £2.5 million, this impressive facility includes the world's largest artificial ice-climbing wall (13.5m) as well as a range of more traditional climbing walls and other facilities such as equipment hire, steam room, sauna and an inexpensive café. Alongside, another part of the aluminium smelter has been transformed into the **Atlas Brewery**, which you can tour on summer evenings (Easter–Sept Mon–Sat 5.30pm; Ⓣ01855/831111). As well as being close to Glen Coe, Kinlochleven stands at the foot of the Mamore hills popular with Munro-baggers; it's also a convenient overnight stop on the **West Highland Way**, with Fort William a day's walk away.

For hikers looking to spend the night in Kinlochleven, the *Blackwater* **hostel** (Ⓣ01855/831253, Ⓦwww.blackwaterhostel.co.uk) beside the river, is decidedly upmarket, with TVs and en-suite facilities in dorms with two, three, four or eight beds, and a communal kitchen/dining area but no separate lounge. For £5 per person you can also camp here. Fine hospitality is to be found at the Edwardian-built *Edencoille Guest House* (Ⓣ01855/831358; ②), while there are two good hotels in Kinlochleven: *MacDonald Hotel* (Ⓣ01855/831539, Ⓦwww.macdonaldhotel.co.uk; ⑤), whose *Bothy Bar* is popular with walkers, and the *Tailrace Inn* on Riverside Road (Ⓣ01855/831777, Ⓦwww.tailraceinn.co.uk; ④), offering reasonable rooms and food, along with regular entertainment.

Loch Ness and around

Twenty-three miles long, unfathomably deep, cold and often moody, **Loch Ness** is bounded by rugged heather-clad mountains rising steeply from a wooded shoreline and attractive glens opening up on either side. Its fame, however, is based overwhelmingly on its legendary inhabitant Nessie, the "Loch Ness monster", whose fame ensures a steady flow of hopeful visitors to the settlements dotted along the loch, in particular **Drumnadrochit**. Nearby, the impressive ruins of **Castle Urquhart** – a favourite monster-spotting location – perch atop a rock on the lochside and attract a deluge of bus parties during the summer. Almost as busy in high season is the village of **Fort Augustus**, at the more scenic southwest tip of Loch Ness, where you can watch queues of boats tackling one of the Caledonian Canal's longest flight of locks.

Away from the lochside, and seeing a fraction of Loch Ness's visitor numbers, the remote glens of **Urquhart** and **Affric** make an appealing contrast, with Affric in particular boasting narrow, winding roads, gushing streams and hillsides dotted with ancient Caledonian pine forests. More commonly encountered is the often bleak high country of **Glen Moriston**, a little to the southwest of Glen Affric, which holds the main road between Inverness and Skye.

Although most visitors use the tree-lined A82 road, which runs along the western shore of Loch Ness, the sinuous single-track B862/B852 (originally a military road built to link Fort Augustus and Fort George) that skirts the eastern shore is quieter and affords far more spectacular views. However, buses from Inverness along this road only run as far south as **Foyers**, so you'll need your own transport to complete the whole loop around the loch, a journey which includes a most impressive stretch between Fort Augustus and the high, hidden **Loch Mhor**, overlooked by the imposing Monadhliath range to the south.

Nessie

The world-famous **Loch Ness monster**, affectionately known as "**Nessie**" (and by serious aficionados as *Nessiteras rhombopteryx*), has been a local celebrity for some time. The first mention of a mystery creature crops up in St Adamnan's seventh-century biography of **St Columba**, who allegedly calmed an aquatic animal which had attacked one of his monks. Present-day interest, however, is probably greater outside Scotland than within the country, and dates from the building of the road along the loch's western shore in the early 1930s. In 1934 the *Daily Mail* published London surgeon R.K. Wilson's sensational photograph of the head and neck of the monster peering up out of the loch, and the hype has hardly diminished since. Recent encounters range from glimpses of ripples by anglers to the famous occasion in 1961 when thirty hotel guests saw a pair of humps break the water's surface and cruise for about half a mile before submerging.

Photographic evidence is showcased in the two "Monster Exhibitions" at Drumnadrochit, but the most impressive of these exhibits – including the renowned black-and-white movie footage of Nessie's humps moving across the water, and Wilson's original head and shoulders shot – have now been exposed as fakes. Indeed, in few other places on earth has watching a rather lifeless and often grey expanse of water seemed so compelling, or have floating logs, otters and boat wakes been photographed so often and with such excitement. Yet while even hi-tech sonar surveys carried out over the past two decades have failed to come up with conclusive evidence, it's hard to dismiss Nessie as pure myth. After all, no one yet knows where the unknown layers of silt and mud at the bottom of the loch begin and end: best estimates say the loch is over 750 feet deep, deeper than much of the North Sea, while others point to the possibilities of underwater caves and undiscovered channels connected to the sea. What scientists have found in the cold, murky depths, including pure white eels and rare arctic char, offers fertile grounds for speculation, with different theories declaring Nessie to be a remnant from the dinosaur age, a giant newt or a huge visiting Baltic sturgeon. With the possibility of a definitive answer sending shivers through the local tourist industry, monster-hunters are these days recruited over the web: Ⓦwww.lochness.co.uk offers round-the-clock **webcams** for views across the loch, while Ⓦwww.lochnessinvestigation.org is packed with research information.

Fort Augustus

FORT AUGUSTUS, a tiny, busy village at the scenic southwestern tip of Loch Ness, was named after George II's son, the chubby lad who later became the "Butcher" Duke of Cumberland of Culloden fame; it was built as a barracks after the 1715 Jacobite rebellion. Today, it's dominated by comings and goings along the Caledonian Canal, which leaves Loch Ness here, and by its large former **Benedictine Abbey**, a campus of grey Victorian buildings founded on the site of the original fort in 1876. Home until relatively recently to a small but active community of monks, it has recently been converted into luxury flats. Traditional Highland culture is the subject of the lively and informative exhibition at the **Clansmen Centre** (Easter to mid-Oct daily 10am–6pm; £3.50), on the banks of the canal. Guides sporting sporrans and rough woollen plaids talk you through the daily life of the region's seventeenth-century inhabitants inside a mock-up of a turf-roofed stone croft, followed by demonstrations of weaponry in the back garden. Rather more sedate is the small **Caledonian Canal Heritage Centre** (July–Sept daily 10am–5pm; free), in Ardchattan House on the northern bank of the canal, where you can view old photographs and records about the history of the canal and watch a black-and-white

Lots and lots of lochs and locks

Surveyed by James Watt in 1773, the **Caledonian Canal** was completed in the early 1800s by Thomas Telford to enable ships to pass between the North Sea and the Atlantic without having to navigate Scotland's treacherous northern coast. There are sixty miles between the west coast entrance to the canal at Corpach, near Fort William, and its exit onto the Moray Firth at Inverness, although strictly speaking only 22 miles of it are bona fide canal – the other 38 exploit the Great Glen's natural string of **freshwater lochs** of Lochy, Oich and Ness.

The most famous piece of canal engineering in Scotland is the series of eight **locks** at Banavie, about a mile from the entrance at Corpach, known as Neptune's Staircase (see p.233). While the canal was originally built for freight-carrying ships and large passenger steamers, these days it is almost exclusively used by small yachts and pleasure boats. Good spots to watch their leisurely progress are Neptune's Staircase and Fort Augustus, where four locks take traffic through the centre of the village into Loch Ness.

If you're interested in the **history of the waterway**, there's the small Caledonian Canal Heritage Centre (see opposite) in Ardchattan House, beside the locks in Fort Augustus. For more active encounters with the canal, you can set off along a section of the Great Glen Way footpath or Great Glen cycleway, both of which follow the **canal towpath** for part of their length (see box on p.225), or you can spend a week **cruising** through the canal on the barge *Fingal of Caledonia* (Ⓣ01397/772167, Ⓦwww.fingal-cruising.co.uk), which organizes a wide range of activities from watersports to mountain biking along the way.

film of the days when paddle-boats and large barges passed through the locks every day. The new *Loch Ness Express* (Easter–Dec £13 one-way, £25 return; Ⓣ0800/3286426, Ⓦwww.lochnessexpress.com) makes speedy daily trips up the length of Loch Ness, while *Cruise Loch Ness* (Mar–Nov; 1hr; £8; Ⓣ01320/366277) provides shorter trips.

Fort Augustus's helpful **tourist office** (daily: April–May 10am–5pm; July & Aug 9am–6pm; June & Sep 9am–5pm; Oct 10am–4.30pm; Ⓣ01320/366779) hands out useful free walking leaflets and stocks maps of the Great Glen Way. They'll also advise on fishing permits for the loch or nearby river. There's **hostel** accommodation at *Morag's Lodge* (Ⓣ01320/366289) above the petrol station on the Loch Ness side of town, where the atmosphere livens up with the daily arrival of backpackers' minibus tours, and at the well-equipped, 30-bed *Stravaigers Lodge* (Ⓣ01320/366257) on Glendoe Road. The *Old Pier* (Ⓣ01320/366418, Ⓔjenny@oldpierhouse.com; ④) is a particularly appealing **B&B** right on the loch at the north side of the village providing two roaring log fires in the evening and the option of hiring two-man Canadian canoes (£10 per day) or even horse riding (min £50 for two people) in the mountains. Of the **hotels**, try either the small, friendly *Caledonian* (Ⓣ01320/366256, Ⓦwww.thecaledonianhotel.com; ④) or the lovely *Lovat Arms Hotel* (Ⓣ01320/366366; ⑤) opposite, built on the site of the 1718 Kilwhimen Barracks.

Either of the above provides reasonable **food**, but for a lively atmosphere in a local pub, the *Lock Inn* has regular music and draws a mixed clientele of locals, yachties and backpackers, as does *Poachers* on the main road. The *Bothy Bite* beside the canal serves Scottish specialities, including a good range of moderately priced fish. There are some good **cycling** routes locally, notably along the Great Glen cycle route. The best place to rent bikes or watersports equipment is at South Laggan, eight miles or so southwest at the head of Loch Lochy, where Monster Activities (Ⓣ01809/501340) rents bikes, speedboats, boats and canoes.

The east side of Loch Ness

The tranquil and scenic **east side** of Loch Ness is skirted by General Wade's old military highway, now the B862/B852. From Fort Augustus, the narrow single-track road swings up, away from the lochside through the near-deserted **Stratherrick** valley, dotted with tiny lochans. It's worth stopping for good-value, home-made food or a pint at the friendly *Whitebridge Hotel* (T01456/486226; 4). Fifty yards further north is the beautifully preserved stone White Bridge built in 1732. From here, the road drops down to rejoin the shores of Loch Ness at **FOYERS**, where there are numerous marked forest trails and an impressive waterfall. Heading north through the village, turn right at the post office and *Waterfall Café* for the friendly *Foyers House* (T01456/486405, W www.foyershouse-lochness.com; 3). This secluded B&B with fabulous views of the loch from its terrace also has a **restaurant** serving up game pie, venison, local salmon and vegetarian options.

Three miles further north at **INVERFARIGAIG** – where a road up a beautiful, steep-sided river valley leads east over to Loch Mhor – stands **Boleskine House**. This was formerly the residence of the self-styled "Great Beast" of black magic, the infamous Satanist and occultist Aleister Crowley, who lived here between 1900 and 1918 amid rumours of devil-worship and human sacrifice. In the 1970s, rock guitarist Jimmy Page bought the place, and it's now the private residence of a Dutch couple. Seven miles along is the sleepy village of **DORES**, nestled at the northeastern end of Loch Ness, where the whitewashed *Dores Inn* makes a pleasant pit stop. Only nine miles southwest of Inverness, the old pub is popular with Invernessians, who trickle out here on summer evenings for a stroll along the grey-pebble beach and some monster-spotting. Note that a local bus from Inverness runs down the east side of the loch to Foyers (3 daily Mon–Fri).

Invermoriston and west

On the other shore, heading north from Fort Augustus along the main A82, which follows the loch's northwestern side, **INVERMORISTON** is a tiny, attractive village just above the loch, from where you can follow well-marked woodland trails past a series of grand waterfalls. Dr Johnson and Boswell spent a couple of nights here in 1773 planning their journey to the Hebrides; you, too, could stay at the delightful *Glenmoriston Arms Hotel* (T01320/351206, W www.glenmoristonarms.co.uk; 6). Established in 1740 as a drovers' inn, the hotel offers high quality though pricey freshly prepared dinners, over 150 malt whiskies and real ale. Alternatively, the SYHA *Loch Ness Hostel* (T0870/004 1138, W www.syha.org.uk; April–Oct), three and a half miles north of Invermoriston is a more economical base with superb loch views.

The A887 leads west from Invermoriston to the west coast (via the A87) on the main commercial route to the Skye Bridge. Rugged and somewhat awesome, the stretch through **Glen Moriston**, beside **Loch Cluanie**, has serious peaks at either side and little sign of human habitation. At the western end of the loch, you'll find the isolated *Cluanie Inn* (T01320/340238, W www.cluanie.co.uk; 4), a popular place with outdoor types serving good food in its real-fire pub: more expensive rooms have a sauna and jacuzzi. West from here, the road drops gradually down **Glen Shiel** into the superb mountainscape of Kintail (see p.278).

Drumnadrochit and around

Situated above a verdant, sheltered bay of Loch Ness fifteen miles southwest of Inverness, **DRUMNADROCHIT** is the southern gateway to remote Glen

Affric and the epicentre of Nessie-hype, complete with a rash of tacky souvenir shops and two rival monster exhibitions whose head-to-head scramble for punters occasionally erupts into acrimonious exchanges, detailed with relish by the local press. Of the pair, the **Loch Ness 2000 Exhibition** (daily: Easter–May 9.30am–5pm; June & Sept 9am–6pm; July & Aug 9am–8pm; Oct–Easter 10am–3.30pm; £5.95), though more expensive, is the better bet, offering an in-depth rundown of eyewitness accounts and information on various research projects that have attempted to shed further light on the mysteries of the loch. The **Original Loch Ness Monster Visitor Centre and Lodge Hotel** (daily: July & Aug 9am–9pm; rest of year 9am–5pm; Dec–March closes 4pm; £5) has a less impressive exhibition though it's a worthwhile stop if only for the delicious array of home baking offered within the adjacent comfortable hotel (❺) and to go in search of the resident ghost within the tartanized interior.

Cruises on the loch aboard *Deep Scan Cruises* run from the Loch Ness 2000 Exhibition (Easter to mid-Oct; 1hr; £10; ⓣ01456/450218), while the *Nessie Hunter* (hourly: Easter–Sept 9am–6pm; Oct–Dec 10am–3pm; 50min; £10; ⓣ01456/450395) can be booked at the Original Loch Ness Visitor Centre. A more relaxing alternative is to head out **fishing** with a local gillie – the boat costs around £20 each (flexible) based on a group of four for two hours; contact Bruce (ⓣ01456/450279; Easter–Sept). If you want to turn your back on all the hype and enjoy the surrounding scenery, you could opt for the well-run **pony trekking** available at the Highland Riding Centre (ⓣ01456/450220), at Borlum Farm (ⓦwww.borlum.com), just two minutes north of Urquhart Castle.

Most photographs allegedly showing the monster have been taken a couple of miles east of Drumnadrochit, around the thirteenth-century ruined lochside **Castle Urquhart** (daily: April–Sept 9.30am–6.30pm; Oct–March 9.30am–4.30pm; HS; £6). Built as a strategic base to guard the Great Glen, the castle was taken by Edward I of England and later held by Robert the Bruce against Edward III, only to be blown up in 1692 to prevent it from falling to the Jacobites. Today it's one of Scotland's classic picture-postcard ruins, crawling with tourists by day but particularly splendid floodlit at night when all the crowds have gone. There's a footpath alongside the A82 road between Drumnadrochit and the castle, though the constant stream of cars, caravans and tour buses doesn't make it a particularly pleasant stroll.

Practicalities

Drumnadrochit's **tourist office** (April–June & Oct Mon–Sat 9am–5pm; July & Aug Mon–Sat 9am–6pm, Sun 10am–4pm; Sept Mon–Sat 9am–5pm, Sun 10am–4pm; Nov–March Mon–Fri 10am–1.30pm; ⓣ01456/459076) shares space with a Highland Council service point in the middle of the main car park in the village. There's a good range of **accommodation** around Drumnadrochit and in the adjoining village of Lewiston. A very welcoming **B&B** is *Gillyflowers* (ⓣ01456/450641, ⓦwww.cali.co.uk/freeway/gillyflowers; ❷), a renovated 1780s farmhouse on a country lane in Lewiston. **Hotels** include the friendly and secluded *Benleva* (ⓣ01456/450080, ⓦwww.benleva.co.uk; ❹) also in Lewiston, where real ale and delicious game and seafood are served by enthusiastic new owners. Two miles west of Drumnadrochit along the Cannich road is a particularly relaxed country-house hotel, *Polmaily House* (ⓣ01456/450343, ⓦwww.polmaily.co.uk; ❼). In addition to offering fine food and comfortable rooms, it's very family-friendly with acres of space including a swimming pool. For **hostel** beds, head to the immaculate and friendly *Loch Ness Backpackers Lodge* (ⓣ01456/450807, ⓦwww.lochness-backpackers.com), at Coiltie Farmhouse in

Lewiston; follow the signs to the left when coming from Drumnadrochit. Facilities include one double and two family rooms (❶) and bike hire, pony trekking and even a special Sunday bus into Glen Affric can be arranged.

Most of the hotels in the area – the *Benleva* in particular – serve good bar **food**; in Drumnadrochit the *Glen Café* has a short and simple menu with basic grills, while the slightly more upmarket *Fiddlers' Café Bar*, next door on the village green, offers local steaks, salmon and hearty lunches.

Glen Affric

Due west of Drumnadrochit is a vast area of high peaks, remote glens and few roads. The reason most folk head this way is to explore the native forests and grand mountains of **Glen Affric**, generally held to be one of Scotland's most beautiful landscapes and heaven for walkers, climbers and mountain-bikers. If you're driving, note that the nearest petrol stations are in Drumnadrochit and in Beauly to the north. On weekdays there's a **bus** three times a day from Inverness to Cannich, but to get right into the heart of Glen Affric you'll need a car or a bike. If you're exploring the area, it's worth getting your hands on the excellent Glen Affric and Strathglass tourist map (ⓦwww.glenaffric.info), which should be available from local businesses and tourist offices.

The approach to the glen is through the small settlement of **CANNICH**, fourteen miles west of Drumnadrochit on the A831. Cannich is a quiet, uninspiring village, but it has an excellent campsite (ⓣ01456/415364) where mountain bikes can be rented and there's the friendly *Glen Affric Backpackers Hostel* (ⓣ01456/415263, ⓦwww.glenaffric.org; year-round) which offers inexpensive twin or four-bed rooms. Check the SYHA website (ⓦwww.syha.org.uk) for updates on the status of the small youth hostel next door, which is to be renovated in 2006. For food, try the modest *Slaters Arms* or buy supplies from the village Spar shop.

Glen Affric itself is an inspiring place, with a rushing river and Caledonian pine and birch woods opening out onto an island-studded loch that was considerably enlarged after the building of a **dam** – one of many hydroelectric schemes hereabouts. Hemmed in by a string of Munros, Glen Affric is great for picnics and pottering, particularly on a calm and sunny day, when the still water of the loch reflects the islands and surrounding hills. From the car park at the head of the single-track road along the glen, ten miles southwest of Cannich, there's a selection of **walks**: the trip round Loch Affric will take you a good five hours but captures the glen, its wildlife and Caledonian pine and birch woods in all their remote splendour. For details for volunteer work weeks based in Glen Affric helping with the restoration of the woodland, get in touch with Trees for Life (ⓦwww.treesforlife.org.uk). You could also do some serious **hiking**. Munro-baggers are normally much in evidence, and it is possible to tramp 25 miles all the way through Glen Affric to Shiel Bridge, on the west coast near Kyle of Lochalsh, which takes at least two full days. The trail is easy to follow, but can get horrendously boggy if there's been a lot of rain, so allow plenty of time and take adequate wet-weather gear, as well as the relevant Ordnance Survey map. The recently revamped *Allt Beithe* SYHA **hostel** (ⓣ0870/155 3255, ⓦwww.syha.org.uk; April–Oct) near the head of Glen Affric, makes a convenient if primitive stopover halfway.

Inverness and around

Inverness, over a hundred miles from any other principal Scottish settlement and with a population of around 80,000, is the only "city" in the Highlands

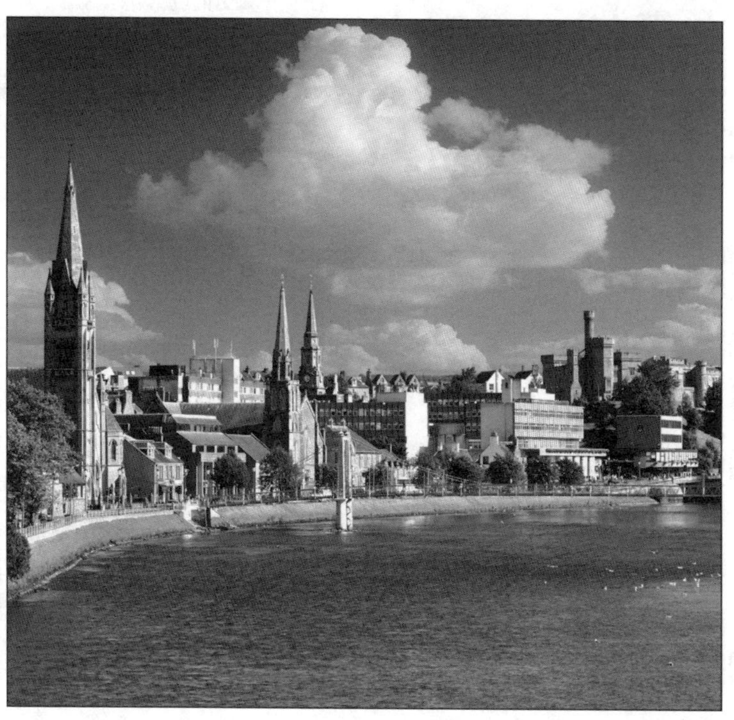

△ Inverness

– an official status conferred in 2000 by the government. A good base for day-trips and a jumping-off point for many of the more remote parts of the region, it is not a compelling place to stay for long and inevitably you are drawn to the attractions of sea and mountains beyond. The approach to the city on the A9 over the barren Monadhliath Mountains from Perth and Aviemore provides a spectacular introduction to the district, with the **Great Glen** to the left, stretching southwestwards towards Fort William and, beyond, the massed peaks of Glen Affric. To the north is the huge, rounded form of Ben Wyvis, whilst to the east lies the **Moray Firth**, which has a lovely coastline boasting some of the region's best castles and historic sites. The gentle, undulating green landscape is well tended and tranquil, a fertile contrast to the windswept moorland and mountains that almost surround it.

A string of worthwhile sights punctuates the approaches to Inverness along the main route from Aberdeen. The low-key holiday resort of **Nairn**, with its long white-sand beaches and championship golf course, stands within striking distance of several monuments, including the whimsical **Cawdor Castle**, featured in Shakespeare's *Macbeth*, and **Fort George**, one of several impressive Hanoverian bastions erected in the wake of the Jacobite rebellion. The infamous battle and ensuing massacre that ended Bonnie Prince Charlie's uprising took place on the outskirts of Inverness at **Culloden**, where a visitor centre and memorial stones beside a heather-clad moor recall the gruesome events of 1746.

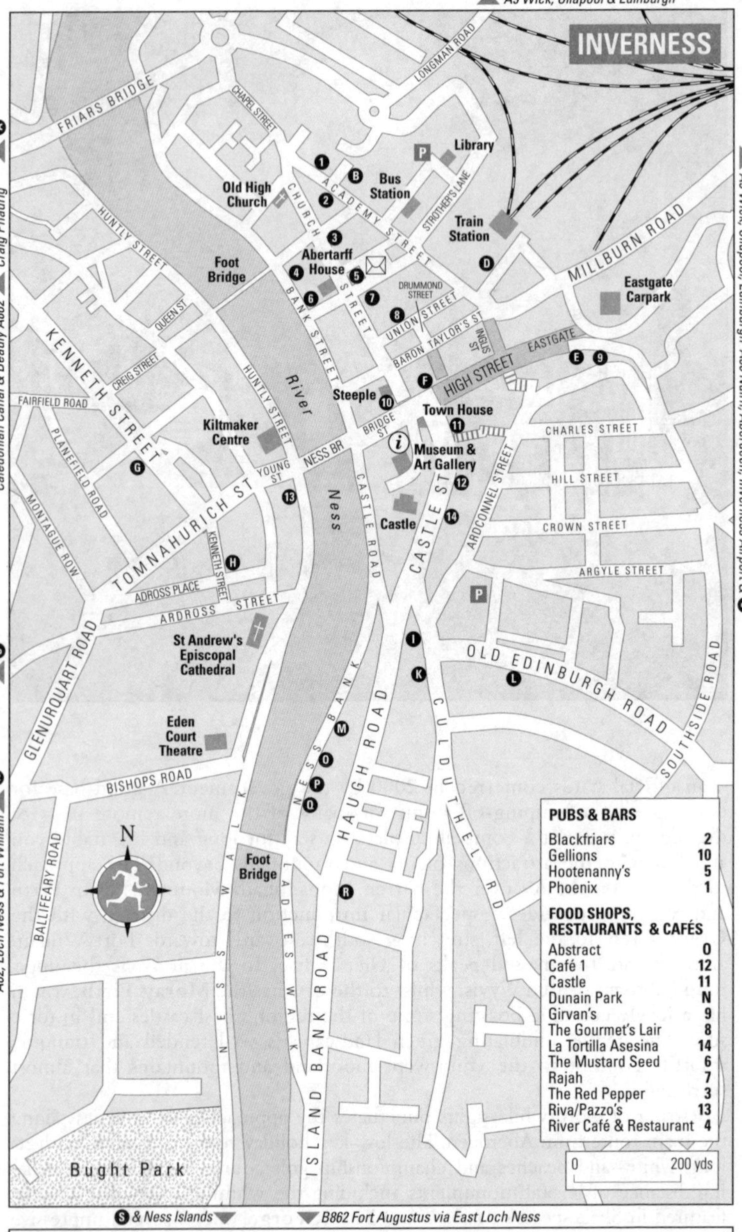
INVERNESS
A9 Wick, Ullapool & Edinburgh
A9 Wick, Ullapool, Edinburgh A96 Nairn, Aberdeen, Inverness Airport & C
Caledonian Canal & Beauly A862 Craig Phadrig A
J
A82, Loch Ness & Fort William N
S & Ness Islands
B862 Fort Augustus via East Loch Ness
FRIARS BRIDGE
CHAPEL STREET
LONGMAN ROAD
Library
Bus Station
Old High Church
CHURCH ST
ACADEMY STREET
STROTHER'S LANE
Train Station
MILLBURN ROAD
Eastgate Carpark
HUNTLY STREET
Foot Bridge
Abertarff House
BANK STREET
DRUMMOND STREET
UNION STREET
BARON TAYLOR'S ST
INGLIS ST
EASTGATE
HIGH STREET
QUEEN ST
KENNETH STREET
CREIG STREET
FAIRFIELD ROAD
HUNTLY STREET
River Ness
Steeple
Town House
Kiltmaker Centre
BRIDGE ST
Museum & Art Gallery
CHARLES STREET
PLANEFIELD ROAD
YOUNG ST
NESS BR
CASTLE ROAD
CASTLE ST
ARDCONNEL STREET
HILL STREET
MONTAGUE ROW
TOMNAHURICH ST
Castle
CROWN STREET
KENNETH STREET
ARGYLE STREET
ADROSS PLACE
ARDROSS STREET
St Andrew's Episcopal Cathedral
GLENURQUART ROAD
OLD EDINBURGH ROAD
SOUTHSIDE ROAD
NESS BANK
HAUGH ROAD
CULDUTHEL RD
Eden Court Theatre
BISHOPS ROAD
BALLIFEARY ROAD
N
Foot Bridge
LADIES WALK
NESS WALK
ISLAND BANK ROAD
Bught Park
0 200 yds
PUBS & BARS
Blackfriars 2
Gellions 10
Hootenanny's 5
Phoenix 1
FOOD SHOPS, RESTAURANTS & CAFÉS
Abstract O
Café 1 12
Castle 11
Dunain Park N
Girvan's 9
The Gourmet's Lair 8
La Tortilla Asesina 14
The Mustard Seed 6
Rajah 7
The Red Pepper 3
Riva/Pazzo's 13
River Café & Restaurant 4
ACCOMMODATION
Bazpackers I
Bught Caravan & Camping Site S
Bunchrew Caravan & Camping Park A
Brae Ness M
Dunain Park N
Eastgate Backpackers E
Edenview Q
Glenmoriston Town House Hostel O
Heathfield H
Ho Ho Hostel F
Inverness Student Hotel K
Inverness Tourist Hostel B
Ivybank Guest House L
Macrae House P
Melrose Villa G
Moyness House J
Riverview House R
Royal Highland D
SYHA hostel C

Inverness

Straddling a nexus of major road and rail routes, **INVERNESS** is the busy and prosperous hub of the Highlands, and an inevitable port of call if you're exploring the region by public transport. **Buses** and **trains** leave for communities right across the far north of Scotland, and it isn't uncommon for people from as far afield as Thurso, Durness and Kyle of Lochalsh to travel down for a day's shopping here – Britain's most northerly chain-store centre. Though boasting few conventional sights, the city's setting on the banks of the River Ness is appealing. Crowned by a pink crenellated **castle** and lavishly decorated with flowers, the compact centre still has some hints of its medieval street layout,

Tours and cruises from Inverness

Inverness is the departure point for a range of day **tours** and **cruises** to nearby attractions, including Loch Ness and the Moray Firth.

City Sightseeing runs an open-topped double-decker **city tour** of **Inverness** (May–Sept daily every 45min; £5.50), which you can hop on and off all day. You can buy tickets on the bus, at the tourist office or at their office in the train station (May–Sept daily 9am–6pm). An entertaining if slightly bizarre **Terror Tour** takes groups on foot around Inverness town centre (daily 7pm from the tourist office; £7), with grisly tales told along the way of ghosts, torture and witches. It ends with a free pint in a haunted pub. Telliesperie (ⓣ01463/233729) also conducts storywalks, leaving daily from Hootananny's on Church Street (1hr; £5) while the Inverness Historic Trail (July & Aug Mon–Sat 11am & 2pm) leaves from the tourist office and provides a great insight to local history.

There are various tours of Loch Ness and Glen Affric leaving from the tourist office lasting from one hour up to a whole day. Loch Ness cruises typically incorporate a visit to the monster exhibition at **Drumnadrochit** and **Urquhart Castle** – try Jacobite Cruises (ⓣ01463/233999, ⓦwww.jacobite.co.uk). Its courtesy bus runs from the tourist office to their dock at Tomnahurich Canal Bridge on Glenurquhart Road, a mile and a half south of Inverness town centre. **Discover Loch Ness** tours (ⓣ01456/450168 or 0800/731 5565, ⓦwww.discoverlochness.com) combine an insightful introduction to the monster-hype with visits to places of geological or historical interest.

The new **Loch Ness Express** also provides a daily return ferry service from Dochgarroch at the eastern end of the loch right down Loch Ness to Fort Augustus. The two-and-a-half-hour trip costs £13 one-way or £25 return (ⓣ0800/328 6426).

Inverness is also about the one place where transport connections allow you to embark on a major **grand tour** of the Highlands. It is possible, cabin fever notwithstanding, to catch the early train to Kyle of Lochalsh, a bus onto Skye and across the island to catch the ferry to Mallaig, which meets the train to Fort William, from where you can take a bus back to Inverness, all in less than twelve hours. Handy for exploring the northwest, Dearman Coaches (April–Sept Mon–Sat; £21; six-day rover ticket £36) has a daily service (bikes accepted) to **Ullapool**, **Lochinver**, **Durness**, **Smoo Cave** and back which stops at several hostels en route.

Enjoyable trips to **John O'Groats** and back in a day, with the chance to see puffins and visit prehistoric sites, are run by Puffin Express (ⓣ01463/717181, ⓦwww.puffinexpress.co.uk); they also put together a package which includes an overnight stop on **Orkney**. You can get to the islands and back with a gruelling full-day whistle-stop tour on the Orkney Bus, which leaves Inverness bus station every day during the summer (£46; advance bookings may be made at the tourist office or on ⓣ01955/611353, ⓦwww.jogferry.co.uk).

See p.254 for details of **dolphin**-spotting cruises on the Moray Firth.

although pedestrianization and some unsightly concrete blocks do a fairly efficient job of masking it. Within walking distance of the centre are peaceful spots along by the Ness, leafy parks and friendly B&Bs located in prosperous-looking stone houses.

The sheltered **harbour** and proximity to the open sea made Inverness an important entrepôt and shipbuilding centre during medieval times. David I, who first imposed a feudal system on Scotland, erected a **castle** on the banks of the Ness to oversee maritime trade in the early twelfth century, promoting it to royal burgh status soon after. Bolstered by receipts from the lucrative export of leather, salmon and timber, the town grew to become the kingdom's most prosperous northern outpost, and an obvious target for the marauding Highlanders who plagued this remote border area. A second wave of growth occurred during the eighteenth century as the Highland cattle trade flourished. The arrival of the **Caledonian Canal** and **rail** links with the east and south brought further prosperity, heralding a tourist boom that reached a fashionable zenith in the Victorian era, fostered by the Royal Family's enthusiasm for all things Scottish. Over the last thirty years, the town has become one of the fastest expanding in Britain, with its population virtually doubling due to the growing tourist industry and improved communications.

Arrival, information and accommodation

Inverness **airport** (Ⓣ01667/464000) is at Dalcross, seven miles east of the city; from here, bus #11 (Mon–Sat every 40min, reduced service Sun; 20min; £3) goes into town, while a taxi costs around £12. The **bus station** (Ⓣ01463/233371) and **train station** (Ⓣ0845/748 4950) both lie just off Academy Street to the northeast of the centre. The **tourist office** (March–May Mon–Sat 9am–5pm; June–Aug 9am–6pm, Sun 10am–4pm; Sept & Oct 9am–5pm, Sun 10am–4pm; Ⓣ0845/225 5121) is in an unsightly 1960s block on Castle Wynd, just five minutes' walk from the train station. It stocks a wide range of literature, including free maps of the city and environs, and the staff can book local accommodation for a £3 fee. There's also a CalMac ferry booking office.

Inverness is one of the few places in the Highlands where you're unlikely to have problems finding **accommodation**, although in July and August you'll have to book ahead. Inverness boasts several good **hotels**, and nearly every street in the older residential areas of town has a sprinkling of **B&Bs**. Good places to look include both banks of the river south of the Ness Bridge, and Kenneth Street and its offshoots on the west side of the river. There are several **hostels** in town, all reasonably central, and a couple of large **campsites**, one near the Ness Islands and the other further out to the west.

Hotels

Brae Ness 17 Ness Bank Ⓣ01463/712266, Ⓦwww.braenesshotel.co.uk. A homely Georgian hotel with only ten rooms (all non-smoking) overlooking the river and St Andrews Cathedral. May–Sept. ❺

Dunain Park Ⓣ01463/230512, Ⓦwww.dunainparkhotel.co.uk. Luxurious country-house hotel off the A82 Fort William road, about three miles west of the centre of town. Excellent food (dinner is around £25 per person) and charming, opulent rooms. ❼

Glenmoriston Town House Hotel 20 Ness Bank Ⓣ01463/223777, Ⓦwww.glenmoriston.com. Classy and stylishly modern hotel harbouring a high-quality French restaurant, *Abstract*. ❼

Royal Highland 18 Academy St Ⓣ01463/231926, Ⓦwww.royalhighlandhotel.co.uk. The old station hotel, dripping with the grandeur of the golden days of Highland travel. The restaurant, *Ash*, provides good food and cocktails. ❼

B&Bs

Edenview 26 Ness Bank Ⓣ01463/234397, Ⓔedenview@clara.co.uk. Very pleasant B&B in a riverside location as good as that of the more expensive hotels, five minutes' walk from the centre. Non-smoking. March–Oct. ❸

Heathfield 2 Kenneth St ⓣ01463/230547. A very comfortable and friendly place at the quiet end of a street packed with B&Bs. All rooms centrally heated and some are en suite. Non-smoking. No credit cards. ❷

Ivybank Guest House 28 Old Edinburgh Rd ⓣ01463/232796, ⓦwww.ivybankguesthouse.com. A grand Georgian home just up the hill from the castle, with open fires and a lovely wooden interior. ❷

Macrae House 24 Ness Bank ⓣ01463/243658, ⓦwww.macraehouse.co.uk. Right on the river, friendly, and with large, comfortable rooms. Non-smoking. ❷

Melrose Villa 35 Kenneth St ⓣ01463/233745, ⓦwww.melrosevilla.com. Very family-friendly, with excellent breakfasts. Three singles as well as doubles and twins, with most rooms en suite. ❸

Moyness House 6 Bruce Gardens ⓣ01463/233836, ⓦwww.moyness.co.uk. Warm, welcoming, upmarket B&B on the west side of Inverness, with original Victorian features and a nice walled garden. ❺

Riverview House 2 Moray Park, Island Bank Rd ⓣ01463/235557. A welcoming B&B in a characterful old house a little further down the river than some pricier guesthouses, but still an easy stroll from the centre. ❸

Hostels

Bazpackers Top of Castle St ⓣ01463/717663. The most cosy and relaxed of the city's hostels, with thirty beds including two double rooms and a twin; some dorms are mixed. Has good views and a garden, which is used for barbecues, as well as the usual cooking facilities. Non-smoking.

Eastgate Backpackers Hostel Eastgate ⓣ01463/718756, ⓦwww.eastgatebackpackers.com. Well-maintained former hotel with single, twin and double room accommodation. Cycle hire, internet access and dorms. Left luggage storage and no curfew.

Ho Ho Hostel 23a High St ⓣ01463/221225, Formerly the grand Highland Club, a town base for lairds. Now a large, rather worn but central hostel with big rooms which tends to attract a partying crowd. They also have cheap twins and doubles (❷) available at a nearby location, called *The Long Lie In*.

Inverness Student Hotel 8 Culduthel Rd ⓣ01463/236556, ⓦwww.scotlands-top-hostels.com. A busy fifty-bed hostel with the usual facilities and fine views over the river. Part of the MacBackpackers group, so expect minibus tours to pull in most days.

Inverness Tourist Hostel 24 Rose Street ⓣ01463/241962. A central, clean, well-equipped 60-bed hostel offering top-notch amenities including wide-screen TVs and internet access.

SYHA hostel Victoria Drive, off Millburn Rd, about three-quarters of a mile east of the centre ⓣ0870/004 1127, ⓦwww.syha.org.uk. One of SYHA's flagship hostels, fully equipped with large kitchens and communal areas, eco-friendly facilities and ten four-bed family rooms among the 166-bed total, but hardly central.

Campsites

Bught Caravan and Camping Site Bught Park ⓣ01463/236920. Inverness's main campsite, on the west bank of the river near the sports centre. Good facilities, but it can get very crowded at the height of the season. Easter to mid-Sept.

Bunchrew Caravan and Camping Park Bunchrew, three miles west of Inverness on the A862 ⓣ01463/237802, ⓦwww.bunchrew-caravanpark.co.uk. Well-equipped site with lots of space for tents on the shores of the Beauly Firth, with hot water, showers, laundry and a shop. Very popular with families. March–Nov.

The Town

The logical place to begin a tour of Inverness is the central **Town House** on the High Street. Built in 1878, this Gothic pile hosted Prime Minister Lloyd George's emergency meeting to discuss the Irish crisis in September 1921, and now accommodates council offices. There's nothing of note inside, but look out for the old **Mercat Cross** next to the main entrance. The cross stands opposite a small square formerly used by merchants and traders and above the ancient *clach-na-cudainn*, or "**stone of tubs**" – so called because washerwomen used to rest their buckets on it on their way back from the river.

Looming above the Town House and dominating the horizon is **Inverness Castle**, a predominantly nineteenth-century red sandstone edifice perched picturesquely above the river. The original castle formed the core of the ancient town, which had rapidly developed as a port trading with Europe after its conversion to Christianity by St Columba in the sixth century. Robert the Bruce wrested it back from the English during the Wars of Independence, destroying it in the process, and while it was held by the Jacobites in both the 1715 and the 1745 rebellions, it was blown up by them to prevent it falling into government hands. Today's edifice houses the Sheriff Court and, in summer, the **Castle Garrison Encounter** (March–Oct Mon–Sat 10am–5pm; £6), an entertaining and noisy interactive exhibition in which the visitor plays the role of a new recruit in the eighteenth-century Hanoverian army. Around 7pm during the summer, a lone piper clad in full Highland garb performs for tourists on the castle esplanade.

Below the castle, the **Inverness Museum and Art Gallery** on Castle Wynd (Mon–Sat 9am–5pm; free) gives a good general overview of the development

The truth about tartan

To much of the world, **tartan** is synonymous with Scotland. It's the natural choice of packaging for Scottish exports from shortbread to Sean Connery, and when the Scottish football team travels abroad to play a fixture, the high-spirited "Tartan Army" of fans are never far behind. Not surprisingly, tartan is big business for the tourist industry, yet the truth is that romantic fiction and commercial interest have enclosed this ancient Highland art form within an almost insurmountable wall of myth.

The original form of tartan, the kind that long ago was called "**Helande**", was a fine, hard and almost showerproof cloth spun in Highland villages from the wool of the native sheep, dyed with preparations of local plants and with patterns woven by artist-weavers. It was worn as a huge single piece of cloth, or **plaid**, which was belted around the waist and draped over the upper body, rather like a knee-length toga. The natural colours of old tartans were clear but soft, and the broken pattern gave superb camouflage, unlike modern versions, where garish, clashing colours are often used to create impact.

The myth-makers were about four centuries ahead of themselves in dressing up the warriors of the film *Braveheart* in plaid: in fact tartan did not become popular in the Lowlands until the beginning of the eighteenth century, when it was adopted as the anti-Union badge of the **Jacobites**. After Culloden, a ban on the wearing of tartan in the Highlands lasted some 25 years; in that time it became a fondly held emblem for emigrant Highlanders in the colonies and was incorporated into the uniforms of the new Highland regiments in the British Army. Then Sir Walter Scott set to work glamorizing the clans, dressing George IV in a kilt (and, just as controversially, flesh-coloured tights) for his visit to Edinburgh in 1822. By the time Queen Victoria set the royal seal of approval on both the Highlands and tartan with her extended annual holidays at Balmoral, the concept of tartan as formal dress rather than rough Highland wear was assured.

Hand in hand with the gentrification of the kilt came "rules" about the correct form of attire and the idea that every clan had its own distinguishing tartan. To have the right to wear tartan, one had to belong, albeit remotely, to a clan, and so the way was paved for the "what's-my-tartan?" lists that appear in tartan picture books and souvenir shops. Great feats of genealogical gymnastics were performed in the concoction of these lists; where these left gaps, a more recent marketing phenomenon of themed tartans developed, with new patterns for different districts, companies and even football teams being produced.

Scotsmen today will commonly wear the **kilt** for weddings and other formal occasions; properly made kilts, however – comprising some four yards of 100 percent wool – are likely to set you back £300 or more, with the rest of the regalia at least doubling that figure. If the contents of your sporran don't stretch that far, most places selling kilts will rent outfits on a daily basis. The best place to find better-quality material is a recognized Highland outfitter rather than a souvenir shop: in Inverness, try the Scottish Kiltmaker Centre at the Highland House of Fraser shop (see opposite).

of the Highlands. Informative sections on geology, geography and history cover the ground floor, while upstairs you'll find a muddled selection of silver, taxidermy, weapons and bagpipes, alongside an art gallery which occasionally attracts worthwhile touring exhibitions.

Leading north from the Town House, medieval **Church Street** is home to the town's oldest-surviving buildings. On the corner with Bridge Street stands the **Steeple** (1791), whose spire had to be straightened after an earth tremor in 1816. Farther down Church Street is **Abertarff House**, reputedly the oldest complete building in Inverness and distinguished by its stepped gables and circular stair tower. It was erected in 1593 and is now owned by the National Trust for Scotland. The **Old High Church**, founded in 1171 and rebuilt on several occasions since, stands just along the street, hemmed in by a walled graveyard. Any Jacobites who survived the massacre of Culloden were brought here and incarcerated prior to their execution in the cemetery. If you look carefully you may see the bullet holes left on gravestones by the firing squads.

Along the River Ness

Just across Ness Bridge from Bridge Street is the **Kiltmaker Centre** in the Highland House of Fraser shop (June to Sept Mon–Sat 9am–9pm, Sun 10am–5pm; rest of year Mon–Sat 9am–5.30pm; £2). Entered through the factory shop, an imaginative small visitor centre, complete with the outfits worn by actors for the *Braveheart* and *Rob Roy* blockbuster films, sets out everything you ever wanted to know about tartan. There's an interesting seven-minute audio-visual film and on weekdays you can watch various tartan products being made in the workshop. The finished products are, of course, on sale in the showroom downstairs, along with all manner of Highland knitwear, woven woollies and Harris tweed.

Rising from the west bank directly opposite the castle, **St Andrews Episcopal Cathedral** was intended by its architects to be one of the grandest buildings in Scotland. However, funds ran out before the giant twin spires of the original design could be completed. The interior is pretty ordinary, too, though it does claim an unusual octagonal chapterhouse. Alongside the cathedral is **Eden Court Theatre** (Ⓦwww.eden-court.co.uk). It's undergoing a multi-million pound refurbishment to make the theatre the largest multi-arts centre in Scotland and will reopen in 2007.

From here, you can wander a mile or so upriver to the peaceful **Ness Islands**, an attractive, informal public park reached and linked by footbridges. Laid out with mature trees and shrubs, the islands are the favourite haunt of local anglers. Further upstream still, the river runs close to the **Caledonian Canal**, designed by Thomas Telford in the early nineteenth century as a link between the east and west coasts, joining lochs Ness, Oich, Lochy and Linnhe. Today its main use is recreational, and there are cruises through part of it to Loch Ness (see p.239), while the towpath provides relaxing walks with good views.

Three miles to the west of the town, on the top of **Craig Phadrig** hill, there's a vitrified **Iron Age fort**, reputed to be where the Pictish King Brude received St Columba in the sixth century. The walls of the fort were built of stone laced with timber and, when the timber was set alight, some of the stone fused to glass, becoming "vitrified". Waymarked forest trails start from the car parks at the bottom of the hill and lead up to the fort, though only the outlines of its perimeter defences are now visible, and recent tree planting is beginning to block some of the views. Stagecoach bus #14 from Church Street (Mon–Sat every 30min) drops you at the foot of Craig Dunain, right beside Craig Phadrig.

Eating and drinking

Inverness has lots of **eating** places, including a few excellent-quality gourmet options, while for the budget-conscious there's no shortage of **pubs**, **cafés** and **restaurants** around the town centre. **Takeaways** cluster on Young Street, just across the river, and at the ends of Eastgate and Academy Street. The best place for **picnic food** is *The Gourmet's Lair*, a well-stocked deli at 8 Union St.

The liveliest **nightlife** revolves around the pubs and, on Friday and Saturday nights at *Bakoo*, the city's main nightclub. The far end of Academy Street has a cluster of good **pubs**; the public bar of the *Phoenix* is the most original town-centre place, though *Blackfriars* across the street has a better atmosphere with entertainment five nights a week, including ceilidhs popular with Australian backpackers searching for their roots. *Hootenanny's* is a popular and lively pub, hosting lots of live gigs and ceilidhs. Over on Bridge Street, the *Gellions* is a legendary local watering hole with several other congenial places in between.

Cafés and restaurants

Abstract 20 Ness Bank ⓣ01463/223777 ⓦwww.abstractrestaurant.com. Best known for its appearance on the TV show *Ramsay's Kitchen Nightmares*, this award-winning and expensive French restaurant positively oozes with style and chic. Closed Mon. Expensive.

Café 1 75 Castle St ⓣ01463/226200. Impressive contemporary Scottish cooking using good local ingredients in a bistro-style setting. Shame about the décor. Closed Sun. Moderate to expensive.

Castle Restaurant 41 Castle St. Classic, 40-year-old family-run café that does a roaring trade in down-to-earth Scottish food – meat pies, chicken and fish, dished up with piles of chips. Open at 8am for breakfast; closed Sun. Inexpensive.

Dunain Park Restaurant Dunain Park ⓣ01463/230512, ⓦwww.dunainparkhotel.co.uk. Scots-French restaurant in a country-house hotel (see p.248) set in lovely gardens just southwest of town; a good choice for a leisurely dinner. Expensive.

Girvan's 2–4 Stephen's Brae ⓣ01463/711900. Offers uncomplicated but decent fare including Scottish meat and fish dishes. Doubles as a daytime patisserie. Inexpensive.

La Tortilla Asesina 99 Castle St ⓣ01463/709809. Simple but lively tapas restaurant, serving all the old favourites as well as some "tartan tapas" majoring on local ingredients. Small portions. Moderate.

The Mustard Seed 16 Fraser St ⓣ01463/220220. The most stylish place in town for an informal meal – an airy converted church with stone walls, smart table settings and an upbeat approach, serving Scottish and European-influenced cuisine and a range of light, bistro-style dishes. Mouthwatering daily specials. Despite the wow factor, it's reasonably priced. Moderate.

Rajah Post Office Ave ⓣ01463/237190. An excellent Indian restaurant, tucked away in a back-street basement. Moderate.

The Red Pepper 74 Church St ⓣ01463/237111. Linked to the Mustard Seed, this is the city's hip coffee-bar hangout with lots of freshly made sandwiches. Takeaway too. Inexpensive.

Riva 4–6 Ness Walk ⓣ01463/237377. Reasonably authentic modern Italian bistro/café beside the river with antipasto, decent mains and good coffee and cakes. Next door is Pazzo's Pizzeria with standard moderately-priced Italian fare. Moderate to expensive.

River Café and Restaurant 10 Bank St ⓣ01463/714884. Healthy wholefood lunches, great high tea with freshly baked cakes and tasty evening meals. Inexpensive to moderate.

Listings

Airport ⓣ01667/464000.

Bike rental Highland Cycles, 16a Telford St ⓣ01463/234789 (8.30am–5.30pm).

Bookshops Leakey's is located in a former church on Church St and filled with almost 100,000 secondhand books and a cosy café. Great spot to browse with a warming wood stove in winter (Mon–Sat 10am–4.30pm). There's also Waterstones at 50–52 High St.

Car rental Budget is on Railway Terrace, behind the train station ⓣ01463/713333; Europcar has an office on Telfer St ⓣ01463/235337; Focus Vehicle Rental is at Shore St ⓣ01463/709517; Aberdeen 4x4 Self-Drive is at 15b Harbour Rd ⓣ01463/871083; and Sharps Reliable Wrecks is based at Inverness train station, Academy St ☎01463/236684 as well as the airport.

Cinemas With the Eden Court Theatre undergoing refurbishment, head for the seven-screen Warner Village complex (☎0870/240 6020), on the A96 Nairn road about two miles from the town centre.

Dentist Contact the Scotland-wide National Health Service Line (☎0800/224488) for local and emergency dentists or The Dental Clinic within Optical Express on High St (☎01463/248871).

Exchange American Express agents Alba Travel are at 43 Church St (Mon–Sat 9am–5pm; ☎01463/239188). The tourist office's bureau de change changes cash and traveller's cheques for a small commission.

Hospital Raigmore Hospital (☎01463/704000) on the southeastern outskirts of town close to the A9.

Internet Highland libraries provide 30min free Internet access. There are also terminals in the tourist office and at Mailbox Etc outside the railway station.

Laundry Young Street Laundrette, 17 Young St (☎01463/242507).

Left luggage Train station lockers cost from £3–5 for 24hr (can only deposit 8am–6.30pm); the left-luggage room in the bus station costs £1 per item (Mon–Sat 8.30am–6pm, Sun 10am–6pm).

Library Inverness library (☎01463/236463), housed in the Neoclassical building on the northeast side of the bus station, has an excellent genealogical research unit (Mon–Fri 10am–1pm & 2–5pm; ext 9). Consultations with the resident genealogist cost £12 per hour, but are free if shorter than ten minutes. An appointment is advisable.

Outdoor supplies Blacks, 3–9 Academy St (☎01463/248617); Graham Tiso, 41 High St (☎01463/716617).

Pharmacy Boots, 1–11 Eastgate Shopping Centre (Mon–Wed & Fri 8.45am–6pm, Thurs 8.45am–7pm, Sat 8.30am–6pm, Sun 11am–5pm; ☎01463/225167).

Post office 14–16 Queensgate (Mon–Sat 9am–5.30pm; ☎0845/722 3344); also noon–5pm at Tesco's.

Public toilets Just behind tourist information on Castle St.

Radio The local radio station is Moray Firth Radio on 97.4FM and 1107AM.

Sports centre Inverness sports centre and Aquadome leisure pool (Mon–Fri 10am–8pm Sat & Sun 9am–5pm; ☎01463/667502), a mile or so south of the town centre off the A82, has a large pool with flumes and waves, also gym, health suite and climbing wall.

Taxis Inverness Taxis ☎01463/220222; Tartan Taxis ☎01463/233033.

East of Inverness

East of Inverness lies the fertile, sheltered coastal strip of the **Moray Firth** and its hinterland, the pastoral countryside contrasting with the scenic splendours you'll encounter once you head further north into the Highlands. Primary target among the sights is **Culloden**, the most poignant battlefield site in Scotland, where Bonnie Prince Charlie's Jacobites were routed in 1746. Further east are **Cawdor Castle** and **Fort George**, two of the best-preserved fortified structures in the Highlands. **Nairn**, the main town of the district, has a pretty harbour as well as appealing walks and cycle routes.

The overloaded A96 traverses this stretch and the region is well served by public transport, with all the historic sights and castles accessible on day-trips from Inverness, or en route to Aberdeen. Highland Country **buses** run from either Queensgate or the main post office to Fort George (#11), Cawdor Castle (#13) and Culloden (#7). You can also purchase a £6 day-rover ticket for these journeys.

Culloden

The windswept moorland of **CULLODEN** (site open all year; free), five miles east of Inverness, witnessed the last-ever battle on British soil when, on April 16, 1746, the Jacobite cause was finally subdued – a turning point in the history of the Scottish nation.

The second Jacobite rebellion had begun on August 19, 1745, with the raising of the Stuarts' standard at **Glenfinnan** on the west coast (see p.270). Shortly after, Edinburgh fell into Jacobite hands, and Bonnie Prince Charlie began his march on London. The English had appointed the ambitious young Duke of Cumberland to command their forces, and his pursuit, together with bad weather and lack of funds, eventually forced the Jacobites to retreat north. They ended up at Culloden, where, ill-fed and exhausted after a pointless night march, they were hopelessly outnumbered by the English. The open, flat ground of Culloden Moor was totally unsuitable for the Highlanders' style of courageous but undisciplined fighting, which needed steep hills and lots of cover to provide the element of surprise, and they were routed. After the battle, in which 1500 Highlanders were slaughtered (many of them as they lay wounded on the battlefield), Bonnie Prince Charlie fled west to the hills and islands, where loyal Highlanders sheltered and protected him. He eventually escaped to France, leaving his erstwhile supporters to their fate – and, in effect, ushering in the end

The dolphins of the Moray Firth

The **Moray Firth**, a great wedge-shaped bay forming the eastern coastline of the Highlands, is one of only three areas of UK waters that supports a resident population of **dolphins**. Over a hundred of these beautiful, intelligent marine mammals live in the estuary, the most northerly breeding ground for this particular species – the bottle-nosed dolphin (*Tursiops truncatus*) – in Europe, and you stand a good chance of spotting a few, either from the shore or a boat.

One of the best places in Scotland, if not in Europe, to look for them is **Chanonry Point**, on the Black Isle (see p.313) – a spit of sand protruding into a narrow, deep channel, where converging currents bring fish close to the surface, and thus the dolphins close to shore; the hour or so before high tide is the most likely time to see them. **Kessock Bridge**, one mile north of Inverness, is another prime dolphin-spotting location. You can go all the way down to the beach at the small village of North Kessock, underneath the road bridge, where there's a decent place to have a drink at the pub in the *North Kessock Hotel*, or you can stop above the village in a car park just off the A9 at the Dolphin visitor centre and listening post (June–Oct 9.30am–4.30pm, free; see p.313) set up by a team of zoologists from Aberdeen University studying the dolphins, where hydrophones allow you to eavesdrop on the clicks and whistles of underwater conversations.

In addition, several companies run dolphin-spotting **boat trips** around the Moray Firth. However, researchers claim that the increased traffic is causing the dolphins unnecessary stress, particularly during the all-important breeding period when passing vessels are thought to force calves underwater for uncomfortably long periods. They have therefore devised a code of conduct for boat operators, based on the experiences of other countries where dolphin-watching has become disruptive. So if you decide to go on a cruise to see the dolphins, which also sometimes holds out the chance of spotting minke whales, porpoises, seals and otters, make sure the operator is a member of the Dolphin Space Programme's Accreditation Scheme (see Ⓦwww.morayfirth-partnership.org and Ⓦwww.wdcs.org). Operators currently accredited include Phoenix, based in Nairn (Ⓣ01667/456078); Moray Firth Cruises, Inverness (Ⓣ01463/717900); and the WDCS Wildlife Centre, Spey Bay (Ⓣ01343/820339). In addition, Dolphin Trips Avoch (Ⓣ01381/622383; Ⓦwww.dolphintripsavoch.co.uk and the highly regarded Ecoventures, Cromarty (Ⓣ01381/600323, Ⓦwww.ecoventures.co.uk) are based on the Black Isle, on the northern side of the firth. Trips cost from £10 for 1hr.

To reach the dolphin sites, hop on the Magic Mini bus (Mon–Sat; £5.10 return) at Inverness (Union Street) to Rosemarkie car park or take the Highland Country Bus (#26; Mon–Fri hourly, irregular Sat) from Inverness bus station to Avoch, Rosemarkie and Cromarty. Bus #12 runs hourly from Inverness Union Street to North Kessock.

of the clan system. The clans were disarmed, the wearing of tartan and playing of bagpipes forbidden, and the chiefs became landlords greedy for higher and higher rents. The battle also unleashed an orgy of violent reprisals on Scotland, as unruly English troops raped and pillaged their way across the region; within a century, the Highland way of life had changed out of all recognition.

The battle site

Today you can walk freely around the battle site; flags show the positions of the two armies, and **clan graves** are marked by simple headstones. The **Field of the English**, for many years unmarked, is a mass grave for the fifty or so English soldiers who died. Half a mile east of the battlefield, just beyond the crossroads on the main road, is the **Cumberland Stone**, thought for many years to have been the point from where the duke watched the battle. It is more likely, however, that he was much further forward and simply used the stone for shelter. Thirty Jacobites were burnt alive outside the old **Leanach cottage** next to the visitor centre; inside, it has been restored to its eighteenth-century appearance.

The **visitor centre** (daily: June, July & Aug 9am–6pm; Feb, March, Nov & Dec 11am–4pm; April, May, Sept & Oct 9am–5.30pm; closed Jan; NTS; £5) provides background information through detailed displays and a film show, as well as a short play set on the day of the battle presented by local actors (June–Sept only; included in admission fee), or you can take the evocative hour-long guided **walking tour** (June–Sept daily; £4). In April, on the Saturday closest to the date of the battle, there's a small commemorative service. The visitor centre has a reference library, and will check for you if you think you have an ancestor who died here. The centre is undergoing an £8m redevelopment which aims to be completed by 2007.

The Clava Cairns

If you're visiting Culloden with your own transport, a short detour is worthwhile to the **Clava Cairns**, an impressive collection of prehistoric burial chambers clustered around the south bank of the River Nairn, a mile southeast of the battlefield. Erected some time before 2000 BC, the cairns, which are encircled by standing stones in a spinney of mature beech trees, are of two different kinds: one large and one very small **ring-cairn**, and two **passage graves**, which have a narrow passageway from edge to centre. Though cremated remains have been found in both types of structure, and unburnt remains in the passage graves, little is known about the nomadic herdsmen who are thought to have built them.

Cawdor Castle

The pretty, if slightly self-satisfied, village of **CAWDOR**, eight miles east of Culloden, is the site of **Cawdor Castle** (May to mid-Oct daily 10am–5.30pm; £7, gardens only £3.70), a setting intimately linked to Shakespeare's *Macbeth*: the fulfilment of the witches' prediction that Macbeth was to become Thane of Cawdor sets off his tragic desire to be king. Though visitors arrive here in their droves each summer because of the site's literary associations, the castle, which dates from the early fourteenth century, could not possibly have witnessed the grisly historical events on which the Bard's drama was based. However, the immaculately restored monument – a fairy-tale affair of towers, turrets, hidden passageways, dungeons, gargoyles and crenellations whimsically shooting off from the original keep – is still well worth a visit.

Six centuries on, the Campbells of Cawdor still spend their winters here, and the castle feels like a family home, albeit one with tapestries, pictures and opulent furniture (all catalogued with mischievous humour). As you explore, look out for the **Thorn Tree Room**, a vaulted chamber complete with the remains of an ancient holly tree that has been carbon-dated to 1372 – an ancient pagan fertility symbol believed to ward off fairies and evil spirits. The **grounds** of the castle are impressive, with an attractive walled garden, a topiarian maze, a small golf course, a putting green and nature trails. It's also worth visiting the village for a drink or meal at the traditional *Cawdor Tavern*, an old inn serving beautifully prepared, though pricey, dinners. To get here, use Highland Country **buses** #7, #12 from Inverness.

Fort George

Eight miles of undulating coastal farmland separate Cawdor Castle from **Fort George** (daily: April–Sept 9.30am–6.30pm; Oct–March 9.30am–4.30pm; HS; £6), an old Hanoverian bastion with walls a mile long, considered by military architectural historians to be one of the finest fortifications in Europe. Crowning a sandy spit that juts into the middle of the Moray Firth, it was built between 1747 and 1769 as a base for George II's army, in case the Highlanders should attempt to rekindle the Jacobite flame. By the time of its completion, however, the uprising had been firmly quashed and the fort has been used ever since as a barracks; note the armed sentries at the main entrance and the periodic crack of live gunfire from the nearby firing ranges.

Apart from the sweeping panoramic views across the Firth from its ramparts, the main incentive to visit Fort George is the **Regimental Museum** of the Queen's Own Highlanders. Displayed in polished glass cases is a predictable array of regimental silver, coins, moth-eaten uniforms and medals, along with some macabre war trophies, ranging from blood-stained nineteenth-century Sudanese battle robes to Iraqi gas masks gleaned in the First Gulf War. The **chapel** is also worth a look – squat and solid outside, and all light and grace within.

Walking on the northern, grass-covered casemates, which look out into the estuary, you may be lucky enough to see the school of bottle-nosed **dolphins** (see box p.254) swimming in with the tide. This is also a good spot for birdwatching: a colony of kittiwakes occupies the fort's slate rooftops. Highland Country **bus** #11 from Queensgate in Inverness serves the fort.

Nairn and around

One of the driest and sunniest places in the whole of Scotland, **NAIRN**, sixteen miles east of Inverness, began its days as a peaceful community of fishermen and farmers. The former spoke Gaelic, the latter English, allowing James VI to boast that a town in his kingdom was so large that people at one end of the main street could not understand those at the other end. Nairn became popular in Victorian times, when the train line offered a convenient link to its revitalizing sea air and mild climate, and today its 11,000 strong population still relies on tourism, with all the ingredients for a traditional seaside holiday – a sandy beach, ice-cream shops and fish-and-chip stalls. It boasts two championship golf courses, and Thomas Telford's **harbour** is filled with leisure craft rather than fishing boats. The **Nairn Museum** (May–Sept Mon–Sat 10am–4.30pm; £2.50) at Viewfield House provides a general insight into the history and prehistory of the area and also hosts the **Fishertown Museum** with interesting exhibits illustrating the parsimonious and puritanical life of the fishing families.

With a good map to help navigate the maze of minor roads, you can explore some pleasant countryside south of Nairn, particularly in the valley of the **River Findhorn**, with **Dulsie Bridge**, on the old military road linking Perth and Fort George, being a favourite local picnic spot. A few miles farther south, the waters of **Lochindorb** surround a ruined thirteenth-century castle. The relative flatness of the land makes these roads ideal for cycling; a bike is also a great way to explore **Culbin Forest**, an unusual area of coastal forest northeast of Nairn where the trees were planted to stabilize an extensive area of sand dune. The forest, a Site of Special Scientific Interest, has a network of paths and information boards, along with picnic spots and plenty of wildlife, including an array of migrating waterfowl at the adjacent RSPB reserve of Culbin Sands.

Nairn no longer has a tourist office. For **accommodation**, *Bracadale House* on Albert Street (ⓣ01667/452547, ⓦwww.bracadalehouse.com; ❸; March–Oct) is grand but affordable and has a Gaelic-speaking owner. *Greenlawns*, 13 Seafield St (ⓣ01667/452738, ⓦwww.greenlawns.uk.com; ❷), is a spacious and friendly B&B with seven en-suite bedrooms. The Swallow *Golf View Hotel* (ⓣ01667/452301, ⓦwww.swallowhotels.com; ❾) overlooks the sea (and, unsurprisingly, the golf course) and serves meals in its restaurant and conservatory. For a reasonably priced meal try the Italian restaurant at the *Aurora Hotel* (ⓣ01667/453551) whilst *The Classroom* is Nairn's fashionable coffee shop serving tasty light bites, lunches and dinners (11am–11pm). Also on High Street is *Ashers Tea-Room*, ideal for those seeking a decent cuppa. **Bike rental** (£9 day) is available from Bike and Buggy (ⓣ01667/455416) at 2 Leopold St.

West of Inverness

West of Inverness, the Moray Firth becomes the **Beauly Firth**, a sheltered sea loch bounded by the Black Isle in the north and the wooded hills of the Aird to the south. At the head of the firth is the medieval village of **Beauly**, seat of the colourful Lovat clan, with the small settlement of **Muir of Ord**, known for its whisky, close by. Most northbound traffic uses Kessock Bridge to cross the Moray Firth from Inverness, so this whole area is quieter, and the A862, which skirts the shoreline and the mud flats, offers a more scenic alternative to the faster A9.

Beauly

The sleepy stone-built village of **BEAULY** lies ten miles west of Inverness, at the point where the Beauly River – one of Scotland's most renowned salmon-fishing streams – flows into the Firth. It's ranged around a single main street that widens into a spacious marketplace, at the north end of which stand the skeletal red sandstone remains of **Beauly Priory** (daily 10am–6pm; free). Founded in 1230 by the Bisset family for the Valliscaulian order, and later becoming Cistercian, it was destroyed during the Reformation and is now in ruins. Beside this, the **Beauly Centre** (daily 10am–6pm; £2) is set up in the manner of an old-time village store, with displays on weaving and the Fraser clan; you can also get local tourist information here and visit the bookshop. The locals will tell you the name Beauly was bestowed on the village by Mary, Queen of Scots, who, when staying at the priory in the summer of 1564, allegedly cried, *"Ah, quel beau lieu!"* ("What a beautiful place!"). In fact, the description "beau lieu" was bestowed by the Lovat family, who came to the region from France with the Normans in the eleventh century.

Beauly has a surprising number of **places to stay**. The most comfortable is the modern *Priory Hotel* (ⓣ01463/782309, ⓦwww.priory-hotel.com; ❻) within the picturesque village square. The *Lovat Arms Hotel* (ⓣ01463/782313, ⓔlovat.arms@cali.co.uk; ❹), at the opposite end of the main street, is more traditional though has a decent restaurant. If you're looking for something cheaper, try the *Heathmount Guest House* (☎01463/782411; ❷), one of several pleasant **B&Bs** in a row of large Victorian houses just south of the *Lovat Arms* on the main road.

Around Beauly

Muir of Ord, a sprawling village four miles north of Beauly, is notable only for the **Glen Ord Distillery** (March–June Mon–Fri 10am–5pm; July–Sept also Sat 10am–5pm & Sun noon–4pm; Oct Mon–Fri 11am–4pm; Nov–Feb Mon–Fri 11.30am–3pm; £4 including discount voucher) on its northern outskirts. Here, as at other distilleries, the mysteries of whisky production are explained with a tour that winds up in the cellars, where you get to sample the 12-year-old Glen Ord single malt. No buses stop outside the distillery, but it's a ten-minute walk from Muir of Ord, which you can reach on the Stagecoach Inverness **bus** #19 from Union Street in Inverness, which travels via Beauly (Mon–Sat hourly); more helpfully, the **train** from Inverness stops at Muir of Ord station (Mon–Sat 6 daily; Sun 2 daily; 20min).

As a change from distilleries, you can visit a **winery** at **Moniack Castle** (Jan–March Mon–Fri 11am–4pm; April–Dec Mon–Sat 10am–5pm; £2), four miles east of Beauly, just off the A862, where you can taste and buy over thirty different home-made products, including silver-birch or meadowsweet wine, sloe-berry liqueur, juniper chutney and rosehip jam.

Travel details

Trains

Fort William to: Crianlarich (Mon–Sat 4 daily, 3 on Sun; 1hr 50min); Glasgow (Mon–Sat 3 daily, 2 on Sun; 3hr 45min); London (Sun–Fri 1 nightly; 12hr); Mallaig (Mon–Sat 3 daily, 2 on Sun; 1hr 25min).

Inverness to: Aberdeen (Mon–Sat 10 daily; 5 on Sun; 2hr 15min); Aviemore (Mon–Sat 9 daily, 5 on Sun; 40min); Edinburgh (Mon–Sat 6 daily, 3 on Sun; 3hr 30min); Kyle of Lochalsh (Mon–Sat 2–3 daily, 1 on Sun; 2hr 30min); London (Mon–Fri & Sun 1 nightly; 11hrs); Thurso (Mon–Sat 2 daily, 1 on Sun; 3hr 25min); Wick (Mon–Sat 2 daily, 1 on Sun; 3hr 45min).

Buses

Fort William to: Drumnadrochit (6 daily; 1hr 30min); Edinburgh (1 direct daily; 4hr); Fort Augustus (6 daily; 1hr); Glasgow (4 daily; 3hr); Inverness (6 daily; 2hr); Mallaig (1 daily; 2hr); Oban (Mon–Sat 4 daily; 1hr 30min); Portree, Skye (1 daily; 3hr).

Inverness to: Aberdeen (hourly; 3hr 40min); Aviemore (10 daily; 45min); Drumnadrochit (8 daily; 25min); Fort Augustus (6 daily; 1hr); Fort William (6 daily; 2hr); Glasgow (6 daily direct; 3hr 35min–4hr 25min); Kyle of Lochalsh (3 daily; 2hr); Nairn (Mon–Sat 4 daily; 50min); Perth (10 daily; 2hr 35min); Portree (3 daily; 3hr); Thurso (Mon–Sat 5 daily, 1 on Sun; 3hr 30min); Ullapool (2 Mon, Tues, Thurs, Sat; 3 Wed, Fri; 2hr 25min); Wick (Mon–Sat 4 daily, 1 on Sun; 3hr).

Flights

Inverness to: Edinburgh (Mon–Fri 4 daily, Sat & Sun 1 daily; 45min); Glasgow (Mon–Fri 1 daily; 50min); Kirkwall (2 Mon–Fri, 1 Sun; 45min); London (Gatwick 3 daily; Luton, Mon–Fri, 1 daily; 1hr 30min); Shetland (Mon–Fri 2 daily; 1hr 40min); Stornoway (Mon–Fri 4 daily, 40min).

4

The north and northwest Highlands

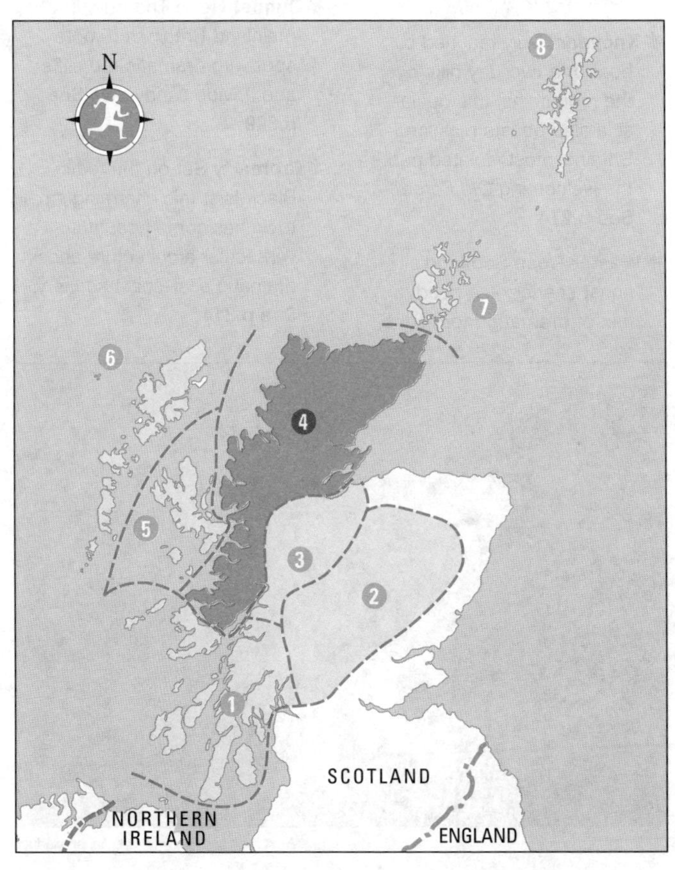

CHAPTER 4

Highlights

✱ **Loch Shiel** This romantic, unspoilt loch is where Bonnie Prince Charlie first raised an army. See p.270

✱ **West Highland Railway** From Glasgow to Mallaig via Fort William; the further north you travel, the more spectacular it gets. See p.271

✱ **Knoydart** Only reached by boat or a two-day hike over the mountains, this peninsula also boasts mainland Britain's most isolated pub, the welcoming *Old Forge*. See p.274

✱ **Wester Ross** Scotland's finest scenery – a heady mix of dramatic mountains, rugged sea lochs, sweeping bays and scattered islands. See p.281

✱ **Ceilidh Place, Ullapool** The best venue for modern Highland culture, with evenings of music, song and dance. See p.291

✱ **Dunnet Head** The true tip of mainland Britain, a remote spot with dramatic red cliffs and a wide sandy bay. See p.309

✱ **Cromarty** Set on the fertile Black Isle, this charming small town has some beautiful vernacular architecture and dramatic east-coast scenery. See p.314

△ West Highland Railway, Glenfinnan viaduct

4

The north and northwest Highlands

The **north and northwest Highlands** – the area beyond the Great Glen – holds some of Scotland's most spectacular scenery: a classic combination of bare mountains, remote glens, dark lochs and tumbling rivers, surrounded on three sides by a magnificently rugged coastline. The inspiring landscape and the tranquillity and space which it offers are without doubt the main attractions of the region. You may be surprised at just how remote much of it still is: the vast peat bogs in the north, for example, are among the most extensive and unspoilt wilderness areas in Europe, while a handful of the west coast's isolated crofting villages can still be reached only by boat.

Exposed to slightly different weather conditions and, to some extent, different historical and cultural influences, each of the three coastlines has its own distinct character. The beautiful **west coast**, with its indented shoreline and dramatic mountains in places like **Torridon** and **Assynt**, is a place whose charm and poetic scenery just about hold their own against the intrusions of the touring hordes in summer. West of Fort William lies the remote and tranquil **Ardnamurchan peninsula** and the "Road to the Isles" to the fishing port of **Mallaig**, railhead of the famous West Highland Railway. From Mallaig ferries cross to Skye, and there's also a service to **Knoydart**, a magical peninsula with no road access that's home to the remotest pub in mainland Britain. The more direct route to Skye is across the famous Skye Bridge at **Kyle of Lochalsh**, not far from which are charming coastal villages such as **Glenelg** and **Plockton**. Between Kyle of Lochalsh and **Ullapool**, the main settlement in the northwest, lies **Wester Ross**, with quintessentially west-coast scenes of sparkling sea lochs, rocky headlands and sandy beaches set against some of Scotland's most dramatic mountains, with Skye and the Western Isles on the horizon.

The little-visited **north coast** stretching from stormy **Cape Wrath**, at the very northwest tip of the mainland, east to **John O'Groats** is yet more rugged than the west, with sheer cliffs and sand-filled bays bearing the brunt of frequently fierce Atlantic storms. The main settlement on this coast is **Thurso**, jumping-off point for the main ferry service to Orkney.

On the fertile **east coast** of the Highland region, stretching north from Inverness to the old herring port of **Wick**, green fields and woodland run down to the sweeping sandy beaches of the **Black Isle** and the **Cromarty** and

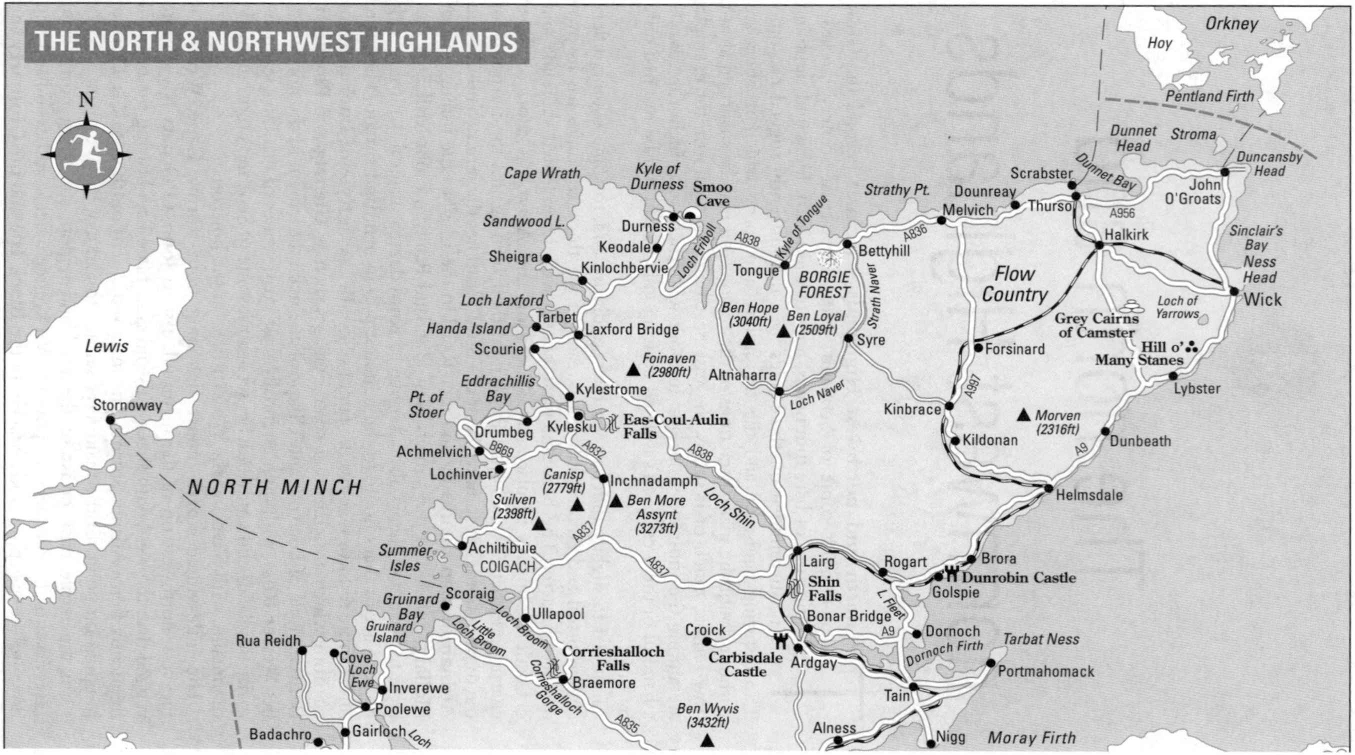

THE NORTH & NORTHWEST HIGHLANDS

N
Orkney
Hoy
Pentland Firth
Dunnet Head
Stroma
Duncansby Head
Dunnet Bay
Scrabster
Thurso
John O'Groats
A956
Halkirk
Sinclair's Bay
Ness Head
Wick
Cape Wrath
Kyle of Durness
Smoo Cave
Strathy Pt.
Dounreay
Melvich
Sandwood L.
Durness
Keodale
Sheigra
Kinlochbervie
Loch Eriboll
A838
Kyle of Tongue
Tongue
Bettyhill
A836
BORGIE FOREST
Strath Naver
Flow Country
Loch of Yarrows
Grey Cairns of Camster
Hill o' Many Stanes
Loch Laxford
Tarbet
Handa Island
Laxford Bridge
Scourie
Ben Hope (3040ft)
Ben Loyal (2509ft)
Syre
Forsinard
Foinaven (2980ft)
Altnaharra
Lewis
Eddrachillis Bay
Kylestrome
Loch Naver
Kinbrace
A997
Lybster
Pt. of Stoer
Stornoway
Drumbeg
Kylesku
Eas-Coul-Aulin Falls
Morven (2316ft)
Kildonan
Dunbeath
Achmelvich
B869
A832
A838
A9
Lochinver
Canisp (2779ft)
Inchnadamph
NORTH MINCH
Suilven (2398ft)
Ben More Assynt (3273ft)
Loch Shin
Helmsdale
A837
Summer Isles
Achiltibuie
COIGACH
A837
Lairg
Rogart
Brora
Shin Falls
Dunrobin Castle
Golspie
L. Fleet
Gruinard Bay
Scoraig
Loch Broom
Ullapool
Bonar Bridge
Gruinard Island
Little Loch Broom
Croick
A9
Dornoch
Tarbat Ness
Rua Reidh
Cove
Loch Ewe
Corrieshalloch Falls
Carbisdale Castle
Ardgay
Dornoch Firth
Portmahomack
Inverewe
Braemore
Corrieshalloch Gorge
Tain
Poolewe
Ben Wyvis (3432ft)
Badachro
Gairloch
Loch
A835
Alness
Nigg
Moray Firth

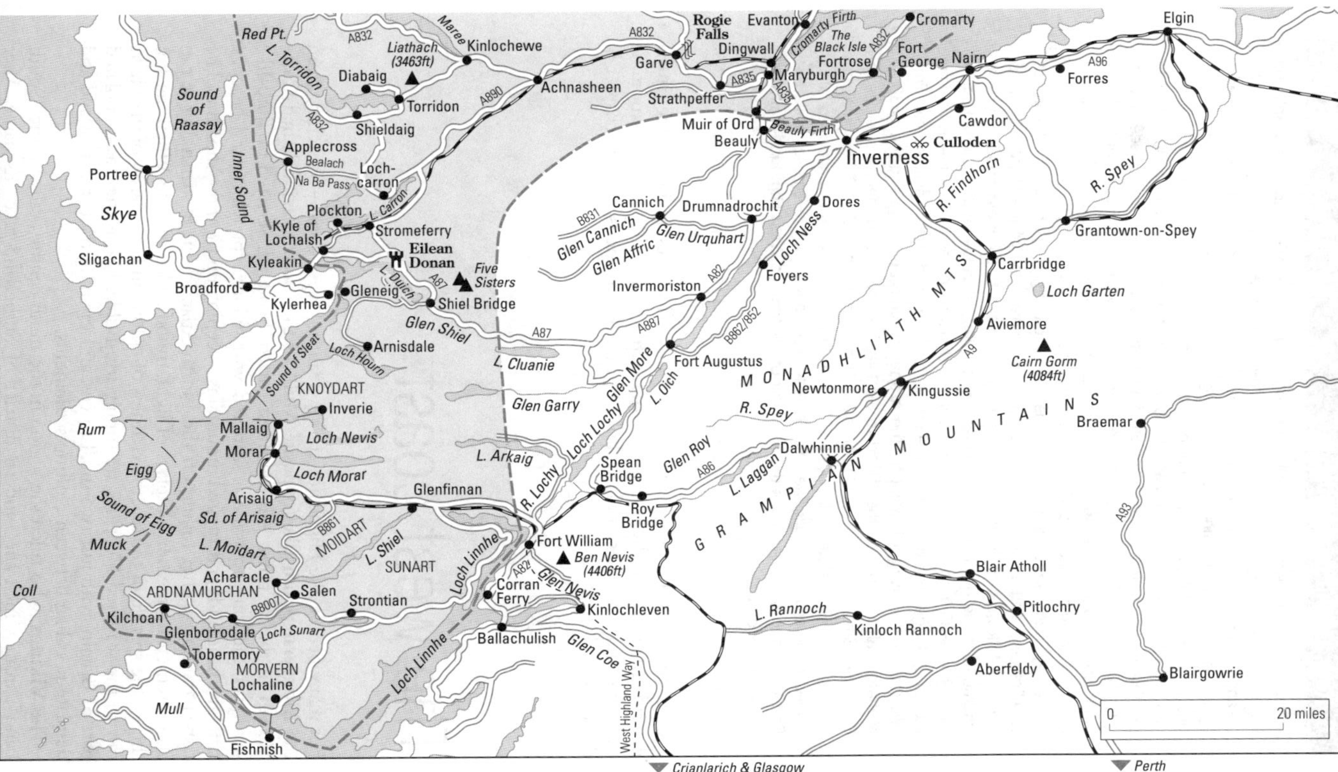
Red Pt.
L. Torridon
A832
Maree
Liathach (3463ft)
Kinlochewe
Diabaig
Torridon
Shieldaig
A890
Achnasheen
Garve
Rogie Falls
Evanton
Cromarty Firth
The Black Isle
Cromarty
Dingwall
Fortrose
Fort George
Nairn
Elgin
A96
Forres
Maryburgh
A835
Strathpeffer
Muir of Ord
Beauly Firth
Beauly
Cawdor
Culloden
Inverness
R. Findhorn
R. Spey
Grantown-on-Spey
Sound of Raasay
Inner Sound
Portree
Skye
Sligachan
Applecross
Bealach Na Ba Pass
Loch-carron
L. Carron
Plockton
Stromeferry
Kyle of Lochalsh
Kyleakin
Eilean Donan
Five Sisters
Broadford
Kylerhea
Glenelg
L. Duich
A87
Shiel Bridge
Glen Shiel
Arnisdale
Loch Hourn
Sound of Sleat
KNOYDART
Inverie
Rum
Mallaig
Loch Nevis
Morar
Loch Morar
Eigg
Arisaig
Sound of Eigg
Sd. of Arisaig
Glenfinnan
B8861
MOIDART
L. Shiel
SUNART
Muck
L. Moidart
Coll
Acharacle
ARDNAMURCHAN
Salen
B8007
Strontian
Kilchoan
Glenborrodale
Loch Sunart
Tobermory
MORVERN
Lochaline
Mull
Fishnish
Loch Linnhe
Cannich
B831
Glen Cannich
Glen Affric
Drumnadrochit
Glen Urquhart
Dores
Loch Ness
Foyers
Invermoriston
A82
A887
B862/852
Fort Augustus
L. Cluanie
Glen More
L. Oich
Glen Garry
Loch Lochy
L. Arkaig
R. Lochy
Spean Bridge
Roy Bridge
Glen Roy
A86
L. Laggan
Fort William
Ben Nevis (4406ft)
A82
Glen Nevis
Corran Ferry
Kinlochleven
Ballachulish
Glen Coe
West Highland Way
MONADHLIATH MTS
Carrbridge
Loch Garten
Aviemore
Cairn Gorm (4084ft)
A9
Newtonmore
Kingussie
R. Spey
GRAMPIAN MOUNTAINS
Braemar
Dalwhinnie
A93
Blair Atholl
L. Rannoch
Kinloch Rannoch
Pitlochry
Aberfeldy
Blairgowrie
0
20 miles
Crianlarich & Glasgow
Perth

Getting around the Highlands

Unless you're prepared to spend weeks on the road, the Highlands are simply too vast to see in a single trip. Most visitors, therefore, base themselves in one or two areas, exploring the coast or hills on foot, and making longer hops across the interior by car, bus or train. Getting around the Highlands, particularly the remoter parts, is obviously easiest if you've got your own transport, but with a little forward planning you can see a surprising amount using **buses** and **trains**, especially if you fill in with **postbuses** (for which you can get timetables at most post offices, or see ⓦwww.postbus.royalmail.com). It is worth remembering, however, that much of the Highlands comes to a halt on **Sundays**, when bus services are sporadic at best and you may well find most shops and restaurants closed.

The key road on the **east coast** is the A9, which hugs the coast from Inverness to **Wick** and **Thurso**, with its connections to Orkney. One of the Highlands' main rail lines follows broadly the same route. Connections to the **west coast** are more fragmented: the quickest way to **Ullapool**, the largest settlement in the region, is along the A835 from Inverness, though with independent transport or plenty of time the much longer approach along the coast from the south is far more scenic. Fort William is the jumping-off point for the **Ardnamurchan** peninsula and the A830 to **Mallaig** – also known as the "Road to the Isles" – from where there are ferries to Skye, the Small Isles and the Outer Isles. The other main route to Skye is along the central A87 to **Kyle of Lochalsh**. Both Kyle of Lochalsh and Mallaig are also served by spectacular train lines: services to Kyle leave from Inverness, while the Fort William to Mallaig route is the final part of the famous **West Highland Railway** line (see box on p.271).

Dornoch firths. This region is rich with historical sites, including the **Sutherland Monument** by Golspie, **Dornoch**'s fourteenth-century sandstone cathedral and a number of places linked to the **Clearances**, a tragic chapter in the Highland story.

The west coast

For many people, the Highlands' starkly beautiful **west coast** – stretching from the **Morvern peninsula** (opposite Mull) in the south to wind-lashed **Cape Wrath** in the far north – is the finest part of Scotland. Serrated by fjord-like sea lochs, the long coastline is scattered with windswept white-sand beaches, cliff-girt headlands and rugged mountains sweeping up from the shoreline. The fast-changing weather rolling off the North Atlantic can be harsh, but it can also often create memorable plays of light, mood and landscape. When the sun shines, the sparkle of the sea, the richness of colour and the clarity of the views out to the scattered Hebrides are simply irresistible. This is the least populated part of Britain, with just two small towns, and yawning tracts of moorland and desolate peat bog between crofting settlements.

The **Vikings**, who ruled the region in the ninth century, called it the "South Land", from which the modern district of Sutherland takes its name. After

Culloden, the Clearances emptied most of the inland glens of the far north, however, and left the population clinging to the coastline, where a herring-fishing industry developed. Today, tourism, crofting, fishing and salmon farming are the mainstay of the local economy, supplemented by EU construction grants and subsidies to farm the sheep you'll encounter everywhere.

For visitors, **cycling** and **walking** are the obvious ways to make the most of the superb scenery, and countless lochans and crystal-clear rivers offer superlative trout and salmon **fishing**. The shattered cliffs of the far northwest are an ornithologist's dream, harbouring some of Europe's largest and most diverse **seabird colonies**, while the area's craggy mountaintops are the haunt of the elusive golden eagle.

The most visited part of the west coast is the stretch between Kyle of Lochalsh and Ullapool. Lying within easy reach of Inverness, this sector boasts the region's more obvious highlights: the awesome mountainscape of **Torridon**, **Gairloch**'s sandy beaches, the famous botanic gardens at **Inverewe** and **Ullapool** itself, a picturesque and bustling fishing town from where ferries leave for the Outer Hebrides. However, press on further north, or south, and you'll get a truer sense of the isolation that makes the west coast so special. Traversed by few roads, the remote northwest corner of Scotland is wild and bleak, receiving the full force of the North Atlantic's frequently ferocious weather. The scattered settlements of the far southwest, meanwhile, tend to be more sheltered, but they are separated by some of the most extensive wilderness areas in Britain – lonely peninsulas with evocative Gaelic names like **Ardnamurchan**, **Knoydart** and **Glenelg**.

Practicalities

Tempered by the Gulf Stream, the west coast's **weather** ranges from stupendous to diabolical. Never count on a sunny morning meaning a fine day; it can rain here at any time, and go on raining for days. Beware, too, of the dreaded **midge**, which drives even the hardiest of locals to distraction on warm summer evenings.

Without your own vehicle, **transport** can be a problem. There's a reasonable **train** service from Inverness to Kyle of Lochalsh and from Fort William to Mallaig, and a useful **summer bus** service connects Inverness to Ullapool, Lochinver, Scourie and Durness. However, services peter out as you venture further afield, where you'll have to rely on **postbuses**, which go just about everywhere, albeit slowly and at odd times of day. **Driving** is a much simpler option: the roads aren't busy, though they are frequently single-track and scattered with sheep. On such routes, you should refuel whenever you can since pumps are few and far between, and make sure your vehicle is in good condition; in a crisis, even if you manage to reach the nearest garage, spares may well have to be sent over from Inverness.

Morvern to Knoydart: the "Rough Bounds"

The remote and sparsely populated southwest corner of the Highlands, from the empty district of **Morvern** to the isolated peninsula of **Knoydart**, is a dramatic, lonely region of mountain and moorland fringed by a rocky, indented coast studded by stunning white beaches which enjoy wonderful views to Mull,

Skye and other islands. Its Gaelic name, *Garbh-chiochan*, translates as the "**Rough Bounds**", implying a region geographically and spiritually apart. Even if you have got a car, you should spend some time here exploring on foot; there are so few roads that some determined hiking is almost inevitable.

The southwest Highlands' main road is the A830, often described as "the Road to the Isles", which winds in tandem with the rail line through the glens from Fort William to the road- and railhead at **Mallaig**, a busy fishing port with ferry connections to Skye. Along the way, the road passes **Glenfinnan**, the much-photographed spot at the head of stunning **Loch Shiel** where Bonnie Prince Charlie gathered the clans to start the doomed Jacobite uprising of 1745. There are regular buses and trains along the main road; elsewhere in the region you'll usually have to rely on daily post- or schoolbuses. If you have your own transport, the five-minute ferry crossing at **Corran Ferry** (every 15min daily summer 7am–9pm; winter 7am–8pm; car and passengers £5.20; foot passengers and bicycles go free), a nine-mile drive south of Fort William down Loch Linnhe, provides a more direct point of entry for Morvern and the rugged **Ardnamurchan** peninsula.

Morvern

Bounded on three sides by sea lochs and in the north by desolate Glen Tarbet, the large, mountainous Morvern peninsula lies at the southwest corner of the Rough Bounds region. Its population is small and widely scattered, and much of the landscape can seem unremittingly bleak and empty – until, that is, you reach the coast which reveals some lovely views over to Mull. Most visitors only travel through here to get to **LOCHALINE** (pronounced "loch-*aa*lin"), a remote community on the **Sound of Mull**, from where a small car ferry chugs to **Fishnish** – the shortest crossing from the mainland (and a cheaper option than the main Oban–Craignure crossing if you're taking a car onto Mull). Lochaline village, little more than a scattering of houses around a small pier, has a diving centre specializing in underwater archeology (Ⓣ01967/421627, Ⓦwww.lochalinedivecentre.co.uk) and is a popular anchorage for yachts cruising the west coast, but holds little else to detain you. For **accommodation**, the dive centre has a bunkhouse with simple twin rooms (❶), or try the straightforward *Lochaline Hotel* (Ⓣ01967/421657; ❶), which has five rooms and serves meals. The best reason to stop here, however, is to **eat** at the superb *White House Restaurant* (Ⓣ01967/421777, Ⓦwww.thewhitehouserestaurant.co.uk; Easter–Oct closed Mon; Oct–Dec Fri & Sat only; Jan–Easter closed), which specializes in delicious, freshly prepared dishes using local meat and seafood. It's a relaxed, friendly place, and not too expensive, particularly if you're in for lunch or coffee and home-baked scones. As you'd expect, **transport** links here (other than the Fishnish ferry) are extremely limited, with a bus running to and from Fort William on a Tuesday, Thursday and Friday only, plus a Saturday service in summer (check times with Shiel Buses Ⓣ01967/431272). By request, the bus goes as far as the road end at **Drimmin** at the northwest corner of Morvern, from where it's possible to organize boat crossings over to Tobermory on Mull or Ardnamurchan through Ardnamurchan Charters (Ⓣ01972/500208).

Sunart and Ardgour

North of Morvern, the predominantly roadless regions of **Sunart** and **Ardgour** make up the country between Loch Shiel, Loch Sunart and Loch Linnhe: the heart of Jacobite support in the mid-eighteenth century and a Catholic stronghold to this day. The area's only real village is sleepy **STRONTIAN**, grouped around a green on an inlet of Loch Sunart. In 1722, lead mines here yielded the first-ever traces of the element **strontium**, which was named after the village. If you're interested, you can pick up a leaflet at the tourist office which explains the history of the mines and details some local routes to see what remains of the workings.

You can get to Strontian on the one **bus** a day (Mon–Sat) which links Fort William with Kilchoan (check times with Shiel Buses ⓣ01967/431272). Strontian's **tourist office** (Easter–May Mon–Sat 10am–5pm; June–Sept Mon–Sat 10am–5/5.30pm, Sun 10am–4pm; Oct Mon–Sat 10am–4pm; ⓣ01967/402382) is by the roadside as you pass through the village. Strontian has a couple of good **hotels**, the *Strontian Hotel* (ⓣ01967/402029, ⓦwww.strontianhotel.supanet.com; ❸), on the main road looking over the water, and luxurious *Kilcamb Lodge* (ⓣ01967/402257, ⓦwww.kilcamblodge.co.uk; ❼), a restored country house set in its own grounds on the lochside, whose **restaurant** serves excellent, if pricey, food. B&B is available at *Heatherbank* (ⓣ01967/402201, ⓦwww.heatherbankbb.co.uk; ❷) and *Craigrowan Croft* (ⓣ01967/402253, ⓦwww.craigrowancroft.co.uk; ❷), both a little way up the Ariundle turn-off. Six miles west of Strontian, only two miles before Salen, *Resipole Farm* (ⓣ01967/431235, ⓦwww.resipole.co.uk; April–Oct) has a great set-up, with a **camping** and caravan park, self-catering accommodation and the *Farm Bar*, serving snacks and unexpectedly good evening meals.

The Ardnamurchan peninsula

The tortuous single-track B8007 road winds west from Salen to the wild **Ardnamurchan peninsula**, the most westerly point on the British mainland. The unspoilt landscape is relatively gentle and wooded at the eastern end, with much of the coastline of long Loch Sunart fringed by ancient oakwoods, which are protected as among the last remnants of the extensive temperate rainforests once common along the Atlantic coast of Europe (ⓦwww.sunartoakwoods.org.uk). The further west you travel, however, the trees disappear and are replaced by a wild, salt-sprayed moorland. The peninsula, which lost most of its inhabitants during the infamous Clearances (see p.505), has only a handful of tiny crofting settlements clinging to its jagged coastline and is sparsely populated – all the more so when you realize that many of the houses are seldom-used holiday cottages. Ardnamurchan, however, can be an inspiring place for its pristine, empty beaches, wonderful vistas of sea and island and the sense of nature all around. With its variety of undisturbed habitats the peninsula harbours a huge variety of birds, animals and wildflowers such as thrift and wild iris, making **walking** an obvious attraction. A variety of routes, from hill climbs to coastal scrambles, are detailed in a comprehensive guide to the peninsula produced annually by the local community (available from tourist offices and most shops on the peninsula, priced around £4), while **guided walks** are also available at most of the nature reserves dotted along the Loch Sunart shoreline; these are run under the auspices of the Highland Council Ranger Service (ⓣ01967/402232). If you want to do some of your own wildlife spotting, it's worth stopping off at the turf-roofed Garbh Eilean hide (free access), not far from the road between Strontian and Salen, from where you can see seals, seabirds and the occasional otter or eagle.

Salen to Glenborrodale

The coastal hamlet of **SALEN** marks the turn-off for Ardnamurchan Point: from here it's a further 25 miles of scenic but slow driving along the single-track road which follows the northern shore of Loch Sunart. Salen is a sheltered anchorage, and yachties often row ashore for a drink at the *Salen Hotel* (Ⓣ01967/4311661, Ⓦwww.salenhotel.co.uk; ❸), which has some neat rooms and serves good bar meals featuring fresh local seafood. There's not much more until you get to the engaging **Glenmore Natural History Centre** (April–Oct Mon–Sat 10.30am–5.30pm, Sun noon–5.30pm; Ⓦwww.ardnamurchannaturalhistorycentre.co.uk; £2.50), which provides an inspiring introduction to the diverse flora, fauna and geology of Ardnamurchan just west of the hamlet of **GLENBORRODALE**. Originally set up by local photographer Michael MacGregor (whose stunning work enlivens postcard stands along the west coast), the centre is housed in a sensitively designed timber building called "The Living Building", complete with turf roof and wildlife ponds. CCTV cameras relay live pictures of the surrounding wildlife, catching the comings and goings of a pine marten's nest, underwater pools in the nearby river and a nearby heronry. The small **café** here serves sandwiches and good home-baked cakes, with evening meals served some evenings in summer (Ⓣ01972/500209). For coastal wildlife and whale-spotting **excursions** – or trips to Tobermory on Mull, the Treshnish Isles or Fingal's Cave – contact Ardnamurchan Charters at Glenborrodale (Ⓣ01972/500208, Ⓦwww.west-scotland-marine.com).

Kilchoan and Ardnamurchan Point

KILCHOAN, nine miles west of the Glenmore Centre, is Ardnamurchan's main village – a straggling but appealing crofting township overlooking the Sound of Mull. A **car ferry** runs from here to Tobermory (Mon–Sat 8am–6.45pm 7 daily, plus June–Aug Sun 10.15am–4.45pm, 5 daily; 35min). The community centre in the village houses a **tourist office** (Easter–Oct daily 9am–5pm; Ⓣ01972/510222, Ⓦwww.ardnamurchan.com), which will help with and book accommodation, though year-round the community centre (and its simple tearoom) are open and will act as an informal source of local advice and assistance. For **boat trips** out of Kilchoan – either wildlife-spotting or fishing – contact Nick Peake (Ⓣ01972/510212, Ⓔactivoutdoors.achnaha.scotland@virgin.net), who also leads guided walks to look for land-based wildlife such as eagles, pine martens and badgers. The only direct **bus** to Kilchoan leaves from Fort William at 1.25pm (Mon–Sat), travelling via the Corran Ferry and arriving two and a half hours later.

The road continues beyond Kilchoan to the rocky, windy **Ardnamurchan Point** and its famous **lighthouse**. The lighthouse buildings house a small café and an absorbing **exhibition** (daily April–Oct 10am–5pm; £5; Ⓣ01972/510210), with well-assembled displays about lighthouses in general, their construction and the people who lived in them. Best of all is the chance to climb up the inside of the Egyptian-style lighthouse tower; at the top, a guide is on hand to tell some of the tall tales relating to the lighthouse and show you around the lighting mechanism. Whales are sometimes seen surfacing in the waters off the point – indeed, the Hebridean Whale and Dolphin Trust, based in Tobermory, often sends volunteers over to the lighthouse to sit by the massive old fog horn and peer out through binoculars counting sightings.

Also worth exploring around the peninsula are the myriad coves, beaches and headlands along the long coastline. The finest of the sandy beaches is about three miles north of the lighthouse at **Sanna Bay**, a shell-strewn strand and series of dunes which offers truly unforgettable vistas of the Small Isles to the north, circled by gulls, terns and guillemots.

Practicalities

Accommodation isn't plentiful in Kilchoan, and in summer you're well advised to book far ahead. You can normally camp in the gardens of the *Kilchoan House Hotel*, and there's also a simple campsite with lovely coastal views by the Ardnamurchan Study Centre (Ⓣ07787/812084, Ⓦwww.ardnamurchanstudycentre.co.uk), about half a mile past the Ferry Stores. For B&B, try *Doirlinn House* (Ⓣ01972/510209, Ⓔdorlinnhouse@yahoo.co.uk; ❷; March–Oct), or *Tigh a'Ghobhainn* (Ⓣ01972/510771, Ⓔmairihunter.kilchoan@virgin.net; ❷; March–Oct), both with lovely views over the Sound of Mull. Along the road between Salen and Kilchoan, at Glenborrodale, there's an exquisite upmarket guesthouse, *Feorag House* (Ⓣ01972/500248, Ⓦwww.feorag.co.uk; ❽ for dinner, B&B), which has three tasteful, modest rooms in a beautifully secluded modern house.

Most of the local hotels offer **food** to non-residents, among them *Kilchoan House Hotel* (Ⓣ01972/510200, Ⓦwww.kilchoanhousehotel.co.uk; ❹) and plain *Sonachan Hotel* (Ⓣ01972/510211, Ⓦwww.sonachan.com; ❶), which despite being hailed as the most westerly hotel on the British mainland is tucked inland away from the coast, halfway between Kilchoan and Ardnamurchan Point. The Ferry Stores in Kilchoan, the only **shop** west of Salen, makes an impressive effort to carry fresh food and local produce when it's available.

Acharacle and around

At the eastern end of Ardnamurchan, just north of Salen where the A861 heads north towards the district of Moidart, the main settlement is **ACHARACLE**, an ancient crofting village set back a few hundred yards from the seaward end of freshwater **Loch Shiel**. Surrounded by gentle hills, it's an attractive place, and being a couple of miles from the sea gives it a different feel to many of the area's other settlements. The pleasant *Loch Shiel House Hotel* (Ⓣ01967/431224, Ⓦwww.lochshielhotel.com; ❺) is a comfortable, friendly place to stay, stop for a drink or eat, while *Ardsheleach Lodge* (Ⓣ01967/431399, Ⓦwww.ardshealach-lodge.co.uk; ❺) is a restaurant with four rooms, serving lunches, afternoon teas and dinner in an attractive house in its own grounds with a great outlook over the loch and hills beyond.

You can get to Acharacle by **boat** from Glenfinnan at the head of Loch Shiel (Wed only; Easter to mid-Oct) with Loch Shiel Cruises (Ⓣ01687/470322, Ⓦwww.highlandcruises.co.uk), or on infrequent **buses** from Mallaig or Fort William. There are plenty of untaxing and attractive **walks** in the local area; Out of Doors, a shop just behind the hotel, stocks a book detailing these. Near this is the Bakehouse with good picnic fodder, which you can supplement with something from the tiny Moidart Smoke House, at Dalnabreac a couple of miles to the north of Acharacle. For evening **entertainment** your best bet is the *Clanranald Hotel* at Mingarry, again just north of Archaracle, which is run by a well-known local accordionist and band leader, Fergie Macdonald.

Castle Tioram

A mile north of Acharacle, a side road running north off the A861 winds for three miles or so past a secluded estuary lined with rhododendron thickets and fishing platforms to **Loch Moidart**, a calm and sheltered sea loch. Perched atop a rocky promontory protruding out into the loch is **Castle Tioram** (pronounced "cheerum"), one of Scotland's most atmospheric historic monuments. Reached via a sandy causeway that's only just above the high tide, the thirteenth-century fortress, whose Gaelic name means "dry land", was the seat of the MacDonalds of Clanranald until it was destroyed by their chief in 1715 to prevent it from falling into Hanoverian hands while he was away fighting for the Jacobites. Today, a certain amount of controversy surrounds the upkeep of the place: while the setting and approach are undoubtedly stunning, large notices and fences keep you from getting too close to the castle due to the danger of falling masonry.

The Road to the Isles

The "**Road to the Isles**" (Ⓦ www.road-to-the-isles.org.uk) from Fort William to Mallaig, followed by the West Highland Railway and the narrow, winding A830, traverses the mountains and glens of the Rough Bounds before breaking out near **Arisaig** onto a spectacularly scenic coast of sheltered inlets, stunning white beaches and wonderful views to the islands of Rùm, Eigg, Muck and Skye. This is country commonly associated with **Bonnie Prince Charlie**, whose adventures of 1745–46 began and ended on this stretch of coast, with his first, defiant gathering of the clans at **Glenfinnan**.

Glenfinnan

GLENFINNAN, nineteen miles west of Fort William at the head of lovely Loch Shiel, was where Bonnie Prince Charlie raised his standard to signal the start of the Jacobite uprising of 1745. Surrounded by no more than two hundred loyal clansmen, the young rebel prince waited here to see if the Cameron of Loch Shiel would join his army. The drone of this powerful chief's pipers drifting up the glen was eagerly awaited, for without him the Stuarts' attempt to claim the English throne would have been sheer folly. Despite strong misgivings, Cameron did decide to support the uprising, and arrived at Glenfinnan on a sunny August 19 with eight hundred men, thereby encouraging other wavering clan leaders to follow suit. Assured of adequate backing, the prince raised his red-and-white silk colour, proclaimed his father as King James III of England and set off on the long march to London – from which only a handful of the soldiers gathered at Glenfinnan would return. The spot is marked by a column

△ Glenfinnan monument, Loch Shiel

The West Highland Railway

Scotland's most famous railway line, and a train journey counted by many as among the world's most scenic, is the brilliantly engineered **West Highland Railway**, running from Glasgow to Mallaig via Fort William. The line is in two sections: the southern part travels from **Glasgow** Queen Street station along the Clyde estuary and up Loch Long before switching to the banks of Loch Lomond on its way to **Crianlarich**, where the train divides, with one section heading for Oban. After climbing around Beinn Odhar on a unique horseshoe-shaped loop of viaducts, the line traverses desolate **Rannoch Moor**, where the track had to be laid on a mattress of tree roots, brushwood and thousands of tons of earth and ashes. By this point the line has diverged from the road, and travels through country which can otherwise be reached only by long-distance footpaths. The train then swings into Glen Roy, passing through the dramatic **Monessie Gorge** and entering **Fort William** from the northeast.

The second leg of the journey, from Fort William to Mallaig, is arguably even more spectacular, and from June to mid-October one of the scheduled services is pulled by the **Jacobite Steam Train** (Mon–Fri, also Sun late July & Aug; departs Fort William 10.20am, departs Mallaig 2.10pm; day-return £26; book on ⓣ01463/239026; ⓦwww.steamtrain.info). Shortly after leaving Fort William the railway crosses the Caledonian Canal beside Neptune's Staircase by way of a swing bridge at **Benavie**, before travelling along the shores of Locheil and crossing the magnificent 21-arch viaduct at **Glenfinnan**, where the steam train, in its "Hogwarts Express" livery, was filmed for the *Harry Potter* movies. At Glenfinnan station there's a small **museum** dedicated to the history of the West Highland line, as well as two old railway carriages which have been converted into a restaurant and a bunkhouse (see below). Not long afterwards the line reaches the coast, where there are unforgettable views of the Small Isles and Skye as it runs past the famous silver sands of **Morar** and up to **Mallaig**, where there are connections to the ferry which crosses to Armadale on Skye.

If you're planning on travelling the West Highland line, and in particular linking it to other train journeys (such as the similarly attractive route between Inverness and Kyle of Lochalsh), it's worth considering one of ScotRail's multiday **rover tickets**, details of which are given on p.39.

(now a little lop-sided, Pisa-like), crowned with a clansman in full battledress, erected as a tribute by Alexander Macdonald of Glenaladale in 1815.

Glenfinnan is a poignant place, a beautiful stage for the opening scene in a brutal drama which was to change the Highlands for ever. The **visitor centre** and café (daily: April, May, Sept & Oct 10am–5pm; June–Aug 9.30am–5.30pm; Nov Sat & Sun 10am–4pm; NTS; £3), opposite the monument, gives an account of the 1745 uprising through to the rout at **Culloden** eight months later (see p.253). A **boat trip** on the loch with Loch Shiel Cruises (ⓣ01687/470322, ⓦwww.highlandcruises.co.uk), which offers a chance to view some very remote scenery and occasionally a golden eagle, is highly recommended.

Glenfinnan is one of the most spectacular parts of the **West Highland Railway** line (see box, above), not only for the glimpse it offers of the monument and graceful Loch Shiel, but also the mighty 21-arched Loch nan Uamh **viaduct** built in 1901 and one of the first-ever large constructions made out of concrete. You can learn more of the history of this section of the railway at the **Glenfinnan Station Museum** (June–Sept daily 9.30am–4.30pm; 50p), set in the old booking office of the station. Right beside the station, two old railway carriages have been pressed into use as a highly original **restaurant** and **bunkhouse**; the *Dining Car* (June–Sept daily 10am–5pm; ⓣ01397/722300) is open for light lunches, home baking and evening meals if you phone ahead to make arrangements, while the *Sleeping Car* (Ⓣ01397/722295; year-round), a converted 1958 camping coach, sleeps ten in bunk beds. The best of the more conventional accommodation options locally is the *Lochailort Inn* (Ⓣ01687/470208, Ⓦwww.lochailortinn.co.uk; ❺), about ten miles on from Glenfinnan towards Arisaig (and also on the train line, although you have to request to stop here).

Arisaig

West of Glenfinnan, the A830 runs alongside captivating Loch Eilt in the district of **Morar**, through Lochailort – where it meets the road from Acharacle – and on to a coast marked by acres of white sands, turquoise seas and rocky islets draped with orange seaweed. **ARISAIG**, scattered round a sandy bay at the west end of the Morar peninsula, makes a good base for exploring this area. A recently constructed **bypass** now whizzes cars (and, more importantly, fish lorries) on their way to Mallaig, but you shouldn't miss out on the slower coast road, which enjoys all the best of the scenery.

The only specific attraction in Arisaig village is the **Land, Sea and Islands Centre** (Easter to mid-Oct Mon–Sat 10am–4pm, Sun noon–4pm, winter closes 3pm; £2), a small, volunteer-run community project relating the social and natural history of the area. The displays include some intriguing detail on local events, including secret operations during World War II and the filming of various movies in the area, along with background on local characters such as the person who inspired Robert Louis Stevenson's pirate Long John Silver. If the weather's fine you could spend hours wandering along the beaches and quiet backroads, and there's a small seal colony at nearby **Rhumach**, reached via the single-track lane leading west out of Arisaig village along the headland. A **boat** also leaves from here daily during the summer for the Small Isles (see p.350), operated by Arisaig Marine (Ⓣ01687/450224, Ⓦwww.arisaig.co.uk). **Accommodation** in the village is plentiful: *Kinloid Farm House* (Ⓣ01687/450366, Ⓦwww.kinloid-arisaig.co.uk; ❸; March–Oct) is one of several pleasant B&Bs with sea views, while the more upmarket *Old Library Lodge* (Ⓣ01687/450651, Ⓦwww.oldlibrary.co.uk; ❺; April–Oct) has a handful of well-appointed rooms, though only two overlook the seafront. For **food**, the restaurant at the *Old Library* is quite upmarket, while there's bar food available at the *Arisaig Hotel*, just along the road.

Morar

Stretching for eight miles or so north of Arisaig is a string of stunning white-sand **beaches** backed by flowery machair, with barren granite hills and moorland rising up behind and wonderful seaward views of Eigg and Rùm. The next settlement of any significance is **MORAR**, where the famous beach scenes from *Local Hero* were shot. Since then, however, a bypass has been built around the village, and the white sands are no longer an unspoilt idyll. Of the string of **campsites** along the coast road try *Camusdarach* (Ⓣ01687/450221, Ⓦwww.road-to-the-isles.org.uk/camusdarach), which isn't quite on the beach but is quieter and less officious than others nearby. **B&B** is also available in the converted billiard room of their attractive main house (❶). Alternatively, you can find B&B at the home of adventurer Tom McClean, Invermorar House (Ⓣ01687/462274; Ⓦwww.road-to-the-isles.org.uk/invermorar.html; ❷; July & Aug only). He runs an adventure school on the north side of nearby **Loch Morar** – rumoured to be the home of a monster called Morag, a lesser-known rival to Nessie – which runs east of Morar village into the heart of a huge wilderness area.

In the footsteps of Bonnie Prince Charlie

Along the Road to the Isles are various places which have great resonance whenever the romantic but ultimately tragic tale of **Bonnie Prince Charlie**'s failed rebellion is told. Having landed on the Western Isles (see p.395), he first set foot on the Scottish mainland on the sparkling sands of **Borrodale** at Loch nan Uamh (Loch of Caves) near Arisaig on July 25, 1745. In his bid to claim the throne of Britain for his father, the Old Pretender, he had been promised 10,000 French troops; instead he arrived with only seven companions – the "Seven Men of Moidart", who are commemorated at Kinlochmoidart by a (now somewhat ravaged) line of beech trees, still distinctive from the roadside. Having stayed a week at Kinlochmoidart, trying to ascertain what support he might muster, the prince took the old hill route (known as the General's Road) to **Dalilea**, on the north shore of Loch Shiel, and the next day, August 19, rowed from Glenalandale to the head of the loch at **Glenfinnan**. Here, surrounded by no more than two hundred loyal clansmen, he awaited the arrival of the clans loyal to the Jacobite cause. At this point, all his ambitions hung by a thread – most of the important local chiefs had turned their back on what they regarded as a desperate enterprise, and it was only when the prince persuaded two younger chiefs to join him late in the day that eight hundred more Highlanders arrived, the standard was raised, and the famous rebellion of 1745 was under way. The tall **Glenfinnan Monument** (see p.270) at the head of Loch Shiel is a poignant memorial both to the inspiring symbolism of that day and the Highlanders who subsequently fought and died for the Prince.

If Charles's original encounter with the Arisaig and Moidart area had been filled with optimism and high ideals, his next visit was far less auspicious. By the summer of 1746 he was on the run, his armies had been routed at Culloden and a price of £30,000 was on his head. It is often noted with admiration that, despite the huge sum on offer, none of the countless Highlanders the prince called on for food, favours or hiding turned him in, and that his fortitude and bravery in those desperate months earned him much more respect than his failure as a leader of men. Fleeing from Culloden down the Great Glen, he passed through Arisaig again on his way to the Western Isles, desperately hoping for the arrival of a French ship to rescue him. It was on South Uist that Flora MacDonald extracted him from a tight situation (see p.349), but still on the run he landed back on the mainland again at **Mallaigvaig**, a short walk from Mallaig. The place was swarming with soldiers, and he went on to **Borrodale** once more, this time hiding in a large cave by the shore. From here Charles set off across Lochaber, dodging patrols and hiding in caves and shelters, including some near **Loch Arkaig** (see p.235) and on the slopes of Ben Alder, by **Loch Ericht** (see p.235). It was here that he got word that a French frigate, *L'Heureux*, was off the west coast, and he made a final dash to Arisaig, departing on September 19, 1746 from a promontory in **Loch nan Uamh**, half a mile east of the spot where he'd landed fourteen months before. Today, a cairn on the shores of the loch beside the A830, between Lochailort and Arisaig village, marks the spot.

Mallaig

A cluttered, noisy port whose pebble-dashed houses struggle for space with great lumps of granite tumbling down to the sea, **MALLAIG**, 47 miles west of Fort William along the A830 (regular buses and trains run this route), is not pretty. Before the railway reached here in 1901, it consisted of only a few cottages, but now it's a busy, bustling place and, as the main ferry stop for Skye, the Small Isles and Knoydart, is always full of visitors. The continuing source of the village's wealth is its **fishing** industry: on the quayside, piles of nets, tackle and ice crates lie scattered around a bustling modern market. When the fleet is in, trawlers encircled by flocks of raucous gulls choke the harbour, and the pubs, among the liveliest on the west coast, host bouts of serious drinking.

Apart from the daily bustle of Mallaig's harbour, the main attraction in town is **Mallaig Marine World**, north of the train station near the harbour (March–Oct daily 9.30am–5.30pm; Nov–Feb Mon–Sat 11am–5.30pm; £3), where tanks of local sea creatures and informative exhibits about the port provide an unpretentious introduction to the local waters. Alongside the train station, the **Mallaig Heritage Centre** (April, May & Oct Mon–Sat 11am–4pm; June–Sept Mon–Sat 9.30am–4.30pm, Sun 1.30–4.30pm; phone for winter hours; ⓣ01687/462085; £1.80), displaying old photographs of the town and its environs, is worth a browse. The walking trail to **Mallaigmore**, a small cove with a white-sand beach and isolated croft, begins at the top of the harbour on East Bay; follow the road north past the tourist office and turn off right when you see the signpost between two houses. The round trip takes about an hour.

Practicalities

Mallaig is a compact place, concentrated around the harbour, where you'll find the **tourist office** (April–Oct Mon–Sat 10am–5pm; Nov–March Mon, Tues & Fri 11am–3pm), which will book accommodation for you, and the **bus** and **train stations**. The CalMac ticket office (ⓣ01687/462403), serving passengers for Skye and the Small Isles, is also nearby, and you can arrange transport to Knoydart by calling Bruce Watt Cruises (ⓣ01687/462320, ⓦwww.knoydart-ferry.co.uk), which sails to Inverie, on the Knoydart peninsula, every morning and afternoon (mid-May to mid-Sept Mon–Fri; otherwise Mon, Wed & Fri); the loch is sheltered, so crossings are rarely cancelled.

There are plenty of **places to stay**. The *West Highland Hotel* (ⓣ01687/462210, ⓦwww.westhighlandhotel.co.uk; ⑤) is a typically bland but comfortable Scottish Highland hotel; some rooms have excellent sea views. For **B&B**, head around the harbour to East Bay, where you'll find the cheery *Western Isles Guest House* (ⓣ01687/462320, ⓦwww.road-to-the-isles.org.uk/western-isles.html; ③). *Sheena's Backpackers' Lodge* (ⓣ01687/462764), a refreshingly laid-back independent **hostel** overlooking the harbour, has mixed dorms, self-catering facilities and a sitting room. For **eating**, the *Fishmarket Restaurant* facing the backpacker lodge features lots of fresh seafood including crab and langoustines, often incorporating various exotic flavours. During the day, the *Tea Garden* at *Sheena's Lodge* is a great place to watch the world go by while you tuck into a bowl of cullen skink (soup made from smoked haddock), a pint of prawns or home-made scones. Also worth seeking out are the freshest of fish and chips – or a portion of scallops and chips if you're feeling decadent – served at the *Cornerstone*, just across the road from the tourist office. To buy fresh or smoked fish, head to Andy Race's fish shop at the harbour.

The Knoydart peninsula

Many people regard the **Knoydart peninsula** as mainland Britain's most dramatic and unspoilt wilderness area. Flanked by **Loch Nevis** ("Loch of Heaven") in the south and the fjord-like inlet of **Loch Hourn** ("Loch of Hell") to the north, Knoydart's knobbly green peaks – three of them Munros – sweep straight out of the sea, shrouded for much of the time in a pall of grey mist. To get to the heart of the peninsula, you must catch a **boat** from Mallaig or Glenelg, or else **hike** for a couple of days across rugged moorland and mountains and sleep rough in old stone bothies (most of which are marked on Ordnance Survey maps). Unsurprisingly, the peninsula tends to attract walkers, lured by the network of well-maintained trails that wind east into the wild interior, where Bonnie Prince Charlie is rumoured to have hidden out after Culloden.

At the end of the eighteenth century, around a thousand people eked out a living from this inhospitable terrain through crofting and fishing. Evictions in 1853 began a dramatic decrease in the population, which continued to dwindle through the twentieth century as a succession of landowners ran the estate as a hunting and shooting playground, prompting a famous land raid in 1948 by a group of crofters known as the "Seven Men of Knoydart", who staked out and claimed ownership of portions of the estate. Although their bid failed, the memory of their cause was invoked when the crofters of Knoydart finally achieved control over the land they lived on in a community buy-out in 1998. These days the peninsula supports around seventy people, most of whom live in the hamlet of **INVERIE**. Nestled beside a sheltered bay on the south side of the peninsula, it has a pint-sized post office, a shop and mainland Britain's most remote pub, the *Old Forge*.

Practicalities

Bruce Watt Cruises' **boat** chugs into Inverie from Mallaig (see p.273). To arrange for a boat crossing from Arnisdale on the Glenelg peninsula to the north coast of Knoydart or Kinloch Hourn, contact Murray Morrison (see p.280).

There are two main **hiking routes** into Knoydart: the trailhead for the first is **KINLOCH HOURN**, a crofting hamlet at the far east end of Loch Hourn which you can get to by road (turn south off the A87 six miles west of Invergarry). From Kinloch Hourn, a well-marked path winds around the coast to Barrisdale and on to Inverie (see ⓦwww.barisdale.com for more). The second path into Knoydart starts at the west side of **Loch Arkaig**, approaching the peninsula via Glen Dessary. These are both long hard slogs over rough, desolate country, so take wet-weather gear, a decent map, plenty of food, warm clothes and a good sleeping bag, and leave your name and expected time of arrival with someone when you set off.

Most of Knoydart's **accommodation** is concentrated in and around Inverie. *Torrie Shieling* (ⓣ01687/462669, ⓔtorrie@knoydart.org; £16 per person), an upmarket independent **hostel** located three-quarters of a mile east of the village on the side of the mountain, is popular with hikers and families, offering top-notch self-catering facilities, comfortable wooden beds in four-person rooms and the cosiness of open fires in the convivial living room. They also have a Land Rover and boat for ferrying guests around the peninsula, and to neighbouring lochs and islands. The Knoydart Foundation (ⓦwww.knoydart-foundation.com) also runs a bunkhouse, with simple but adequate facilities, in some old steadings not far from *Torrie Shieling*. To book this call the foundation office (ⓣ01687/462242). In Inverie itself there's just one guesthouse, the *Pier House* (ⓣ01687/462347, ⓦwww.thepierhouseknoydart.co.uk; ❻ for dinner, B&B), a great place to stay: they have their own **restaurant** serving à la carte evening meals, including some good veggie options. Dinner is available to non-residents (three courses from around £15). If you want total isolation and all the creature comforts book into the beautiful *Doune Stone Lodges* (ⓣ01687/462667, ⓦwww.doune-knoydart.co.uk; full board ❼; min 3 nights), on the remote north side of the peninsula. Rebuilt from ruined crofts, this place has pine-fitted en-suite double rooms right on the shore; alongside the Doune dining room serves hearty meals. It's not easy to get to Doune by land, so you'll have to get them to pick you up by boat from Mallaig. The *Old Forge* is one of Scotland's finer pubs, with a convivial atmosphere where visitors and locals mix, generous bar meals often featuring recently caught seafood, real ales, an open fire and a good chance of live music of an evening. You can rent **mountain bikes** from *Pier House*; they've established various mountain-bike trails in the area, and offer mountain walks for groups of four or more.

Kyle of Lochalsh and around

As the main gateway to Skye, **Kyle of Lochalsh** used to be an important transit point for tourists, locals and services. However, with the building of the Skye Bridge in 1995, Kyle was left as merely the terminus for the train route from Inverness, with little else to offer. Of much more interest to most visitors is nearby **Eilean Donan Castle**, one of Scotland's most famous and popular sights, perched at the end of a stone causeway on the shores of **Loch Duich**. It's not hard, however, to step off the tourist trail, with the **Glenelg** peninsula on the south side of Loch Duich testimony to how quickly the west coast can seem remote and undiscovered. A few miles north of Kyle of Lochalsh, the delightful village of **Plockton** is a refreshing alternative to its utilitarian neighbour, with cottages grouped around a yacht-filled bay and Highland cattle wandering the streets. Plockton lies on the southern shore of **Loch Carron**, a long inlet which, together with **Strathcarron** at the head of the loch, acts as a dividing line between the Kyle of Lochalsh district and the scenic splendours of Wester Ross to the north.

Kyle of Lochalsh

KYLE OF LOCHALSH is not particularly attractive and is ideally somewhere to pass through rather than linger in. With the building of the **Skye road bridge**, traffic has little reason to stop before rumbling over the channel a mile to the west, leaving Kyle's shopkeepers bereft of the passing trade they used to enjoy. Just about the only reason to pause in Kyle is to take a ride on the *Atlantis* (Ⓣ01471/822716 or 0800/980 4846, Ⓦwww.seaprobe.freeserve.co.uk), the UK's only semi-submersible glass-bottomed **boat**, aboard which you can visit the protected seal and bird colonies on Seal Island or see the World War II wreck of *HMS Port Napier* (Easter to Oct; £6.50).

Buses run to Kyle of Lochalsh from Glasgow via Fort William and Invergarry (3 daily; 5hr 10min–6hr) and from Inverness via Invermoriston (3 daily; 2hr–2hr 30min). Book in advance for all of them (Ⓣ0870/550 5050, Ⓦwww.citylink.co.uk). All continue at least as far as Portree on Skye. Buses also shuttle across the bridge to Kyleakin on Skye every thirty minutes or so. **Trains** run to Kyle of Lochalsh from Inverness (Mon–Sat 3 daily, 1 on Sun; 2hr 30min); curving north through Achnasheen and Glen Carron, the train line is a rail enthusiast's dream, even if scenically it doesn't quite match the West Highland line to Mallaig.

Kyle's **tourist office** (April–June, Sept & Oct Mon–Sat 9.30am–5pm; July & Aug Mon–Sat 9.30am–6pm, Sun 10am–4pm), on top of the small hill near the old ferry jetty, can book **accommodation** – a useful service as there are surprisingly few options. The best hotel is probably the welcoming *Kyle Hotel* in Main Street, with a menu including fresh seafood and game (Ⓣ01599/534204, Ⓦwww.kylehotel.co.uk; ⑤). One of the most pleasant **B&Bs** in the area is the *Old Schoolhouse* at Erbusaig, built in the 1820s and located two miles north of Kyle towards Plockton (Ⓣ01599/534369, Ⓦwww.oldschoolhouse87.co.uk; ④). There's a simple bunkhouse in town, *Cúchulainn's* (Ⓣ01599/534492), above a pub across the main street from the tourist office. To **eat**, sample the steak and home-made puddings at the *Waverley Restaurant* (5.30–9.30pm, closed Thurs; ⓣ01599/534337) or for a snack visit *Sheila's Café* opposite the tourist office.

Loch Duich

Skirted on its northern shore by the A87, **Loch Duich**, the boot-shaped inlet just to the south of Kyle of Lochalsh, features prominently on the tourist trail, with buses from all over Europe thundering down the sixteen miles from **SHIEL BRIDGE** to Kyle of Lochalsh on their way to Skye. The main road, which connects to the Great Glen at Invermoriston (see p.242) and Invergarry, makes for a dramatic approach to the loch out of Glen Shiel, where, to the north, the much-photographed mountains known as the **Five Sisters of Kintail** surge impressively up to heights of 3000ft. With steep-sided hills hemming in both sides of the loch, it's sometimes hard to remember that this is, in fact, the sea. There's comfortable **accommodation** to be had in Shiel Bridge itself at the *Kintail Lodge Hotel* (ⓣ01599/511275, ⓦwww.kintaillodgehotel.co.uk; ⑥); the hotel also offers **hostel** accommodation, dorm-style in the appropriately named *Wee Bunkhouse* and in twins and singles in the *Trekkers' Lodge*. At **RATAGAN**, a mile or so up the southern shore from Shiel Bridge, there's also an excellent SYHA **hostel** (ⓣ0870/004 1147, ⓦwww.syha.org.uk; March–Oct), popular with walkers newly arrived off the Glen Affric trek from Cannich (see p.244).

Eilean Donan Castle

After Edinburgh's hilltop fortress, **Eilean Donan Castle** (March & Nov 10am–4pm; April–Oct daily 10am–5.30pm; £4.75), ten miles north of Shiel Bridge on the A87, has to be Scotland's most photographed monument. Presiding over the once strategically important confluence of lochs Alsh, Long and Duich, the forbidding crenellated tower rises from the water's edge, joined to the shore by a narrow stone bridge and with sheer mountains as a backdrop. The original castle was established in 1230 by Alexander II to protect the area

△ Eilean Donan Castle

Hiking in Glen Shiel

Ordnance Survey Explorer map no. 414.

The mountains of **Glen Shiel**, sweeping southeast from Loch Duich, offer some of the best hiking routes in Scotland. Rising dramatically from sea level to over 3000ft in less than a couple of miles, they are also exposed to the worst of the west coast's notoriously fickle weather. Don't underestimate either of these two routes. Tracing the paths on a map, they can appear short and easy to follow; nonetheless, unwary walkers die here every year, often because they failed to allow enough time to get off the mountain by nightfall, or because of a sudden change in the weather. Only attempt these routes if you're confident in your walking experience, and have a map, a compass and a detailed trekking guide – the SMC's *Hill Walks in Northwest Scotland* is recommended. Also make sure to follow the usual safety precautions outlined on p.59.

Taking in a bumper crop of Munros, the **Five Sisters traverse** is deservedly the most popular trek in the area. Allow a full day to complete the whole route, which begins at the first fire break on the left-hand side as you head southeast down the glen on the A87. Strike straight up from here and follow the ridge north along to Scurr na Moraich (2874ft), dropping down the other side to Morvich on the valley floor.

The distinctive chain of mountains across the glen from the Five Sisters is the **Kintail Ridge**, crossed by another famous hiking route that begins at the *Cluanie Inn* (see p.242) on the A87. From here, follow the well-worn path south around the base of the mountain until it meets up with a stalkers' trail, which winds steeply up Creag a' Mhaim (3108ft) and then west along the ridgeway, with breathtaking views south across Knoydart and the Hebridean Sea.

from the Vikings. Later, during a Jacobite uprising in 1719, it was occupied by troops dispatched by the King of Spain to help the "**Old Pretender**", James Stuart. However, when King George heard of their whereabouts, he sent frigates to take the Spaniards out, and the castle was blown up with their stocks of gunpowder. Thereafter, it lay in ruins until John Macrae-Gilstrap had it rebuilt between 1912 and 1932. Eilean Donan has since featured in several major **films**, including *Highlander*, *Entrapment* and the James Bond adventure *The World is Not Enough*. Three floors, including the banqueting hall, the bedrooms and the troops' quarters are open to the public, with various Jacobite and clan relics also on display, though like many of the region's most popular castles, the large numbers of people passing through make it hard to appreciate the real charm of the place.

There are several places to **stay** less than a mile away from the castle in the hamlet of **DORNIE**. The *Dornie Hotel*, Francis Street (Ⓣ01599/555205; ❺), provides comfortable unpretentious rooms, while the *Loch Duich Hotel* (Ⓣ01599/555213; ❺) has splendid doubles overlooking the loch; ask for the four-poster bed. Its small **restaurant** serves tasty bar snacks and evening meals. On Sunday nights they have a popular **folk music** session in the bar. Along from the *Dornie Hotel*, an eclectic bar meal menu is offered at the *Clachan Pub*.

The Glenelg peninsula

South of Loch Duich, the **Glenelg peninsula**, jutting out into the Sound of Sleat, is the isolated and little-known crofting area featured in Gavin Maxwell's otter novel *Ring of Bright Water*. Maxwell disguised the identity of this pristine stretch of coast by calling it "Camusfearnà", and it has remained a tranquil backwater in spite of the traffic that trickles through during the summer for the

Kylerhea ferry to Skye (see p.335 for details of the wildlife sanctuary at Eilean Ban, once Maxwell's home).

The landward approach to the peninsula is from the east by turning off the fast A87 at Shiel Bridge on Loch Duich, from where a narrow single-track road climbs a tortuous series of switchbacks to the Mam Ratagan Pass (1115ft), affording spectacular views over the awesome **Five Sisters** massif. There's a terrific picnic stop half-way up the road. Following the route of an old drovers' trail, the road, covered weekdays from Kyle of Lochalsh by both the postbus and Skyeways bus service, drops down the other side through Glen More, with the magnificent Kintail Ridge visible to the southeast, towards the peninsula's main settlement, **GLENELG**, on the Sound of Sleat. One mile east of the village is Glenelg Candles and Coffee Shop (March–Oct daily) where, within the delightful walled garden of a Georgian manse, you'll receive a warm welcome and organic coffee from candle-maker Donna Stiven.

Glenelg itself is comprised of a row of picturesque whitewashed houses, surrounded by trees. The *Glenelg Inn* (ⓣ01599/522273, ⓦwww.glenelg-inn.com; ⑤) is a wonderful spot, boasting seven luxurious (en-suite) **rooms** overlooking the bay, moderately priced fresh food that's served all day and where, aside from its handy bank machine, there's also a good chance of finding live music from any local musicians who happen to be in the **pub**.

The six-car **Glenelg–Kylerhea ferry** shuttles across the Sound of Sleat and one of the fastest tidal races in the UK from a jetty northwest of the village. At the time of writing, the ferry is for sale but expected to continue running. Call the tourist office in Kyle of Lochalsh for information (ⓣ01599/534390). In former times, this choppy channel where minke whale and dolphins may be spotted used to be an important drovers' crossing: 8000 cattle each year were herded head to tail across from Skye to the mainland.

One and a half miles south of Glenelg village, a left turn up Glen Beag leads to the **Glenelg Brochs**, some of the best-preserved Iron Age monuments in the country. Standing in a sheltered stream valley, the circular towers – Dun Telve and Dun Troddan – are thought to have been erected around 2000 years ago to protect the surrounding settlements from raiders. About a third of each main structure remains, with the curving dry-stone walls and internal passages still impressively intact.

Arnisdale

A narrow backroad snakes its way southwest beyond Glenelg village through a scattering of old crofting hamlets and timber forests. The views across the Sound of Sleat to Knoydart grow more spectacular at each bend, reaching a high point at a windy pass that takes in a vast sweep of sea, loch and islands. Below the road at **Sandaig** is where Gavin Maxwell and his otters lived in the 1950s: the site of his house is now marked by a cairn.

Swinging east, the road winds down to the waterside again, following the north shore of Loch Hourn as far as **ARNISDALE**, departure point for the boat to Knoydart (see p.274). Arnisdale is made up of the two hamlets of **Camusbane** and **Corran**, the former consisting of a single row of old cottages ranged behind a long pebble beach, with a massive scree slope behind, while the latter, a mile along the road, is a minuscule whitewashed fishing hamlet at the water's edge. Aside from the arrival of electricity and a red telephone box, the only major addition to this gorgeous hamlet in the last hundred years has been Mrs Nash's **B&B** and tea hut (ⓣ01599/522336; ①), where you can enjoy hot drinks and home-baked cake in a "shell garden", with breathtaking views on all sides.

From Monday to Saturday, you can get to Arnisdale on the 10am **postbus** from Kyle of Lochalsh (4hr 50min), returning on the 7.10am postbus from Arnisdale, or you can use the Skyeways bus service (Ⓣ01599/555477, Ⓦwww.skyeways.co.uk; Mon–Fri 1hr; £5.90 return) that operates a service between Kyle, Ratagan hostel and Glenelg post office. On request, the bus will go on to Arnisdale and Corran; similarly, the return bus from Glenelg can make arrangements to meet the Inverness or Glasgow buses at Kyle.

Murray Morrison's year-round **passenger ferry** from Arnisdale across Loch Hourn to Barrisdale (and to Kinloch Hourn) provides an excellent means for walkers and cyclists to explore the most inaccessible parts of the Knoydart Peninsula (Ⓣ01599/522774, Ⓦwww.arnisdaleferryservice.com; £10 single).

Plockton

A fifteen-minute train ride north of Kyle at the seaward end of islet-studded Loch Carron lies the unbelievably picturesque village of **PLOCKTON**: a chocolate-box row of neatly painted cottages ranged around the curve of a tiny harbour and backed by a craggy landscape of heather and pine. Originally known as Am Ploc, the settlement was a crofting hamlet until the end of the eighteenth century, when a local laird transformed it into a prosperous fishery, renaming it "Plocktown". Its fifteen minutes of fame came in the mid-1990s, when the BBC chose the village as the setting for the TV drama *Hamish Macbeth*. Though the resulting spin-off has since quietened, in high season it's packed full of tourists, yachties and second-home owners. The unique brilliance of Plockton's light has also made it something of an artists' hangout, and during the summer the waterfront, with its row of shaggy palm trees, even shaggier Highland cattle, flower gardens and pleasure boats, is invariably dotted with painters dabbing at their easels.

The friendly, cosy *Haven Hotel*, on Innes Street (Ⓣ01599/544223; ❼), has king-size beds and is renowned for its excellent food, whilst the family-run *Plockton Inn*, also on Innes Street (Ⓣ01599/544222, Ⓦwww.plocktoninn.co.uk; ❺) is an equally friendly and informal alternative. The *Plockton Hotel*, Harbour Street (Ⓣ01599/544274, Ⓦwww.plocktonhotel.co.uk; ❻), overlooking the harbour with some rooms in a nearby cottage, also serves excellent seafood. Of the fifteen or so **B&Bs**, *The Shieling* (Ⓣ01599/544282; ❷) has a great location on a tiny headland at the top of the harbour, and the nearby *Heron's Flight* (Ⓣ01599/544220; ❸; March-Nov) enjoys uninterrupted views across the loch from its two upstairs bedrooms. At the cosy main-street retreat *An Caladh*, "the resting place on the shore" (Ⓣ01599/544356; ❷), guests have the free use of two wooden sailing dinghies and can even watch the owner sail in with the morning catch of prawns. On the outskirts of Plockton, there's the attractive *Station Bunkhouse* (Ⓣ01599/544235) built in the shape of a signal box next to the railway station and featuring four- and six-person dorms and a cosy open-plan kitchen and living area.

There's a wealth of good places to **eat**: *The Haven*, the *Plockton Inn* and the *Plockton Hotel* all have excellent seafood **restaurants**, while *Off the Rails Restaurant and Tearoom* (Ⓦwww.off-the-rails.co.uk), in the train station, serves evening fare that includes local shellfish and game. *The Buttery*, part of Plockton Stores on the seafront, is also open all day for snacks and inexpensive meals. Beside Plockton Stores, Calum's Seal Trips (Ⓣ01599/544306 or 07761/263828; Easter–Oct daily; £6) provides an interesting one-hour excursion. He also hires out rowing boats and canoes. **Bike rental** is available from Plockton Craft Shop (Ⓣ01599/544255) on the seafront.

Strathcarron and Kishorn

The sea lochs immediately north of Plockton are the dual inlets of **Loch Kishorn**, so deep it was once used as an oil-rig construction site, and **Loch Carron**, which cuts inland to **STRATHCARRON**, a useful linking point between the Kyle of Lochalsh and the Torridon area to the north. Strathcarron has a station on the Kyle–Inverness line and provides a postbus connection to Sheildaig and Torridon (Mon–Sat 10am). Duncan MacLennan's bus also provides a regular service to Torridon (12.30pm). Right by the station, housed in the old station building, is the Strathcarron **tourist information, shop and post office** (Mon–Wed & Fri 9am–12.30pm & 1.30–5.30pm, Thurs 9am–1pm, Sat 9am–12.30pm; ⓣ01520/722218). Next door, the *Strathcarron Hotel* (ⓣ01520/722227; ❸) serves bar meals and several real ales. A mile back, along the road to Kyle, the *Carron Pottery, Crafts and Restaurant* (ⓣ01520/722488) serves up excellent food and offers some fine crafts.

There are several more **accommodation** options two or three miles away in **LOCHCARRON** (ⓦwww.lochcarron.org.uk), a pretty little village of whitewashed cottages stretched out along the northern shore of the loch. One of the best is *Rockvilla Hotel* (ⓣ01520/722379; ❹), a small, biker-friendly hotel in the centre of the village that serves huge breakfasts, organic yoghurts and breads and local produce. There are numerous B&Bs to choose from, including the very friendly *Old Manse* (ⓣ01520/722208, ⓦwww.theoldmanselochcarron.com; ❸), just off the road to Strome Castle. **Camping** is possible at the simple *Wee Campsite* (ⓣ01520/722245), above the village. Further down towards Strome Castle is the much-heralded **Lochcarron Weavers**, housed in an old-fashioned timber-clad workshop, where you can watch weaving demonstrations (Mon–Thurs 9.30am, 11.30am, 1.30pm & 2.30pm, Fri 10.30am & 11.30am; ⓦwww.lochcarron.com). Another wet-weather option is the **Lochcarron Smithy Heritage Centre** (ⓣ01520/722722; April–Oct daily 10am–5.30pm; free), a restored smithy and forge on the road between Strathcarron and Lochcarron, which houses a small exhibition and video on the local history.

A single-track road leads over the hillside to **KISHORN**, at the head of the loch of the same name. The wooden chalet of the *Kishorn Seafood Bar* (ⓣ01520/733240) is worth a stop for indulging in **fresh local shellfish** or coffee, home-baking and bacon rolls.

Wester Ross

Wester Ross, the western seaboard of the old county of Ross-shire, is widely regarded as the most glamorous stretch of this coast. Here all the classic elements of Scotland's **coastal scenery** – dramatic mountains, sandy beaches, whitewashed crofting cottages and shimmering island views – come together in spectacular fashion. Though popular with generations of adventurous Scottish holiday-makers, only one or two places feel blighted by tourist numbers, with places such as **Applecross** and the peninsulas north and south of **Gairloch** maintaining an endearing simplicity and sense of isolation. There is some tough but wonderful **hiking** to be had in the mountains around **Torridon** and **Coigach**, while **boat trips** out among the islands and the prolific sea- and birdlife of the coast are another draw. The main settlement is the attractive fishing town of **Ullapool**, port for ferry services to Stornoway in the Western Isles, but a pleasant enough place to use as a base, not least for its active social and cultural scene.

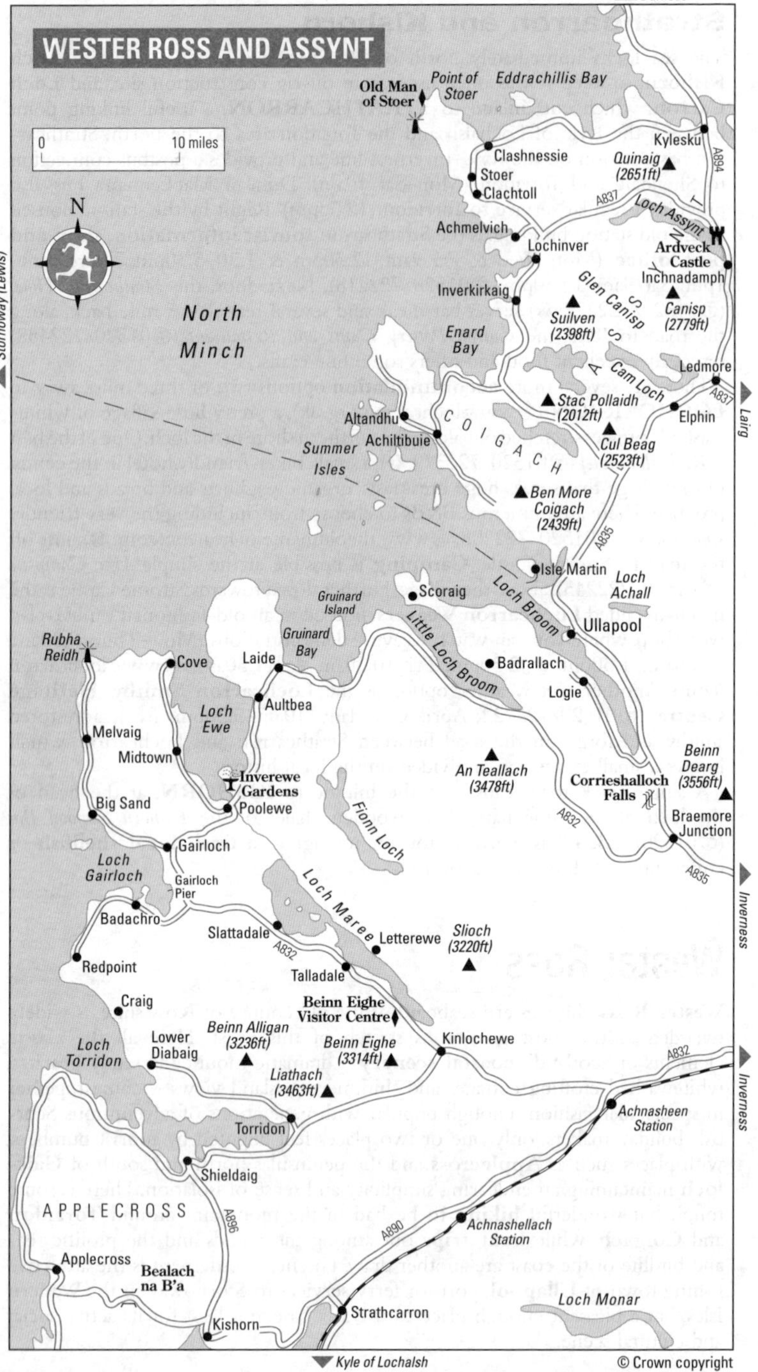
WESTER ROSS AND ASSYNT
0
10 miles
N
Durness
Old Man of Stoer
Point of Stoer
Eddrachillis Bay
Kylesku
A894
Clashnessie
Quinaig (2651ft)
Stoer
Clachtoll
A837
Loch Assynt
Achmelvich
Lochinver
Ardveck Castle
Inchnadamph
Glen Canisp
ASSYNT
Inverkirkaig
Suilven (2398ft)
Canisp (2779ft)
North Minch
Enard Bay
Cam Loch
Ledmore
A837
Stac Pollaidh (2012ft)
Elphin
Lairg
Altandhu
Achiltibuie
COIGACH
Summer Isles
Cul Beag (2523ft)
Ben More Coigach (2439ft)
Stornoway (Lewis)
A835
Isle Martin
Loch Achall
Scoraig
Loch Broom
Gruinard Island
Gruinard Bay
Ullapool
Little Loch Broom
Rubha Reidh
Cove
Laide
Badrallach
Logie
Aultbea
Loch Ewe
Melvaig
Midtown
An Teallach (3478ft)
Beinn Dearg (3556ft)
Inverewe Gardens
Corrieshalloch Falls
Big Sand
Poolewe
A832
Braemore Junction
Fionn Loch
Gairloch
A835
Loch Gairloch
Gairloch Pier
Inverness
Loch Maree
Badachro
Slattadale
Letterewe
Slioch (3220ft)
A832
Redpoint
Talladale
Craig
Beinn Eighe Visitor Centre
Beinn Alligan (3236ft)
Loch Torridon
Lower Diabaig
Beinn Eighe (3314ft)
Kinlochewe
A832
Liathach (3463ft)
Achnasheen Station
Inverness
Torridon
Shieldaig
APPLECROSS
A896
Achnashellach Station
A890
Applecross
Bealach na B'a
Strathcarron
Loch Monar
Kishorn
Kyle of Lochalsh

The Applecross peninsula

The most dramatic approach to the **Applecross peninsula** (the English-sounding name is a corruption of the Gaelic *Apor Crosan*, meaning "estuary") is from the south, up a classic glacial U-shaped valley and over the infamous **Bealach na Bà** (literally "Pass of the Cattle"). Crossing the forbidding hills behind Kishorn and rising to 2053ft, with a gradient and switchback bends worthy of the Alps, this route – a popular cycling piste – is hair-raising in places, but the panoramic views across the Minch to Raasay and Skye more than compensate. The other way in is from the north: a beautiful coast road that meanders slowly from Shieldaig on Loch Torridon, with tantalizing glimpses of the Skye Cuillin to the south. This is the route the 11.30am postbus takes from Shieldaig on Loch Torridon; to reach Shieldaig, you need to catch the 10am postie from Strathcarron train station. No buses run over the Bealach na Bà.

The sheltered, fertile coast around **APPLECROSS** village (Ⓦwww.applecross.info), where the Irish missionary monk Maelrhuba founded a monastery in 673 AD, comes as a surprise after the bleakness of the moorland approach. Maybe it's the journey, but Applecross feels like an idyllic place: you can wander along lanes banked with wild iris and orchids, and explore beaches and rock pools on the shore. There's a small **Heritage Centre** (April–Oct Mon–Sat noon–4pm; Ⓦwww.applecrossheritage.org.uk) overlooking Clachan church and graveyard, and a number of short **waymarked trails** along the shore – great for walking off a pub lunch. If you're interested in something more exerting, contact the local experts Applecross Mountain & Sea (Ⓣ01520/744394, Ⓦwww.applecross.uk.com), which organizes mountain expeditions and sea kayaking around the coast.

The old, tastefully refurbished and family-run *Applecross Inn* (Ⓣ01520/744262, Ⓦwww.applecross.info; ❹), right beside the sea, is the focal point of the community, with **rooms** upstairs, and a lively bar that serves delicious, freshly prepared local seafood and produce (noon–9pm). Busy during the annual Fish Festival (June), the inn is the first stop for most folk coming here, but there are several excellent B&Bs on the peninsula. *Tigh na Mara* (Ⓣ01520/744277; ❸) at Lonbain provides views of Raasay whilst, nearer Shieldaig, *Tigh a' Chracaich* (Ⓣ01520/755367; ❸) is a great alternative. **Camping** is provided as you come into the village from the pass at the *Applecross Campsite* (Ⓣ01520/744268), within which is the *Flower Tunnel* café-bar (daily 11am–9.30pm).

Loch Torridon

Loch Torridon marks the northern boundary of the Applecross peninsula, its awe-inspiring setting backed by the appealingly rugged mountains of **Liathach** and **Beinn Eighe**, tipped by streaks of white quartzite. The greater part of this area is composed of the reddish 750-million-year-old Torridonian sandstone, and some 15,000 acres of the massif are under the protection of the National Trust for Scotland. The trust looks after **Shieldaig Island**, where a heronry has been established among the tall Scots pines. The island lies in a sheltered bay off the prim but pretty village of **SHIELDAIG** ("herring bay") on the southern shore of Loch Torridon, where at the beginning of August the popular Shieldaig Fete is annually held. There's an attractive small **hotel** and friendly snug bar by the shore in the village, *Tigh-an-Eilean* (Ⓣ01520/755251; March–Oct; ❼), the close-by *Rivendell* B&B (Ⓣ01520/755250; ❷) and a simple **campsite** affording terrific loch views a little way up the hill. Out of the village at Doireaonor, on the southwest side of Loch Shieldaig, west of Shieldaig across the inlet, *Tigh Fada* (Ⓣ01520/755248) offers self-catering accommodation in a delightful log cabin.

Loch Torridon prides itself on its **seafood**, either caught or farmed locally. *Tigh an Eilean* at Shieldaig serves impressive meals, while the very friendly *Loch Torridon Smoke House* (ⓣ01520/755230), on the bypass behind Shieldaig, dishes up tea and home-baking and a mouth-watering range of seafoods including hot smoked salmon.

At **TORRIDON** village, at the east end of the loch, the main road heads inland through Glen Torridon, while the minor road runs through the village along the northern shore of the loch. At the road junction, past the Torridon Mountain Rescue post, the National Trust for Scotland runs a **Countryside Centre** (Easter to end Sept Mon–Sat 10am–6pm; £3), where you can call in and learn a bit more about the local geology, flora and fauna. Nearby is a small but informative NTS Deer Museum (same hours as Countryside Centre). Oyster-catchers and otters may be spotted from the wildlife hide on the shore. The road, which continues beyond Torridon, is scenic and dramatic, winding first along the shore, then climbing and twisting past lochans, cliffs and gorges, past tiny **INVERALLIGIN** (good for free-range eggs and camping) and terminating at the green wooded slopes around **LOWER DIABAIG**. On the south side of the loch stands one of the area's grandest **hotels**, the smart, rambling Victorian *Loch Torridon Hotel* (ⓣ01445/791242, ⓦwww.lochtorridonhotel.com; ⑧), set amid well-tended lochside grounds. The hotel also runs the adjacent *Ben*

Walks around Torridon

Ordnance Survey Explorer map no. 433.

With the support of Scottish Natural Heritage (SNH), large tracts of Torridon's Beinn Eighe National Nature Reserve are being replanted with native trees including birch, Scots pine and rowan. There can be difficult conditions on virtually all hiking routes around Torridon, and the weather can change very rapidly. If you're relatively inexperienced but want to do the magnificent ridge walk along the **Liathach** (pronounced "lee-ach") massif, or the strenuous traverse of **Beinn Eighe** (pronounced "ben ay"), you can join a National Trust Ranger Service guided hike (July & Aug; Torridon Countryside Centre; ⓣ01445/791221).

For those confident to go it alone, one of many possible routes takes you behind Liathach and down the pass, **Coire Dubh**, to the main road in Glen Torridon. This is a great, straightforward walk if you're properly equipped (see p.59), covering thirteen miles and taking in superb landscapes. Allow yourself the whole day. Start at the stone bridge on the Diabaig road along the north side of Loch Torridon. Follow the Abhainn Coire Mhic Nobuil burn up to the fork at the wooden bridge and take the track east to the pass (a rather indistinct watershed) between Liathach and Beinn Eighe. The path becomes a little lost in the boggy area studded with lochans at the top of the pass, but the route is clear and, once over the watershed, the path is easy to follow. At this point you can, weather permitting, make the rewarding diversion up to the **Coire Mhic Fhearchair**, widely regarded as the most spectacular corrie in Scotland; otherwise continue down the Coire Dubh stream, ford the burn and follow its west bank down to the Torridon road, from where it's about four miles back to Loch Torridon.

A rewarding walk even in rough weather is the seven-mile hike up the coast from **Lower Diabaig**, ten miles northwest of Torridon village, to **Redpoint**. On a clear day, the views across to Raasay and Applecross from this gentle undulating path are superlative, but you'll have to return along the same trail, or else make your way back via Loch Maree on the A832. If you're staying in Shieldaig, the track that winds up the peninsula running north from the village makes a pleasant ninety-minute round walk.

Damph Lodge (March–Oct; ❺), a cyclist- and walker-friendly modern conversion of an old farmstead with neat twins and doubles and a bistro-bar. Torridon Activities, run from the hotel, offers residents and non-residents alike pursuits including hill walking, mountain biking and sea kayaking. Close to the Countryside Centre is a rather unsightly SYHA **hostel** (ⓣ0870/004 1154, ⓦwww.syha.org.uk; March–Oct, and a council-run **campsite**. Donnie and Morag MacDonald operate the well-stocked Torridon Stores (ⓣ01445/791400) in Torridon village. The area's only shop, it sells everything from camping gas and midgy nets to fruit and veg and secondhand books.

Note that the chief transport connection with the Torridon region is **Achnasheen**, 18 miles northeast of Strathcarron at the head of Glen Carron. Another stop on the Kyle train line, Achnasheen marks a fork in the road from Inverness: one branch, the A890, follows the railway towards Strathcarron and Kyle; the other, the A832, snakes through the mountains to Kinlochewe, beside the Torridon hills. There are postbus links from the railway through to Torridon.

Loch Maree

About eight miles north of Loch Torridon, **Loch Maree**, dotted with Caledonian pine-covered islands, is one of the west's scenic highlights, best viewed from the A832 road that drops down to its southeastern tip through Glen Docherty. At the southeastern end of the loch, the A896 from Torridon meets the A832 from Achnasheen at the small settlement of **KINLOCHEWE** (ⓦwww.torridon-mountains.com), a good base if you're heading into the hills. There is a plain **bunkhouse** as well as good meals at the *Kinlochewe Hotel* (ⓣ01445/760253, ⓦwww.kinlochewehotel.co.uk; ❹), but for a little extra head a mile southwest along the road towards Torridon to *Cromasaig* B&B (ⓣ01455/760234, ⓦwww.cromasaig.com; ❷), a great place for hill walkers set in the forest right at the foot of the track up Beinn Eighe. The *Cromasaig* folk also run the Moru outdoor shop at the old petrol station opposite the hotel and will furnish you with maps and guidebooks, as well as equipment and the weather forecast. The friendly Kinlochewe Store opposite the hotel contains the post office (which opens Mon–Sat 9–11am) and the *Teapot Café*, whilst 400yd up the road towards Gairloch is the petrol station and *Tipsy Laird* tearoom.

The A832 skirts the southern shore of Loch Maree, passing the **Beinn Eighe Nature Reserve**, the UK's oldest wildlife sanctuary. Parts of the Beinn Eighe reserve are forested with Caledonian pinewood, which once covered the whole of the country, and it is home to wildlife that includes pine martens, wildcats, buzzards and golden eagles. A mile north of Kinlochewe, the well-run **Beinn Eighe Visitor Centre** (Easter & May–Oct daily 10am–5pm) on the A832, uses excellent audiovisual presentations and child-friendly displays to inform visitors about the area's rare species. Outside, the "talking trails" are an imaginative innovation and provide an easy walk through the vicinity. Several interesting **walks** start from the car park, a mile north of the visitor centre.

Loch Maree is surrounded by some of Scotland's finest **deerstalking** country: the remote, privately owned Letterewe Lodge on the north shore, accessible only by helicopter or boat, lies at the heart of a famous deer forest. In 1877, Queen Victoria stayed for a few days at the wonderfully sited *Loch Maree Hotel*; it offers dinner and B&B to guests (ⓣ01445/760288; ❼), when not rented out as an exclusive self-catering lodge. An even better place **to stay** nearby is *The Old Mill* (ⓣ01445/760271; ❽), a beautiful Highland lodge where rates include an absolutely fabulous dinner, bed and breakfast.

Gairloch and around

GAIRLOCH spreads itself around the northeastern corner of the wide sheltered bay of Loch Gairloch, with its sometimes sandy, sometimes rocky shores. During the summer, Gairloch thrives as a low-key holiday resort with several tempting sandy beaches and some excellent coastal walks within easy reach. The township is divided into several, pretty distinct areas spread over nearly two miles of shoreline: to the south, in **Flowerdale Bay**, are the old pier and harbour; past the bank, at the turn-off to Melvaig is **Achtercairn**, the centre of Gairloch, and along the north side of the bay, on the road to Melvaig, is **Strath**. The main supermarket and **tourist office** (June–Sept daily 9am–5.30pm; Oct Mon–Sat 9am–5.30pm; Nov–May Mon–Sat 10am–4pm) are in Achtercairn, right by the **Gairloch Heritage Museum** (March–Sept daily 10am–5pm; Oct Mon–Sat 10am–1pm); £3) has eclectic, appealing displays covering geology, archeology, fishing and farming that range from a mock-up of a croft house to an early knitting machine. Probably the most interesting section is the archive made by elderly locals – an array of photographs, maps, genealogies, lists of place names and taped recollections, mostly in Gaelic.

Gairloch has a good choice of **accommodation**, but you might prefer to stay out along the road north to Melvaig or south to Redpoint (see opposite). In Achtercairn, opposite the post office, a room-only option can be found at the *Mountain Lodge* (Ⓣ01445/712316; ❷; March–Dec). Next door, you can indulge in good coffee and fresh, though pricey, scones at the laid-back *Mountain Café*, which also features good views over the bay. There are also some very good **B&Bs**: in Strath, try Gaelic-speaking Miss Mackenzie's *Duisary* (Ⓣ01445/712252, Ⓦwww.duisary.freeserve.co.uk; ❷; April–Oct); near the pier, head for *Heatherdale* (Ⓣ01445/712388, ⒺBrochod1@aol.com; ❸; March to end Oct); and further south still, just before the turn-off to Badachro, there's the atmospheric and tastefully furnished *Kerrysdale House* (Ⓣ01445/712292, Ⓦwww.kerrysdalehouse.co.uk; ❷) set back in its own lovely gardens.

For **food**, head for the harbour where the *Old Inn* (Ⓦwww.theoldinn.co.uk) offers seafood on its bar menu and a very good range of Scottish real ales. There's also the *Harbour Lights Café* for those in search of reasonably priced snacks and evening meals. Nearby, the *Creel Restaurant* offers delicious fare whilst the *Steading Restaurant*, tucked beside the Gairloch Museum, is another popular eatery. For **snacks**, try the *Mountain Lodge* or the bistro-style *Café Blueprint* across the road where you'll also find the chip shop.

One leisurely way to explore the coast is on a wildlife-spotting **cruise**. There are several operators but try Gairloch Marine Life Centre & Cruises (Easter–Oct; Ⓣ01445/712636); pier-based, they run informative and enjoyable boat trips across the bay in search of dolphins, seals and even the odd whale. They also deploy a mini-sub that sends underwater pictures back to the boat whilst a hydrophone picks up audio from the sea life. You can **rent a boat** for the day through the Gairloch Chandlery (Ⓣ01445/712458), at the pier, or go **pony trekking** with Gairloch Trekking Centre (Ⓣ01445/712652; closed Thurs). There's also the scenic and testing nine-hole Gairloch golf course (Ⓣ01445/712407; £20). From the car park on the north side of the Flowerdale river, a sheltered glen enables walkers to enjoy a scenic woodland walk. Ask at the tourist office for directions.

Rubha Reidh and around

The area's real attraction, however, is its beautiful **coastline**. To get to one of the most impressive stretches, head around the north side of the bay and follow the single-track B8021 to **BIG SAND**, which has a cleaner and quieter **beach** than the one in Gairloch. An excellent **campsite** sits above the beach (Ⓣ01445/712152). Just before Big Sand, there's an SYHA **hostel** at Carn Dearg (Ⓣ0870/004 1110, Ⓦwww.syha.org.uk; April–Sept), spectacularly set on the edge of a cliff with views to Skye. The B8021, and the postbus from Gairloch, terminate at the tiny crofting hamlet of Melvaig where a white-stone former Free Church provides a rustic setting for fabulous freshly prepared food at the *Mustn't Grumble* restaurant (Ⓣ01445/771212, Ⓦwww.mustnt-grumble.com). The proprietor even runs a stretch limo and minibus service from Gairloch.

From Melvaig, it's another three miles out to **Rubha Reidh** (pronounced "roo-a-ray"). You can stay at the headland's still operational Stevenson-designed *Rua Reidh Lighthouse* (Ⓣ01445/771263, Ⓦwww.ruareidh.co.uk; ❶), which looks straight out to the Outer Hebrides. Comfortable accommodation options include a bunkhouse, double and family rooms (meals extra; book ahead in high season). Fran, the cheerful owner, serves slap-up **afternoon teas** and home-made cakes (Tues & Thurs 11am–5pm), pre-booked evening meals are available and guided walking and climbing courses are offered.

Around the headland from Rubha Reidh lies the secluded and beautiful **Camas Mor** beach. For a great half-day walk, follow the marked footpath inland (southeast) from here along the base of a sheer scarp slope, and past a string of lochans, ruined crofts and a remote wood to **MIDTOWN** on the east side of the peninsula, four miles north of Poolewe on the B8057. However, unless you leave a car at the end of the trail or arrange to be picked up, you'll have to walk or hitch back to Gairloch, as the only transport along this road is an early-morning post van.

Badachro and Redpoint

Three miles south of Gairloch, a narrow single-track lane (built with the Destitution Funds raised during the nineteenth-century potato famine) winds west from the main A832, past wooded coves and inlets on its way south of the loch to **BADACHRO**, a sleepy former fishing village in a very attractive setting with a wonderful pub, the *Badachro Inn* (Ⓦwww.badachroinn.com), right by the water's edge, where you can sit in the beer garden watching the boats come and go and tuck into deliciously fresh seafood with a real ale. Some 300yd away, seek out the secluded *Shieldaig Lodge Hotel* (Ⓣ01445/741250, Ⓦwww.shieldaiglodge.com; ❸) for comfortable accommodation in a former Victorian shooting lodge. Accessed via a floating bridge and a short drive away, *Dry Island* provides visitors to Badachro with a great B&B or self-catering option (Ⓣ01445/741263, Ⓦwww.dryisland.co.uk; ❹). The owner will even run trips on his traditional fishing boat on which visitors can help haul in the creels.

Beyond Badachro, the road winds for five more miles along the shore to **REDPOINT**, a straggling hamlet with beautiful beaches of peach-coloured sand and great views to Raasay, Skye and the Western Isles. It also marks the trailhead for the wonderful coast walk to Lower Diabaig (see box on p.284). Even if you don't fancy a full-blown hike, following the path a mile or so brings you to the exquisite **beach** hidden on the south side of the headland, which you'll often have all to yourself.

Poolewe and around

It's a fifteen-minute hop by bus over the headland from Gairloch to the trim little village of **POOLEWE** which sits by a small bay at the sheltered southern end of Loch Ewe, where the (very short) River Ewe rushes down from Loch

Maree. One of the area's best **walks** begins near here, signposted from the layby-cum-viewpoint on the main A832, a mile south of the village. It takes a couple of hours to follow the easy trail across open craggy moorland to the shores of **Loch Maree** (see p.285), and thence to the car park at Slattadale, seven miles southeast of Gairloch. If you reach Slattadale just before 7pm on a Tuesday, Thursday or Friday, you should be able to pick up the Wester bus from Inverness back to Poolewe or Aultbea.

Also worthwhile is the ten-mile drive along the small side road running along the west shore of Loch Ewe to **COVE**. Here you'll find an atmospheric cave that was used by the severe Presbyterian "Wee Frees" as a church into the twentieth century; it's quite a perilous scramble up, however, and there's little to see once you're there.

For **accommodation** Poolewe has a popular and well-equipped **campsite** (Ⓣ01445/781249; May–Oct), whilst the family-run and refurbished *Poolewe Hotel* (Ⓣ01445/781241, Ⓦwww.poolewehotel.co.uk; ❺), on the Cove road, serves tasty dinners that include award-winning black pudding and fresh seafood. For a taste of luxury, relax at the award-winning *Pool House Hotel* (Ⓣ01445/781272, Ⓦwww.poolhousehotel.com; ❽) which once belonged to Osgood MacKenzie (see below). At Aultbea, *Cartmel* (Ⓣ01445/731375, Ⓦwww.cartmelguesthouse.com; ❸) is a very professional place with charming hosts. Four miles north of Poolewe at Inverasdale, *Bruach Ard* offers comfortable B&B lodging (Ⓣ01445/781765). In Poolewe itself, *The Bridge Cottage Coffee Shop and Gallery*, just up the Cove road from the village crossroads, is a cosy snack stop.

Inverewe Gardens

Half a mile across the bay from Poolewe on the A832, **Inverewe Gardens** (daily: April–Oct 9.30am–9pm or dusk; Nov–March 9.30am–4pm; NTS; £8), a verdant oasis of foliage and riotously colourful flower collections, forms a vivid contrast to the wild, heathery crags of the adjoining coast. The gardens were the brainchild of **Osgood MacKenzie**, who inherited the surrounding 12,000-acre estate from his stepfather, the laird of Gairloch, in 1862. Taking advantage of the area's famously temperate climate (a consequence of the Gulf Stream, which draws a warm sea current from Mexico to within a stone's throw of these shores), Mackenzie collected plants from all over the world for his walled garden, which still forms the nucleus of the complex. Protected from Loch Ewe's corrosive salt breezes by a dense brake of Scots pine, rowan, oak, beech and birch trees, the fragile plants flourished on rich soil brought here as ballast on Irish ships to overlay the previously infertile beach gravel and sea grass. By the time MacKenzie died in 1922, his garden sprawled over the whole peninsula, surrounded by a hundred acres of woodland. Today the National Trust for Scotland strives to develop the place along the lines envisaged by its founder.

Thousands of visitors pour through here annually, but the place rarely feels overcrowded. Interconnected by a labyrinthine network of twisting paths and walkways, a few accessible by wheelchair, more than a dozen gardens feature exotic plant collections from as far afield as Chile, China, Tasmania and the Himalayas. Strolling around the lotus ponds, palm trees and borders ablaze with exotic blooms, it's amazing to think you're at the same latitude as Hudson Bay. Mid-May to mid-June is the best time to see the rhododendrons and azaleas, while the herbaceous garden reaches its peak in July and August, as does the wonderful Victorian vegetable and flower garden beside the sea. Look out, too, for the grand old eucalyptus in the Peace Plot, which is the largest in the northern hemisphere, and the nearby Ghost Tree (*Davidia involucrata*), representing the earliest evolutionary stages of flowering trees. You'll need at least a couple of hours, particularly if you explore the Pinewood Trail and still leave time for the **visitor centre** (April–Sept daily 9.30am–5pm), which houses an informative display on the history of the garden and is the starting point for **guided walks** (May–Sept). The **restaurant** serves good food.

Gruinard Bay and Little Loch Broom

At **LAIDE**, ten miles north of Poolewe, the road skirts the shores of **Gruinard Bay**, offering fabulous views and, at the inner end of the bay, some excellent sandy beaches. During World War II, **Gruinard Island**, in the bay, was used as a testing ground for biological warfare, and for years was ringed by huge signs warning the public not to land. The **anthrax** spores released during the testing can live in the soil for up to a thousand years, but in 1987, after much protest, the Ministry of Defence had the island decontaminated and it was finally declared "safe" in 1990. As befits the stunning scenery, there are some lovely **accommodation** choices all along this stretch, including a reasonable campsite (ⓣ01445/731225) and the welcoming *Old Smiddy Guest House* (ⓣ01445/731696, ⓦwww.oldsmiddyguesthouse.co.uk; ③) on the main road in Laide and not to be confused with the well-run self-catering *Old Smiddy Cottages* run by Kate Macdonald (ⓣ01445/731425). Another option is the remote but hospitable *Sheiling* B&B at Achgarve (ⓣ01445/731487; ③). To reach it, turn left at Laide post office and travel 1.5 miles down the road towards Mellon Udrigle. **Transport** is very patchy in these parts. On a Thursday only, a bus departs Gairloch (9am) and passes through Poolewe, Laide (post office; 9.40am) and Dundonnell en route to Ullapool.

To the east of Gruinard Bay lies **Little Loch Broom**, a narrow sea loch surrounded by a salt marsh that is covered with flowers in early summer. To the south, the loch is overlooked by the mass of **An Teallach** (3478ft); to the north, it is divided from Loch Broom by the rugged **Scoraig peninsula**, one of the remotest places on the British mainland, accessible only by boat or on foot. Formerly dotted with crofting townships, it is now deserted apart from tiny **SCORAIG** village, where a mostly self-sufficient community has established itself, complete with windmills, organic vegetable gardens and a thriving primary school. Understandably, Scoraig's inhabitants would rather not be regarded as tourist curiosities, so you should only venture out here if you're sympathetic to such a community. To reach Scoraig, you have two main options: you can drive to **BADRALLACH**, on the north side of Little Loch Broom, and walk from there, or try to plan a trip for when the postboat crosses the loch (ⓣ01854/633333; Mon, Wed & Fri 11am). The boat is weather-dependent, so you should always call and check if it's running.

Accommodation in the area is limited, but there's the small *Northern Lights* **campsite** at Badcaul before which you will find the *Sail Mhor Croft* (ⓣ01854/633224, ⓦwww.sailmhor.co.uk), a small independent **hostel** in Camusnagaul in a lovely location on the lochside. Alternatively, heading two miles east you could stay at the head of Little Loch Broom, at the *Dundonnell* (ⓣ01854/633204, ⓦwww.dundonnellhotel.com; ⑦), a smart, comfortable **hotel** which serves bar meals. Dundonnell is also where you'll find the nearest petrol station for miles around, the home of the An Teallach micro-brewery and the mountain rescue post. Heading on past the hotel, turn left and seven miles up the single-track road you'll find the very remote *Badrallach* campsite and bothy (ⓣ01854/633281, ⓦwww.badrallach.com; ①). Take plenty of food if visiting this remote area.

Falls of Measach

The road heads inland before joining the A835, the main Inverness–Ullapool road, at **Braemore Junction**, above the head of Loch Broom. Just nearby, and easily accessible from a layby on the A835, are the spectacular 164ft **Falls of Measach**, which plunge through the mile-long Corrieshalloch Gorge, formed by glacial melt-waters. You can overlook the cascades from a precarious observation platform, or from the impressive, wobbly Victorian suspension bridge that spans the chasm, whose 197ft vertical sides are draped in a rich array of plantlife, with thickets of wych elm, goat willow and bird cherry miraculously thriving on the cliffs. The A835 from the head of Loch Broom to Ullapool is one of the so-called **Destitution Roads**, built to give employment to local people during the nineteenth-century potato famines.

Ullapool

ULLAPOOL (Ⓦwww.ullapool.co.uk), the northwest's principal centre of population, was founded at the height of the herring boom in 1788 by the British Fisheries Society, on a sheltered arm of land jutting into Loch Broom. The grid-plan town is still an important fishing centre, though the **ferry** link to Stornoway on Lewis (see p.368) means that in high season its personality is practically swamped by visitors. Note that visitors can now make a day-long return ferry/bus visit to Lewis with Caledonian MacBrayne (Ⓣ0870/565 0000; £26.25). Though busy, Ullapool remains a hugely appealing place and a good base for exploring the northwest Highlands. Regular **buses** run from here

Ceilidhs

The **ceilidh** is essentially an informal, homespun kind of entertainment, the word being Gaelic for a "visit". In remote Highland communities, talents and resources were pooled, people gathering to play music, sing, recite poems and dance. The dances themselves are thought to be ancient in origin; the Romans wrote that the Caledonians danced with abandon round swords stuck in the ground, a practice echoed in today's formalized sword dance, where the weapons are crossed on the floor and a quick-stepping dancer skips over and around them.

Highland ceilidhs, fuelled by whisky and largely extemporized, must have been an intoxicating, riotous means of fending off winter gloom. Like much of clan culture, however, the traditions died or were forced underground after the defeat of the Highlanders at Culloden and the passing of the 1747 Act of Proscription, which forbade the wearing of the plaid and other expressions of Highland identity.

Ceilidhs were enthusiastically revived in the reign of tartan-fetishist Queen Victoria, and in the twentieth century became the preserve of the village hall and hotel ballroom, buoyed to some extent by the popularity of jaunty 1950s TV programmes such as *The White Heather Club*, which showed rather prim demonstrations of Scottish country dancing and made a star out of master accordionist Jimmy Shand. More recently, though, the ceilidh has thrown off some of these stale associations, with places such as the *Ceilidh Place* in Ullapool and the *Taybank Hotel* in Dunkeld (see p.368) restoring some of its spontaneous, infectious fun to a night of Scottish music and dancing. Whether performed by a band of skilled traditional musicians or in freer form by lively, younger players, ceilidh music is pretty irresistible, and it's quite common to find all generations gathering for an evening's entertainment. Ceilidh dances can look complex and often involve you being whirled breathlessly round the room, though in fact most of the popular ones, like the "Gay Gordons" and eightsome reel, are reasonably simple and are commonly explained or "called" beforehand by the bandleader.

to Inverness and Durness, while there's an early-morning run through to the remote train station at Lairg. Accommodation is plentiful and Ullapool is an obvious hideaway if the weather is bad, with cosy pubs, a swimming pool and a lively **arts centre**, the *Ceilidh Place*.

Arrival, information and accommodation

Forming the backbone of its grid plan, Ullapool's two main arteries are the lochside **Shore Street** and, parallel to it, **Argyle Street**, further inland. **Buses** stop at the pier, in the town centre near the ferry dock, from where it's easy to get your bearings. The well-run **tourist office** (April, May & Sept Mon–Sat 9.30am–5pm; June–Aug Mon–Sat 9am–5pm, Sun 10am–4pm; Oct Mon–Fri 10am–5pm; Nov & Dec Mon–Fri 2–5.30pm), on Argyle Street, offers an accommodation booking service.

Ullapool has all kinds of **accommodation**, including a couple of welcoming hostels and some decent guesthouses and B&Bs, though it's worth booking ahead to get any of the places listed below.

Hotels, guesthouses and B&Bs

The Ceilidh Place West Argyle St ⓣ01854/612103, ⓦwww.theceilidhplace.com. Tasteful and popular hotel, with the west coast's best bookshop, a relaxing first-floor lounge, a great bar/restaurant, sea views and a laid-back atmosphere. Also has a good-value bunkhouse for £15 per person. 6

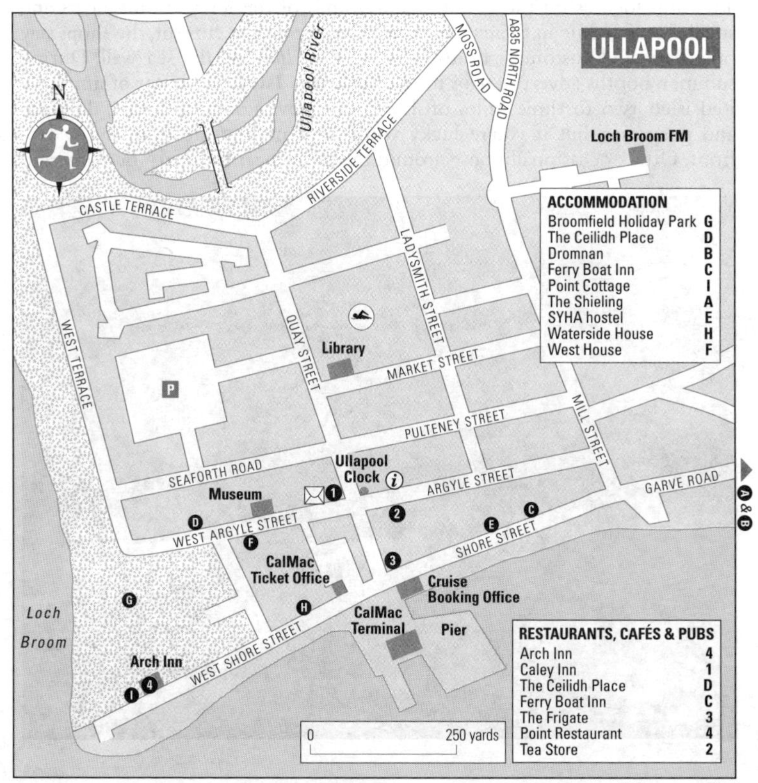

Dromnan Garve Rd ⓣ01854/612333, ⓦwww.dromnan.co.uk. Excellent B&B run by very friendly hosts, who serve up a hearty breakfast. ③

Ferry Boat Inn Shore St ⓣ01854/612366, ⓦwww.ferryboat-inn.com. Traditional inn right on the waterfront with a friendly atmosphere and reasonable food. ⑤

Point Cottage 22 West Shore St ⓣ01854/612494, ⓦwww.pointcottage.co.uk. Rustic, very well-equipped and friendly B&B at the quieter end of the seafront. Guests can borrow OS maps that have been already marked up with walking routes. ③

The Shieling Garve Rd ⓣ01854/612947. Another very friendly, comfortable guesthouse overlooking the loch, with immaculate, spacious rooms (nos. 4 and 5 have the best views), superb breakfasts (try their home-made venison and leek sausages) and a sauna. ③

Waterside House 6 West Shore St ⓣ01854/612140, ⓦwww.waterside.uk.net. Three tastefully furnished en-suite rooms in a very pleasant, seafront B&B. ③

Hostels and campsite

Broomfield Holiday Park West Shore St ⓣ01854/612020. Modest, good-value campsite, five minutes' walk from town. Exposed to the wind off Loch Broom but offers great views and warm showers.

SYHA hostel Shore St ⓣ0870/004 1156, ⓦwww.syha.org.uk. Busy hostel on the front, with Internet access, laundry and lots of good information about local walks. March–Oct.

West House West Argyle St ⓣ01854/613126, ⓦwww.scotpackers-hostels.co.uk. Lively, welcoming hostel with four- to six-bed dorms; some en suite. Internet access (£1). Bike rental available (£10 per day).

The Town

Day or night, most of the action in Ullapool centres on the **harbour**, which has an authentic and salty air, especially when the boats are in. By day, attention focuses on the comings and goings of the ferry, fishing boats and smaller craft, while in the evening, yachts swing on the current, the shops stay open late, and customers from the *Ferry Boat Inn* line the sea wall. During summer, booths advertise trips to the **Summer Isles** – a cluster of uninhabited islets two to three miles offshore – to view seabird colonies, dolphins and porpoises, but if you're lucky you'll spot marine life from the waterfront. Otters occasionally nose around the rocks near the *Ferry Boat Inn*, and

△ Ullapool

seals swim past begging scraps from the boats moored in the middle of the loch.

The only conventional attraction in town is the award-winning **museum**, in the old parish church on West Argyle Street (April–Oct Mon–Sat 10am–5pm; Nov–March Sat 10am–4pm; £4), where photographs, audiovisual and touch-screen displays provide an insight into life in a Highland community, including crofting, fishing, local religion and emigration. During the Clearances, Ullapool was one of the ports through which evicted crofters left to start new lives abroad.

Eating, drinking and entertainment

The two best **pubs** in Ullapool are the *Arch Inn*, home of the Ullapool football team, and the *Ferry Boat Inn* (known as the "FBI"), where you can enjoy a pint of real ale at the lochside – midges permitting. **Live Scottish folk music** is a special feature at *The Ceilidh Place* or on Thursday nights at the *FBI*. The atmospheric *Ceilidh Place* also runs a monthly art exhibition as part of its regular entertainment. All three pubs serve bar meals – the *FBI* is possibly the pick of the bunch.

There are several great places to eat in the town. Those in search of delicious fine dining should seek out the *Point Restaurant* (March–Oct Tues–Sat) above the *Arch Inn* on the shore where the emphasis is on fresh, home-made dishes with local hot-smoked salmon and haggis among the treats. The *Caley Inn* on

Walks and hikes around Ullapool

Ordnance Survey Explorer map nos. 439, 436 & 435.

Ullapool lies at the start of several excellent **hiking trails**, ranging from sedate shoreside ambles to long and strenuous ascents of Munros. However, the weather here can change very quickly, so take the necessary precautions (see p.59). More detailed descriptions of the routes outlined below are available from the hostel on Shore Street; hostellers can also rent the relevant up-to-date OS maps – essential for the hill walks.

An easy **half-day ramble** begins at the north end of Quay Street: cross the walkway/footbridge here and follow the river bank on the far side left towards the sea. Walk past the golf course and follow the shoreline as best you can for around two miles until you reach a hilltop lighthouse, from where you gain fine views across the sea to the Summer Isles. Return the same way or via the main A835 road.

For a harder **half-day hike**, head north along Mill Street on the east edge of town to Broom Court retirement home, trailhead for the Ullapool hill walk (look for the sign next to the electricity substation). A rocky path zigzags steeply up from the roadside to the summit of **Meall Mor** (886ft), where there are great views of the area's major peaks. This is also a prime spot for botanists, with a rich array of plants and flowers, including two insect-eating species: sundew and butterwort. The path then drops sharply down the heather-clad northeast side of Meall Mor into **Glen Achall**, where you turn left onto the surfaced road running past the limestone quarry; the main road back to Ullapool lies a further thirty-minute walk west.

A right turn where the path meets the road will take you through the **Rhidorroch** estate to Loch Achall and the start of a **two-day hike** along an old drovers' trail across the wilderness of the Highlands to **Croick** (see p.320). At the East Rhidorroch Lodge, if you ignore the suspension bridge and strike up the steep hill ahead onto open moorland, you'll make it to secluded Loch nan Daimh, where there's the small, well-maintained **Knockdamph bothy**, the midway point of this long-distance hike, which should not be undertaken alone or without proper gear.

Quay Street combines Scottish fusion cuisine with the chance to sample several real ales whilst the nearby *Ceilidh Place* is another popular destination where modestly priced lunches, snacks and dinners are served in a pleasant bistro area. *The Frigate*, an airy café on the seafront, serves good coffee but many a local seeks out the well-run *Tea Store*, on Argyll Street opposite the tourist information, for a tasty, inexpensive sandwich and refreshing cuppa.

Assynt

If you've come as far as Ullapool it really is worth continuing further north into the ever-more dramatic, remote and highly distinctive hills of **Assynt** (Ⓦwww.assynt.co.uk), which marks the transition from Wester Ross into Sutherland. One of the least populated areas in Europe, this is a landscape not of mountain ranges but of extraordinary peaks rising individually from the moorland. It's an area of peaceful, slow backroads, which, after twisting through idyllic crofts, invariably end up at a deserted beach or windswept headland with superb clear-day views west to the Outer Hebrides. **Lochinver**, midway along the west coast, is the main settlement, though you're unlikely to want to stay here. Head, instead, for one of the crofting villages along the coast, like those around **Achiltibuie**, or – if you're keen to climb the mountains – head for **Inchnadamph**, which sits below the region's two Munros.

Coigach

Coigach (Ⓦwww.coigach.com) is the peninsula immediately to the north of Loch Broom, accessible via a slow, winding, single-track road that leaves the A835 ten miles north of Ullapool, squeezing between the northern shore of Loch Lurgainn, the lower slopes of **Cul Beag** (2523ft) and craggy, **Stac Pollaidh** (2012ft). To the south, the awesome bulk of **Ben More Coigach** (2439ft) presides over the district, which contains some spectacular coastal scenery including a string of sandy beaches and the Summer Isles, scattered just offshore. Coigach's main settlement is **ACHILTIBUIE**, an old crofting village scattered across the hillside above a series of white-sand coves and rocks tapering into the Atlantic, from where a fleet of small fishing boats carries sheep and tourists to the enticing pastures of the **Summer Isles** which lie a little way offshore. For **boat** trips round the isles, including some time ashore on the largest, Tanera Mor, Ian Macleod's boat *Hectoria* (Ⓣ01854/622200) usually runs twice a day from the pier (Easter–Oct).

The village attracts gardening enthusiasts, thanks to the unlikely presence of the **Hydroponicum** (April–Sept daily 10am–6pm; Oct Mon–Fri 11.30am–3.30pm; Ⓦwww.thehydroponicum.com; £4.95; tours on the hour), a cross between a giant greenhouse and a futuristic scientific research station, and, it has to be said, something of an eyesore. Dubbed "The Garden of the Future", all kinds of flowers, fruits and vegetables are grown without using soil in conditions that concentrate the sun's heat while protecting the plants from winter (and summer) chill. Bumper crops of strawberries, salad leaves, figs and even bananas result – guided tours explain how it's all done and show you round the different "climate zones". You can taste whatever's being harvested in the subtropical setting of the functional *Lilypond Café*, which serves snacks and meals, including weekend evenings (7–9pm).

If in need of fuel or provisions, visit the well-stocked Achiltibuie Store, while for **accommodation**, the wonderfully understated *Summer Isles Hotel*

(Ⓣ01854/622282, Ⓔinfo@summerisleshotel.co.uk; ❼; Easter–Oct), just up the road from the Hydroponicum, enjoys a perfect setting with views over the islands. The hotel buys in Hydroponicum fruit and vegetables and has its own chicken run. An excellent set dinner in the **restaurant** costs about £40, although superb bar snacks and lunches feature crab, langoustines and smoked mackerel starting from £4. Note that children under 14 are not allowed in the bar area. Of Achiltibuie's several **B&Bs**, *Dornie House* (Ⓣ01854/622271, Ⓔdorniehousebandb@aol.com; ❶; Easter–Nov), halfway to Altandhu, is welcoming and provides huge breakfasts.

Also worth a visit is the **Achiltibuie Smokehouse** (Ⓣ01854/622353; April–Sept Mon–Sat 9.30am–5pm; free), five miles northwest of the Hydroponicum at **ALTANDHU**, where you can see meat, fish and game being cured in the traditional way and can buy some afterwards. Next to this, the *Fuaran* bar serves lunches, snacks and evening meals, including fresh hand-dived scallops, and like everywhere else along this stretch, enjoys terrific views over to the Summer Isles.

There's also a beautifully situated twenty-bed SYHA **hostel** (Ⓣ0870/004 1101, Ⓦwww.syha.org.uk; May–Sept), three miles southeast of Achiltibuie down the coast at **ACHININVER**, which is handy for accessing Coigach's mountain hikes. If you're reasonably experienced and can use a map and compass, you can walk to the hostel from Ullapool. The rock path, which winds along one of the region's most beautiful and unspoilt stretches of coastline, is over ten miles long, easy to follow in good weather, but very boggy and slippery when wet. Sound footwear, fluid, waterproofs and a map are essential.

Lochinver and around

The potholed and narrow road north from Achiltibuie through Inverkirkaig is unremittingly spectacular, threading its way through a tumultuous landscape of secret valleys, moorland and bare rock, past the startling shapes of Cul Beag (2523ft), Cul Mor (2785ft) and the distinctive sugar-loaf **Suilven** (2398ft). You pass thick-walled, idyllic crofts and the start of several community woodland walking trails established by Little Assynt Estate, and then a sheltered bay heralds your arrival at **LOCHINVER**, sixteen miles due north of Ullapool (although more than thirty by road). One of the busiest fishing harbours in Scotland, it's a workaday place from where large trucks head off for the continent. Like Gairloch, Lochinver is divided into quite distinct areas, with the harbour to the south, the centre of the village at the road junction half a mile or so to the north and Baddidarrach further west along the northern shore of Loch Inver. Halfway between the two is the **tourist office** (April to end Oct Mon–Sat 10am–5pm, June–Sept also Sun 10am–4pm), within the excellent **Assynt Visitor Centre**, which gives an interesting rundown on the area's geology, wildlife and history and has a CCTV link to a nearby heronry; a countryside ranger is available for advice, and there are a whole series of guided walks and activities put on from May to September. The area is popular with **fishing** enthusiasts. You can get information on permits at the tourist office or post office and at The Cottage, Culag Square (Ⓣ01571/844076), where boats are also rented.

Lochinver has a wide choice of good **B&Bs**: on the north side of the loch, *Ardglas House* (Ⓣ01571/844257, Ⓔguide@ardglas.co.uk; ❶) has superb views, whilst next-door *Davar* (Ⓣ01571/844501, Ⓔjean@davar36.fsnet.co.uk; ❷; March–Oct) is very welcoming. More central, close to the tourist office, comfortable *Polcraig* (Ⓣ01571/844429, Ⓔcathelmac@aol.com; ❷) serves up fabulous breakfasts and can arrange fishing. Combining fine dining with a relaxed, upmarket stay is the beautifully appointed *Albannach Hotel* at Baddidarrach (Ⓣ01571/844407, Ⓦwww.thealbannach.co.uk; ⑨; March–Nov; no children under 12). An attractive nineteenth-century building set in a walled garden, its five-course menu includes fresh game and seafood. Lochinver's most popular **food** halt is the *Larder Riverside Bistro* on the main street: it is perhaps best known for excellent, though pricey, home-made pies such as wild boar, port and prune. Decent bar meals are available at the *Caberfeidh* next door, which is also the most convivial place to head for a drink, while the *Seamen's Mission*, down at the harbour, is a good option for the budget-conscious traveller. The local football team meet at the *Wayfarers Pub* at the pier.

Inverkirkaig Falls

Approaching Lochinver from the south, the road bends sharply through a wooded valley where a signpost for **Inverkirkaig Falls** marks the start of a long but gentle **walk** to the base of **Suilven** – the most distinctive mountain in

Walks in Coigach and Assynt

Ordnance Survey Explorer map no. 442.

Of Coigach and Assynt's spectacular array of idiosyncratic peaks, **Stac Pollaidh** (2012ft) counts as the most accessible and popular hike – so much so, in fact, that Inverpolly National Nature Reserve have had to extensively repair and re-route the main path up the mountain from the car park on the Achiltibuie road. The path now leads walkers around to the northern side of the hill before climbing steeply. You'll need a head for heights to explore the jagged summit ridge extensively, and this is one hill where you should turn back from bagging the summit if you feel uncertain doing some basic rock climbing.

Suilven (2399ft), described by poet Norman McCaig as "one sandstone chord that holds up time in space", is the most memorable of the Assynt peaks to look at, though the ascent is a tough eight-hour outing, including the boggy five-mile walk to its base. From the A837 at Elphin, head round the north of Cam Loch then through the glen between Canisp and Suilven, until you pick up the path that aims for the saddle – Bealach Mor – in the middle of Suilven's summit ridge, from where the path to the top is straightforward. The return is by the same route, although at the saddle you could choose to turn southwest for the route to Inverkirkaig, while a descent down the northwestern side can lead either back to Elphin or west to Lochinver by way of Glen Canisp.

The highest peaks in Assynt are the neighbouring **Conival** and **Ben More Assynt**, often climbed for their status as Munros (see p.58), despite the fact that they're less distinctive than their neighbours, and are generally known for their rough harshness and bleak landscape. The route follows the track up Glen Dubh from Inchnadamph, staying to the north of the river as you aim for the saddle between Conival and the peak to the north, Beinn an Fhurain. Once on the ridge, turn southeast to climb to the top of Conival then turn east along a high, exposed ridge to the top of Ben More. The entire walk, including the return to Inchnadamph, takes five to six hours.

If you're looking for something less testing, there are some classic **coastal walks** immediately north of Lochinver. From **Baddidarrach**, opposite Lochinver village on the north side of the rivermouth, a path with fantastic views of the Assynt peaks leads over heather slopes to Loch Dubh and down to **Achmelvich** (a 1hr walk). From here there's a sporadically signposted but reasonable path to **Clachtoll** (about 2hr) past delightful sandy coves, grassy knolls, and rocks to clamber across at low tide. At Clachtoll there's a dramatic split rock (after which the crofting hamlet is named) and an Iron Age fort. More dramatic is the ninety-minute cliff-top walk from Stoer lighthouse along to the famous stack, **The Old Man of Stoer** (220ft).

Scotland, its huge sandstone dome rising above the heather boglands of Assynt. Serious hikers use the path to approach the mighty peak, but you can follow it for an easy three-to-four-hour ramble, taking in a waterfall and a tour of a secluded loch. Just by the start of the trail but tucked away among the dark pine trees, **Achins Bookshop** must rate as the Highland's best-hidden nook. You can browse the shelves of heavyweight classics and local-interest titles, then shuffle into the adjoining **coffee shop** for a bowl of soup or some home-baking.

North of Lochinver

Heading **north** from Lochinver, there are two possible routes: the fast A837, which runs eastwards along the shore of Loch Assynt (see below) to join the northbound A894, or the narrow, more scenic B869 **coast road** that locals dub "The Breakdown Zone", because its ups and downs claim so many victims during summer. Hugging the indented shoreline, this route offers superb views of the Summer Isles, as well as a number of rewarding side-trips to beaches and dramatic cliffs. Post- and schoolbuses from Lochinver cover the route as far as Ardvar or Drumbeg (Mon–Sat).

Unusually, most of the land and lochs around here are owned by local crofters rather than wealthy landlords. Helped by grants and private donations, the **Assynt Crofters' Trust** (Ⓦwww.assyntcrofters.co.uk) made history in 1993 when it pulled off the first-ever community buyout of estate land in Scotland. Subsequent agreements have now given Little Assynt Estate over 1200 hectares of the Assynt hinterland to carefully nurture and manage. The Trust owns some of the lucrative fishing rights to the area, too, selling permits through local post offices and the Lochinver tourist office.

The first village worthy of a detour is **ACHMELVICH**, three miles northwest of Lochinver, where a tiny bay cradles a stunning white-sand beach lapped by startlingly turquoise water. There's a **campsite** and a basic 36-bed SYHA **hostel** (Ⓣ0870/004 1102, Ⓦwww.syha.org.uk; April–Sept) just behind the largest beach. However, for total peace and quiet, head to other, equally seductive beaches beyond the headlands. Back to the B869, the giant peak of Suilven dominates the skyline. Further west, the crofting hamlet of Clachtoll is dominated by another beautiful bay with a campsite, and nearby which you'll find the former Clachtoll Salmon Station, now preserved by the Assynt Historical Society.

The side road that branches north off the B869 between **STOER** and **CLASHNESSIE** ends abruptly by the automatic lighthouse at **Raffin**, Steveson-built in 1870. You can continue for two miles along a boggy, slightly tricky track to the Point of Stoer, named after the colossal rock pillar that stands offshore known as "**The Old Man of Stoer**", surrounded by sheer cliffs and splashed with guano from the seabird colonies that nest on its 200ft sides. Some five miles east of Clashnessie you could treat yourself to a **room** and delicious food at the *Drumbeg Hotel* (Ⓣ01571/833236, Ⓦwww.drumbeghotel.com; ③).

Loch Assynt, Inchnadamph and around

The area east of Lochinver, traversed by the A837, centred on **Loch Assynt** and bounded by the gnarled peaks of the Ben More Assynt massif, is a wilderness of mountains, moorland, mist and scree. Dotted with lochs and lochans, it's also an angler's paradise, home to the only non-migratory fish in northern Scotland, the brown trout, and numerous other sought-after species, including the Atlantic salmon, sea trout, arctic char and a massive prize strain of cannibal ferox.

On a rocky promontory pushing out into Loch Assynt stand the jagged remnants of **Ardveck Castle** (free access), a MacLeod stronghold from 1597 that fell to the Seaforth Mackenzies after a siege in 1691. Previously, the Marquis of Montrose had been imprisoned here after his defeat at Carbisdale in 1650. The rebel duke, whom the local laird had betrayed to the government for £20,000 and four hundred bowls of sour meal, was eventually led away to be executed in Edinburgh, lashed back to front on his horse.

At **INCHNADAMPH** at the southeastern tip of Loch Assynt, the *Inchnadamph Hotel* (Ⓣ01571/822202, Ⓦwww.inchnadamphhotel.co.uk; ❺), is a seventeenth-century coaching inn which makes for a wonderful Highland retreat; inside, the walls are covered with the stuffed catches of past guests. The hotel offers fine old-fashioned cooking, usually with good vegetarian options, in its moderately priced restaurant and bar. It's popular with anglers, who get free fishing rights to Loch Assynt, as well as several hill lochs backing onto Ben More, haunts of the infamous ferox trout. Just along the road, the Assynt Field Centre or *Inchnadamph Lodge* (Ⓣ01571/822218, Ⓦwww.inch-lodge.co.uk; ❶) has basic, comfortable bunk rooms and spacious B&B accommodation. The lodge also serves as a study resource centre for groups interested in the area's fascinating geology, fauna and flora.

The displays within the grass-roofed, unstaffed **Knockan Crag** (Creag a' Chnocain; Ⓦwww.knockan-crag.co.uk) visitor centre, nine miles south of Loch Assynt on the A835 to Ullapool and part of the Inverpolly National Nature Reserve, outline why this is one of the most important geological sites in the world. In 1859, the theory of thrust faults was developed by eminent geologist James Nicol, and two interpretive **trails** (one 15min, the other 1hr) show you how to detect the movement of rock plates in the nearby cliffs. A few miles further on in the village of Knockan itself, the *Birchbank Lodge* (Ⓣ01854/666215; ❸) is an excellent base if you're planning to fish in an area renowned for its wild brown trout lochs. The proprietors can advise both fishing enthusiasts and hill-walking guests.

Kylesku and around

KYLESKU, 33 miles north of Ullapool on the main A894 road, is the point where a curvaceous road bridge sweeps over the mouth of lochs Glencoul and Glendhu. Kylesku is a small, peaceful backwater where during World War II the deep lochs provided a secret training base for the brave crews of the x-craft mini-submarines. A small, poignant memorial to the crews stands in the car park at the northern end of the Kylesku road bridge.

The congenial *Kylesku Hotel* (Ⓣ01971/502231; ❺; March–Oct) by the water's edge above the old ferry slipway, has a welcoming bar popular with locals, and serves **fresh seafood** including lobsters, langoustines, mussels and local salmon. Alternatively, *Newton Lodge* (Ⓣ01971/502070, Ⓔinfo@newtonlodge.co.uk; ❺; May–Sept) is a modern, friendly and comfortable small **hotel** a mile or so up the road towards Ullapool, with superb views over the loch and small seal colony. Self-catering accommodation is available at *Kylesku Lodges* (Ⓣ01971/502003, Ⓦwww.kyleskulodges.co.uk), where three-bedroom lodges offer great views to Quinaig (coo-in-yag) mountain and out to sea.

Statesman Cruises runs entertaining **boat trips** (March–Oct twice daily except Sat; round trip 2hr; £12.50; Ⓣ01571/844446 or 01971/502345) from the jetty below the *Kylesku Hotel* to the 650ft **Eas-Coul-Aulin**, Britain's highest waterfall, located at the head of Loch Glencoul; otters, seals, porpoises and minke whales can occasionally be spotted along the way; you can also get dropped off in the morning and/or picked up in the afternoon if you arrange it beforehand. The boat also makes regular trips out to **Kerracher Gardens** (mid-May to mid-Sept Tues, Thurs & Sun; boat departs 1pm; £12.50) which are only accessible from the sea; this remarkable west-coast garden harnesses the Gulf Stream weather to create a riot of colour and exotic vegetation in the rugged Highland scenery. It's also possible to reach the waterfall **on foot**: a rough four-mile trail (3hr) leaves the A894 three miles south of Kylesku, skirting the south shore of Loch na Gainmhich (known locally as the "sandy loch") to approach the falls from above. Great care should be taken here as the path above the cliffs can get very slippery when wet; the rest of the route is also difficult to follow, particularly in bad weather, and should only be attempted by experienced, properly equipped and compass-literate hikers.

The far northwest coast

The Sutherland coastline north of Kylesku is a bridge too far for some, yet for others the stark, elemental beauty of the Highlands is to be found on the **far northwest coast** as nowhere else. Here, the peaks become more widely spaced and settlements smaller and fewer, linked by twisting single-track roads and shoreside footpaths that make excellent hiking trails. From the Kylesku bridge to the beautiful strip of sand at **Sandwood Bay**, a day's hike from Cape Wrath, the area retains an exhilarating essence of wildness. One of the few conventional tourist attractions is the simple ferry that takes folk to see the puffins of the island wildlife reserve of **Handa**. Places to stay and eat can be thin on the ground, particularly out of season, but the lack of infrastructure is testimony to the isolation which this corner of Scotland delivers in such sweeping style.

Scourie and around

Ten miles north of Kylesku, the widely scattered crofting community of **SCOURIE**, on a bluff above the main road, surrounds a beautiful sandy beach whose safe bathing has made it a popular holiday destination for families; there's plenty to do for walkers and trout anglers, too. The mobile bank visits the area on Tuesday and Thursday afternoons. Scourie itself has some good **accommodation**, including the charming *Scourie Lodge* (ⓣ01971/502248; ❺; March–Oct), an old shooting retreat surrounded by trees on the north side of the sandy bay, with a lovely garden and its own hens and ducks; the welcoming owners do great evening meals. There's a decent **campsite** by the bay, the *Scourie Caravan and Camping Park* (ⓣ01971/502060), with the simple *Anchorage* café bar and adjoining hotel and a small supermarket. There's also a petrol station.

Even more remote is **UPPER BADCALL** village, three miles south of Scourie, with a couple of **B&Bs**, including *Stoer View* (ⓣ01971/502411, ⓦwww.badcall.supanet.com; ❷), whose clean and comfortable rooms look over Badcall and Eddrachillis Bay to Stoer Point. The *Eddrachilles Hotel* (ⓣ01971/502080, ⓦwww.eddrachilles.com; ❻), a homely former 1700s manse hidden behind trees and just south of the turning to Upper Badcall, combines a warm welcome with comfortable rooms (the family room includes a separate bedroom for the kids), delicious dinners in a rustic setting and the chance to enjoy great sea views while sampling one of the bar's 103 malt whiskies.

Tarbet and Handa Island

Visible just offshore to the north of Scourie is **Handa Island**, a huge chunk of red Torridon sandstone surrounded by sheer cliffs, carpeted with machair and purple-tinged moorland, and teeming with seabirds. A **wildlife reserve** administered by the Scottish Wildlife Trust (Ⓦwww.swt.org.uk), Handa Island supports one of the largest seabird colonies in northwest Europe. It's a real treat for ornithologists, with razorbills and guillemots breeding on its guano-splashed cliffs during summer. From late May to mid-July, large numbers of puffins waddle comically over the turf-covered clifftops where they dig their burrows. Until the mid-nineteenth century, Handa supported a thriving, if somewhat eccentric, community of crofters, who survived on a diet of fish, potatoes and seabirds. The islanders, whose ruined cottages still cling to the slopes by the jetty, devised their own system of government, with a "queen" (Handa's oldest widow) and "parliament" (a council of men who met each morning to discuss the day's business). Uprooted by the 1846 potato famine, most of the villagers eventually emigrated to Canada's Cape Breton.

Weather permitting, **boats** (Ⓣ01971/502347) leave for Handa throughout the day (Easter to Sept Mon–Sat; £8) from the tiny cove of **TARBET**, three miles northwest of the main road and accessible by postbus from Scourie, where there's a small car park and jetty. You're encouraged to make a donation towards Handa's upkeep. You'll need about three hours to follow the **footpath** around the island – an easy and enjoyable walk taking in the north shore's Great Stack rock pillar and some fine views across the Minch: a detailed route guide is featured in the SWT's free leaflet, available from the warden's office when you arrive. Camping is not allowed on the island, but the SWT is currently revamping what is a popular **bothy** for bird-watchers (reservations essential on Ⓣ01463/714746). In Tarbet, the *Croft House* (Ⓣ01971/502098; ❶) is a comfortable little **B&B** overlooking the bay. For **food**, Tarbet's unexpected *Seafood Restaurant* (Mon–Sat noon–8pm) serves delicious, moderately priced fish and vegetarian dishes, and a good selection of home-made cakes and desserts, in its conservatory just above the jetty.

Loch Laxford to Sandwood Bay

North of Scourie, the road sweeps inland through the starkest part of the Highlands; rocks piled on rocks, bog and water create an almost alien landscape, and the astonishingly bare, stony coastline looks increasingly inhospitable. Here, on the Ardmore peninsula, an outdoor school was established in the 1960s by adventurer John Ridgway. Now, on an isolated sea loch, off **Loch Laxford**, his daughter Rebecca, and her husband Will, have set up Cape Adventure International (Ⓣ01971/521006, Ⓦwww.capeventure.com), where you can get stuck into all sorts of outdoor thrills and spills, including sea kayaking, rock-climbing and land yachting. While they run residential courses and "castaway" weekends, if you're only in the area for a short period you can also join in any of the activities as a day-course.

Further north still, near the road junction at **RHICHONICH** and under the shadow of **Foinaven** (2980ft), a comfortable stay can be enjoyed at the *Rhichonich Hotel* (Ⓣ01971/521224; ❺). The hotel has the fishing rights to the local estate and can organize deer-stalking, walking and bird-watching. A mile up the road, the B801 side road branches off to **KINLOCHBERVIE**, which for all the world seems to be a typical, straggling West Highland crofting community with a hotel (Ⓣ01971/521275; ❺) – until you turn a corner and encounter an incongruously huge fish market and modern concrete harbour. Trucks from all over Europe pick up cod and shellfish from here. There's a mobile bank and petrol pump and if you're in need of sustenance, try the **fish and chips** at the *Fishermen's Mission* (closed Sat & Sun); otherwise press on towards Oldshoremore.

△ Sandwood Bay

A single-track road continues northwest of Kinlochbervie through isolated **OLDSHOREMORE**, a working crofters' village scattered above a stunning white-sand beach, to **BLAIRMORE**, where the enlarged car park is testament to the growing number of visitors making the four-mile walk across peaty moorland to **Sandwood Bay**. After an unremarkable walk-in, the shell-white sandy **beach** at the end of the rough track is a breathtaking sight and one of the most beautiful in Scotland. Flanked by rolling dunes and lashed by fierce gales for much of the year, the dramatic leaning rock stack to the south is said to be haunted by a bearded mariner – one of many sailors to have perished on this notoriously dangerous stretch of coast since the Vikings first navigated it over a millennium ago. Around the start of the twentieth century, the beach, whose treacherous undercurrents make it unsuitable for swimming, also witnessed Britain's most recent recorded sighting of a **mermaid**. Turning back and past Blairmore at **SHEIGRA**, where the road ends, you can camp behind the beach, whilst provisions can be bought in the small store at Oldshoremore.

It's possible to trek overland from Sandwood Bay north to Cape Wrath, the most northwesterly point in mainland Britain, a full day's walk away. If you're planning to meet the Cape Wrath minibus (see p.304) to Durness, contact them first since it won't run if the weather turns bad, leaving you stranded.

The north coast

Though a constant stream of sponsored walkers, caravans and tour groups makes it to the dull town of **John O'Groats**, surprisingly few visitors travel the whole length of the Highlands' wild **north coast**. Those that do, however, rarely return disappointed. Pounded by one of the world's most ferocious seaways, Scotland's rugged northern shore is backed by barren mountains in the west, and in the east by lochs and open rolling grasslands. Between its far ends, mile upon mile of crumbling cliffs and sheer rocky headlands shelter bays whose perfect white beaches are nearly always deserted, even in the height of summer – though, somewhat incongruously, they're also home to Scotland's best surfing waves (see p.63).

Though only a wee place, **Durness** is a good jumping-off point for nearby Balnakeil beach, one of the area's most beautiful sandy strands, and for rugged **Cape Wrath**, the windswept promontory at Scotland's northwest tip, which has retained an end-of-the-world mystique lost long ago by John O'Groats. Continuing east, **Loch Eriboll** is probably the most spectacular of the north-coast sea lochs, and **Tongue**, the most picturesque of the small crofting villages. **Thurso**, the largest town on the north coast, is really only visited by those en route to Orkney. More enticing are the huge seabird colonies clustered in clefts and on remote stacks at **Dunnet Head** and **Duncansby Head**, to the east of Thurso.

Public transport around this stretch of coast can be a slow and frustrating business: Thurso, the area's main town and springboard for Orkney, is well connected by **bus** and **train** with Inverness, but further west, after the main A836 peters out into a single-track road, you have to rely on **postbus** connections.

Durness and around

Scattered around a string of sheltered sandy coves and grassy clifftops, **DURNESS** (ⓦwww.durness.org), the most northwesterly village on the British mainland, straddles the turning point on the main A838 road as it swings east from the inland peat bogs of the interior to the north coast's fertile strip of limestone machair. First settled by the Picts around 400 BC, the area has been farmed ever since, its crofters being among the few not cleared off estate land during the nineteenth century. Today, Durness is the centre for several crofting communities and an unexpectedly pleasant base for a couple of days, with some good walks.

Durness village itself sits above its own sandy bay, Sango Sands, while half a mile to the east is **SMOO**, which used to be an RAF station. In between Durness and Smoo is the millennial village hall, which features a windblown and rather forlorn community garden that harbours a memorial commemorating the Beatle **John Lennon**, who used to come to Durness on family holidays as a kid (and even revisited the place in the 1960s with Yoko). It's worth pausing at Smoo to see the 200ft-long **Smoo Cave,** a gaping hole in a sheer limestone cliff formed partly by the action of the sea and partly by the small burn that flows through it. Tucked away at the end of a narrow sheer-sided sea cove, the main chamber is accessible via steps from the car park by the A838. The much-hyped rock formations are less memorable than the short rubber-dinghy trip you have to make in the other two caverns, where the whole experience is enlivened after wet weather by a waterfall that crashes through the middle of the cavern. **Boat trips** (May–Sept) are run on request and weather permitting by Colin Coventry (ⓣ01971/511704).

A narrow road winds a mile or so northwest of Durness to **BALNAKEIL**, passing **Balnakeil Craft Village** en route. Disabuse yourself of any notion of quaint cottages, as the craft village is housed in a grim 1940s military base, transformed in the 1960s into a sort of industrial estate for arts and crafts, thanks to the carrot of cheap rents for studio and living quarters. It's come a long way since those idealistic days. A dozen or so workshops continue to function, including a woodwind-instrument maker, a picture framer, painters, potters and leather-workers. There's also the friendly *Loch Croispol* bookshop which runs an excellent daytime café (daily 10am–5pm, but restricted winter opening; ⓣ01971/511777) and serves Sunday lunch.

In tiny Balnakeil itself, a seventeenth-century **ruined chapel** overlooks the remote hamlet, but a church has stood here for at least 1200 years. A skull-and-crossbones stone set in the south wall marks the grave of Donald MacMurchow, a seventeenth-century highwayman and contract killer who murdered eighteen people for his clan chief (allegedly by throwing them from the top of the Smoo Cave). The "half-in, half-out" position of his grave was apparently a compromise between his grateful employer and the local clergy, who initially refused to allow such an evil man to be buried on church ground.

Balnakeil is also known for its **golf course**, whose ninth and final hole involves a well-judged drive over the Atlantic; you can rent equipment from the clubhouse. The white-sand beach on the east side of **Balnakeil Bay** is a stunning sight in any weather, but most spectacular on sunny days when the water turns to brilliant turquoise. For the best views, walk along the path that winds north through the dunes (pockmarked from occasional naval bombing exercises) behind it; this eventually leads to **Faraid Head** – from the Gaelic *Fear Ard* (High Fellow) – where there's a very small colony of nesting puffins (ask the tourist office for directions). The fine views east to the mouth of Loch Eriboll and west to Cape Wrath make this round walk (3–4hr) the best in the Durness area.

Practicalities

Public transport is sparse; the key service is the Dearman Coaches link (May–Sept Mon–Sat 1 daily) from Inverness via Ullapool and Lochinver. The bus has a cycle carrier. Postbuses provide a more complicated year-round alternative and meet trains at Lairg; check schedules at the post office or tourist office. The helpful Durness **tourist office** (March–Oct Mon–Sat 10am–5pm; July & Aug also Sun 10am–4pm; Nov–Feb, Mon–Fri, 10am–1.30pm) has a small **visitor centre** that features excellent interpretive panels detailing the area's history, geology, flora and fauna, with insights into the daily life of the community.

In terms of **accommodation**, *Mackays Room and Restaurant*, at the western edge of the village, stands out for its welcome, tasteful Highland decor and an emphasis on freshly prepared cooking with the personal touch (ⓣ01971/511202, ⓦwww.visitmackays.com; ❺). The proprietor also runs the clean and popular *Lazy Crofter Bunkhouse* (ⓣ01971/511202, ⓦwww.durnesshostel.com) next door. The village has a basic SYHA **hostel** (ⓣ0870/004 1113, ⓦwww.syha.org.uk; March–Oct), beside the Smoo Cave car park half a mile east of the village. Of the **B&Bs**, *Puffin Cottage* (ⓣ01971/511208, ⓦwww.puffincottage.com; ❶, April–Sept) is very pleasant. There's a **campsite** (ⓣ01971/511222), on an exposed spot near the tourist office, with views over Sango Sands; close by is the local village **pub.** In addition to *Mackays* and the restaurant at Loch Eriboll's *Port-Na-Con* guesthouse (see p.304), the *Seafood Platter* on the outskirts of the village towards Tongue is great value, serving the freshest of seafood and succulent steaks in a small, cosy restaurant. Opposite the tourist office is Wax and Wines, a delightful shop with candles and a host of **local wines** and spirits from flowers, fruit and herbs.

Cape Wrath

An excellent day-trip from Durness begins two miles southwest of Durness at **KEOLDALE**, where (tides and MOD permitting) a foot-passenger **ferry** (daily: May & Sept 11am & 1.30pm; June–Aug 9.30am, 11am & 1.30pm; ☎01971/511376 for ferry; £7 return) crosses the spectacular Kyle of Durness estuary to link up with a **minibus** (☎01971/511343; May–Sept) that runs the eleven miles out to **Cape Wrath**, the British mainland's most northwesterly point. Note that Garvie Island (An Garbh-eilean) is an air bombing range, and the military regularly close the road to Cape Wrath, so check with Durness tourist office or the MOD advisory line (☎0800/833300). The headland takes its name not from the stormy seas that crash against it for most of the year, but from the Norse word *hvarf*, meaning "turning place" – a throwback to the days when Viking warships used it as a navigation point during raids on the Scottish coast. These days, a Stevenson lighthouse warns ships away from the treacherous rocks; looking east to Orkney and west to the Outer Hebrides, it stands above the famous **Clo Mor cliffs**, the highest sea cliffs in Britain and a prime breeding site for seabirds. You can walk from here to remote Sandwood Bay (see p.301), visible to the south, although the route, which cuts inland across lochan-dotted moorland, is hard to follow in places. Hikers generally continue south from Sandwood to the trail end at Blairmore; if you hitch or walk the six miles from here to Kinlochbervie you can, with careful planning, catch a bus back to Durness.

Loch Eriboll

The road east of Durness passes several spectacular sandy bays en route to deep and sheltered **Loch Eriboll**, the north coast's most spectacular sea loch, ringed by ghost-like limestone mountains. Servicemen stationed here during World War II to protect passing Russian convoys nicknamed it "Loch 'Orrible", but if you're looking for somewhere wild and unspoilt, you'll find this a perfect spot. Porpoises and otters are a common sight along the rocky shore, and minke whales occasionally swim in from the open sea.

Overlooking its own landing stage at the water's edge, *Port-Na-Con* (☎01971/511367; ❷; Feb–Oct, otherwise by arrangement), seven miles from Durness on the west side of the loch, is a wonderful **B&B**. Top-notch food is served in its small **restaurant** (open all year), with a choice of vegetarian haggis, local kippers, fruit compote and home-made croissants for breakfast, and adventurous three-course evening meals for around £14; the menu always includes a gourmet vegetarian dish. Non-residents are welcome, although you'll need to book.

Tongue to Thurso

There's great drama in the landscape between Tongue and Thurso, as the A836 – still single-track for much of the way – wends its way over bleak and often totally uninhabited rocky moorland, intercut with sandy sea lochs. Tiny little **Tongue** is pleasant enough, as is the equally small settlement of **Bettyhill**, to the east, but the real reason to venture this far is to explore the countryside: **Ben Hope** (3040ft), the most northerly Munro, and the fascinating blanket bog of the **Flow Country** even further inland.

Tongue and around

The road takes a wonderfully slow and circuitous route around Loch Eriboll and east over the top of A' Mhoine moor to the pretty crofting township of **TONGUE**. Dominated by the ruins of **Castle Varrich** (Caisteal Bharraich), a medieval stronghold of the Mackays (three-mile return walk), the village is strewn above the east shore of the **Kyle of Tongue**, which you can cross

Jacobites in the Kyle of Tongue

In 1746, the Kyle of Tongue was the scene of a naval engagement reputed to have sealed the fate of Bonnie Prince Charlie's **Jacobite rebellion**. In response to a plea for help from the prince, the King of France dispatched a sloop and £13,600 in gold coins to Scotland. However, the Jacobite ship (formerly HMS *Hazard*, now the *Prince Charles*) was spotted by the English frigate HMS *Sheerness*, and fled into the Kyle, hoping that the larger enemy vessel would not be able to follow. It did, though, and soon forced the *Hazard* aground. Pounded by English cannon fire, its Jacobite crew slipped ashore under cover of darkness in an attempt to smuggle the treasure to Inverness. The next morning, however, the rebels fell into an ambush laid by the anti-Jacobite MacKay clan, and, hopelessly outnumbered and outgunned, began throwing the gold into **Lochan Hakel**, southwest of Tongue (most of it was recovered later). The prince, meanwhile, instructed Lord Cromartie to send 1500 of his men north to rescue the treasure, but these too were defeated and taken prisoner en route; historians debate whether the missing men might have altered the outcome of the Battle of Culloden three weeks later. Locals maintain that cows still occasionally wander out of the loch's shallows with gold pieces stuck in their hooves.

either via a new causeway, or by following the longer and more scenic single-track road around its southern side. When the tide recedes, this shallow estuary becomes a mass of golden sand flats, superb on sunny days, with the sharp profiles of **Ben Hope** (3040ft) and **Ben Loyal** (2509ft) looming like twin sentinels to the south, and the Rabbit Islands a short way out to sea. Tongue's relatively temperate maritime climate even allows it to claim Britain's most northerly palm tree.

The best **accommodation** in Tongue is the *Tongue Hotel* (ⓣ01847/611206, ⓦwww.tonguehotel.co.uk; ❻; April–Oct), the plush former hunting lodge of the Duke of Sutherland, which serves delicious food, and has a cosy downstairs bar. Close by is the modern *Ben Loyal Hotel* and the modest *Tign-Nan-Ubhal* guesthouse (ⓣ01847/611281; ❸). A half-mile south of the post office, a comfortable stay can be had at the *Rhian* guesthouse (ⓣ01847/611257, ⓦwww.rhiancottage.co.uk; ❸). The SYHA **hostel** (ⓦwww.syha.org.uk), right beside the causeway a mile north of the village centre on the Kyle's east shore is currently closed but expected to reopen in 2006.

Over on the western side of the Kyle, five miles away at **TALMINE**, a converted nineteenth-century church with great views out towards the Orkney Islands is the home of the popular *Cloisters* B&B (ⓣ01847/601286, ⓦwww.cloistertal.demon.co.uk; ❷). There is also a very basic **campsite** opposite the sandy beach.

Three miles east of Tongue sits the delightful and friendly *Strathtongue Old Manse* B&B (ⓣ01847/611252, ⓦwww.strathtongue.co.uk; ❸).

Bettyhill and around

Twelve miles east of Tongue, **BETTYHILL** is a major crofting village, set among rocky green hills. In Gaelic, it was known as *Am Blàran Odhar* (Little Dun-coloured Field), but the origins of the English name are unknown; however, it was definitely not named after Elizabeth, Countess of Sutherland, who presided over the Strathnaver Clearances. The story of those terrible times is told by local schoolchildren at the delightful and loyally maintained **Strathnaver Museum** (April–Oct, Mon–Sat 10am–1pm & 2–5pm; £1.90), housed in the old Farr church, set apart from the main village. Inside, you can

North coast walking and cycling

Ordnance Survey Explorer map nos. 447 & 448.

A pair of peaks rising up from the southern end of the Kyle of Tongue, Ben Hope and Ben Loyal offer moderate to hard walks, rewarded on a decent day by vast views over the harsh north coast and empty Sutherland landscape. **Ben Hope** (3040ft), which was given its name ("Hill of the Bay") by the Vikings, is the most northerly of Scotland's Munros. The best approach, a four-hour round-trip, is from the road that runs down the west side of Loch Hope. Start at a sheep shed by the roadside just under two miles beyond the southern end of Loch Hope, following the tributary of the stream that descends through an obvious break in the imposing-looking cliffline. Once on top of the cliffs, it's a relatively easy but inspiring walk along them to the summit.

Ben Loyal (2509ft), though lower, is a longer hike, at around six hours. To avoid the worst of the bogs, follow the northern spur from Ribigill Farm, a mile south of Tongue. At the end of the southbound farm track, a path emerges; follow this up a steepish slope to gain the first peak on the ridge. It's not the summit, but the views are rewarding, and from here to the top the walking is easier.

For those looking for **shorter walks** or **cycles**, there are well-marked woodland trails at **Borgie Forest**, six miles west of Tongue, and **Truderscraig Forest** by Syre, twelve miles south of Bettyhill on the B871. If you follow the signs to "**Rosal Pre-Clearance Village**", you'll find an area clear of trees with various ruins that stand as a memorial to the brutality of the Highland Clearances. Various boards provide details about the way of life of the inhabitants in the eighteenth century before the upheavals, which saw them scattered to bleak coastal settlements or onto the emigration ships leaving for Canada and America.

see some Pictish stones and a 3800-year-old early Bronze Age beaker. In the churchyard that lies to the west of the church stands the mysterious **Farr Stone**, a six-foot-high Pictish cross decorated with intricate interlacing and dating from around 800. The 24-mile Strathnaver Trail, running south from Bettyhill along the B873 to Altnaharra, highlights numerous historical sites from the Neolithic, Bronze and Iron Age periods.

A short stroll north of the church is the splendid sheltered **Farr beach**, which forms an unbroken arc of pure white sand between the Naver and Borgie rivers. Even more visually impressive is the River Naver's narrow tidal estuary, to the west of Bettyhill, and **Torrisdale beach** (popular with surfers; access off the road to Borgie five miles west of Bettyhill), which ends in a smooth white spit that forms part of the **Invernaver Nature Reserve**. During summer, arctic terns nest here on the riverbanks, which are dotted with clumps of rare Scottish primroses, and you stand a good chance of spotting an otter or two.

At the eastern end of Bettyhill, in the museum car park, the small **tourist office** (April–May & Sept–Oct Mon–Sat 10.30am–5pm; June, July & Aug daily 10.30am–5pm plus 8pm Fri & Sat) also runs *Elizabeth's Café*, a decent eating option. Nearby, the *Farr Bay Inn*, known locally as the "FBI", also serves good meals. The *Bettyhill Hotel* (ⓣ01641/521352; ❷) provides good-value accommodation and bar meals whilst 100yd further east, *Dunveaden Guest House* ⓣ01641/521273; ❷) can organize fishing for guests. Bettyhill's large campsite affords excellent views over the bay. The most bizarre sight is a road sign proclaiming the village store to be "open 8 days per week". Sheltered in woods four or five miles west of Bettyhill, the *Borgie Lodge Hotel* (ⓣ01641/521332, ⓦwww.borgielodgehotel.co.uk; ❻; Feb–Nov) is an upmarket base that's popular for salmon- and sea-fishing and boasts an excellent restaurant.

Melvich and Dounreay

As you move east from Bettyhill, the north coast changes dramatically as the hills on the horizon recede to be replaced by fields fringed with flagstone walls. At the hamlet of **MELVICH**, twelve miles east of Bettyhill, the A897 cuts south through Strath Halladale, the Flow Country (see below) and the Strath of Kildonan to Helmsdale on the east coast (see p.324). Melvich has some good **accommodation**, notably the wonderfully hospitable *Sheiling Guesthouse* (⊕01641/531256, ⓦwww.thesheiling.co.uk; ❹; May–Sept) by the main road, whose impressive breakfasts feature locally smoked haddock and fresh herring. Good bar meals are on offer at the *Halladale Inn*, half-a-mile further east whilst the slightly run-down *Melvich Hotel* brews "Fast Reactor" ale on its premises. The *Strathy Inn* in Strathy is another good food stop on this stretch.

Five miles further east of Melvich, golfers can enjoy a round at Reay before continuing on the A836 past **Dounreay Nuclear Power Station** (ⓦwww.ukaea.org.uk/dounreay), a surreal collection of chimney stacks and box-like buildings, plus the famous golf-ball-shaped DFR (Dounreay Fast Reactor). Established back in 1955, Dounreay pioneered the development of fast reactor technology and was the first reactor in the world to provide mains electricity. The reactors themselves have long since closed, though Dounreay remains by far the biggest employer on the north coast, with decommissioning estimated to take another 30 years at a cost of £2.7 billion. In recent years, an oyster-catcher has created its nest (May–June) outside the tiny teabar beside the helpful **visitor centre** (Easter to end Oct daily 10am–4pm; free). The centre details the processes (and, unsurprisingly, the benefits) of nuclear power, and seeks to offer explanations for a range of issues such as the area's "leukaemia cluster" (allegedly not connected with radiation), and the radioactive particles that continue to be found on the nearby beaches. A more green activity can be enjoyed walking along the short Achvarasdal woodland trail, half a mile south of Reay.

The Flow Country

From Melvich, you can head forty miles or so south towards Helmsdale on the A897, through the **Flow Country**, whose name comes from *flói*, an Old Norse word meaning "marshy ground". This huge expanse of "blanket bog" is a valuable "carbon sink" and home to a wide variety of wildlife. At the train station at **FORSINARD**, fourteen miles south of Melvich and easily accessible from Thurso, Wick and the south by train, there is an RSPB **visitor centre** (April–Oct daily 9am–6pm; ⊕01641/571225), with CCTV coverage of hen harriers nesting, and also a **Peatland Centre**, which explains the wonders of peat. To get to grips with the whole concept of blanket bog, take a leaflet and follow the short **Dubh Lochan Trail** that's been laid out over the flagstones, through peat banks to some nearby black lochans. En route, you get to see bog asphodel, bogbean, sphagnum moss and the insect-trapping sundew and butterwort; you've also got a good chance of seeing greenshanks, golden plovers and hen harriers. There are also regular guided walks through the area from the visitor centre. The *Forsinard Hotel* (closed Feb), opposite the station, is popular with anglers and does standard **bar food**, but Sue Grimshaw's **B&B** (⊕01641/571262; ❷), described by one guest as "heaven on earth", offers guests a comfortable stay and three-course evening meals made with local produce.

Thurso

Approached from the isolation of the west, **THURSO** feels like a metropolis. In reality, it's a relatively small service centre visited mostly by people passing through to the adjoining port of **Scrabster** to catch the ferry to Orkney or by increasing numbers of surfers attracted to the waves on the north coast. The birthplace in 1854 of William Smith, founder of the international Boys' Brigade, the town's name derives from the Norse word *Thorsa*, literally "River of the God Thor", and in Viking times this was a major gateway to the mainland. Later, ships set sail from here for the Baltic and Scandinavian ports loaded with meal, beef, hides and fish. Much of the town, however, dates from the 1790s, when Sir John Sinclair built a large new extension to the old fishing port. The nearby Dounreay Nuclear Power Station ensured continuing prosperity after World War II, tripling the population when workers from the plant (dubbed "atomics" by the locals) settled in Thurso.

Thurso's grid-plan streets boast some rather handsome Victorian architecture in the local, greyish sandstone, though there's nothing really specific to detain you. **Traill Street** is the main drag, turning into the pedestrianized Rotterdam Street and High Street precinct at its northern end. On the High Street, by the side of the old Victorian town hall, is **Thurso Heritage Museum** (June–Sept Mon–Sat 10am–1pm, 2–5pm; £1) whose most intriguing exhibits are the Ulbster Stone in the entrance, which features elephants, fish and other beasts,

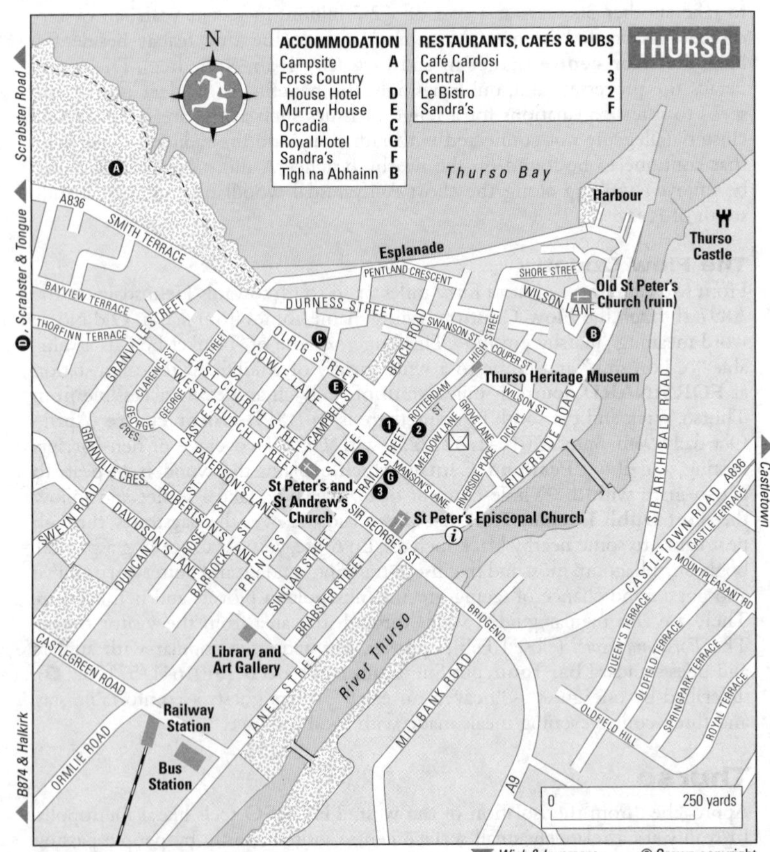

and the Skinnet Stone, intricately carved with enigmatic symbols and a runic cross. If you continue north up the High Street, you'll reach **Old St Peter's Church**, a substantial ruin with origins in the thirteenth century, and the old part of town, near the harbour.

Practicalities

Trains from Inverness (all of which go via Wick) arrive at Thurso **train station**, adjacent to the **bus station**, both a ten-minute walk down Princes Street and Sir George's Street to the helpful riverside **tourist office** (April–May & Oct Mon–Sat 10am–5pm; June–Sept Mon–Sat 10am–5pm, Sun 10am–4pm; closed Nov–Easter). The **Scrabster ferry terminal** is a mile or so northwest of town, with regular buses from the train station in the morning, and from Olrig Street in the afternoon. For more on **ferries to Orkney** from Scrabster, Gills Bay and John O' Groats, see p.328. Note that ferry tickets cannot be booked at the tourist office.

Thurso is well stocked with **accommodation**, including several **hostels**, the best of which is *Sandra's*, 24/26 Princes St (ⓣ01847/894575, ⓦwww.sandras-backpackers.ukf.net), a refurbished, clean and well-run place owned by the popular chippie downstairs. They also offer **bike rental** (£14) and **Internet** access. Aside from the upmarket *Forss Country House Hotel* (ⓣ01847/861201; ❻), three miles west of Thurso on the A836, the *Royal Hotel* (ⓣ01847/893191, ⓦwww.british-trust-hotels.com; ❻) on Traill Street is among several comfortable and central hotels. Of the **B&Bs**, *Murray House*, 1 Campbell St (ⓣ01847/895759, ⓦwww.murrayhousebb.com; ❷), is central, comfortable and friendly; there's also *Tigh na Abhainn*, an old house by the river (ⓣ01847/893443; ❷), or the long-established *Orcadia*, 27 Olrig St (ⓣ01847/894395; ❶). The nearest **campsite** (ⓣ01847/805503) sits out towards Scrabster alongside the main road, though there's a much nicer one at Dunnet Bay, a few miles east (see below).

By far the best place **to eat** in Thurso is the popular *Le Bistro*, 2 Traill St (ⓣ01847/893737; Tues–Sat), where the reasonably priced menu includes traditional fare such as Cullen skink soup. For fresh seafood, head for Scrabster and *The Captain's Galley* but if you're cooking your own supper there's a decent fishmonger and a bakery in Thurso's Rotterdam Street. Across from *Le Bistro*, the younger crowd may prefer a coffee at *Café Cardosi* or a pint in the *Central*, on Traill Street and there's always *Skinnandi's Nightclub* on Sir George's Street (Thurs–Sun). Thurso also has its very own entertainment complex, the *All St@r Factory*, down the Ormlie Road beyond the train station, with a two-screen **cinema**, a ten-pin bowling alley and a popular "night spot".

If you're coming to **surf**, Andy Bain of Thurso Surf offers surf lessons and advice (ⓣ01847/831866, ⓦwww.thursosurf.com; April–Sept) or you can try Tempest Surf (ⓣ01847/892500) on Riverside Road.

Dunnet Head and the Castle of Mey

Thurso doesn't have much of a beach, so if you want to sink your toes into sand, head five miles east along the A836 to **Dunnet Bay**, a vast golden beach backed by huge dunes. The bay is popular with surfers, and even in the winter you can usually spot intrepid figures far out in the Pentland Firth's breakers. On the south side of the bay is an abandoned flagstone quarry, which employed up to five hundred people before it closed in 1912. The old harbour, workers' cottages, quarry offices and windmill – all made out of the local Caithness flagstone – are now overgrown with wild flowers, but the informative **Castlehill Flagstone Trail** tells you about the place, and a sculpture trail links the site with the nearby village of Castletown. At the northeast end of the bay, there's a **Ranger Centre** (April–Sept Tues–Fri & Sun 2–5pm) beside the excellent campsite, where you can pick up information on good local history and nature walks, including a short self-guided trail into nearby **Dunnet Forest**, a failed plantation which has been left to go – literally – to seed, allowing a rich range of plant and animal life to thrive. To the north of the bay is the small village of **Dunnet**, where it's worth stopping in at **Mary-Ann's Cottage** (June–Sept Tues–Sun 2–4.30pm; £2), a farming croft vacated in 1990 by 93-year-old Mary-Ann Calder, whose grandfather had built the cottage, and maintained just as she left it, full of reminders of the three generations who lived and worked here over the last 150 years.

Despite the publicity that John O'Groats customarily receives, mainland Britain's most northerly point is in fact **Dunnet Head**, north of Dunnet along the B855, which runs for four miles over bleak heather and bog to the tip of the headland, crowned with a Stevenson lighthouse. At 345ft above sea-level, stones hurled up from the sea have been known to break its windows. In early summer, puffins may be spotted on the impressive red cliffs whilst seals bathe off rocks below the weirdly eroded rock stacks. On a clear day you can see the whole northern coastline from Cape Wrath to Duncansby Head, and across the treacherous Pentland Firth to Orkney. In Brough, en route to the lighthouse, there's a small tearoom in the *Dunnet Head Educational Trust* (Easter–Sept 11am–5pm, closed Wed; ⓣ01847/851991, ⓦwww.dunnethead.com). Aside from information on the area's archeology, wildlife and transport links, behind the cottage a path leads to a seal-viewing area. Next door is *Windhaven Cottage* **B&B** (ⓣ01847/851774; ❷; Easter–Sept).

Roughly fifteen miles east of Thurso, just off the A836, lies the late Queen Mother's former Scottish home and the most northerly castle on the UK mainland: the **Castle of Mey** (May to end July & mid-Aug to end Sept; Sat–Thurs 10.30am–4pm; £7; ⓦwww.castleofmey.org.uk). It's a modest little place, hidden behind high flagstone walls, with great views north to Orkney and a herd of the Queen Mum's beloved Aberdeen Angus grazing out front. The original castle was a sixteenth-century Z-plan affair, owned by the earls of Caithness until 1889, and bought in a state of disrepair the year her husband, George VI died. The Queen Mum used to spend every August here, and unusually for a royal palace, it's remarkably unstuffy inside, the walls hung with works by local amateur artists (and watercolours by Prince Charles), the sideboards cluttered with tacky joke ornaments and the video library well stocked with copies of *Fawlty Towers* and *Dad's Army*.

John O'Groats and around

Romantics expecting to find a magical meeting of land and water at **JOHN O'GROATS** (ⓦwww.visitjohnogroats.com) are invariably disappointed – sadly it remains an uninspiring tourist trap. The views north to Orkney are fine enough, but the village offers little more than a string of souvenir and craft shops and several refreshment stops thronged with coach parties. The village gets its name from the Dutchman, Jan de Groot, who obtained the ferry contract for the hazardous crossing to Orkney in 1496. The eight-sided house he built for his eight quarrelling sons (so that each one could enter by his own door) is echoed in the octagonal tower of the much-photographed but neglected *John O'Groats Hotel*. Aside from regular **buses** to Wick and Thurso, there are frequent if irregular links with Land's End (the far southwest tip of England), maintained by a succession of walkers, cyclists, vintage-car drivers and pushers of baths.

The **tourist office** (daily: May & Oct 10am–5pm; June 9.30am–6pm; July–Aug 9am–7pm; Sept 9am–6pm) is by the car park. One of the best **B&Bs** in the area is *Bencorragh House* (ⓣ01955/611449, ⓦwww.bencorraghhouse.com; ❷; March–Oct), which has very pleasant farmhouse accommodation and spectacular views at Upper Gills near Canisbay, three miles southwest of John O'Groats. The small SYHA **hostel** (ⓣ0870/004 1129, ⓦwww.syha.org.uk; April–Sept) is in Canisbay itself. Of the two local **campsites**, *Stroma View* (ⓣ01955/611313; March–Sept), one mile along the Thurso road, is less exposed than the windswept but well-equipped John O'Groats campsite (ⓣ01955/611329). There are several **boat trips** to be had: John O'Groats Ferries (ⓣ01955/611353, ⓦwww.jogferry.co.uk) offers a leisurely afternoon cruise, which will take you round the seabird colonies and stacks of Duncansby Head or the seal colonies of Stroma (mid-June to Aug daily 2.30pm; 1hr 30min; £14); North Coast Marine Adventures (Easter to Oct daily; ⓣ01955/611797, ⓦwww.northcoast-marine-adventures.co.uk) offers rather more high-adrenalin half-hour trips in a rigid inflatable (£13) and a one-hour wildlife scenic tour (£16).

If you're disappointed by John O'Groats, press on a couple of miles further east to **Duncansby Head**, which, with its lighthouse, dramatic cliffs and well-worn coastal path, has a lot more to offer. The birdlife here is prolific, and south

The Pentland Firth and Stroma

The Caithness coastline is a good place from which to view Orkney. Dividing the islands from the mainland is the infamous **Pentland Firth**, one of the world's most treacherous waterways. Only seven miles across, it forms a narrow channel between the Atlantic Ocean and North Sea, and for fourteen hours each day the tide rips through here from west to east at a rate of ten knots or more, flooding back in the opposite direction for the remaining ten hours. Combined with the rocky seabed and a high wind, this can cause deep whirlpools and terrifying 30-foot or 40-foot towers of water when the ebbing tide crashes across the reefs offshore. The latter, known as the "Bores of Duncansby", are the subject of many old mariners' myths from the time of the Vikings onwards. Ever-increasing numbers of oil tankers are braving the Pentland Firth to save time on the longer passage north of the Orkneys – an environmental catastrophe waiting to happen, according to locals.

Obstructing the flow of the Pentland Firth and, as a result, surrounded by turbulent seas, is **Stroma** (from the Norse *staum-øy* or "tidal stream"), a flat island visible a few miles north of Gills Bay, terminal for the Pentland Ferries to Orkney (see p.328). Part of Caithness, and not counted as one of the nearby Orkney islands, Stroma had a population of well over three hundred in the late nineteenth century, which had dwindled to around eighty by the 1950s. To help stem the depopulation, a new harbour was constructed in 1955 at great expense. The contractors employed the locals as the workforce, paying such good wages that many of the islanders used the money to move to the mainland. Within a few years, just the lighthouse keepers remained, and nowadays only sheep make use of the buildings and the single road. John O'Groats Ferries (ⓣ01955/611353, ⓦwww.jogferry.co.uk) offers a leisurely afternoon **wildlife cruise**, which (depending on the tides) will take you round the seabird colonies and stacks of Duncansby Head or the seal colonies of Stroma (mid-June to Aug daily; 1hr 30min; £14). North Coast Marine Adventures (ⓣ01955/611797, ⓦwww.northcoast-marine-adventures.co.uk) offer rather more high-adrenalin trips in a rigid inflatable, but only Mr Simpson (ⓣ01955/611394), who actually owns Stroma, will occasionally and on request take groups across to the island in his boat.

of the headland lie some spectacular 200ft cliffs, cut by sheer-sided clefts known locally as *geos*, and several impressive sea stacks, including a very photogenic triangular one.

The east coast

The **east coast** of the Highlands, between Inverness and Wick, is nowhere near as spectacular as the west, with gently undulating moors, grassland and low cliffs where you might otherwise expect to find sea lochs and mountains. Washed by the cold waters of the North Sea, it's markedly cooler, too, although less prone to spells of permadrizzle and midges.

While many visitors speed up the main A9 road through this region in a headlong rush to the Orkneys' prehistoric sites, those who choose to dally will find a wealth of brochs, cairns and standing stones, many in remarkable condition. The area around the Black Isle and the Tain was a Pictish heartland, and has yielded many important finds. Further north, from around the ninth century AD onwards, the **Norse** influence was more keenly felt than in any other part of mainland Britain, and dozens of Scandinavian-sounding names recall the era when this was a Viking kingdom.

Culturally and scenically, much of the east coast is more lowland than highland, and Caithness in particular evolved more or less separately from the Highlands, avoiding the bloody tribal feuds that wrought such havoc further south and west. Later, however, the nineteenth-century **Clearances** hit the region hard, as countless ruined cottages and empty glens show. To make way for sheep, hundreds of thousands of crofters were evicted and forced to emigrate to New Zealand, Canada and Australia, or else take up fishing in one of the numerous herring ports established on the coast. The fishing heritage is a recurring theme along this coast, though there are only a handful of working boats scattered around the harbours today, and while the oil boom has brought a transient prosperity to one or two places over the past few decades, the area remains one of the country's poorest, reliant on relatively thin pickings from sheep farming, fishing and tourism.

The one stretch of the east coast that's always been relatively rich is the **Black Isle** just over the Kessock Bridge heading north out of Inverness, whose main village, **Cromarty**, is the region's undisputed highlight, with a crop of elegant mansions and appealing fishermen's cottages clustered near the entrance to the Cromarty Firth. In late medieval times, pilgrims, including James IV of Scotland, poured through here en route to the red sandstone town of **Tain** to worship at the shrine of St Duthus, where the former sacred enclave has now been converted into one of the many "heritage centres" that punctuate the route north. Beyond **Dornoch**, a renowned golfing resort recently famous as the site of Madonna's wedding, the ersatz-Loire château **Dunrobin Castle** is the main tourist attraction, a monument as much to the iniquities of the Clearances as to the eccentricity of Victorian taste. The award-winning **Timespan Heritage Centre**, further north at Helmsdale, recounts the human cost of the landlords' greed, while the area around the port of **Lybster** is littered with the remains of more ancient civilizations. **Wick**, the largest town on this section of coast, has an interesting past inevitably entwined with the fishing industry, whose story is told in another good heritage centre, but is otherwise uninspiring. The relatively flat landscapes of this northeast corner – windswept peat bog and farmland dotted with lochans and grey-and-white crofts – are a surprising contrast to the more rugged country south and west of here.

The Black Isle and around

Sandwiched between the Cromarty Firth to the north and, to the south, the Moray and Beauly firths which separate it from Inverness, the **Black Isle** is not an island at all, but a fertile peninsula whose rolling hills, prosperous farms and stands of deciduous woodland make it more reminiscent of Dorset or Sussex than the Highlands. It probably gained its name because of its mild climate: there's rarely frost, which leaves the fields "black" all winter; another explanation is that the name derives from the Gaelic word for black, *dubh* – a possible corruption of St Duthus (see p.318).

The Black Isle is littered with dozens of **prehistoric sites**, but the main incentive to make the detour east from the A9 is to visit the picturesque eighteenth-century town of **Cromarty**, huddled at the northeast tip of the peninsula. A string of villages along the south coast is also worth stopping off in en route, and one of them, Rosemarkie, has an outstanding small **museum** devoted to Pictish culture. Nearby Chanonry Point is among the best **dolphin-spotting** sites in Europe.

The southern Black Isle

Just across the Kessock Bridge from Inverness is a roadside lay-by which hosts a **tourist office** (Easter–Oct Mon–Sat 10am–5pm, Sun 10am–4pm; July & Aug Mon–Sat until 6pm; ⓣ01463/731505), as well as a small **dolphin and seal centre** (June–Sept daily 9.30am–4.30pm; free), which offers the chance to observe (and listen to) these popular creatures.

The most rewarding approach to Cromarty is along the south side of the Black Isle on the A832, which passes a **clootie well** just north of Munlochy, where a colourful, if somewhat motley, collection of rags has been hung on overhanging branches to bring luck and health. Ailing children used to be left here alone overnight in hopes of a miracle cure. Just south of Munlochy, kids not yet abandoned by their parents will enjoy the Black Isle Wildlife and Country Park (April–Oct daily 10am–6pm; £4), while the simple farm steading premises of the nearby **Black Isle Brewery** produces tasty organic ales and lager (tours Mon–Sat 10am–6pm, April–Oct also Sun 11.30am–5.30pm; free).

Fortrose and Rosemarkie

FORTROSE, six miles east of Munlochy, is a quietly elegant village dominated by the beautiful ruins of an early thirteenth-century **cathedral** (daily 9am–8pm; free access). Founded by King David I, it now languishes on a lovely green bordered by red sandstone and colourwashed houses, where a hoard of gold coins dating from the time of Robert III was unearthed in 1880. There's also a memorial to the Seaforth family, whose demise the Brahan Seer famously predicted (see box on p.314).

There's a memorial plaque to the seer at nearby **Chanonry Point**, reached by a backroad from the north end of Fortrose; the thirteenth hole of the golf

The Brahan Seer

A memorial plaque in Fortrose remembers the seventeenth-century visionary **Cùinneach Odhar** (Kenneth MacKenzie), known as the Brahan Seer, who was born at Uig on Skye and lived and worked on the estate of the Count and Countess of Seaforth. Legend has it that he derived his powers of second sight from a small white divination stone passed on to him, through his mother, from a Viking princess. With the pebble pressed against his eye, Cùinneach foretold everything from outbreaks of measles in the village to the building of the Caledonian Canal, the Clearances and World War II. His visions brought him widespread fame, but also resulted in his untimely death. In 1660, Countess Seaforth, wife of the local laird, summoned the seer after her husband was late home from a trip to France. Reluctantly – when pressurized – he told the Countess that he had seen the earl "on his knees before a fair lady, his arm round her waist and her hand pressed to his lips". At this, she flew into a rage, accused him of sullying the family name and ordered him to be thrown head first into a barrel of boiling tar. However, just before the gruesome execution, which took place near Brahan Castle on Chanonry Point, Cùinneach made his last prediction: when a deaf and dumb earl inherited the estate, the Seaforth line would end. His prediction finally came true in 1815 when the last earl died.

course here marks the spot where he met his death. Jutting into a narrow channel in the Moray Firth (deepened to allow warships into the estuary during World War II), the point, fringed on one side by a beach of golden sand and shingle, is an excellent place to look for **dolphins** (see box on p.254). Come here when the tide is rising and you stand the best chance of spotting a couple leaping through the surf in search of fish brought to the surface by converging currents.

ROSEMARKIE, a lovely one-street village a mile north of Fortrose at the opposite (northwest) end of the beach, is thought to have been evangelized by St Boniface in the early eighth century. The cosy **Groam House Museum** (May–Sept Mon–Sat 10am–5pm, Sun 2–4.30pm; Oct–April Sat & Sun 2–4pm; free), at the bottom of the village, displays a bumper crop of intricately carved Pictish standing stones (among them the famous Rosemarkie Cross Slab), and shows an informative video highlighting Pictish sites in the region. A lovely mile-and-a-half **woodland walk**, along the banks of a sparkling burn to Fairy Glen, begins at the car park just beyond the village on the road to Cromarty. Good **bar food** in this area is available at the *Plough Inn*, just down the main street from the museum in Rosemarkie, or at *The Anderson* (Ⓣ01381/620236, Ⓦwww.theanderson.co.uk), a pleasantly individual hotel just around the corner from the cathedral in Fortrose.

Cromarty

An ancient legend recalls that the twin headlands flanking the entrance to the **Cromarty Firth**, known as The Sutors (from the Gaelic word for shoemaker), were once a pair of giant cobblers who used to protect the Black Isle from pirates. Nowadays, however, the only giants in the area are Nigg and Invergordon's colossal oil rigs, marooned in the estuary like metal monsters marching out to sea. Built and serviced here for the Forties oil field in the North Sea, they form a surreal counterpoint to the web of tiny streets and chocolate-box workers' cottages of **CROMARTY**, the Black Isle's main settlement. The town, an ancient ferry crossing-point on the pilgrimage trail to St Duthus's shrine in Tain, lost much of its trade during the nineteenth century to places served by the railway; a branch line to the town was begun but never completed. Although a royal burgh since the fourth century, Cromarty didn't became a prominent port until 1772 when the entrepreneurial local landlord, George Ross, founded a hemp mill here, fuelling a period of prosperity during which Cromarty acquired some of Scotland's finest Georgian houses; these, together with the terraced fishers' cottages of the nineteenth-century herring boom, have left the town with a wonderfully well-preserved concentration of Scottish domestic architecture.

To get a sense of Cromarty's past, wander through the town's pretty streets to the **museum** housed in the old **Courthouse** on Church Street (daily: April–Oct 10am–5pm; Nov–Dec noon–4pm; £3.50), which tells the history of the town using audiovisuals and animated figures, including one of Sir Thomas Urquhart, an eccentric local laird who traced his ancestry back to Adam and Eve, and reportedly died laughing on hearing of the restoration of Charles II. You are also issued with an audio handset and a map for a walking tour around the town. **Hugh Miller**, a nineteenth-century stonemason turned author, geologist, folklorist and Free Church campaigner, was born in Cromarty, and his **birthplace** (Easter–Sept daily noon–5pm; Oct Sun–Wed noon–5pm; NTS; £5), a modest thatched cottage on Church Street, has been restored to give an idea of what Cromarty must have been like in his day.

Aside from any formal sights, Cromarty is a pleasant place just to wander around, and there's an excellent **walk** out to the south Sutor stacks. You can pick up the path by leaving town on Miller Road, and turning right when the lane becomes "The Causeway". Follow this through the woods and past eighteenth-century Cromarty House until you reach the junction at Mains Farm; a left turn here takes you across open fields and through woods to the top of the headland, from where there are superb views across the Moray Firth. You can return via the beach and along Shore Street.

Dolphin- and other wildlife-spotting trips are offered locally by *Ecoventures* (Ⓣ01381/600323, Ⓦwww.ecoventures.co.uk), who blast out through

△ Hugh Miller's cottage

the Soutars to the Moray Firth in a powerful RIB. The tiny two-car Nigg–Cromarty **ferry** (June–Oct daily 8am–6.15pm), Scotland's smallest, also doubles up as a cruiser on Wednesday evenings in summer; you can catch it from the jetty near the lighthouse.

Practicalities

Nine **buses** a day run to Cromarty from Inverness (55min), returning from the car park at the bottom of Forsyth Place. During summer, **accommodation** is in short supply. Most upmarket is the traditional *Royal Hotel* (Ⓣ01381/600217, Ⓦwww.royalcromartyhotel.co.uk; ❹), down at the harbour, which has rather small but richly furnished rooms overlooking the Firth. For **B&B**, try one of the attractive old houses on Church Street, such as Mrs Robinson's at no. 7 (Ⓣ01381/600488; ❶), where you can also **rent bikes**. A little way out of the town in the direction of Dingwall, *Newfield B&B* (Ⓣ01381/610325, Ⓦwww.newfield-bb.co.uk; ❷) is also a pleasant option.

For something **to eat**, there are few more down-to-earth but satisfying restaurants in the Highlands than *Sutor Creek* at 21 Bank St (Ⓣ01381/600855, Ⓦwww.sutorcreek.co.uk; closed Mon–Wed in winter). A small but friendly place run as a local cooperative, it serves delicious fresh pizza cooked in a wood-fired oven, though the imaginative toppings (and the daily blackboard specials) are local and seasonal rather than conventionally Italian.

Dingwall and the Cromarty Firth

Most traffic nowadays takes the upgraded A9 north from Inverness, bypassing the small market town of **DINGWALL** (from the Norse *thing*, "parliament", and *vollr*, "field"), a royal burgh since 1226 and former port that was left high and dry when the river receded during the nineteenth century. Today, it has succumbed to the curse of British provincial towns and acquired an ugly business park and characterless pedestrian shopping street. Dingwall's only real claim to fame is that it was the birthplace of Macbeth, whose family occupied the now ruined castle on Castle Street. You're unlikely to want to hang around here for long – for somewhere pleasant to stay move on to Strathpeffer or push on north.

Northeast of Dingwall, the **Cromarty Firth** has always been recognized as a perfect natural harbour. During World War I it was a major **naval base**, and today its sheltered waters are used as a centre for repairing North Sea oil rigs. The A862 road from Dingwall rejoins the A9 just after the main road crosses the firth on a long causeway; a few miles further along, look out for the extraordinary edifice on the hill behind **EVANTON**. This is the **Fyrish Monument**, built by a certain Sir Hector Munro, partly to give employment to the area and partly to commemorate his own capture of the Indian town of Seringapatam in 1781 – hence the design, resembling an Indian gateway. If you want to get a close-up look, it's a tough two-hour walk through pine woods to the top. An easier, but no less dramatic walk from the village is to follow the Allt Graad river to the mile-long **Black Rock** gorge, an unexpected chasm which is a giddy 100ft deep in places but only 12–15ft wide. The best approach to the gorge is a half-hour walk along a track which leaves from *Black Rock Caravan Park*, set in a peaceful grassy glen, where there's also a simple but neat bunkhouse (Ⓣ01349/830917, Ⓦwww.blackrockscotland.co.uk).

Strathpeffer

STRATHPEFFER, a mannered and leafy Victorian spa town surrounded by wooded hills four miles west of Dingwall, is pleasant enough but does suffer from a high density of coach parties. During its heyday, this was a renowned European **health resort** reached by the tongue-twisting Strathpeffer Spa Express train from Aviemore. A recent face-lift has seen the town's attractive grand pavilion transformed into a performing arts centre, the Strathpeffer Pavilion (Ⓦwww.strathpefferpavilion.org) and the nearby **Pump Room** (March–Oct Mon–Sat 10am–6pm, Sun 2–5pm; £2), converted into a visitors' centre, where displays and videos tell the history of the resort and you can sample water from five different local wells which were supposed to treat all manner of ailments – most of today's visitors, however, find the sulphurous-smelling liquid more masochistic than medicinal.

Also making the most of the Victorian theme is the **Highland Museum of Childhood** (April–Oct Mon–Sat 10am–5pm, Sun 2–5pm; £2), located at the restored Victorian train station half a mile east of the main square. The museum looks at growing up in the Highlands, from home- and school-life to folklore and festivals, with some well-displayed photographs, display cabinets with toys and games and a colourful series of commissioned murals. In other parts of the station are a pleasant café and craft workshops.

Strathpeffer is within striking distance of the bleak **Ben Wyvis**, and so is also a popular base for walkers. One of the best hikes in the area is up the hill of Cnoc Mor, where the vitrified Iron Age hill fort of **Knock Farrel** affords superb panoramic views to the Cromarty Firth and the surrounding mountains.

Walks around Strathpeffer

Ordnance Survey Explorer map no. 437.

From the former youth hostel at the southern end of Strathpeffer, a two- to three-hour walk leads to the remains of a vitrified Iron Age fort at **Knock Farril**. The first part of the walk follows woodland trails; rather less than a mile further on, turn up onto the ridge above you and follow it in a northeasterly direction along the crest of the hill known as the Cat's Back. Past some fine old Scots pines, the trees begin to thin out, and as you reach the hill fort great views of the Cromarty Firth begin to show to the east. Before you get to the ridge, look out for the unusual **Touchstone Maze**, which was built as a local arts project in 1992 and includes around eighty stones set in circles representing the major rock types from around the Highlands. A path also leads directly to the maze from near the old train station in Strathpeffer. When you reach the fort, it is possible to pick up a minor road and continue along the ridge to Dingwall, from where there are buses back to Strathpeffer. A shorter route drops back down from Knock Farril to the main road and back to the village that way.

A little further out of the village, two miles north of Contin on the main A835 to Braemore, are the **Rogie Falls**. It's only a short walk from the car park to the spot where you can see the Black Water come frothing down a long stretch of rocks and mini-gorges, in one place plunging down a 25-foot drop. Salmon leap upriver in summer, particularly at the fish ladder built to offer an alternative route up the toughest of the rapids. A suspension bridge over the river leads to some waymarked forest trails – including a five-mile loop to **View Rock**, at a point only 160ft above sea-level but which has great views of the local area.

The most ambitious hike in this area is up **Ben Wyvis**, a huge mass of mountain clearly seen from Inverness. The high point is Glas Lethad Mor (3432ft), which means, rather prosaically, "Big Greenish-Grey Slope". The most common route is through Garbat Forest, leaving the road just south of Garbat itself, staying on the north bank of the Allt a'Bhealaich Mhoir stream to get onto the southwestern end of the long summit ridge at the minor peak of An Cabar.

Buses run regularly between Dingwall and Strathpeffer (11 daily Mon–Sat), dropping passengers in the square. **Tourist information** is available in the front section of the Pump Room (see p.317 for opening hours). The large **hotels** in the village are very popular with bus tours, so try one of the smaller places such as *Brunstane Lodge* (ⓣ01997/421261, ⓦwww.brunstanelodge.com; ❺); there's also **B&B** at the upmarket *Craigvar* (ⓣ01997/421622, ⓦwww.craigvar.com; ❹), which overlooks the square, or the hospitable and spacious *Dunraven Lodge* on Golf Course Road (ⓣ01997/421210, ⓦwww.dunravenlodge.co.uk; ❸). For **food**, cheap bar meals can be had at the *Strathpeffer Hotel*, while the *Richmond Hotel* offers similar fare. Anyone with a sweet tooth might enjoy paying a visit to *Mya* on Main Street, just across from the Pump Room, an attractive café (closed Sun & Mon) and artisan chocolate factory with a viewing window through to the production area where you can sometimes see the Belgian proprietor at work. There's also an excellent **bike** shop right on the Square, called *Square Wheels* (ⓣ01997/421000; closed Tues) which rents out bikes and offers good advice on some enjoyable local routes.

The Dornoch Firth and around

North of the Cromarty Firth, the hammer-shaped **Fearn peninsula** can still be approached from the south by the ancient ferry crossing from Cromarty to Nigg, though to the north the link is a more recent causeway over the **Dornoch Firth**, the inlet which marks the northern boundary of the peninsula. On the southern edge of the Dornoch Firth the A9 bypasses the quiet town of **Tain**, probably best known as the home of Glenmorangie whisky. Inland, at the head of the firth, there's not much to the village of **Bonar Bridge**, but fans of unusual hostels travel from far and wide to spend a night with the ghosts at the Duchess of Sutherland's imposing former home, **Carbisdale Castle**. Further inland, the rather lonely village of **Lairg** is a connection point between west and east coasts, with roads spearing through the glens from northwest Sutherland and the railway making a laboured detour in from the east coast. Back on the coast, on the north side of the Dornoch Firth, the neat town of **Dornoch** itself, long known for its impressive cathedral and well-manicured golf courses, found renewed fame in 2000 as the venue for an outbreak of Madonna-mania, when it hosted the pop star's wedding to Guy Ritchie.

Tain

The peninsula's largest settlement is **TAIN**, an attractive if old-fashioned small town of grand whisky-coloured sandstone buildings that was the birthplace of **St Duthus**, an eleventh-century missionary who inspired great devotion in the Middle Ages. His miracle-working relics were enshrined in a sanctuary here in the eleventh century, and in 1360 St Duthus Collegiate Church was built, visited annually by James IV, who usually arrived here fresh from the arms of his mistress, Janet Kennedy, whom he had conveniently installed in nearby Moray. A good place to get to grips with the peninsula's past is the **Tain Through Time** exhibition (April–Oct Mon–Sat 10am–5pm, July & Aug till 6pm; £3.50), which makes creative use of three old buildings around the church and graveyard, leading you round using an audio-guide. The ticket price also includes a walking tour of the town and neighbouring **museum** on Castle Brae (just off the High St), housing an interesting display of the much-sought-after work of the Tain silversmiths, along with mediocre archeological finds and clan memorabilia. There's not a great deal more to see in the centre of Tain, but check out the High Street's castellated eighteenth-century **Tolbooth**, with its stone turrets and old curfew bell. Tain's other main attraction is the **Glenmorangie whisky distillery** where the highly rated malt is produced (ⓣ01862/892477; shop Mon–Fri 9am–5pm, April–Oct also Sat 10am–4pm, June–Aug also Sun noon–4pm; tours Mon–Fri 10.30am–3.30pm, Sat 10.30am–2.30pm, Sun 12.30–2.30pm; £2.50 including discount voucher); it lies beside the A9 on the north side of town. Booking is recommended for the tours.

For **accommodation**, the *Carnegie Lodge Hotel* (ⓣ01862/894039, ⓦwww.carnegiehotel.co.uk; ❹) on Viewfield Road, tucked away behind a housing estate on the west side of the A9 from the main part of Tain, looks and feels a bit like a golf clubhouse but offers decent and reasonably priced rooms. The more modest *Golf View House* (ⓣ01862/892856, ⓦwww.golf-view.co.uk; Feb–Nov; ❸), three minutes' drive south of the town centre on Knockbreck Road, offers comfortable B&B, as does *Carringtons*, Morangie Road (ⓣ01862/892635, ⓦwww.stelogic.com/carringtons; ❷). The best option for **food** in Tain is the bistro at the *Carnegie Lodge Hotel*, while the *Royal Hotel* (ⓣ01862/892013; ❺), a lovely sandstone building at the western end of the main street, does reasonable bar food. There's a decent deli in town, Food Frenzi on Market Street, for lunchtime sandwiches or picnic fare.

Portmahomack

Unless you're making use of the Cromarty–Nigg ferry, not many people visit the Fearn peninsula to the east of Tain. It has a couple of delightful discoveries, however, including the green, windswept village of **PORTMAHOMACK**, which huddles around a curving sandy beach. On the edge of the village the **Tarbat Discovery Centre** (April & Oct daily 2–5pm; May–Sept daily 10am–5pm; Nov Fri & Sat 2–4pm; £3.50) deals with the archeology of the Picts in the area, and has many original and replica examples of sculpture. From Portmahomack, narrow roads run through fertile farmland to the gorse-covered point at **Tarbat Ness**, where there's a lighthouse – one of the highest in Britain. A good seven-mile **walk** starts here (2–3hr round trip): head south from Tarbat Ness for three miles, following the narrow passage between the foot of the cliffs and the foreshore, until you get to the hamlet of Rockfield. A path leads past a row of fishermen's cottages from here to Portmahomack, then joins the tarmac road running northeast back to the lighthouse. Further south on the peninsula there are impressive Pictish **standing stones** at Hilton and at Shandwick, while near Fearn village is the unexpectedly well-groomed factory shop for Anta (April–Dec Mon–Sat 9.30am–5.30pm, Sun 11am–5pm; ⓦwww.anta.co.uk; free), which sells attractive modern tweed and tartan fabrics, as well as pottery. There's a nice wee **café** inside.

In Portmahomack, the *Oystercatcher* on Main Street (ⓣ01862/871560, ⓦwww.the-oystercatcher.co.uk; closed Mon & Tues) is one of the **restaurant** highlights of this stretch of the east coast, serving a big selection of sumptuous seafood dishes. For **accommodation**, the *Oystercatcher* has a small double (❷) and a larger en-suite double (❺) above the restaurant, or try the *Caledonian Hotel* (ⓣ01862/871345, ⓦwww.caleyhotel.co.uk; ❹) further along Main Street with views out over the Dornoch Firth.

Bonar Bridge and around

Before the causeway was built across the Dornoch Firth, traffic heading along the coast used to skirt west around the estuary, crossing the Kyle of Sutherland at the village of **BONAR BRIDGE**. In the fourteenth and fifteenth centuries, the village harboured a large iron foundry. Ore was brought across the peat moors of the central Highlands from the west coast on sledges, and fuel for smelting came from the oak forest draped over the northern shores of the nearby kyle. However, James IV, passing through here on his way to Tain, was shocked to find the forest virtually clear-felled and ordered that oak saplings be planted in the gaps. Although now hemmed in by spruce plantations, the beautiful ancient woodland east of Bonar Bridge dates from this era.

Bonar Bridge has struggled since it was bypassed: there's little of note here other than the **bridge** itself, which has had three incarnations up to the present steel construction of 1973, all recalled on a stone plinth on the north side.

Carbisdale Castle

Towering high above the River Shin, three miles northwest of Bonar Bridge, the daunting neo-Gothic profile of **Carbisdale Castle** overlooks the Kyle of Sutherland, as well as the battlefield where the gallant Marquis of Montrose was defeated in 1650, finally forcing Charles II to accede to the Scots' demand for Presbyterianism. The castle was erected between 1906 and 1917 for the dowager Duchess of Sutherland, following a protracted family feud, during which the Duchess was found in contempt of court for destroying important documents pertinent to a legal case, and locked up in London's Holloway prison for six weeks. However, by way of compensation, a castle was built for the Duchess worthy of her rank. Designed in three distinct styles (to give the impression it was added to over a long period of time), Carbisdale was eventually acquired by a Norwegian shipping magnate in 1933, and finally gifted, along with its entire contents and estate, to the Scottish Youth Hostels Association, which has turned it into what must be one of the most opulent **hostels** in the world, full of white Italian marble sculptures, huge gilt-framed portraits, sweeping staircases and magnificent drawing rooms alongside standard facilities such as self-catering kitchens, games rooms, TV rooms and thirty dorms, including some recently upgraded four-bed family rooms (Ⓣ0870/004 1109, Ⓦwww.carbisdale.org; March–Oct), often booked out by groups. The best way to get here by public transport is to take a **train** to nearby Culrain station, which lies within easy walking distance of the castle. **Buses** from Inverness (3 daily; 1hr 30min) and Tain (4 daily; 25min) only stop at **Ardgay**, three miles south.

Croick Church

A mile or so southwest of Bonar Bridge, the scattered village of **ARDGAY** stands at the mouth of Strath Carron, a wooded river valley winding west into the heart of the Highlands. It's worth heading ten miles up the strath to **Croick Church**, which harbours one of Scotland's most poignant and emotive reminders of the Clearances. Huddled behind a brake of wind-bent trees, the graveyard surrounding the tiny grey chapel sheltered eighteen families (92 individuals) evicted from nearby Glen Calvie during the spring of 1845 to make way for flocks of Cheviot sheep, introduced by the Duke of Sutherland as a money earner. An evocative written record of the event is preserved on the diamond-shaped panes of the chapel windows, where the villagers scratched **graffiti memorials** still legible today: "Glen Calvie people was in the churchyard May 24th 1845", "Glen Calvie people the wicked generation", and "This place needs cleaning".

Lairg and around

North of Bonar Bridge, the A836 parallels the River Shin for eleven miles to **LAIRG** (Ⓦwww.lairghighlands.org.uk), a bleak and scattered settlement at the eastern end of lonely **Loch Shin**. On fine days, the vast wastes of heather and deergrass surrounding the village can be beautiful, but in the rain it can be a deeply depressing landscape. Lairg is predominantly a transport hub and the railhead for a huge area to the northwest; there's nothing much to see in town. The Ferrycroft Countryside Centre and **tourist office**, on the west side of the river (daily: April–Oct 10am–4pm; June–Aug 10am–5pm; ⓣ01549/402160), is friendly and helpful, and has a good free display on the woodlands and history of the area; it's also the starting point for forest walks and an archeological trail. There's a simple café with Internet access at the centre. Four miles south of Lairg, on the opposite side of the river – along the A836, then the B864 – the **Falls of Shin** is one of the best places in Scotland to see **salmon** leaping on their upstream migration; there's a viewing platform, and an overpriced café/shop by the car park catering to bus parties. Oddly enough, you'll find a few lines in the shop which have come direct from Harrods – the reason being that the owner of the London store, Mohammed al-Fayed, owns a grand Highland estate nearby. More prosaically, Lairg hosts an annual lamb sale every August, the biggest one-day livestock market in Europe, when sheep from all over the north of Scotland are bought and sold.

Lairg's train station is a mile south of town on the road to Bonar Bridge; buses stop right on the lochside. Should you want to **stay**, *Ambleside* B&B (ⓣ01549/402130; ❶) offers good views, as does the grander *Park House* (ⓣ01549/402208, ⓦwww.fishinscotland.net/parkhouse; ❸) on Station Road, overlooking Loch Shin, which is a welcoming spot if you're planning on doing some walking, fishing or cycling in the area. In Lairg, the best bet for **food** is the bar menu at the *Nip Inn*, next to the post office, though *Park House* serves meals to residents.

Dornoch

DORNOCH, a genteel and appealing town eight miles north of Tain, lies on a flattish headland overlooking the **Dornoch Firth**. Surrounded by sand dunes and blessed with an exceptionally sunny climate by Scottish standards, it's something of a middle-class holiday resort, with solid Edwardian hotels, trees and flowers in profusion, and miles of sandy beaches giving good views across the estuary to the Fearn peninsula. The town is also renowned for its championship **golf course**, Scotland's most northerly first-class course. Dornoch was the scene for Scotland's most prestigious rock'n'roll wedding of recent times, when Madonna married Guy Ritchie at nearby Skibo Castle and had her son baptized in Dornoch cathedral. *Skibo*, an exclusive, private hotel used as a hideaway of the world's rich and powerful, is just to the west of Dornoch. Only members of the hugely expensive Carnegie Club (ⓦwww.carnegieclub.co.uk) or their guests, however, will get anywhere near the place.

Dating from the twelfth century, Dornoch became a royal burgh in 1628. Among its oldest buildings, which are all grouped round the spacious square, the exquisite **cathedral** was founded in 1224 and built of local sandstone. The original building was horribly damaged by marauding Mackays in 1570, and much of what you see today was restored by the Countess of Sutherland in 1835, though her worst Victorian excesses were removed in the twentieth century, when the interior stonework was returned to its original state. The vaulted roof is particularly appealing; the stained-glass windows in the north wall were later additions, endowed by the expat Andrew Carnegie. Opposite, the fortified sixteenth-century **Bishop's Palace**, a fine example of vernacular architecture with stepped gables and towers, has been refurbished as a hotel (see below). Next door, the castellated **Old Town Jail** is home to a series of upmarket craft shops under the banner Jail Dornoch, while tucked in behind the *Castle Hotel* is the local **Historylinks Museum** (April & May Mon–Fri 10am–4pm; June–Sept daily 10am–4pm; £2), which tells the story of Dornoch, from local saints to the Madonna herself.

Practicalities

Local **tourist information** can be found beside the *Coffee Shop* in the cluster of buildings near the Cathedral (April–Sept daily 9.30am–5.30pm; Oct–March Mon–Sat 10am–5pm, Sun 11am–5pm), where there's also bike rental available. There's no shortage of **accommodation**: *Tordarroch B&B* (Ⓣ01862/810855; ❷; March–Oct) has a great location opposite the cathedral, as does the *Trevose* (Ⓣ01862/810269; ❷; March–Sept), which is swathed in roses. The characterful *Dornoch Castle Hotel* (Ⓣ01862/810216, Ⓦwww.dornochcastlehotel.com; ❺), in the Bishop's Palace on the Square, has a cosy old-style bar and relaxing tea garden. The *Caravan Park* (Ⓣ01862/810423, Ⓦwww.dornochcaravans.co.uk; April–Oct) is attractively set between the manicured golf course and the uncombed vegetation of the sand dunes which fringe the beach; it also offers **camping** although the site does get busy with caravans in July and August.

Expensive gourmet meals are available at the *2 Quail* **restaurant** (Ⓣ01862/811811; May–Sept Tues–Sat; Oct–April Thurs–Sat) on Castle Street, which also has tasteful rooms (❺); otherwise, try *Luigi's* on Castle Street, which is open during the day and in summer stays open into weekend evenings serving familiar but decent Italian-style snacks and meals.

North to Wick

North of Dornoch, the A9 hugs the coastline for most of the sixty or so miles to **Wick**, the principal settlement in the far north of the mainland. Perhaps the most important landmark in the whole stretch is the **Sutherland Monument** near Golspie, erected in memory of the first Duke of Sutherland, the landowner who oversaw the eviction of thousands of his tenants in a process known as the Clearances. The bitter memory of those times resonates through most of the small towns and villages on this stretch, including **Brora**, the gold-prospecting village of **Helmsdale**, **Dunbeath** and **Lybster**. With sites dotted around recalling Iron-Age settlers and Viking rule, many of these settlements also hark back to the days of a thriving fishing trade, none more so than the main town of Wick, once the busiest herring port in Europe.

Golspie and around

Ten miles north of Dornoch on the A9 lies the straggling red sandstone town of **GOLSPIE**, whose status as an administrative centre does little to relieve its dullness. It does, however, boast an eighteen-hole golf course and a sandy beach, while half a mile further up the coast, the **Big Burn** has several rapids and waterfalls that can be seen from an attractive **woodland trail** beginning at the *Sutherland Arms Hotel*.

Dunrobin Castle

The main reason to stop in Golspie is to look around **Dunrobin Castle** (April–May & early Oct Mon–Sat 10.30am–4.30pm, Sun noon–4.30pm; June–Sept daily 10.30am–5.30pm; £6.70), overlooking the sea a mile north of town.

Approached via a long tree-lined drive, this fairy-tale confection of turrets and pointed roofs – modelled by the architect Sir Charles Barry (designer of London's Houses of Parliament) on a Loire château – is the seat of the infamous Sutherland family, at one time Europe's biggest landowners, with a staggering 1.3 million acres, and the principal driving force behind the Clearances in this area. The castle is on a correspondingly vast scale, boasting 189 furnished rooms, of which the tour takes in only seventeen. Staring up at the pile from the midst of its elaborate **formal gardens**, it's worth remembering that such extravagance was paid for by uprooting literally thousands of crofters from the surrounding glens.

The castle's opulent **interior** is crammed full of fine furniture, paintings (including works by Landseer, Allan Ramsay and Sir Joshua Reynolds), tapestries and *objets d'art*. The attractive gardens are pleasant to wander around, and it's worth diverting through them to get to Dunrobin's unusual **museum**, housed in an eighteenth-century building at the edge of the garden. Inside, hundreds of disembodied animals' heads and horns peer down from the walls, alongside other more macabre appendages, from elephants' toes to rhinos' tails. Bagged mainly by the fifth Duke and Duchess of Sutherland, the trophies vie for space with other fascinating family memorabilia, including one of John O'Groat's bones, Chinese opium pipes and such curiosities as a "picnic gong from the South Pacific". Nearby, one corner of the gardens is home to various trained birds of prey; you can see them on their perches at any time or hang around for one of the flying falconry displays which take place three times daily.

Conveniently, the castle has its own **train** station on the main Inverness–Wick line; this is no surprise, really, as the duke built the railway.

The Sutherland Monument

Approaching Golspie, you can't miss the 100ft **monument** to the first Duke of Sutherland, which peers proprietorially down from the summit of the 1293ft **Beinn a'Bhragaidh** (Ben Bhraggie). An inscription cut into its base recalls that the statue was erected in 1834 by "a mourning and grateful tenantry [to] a judicious, kind and liberal landlord [who would] open his hands to the distress of the widow, the sick and the traveller". Unsurprisingly, there's no reference to the fact that the duke, widely regarded as Scotland's own Josef Stalin, forcibly evicted 15,000 crofters from his million-acre estate – a fact which, in the words of one local historian, makes the monument "a grotesque representation of the many forces that destroyed the Highlands". The campaign to have the statue smashed and scattered over the hillside has largely died down; the general attitude now seems to be that the statue now stands as a useful reminder of the duke's infamy as much as his achievements.

It's worth the stiff **climb** to the top of the hill (round trip 1hr 30min) for the wonderful views south along the coast past Dornoch to the Moray Firth and west towards Lairg and Loch Shin. The path is steep and strenuous in places, however, and there's no view until you're out of the trees, about twenty minutes from the top. Head up Fountain Road about half-way along Golspie's main street; after crossing the railway line and passing through Rhives farm steading, follow the Beinn a'Bhragaidh footpath (BBFP) signs along the path into the woods.

Loch Fleet and Rogart

Just to the south of Golspie, the A9 fringes a tidal estuary on a causeway that was constructed in 1816 by Thomas Telford. The inlet, **Loch Fleet**, is part of a large nature reserve (open access) harbouring some delicate coastal and woodland vegetation, including Britain's greatest concentration of one-flowered wintergreen, also known as St Olaf's candlestick, as well as a range of birdlife including greylag geese and arctic terns, and sealife such as seals and otters. You can walk in the reserve by following the minor road south out of Golspie for three miles; from Balblair Bay a path leads into pine-forested Balblair Wood, while from Littleferry there are walks along the coastal heathland to the Moray Firth beaches.

Four miles northwest of Loch Fleet on the A839 to Lairg is one of Scotland's most unusual and imaginative **hostels**, *Sleeperzzz.com* (Ⓣ01408/641343, Ⓦwww.sleeperzzz.com), where you can stay in one of two first-class railway carriages parked in a siding beside the station on the Inverness–Thurso line in the tiny settlement of **ROGART**. Each of the comfortable compartments has a bunk-bed on one side and the original seats on the other, while the two end compartments are used as a kitchen and common room. The owners have free **mountain bikes** available to let you explore the local countryside, and the place stands 100yd from a convivial local **pub**, the *Pittentrail Inn*, which serves warming evening meals. A small reduction is even offered to those arriving by train or bicycle.

Brora

BRORA, on the coast six miles north of Golspie, once boasted the only bridge in the region – hence the name, which means "River of the Bridge" in Norse. Until the 1960s, it was the only coal-mining village in the Highlands, having played host to the industry for four hundred years. These days, however, the small grey town holds little of interest, although as with all these towns the old harbour has a intriguing if rather woebegone feel to it. Three miles south of the town is the remarkably well-preserved Iron Age broch of **Carn Liath**, with great twelve-foot-thick walls and a number of obvious features intact, such as a staircase and entrance passage. The car park for the site is on the inland side of the A9, just before the broch if you're travelling north. A more interesting way to reach it is by walking along the coastal path which links Golspie and Brora. A mile or so north of town, the **Clynelish Distillery** (April–Sept Mon–Fri 10am–5pm; Oct 11am–4pm; Nov–March by appointment; £2; Ⓣ01408/623000), will give you a guided tour and a sample dram.

There are a couple of good **B&Bs** in the area. The *Selkie* (Ⓣ01408/621717, Ⓦwww.selkiebrora.co.uk; ❷; April–Oct), on Harbour Road, is superbly located where the river meets the sea – otters and seals are frequent sights from the garden. *Clynelish Farm* (Ⓣ01408/621265, Ⓦwww.scotland2000.com/clynelish; ❷; March–Oct) – turn left after the petrol station – is a working Victorian stone farmhouse with en-suite rooms, built to provide employment for dispossessed crofters after the Clearances. The rooms here are spacious, with views over the fields to the Moray Firth, and evening meals are available by arrangement. The best place to **eat** in Brora is *The Quiet Piggy* (Ⓣ01408/622011, Ⓦwww.thequietpiggy.com) on Station Square, which serves light, contemporary lunches and grander, expensive evening meals based around beef, fish and game.

Helmsdale and around

Eleven scenic miles north along the A9 from Golspie, **HELMSDALE** is an old herring port, founded in the nineteenth century to house the evicted inhabitants of Strath Kildonan, which lies behind it. Today, the main draw in the sleepy grey village is the attractively designed **Timespan Heritage Centre** beside the river (April–Oct Mon–Sat 10am–5pm, Sun noon–5pm; £4). It's an ambitious venture for a place of this size, telling the local story of Viking raids, witch-burning, Clearances, fishing and gold-prospecting through high-tech displays, sound effects and an audiovisual programme. The centre also has an art gallery and a plain café.

There's no official tourism office in town, but you'll pick up local information at Strath Ullie Crafts on the harbour. At the end of Dunrobin Street is the *Bridge Hotel* (ⓣ01431/821100, ⓦwww.bridgehotel.net; ❺), a pleasantly grand and comfortable **hotel** with big open fireplaces and mounted antlers lining the walls. There are several good-value **B&Bs**, including *Broomhill House* on Navidale Road (ⓣ01431/821259, ⓦwww.blancebroomhill.com; ❷), which has bedrooms in a turret added to the former croft by a miner who struck it lucky in the Kildonan gold rush (see below). Alternatively, try *Bayview* (ⓣ01431/821679, ⓦwww.bayview-helmsdale.org.uk; ❶), just south of Helmsdale at Portgower. There's also a small SYHA **youth hostel** (ⓣ0870/004 1124, ⓦwww.syha.org.uk; April–Sept), beside the A9 as it climbs north up from the harbour.

If you're looking for somewhere to **eat** in Helmsdale, your eye may well be drawn to the bizarre *Mirage* restaurant (ⓦwww.lamirage.org) on Dunrobin Street. The former proprietor of the *Mirage* became something of a local celebrity, modelling herself on the romantic novelist Barbara Cartland. The fittings and furnishings are suitably garish, complemented by framed photographs of visiting personalities covering the walls. There's a long menu, which includes large helpings of fish and chips. Immediately opposite, the *Wayfarer* offers a more conservative approach to bistro dining.

Baile an Or

From Helmsdale the single-track A897 runs up Strath Kildonan and across the Flow Country (see p.307) to the north coast, at first following the River Helmsdale, a strictly controlled and exclusive salmon river frequented by the Royal Family. Some eight miles up the Strath at **BAILE AN OR** (Gaelic for "goldfield"), gold was discovered in the bed of the Kildonan Burn in 1869; a **gold rush** ensued, hardly on the scale of the Yukon, but quite bizarre in the Scottish Highlands. A tiny amount of gold is still found by some hardy prospectors every year: should you fancy **gold-panning** yourself, you can rent the relevant equipment for £2.50 from Strath Ullie Crafts, which also sells a booklet with a few basic tips.

Dunbeath and around

Just north of Helmsdale, the A9 begins its long haul up the **Ord of Caithness**. This steep hill used to form a pretty impregnable obstacle, and the desolate road still gets blocked during winter snowstorms. Once over the pass, the landscape changes dramatically as heather-clad moors give way to miles of treeless green grazing lands, peppered with derelict crofts and latticed by long dry-stone walls. As you come over the pass, look out for signs to the ruined village of **Badbea**, reached via a ten-minute walk from the car park at the side of the A9. Built by tenants cleared from nearby Ousdale, the settlement now lies deserted, although its ruined hovels show what hardship the crofters had to endure: the cottages stood so near the windy cliff edge that children had to be tethered to prevent them from being blown into the sea.

DUNBEATH, hidden at the mouth of a small strath twelve miles north of Ord of Caithness, was another village founded to provide work in the wake of the Clearances. The local landlord built a harbour here in 1800, at the start of the herring boom, and the settlement briefly flourished. Today it's a sleepy place, with lobster pots stacked at the quayside and views of windswept Dunbeath Castle (no public access) on the opposite side of the bay. The novelist Neil Gunn was born here, in one of the terraced houses under the flyover that now swoops above the village; you can find out more about him at the **Dunbeath Heritage Centre** (April–Oct daily 10am–5pm; Nov–March Mon–Fri 11am–3pm; £2), signposted from the road. The staff can advise you on several good walks along the *Highland River* of Gunn's novel; his other famous book, *The Silver Darlings*, was also set on this coastline. The best of the handful of modest **B&Bs** here is *Tormore Farm* (ⓣ01593/731240; ❶; May–Oct), a large farmhouse with four comfortable rooms, half a mile north of the harbour on the A9.

Just north of Dunbeath is the simple but moving **Laidhay Croft Museum** (Easter–Oct daily 10am–6pm; £2), which offers a useful perspective on the sometimes over-romanticized life of the Highlander before the Clearances. A little further up the coast, the **Clan Gunn Heritage Centre and Museum** (June–Sept Mon–Sat 11am–1pm & 2–4pm; £2) is mainly a place for members of the Clan Gunn and its septs, although it also doles out a bit more local history and a few titbits for those on the trail of Neil Gunn.

Lybster and around

The final stretch of road before Wick gives great views out to sea to the oil rigs perched on the horizon. The spectacular series of green-topped cliffs and churning bays are gorgeous in the sun and impressively bleak in bad weather. The planned village of **LYBSTER** (pronounced "libe-ster"), established at the height of the nineteenth-century herring boom, once had two hundred-odd boats working out of its harbour: now there are just one or two. The **Water Lines** heritage centre by the harbour (May–Sept daily 11am–5pm; £2.50) is an attractive modern display about the "silver darlings" and the fishermen that pursued them; there's a snug café downstairs. There's not much else to see here apart from the harbour area; the upper town is a grim collection of grey pebble-dashed bungalows centred on a broad main street.

The **Grey Cairns of Camster**, seven miles due north and one of the most memorable sights on the northeast coast, are a different story. Surrounded by bleak moorland, these two enormous reconstructed prehistoric burial chambers, originally built four or five thousand years ago, were immaculately designed, with corbelled dry-stone roofs in their hidden chambers, which you can crawl into through narrow passageways. More extraordinary ancient remains lie at **East Clyth**, two miles north of Lybster on the A99, where a path leads to the "**Hill o'Many Stanes**". Some two hundred boulders stand in the ground here, forming 22 parallel rows that run north to south; no one has yet worked out what they were used for, although archeological studies have shown there were once six hundred stones in place. A fourteen-mile track waymarked as a cycle path leads between the two sites, entering the forest at a car park half a mile south of the Camster Cairns and emerging near the single-track road which passes the Hill o'Many Stanes and connects with the A99.

Another relatively unknown historic site in the area is the **Whaligoe staircase**, ten miles north of Lybster on the A99 at the north end of the village of Ulbster. The stairway, which has 365 steps constructed out of the distinctive local slab stone, leads steeply down from the side of the house beside the car park to a natural harbour surrounded by cliffs. At the bottom you'll see a few remnants of the harbour used by herring fishermen in the last century, as well as vast numbers of seabirds, including cormorants, skuas and puffins; the daunting climb back up is made a little bit easier by the thought that, unlike the women of Ulbster, you don't have a creel full of herring to carry all the way to the top. The stairway is steep and uneven for much of the way down, so be particularly careful if the steps are wet. To get to the stairway, turn off towards the sea at the junction signposted on its landward side to the "Cairn o'Get".

Wick

Originally a Viking settlement named *Vik* (meaning "bay"), **WICK** has been a royal burgh since 1589. It's actually two towns: Wick proper, and **Pultneytown**, immediately south across the river, a messy, rather run-down community planned by Thomas Telford in 1806 for the British Fisheries Society to encourage evicted crofters to take up fishing. Wick's heyday was in the mid-nineteenth century, when it was the busiest herring port in Europe, with a fleet of over 1100 boats, exporting tons of fish to Russia, Scandinavia and the West Indian slave plantations. Robert Louis Stevenson described it as "the meanest of man's towns, situated on the baldest of God's bays", and something of that down-at-heel atmosphere is apparent today. It's not somewhere you're likely to linger; if you're here for a few hours, the area around the harbour in Pultneytown, lined with rows of fishermen's cottages, is most worth a wander, with the acres of largely derelict net-mending sheds, stores and cooperages around the harbour giving some idea of the former scale of the fishing trade.

The town's story is told in the loyally maintained, but far from slick **Wick Heritage Centre** in Bank Row, Pultneytown (Easter–Oct Mon–Sat 10am–5pm; £2), which contains a fascinating array of artefacts from the old fishing days which verges on a jumble, including fully-rigged boats, original boat models, the old Noss Head lighthouse light and a great photographic collection dating from the 1880s. The other visitor attraction nearby is the fairly simple **Pulteney Distillery** (Mon–Fri 10am–1pm & 2pm–4pm; tours at 11am & 2pm or by arrangement ⓣ01955/602371; £3.50 includes discount voucher) on Huddart Street, a few blocks back from the sea. Much is made here of the maritime character of both the distillery and the whisky – the coopers who made barrels for the distillery, for example, also made them for storing cured herrings bound for Russia and Germany.

The **train** station and **bus** stops are next to each other immediately south and west of the bridge which crosses the Wick River in the centre of town. Frequent local buses run to Thurso and up the coast to John O'Groats. Wick also has an **airport** (ⓣ01955/602215), a couple of miles north of the town, with direct flights from Edinburgh and Aberdeen.

There's no tourist office. The best of the **hotels** is *Mackay's*, on the south side of the river in the town centre (ⓣ01955/602323, ⓦwww.mackayshotel.co.uk;

Walks and cycles around Wick

Ordnance Survey Explorer map no. 450.

There's a good **clifftop walk** to the dramatic fifteenth- to seventeenth-century ruins of **Sinclair** and **Girnigoe castles**, rising steeply from a needle-thin promontory three miles north of Wick, which functioned as a single stronghold for the earls of Caithness. In 1570 the fourth earl, suspecting his son of trying to murder him, imprisoned him in the dungeon here until he died of starvation. From the tiny fishing village of **Staxigoe**, head north from the harbour to Field of Noss farm and follow the line of the cliffs, where you'll encounter all sorts of seabirds, including puffins. At Noss Head lighthouse, head along the access road to a car park, where a path leads out to the castles on the north-facing coastline. **Cycling** is a good way to get to the castles: the roads near Noss Head are flat and straight, though you should think twice about setting off if the wind is too strong.

A longer ride (a fourteen-mile two-way trip) is along the backroads southwest of Wick through Newton Row and Tannach to the short archeological walking trail at the **Loch of Yarrows**, which includes remains of a lochside broch, a hilltop fort and chambered cairns.

❺), while reasonable **B&B** options include *Quayside*, 25 Harbour Quay (Ⓣ01955/603229, Ⓦwww.quaysidewick.co.uk; ❷), and *The Clachan*, 13 Randolph Place on South Road (Ⓣ01955/605384, Ⓦwww.theclachan.co.uk; ❷). Five miles towards Thurso is lovely *Bilbster House* (Ⓣ01955/621212, Ⓦwww.accommodation bilbster.com; ❷; April–Oct, in winter by arrangement).

Good **eating** options don't abound, though the moderately priced *Bord de l'Eau* (Ⓣ01955/604400; closed Mon) on Market Street, which runs along the north side of the river, offers a reasonable menu of classic French standards. Among the local **pubs**, try the *Alexander Bain* (named after the inventor of the fax machine, who lived locally) in Market Place, or the bar in *Mackay's Hotel*.

Travel details

Trains

Inverness to: Dingwall (Mon–Sat 7–8 daily, 2–4 on Sun; 25min); Helmsdale (Mon–Sat 3 daily, 1 on Sun; 2hr 20min); Kyle of Lochalsh (Mon–Sat 3–4 daily, 1–2 on Sun; 2hr 40min); Lairg (Mon–Sat 3–4 daily, 1–2 on Sun; 1hr 40min); Plockton (Mon–Sat 3–4 daily, 1–2 on Sun; 2hr 15min); Thurso (Mon–Sat 3 daily, 1 on Sun; 3hr 25min); Wick (Mon–Sat 3 daily, 1 on Sun; 3hr 45min).
Fort William to: Arisaig (Mon–Sat 4 daily, 1 on Sun; 1hr 10min); Glenfinnan (Mon–Sat 4 daily, 1 on Sun; 35min); Mallaig (Mon–Sat 4 daily, 1 on Sun; 1hr 25min).
Kyle of Lochalsh to: Dingwall (Mon–Sat 3–4 daily, 1–2 on Sun; 2hr); Inverness (Mon–Sat 3–4 daily, 1–2 on Sun; 2hr 40min); Plockton (Mon–Sat 3–4 daily, 1–2 on Sun; 15min).
Thurso to: Dingwall (Mon–Sat 3 daily, 1–2 on Sun; 3hr); Inverness (Mon–Sat 3 daily, 1–2 on Sun; 3hr 20min); Lairg (Mon–Sat 3 daily, 1–2 on Sun; 1hr 50min), Wick (Mon–Sat 3 daily, 1–2 on Sun; 35min).
Wick to: Dingwall (Mon–Sat 3 daily, 1–2 on Sun; 3hr 30min); Inverness (Mon–Sat 3 daily, 1–2 on Sun; 4hr); Lairg (Mon–Sat 3 daily, 1–2 on Sun; 2hr 20min).

Buses

Fort William to: Acharacle (Mon–Sat 2–3 daily; 1hr 30min); Inverness (6 daily; 2hr 15min); Kilchoan (1 daily; 3hr 35min); Mallaig (Mon–Fri 1 daily; 1hr 30min).
Gairloch to: Inverness (Mon–Sat 1 daily; 2hr 45min); Redpoint (Mon–Fri 1–2 daily during school term only; 1hr 35min).
Inverness to: Durness (Mon–Sat 1 daily, May–Sept only; 5hr); Thurso (Mon–Sat 5 daily, 4 on Sun; 3hr 35min); Wick (Mon–Sat 5 daily, 4 on Sun; 2hr 55min).
Kyle of Lochalsh to: Fort William (3 daily; 1hr 50min); Glasgow (3 daily; 5hr); Inverness (2 daily; 2hr).
Lochinver to: Inverness (Easter–Sept 1 daily; 3hr 10min); Ullapool (Mon–Sat 2 daily; 1hr).
Thurso to: Inverness (4–5 daily; 3hr 30min); John O' Groats (Mon–Fri 5 daily, 2 on Sat; 1hr); Wick (Mon–Fri hourly, Sat & Sun 6 daily; 35min).
Ullapool to: Durness (Mon–Sat 1 daily, Easter–Sept only; 3hr); Inverness (Mon–Sat 2–3 daily; 1hr 30min).
Wick to: John O' Groats (4 daily Mon–Sat; 50min).

Ferries

To Lewis: Ullapool–Stornoway (Mon–Sat 2 daily; 2hr 45min).
To Mull: Kilchoan–Tobermory (Mon–Sat 7 daily; June–Aug also Sun 5 daily; 35min); Lochaline–Fishnish (Mon–Sat every 50min, Sun hourly; 15min).
To Orkney: Gill's Bay–St Margaret's Hope (3 daily; 1hr); John O'Groats–Burwick (passengers only; 2–4 daily; 40min); Scrabster–Stromness (2–3 daily; 2hr).
To Skye: Glenelg–Kylerhea (daily frequently; 15min); Mallaig–Armadale (Mon–Sat 8–9 daily; mid-May to mid-Sept also Sun; 30min).
To the Small Isles: Mallaig to Eigg, Rùm, Mùck and Canna, see p.358.

Flights

Wick to: Edinburgh (Mon–Sat 1 daily; 1hr 10min); Inverness (Mon–Fri 2 daily; 35min); Kirkwall (Mon–Sat 1 daily; 25min).

5

Skye and the Small Isles

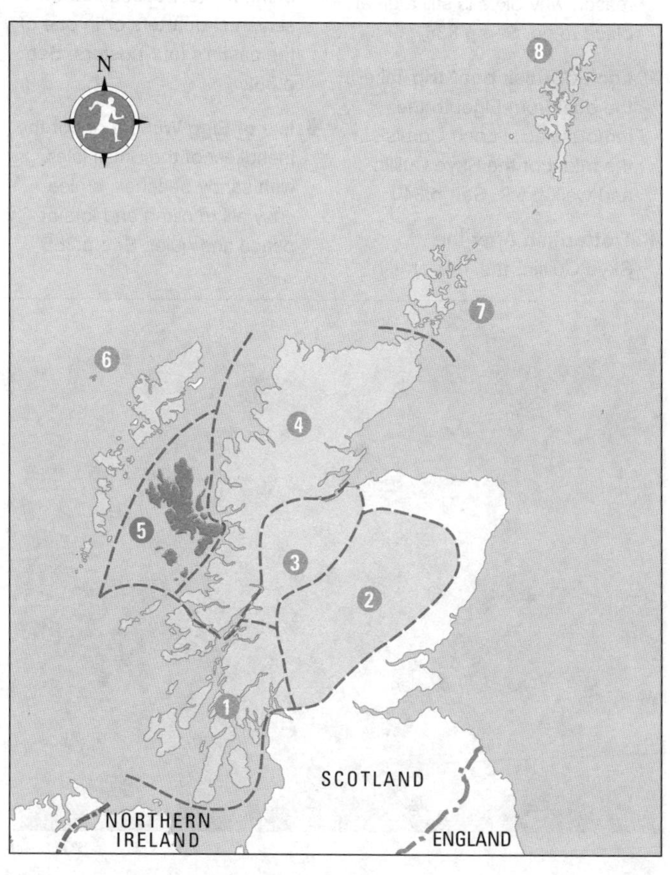

CHAPTER 5

Highlights

✱ **Isle of Raasay** Just off the coast of Skye, Raasay is well of the beaten track, yet offers a wide variety of outdoor pursuits from windsurfing to hill-walking. See p.337

✱ **Skye Cuillin** The jagged peaks of the Skye Cuillin are the real reason why Skye is still a great place to go. See p.338

✱ **Loch Coruisk boat trip** Take the boat from Elgol to the remote glacial Loch Coruisk in the midst of the Skye Cuillin, and walk back. See p.340

✱ **Trotternish** After the Skye Cuillin, the Trotternish peninsula is the most distinctive landscape on Skye, with its basalt intrusions and massive landslides. See p.347

✱ **Kinloch Castle, Isle of Rùm** Visit the outrageous Edwardian pile or, better still, stay in the hostel housed in the servants' quarters or in one of the castle's four-posters. See p.352

✱ **Isle of Eigg** Without doubt the friendliest of the Small Isles, with sandy beaches, a nice easy hill to climb and lots of peace and quiet. See p.355

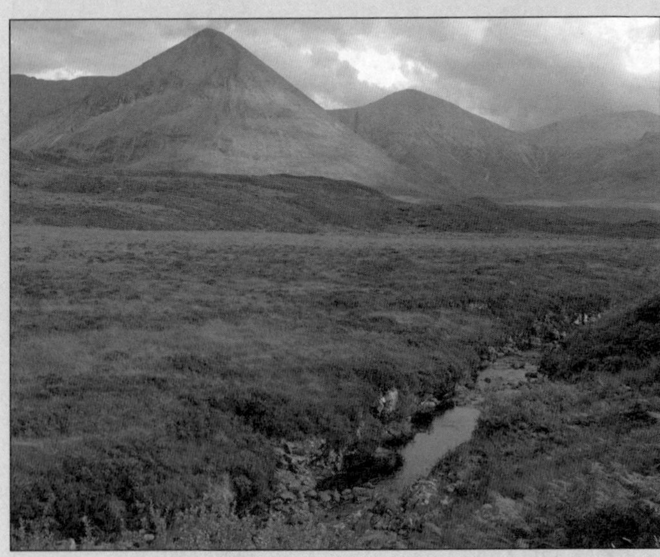

△ Skye Cuillin

5

Skye and the Small Isles

Some say the **Isle of Skye** (An t-Eilean Sgiathanach) was named after the Old Norse word for "cloud" (*skuy*), earning itself the Gaelic moniker *Eilean a Cheo* (Island of Mist). Yet, despite the unpredictability of the weather, tourism has been an important part of the island's economy for more than a hundred years, since the train line pushed through to Kyle of Lochalsh in the western Highlands in 1897. From here, it was the briefest of boat trips across to Skye, and the Edwardian bourgeoisie was soon swarming over to walk its mountains, whose beauty had been proclaimed by an earlier generation of Victorian climbers. Since the opening of the Skye Bridge, the island has been busier than ever, and at the height of the summer the road system often begins to bottleneck with coach tours, minibuses and caravans. Yet Skye is a deceptively large island, and you'll get the most out of it – and escape the worst of the crowds – if you take the time to explore the more remote parts of the island.

The Clearances saw an estimated 30,000 indigenous *Sgiathanachs* (pronounced "ski-anaks") emigrate in the mid-nineteenth century, leaving a population today of around 9000. Nevertheless, Skye remains the most important centre for **Gaelic culture** and language outside of the Western Isles. Over a third of the population is fluent in Gaelic, the Gaelic college on Sleat is the most important in Scotland, and the Free Church (see p.364) maintains a strong presence. Yet tourism is by far the island's biggest earner and has attracted several thousand "white settlers" over the last couple of decades. As an English-speaking visitor, it's as well to be aware of the tensions that exist between these two communities within this idyllic island, even if you never experience them firsthand. For a taste of the resurgence of Gaelic culture, try and get here in time for the Skye and Lochalsh Festival, *Feis an Eilein* (Ⓦwww.feisaneilein.com), which takes place over two weeks beginning in late July. A good way of finding out what's going on in the region is to read the weekly *West Highland Free Press*, a refreshingly vociferous campaigning newspaper published in Broadford.

One way to avoid the crowds on Skye is to head off to the so-called **Small Isles** – the improbably named **Rùm**, **Eigg**, **Muck** and **Canna** – to the south. Each with a population of far less than a hundred, they are easily accessible by ferry from Mallaig and Arisaig, though with limited accommodation available it's as well to do a bit of forward planning.

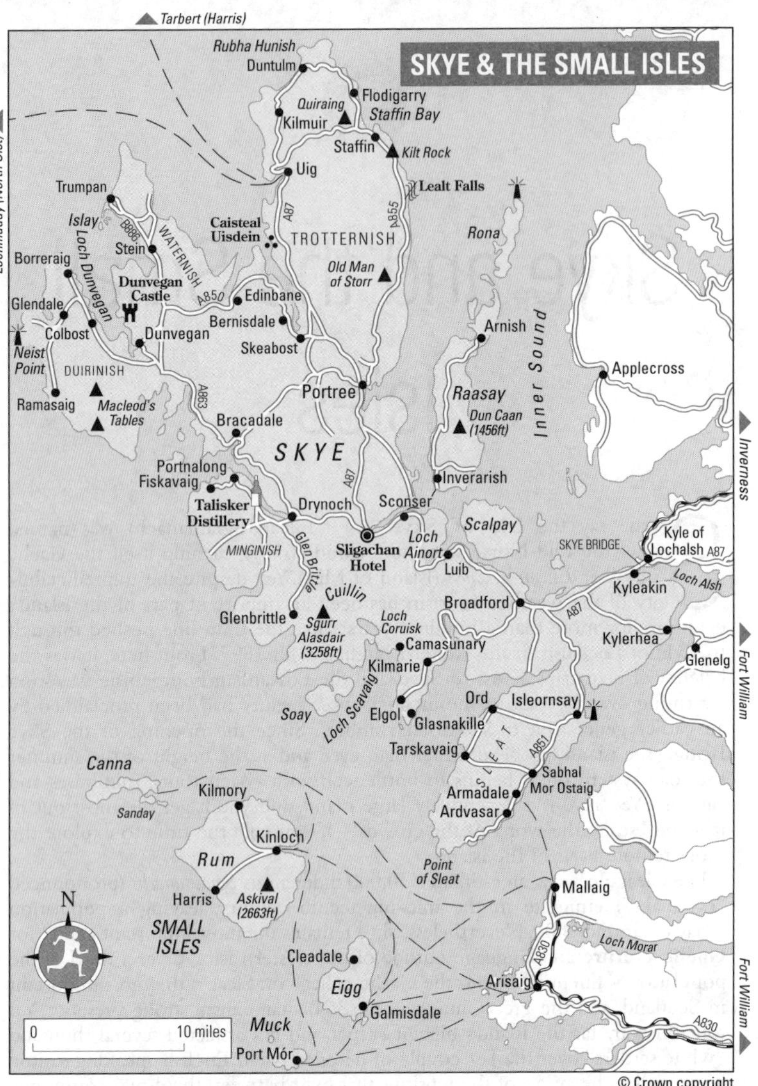

Skye

Jutting out from the mainland like a giant butterfly – *sgiath* means "winged" – the bare and bony promontories of **Skye** (ⓦwww.skye.co.uk) fringe a deeply indented coastline. The island's most popular destination is the **Cuillin** ridge, whose jagged peaks dominate the island during clear weather; to explore them at close quarters you'll need to be a fairly experienced and determined walker. More accessible and equally dramatic in their own way are the rock formations of the **Trotternish** peninsula, in the north, from which there are inspirational views across to the Western Isles. If you want to escape the summer crush, shuffle off to **Glendale** and the cliffs of Neist Point or head for the **Isle of Raasay**, off Skye's east coast. Of the two main settlements, Portree is the only one with any charm, and a useful base for exploring the Trotternish; however, neither Portree nor Broadford are practical as jumping-off points for the Cuillin, for which you need to head for Glenbrittle, Sligachan or Elgol.

Most visitors still reach Skye via Kyle of Lochalsh, linked with Inverness by train, and Kyleakin, on the eastern tip of the island, via the **Skye Bridge**. This southeast corner of Skye is relatively dull, and the more scenic approach is by **ferry** from **Mallaig**, further south on the Morar peninsula (see p.273). Linked by **train** with Glasgow, the Mallaig boat takes thirty minutes to cross to **Armadale**, on the gentle southern slopes of the **Sleat peninsula**. A third option is the privately operated **car ferry** which leaves the mainland at Glenelg, south of Kyle of Lochalsh, to arrive at **Kylerhea**, from where the road heads inland towards Portree. If you're carrying on to the Western Isles, be aware that it's 57 miles from Armadale and 49 miles from Kyleakin to Uig, at the opposite end of Skye, where ferries leave for Tarbert on Harris and Lochmaddy on North Uist.

Skye has several substantial **campsites**, and numerous **hostels** or bunkhouses – all of which recommend advance bookings, particularly in July and August – along with plenty of B&Bs and a string of pricey, but excellent **hotels**. Most visitors arrive by car, as the **bus** services, while adequate between the villages, peter out in the more remote areas, and virtually close down on Sundays.

Sleat

Ferry services (Mon–Sat 8–9 daily; mid-May to mid-Sept also Sun; 30min) from Mallaig connect with the **Sleat** (pronounced "slate") **peninsula**, Skye's southern tip, an uncharacteristically fertile area that has earned it the sobriquet "The Garden of Skye". The CalMac ferry terminal is at **ARMADALE** (Armadal), an elongated hamlet stretching along the wooded shoreline. If you've time to kill waiting for the ferry, take a look at the huge variety of Scottish and Irish knitwear on offer at Ragamuffin by the pier or, if you need a bite **to eat**, pop into the *Pasta Shed* next door, which does a great seafood pizza (eat-in or takeaway).

If you're leaving Skye on the early-morning ferry or you arrive late and need to stay near Armadale, your best bet is one of the **hostels** on the peninsula: Armadale SYHA **hostel** (Ⓣ0870/004 1103; April–Sept) is a convenient ten-minute walk up the A851 towards Broadford and has a good position overlooking the bay; the *Flora MacDonald Hostel* (Ⓣ0783/447 6378, Ⓦwww.isle-of-skye-tour-guide.co.uk), two miles further up the same road, beyond Sabhal Mòr Ostaig, is a converted barn with bunkbeds, family rooms and even B&B (❸); they will fetch you from the ferry. There are also two luxury options: a mile southwest to neighbouring Ardvasar, the traditional, whitewashed *Ardvasar Hotel* (Ⓣ01471/844223, Ⓦwww.ardvasarhotel.com; ❻) has a good restaurant specializing in local seafood, and six miles up the A851, overlooking Knock Bay, the *Toravaig House Hotel* (Ⓣ01471/833231, Ⓦwww.skyehotel.co.uk; ❻) has immaculate, stylish, en-suite rooms and a smart, pricey restaurant. **Bike rental** is available from the SYHA hostel or the local petrol station (Ⓣ01471/844249), close to the pier; **boat trips** operate from Armadale with Seafari Adventures (Ⓣ01471/833316, Ⓦwww.seafari.co.uk), who also have a shop on the pier; alternatively, you can go **horse riding** on Clydesdale and Shire horses with West Highland Heavy Horses (Ⓣ0776/958 8565, Ⓦwww.westhighlandheavyhorses.com).

A little further along the A851, past the youth hostel, you'll find one of the best tourist attractions on the island, the **Armadale Castle Gardens** (April–Oct daily 9.30am–5.30pm; £4.80; Ⓦwww.clandonald.com). Within the handsome forty-acre gardens lies the shell of the MacDonalds' neo-Gothic castle, a café and a library for those who want to chase up their ancestral Donald connections. The gardens' slick, purpose-built **Clan Donald Museum** has a good section on the Jacobite period and its aftermath, featuring a few Bonnie Prince Charlie objects and a couple of cannonballs fired at the castle by HMS *Dartmouth*, sent by William and Mary to shell the castle which "sent them scampering to the hills" (those who surrendered were hanged). There's also one or two top-notch works of art: a splendid portrait of a young, theatrical Glengarry (on whom Walter Scott modelled the hero of the Waverley novels) by Angelika Kauffman, and a portrait of his more conventional brother, MacDonell, by Raeburn.

A couple of miles up the road in an old MacDonald farm is the **Sabhal Mòr Ostaig** (Ⓣ01471/844373, Ⓦwww.smo.uhi.ac.uk), a modern Gaelic college of further education founded by Sir Iain Noble, an Edinburgh merchant banker, who owns a large chunk of the peninsula and is an untiring Gaelic enthusiast. The college is part of the University of the Highlands and Islands and runs a variety of extremely popular short courses in Gaelic language, music and culture, and longer full-time courses in Gaelic business, computing and media. If you're looking for a book and tape on beginners' Gaelic, the college bookshop has a good selection.

The loveliest part of the Sleat peninsula, by far, is the west coast: take the fiercely winding single-track road over to the scattered settlement of **TARSKAVAIG**, with its little sandy beach looking out over to the Small Isles. Further north along the coast, through some ancient deciduous woods, you come to **Tokavaig**, where a stony, seaweedy beach overlooked by the ruined Dunscaith Castle boasts views over the entire Cuillin range – this, and neighbouring **ORD**, with a pleasant sandy beach, are the two best places on the whole of Skye from which to view the mountains in fine weather.

Continuing northeast, it's another six miles to **ISLEORNSAY** (Eilean Iarmain), a secluded little village of whitewashed cottages that was once Skye's main fishing port. With the mountains of the mainland on the horizon, the views out across the bay are wonderful, overlooking a necklace of seaweed-encrusted rocks and the tidal **Isle of Ornsay**, which sports a trim lighthouse built by Robert Louis Stevenson's father. You can **stay** at another of Sir Iain Noble's enterprises, the mid-nineteenth-century *Isleornsay Hotel* – also known by its Gaelic name *Hotel Eilean Iarmain* – a pricey place with excellent service, whose **restaurant** serves great seafood (Ⓣ01471/833332, Ⓦwww.eilean-iarmain.com; ⑦); you could just have a good bar meal by an open fire. There are various enterprises based in Isleornsay, including Sir Iain's Gaelic whisky company, Pràban na Linne, which markets a number of unpronounceable Gaelic-named blended and single malt whiskies; the company offers tastings at its head office (phone Ⓣ01471/833496 for opening hours). Another couple of miles brings you to the turning for *Kinloch Lodge Hotel* (Ⓣ01471/833333, Ⓦwww.claire-macdonald.com; dinner, bed & breakfast only ⑧) and shop, centred on an old hunting lodge still in the possession of Lord Macdonald of Macdonald, with excellent food guaranteed by wife Claire whose cookery books are internationally famous. If you need to work off the calories, you can go **sea kayaking** with *Skyak Adventures* (Ⓣ01471/833428, Ⓦwww.skyakadventures.com), based at the bay to the south of Isleornsay.

Kyleakin and Kylerhea

The aforementioned Sir Iain Noble was also one of the leading advocates of (and investors in) the (now toll-free) **Skye Bridge**, which links the tidy hamlet of **KYLEAKIN** (Caol Acain – pronounced "ka*la*kin", with the stress on the second syllable) with the Kyle of Lochalsh (see p.276), just half a mile away on the mainland. Built in 1995 for a cool £30 million, the Skye Bridge was the most expensive toll bridge in Europe, and no cheaper than the ferry it replaced. Protests and non-payment eventually persuaded the Scottish Executive to buy out the firm (for £27 million) in 2004 and abolish the tolls. Strictly speaking there are, in fact, two bridges with an island in the middle, **Eilean Bàn**, whose lighthouse cottages were once the home of author and naturalist Gavin Maxwell. One of the houses is now a museum, and can be visited, along with the lighthouse, on a guided tour (£6); numbers are limited and must be booked in advance through the **Bright Water Visitor Centre** in Kyleakin (April–Oct Mon–Fri 10am–5pm; free; ⓣ01599/530040, ⓦwww.eileanban.org). The centre itself is well worth a visit, as it's full of hands-on things for kids of all ages.

The other sight in Kyleakin is the scant remains of **Castle Moil**, a fourteenth-century keep poking out into the straits on top of a diminutive rocky knoll, which looks romantic when floodlit. One of its earliest inhabitants, an entrepreneurial Norwegian princess married to a MacDonald chief, hung a chain across the water and exacted a toll from every passing boat. With its ferry now defunct, Kyleakin has reinvented itself as something of a backpackers' hangout – to the consternation of some villagers (in summer, the population more than doubles). If you're looking for a party atmosphere, then head for *Saucy Mary's* (ⓣ01599/534845, ⓦwww.saucymarys.com), a **pub and hostel** where there's often live music until the early hours; alternatively, snuggle down at the cosy *Dun Caan Hostel* (ⓣ01599/534087, ⓦwww.skyerover.co.uk), or nearby *Skye Backpackers* (ⓣ01599/534510, ⓦwww.scotlands-top-hostels.com), part of the MacBackpackers' circuit of hostels; there's also an SYHA hostel (ⓣ0870/004 1134) in an ugly, modern building a couple of hundred yards from the old pier. **Bike rental** is available from *Dun Caan* and Skye Bikes (ⓣ01599/534795) on the pier.

You can still go "over the sea to Skye" by taking the small **car ferry** (Easter to mid-May Mon–Sat 9am–5.45pm; mid-May to Aug Mon–Sat 9am–7.45pm, Sun 10am–5.45pm; Sept Mon–Sat 9am–5.45pm Sun 10am–5.45pm; ⓣ01599/511302, ⓦwww.skyeferry.co.uk) which sets off every quarter or half hour from Glenelg and takes just five minutes to reach **KYLERHEA** (pronounced "kile-ray"), a peaceful little place some four miles down the coast from Kyleakin. From here you can walk half an hour up the coast to the Forestry Commission **Otter Hide**, where, if you're lucky, you may be able to spot one of these elusive creatures.

Broadford

Heading west out of Kyleakin or Kylerhea brings you eventually to the island's second-largest village, charmless **BROADFORD** (An t-Ath Leathann), whose mile-long main street curves round a wide bay. Despite its rather unlovely appearance, Broadford makes a useful base for exploring the southern half of Skye, and has one of the island's best wet-weather retreats, the unusual **Skye Serpentarium** (Easter–Oct Mon–Sat 10am–5pm; July & Aug daily; £2.50; ⓦwww.skyeserpentarium.org.uk), housed in an old mill by the main road heading east out of town. There are over fifty animals on display, all of them abandoned or rescued, ranging from tiny tree frogs to large iguanas and there's usually a snake you can handle. Another popular activity in Broadford is to take a **boat trip** either on *Family's Pride II* (Ⓣ0800/783 2175, Ⓦwww.glassbottomboat.co.uk), a glass-bottomed boat, or in a RIB, both of which set off from Broadford pier.

Broadford's **tourist office** (Easter–Oct Mon–Fri 9.30am–5pm; June–Aug Mon–Fri 9.30am–5pm, Sat & Sun 9.30am–4pm; Ⓣ01471/822713) is by the 24-hour garage on the main road, where there's a laundry, small shop and bureau de change. At the west end of the village there's a bank, a bakery, a tearoom and a post office. The SYHA **hostel** is on the west shore of Broadford Bay (Ⓣ0870/004 1106; March–Oct). Two **B&Bs** which stand out are the delightful old croft-house *Lime Stone Cottage*, 4 Lime Park (Ⓣ01471/822142, Ⓦwww.limestonecottage.co.uk; ❸), near the Serpentarium, and the modern, comfortable *Ptarmigan* (Ⓣ01471/822744, Ⓦwww.ptarmigan-cottage.com; ❸), on the main road, with views over the bay. If you want a bite **to eat**, try the justifiably popular *Creelers Seafood Restaurant* (Ⓣ01471/822281, Ⓦwww.skye-seafood-restaurant.co.uk) at the south end of the bay, which also does takeaway round the back. For top-notch French seafood, head for the award-winning *Rendezvous* on the main road at Breakish (booking advisable, on Ⓣ01471/822001), a mile or so east of Broadford. **Bike rental** is available from the SYHA hostel or from *Fairwinds*, (Ⓣ01471/822270), just past the *Broadford Hotel*.

Scalpay and The Braes

The A87 from Broadford to Portree continues to hug the coast for the next ten miles, giving out views across Loch na Cairidh to the **Isle of Scalpay**, a huge heather-backed lump that looks something like a giant scone, rising to 1298ft at the peak of Mullach na Carn. The island is part red-deer farm, part forestry plantation, and is currently owned by a merchant banker. Close by the boat slip in **ARD DORCH** that serves Scalpay is *The Picture House* (Ⓣ01471/822531, Ⓦwww.skyepicturehouse.co.uk; ❷), a **B&B** with stunning views of the Inner Sound, which doubles as a photographic gallery (not a cinema as you might think).

From the head of Loch Ainort, the main road takes a steep short cut across a pass to Loch Sligachan, while a prettier, minor road meanders round the coast – either way, you'll reach **SCONSER**, departure point for the car ferry to Raasay (see below), and home to a nine-hole **golf course**, with superb views. There's a good **B&B** here by the shore in a modern croft house, *Loch Aluinn* (Ⓣ01478/650288; March–Oct; ❸).

On the opposite side of Loch Sligachan are the crofting communities of **The Braes**, whose inhabitants staged a successful rent strike in 1881 against their landlords, the MacDonalds. After eviction summonses were burnt by the crofters, a detachment of fifty Glasgow policemen were drafted in and took part in a "battle", which aroused a great deal of publicity for the crofters' cause (for more on which, see p.343).

Isle of Raasay

I will wait for the birch wood
Until it comes up by the cairn,
Until the whole ridge from Beinn na Lice
Will be under its shade.

If it does not, I will go down to Hallaig,
To the Sabbath of the dead,

When the people are frequenting,
Every single generation gone.

They are still in Hallaig,
MacLeans and MacLeods,
All who were there in the time of Mac Gille Chaluim
The dead have been seen alive.

The men lying on the green
At the end of every house that was,
The girls a wood of birches,
Straight their backs, bent their heads.

from *Hallaig* by Sorley MacLean

Despite lying less than a mile offshore, the long, hilly island of **Raasay** sees surprisingly few visitors. For much of its history, Raasay was the property of a branch of the staunchly Jacobite MacLeods of Lewis, and the island sent 100 men and 26 pipers to Culloden, as a consequence of which it was practically destroyed by government troops in the aftermath of the 1745 uprising. Bonnie Prince Charlie spent a miserable night in a "mean low hut" on Raasay during his flight and swore to replace the burnt turf cottages with proper stone houses (he never did). When the MacLeods were finally forced to sell up in 1843, the Clearances started in earnest, a period of the island's history immortalized in verse by Raasay poet Sorley MacLean (Somhairle MacGill Eathain). In 1921, seven ex-servicemen and their families from the neighbouring isle of **Rona** (see box, p.338) illegally squatted crofts on Raasay, and were imprisoned, causing a public outcry. As a result, both islands were bought by the government the following year. Rona now has one permanent resident while Raasay's population stands at around two hundred, many of them members of the Free Presbyterian Church (see p.364). Strict observance of the Sabbath is the most obvious manifestation for visitors, who should respect the islanders' feelings.

The ferry docks at the southern tip of the island, an easy fifteen-minute walk from **INVERARISH**, a tiny village set within thick woods on the island's southwest coast. If your time is limited there are several walks in these woods: you can follow the miners' trail, which traces the route of the railway constructed to carry iron ore to the jetty, built by German POWs in 1914. The grand Georgian mansion of **Raasay House** (now an outdoor centre) was built by the MacLeods in the late 1740s, to be all but ruined by government troops a few years later. The grounds slope down to a tiny **harbour**, overlooked by two weathered stone mermaids stuck on top of the remains of a battery armed in the Napoleonic era with several cannons. The house's stable clock stopped on the day in 1914 when 36 men of Raasay went to war – only 14 returned. Also in the grounds, there are Pictish symbol stones and the charming ruined thirteenth-century Chapel of St Moluag.

The interior of Raasay is starkly barren, a rugged and rocky terrain of sandstone in the south and gneiss in the north, with the most obvious feature being the curiously truncated basalt cap on top of **Dun Caan** (1456ft), where Boswell "danced a Highland dance" on his visit to the island with Dr Johnson in 1773 – you may feel like doing the same if you're rewarded with a clear view over to the Cuillin and the Outer Hebrides. The trail to the top of the peak is fairly easy to follow, a splendid five-mile trek up through the forest and along the burn behind Inverarish. The quickest return is made down the northwest slope of Dun Caan, but – by going a couple of miles further – you can get back to the ferry along the path by the southeast shore, passing the abandoned crofters'

Isle of Rona

To the north of Raasay is the **Isle of Rona** (Ⓦwww.isleofrona.com) – sometimes called South Rona to distinguish it from North Rona (see p.376) – ancestral home of the family of Billy Graham, the American evangelist. Uninhabited, apart from its lighthouse keepers and NATO personnel, since 1943, only Rona Lodge, above the sheltered harbour of Acairseid Mhór, is permanently inhabited. However, if you can reach the island, there is **accommodation**: you can camp with permission, there's a bunkhouse, two self-catering cottages, and you can even get dinner, bed and breakfast at Rona Lodge (Ⓣ0777/559 3055). The only regular **ferry** is a boat that occasionally comes over from Portree (Wed & Sat 2pm; Ⓣ0779/874 3858).

village of Hallaig, whose steep incline led mothers to tether their children to stakes to prevent them rolling onto the shore.

If you want to explore the north of the island you need a fine day to appreciate the views across to the Skye Cuillin, Portree and the Trotternish peninsula. Where the road dips to the east coast the stark remains of fifteenth-century **Brochel Castle** stand overlooking the shore. The last two miles of the road to Arnish is known as **Calum's Road**: in the 1960s the council refused to extend the road to the village, so Calum MacLeod decided to build it himself. It took him ten years, and by the time he'd finished he and his wife were the only people left in the village. You can walk on a boggy path to the north end and on to **Eilean Tigh** at low tide, or there's a shorter walk on to **Eilean Fladday**, which is also tidal. Raasay is rich in flora and fauna, and it's at the north end that you're more likely to see a golden eagle, snipe, orchids and perhaps the unique Raasay vole.

Practicalities

The CalMac **car ferry** departs for Raasay from Sconser (Mon–Sat 9–11 daily, Sun 2 daily; 15min). Many visitors go for the day, since there's plenty to do within walking distance of the pier – if you do take a car, be warned, as there's no petrol on the island. Comfortable **accommodation** in pleasantly casual rooms is available at the *Raasay Outdoor Centre* (Ⓣ01478/660266, Ⓦwww.raasay-house.co.uk; ❶), where Boswell and Johnson stayed; there is also a café, open to all, with live music in the evenings. You can also **camp** in the grounds or stay in the bunkhouse, and they'll happily collect you from the ferry terminal. In addition, you can join in the centre's activity programme (£12–65): anything from sailing, windsurfing and canoeing, to climbing and hill walking to suit all ages. Close by is the welcoming *Isle of Raasay Hotel* (Ⓣ01478/660222, Ⓦwww.isleofraasayhotel.co.uk; ❹), which serves traditional Scottish food and where the view of the Cuillin surpasses any other. A rough track cuts up the steep hillside from the village to Raasay's isolated but beautifully placed SYHA **hostel** (Ⓣ0870/004 1146; May–Sept).

The Cuillin and the Red Hills

For many people, the **Cuillin**, whose sharp snowcapped peaks rise mirage-like from the flatness of the surrounding terrain, are Skye's *raison d'être*. When the clouds finally disperse, they are the dominating feature of the island, visible from every other peninsula on Skye. There are basically three approaches to the Cuillin: from the south, by foot or by boat from Elgol; from the *Sligachan Hotel* to the north; or from Glen Brittle to the west of the mountains. Glen Sligachan is one of the most popular routes, dividing as it does the granite of the round-topped **Red Hills** (sometimes known as the Red Cuillin) to the east from the dark, coarse-grained jagged-edged gabbro of the real Cuillin (also known as the Black Cuillin) to the west. With some twenty Munros between them, these are mountains to be taken seriously, and many routes through the Cuillin are for experienced climbers only (for more on safety, see p.59).

Elgol, Loch Coruisk and Glen Sligachan

The road to **ELGOL** (Ealaghol), fourteen miles southwest of Broadford at the tip of the Strathaird peninsula, is one of the most dramatic on the island, leading right into the heart of the Red Hills and then down a precipitous slope, with a stunning view from the top down to Elgol pier. On the way you pass the ruins of a pre-Reformation church and graveyard at Kilchrist, where there are also traces of marble quarries which flourished for a while, employing Belgian experts and running the marble on a small railway to Broadford pier. Further down the road at Torrin you'll see the modern quarry with its white gleaming gash in the hillside; the brilliance of the stone has been compared favourably with Carrara, but it is too hard to work and mostly graces local driveways as chippings.

Walking in the Cuillin

Ordnance Survey Explorer map no. 411.

For many walkers and climbers, there's nowhere in Britain to beat the **Cuillin**. The main ridge is just eight miles long, but with its immediate neighbours it is made up of over thirty peaks, including twelve Munros. Those intent on doing a complete traverse of the Cuillin ridge usually start at Gars-bheinn, at the southeastern tip, and finish off at Sgurr nan Gillean (3167ft), descending on the famous *Sligachan Hotel* for a well-earned pint. The entire journey takes a minimum of sixteen hours, which either means a very long day, or two days and a bivouac. A period of settled weather is pretty much essential, and only experienced walkers and climbers should attempt it. Before setting out on any of the walks below, you should not only take note of all the usual safety precautions (see p.59), but should also be aware of the fact that **compasses** are unreliable in the Cuillin, due to the magnetic nature of the rocks. If you want to hire a guide, or take a course in mountain climbing and walking, contact Skye Guides (Ⓣ01471/822116, Ⓦwww.skyeguides.co.uk).

If you're based in Glenbrittle, and simply want to bag one or two of the peaks, there are several corries that provide relatively straightforward approaches to the most central Munros. From the SYHA hostel, a path heads west along the southern bank of the stream that tumbles down from the **Coire a' Ghreadaidh**. From the corrie, you can climb up to An Dorus, the most obvious gap in the ridge ahead, from which you can either ascend Sgurr a' Mhadaidh (3012ft), to the north, or Sgurr a' Ghreadaidh (3192ft). Alternatively, before you reach Coire a' Ghreadaidh, you can head south to the **Coir' an Eich**, from which you can easily climb Sgurr na Banachdich (3166ft) via its western ridge. To the south of the youth hostel, the road crosses another stream, with another path along its southern banks. This path heads west past the impressive Eas Mór (Great Waterfall), before heading up to the **Coire na Banachdich**. The pass above the corrie is the main one over to Loch Coruisk, but also gives access to Sgurr Dearg, best known for its great view of the Inaccessible Pinnacle (3235ft), Scotland's most difficult Munro to conquer, since it requires considerable rock-climbing skills. Back at Eas Mór, paths head off for **Coire Lagan**, by far the most popular corrie thanks to its steep sides and tiny lochan. A laborious slog up the Great Stone Chute is the easiest approach if you want to reach the top of Sgurr Alasdair (3258ft).

The chief reason for visiting Elgol is, weather permitting, to take a boat across Loch Scavaig (March–Sept 2 daily; £20–30 return), past a seal colony, to a jetty near the entrance of **Loch Coruisk** (from *coire uish*, "cauldron of water"). An isolated, glacial loch, this needle-like shaft of water, nearly two miles long but only a couple of hundred yards wide, lies in the shadow of the highest peaks of the Black Cuillin, a wonderfully overpowering landscape.

The journey by sea takes forty-five minutes and passengers are dropped to spend about one and a half (or six and a half) hours ashore. It's essential to book ahead online or over the phone between 7.30am to 10am (Ⓣ0800/731 3089, Ⓦwww.bellajane.co.uk); RIB trips are also offered to the Small Isles. Walkers can use the boat on a one-way trip (£15) simply to get to Loch Coruisk, from where there are numerous possibilities for hiking amidst the Red Hills, the most popular (and gentle) of which is the eight-mile trek north over the pass into **Glen Sligachan**. Alternatively, you could walk round the coast to the sandy bay of **Camasunary**, over two miles to the east – a difficult walk that involves a tricky river crossing and negotiating "The Bad Step", an overhanging rock with a thirty-foot drop to the sea – and either head north to Glen Sligachan, continue south three miles along the coast to Elgol or continue east to the Am Mam shoulder, for a stunning view of mountains and the islands of Soay, Rùm and Canna. From Am Mam, the path leads down to the Elgol road, joining it at Kilmarie.

The only public transport is the **postbus** from Broadford (Mon–Fri 2 daily, 1 on Sat), which delivers the post en route and takes over two hours to reach Elgol in the morning. If you want a bite to eat, there's a coffee shop, or the excellent seafood **restaurant** in *Coruisk House* (Ⓣ01471/866330, Ⓦwww.seafood-skye.co.uk; April–Oct; ⑤), which also offers **B&B** in its bright and cheerful rooms If you don't want to stay in Elgol, head for *Rowan Cottage* (Ⓣ01471/866287, Ⓦwww.rowancottage-skye.co.uk; March–Oct; ④), a lovely **B&B** a mile or so east in Glasnakille.

By far the most popular place to stay, though, is the **campsite** (April–Oct) by the *Sligachan Hotel* (Ⓣ01478/650204, Ⓦwww.sligachan.co.uk; ⑤) on the A87, at the northern end of Glen Sligachan; the hotel also has a **bunkhouse**. Its huge *Seamus Bar* serves food for weary walkers until 11pm, and quenches their thirst with its own real ales, and often has live bands; there's also a more formal restaurant with splendid food.

Glen Brittle

Six miles along the A863 to Dunvegan from the *Sligachan Hotel*, a turning signed "Carbost and Portnalong" quickly leads to the entrance to stony **Glen Brittle**, edging the most spectacular peaks of the Cuillin; at the end of the glen, idyllically situated by the sea, is the village of **GLENBRITTLE**. Climbers and serious walkers tend to congregate at the SYHA **hostel** (Ⓣ0870/004 1121; April–Sept) or the beautifully situated **campsite** (Ⓣ01478/640404, Ⓦwww.dunvegancastle.com; April–Oct), a mile or so further south behind the wide sandy beach at the foot of the glen. From mid-May to September, two buses a day (Mon–Sat only) from Portree make it to Glenbrittle; both the hostel and the campsite have grocery stores, the only ones for miles.

From the valley a score of difficult and strenuous trails lead east into the **Black Cuillin**, a rough semicircle of peaks rising to about 3000ft, which surround Loch Coruisk. One of the easiest walks is the five-mile round-trip from the campsite up **Coire Lagan**, to a crystal-cold lochan squeezed in among the sternest of rockfaces. Above the lochan is Skye's highest peak, **Sgurr Alasdair** (3258ft), one of the more difficult Munros, while Sgurr na Banachdich

(3166ft) is considered the most easily accessible Munro in the Cuillin (for the usual walking safety precautions, see p.59). The Mountain Rescue Service has produced a book of walks for those who are not climbers, available locally.

Minginish

If the Cuillin has disappeared into the mist for the day, you could while away an afternoon exploring the nearby **Minginish** peninsula, to the north of Glen Brittle. One wet-weather activity is to visit the **Talisker whisky distillery** (Mon-Sat 9.30am–5pm; ⓣ01478/614308), which produces a very smoky, peaty single malt. The island's only distillery, Talisker is situated on the shores of Loch Harport at **CARBOST** (and not, confusingly, at the village of Talisker itself, which lies on the west coast of Minginish). Hostellers might like to know that there are several year-round **bunkhouses** in Carbost and **PORTNALONG**, a couple of miles north: the *Waterfront Bunkhouse* is next to (and owned by) the *Old Inn* in Carbost (ⓣ01478/640205, ⓦwww.carbost.f9.co.uk; ❸), which does good bar meals; the *Croft Bunkhouse and Bothies* (ⓣ01478/640254, ⓦwww.skye-hostels.com), with good family accommodation and **camping**, is signposted just before you get to Portnalong; while the *Skyewalker Independent Hostel* (ⓣ01478/640250, ⓦfreespace.virgin.net/skyewalker.hostel) is a converted school building beyond Portnalong, en route to Fiskavaig – it also has a campsite, shop and an excellent café that welcomes passers-by. There's also the friendly *Taigh Ailean Hotel,* which serves good meals in the evening. Of course, if money's not a problem, then you can make your way over to *Ullinish Country Lodge* (ⓣ01470/572214, ⓦwww.theisleofskye.co.uk; ❼), a **hotel** which overlooks Portnalong from the north; to get there head eight miles up the A863 to Dunvegan and follow the signs. The building itself dates back to the mid-eighteenth century and has lots of character – you can sleep in a super king-size half-tester bed in the room once occupied by Dr Johnson – and the hotel offers five course dinners for around £40 a head.

Dunvegan, Duirinish and Waternish

After the Portnalong and Glen Brittle turning, the A863 slips across bare rounded hills to skirt the bony sea cliffs and stacks of the west coast twenty miles or so north to **DUNVEGAN** (Dùn Bheagain). It's an unimpressive place, strung out along the east shore of the sea loch of the same name, though it does make quite a good base for exploring two interesting peninsulas: **Duirinish** and **Waternish**.

The main tourist trap in the village is **Dunvegan Castle** (daily: mid-March to Oct 10am–5pm; Nov to mid-March 11am–4pm; £7, gardens only £5; ⓦwww.dunvegancastle.com), which sprawls on top of a rocky outcrop, sandwiched between the sea and several acres of beautifully maintained gardens. It's been the seat of the Clan MacLeod since the thirteenth century, but the present greying, rectangular fortress, with its uniform battlements and dummy pepper pots, dates from the 1840s. Inside, you don't get a lot of castle for your money and the contents are far from stunning, but there are three famous items, the most intriguing of which is the battered remnants of the **Fairy Flag** in the drawing room. This yellow silken flag from the Middle East may have been the battle standard of the Norwegian king Harald Hardrada, who had been the commander of the imperial guard in Constantinople. Hardrada died trying to seize the English throne at the Battle of Stamford Bridge in 1066, after which his flag was allegedly carried back to Skye by his Gaelic boatmen. More fancifully, MacLeod family tradition asserts that the flag was the gift of the fairies, blessed with the power to protect the clan in times of danger – as late as World

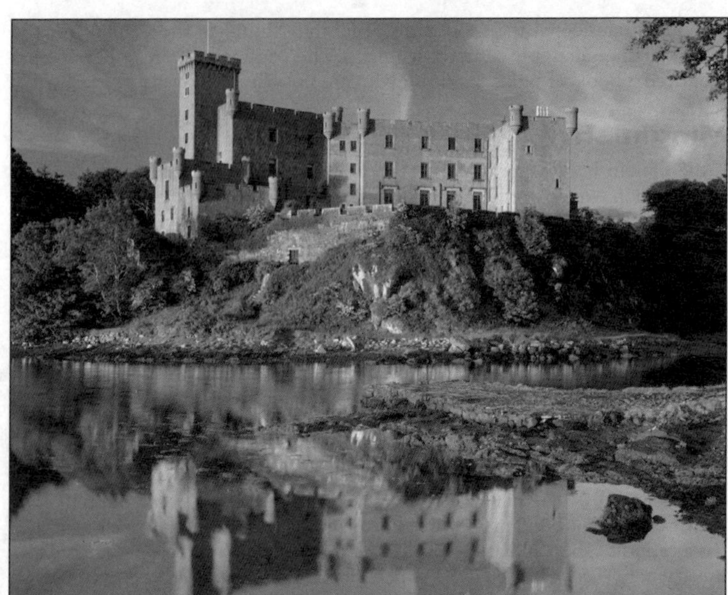
△ Dunvegan Castle

War II, MacLeod pilots carried pictures of it for luck. The other two items are **Rory Mor's Horn**, a drinking vessel made from the horn of a mad bull and capable of holding half a gallon, which each new chief still has to drain at one draught "without setting down or falling down", and the **Dunvegan Cup**, made of bog oak covered in medieval silver filigree, and believed to have been given to Rory Mor by the O'Neils of Ulster in return for his help against England. Among the Jacobite mementoes are a lock of hair and cream waistcoat belonging to Bonnie Prince Charlie (whom the MacLeods, in fact, fought against) and Flora MacDonald's corsets. Elsewhere there's a "virtual" consumptive in the dungeon and an interesting display on the remote archipelago of St Kilda (see p.391), long the fiefdom of the MacLeods.

From the jetty outside the castle there are regular seal-spotting **boat trips** out along Loch Dunvegan, as well as longer and less frequent sea cruises to the small islands of Mingay, Isay and Clett, which were cleared of the last crofters in 1860. Outside in the car park you can buy sandwiches from a kiosk or have a more substantial snack in the castle restaurant.

On a wet day you might scrape up some enthusiasm for Dunvegan's newest tourist attraction, the **Giant Angus MacAskill Museum** (Easter–Nov daily 10am–6pm; £1.50), housed in a restored thatched smithy. The museum's eponymous hero was born in the Outer Hebrides in 1825 and emigrated to Nova Scotia when he was just 6. He eventually grew to 7 feet 9 inches and, until his untimely death of a fever at the age of 38, toured with the midget Tom Thumb, who, it is said, used to dance on Angus's outstretched hand.

Duirinish and Glen Dale

The hammerhead **Duirinish peninsula** lies to the west of Dunvegan, much of it inaccessible to all except walkers prepared to scale or skirt the area's twin flat-topped basalt peaks: Healabhal Bheag (1600ft) and Healabhal Mhor (1538ft). The mountains are better known as **MacLeod's Tables**, for legend has it that the MacLeod chief held an open-air royal feast on the lower of the two for James V.

The main areas of habitation lie to the north, along the western shores of Loch Dunvegan, and in the broad green sweep of **Glen Dale** (Ⓦwww.glendale-skye.org.uk), attractively dotted with white farmhouses and dubbed "Little England" by the locals, due to its high percentage of "white settlers", English incomers searching for a better life. Glen Dale's current predicament is doubly ironic given its history, for it was here in 1882 that local crofters, following the example of their brethren in The Braes (see p.336), staged a rent strike against their landlords, the MacLeods. Five locals – who became known as the "Glen Dale Martyrs" – were given two-month prison sentences, and eventually, in 1904, the crofters became the first owner-occupiers in the Highlands. All this, and a great deal more about nineteenth-century crofting, is told through fascinating contemporary news cuttings at **Colbost Folk Museum** (Easter–Oct daily 9am–6pm; £1.50), situated in a restored blackhouse, four miles up the road from Dunvegan. A guide is usually on hand to answer questions, the peat fire smokes all day, and there's a restored illegal whisky still round the back.

Just off the road to **BORRERAIG** is **Borreraig Park** (daily 10am–6pm; £2), a piping heritage centre that tells the story of the MacCrimmons, hereditary pipers to the MacLeod chiefs for three centuries, until they were sent packing in the 1770s. The plaintive sounds of the *piobaireachd* of the MacCrimmons, the founding family of Scottish piping, fill this museum, a sound as melancholy as the sight of dusty worm-eaten rat skeletons and artefacts from a bygone way of life. To hear the real thing, go to the annual recital held in Dunvegan Castle (see p.341) early in August.

If you've got kids, you might like to pay a visit to the **Toy Museum** (Mon–Sat 10am–6pm; £2.50; Ⓦwww.toy-museum.co.uk), in **GLENDALE** itself, which has everything from early Meccano sets to a fully equipped mini-crofters' kitchen, plus innumerable Sasha dolls and Marie and Donny Osmond string puppets. Beyond Glendale, a bumpy road leads to Ramasaig, and beyond for another five miles to the deserted village of Lorgill where, on August 4, 1830, life came to an end when every crofter was ordered to board the *Midlothian* in Loch Snizort to go to Nova Scotia or go to prison (those over the age of 70 were sent to the poorhouse). As a result of such Clearances, the west coast of Duirinish is mostly uninhabited now. For walkers, though, it's a great area to explore, with blustery but easy footpaths leading to the dramatically sited lighthouse on **Neist Point**, Skye's most westerly spot, which features some fearsome sea cliffs, and wonderful views across the sea to the Western Isles. Despite the fact that the present owner has put up "Keep Out!" notices, the locals continue to exert their right to roam right up to the lighthouse. Alternatively, you could head north for the sheer 1000-foot cliffs of **Biod an Athair** near Dunvegan Head, though there's no path, and it's a bit of a slog.

Waternish

Waternish is a thin and little-visited peninsula to the north of Dunvegan. It's not as spectacular as either Duirinish or Trotternish, but it provides equally great views over to the Western Isles on a good day. Before you can explore the peninsula, however, you have to cross the **Fairy Bridge**, at the junction of the B886, where legend has it that a MacLeod chief, foolishly married to a fairy, was forced to say farewell when she decided to go home to her mother. More likely its significance lies in the fact that it's at the meeting of three roads and was the scene of religious assemblies of the Free Church and, later, of rebellious crofters led by John MacPherson, one of the "Glen Dale Martyrs".

Waternish's prettiest village is **STEIN**, on the west coast looking out over Loch Bay and over the Western Isles. As you descend through the settlement, you eventually reach a row of whitewashed cottages built in 1787 by the British Fisheries Society. The place never really took off and by 1837 had been more or less abandoned. Today, however, it's coming back to life, particularly the pub, the sixteenth-century *Stein Inn*, which is well worth a visit. Along the road north, there are a number of interesting craft enterprises: just above Stein, a **tannery** at Skyeskyns (Ⓦwww.skyeskyns.co.uk) displays beautiful fleeces and gives free guided tours of the workshop; at **HALISTRA**, a mile or two north of Stein, there's a pottery and, further on, an exhibition of wool dyeing using natural colours.

At the end of the road is **Trumpan Church**, an evocative medieval ruin on a clifftop looking out to the Western Isles. This peaceful site was the scene of one of the bloodiest episodes in Skye history, when, in a revenge attack in 1578, the MacDonalds of Uist set fire to the church while numerous MacLeods were attending a service inside. Everyone perished except one young girl, who escaped by squeezing through a window, severing one of her breasts in the process. She raised the alarm, and the rest of the MacLeods quickly rallied and, bearing their famous Fairy Flag (see p.341), attacked the MacDonalds as they were launching their galleys. Every MacDonald was slaughtered and their bodies were thrown in a nearby dyke. In the churchyard, along with two medieval gravestones, you can also see the **Trial Stone**, a four-foot-high pillar with a hole drilled in it. Anyone accused of a crime was blindfolded and had to attempt to put their finger in it: success meant innocence, failure signified death. Back on the A850, heading for Portree, Edinbane **pottery** is well worth a visit, and a couple of miles before the junction with the A87, in **Bernisdale**, there are daily **sheepdog demonstrations** by a past finalist from the BBC's *One Man and his Dog* series; they're very popular, so booking is essential (Ⓣ01470/532331).

Practicalities

Dunvegan is by no means the most picturesque place on Skye, but it's a useful alternative base to Portree. It has a **tourist office** (Easter to mid-Oct Mon–Sat 9am–5.30pm; mid-Oct to Easter Mon–Fri 10am–1.30pm; Ⓣ01470/521581) and boasts several good **hotels** and **B&Bs** dotted along the main road, such as the converted traditional croft *Roskhill House* (Ⓣ01470/521317, Ⓦwww.roskhillhouse.co.uk; March–Nov; ④) or the beautifully situated *Silverdale Guesthouse* (Ⓣ01470/521251, Ⓦwww.silverdaleskye.com; ③), just before you get to Colbost. There are a couple of excellent lochside **campsites**: one at Loch Greshornish, a mile north of Edinbane on the A850 (Ⓣ01470/582230, Ⓦwww.skyecamp.com; April–Sept; bike and canoe rental available) and another on Loch Dunvegan (Ⓣ01470/521531, Ⓦwww.kinloch-campsite.co.uk; April–Nov), off the road to Colbost.

The culinary mecca in the area is the expensive *Three Chimneys* **restaurant** (Ⓣ01470/511258, Ⓦwww.threechimneys.co.uk; closed Sun lunch), located beside Colbost Folk Museum, which serves sublime three-course meals at £45 a head; the restaurant also has six fabulous rooms at the restaurant's adjacent *House Over-By* (⑨), which cost £240 bed and breakfast. A good place to stay, with welcoming fires and good pub food is the sixteenth-century *Stein Inn* (Ⓣ01470/592362, Ⓦwww.steininn.co.uk; ③), in Stein – next door is the much pricier *Lochbay Seafood Restaurant* (Ⓣ01470/592235; Easter–Oct closed Sat & Sun; Aug closed Sun), where you'll need to book ahead. Without doubt, the best place to eat in Dunvegan is *The Old School* (ⓣ01470/521421) whose excellent food belies its appearance from outside. Otherwise, all the hotels do dinner and, on a more modest scale, there is a snug **café** attached to *Dunvegan Bakery* (confusingly the sign simply says "fish and chips").

Portree

Although referred to by the locals as "the village", **PORTREE** is the only real town on Skye, with a population of around two thousand. It's also one of the most attractive fishing ports in northwest Scotland, its deep, cliff-edged harbour filled with fishing boats and circled by multicoloured restaurants and guesthouses. Originally known as *Kiltragleann* (the church at the foot of the glen), it takes its current name – some say – from *Portrigh* (Port of the King), after the state visit James V made in 1540 to assert his authority over the chieftains of Skye.

Information and accommodation

Hours vary enormously at Portree's **tourist office**, just off Bridge Street, so the ones here are just a guideline (April–Oct Mon–Sat 9am–8pm, Sun 10am–4pm; Nov–March Mon–Sat 9am–5.30pm; ⓣ01478/612137). The office will, for a small fee, book **accommodation** for you – especially useful if you haven't booked ahead, and you can go online here. Accommodation prices tend to be higher in Portree than elsewhere on the island, especially in the town itself, though B&Bs on the outskirts are usually cheaper. The only **hostel** in Portree is the clean and smart *Portree Independent Hostel* (ⓣ01478/613737, ⓦwww.portreehostel.f9.co.uk) housed in the Old Post Office on the Green. *Torvaig* **campsite** (ⓣ01478/612209; April–Oct) is clean, well-kept, with a friendly owner, and lies a mile and a half north of town off the A855 Staffin road.

Balloch Viewfield Road ⓣ01478/612093, ⓦwww.balloch-skye.co.uk. Perfectly ordinary, reliable B&B (once visited by the Queen) just off the main road into Portree from the south. Open Easter–Oct. ❷

Bosville Bosville Terrace ⓣ01478/612846, ⓦwww.bosvillehotel.co.uk. Commands a good view of the harbour, and has a gourmet seafood restaurant. ❼

Cuillin Hills ten minutes' walk out of town along the northern shore of the bay ⓣ01478/612003, ⓦwww.cuillinhills-hotel-skye.co.uk. Very comfortable hotel, with a splendid view over the harbour and reasonably priced bar snacks. ❽

Medina Coolin Hills Gardens ⓣ01478/612821, ⓦwww.medinaskye.co.uk. Well-run B&B, with tasty breakfasts, in a quiet spot near the *Cuillin Hills Hotel.* ❸

Portree House Home Farm Road ⓣ01478/613713, ⓦwww.portreehouse.co.uk. Built in 1810s by the MacDonalds, and set in lovely mature gardens, this hotel is just a few minutes' walk from the town centre. ❺

Skeabost House near Portree ⓣ01470/532202, ⓦwww.skeabostcountryhouse.com. Late Victorian pile, five miles northwest in Skeabost, which offers the life of a country gent in the main building with an original billiard room and, outdoors, fishing, golf and extensive gardens. Open March–Oct. ❽

Viewfield House ⓣ01478/612217, ⓦwww.viewfieldhouse.com. For real atmosphere and elegance, it's hard to beat this hotel on the southern outskirts of town, which has been in the hands of the MacDonalds for over two hundred years, and has a wonderful Victorian air, stuffed polecats and antiques. Open mid-April to mid-Oct. ❻

The Town

The **harbour** is well worth a stroll, with its attractive pier built by Thomas Telford in the early nineteenth century. Fishing boats still land a modest catch, some of which is sold through Anchor Seafoods (Tues–Fri only) at the end of the pier. The harbour is overlooked by **The Lump**, a steep and stumpy peninsula with a flagpole on it that was once the site of public hangings on the island, attracting crowds of up to 5000; it also sports a folly built by the celebrated Dr Ban, a visionary who wanted to make Portree into a second Oban (see p.87). Up above the harbour is the spick-and-span town centre, spreading out from **Somerled Square**, built in the late eighteenth century as the island's administrative and commercial centre, and now housing the bus station and car park. The **Royal Hotel** on Bank Street occupies the site of the *McNab's Inn* where Bonnie Prince Charlie took leave of Flora MacDonald (see p.349), and where, 27 years later, Boswell and Johnson had "a very good dinner, porter, port and punch".

A mile or so out of town on the Sligachan road is the **Aros Centre** (daily 9am–6pm; open later in summer; Ⓦwww.aros.co.uk), one of Skye's most successful tourist attractions despite the fact that it's little more than one enormous souvenir shop. If it's wet, you can grab a live RSPB webcam centred on sea eagles' nests and an audiovisual roam around the island (£4). The best bit about Aros is that it hosts gigs (see below) and contains a **cinema**, a modern exhibition space, a licensed bar and a popular café, and there's a special play area for small kids. If it's fine, there are easy waymarked forest walks from the car park.

For a view of the contemporary visual arts scene, it's well worth seeking out **An Tuireann**, an arts centre housed in a converted fever hospital on the Struan road (Mon–Sat 10am–5pm; free; Ⓦwww.antuireann.org.uk), which puts on exhibitions, stages concerts, and has an excellent small licensed café (Tues–Sat only) where even the counter is a work of art, with an imaginative range of food on offer.

Eating, drinking and nightlife

Eating out can be pretty pricey in Portree, with the likes of the *Bosville Hotel*'s outstanding *Chandlery* restaurant (eves only) offering set menus from £28 a head, although the *Bosville Bistro* is much cheaper. Other options include *Harbour View* (Ⓣ01478/612069, Ⓦwww.harbourviewskye.co.uk; closed Wed), a seafood restaurant, also on Bosville Terrace, with candlelit ambience and very fresh fish on the menu. The popular *Lower Deck Seafood Restaurant* (Ⓣ01478/613611) on the harbour has a wood-panelled warmth to it, and is reasonably priced at lunchtime (less so in the evenings, when booking is essential); for good **fish and chips**, pop next door to their excellent chippy. If you're looking for somewhere a bit more relaxed, look no further than *Café Arriba*, at the top of the road down to the harbour, which offers an array of reasonably priced Mediterranean dishes. For a simple cuppa and a cake, there's the *Granary* bakery's **teashop** on Somerled Square. The *Café*, an ice-cream parlour on Wentworth Street, serves a selection of cakes, toasties and paninis. As for **pubs**, the bar of the *Pier Hotel* on the quayside is the fishermen's drinking hole, and the *Tongadale* on Wentworth Street is lively. Currently the most popular evening venue by far, though, is the *Isles Inn* on Somerled Square, which has excellent bar meals as well as live music.

The aforementioned Aros Centre has a **theatre**, which shows films and hosts Gaelic **concerts** (for more details phone Ⓣ01471/613649); concerts and events also go on at An Tuireann (see above), and it's also worth checking out what's on at the Portree Community Centre (Ⓣ01478/613736), which hosts ceilidhs and so forth. For **bike rental**, go to Island Cycles (closed Sun; Ⓣ01478/613121) below The Green; for **horse riding**, head for the Portree Riding Stables off the B885 to Struan, signposted "Peiness" (Ⓣ01478/613124, Ⓦwww.portreeriding.co.uk). Day or half-day **boat trips** leave the pier for daily excursions to Raasay and Rona (Ⓣ01478/613718); **diving** can be organized through

Dive-and-Sea the Hebrides in Lochbay, towards Dunvegan (Ⓣ01470/592219, Ⓦwww.dive-and-sea-the-hebrides.co.uk). Look out, too, for occasional **bird of prey displays** organized by the local Isle of Skye Falconry (Ⓣ01470/532489, Ⓦwww.isleofskye-falconry.co.uk), who also run courses.

Trotternish

Protruding twenty miles north from Portree, the **Trotternish peninsula** boasts some of the island's most bizarre scenery, particularly on the east coast, where volcanic basalt has pressed down on the softer sandstone and limestone underneath, causing massive landslides. These, in turn, have created sheer cliffs, peppered with outcrops of hard, wizened basalt, which run the full length of the peninsula. These pinnacles and pillars are at their most eccentric in the **Quiraing**, above Staffin Bay, on the east coast. Trotternish is best explored with your own transport, but an occasional bus service (Mon–Sat 2–4 daily) along the road encircling the peninsula gives access to almost all the coast.

The east coast

The first geological eccentricity on the **Trotternish** peninsula, six miles north of Portree along the A855, is the **Old Man of Storr**, a distinctive column of rock, shaped like a willow leaf, which, along with its neighbours, is part of a massive landslip. Huge blocks of stone still occasionally break off the cliff face of the Storr (2358ft) above, and slide downhill. At 165ft, the Old Man is a real challenge for climbers; less difficult is the half-hour trek up the new footpath to the foot of the column from the woods beside the car park.

Five miles further north, there's another turn-off to the **Lealt Falls**, at the head of a gorge which spends most of its day in shadow (and is home to a fiendish collection of midges). Walking all the way down to the falls is fairly pointless, but the views across to Wester Ross from the first stage of the path are spectacular (weather permitting). The coast here is worth exploring, however, especially the track leading to **Rubha nam Brathairean** (Brothers' Point), where the Glasgow provision boat used to put in, and where fossil hunters can also follow the road that turns off at Dunans down to the end and try their luck on the beach at low tide.

Another car park a few miles up the road gives access to **Kilt Rock**, whose tubelike, basaltic columns rise precipitously from the sea, set amongst sea cliffs dotted with nests for fulmars and kittiwakes. There is a spectacular waterfall which drops 300ft to the sea, and a small loch by the car park alive with wildlife. Close by, near the turn-off to Elishader, is the slate-roofed **Staffin Museum** (sporadic opening hours; £1.50), which contains fossil finds from the area, and a dinosaur bone discovered here in 1994.

Over the brow of the next hill, **Staffin Bay**, where several fossilized dinosaur footprints were discovered in 1996, is spread out before you, dotted with whitewashed and "spotty" houses. **STAFFIN** itself is a lively, largely Gaelic-speaking community where crofts have been handed down the generations. It's also the unlikely home of the **Columba 1400** centre (Ⓦwww.columba1400.com), which runs courses for all sorts of groups from headteachers to disadvantaged youth, "releasing the leadership potential of young people from tough realities", in their own words, and whose new purpose-built headquarters are hard to miss.

A single-track road cuts across the peninsula from the north end of the bay, allowing access to the **Quiraing**, a spectacular forest of mighty pinnacles and savage rock formations. There are two car parks: from the first, beside a cemetery, it's a steep half-hour climb to the rocks; from the second, on the saddle it's a longer, but more gentle traverse. Once you're in the midst of the rocks, you should be able to make out the Prison to your right, and the 120-foot Needle, to your left; the Table, a great sunken platform where locals used to play shinty, lies above and beyond the Needle, another fifteen-minute scramble up the rocks; legend also maintains that a local warrior named Fraing hid his cattle there from the invading Norsemen.

Most **accommodation** choices on the east coast enjoy fantastic views out over the sea. Just beyond the Lealt Falls there's the very welcoming and comfortable *Glenview Inn* (ⓣ01470/562248, ⓦwww.glenview-skye.co.uk; ④), with an excellent restaurant, and a **campsite** (ⓣ01470/562213; April–Sept) south of Staffin Bay. In fine weather, you can enjoy good bar snacks on the castellated terrace of the stylish *Flodigarry Country House Hotel* (ⓣ01470/552203, ⓦwww.flodigarry.co.uk; ⑥), three miles up the coast from Staffin. Behind the hotel (and now part of it) is the cottage where local heroine Flora MacDonald lived, and had six of her seven children, from 1751 to 1759. If the hotel's rooms are beyond your means, you can **camp** or stay at the neat and attractive *Dun Flodigarry* **hostel** (ⓣ01470/552212), a couple of minutes' walk away. For **boat trips** from Staffin up the coast, contact Staffin Bay Cruises (ⓣ01470/562217, ⓦwww.trotternish.co.uk; April–Oct).

Duntulm and Kilmuir

Beyond Flodigarry, at the tip of the Trotternish peninsula, by the road to Shulista, a public footpath leads past the ruins of a cleared hamlet to the spectacular sea stacks of **Rubha Hunish**, the most northerly point on Skye. A couple of miles further along the A855 lies **DUNTULM** (Duntuilm), whose heyday as a major MacDonald power base is recalled by the shattered remains of a headland fortress abandoned by the clan in 1732 after a clumsy nurse dropped the baby son and heir from a window onto the rocks below; on these same rocks, it is said, can be seen the keel marks of Viking longships. The imposing *Duntulm Castle Hotel* (March–Nov) is close by, and provides good pub food as well as wonderful views across the Minch to the Western Isles.

△ Blackhouse, Skye Museum of Island Life

Bonnie Prince Charlie

Prince Charles Edward Stuart – better known as **Bonnie Prince Charlie** or "The Young Pretender" – was born in Rome in 1720, where his father, "The Old Pretender", claimant to the British throne, was living in exile. At the age of 25, having little military experience, no knowledge of Gaelic, an imperfect grasp of English and a strong attachment to the Catholic faith, the prince set out for Scotland on a French ship, disguised as a seminarist from the Scots College in Paris. He arrived on the Outer Hebridean island of Eriskay (see p.395) on July 23, 1745, and was immediately implored to return to France by the clan chiefs, who were singularly unimpressed by his lack of army. Charles was unmoved and went on to raise the royal standard at Glenfinnan (see p.270), gather together a Highland army, win the Battle of Prestonpans, march on London and reach Derby, before finally (and foolishly) agreeing to retreat. Back in Scotland, he won one last victory, at Falkirk, before the final disaster at Culloden in April 1746.

The prince spent the following five months in hiding, with a price of £30,000 on his head, and literally thousands of government troops searching for him. He certainly endured his fair share of cold and hunger whilst on the run, but the real price was paid by the Highlanders themselves, who risked their lives (and often paid for it with them) by aiding and abetting the prince. The most famous of these was, of course, 23-year-old **Flora MacDonald**, whom Charles met on South Uist in June 1746. Flora was persuaded – either by his beauty or her relatives, depending on which account you believe – to convey Charles "over the sea to Skye", disguised as an Irish servant girl by the name of Betty Burke. She was arrested just seven days after parting with the prince in Portree, and held in the Tower of London until July 1747. She went on to marry a local man, had seven children, and in 1774 emigrated to America, where her husband was taken prisoner during the American War of Independence. Flora returned to Scotland and was reunited with her husband on his release; they resettled in Skye and she died at the age of 68.

Charles eventually boarded a ship back to France in September 1746, but, despite his promises – "for all that has happened, Madam, I hope we shall meet in St James's yet" – never returned to Scotland, nor did he ever see Flora again. After mistreating a string of mistresses, he eventually got married at the age of 52 to the 19-year-old Princess of Stolberg, in an effort to produce a Stuart heir. They had no children, and she eventually fled from his violent drunkenness; in 1788, a none-too-"bonnie" Prince Charles died in the arms of his illegitimate daughter in Rome. Bonnie Prince Charlie became a legend in his own lifetime, but it was the Victorians who really milked the myth for all its sentimentality, conveniently overlooking the fact that the real consequence of 1745 was the virtual annihilation of the Highland way of life.

Heading down the west shore of the Trotternish, it's two miles to the **Skye Museum of Island Life** (April–Oct Mon–Sat 9am–5.30pm; £1.75; Ⓦwww.skyemuseum.co.uk), an impressive cluster of thatched blackhouses on an exposed hill overlooking Harris. The museum, run by locals, gives a fascinating insight into a way of life that was commonplace on Skye a hundred years ago. The blackhouse, now home to the ticket office, is much as it was when it was last inhabited in 1957, while the two houses to the east contain interesting snippets of local history. Behind the museum in the cemetery up the hill are the graves of **Flora MacDonald** and her husband. Thousands turned out for her funeral in 1790, creating a funeral procession a mile long – indeed, so widespread was her fame that the original family mausoleum fell victim to souvenir hunters and had to be replaced. The Celtic cross headstone is inscribed with a simple tribute by Dr Johnson, who visited her in 1773:

"Her name will be mentioned in history, if courage and fidelity be virtues, mentioned with honour."

The land around **KILMUIR**, a mile or so to the south, used to be called the "Granary of Skye", since every inch was cultivated: even St Columba's Loch, where there are still indistinct remains of beehive cells and a chapel, was drained and the land eagerly reclaimed by crofters. **Accommodation** is available in the attractive *Kilmuir House*, previously the old manse (Ⓣ01470/542262, Ⓦwww.kilmuir-skye.co.uk; ❷). If you're looking for action, contact Whitewave (Ⓣ01470/542414, Ⓦwww.white-wave.co.uk), in Linicro; they also organize everything from **windsurfing** and **sea kayaking** to **hill walking** and **archery**.

Uig

A further four miles south of Kilmuir is the ferry port of **UIG** (Uige), which curves its way round a dramatic, horseshoe-shaped bay, and is the arrival point for CalMac ferries from Tarbert (Harris) and Lochmaddy (North Uist); if you've time to spare while waiting for a ferry, pop into Uig Pottery (Ⓦwww.uigpottery.co.uk), next to the pier car park. Most folk come to Uig to take the ferry to the Western Isles, but if you need to stay near the ferry terminal, there are a couple of decent inexpensive **B&Bs**: *Orasay*, 14 Idrigill (Ⓣ01470/542316, Ⓦwww.orasay.freeserve.co.uk; ❶), a minute's walk from the pier, and *Braigh-uige* (Ⓣ01470/542228, Ⓦwww.uig-skye.co.uk; March–Oct; ❶), on the other side of the bay near the church. The **campsite**, on a sloping field very close to the pier (Ⓣ01470/542714, Ⓦwww.uig-camping-skye.co.uk), is open all year and also offers **bike rental**. By contrast, the SYHA **hostel** (Ⓣ0870/004 1155; April–Oct) is a fifteen-minute walk away, high up on the south side of the village, with exhilarating views over the bay. The *Pub at the Pier* offers basic meals, and serves beers from the Outer Hebrides and from the nearby brewery (Mon–Fri tours by appointment; Ⓣ01470/542477, Ⓦwww.skyebrewery.co.uk).

The prettiest place for a fair-weather stroll and picnic around Uig is the **Fairy Glen**, reached by taking the minor road up to Balnaknock. Another good walk is to the intriguing ruined castle with no door called **Caisteal Uisdein**, built by Hugh MacDonald of Sleat in the seventeenth century. Take the turning to Cuidrach and continue to the end of the road; walk through the village and then follow the posts, but you'll have to climb in through a window – in spring, the castle is filled with primroses. When Hugh's clan chief found he'd been plotting against him, he walled him up in here with a piece of salt beef and an empty water jug.

The Small Isles

The history of the **Small Isles**, which lie to the south of Skye, is typical of the Hebrides: early Christianization, followed by a period of Norwegian rule that ended in 1266, when the islands fell into Scottish hands. Their support for the Jacobite cause resulted in hard times after the failed rebellion of 1745, but the biggest problems came with the introduction of the **potato** in the mid-eighteenth century. The consequences were as dramatic as they were unforeseen: the success of the crop and its nutritional value – when grown in conjunction with traditional cereals – eliminated famine at a stroke, prompting a population explosion. In 1750, there were a thousand islanders, but by 1800 their numbers had almost doubled.

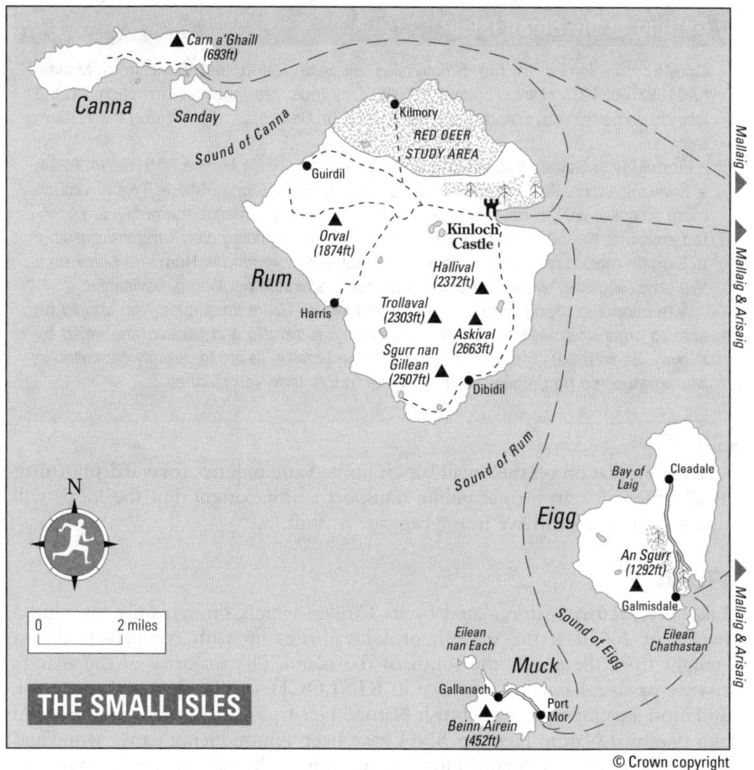

At first, the problem of overcrowding was camouflaged by the **kelp** boom, in which the islanders were employed, and the islands' owners made a fortune, gathering and burning local seaweed to sell for use in the manufacture of gunpowder, soap and glass. But the economic bubble burst with the end of the Napoleonic Wars and, to maintain their profit margins, the owners resorted to drastic action. The first to sell up was Alexander MacLean, who sold Rùm as grazing land for **sheep**, got quotations for shipping its people to Nova Scotia, and gave them a year's notice to quit. He also cleared Muck to graze cattle, as did the MacNeills on Canna. Only on Eigg was some compassion shown: the new owner, a certain Hugh MacPherson, who bought the island from the Clanranalds in 1827, actually gave some of his tenants extended leases.

Since the Clearances, each of the islands has been bought and sold several times, though only **Muck** is now privately owned by the benevolent laird, Lawrence MacEwen. **Eigg** hit the headlines in 1997, when the islanders finally managed to buy the island themselves and put an end to more than 150 years of property speculation. The other islands were bequeathed to national agencies: **Rùm**, by far the largest and most-visited of the group, possessing a cluster of formidable volcanic peaks and the architecturally remarkable Kinloch Castle, passed to the Nature Conservancy Council (now Scottish Natural Heritage) in 1957; and **Canna**, in many ways the prettiest of the isles, with its high basalt cliffs, has been in the hands of the National Trust for Scotland since 1981.

Getting to the Small Isles

CalMac run ferries to the Small Isles all year round (not Sun) from Mallaig (ⓣ01687/462403, ⓦwww.calmac.co.uk). Day-trips are possible to each of the islands on certain days, and to all four islands on Saturdays, if you catch the 7.30am ferry.

From May to September, the **Sheerwater**, run by Arisaig Marine (ⓣ01687/450224, ⓦwww.arisaig.co.uk), operates a daily service to Rùm, Eigg or Muck. This is a much more pleasant way to get there, not least because if any marine mammals are spotted en route, the boat will pause for a bit of whale-watching. Day-trips are possible to Eigg on most days, allowing four to five hours ashore, and to Rùm and Muck on a few days, allowing two to three hours ashore – advance booking is advisable.

With careful studying of both CalMac and Murdo Grant timetables, you should be able to organize a visit to suit you, especially as Arisaig and Mallaig are linked by railway. Be warned, however, that boats to the Small Isles are frequently cancelled in bad weather, so be prepared to holiday for longer than you planned.

Accommodation on the Small Isles is limited and requires **forward planning** at all times of year; formal public transport is nonexistent, but the locals will usually oblige if you have heavy baggage to shift.

Rùm

Like Skye, **Rùm** is dominated by its Cuillin, which, though only reaching a height of 2663ft at the summit of Askival, rises up with comparable drama straight from the sea in the south of the island. The majority of the island's twenty or so inhabitants now live in **KINLOCH**, on the sheltered east coast, and most are employed by Scottish Natural Heritage (SNH), who run the island as a National Nature Reserve. SNH have been reintroducing native woodland to the island, and overseeing a long-term study of the vast red-deer population. However, the organization's most notable achievement to date is the reintroduction of **white-tailed (sea) eagles**, whose wingspan is even greater than that of the golden eagle. These magnificent birds of prey were last known to have bred on the Isle of Skye in 1916. After a caesura of some seventy years, the eagles returned, and have since mostly abandoned Rùm in favour of neighbouring islands. You can learn more about the history of the island, and its flora and fauna, in the small **museum** near the old pier.

Rùm's chief formal attraction is **Kinloch Castle** (guided tours most days around 2pm; £5), a squat red-sandstone edifice fronted by colonnades and topped by crenellations and turrets, which dominates the village of Kinloch. Completed at enormous expense in 1900 – the red sandstone was shipped in from Dumfriesshire, and the soil for the gardens from Ayrshire – and now in need of some serious restoration, its interior is a perfectly preserved example of Edwardian decadence, "a living memorial of the stalking, the fishing and the sailing, the tenantry and plenty of the days before 1914". From the galleried hall, with its tiger rugs, stags' heads and giant Japanese incense burners, to the "Extra Low Fast Cushion" of the Soho snooker table in the Billiard Room, the interior is packed with knick-knacks and technical gizmos accumulated by **Sir George Bullough** (1870–1939), the spendthrift son of self-made millionaire, Sir John Bullough, who bought the island as a sporting estate in 1888. As such, it was only really used for a few weeks each autumn, during the "season", yet employed an island workforce of one hundred all year round. Bullough's guests were woken at eight each morning by a piper; later on, an orchestrion, an electrically driven barrel organ (originally destined for Balmoral), crammed in under the stairs, would grind out an eccentric mixture of pre-dinner tunes – *The Ride of the Valkyries* and *Ma Blushin' Rosie* among others (a demo is included in the tour). The ballroom has a sprung floor, the library features a gruesome photographic collection from the Bulloughs' world tours, but the *pièce de résistance* has to be Bullough's **Edwardian bathrooms**, whose baths have hooded walnut shower cabinets, fitted with two taps and four dials, which allow the bathers to fire high-pressure water at their body from every angle.

For those with limited time or energy, there are two gentle waymarked **trails**, both of which start from Kinloch, and take around two hours to complete. For longer walks, you must fill in route cards and pop them into the *White House* (Mon–Fri 9am–12.30pm), where the reserve manager can give useful advice.

Sir George Bullough

Scotland has had more than its fair share of eccentric rich landlords, but few come close to **Sir George Bullough** (1870–1939), heir to a fortune accumulated by his father and grandfather, whose Lancashire factories produced textile machinery. When his father died, George was on a two-year world tour, three days short of his 21st birthday; rumour had it he'd been sent off to keep him away from his young stepmother, with whom he'd had a rather "close relationship". In 1899, at the time of the Second Boer War, Bullough, at his own expense, kitted out and staffed his recently acquired 221-foot-long steam yacht, *Rhouma*, as a hospital ship, and sent it off to South Africa. For this act of "patriotic devotion", he was rewarded with a knighthood, though allegedly he actually received his title for agreeing to be named in the divorce proceedings between Charles Charrington and his wife, Monica, in order to avoid King Edward VII being named. There is, however, no evidence that Monica was ever the king's mistress, and once the divorce came through she and George Bullough were married.

Meanwhile, in 1897, work began on George Bullough's ultimate dream: his very own Scottish castle. For three years, 300 men were employed to build **Kinloch Castle** on Rùm – or, as George preferred it to be known, "Rhum" – and paid an extra shilling a week to wear Rùm tartan kilts; smokers were also given a daily bonus of twopence "to keep the midges away". The castle's heyday was the Edwardian era, when Rùm was fitted out with the biggest, the best and the most technologically advanced mod cons money could buy: it was double-glazed, centrally heated, was the first place in Scotland to be lit by electricity (after Glasgow) and the first private house in Scotland to have an internal telephone system. There was a nine-hole golf course, a bowling green, a huge walled garden (350ft by 200ft), with fourteen greenhouses producing exotic fruit for the guests, and six domed palm-houses, alive with hummingbirds (they died when the heating broke down and can now be found stuffed in the house), and fitted with heated pools stocked with giant turtles and alligators, though these were eventually removed at the insistence of the terrified staff. There were twelve full-time gardeners and fourteen full-time roadmen, whose job it was to keep Rùm's roads carefully raked so that George and his chums could race their sports cars across the island. In the bay, the Bulloughs would moor the *Rhouma*, whose band would come ashore to play from the castle ballroom's minstrels' gallery.

The outbreak of World War I signalled the end of the world of opulence in which the Bulloughs had excelled. Sir George was elevated to the baronetcy in 1916, after having loaned £50,000 interest-free to the government, but after the war he and the family visited Rùm less and less. The house was barely used when Sir George died of a heart attack while playing golf on holiday in France in 1939. Lady Bullough eventually sold Rùm in 1957; she died ten years later, and was buried, along with her husband, in the Bullough Mausoleum in Harris.

They also occasionally offer **guided walks** around the island, including a night-time hike to see the shearwaters on the slopes of Hallival.

The island's best beach is at **KILMORY**, to the north (5hr return), where students get eaten alive by midges while studying red deer. When the island's human head count peaked at 450 in 1791, the hamlet of **HARRIS** on the southwest coast (6hr return) housed a large crofting community – all that remains now are several ruined blackhouses and the extravagant **Bullough Mausoleum**, built by Sir George to house the remains of his father in the style of a Greek Doric temple, overlooking the sea. This is, in fact, the second one to be constructed here: the first was lined with Italian marble mosaics, but when a friend remarked that it looked like a public lavatory Bullough had it dynamited and the current Neoclassical one erected.

Practicalities

Until Rùm passed into the hands of the SNH, it was known as the "Forbidden Isle" because of its exclusive use as a sporting estate for the rich – nowadays, visitors are made very welcome by the SNH staff. Day-trips are possible more or less daily in the summer, either via CalMac or the Sheerwater (see box, p.352). If you plan to stay the night, you do need to book in advance, as **accommodation** is fairly limited. Kinloch Castle was a luxury hotel until the early 1990s, and still lets a few of its four-poster rooms (5), but it's basically run

Hiking in the Rùm Cuillin

Ordnance Survey Explorer map no. 397.

Rùm's Cuillin may not be as famous as Skye's, but if the weather's fine there are equally exhilarating **hiking** possibilities. Whatever route you choose, be sure to take all the usual safety precautions, described on p.59.

The most popular walk is to traverse most or part of the **Cuillin Ridge**, which takes between eight and twelve hours round-trip from Kinloch. The most frequent route is up past the old dams to Coire Dubh, and then on to the saddle of Bealach Bairc-mheall. From here, you can either climb Barkeval itself, to the west, or go straight for **Hallival** (2372ft) to the southeast, which looks daunting but is no more than a mild rock scramble. South of Hallival, the ridge is grassy, but the rocky north ridge of **Askival** (2663ft) needs to be taken quite carefully, sticking to the east side for safety. Askival is the highest mountain on Rùm, and if you're thinking of heading back, or the weather's closing in, Glen Dibidil provides an easy means of descent, after which you can follow the track back to Kinloch.

To continue along the ridge, head west to the double peak of **Trollaval** (or Trallval), the furthest of which is the highest. The descent to Bealach an Fhuarain is steep, after which it's another scramble to reach the top of **Ainshval**. Depending on the time and weather, you can continue along the ridge to **Sgurr nan Gillean**, descend via Glen Dibidil and take the coastal path back to Kinloch, or skip the Sgurr and go straight on to the last peak of the ridge, **Ruinsival**, descend via the Fiachanis basin to Harris, and then slog it back to Kinloch along the road.

On your walks, look out for the island's **native ponies**, which feed mainly in Kilmory Glen and Kinloch Glen, and are used for the stag cull in July; the **Highland cattle**, who live in Harris, except during July and August, when they're moved in Guirdil; and the multicoloured **wild goats**, which stick to the coastal areas between Kilmory, Harris and Dibidil. However, if you want to see the **Manx shearwater**, which nest in burrows on the slopes of Hallival, you'll need to be there around dusk or dawn, as this is the only time the birds return to their nests – SNH organise regular night-time hikes to go and see the birds.

as an independent **hostel** (☎01687/462037), with dormitories in the old servants' quarters. B&B is sometimes available on the island – ask at the hostel for the latest situation. There are also two simple mountain **bothies** (three nights maximum stay), in Dibidil and Guirdil, and basic **camping** (toilets and a standpipe) on the foreshore near the old pier. You need to book ahead for both by contacting the reserve manager at the *White House* (☎01687/462026).

Wherever you're staying, you can either do self-catering – hostellers can use the hostel kitchen – or eat in the hostel's licensed **bistro**, which serves full breakfasts, offers packed lunches and charges just over £10 a head for a tasty three-course evening meal (advance booking essential). There is also a small shop/off-licence/post office on the north side of the bay. Bear in mind that Rùm is the wettest of the Small Isles, and is known for having some of the worst **midges** (see p.57) in Scotland – come prepared for both. Finally, note that overnight visitors cannot bring dogs, but day-trippers can.

Eigg

Eigg (Ⓦwww.isleofeigg.org) is without doubt the most easily distinguishable of the Small Isles from a distance, since the island is mostly made up of a basalt plateau 1000ft above sea level, and a great stump of columnar pitchstone lava, known as An Sgurr, rising out of the plateau another 290ft. It's also by far the most vibrant, populous and welcoming of the Small Isles, with a real strong sense of community. This was given an enormous boost by the 1997 buyout by the seventy-odd islanders (along with the local council and the Scottish Wildlife Trust), which ended Eigg's unhappy history of private ownership, most notoriously with the Olympic bobsleigher and gelatine heir Keith Schellenberg. The anniversary of the buyout is celebrated every year with an all-night ceilidh on the weekend nearest to June 12.

Ferries arrive at the new causeway, which juts out into **Galmisdale Bay**, at the southeast corner of the island – which measures just five miles by three – where **An Laimhrig** (The Anchorage), the island's community centre, stands, housing a shop, post office, licensed tearoom and information centre. Davie's minibus meets incoming ferries, and will take you to wherever you need to go on the island (☎01687/482494; £2). If time is limited, you could simply head through the woods for the nearby **Lodge**, the former laird's house and gardens, which the islanders plan to renovate in the future. With the island's great landmark, **An Sgurr** (1292ft), watching over you wherever you go, many folk feel duty-bound to climb it, and enjoy the wonderful views over to Muck and Rùm. The easiest approach is to take the path that skirts the summit to the north, and ascend from the saddle to the west (3–4hr return).

Many visitors head off to **CLEADALE**, the main crofting settlement in the north of the island, where the beach, known as Camas Sgiotaig, or the **Singing Sands**, is comprised of quartz, which squeaks underfoot when dry (hence the name). The steep climb up to the ridge of **Ben Bhuidhe**, to the east, is hard going underfoot, but worth it for the views across to Rùm and Skye. A large colony of **Manx shearwater** nests in burrows around the base of Ben Bhuidhe; to view the birds, you need to be there just after dusk.

If you're just here for the day, make sure you pop into the **tearoom**, which has a lovely terrace looking out to sea. The nicest place **to stay** on Eigg is *Kildonan House* (☎01687/482446; full board ④), an eighteenth-century, wood-panelled house beautifully situated on the north side of Galmisdale Bay, with good home cooking. There are several **self-catering** options, which you can get off the island's website, plus *Glebe Barn* (☎01687/482417), a very

△ An Sgurr, Eigg

comfortable **bunkhouse** where you must book ahead. Wild **camping** is also possible at Galmisdale Bay and in Cleadale with Sue Hollands (Ⓣ01687/482480, Ⓔsuehollands@talk21.com), who also rents out a bothy. **Bike rental** is available from Eigg Bikes (Ⓣ01687/482432), by the pier. You'll probably notice, as you walk around the island, that Eigg has no mains electricity; some houses have water-generated electricity, but others still run off noisy diesel generators.

Muck

Smallest and most southerly of the Small Isles, **Muck** (Ⓦwww.islemuck.com) is low-lying, mostly treeless and extremely fertile, and as such shares more characteristics with the likes of Coll and Tiree (see p.115) than its nearest neighbours. Its name derives from *muc*, the Gaelic for "pig" – or, as some would have it, *muc mara*, "sea pig" or porpoise, which abound in the surrounding waters – and has long caused much embarrassment to generations of lairds who preferred to call it the "Isle of Monk", because it had briefly belonged to the medieval church.

PORT MÓR, the village on the southeast corner of the island, is where visitors arrive and where most of the thirty or so residents live. The prominent memorial in the local graveyard commemorates two islanders and a visiting student who were drowned shooting shags near Eilean nan Each (Horse Island). A road, just over a mile in length, connects Port Mór with the island's main farm, **GALLANACH**, which overlooks the rocky seal-strewn skerries on the north side of the island. The nicest sandy beach is Camas na Cairidh, to the east of Gallanach. Despite being only 452ft above sea-level, it really is worth climbing **Beinn Airein**, in the southwest corner of the island, for the 360-degree panoramic view of the surrounding islands; the return journey from Port Mór takes around two hours.

You can **stay** with one of the MacEwen family, who have owned the island since 1896, at *Port Mór House* (Ⓣ01687/462365; full board ④); the rooms are pine-clad and enjoy great views, and the food is delicious. Alternatively, you can stay at the island's **bunkhouse** (Ⓣ01687/462362), a characterful, wood-panelled bothy heated by a Rayburn stove – it's a seven-bed hostel, with three rooms, but can be booked exclusively as a self-catering unit. You can also hire the island **yurt** or the **tipi** (Ⓣ01687/462362, Ⓔjenny@isleofmuck.fsnet.co.uk), or **camp rough** on the island for free; ask at the craft shop for where to camp, and bring supplies with you, as there is no shop. For more **self-catering** options, including the island's yurt, visit the island website.

The craft shop in Port Mór springs into life when day-trippers arrive, and doubles as a licensed **restaurant**. Willow basketmaking courses are an island speciality (contact details same as yurt hire).

Canna

Measuring a mere five miles by one, and with just a handful of full-time residents, **Canna** is run as a single farm and bird sanctuary by the National Trust for Scotland (NTS). The island enjoys the best harbour in the Small Isles, a horn-shaped haven at its southeastern corner protected by the tidal island of Sanday, now linked to Canna by a wooden footbridge. For visitors, the chief pastime is walking: from the dock it's about a mile across a grassy basalt plateau to the bony sea cliffs of the north shore, which rise to a peak around Compass Hill (458ft) – so called because its high metal content distorts compasses – in the northeastern corner of the island, from where you get great views across to Rùm and Skye. The cliffs of the buffeted western half of the island are a breeding ground for both Manx shearwater and puffin, though both have suffered from the island's rat infestation. Some seven miles offshore stands the **Heiskeir of Canna**, a curious mass of stone columns sticking up 30ft above the water.

Accommodation is extremely limited. With permission from the NTS, you may **camp rough** on Canna, though you need to bring your own supplies, as there's no real shop to speak of. The NTS runs **self-catering** cottages, *Tighard*, a Victorian house half a mile from the jetty, which sleeps a maximum of ten people, and *Kate's Cottage*, a much simpler (and cheaper) bothy, which sleeps six, plus a hostel for groups in the distinctive St Edward's Church on Sanday. All the above should be booked through the NTS holidays department (Ⓣ0131/243 9300, Ⓦwww.nts.org.uk). The NTS rep on Canna is Wendy MacKinnon, who can help answer most queries (Ⓣ01687/462465, Ⓦwww.harbourview-canna.co.uk) and runs the *Harbour View* licensed **tearoom**, which serves lunch and dinner (March–Oct; advance booking essential).

Travel details

Trains

Aberdeen to: Kyle of Lochalsh (Mon–Sat 3 daily, 1 on Sun; 5hr).
Fort William to: Mallaig (4–5 daily; 1hr 25min).
Glasgow (Queen St) to: Mallaig (Mon–Sat 4 daily, 2 on Sun; 5hr 20min).
Inverness to: Kyle of Lochalsh (Mon–Sat 3–4 daily, 1–2 on Sun; 2hr 30min).

Buses

Mainland

Glasgow to: Broadford (3–4 daily; 5hr 25min); Portree (3–4 daily; 6hr–6hr 30min); Uig (Mon–Sat 3–4 daily; 7hr 40min).
Inverness to: Broadford (2 daily; 2hr 50min); Portree (2 daily; 3hr 15min).
Kyle of Lochalsh to: Kyleakin (every 30min; 10min).

Skye

Armadale to: Broadford (Mon–Sat 3–10 daily; 45min); Portree (Mon–Sat 3–10 daily; 1hr 20min); Sligachan (Mon–Sat 3–10 daily; 1hr 10min).
Broadford to: Portree (Mon–Sat 5–10 daily; 40min).
Dunvegan to: Glendale (Mon–Sat 1–2 daily; 30min).
Kyleakin to: Broadford (Mon–Sat 4–10 daily, 3–5 on Sun; 15min); Portree (Mon–Sat 4 daily, 3–5 on Sun; 1hr); Sligachan (Mon–Sat 7–8 daily, 5 on Sun; 45min); Uig (Mon–Sat 2 daily; 1hr 20min).
Portree to: Carbost (Mon–Fri 4–5 daily, 1 on Sun; 35min); Duntulm (Mon–Sat 2–4 daily; 1hr); Dunvegan (Mon–Sat 2–4 daily; 50min); Staffin (Mon–Sat 2–4 daily; 40min); Uig (Mon–Sat 4–5 daily; 30min).

CalMac ferries

Summer timetable only.
To Canna: Eigg–Canna (Mon & Sat; 2hr 15min); Mallaig–Canna (Mon, Wed, Fri & Sat; 2hr 40min–3hr 50min); Muck–Canna (Sat; 1hr 35min); Rùm–Canna (Mon, Wed, Fri & Sat; 55min).
To Eigg: Canna–Eigg (Mon & Sat; 2hr 15min); Mallaig–Eigg (Mon, Tues & Thurs–Sat; 1hr 15min–2hr 25min); Muck–Eigg (Tues & Thurs–Sat; 30min); Rùm–Eigg (Mon & Sat; 1hr–3hr 30min).
To Muck: Canna–Muck (Sat; 1hr 35min); Eigg–Muck (Tues, Thurs & Sat; 30min); Mallaig–Muck (Tues, Thurs, Fri & Sat; 1hr 40min–4hr 20min); Rùm–Muck (Sat; 2hr 45min).
To Raasay: Sconser–Raasay (Mon–Sat 9–11 daily, 2 on Sun; 15min).
To Rùm: Canna–Rùm (Mon, Wed, Fri & Sat; 55min); Eigg–Rùm (Mon & Sat; 1hr–3hr 30min); Mallaig–Rùm (Mon, Wed, Fri & Sat; 1hr 20min–2hr 30min); Muck–Rùm (Sat; 1hr 10min).
To Skye: Glenelg–Kylerhea (daily frequently; 15min); Mallaig–Armadale (Mon–Sat 8–9 daily; mid-May to mid-Sept also Sun; 30min).

6

The Western Isles

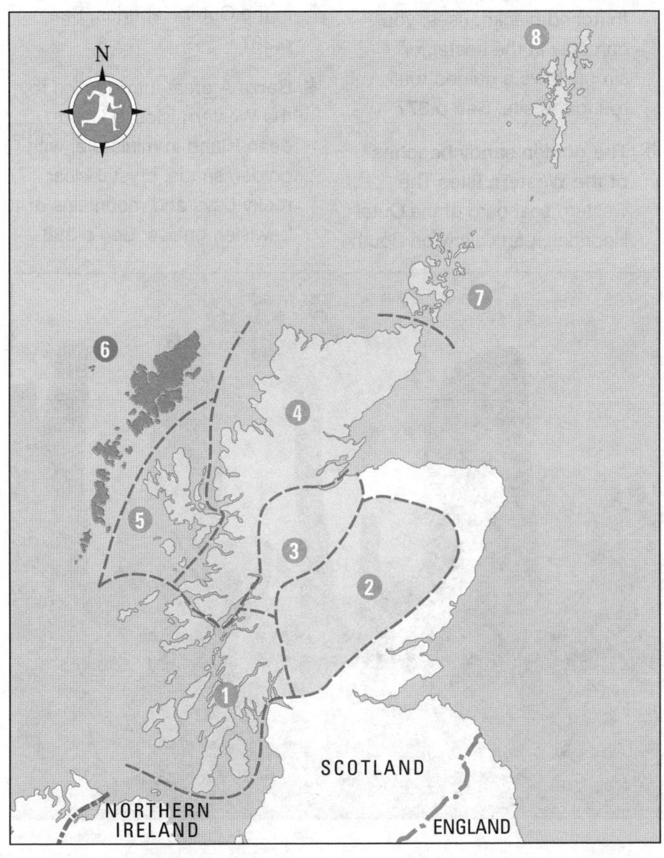

CHAPTER 6

Highlights

* **Calanais (Callanish) standing stones** Scotland's finest standing stones are in a serene lochside setting on the west coast of the Isle of Lewis. See p.377

* **Gearrannan (Garenin), Isle of Lewis** A crofting village of painstakingly restored thatched blackhouses: you can stay in the hostel, or simply have a guided tour round the site. See p.377

* **The golden sandy beaches of the Western Isles** The western seaboard of the Outer Hebrides, particularly on South Harris and the Uists, is strewn with stunning, deserted, beaches backed by flower-strewn machair. See p.384

* **Roghadal (Rodel) Church, Isle of Harris** Roghadal's pre-Reformation St Clement's Church boasts the most ornate sculptural decoration in the Outer Hebrides. See p.387

* **Barra** A great introduction to the Western Isles: a Hebridean island in miniature, with golden sands, crystal-clear rocky bays and mountains of Lewisian gneiss. See p.396

△ Calanais standing stones, Lewis

6

The Western Isles

Beyond Skye, across the unpredictable waters of the Minch, lie the wild and windy Outer Hebrides or Outer Isles, also known as the **Western Isles** (Ⓦwww.witb.co.uk), a 130-mile-long archipelago stretching from Lewis and Harris in the north to the Uists and Barra in the south. An elemental beauty pervades each of the more than two hundred islands that make up the Long Isle, as it's sometimes known, though only a handful are actually inhabited by a total population of just under 27,000 people. This is truly a land on the edge, where the turbulent seas of the Atlantic smash up against a geologically complex terrain whose rough rocks and mighty sea cliffs are interrupted by a thousand sheltered bays and, in the far west, a long line of sweeping sandy beaches. The islands' interiors are equally dramatic, a series of formidable mountain ranges soaring high above great chunks of flat, boggy peat moor, a barren wilderness enclosing a host of tiny lakes, or lochans.

However, the most significant difference between the Western Isles and the rest of the Hebrides is that here tourism is much less important to the islands' fragile economy, which is still mainly concentrated around crofting, fishing and weaving, and the percentage of "white settlers" is fairly low. In fact, the Outer Hebrides remain the heartland of **Gaelic** culture, with the language spoken by the vast majority of islanders, though its everyday usage remains under constant threat from the national dominance of English. Its survival is, in no small part, due to the efforts of the Western Islands Council and the Scottish Executive, and down to the influence of the Church in the region: the Free Church and its various offshoots in Lewis, Harris and North Uist and the Roman Catholic church in South Uist and Barra.

The interior of the northernmost island, **Lewis**, is mostly peat moor, a barren and marshy tract that gives way abruptly to the bare peaks of **North Harris**. Across a narrow isthmus lies **South Harris**, presenting some of the finest scenery in Scotland, with wide beaches of golden sand trimming the Atlantic in full view of the mountains and a rough boulder-strewn interior lying to the east. Across the Sound of Harris, to the south, a string of tiny, flatter isles – **North Uist**, **Benbecula**, **South Uist** – linked by causeways, offer breezy beaches, whose fine sands front a narrow band of boggy farmland, which, in turn, is mostly bordered by a lower range of hills to the east. Finally, tiny **Barra** contains all the above landscapes in one small Hebridean package.

In direct contrast to their wonderful landscapes, villages in the Western Isles are rarely very picturesque in themselves, and are usually made up of scattered, relatively modern crofthouses dotted about the elementary road system. **Stornoway**, the only real town in the Outer Hebrides, is eminently unappealing.

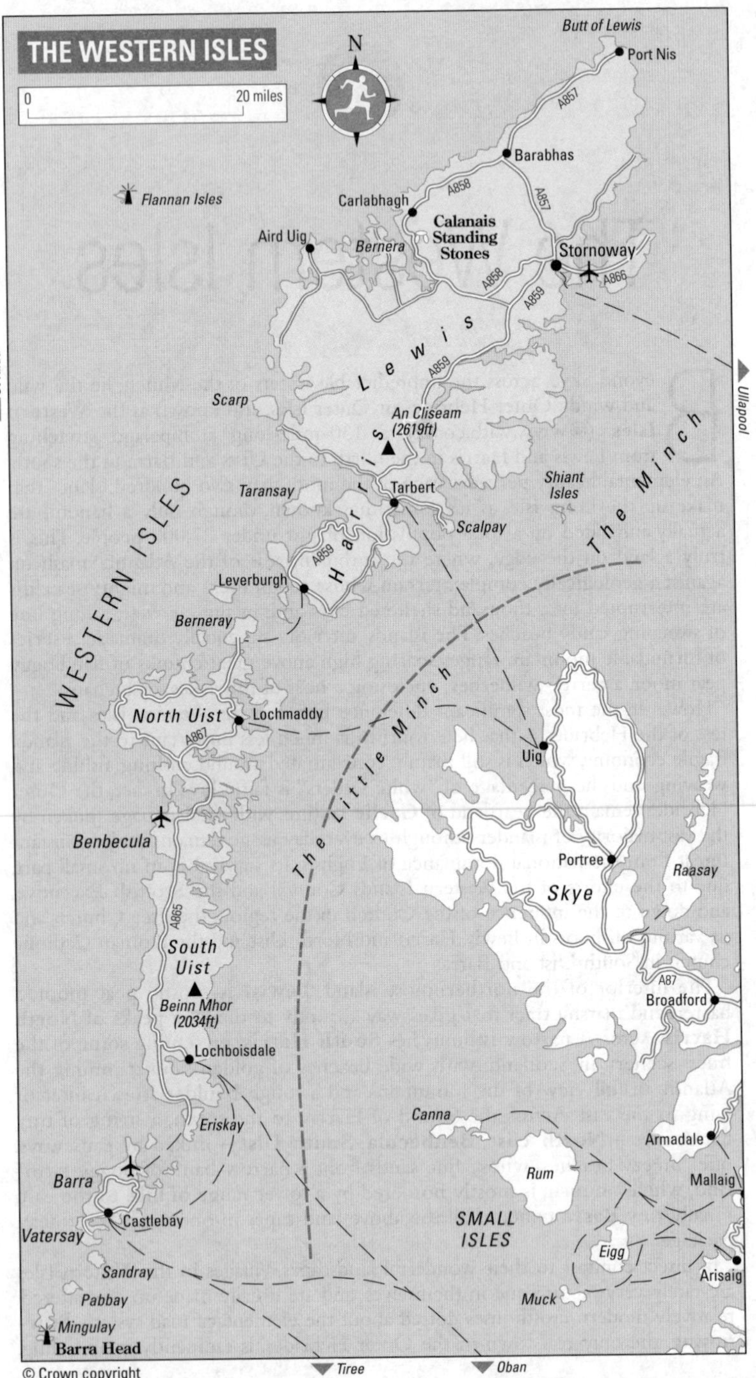
THE WESTERN ISLES
0
20 miles
N
Butt of Lewis
Port Nis
A857
Barabhas
Flannan Isles
Carlabhagh
A858
A857
Calanais
Standing
Stones
Aird Uig
Bernera
Stornoway
A866
A858
A859
Lewis
A859
St Kilda
Ullapool
Scarp
An Cliseam
(2619ft)
Harris
The Minch
Shiant
Isles
Taransay
Tarbert
Scalpay
WESTERN ISLES
A859
Leverburgh
Berneray
North Uist
Lochmaddy
A867
The Little Minch
Uig
Benbecula
Portree
Raasay
Skye
A865
South
Uist
Beinn Mhor
(2034ft)
A87
Broadford
Lochboisdale
Eriskay
Canna
Armadale
Barra
Rum
Mallaig
Castlebay
SMALL
ISLES
Vatersay
Eigg
Arisaig
Sandray
Pabbay
Muck
Mingulay
Barra Head
Tiree
Oban

Gaelic in the Western Isles

Except in Stornoway, and Balivanich on Benbecula, **road signs** are now almost exclusively in **Gaelic**, a difficult language to the English-speaker's eye, with complex pronunciation (see p.541), though as a (very) general rule, the English names often provide a rough pronunciation guide. Particularly if you're driving, it's a good idea to buy the bilingual Western Isles **map**, produced by the local tourist board, Bord Turasachd nan Eilean, and available at most tourist offices. To reflect the signposting, we've put the Gaelic first in the text, with the English equivalent in brackets. Thereafter we've stuck to the Gaelic names, to try to familiarize readers with their (albeit variable) spellings – the only exceptions are in the names of islands and ferry terminals, where we've stuck to the English names (with the Gaelic in brackets), partly to reflect CalMac's own policy.

Many visitors, walkers and nature watchers forsake the main settlements altogether and retreat to secluded cottages, simple hostels and B&Bs.

Some history

The Western Isles were first settled by Neolithic farming peoples in around 4000 BC. They lived along the coast, where they are remembered by scores of remains, from passage graves through to stone circles – most famously at **Calanais** (Callanish) on Lewis. Viking colonization gathered pace from 700 AD onwards – on Lewis four out of every five place names is of Norse origin – and it was only in 1266 that the islands were returned to the Scottish crown. James VI (and I of England), a Stuart and a Scot, though no Gaelic-speaker, was the first to put forward the idea of clearing the Hebrides, though it wasn't until after the Jacobite uprisings, in which many Highland clans disastrously backed the wrong side, that the **Clearances** began in earnest.

The isolation of the Outer Hebrides exposed them to the whims and fancies of the various merchants and aristocrats who caught "island fever" and bought them up. Time and again, from the mid-eighteenth century to the present day, both the land and its people were sold to the highest bidder. Some proprietors were well-meaning, but insensitive – like **Lord Leverhulme**, who had no time for crofting and wanted to turn Lewis into a centre of the fishing industry in the 1920s – while others were simply autocratic – such as **Colonel Gordon of Cluny**, who bought Benbecula, South Uist, Eriskay and Barra, and forced the inhabitants onto ships bound for North America at gunpoint. Almost everywhere crofters were driven from their ancestral homes, robbing them of their particular sense of place. Today, memorials and cairns dot the landscape commemorating the often violent struggle which accompanied this period.

Visiting the Western Isles

Several airlines operate fast and frequent daily **flights** from Glasgow, Edinburgh and Inverness to Stornoway on Lewis, and from Glasgow to Barra and Benbecula (Mon–Sat only). But be warned: the weather conditions on the islands are notoriously changeable, making flights prone to cancellation, delay and stomach-churning bumpiness. On Barra, the other complication is that you land on the beach, so the timetable is adjusted with the tides. CalMac **car ferries** run from Ullapool in the Highlands to Stornoway (Mon–Sat only); from Uig, on Skye, to Tarbert (Mon–Sat) and Lochmaddy (daily); and from Oban to South Uist and Barra (daily), via Tiree (Thurs only). There's also an **inter-island ferry** from Leverburgh, on Harris, to Berneray (Mon–Sat only), and thence to the

Religion in the Western Isles

It is difficult to overestimate the importance of **religion** in the Western Isles, which are divided – with very little enmity – between the Catholic southern isles of Barra and South Uist, and the Protestant islands of North Uist, Harris and Lewis. Church attendance is higher here than anywhere else in Britain and in fact, Barra, Eriskay and South Uist are the only parts of Britain where Roman Catholics are in a majority, and where you'll see statues of the Madonna by the roadside. In the Presbyterian north, the creed of **Sabbatarianism** is very strong. Here, Sunday is the Lord's Day, and pretty much the whole community (irrespective of their degree of piety) stops work – shops close, pubs close, garages close and there's no public transport. Even the swings in the children's playgrounds used to be padlocked, though that is no longer the case. In fact, in recent years Sunday flights have appeared, at least one garage opens and you can have a drink (with food) on the Sabbath. Nevertheless, it's advisable for visitors not to arrive at or leave their accommodation on a Sunday, to avoid causing offence.

The main area of division is, paradoxically, within the Protestant Church itself. Scotland is unusual in that the national church, the **Church of Scotland** (ⓦwww.churchofscotland.org.uk), is Presbyterian (ruled by the ministers and elders of the church) rather than Episcopal (ruled by bishops). At the time of the main split in the Presbyterian Church – the so-called **1843 Disruption** – a third of its ministers left the Church of Scotland, protesting at a law that allowed landlords to impose ministers against parishioners' wishes, and formed the breakaway **Free Church of Scotland** (ⓦwww.freechurch.org). Since those days there have been several amalgamations, reconciliations, and further splits. In 1893, for example, a minority of the Free Church became the Free Presbyterian Church of Scotland (ⓦwww.fpchurch.org.uk); meanwhile, others slowly made their way back to the Church of Scotland. To confuse matters further, both the Free Church and the Free Presbyterians are referred to as "**Wee Frees**". In recent years, there have been still more schisms within the Wee Frees: in 1988 the Free Presbyterian Church split over a minister, Lord Mackay of Clashfern, who attended a Requiem Mass during a Catholic funeral of a friend – he and his supporters went on to form the breakaway Associated Presbyterian Churches (ⓦwww.apchurches.org). More recently still, the Free Church split over the "heresies" of Professor Donald MacLeod, one of its more liberal members, who writes a regular column in the *West Highland Free Press*. A minority within the church went on to form the Free Church of Scotland (Continuing) (ⓦwww.freechurchcontinuing.co.uk), accompanied by the usual battles over church buildings and congregations.

The various brands and subdivisions of the Presbyterian Church may appear trivial to outsiders, but to the churchgoers of Lewis, Harris and North Uist (as well as much of Skye and Raasay) they are still keenly felt. In part, this is due to social and cultural reasons: Free Church elders helped organize resistance to the Clearances, and the Wee Frees have contributed greatly to preserving the Gaelic language. A Free Church service is a memorable experience, and in some villages it takes place every evening (and twice on Sunday): there's no set service or prayer book and no hymns; only biblical readings, psalm singing and a fiery sermon all in Gaelic; the pulpit is the architectural focus of the church, not the altar, and communion is taken only on special occasions. If you want to attend one, the Free Church on Kenneth Street in Stornoway has reputedly the largest Sunday evening congregation in the UK, with up to 1500 people attending.

Uists, and daily between Eriskay, at the foot of the Uists, and Barra (for more on ferry services, see "Travel details" on p.400).

Although travelling around the islands is time-consuming, for many people this is part of their charm. A series of inter-island causeways makes it possible to drive from one end of the Western Isles to the other with just two interruptions – the CalMac **ferry** trip from Harris to Berneray, and the one from Eriskay to Barra. The islands boast an efficient **bus** service, but there are absolutely no buses on Sundays. Note, however, local companies often offer very reasonable **car rental** rates though you're not permitted to take their vehicles off the Western Isles. Cycle tourism is surprisingly popular: it's true that traffic is very light but the (prevailing southwest) wind makes cycling something of a challenge even for the fit and healthy. Limited **bike rental** is available throughout the archipelago.

The islands' **hostels** are geared up for the outdoor life, occupying remote locations on or near the coast. Several of them are run by the Gatliff Hebridean Hostels Trust or GHHT (Ⓦwww.gatliff.org.uk), which has renovated several isolated cottages. None of these has phones, so you can't book in advance – in the height of summer it's best to get there early to be sure of a bed, though it's also possible to camp at the hostels; each hostel has hot water and a simple kitchen. If you're after a little more comfort, then the islands have a generous sprinkling of reasonably priced **B&Bs** and **guesthouses** – many of which are a lot better value than the hotels, allow you to meet local folk and can be easily booked over the phone, or through the tourist offices for a small fee – again, in the height of summer it's best to book in advance.

The influence of the Atlantic Gulf Stream ensures a mild but moist climate, though you can expect the **strong Atlantic winds** to blow in rain on two out of every three days even in summer. Weather fronts, however, come and go at such dramatic speed in these parts that there's little chance of mist or fog settling for long and few problems with midges. Lastly, a good way to get acquainted with local life is to read the **local papers**; the old fashioned *Stornoway Gazette* and, in particular, the weekly *West Highland Free Press* (Ⓦwww.whfp.com), a refreshingly vociferous campaigning paper, published in Broadford on Skye, but covering events in the whole of the Western Isles and Highland region.

Lewis (Leodhas)

Shaped rather like the top of an ice-cream cone, **Lewis** is the largest and by far the most populous of the Western Isles and the northernmost island in the Hebridean archipelago. Most of the island's 20,000 inhabitants – two-thirds of the Western Isles' total population – now live in the crofting and fishing villages strung out along the northwest coast, between **Calanais** and **Port Nis**, in one of the most densely populated rural areas in the country. On this coast you'll also find the islands' best-preserved **prehistoric remains** – Dùn Charlabhaigh broch and the Calanais standing stones – as well as a smattering of ancient crofters' houses in various stages of abandonment. The landscape is mostly flat peat bog – hence the island's name, derived from the Gaelic *leogach* (marshy) – but the shoreline is more dramatic especially around Rubha Robhanais (Butt of Lewis), a group of rough rocks on the island's northernmost tip, near Port Nis. To the south, where Lewis is physically joined with Harris, the land rises to just over 1800ft, providing an exhilarating backdrop for the excellent beaches that pepper the isolated coastline of **Uig**, to the west of Calanais. **Stornoway**, on the east coast, is the only real town in the Western Isles, but it's really only useful for stocking up on provisions and/or catching the bus: there are regular services to all parts of the island, and most usefully to Port Nis and Tarbert, and along the 45-mile round trip from Stornoway to Calanais, Carlabhagh, Arnol and back.

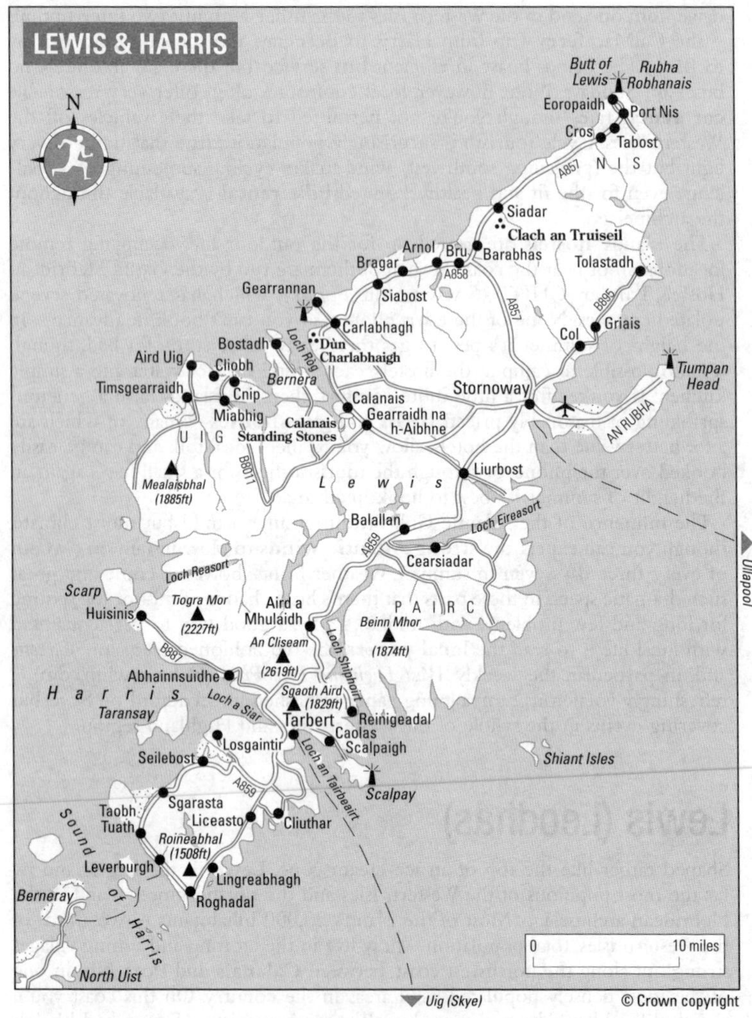

Some history

After Viking rule ended in 1266, Lewis became a virtually independent state, ruled over by the **MacLeod clan** for several centuries. King James VI, however, had other ideas: he declared the folk of Lewis to be "void of religion", and attempted to establish a colony, as in Ulster, by sending Fife Adventurers to attack Lewis. They were met with armed resistance by the MacLeods; so, in retaliation, James VI granted the lands to their archrivals, the MacKenzies of Kintail. The MacKenzie chiefs – the Earls of Seaforth – chose to remain absentee landlords until 1844, when they sold Lewis to **Sir James Matheson**, who'd made a fortune from pushing opium on the Chinese. Matheson invested heavily in the island's infrastructure, though, as his critics point out, he made sure he recouped his money through tax or rent. He was relatively benevolent when the island was hit by potato famine in the mid-1840s, but ultimately opted for solving the problem through eviction and emigration. His chief factor, Donald Munro, was utterly ruthless, and was only removed after the celebrated Bernera Riot of 1874 (see p.379). The 1886 Crofters' Act greatly curtailed the power of the Mathesons; it did not, however, right any of the wrongs of the past. Protests, such as the Pairc Deer Raid of 1887, in which starving crofters killed 200 deer from one of the sporting estates, and the Aignish land raids of the following year, continued against the Clearances of earlier that century.

When **Lord Leverhulme**, founder of the soap empire Unilever, acquired the island (along with Harris) in 1918, he was determined to drag Lewis out of its cycle of poverty by establishing an integrated fishing industry. To this end he founded MacFisheries, a nationwide chain of retail outlets for the fish which would be caught and processed on the islands: he built a cannery, an ice factory, roads, bridges and a light railway; he bought boats, and planned to use spotter planes to locate the shoals of herring. But the dream never came to fruition. Unfortunately, Leverhulme was implacably opposed to the island's centuries-old tradition of crofting, which he regarded as inefficient and "an entirely impossible way of life". He became involved in a long, drawn-out dispute over the distribution of land to returning ex-servicemen, the "land fit for heroes" promised by the Board of Agriculture.

Peat

One of the characteristic features of the landscape of the Scottish Highlands and Islands is **peat** (*mòine*) – and nowhere is its presence more keenly felt than on Lewis. Virtually the whole interior of the island is made up of one, vast blanket bog, scarred with lines of peat banks old and new, while the pungent smell of peat smoke hits you as you drive through the villages. Essentially, peat is made up of dead vegetation that has failed to rot completely because the sheer volume of rainfall has caused the soil acidity to reach such a level that it acts as a preservative. In other words, organic matter – such as sphagnum moss, rushes, sedges and reeds – is dying at a faster rate than it is decomposing. This means, of course, that peat is still (very slowly) forming in certain parts of Scotland, at around an inch or less every fifty years. In the mostly treeless Scottish Islands, peat provided an important source of fuel, and the cutting and stacking of peats in the spring was part of the annual cycle of crofting life. As a result, peat cutting remains embedded in island culture, and is still practised on a large scale particularly in the Hebrides and Shetland. It's a social occasion as much as anything else, which heralds the arrival of the warmer, drier days of late spring.

Great pride is taken in the artistry and neatness of the peat banks and stacks. In some parts, the peat lies up to thirty feet deep, but peat banks are usually only cut to a depth of around six or seven feet. Once the top layer of turf has been removed, the peat is cut into slabs between two and four peats deep, using a traditional *tairsgeir* (pronounced "tushkar"). Since peat is ninety percent water in its natural state, it has to be carefully "lifted" in order to dry out. Peats tend to be piled up either vertically in "rooks", or crisscrossed in "windows"; either way the peat will lose around 75 percent of its water content, and shrink by about a quarter. Many folk wonder how on earth the peat can dry out when it seems to rain the whole time, but the wind helps, and eventually a skin is formed that stops any further water from entering the peats. After three or four weeks, the peats are skilfully "grieved", rather like the slates on a roof, into round-humped stacks or onto carts that can be brought home. Traditionally, the peat would be carried from the peat banks by women using "creels", baskets that were strapped on the back. Correctly grieved peats allow the rain to run off, and therefore stay dry for a year or more outside the croft.

In the end, however, it was actually financial difficulties which prompted Leverhulme to pull out of Lewis in 1923 and concentrate on Harris. He generously gifted Lews Castle and Stornoway to its inhabitants and offered free crofts to those islanders who had not been involved in land raids. In the event, few crofters took up the offer – all they wanted was security of tenure, not ownership. Whatever the merits of Leverhulme's plans, his departure left a huge gap in the non-crofting economy, and between the wars thousands more emigrated.

Stornoway (Steornabhagh)

In these parts, **STORNOWAY** is a buzzing metropolis, with over 6000 inhabitants, a one-way system, pedestrian precinct with CCTV and all the trappings of a large town. It's a centre for employment, a social hub for the island and, perhaps most importantly of all, home to the Western Isles Council or **Comhairle nan Eilean Siar** (Ⓦwww.cne-siar.gov.uk), set up in 1974, which has done so much to promote Gaelic language and culture and to try to stem the tide of anglicization. For the visitor, however, the town is unlikely to win any great praise – aesthetics are not its strong point, and the urban pleasures on offer are limited.

Information and accommodation

The best thing about Stornoway is the convenience of its services. The island's **airport** (Ⓣ01851/707400, Ⓦwww.hial.co.uk) is four miles east of the town centre: the hourly bus takes fifteen minutes, or else it's a £5 taxi ride into town. The swanky octagonal CalMac **ferry terminal** (Ⓣ01851/702361) is on South Beach, close to the **bus station** (Ⓣ01851/704327). You can get bus timetables, a map of the town, a parking disc and other useful information from the **tourist office**, near North Beach at 26 Cromwell St (April to mid-Oct Mon–Sat 9am–6pm, open 8–9pm to meet the evening ferry; mid-Oct to March Mon–Fri 9am–5pm; Ⓣ01851/703088).

Of the **hotels**, the *Royal Hotel* on Cromwell Street (Ⓣ01851/702109, Ⓦwww.calahotels.com; ⑤) is your best bet. Better value by far, however, is the *Park Guest House* (Ⓣ01851/702485; ④) on James Street, where the public areas have bags of lugubrious late Victorian character (the bedrooms significantly less), or the *Hebridean Guest House*, 61 Bayhead St (Ⓣ01851/702268, Ⓦwww.hebrideanguesthouse.co.uk; ④), whose rooms are newly furnished in pine. Of the **B&Bs**, try *Fernlea*, a listed Victorian house, along leafy Matheson Road, at no. 9 (Ⓣ01851/702125, Ⓔmaureenmacmillan@amserve.com; ③), or *Hal O The Wynd*, 2 Newton St (Ⓣ01851/706073; ③), conveniently situated right opposite the ferry terminal.

Fair Haven, 28 Francis St (Ⓣ01851/705862, Ⓦwww.hebrideansurf.co.uk; ①), is primarily a **hostel** for surfers, but welcomes all; accommodation consists of bunk, family and single rooms and there's a good restaurant too. If you're **camping**, head out of Stornoway, unless you need to stay near town, in which case *Laxdale Holiday Park* (Ⓣ01851/703234, Ⓦwww.laxdaleholidaypark.com) lies a mile or so along the road to Barabhas, on Laxdale Lane; the campsite has holiday caravans (short breaks available), a self-catering bungalow and a purpose-built **bunkhouse**, as well as a nice sheltered spot for tents.

The Town

For centuries, life in Stornoway has focused on its **harbour**, whose quayside was filled with barrels of pickled herring, and whose deep and sheltered waters were thronged with coastal steamers and fishing boats in their nineteenth-century heyday, when more than a thousand boats were based at the port. Today,

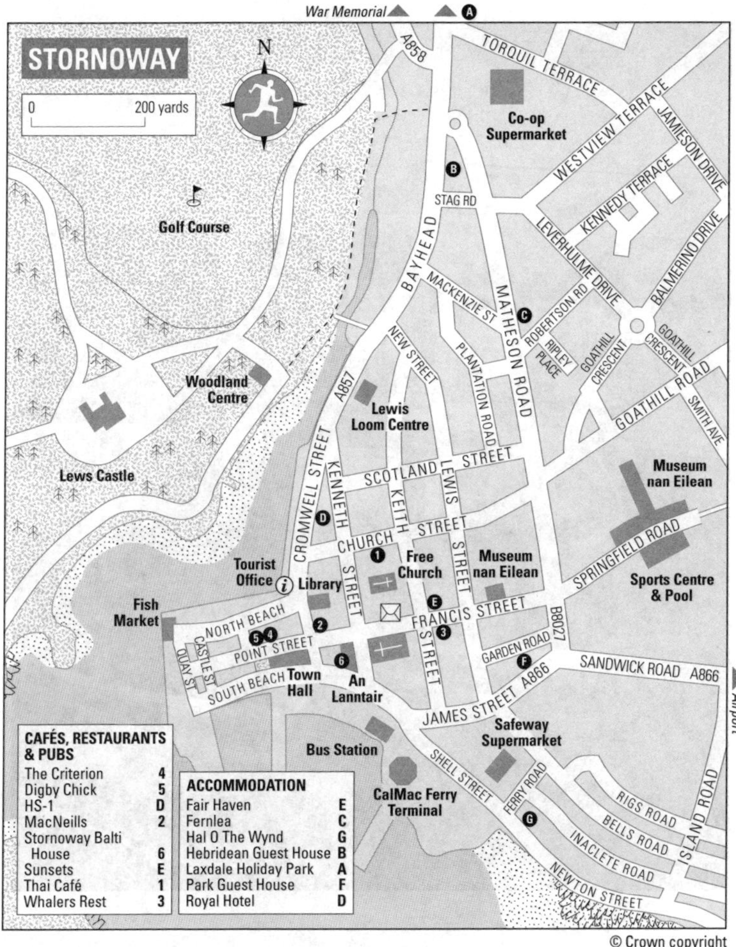

most of the catch is landed on the mainland, and, despite the daily comings and goings of the CalMac ferry from Ullapool, the harbour is a shadow of its former commercial self. The nicest section of it is Cromwell Street Quay, by the tourist office, where the remaining fishing fleet ties up for the night.

Stornoway's commercial centre, to the east, is little more than a string of unprepossessing shops and bars. The one exception is the old **Town Hall** on South Beach, a splendid Scots Baronial building, its rooftop peppered with conical towers, above which a central clocktower rises. One block east along South Beach, and looking rather like a modern church, you'll find **An Lanntair** (Mon–Sat 10am–10pm; free; Ⓦwww.lanntair.com) – Gaelic for "lantern" – Stornoway's long-awaited new arts centre, which houses a 250-seat auditorium and cinema, and gallery space for temporary exhibitions, plus a very pleasant café-bar.

At the eastern end of Francis Street is the **Museum nan Eilean** (April–Sept Mon–Sat 10am–5.30pm; Oct–March Tues–Fri 10am–5pm, Sat

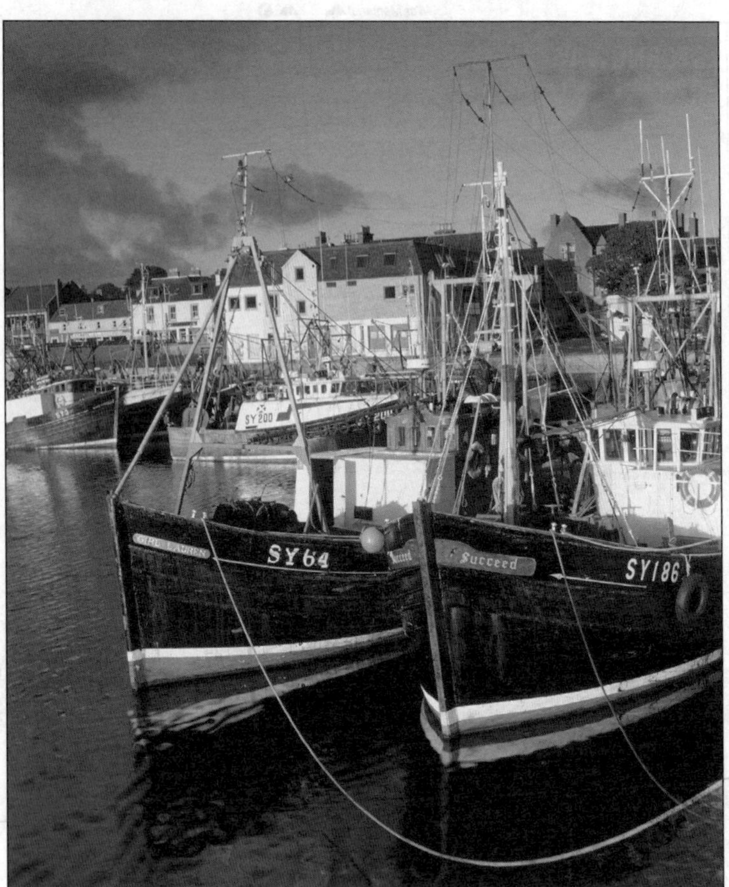

△ Stornoway harbour

10am–1pm; free; Ⓦ www.cne-siar.gov.uk), in the Victorian school buildings that used to house the Nicolson Institute. The ground-floor gallery explores the island's history until the MacKenzie takeover in 1613, and is full of artefacts found during peat-cutting, including silver jewellery, a large Viking dish made from alderwood and a plaque fashioned from a fragment of whalebone. The first-floor gallery concentrates on the herring and weaving industries and houses an old loom shed with one of the semi-automatic looms introduced by Lord Leverhulme in the 1920s. There's also a blackhouse interior, press cuttings on the Rocket Mail (see p.384) and a silent film of crofting life shot on Lewis in 1937.

Anyone remotely interested in Harris tweed should head for the **Lewis Loom Centre** (Mon–Sat 9am–6pm; £1; Ⓦ www.lewisloomcentre.co.uk), run by an eccentric and engaging man, and located at the far end of Cromwell Street, in the Old Grainstore off Bayhead. There's an exhibition on the cloth, a shop, and three looms, one of which is a Hattersley, which you may catch going through its paces.

To the northwest of the town centre, across the bay, stands **Lews Castle** (Ⓦwww.lews-castle.com), a castellated pomposity built by Sir James Matheson in 1863 after resettling the crofters who used to live here. As the former laird's pad, it is seen as a symbol of old oppression by many: it was here, in the house's now defunct conservatory, that Lady Matheson famously gave tea to the Bernera protesters, when they marched on Stornoway prior to the riot (see p.379); when the eccentric Lord Leverhulme took up residence, he had unglazed bedroom windows which allowed the wind and rain to enter, and gutters in the asphalt floor to carry off the residue. The building is currently in a state of some disrepair, and looks set to stay that way for some time still as it would take millions to renovate the place. In the meantime, its chief attraction is its mature wooded grounds, a unique sight on the Western Isles, for which Matheson had to import thousands of tons of soil from the mainland. Hidden in amongst the trees is the **Woodland Centre** (Mon–Sat 10am–5pm; free), which has a straightforward exhibition on the history of the castle and the island upstairs, with a live CCTV link to a nearby nest box, and a decent **café** serving soup, salads and cakes downstairs.

If you enter or exit Stornoway via Willowglen Road (A858), you'll see the town **War Memorial**, a castle tower set high above the town amidst gorse bushes, and a good place to take in the sprawl that is Stornoway.

Eating, drinking and nightlife

Food options have improved in Stornoway over the last couple of years. The best option is the *Thai Café*, 27 Church St, which serves inexpensive but authentic Thai food – reserve ahead if you can (Ⓣ01851/701811; closed Sun). *HS-1*, the café-bar in the *Royal Hotel*, is a stylish, modern place, offering everything from simple fare like baked potatoes to stir-fries and curry. *Sunsets*, the smart, modern restaurant below the *Fair Haven* surfers' hostel, serves good local food, as does the even more formal *Digby Chick*, on the corner of Bank Street and Point Street (Ⓣ01851/700026) – both are expensive, but *Digby Chick* offers more reasonably priced lunch and early evening menus. The *Stornoway Balti House*, near the bus station on South Beach, is a good option on any night, but particularly on Sunday evenings, when most places are closed.

As for **pubs**, *MacNeills* on Cromwell Street is the liveliest central pub, with a mixed clientele of keen drinkers. *The Criterion*, a tiny wee pub on Point Street, is another option. There's sometimes **live music** at the Royal British Legion, opposite the ferry terminal, or the *Whalers Rest*, on Francis Street, and a regular programme of **gigs and films** at *An Lanntair*. Stornoway is also the focus of the annual **Hebridean Celtic Festival** (Ⓦwww.hebceltfest.com), in mid-July, a jamboree of music with a festival tent in Lews Castle grounds, and other events in Stornoway and elsewhere on Lewis and Harris. Needless to say, nearly all pubs are closed on Sundays, though some hotel bars will serve food and drink to non-residents.

Listings

Bakery Stag Bakery, Cromwell St; next door is Nature's Store, a health-food shop.
Bike rental Alex Dan's, 67 Kenneth St Ⓣ01851/704025, Ⓦwww.hebrideancycles.co.uk (closed Sun).
Black puddings The Stornoway black puddings (and the white and fruit ones) are famous, and made to a secret family recipe by local butcher, Charles MacLeod, who has a shop at Ropework Park (Ⓣ01851/702445, Ⓦwww.charlesmacleod.co.uk).
Bookshops Baltic Bookshop, 8–10 Cromwell St.
Brewery The Hebridean Brewing Company, at 18 Bells Rd, produce their own beers and their premises can be toured by phoning Ⓣ01851/700123, Ⓦwww.hebridean-brewery.co.uk.

The Iolaire disaster

Of the 6200 men from the Western Isles who served in World War I, around 1000 died. Yet, on New Year's Day 1919, in the single most terrible tragedy to befall Lewis, another 208 more perished. On New Year's Eve some 530 servicemen were gathered at Kyle of Lochalsh to return home to Lewis and their families on the mailboat. However, as there were so many of them, an extra boat was called into service, the **Iolaire**, originally built as a luxury yacht in 1881. The boat left at 7.30pm heavily overloaded, carrying 284 men, young men and veterans, friends and relatives, to cross the Minch. In the early hours of the morning as the boat approached Stornoway harbour, she struck a group of rocks called Blastan Thuilm (Beasts of Holm). In the darkness, it was impossible for those on board to see that they were in fact only twenty yards from the shore.

One man, a boatbuilder from Nis (Ness), a village that was to lose 21 men that night, fought his way ashore with a lifeline which saved the lives of forty others. Another was saved by clinging to the mast for seven hours, but he lost his elder brother, who'd postponed his return so that they could come back together. Another man, when on active service, had spent 36 hours in the sea, sole survivor of his torpedoed ship; now he drowned within sight of his home. Every village in Lewis lost at least one returning loved one, and this, together with the losses in the war and the mass emigration that followed, cast a shadow over life on Lewis for many years. It was the worst peacetime shipping disaster in home waters that century. There's a monument at Rubha Thuilm (Holm Point) and the ship's bell is in the Museum nan Eilean in Stornoway.

Car rental Lewis Car Rentals, 52 Bayhead St (☎01851/703760, Ⓦwww.lewis-car-rental.co.uk), will deliver locally for free, as will Mackinnon Self-Drive, southeast of the town centre, at 18 Inaclete Rd (☎01851/702984, Ⓦwww.mackinnonselfdrive.co.uk).

Internet Stornoway Library, 19 Cromwell St ☎01851/703064 (closed Sun).

Pharmacy Boots is on the corner of Cromwell St and Point St.

Taxis Radio Cabs, 14a New St ☎01851/702092.

The road to Tolastadh (Tolsta)

Given the relative paucity of attractions in Stornoway, the dead-end B895 to **TOLASTADH**, twelve miles north along the east coast, is a good road to head out on. It boasts several excellent golden beaches and marks the starting point of a lovely coastal walk to Nis – at least, for the moment, though the locals have plans to blast a road through here, just as Lord Leverhulme once envisaged (see below).

The legacy of Lord Leverhulme's brief ownership of Lewis is recalled by the striking **Griais Memorial** to the Lewis land-raiders, situated by Griais Bridge, above Gress Sands. It was here that Leverhulme's plans came unstuck: he wanted to turn the surrounding crofting land into three big farms, which would provide milk for the workers of his fish-canning factory; the local crofters just wanted to return to their traditional way of life. Such was Leverhulme's fury at the land-raiders from Griais (Gress) and nearby Col (Coll), a mile to the south, that, when he offered to gift the crofts of Lewis to their owners, he made sure the offer didn't include Griais and Col. The stone-built memorial is a symbolic croft split asunder by Leverhulme's interventions.

Further north, beyond Tolastadh, is probably the finest of the coast's sandy beaches, Gheardha (Garry), and the beginning of the footpath to Nis. Shortly after leaving the bay, the path crosses the **Bridge to Nowhere**, built by Leverhulme as part of an unrealized plan to forge a new road right along the east coast. A little further along the track, there's a fine waterfall on the Abhainn na Cloich (River of Stones). The makeshift road peters out, but a waymarked path continues for another ten miles via the old sheiling village of Diobadail, to Nis (see p.374). It's very boggy, and badly churned up in places due to its popularity with local quad-bikers, so make sure you've got proper footwear. If you're in search of a cuppa, try the **pottery** back in Col.

The road to Barabhas (Barvas) and Nis (Ness)

Northwest of Stornoway, the A857 crosses the vast, barren **peat bog** of the Lewis interior, an empty, undulating wilderness riddled with stretchmarks formed by peat cuttings and pockmarked with freshwater lochans. The whole area was once covered by forests, but these disappeared long ago, leaving a smothering deposit of peat that is, on average, six feet thick, and is still being formed in certain places. For the people of Lewis, the peat continues to serve as a valuable energy resource, with each crofter being assigned a slice of the bog. The islanders spend several very sociable weeks each spring cutting the peat, turning it over and leaving it neatly laid out in the open air to dry, returning in summer to collect the dried sods and stack them outside their houses. Though tempting to take home as souvenirs, these piles are the fruits of hard labour, and remain the island's main source of domestic fuel, its pungent smoke one of the most characteristic smells of the Western Isles.

Twelve miles across the peat bog the road approaches the west coast of Lewis and divides, heading southwest towards Calanais (see p.377), or northeast through **BARABHAS** (Barvas), and a whole string of bleak and fervently Presbyterian crofting and weaving villages. These scattered settlements have none of the photogenic qualities of Skye's whitewashed villages: the churches are plain and unadorned; the crofters' houses relatively modern and smothered in grey pebble-dash rendering or harling; the stone cottages and enclosures of their forebears often lie half-abandoned in the front garden; a rusting assortment of

Lewis Wind Farm

Tourists tend to cross the barren, almost intimidating, landscape of the Lewis **peat bog** at some speed – even the locals spend little time on the moor except to gather peat. Yet these natural wetlands have been identified as important "carbon sinks", which soak up greenhouse gases, and as a vital breeding ground for species such as red- and black-throated diver, golden plover, dunlin and greenshank. In a tricky little clash of ecological interests, however, plans are afoot to build the world's largest onshore **wind farm** (®www.lewiswind.com), with over two hundred wind turbines, each standing 400ft high, harnessing a renewable resource which Lewis has in vast quantities. Understandably, many locals are in favour of the project, which should create three hundred jobs, provide electricity for over a million people, and pump millions into the local economy. However, an equal number are concerned about the inevitable visual and environmental impact: over 100 miles of roads will need to be built, along with 40 miles of overhead cables, over 200 pylons, 9 electrical substations and at least 5 quarries. The council received around 5000 objections to the proposal, including ones from the RSPB, the Scottish Wildlife Trust and the John Muir Trust, but unanimously passed the planning application. Ultimately, it will be down to the Scottish ministers who will make a decision in 2006, and, after that, the European Commission.

discarded cars and vans store peat bags and the like. Just beyond Barabhas, a signpost points to the pleasant **Morven Gallery** (Easter–Oct Mon–Sat 10.30am–5pm; free; Ⓦwww.morvengallery.com/prints.asp), which hosts exhibitions by local artists and photographers and has a handy café to hole up in during bad weather. Three miles further up the road, you pass the twenty-foot monolith of **Clach an Truiseil**, the first of a series of prehistoric sights between the crofting and weaving settlements of **Baile an Truiseil** (Ballantrushal) and **Siadar** (Shader). Beyond Siadar, anyone with a passing interest in pottery should visit **Borgh Pottery** (Mon–Sat 9.30am–6pm; free; Ⓦwww.borgh-pottery.com), where you can watch the husband-and-wife team creating hand-thrown pots.

Nis (Ness)

The main road continues through a string of straggling villages, until you reach the various densely populated settlements that make up the parish of **NIS** (Ness), at the northern tip of Lewis. Nis has the highest percentage of Gaelic speakers in the country, at over ninety percent, but the locals are perhaps best known for their annual culling of young gannets on Sula Sgeir (see box, p.376). For an insight into the social history of the area, take a look inside Ness Heritage Centre or **Comunn Eachdraidh Nis** (Oct–May Mon–Fri 10am–5pm; June–Sept Mon–Sat; free; Ⓦwww.c-e-n.org), on the left as you pass through **TABOST** (Habost). The museum, housed in an unlikely-looking building, contains a huge collection of photographs, but its prize possession is a diminutive sixth- or seventh-century cross from the Isle of Rona (see box, p.376), decorated with a much-eroded nude male figure, and thought by some to have been St Ronan's gravestone; you can have tea and coffee here too. The road terminates at the fishing village of **PORT NIS** (Port of Ness), with a tiny harbour and lovely golden beach.

Shortly before you reach Port Nis, a minor road heads two miles northwest to the hamlet of **EOROPAIDH** (Europie) – pronounced "Yor-erpee". Here, by the road junction that leads to the Butt of Lewis, the simple stone structure of **Teampull Mholuaidh** (St Moluag's Church) stands amidst the runrig fields, which now act as sheep runs. Thought to date from the twelfth century, when the islands were still under Norse rule, but restored in 1912 (and now used once a month by the Scottish Episcopal Church for sung Communion), the church features a strange south chapel with only a squint window connecting it to the nave. In the late seventeenth century, the traveller Martin Martin noted: "they all went to church … and then standing silent for a little time, one of them gave a signal … and immediately all of them went into the fields, where they fell a drinking their ale and spent the remainder of the night in dancing and singing, etc". Church services aren't what they used to be.

From Eoropaidh, a narrow road twists to the bleak and blustery northern tip of the island, **Rubha Robhanais** – well-known to devotees of the BBC shipping forecast as the **Butt of Lewis** – where a redbrick lighthouse sticks up above a series of sheer cliffs and stacks, alive with kittiwakes, fulmars and cormorants, with skuas and gannets feeding offshore; it's a great place for marine mammal-spotting. The lighthouse is closed to the public, and there's no way down to the sea, but backtrack half a mile or so, and there's a path down to the tiny sandy bay of **Port Sto**, a more sheltered spot for a picnic than the Butt itself. From Eoropaidh, you can also gain access to the dunes and machair of the nearby coastline that stretches for two or three miles to the southwest.

Practicalities

There are between four and six buses a day from Stornoway to Port Nis, Sundays excepted, and one or two **accommodation** possibilities. The best place to stay is *Galson Farm Guest House* (Ⓣ01851/850492, Ⓦwww.galsonfarm.freeserve .co.uk; ❹), an eighteenth-century farmhouse in Gabhsann Bho Dheas (South Galson), halfway between Barabhas and Port Nis, that was once the home of the Mathesons' much-hated factor, Donald Munro; it also runs a **bunkhouse** in a nearby converted barn (phone number as above). There are also a couple of very comfortable and welcoming **B&Bs**: *Tom Gorm* (Ⓣ01851/810661; ❷), a modern house in Nis, and *Heatherview* (Ⓣ01851/850781; ❸), a much older crofthouse in Gabhsann Bho Thuath (North Galson). There are few shops (supplemented by mobile ones) in these parts, so it's as well to stock up in Stornoway before you set out. The *Cross Inn* in Cros is about the only **pub** in the area, but look out for any **live music** or other events going on at *Taigh Dhonnchaidh* (Ⓦwww .taighdhonnchaidh.com), an arts and music centre in Tabost.

Bru (Brue), Arnol and Siabost (Shawbost)

Heading southwest from the crossroads near Barabhas brings you to several villages that meander down towards the sea. The first is **BRU** (Brue), where you'll find the **Oiseval Gallery** (Mon–Sat 10.30am–5.30pm; free; Ⓦwww .oiseval.co.uk), a photographic gallery that's worth a look. In the neighbouring village of **ARNOL**, the remains of numerous blackhouses lie abandoned by the roadside; at the north end of the village, no. 42 has been preserved as the **Arnol Blackhouse** (Mon–Sat: April–Sept 9.30am–6.30pm; Oct–March 9.30am–4.30pm; HS; £4) to show exactly how a true blackhouse, or *taigh dubh*, would have been. The dark interior is lit and heated by a small peat fire, which is kept alight in the central hearth of bare earth, and is usually fairly smoky as there is no chimney; instead, smoke drifts through the thatch, helping to kill any creepy-crawlies, keep out the midges and turn the heathery sods and oat-straw thatch itself into next year's fertilizer. The animals slept in the byre, separated from the living quarters only by a low partition, while potatoes and grain were stored in the adjacent barn. The old woman who lived here moved out only very reluctantly in 1964, and even then only after the council had agreed to build a house with a byre for her animals (the building now houses the ticket office). Across the road is a ruined blackhouse, abandoned in 1920 when the family moved into the white house, or *taigh geal*, next door.

Returning to the main road, it's about a mile or so to **BRAGAR**, where it's difficult to miss the stark arch formed by the jawbone of a blue whale, washed up on the nearby coast in 1920. The spear sticking through the bone is the harpoon, which only went off when the local blacksmith was trying to remove it, badly injuring him. Another two miles on at **SIABOST** (Shawbost), you'll find the **Shawbost Museum** (April–Sept Mon–Sat 9am–6pm; free) in the new community centre, Ionad na Seann Sgoil, to the north of the school. The exhibits – most of them donated by locals – include a rare Lewis brick from the short-lived factory set up by Lord Leverhulme, an old hand-driven loom and a reconstructed living room with a traditional box bed. There's a great **B&B** in Siabost Bho Deas (South Shawbost) at *Airigh* (Ⓣ01851/710478; ❷), and behind the church is the *Eilean Fraoich* **campsite** (Ⓣ01851/710504; April–Oct). You can grab a bite to eat at the *Shawbost Inn*.

Just outside Siabost, to the west, there's a sign to the newly restored **Norse Mill and Kiln**. It's a ten-minute walk over a small hill to the two thatched bothies beside a little stream; the nearer one's the kiln, the further one's the horizontal mill. Mills and kilns of this kind were common in Lewis up until the 1930s, and despite the name are thought to have been introduced here

Offshore islands

Though three men dwell on Flannan Isle
To keep the lamp alight,
As we steer'd under the lee, we caught
No glimmer through the night.

Flannan Isle by Wilfred Wilson Gibson

On December 15, 1900, a passing ship reported that the lighthouse on the **Flannan Isles**, built the previous year by the Stevensons some 21 miles west of Aird Uig on Lewis, was not working. Gibson's poem goes on to recount the arrival of the relief boat from Oban on Boxing Day, whose crew found no trace of the three keepers. More mysteriously still, a full meal lay untouched on the table, one chair was knocked over, and only two oilskins were missing. Subsequent lightkeepers doubtless spent many lonely nights trying in vain to figure out what happened, until the lighthouse went automatic in 1971.

Equally famous, but for different reasons, is the tiny island of **Sula Sgeir**, 41 miles due north of the Butt of Lewis. Every August since anyone can remember, the men of Nis (known as Niseachs) have set sail from Port Nis to harvest the young gannet or guga that nest in their thousands high up on the islet's sea cliffs. It's a dangerous activity, but boiled gannet and potato continues to be a popular Lewis delicacy (the harvest has to be strictly rationed), and there's never any shortage of eager volunteers for the annual cull. For the moment, the Niseachs have a licence to harvest no more than two thousand birds, and Scottish Natural Heritage and the RSPB have accepted the cull as sustainable; other animal rights groups beg to differ.

Somewhat incredibly, the island of **Rona** (sometimes referred to as North Rona), ten miles east of Sula Sgeir, was inhabited on and off until the nineteenth century, despite being less than a mile across. The island's St Ronan's Chapel is one of the oldest Celtic Christian ruins in the country. St Ronan was, according to legend, the first inhabitant, moving here in the eighth century with his two sisters, Miriceal and Brianuil, until one day he turned to Brianuil and said, "My dear sister, it is yourself that is handsome, what beautiful legs you have." She apparently replied that it was time for her to leave the island, and made her way to neighbouring Sula Sgeir where she was later found dead with a shag's nest in her ribcage. Rona is now in the care of Scottish Natural Heritage (Ⓣ01870/705258), from whom you must get permission before landing.

Clearly visible from the ferry to Lewis and Harris, the **Shiant Islands**, whose name translates as "the enchanted islands", sit right in the middle of the Minch, twenty miles or so due south of Stornoway but just five miles off the east coast of Lewis. Inhabited on and off until the beginning of the last century, the islands were bought by the author Sir Compton MacKenzie in 1925, and then sold on to the publisher, Nigel Nicolson, whose family still owns them. The Shiants have wonderful cliffs of fluted basalt columns that shelter thousands of seabirds, including puffin, in the breeding season.

Boat operators such as the excellent Island Cruising (Ⓣ01851/672381, Ⓦwww.island-cruising.com), based in Uig, will take folk out in their former marine research vessel on day-trips to the Shiants or Flannan Isles or, on longer trips out to Sula Sgeir and even **St Kilda** (see p.391); Kilda Cruises, (Ⓣ01859/502060, Ⓦwww.kildacruises.co.uk) have a motor cruiser that leaves from Leverburgh for day-trips to similar destinations and takes just under three hours to reach St Kilda; Sea Trek (Ⓣ01851/672464, Ⓦseatrek.co.uk), also based in Uig, offer RIB day-trips as far afield as St Kilda.

from Ireland as early as the sixth century. To the east beyond Siabost is lovely Dalbeg Bay, where there is a **tearoom**, *The Copper Kettle*, with a terrace for sunny days.

Carlabhagh (Carloway) and Gearrannan (Garenin)

The landscape becomes less monotonous as you approach the parish of **CARLABHAGH** (Carloway), with its crofthouses, boulders and hillocks rising out of the peat moor. A mile-long road leads off north to the beautifully remote coastal settlement of **GEARRANNAN** (Garenin), where nine thatched crofters' houses – the last of which was abandoned in 1974 – have been restored and give a great impression of what a **Baile Tughaidh**, or blackhouse village (Mon–Sat 9.30am–5.30pm; £2.50) must have been like. The first house you come to houses a **café**, serving cheap and cheerful fare during the day and classic Scottish three-course meals for £25 a head in the evening (Wed–Sat only; phone ahead ⓣ01851/643416). The second house has been restored to its condition at the time of abandonment, so there's electricity, but no running water, lino flooring, but a peat fire and box beds – and a weaving machine in the byre. The third house has interpretive panels and a touch-screen computer telling the history of the village and the folk who lived here. Next door, there are public toilets and opposite is the GHHT **hostel** (ⓦwww.gatliff.org.uk); several others have been converted into **self-catering** houses (ⓦwww.gearrannan.com). A waymarked path leads four miles east to Dail Beag (Dalbeg), affording spectacular views along the coast and passing two lovely **sandy bays** – a mile beyond is the Norse Mill and Kiln (see p.375). In the opposite direction, it's a mile and a half along the cliffs to Laimishader lighthouse.

Just beyond Carlabhagh, about 400yd from the road, **Dùn Charlabhaigh Broch** perches on top of a conspicuous rocky outcrop overlooking the sea. Scotland's Atlantic coast is strewn with the remains of over five hundred brochs, or fortified towers, but this is one of the best-preserved, its dry-stone circular walls reaching a height of more than 30ft on one side. The broch consists of two concentric walls, the inner one perpendicular, the outer one slanting inwards, the two originally fastened together by roughly hewn flagstones, which also served as lookout galleries reached via a narrow stairwell. The only entrance to the roofless inner yard is through a low doorway set beside a crude and cramped guard cell. As at Calanais (see below), there have been all sorts of theories about the purpose of the brochs, which date from between 100 BC and 100 AD; the most likely explanation is that they were built to provide protection from Roman slave-traders.

Dùn Charlabhaigh now has its very own **Doune Broch Centre** (June–Sept Mon–Sat 10am–6pm; free), situated at a discreet distance, stone-built and sporting a turf roof. It's a good wet-weather retreat, and fun for kids, who can walk through the hay-strewn mock-up of the broch as it might have been. A mile or so beyond the broch, beside a lochan, is the *Doune Braes Hotel* (ⓣ01851/643252, ⓦwww.doune-braes.co.uk; ⑤), a friendly, unpretentious former schoolhouse, whose bar serves up tasty seafood dishes.

Calanais (Callanish)

Five miles south of Carlabhagh lies the village of **CALANAIS** (Callanish), site of the islands' most dramatic prehistoric ruins, the **Calanais standing stones**, whose monoliths – nearly fifty of them – occupy a serene lochside setting. There's been years of heated debate about the origin and function of the stones – slabs of gnarled and finely grained gneiss up to 15ft high – though almost everyone agrees that they were lugged here by Neolithic peoples between 3000 and 1500 BC. It's also obvious that the planning and construction of the site

– as well as several other lesser circles nearby – were spread over many generations. Such an endeavour could, it's been argued, only be prompted by the desire to predict the seasonal cycle upon which these early farmers were entirely dependent, and indeed many of the stones are aligned with the positions of the sun and the stars. This rational explanation, based on clear evidence that this part of Lewis was once a fertile farming area, dismisses as coincidence the ground plan of the site, which resembles a colossal Celtic cross, and explains away the central burial chamber as a later addition of no special significance. These two features have, however, fuelled all sorts of theories ranging from alien intervention to human sacrifice.

A blackhouse adjacent to the main stone circle has been refurbished as a **tearoom** – it has limited snacks but bags more atmosphere than the **Calanais Visitor Centre** (Mon–Sat: April–Sept 10am–6pm; Oct–March 10am–4pm; museum £1.75) on the other side of the stones (and thankfully out of view), to which all the signs direct you from the road. The centre runs a decent restaurant and a small museum on the site, but with so much information on the panels beside the stones there's little reason to visit it. You're politely asked not to walk between the stones, only along the path that surrounds them, though everyone ignores this. If you want to commune with standing stones in solitude, head for the smaller circles in more natural surroundings a mile or two southeast of Calanais, around Gearraidh na h-Aibhne (Garynahine).

There are several good **places to stay** in Calanais: try the modern *Eshcol Guest House* (Ⓣ01851/621357, Ⓦwww.eshcol.com; ④), no beauty from the outside, but very well run and comfortable within, or the newly built *Leumadair Guest House* (Ⓣ01851/612706, Ⓦwww.leumadair.co.uk; ④). If it's just **food** you want, *Tigh Mealros* (Ⓣ01851/621333; closed Sun), in Gearraidh na h-Aibhne, serves good, inexpensive lunches and evening meals, featuring local seafood.

Bernera (Bearnaraigh)

From Gearraidh na h-Aibhne, the main road leads back to Stornoway, while the B8011 heads off west to Uig (see opposite), and, a few miles on, the B8059 sets off north to the island of Great Bernera, usually referred to simply as **Bernera**.

△ Iron Age House at Bostadh

Joined to the mainland since 1953 via a narrow bridge that spans a small sea channel, Bernera is a rocky island, dotted with lochans, fringed by a few small lobster-fishing settlements and currently owned by Comte Robin de la Lanne Mirrlees, the Queen's former herald – the inspiration, it is said, for Ian Fleming's James Bond, who also claims the title, Prince of Incoronata (an area of former Yugoslavia gifted to the count by the country's late King Peter II).

Bernera has an important place in Lewis history due to the **Bernera Riot** of 1874, when local crofters successfully defied the eviction orders delivered to them by the landlord, Sir James Matheson. In truth, there wasn't much of riot, but three Bernera men were arrested and charged with assault. The crofters marched on the laird's house, Lews Castle in Stornoway, and demanded an audience with Matheson, who claimed to have no knowledge of what his factor, Donald Munro, was doing. In the subsequent trial, Munro was exposed as a ruthless tyrant, and the crofters were acquitted. A stone-built cairn now stands as a memorial to the riot, at the crossroads beyond the central settlement of **BREACLEIT** (Breaclete), which sits beside one of the island's many lochs. Here, you'll find the **Bernera Museum** (June–Sept Mon–Sat 11am–6pm; £1.50), housed in the local community centre. There's a small exhibition on lobster fishing, a St Kilda mailboat and a mysterious 5000-year-old Neolithic stone tennis ball, and you can trace your ancestry.

Much more interesting is the replica **Iron Age House** (times vary so contact the tourist office) that has been built above a precious little bay of golden sand beyond the cemetery at **BOSTADH** (Bosta), three miles north of Breacleit – follow the signs "to the shore". In 1992, gale-force winds revealed an entire late Iron Age or Pictish settlement hidden under the sand; due to its exposed position, the site has been refilled with sand, and a full-scale mock-up built instead, based on the "jelly baby" houses – after the shape – that were excavated. Inside, the house is incredibly spacious, and very dark, illuminated only by a central hearth and a few chinks of sunlight. If the weather's fine and you climb to the top of the nearby hills, you should get a good view over the forty or so islands in Loch Roag, and maybe even the Flannan Isles (see p.376) on the horizon.

If you want to stay, there are a couple of simple **B&Bs** on the island: *Kelvindale* (Ⓣ01851/612347; ❷; April–Oct) in Tobson, a couple of miles northwest of Breacleit, and *Garymilis* (Ⓣ01851/612341, Ⓔgarymilis@talk21.com; ❷; Feb–Nov), in Circebost (Kirkibost), on the southeastern corner of the island.

Uig

It's a long drive along the partially upgraded B8011 to the remote parish of **UIG**, one of the areas of Lewis that suffered really badly from the Clearances. The landscape here is hillier, and more dramatic than elsewhere, a combination of myriad islets, wild cliff scenery and patches of pristine golden sand.

At the crossroads to **MIABHAIG** (Miavaig), you have a choice of either heading straight for the Uig Sands (see below), or veering off the main road, and heading along a dramatic little road northeast to **CLIOBH** (Cliff). The Atlantic breakers that roll onto the beach below the village are often spectacular, but make it unsafe for swimmers, who should continue another mile to **CNÌP** (Kneep), to the southeast of which is **Tràigh na Beirghe**, a glorious strand of shell sand, backed by dunes and machair, where there's a small primitive **campsite** (Ⓣ01851/672265; mid-April to mid-Sept).

The other route from Miabhaig is to continue along the main road through the narrow canyon of Glèann Bhaltois (Glen Valtos) to **TIMSGEARRAIDH** (Timsgarry), which overlooks **Uig Sands** (Tràigh Uuige), the largest and most prized of all the golden strands on Lewis, where the sea goes out for miles at low tide; the best access point is from the car park near the cemetery in Eadar Dha Fhadhail. It was here in 1831 that a local cow rubbed itself against a sandbank and stumbled across the **Lewis Chessmen**, 78 twelfth-century Viking chesspieces carved from walrus ivory that now reside in Edinburgh's Royal Museum of Scotland and the British Museum in London. You can see replicas of the chessmen in the **Uig Heritage Centre** (Mon–Sat noon–5pm; £1), housed in Uig School in Timsgearraidh. As well as putting on some excellent temporary exhibitions, the museum has bits and bobs from blackhouses and is staffed by locals, who are happy to answer any queries you have; there's also a welcome **tearoom** in the adjacent nursery during the holidays.

The most intriguing **place to stay** is *Baile na Cille* (Ⓣ01851/672242, Ⓦwww.bailenacille.com; ❹; Easter–Oct), in an idyllic setting overlooking the Uig Sands in Timsgearraidh. It's a chaotic kind of place, run by an eccentric couple, who are very welcoming to families – the Blairs have stayed here – and dish up wonderful, though expensive, set-menu dinners for £30 a head. The best B&B in the area is *Suainaval* (Ⓣ01851/672386, Ⓦwww.suainaval.com; ❷), in Cradhlastadh (Crowlista), run by a truly welcoming couple, and boasting superb views over Uig bay from the north.

An entirely different (but equally unusual) experience is to stay at the old RAF station in **AIRD UIG**, three miles north of Timsgearraidh. The concrete buildings themselves are something of an eyesore, but the position, overlooking a rocky inlet beside Gallan Head, is superb. An enterprising Irish-Breton couple offer **B&B** (Ⓣ01851/672474, Ⓦwww.bonaventurelewis.co.uk; ❷) and run the popular *Bonaventure* **restaurant** (booking advisable), which serves up outstanding French/Scottish three-course meals at around £25 a head. Alternatively, you can stay over in another part of the old barracks with the Western Isles Kite Company (WiKc), who run kite-surfing courses and also offer B&B (Ⓣ01851/672771, Ⓦwww.powerkitesales.co.uk; ❷).

Harris (Na Hearadh)

Harris, whose name derives from the old Norse for "high land", is much hillier, more dramatic and much more immediately appealing, its boulder-strewn slopes descending to aquamarine bays of dazzling, white sand. The shift from Lewis to Harris is almost imperceptible, as the two are, in fact, one island, the "division" between them embedded in a historical split in the MacLeod clan, lost in the mists of time. The border was also, somewhat crazily, a county boundary until 1975, with Harris lying in Invernessshire, and Lewis belonging to Ross and Cromarty. Nowadays, the dividing line is rarely marked even on maps; for the record, it comprises Loch Reasort in the west, Loch Shìphoirt (Loch Seaforth) in the east, and the six miles in between. Harris itself is more clearly divided by a minuscule isthmus, into the wild, inhospitable mountains of **North Harris** and the gentler landscape and sandy shores of **South Harris**.

Along with Lewis, Harris was purchased in 1918 by **Lord Leverhulme**, and after 1923, when he pulled out of Lewis, all his efforts were concentrated here. In contrast to Lewis, though, Leverhulme and his ambitious projects were broadly welcomed by the people of Harris. His most grandiose plans were drawn up for Leverburgh (see p.386), but he also purchased an old Norwegian whaling station in Bun Abhain Eadara in 1922, built a spinning mill at Geocrab and began the construction of four roads. Financial difficulties, a slump in the

Harris tweed

Far from being a picturesque cottage industry, as it's sometimes presented, the production of **Harris tweed** is vital to the local economy, with a well-organized and unionized workforce. Traditionally the tweed was made by women, from the wool of their own sheep, to provide clothing for their families, using a 2500-year-old process. Each woman was responsible for plucking the wool by hand, washing and scouring it, dyeing it with lichen, heather flowers or ragwort, carding (smoothing and straightening the wool, often adding butter to grease it), spinning and weaving. Finally the cloth was dipped in stale urine and "waulked" by a group of women, who beat the cloth on a table to soften and shrink it whilst singing Gaelic waulking songs. Harris tweed was originally made all over the islands, and was known simply as *clò mór* (big cloth).

In the mid-nineteenth century, the Countess of Dunmore, who owned a large part of Harris, started to sell surplus cloth to her aristocratic friends; she then sent two sisters from Srannda (Strond) to Paisley to learn the trade. On their return, they formed the genesis of the modern industry, which continues to serve as a vital source of employment, though demand (and therefore employment levels) can fluctuate wildly as fashions change. To earn the official Harris Tweed Association trademark of the Orb and the Maltese Cross – taken from the Countess of Dunmore's coat of arms – the fabric has to be hand-woven on the Outer Hebrides from 100 percent pure new Scottish wool, while the other parts of the manufacturing process must take place only in the local mills.

The main centre of production is now Lewis, where the wool is dyed, carded and spun; you can see all these processes by visiting the **Lewis Loom Centre** in Stornoway (see p.370). In the last few decades, there has been a revival of traditional tweed-making techniques, with several small producers following old methods. One such place is Soay Studio at the western end of Tarbert (May–Sept Tues–Thurs 9am–12.30pm & 1.30–4pm; ⓣ01859/502361), which uses indigenous plants and bushes to dye the cloth: yellow comes from rocket and broom; green from heather; grey and black from iris and oak; and, most popular of all, reddish brown from crotal, a flat grey lichen scraped off rocks.

tweed industry and the lack of market for whale products meant that none of the schemes was a wholehearted success, and when he died in 1925 the plug was pulled on all of them by his executors.

Since the Leverhulme era, unemployment has been a constant problem in Harris. Crofting continues on a small scale, supplemented by the Harris tweed industry, though the main focus of this has, in fact, shifted to Lewis. The fishing industry continues to thrive on **Scalpay**, while the rest of the population gets by on whatever employment is available: roadworks, crafts, hunting and fishing and, of course, tourism. There's a regular **bus** connection between Stornoway and **Tarbert**, and an occasional service which circumnavigates South Harris (see also "Travel details" on p.399).

Tarbert (An Tairbeart)

The largest place on Harris is the ferry port of **TARBERT**, sheltered in a green valley on the narrow isthmus that marks the border between North and South Harris. The town's mountainous backdrop is impressive, and the town is attractively laid out on steep terraces sloping up from the dock. However, it does boast the only **tourist office** (April–Oct Mon–Fri 9am–5pm, Sat 9am–1pm & 2–5pm; also open to greet the evening ferry; winter hours variable;

Ⓣ01859/502011) on Harris, close to the ferry terminal. The office can arrange modest, inexpensive B&B **accommodation** and has a full set of bus timetables, but its real value is as a source of information on local walks.

If you wish to base yourself in Tarbert there's an excellent **hostel** called the *Rockview Bunkhouse* (Ⓣ01859/502626), on Main Street, which has laundry facilities and also offers **bike rental**. If you're looking for **accommodation** close to the ferry terminal, there's a very good **B&B**, *Tigh na Mara* (Ⓣ01859/502270, Ⓦwww.tigh-na-mara.co.uk; ❷), or the long-established, but recently refurbished *Harris Hotel* (Ⓣ01859/502154, Ⓦwww.harrishotel.com; ❺), five minutes' walk away. Another option is *Ardhasaig House* (Ⓣ01859/502066, Ⓦwww.ardhasaig.co.uk; ❻), a small hotel up the Stornoway road, looking out over North Harris – it's newly modernized inside and TV-free. The lounge and bar of the *Harris Hotel* act as the local social centre, but the best **fish and chips** are actually dispensed by *Ad's Take-Away* (April–Oct; closed Sun), next to the hostel. Otherwise, you're best off heading for the very pleasant *First Fruits* **tearoom** (April–Sept; closed Sun), behind the tourist office, housed in an old stone-built cottage and serving real coffee, home-made cakes, toasties and so forth, plus evening meals (Tues–Fri).

North Harris (Ceann a Tuath na Hearadh)

Mountainous **North Harris** was run like some minor fuedal fiefdom until 2003, when the locals were given the right to buy the 22,000-acre estate for a knock-down £2 million. If you're coming from Stornoway on the A859, it's a spectacular introduction to Harris, its bulging, pyramidal mountains of gneiss looming over the dramatic fjord-like **Loch Shìphoirt** (Loch Seaforth). From **AIRD A' MHULAIDH** (Ardvourlie), you weave your way over a boulder-strewn saddle between mighty **Sgaoth Aird** (1829ft) and An Cliseam or the **Clisham** (2619ft), the highest peak in the Western Isles. This bitter terrain, littered with debris left behind by retreating glaciers, offers but the barest of vegetation, with an occasional cluster of crofters' houses sitting in the shadow of a host of pointed peaks, anywhere between 1000ft and 2500ft high.

Other than self-catering cottages, the only place to stay in this area is the GHHT **hostel** (Ⓦwww.gatliff.org.uk), in the lonely coastal hamlet of **REINIGEADAL** (Rhenigdale), until the 1990s only accessible by foot or boat. Nowadays, there's a road, and even a bus service, though this must be booked in advance (Ⓣ01859/502221). To reach the hostel on foot, walk east along the wonderfully undulating road to Caolas Scalpaigh (Kyles Scalpay). After a couple of miles, watch for the sign marking the start of the path which threads its way for three miles over the rocky landscape to Reinigeadal. It's a magnificent hike, with superb views out along the coast and over the mountains, but you'll need to be properly equipped (see p.59) and should allow three hours for the one-way trip.

Scalpay (Scalpaigh)

Caolas Scalpaigh looks out across Loch an Tairbeairt to the island of **Scalpay** (Scalpaigh) – from the Norse *skalp-ray* (the island shaped like a boat) – now accessible via a single-track bridge erected in 1997. Traditionally, Scalpay is the place where Bonnie Prince Charlie tried unsuccessfully to get a boat to take him back to France after the defeat at Culloden. Today this tightly knit community is surprisingly buoyant, maintaining a relatively large population of around four hundred, thanks to its fishing fleet and fish-processing factory. On a good day, it's a pleasant and fairly easy three-mile hike along the island's north coast to the **Eilean Glas** lighthouse, which looks out over to Skye. Alternatively, you can drive to the end of the road and enjoy a shorter walk along the southern coastline; both paths are waymarked. Eilean Glas was the first lighthouse to be erected in Scotland, in 1789, though the present Stevenson-designed granite tower dates from 1824 and is currently inaccessible. There are several B&Bs on the island: *Hirta House* (ⓣ01859/540394, ⓔm.mackenzie@tiscali.co.uk; ❷) is a Victorian house near the bridge with a great conservatory looking

Walking in North Harris

Ordnance Survey Explorer map no. 456.

Harris is great walking country. The crowds that flock to the Skye Cuillin are absent, there are no Munro-baggers, and the landscape is wonderfully lunaresque. It's also one of the largest continuously mountainous regions in the country, made up of ancient **Lewisian gneiss**, among the oldest rocks in the world formed almost 3000 million years ago. As always, if you're walking, you should take note of safety precautions (see p.59), and be particularly conscious of the weather conditions, which can change rapidly in these parts.

As the highest mountain in the Western Isles, Clisham or **An Cliseam** (2619ft) is an obvious objective for walkers, and can be easily climbed from the parking space on the A859, where the road crosses the Abhainn Mhàraig. There isn't a path as such, but if you follow the river, and approach the mountain from its southeast ridge, an ascent should be fairly straightforward (2–3hr return). Clisham forms part of a horseshoe ridge that extends from Mullach an Langa in the northwest to Tomnabhal in the east. In order to climb the whole ridge, you're better off starting off from near where the A859 crosses the Abhainn Scaladail, just before Aird a' Mhulaidh. There's an old drovers' road, half a mile before the bridge, which heads south, skirting Caisteal Ard and Cleit Ard; from the track you get a gentle approach to the southeastern ridge of Tomnabhal. At the other end of the ridge, you can return to Aird a' Mhulaidh, via Loch Mhisteam and the Abhainn Scaladail. The entire circuit of the ridge should take around five hours. If you're based in Tarbert and don't have your own transport, it's roughly an hour's walk to Bun Abhainn Eadarra.

If weather conditions are fairly poor, there are several low-level walks that take you right through the heart of the mountains of North Harris. None of them is circular, so unless you study the bus timetables carefully you'll probably have to backtrack. The first route takes the aforementioned path from Bun Abhainn Eadarra, and then continues up to Loch a' Sgàil, and, over the narrow pass into **Glen Langadale**, from which a path eventually heads east to the A859 just north of Aird a' Mhulaidh, a total distance of eight miles (4hr). A longer and more rewarding ten-mile walk (5–6hr) is along **Gleann Mhiabhaig** via Loch Scourst and Loch Bhoisimid, and then east to the A859 just north of Aird a' Mhulaidh; an interesting detour can also be made to Gleann and Loch Stuladail, which are surrounded by crags. The most impressive low-level walk, however, is along **Gleann Ulladail**, where Loch Ulladail is overlooked by the rocky headland of Sron Ulladail. There's a decent path all the way from the dam on the B887, just before Abhainn Suidhe, to Loch Ulladail, a distance of under five miles; the return journey takes four to five hours. If you've energy, and the weather's good, you can use the above low-level walk as a return route, after climbing the ridge of peaks that starts with Cleiseabhal in the south, and ends with Ullabhal in the north.

Unfortunately, the Reinigeadal GHHT hostel is too far east to use as a base for any of these walks. However, you can console yourself by climbing the nearby peak of **Tòdun** (1732ft), which can be easily approached along its north or south ridge. The return trip will probably only take a couple of hours, so for a longer day's hike you could aim for a circuit of the trio of mountains further west: Sgaoth Iosal (1740ft), Sgaoth Aird (1829ft) and Gillaval Glas (1544ft).

out over Loch an Tairbeairt; while close by *New Haven* (Ⓣ01859/540325, Ⓔnewhaven@madasafish.com; ❷) is a modern crofthouse looking out over the village.

The road to Huisinis (Hushinish)

The only other road on North Harris is the winding, single-track B887, which clings to the northern shores of Loch a Siar (West Loch Tarbert), and gives easy access to the awesome mountain range of the (treeless) Forest of Harris to the north. Immediately as you turn down the B887, you pass through **Bun Abhàinn Eadarra** (Bunavoneadar), where some Norwegians established a short-lived whaling station – the slipways and distinctive red-brick chimney can still be seen. Seven miles further on, the road takes you through the gates of **Amhuinnsuidhe Castle** (pronounced "avan-soo-ee"), built in Scottish Baronial style in 1868 by the Earl of Dunmore, and right past the front door, much to the annoyance of the castle's succession owners. As it is, you have time to admire the lovely salmon-leap waterfalls and pristine castle grounds.

It's another five miles to the end of the road at the small crofting community of **HUISINIS** (Hushinish), where you are rewarded with a south-facing beach of shell sand that looks across to South Harris. A slipway to the north of the bay serves the nearby island of **Scarp**, a hulking mass of rock rising to over 1000ft, once home to more than two hundred people and abandoned as recently as 1971 (it's now a private holiday hideaway). The most bizarre moment in its history – and the subject of the recent film *The Rocket Post* – was undoubtedly in 1934, when the German scientist Gerhardt Zucher conducted an experiment at sending mail by rocket. Zucher made two attempts at launching his rocket from Scarp, but the letter-laden missile exploded before it even got off the ground, and the idea was shelved.

South Harris (Ceann a Deas na Hearadh)

The mountains of **South Harris** are less dramatic than in the north, but the scenery is equally breathtaking. There's a choice of routes from Tarbert to the ferry port of **Leverburgh**, which connects with North Uist: the east coast, known as **Na Baigh** (The Bays), is rugged and seemingly inhospitable, while the **west coast** is endowed with some of the finest stretches of golden sand in the whole of the archipelago, buffeted by the Atlantic winds.

Na Baigh (The Bays)

Paradoxically, most people on South Harris live along the harsh eastern coastline of **The Bays** rather than the more fertile west side. But not by choice – they were evicted from their original crofts to make way for sheep-grazing. Despite the uncompromising lunar landscape – mostly bare grey gneiss and heather – the crofters managed to establish "lazybeds" (small labour-intensive raised plots between the rocks fertilized by seaweed and peat), a few of which are still in use even today. The narrow sea lochs provide shelter for fishing boats, while the interior is speckled with freshwater lochans, and the whole coast is now served by the endlessly meandering **Bays Road**, often wrongly referred to as the "Golden Road", though this, in fact, was the name given to the sideroad to Scadabhagh (Scadabay), coined by a local councillor who disapproved of the expense.

There are just a few **places to stay** along the coast, the most obvious being the independent *Drinishader* **bunkhouse** (Ⓣ01851/511255, Ⓔroddy@drinishader.freeserve.co.uk; April–Nov), a converted cottage three miles south of Tarbert in Drinisiadar (Drinishader); alternatively, there's the very welcoming *Dunvegan*

View (Ⓣ01859/530294, Ⓦwww.dunveganview.co.uk; ❷), a good **B&B** in Cliuthar (Cluer), with wonderful views over the Minch and bikes to rent. If you're looking for somewhere to stop and have home-made soup, baguettes and cakes, head for *Skoon* **café** and art gallery in Geocrab, which also has internet access (Ⓦwww.skoon.co.uk; closed Mon & Sun).

Six miles beyond Liceasto at **Lingreabhagh** (Lingerabay), the road skirts the foot of **Roineabhal** (1508ft), the southernmost mountain of the island. The locals wanted to reopen and expand a quarry here to provide a dozen or so jobs in an area of high unemployment and emigration. Instead, what was proposed was one of Europe's largest superquarries, which would have demolished virtually the entire mountain over the course of seventy years. After the longest public enquiry in British legal history, the proposal was eventually dropped in 2004. As the *West Highland Free Press* succinctly put it: "The project was too big, the opposition too selfish and the process far, far, far too long".

The west coast

The main road from Tarbert into South Harris snakes its way west for ten miles across the boulder-strewn interior to reach the coast. Once there, you get a view of the most stunning **beach**, the vast golden strand of **Tràigh Losgaintir**. The road continues to ride above a chain of sweeping sands, backed by rich **machair**, that stretches for nine miles along the Atlantic coast. In good weather, the scenery is particularly impressive, foaming breakers rolling along the golden sands set against the rounded peaks of the mountains to the north and the islet-studded turquoise sea to the west – and even on the dullest day the sand manages to glow beneath the waves. A short distance out to sea is the large island of **Taransay** (Tarasaigh), which once held a population of nearly a hundred, but was abandoned as recently as 1974. In 2000 it was the scene of the BBC series *Castaway*, in which thirty-odd contestants were filmed living on

Machair

Machair is the Gaelic term used to describe the sand-enriched coastal grasslands of the Hebrides and the Northern Isles. At first sight, machair might not look very different from your average slice of green pasture, but it is, in fact, miraculous stuff. For a start, in contrast to the links of Scotland's eastern coast, the sand blown onto the machair by the prevailing westerly wind has a very high shell content (up to eighty to ninety percent) and the calcium has a liming effect on the soil. This makes machair exceptionally rich pasture, a point not lost on settlers in these parts, who have cultivated the grasslands since Neolithic times, using seaweed as manure. Indeed, the continued small-scale cultivation of machair, such as that practised by traditional crofters, is essential for minimizing erosion and ensuring the machair's long-term fertility.

For visitors, machair is celebrated primarily for its astonishing carpet of **wild flowers** that appear each year in May, June and July. Buttercups, red and white clover, tiny eyebright, vetch, selfheal and daisies predominate in this sea of flowers, but you'll also regularly find lady's bedstraw, "eggs and bacon", ragged robin, wild thyme, bog asphodel and – if you're lucky – spotted orchids. Machair is also rich in invertebrates and, consequently, birdlife; in particular, waders such as lapwing, redshank, snipe, dunlin, ringed plover, oystercatchers, corn buntings and corncrakes. Almost half the Scottish machair occurs in the Western Isles, and nowhere has larger uninterrupted swaths of the stuff than the Uists and Benbecula, where shell-sand beaches extend along the entire west coast. Other places with extensive machair include Barra, Coll, Tiree, Colonsay, South Harris, and parts of Lewis, Orkney and Shetland.

the island for the best part of a year. Day-trips are possible to the island from Horgabost beach (Mon–Fri; £15); the island also has self-catering cottages (ⓣ01859/550260, ⓦwww.visit-taransay.com; April–Oct).

Beul-na-Mara (ⓣ01859/550205, ⓦwww.beulnamara.co.uk; ❸) is a very good modern **B&B** in Seilebost, overlooking the sands of Tràigh Losgaintir, but the most luxurious **guesthouse** in the area is five miles further south in Sgarasta (Scarista), where one of the first of the Hebridean Clearances took place in 1828, when thirty families were evicted and their homes burnt. Here, the beautifully furnished rooms of the Georgian former manse of *Scarista House* (ⓣ01859/550238, ⓦwww.scaristahouse.com; ❽) overlook yet more golden sands; the restaurant's meat and seafood are among the freshest and finest on the Western Isles, and among the most expensive, at nearly £40 a head.

There's a particularly magnificent stretch of machair, by the golden sands close to the village of **TAOBH TUATH** (Northton), a lovely spot overlooked by the round-topped hill of Chaipabhal at the southwesternmost tip of the island. Taobh Tuath itself is no picture postcard, with the exception of the award-winning **MacGillivray Centre** (open all year at any time), whose design was inspired by the Hebridean blackhouse; though clearly the building won the accolades and not the centre, which contains precious little information on the naturalist, William MacGillivray (1796–1852), after whom it's named, and only a little on crofting and machair. There's more information on geology, flora and fauna to be found in **Seallam!** (Mon–Sat 10am–5pm; £2.50; ⓦwww.seallam.com), on the main road, primarily a centre for eager ancestor hunters, but also providing interest for kids, literally at their level.

Leverburgh (An t-Ob)

From Taobh Tuath the road veers to the southeast to trim the island's south shore, eventually reaching the sprawling settlement of **LEVERBURGH** (An t-Ob), where a series of brown clapboard houses strikes an odd Scandinavian note. Named after Lord Leverhulme, who planned to turn the place into the largest fishing port on the west coast of Scotland, it's a place that has languished for quite some time, but has picked up quite a bit since the establishment of the CalMac **car ferry** service to Berneray and the Uists. The hour-long journey across the skerry-strewn Sound of Harris is one of Scotland's most tortuous ferry routes, with the ship taking part in a virtual slalom race to avoid numerous hidden rocks – it's also a great crossing from which to spot seabirds and sea mammals. If you want an even closer look at the wildlife, contact Strond Wildlife Charters (ⓣ01859/520204), who organise **boat trips** to the islands in the Sound.

There's a good choice of **accommodation** in Leverburgh: try *Caberfeidh House* (ⓣ01859/520276; ❷), a lovely stone-built Victorian building by the turn-off to the ferry, or *Sorrel Cottage* (ⓣ01859/520319, ⓦwww.sorrelcottage.co.uk; ❷), which specializes in vegetarian and seafood cooking and offers **bike rental**. A cheaper alternative is the quirky, timber-clad *Am Bothan* (ⓣ01859/520251, ⓦwww.ambothan.com), a luxurious **bunkhouse** that's very welcoming, has great facilities and is only a few minutes' walk from the ferry. On the north side of the bay is the *An Clachan* co-op store which houses a small **information office**. For some local langoustines, home-made cakes and the usual comfort **food**, head for *The Anchorage*, over by the ferry slipway, and look out for the occasional live music night.

Roghadal (Rodel)

A mile or so from Rubha Reanais (Renish Point), the southern tip of Harris, is the old port of **ROGHADAL** (Rodel), where a smattering of ancient stone houses lies among the hillocks surrounding the dilapidated harbour where the ferry from Skye used to arrive. On top of one of these grassy humps, with sheep grazing in the graveyard, is **St Clement's Church** (Tur Chliamainn), burial place of the MacLeods of Harris and Dunvegan in Skye. Dating from the 1520s – in other words pre-Reformation, hence the big castellated tower (which you can climb) – the church was saved from ruination in the eighteenth century, and fully restored in 1873 by the Countess of Dunmore. The bare interior is distinguished by its wall tombs, notably that of the founder, Alasdair Crotach (also known as Alexander MacLeod), whose heavily weathered effigy lies beneath an intriguing backdrop and canopy of sculpted reliefs depicting vernacular and religious scenes – elemental representations of, among others, a stag hunt, the Holy Trinity, St Michael and the devil and an angel weighing the souls of the dead. Look out, too, for the sheila-na-gig halfway up the south side of the church tower; unusually, she has a brother displaying his genitalia, below a carving of St Clement on the west face. Beyond the church, tucked away by a quiet harbour, the harling-smothered *Rodel Hotel* (ⓣ01859/520210, ⓦwww.rodelhotel.co.uk; ❻) has been totally refurbished inside and serves decent bar meals.

North Uist (Uibhist a Tuath)

Compared to the mountainous scenery of Harris, **North Uist** – seventeen miles long and thirteen miles wide – is much flatter and for some comes as something of an anticlimax. Over half the surface area is covered by water, creating a distinctive peaty-brown lochan-studded "drowned landscape". Most visitors come here for the trout and salmon fishing and the deerstalking, both of which (along with poaching) are critical to the survival of the island's economy. Others come for the smattering of prehistoric sites, the birds, or the sheer peace of this windy isle and the solitude of North Uist's vast sandy beaches, which extend – almost without interruption – along the north and west coast.

There are two **car ferry** services to North Uist: the first is from Leverburgh on Harris to Berneray (Mon–Sat 3–4 daily, subject to tides; 1hr), from where there are regular **buses** to Lochmaddy, the principal village on the east coast; the second is from Uig on Skye (2 daily; 1hr 45min) and docks at Lochmaddy itself. Five or six daily buses leave for Lochboisdale in South Uist along the main road, and several buses travel some way round the coastal road. There is no public transport on Sundays.

Lochmaddy (Loch nam Madadh) and around

Despite being situated on the east coast, some distance away from any beach, the ferry port of **LOCHMADDY** – "Loch of the Dogs" – makes a good base for exploring the island. Occupying a narrow, bumpy promontory and overlooked by the brooding mountains of Lì a Tuath (North Lee) and Lì a Deas (South Lee) to the southeast, it's difficult to believe that this sleepy settlement was a large herring port as far back as the seventeenth century. Its most salient feature now is the sixteen incongruous brown weatherboarded houses, which arrived from Sweden in 1948.

The only thing to keep you in Lochmaddy is **Taigh Chearsabhagh** (Mon–Sat 10am–5pm; ⓦwww.taigh-chearsabhagh.org) a converted eighteenth-century merchant's house, now home to a vibrant community arts centre, with a simple

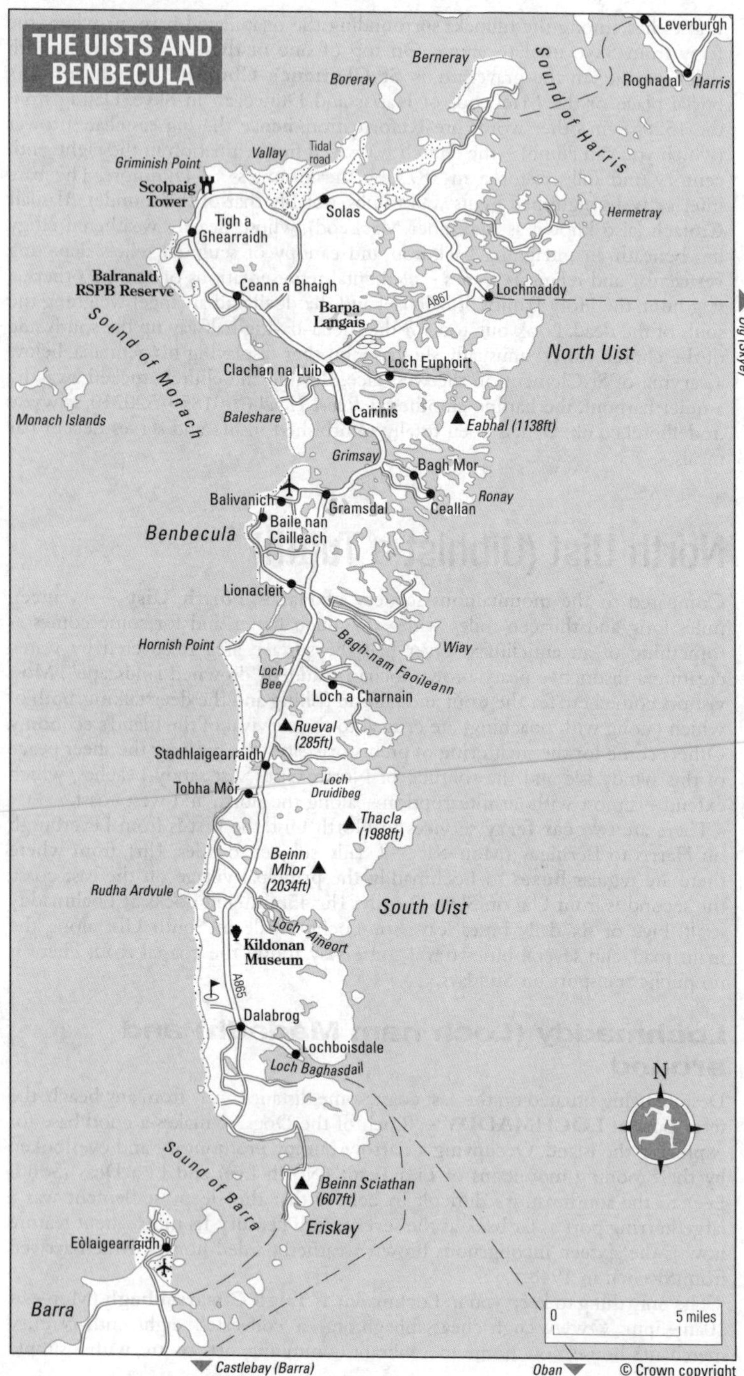
THE UISTS AND BENBECULA
Leverburgh
Berneray
Boreray
Roghadal
Harris
Sound of Harris
Vallay
Tidal road
Griminish Point
Scolpaig Tower
Solas
Tigh a Ghearraidh
Hermetray
Balranald RSPB Reserve
Ceann a Bhaigh
Lochmaddy
Barpa Langais
A867
Sound of Monach
Uig (Skye)
North Uist
Clachan na Luib
Loch Euphoirt
Cairinis
Monach Islands
Baleshare
Eabhal (1138ft)
Grimsay
Bagh Mor
Balivanich
Gramsdal
Ceallan
Ronay
Baile nan Cailleach
Benbecula
Lionacleit
Bagh-nam Faoileann
Hornish Point
Wiay
Loch Bee
Loch a Charnain
Rueval (285ft)
Stadhlaigearraidh
Loch Druidibeg
Tobha Mòr
Thacla (1988ft)
Beinn Mhor (2034ft)
Rudha Ardvule
South Uist
Loch Aineort
Kildonan Museum
A865
Dalabrog
Lochboisdale
Loch Baghasdail
N
Sound of Barra
Beinn Sciathan (607ft)
Eriskay
Eòlaigearraidh
Barra
0
5 miles
Castlebay (Barra)
Oban
© Crown copyright

airy café, post office, shop and excellent museum, which puts on some seriously innovative exhibitions. Taigh Chearsabhagh was one of the prime movers behind the commissioning of a series of seven sculptures dotted about the Uists. Ask at the arts centre for directions to the ones in and around Lochmaddy, the most interesting of which is the **Both nam Faileas** (Hut of the Shadow), 1km north of the town. The hut is an ingenious dry-stone, turf-roofed camera obscura built by sculptor Chris Drury that projects the nearby land, sea and skyscape onto its back wall – take time to allow your eyes to adjust to the light. On the way back keep a look out for otters, who love the tidal rapids hereabouts.

The **tourist office** (April to mid-Oct Mon–Sat 9am–5pm; also open for an hour to greet the evening ferry; ⓣ01876/500321), near the quayside, has local bus and ferry timetables and can help with **accommodation**. Lochmaddy itself doesn't have the best options: the long-established *Lochmaddy Hotel* (ⓣ01876/500331, ⓦwww.lochmaddyhotel.co.uk; ❺) is the anglers' HQ, and has been fairly recently refurbished; the Georgian *Old Courthouse* (ⓣ01876/500358, ⓔmjohnson@oldcourthouse.fsnet.co.uk; ❸), the Uists' former jail, retains more character. A little further north is Lochmaddy's newest hotel, *Tigh Dearg* (ⓣ01876/500700, ⓦwww.tighdearghotel.co.uk; ❼), whose stylish modernity comes as something of a culture shock compared to anything else on the Uists; guests also get free use of the hotel's gym, sauna and steam room. Beyond lies the *Uist Outdoor Centre* (ⓣ01876/500480, ⓦwww.uistoutdoor centre.co.uk), which has **hostel** accommodation in four-person bunk rooms and offers a wide range of outdoor activities, from canoeing round the indented coastline to "rubber tubing" for residents and non-residents alike.

The bar in the *Lochmaddy Hotel* is the lively local **pub**, but the *Tigh Dearg* offers more imaginative bar **food** (as well as formal four-course à la carte for £25 a head). The island's only **bank** is further inland from the tourist office. There is a small **general store**, petrol, a post office in Taigh Chearsabhagh, but the nearest large supermarket is in Solas (see p.390).

Nearby Neolithic sites

Several prehistoric sites lie in the vicinity of Lochmaddy. The most remarkable is **Barpa Langais**, a huge, chambered burial cairn a short walk from the A867, seven barren miles southwest. The stones are visible from the road and, unless the weather's good, it's not worth making a closer inspection as the chamber has collapsed and is now too dangerous to enter. A mile further down the A867, a side-road leads off to *Langass Lodge* (ⓣ01876/580285, ⓦwww.langasslodge .co.uk; ❻), a small **hotel** whose restaurant and bar snacks feature excellent local seafood. Beside the hotel, a rough track leads to the small stone circle of **Pobull Fhinn** (Finn's People), which enjoys a much more picturesque location overlooking a narrow loch. The circle covers a large area and, although the stones are not that huge, they occupy an intriguing amphitheatre cut into the hillside. For those interested in wildlife, the RSPB runs **otter walks** (May–Aug Wed 10am; £4; booking essential ⓣ01876/560284), which set off from the car park at *Langass Lodge*. Three miles northwest of Lochmaddy along the A865 you'll find **Na Fir Bhreige** (The Three False Men), three standing stones which, depending on your legend, mark the graves of three spies buried alive or three men who deserted their wives and were turned to stone by a witch.

Berneray (Bhearnaraigh)

The ferry connection with Harris now leaves from the very southeastern point of **Berneray** (ⓦwww.isleofberneray.com), a low-lying island immediately to

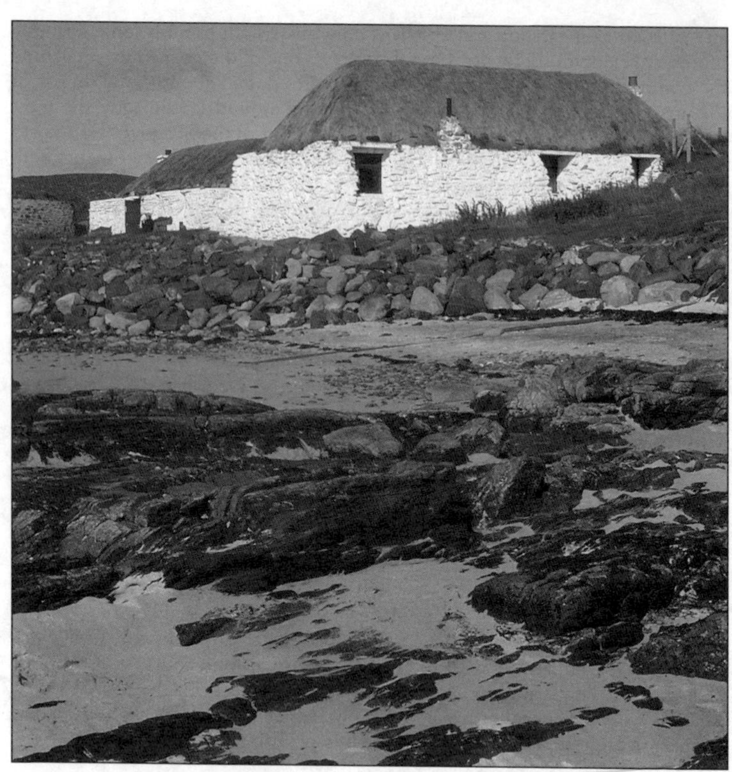
△ Berneray hostel

the north of North Uist and connected to the latter via a causeway. Two miles by three, with a population of just over a hundred, the island has a superb three-mile-long sandy beach on the west and north coast, backed by rabbit-free dunes and machair. Prince Charles, lover of Gaelic culture, was a frequent visitor at one time, and was memorably filmed helping local crofter "Splash" MacKillop pick potatoes. The other great draw is the wonderful GHHT **hostel** (Ⓦwww.gatliff.org.uk), which occupies a pair of thatched blackhouses in a lovely spot by a beach, beyond Loch a Bhàigh and the main village. Alternatively you can follow in the prince's footsteps and stay (and help out) at "Splash" MacKillop's *Burnside Croft* **B&B** (Ⓣ01876/540235, Ⓦwww.burnsidecroft.fsnet.co.uk; ❷; Feb–Nov), in Borgh (Borve), overlooking the machair and dunes, and enjoy "storytelling evenings"; **bike rental** is also available. There's a **tearoom** called *The Lobster Pot* in the shop on the main road, near the junction, and a **bus** connection with Lochmaddy.

The coastal road via Solas (Sollas)

The A865, which skirts the northern and western shoreline of North Uist for more than thirty miles, takes you through the most scenic sections of the island. Once you've left the boggy east coast and passed the turning to Berneray and the Harris Ferry, the road reaches the parish of **SOLAS** (Sollas), which stands at the centre of a couple of superb tidal strands – sea green at high tide, golden sand at low tide – backed by large tracts of machair that are blanketed with wild flowers in summer. A new memorial opposite the local co-op recalls the appallingly brutal Clearances undertaken by Lord MacDonald of Sleat in Solas. The current laird, Lord Granville, who owns much of North Uist, occupies the large house on the tidal island of **Vallay** (Bhalaigh), which is connected by a road that crosses the largest of the two strands. For a comfortable, friendly **B&B** with great views across Vallay Strand, head for *Struan House* (Ⓣ01876/560282; ❶; April–Sept), also known as *Struan Ruadh*.

Beyond Solas, the rolling hills that occupy the centre of North Uist slope down to the sea. Here, in the northwest corner of the island, you'll find **Scolpaig Tower**, a castellated folly on an islet in Loch Scolpaig, erected as a famine-relief project in the nineteenth century – you can reach it, with some difficulty, across stepping stones. A tarmac track leads down past the loch and tower to Scolpaig Bay, beyond which lies the rocky shoreline of **Griminish Point**, the closest landfall to St Kilda (see box, below), which is clearly visible on the horizon in fine weather, looming like some giant dinosaur's skeleton emerging from the sea.

Roughly three miles south of Scolpaig Tower, through the sand dunes, is the **Balranald RSPB Reserve**, where if you're lucky you should be able to encounter corncrakes, once common throughout the British countryside, but now among the country's rarest birds. Unfortunately, the birds are very good at hiding in long grass, so you're unlikely to see one; however, the males' loud "craking" is relatively easy to hear from May to July throughout the Uists and Barra. In fact, there are usually one or two making a loud noise right outside the RSPB **visitor centre**, from which you can pick up a leaflet outlining a two-hour walk along the headland, marked by posts. A wonderful carpet of flowers covers the machair in summer, and there are usually corn buntings and arctic

St Kilda

Britain's westernmost island chain is the NTS-owned **St Kilda** archipelago (Ⓦwww.kilda.org.uk), roughly a hundred miles west southwest of the Butt of Lewis and over forty miles from its nearest landfall, Griminish Point on North Uist. Dominated by the highest cliffs and sea stacks in Britain, Hirta, St Kilda's main island, was occupied on and off for some two thousand years, with the last 36 Gaelic-speaking inhabitants evacuated at their own request in 1930. Immediately after evacuation, the island was bought by the Marquess of Bute, who was keen to protect the island's population of somewhere between one and two million puffins, gannets, petrels and other seabirds. In 1957, having agreed to allow the army to build a missile-tracking radar station here linked to South Uist, the Marquess bequeathed the island to the NTS (Ⓣ01463/232034, Ⓦwww.nts.org.uk). Despite its inaccessibility, several thousand visitors make it out to St Kilda each year; the resident NTS ranger usually gives a little talk, you get to see the museum, send a postcard and enjoy a drink at the army's pub, the *Puff Inn*. If you have your own yacht, you must have permission in order to land; several boat companies also offer **day-trips** to St Kilda for around £125 per person (see p.376). Between mid-May and mid-August, the NTS organizes volunteer **work parties**, which either restore and maintain the old buildings or take part in archeological digs. Volunteers are expected to work 24–36 hours a week for two weeks, for which they must pay around £500 per person, though, with only twelve people on each party and more applications than there are places, there's no guarantee you'll get on one. Volunteers meet at Oban, and should be prepared for a rough, fifteen-hour overnight crossing. For the armchair traveller, the best general book on St Kilda is Tom Steel's *The Life and Death of St Kilda*.

terns inland, and gannets, Manx shearwaters and skuas out to sea. On a clear day you can see the unmistakable shape of St Kilda, seeming miraculously near.

A couple of miles down the main road from Balranald, the **Claddach Kirkibost Centre** has an excellent café in a conservatory with sea views, which uses local produce and has internet facilities (Mon–Fri 11am–5pm). Half a mile further on, you can get peat-smoked salmon and other seafood delights by the roadside from the *Hebridean Smokehouse* (Mon–Fri 9am–5pm; mid-May to Oct also Sat 9am–5pm; Ⓦwww.hebrideansmokehouse.com).

Clachan to Grimsay (Griomasaigh)

At **CLACHAN NA LUIB**, by the crossroads with the A867 from Lochmaddy, there's a post office and general store. Offshore, to the southwest, lie two flat, tidal, dune and machair islands, the largest of which is **Baleshare** (Baile Sear), with its fantastic three-mile-long beach, connected by causeway to North Uist. In Gaelic the island's name means "east village", its twin "west village" having disappeared under the sea during a freak storm in the fifteenth or sixteenth century. The storm also isolated the **Monarch Islands** (also known by their old Norse name of Heisgeir or Heisker), once joined to North Uist at low tide, now eight miles out to sea. The islands, which are connected with each other at low tide, were inhabited until the 1930s, when the last remaining families moved to Solas in North Uist. For a superb overview of North Uist's watery landscape, it's a boggy, but relatively straightforward climb up Baleshare's highest hill, **Eabhal** (1138ft). The best starting point is the end of the B894 to Loch Euphoirt: skirt round the east side of Loch Obasaraigh and approach the summit from the northeast (return trip 3–4 hr).

There are several decent **accommodation** options in the Clachan area: *Temple View Hotel* (Ⓣ01876/580676, Ⓦwww.templeviewhotel.co.uk; ❻) is a friendly family-run, small hotel overlooking the medieval ruined church of **Teampull na Trionaid**; the nearby local pub, *Carinish Inn* (Ⓣ01876/580673, Ⓦwww.macinnesbros.co.uk; ❺), offers a wide range of bar meals, and occasionally has live music. In an isolated position, overlooking Baleshare, is *Taigh mo Sheanair* (Ⓣ01876/580246, Ⓔcarnach@amserve.net), a very welcoming, family-run **hostel**, with bunk beds, en-suite rooms and a peat fire – you can also **camp**. The hostel is clearly signposted from the main road, from which it's a good fifteen-minute walk.

On leaving North Uist the main road squeezes along a series of single-track causeways, built by the military in 1960, that cross the tidal rapids separating North Uist from Benbecula. The causeways trim the west edge of **Grimsay** (Griomasaigh), a peaceful, little-visited, rocky island that's really quite pretty, especially around **BAGH MOR** (Baymore). The main source of employment is fishing for langoustines, lobsters and the like, which takes place at the modern pier in **CEALLAN** (Kallin), where you can usually buy some shellfish on Saturday mornings; there's also an excellent little B&B, *Glendale* (Ⓣ01870/602029, Ⓔglendale@ecosse.net; ❶). Ceallan is also home to the **Grimsay Boatshed** (Mon–Sat 9am–4pm; free), where there's a display of old and new Grimsay Boats, the clinker-built open boats that were perfectly designed for negotiating the local watery labyrinth.

Benbecula (Beinn na Faoghla)

Blink and you could miss the pancake-flat island of **Benbecula** (put the stress on the second syllable), sandwiched between Protestant North Uist and Catholic South Uist. Most visitors simply trundle along the main road that cuts across the middle of the island in less than five miles – not such a bad idea, since the island is scarred from the postwar presence of the Royal Artillery, who until recently used to make up half the local population. Economically, of course, the area benefited enormously from the military presence, though the impact on the environment and the local Gaelic culture (with so many English speakers around) has been less positive.

The legacy of Benbecula's military past is only too evident in the depressing, barracks-like housing developments of **BALIVANICH** (Baile a Mhanaich), the grim, grey capital of Benbecula in the northwest. The only reason to come here at all is if you happen to be flying into or out of **Benbecula airport** (direct flights to Glasgow, Barra and Stornoway), need to take money out of the Bank of Scotland ATM (the only one on Benbecula and South Uist) or want to do some laundry (the laundry is behind the bank) or stock up on provisions, best done at the old NAAFI store (now a Spar supermarket; open daily), to the west of the post office. There's no tourist office and no real need **to stay** here, but if you've time to kill, you could head down to MacGillivray's, a long-established, old-fashioned shop selling everything from local tweeds to books, within easy walking distance of the airport, on the road to North Uist. If you need a bite to eat, *Stepping Stone* (closed Mon eve), a purpose-built **café/restaurant**, is divided into the *Food Base* café, which serves up cheap filled rolls, hot meals, and chips with everything; and the underwhelming £20-a-head *Sinteag* restaurant (evenings only), up the steps. **Car rental** is available at the airport from Ask Car Hire (ⓣ01870/602818).

The chief **campsite** on the Uists is *Shell Bay* (ⓣ01870/602447; April–Oct), in the south of the island at **LIONACLEIT** (Liniclate). Adjacent is the modern **Sgoil Lionacleit**, the only secondary school (and public swimming pool) on the Uists and Benbecula, and home to a small **Museum nan Eilean** (Mon–Sat only; phone for times; ⓣ01870/602864), which puts on temporary exhibitions on the history of the islands, as well as occasional live music and other events. Close to the school, **accommodation** is available at the comfortable *Lionacleit Guest House* (ⓣ01870/602176, ⓦwww.lionacleit-guesthouse.com; ④), and, just across the water in South Uist, the *Orasay Inn* (see p.394). If you're passing along the west side of the island, pop into Baile nan Cailleach, better known as the **Nunton Steadings**, an unusual three-sided eighteenth-century farm building with a cobbled courtyard, and a small belltower (used to call the workers in from the fields), where there are occasional exhibitions and a weekend **café** in the summer.

South Uist (Uibhist a Deas)

To the south of Benbecula, the island of **South Uist** is the largest and most varied of the southern chain of islands. The west coast boasts some of the region's finest machair and beaches – a necklace of gold and grey sand strung twenty miles from one end to the other – while the east coast features a ridge of high mountains rising to 2034ft at the summit of Beinn Mhor. Whatever you do, don't make the mistake of simply driving down the main A865 road, which runs down the centre of the island like a backbone. To reach the beaches (or even see them), you have to get off the main road and pass through the old crofters' villages that straggle along the west coast; to climb the mountains in the east, you need a detailed 1:25,000 Explorer map, in order to negotiate the island's maze of lochans. The only blot on South Uist's landscape is the old

Royal Artillery missile range, which dominates the northwest corner of the island.

Loch Druidibeg, Tobha Mòr (Howmore) and around

The Reformation never took a strong hold in South Uist (or Barra), and the island remains Roman Catholic, as is evident from the various roadside shrines and the slender modern Madonna, *Our Lady of the Isles*, that stands by the main road below the small hill of **Rueval**, known to the locals as "Space City" for its forest of aerials and giant "golf balls", which help track the missiles heading out into the Atlantic. To the south of Rueval is the freshwater **Loch Druidibeg**, now at the centre of one of the country's National Nature Reserves. The area is comprised of diverse habitats, from brackish lagoons and peaty moorland in the east to dune and machair in the west. Apart from a few over-friendly Shetland ponies, though, it's not exactly teeming with wildlife in summer, but it's lovely countryside, and, as in most of the Uists, there's the chance of seeing some raptors hunting over the moorland, including hen harriers and golden eagle; there's a waymarked path through the reserve that begins just by the telephone box on the main road in **Stadhlaigearraidh** (Stilligarry); a map is available from the tourist office.

One of the best places to gain access to the sandy shoreline is at **TOBHA MÒR** (Howmore), a pretty little crofting settlement with a fair number of restored houses, many still thatched, including one distinctively roofed in brown heather. A GHHT **hostel** (Ⓦwww.gatliff.org.uk) occupies one such house near the village church, from where it's an easy walk across the flower-strewn machair to the gorgeous beach. Close by the hostel are the shattered, lichen-encrusted remains of no fewer than four medieval churches and chapels, and a burial ground now harbouring just a few scattered graves. The sixteenth-century **Clanranald Stone**, carved with the arms of the clan who ruled over South Uist from 1370 until 1839, used to lie here. It's now displayed in the nearby Kildonan Museum (see below), after it was stolen in 1990 and removed to London by a Canadian artist, Lawren Maben. It took three months before anyone noticed it had disappeared. Five years later, it was discovered by the artist's father in a bedsit near Euston station, as he sorted out his son's belongings, following his "death by misadventure".

There's much more besides the aforementioned stone at the **Taigh-tasgaidh Chill Donnain** – or Kildonan Museum (April & May Mon–Sat 11am–4pm; June–Sept Mon–Sat 10am–5pm, Sun 2–5pm; £1.50), on the main road five miles south of Tobha Mòr. Mock-ups of Hebridean kitchens through the ages, two lovely box beds and an impressive selection of old photos are accompanied by a firmly unsentimental yet poetic written text on crofting life in the last two centuries. Among the more unusual exhibits is a pair of ornamental shoes made of deer hooves. The museum also runs a café serving sandwiches and home-made cakes, and has a choice of historical videos for those really wet and windy days. A little to the south of the museum, the road passes a cairn that sits amongst the foundations of **Flora MacDonald**'s childhood home; she was born nearby, but the house no longer stands.

Apart from the aforementioned hostel, there's the *Orasay Inn* (Ⓣ01870/610298, Ⓔorasayinn@btinternet.com; ④), a **hotel** in a peaceful spot off the road to Loch a Charnain (Lochcarnan), in the northeastern corner of the island. If you get a room looking east out towards the Minch, you can enjoy a bit of birdwatching from your balcony; the bar meals are also good value and the breakfasts are great. If you're amassing a picnic, try some "flaky smoked salmon", available throughout the Western Isles, as well as straight from its source, *Salar* (closed Sat & Sun), further along the road to Loch a Charnain, beyond the *Orasay Inn* turn-off. Further south, you can stay at two inexpensive **B&Bs**: the modern farmhouse *Tigh-an-Droma* (ⓣ01870/620292, ⓔtighandroma@aol.com; ❶), overlooking Loch Druidibeg, or in the *Old Croft House* (ⓣ01870/620292, ⓔmmack6k@aol.com; ❷) in Cill Donnain (Kildonan). **Bike rental** (and repair) is available from Rothan Cycles (ⓣ01870/620283), on the main road in Tobha Mòr (Howmore).

Lochboisdale (Loch Baghasdail) and around

Although it is South Uist's chief settlement and ferry port, **LOCHBOISDALE**, occupying a narrow, bumpy promontory on the east coast, has less to offer than Lochmaddy. If you're arriving here late at night on the boat from Oban (or from Barra or Tiree), you should try to book accommodation in advance; otherwise, head for the **tourist office** (Easter to mid-Oct Mon–Sat 9am–5pm; open for an hour to meet the ferry; ⓣ01878/700286); next door is a useful coin-operated shower and toilet block (daily 9am–6pm). The town's only **hotel**, the *Lochboisdale* (ⓣ01878/700332, ⓦwww.lochboisdale.com; ❹) has been refurbished, and does decent bar meals, including succulent local cockles. There are also several small, perfectly friendly **B&Bs** within comfortable walking distance of the dock, one of the best (and nearest) being *Brae Lea House* (ⓣ01878/700497, ⓔbraelea@supanet.com; ❸). There's a bank, but the shops in Lochboisdale are pretty limited; the nearest supermarket is three miles west in Dalabrog (Daliburgh). Another place you could hole up in is the *Polochar Inn* (ⓣ01878/700215, ⓦwww.macinnesbros.co.uk; ❺), eight miles from Lochboisdale, right on the south coast overlooking the Sound of Barra, and with its own sandy beach close by.

Eriskay (Eiriosgaigh)

Famous for its patterned jerseys and a peculiar breed of pony, originally used for carrying peat and seaweed, the barren, hilly island of **Eriskay** is connected to the south of South Uist by a causeway, built in 2001. The island, which measures just over two miles by one, and shelters a small fishing community of about 150, makes a great day-trip from South Uist.

For a small island, Eriskay has had more than its fair share of historical headlines. The island's main beach on the west coast, Coilleag a Phrionnsa (Prince's Cockle Strand), was where **Bonnie Prince Charlie** landed on Scottish soil on July 23, 1745 – the sea bindweed that grows here to this day is said to have sprung from the seeds Charles brought with him from France. The prince, as yet unaccustomed to hardship, spent his first night in a local blackhouse and ate a couple of flounders, though he apparently couldn't take the peat smoke and chose to sleep sitting up rather than endure the damp bed.

Eriskay's other claim to fame came in 1941 when the 8000-ton **SS Politician** or "*Polly*" as it's fondly known, sank on its way from Liverpool to Jamaica, along with its cargo of bicycle parts, £3 million in Jamaican currency and 264,000 bottles of whisky, inspiring Compton MacKenzie's book, and the Ealing comedy (filmed on Barra in 1948), *Whisky Galore!* (released as *Tight Little Island* in the US). The real story was somewhat less romantic, especially for the 36 islanders who were charged with illegal possession by the Customs and Excise officers, 19 of whom were found guilty and imprisoned in Inverness. The ship's stern can still be seen at low tide northwest of Calvay Island in the Sound of Eriskay, and one of the original bottles (and lots of other related memorabilia) is on show in *Am Politician*, the island's purpose-built pub near the two cemeteries on the west coast where you can get something to eat when the bar's open (times vary).

Built in 1903, in a vaguely Spanish style on raised ground above the harbour, is **St Michael's Church**. Its most striking features are the bell, which sits outside the church and comes from the World War I battle cruiser *Derfflinger*, the last of the scuttled German fleet to be salvaged from Scapa Flow (see p.425), and the altar, which is made from the bow of a lifeboat. From the church, it's a short walk to the **community centre** (Mon–Sat 11am–3pm), which serves tea and snacks in summer, and sells jumpers and occasionally hosts exhibitions. The walk up to the island's highest point, **Ben Sciathan** (607ft), is well worth the effort on a clear day, as you can see the whole island, plus Barra, South Uist, and across the sea to Skye, Rùm, Coll and Tiree (2hr return from the village). On the way up or down, look out for the diminutive Eriskay ponies, which roam free on the hills but tend to graze around Loch Crakavaig, the island's freshwater source.

Apart from one self-catering option (Ⓣ01878/720274), the only way to stay here is to **camp rough** (with permission). CalMac now runs a **car ferry to Barra** (4–5 daily; 40min) from a new harbour on the southwest coast of Eriskay.

Barra (Barraigh)

Just four miles wide and eight miles long, **Barra** (Ⓦwww.isleofbarra.com) has a well-deserved reputation for being the Western Isles in miniature. It has sandy beaches, backed by machair, mountains of Lewisian gneiss, prehistoric ruins, Gaelic culture and a laid-back, welcoming Catholic population of just over 1300. Like some miniature feudal island state, it was ruled over for centuries, with relative benevolence, by the MacNeils. Unfortunately, however, the family sold the island in 1838 to Colonel Gordon of Cluny, who had also bought Benbecula, South Uist and Eriskay. The colonel deemed the starving crofters "redundant", and offered to turn Barra into a state penal colony. The government declined, so the colonel called in the police and proceeded with some of the cruelest forced Clearances in the Hebrides. In 1937, the 45th chief of the MacNeil clan bought back most of the island, and the island returned with relief to its more familiar, feudal roots.

Castlebay (Bàgh a Chaisteil)

The only settlement of any size is **CASTLEBAY** (Bàgh a Chaisteil), which curves around the barren rocky hills of a beautiful wide bay on the south side of the island. It's difficult to imagine it now, but Castlebay was a herring port of some significance back in the nineteenth century, with up to four hundred boats in the harbour and curing and packing factories ashore. Barra's religious allegiance is immediately announced by the large Catholic church, Our Lady, Star of the Sea, which overlooks the bay; to underline the point, there's a Madonna and Child on the slopes of **Sheabhal** (1260ft), the largest peak on Barra, and a fairly easy hike from the bay.

As its name suggests, Castlebay has a castle in its bay, the picturesque medieval islet-fortress of Caisteal Chiosmuil, or **Kisimul Castle** (April–Sept daily

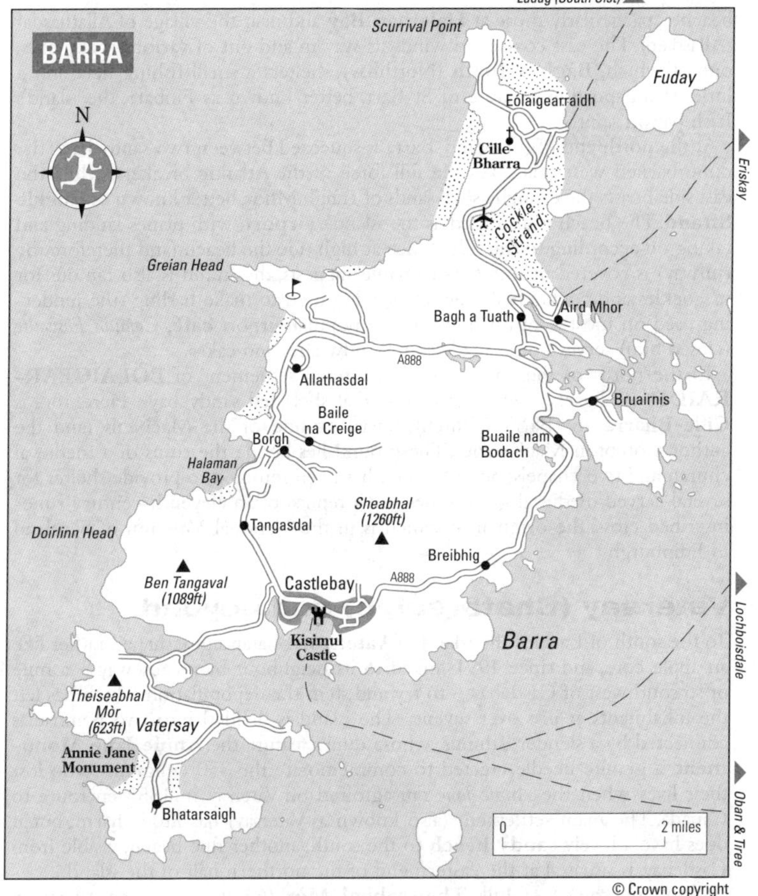

9.30am–6.30pm; HS; £3.30), ancestral home of the MacNeil clan. The castle burnt down in the eighteenth century, but when the 45th MacNeil chief – conveniently enough, a wealthy American and trained architect – bought the island back in 1937, he set about restoring the castle. There's nothing much to see inside, but the whole experience is fun – head down to the slipway at the bottom of Main Street, where the HS ferryman will take you over (weather permitting; ⓣ01871/810313).

To learn more about the history of the island, and about the postal system of the Western Isles, it's worth paying a visit to the Barra Heritage Centre, known as **Dualchas** (March, April & Sept Mon, Wed & Fri 11am–4pm; May–Aug Mon–Sat 11am–4pm; £2; ⓦwww.barraheritage.com), on the road that leads west out of town; the museum also has a handy **café** serving soup, toasties and cakes.

North to Cockle Strand and Eòlaigearraidh

If you head north from Castlebay, basically you have a choice of taking the west or the east coast road. The west coast road takes you past the island's finest sandy beaches, particularly those at **Halaman Bay** and near the village of Allathasdal (Allasdale). The east coast road winds its way in and out of various rocky bays, one of which, **Bàgh a Tuath** (Northbay), shelters a small fishing fleet and a little island sporting a statue of St Barr, better known as Finbarr, the island's Irish patron saint.

At the north end of the island, Barra is squeezed between two sandy bays: the dune-backed west side takes the full force of the Atlantic breakers, while the east side boasts the crunchy shell sands of Tràigh Mhòr, better known as **Cockle Strand**. The beach is also used as the island's **airport**, with planes landing and taking off according to the tides, since at high tide the beach (and therefore the runway) is covered in water. As its name suggests, the strand is also famous for its cockles and cockleshells, the latter being used to make harling (the rendering used on most Scottish houses). The popular airport **café**, *Cafaidh Fosgailte* (closed Sun) serves home-made soup, sandwiches and cakes.

To the north of the airport is the scattered settlement of **EÒLAIGEARRAIDH** (Eoligarry), which boasts several sheltered sandy bays. Here, too, is **Cille-Bharra** (St Barr's Church), burial ground of the MacNeils (and the author Compton MacKenzie). The ground lies beside the ruins of a medieval church and two chapels, one of which has been reroofed to provide shelter for several carved medieval gravestones and a replica of an eleventh-century rune-inscribed cross, the original of which is in the National Museum of Scotland in Edinburgh.

Vatersay (Bhatarsaigh) and beyond

To the south of Barra is the island of **Vatersay** (Bhatarsaigh), shaped rather like an apple core, and since 1991 linked to its neighbour by a causeway – a mile or so southwest of Castlebay – to try and stem the depopulation which has left the inhabitants at just over seventy. The island is divided into two peninsulas connected by a slender isthmus, whose dunes feature the **Annie Jane Monument**, a granite needle erected to commemorate the 350 emigrants who lost their lives when the *Annie Jane* ran aground off Vatersay in 1853 en route to Canada. The main settlement (also known as Vatersay) has little charm, but it does have a lovely **sandy beach** to the south; another fine beach, visible from Castlebay, is situated at the eastern end of the northern half of the island.

Climb up the chief hill, **Theiseabhal Mòr** (623ft), to get an overview of Vatersay and the Bishop's Isles to the south, all of which were inhabited up until just before World War II. The largest of the islands is **Mingulay** (Miùghlaigh), which once had a population of 160 and with its large seabird colonies, spectacular sea cliffs and stacks, is often compared to St Kilda (see box, p.376). The crofters of Mingulay began a series of land raids on Vatersay from 1906 and by 1912 the island had been abandoned, with none of the publicity later given to St Kilda. The most southerly of the Western Isles is Berneray (Bearnaraigh) – not to be confused with the Berneray north of North Uist – best known for its lighthouse, **Barra Head**, which stands on cliffs over 620ft high. For details of boat trips to the island, phone Barra Fishing Charters below.

Practicalities

There are two **ferry terminals** on Barra: from Eriskay, you arrive at an uninhabited spot called Aird Mhòr, on the northeast of the island; from Oban, Lochboisdale or Tiree, you arrive at the main terminal in Castlebay itself. Barra Car Hire (☎01871/810243) will deliver **cars** to either terminal or the airport, and Barra Cycle Hire (Ⓣ01871/810438) will do the same with **bikes**. There's also a fairly decent **bus/postbus** service, which does the rounds of the island (Mon–Sat). Barra's **tourist office** (April–Oct Mon–Sat 9am–1pm & 2–5pm; also open to greet the ferry; Ⓣ01871/810336) is situated on Main Street in Castlebay just round from the pier, and can help book accommodation, though it's as well to book in advance for B&Bs and hotels. Guided **sea kayaking** is available from the *Dunard Hostel* (Ⓦwww.clearwaterpaddling.com), and those interested in a **boat trip** to any of the islands around Barra, including **Mingulay**, should phone Donald (Ⓣ01871/890384, Ⓦwww.barrafishingcharters.com) or enquire at the tourist office.

For **accommodation** in Castlebay itself, the *Castlebay Hotel* (Ⓣ01871/810223, Ⓦwww.castlebay-hotel.co.uk; ❺) is the more welcoming of the town's two hotels, followed by *Tigh-na-Mara* (Ⓣ01871/810304, Ⓔtighnamara@aol.com; ❷), a Victorian guesthouse a couple of minutes' walk from the pier, overlooking the sea. Although architecturally something of a 1970s monstrosity, the *Isle of Barra Hotel* (Ⓣ01871/810383, Ⓦwww.isleofbarra.com/iob.html; ❺; Easter–early Oct) enjoys a classic location overlooking Halaman Bay. However, the best option outside Castlebay is *Northbay House* (Ⓣ01871/890255, Ⓦwww.barraholidays.co.uk; ❸; April–Oct), a very nicely converted old school in Buaile nam Bodach (Balnabodach), or the *Old Croft House* (Ⓣ01871/890799, Ⓔbernieandpaddy@tiscali.co.uk; ❷), half a mile further north in Bruairnis (Bruernish). Lastly, there's *Dunard Hostel* (Ⓣ01871/810443, Ⓦwww.dunardhostel.co.uk), a relaxed, family-run place just 200yd west of the ferry terminal in Castlebay.

On Main Street, the *Kisimul* **café** (closed Sun) serves breakfast all day, and specializes in cheap-and-cheerful Scottish fry-ups. For more fancy fare, head to the *Castlebay Hotel*'s cosy **bar**, which regularly has cockles, crabs and scallops on its menu, and good views out over the bay. The only two watering holes in the north of the island are the airport terminal café (see p.398) and the *Heathbank Hotel*, a pub in Bagh a Tuath (Northbay). **Films** are occasionally shown on Saturday evenings at the local school – look out for the posters – where there is also a swimming pool (Tues–Sun), library and sports centre, all of which are open to the general public.

Travel details

Buses

Lewis/Harris

Information at Ⓦwww.cne-siar.gov.uk/travel.

Stornoway to: Arnol (Mon–Sat 4–6 daily; 35min); Barabhas (Mon–Sat 8–12 daily; 25min); Calanais (Mon–Sat 4–6 daily; 40min); Carlabhagh (Mon–Sat 4–6 daily; 1hr); Great Bernera (Mon–Sat 4 daily; 1hr); Leverburgh (Mon–Sat 4–5 daily; 1hr 55min); Port Nis (Mon–Sat 4–6 daily; 1hr); Siabost (Mon–Sat 4–6 daily; 45min); Tarbert (Mon–Sat 4–5 daily; 1hr 5min); Tolsta (Mon–Sat hourly; 40min); Uig (Mon–Sat 3–4 daily; 1hr–1hr 30min).

Tarbert to: Huisinis (schooldays Mon–Fri 2–3 daily; school holidays Tues & Fri 3 daily; 45min); Leverburgh (Mon–Sat 6–7 daily; 45min–1hr); Leverburgh via the Bays (Mon–Sat 3–4 daily; 1hr); Rhenigadale (Mon–Sat 2 daily; 30min); Scalpay (Mon–Sat 4–5 daily; 20min).

Uists & Benbecula

Berneray to: Lochmaddy (Mon–Sat 6–7 daily; 20–50min).

Lochboisdale to: Eriskay (Mon–Sat 6–7 daily; 35min).

Lochmaddy to: Balivanich (Mon–Sat 5–6 daily; 45min–2hr); Balranald (Mon–Sat 3 daily; 50min); Lochboisdale (Mon–Sat 5–6 daily; 2hr).

Barra

Castlebay to: airport/ferry for Eriskay (Mon–Sat 6–7 daily; 35min–45min); Vatersay (Mon–Sat 3–4 daily; 20min).

Ferries

Summer timetable only.

To Barra: Eriskay–Barra (5 daily; 40min); Lochboisdale–Castlebay (Mon & Tues; 1hr 30min); Oban–Castlebay (1 daily; 4hr 50min); Tiree–Castlebay (Thurs; 3hr).

To Harris: Berneray–Leverburgh (Mon–Sat 3–4 daily; 1hr); Uig–Tarbert (Mon–Sat 2 daily; 1hr 45min).

To Lewis: Ullapool–Stornoway (Mon–Sat 2–3 daily; 2hr 45min).

To North Uist: Leverburgh–Berneray (Mon–Sat 3–4 daily; 1hr); Uig–Lochmaddy (1–2 daily; 1hr 40min).

To South Uist: Castlebay–Lochboisdale (Mon, Tues & Fri–Sun; 1hr 40min); Oban–Lochboisdale (daily except Wed; 4hr 50min–6hr 40min).

Flights

Benbecula to: Barra (Mon–Fri 1 daily; 20min); Stornoway (Mon–Fri 2 daily; 30min).

Edinburgh to: Stornoway (Mon–Fri 3 daily, Sat & Sun 1–2 daily; 1hr).

Glasgow to: Barra (Mon–Sat 1 daily; 1hr 5min); Benbecula (Mon–Fri 2 daily, Sat & Sun 1 daily; 1hr); Stornoway (daily; 1hr 10min).

Inverness to: Stornoway (Mon–Fri 4 daily, Sat & Sun 1–2 daily; 35–40min).

7

Orkney

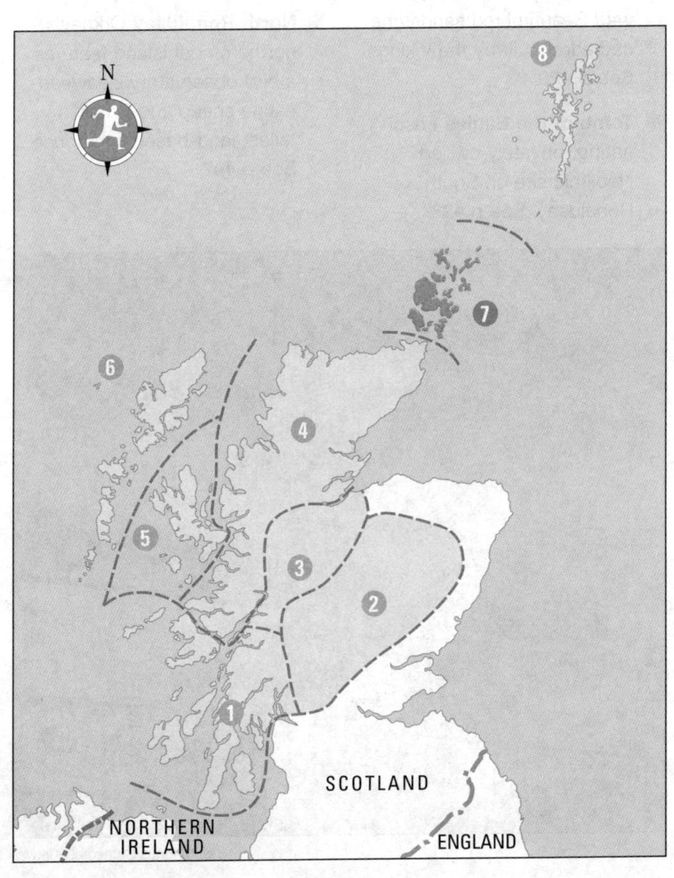

CHAPTER 7

Highlights

* **Maes Howe** Orkney's, and Europe's, finest Neolithic chambered tomb. See p.412
* **Skara Brae** Mesmerizing Neolithic homes, crammed with domestic detail. See p.413
* **St Magnus Cathedral, Kirkwall** Beautiful red sandstone cathedral built by the Vikings. See p.420
* **Tomb of the Eagles** Fascinating, privately owned Neolithic site on South Ronaldsay. See p.428
* **Balfour Castle** Eat, sleep and live like a king in Orkney's most sumptuous castle hotel. See p.434
* **Westray** Thriving Orkney island with seabird colonies, sandy beaches and a ruined castle. See p.437
* **North Ronaldsay** Orkney's northernmost island features a bird observatory, seaweed-eating sheep and Britain's tallest land-based lighthouse. See p.447

△ St Magnus Cathedral, Kirkwall

7

Orkney

Just a short step from John O'Groats, **Orkney** is a unique and fiercely independent archipelago made up of seventy or so islands, seventeen of which share a population of less than 20,000. With the major exception of Hoy, which is high and rugged, the islands are mostly low-lying, gently sloping and richly fertile, and for centuries have provided a reasonably secure living for their inhabitants from farming and, to a much lesser extent, fishing. The locals tend to refer to themselves first as Orcadians, regarding Scotland as a separate entity, and proudly flying their own unofficial flag. For an Orcadian, the "Mainland" invariably means the largest island in Orkney rather than the rest of Scotland, and throughout their distinctive history they've been linked to lands much further afield, principally Scandinavia.

There is a peaceful continuity to Orcadian life reflected not only in the well-preserved treasury of Stone Age remains, but also in the rather conservative nature of society here today. For the visitor, the best time to come is in spring and summer, when the days are long, the sandy beaches dazzling, the cliffs packed with seabirds and the meadows thick with wild flowers. In autumn and winter, the islands are often battered by gale-force winds and daylight is scarce, but the temperature stays remarkably mild thanks to the ameliorating effect of the Gulf Stream. Wind is, of course, a factor throughout the year, though its almost constant presence does mean that midges are less of a problem, except on Hoy.

Some history

Orkney lay athwart a great sea-way
from Viking times onwards, and its lore
is crowded with sailors, merchants, adventurers,
pilgrims, smugglers, storms and sea-changes.
The shores are strewn with wrack, jetsam,
occasional treasure.

George Mackay Brown

Small communities began to settle in the islands around 4000 BC, and the village at **Skara Brae** on the Mainland is one of the best-preserved Stone Age settlements in Europe. This and many of the other older archeological sites, including the **Stones of Stenness** and **Maes Howe**, are concentrated in West Mainland. Elsewhere the islands are scattered with chambered tombs and stone circles, a tribute to the well-developed religious and ceremonial practices taking place here from around 2000 BC. More sophisticated **Iron Age** inhabitants built fortified villages incorporating stone towers known as brochs, protected by walls and ramparts, the finest of which is the **Broch of Gurness**. Later, **Pictish**

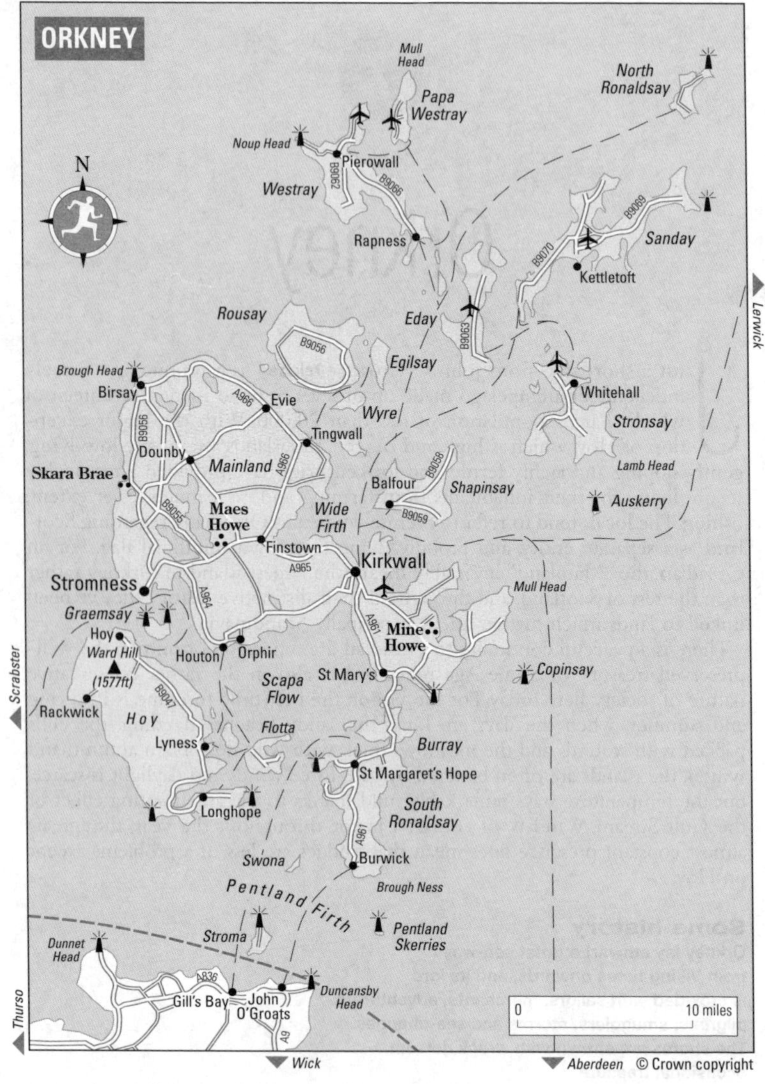

7 ORKNEY

culture spread to Orkney and the remains of several of their early Christian settlements can still be seen, the best at the **Brough of Birsay**, where a group of small houses is clustered around the remains of an early church. In the ninth century or thereabouts, **Norse** settlers from Scandinavia arrived and the islands became Norse earldoms, forming an outpost of a powerful, expansive culture which was gradually forcing its way south. The last of the Norse earls was killed in 1231, but they had a lasting impact on the islands, leaving behind not only their language but also the great **St Magnus Cathedral** in Kirkwall, one of Scotland's outstanding examples of medieval architecture.

After the end of Norse rule, the islands became the preserve of **Scottish earls**, who exploited and abused the islanders, although a steady increase in sea trade did offer some chance of escape. French and Spanish ships sheltered here in the sixteenth century, and the ships of the **Hudson's Bay Company** recruited hundreds of Orcadians to work in the Canadian fur trade. The islands were also an important staging post in the **whaling industry** and the herring boom, which drew great numbers of small Dutch, French and Scottish boats. More recently, the choice of **Scapa Flow**, Orkney's natural harbour, as the Royal Navy's main base brought plenty of money and activity during both world wars, and left the clifftops dotted with gun emplacements and the seabed scattered with wrecks – which these days make for wonderful diving opportunities.

After the war, things quietened down somewhat, although since the mid-1970s the large **oil terminal** on the island of Flotta, the establishment of the Orkney Islands Council (OIC), combined with EU development grants, have brought surprise windfalls, stemming the exodus of young people. Meanwhile, many disenchanted southerners have become "ferryloupers" (incomers), moving to Orkney in search of peace and the apparent simplicity of island life.

Orientation and information

Orkney **Mainland** has two main settlements: the old port of **Stromness**, an attractive old fishing town on the far southwestern shore, and the central capital of **Kirkwall**, which stands at the dividing point between East and West Mainland. The whole of Mainland is relatively heavily populated and farmed throughout, and is joined by causeways to a string of southern islands. The island of **Hoy**, the second-largest in the archipelago, to the south of Mainland, presents a superbly dramatic landscape, with some of the highest sea-cliffs in the country. Hoy, however, is atypical: Orkney's smaller, much quieter **northern islands** are low-lying, elemental but fertile outcrops of rock and sand, scattered across the ocean. The islands' tourist board at Ⓦwww.visitorkney.com has plenty of information, and most of the islands have their own website.

Rolling out of the sea "like the backs of sleeping whales" (Mackay Brown again), the Orkney isles offer excellent coastal **walking**, abundant birdlife and beautiful sweeping white-sand beaches. Orkney's rivers and lochs also provide some of the best trout and sea-trout fishing in Britain. The two main cultural celebrations are the popular four-day **Orkney Folk Festival** (Ⓦwww.orkneyfolkfestival.com), held in Stromness in May, and the week-long **St Magnus Festival** (Ⓦwww.stmagnusfestival.com), a superb arts festival based in Kirkwall. July is peppered with several island regattas, followed by numerous agricultural shows, culminating in the County Show held in the middle of August in Kirkwall. To find out **what's on** (and what the weather's going to be like), tune in to Radio Orkney on 93.7FM, and buy yourself a copy of *The Orcadian*, the local newspaper, which comes out on a Thursday (Ⓦwww.orcadian.co.uk).

Arrival

Orkney is connected to the Scottish mainland by several **ferry** routes – and if you're coming by car, you should book your return journey in advance. Pentland Ferries (Ⓣ01856/831226, Ⓦwww.pentlandferries.co.uk) operates the shortest car ferry crossing from **Gills Bay**, on the north coast near John O'Groats (and linked by bus to Wick and Thurso) to **St Margaret's Hope** on South Ronaldsay (3–4 daily; 1hr). Services to **Stromness** from **Scrabster** (2–3 daily; 1hr 30min), which is connected to nearby Thurso by a shuttle bus, are

△ Orkney Folk Festival, Stromness

run by Northlink Ferries (Ⓣ0845/600 0449, Ⓦwww.northlinkferries.co.uk), which also operates ferries to **Kirkwall** from **Aberdeen** (4 weekly; 6hr) and from **Lerwick** in Shetland (3 weekly; 5hr 30min).

John O'Groats Ferries (Ⓣ01955/611353, Ⓦwww.jogferry.co.uk) runs a passenger ferry from **John O'Groats** to **Burwick** on South Ronaldsay (May & Sept 2 daily; June–Aug 4 daily; 40min), its departure timed to connect with the arrival of the Orkney Bus from Inverness; there's also a free taxi service from Thurso train station. The ferry is small and, except in fine weather, is recommended only for those with strong stomachs.

Direct **flights** serve Kirkwall airport from Sumburgh in Shetland, Wick, Inverness and Aberdeen, and there are good connections from Edinburgh, Glasgow, Manchester, Birmingham and London. All can be booked through British Airways (Ⓣ0870/850 9850, Ⓦwww.britishairways.com).

Island transport

Bus services on the Orkney Mainland are infrequent, and skeletal on Sundays, making a Day Rover (£6) or Three-Day Rover (£15) of limited value (see Ⓦwww.rapsons.co.uk for more details) – a free timetable is available from the tourist office. On the smaller islands, a minibus usually meets the ferry and will take you to your destination. **Cycling** is not a bad option if the weather holds, since there are few steep hills and distances are modest, though the wind can make it hard going. You can rent bikes in Kirkwall, Stromness and on most of the smaller islands.

Bringing a **car** to Orkney is straightforward but expensive; alternatively, you can **rent** a car in Kirkwall, Stromness or on several of the islands (details are given in the text). If your time is limited, you may want to consider one of the informative bus or minibus **tours** on offer: Wildabout Orkney Tours (Ⓣ01856/851011, Ⓦwww.orknet.co.uk/wildabout; March–Oct) has good-value tours of the chief sights on the Mainland and Hoy; other tours for specific islands are detailed in the text.

Getting to the other islands from the Mainland isn't difficult, though it is expensive: Orkney Ferries (Ⓣ01856/872044, Ⓦwww.orkneyferries.co.uk) operates several **ferries** daily to Hoy, Shapinsay and Rousay, and between one and three a day, depending on route and season, to all the others except North Ronaldsay, which has a weekly boat on Fridays. If you're taking a car on any of the ferries, it is sensible to book your ticket well in advance. There are also a growing number of **boat trips** on offer: Explorer Fast Sea Charters (Ⓣ01856/741472, Ⓦwww.explorercharters.co.uk) is based in Kirkwall and uses high-adrenalin RIBs to reach the outer isles, while Out West Charters (Ⓣ01856/850621, Ⓦwww.outwestcharters.co.uk) uses a more sedate motor-boat to take folk out from Stromness to see the sea cliffs of Hoy.

There are **flights** from Kirkwall to Eday, North Ronaldsay, Westray, Papa Westray, Sanday and Stronsay, operated by Loganair (Ⓣ01856/872494, Ⓦwww.loganair.co.uk), using a tiny eight-seater plane. Loganair also offers **sightseeing flights** over Orkney, which are spectacular in fine weather (but cancelled in bad), as well as a discounted **Orkney Adventure** ticket, which allows you return tickets to three islands for around £70, and a special £12 offer on return flights to North Ronaldsay or Papa Westray if you stay over.

Travel between individual islands by sea or air isn't so straightforward, but careful study of timetables can sometimes reduce the need to come all the way back to Kirkwall. It's worth enquiring from Orkney Ferries about their **additional Sunday sailings** in summer, which often make useful inter-island connections.

Stromness

STROMNESS has to be one of the most enchanting ports at which to arrive by boat, its picturesque waterfront a procession of tiny sandstone jetties and slate roofs nestling below the green hill of Brinkies Brae. As one of Orkney's main points of arrival, Stromness is a great introduction, and one that's well worth spending a day exploring, or using as a base in preference to Kirkwall. Its natural sheltered harbour (known as Hamnavoe) must have been used in Viking times, but the town itself only really took off in the eighteenth century. At that time, European conflicts made it safer for ships heading across the Atlantic to travel around the north of Scotland rather than through the English Channel,

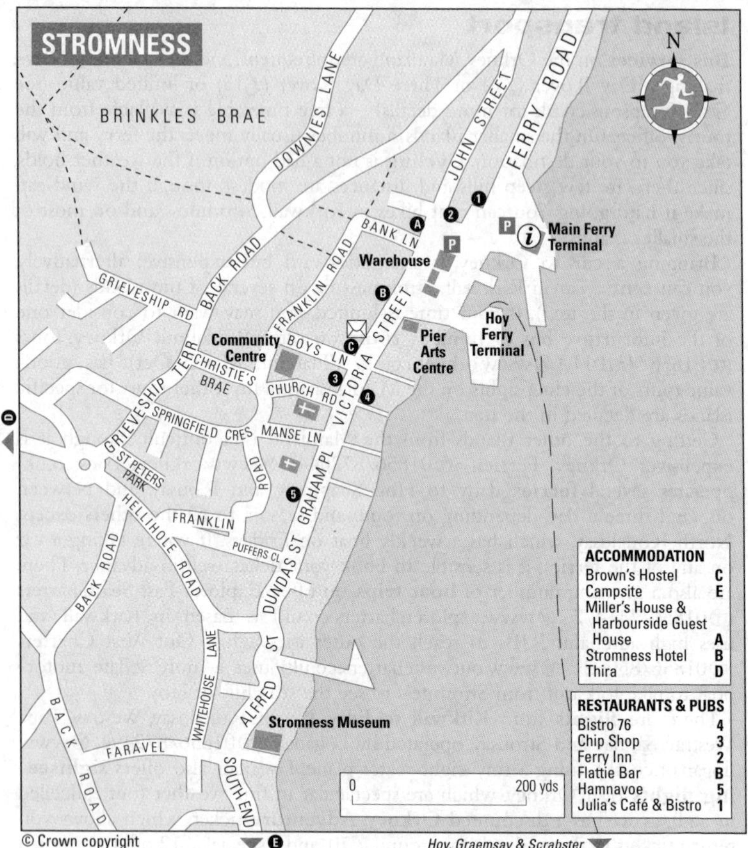

and many of them called in to Stromness to take on food, water and crew. The Hudson's Bay Company made Stromness its main base from which to make the long journey across the North Atlantic, and crews from Stromness were also hired for herring and whaling expeditions – and, of course, press-ganged into the Royal Navy.

By 1842, the town boasted forty or so pubs, and reports circulated of "outrageous and turbulent proceedings of seamen and others who frequent the harbour". The herring boom brought large numbers of small boats to the town, along with thousands of young women who gutted, pickled and packed the fish in barrels. Things got so rowdy by World War I that the town voted in a referendum to ban the sale of alcohol, leaving Stromness dry from 1920 until 1947. Nowadays, Stromness is very quiet, though it remains an important harbour and fishing port, serving as Orkney's main ferry terminal for the Scottish mainland.

Information and accommodation

Arriving by ferry, you'll disembark at the modern ferry terminal, which also houses the **tourist office** (April–Oct Mon–Fri 8am–5pm, Sat 9am–4pm, Sun

10am–3pm; Nov–March Mon–Fri 9am–5pm; ⓣ01856/850716). **Accommodation** is actually quite thin on the ground in Stromness. As far as hotels go, the venerable Victorian *Stromness Hotel* (ⓣ01856/850298, ⓦwww.stromnesshotel.com; ❻) – the town's first – is probably your best bet. For something with more character, head for the *Miller's House and Harbourside Guest House*, at 7 & 13 John St (ⓣ01856/851969, ⓦwww.orkneyisles.co.uk/millershouse; ❷), in the town's oldest property (and a near neighbour). If you've your own transport, you might also consider *Thira* (ⓣ01856/851181, ⓦwww.thiraorkney.co.uk; ❸), a modern house on the hill above town, boasting great views overlooking Hoy and good breakfasts.

The SYHA **hostel** in Stromness is undergoing much-needed refurbishment, with no date set for completion. The alternative is the laid-back family-run *Brown's Hostel*, 45–47 Victoria St (ⓣ01856/850661, ⓦwww.brownshostel.co.uk), with bunk beds in very small, shared rooms and kitchen facilities. There's also a **campsite** (ⓣ01856/873535; May to mid-Sept) in a superb setting a mile south of the ferry terminal at Point of Ness, with views out to Hoy; it's well equipped and even has its own lounge, but is extremely exposed, especially if a southwesterly is blowing.

The Town

Stromness still has a few reminders of its trading heyday, starting with the **Warehouse**, situated diagonally opposite the new ferry terminal. Though it may not look like it, the building was constructed in the 1760s – just too late to catch the trade in American rice. More eye-catching is the **Stromness Hotel**, a tall and imposing sandstone building behind the Warehouse; during World War II, Gracie Fields sang from its balcony, when it served as the headquarters of the Orkney and Shetland Defence ("OS Def").

Unlike Kirkwall, the old town of Stromness – famously described by Sir Walter Scott as "a dirty, straggling town" – still hugs the shoreline, its one and only street, a narrow winding affair, built long before the advent of the motor car, still paved with great flagstones and fed by a tight network of alleyways or closes. The central section, which begins at the *Stromness Hotel*, is known as **Victoria Street**, though in fact it takes on several other names – Graham Place, Dundas Street, Alfred Street and South End – as it threads its way southwards. On the east side of the street the houses are gable-end-on to the waterfront, and originally each one would have had its own pier, from which merchants would trade with passing ships.

You can visit the first of the old jetties, to the south of the modern harbour, since it now houses the **Pier Arts Centre** (Tues–Sat 10.30am–12.30pm & 1.30–5pm; free). The art gallery hosts temporary exhibitions, often featuring painting and sculpture by local artists, as well as having a remarkable permanent display of twentieth-century British art. At first it comes as a shock to see abstract works executed by members of the Cornish art scene such as Barbara Hepworth, Ben Nicholson, Terry Frost and Patrick Heron, but the marine themes of many of the works, and in particular the primitive scenes by Alfred Wallis, have a special resonance in this seaport.

Ten minutes' walk down the main street, at the junction of Alfred Street and South End, is the **Stromness Museum** (April–Sept daily 10am–5pm; Oct–March Mon–Sat 11am–3.30pm; £2.50), built in 1858, partly to house the collections of the local natural history society. The natural history collection is still here – don't miss the pull-out drawers of birds' eggs, butterflies and moths by the ticket desk – and has now taken up the whole of the upper floor with its cabinets of stuffed birds and shell displays. On the ground floor, meanwhile,

Orkney's Neolithic top five

Stones of Stenness, West Mainland (see p.412). Orkney's finest stone circle.

Skara Brae, West Mainland (see p.413). The best preserved and most extensive Neolithic settlement.

Maes Howe, West Mainland (see p.412). The mother of all Neolithic burial chambers.

Dwarfie Stane, Hoy (see p.430). Wonderful isolated location and Persian graffiti set this unusual chambered tomb apart.

Tomb of the Eagles, South Ronaldsay (see p.428). Family-run Neolithic site where you get to ride on a trolley to enter the chambered cairn.

there's a Halkett cloth boat, an early inflatable like the one used by John Rae, the Stromness-born Arctic explorer, whose fiddle, octant and shotgun are also on display. Amidst the beaver furs and model boats, there are also numerous salty artefacts gathered from shipwrecks, including some barnacle-encrusted crockery from the German High Seas Fleet that was sunk in Scapa Flow. As a plaque recalls, the Stromness-born poet **George Mackay Brown** (1921–96) lived out the last twenty years of his life in the house diagonally opposite the museum.

The **cannon**, further south down South End by the shore, was fired to announce the arrival of a ship from the Hudson's Bay Company. Today the trade in American rice and Canadian fur has gone, but the site of the cannon still gives magnificent views of the harbour. Further south along Ness Road, jutting out into the bay, **The Doubles**, a large pair of houses on a raised platform, were built in the early nineteenth century as a home by Mrs Christian Robertson with the proceeds of her shipping agency, which sent as many as eight hundred men on whaling expeditions in one year.

Eating and drinking

Stromness has several decent **places to eat**, starting with *Julia's Café and Bistro* (summer also Fri–Sun eve), situated opposite the ferry terminal, with a sunny conservatory, serving tasty meals and delicious cakes. The moderately expensive, evening-only *Hamnavoe Restaurant*, at 35 Graham Place (Ⓣ01856/850606; April–Sept; closed Mon), offers the town's most ambitious cooking, using local produce including shellfish, fish and beef, and offering some delicious vegetarian dishes, in a formal setting. *Bistro 76*, part of the *Orca Hotel* on Victoria Street, serves imaginative food in snug surroundings (booking advisable; Ⓣ01856/851803; closed Sun).

For **takeaways**, head for the *Chip Shop* on the main street (closed Thurs eve, Sat lunch & Sun). The downstairs *Flattie Bar* of the *Stromness Hotel* is a congenial place to warm yourself by a real fire (or, depending on the season, sit outside) with a **drink**; the most popular pub is, however, the *Ferry Inn*, opposite the terminal. Argo's Bakery, on Victoria Street, has a wide range of **picnic** basics, while The Original Orkney Hamper Company, a few doors down, sells local ice cream and delicious made-to-order sandwiches, with local seafood a speciality.

Listings

Banks There are branches of the Bank of Scotland and Royal Bank of Scotland on the main street, both with ATMs.

Bike rental Stromness Cycle Hire, opposite the ferry terminal Ⓣ01856/850750; Orkney Cycle Hire, 54 Dundas St Ⓣ01856/850255.

Bookshops J.L. Broom is the best of the bookshops on the main street, and probably the best in the whole of Orkney.

Car rental Brass's Self Drive, Blue Star Garage, North End Rd ☎01856/850850; Stromness Car Hire, 75 John St ☎01856/850973.

Internet access You can get Intermet access for free at the library, opposite the museum.

West Mainland

Stromness sits in the southwesternmost corner of the **West Mainland** – west of Kirkwall, that is – the great bulk of which is fertile, productive farmland, fenced off into a patchwork of fields used either to produce crops or for cattle-grazing. Fringed by some spectacular coastline, particularly in the west, West Mainland is littered with some of the island's most impressive prehistoric sites, such as the village of **Skara Brae**, the standing **Stones of Stenness**, the chambered tomb of **Maes Howe** and the **Broch of Gurness**, as well as one of Orkney's best preserved medieval castles at **Birsay**. Despite the intensive farming, there are still some areas which are too barren to cultivate, and the high ground and wild coastline are protected by several interesting **wildlife reserves**.

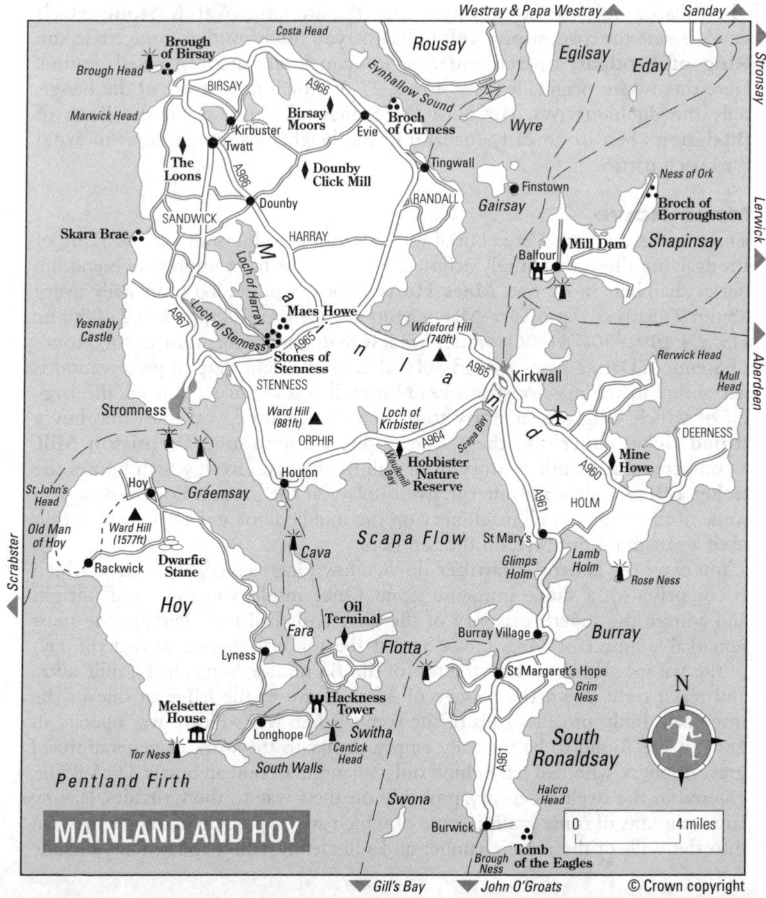

Stenness

The parish of **Stenness**, northeast of Stromness along the main road to Kirkwall, slopes down from Ward Hill (881ft) to the lochs of Stenness and Harray, the first of which is tidal, the second of which is Orkney's most famous freshwater trout loch. The two lochs are separated by a couple of promontories, now joined by a short causeway that may well have been a narrow isthmus around 3000 BC, when it stood at the heart of Orkney's most important Neolithic ceremonial complex, centred on the burial chamber of **Maes Howe**.

The Stones of Stenness and the Ring of Brodgar

The most visible part of the complex between lochs Stenness and Harray is the **Stones of Stenness**, originally a circle of twelve rock slabs, now just four, the tallest of which is a real monster at over 16ft, though it's more remarkable for its incredible thinness. A broken table-top lies within the circle, which is surrounded by a much-diminished henge (a circular bank of earth and a ditch) with a couple of entrance causeways. A path leads east from the stones to the **Barnhouse Settlement**, where the foundations of a Neolithic village contemporary with the stones are marked out on the ground.

Less than a mile to the northwest, past the awesome **Watch Stone** which stands beside the road, at over 18ft in height, you reach another stone circle, the **Ring of Brodgar**, a much wider circle dramatically sited on raised ground. Here there were originally sixty stones, 27 of which now stand; of the henge, only the ditch survives. For both the Stones of Stenness and the Ring of Brodgar, it's best to go early (or late) in the height of summer, so as to avoid the coach parties.

Maes Howe

There are several quite large burial mounds visible to the south of the Ring of Brodgar, but these are entirely eclipsed by one of the most impressive Neolithic burial chambers in Europe, **Maes Howe** (April–Sept guided tours daily every 45min 9.45am–5.15pm; Oct–March Mon–Sat 9.45am–3.45pm, Sun 2–4.30pm; HS; £4; ⓣ01856/761606), which lies less than a mile northeast of the Stones of Stenness. Dating from around 3000 BC, its excellent state of preservation is partly due to the massive slabs of sandstone it was constructed from, the largest of which weighs over thirty tons. To visit the tomb, you must first buy a **timed ticket** either over the phone or direct from nearby **Tormiston Mill**, a converted nineteenth-century meal mill by the main road, which houses the **ticket office**, toilets and interpretive display on the ground floor, a shop and some of the original mill machinery on the middle floor and a café, which calls itself a restaurant but isn't, on the top floor.

You enter the **central chamber** down a low, long passage, one wall of which is comprised of a single immense stone. Once inside, you can stand upright and admire the superb masonry of the lofty corbelled roof. Perhaps the most remarkable aspect of Maes Howe is that the tomb is aligned so that the rays of the winter solstice sun hit the top of the Barnhouse Stone, half a mile away, and reach right down the passage of Maes Howe to the ledge of one of the three cells built into the walls of the tomb. When Maes Howe was opened in 1861, it was found to be virtually empty, thanks to the work of generations of grave-robbers, who had left behind only a handful of human bones. The Vikings entered in the twelfth century, probably on their way to the Crusades, leaving large amounts of runic graffiti, some of which are cryptographic twig runes, cut into the walls of the main chamber and still clearly visible today. They include

Orkney's Historic Scotland sights

If you're planning on visiting more than one of Orkney's Historic Scotland sights, it might be worth buying the **Orkney Explorer Pass**, which costs £12 and covers entry to Maes Howe, Skara Brae, the Broch of Gurness (p.416), and the Bishop's and Earl's palaces in Kirkwall (p.421).

phrases such as "many a beautiful woman has stooped in here, however pompous she might be", and "these runes were carved by the man most skilled in runes in the entire western ocean", to the more prosaic "Thor and I bedded Helga".

Practicalities

Given the density of prehistoric sites around Stenness, and its central position on the Mainland, it's not a bad area in which to base yourself. For **accommodation** look no further than the carefully converted *Mill of Eyrland* (Ⓣ01856/850136, Ⓦwww.millofeyrland.co.uk; ③), in a delightful setting by a mill stream on the A964 to Orphir; it's filled with wonderful antiques, old mill machinery plus all mod cons, and serves enormous breakfasts. Alternatively, you could stay at *Holland House* (Ⓣ01856/771400, Ⓦwww.hollandhouseorkney.co.uk; ③), a former manse halfway along the A986 to Dounby, that's tastefully furnished and serves up very good breakfasts (and dinners if required). Both the hotels in the area attract large numbers of anglers: the *Standing Stones* (Ⓣ01856/850449; ④), on the southern shore of the Loch of Stenness, has been pretty ruthlessly modernized, though it's certainly comfortable; the *Merkister* (Ⓣ01856/771366, Ⓦwww.smoothhound.co.uk/hotels/merkister; ③), on the northeastern shore of the Loch of Harray, is a bit more dowdy, but its **bar meals** are very popular with the locals

Skara Brae and around

Around seven miles north of Stromness, the parish of Sandwick contains the best known of Orkney's prehistoric monuments, the Neolithic village of **Skara Brae** (April–Sept daily 9.30am–6.30pm; Oct–March Mon–Sat 9.30am–4.30pm, Sun 2–4.30pm; HS; £6), beautifully situated beside the white curve of the Bay of Skaill. Here, the extensive remains of a small Neolithic fishing and farming village, dating back to 3000 BC, were discovered in 1850 after a fierce storm ripped off the dunes covering them. The village is amazingly well preserved, its houses huddled together and connected by narrow passages, which would originally have been covered over with turf. The houses themselves consist of a single, spacious living room, filled with domestic detail, including dressers, fireplaces, built-in cupboards, beds and boxes, all ingeniously constructed from slabs of stone.

Before you reach the site you must buy a ticket from the **visitor centre**, which houses an excellent **café/restaurant,** where you can also get takeaway sandwiches to order. If you want to, you can pay a visit to the small introductory **exhibition**, with a few replica finds, and some hands-on stuff for kids. You then proceed to a full-scale replica of House 7 (the best-preserved house), complete with a fake wood and skin roof. It's all a tad neat and tidy, with fetching uplighting – rather than dark, smoky and smelly – but it'll give you the general idea. Unfortunately, the sheer numbers now visiting Skara Brae mean that you can no longer explore the site itself properly, but only look down from the outer walls. Sadly, too, House 7 now sports a glass roof to protect it from the elements; however, House 1, which also contains a dresser, as yet does not. A short video, in the little building at the far end of the site, helps put the site in context.

In the summer months, your ticket to Skara Brae also covers entry to nearby **Skaill House**, an extensive range of buildings 300yd inland, home of the laird of Skaill. The original house was a simple two-storey block with a small courtyard, built for Bishop George Graham in the 1620s, but it has since been much extended. The house's prize possession is Captain Cook's dinner service from the *Resolution*, which was delivered after Cook's death when the *Resolution* and the *Discovery* sailed into Stromness in 1780. The last occupant of the house was Mrs Kathleen Scarth, who died in 1991; her bedroom has been left as it was, and is filled with old frocks, an ostrich feather fan and a "twist and slim exerciser". The house also has a couple of self-catering flats available for rent (ⓣ01856/841501, ⓦwww.skaillhouse.com).

The other good reason for exploring the area around Skara Brae are the cliffs to the north and south of the Bay of Skaill, which provide some of the most spectacularly rugged **coastal walks** on Orkney's Mainland. The best place to head for is **Yesnaby**, to the south of the Bay of Skaill, where the sandstone cliffs have been savagely eroded into stacks and geos by the force of the Atlantic. Come here during a westerly gale and you'll see the waves sending sea spray shooting over the wartime buildings and the neighbouring fields. As a result, the clifftops support a unique plantlife, which thrives on the salt spray, including the rare and very small purple Scottish primrose, which flowers in May and from July to late September. The walk south along the coast from here is exhilarating: the Old Man of Hoy is visible in the distance and, after a mile and a half, you come to West Mainland's own version of the Old Man, known as **Yesnaby Castle**.

Practicalities

With only infrequent bus connections, you really need your own transport to reach Sandwick parish. There's no main settlement as such, though there are a couple of **accommodation** options in the vicinity: try *Netherstove* (ⓣ01856/841625, ⓦwww.netherstove.com; ❷; May–Oct), a friendly modern farmhouse B&B a mile north of Skara Brae, or *Via House* (ⓣ01856/841207, ⓦwww.orkneyimages.com; ❷), a bohemian Orcadian farmhouse on the A967 just past the Loch of Stenness, which hosts regular evening **storytelling** sessions by the peatfire (Tues, Fri & Sun; advance booking essential).

Birsay and around

Occupying the northwest corner of the Mainland, the parish of **BIRSAY** (ⓦwww.birsay.org.uk) was the centre of Norse power in Orkney for several centuries before the earls moved to Kirkwall, some time after the construction of its cathedral. Today a tiny cluster of homes is gathered around the imposing sandstone ruins of the **Earl's Palace**, which was built in the second half of the sixteenth century by Robert Stewart, Earl of Orkney, using the forced labour of the islanders, who weren't even given food and drink for their work. By all accounts, it was a "sumptuous and stately dwelling", built in four wings around a central courtyard, its upper rooms decorated with painted ceilings and rich furnishings; surrounding the palace were flower and herb gardens, a bowling green and archery butts. The palace appears to have lasted barely a century before falling into rack and ruin; the crumbling walls and turrets retain much of their grandeur, although inside there is little remaining domestic detail. However, its vast scale makes the Earl's Palace in Kirkwall seem almost humble in comparison.

Half a mile southeast of the palace, up the burn, is the **Barony Mills** (April–Sept daily 10am–1pm & 2–5pm; free), Orkney's only working nineteenth-century water mill to survive into the modern era. The mill specializes in producing traditional stoneground beremeal, essential for making bere bannocks. Bere is a four-kernel barley crop with a very short growing season perfectly suited for the local climate and was once the staple diet in these parts. The miller on duty will give you a guided tour and show you the machinery going through its paces, though milling only takes place in the autumn.

Brough of Birsay

Just over half a mile northwest of the palace is the **Brough of Birsay**, a substantial Pictish settlement on a small tidal island that is only accessible during the two hours each side of low tide. Stromness and Kirkwall tourist offices have the tide times and Radio Orkney broadcasts them (93.7FM; Mon–Fri 7.30–8am). Once you reach the island, there's a small ticket office, where you must pay your **entrance fee** (mid-June to Sept daily; £2), and where you can see a few artefacts gathered from the site, including a game made from whalebone and an antler pin. Coastal erosion over the last eight centuries means that some of the site has disappeared off the side of the low cliffs, and concrete sea defences are currently in place to try and stem the tide.

The focus of the village was – and still is – the sandstone-built twelfth-century **St Peter's Church**, which stands higher than the surrounding buildings; the stone seating along the walls is still in place, and there are a couple of semicircular recesses for altars, and a semicircular apse. The church is thought to have stood at the centre of a monastic complex of some sort – the foundations of a courtyard and outer buildings can be made out to the west. Close by is a large complex of Viking-era buildings, including several houses, a sauna and some sophisticated stone drains.

The Brough of Birsay is a popular day-trip, partly due to the fun of dodging the tides, but few folk bother to explore the rest of the island, whose gentle green slopes, when viewed from the mainland, belie the dramatic, rugged cliffs that characterize the rest of the coastline. In winter, sea spray from the waves crashing against the cliffs can envelop the entire island. In summer, the cliffs are home to various seabirds, including a few puffins, making the half-mile walk to the island's castellated **lighthouse** and back along the northern coastline well worth the effort. If you make it out here, spare a thought for the lighthouse keepers who used to man the **Sule Skerry** lighthouse – the most isolated in Britain – which lies on a piece of bare rock barely visible some 37 miles out to sea, and whose only contact with the outside world was via carrier pigeon.

Marwick Head and The Loons

The best of Birsay's coastal scenery lies to the south of Birsay Bay around **Marwick Head**. The headland itself is clearly visible on the horizon thanks to the huge castellated tower of the **Kitchener Memorial**, raised by the people of Orkney to commemorate the Minister of War, Lord Kitchener, who drowned along with all but twelve of the 655 men of the 11,000-ton cruiser HMS *Hampshire* when the ship struck a mine just off the coast on June 5, 1916. There has been much speculation about the incident over the years, due to the fact that Kitchener was on a secret mission to Russia to hold talks with the Tsar. As a result, salvage operations were closely controlled by the Admiralty and the findings of the naval court of enquiry kept secret, fanning the rumours that Kitchener had been deliberately sent to his death (he was extremely unpopular at the time). In reality, it appears to have been a simple case of naval incompetence: a weather forecast from the Admiralty warning of severe northwesterly gales was ignored, as were the reports of submarine activity in the area.

Marwick Head is also an **RSPB reserve** and, during the nesting season, there are numerous fulmar, kittiwakes, guillemots and razorbills in residence on the 200-foot cliffs; at that time, the sight and smell is quite overwhelming. A mile or so inland, another RSPB reserve is centred on the wetlands of **The Loons**. There's no public access to the area, but you can watch the waterfowl, snipe, curlews and even the odd short-eared owl from the hide on the northwest side of the reserve on the road to Twatt.

Kirbuster and Corrigall farm museums

Lying between the Loch of Boardhouse and the Loch of Hundland, the **Kirbuster Farm Museum** (March–Oct Mon–Sat 10.30am–1pm & 2–5pm, Sun 2–7pm; free) offers an interesting insight into life on an Orkney farmsteading in the mid-nineteenth century. Built in 1723, the farm is made up of a typical collection of flagstone buildings, though Kirbuster is more substantial than most, and boasts its own, very beautiful, garden. Ducks, geese and sheep wander around the grassy open yard, which is entered through a whalebone archway. The most remarkable thing about Kirbuster, however, is that, despite being inhabited until as late as 1961, it has retained its firehoose, in which the smoke from the central peat fire is used to dry fish fillets, and eventually allowed simply to drift up towards a hole in the ceiling; the room even retains the old neuk-beds, simple recesses in the stone walls, which would have originally been lined with wood.

If you've enjoyed your time at Kirbuster – and kids almost certainly will – then it's definitely worth visiting **Corrigall Farm Museum** (same times), another eighteenth-century farmstead some five miles southeast of Kirbuster, beyond Dounby in the parish of Harray. There are lovely views west and south from the honeysuckle-draped shop, as well as hens and sheep scampering around the farmyard. Be sure to check out the well-preserved flagstone byre, and the stable, which has a characteristic beehive-shaped kiln for drying grain at one end.

Practicalities

The best **accommodation** in Birsay is at *Linkshouse* (Ⓣ01856/721221, Ⓦwww.ewaf.co.uk; ❷), a B&B in an old house with a bit of character close to Birsay village itself. The nearest watering hole is the bar of the *Barony Hotel*, overlooking the Loch of Boardhouse, to the southeast of Birsay village.

Evie and the Broch of Gurness

The village and parish of **EVIE**, on the north coast, look out across the turbulent waters of Eynhallow Sound towards the island of Rousay. Its chief draw is the **Broch of Gurness** (April–Sept daily 9.30am–6.30pm; HS; £3.30), the best-preserved broch on an archipelago replete with them, and one which is still surrounded by a remarkable complex of later buildings. As at Birsay, the sea has eaten away half the site, but the broch itself, dating from around 100 BC, still stands, its walls reaching a height of 12ft in places, its inner cells still intact. The compact group of homes clustered around the broch has also survived amazingly well, with much of their original and ingenious stone shelving and fireplaces still in place. The best view of the site is from the east, where you can clearly make out the "main street" leading towards the broch. The **visitor centre** where you buy your ticket is also worth a quick once-over, especially for those with kids, who will enjoy using the quernstone corn grinder. The broch is clearly signposted from Evie, the road skirting the pristinely white **Sands of Evie**, a perfect picnic spot in fine weather.

A large section of the hills to the southwest of Evie now forms the **RSPB Birsay Moors Reserve**, whose heather-coated ground provides good hunting for kestrels, merlins and hen harriers. **Lowrie's Water**, on Burgar Hill itself, meanwhile, is regularly used as a nesting site by red-throated divers; there's a hide from which you can view the loch at the top of the rough track leading to the three **aerogenerators**, first built here in the 1980s in order to carry out research into wind power. The moor is also a source of more traditional fuel, and if you take the B9057 towards Dounby you can make out the areas in which peat is cut, with small stacks often drying on the hillside.

Before you reach Dounby itself, a sign points across a field to the turf-roofed **Dounby Click Mill**, the only surviving example of a horizontal water mill in Orkney. With only limited water power available, this type of mill was a simple but effective way of grinding flour for two to three families. The mechanism inside has been fully restored, and you can see the wheel underneath the building.

Practicalities

One of the most secluded **accommodation** options on the Mainland is the artfully decorated *Woodwick House* (Ⓣ01856/751330, Ⓦwww.woodwickhouse.co.uk; ④), southeast of the main village. The cheaper rooms have shared, slightly ancient bathrooms, but there are two residents' lounges, both with real fires and the wooded grounds are delightful (and feature a seventeenth-century doocot). At the other end of the scale, you can stay in the simple *Eviedale* **campsite**, run by Dale Farm (Ⓣ01856/751270, Ⓦwww.creviedale.orknet.co.uk; April–Oct) and situated in a sheltered spot right by the junction of the road to Dounby. The local shop and post office are close by.

Orphir

The southern shores of the West Mainland, overlooking Scapa Flow, are much gentler than the rest of the coastline, and have fewer of Orkney's premier-league sights. However, if you've time to spare, or you're heading for Hoy from the car ferry terminal at Houton, there are a couple of points of interest in the neighbouring parish of **ORPHIR**. Here, beside the parish cemetery, the council have built a new **Orkneyinga Saga Centre** (daily 9am–5pm; free), where there's a small exhibition and a fifteen-minute audiovisual show which gives you a taste of the *Orkneyinga Saga*, the bloodthirsty Viking tale written around 1200 AD by an unnamed Icelandic author, which described the conquest of the Northern Isles by the Norsemen. The **Earl's Bu** at Orphir features in the saga as the

Orkney Boat Museum

"Such a famous house – and so gracious too, even in decay – ought to be preserved as a keystone in our heritage". George Mackay Brown

A couple of miles north of Orphir along the A964 is the **Hall of Clestrain**. Built around 1769, it was the childhood home of the Arctic explorer John Rae (1813–1893), who discovered the ultimate fate of the Franklin expedition which had set off to find the Northwest Passage. Once the money has been raised, the house is earmarked to be restored and converted into the **Orkney Boat Museum** (Ⓦwww.orkneyboatmuseum.org.uk).

home of Earl Thorfinn the Mighty, Earl Paul and his son, Haakon, who ordered the murder of Earl (later St) Magnus on Egilsay (see p.436). The foundations of what is presumed to have been the Earl's Bu have been uncovered just outside the cemetery gates, while inside the cemetery is a section of the round church, built by Haakon after his pilgrimage in penance to Jerusalem, and in which further murder was done.

Further east along the A954 towards Kirkwall lies the **Hobbister RSPB reserve**, a mixture of moorland, sea cliffs, salt marsh and sand flats that's great for spotting a wide variety of birdlife and, at the sandy Waulkmill Bay, a relatively warm place in which to swim, and a favourite beach with visitors in the know.

Kirkwall

Initial impressions of **KIRKWALL**, Orkney's capital, are not always favourable. It has nothing to match the picturesque harbour of Stromness, and its residential sprawl is far less appealing. However, it does have one great redeeming feature – its sandstone **cathedral**, without doubt the finest medieval building in the north of Scotland. In any case, if you're staying any length of time in Orkney you're more or less bound to find yourself in Kirkwall at some point, as the town is home to the islands' better-stocked shops, including the only large supermarket, and is the departure point for most of the ferries to Orkney's northern isles.

Part of the reason for Kirkwall's disappointing waterfront is that today's harbour is a largely modern invention; in the mid-nineteenth century, the shoreline ran along Junction Road, and before that it was flush with the west side of Broad Street. Nowadays, the town is very much divided into two main focal points: the old **harbour**, at the north end of the town, where visiting yachts moor and the small inter-island ferries come and go all year round; and the flagstoned **main street**, which changes its name four times as it twists its way south from the harbour past the cathedral.

Arrival, information and accommodation

Northlink **ferries** from Shetland and Aberdeen (and all cruise ships) dock at the new Hatston terminal, a mile or so northwest of town; the buses waiting at Hatston will take you to Stromness, or into the centre of Kirkwall. Kirkwall **airport** is about three miles southeast of town on the A960; a bus (Mon–Sat 7–8 daily; 15min) will take you to Broad Street in the town centre, before terminating at the **bus station**, a few minutes' walk west of the centre.

Kirkwall is an easy place in which to orientate yourself, despite its **main street** taking four different names – Bridge Street, Albert Street, Broad Street and Victoria Street – as it winds through the town, with the prominent spire of St Magnus Cathedral clearly marking the town centre. The helpful **tourist office**, on Broad Street beside the cathedral graveyard (April–Sept daily 8.30am–8pm; Oct–March Mon–Sat 9.30am–5pm; ⓣ01856/872856), books accommodation, changes money and gives out a free plan of the town.

Accommodation

As for **accommodation**, Kirkwall has plenty of small rooms in ordinary B&Bs, and a host of blandly refurbished hotels, but nothing exceptional, so unless you're reliant on public transport, or have business in town, there's really no

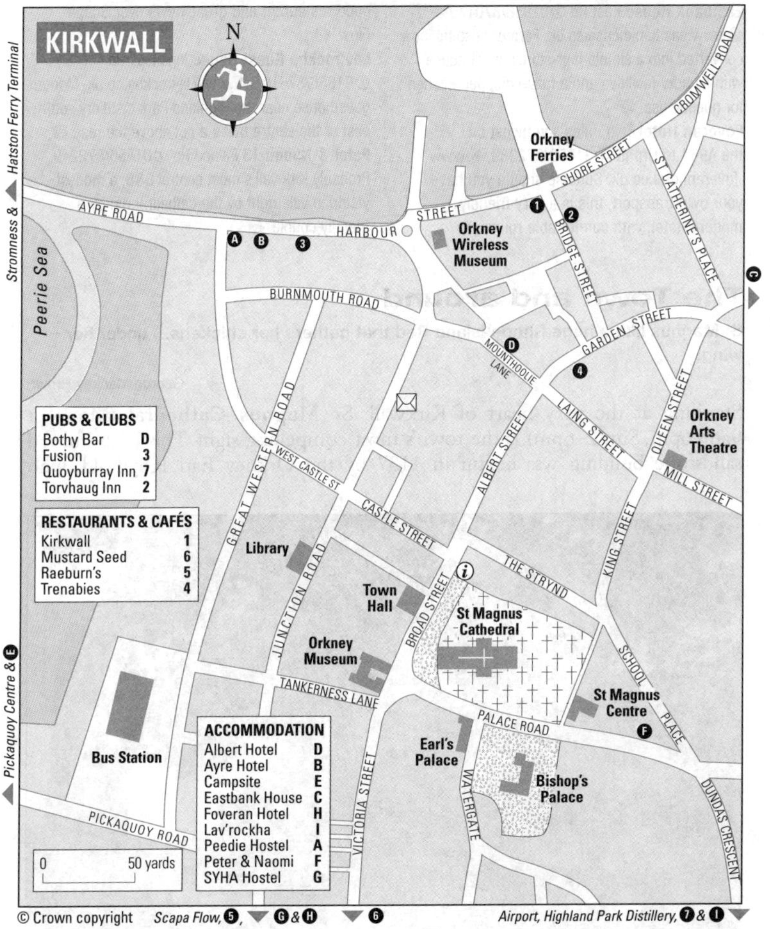

strong reason to base yourself here. Instead, head out into Orkney's wonderful countryside.

The SYHA **hostel** (Ⓣ0870/004 1133, Ⓦwww.syha.org.uk; April–Sept) is a good ten minutes' walk out of the centre on the road to Orphir, and is no beauty outside or in. A more central and more comfortable option is the small privately run *Peedie Hostel* (Ⓣ01856/875477), on the waterfront next door to the *Ayre Hotel*. There's also a **campsite** (Ⓣ01856/879900; mid-May to mid-Sept) behind the Pickaquoy Leisure Centre, five minutes' walk west of the bus station; the site is well equipped with laundry facilities, but it's hardly what you'd call picturesque.

Hotels and B&Bs

Albert Hotel Mounthoolie Lane Ⓣ01856/876000, Ⓦwww.alberthotel.co.uk. Great central location, lively bar (with disco attached), and completely refurbished inside, this is a comfortable option. ③

Ayre Hotel Ayre Rd Ⓣ01856/873001, Ⓦwww.ayrehotel.co.uk. Despite harbourfront appearances – the hotel entrance is round the back – this is probably the smartest option in town, as well as being home to the local accordion and fiddle club (Wed). ⑥

Eastbank House East Rd ⓣ01856/870179, ⓦwww.eastbankhouse.co.uk. Former hospital, now converted into a simple four-storey guest house, with laundry facilities and a fully-equipped kitchen for guests' use. ❸

Foveran Hotel Two miles southwest on the A964 to Orphir ⓣ01856/872389, ⓦwww.foveranhotel.co.uk. Suitable should you have your own transport, this is a very friendly modern hotel, with comfortable rooms, a good restaurant and great views over Scapa Flow. ❻

Lav'rockha Guest House Inganess Rd ⓣ01856/876103, ⓦwww.lavrockha.co.uk. Modern guesthouse near the Highland Park distillery south-east of the centre that's a cut above the rest. ❷

Peter & Naomi 13 Palace Rd ⓣ01856/872249. Probably Kirkwall's most central B&B, a modest Victorian villa right by the cathedral run by a friendly couple. ❸

The Town and around

St Magnus like a huge Rhode Island Red that gathers her chickens... under her wing.

George Mackay Brown

Standing at the very heart of Kirkwall, **St Magnus Cathedral** (Mon–Sat 9am–6pm, Sun 2–6pm) is the town's most compelling sight. This beautiful red sandstone building was begun in 1137 by the Orkney Earl Rognvald, who

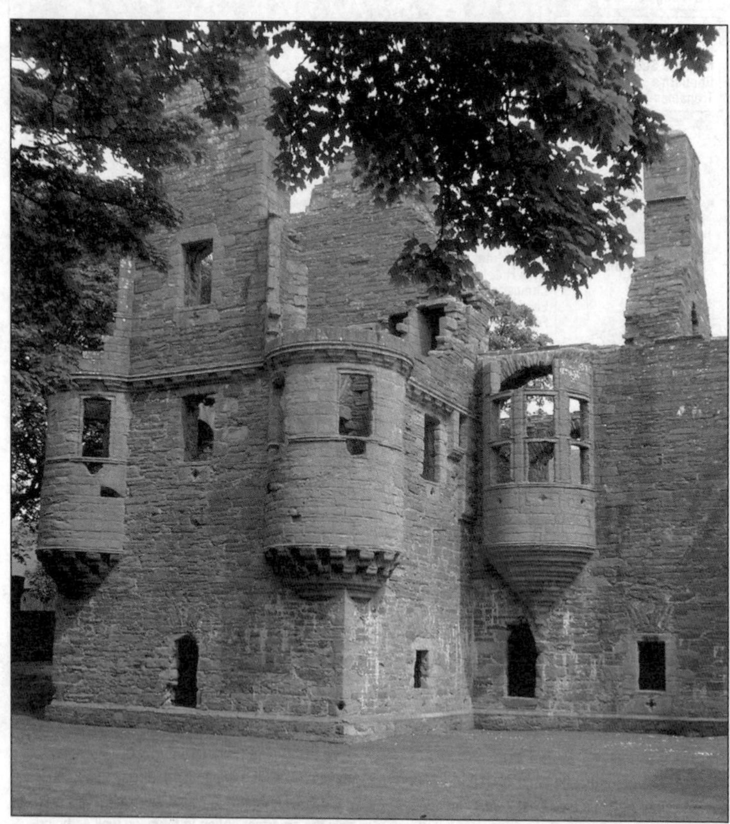

△ Earl's Palace, Kirkwall

decided to make full use of a growing cult surrounding the figure of his uncle Magnus, killed on the orders of his cousin Haakon in 1117 (see p.436). When Magnus's body was buried in Birsay, a heavenly light was said to have shone overhead, and his grave soon became a place of pilgrimage attributed with miraculous powers that drew pilgrims from far afield. When Rognvald finally took over the earldom, he built the cathedral in his uncle's honour, moving the centre of religious and secular power from Birsay to Kirkwall.

The first version of the cathedral, built using yellow sandstone from Eday and red sandstone from the Mainland, was somewhat smaller than today's structure, which has been added to over the centuries, with a new east window in the thirteenth century, the extension of the nave in the fifteenth century, and a new west window to mark the building's 850th anniversary in 1987. Today much of the detail in the soft sandstone has worn away – the capitals around the main doors are reduced to artistically gnarled stumps – but it's still an immensely impressive building, its shape and style echoing the great cathedrals of Europe. Inside, the atmosphere is surprisingly intimate, the bulky sandstone columns drawing your eye up to the exposed brickwork arches, while around the walls is a series of mostly seventeenth-century tombstones, many carved with a skull and crossbones and other emblems of mortality, alongside chilling inscriptions calling on the reader to "remember death waits us all, the hour none knows".

In the square pillars on either side of the high altar, the bones of Magnus and Rognvald are buried. In the southeastern corner of the cathedral lies the tomb of the Stromness-born Arctic explorer John Rae, who went off to try and find Sir John Franklin's expedition; he is depicted asleep, dressed in moleskins and furs, his rifle and Bible by his side. Beside Rae's tomb is Orkney's own poets' corner, with memorials to, among others, George Mackay Brown, Eric Linklater, Edwin Muir and Robert Rendall (who was also an eminent conchologist). Another poignant monument is the one to the dead of HMS *Royal Oak*, which was torpedoed in Scapa Flow in 1939 with the loss of 833 men (see p.423).

If you want to learn more about the life of St Magnus, pop into the **St Magnus Centre** (April-Oct Mon–Sat 9.30am–5.30pm, Sun 1.30–5.30pm; Oct–March Mon–Sat 12.30–2pm; free), behind the cathedral, where you can watch a short video on his martyrdom and the history of the cathedral, and consult some of the books in the study/library, and afterwards have coffee and cake.

To the south of the cathedral are the ruined remains of the **Bishop's Palace** (April–Sept daily 9.30am–6.30pm; Oct & Nov Mon–Sat 9.30am–4.30pm, Sun 2–4.30pm; HS; £2.50), residence of the Bishop of Orkney since the twelfth century. It was here that the Norwegian King Haakon died in 1263 on his return from defeat at the Battle of Largs. Most of what you see now, however, dates from the time of Bishop Robert Reid, the founder of Edinburgh University, in the mid-sixteenth century. The walls still stand, as does the tall round tower in which the bishop had his private chambers; a narrow spiral staircase takes you to the top for a good view of the cathedral and across Kirkwall's rooftops.

The ticket for the Bishop's Palace also covers entry to the neighbouring **Earl's Palace**, built by the infamous Earl Patrick Stewart around 1600 using forced labour, which is rather better preserved and a lot more fun to explore. With its grand entrance, fancy oriel windows, dank dungeons, massive fireplaces and magnificent central hall, it has a confident solidity, and is reckoned to be one of the finest examples of Renaissance architecture in Scotland. The roof may be missing, but many domestic details remain, including a set of toilets and the

Orcadian wedding traditions

If you're passing through Kirkwall, particularly during the summer, you may come across a bunch of locals sitting in the back of a truck, banging drums and pots and pans and drinking alcohol. What you are witnessing is the strange local custom known as **"the Blackening"**. Not for the faint-hearted (nor the politically correct), the blackening takes place in the build-up to a wedding. The groom's "friends" hire a lorry and ambush him, strip him naked and then tar and feather him. They then set off on a tour of the town, possibly a pub-crawl, and often a dip in sea. No one knows the origin of the Blackening, though the din may have originally been made to ward off evil spirits. Occasionally, you may even see a bride subjected to the same humiliations.

stone shelves used by the clerk to do his filing. Earl Patrick enjoyed his palace for only a very short time before he was imprisoned and charged with treason. The earl might have been acquitted, but he foolishly ordered his son, Robert, to organize an insurrection; he held out four days in the palace against the Earl of Caithness, before being captured, sent to Edinburgh and hanged there; his father was beheaded at the same place five weeks later.

Opposite the cathedral stands the sixteenth-century Tankerness House, a former home for the clergy. It has been renovated countless times over the years, most recently in the 1960s in order to provide a home for the **Orkney Museum** (Mon–Sat 10.30am–5pm; May–Sept also Sun 2–5pm; free). A couple of rooms have been restored to how they would have been in 1820, when the building was a private home for the Baikie family. The rest house some of the islands' most treasured finds; among the more unusual of which are a witch's spell box, and a lovely whalebone plaque from a Viking boat grave discovered on Sanday. On a warm summer afternoon, the museum **gardens** (which can be entered either from the house itself or from a gate on Tankerness Lane) are thick with the buzz of bees and vibrantly coloured flora. In wet weather, you can stay inside and watch a video of the traditional Orkney ball game, **The Ba'**, played at Christmas and New Year. Beginning at 1pm at the Mercat Cross outside the cathedral, the "Uppies" and the "Doonies" attempt to get the ba' (ball) into the other's goal (a wall to the south and the harbour respectively). There's no restriction on numbers, and the game can take hours – spectators (and participants) rarely get a glimpse of the ball, which is usually stuck tight in a heaving, steaming scrum of men.

At the harbour end of Junction Road, at Kiln Corner, you can browse around the tiny **Orkney Wireless Museum** (April–Sept Mon–Sat 10am–4.30pm, Sun 2–4.30pm; £2; Ⓦwww.owm.org.uk), a single room packed to the roof with every variety of antique radio equipment you can imagine. The museum is particularly strong on technical flotsam from the two world wars, and there's even a working crystal set which you can listen to.

Out of the centre

Further afield, a mile or so south of the town centre on the A961 to South Ronaldsay, is the **Highland Park distillery** (April–Oct tours every 30min Mon–Fri 10am–5pm; July–Sept also Sat 10am–5pm & Sun noon–5pm; Nov–March Mon–Fri tours at 2pm; £3; Ⓣ01856/874619, Ⓦwww.highlandpark.co.uk), billed as "the most northerly legal distillery in Scotland". It's been in operation for more than two hundred years, and still has its own maltings, although it was closed during World War II, when the army used it as a food store and the huge vats served as communal baths. You can decide for yourself whether the taste still lingers by partaking of the customary dram after one of the regular guided tours of the beautiful old buildings.

If the weather happens to be unusually good and you're moved to consider taking the plunge for a dip, do as the locals do and head one mile south of town on the B9148 to **Scapa Bay**, Kirkwall's very own sandy beach. Briefly a naval headquarters at the outbreak of World War I, Scapa's pier is now used by the council tugs and pilot launches servicing the oil tankers out in Scapa Flow. Visible from the beach is the green Admiralty wreck buoy marking the position of **HMS Royal Oak**, which was torpedoed by a German U-boat on October 14, 1939, with the loss of 833 men (out of a total crew of around 1400). A small display shed at the eastern end of the bay tells the full story, and has photos of the wreck (still an official war grave) as it looks today.

If you've time to kill and the weather's not so good, you could search out one of Kirkwall's more unusual sights, the **Grain Earth House**, a food cellar dating back to the first millennium BC, now hidden in the industrial estate northwest of the town centre. Collect the key (and a torch) from Ortak jewellers, at the entrance to the estate, and head round the corner. Steep steps lead down to a long, dark, curving passageway, which ends at a stone-clad cellar held up by large stone pillars; now you know what it felt like to be an Iron Age bere bannock.

Eating, drinking and entertainment

Given the quality of Orkney beef, and the quantity of shellfish caught in the vicinity, Kirkwall's **food** options are pretty disappointing. The best **café** in town is the venerable *Trenabies* on Albert Street, which does high teas, and more adventurous bistro fare in the evening. Another good café for lunch is the *Mustard Seed* (closed Wed & Sun), in the small Christian bookshop at 86 Victoria St, which serves home-made soups and imaginative, inexpensive main courses. Otherwise, there's nothing for it but to head for one of the town's hotels: the *Kirkwall*, on Harbour Street, is probably the best option, as it offers both **bar meals** and reasonable à la carte, though the bar meals at the *Albert* are OK, too. The best **fish and chips** is from *Raeburn's* at the corner of Union Street and Junction Road.

Kirkwall has its very own state-of-the-art **nightclub**, *Fusion* (Thurs–Sat), which occasionally attracts top-name DJs and also stages live gigs. The liveliest **pub** is the *Torvhaug Inn* at the harbour end of Bridge Street; another good place to try is the *Bothy Bar* in the *Albert Hotel*, which sometimes has live music. The *Ayre Hotel* has regular Orkney Accordion & Fiddle Club nights on Wednesdays, and there's sometimes live music at the *Quoyburray Inn*, a couple of miles beyond the airport on the A960, and at other hotels in Kirkwall. Check the *Orcadian* listings for the latest (Ⓦwww.orcadian.co.uk).

Kirkwall's new **Pickaquoy Leisure Centre** (Ⓦwww.pickaquoy.com) – known locally as the "Picky" – is a short walk west of the town centre, up Pickaquoy Road past the supermarket. It now serves as one of the town's main large-scale venues, and also contains the New Phoenix **cinema** (Ⓣ01856/879900). There's a swimming pool on the other side of town, on Thomas Street.

Listings

Airport Ⓣ01856/872494, Ⓦwww.loganair.com.
Banks The main street has branches of the big Scottish banks, all with ATMs.
Bike rental Cycle Orkney, Tankerness Lane Ⓣ01856/875777.
Bookshops Leonard's at the corner of Bridge St

and Albert St, and The Orcadian Bookshop, 50 Albert St (Ⓦ www.orcadian.co.uk), are the best stocked.

Camping gear and outdoor sports Eric Kemp, 31–33 Bridge St Ⓣ 01856/872137.

Car rental Peace's Car Hire, Junction Rd Ⓣ 01856/872866, Ⓦ www.orkneycarhire.co.uk; W.R. Tullock, Castle St and Kirkwall Airport Ⓣ 01856/876262, Ⓦ www.orkneyairportcarhire.co.uk.

Consulates Denmark and Germany, J. Robertson, Shore St Ⓣ 01856/872961; Norway, J. Jolly, 21 Bridge St Ⓣ 01856/872268.

Exchange In addition to the banks, the tourist office in Broad St runs an exchange service (summer daily 8.30am–8pm).

Ferries Orkney Ferries, Shore St Ⓣ 01856/872044, Ⓦ www.orkneyferries.co.uk (Mon–Fri 7am–5pm, Sat 7am–noon & 1–3pm); Northlink Ferries, Hatston Ⓣ 0845/600 0449, Ⓦ www.northlinkferries.co.uk.

Fishing Orkney Trout Fishing Association, Ⓣ 01856/761586, Ⓦ www.orkneytroutfishing.co.uk.

Internet access Support Training Ltd, West Tankerness Lane Ⓣ 01856/873582, Ⓦ www.support-training-orkney.co.uk (Mon–Fri 8.30am–7pm, Tues closes 9.30pm, Sat 10am–5pm).

Laundry Launderama, 47 Albert St (Mon–Fri 8.30am–5.30pm, Sat 9am–5.30pm).

Medical care Balfour Hospital, Kirkwall Health Centre and Dental Clinic, New Scapa Rd Ⓣ 01856/885425.

Post office Junction Rd (Mon–Fri 9am–5pm, Sat 9.30am–12.30pm).

Taxi Bob's Taxis, Hatston, Kirkwall, Ⓣ 01856/876543.

East Mainland and South Ronaldsay

Southeast from Kirkwall, the narrow spur of the **East Mainland** juts out into the North Sea and is joined, thanks to the remarkable Churchill Barriers, to several smaller islands, the largest of which are **Burray** and **South Ronaldsay**. As with the West Mainland, the land here is relatively densely populated and heavily farmed, but contains few of Orkney's more famous sights. Nevertheless, there are several interesting fishing villages, some good coastal walks to enjoy, an unusual new Iron Age site to explore at **Mine Howe** and, at the **Tomb of the Eagles**, one of the most enjoyable and memorable of Orkney's prehistoric sites.

East Mainland

The northern side of the **East Mainland** consists of three exposed peninsulas that jut out like giant claws. The most intriguing peninsula is the easternmost one of Deerness (see below), but before you reach it you should pay a quick visit to the recently excavated Iron Age mound of **Mine Howe** (May Wed & Sun 11am–3pm; June to early Sept daily 11am–5pm; rest of Sept Wed & Sun 11am–2pm; £2.50), just off the A960 in the Tankerness peninsula, beyond the airport. Originally Mine Howe would have been a large mound surrounded by a deep ditch, but only a small section has been excavated. At the top of the mound a series of steps leads steeply down to a half-landing, and then plunges down even deeper to a small chamber some twenty feet below the surface. Visitors don a hard hat and grab a torch, before heading underground. The whole layout is unique and has left archeologists totally baffled, though, naturally, numerous theories as to its purpose abound, from execution by ritual drowning to a temple to the god of the underworld. Mine Howe's relationship to the nearby mound and broch of Longhowe remains a mystery too. A survey has revealed a ditch with a single entrance encompassing the site, beyond which are signs of a settlement, probably of Pictish origin.

The easternmost peninsula of **Deerness** is joined to the Mainland only by a narrow, sandy isthmus. Its northeastern corner, around the sea cliffs of **Mull**

Head, boasts a large colony of nesting seabirds from May to August, including fulmars, kittiwakes, guillemots, razorbills and puffins, plus, inland, arctic terns that swoop and screech threateningly. The only way to reach Mull Head is to walk from the car park, located a mile or so to the south. On a short walk east of the car park you can also view **The Gloup**, an impressive collapsed sea cave, the name of which stems from the Old Norse *gluppa*, or "chasm"; the tide still flows in and out through a natural arch, making strange gurgling noises. Half a mile north of the Gloup is the **Brough of Deerness**, a grassy promontory whose narrow land bridge has collapsed, and which is now accessible only via a precipitous path; the ruins are thought to have once been a Norse or Pictish monastic site.

Scapa Flow

Apart from a few oil tankers, there's generally very little activity in the great natural harbour of **Scapa Flow**, yet for the first half of the twentieth century, the Flow served as the main base of the Royal Navy, with over a hundred warships anchored here at any one time. The coastal defences required to make Scapa Flow safe to use as the country's chief naval headquarters were considerable and many are still visible all over Orkney, ranging from half-sunk blockships to the Churchill Barriers (see p.426) and the gun batteries that pepper the coastline. Unfortunately, these defences weren't sufficient to save **HMS Royal Oak** from being torpedoed by a German U-boat in October 1939 (see p.423), but they withstood several heavy German air raids during the course of 1940. Ironically, the worst disaster the Flow has ever witnessed was self-inflicted, when **HMS Vanguard** sank on July 9, 1917, after suffering an internal explosion, taking over a thousand of her crew with her and leaving only two survivors.

Scapa Flow's most celebrated moment in naval history, however, was when the entire **German High Seas Fleet** was interned here immediately after the end of World War I. A total of 74 ships, manned by several thousand German sailors, was anchored off the island of Cava awaiting the outcome of the Versailles Peace Conference. At around noon on Midsummer's Day 1919, believing either that the majority of the German fleet was to be handed over, or that hostilities were about to resume, the commanding officer, Admiral von Reuter, ordered the fleet to be scuttled. By 5pm, every ship was beached or had sunk and nine German sailors had lost their lives, shot by outraged British servicemen. The British government was publicly indignant, but privately relieved since the scuttling avoided the diplomatic nightmare of dividing up the fleet between the Allies.

Between the wars, the largest **salvage operation** in history took place in Scapa Flow, with the firm of Cox & Danks alone raising twenty-six destroyers, one light cruiser, four battlecruisers and two battleships. Despite this, seven large German ships – three battleships and four light cruisers – remain on the seabed of Scapa Flow, along with four destroyers and a U-boat. Although the remaining vessels can only be salvaged on a piecemeal basis, their pre-atomic era steel is still extremely valuable as it is radiation-free and is in great demand in the space and nuclear industries. Scapa Flow is also considered one of the world's greatest dive sites. Scapa Scuba (Ⓣ01856/851218, Ⓦwww.scapascuba.co.uk), based in Stromness, offers one-to-one **scuba-diving** tuition for beginners, lasting three hours, diving on one of the blockships sunk by the Churchill Barriers; they also offer wreck diving for those with more experience. If you don't want to get your feet wet, Roving Eye Enterprises (Ⓣ01856/811309, Ⓦwww.rovingeye.co.uk) runs a boat fitted with an underwater camera, which does the diving for you, while you sit back and watch the video screen; their trip leaves from Houton Pier at 1.20pm, takes three hours, costs £25 and includes a visit to the Scapa Flow Visitor Centre in Lyness (see p.431).

Visible across the sea to the north are Auskerry and Stronsay and, to the southeast, the uninhabited island of **Copinsay**, with its lighthouse, perched on yet more seabird-infested cliffs. Copinsay is now an RSPB reserve, with huge seabird colonies nesting on its cliffs in season; boat trips are possible.

On the south coast, just before you hit the Churchill Barriers, stands **ST MARY'S**, an old fishing village whose livelihood was destroyed by the building of the causeways. Just east of St Mary's, you'll find **Norwood Antiques** (May–Sept Tues–Thurs & Sun 2–5pm; also by arrangement ⓣ01856/781217; £3), a display of antiques collected by local stonemason Norrie Wood from the age of 13. Only about half of the collection is on display, but it's a fascinating and eccentric selection of bits and pieces from around the world, including pottery, painting, medals, furniture, cutlery, clocks, even a narwhal's tusk, all housed in a grand Orkney home.

The Churchill Barriers

To the south of St Mary's is the first of four causeways known as the **Churchill Barriers**, since they were given the go-ahead by Churchill when he was First Lord of the Admiralty. They were built during World War II as anti-submarine barriers, which would seal the waters between the Mainland and the string of islands to the south, and thus protect the Royal Navy, based in Scapa Flow at the time, from German U-boat attack. However, the Admiralty was only prompted into action by the sinking of the battleship HMS *Royal Oak* on October 14, 1939 (see p.423). Despite the presence of blockships, deliberately sunk during World War I in order to close off the eastern approaches, one German U-boat captain managed to get through and torpedo the *Royal Oak*, before returning to a hero's welcome in Germany. He claimed to have acquired local knowledge while fishing in the islands before the war. As you cross the barriers – don't cross them during high winds – you can still see the blockships, rusting away, an eerie reminder of Orkney's important wartime role.

The barriers – an astonishing feat of engineering when you bear in mind the strength of Orkney tides – were an incredibly expensive undertaking, costing an estimated £2.5 million. Special camps were built on the uninhabited island of Lamb Holm, in order to accommodate the 1700 men involved in the project, 1200 of whom were Italian POWs. The camps have long since disappeared, but the Italians left behind the extraordinary **Italian Chapel** (daily dawn–dusk; free) on Lamb Holm. This, the so-called "miracle of Camp 60", must be one of the greatest adaptations ever, made from two Nissen huts, concrete, barbed wire and parts of a rusting blockship. It has a great false facade, and colourful trompe-l'oeil decor, lovingly restored by the chapel's principal architect, Domenico Chiocchetti, who returned in 1960. Mass is still said regularly.

Burray

If you're travelling with children, you may like to stop off on the island of **Burray** in order to visit the **Orkney Fossil and Heritage Centre** (April–Sept daily 10am–6pm; £2.50), housed in a converted farm on the main road across the island. Most of the fossils on display downstairs have been found locally, so they tend to be of fish and sea creatures, since Orkney was at the bottom of a tropical sea in Devonian times. The UV room, where the rocks reveal their iridescent colours, is a particular favourite with kids. Upstairs, there's a lot of wartime memorabilia, books to read, a rocking horse to play on and a comfy chair and binoculars with which to spot the birdlife down by the shore. There's also a tearoom attached to the museum.

BURRAY VILLAGE, on the south coast of the island, expanded in the nineteenth century during the boom years of the herring industry, but was badly affected by the sinking of the blockships during World War I. The two-storey warehouse, built in 1860 in order to cure and pack the herring, has since been converted into the *Sands Hotel* (Ⓣ01856/731298, Ⓦwww.thesandshotel.co.uk; ❸), where you can find freshly caught local fish on the menu and six nicely refurbished **hotel** rooms. Alternatively, head for *Vestlaybanks* (Ⓣ01856/731305, Ⓦwww.vestlaybanks.co.uk; ❷), a very comfortable **B&B** along the road to Littlequoy, which boasts great views over Scapa Flow.

South Ronaldsay

At the southern end of the series of four barriers is low-lying **South Ronaldsay**, the largest of the islands linked to the Mainland and, like the latter, rich farming country. It was traditionally the chief crossing point to the Scottish mainland, as it's only six miles across the Pentland Firth from Caithness. Car **ferries** currently arrive at St Margaret's Hope, and there's a small passenger ferry between John O'Groats and Burwick, on the southernmost tip of the island (see p.406 for details).

St Margaret's Hope

The main settlement on South Ronaldsay is **ST MARGARET'S HOPE**, which local tradition says takes its name from Margaret, the Maid of Norway and daughter of the King of Norway, who is thought to have died here at the age of 8 in November 1290. As the granddaughter of Alexander III, Margaret had already been proclaimed Queen of Scotland and was on her way to marry the English prince Edward (later Edward II), thereby unifying the two countries. Today, St Margaret's Hope – or "The Hope", as it's known locally (from the Norse *hyop* meaning "bay") – is a pleasing little gathering of stone-built houses overlooking a sheltered bay, and is by far the best base from which to explore the area. As is obvious from the architecture, and the piers, The Hope was once a thriving port. Nowadays, despite the presence of the Pentland Ferries terminal, it remains a very peaceful place.

The village smithy on Cromarty Square has been turned into a **Smiddy Museum** (June–Aug daily noon–4pm; May & Sept daily 2–4pm; Oct Sun 2–4pm; free), which is particularly fun for kids, who enjoy getting hands-on with the old tools, drills and giant bellows. There's also a small exhibition on the annual **Boys' Ploughing Match**, in which local boys compete with miniature hand-held ploughs. The competition, which is taken extremely seriously by all those involved, happens on the third Saturday in August, at the beautiful golden beach at the **Sands O'Right** in Hoxa, a couple of miles west of The Hope. At the same time a **Festival of the Horse** takes place, with the local children dressing up in spectacular costumes and harnesses.

If you want **to stay** in St Margaret's Hope itself you should head for *The Creel* (Ⓣ01856/831311, Ⓦwww.thecreel.co.uk; ❻) on the harbourfront, with a view over the bay, and one of the best **restaurants** in Scotland and a winner of all sorts of awards. At around £25 for two courses, it's expensive, but also friendly and relaxed. More modest bar meals are available from the *Murray Arms Hotel* (Ⓣ01856/831205, Ⓦwww.murrayarmshotel.com; ❹), on Back Road, which has rooms above the pub and a backpackers' **hostel** round the side.

Outside St Margaret's Hope, you're spoilt for choice with *Shoreside* (Ⓣ01856/831560, Ⓦwww.orkneyholiday.com; ❸), a **B&B** back down the road to Kirkwall, where you're guaranteed fresh fish and shellfish as the stuff comes from their own fishing boat, and *Roeberry House* (ⓣ01856/831838; ⓦwww.roeberry.co.uk; ❸), an imposing country house two miles west of The Hope along the B9043. Guests have their own flat, complete with lounge and kitchen, the Sands O' Right beach is nearby and the views are great. For a **hostel** with some character, head for *Wheems* (ⓣ01856/831537; April–Oct), on the eastern side of South Ronaldsay, a mile and a half from the war memorial on the main road outside The Hope. Mattresses and clean linen are provided, and seasonal produce from the croft is on sale: **camping** is also possible.

The Tomb of the Eagles

One of the most enjoyable archeological sights on Orkney is the Isbister chambered cairn at the southeastern corner of South Ronaldsay, known as the **Tomb of the Eagles** (daily: March 10am–noon; April–Oct 9.30am–6pm; Nov–March by appointment; £5; ⓣ01856/831339, ⓦwww.tomboftheeagles.co.uk). The cairn was discovered and excavated by a local farmer, Ronald Simison of Liddle, who still owns it, so a visit here makes a refreshing change from the usual interpretive centre. First off, you get to look round the family's private museum of prehistoric artefacts; this is the original hands-on museum, so visitors can actually touch and admire the painstaking craftsmanship of Neolithic folk, and examine a skull. Next you get a brief guided tour of a nearby Bronze Age **burnt mound**, which is basically a Neolithic rubbish dump, beside which there was a large trough, where joints of meat were boiled by throwing in rocks from the fire. Finally you get to walk out to the **chambered cairn**, by the cliff's edge, where human remains were found alongside talons and carcasses of sea eagles. To enter the cairn, you must lie on a trolley and pull yourself in using an overhead rope – something that's guaranteed to put a smile on every visitor's face. The cairn's clifftop location is spectacular, and walking along the coast in either direction is rewarding: south to the sea inlet of Ham Geo, or north to Halcro Head, and beyond to Wind Wick Bay, where seals and their pups can be seen in the autumn.

Hoy

Hoy, Orkney's second-largest island, rises sharply out of the sea to the southwest of the Mainland. The least typical of the islands, but certainly the most dramatic, its north and west sides are made up of great glacial valleys and mountainous moorland rising to over 1500ft, dropping into the sea off the red sandstone cliffs of St John's Head, and, to the south, forming the landmark sea stack known as the **Old Man of Hoy**. The northern half of Hoy, though a huge expanse, is virtually uninhabited, with just the village of Hoy opposite Stromness, and the cluster of houses at **Rackwick** nestling dramatically in a bay between the cliffs. Meanwhile, most of Hoy's four hundred or so residents live on the gentler, more fertile land in the southeast, in and around the villages of **Lyness** and **Longhope**. This part of the island is littered with buildings dating from the two world wars, when Scapa Flow served as the main base for the Royal Navy (see p.425).

Two **ferry services** run to Hoy: a passenger ferry from Stromness to Moaness Pier, by Hoy village (Mon–Fri 4–5 daily, Sat & Sun 2 daily; 25min; ⓣ01856/850624), which also serves the small island of Graemsay; and the roll-on/roll-off car ferry from Houton on the Mainland to Lyness (Mon–Fri 6 daily, Sat & Sun 2–4 daily; 45min–1hr 25min; ⓣ01856/811397), which sometimes calls in at the oil terminal island of Flotta (see p.431), and begins and ends its daily schedule at Longhope. There's no bus service on Hoy, but those arriving on the passenger ferry from Stromness should find a **minibus** waiting to take them to Rackwick.

North Hoy

Much of Hoy's magnificent landscape is made up of rough grasses and heather, which harbour a cluster of arctic plants and a healthy population of mountain hares, as well as numerous great skuas, plus a few merlins, kestrels and peregrine falcons, while the more sheltered valleys are nesting sites for snipe and arctic skua. Walkers arriving by passenger ferry from Stromness at Moaness Pier, near the tiny village of **HOY**, and heading for Rackwick (four miles southwest), can either catch the minibus or take the well-marked footpath that goes past Sandy

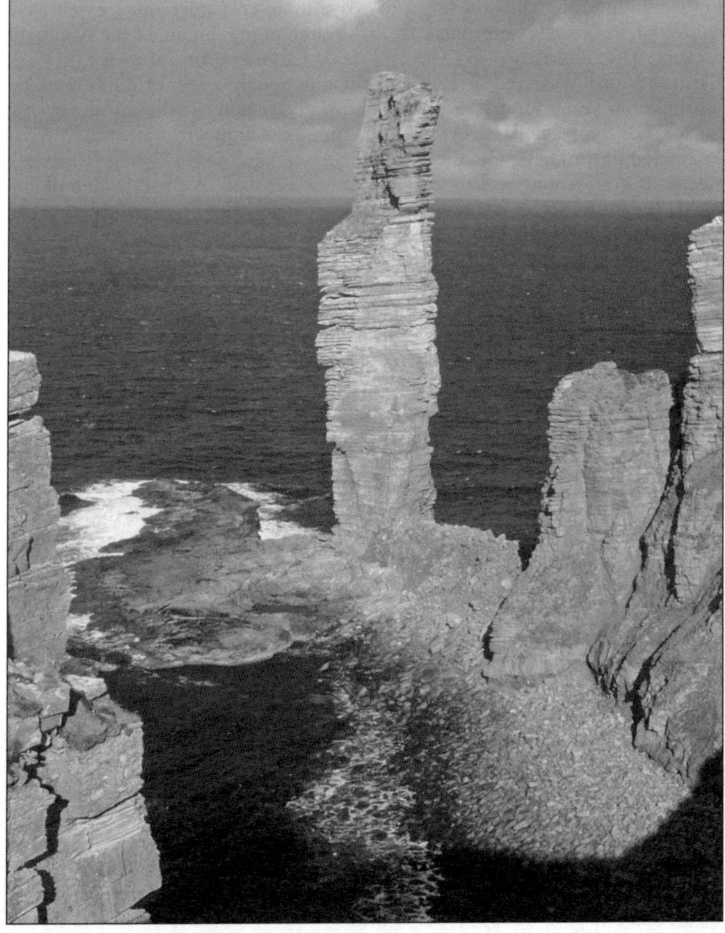

△ Old Man of Hoy

Loch and along the large open valley beyond. On the western side of this valley is the narrow gully of **Berriedale**, which supports Britain's most northerly native woodland, a huddle of birch, hazel and honeysuckle.

The minibus route to Rackwick is via the single-track road along another valley to the south. En route, duckboards head across the heather to the **Dwarfie Stane**, Orkney's most unusual chambered tomb, cut from a solid block of sandstone and dating back to 3000 BC. The sheer effort that must have been involved in carving out this tomb, with its two side-cells, is staggering and, as you crawl inside, the marks of the tools used by the Neolithic builders on the ceiling are still visible. The tomb is also decorated with copious Victorian graffiti, the most interesting of which is to be found on the northern exterior, where Major Mouncey, a former British spy in Persia and a confirmed eccentric who dressed in Persian garb, carved his name backwards in Latin, and also carved in Persian the words "I have sat two nights and so learnt patience."

RACKWICK is an old crofting and fishing village squeezed between towering sandstone cliffs on the west coast. In an area once quite extensively cultivated, Rackwick went into a steady decline in the middle of the twentieth century: its school closed in 1953 and the last fishing boat put to sea in 1963. Electricity finally arrived in 1980 but these days only a few of the houses are inhabited all year round (the rest serve as holiday homes), though the savage isolation of the place has provided inspiration to a number of artists and writers, including Orkney's George Mackay Brown, who wrote "when Rackwick weeps, its grief is long and forlorn and utterly desolate." A small farm building beside the hostel serves as a tiny **museum** (open any time; free), with a few old photos and a brief rundown of Rackwick's rough history. Take the time, too, to stroll down to the sandy beach, backed by giant sandstone pebbles washed smooth by the sea, which make a thunderous noise when the wind gets up.

Despite its isolation, Rackwick has a steady stream of walkers and climbers passing through it en route to the **Old Man of Hoy**, a great sandstone column some 450ft high, perched on an old lava flow which protects it from the erosive power of the sea. The Old Man is a popular challenge for rock-climbers, and a 1966 ascent, led by the mountaineer Chris Bonington, was the first televised climb in Britain. The well-trodden footpath from Rackwick is an easy three-mile walk (3hr round trip) – the great skuas will dive-bomb you only during the nesting season – and gives the reward of a great view of the stack. The surrounding cliffs provide ideal rocky ledges for the nests of thousands of seabirds, including guillemots, kittiwakes, razorbills, puffins and shags.

Continuing north along the clifftops, the path peters out before **St John's Head** which, at 1136ft, is one of the highest sea cliffs in the country and mostly too sheer even for nesting seabirds. Another, safer, option is to hike to the top of **Ward Hill** (1577ft), the highest mountain in Orkney, from which on a fine day you can see the whole archipelago laid out before you.

Practicalities

There are only a few places to stay in North Hoy. Luckily one of them is *The Glen* (☎01856/791262; ❷), in Rackwick, run by a friendly couple whose family have lived on the island for centuries; they also offer dinner and will collect guests from Hoy. In addition, there are two council-run, SYHA-affiliated **hostels**, housed in converted schools; to book ahead, you must contact the education department at the Orkney Islands Council (☎01856/873535 ext 2415). The *North Hoy Hostel* (May to mid-Sept) in Hoy village is the larger of the two, but the *Rackwick Hostel* (mid-March to mid-Sept), with just eight beds, enjoys a better location. You can **camp** in Rackwick, either behind the

Flotta

It comes as something of a shock when you first catch sight of the 223-foot flare stack that rises like a giant Bunsen burner from the oil terminal island of **Flotta**, east of Hoy in Scapa Flow. However, it's also a testament to the success of the local council, which, in confining the **oil industry** to the island of Flotta, has managed to minimize the impact it's had on the Mainland community. That said, it's difficult to underestimate the significance of the discovery of North Sea oil on Orkney, not only in providing several hundred well-paid jobs, but also in terms of pumping money into the local economy. Oil production has passed its peak, though it still has some years to run, and supertankers from all over the world remain a constant, slightly menacing sight in Scapa Flow.

It may seem perverse to visit an island dominated by an oil terminal, but Flotta does have one or two points of interest, and is very easily accessible, with frequent car ferries from both Hoy and the Mainland. Like Lyness, Flotta was an important naval base during both world wars, and there are a lot of wartime relics dotted over the island, including gun and rocket batteries, a signal station, and the huge ruin of an old YMCA, built in local stone during World War I. For a panoramic **view** of the island, and the whole of Scapa Flow, climb up West Hill (190ft), Flotta's highest point.

hostel, down by the unusually attractive public toilets, or beside *Burnside Cottage* (Ⓣ01856/791316), the heather-thatched **bothy** in a beautiful setting right by the beach, which has no mattresses or kitchen facilities. **Bike rental** is available from Hoy's Moaness Pier Ⓣ01856/791225). However, there's no shop in Rackwick, so take all your supplies with you; the post office shop in Hoy only sells chocolate, but the *Hoy Inn*, near the post office, serves very good **bar meals** in season. Be warned, too, that North Hoy is probably the worst place on Orkney for midges.

Lyness and Longhope

Along the sheltered eastern shore of Hoy, high moorland gives way to a gentler environment similar to that on the rest of Orkney. Hoy defines the western boundary of Scapa Flow, and **LYNESS** played a major role for the Royal Navy during both world wars. Many of the old wartime buildings have been cleared away over the last few decades, but the harbour and hills around Lyness are still scarred with the scattered remains of concrete structures that once served as hangars and storehouses during World War II, and are now used as barns and cowsheds. Among these are the remains of what was – incredibly – the largest cinema in Europe, but perhaps the most unusual remaining building is the monochrome Art Deco facade of the old **Garrison Theatre**, on the main road south of Lyness, now a private home. Lyness also has a large **naval cemetery**, where many of the victims of the various disasters that have occurred in the Flow, such as the sinking of the *Royal Oak* (see p.423), now lie, alongside a handful of German graves.

The old oil pumphouse, which still stands opposite the Lyness ferry terminal, has been turned into the **Scapa Flow Visitor Centre & Museum** (April–Oct Mon–Sat 9am–4.30pm, Sun 10.30am–4pm; July–Sept Sun until 6.15pm; Nov–March Mon–Fri only; free), a fascinating insight into wartime Orkney. As well as the usual old photos, torpedoes, flags, guns and propellers, there's a paratrooper's folding bicycle, and a whole section devoted to the scuttling of the German High Seas Fleet and the sinking of the *Royal Oak*. The pumphouse itself retains much of its old equipment – you can even ask for a working demo of one of the oil-fired boilers – used to pump oil off tankers moored at Lyness into sixteen tanks, and from there into underground reservoirs cut into the neighbouring hillside. On request, an audiovisual show on the history of Scapa Flow is screened in the sole surviving tank, which has incredible acoustics. Even the **café** has an old NAAFI feel about it.

Melsetter House

The finest architecture on Hoy is to be found at **Melsetter House** (Thurs, Sat & Sun by appointment; ⓣ01856/791352), four miles southwest of Lyness, overlooking the deep inlet of North Bay. Originally built in 1738, it was bought by Thomas Middlemore, heir to a Birmingham leather tycoon, who commissioned the Arts and Crafts architect William Lethaby to transform the house in 1898. The charming owners will happily take you round a handful of the thoroughly lived-in rooms in the house itself, all of which are simply decorated with white wood panelling, floral plasterwork and William Morris-style fabrics, and leave you to wander freely around the house's very beautiful grounds. Don't miss the little **Chapel of St Margaret and St Colm** that Lethaby fashioned from the Melsetter's outhouses, which features some characteristic symbolic touches, and four tiny, stained-glass windows by, among others, Ford Madox Brown and Burne-Jones. The walk along the cliffs of the west coast to Rackwick is spectacular and takes about six hours.

South Walls

To the east of Melsetter House, a causeway built during World War II connects Hoy with **South Walls** (pronounced "Waas"), a fertile tidal island which is more densely populated with farms and homes than Hoy. On the north side of South Walls is the main settlement of **LONGHOPE** (ⓦwww.longhope.co.uk), an important safe anchorage during the Napoleonic Wars and World War I, but since then overshadowed by Lyness and Flotta. The **Longhope Lifeboat** capsized in strong gale-force winds in 1969 on its way to the aid of a Liberian freighter. The entire eight-man crew was killed, leaving seven widows and ten fatherless children; the crew of the freighter, by contrast, survived. There's a moving memorial to the men – six of whom came from just two families – in **Kirkhope Churchyard** on the road to Cantick Head Lighthouse. Just up the road before the causeway is the **Longhope Lifeboat Museum** (daily dawn–dusk; free) which houses the *Thomas McCunn*, a lifeboat in service from 1933 to 1962 and still launched for high days and holidays.

Evidence of Longhope's strategic importance during the Napoleonic Wars lies to the east of the village at the Point of Hackness, where the **Hackness Martello Tower** stands guard over the entrance to the bay, with a matching tower on the opposite promontory of Crockness. Built in 1815, these two circular sandstone Martello towers are the northernmost in Britain, and were built to protect merchant ships waiting for a Royal Navy escort from American and French privateers. You can visit Hackness Tower (if it's locked, a sign will tell you where to pick up the key) via a steep ladder connected to the upper floor, where nine men and one officer shared the circular room. Originally a portable ladder would have been used and retracted, making the place pretty much impregnable: the walls are up to 9ft high on the seaward side, and the tower even had its own water supply. Overlooking the bay at the nearby **Hackness Battery**, positioned closer to the shore, yet more cannon were trained on the horizon.

Practicalities

South Hoy has a handful of good **accommodation** options, including *St John's Manse* (ⓣ01856/791240; ③), south of Lyness, overlooking Longhope; in

Longhope itself is the welcoming *Stromabank Hotel* (Ⓣ01856/701494, Ⓦwww.stromabank.co.uk; ❸), a nicely converted old schoolhouse, which also does good bar **food** (closed Thurs). **Self-catering** options include the Cantick Head lighthouse cottages (Ⓣ01856/701255; 4–6 people; £375–500 per week). There are two shops: one round the back of the *Hoy Hotel*, and one by the pier in Longhope.

Shapinsay

Just a few miles northeast of Kirkwall, **Shapinsay** is the most accessible of Orkney's northern isles. A gently undulating grid-plan patchwork of rich farmland, it's a bit like an island suburb of Kirkwall, which is clearly visible across the bay. Its chief attraction for visitors is **Balfour Castle** (May–Aug guided tours Sun 3pm; see below for details of the all-inclusive ticket), the imposing baronial pile designed by David Bryce and completed in 1848 by the Balfour family of Westray, who had made a small fortune in India the previous century. The Balfours died out in 1960 and the castle was bought by a Polish cavalry officer, Captain Tadeusz Zawadski, whose family now run the place as a hotel. The **guided tours** are great fun, and go down very well with children too, as they finish off with complimentary tea and home-made cakes in the servants' quarters. Before you enter the castle, you get to walk through the wooded grounds and view the vast kitchen gardens, which are surrounded by fifteen-foot-high walls, and once had coal-fired greenhouses to produce fruit and vegetables out of season. The interior of the castle is not that magnificent, though it has an attractively lived-in ambience and is pretty grand for Orkney; decorative otters crop up all over the place, as they feature prominently in the Balfour family crest.

The Balfours also reformed the island's agricultural system and built **BALFOUR** village, a neat and disciplined cottage development, to house their estate workers. The family's grandiose efforts in estate management have left some appealingly eccentric relics. Melodramatic fortifications around the harbour include the huge and ornate **Gatehouse**, which now serves as the local pub. There's also a stone-built coal-fired **Gasometer**, which once supplied castle and harbour with electricity and, southwest of the pier, the castellated **Dishan Tower**, a seventeenth-century doocot that was converted into a salt-water toilet in Victorian times. The old smiddy, halfway along the village street, houses the **Shapinsay Heritage Centre** (May–Sept Mon–Fri 11am–4.30pm, Sat & Sun 11am–6pm; free), where you can learn everything you ever wanted to know about the island, before availing yourself of its excellent café.

Most folk visit Shapinsay on a day-trip, but if you're staying here for a few days you'd do well to explore one or two points of interest beyond the castle and village. One mile north of Balfour village is the small **Mill Dam**, a breeding ground for black-headed gulls, with a hide to the west from which you can also look down on wigeon, teal, shovellers and (if you're really lucky) pintails. The east coast from the Bay of Linton to the Foot of Shapinsay has the most interesting cliffs and sea caves and is backed by the only open moorland on the island. On the far northeastern peninsula is Shapinsay's most striking ancient monument, the **Broch of Burroughston**, a well-preserved strongly fortified Iron Age broch with the substantial remains of living quarters within, a bar hole to make fast the door, and a guard-cell. This bit of the coast is also a good spot for watching **seals** sunning themselves on the nearby rocks. The finest stretch of sandy beach is at the sweeping curve of **Sandgarth Bay**, in the southeast.

Practicalities

Less than thirty minutes from Kirkwall by **ferry** (Mon–Fri 5 daily, Sat & Sun 4 daily), Shapinsay is an easy day-trip. If you want to visit the castle, you should phone ahead and book an **all-inclusive ticket** from Balfour Castle (£18), which includes a return ferry ticket. The ferry for the guided tour leaves at 2.15pm, but you can catch an earlier ferry if you want to have some time to explore the rest of the island. It's also possible **to stay** for dinner, bed and breakfast in lord-of-the-manor style at the *Balfour Castle Hotel* (ⓣ01856/711282, ⓦwww.balfourcastle.co.uk; ⑨); the rooms are vast and beautifully furnished, and you also get use of the library and the other public rooms. More modest **B&B** is available at *Girnigoe* (ⓣ01856/711256, ⓦwww.girnigoe.net; ②), a very comfortable Orcadian croft close to the north shore of Veantro Bay that offers optional full board. Even if you're just coming for the day, it's worth popping into *The Smithy* (May–Sept; ⓣ01856/711722, ⓦwww.shapinsaysmithy.com), the wonderfully cosy licensed **café** below the heritage centre, which serves delicious food (daily lunchtime plus Fri & Sat eve) and also offers **bike rental**.

Rousay, Egilsay and Wyre

Just over half a mile from the Mainland's northern shore, the hilly island of **Rousay** (ⓦwww.visitrousay.co.uk) is one of the more accessible northern isles as well as being home to a number of intriguing prehistoric sites. The group of a dozen or so houses above the ferry terminal is the only settlement of any size, but a single road runs around the edge of the island, connecting a string of small farms which make use of the more cultivable coastal fringes. Many visitors

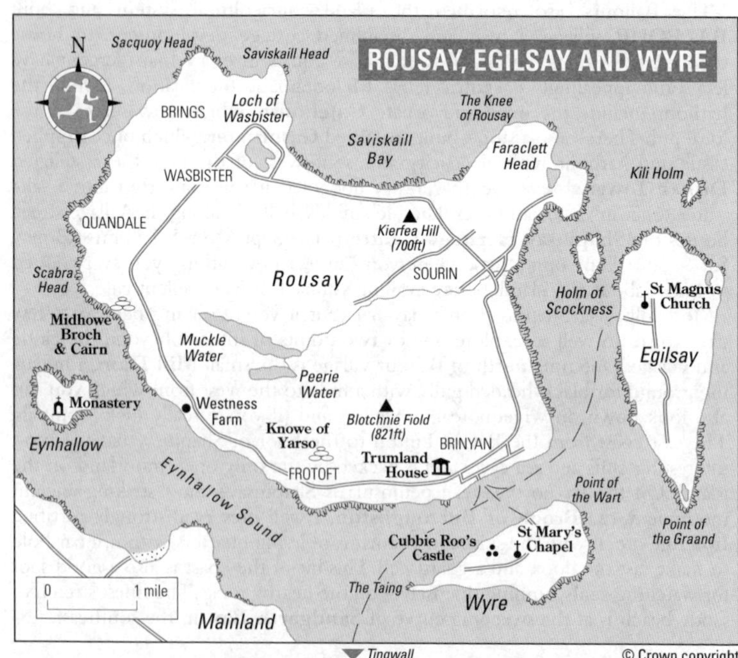

© Crown copyright

come on a day-trip, as it's easy enough to reach the main points of archeological interest on the south coast by foot from the ferry terminal.

Rousay's diminutive neighbours, **Egilsay** and **Wyre**, contain a few medieval attractions of their own, which can either be visited on a day-trip from Rousay itself, or from the mainland.

Trumland House to the Knowe of Yarso

Despite its long history of settlement, Rousay is today home to little more than two hundred people (many of them incomers), as this was one of the few parts of Orkney to suffer Highland-style Clearances, initially by George William Traill at Quandale in the northwest. His successor and nephew, Lieutenant General Traill-Burroughs, built a wall to force crofters onto a narrow coastal strip and eventually provoked so much distress and anger that a gunboat had to be sent to restore order. You can learn about the history and wildlife of the island from the well-laid-out display room of the **Rousay Heritage Centre** housed in the back of the ferry waiting room.

It was the aforementioned Burroughs who built **Trumland House**, the forbidding Jacobean-style pile designed by David Bryce in 1873, and hidden in the trees half a mile northwest of the ferry terminal. The house is currently undergoing much-needed restoration, as are the **gardens**, which can be visited (May–Sept Mon–Fri 10am–5pm; £2). The road west from Trumland House is bordered over the next couple of miles by a trio of intriguing prehistoric cairns, starting with **Taversoe Tuick**, discovered by workers during the building of a Victorian viewpoint. Dating back to 3500 BC, it's remarkable in that it exploits its sloping site by having two storeys, one entered from the upper side and one from the lower. A little further west is the **Blackhammar Cairn**, which is more promising inside than it looks from the outside. You enter through the roof via a ladder; the long interior is divided into "stalls" by large flagstones, rather like the more famous cairn at Midhowe (see below). Finally, there's the **Knowe of Yarso**, another stalled cairn dating from the same period that's a stiff climb up the hill from the road, but worth it, if only for the magnificent view. The remains of 29 individuals were found inside, with the skulls neatly arranged around the walls; the bones of 36 deer were also buried here.

A footpath sets off from beside the Taversoe Tuick tomb into the **RSPB reserve** that encompasses a large section of the nearby heather-backed hills, the highest of which is **Blotchnie Fiold** (821ft). This high ground offers good hill walking, with superb panoramic views of the surrounding islands, as well as excellent bird-watching. If you're lucky, you may well catch a glimpse of merlins, hen harriers, short-eared owls and red-throated divers, although the latter are more widespread just outside the reserve on one of the island's three freshwater lochs, which also offer good trout fishing.

Midhowe Cairn and Broch

The southwestern side of Rousay is home to the most significant and impressive of the island's archeological remains, strung out along the shores of the tide races of Eynhallow Sound, which runs between the island and the Mainland. Most lie on the mile-long **Westness Walk** that begins at Westness Farm, four miles west of the ferry terminal. This scramble along the shore is rewarded with a kaleidoscope of history, with remains of an Iron Age cairn, a Viking farm, a post-Reformation church, a medieval tower, and crofts from which the tenants were evicted in the nineteenth century. At the end stands the **Midhowe Cairn**, which comes as something of a surprise, both for its immense size – it's known as "the great ship of death" and measures nearly 100ft in length – and for the fact that it's now entirely surrounded by a stone-walled barn with a corrugated roof. Unfortunately, you can't actually explore the roofless communal burial chamber, dating back to 3500 BC, but only look down from the overhead walkway. The central corridor, 25yd long, is partitioned with slabs of rock, with twelve compartments on each side, where the remains of 25 people were discovered in a crouched position with their backs to the wall.

A couple of hundred yards beyond Midhowe Cairn is Rousay's finest archeological site, **Midhowe Broch**, whose compact layout suggests that it was originally built as a sort of fortified family house, surrounded by a complex series of ditches and ramparts. These are now partially obscured by later houses, many of which have shelving and stairs still intact. The broch itself looks as though it's about to slip into the sea: it was obviously shored up with flagstone buttresses back in the Iron Age, and has more recently been given extra sea defences by Historic Scotland. The interior of the broch, entered through an impressive doorway, is divided into two separate rooms, each with its own hearth, water tank and quernstone, all of which date from the final phase of occupation around the second century AD.

From Midhowe Broch you get a good view of the nearby small island of **Eynhallow**, which is surrounded by the most ferocious tides. The island was cleared in 1851, at which point it was discovered that one of the houses was in fact a converted church, possibly part of a monastery, dating back to at least the twelfth century. Beyond Midhowe, a walk along the clifftops will take you past the impressive scenery around **Scabra Head**, where numerous seabirds nest in summer. Inland, the heathland of Quandale and Brings provides yet more birdwatching, with arctic terns and arctic skuas in abundance. To the north is a fine sandy beach at Saviskaill Bay, where seals "hang" out.

Egilsay and Wyre

Egilsay, the largest of the low-lying islands sheltering close to the eastern shore of Rousay, makes for an easy day-trip. The island is dominated by the ruins of **St Magnus Church**, with its distinctive round tower. Built around the twelfth century in a prominent position in the middle of the island, probably on the site of a much earlier version, the roofless church is the only surviving example of the traditional round-towered churches of Orkney and Shetland. It is possible that it was built as a shrine to Earl (later Saint) Magnus, who arranged to meet his cousin Haakon here in 1117, only to be treacherously killed on Haakon's orders by the latter's cook, Lifolf. A cenotaph marks the spot where the murder took place, about a quarter of a mile southeast of the church. Egilsay is almost entirely inhabited by incomers, and a large slice of the island's farmland is managed by the RSPB in a vain attempt to encourage corncrakes. If you're just here for the day, walk due east from the ferry terminal to the coast, where there's a beautiful sandy bay overlooking Eday.

The tiny, neighbouring island of **Wyre**, to the southwest, directly opposite Rousay's ferry terminal, is another possible day-trip, and is best known for **Cubbie Roo's Castle**, the "fine stone fort" and "really solid stronghold" mentioned in the *Orkneyinga Saga*, and built around 1150 by local farmer Kolbein Hruga. The castle gets another mention in *Haakon's Saga*, when those inside successfully withstood all attacks. The outer defences have survived well on three sides of the castle, which has a central keep, with walls to a height of around six feet, its central water tank still intact. Close by the castle stands **St Mary's Chapel**, a roofless twelfth-century church founded either by Kolbein or his son, Bjarni the Poet, who was Bishop of Orkney. Kolbein's permanent residence or Bu is recalled in the name of the nearby farm, the Bu of Wyre, where the poet **Edwin Muir** (1887–1959) spent his childhood, described in detail in his autobiography. To learn more about Muir, Cubbie Roo or any other aspect of Wyre's history, pop into the **Wyre Heritage Centre**, near the chapel. If you walk to the very western tip of Wyre, known as **The Taing**, you're pretty much guaranteed to see large numbers of grey and common **seals** basking on the rocks.

Practicalities

Rousay makes a good day-trip from the Mainland, with regular **car ferry** sailings from Tingwall (30min), linked to Kirkwall by buses. Most ferries also call in at Egilsay and Wyre, but some need to be booked the day before at the Tingwall ferry terminal (ⓣ01856/751360). Alternatively, you can join one of the very informative **minibus tours** run by Rousay Traveller (June–Aug Tues–Fri; £16; ⓣ01856/821234), which connect with ferries and last between two and six hours, the longer ones allowing extended walks.

Accommodation on Rousay is limited. If you want to be near the ancient sites, your best bet is the **hostel** at *Trumland Farm* (ⓣ01856/821252), a working organic farm half a mile or so west of the terminal. As well as a couple of dorms, you can also camp here, and they offer **bike rental**. The *Taversoe Inn*, further along the road, offers unpretentious accommodation (ⓣ01856/821325, ⓔTaversoeHotel@aol.com; ❶) and does good bar meals. If you're up for exploring more of the island, head for *Ervadale* (ⓣ01856/821351, ⓔervadale@aol.com; ❷), a traditional Orcadian crofthouse **B&B** in the northeastern corner of the island, below Kierfea Hill. *The Pier* **pub**, right beside the terminal, serves bar meals at lunchtime and will make up some fresh crab sandwiches if you phone in advance (ⓣ01856/821359). Don't arrive expecting to be able to buy yourself many provisions, though, as Marion's Shop, the island's main general store, is in the northeastern corner of the island.

Westray

Although exposed to the full force of the Atlantic weather in the far northwest of Orkney, **Westray** (ⓦwww.westray-orkney.co.uk or ⓦwww.westraypapawestray.com) shelters one of the most tightly knit, prosperous and independent island communities. It has a fairly stable population of six hundred or so, producing superb beef, scallops, shellfish and a large catch of white fish, with its own small fish-processing factory and an organic salmon farm. Old Orcadian families still dominate every aspect of life, giving the island a strong individual character.

The landscape is very varied, with sea cliffs and a trio of hills in the west, and rich low-lying pastureland and sandy bays elsewhere. However, given that distances are fairly large – it's about twelve miles from the ferry terminal in the south to the cliffs of Noup Head in the far northwest – and that the boat from Kirkwall takes nearly an hour and a half, Westray is an island that repays a longer stay, especially as there's lots of good accommodation and the locals are extremely welcoming and genuinely interested in visitors.

The main village and harbour is **PIEROWALL** set around a wide bay in the north of the island, a good eight miles from the Rapness ferry terminal on the southernmost tip of the island. Pierowall is a place of some considerable size, relatively speaking, with a school, several shops, a bakery (Orkney's only one off

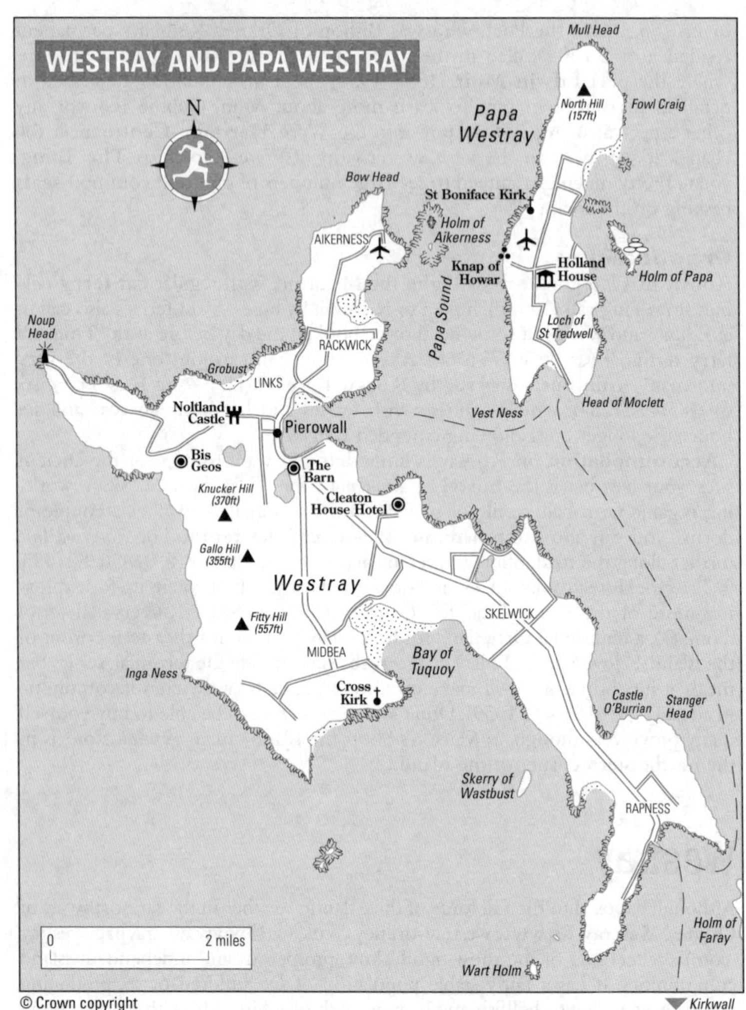

the Mainland), and the excellent **Westray Heritage Centre** (May–Sept Mon & Sun 11.30am–5pm, Tues–Sat 2–5pm; July & Aug also Tues–Fri 10am–noon; £2), a tiny building hidden up a lane flanked by fuchsias. This is a very welcoming wet-weather retreat, with a great mock-up of the sea cliffs of Noup Head (see below), a really imaginative range of hands-on exhibits for kids and a good place for a cup of tea. Pierowall also boasts the **Lady Kirk**, a ruined chapel sporting a diminutive belfry, to the north of the village centre, which contains two very fine seventeenth-century tombstones.

The island's most impressive ruin, however, is the colossal sandstone hulk of **Noltland Castle**, which stands above the village half a mile west up the road to Noup Head. This Z-plan castle, pockmarked with over seventy gun loops, was begun around 1560 by Gilbert Balfour, a shady character from Fife, who was

Master of the Household to Mary, Queen of Scots, and was implicated in the murder of her husband, Lord Darnley, in 1567. Mary was deposed before she could make her planned visit to Noltland, and Balfour, having joined an unsuccessful uprising in favour of the exiled queen, was forced to flee to Sweden. There he was found guilty of plotting to murder the Swedish king and was executed in 1576. Somewhat miraculously, the Balfour family managed to hold on to Noltland (and Westray), eventually shifting their seat to Shapinsay (see p.433). To explore the castle, you must first pick up the key, which hangs outside the back door of the nearby farm. The most striking features of the interior are the huge, carved stone newel at the top of the grand, main staircase, and the secret compartments built into the sills of two of the windows.

The northwestern tip of Westray rises up sharply, culminating in the dramatic sea cliffs of **Noup Head**, which are particularly spectacular when a good westerly swell is up. During the summer months, the guano-covered rock ledges are packed with over 100,000 nesting seabirds, primarily guillemots, razorbills, kittiwakes and fulmars, with puffins as well: a truly awesome sight, sound and smell. There's a great viewpoint just to the northwest of the lighthouse, and another at Lawrence's Piece, half a mile to the south, where a narrow rocky ledge juts out into the sea. The open ground above the cliffs, which is grazed by sheep, is superb maritime heath and grassland, carpeted with yellow, white and purple flowers, and a favourite breeding ground for arctic terns and arctic skuas.

The four-mile coastal walk along the top of Westray's red sandstone cliffs from Noup Head south to Inga Ness is thoroughly recommended, as is a quick ascent of **Fitty Hill** (557ft), Westray's highest point. Also in the south of the island is the tiny **Cross Kirk** which, although ruined, retains an original Romanesque arch, door and window. It's right by the sea, and on a fine day the nearby sandy beach is a lovely spot for a picnic, with views over to the north side of Rousay. The sea cliffs in the southeast of the island around **Stanger Head** are not quite as spectacular as at Noup Head, but it's here that you'll find **Castle o'Burrian**, a sea stack that was once an early Christian hermitage. It's now the best place on Westray at which to see **puffins** nesting; there's even a signpost to the puffins from the main road.

Practicalities

Westray is served by car **ferry** from Kirkwall (2–3 daily; 1hr 25min; ⓣ01856/872044), or you can **fly** on Loganair's tiny eight-seater plane from Kirkwall to Westray (Mon–Sat 2 daily; 12min). **Guided tours** of the island by minibus or bike can also be arranged with Westraak (ⓣ01857/677777, ⓦwww.westraak.co.uk), who will meet you at the ferry. J&M Harcus of Pierowall (ⓣ01857/677450) runs a **bus service** that will take you from Rapness to Pierowall, though you should phone ahead to check it's running. For **bike rental**, contact either of the hostels (see p.440).

Westray's finest **accommodation** is at the *Cleaton House Hotel* (ⓣ01857/677508, ⓦwww.cleatonhouse.co.uk; ⑤), a whitewashed Victorian manse about two miles southeast of Pierowall, with great views over to Papa Westray. *Cleaton House* is also the place to sample Westray's organic salmon, either in the **restaurant** or in the hotel's congenial **bar**, which serves real ale. Somewhat bizarrely, the hotel also has a **pétanque** pitch, which residents and non-residents alike are welcome to use. The *Pierowall Hotel* (ⓣ01857/677472, ⓦwww.orknet.co.uk/pierowall; ③), in Pierowall itself, is less stylish and less expensive, but equally welcoming, with a popular bar and a well-justified reputation for excellent **fish and chips**, fresh off the boats (much of it you're unlikely to have heard of) – you can buy fresh fish from the hotel, too.

B&B is available at *No. 1 Broughton* (Ⓣ01857/677726, Ⓦwww.no1broughton.co.uk; ③), a recently renovated mid-nineteenth-century house by the southern shore of Gill Bay, on the edge of Pierowall. Westray is positively spoilt for **hostels**: *Bis Geos* (Ⓣ01857/677420, Ⓦwww.bisgeos.co.uk), on the road to Noup Head, has unbeatable views along the cliffs and out to sea; inside, it's beautifully furnished, and there are also a couple of very good **self-catering** cottages. *The Barn* (Ⓣ01857/677214, Ⓦwww.thebarnwestray.co.uk) is situated in an old farm at the southern edge of Pierowall; it's luxurious inside, is easier to get to, has a small **campsite** adjacent to it and a games room and genuinely friendly hosts. You can rent clubs from Tulloch's shop (Ⓣ01857/677373) to play the somewhat eccentric **golf course** on the links northwest of Pierowall, near the island's best beach. To find out when the local **swimming pool** is available, phone Ⓣ01857/677750.

Papa Westray

Across the short Papa Sound from Westray is the island of **Papa Westray**, known locally as "Papay" (Ⓦwww.papawestray.co.uk). With a population hovering precariously around seventy, Papay has had to fight hard to keep itself viable over the last couple of decades, helped by a hefty influx of outsiders.

△ Puffin, Orkney

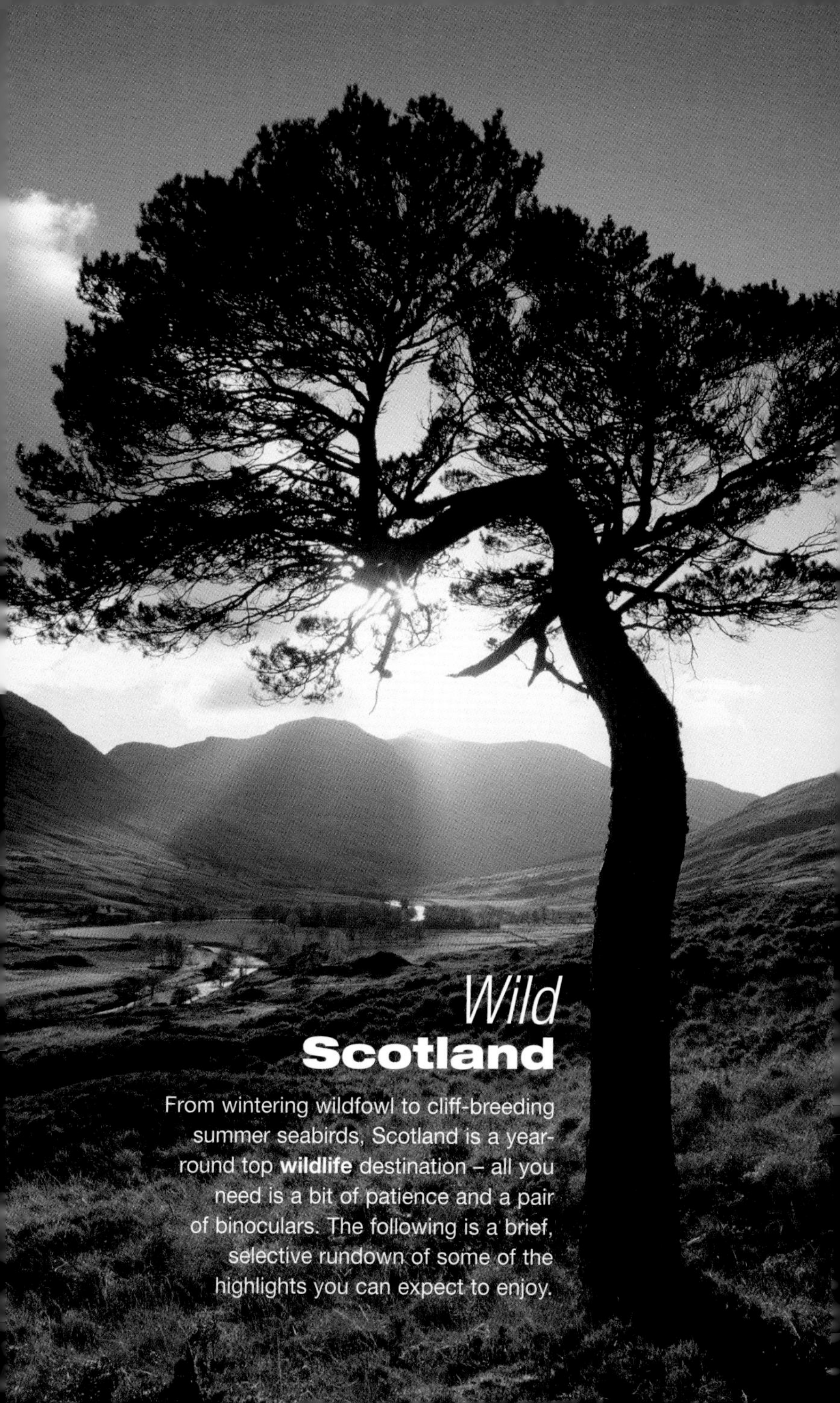

Wild
Scotland
From wintering wildfowl to cliff-breeding summer seabirds, Scotland is a year-round top wildlife destination – all you need is a bit of patience and a pair of binoculars. The following is a brief, selective rundown of some of the highlights you can expect to enjoy.

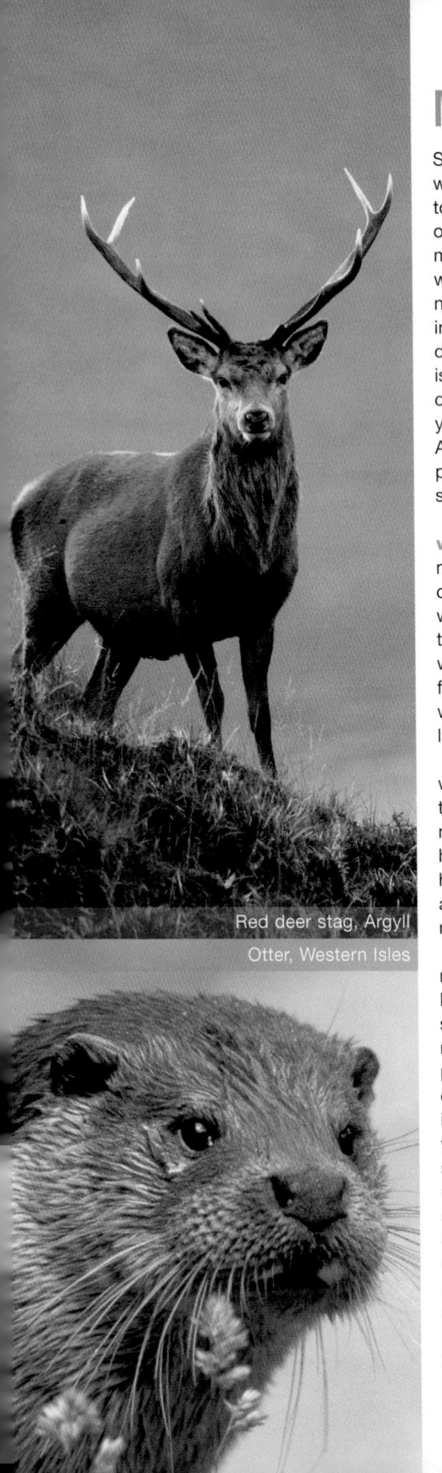
Red deer stag, Argyll

Otter, Western Isles

Mammals and fish

Scotland's largest wild mammal is the **red deer**, which, despite culling and stalking, continues to grow in numbers. You've got a good chance of seeing red deer all year round but they're most obvious in the snowy depths of winter, when, forced downhill in search of food, large numbers may be seen by road or rail travellers in the Highlands. Scotland's most popular domesticated mammal with visitors, however, is the shaggy auburn **Highland cow**, which can survive in snowy conditions for fifty days a year, and is always happy to pose for a photo. Another favourite is Britain's smallest native pony, the **Shetland pony**, which still roams semi-wild in its homeland.

Among the more elusive mammals are the **wildcat** and **pine marten** which hide away in the moors and forests. You've a slightly better chance of encountering an **otter**, most likely along the west coast and on the islands, where it hunts the seashore for crabs and fish. Easily confused with the otter is the feral **mink**, a fugitive from fur farms and now successfully established in the wild, where it causes merry havoc, destroying livestock and groundnesting birds.

Of course, Scotland once boasted a much wider variety of mammals, from the Scottish wolf to the elk, most of which had disappeared by the mid-eighteenth century. Since then, a semi-wild herd of **reindeer** (wiped out in the twelfth century) has returned to the slopes of the Cairngorms above Aviemore and the **beaver** is currently being reintroduced to the forests of Argyll.

After the Loch Ness Monster, Scotland's most famous aquatic creature is the **salmon**. Ninety-nine percent of the Scottish salmon sold worldwide comes from offshore fish farms; meanwhile the population of wild salmon has plummeted. Nevertheless, in June and July you can still see them heading upstream to breed in their ancestral gravel headwaters, leaping waterfalls on the way. Scotland also has the second largest **seal** population in the world, mostly grey seals, but also (the rarer) common seal. These creatures are easy to see in most Scottish bays and even some harbours; to catch a glimpse of the country's other sea mammals, you need to take to the water. The easiest cetacean to spot is the **porpoise**, but **dolphins** and **whales** are also frequent visitors to Scotland's coastal waters particularly in the summer and autumn.

Osprey, Cairngorms

Birdlife

Scotland's most distinctive bird is now one of the rarest and most endangered in the country. The **capercaillie** was eradicated in Scotland once before, in 1785, but reintroduced in the nineteenth century. It's an unexpectedly large, turkey-like bird, about 3ft from bill to tail, and, like the **black grouse**, has a flamboyant communal courting display known as a "lek". Capercaillies are more or less confined to the last remaining native pine forest in the Highlands, as are the **crested tit** and the parrot-like **Scottish crossbill** – the UK's only endemic bird species – which uses its overlapping bill to prise open pine cones.

The bird that most visitors are keen to see is the **golden eagle**, whose wingspan can reach over seven feet. However, with only around four hundred pairs resident in the Highlands and the Hebrides, you're much more likely to see a **buzzard**, easily mistaken for an eagle when soaring high above you. Even larger (and rarer) than the golden eagle is the **white-tailed eagle** or "fish eagle", reintroduced in the 1970s after a seventy-year absence. Some thirty pairs have established themselves and are regularly seen hunting over the waters around the Inner Hebrides. After forty years' absence, the **osprey** returned of its own accord in the 1950s, and more than a hundred pairs now breed in lochs right across the Highlands.

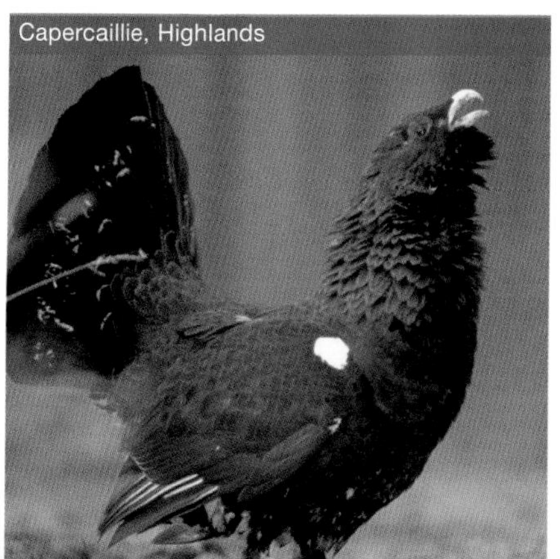
Capercaillie, Highlands

Not unsurprisingly, Scotland is big on seabirds. Among the most celebrated are the superbly streamlined fish-eating **divers** which nest on inland lochs but go fishing at sea. The most spectacular sight, though, are the remote cliffs that attract vast colonies of **gannets**, **puffins**, **guillemots**, **razorbills**, **fulmars**, **shags** and **kittiwakes**, or the isolated colonies of **Manx shearwaters** on Rùm or the **storm petrels** on Mousa in Shetland.

Sundew

Scotland's **top ten** wild hot spots

OSPREYS. Loch Garten, Speyside. The best place to spot this rare, fish-eating summer visitor. See p.211.

CAPERCAILLIE LEK, Abernethy Forest, Strathspey. An early start in April and May is necessary to see capercaillie's fierce mating rituals. See p.211.

BOTTLE-NOSED DOLPHINS, Moray Firth. June and August are the best times to see these aquatic gymnasts. See p.254.

WINTERING WILDFOWL, Isle of Islay. Thousands of barnacle and white-fronted geese fly from Greenland to winter here. See p.144.

SCOTS PINE, Cairngorms. One of the largest tracts of ancient Caledonian Forest is in Rothiemurchus. See p.206.

PUFFINS, Shetland. Scotland's favourite seabird is at its most abundant in these northern isles. See p.467.

SALMON LADDER, Pitlochry, Perthshire. The most celebrated place to watch salmon leaping upstream in summer to spawn.

STORM PETRELS, Mousa Broch, Shetland. As darkness falls, watch thousands of storm petrels return to their nests. See p.465.

WILD FLOWERS, Western Isles. The sand-enriched coastal grasslands (known locally as machair) are carpeted in wildflowers from May to July. See p.385.

RED-THROATED DIVERS, Isle of Eday, Orkney. The hide overlooking Mill Loch is home to several pairs of nesting red-throated divers. See p.442.

Trees and **flowers**

Scotland has more **trees** than either England or Wales, with fifteen percent of the country covered by forest. Unfortunately, much of what you'll see is slab plantations of Sitka spruce. Only rarely will you catch sight of the most distinctive native tree, the **Scots pine**, which once formed the backbone of the land's great Caledonian Forest, a vast mosaic of trees, including birch, willow, alder, elm, ash, and oak. Only one percent of this ancient forest now remains in areas such as the Black Wood of Rannoch and Rothiemurchus Forest below the Cairngorms.

Almost three-quarters of the country is uncultivated **peat bog**, rock and **heather**, which turns the country's hillsides purple in the late summer. The wettest areas give rise to specialized plants such as **butterwort** and the **sundews**, which gain nutrients in these poor surroundings by trapping midges. In the far north there are **lichens** and **mosses** found nowhere else in Britain. Although the thistle is commonly associated with Scotland, the national flower is actually the **Scottish bluebell**, known to the English as the harebell (the English "bluebell" is known as wild hyacinth in Scotland). Equally characteristic now are introduced species such as the **rhododendron** and **azalea** which flourish in the damp, frost-free climate on the west coast, producing spectacular bursts of colour in May and June.

With one of Orkney's best-preserved Neolithic settlements, and a large nesting seabird population, Papay is worthy of a stay in its own right or an easy day-trip from its neighbour.

As the name suggests – *papøy* is Old Norse for "priest" – the island was once a medieval pilgrimage centre, focused on a chapel dedicated to **St Tredwell**, which is now reduced to a pile of rubble on a promontory on the loch of the same name just inland from the ferry terminal. St Tredwell (Triduana) was a plucky young local girl who gouged out her eyes and handed them to the eighth-century Pictish King Nechtan when he attempted to rape her. By the twelfth century, the chapel had become a place of pilgrimage for those suffering from eye complaints.

The island's visual focus is **Holland House**, occupying the high central point of the island and once seat of the local lairds, the Traill family, who ruled over Papay for three centuries. The main house, with its crow-stepped gables, is still in private hands, but the current owners are perfectly happy for visitors to explore the old buildings of the home farm, on the west side of the road, which include a kiln, a doocot and a horse-powered threshing mill. An old bothy for single male servants, decorated with red horse yokes, has even been restored and made into a small **museum** (open anytime; free), filled with bygone bits and bobs, from a wooden flea trap to a box bed.

A road leads down from Holland House to the western shore, where Papay's prime prehistoric site, the **Knap of Howar**, stands overlooking Westray. Dating from around 3500 BC, this Neolithic farm building makes a fair claim to being the oldest-standing house in Europe. It's made up of two roofless buildings, linked by a little passageway; one has a hearth and copious stone shelves, and is thought to have been some kind of storehouse. Half a mile north along the coast from the Knap of Howar is **St Boniface Kirk**, a pre-Reformation church that has recently been restored. Inside, it's beautifully simple, with a bare flagstone floor, dry-stone walls, a little wooden gallery and just a couple of surviving box pews. The church is known to have seated at least 220, which meant they would have been squashed in, fourteen to a pew. In the surrounding graveyard there's a Viking **hogback grave**, decorated with carvings in imitation of the wooden shingles on the roof of a Viking longhouse.

The northern tip of the island around **North Hill** (157ft) is now an RSPB reserve. During the breeding season, you're asked to keep to the coastal fringe, where razorbills, guillemots, fulmars, kittiwakes and puffins nest, particularly around Fowl Craig on the east coast, where you can also view the rare Scottish primrose, which flowers in May and from July to late September. If you want to explore the interior of the reserve, which plays host to one of the largest arctic tern colonies in Europe as well as numerous arctic skuas, contact the warden (Ⓣ01857/644240), who conducts regular escorted walks.

If you're here for more than a day, it's worth considering renting a boat to take you over to the **Holm of Papay**, an islet off the east coast. Despite its tiny size, the Holm boasts several Neolithic chambered cairns, one of which, occupying the highest point, is extremely impressive. Descending into the tomb via a ladder, you enter the main rectangular chamber, which is nearly 70ft in length, with no fewer than twelve side-cells, each with its own lintelled entrance. To arrange a boat, contact the Community Co-operative (see over).

Practicalities

Papay is an easy day-trip from Westray, with a regular **passenger ferry** service from Gill Pier in Pierowall (2–5 daily; 25min), which also takes bicycles. However, it's just as easy to stay on Papay and take a day-trip to Westray instead.

On Tuesdays and Fridays, the **car ferry** from Kirkwall to Westray continues on to Papa Westray; at other times, a bus (which accepts a limited number of bicycles) from Rapness connects with the Pierowall passenger ferry. Papay is also connected to Westray by the **world's shortest scheduled flight** – two minutes in duration, or less with a following wind. You can also fly direct from Kirkwall to Papa Westray (Mon–Sat 2–3 daily, 1 on Sun) for a special return fare of £12 if you stay overnight.

Papay's Community Co-operative has a **minibus**, which will take you from the pier to wherever you want on the island, and can arrange a Papay Peedie Tour (mid-May to mid-Sept Tues, Thurs & Sat; £33; ⓣ01857/644321). It also runs a shop, a sixteen-bed SYHA-affiliated **hostel** (ⓦwww.syha.org.uk) and the *Beltane House* **B&B** (ⓣ01857/644267, ⓔpapaybeltane2@hotmail.com; ③), all housed within the old estate workers' cottages at Beltane, east of Holland House.

Eday

A long, thin island at the centre of Orkney's northern isles, **Eday** shares more characteristics with Rousay and Hoy than with its immediate neighbours, dominated as it is by a great block of heather-covered upland, with farmland confined to a narrow strip of coastal ground. However, Eday's hills have proved useful in their own way, providing huge quantities of peat, which has been exported to the other peatless northern isles for fuel, and was even, for a time, exported to various whisky distillers. Eday's yellow sandstone has also been extensively quarried, and was used to build the St Magnus Cathedral in Kirkwall.

Eday is sparsely inhabited, with a population of around 130, the majority of them incomers, and there's no real village as such. The island is almost divided in two by its thin waist, flanked on either side by sandy bays, between which lies the airfield (known as London Airport). Eday has Orkney's only resident population of whimbrels, which nest around Flaughton Hill (328ft), a mile or so to the south, but the chief points of interest are all in the northern half of the island, beyond the post office, petrol pump and community shop (closed Sun) on the main road. This marks the beginning of the signposted **Eday Heritage Walk**, which covers all the main sights and takes about three hours to complete. The walk initially follows the road heading northwest, past the bird hide overlooking **Mill Loch**, where several pairs of red-throated divers regularly breed.

Clearly visible to the north of the road is the fifteen-foot **Stone of Setter**, Orkney's most distinctive standing stone, weathered into three thick, lichen-encrusted fingers. The stone clearly held centre stage in the Neolithic landscape, and is visible from the other nearby prehistoric sites. From here, passing the less spectacular Braeside and Huntersquoy chambered cairns en route, you can climb the hill to reach Eday's finest, the **Vinquoy Chambered Cairn**, which has a similar structure to that of Maes Howe. You can crawl into the tomb through the narrow entrance: a skylight inside lets light into the main, beehive chamber, now home to some lovely ferns, but not into the four side-cells. From the cairn, you can continue north to the viewpoint on the summit of **Vinquoy Hill** (248ft), and on to the very northernmost tip of the island, where lie the dramatic red sandstone sea cliffs of **Red Head**, where guillemots, razorbills, puffins and other seabirds nest in summer.

Visible on the east coast is **Carrick House**, the grandest home on Eday (Sun 2pm or by appointment ⓣ01857/622260; £2.50). Built by the Laird of Eday

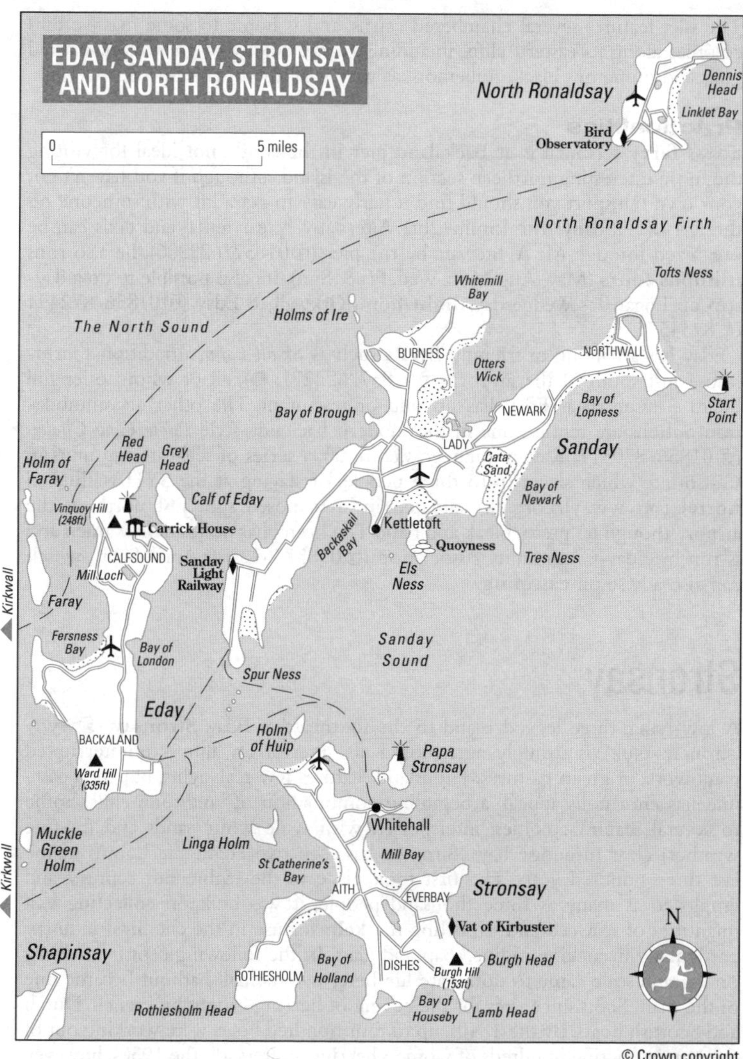

in 1633, it was extended in the original style by successive owners, but is best known for its associations with the pirate **John Gow** – on whom Sir Walter Scott's novel *The Pirate* is based – whose ship *The Revenge* ran aground on the Calf of Eday in 1725. He asked for help from the local laird, but was taken prisoner in Carrick House, before eventually being sent off to London, where he was tortured and executed. Highlight of the languid tour is the bloodstain on the floor of the living room, where John Gow was detained and stabbed whilst trying to escape.

From Carrick House, the uninhabited island of the **Calf of Eday** is only a stone's throw away. If you're keen to visit the island, contact Carrick House.

The islet features several chambered cairns, and is home to some massive bird colonies along its eastern cliffs, including a large colony of great black-backed gulls and numerous black guillemots, as well as all the usual suspects.

Practicalities

Eday's **ferry** terminal is at Backaland pier in the south, not ideal for visiting the more interesting northern section of the island, although if you haven't got your own transport you should find it fairly easy to get a lift with someone off the ferry (1–2 daily; 1hr 15min–2hr). Alternatively, car rental and taxis can be organized through Mr A. Stewart by the pier (Ⓣ01857/622206); he also runs **minibus tours** (May–Aug Mon, Wed, Fri & Sun). It's also possible to do a day-trip on Loganair's Wednesday **flight** from Kirkwall to Eday (Ⓣ01856/872494 or 873457).

Eday has a handful of friendly **B&Bs** such as *Skaill Farm*, a traditional farmhouse just south of the airport (Ⓣ01857/622271; ③), all of whom offer full board – essential as Eday has no pub or restaurant. The other accommodation options are renting one of the modern hacienda-style *Pirate Gow Chalets* (Ⓣ01856/879517, Ⓦwww.pirategow.com; ①), a series of self-catering units in Calfsound, which sleep up to three people, or staying at the SYHA-affiliated **hostel** (Ⓦwww.syha.org.uk), situated in an exposed spot just north of the airport, though it's pretty bleak and basic. The hostel has no resident warden and is run by Eday Community Association (Ⓣ01857/622206; April–Sept), which can also advise on **camping**.

Stronsay

A low-lying, three-legged island to the southeast of Eday, **Stronsay** (Ⓦwww.stronsay.co.uk) is strongly agricultural, its interior an almost uninterrupted patchwork of green pastures. The island features few real sights, but the coastline has enormous appeal: a beguiling combination of sandstone cliffs, home to several seabird colonies, interspersed with wide white sands and (in fine weather) clear turquoise bays. Stronsay has seen two economic booms in the last three hundred years. The first took place in the eighteenth century, and employed as many as three thousand people; it was built on collecting vast quantities of seaweed and exporting the **kelp** for use in the chemical industry, particularly in making iodine, soap and glass. In the following century, **fishing** on a grand scale came to dominate life here, as Whitehall harbour became one of the main Scottish centres for the curing of herring caught by French, Dutch and Scottish boats. By the 1840s, up to four hundred boats were working out of the port, attracting hundreds of women herring-gutters. By the 1930s, however, the herring stocks had been severely depleted and the industry began a long decline.

WHITEHALL, in the north of the island, is the only real village on Stronsay, made up of rows of stone-built fishermen's cottages set between two large piers. Wandering along the tranquil, rather forlorn harbourfront today, you'll find it hard to believe that the village once supported five thousand people in the fishing industry during the summer season, as well as a small army of coopers, coal merchants, butchers, bakers, several Italian ice-cream parlours and a cinema. It was said that, on a Sunday, you could walk across the decks of the boats all the way to **Papa Stronsay**, the tiny island that shelters Whitehall from the north, on which a new monastery has been built (see box on p.445). The old fish

Papa Stronsay

Clearly visible from the harbourfront at Whitehall is the tiny island of **Papa Stronsay** (Ⓦwww.papastronsay.com). The island features in the *Orkneyinga Saga* as the place where Earl Rognvald Brusason was murdered by Earl Thorfinn Sigurdarson. Later, during the herring boom, it was home to no fewer than five fish-curing stations. As the name suggests, the island is thought originally to have been a monastic retreat, a theory given extra weight by the discovery of an eighth-century chapel during recent excavations. Since 2000, the island has been in the hands of the **Roman Catholic Order of Transalpine Redemptorists**, who were founded in 1988, after breaking with the Vatican over their refusal to stop celebrating Mass in Latin. They are anti-ecumenical, and are actively involved in trying to convert the Orthodox believers of the former Soviet Union to Roman Catholicism. On Papa Stronsay, "a desert in the sea", they hope to revive the lost tradition of Celtic monasticism. They have built themselves the multi-million-pound Golgotha Monastery, with a creamery for making their Monastery Cheese. The black-robed monks are happy to take visitors across to (and around) the island by boat, by prior arrangement (answerphone Ⓣ01857/616389).

market by the pier houses a small **museum**, with a few photos and artefacts from the herring days – ask at the adjacent café.

If the weather's fine, you can choose which of the island's many arching, dazzlingly white beaches to relax on. The most dramatic section of coastline, featuring great, layered slices of sandstone, lies in the southeast corner of the island. Signposts show the way to Orkney's biggest and most dramatic natural arch, the **Vat of Kirbuster**. Before you reach the arch there's a seaweedy, shallow pool in a natural sandstone amphitheatre, where the water is warmed by the sun and kids and adults can safely wallow: close by is a rocky inlet for those who prefer colder, more adventurous swimming. You'll find progressively more nesting seabirds, including a few puffins, as you approach **Burgh Head**, further along down the coast. Meanwhile, at the promontory of **Lamb Head**, there are usually loads of seals, a large colony of arctic terns, and good views out to the lighthouse on the outlying island of **Auskerry**, to the south.

Practicalities

Stronsay is served by a regular car **ferry** service from Kirkwall to Whitehall (2 daily; 1hr 40min–2hr), and weekday Loganair **flights**, also from Kirkwall (Mon–Sat 2 daily; 25min). There's no bus service, but D.S. Peace (Ⓣ01857/616335) operates taxis and offers **car rental**.

Of the few **accommodation** options, a good choice is the *Stronsay Fish Mart* **hostel** (Ⓣ01857/616346) in the old fish market by the pier, with a well-equipped kitchen, washing machine and comfortable bunk-bedded rooms. The pub opposite is the refurbished *Stronsay Hotel* (Ⓣ01857/616213, Ⓦwww.stronsay.co.uk/stronsayhotel; ❸), which once boasted the longest bar in the north of Scotland. Alternatively, head for the *Stronsay Bird Reserve* (Ⓣ01857/616363; ❷), a nicely positioned **B&B** in a lovely old crofthouse, which also tolerates **camping** on the shores of Mill Bay; the folk who run it are bird enthusiasts and keep a record of the astonishing number of rare migrants which regularly turn up on the island. Lastly, there's the very basic *Torness Camping Barn,* by the sea near Holland House (Ⓣ01857/616314), at the southernmost tip of the island.

The *Stronsay Hotel* does good pub **food** – try the seafood taster – but otherwise you'll need to bring your own supplies and make use of the island's two shops.

There's a **swimming pool** behind the school which is available for public use, but it's operated on a voluntary basis, so check first at the shop in Whitehall.

Sanday

Sanday (Ⓦwww.sanday.co.uk), though the largest of the northern isles, and the most populous after Westray, is also the most insubstantial, a great low-lying, drifting dune strung out between several rocky points. The island's sweeping aquamarine bays and vast stretches of clean white sand are the finest in Orkney, and in dry, clear weather it's a superb place to spend a day or two. The sandy soil is, in fact, very fertile, and the island remains predominantly agricultural even today, holding its very own agricultural show each year at the beginning of August.

The island has a long history as a shipping hazard, with many wrecks smashed against its shores, although the construction of the **Start Point Lighthouse** in 1802 on the island's exposed eastern tip reduced the risk for seafarers. Shipwrecks were, in fact, not an unwelcome sight on Sanday, as the island has no peat, and driftwood was the only source of fuel other than cow dung – it's even said that the locals used to pray for shipwrecks in church. The present Stevenson lighthouse, which dates from 1870, now sports very natty vertical black and white stripes. It actually stands on a tidal island, which is accessible only either side of low tide, so ask locally for the tide times before setting out (it takes an hour to walk there and back).

The shoreline supports a healthy seal, otter and wading bird population, and behind the splendid sandy beaches are stretches of beautiful open machair and grassland, thick with wild flowers during the spring and summer. The entire coastline presents the opportunity for superb walks, with particularly spectacular sand dunes to the south of the vast, shallow, tidal bay of **Cata Sand**. Sanday is also rich in archeology, with hundreds of mostly unexcavated sites including cairns, brochs and burnt mounds. The most impressive is **Quoyness Chambered Cairn**, on the fertile farmland of Els Ness peninsula. The tomb, which dates from before 2000 BC, has been partially reconstructed, and rises to a height of around thirteen feet. The imposing, narrow entrance, flanked by high dry-stone walls, would originally have been roofed for the whole of the way into the thirteen-foot-long main chamber, where bones and skulls were discovered in the six small side-cells.

Sanday also has two rather unusual attractions. Nearest the ferry terminal is the **Sanday Light Railway** (Ⓣ01857/600700, Ⓦwww.sandaylightrailway.co.uk), a passenger-carrying seven-and-a-quarter-inch-gauge railway that winds its way round the farmhouse of Strangquoy in a lovely position looking over to Eday; phone to confirm it's running. Sanday's **Orkney Angora** craft shop (Ⓣ01857/600421, Ⓦwww.orkneyangora.co.uk) is in Upper Breckan in the parish of Burness. The owner will usually oblige with a quick look and a stroke of one of the comically long-haired albino rabbits that supply the wool. Close by is the stone tower of an old windmill, which belonged to the neighbouring farmstead and house of **Scar**, where you can still see the chimney from the farm's old steam-powered meal mill.

Practicalities

Ferries to Sanday arrive at the Loth terminal at the southern tip of the island and are met by the **minibus** (book on Ⓣ01857/600284), which will take you to most points. The airfield is in the centre of the island and there are regular Loganair **flights** to Kirkwall (Mon–Sat 1–2 daily; 10min). The fishing port of **Kettletoft** is where the ferry used to dock, and where you'll find the island's two **hotels**. Of the two, *The Belsair* (Ⓣ01857/600206, Ⓔlaura@belsair.fsnet.co.uk; ❶) has the slightly more adventurous restaurant menu; the *Kettletoft* has a lively bar that's popular with the locals. Of the numerous **B&Bs**, try the *Marygarth Manse* (Ⓣ01857/600467; ❶), in Broughtown, who can also organize car and bike rental. If you're on a budget, head for nearby *Ayre's Rock* (Ⓣ01857/600410, Ⓔdiane@ayresrock.fsnet.co.uk), a well-equipped **hostel** and **campsite** by the Bay of Brough with washing and laundry facilities, a chip shop (Sat only) and bike rental.

North Ronaldsay

North Ronaldsay – or "North Ron" as it's fondly known – is Orkney's most northerly island. Separated from Sanday by the treacherous waters of the North Ronaldsay Firth, it has a unique outpost atmosphere, brought about by its extreme isolation. Measuring just three miles by one, and rising only 66ft above sea level, the island is almost overwhelmed by the enormity of the sky, the strength of wind and the ferocity of the sea – so much so that its very existence seems an act of tenacious defiance. Despite these adverse conditions, North Ronaldsay has been inhabited for centuries, and continues to be heavily farmed, from old-style crofts whose roofs are made from huge local flagstones. With no natural harbours and precious little farmland, the islanders have been forced to make the most of what they have, and **seaweed** has played an important role in the local economy. During the eighteenth century, kelp was gathered here, burnt in pits and sent south for use in the chemicals industry.

The island's **sheep** are a unique, tough, goatlike breed, who feed mostly on seaweed, giving their flesh a dark tone and a rich, gamey taste, and making their thick wool highly prized. A high **dry-stone dyke**, completed in the mid-nineteenth century and running the thirteen miles around the edge of the island, keeps them off the farmland, except during lambing season, when the ewes are allowed onto the pastureland. North Ronaldsay sheep are also unusual in that they can't be rounded up by sheepdogs like ordinary sheep, but scatter far and wide at some considerable speed. Instead, once a year the islanders herd the sheep communally into a series of **dry-stone "punds"** near Dennis Head, for clipping and dipping, in what is one of the last acts of communal farming practised in Orkney.

The most frequent visitors to the island are ornithologists, who come in considerable numbers to catch a glimpse of the rare migrants who land here briefly on their spring and autumn migrations. The peak times of year for migrants are from late March to early June, and from mid-August to early November, although there are also many breeding species which spend the spring and summer here, including gulls, terns, waders, black guillemots, cormorants and even the odd corncrake. As on Fair Isle (see p.468), there's a permanent **Bird Observatory**, established in 1987 by adapting a croft situated in the southwest corner of the island to wind and solar power; they can give advice as to what birds have recently been sighted.

Holland House – built by the Traill family, who bought the island in 1727 – and the two lighthouses at Dennis Head are the only features to interrupt the flat horizon. The attractive, stone-built **Old Beacon** was first lit in 1789, but the lantern was replaced by the huge bauble of masonry you now see as long ago as 1809. The **New Lighthouse** (May–Sept Sun 12.30–5.30pm; at other times by appointment; Ⓣ01857/633257; £3), designed by Alan Stevenson in 1854 half a mile to the north, is the tallest land-based lighthouse in Britain, rising to a height of over 100ft. You can climb to the top of the lighthouse, don white gloves (to protect the brass) and admire the view – on a clear day you can see Fair Isle, and even Sumburgh and Fitful Head on Shetland.

Practicalities

The **ferry** from Kirkwall to North Ronaldsay runs only once a week (usually Fri; 2hr 40min–3hr), though day-trips are possible on occasional Sundays between late May and early September (phone ⓣ01856/872044 for details). Your best bet is to catch a Loganair **flight** from Kirkwall (2–3 daily; 15min): if you stay the night on the island, you're eligible for a bargain £12 return fare. A **minibus** usually meets the ferries and planes (phone ⓣ01857/633244) and will take you off to the lighthouse. You can **stay** at the eco-friendly *Bird Observatory* (ⓣ01857/633200, ⓦwww.nrbo.f2s.com), which offers full board either in private guestrooms (❸) or in a **bunkhouse**; the observatory's *Obscafé* is a sort of pub/restaurant and serves decent meals. Full-board accommodation is also available at *Garso*, in the northeast (ⓣ01857/633244, ⓔchristine@garso.fsnet.co.uk; ❸). The *Burrian Inn*, to the southeast of the war memorial, is the island's small **pub**, and does hot food. As part of an initiative to help regenerate the island, North Ron now stages its own annual **Rinansay Folk Festival**, over one weekend in June, with a return ferry fare included in the ticket price.

Travel details

Ferries to Orkney

Summer timetable only.

Aberdeen to: Kirkwall (4 weekly; 6hr).

Gills Bay to: St Margaret's Hope (3 daily; 1hr).

John O'Groats to: Burwick (passengers only; 2–4 daily; 40min).

Lerwick to: Kirkwall (3 weekly; 5hr 30min).

Scrabster to: Stromness (2–3 daily; 1hr 30min).

Inter-island ferries

Summer timetable only.

To Eday: Kirkwall–Eday (1–2 daily; 1hr 15min–2hr).

To Egilsay: Tingwall–Egilsay (3–4 daily; 50min–1hr 45min).

To Flotta: Houton–Flotta (Mon–Fri 4 daily, Sat & Sun 2–3 daily; 45min–1hr).

To Hoy: Houton–Lyness (Mon–Fri 6 daily, Sat & Sun 2–4 daily; 45min–1hr 25min); Stromness–Hoy (passengers only; Mon–Fri 4–5 daily, Sat & Sun 2 daily; 25min).

To North Ronaldsay: Kirkwall–North Ronaldsay (1 weekly, usually Fri; 2hr 40min–3hr).

To Papa Westray: Kirkwall–Papa Westray (Tues & Fri; 2hr 15min); Pierowall (Westray)–Papa Westray (passengers only; 2–5 daily; 25min).

To Rousay: Tingwall–Rousay (5–6 daily; 30min).

To Sanday: Kirkwall–Sanday (2 daily; 1hr 25min).

To Shapinsay: Kirkwall–Shapinsay (Mon–Fri 5 daily, Sat & Sun 4 daily; 45min).

To Stronsay: Kirkwall–Whitehall (2 daily; 1hr 35min–2hr).

To Westray: Kirkwall–Westray (2–3 daily; 1hr 25min).

To Wyre: Rousay–Wyre (5–7 daily; 10–20min).

Inter-island flights

Kirkwall to: Eday (Wed; 8–26min); North Ronaldsay (2–3 daily; 15min); Papa Westray (Mon–Sat 2–3 daily, 1 on Sun; 12–19min); Sanday (Mon–Sat 1–2 daily; 10min); Stronsay (Mon–Sat 2 daily; 25min); Westray (Mon–Sat 2 daily; 12min).

Buses on Orkney Mainland

Kirkwall to: Burwick (3–4 daily; 50min); Birsay (Mon–Fri 2 daily; 45min); Deerness (Mon–Fri 4 daily, 2 on Sat; 30min); Evie (Mon–Sat 4 daily; 30min); Houton (Mon–Fri 5 daily, 3 on Sat; 30min); St Margaret's Hope (Mon–Fri 4 daily, 2 on Sat; 40min); Skara Brae (June–Aug Mon–Fri 2 daily; 1hr 15min); Stromness (Mon–Fri hourly, 8 on Sat, 4 on Sun; 30min); Tingwall (Mon–Fri 4 daily, Sat & Sun 2–3 daily; 35min).

Stromness to: Skara Brae (3–4 daily; 20min); Tingwall (Wed & Fri 2 daily; 1hr).

Shetland

N

8

7

6

4

5

3

2

1

SCOTLAND

NORTHERN IRELAND

ENGLAND

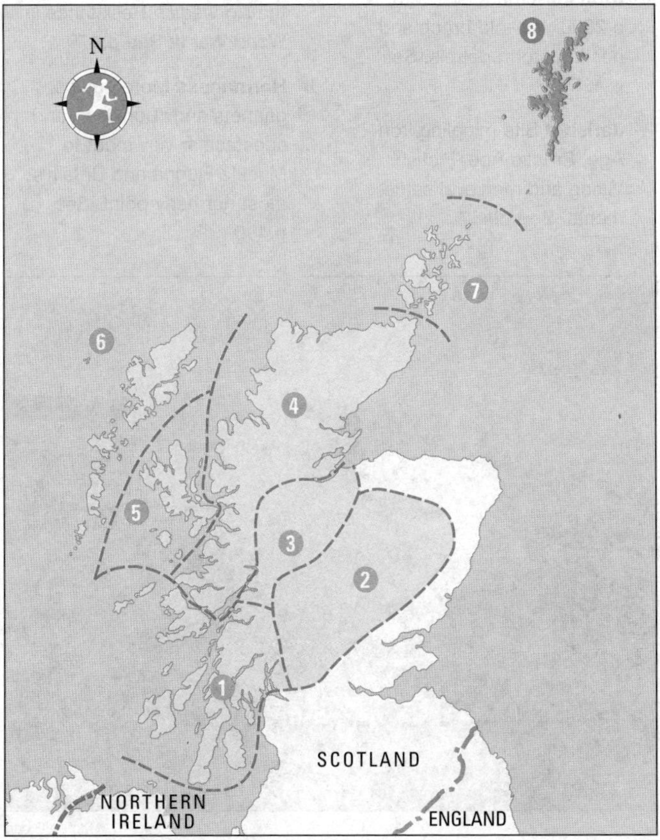

CHAPTER 8

Highlights

* **Traditional music** Catch some local music at the weekly Simmer 'n Sessions in Lerwick, or the annual Shetland Folk Festival. See p.461

* **Isle of Noss** Guaranteed seals, puffins and dive-bombing "bonxies". See p.463

* **Mousa** Remote islet with a 2000-year-old broch and nesting storm petrels. See p.465

* **Jarlshof** Site mingling Iron Age, Bronze Age, Pictish, Viking and medieval settlements. See p.467

* **Fair Isle** Magical little island half-way between Shetland and Orkney, with a lighthouse at each end and a world-famous bird observatory in the middle. See p.468

* **Lunna House** Superb B&B in an old laird's house that was used as the headquarters of the Norwegian Resistance in World War II. See p.479

* **Hermaness** More puffins, gannets and "bonxies", and spectacular views out to Muckle Flugga and Britain's most northerly point. See p.490

△ Mousa Broch

8

Shetland

Shetland is, in nearly all respects, a complete contrast with Orkney. Orkney lies within sight of the Scottish mainland, whereas Shetland lies beyond the horizon. Most maps plonk the islands in a box somewhere off Aberdeen, but in fact they're a lot closer to Bergen in Norway than Edinburgh, and to the Arctic Circle than Manchester. With little fertile ground, Shetlanders have traditionally been crofters rather than farmers, often looking to the sea for an uncertain living in fishing and whaling or the naval and merchant services. The 20,000 or so islanders tend to refer to themselves as Shetlanders first, and, with the unofficial Shetland flag widely displayed, they regard Scotland as a separate and quite distant entity. As in Orkney, "the mainland" is the one in their own archipelago, not the Scottish mainland.

The islands' capital, **Lerwick**, is a busy little port, and, as in Orkney, there are spectacular prehistoric sites to visit such as Jarlshof and Mousa Broch. However, most folk come here for the islands' unique wildlife and **landscape**, a product of the struggle between rock and the forces of water and ice that have, over millennia, tried to break it to pieces. Smoothed by the last glaciation, the surviving land has been exposed to the most violent weather experienced in the British Isles; it isn't for nothing that Shetlanders call the place "the Old Rock", and the coastline, a crust of cliffs with caves, blow-holes and stacks, testifies to the continuing battle. Inland (a relative term, since you're never more than three miles from the sea), the terrain is a barren mix of moorland, often studded with peaty lochs which glitter a brilliant blue when the sun shines, and the occasional patch of green farmland, dotted with hardy, multicoloured sheep and diminutive ponies.

It's impossible to underestimate the influence of the **weather** in these parts. In winter, gales are routine and Shetlanders take even the occasional hurricane in their stride, marking a calm fine day as "a day atween weathers". Even in the summer months, more often than not, it will be windy and rainy; though, as they say in the nearby Faroes, you can have all four seasons in one day. The wind-chill factor is not to be taken lightly, and there is often a dampness or drizzle in the air, even when it's not actually raining. Of course, there are some good spells of dry, sunny weather (which often brings in sea mist) from May to September, but it's the "**simmer dim**", the twilight which lingers through the small hours at this latitude, which makes Shetland summers so memorable; in June especially, the northern sky is an unfinished sunset of blue and burnished copper. Insomniac sheep and seabirds barely settle, and golfers, similarly afflicted, play midnight tournaments.

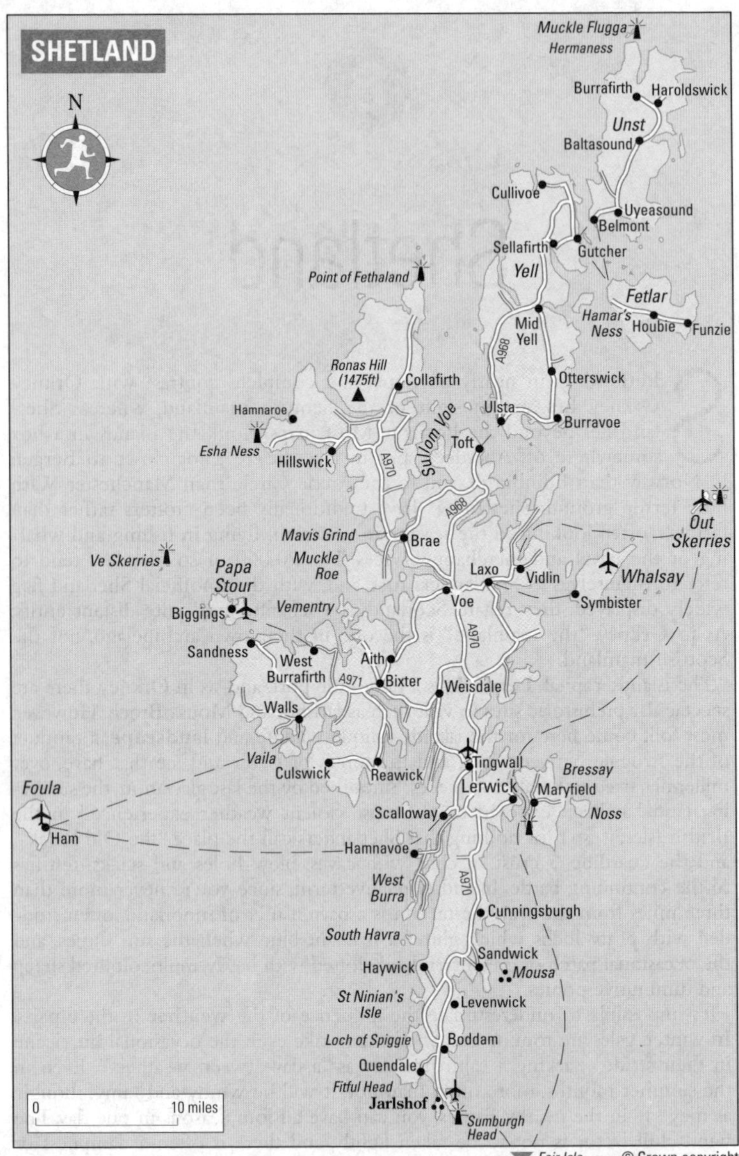

Some history

Since people first began to explore the North Atlantic, Shetland has been a stepping stone on routes between Britain, Ireland and Scandinavia, and people have lived here since **prehistoric times**, certainly from about 3500 BC. The **Norse settlers**, who began to arrive from about 800 AD, with substantial migration from around 900 AD, left the islands with a unique cultural character.

Shetland started out as part of the Orkney earldom, but was ruled directly from Norway for nearly three hundred years after 1195. The Norse legacy is clearly evident today in place names and in the **dialect** (for more on which, see p.545); Shetland was never part of the Gaelic-speaking culture of Highland Scotland, and the later Scottish influence is essentially a Lowland one.

In 1469, Shetland followed Orkney in being **mortgaged to Scotland**, King Christian I of Norway being unable to raise the dowry for the marriage of his daughter, Margaret, to King James III. The Scottish king annexed Shetland in 1472 and the mortgage was never redeemed. Though Shetland retained links with other North Sea communities, religious and administrative practice gradually become Scottish, and **mainland lairds** set about grabbing what land and power they could. The economy soon fell increasingly into the hands of **merchant lairds**; they controlled the fish trade and the tenants who supplied it through a system of truck, or forced barter. It wasn't until the 1886 Crofters' Act and the simultaneous rise of **herring fishing** that ordinary Shetlanders gained some security. However, the boom and the prosperity it brought were short-lived and the economy soon slipped into depression.

During the two world wars, Shetland's role as gatekeeper between the North Sea and North Atlantic meant that the defence of the islands and control of the seas around them were critical: thousands of naval, army and air force personnel were drafted in and some notable relics, such as huge coastal guns, remain. **World War II** also cemented the old links with Norway, Shetland playing a remarkable role in supporting the Norwegian Resistance (see box on p.470). With a rebirth of the local economy in the 1960s, Shetland was able to claim, in the following decade, that the **oil industry** needed the islands more than they needed it. Careful negotiation, backed up by pioneering local legislation, produced a substantial income from oil, which the Shetland Islands Council (SIC) reinvested in the community, building roads, improving housing, keeping the price of ferry tickets down and pouring money into the outlying islands. However, it's clear that the oil boom days are over, and the islanders are having to think afresh how to carve out a living in the new millennium. **Tourism**,

Shetland ponies, sheep and sheepdogs

Shetland is famous for its diminutive **ponies**, but it is still something of a surprise to find so many of the wee beasts on the islands. Traditionally they were used exclusively as pack animals (although a ninth-century carving on Bressay shows a hooded priest riding a very small pony), and their tails were essential for making fishing nets. During the Industrial Revolution, Shetland ponies were exported to work in the mines in England, since they were the only animals small enough to cope with the low galleries. Shetlands then became the playthings of the English upper classes (the Queen Mother was Patron of the Shetland Pony Stud Book Society) and they still enjoy the limelight at the Horse of the Year show.

It's not just the ponies that are small on Shetland either; the native **sheep** are also less substantial than their mainland counterparts. Thought to be descended from those brought by the Vikings, their wool comes in a wide range of colours, is very fine and is used to make the famous "Fair Isle" patterns and shawls so gossamer-thin that they can be passed through a wedding ring. To round up Shetland's small sheep, an even smaller **sheepdog** was bred, crossed with rough-coated collies. These dogs are now recognized as a separate breed, called "shelties", known for their gentleness and devotion as well as their working characteristics of agility and obedience. Their coat is distinctive, being long, straight and rough over a dense furry undercoat – their own thermal wear for Shetland weather conditions.

which has traditionally played only a minor role in the local economy, is beginning to develop slowly. For the moment, however, comparatively few travellers make it out here, and those that do are as likely to be Faroese or Norwegian as British.

Orientation and information

Whatever else you do in Shetland you're sure to find yourself, at some point or other, in the lively port of **Lerwick**, the only town of any size, and the hub of all transport and communications. Many parts of Shetland can be reached from here on a day-trip. **South Mainland**, south of Lerwick, is a narrow finger of land that runs some 25 miles to **Sumburgh Head**; this area is particularly rich in archeological remains, including the Iron Age **Mousa Broch** and the ancient settlement of **Jarlshof**. A further 25 miles south of Sumburgh Head is the remote but thriving **Fair Isle**, synonymous with knitwear and exceptional birdlife.

The **Westside** of Mainland is bleaker and more sparsely inhabited, as is **North Mainland**, although the landscape, particularly to the north, opens out in scale and grandeur as it comes face to face with the Atlantic. Off the west coast, **Papa Stour** lies just a mile from Sandness and boasts some spectacular caves and stacks; much further out are the distinctive peaks and precipitous cliffs of the remote island of **Foula**. Shetland's three **North Isles** bring Britain to a dramatic, windswept end. Their landscapes and seascapes have been shaped by centuries of fierce storms and have an elemental beauty. Nevertheless, they differ markedly from one another: **Yell** has the largest population of otters in Shetland; **Fetlar** is home to the rare red-necked phalarope; north of **Unst**, there's nothing until you reach the North Pole

Supporting an impressive array of **birds and wildlife**, the islands offer excellent bird-watching and coastal walking. The **fishing** is good, too, with lochs well stocked with brown trout, sea trout in the voes and the chance to go sea angling for ling, mackerel or even shark and halibut.

Arrival and island transport

NorthLink Orkney & Shetland Ferries (ⓣ0845/600 0449, ⓦwww.northlinkferries.co.uk) operates a daily overnight **car ferry** from **Aberdeen** to Lerwick, either direct (12hr) or via Kirkwall (13hr). British Airways (ⓣ0870/850 9850) runs **flights** nonstop to Shetland from Aberdeen, Inverness, Kirkwall and Wick, with connections into those airports from Edinburgh, Glasgow, Birmingham, Manchester and London; Highland Airways (ⓣ0845/450 2245) also operates a daily Inverness to Shetland flight and Atlantic Airways runs a summer-only service from London Stansted and the Faroes (ⓣ01737/214255). Shetland's main airport is at **Sumburgh** (ⓣ01950/461000), from where buses make short work of the 25-mile journey north to Lerwick. Standard airfares are high, but various cheaper tickets and special offers are sometimes available (see p.462).

Public transport is pretty good in Shetland, with **buses** fanning out from Lerwick to just about every corner of Mainland, and even via ferries across to Yell and Unst. You can buy the full timetable (£1), which includes all ferries and flights, from Lerwick tourist office. Various **tours** are also available from specialists such as Shetland Wildlife (ⓣ01950/422483, ⓦwww.shetlandwildlife.co.uk). Given the price of bringing a car on the ferry, it might be worth considering using a local **car rental** firm once on the islands (see p.462). **Hitching** is viable and pretty safe, but **cycling** is hard going due to the almost constant wind.

Onwards from Shetland

Thanks to the historical ties and the attraction of a short hop to continental Europe, **Norway** is a popular destination for Shetlanders and Orcadians. Norwegians often think of Shetland and Orkney as their western isles and, particularly in west Norway, old wartime bonds with Shetland are still strong. Norwegian yachts and sail-training vessels are frequent visitors to Lerwick and Kirkwall. Shetlanders can also go by ferry to the **Faroe Islands** – steep, angular shapes rising out of the North Atlantic – and on to **Iceland**.

From late May to early September the large, comfortable and fast Faroese car **ferry** *Norröna,* run by the Smyril Line (Ⓦwww.smyril-line.com), makes weekly return trips from her home port in the Faroe Islands to Shetland, Norway, Iceland and Denmark. From Shetland, the voyages to **Bergen** in Norway or **Tórshavn** in the Faroe Islands both take around thirteen hours; to **Seydisfjördur** in Iceland, it takes thirty hours including a brief stop in the Faroes; on the way back there's a two-day stopover in Faroes while the ship makes a return trip to **Hanstholm** in Denmark.

The council-run **inter-island ferries** are excellent: journey times are mostly less than half an hour, and fares are much cheaper than those in Orkney or the Hebrides. Adults pay around £3 return on most routes, and a car plus driver can cross for around £10 return. There are also British Airways **flights** linking Tingwall airport, five miles west of Lerwick, to Fair Isle and less frequent Loganair flights to Whalsay, Out Skerries, Papa Stour and Foula. (Some Fair Isle flights leave from Sumburgh Airport.) Sample one-way fares include £25 Tingwall to Foula, and £28 Tingwall to Fair Isle; be sure to book well in advance, however, as the planes only take around eight passengers, and be prepared to be flexible, as flights are often cancelled due to the weather. It's also possible to take **boat trips** for pleasure, to explore the coastline and spot birds, seals, porpoises, dolphins and whales; operators include Shetland Wildlife (see opposite), Seabirds-and-Seals (Ⓣ01595/693434, Ⓦwww.seabirds-and-seals.com), and Tom Jamieson from Sandwick for the Broch of Mousa (Ⓣ01950/431367, Ⓦwww.mousaboattrips.co.uk). Specialist services for **diving** or **sea angling** can be tracked down through the Lerwick tourist office.

Lerwick

For Shetlanders, there's only one place to stop, meet and do business, and that's "da toon", **LERWICK**. Very much the focus of Shetland's commercial life, Lerwick is home to about 6600 people, just less than a third of the islands' population. All year, its sheltered **harbour** at the heart of the town is busy with ferries, fishing boats, oil-rig supply vessels and a variety of more specialized craft including seismic survey and naval vessels from all round the North Sea. In summer, the quayside comes alive with local pleasure craft, visiting yachts, cruise liners, historic vessels such as the restored *Swan* and the occasional tall sailing ship. Behind the old harbour is the compact town centre, made up of one long main street, Commercial Street; from here, narrow lanes, known as "**closses**", rise westwards to the late Victorian new town.

Leir Vik ("Muddy Bay") began life as a temporary settlement, catering to the **Dutch** herring fleet in the seventeenth century, which brought in as many as twenty thousand men. It was burnt down in 1614 and 1625 by the jealous and disapproving folk of Scalloway, and again in 1702 by the French fleet. During the

△ Lerwick harbour

nineteenth century, with the presence of ever-larger Scottish, English and Scandinavian boats, it became a major **fishing** centre, and whalers called to pick up crews on their way to the northern hunting grounds. In 1839, the visiting Danish governor of the Faroes declared that "everything made me feel that I had come to the land of opulence". Business was conducted largely from buildings known as **lodberries** (from the Old Norse for "loading rock"), each typically having a store, a house and small yard on a private jetty. **Smuggling** was part of the daily routine, and secret tunnels – some of which still exist – connected the lodberries to illicit stores. During the late nineteenth century, the construction of the Esplanade along the shore isolated several lodberries from the sea, but further south beyond the *Queen's Hotel* are some that still show their original form. Lerwick expanded considerably at this time and the large houses and grand public buildings established then still dominate, notably the **Town Hall**, which remains the most prominent landmark. Another period of rapid growth began during the oil boom of the 1970s, with the farmland to the southwest disappearing under a suburban sprawl, and the town's northern approaches becoming an industrial estate.

Arrival, information and accommodation

First impressions of Lerwick are very much dependent on the weather (and, if you arrive by boat, the crossing you've just experienced). The **ferry terminal** is situated in the unprepossessing north harbour, about a mile from the town centre: just walk south down Holmsgarth Road, east along North Road and on into Commercial Road. **Flying** into Sumburgh Airport, you can take one of the regular buses to Lerwick; taxis (around £25) and car rental are also available. Buses stop on the Esplanade, very close to the old harbour and Market Cross, or at the Viking bus station on Commercial Road, a little to the north of the town centre. Orientation within Lerwick is straightforward: the town is small and everything is within easy walking distance.

The **tourist office**, at the Market Cross on Commercial Street (May–Sept Mon–Sat 8am–6pm, Sun 10am–1pm; Oct–April Mon–Fri 9am–5pm;

Ⓣ01595/693434, Ⓦwww.visitshetland.com), is a good source of information, and will book accommodation for a small fee. At any time in the summer and over the Folk Festival weekend in April, accommodation can be in short supply, so it's a good idea to book in advance. Once you're here, pick up a copy of the annual *Shetland Visitor* magazine, and the weekly *Shetland Times*, to get an idea of what's going on.

Accommodation

Shetland's best **hotels** are not to be found in Lerwick, which has been spoilt in the past by the steady supply of visitors in the oil business. The town's **B&Bs** and **guesthouses** are usually better value for money, and will allow you to get closer to Shetland life.

The SYHA **hostel** (Ⓣ01595/692114, Ⓦwww.islesburgh.org.uk; Easter–Sept) at Islesburgh House on King Harald Street, offers unusually comfortable surroundings and has family rooms, a café and useful laundry facilities. The *Clickimin* **campsite** (Ⓣ01595/741000, Ⓦwww.srt.org.uk; May–Sept) enjoys the excellent facilities of the neighbouring Clickimin leisure centre, including good hot showers, but its sheltered suburban location is far from idyllic.

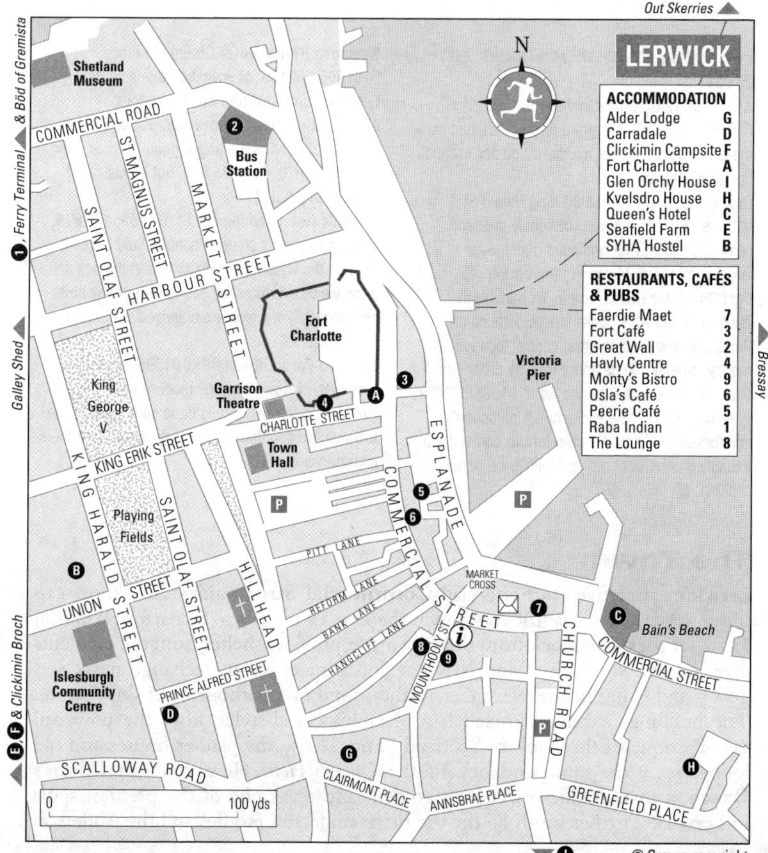

Böds

With only one official SYHA hostel in the whole of Shetland, it's worth knowing about the islands' unique network of **camping böds**, which are open from April to September. Traditionally, a böd was a small building beside the shore, where fishermen used to house their gear and occasionally sleep; the word was also applied to trading posts established by merchants of the Hanseatic League. Today, the tourist board uses the term pretty loosely: none of the places they run is strictly speaking a böd, ranging instead from stone-built cottages to weatherboarded sail lofts. In order to stay at a böd, you must **book in advance** through Shetland Amenity Trust (ⓣ01595/694688, ⓦwww.camping-bods.com), as there are no live-in wardens. All the böds have some form of (primitive) heating system, cold water, toilets, a kitchen (though no stove or cooking utensils) and bunk beds (but as yet no mattresses), so a sleeping bag and bedding mat are pretty much essential. If you're on a camping trip, they're a great way to escape the wind and rain for a night or two; they're also remarkably good value, at around £5 per person per night. Except in June, July and August, it's even possible to pay for exclusive use of any of the böds; prices range from £35 to £90 per night depending on the size of the böd. **Camping rough** is also possible in Shetland, with the landowner's permission, but make sure you're fully equipped for the Shetland wind.

Hotels, guesthouses and B&Bs

Alder Lodge Guest House 6 Clairmont Place ⓣ01595/695705. Converted former Victorian bank that's probably the best middle-range accommodation available. ③

Carradale Guest House 36 King Harald St ⓣ01595/692251, ⓦwww.carradale.shetland.co.uk. Spacious, well-equipped guesthouse in a large, comfortable Victorian family home. ②

Fort Charlotte Guest House 1 Charlotte St ⓣ01595/692140, ⓦwww.fortcharlotte.co.uk. Small guesthouse with great central location, mostly en-suite rooms and a friendly proprietor. ③

Glen Orchy House 20 Knab Rd ⓣ01595/692031, ⓦwww.guesthouselerwick.com. A particularly comfortable, fully modernized former convent that's virtually a hotel, licensed and with good home-cooking. ⑤

Kvelsdro House Hotel Greenfield Place ⓣ01595/692195, ⓦwww.kgqhotels.co.uk. Lerwick's smartest and most luxurious establishment (pronounced "kelro"), with immaculate bedrooms and a good harbour view from the bar. It's hard to find, but locals can usually help out. ⑥

Queen's Hotel Commercial St ⓣ01595/692826, ⓦwww.kgqhotels.co.uk. A beautiful old building right on the waterfront with its feet in the sea and great views over Bressay Sound from many of its bedrooms, all of which are equipped with modern furnishings. ⑥

Seafield Farm Off Sea Rd ⓣ01595/693853. A very friendly B&B in a huge modern farmhouse overlooking the sea, a mile or so southwest of the town centre and therefore best for those with their own transport. ②

The Town

Lerwick's attractive, flagstone-clad **Commercial Street**, universally known to locals as "da street", is still very much the core of the town. Its narrow, winding form, set back one block from the Esplanade, provides shelter from the elements even on the worst days, and is where locals meet, shop, exchange news and gossip and bring in the New Year to the sound of a harbourful of ships' sirens. The buildings exhibit a mixed bag of architectural styles, from the powerful neo-Baroque of the Bank of Scotland at no. 117 to the plainer houses and old lodberries at the south end, beyond the *Queen's Hotel*. Here, you'll find **Bain's Beach**, a small, hidden stretch of golden sand that's one of the prettiest spots in Lerwick. Further south lie the Victorian Anderson Homes and the Anderson

High School, the latter's ornate, Franco-Scottish towers and dormers now unfortunately rather lost among later additions. Both were the gift of **Arthur Anderson** (1792–1868), co-founder of the Peninsular and Oriental Steam Navigation Company (P&O), for more on whom see p.460.

The Street's northern end is marked by the towering walls of **Fort Charlotte** (daily: June–Sept 9am–10pm; Oct–May 9am–4pm; free), which once stood directly above the beach. Begun for Charles II in 1665 during the wars with the Dutch, the fort was attacked and burnt down by the Dutch fleet in August 1673. In the 1780s it was repaired and given its name in honour of George III's queen. Since then, it's served as a prison and a Royal Navy training centre; it's now open to the public, except on rare occasions when it's used by the Territorial Army. The fort affords good views from its solid battlements, and has four replica eighteenth-century cannons pointing out across Bressay Sound.

Although the narrow lanes or **closses** that connect the Street to Hillhead are now a desirable place to live, it's not so long ago that they were regarded as slumlike dens of iniquity, from which the better-off escaped to the Victorian new town laid out to the west on a grid plan. The steep stone-flagged lanes are now fun to explore, each one lined by tall houses with trees, fuchsias, flowering currants and honeysuckle pouring over the garden walls. If you look at the street signs, you can see that all the closses have two names: their former ones and their current titles, chosen in 1845 by the Police Commissioners – Reform, Fox and Pitt, reflecting the liberal political culture of the period – or derived from the writings of Sir Walter Scott.

Hillhead, up in the Victorian new town, is dominated by the splendid **Town Hall** (Mon–Thurs 9am–5pm, Fri 9am–4pm; free), a Scottish Baronial monument

Up Helly-Aa

On the last Tuesday in January, whatever the weather, Lerwick's new town is the setting for the most spectacular part of the **Up Helly-Aa**, a huge fire festival, the largest of several held in Shetland from January to March. Around nine hundred torchbearing participants, all male and all in extraordinary costumes, march in procession behind a grand Viking longship. The annually appointed Guizer Jarl and his "squad" appear as Vikings and brandish shields and silver axes; each of the forty or so other squads is dressed for their part in the subsequent entertainment, perhaps as giant insects, space invaders or ballet dancers. Their circuitous route leads to the King George V Playing Field where, after due ceremony, all the torches are thrown into the longship, creating an enormous bonfire. A firework display follows, then the participants, known as "guizers", set off in their squads to do the rounds of more than a dozen "halls" (which usually include at least one hotel and the Town Hall) from around 8.30pm in the evening until 8am the next morning, performing some kind of act – usually a comedy routine – at each.

Up Helly-Aa itself is not that ancient, dating only from Victorian times, when it was introduced to replace the much older Christmas tradition of rolling burning tar barrels through the streets, which was banned in 1874. Seven years later a torchlight procession took place, which eventually developed into a full-blown Viking celebration, known as "Up Helly-Aa". Although this is essentially a community event with entry to halls by invitation only, visitors are welcome at the Town Hall, for which tickets are sold in early January; contact the tourist office well in advance. To catch some of the atmosphere of the event, check out the annual Up Helly-Aa exhibition in the **Galley Shed** on St Sunniva Street (mid-May to mid-Sept Tues 2–4pm & 7–9pm, Fri 7–9pm, Sat 2–4pm; £3), where you can see a full-size longship, costumes, shields and photographs.

to civic pride, built by public subscription. Visitors are free to wander round the building (providing there are no functions going on), to admire the wonderful stained-glass windows in the main hall, which celebrate Shetland's history, and to climb the castellated central tower that occupies the town's highest point.

Lerwick's one other tourist sight is the **Shetland Museum** (Wed–Sat 10am–5pm; free; ⓦwww.shetland-museum.org.uk), which has recently moved to its new purpose-built waterfront premises at Hay's Dock, off Commercial Road. The museum was closed at the time of going to print, but will house the museum's wonderful collection of nauticalia. More unusual exhibits include Shetland's oldest telephone, fitted with a ceramic mouthpiece, and a carved head of Goliath by Adam Christie (1869–1950), a Shetlander who spent much of his life in Montrose Asylum, and who is perhaps best known for his application to patent a submarine built of glass, which would thus be invisible to enemies.

Clickimin Broch and the Böd of Gremista

A mile or so southwest of the town centre on the road leading to Sumburgh, the much-restored **Clickimin Broch** stands on what was once a small island in Loch Clickimin. The settlement here began as a small farmstead around 700 BC and was later enclosed by a defensive wall. The main tower served as a castle and probably rose to around 40ft, as at Mousa (see p.465), though the remains are now not much more than 10ft high. There are two small entrances, one at ground level and the other on the first floor, which are carefully protected by outer defences and smaller walls. With the modern housing in the middle distance, it's pretty hard to imagine the original setting or sense the magical atmosphere of the place. Excavation of the site has unearthed an array of domestic goods that suggest international trade, including a Roman glass bowl thought to have been made in Alexandria around 100 AD.

In earlier times the seasonal nature of the Shetland fishing industry led to the establishment of small stores, known as **böds** (see box on p.458), often incorporating sleeping accommodation, beside the beaches where fish were landed and dried. Just beyond Lerwick's main ferry terminal, a mile and a half north of the town centre, stands the **Böd of Gremista** (May to mid-Sept Wed–Sun 10am–1pm & 2–5pm; free; ⓦwww.shetland-museum.org.uk), the birthplace of **Arthur Anderson** (1792–1868). Though almost lost among the surrounding industrial estate, the building has been completely restored and the displays explore Anderson's life as beach boy (helping to cure and dry fish), naval seaman, businessman, philanthropist, Shetland's first native MP and founder of Shetland's first newspaper, the *Shetland Journal*. Built at the end of the eighteenth century for Anderson's father, the ground floor was originally used as an office and fish-curing station, while the trader and his family resided permanently upstairs.

Eating

Shetland produces a huge harvest of fresh fish from the surrounding seas, including shellfish and salmon, and from the land there's superb lamb and even local tomatoes, cucumbers and peppers, grown under glass. The most celebrated local delicacy is *reestit* mutton: steeped in brine, then air-dried, it's the base for a potato soup cooked and adored by the locals around New Year. Unfortunately, the **food** on offer in the majority of Lerwick's hotels and pubs doesn't do these ingredients justice. It's not even possible to assemble a decent picnic without resorting to a visit to the supermarket, situated a mile or so southwest of town, opposite the Clickimin Broch.

Daytime cafés

Faerdie-Maet Commercial St (by the post office). Cosy café serving generously filled rolls to eat in or take away, as well as cakes, teas, real cappuccino and good ice cream. No smoking. Closed Sun.

Havly Centre 9 Charlotte St. Spacious Norwegian lunchtime café, with big comfy sofas and armchairs and a kids' corner; it offers home-made cakes, bread and pizzas. Closed Sun.

Osla's Café Commercial St. Situated opposite the *Grand Hotel*, the downstairs café-bar specializes in savoury and sweet pancakes; upstairs is the evening-only *La Piazza*, serving up pizza and pasta. Closed Sun.

Peerie Café Esplanade. Funky designer shop/gallery/café in an old lodberry, with imaginative cakes, soup and sandwiches, and what is probably Britain's northernmost latte. Closed Sun.

Restaurants

Fort Café 2 Commercial St. Lerwick's best fish-and-chip shop, situated below Fort Charlotte: take away or eat inside in the small café. Closed Sun lunch. Inexpensive.

Great Wall Viking Bus Station ⓣ01595/693988. A Chinese/Thai restaurant located above the bus station. Highly rated by the locals. Moderate.

Kvelsdro House Hotel Greenfield Place ⓣ01595/692195. The traditional bar meals or table d'hôte, served in the modern cocktail bar overlooking Bressay Sound, are above average in price and quality. Moderate to expensive.

Monty's Bistro 5 Mounthooly St ⓣ01595/696555. Unpretentious place serving inexpensive and delicious meals and snacks at lunchtimes, and accomplished contemporary cooking – the best in Lerwick – in the evening, with friendly service. Closed Sun & Mon. Moderate.

Raba Indian Restaurant 26 Commercial Rd ⓣ01595/695585. A consistently excellent curry house, with cheerful, efficient service and reasonable prices. Moderate.

Drinking, nightlife and entertainment

The friendliest **pub** in town is the upstairs bar in *The Lounge*, up Mounthooly Street, where local musicians often do sessions. If you're desperate to keep going until the early hours, you have a choice of two main discos: *Posers* (Wed & Fri), a small **nightclub** at the back of the *Grand Hotel* on Commercial Street, or the *North Star* up Harbour Street (Sat only). The Garrison Theatre (ⓣ01595/692114, ⓦwww.islesburgh.org.uk), by the Town Hall, shows occasional **films** as well as putting on theatre productions, comedy acts and live gigs. The Islesburgh Community Centre has introduced regular **crafts and culture evenings** (late May to early Sept Mon & Wed 7–9.30pm), where you can buy local knitwear, chat to some locals and listen to traditional music.

Music features very strongly in Shetland life and every style has an enthusiastic following. The emphasis in traditional music is firmly instrumental, not vocal, with substantial numbers of young people learning the fiddle. In late April or early May, musicians from all over the world converge on Shetland for the excellent four-day **Shetland Folk Festival** (ⓣ01595/694757, ⓦwww.shetlandfolkfestival.com), which embraces a wider range of musical styles than the title might suggest; there are concerts and dances in every corner of the islands. There are further musical gatherings in mid-June, when the newly founded three-day **Blues Festival** (ⓦwww.lerwick.plus.com/sbf/frameset.html) takes place, and in mid-October, there's an **Accordion and Fiddle Festival** (ⓦwww.shetlandaccordionandfiddle.com.

As well as the regular musical offerings at the Islesburgh (see above), there are **informal sessions**, held regularly over the summer in *The Lounge* (Wed & Fri eves & Sat), and *Da Noost* (Fri) two pubs on Commercial Street in Lerwick, on visiting cruise ships, and in various other venues on the islands (ⓦwww.shetland-music.com). Throughout the year, there are also **traditional dances** in local halls all over Shetland; the whole community turns up and you can watch, or join in with, dances like the Boston Two-Step, quadrilles or the Foula Reel. There are also full-on **gigs** featuring a surprising number of accomplished local groups: legendary local fiddler Aly Bain (see p.511) and the likes of Fiddlers Bid make occasional appearances on the islands. For details of **what's on**, listen in to *Good Evening Shetland* on BBC Radio Shetland, 92.7FM (Mon–Fri 5.30pm),or buy the *Shetland Times* on Fridays (Ⓦwww.shetlandtoday.co.uk). Some events are also advertised on Shetland's independent radio station SIBC, 96.2FM. To pick up a CD or cassette of traditional Shetland music, head for High Level Music, up the steps by the chemists on the Market Cross.

Not surprisingly, another Shetland passion is **boating and yachting**, and regattas take place most summer weekends, in different venues throughout the islands. The sport of **yoal racing** has a big following, too, and teams from different districts compete passionately in large six-oared boats which used to serve as the backbone of Shetland's fishing industry. If you plan ahead, you could take a trip on the *Swan* (Ⓣ01595/697406, Ⓦwww.theswan.shetland.co.uk), a 67ft restored wooden **sailing ship** built locally as a fishing smack in 1900, which undertakes various trips, from one to nine days long, as far afield as Norway and the Faroes.

Listings

Airports Tingwall airport Ⓣ01595/840246; Sumburgh airport Ⓣ01950/460654.
Banks Clydesdale, Bank of Scotland and Royal Bank of Scotland are all on Commercial St; Lloyds TSB is the gleaming and locally controversial structure on the Esplanade.
Bike rental Grantfield Garage, Commercial Rd Ⓣ01595/692709, Ⓦwww.grantfieldgarage.co.uk.
Bookshops Shetland Times Bookshop, 71–79 Commercial St (Ⓣ01595/695531, Ⓦwww.shetlandtoday.co.uk; closed Sun).
Bus information Ⓣ01595/694100.
Car rental Bolts Car Hire, 26 North Rd Ⓣ01595/693636, Ⓦwww.boltscarhire.co.uk; John Leask & Sons, Esplanade Ⓣ01595/693162, Ⓦwww.leaskstravel.co.uk; Star Rent-a-Car, 22 Commercial Rd Ⓣ01595/692075, Ⓦwww.starrentacar.co.uk. All of these also have offices at Sumburgh airport.
Consulates Denmark, Iceland and Sweden: Hay & Co, 66 Commercial Rd Ⓣ01595/692533; Finland, France, Germany and Norway: Shearer Shipping Services, Garthspool Ⓣ01595/692556.
Internet access At the tourist office or the SYIS opposite.
Laundry For self-service laundry head for Manson's Dry Cleaners (closed Sat lunch & Sun), behind the garage, west of the roundabout by the Somerfield supermarket.
Medical care The Gilbert Bain Hospital Ⓣ01595/743000, and the Lerwick Health Centre Ⓣ01595/693201, are opposite each other on Scalloway Rd.
Sports centre The large, modern Clickimin Leisure Centre is in Lochside, on the west side of town by Loch Clickimin (Ⓣ01595/694555, Ⓦwww.srt.org.uk), with a superb leisure pool, bowling, a café and bar.

Bressay and Noss

Shielding Lerwick from the full force of the North Sea is the island of **Bressay**, dominated at its southern end by the conical Ward Hill (744ft) – "da Wart" – and accessible on an hourly car and passenger ferry from Lerwick (takes 5min). At the end of the nineteenth century, Bressay had a population of around eight hundred, due mostly to the prosperity brought by the Dutch herring fleet; now about four hundred people live here. If you've time to kill before the ferry, pop into the **Bressay Heritage Centre** (Tues, Wed, Fri & Sat 10am–4pm, Sun 11am–5.30pm; free; Ⓦwww.bressay-history-group.org), by the ferry terminal in **MARYFIELD**, where the local history group puts on temporary exhibitions. A short distance to the north lies **Gardie House**, built in 1724 and, in its Neoclassical detail, one of the finest of Shetland's laird houses, where the likes of Sir Walter Scott and minor royalty once stayed, and now home to the Lord Lieutenant of Shetland.

In 1917, convoys of merchant ships would gather in Bressay Sound before travelling under naval escort across the Atlantic. Huge World War I gun batteries at Score Hill on Aith Ness in the north, and on Bard Head in the south, were constructed, and now provide a focus for a couple of interesting cliff and coastal walks. Another fine walk can be made to **Bressay Lighthouse**, three miles south of the ferry terminal at Kirkibuster Ness, built by the Stevensons in the 1850s. The lighthouse contains several self-catering cottages and will eventually house a **camping böd** (call Shetland Amenity Trust ⓣ01595/694688 for the latest). **Accommodation** is available at *Maryfield House* near the ferry terminal (ⓣ01595/820207; ④), the island's unremarkable hotel and pub.

Noss

The chief reason most visitors pass through Bressay is in order to visit the tiny but spectacular island of **Noss** – the name means "a point of rock" – just off Bressay's eastern shore. Sloping gently into the sea at its western end, and

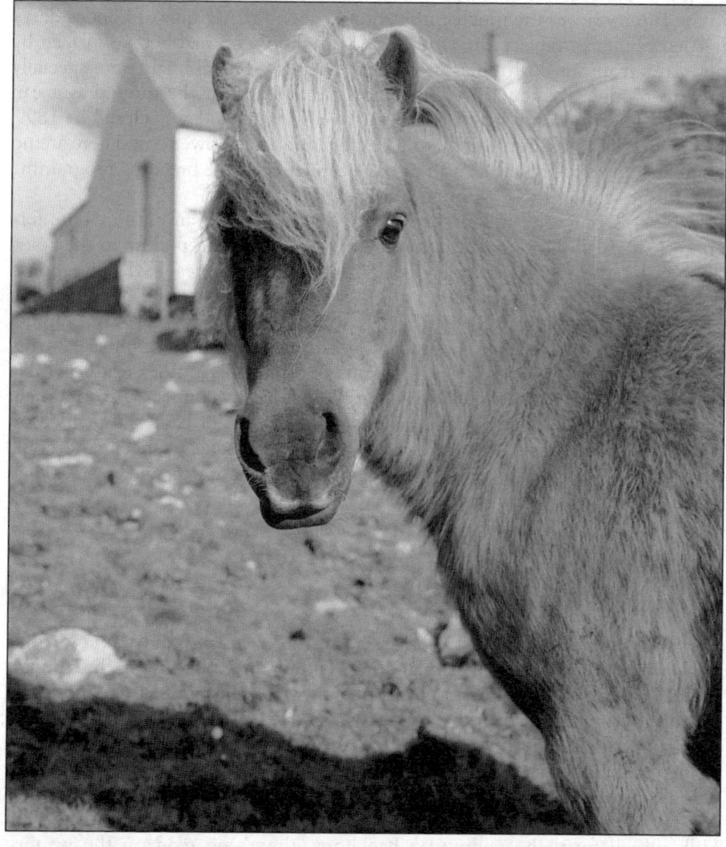

△ Shetland pony

plunging vertically from over 500ft at its eastern end, Noss has the dramatic and distinctive outline of a half-sunk ocean liner. The island was inhabited until World War II but is now a nature reserve and sheep farm, partly managed by Scottish Natural Heritage, who operate an inflatable as a **ferry** from Bressay (May–Aug Tues, Wed & Fri–Sun; £3 return; phone ⓣ0800/107 7818). The ferry departs from the landing stage below the car park overlooking Noss Sound, two miles from Maryfield – an easy stroll or short journey on bikes rented in Lerwick beforehand. A morning postcar takes over two hours to reach Noss Sound from Maryfield. If the weather is abnormally windy, check to make sure the Noss ferry is running before setting off.

A more convenient, but more expensive alternative is to join one of the **boat trips** that set out from Lerwick to see the rock arches and caves of Bressay and the cliffs and nesting seabirds on Noss: try Seabirds and Seals (May–Aug 2 daily; £30; ⓣ01595/693434, ⓦwww.seabirds-and-seals.com).

On the island, the old farmhouse, or Haa of Gungstie, contains a small **visitor centre** (open whenever the ferry is operating), where the warden will give you a quick briefing and a free map and guide. Nearby is a sandy beach, perfect for a picnic in fine weather, while behind the Haa is a **Pony Pund**, a square stone enclosure built for the breeding of Shetland ponies. A stud was established here in the latter years of the nineteenth century, when the Marquis of Londonderry needed ponies to replace the women and children who had been displaced by new laws from his coal mines in County Durham. The animals were specially bred to produce "as much weight as possible and as near the ground as it can be got". The stud only lasted for about twenty years and was closed in 1899, superseded by English studs able to meet the demand at lower cost. There are no ponies on Noss today, but it's said that the influence of the breeding programme can still be seen in those roaming other parts of Shetland.

As Noss is only one mile wide, it's easy enough to do an entire circumference of the island in one day. If you do, make sure you keep close to the coast, since otherwise the great skuas (locally known as "bonxies") will dive-bomb you. The most memorable feature of Noss is its eastern coastline of cliffs, rising to a peak at the massive **Noup** (500ft), from which can be seen vast colonies of cliff-nesting gannets, puffins, guillemots, shags, razorbills and fulmars: a truly wonderful sight and one of the highlights of Shetland. Another feature visible on the walk is the **Holm of Noss**; until 1864, it was connected to the main island by an extraordinary device called a cradle, a sort of basket suspended on ropes which was intended to allow access for the grazing of sheep. The Foula man who allegedly installed it in the seventeenth century is said to have died when, preferring to climb back down the cliffs, he fell.

South Mainland

Shetland's **South Mainland** is a long, thin finger of land, only three or four miles wide, but twenty-five miles long, ending in the cliffs of **Sumburgh Head** and **Fitful Head**. It's a beautiful area with wild undulating landscapes, lots of good green farmland, fabulous views out to sea and the mother of all brochs on the island of **Mousa**, just off the east coast. The most concentrated points of interest are at the southern end of the peninsula, with its seabird colonies, crofting museum and, in particular, **Jarlshof**, Shetland's most impressive archeological treasure. The main road hugs the eastern side of the Clift Hills which form the peninsula's backbone; there's no road on the western side between Scalloway and Maywick, except for a short spur from Easter to Wester Quarff.

Sandwick and Mousa

Halfway down the South Mainland, opposite the parish of **SANDWICK**, the island of **Mousa** boasts the most amazingly well-preserved broch in the whole of Scotland. Rising to more than 40ft, and looking rather like a Stone Age cooling tower, **Mousa Broch** has a remarkable presence, and features in both *Egil's Saga* and the *Orkneyinga Saga*, contemporary chronicles of Norse exploration and settlement. In the former, a couple eloping from Norway to Iceland around 900 AD take refuge in it after being shipwrecked, while in the latter the broch is besieged by an Earl Harald Maddadarson when his mother is abducted and brought here from Orkney by Erlend the Young, who wanted to marry her. To get to the broch, simply head south from the jetty along the western coastline for about half a mile. The low entrance passage leads through two concentric walls to a central courtyard, divided into separate beehive chambers. Between the walls, a rough (very dark) staircase leads to the top parapet; a torch is provided for visitors.

To reach Mousa, take the small **passenger ferry** from Leebotton in the district of Sandwick (mid-April to mid-Sept 2 daily; takes 15min; £8 return; ⓣ01950/431367, ⓦwww.mousaboattrips.co.uk), though it's best to ring ahead to check the current schedule. Mousa is only a mile wide, but if the weather's not too bad it's easy enough to spend the whole day here. For a start, there are usually lots of grey and common **seals** sunning themselves on the rocks by the East and West Pool, at the southeastern corner of the island, plus black guillemots (or "tysties" as they're known in Shetland) breeding along the low-lying coast, and arctic tern colonies inland. Elsewhere, there are the remains of several buildings, some of which were inhabited until the mid-nineteenth century. From late May to mid-July, a large colony of around six thousand **storm petrels** breeds in and around the broch walls, fishing out at sea during the day and only returning to the nests after dark. The ferry also runs special late-night trips (Wed & Sat weather permitting), setting off in the "simmer dim" twilight around 11pm. Even if you've no interest in the storm petrels, which appear like bats as they flit about in the half-light, the chance to explore the broch at midnight is worth it alone.

In Hoswick, a mile or so southwest of Leebotton, is **Hoswick Visitor Centre** (May–Sept Mon–Sat 10am–5pm, Sun 11am–5pm; free), with a permanent exhibition on crofting, haaf fishing, whaling, old radios and the copper and iron mines beyond Sand Lodge. The Betty Mouat story (see p.466) is also told here and there's a café serving cakes, tea and coffee.

St Ninian's Isle to Quendale

A little beyond Sandwick, on the main road south, it's possible to cross to **BIGTON**, on the west coast of the South Mainland. From the village, a signposted track leads down to a spectacular sandy causeway, or **tombolo**, leading to **St Ninian's Isle**. The tombolo – a concave strip of shell sand with Atlantic breakers crashing on either side, the best example of its kind in Britain – is usually exposed; you can walk over to the island, where there are the ruins of a church probably dating from the twelfth century and built on the site of an earlier, Pictish, one. The site was excavated in the 1950s and **treasure**, a hoard of 28 objects of Pictish silver, was found hidden in a larch box beneath a slab in the earlier building's floor; the larch probably came from the European mainland, as it didn't grow in Britain at that time. The treasure included bowls, a spoon and brooches and is thought to date from around 800 AD; it may have been hastily hidden during a Norse raid. Replicas are in the Shetland Museum in Lerwick and the originals can be seen in the Museum of Scotland in Edinburgh.

South of Bigton, the coast is attractive: cliffs alternate with beaches and the vivid greens and yellows of the farmland contrast with black rocks and a sea which may be grey, deep blue or turquoise. The **Loch of Spiggie**, which used to be a sea inlet, attracts large autumn flocks of some four hundred whooper swans; it's pretty quiet the rest of the year, though you've a chance of spotting red-throated divers. A track leads from the east side of the loch to a long, reasonably sheltered sandy beach known as the **Scousburgh Sands**.

Over on the east coast, a back road winds around to the **Croft House Museum** (May–Sept daily 10am–1pm & 2–5pm; free; ⓦ www.shetland-museum.org.uk) in Southvoe. Housed in a fairly well-to-do thatched croft built around 1870, the museum tries to recreate the feel of late nineteenth-century crofting life, with a peat fire, traditional box beds and so forth. Adjacent to the living quarters is the byre for the cows and tatties, and the kiln for drying the grain. Crofting was mostly done by women in Shetland, while the men went out haaf fishing for the laird. Down by the nearby burn, there's also a restored thatched horizontal mill.

A few miles south of Loch Spiggie lies **QUENDALE**, overlooking a sandy south-facing bay. The village contains the beautifully restored full-size **Quendale Watermill** (mid-April to mid-Oct daily 10am–5pm; £2; ⓦ www.quendalemill.shetland.co.uk), built in the 1860s but not in operation since the early 1970s. You can explore the interior and watch a short video of the mill working, and there's a tearoom attached. Not far from Quendale, near the head of the rocky inlet of Cro Geo, on the other side of Garths Ness, lies a rusting ship's bow, all that remains of the **Braer oil tanker**, a Liberian-registered, American-owned ship that ran onto the rocks here at 11.13am on January 5, 1993, a wild Tuesday morning etched in the memory of every Shetlander. Although the *Braer* released twice the quantity of oil spilt even by the *Exxon Valdez* in Alaska, the damage was less serious than it might have been, due to the oil being churned and ultimately cleansed by huge waves driven by hurricane-force winds which, unusually even for Shetland, blew for most of January.

Sumburgh

Shetland's southernmost parish is known as **Dunrossness** or "The Ness", a rolling agricultural landscape (one often compared with that of Orkney), dominated from the west by the great brooding mass of Fitful Head (929ft). The main road leads to **SUMBURGH**, whose **airport** is busy with helicopters and aircraft shuttling to and from the North Sea oilfields, as well as passenger services, and **GRUTNESS**, the minuscule ferry terminal for Fair Isle.

By the main road, just west of the airport, excavations are currently under way at **Old Scatness Broch & Iron Age Village** (May–Oct daily except Fri & Sat 10am–5.30pm; £2), where a vast Iron Age settlement is currently being excavated. First off, you get a guided tour of the site from a viewing platform, followed by a taste of life in a restored wheel-house in Norse and Pictish times, provided by costumed guides and a weaving demonstration.

In the nearby village of Scatness itself is **Betty Mouat's Cottage** (now restored as a camping böd). Betty Mouat was quite a character. In January 1886, at the age of 60, she set off for Lerwick in the smack *Columbine*, crewed by three local men. A storm swept the skipper overboard and the other two jumped in to try to rescue him; they failed, the skipper drowned and the two men, though they survived, lost contact with the smack. Betty and her boat were battered by the storm for nine days and nights, finally running ashore north of Aalesund in Norway. Astonishingly, she survived this experience, existing on some milk which she had with her. She returned to Shetland to become a celebrity, living into her nineties.

The Mainland comes to a dramatic end at **Sumburgh Head** (262ft), which rises sharply out of the land only to drop vertically into the sea about a mile or so southeast of Jarlshof. The **lighthouse**, on the top of the cliff, was built by Robert Stevenson in 1821, and is not open to the public. However, its grounds offer great views northwards to Noss and south to Fair Isle, as well as being the perfect site for watching nesting seabirds such as kittiwakes, fulmars, shags, razorbills and guillemots, not to mention gannets diving for fish. This is also the easiest place in Shetland to get close to **puffins**: during the nesting season (May to early Aug), you simply need to look over the western wall, just before you enter the lighthouse complex, to see them arriving at their burrows a few yards below with beakfuls of sand eels or giving flying lessons to their offspring.

Jarlshof

Of all the archeological sites in Shetland, **Jarlshof** (April–Sept daily 9.30am–6.30pm; HS; £3.30; Oct–March open access to grounds; free) is the largest and most impressive. What makes Jarlshof so amazing is the fact that you can walk right into a house built 1600 years ago, which is still intact to above head height. The site is big and confusing, scattered with the ruins of buildings dating from the Stone Age to the early seventeenth century. The name, which is misleading as it is not primarily a Viking site, was coined by Sir Walter Scott, who decided to use the ruins of the Old House in his novel *The Pirate*. However, it was only at the end of the nineteenth century that the Bronze Age, Iron Age and Viking settlements you see now were discovered, after a violent storm ripped off the top layer of turf.

The site guidebook, available from the small **visitor centre** where you buy tickets, is very badly designed, and you'd be just as well off using the information panels. The Bronze Age smithy and Iron Age dwellings nearest the entrance, dating from the second and first millennia BC, are nothing compared with the cells which cluster around the **broch**, close to the sea. Only half of the original broch survives, and its courtyard is now an Iron Age aisled roundhouse, with stone piers. However, it's difficult to distinguish the broch from the later Pictish **wheelhouses** which now surround it. Still, it's all great fun to explore, as, unlike at Skara Brae in Orkney, you're free to roam around the cells, checking out the in-built stone shelving, water tanks, beds and so on. Inland lies the maze of grass-topped foundations marking out the **Viking longhouses**, dating from the ninth century AD and covering a much larger area than the earlier structures. Towering over the whole complex are the ruins of the laird's house, built by Robert Stewart, Earl of Orkney and Lord of Shetland, in the late sixteenth century, and the **Old House of Sumburgh**, built by his son, Earl Patrick.

South Mainland practicalities

Accommodation in the South Mainland is provided by several comfortable modern B&Bs, such as *Setterbrae* (Ⓣ01950/440468, Ⓦwww.setterbrae.co.uk; ❸), located a stone's throw from the *Spiggie Hotel* (Ⓣ01950/460563, Ⓦwww.thespiggiehotel.co.uk; ❺), which has a lively bar serving real ales and a **restaurant**

with great views over the Loch of Spiggie and out to Foula; both serve very reasonably priced and well-presented dishes. Over in Bigton, you can get soup and simple sandwiches at the *St Ninian's Isle Café* (closed Tues), whilst enjoying the views out to Foula. There's **hostel** accommodation at the modern *Cunningsburgh Village Club* (ⓣ01950/477241; June–Aug), some ten miles south of Lerwick, and a **camping böd** in *Betty Mouat's Cottage* (ⓣ01595/694688, ⓦwww.camping-bods.com; April–Sept), in Scatness, at the tip of the peninsula, close to the airport. At Levenwick, around eighteen miles south of Lerwick, a small, terraced **campsite** is run by the local community (ⓣ01950/422207, ⓦwww.levenwick.shetland.co.uk; May–Sept), with hot showers, a tennis court and a superb view over the east coast.

Fair Isle

Fair Isle (ⓦwww.fairisle.org.uk) measures just three miles by one-and-a-half, marooned in the sea half-way between Shetland and Orkney and very different from both. The weather reflects its isolated position: you can almost guarantee that it'll be windy, though if you're lucky your visit might coincide with fine

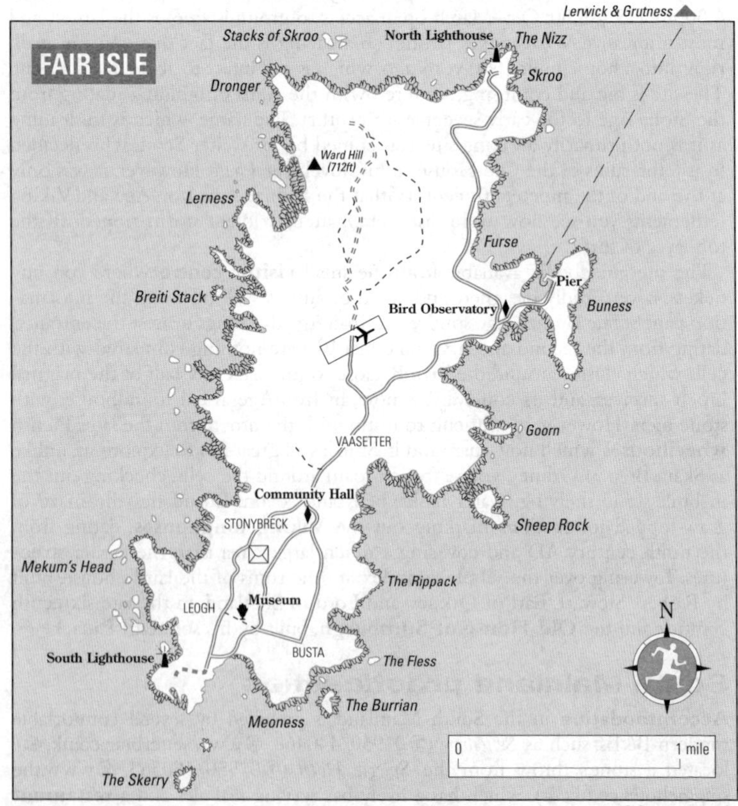

weather – what the islanders call "a given day". At one time Fair Isle's population was not far short of four hundred, but Clearances forced emigration from the middle of the nineteenth century. By the 1950s, the population had shrunk to just 44, a point at which evacuation and abandonment of the island were seriously considered. **George Waterston**, who'd bought the island and set up a bird observatory in 1948, passed it into the care of the NTS in 1954 and rejuvenation began. Since then, islanders, the Trust and the Shetland Islands Council have invested in many improvements to housing, the harbour and basic services, including an advanced electricity system integrating wind and diesel generation. Crafts including boatbuilding, the making of fiddles, felt and stained glass have been developed, and today Fair Isle supports a vibrant community of around seventy people.

The north end of the island rises like a wall, while the Sheep Rock, a sculpted stack of rock and grass on the east side, is another dramatic feature. The croft land and the island's scattered (exclusively white) houses are concentrated in the south, but the focus for many visitors is the **Bird Observatory**, a military-looking building just above the sandy bay of North Haven, where the ferry from Shetland Mainland arrives. It's one of the major European centres for ornithology, and its work in watching, trapping, recording and ringing birds goes on all year. Fair Isle is a landfall for a huge number and range of migrant birds during the spring and autumn passages. Migration routes converge here and more than 345 species, including many rarities, have been noted. As a result, Fair Isle is a haven for twitchers, who descend on the island in planes and boats whenever a major rarity is spotted; for more casual birders, however, there's also plenty of summer resident birdlife to enjoy. The high-pitched screeching that fills the sky above the airstrip comes from hundreds of arctic terns, and arctic skuas can also be seen here. Those in search of puffins should head for the cliffs around Furse, while to find gannets aim for the spectacular Stacks of Scroo.

Fair Isle is, of course, even better known for its **knitting** patterns, still produced with great skill by the local knitwear cooperative, though not in the quantities which you might imagine from a walk around city department stores; from time to time there are displays at the Community Hall, by the island school (usually on a Monday, or when a cruise ship calls by). If the Hall is closed, then you'll have to make do with the samples on display at the island's **museum** (Mon 2–5pm, Wed 10am–noon, Fri 2–4.30pm; free; ⓣ01595/760244), which is named after George Waterston and situated next door to the island's Methodist Chapel. Particularly memorable are stories of shipwrecks; in 1868 the islanders undertook a heroic rescue of all 465 German emigrants aboard the *Lessing*. More famously, the *El Gran Grifon*, part of the retreating Spanish Armada, was lost here in 1588 and three hundred Spanish seamen were washed up on the island. Food was in such short supply that fifty died of starvation before help could be summoned from Shetland. The idea that the islanders borrowed all their patterns from the shipwrecked Spanish seamen is nowadays regarded as a patronizing myth.

Fair Isle has two **lighthouses**, one at either end of the island, both designed by the Stevenson family and erected in 1892. Before that, the Vikings used to light beacons to signal an enemy fleet advancing, and in the nineteenth century a semaphore consisting of a tall wooden pole was used; it can still be seen on the hill above South Lighthouse. The North Lighthouse was considered to be on such an exposed spot that the foghorn was operated from within. Both lighthouses were automated in 1998, and the South Lighthouse had the distinction of being the last manned lighthouse in the country.

Practicalities

For matters of administration and transport, Fair Isle is linked to Shetland. The passenger **ferry** connects Fair Isle with either Lerwick (on alternate Thurs; 4hr 30min) or Grutness in Sumburgh (Tues, Sat & alternate Thurs; 3hr); since the boat only takes a limited number of passengers, it's advisable to book in advance (Ⓣ01595/760222). The crossing can be very rough at times, so if you're at all susceptible to seasickness it might be worth considering catching a **flight** from Tingwall (Mon, Wed, Fri & Sat) or Sumburgh (Sat); a one-way ticket costs £28, and day-trips are possible (Mon, Wed & Fri).

Camping is not permitted, but there is full-board **accommodation** at the *Fair Isle Lodge & Bird Observatory* (Ⓣ01595/760258, Ⓦwww.fairislebirdobs.co.uk; full board ⑤), in twins and singles or hostel-style dorms. To guests and visitors alike, the Bird Observatory offers tea, coffee and good home cooking for lunch and dinner; you might even be able to lend a hand with the observatory's research programme. A good **B&B** alternative – with full-board option – is *Upper Leogh* in the south of the island (Ⓣ01595/760248; ②), where you'll be well looked after. There is a shop/post office nearby (closed Thurs & Sun).

Central Mainland

The districts of Tingwall and Weisdale, plus the old capital of **Scalloway**, make up the **Central Mainland**, an area of minor interest in the grand scheme of things, but one that is very easy to reach from Lerwick. In fine weather, it's a captivating mix of farms, moors and lochs, and includes Shetland's only significant woodland; the scale of the scenery ranges from the intimate to the vast, with particularly spectacular views from high points above Whiteness and Weisdale. The area also holds strong historical associations, with the

The Shetland Bus

The story of the **Shetland Bus**, the link between Shetland and Norway that helped to sustain the Norwegian Resistance through the years of Nazi occupation, is quite extraordinary. Constantly under threat of attack by enemy aircraft or naval action, small Norwegian fishing boats set out from Shetland to run arms and resistance workers into lonely fjords. The trip took at least 24 hours and on the return journey boats brought back Norwegians in danger of arrest by the Gestapo, or those who wanted to join Norwegian forces fighting with the Allies. For three years, through careful planning, the operation was remarkably successful: instructions to boats were passed in cryptic messages in BBC news broadcasts. Although local people knew what was going on, the secret was generally well kept. In total, 350 refugees were evacuated, and more than four hundred tons of arms, large amounts of explosives and sixty radio transmitters were landed in Norway.

Originally established at **Lunna** in the northeast of the Mainland, the service moved to **Scalloway** in 1942, partly because the village could offer good marine engineering facilities at Moore's Shipyard at the west end of Main Street, where a plaque records the morale-boosting visit of the Norwegian Crown Prince Olav. Many buildings in Scalloway were pressed into use to support the work: explosives and weapons were stored in the castle. **Kergord House** in Weisdale was used as a safe house and training centre for intelligence personnel and saboteurs. The hazards, tragedies and elations of the exercise are brilliantly described in David Howarth's book, *The Shetland Bus*; their legacy today is a heartfelt closeness between Shetland and Norway.

Norse parliament at **Law Ting Holm** and unhappy memories of Earl Patrick Stewart's harsh rule at Scalloway and of nineteenth-century Clearances at Weisdale.

Scalloway

Approaching **SCALLOWAY** from the shoulder of the steep hill to the east known as the **Scord**, there's a dramatic view over the town and the islands to the south and west. Once the capital of Shetland, Scalloway's importance waned through the eighteenth century as Lerwick, just six miles to the east, grew in trading success and status. Nowadays, Scalloway is fairly sleepy, though its prosperity, always closely linked to the fluctuations of the fishing industry, has recently been given a boost with investment in fish-processing factories, and in the impressive North Atlantic Fisheries College on the west side of the busy harbour.

In spite of modern developments nearby, Scalloway is dominated by the imposing shell of **Scalloway Castle**, a classic fortified tower house built with forced labour in 1600 by the infamous Earl Patrick Stewart, and thus seen as a powerful symbol of oppression. Stewart, who'd succeeded his father Robert to the Earldom of Orkney and Lordship of Shetland in 1592, held court in the castle and gained a reputation for enhancing his own power and wealth through the calculated use of harsh justice, frequently including confiscation of assets. He was eventually arrested and imprisoned in 1609, not for his ill-treatment of Shetlanders, but for his aggressive behaviour toward his fellow landowners; his son, Robert, attempted an insurrection and both were executed in Edinburgh in 1615. The castle was used for a time by Cromwell's army, but had fallen into disrepair by 1700 and is nowadays in the hands of Historic Scotland. The castle itself is well preserved and fun to explore; if the door is locked, the key can be borrowed from the *Scalloway Hotel*.

On Main Street, the small **Scalloway Museum** (May–Sept Mon 9.30–11.30am & 2–4.30pm, Tues–Fri 10am–noon & 2–4.30pm, Sat 10am–12.30pm & 2–4.30pm; free), run by volunteers, holds a few local relics. It explains the importance of fishing and attempts to tell the story of the **Shetland Bus** (see box opposite), a memorial for which stands along the harbour at Mid Shore. From the northern outskirts of Scalloway, there's a pleasant, if energetic, walk (2–3hr return) up the Gallows or Witches Hill, where alleged witches were put to death, and then on to the hamlet of **Burwick**, a former fishing settlement.

Scalloway has very little **accommodation** apart from the *Scalloway Hotel* (Ⓣ01595/880444; ⑤), on the harbourfront, whose bar acts as the local pub. For **food**, head for *Da Haaf* (Ⓣ01595/880747; closed Sat & Sun), the unpretentious licensed restaurant in the North Atlantic Fisheries College, which serves a wide range of fresh fish, simply prepared, with broad harbour views to enjoy as well.

Trondra and Burra

Southwest of Scalloway – and connected to the Mainland by a bridge since 1971 – is the island of **Trondra**, where you can visit a working crofthouse, situated in a lovely spot in the centre of the island. Pick up a leaflet and a bucket of feed for the hens from the barn, and head off along the **Croft Trail**, which takes you to see the ducks, down to the shore (a good picnic spot), over to a restored watermill and then through a field of orchids, buttercups and other flowers.

Further south, the Burra Bridge connects Trondra with the twin islands of East and West **Burra**, which have some beautiful beaches and some fairly gentle coastal walks. West Burra has the largest settlement in the area, **HAMNAVOE**, a planned fishing settlement unlike any other in Shetland. Just south of Hamnavoe, a small path leads down from the road to the white sandy beach at **Meal**, deservedly popular on warm summer days. At the southern end of West Burra, at **Banna Minn**, there's another fine beach, with excellent walking nearby on the cliffs of Kettla Ness, linked to the rest of West Burra only by a sliver of tombolo.

East Burra, joined to West Burra at the middle like a Siamese twin, ends at the hamlet of **HOUSS**, distinguished by the tall, ruined laird's house or Haa. From the turning place outside the cattlegrid, continue walking southwards, following the track to the left, down the hill and across the beach, and after about a mile you'll reach the deserted settlement of **Symbister**, inhabited until the 1940s. You can now see ancient field boundaries and, just south of the ruins, a **burnt mound** (an overgrown pile of Neolithic cooking stones dumped when no longer usable). Half a mile further south, the island ends in cliffs, caves and wheeling fulmars. From there, the islet of **South Havra**, topped by the ruins of Shetland's only **windmill**, is just to the southwest. Once supporting a small fishing community, the islet was abandoned, except for the grazing of sheep, by the last eight families in 1923; it was such a perilous existence that children as well as animals had to be tethered to prevent them from falling over the cliffs.

Tingwall

TINGWALL, the name for the loch-studded, fertile valley to the north of Scalloway, takes its name from the **Lawting** or Althing (from *thing*, the Old Norse for "parliament"), in existence from the eleventh to the sixteenth century, where local people and officials gathered to make or amend laws and discuss evidence. From the late thirteenth century, Shetland's laws were based on the udal law of the Norwegian king Magnus the Lawmender; after the sixteenth century, judicial affairs were dealt with in Patrick Stewart's new castle at Scalloway. The Lawting was situated at **Law Ting Holm**, the small peninsula at the northern end of Loch Tingwall that was once an island linked to the shore by a causeway. Although structures on the holm have long since vanished, there's an information board which helps in visualizing the scene. At the southwest corner of the loch, a seven-foot **standing stone** by the roadside is said to mark the spot where, after a dispute at the Lawting in 1389, Earl Henry Sinclair killed his cousin and rival, Marise Sperra, together with seven of his followers.

Just north of the loch is **Tingwall Kirk**, unexceptional from the outside, but preserving its attractive late eighteenth-century interior. In the burial ground, there's a dank, turf-covered **burial aisle** from the old medieval church that was demolished in 1788. Inside are several very old gravestones, including one to a local official called a *Foud* – a representative of the king – who died in 1603. The ornate seventeenth-century sarcophagus in the graveyard was used as a social meeting point and resting place by locals who arrived early for the Sunday service.

Most of Shetland's inter-island flights leave from **Tingwall airport** (ⓣ01595/840246); taxis from Lerwick bus station cost just £1, but must be booked 24 hours in advance (ⓣ01595/694617). If you're looking for somewhere to **stay** within easy striking distance of the airstrip, try the distinctive red *Herrislea House Hotel* (ⓣ01595/840208; ❺), overlooking the airstrip by the main crossroads; its spacious **bar**, the idiosyncratically decorated *Starboard Tack*, doubles as Tingwall's social centre, serves good pub food and regularly features live **traditional music.** You can eat, or enjoy some draught Shetland ale whilst enjoying the view down Whiteness Voe, at the *Inn on the Hill*, on the A971.

Weisdale

Weisdale, five miles or so northwest of Tingwall, is notable primarily for **Weisdale Mill** (Tues–Sat 10.30am–4.30pm, Sun noon–4.30pm; free), situated up the B9075 from the head of Weisdale Voe. Built for milling grain in 1855, this is now an attractively converted arts centre, housing the small, beautifully designed **Bonhoga Gallery**, in which touring and local exhibitions of painting, sculpture and other media are shown. Don't miss the small but fascinating **Shetland Textile Working Museum** (£1) in the basement, which puts on temporary exhibitions, and has pull-out drawers showing the knitted patterns unique to Shetland and Fair Isle. There's also a very pleasant café, serving soup, scones and snacks in the south-facing conservatory overlooking the stream.

Weisdale is an evocative name in Shetland, for in this valley some of the cruelest Clearances of people in favour of sheep took place in the middle of the nineteenth century. The perpetrator was David Dakers Black, a farmer from the county of Angus who began buying land in 1843. Hundreds of tenants were dispossessed, and in 1850 the large **Kergord House**, then called Flemington, was built towards the northern end of the valley from the stones of some of the older houses. The ruined shells of some of the rest still stand on the valley sides; local writers, particularly John J. Graham, have recounted the period in novels (notably his *Shadowed Valley*) and drama.

Around Kergord House and on the upper valley sides there are several **tree plantations** dating mainly from around 1920 but with a later experimental addition by the Forestry Commission. An amazing range of species is present, from the sycamores and willows which thrive in many Shetland gardens to examples of chestnut, copper beech, monkey puzzle and much else besides. Along with the trees comes a woodland ecosystem, with foxgloves, Britain's most northerly rookery and a reliable cuckoo. During the war, Kergord House played a role in the Shetland Bus operation (see box, p.470); the saboteurs who trained here are said to have amused visitors by demonstrating booby traps and incendiary devices in the garden.

South of Kergord House and Weisdale Mill on the west shore of Weisdale Voe, among trees near the voe's narrowest point, is the ruined house once occupied by **John Cluness Ross** (1786–1853). Ross travelled to the Indian Ocean and settled in the Cocos Islands, going into coconut farming and appointing himself king; he was the first in a family dynasty of three which ruled – some would say oppressed – the Cocos islanders for decades.

The Westside

The western Mainland of Shetland – known as the **Westside** (Ⓦwww.walls.shetland.co.uk) – stretches west from Weisdale and Voe to Sandness. Although there are some important archeological remains and wildlife in the area, the area's greatest appeal lies in its outstanding **coastal scenery** and walks. At its heart, the Westside's rolling brown and purple moorland, dotted with patches of bright-green reseeded land, glistens with dozens of small, picturesque blue or silver lochs. On the west coast the rounded form of Sandness Hill (750ft) falls steeply away into the Atlantic. The coastal scenery, cut by several deep voes, is very varied; aside from dramatic cliffs, there are intimate coves and some fine beaches, as well as, just offshore, the stunning island of **Papa Stour**.

Bixter and around

Having left Weisdale, the first settlement you come to on the A971 is **TRESTA**, at the head of Sandsound Voe. If you're keen on plants, it's worth having a peek round **Lea Gardens** (Wed & Sat 11am–8pm, Sun 2–6pm; also at other times if they're in), where one family have put a great deal of energy into their cottage garden, growing a huge variety of plants that enjoy the moist, frost-free Shetland climate.

The chief crossroads for the area is a few miles further on at **BIXTER**, a place of no particular consequence from where you can travel south to Skeld and Reawick, west to Walls, West Burrafirth and Sandness, or northwest along a scenic winding road towards **AITH** and eventually Voe (see p.479). There isn't a lot at Aith either, except a shop and school, and an attractive little harbour that serves as the base for the west of Shetland lifeboat. Northwest of Aith, the road ends at the farm of **Vementry**, also, confusingly, the name of the nearby island that boasts the best-preserved **heel-shaped cairn** in Shetland, right on top of the highest hill, Muckle Ward (298ft). There are also two excellently preserved **six-inch guns** from World War I on Swarbucks Head, in the north of the island. To reach the island, enquire locally or through Lerwick tourist office (see p.456).

Southwest of Bixter, on the picturesque Sandsting peninsula, there are two beautiful terracotta-coloured **sandy bays** at **REAWICK**, and excellent **coastal walks** to be had along the coast around Westerwick and Culswick, past red-granite cliffs, caves and stacks. There's also a **camping böd** (ⓣ01595/694688, ⓦwww.camping-bods.com; April–Sept) and **campsite** at **SKELD**, by the pier and marina in the sheltered Skelda Voe, between Reawick and Westerwick.

Three miles southwest of Bixter lies the finest Neolithic structure in the Westside, dubbed the **Staneydale Temple** by the archeologist who excavated it because it resembled a temple on Malta. Whatever its true function, it was twice as large as the surrounding oval-shaped houses (now in ruins) and was certainly of great importance, perhaps as some kind of community centre. The horseshoe-shaped foundations measure more than 40ft by 20ft internally, with immensely thick walls, still around 4ft high, whose roof would have been supported by spruce posts (two postholes can still be clearly seen). To reach the temple, take the path marked out by black-and-white poles across the moorland for half a mile from the road.

Walls and Sandness

Once an important fishing port, **WALLS** (pronounced *waas*), appealingly set round its harbour, is now a quiet village which comes alive once a year in the middle of August for the Walls Agricultural Show, the biggest farming bash on the island. If you're just passing by, you might like to stop by the **bakery and tearoom**, but Walls also has several good **accommodation** options: the nicely restored *Voe House* (ⓣ01595/694688, ⓦwww.camping-bods.com; April–Sept), the largest **camping böd** on Shetland, with its own peat fire, and the wonderfully welcoming *Skeoverick* (ⓣ01595/809349; ❷), a lovely modern crofthouse B&B which lies a mile or so north of Walls. The only **guesthouse** in the area is *Burrastow House* (ⓣ01595/809307, ⓦwww.users.zetnet.co.uk/burrastow-house-hotel; ❺; April–Oct), beautifully situated about three miles southwest of Walls; parts of the house date back to 1759, and have real character, others are more modern. With fresh Shetland ingredients and a French chef, the cooking is superb, with **dinner** available to non-residents at the weekend.

A short distance across the sea lies the island of **Vaila**, from where in 1837 Lerwick philanthropist Arthur Anderson operated a fishing station in an unsuccessful attempt to break down the system of fishing tenures under which tenants were forced to fish for the landlords under pain of eviction. The ruins of Anderson's fishing station still stand on the shore, but the most conspicuous monument is **Vaila Hall**, the largest laird's house on Shetland, originally built in 1696, but massively enlarged by a wealthy Yorkshire mill-owner, Herbert Anderton, who bought the island in 1893. Anderton also restored the island's ancient watchtower of Mucklaberry Castle, built a Buddhist temple (now sadly in ruins), and had a cannon fired whenever he arrived on the island. The island is currently owned by an eccentric Polish woman and her partner; if you wish to visit, enquire at *Burrastow House*.

At the end of a long winding road across an undulating, uninhabited, boulder-strewn landscape, you eventually reach the fertile scattered crofting settlement of **SANDNESS** (pronounced "saaness"), which you can also reach by walking along the coast from Walls past the dramatic Deepdale and across Sandness Hill. It's an oasis of green meadows in the peat moorland, with a nice beach, too. The modern **Jamieson's Spinning Mill** at Sandness (Mon–Fri 8am–5pm; free) is the only one on Shetland producing pure Shetland wool; the factory welcomes visitors, and you can watch how workers take the fleece and then wash, card and spin the exceptionally fine Shetland wool into yarn.

There's nowhere to stay in Sandness, but there is a croft B&B with great sea views: *Snarraness House* (Ⓣ01595/809375; ❷), in **WEST BURRAFIRTH**, the ferry terminal for Papa Stour, five miles or so north of Walls.

Papa Stour

A mile offshore from Sandness is the rocky island of **Papa Stour** (Ⓦwww.papastour.shetland.co.uk), created out of volcanic lava and ash, which has subsequently been eroded into some of the most impressive coastal scenery in Shetland. In good weather, it makes for a perfect day-trip, but in foul weather or a sea mist it

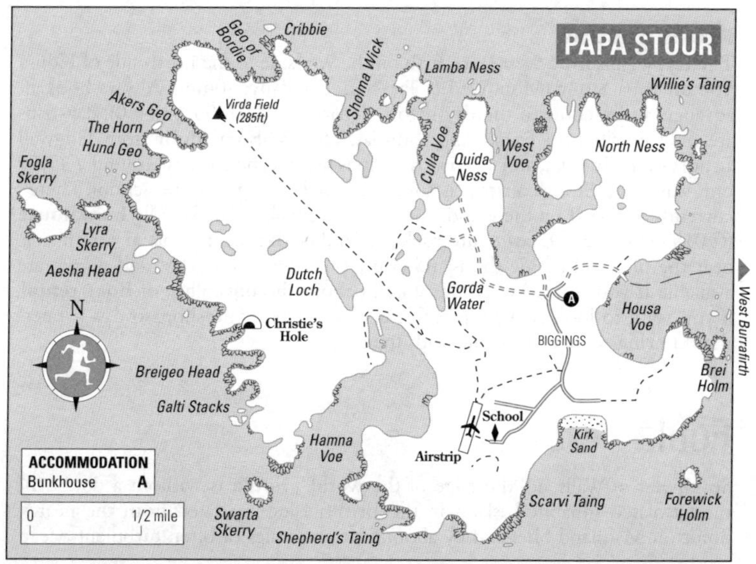

can certainly appear pretty bleak. Its name, which means "big island of the priests", derives from its early Celtic Christian connections, and the island was home, in the eighteenth century, to people who were mistakenly believed to have been lepers (though in fact they were suffering from a hereditary skin disease caused by severe malnutrition). The land is very fertile, and in the nineteenth century Papa Stour supported around three hundred inhabitants, but by the early 1970s there was a population crisis: the island's school closed, and the remaining sixteen inhabitants were all past child-bearing age; worse still, it looked like the post office would close and the mailboat be withdrawn. The islanders made appeals for new blood to revive the fragile economy and managed to stage a dramatic recovery, releasing croft land to young settlers from Britain and overseas. Papa Stour was briefly dubbed "the hippie isle", but eventually most of the newcomers moved on, often to other parts of Shetland, making a further appeal necessary in the early 1990s. The school closed for a while in 2002 due to a lack of pupils, and today the island struggles to sustain a community of twenty-five or so.

Papa Stour's main settlement, **BIGGINGS**, lies in the east near the pier, and it was here that excavation in the early 1980s revealed the remains of a thirteenth-century Norse house, which is thought to have belonged to Duke Haakon, heir to the Norwegian throne. There's an explanatory panel, but nothing much to see – in any case, the chief reason to come to Papa Stour is to go **walking**; to reach the best of the coastal scenery, head for the far west of the island. From **Virda Field** (285ft), the highest point, in the far northwest, you can see the treacherous rocks of Ve Skerries, three miles or so northwest off the coast, where a lighthouse was erected as recently as 1979. The couple of miles of coastline from here southeast to Hamna Voe has some of the island's best stacks, blow-holes and natural arches. Probably the most spectacular formation of all is the **Christie's Hole**, a gloup or partly roofed cleft, which extends far inland from the cliff line, and where shags nest on precipitous ledges. Other points of interest include a couple of defunct horizontal click-mills, below Dutch Loch, and the remains of a "meal road", so called because the workmen were paid in oatmeal or flour. In addition, several pairs of red-throated divers regularly breed on inland lochs such as Gorda Water.

Practicalities

The **ferry** runs from West Burrafirth on the Westside to the north side of Housa Voe on Papa Stour (Mon, Wed & Fri–Sun 1–2 daily; 40min). Always book in advance, and reconfirm the day before departure (Ⓣ01595/810460); day-trips are only possible on Friday and Saturday. There's also a **flight** from Tingwall airport every Tuesday, and again a day-trip is feasible; tickets cost around £17.50 one way. Papa Stour's airstrip is southwest of Biggings, by the school. There's currently no B&B on the island, but there is a small, clean, friendly **bunkhouse** (Ⓣ01595/873229, Ⓔfay@hurdiback.shetland.co.uk; April–Sept) at Hurdiback, near the pier and beside the island's only phone box; breakfast and dinner are available if you want. Ask around locally about the possibility of **boat rental**, if you want to look at the stacks from the sea. There's no shop, so day-trippers should bring their own picnic with them.

Foula

Southwest of Walls, at "the edge of the world", **Foula** is without a doubt the most isolated inhabited island in the British Isles, separated from the nearest point on Mainland Shetland by about fourteen miles of often turbulent ocean.

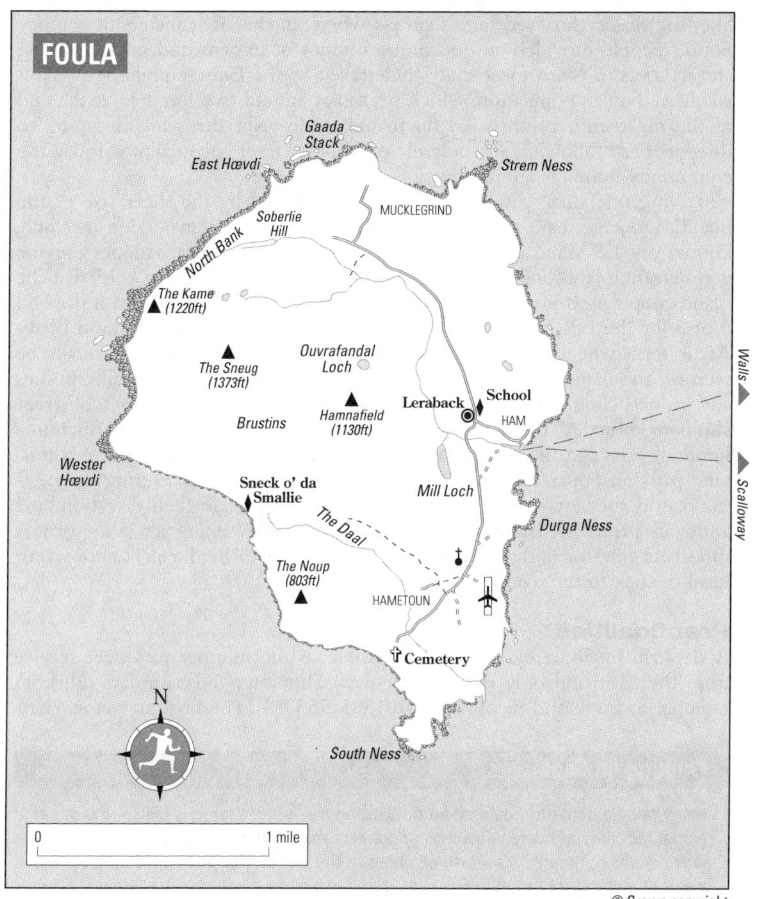

Seen from the Mainland, its distinctive mountainous form changes subtly, depending upon the vantage point, but the outline is unforgettable. Its western **cliffs**, the second highest in Britain after those of St Kilda, rise at **The Kame** to some 1220ft above sea level; a clear day at The Kame offers a magnificent panorama stretching from Unst to Fair Isle. On a bad day, the exposure is complete and the cliffs generate turbulent blasts of wind known in Shetland as "flans", which rip through the hills with tremendous force.

Foula has been inhabited since prehistoric times, and the people here take pride in their separateness from Shetland, cherishing local traditions such as the observance of the **Julian calendar**, officially dropped in Britain in 1752, where Old Yule is celebrated on January 6 and the New Year doesn't arrive until January 13. The folk of Foula were still using Norse **udal law** in the late seventeenth century, seemingly unaware that it had been superseded by Scots law in the rest of the country. Foula was also the last place that **Norn**, the old Norse language of Orkney and Shetland, was spoken as a first language, in the eighteenth century. Likewise, the island's isolation meant that more of the

Shetland dialect survived here than elsewhere; in the late nineteenth century, Foula's people provided an enormous amount of information on the dialect and its roots in Norn for a study undertaken by the Faroese philologist Jakob Jakobsen. Foula's population, which peaked at around two hundred at the end of the nineteenth century, has fluctuated wildly over the years, dropping to three in 1720 following an epidemic of "muckle fever" or smallpox. Today, the community numbers around thirty.

Arriving on Foula, you can't help but be amazed by the sheer size of the island's immense, bare mountains, whose summits are often hidden in cloud, known on the Mainland as "Foula's hat". The gentler eastern slopes provide good crofting land, and plentiful peat, and it is along this "green belt" that the island's population is scattered. The island, whose name is derived from the Old Norse for "bird island", also provides a home for a quarter of a million **birds**. Arctic terns wheel overhead at the airstrip, red-throated divers can usually be seen on the island's smaller lochs, while fulmars, guillemots, razorbills, puffins and gannets cling to the rock ledges. However, it is the island's colony of **great skuas** or "bonxies" that you can't fail to notice. From the edge of extinction a hundred years ago, the bonxies are now thriving, with an estimated three thousand pairs on Foula, making it the largest colony in Britain. During the nesting season, they attack anyone who comes near. Although their dive-bombing antics are primarily meant as a threat, they can make walking across the island's moorland interior fairly stressful: the best advice is to hold a stick above your head or stick to the road and the coast.

Practicalities

A day-trip to Foula by **ferry** isn't possible, as the summer passenger service from the Mainland only runs on Tuesdays, Thursdays and Saturdays (2hr); it's essential to book and reconfirm (ⓣ01595/753254). The boat arrives at Ham,

Walking on Foula

Many people come to Foula intent on viewing the island's famous cliffs – though in actual fact they are very difficult to appreciate except from the air or the sea. If the weather's fine, though, it's worth climbing to the top of **The Sneug** (1373ft), for the views stretching from Unst to Fair Isle. From the airstrip, climb up the southeast ridge of **Hamnafield** (1130ft), and then continue along the ridge of Brustins to The Sneug itself. From The Sneug, drop down to **The Kame** (1220ft), Foula's sheer cliff, the best view of which is from Nebbiefield, to the south. Return via Da Nort Bank to Soberlie Hill, from where you can pick up the island's road. All in all, it's only a walk of five or six miles, but it'll take three to four hours. If you're coming from the ferry at Ham, it's probably best to do the circuit in reverse, which is no bad thing, as the climb from Soberlie Hill up Da Nort Bank is one of the most exhilarating on the island; the edge of the hill is an ever-increasing vertical drop.

There are other more gentle walks possible on Foula, too. The coastal scenery to the north of the island, beyond Mucklegrind, features several stacks and natural arches, with the waves crashing over skerries, and seals sunning themselves. One of the easiest places to spot seabirds is from beyond the graveyard in Biggings, beyond Hametoun. The nearby hill of **The Noup** (803ft) is a relatively easy climb, compared to The Sneug, and, if you descend to the northwest, brings you to **Sneck o' da Smallie**, where there's a narrow slit in the cliffs, some 200ft high. You can return to the airstrip by heading back down the valley known as The Daal, although the bonxies are pretty thick on the ground. All Foula's cliffs are potentially lethal, especially in wet weather, and all the usual safety precautions should be taken (see p.59).

in the middle of Foula's east coast, and has to be winched up onto the pier to protect it. However, there are regular **flights** from Tingwall (Mon–Wed & Fri; ⓣ01595/753226); tickets cost around £25 one way and day-trips are possible on Wednesdays (mid-Feb to mid-Oct) and Fridays. From May to September, Foula has its own resident part-time ranger, who usually greets new arrivals and offers local advice; it's also possible to arrange for guided walks (ⓣ01595/753228). Foula's only **B&B** is *Leraback* (ⓣ01595/753226, ⓦwww.originart.com; ❸), near Ham, which does full board only, though they can also rent out a self-catering cottage on a daily basis; they will collect you from the airstrip or pier. There's no shop, so you'll need to take all your food and supplies with you. There's just one road, which runs along the eastern side of the island, and is used by Foula's remarkable fleet of clapped-out vehicles.

North Mainland

The **North Mainland**, stretching more than thirty miles north from the Central Belt around Lerwick, is wilder than much of Shetland, with almost relentlessly bleak moorland and some rugged and dramatic coastal scenery. It is all but split in two by the isthmus of Mavis Grind: to the south are the districts of Delting, home to Shetland's oil terminal (Sullom Voe) and town (Brae), Lunnasting (gateway to the islands of Whalsay and Out Skerries) and Nesting; to the north is the remote region of Northmavine, which boasts some of the most scenic cliffs in Shetland.

Voe and Lunnasting

If you're travelling north, you're bound to pass by **VOE**, as it sits at the main crossroads of the North Mainland: to the east, the road leads to Vidlin and Laxo, ferry terminals for Whalsay and Out Skerries; to the northeast, the road cuts across to Toft, where the ferry departs for Yell; to the northwest, it continues on to Brae and Northmavine. If you stay on the main road, it's easy to miss the picturesque old village, a tight huddle of homes and workshops down below the road around the pier (and signposted "Lower Voe"). Set at the head of a deep, sheltered, sea loch, Voe has a Scandinavian appearance, helped by the presence of the **Sail Loft**, painted in a rich, deep red. The building was originally used by fishermen and whalers for storing their gear; later, it became a knitwear workshop, and it was here that woollen jumpers were knitted for the 1953 Mount Everest expedition. Today, the building has been converted into a large **camping böd** (ⓣ01595/694688, ⓦwww.camping-bods.com; April–Sept); it has hot showers, a kitchen, and a solid-fuel heater in the smaller of the bedrooms. Across the road, the old butcher's is now the *Pierhead Restaurant & Bar*: the cosy wood-panelled **pub** has a real fire, occasional live music and offers a good bar menu, a longer version of which is on offer in the upstairs restaurant, featuring local mussels and the odd catch from the fishing boats.

LAXO, the ferry terminal for Whalsay (see p.482), lies two miles east of Voe. If you continue along the B9071 past the village, you'll pass **The Cabin** (open when the flag flies, which is mostly daily 10am–5pm; free; ⓣ01806/577243), a glorified garden shed packed to the rafters with wartime memorabilia collected over many years by the very welcoming proprietor, Andy Robertson. You can try on some of the uniforms and caps or pore over the many personal accounts of the war written by locals. Three miles or so further north past Vidlin, the departure point for the Out Skerries (see p.483), is **Lunna House**

(Ⓣ01806/577311, Ⓦwww.lunnahouse.co.uk; ❷), with its distinctive red window surrounds, set above a sheltered harbour nine miles northeast of Voe. The house was originally built in 1660 by the Hunter family, but is best known as the initial headquarters from which the Shetland Bus resistance operation was conducted during World War II (see box, p.470). It's now a wonderful **place to stay**, with spacious bedrooms, lovely views and a top-class breakfast.

Down the hill lies the little whitewashed **Lunna Kirk**, built in 1753, with a simple tiny interior including a carved hexagonal pulpit. Among its more peculiar features is a "lepers' squint" on the outside wall, through which those believed to have the disease could participate in the service without risk of infecting the congregation; there was, however, no leprosy here, the outcasts in fact suffering from a hereditary, non-infectious skin condition brought on by malnutrition. In the graveyard, several unidentified Norwegian sailors, torpedoed by the Nazis, are buried.

Brae and Sullom Voe

BRAE, a sprawling settlement that still has the feel of a frontier town, was one of four expanded in some haste in the 1970s to accommodate the workforce for the huge **Sullom Voe Oil Terminal**, just to the northeast. Sullom Voe is the longest sea loch in Shetland and has always attracted the interest of outsiders in search of a deep-water harbour. During World War II it was home to the Norwegian Air Force and a base for RAF seaplanes. Although the oil terminal, built between 1975 and 1982, has passed its production peak, it is still the largest of its kind in Europe. Its size, however, isn't obvious from beyond the site boundary and few clues remain to the extraordinary scale of the construction effort, which for several years involved a workforce of six thousand, accommodated in two large "construction villages" and two ships.

Brae may not, at first sight, appear to be somewhere to spend the night, but it does boast one of Shetland's finest **hotels**, *Busta House* (Ⓣ01806/522506, Ⓦwww.bustahouse.com; ❻), a lovely laird's house with stepped gables that has been tastefully enlarged over the last four hundred years and which sits across the bay of Busta Voe from the modern sprawl of Brae. Even if you're not staying the night here, it's worth coming for afternoon tea in the Long Room, for a stroll around the lovely wooded grounds, or for a drink and an excellent bar meal in the hotel's pub-like bar. A cheaper alternative is the modern crofthouse **B&B** of *Westayre* (Ⓣ01806/522368, Ⓦwww.westayre.shetland.co.uk; ❷), beyond Busta, overlooking a red sandy bay on the peaceful island of Muckle Roe, which is linked to the mainland by a bridge.

Northmavine

Northmavine, the northwest peninsula of North Mainland, is unquestionably one of the most picturesque areas of Shetland, with its often rugged scenery, magnificent coastline and wide open spaces. The peninsula begins a mile west of Brae at **Mavis Grind**, a narrow isthmus at which it's said you can throw a stone from the Atlantic to the North Sea, or at least to Sullom Voe. Three miles north of the isthmus, it's worth abandoning the main road to explore the remoter corners; the twisting side road west to Gunnister and Nibon travels through a wonderful tumbled landscape of pink and grey rock where abandoned fields and broken shells of crofthouses provide abundant evidence of past human struggles to make a living. Where the road ends, at Nibon, you can view a jigsaw of islands and rocky headlands which, even on a relatively calm day, smash the Atlantic into streams of white foam.

Hillswick

HILLSWICK, the main settlement in the area, was once served by the steamboats of the North of Scotland, Orkney & Shetland Steam Navigation Company, and in the early 1900s the firm built the **St Magnus Hotel** to house their customers, importing it in the form of a timber kit from Norway. Despite various alterations over the years, it still stands overlooking St Magnus Bay, rather magnificently clad in black timber-framing and white weatherboarding. Nearer the shore is the much older Hillswick House and, attached to it, **Da Böd**, once the oldest pub in Shetland, said to have been founded by a German merchant in 1684, now an alternative veggie café and wildlife sanctuary called *The Booth* (ⓣ01806/503348; June–Sept; closed Mon).

The *St Magnus Hotel* is full to the rafters with contractors working at Sullom Voe, so if you want a decent **B&B** in the vicinity, look to *Almara* (ⓣ01806/503261, ⓦwww.almara.shetland.co.uk; ❸), a mile or two back down the road in Upper Urafirth, which will present you with good food, a family welcome and excellent views. The nicest sandiest **beach** to collapse on is on the west side of the Hillswick isthmus, overlooking Dore Holm (see below), a short walk across the fields from the hotel.

Esha Ness

Just outside Hillswick, a side-road leads west to the exposed headland of **Esha Ness** (pronounced "*Ay*sha Ness"), celebrated for its splendid coastline views. Spectacular red-granite **cliffs**, eaten away to form fantastic shapes by the elements, are spread out before you as the road climbs away from Hillswick: in the foreground are the stacks known as **The Drongs** off the Ness of Hillswick, while in the distance the Westside and Papa Stour are visible.

A mile or so south off the main road is the **Tangwick Haa Museum** (May–Sept Mon–Fri 1–5pm, Sat & Sun 11am–7pm; free), housed in a seventeenth-century building, which, through photographs, old documents and fishing gear, tells the often moving story of this remote corner of Shetland and its role in the dangerous trade of deep-sea fishing and whaling. Kids and adults alike will also enjoy the shells, the Shetland wool and sand samples, and the prize exhibit, the Gunnister Man, who was found preserved in peat in 1951. Over 250 years old now, he's down to his bones, for the most part, but his clothes are in good condition, as is his knitted purse, which contained three coins: two Dutch and one Swedish.

Just before it finally peters out, the road divides, with the southern branch leading to the remains of **Stenness fishing station**, which was once one of the most important deep-sea or haaf fishing stations in Shetland. The remains of a few of the böds used by the fishermen are still visible along the sloping pebbly beach where they would dry their catch. At the peak of operations, in the early nineteenth century, as many as eighteen trips a year were made in up to seventy open, six-oared boats, known as "sixareens", to the fishing grounds thirty or forty miles to the west. A Shetland folk song, *Rowin' Foula Doon*, recalls how the crews rowed so far west that the island of Foula began to sink below the eastern horizon. Visible half a mile offshore to the south is **Dore Holm** or the "Drinking Horse", an impressive island with a natural arch.

The northern branch of the road ends at the **Esha Ness Lighthouse**, a great place to view the red-sandstone cliffs, stacks and blow-holes of this stretch of coast. A useful information board at the lighthouse details some of the dramatic geological features here and, if the weather's a bit rough, you should be treated to some spectacular crashing waves. One of the features to beware of at Esha Ness are the blow-holes, some of which are hidden far inland. The best example is the **Holes of Scraada**, a partly roofed cleft where the sea suddenly appears 300yd inland from the cliff line. The incredible power of the sea can be seen in the various giant boulder fields above the cliffs: these **storm beaches** are formed by rocks torn from the cliffs in storms and deposited inland.

One of the few places to stay in Esha Ness is *Johnnie Notions* **camping böd** (Ⓣ01595/694688, Ⓦwww.camping-bods.com; April–Sept; no electricity), up a turning north off the main road, in the hamlet of **HAMNAVOE**. The house was originally the birthplace of Johnnie "Notions" Williamson (1740–1803), a man of many talents, including blacksmithing and weaving, whose fame rests on his work in protecting several thousand of the population against smallpox using a serum and a method of inoculation he'd invented himself, to the amazement of the medical profession. He used a scalpel to lift a flap of skin without drawing blood, then placed the serum he'd prepared underneath, dressing it with a cabbage leaf and a bandage.

Ronas Hill

North of Ronas Voe, by the shores of Colla Firth, an unmarked road leads up **Collafirth Hill**, at the top of which are the crumbling remains of a NATO radio station. The natural landscape is much more impressive, with tremendous views on a clear day, and a foreground of large, scattered stones with hardly any vegetation. Though the walk isn't quite as straightforward as it looks, scale and distance being hard to judge in this setting, Collafirth Hill is the easiest place from which to approach the rounded contours of **Ronas Hill**, Shetland's highest point (1475ft). The climb, with no obvious path, is exhausting but rewarding (4hr round trip; be aware of the safety precautions on p.59): from the top you can look west to one of the most beautifully sculpted parts of the Shetland coast, as the steep slope of the hill drops down to the arching sand and shingle beach called the **Lang Ayre**, south and east over all of the Mainland, north along the coast of Yell, or out into the daunting expanse of the Atlantic. Also at the summit, among subarctic vegetation and block-fields of granite boulders formed by intense frost and wind, is a Neolithic or Bronze Age **chambered cairn**, one of the best preserved in Shetland and useful as a shelter from the wind.

Whalsay and Out Skerries

The island of **Whalsay**, known in Shetland as the "Bonnie Isle", is a friendly community of over a thousand, devoted almost entirely to fishing. The islands' crews operate a very successful pelagic fleet of immense super-trawlers which can fish far afield in all weathers and catch a wide range of species. The island is, in addition, extremely fertile, but crofting takes second place to fishing here; there are also plentiful supplies of peat, which can be seen in spring and summer, stacked neatly to dry out above huge peat banks, ready to be bagged for the winter.

Ferries from the Mainland arrive at the island's chief town, **SYMBISTER**, in the southwest, whose harbour is usually dominated by the presence of several of the island's sophisticated, multi-million-pound purse-netters, some over 180ft long; you'll also see smaller fishing boats and probably a few "fourareens", which the locals race regularly in the summer months. Across the busy harbour from the ferry berth stands the tiny grey-granite **Pier House** (Mon–Sat 9am–1pm & 2–5pm, Sun 2–4pm; free), the key for which resides in the shop opposite. This picturesque little building, with a hoist built into one side, is thought to have been a Hanseatic merchants' store, and contains a good display on how the Germans traded salt, tobacco, spirits and cloth for Whalsay's salted, dried fish from medieval times until the eighteenth century; close by is the Harbour View house that is thought to have been a Hanseatic storehouse or booth. On a hill overlooking the town is the imposing Georgian mansion of **Symbister House**, built in grey granite and boasting a Neoclassical portico. It was built in the 1830s at great expense by Robert Bruce, not because he wanted to live on Whalsay but, so the story goes, because he wanted to deprive his heirs of his fortune. Since the 1940s it has served as the local school and, in the process, has lost some of its grandeur.

About half a mile east of Symbister at the hamlet of **SODOM** – an anglicized version of Sudheim, meaning "South House" – is **Grieve House** (now a camping böd; see below), the modest former home of celebrated Scots poet, writer and republican **Hugh MacDiarmid** (1892–1978), born Christopher Grieve in the Borders town of Langholm. He stayed here from 1933 until 1942, writing about half of his output, including much of his best work: lonely, contemplative poems honouring fishing and fishermen, with whom he sometimes went out to sea. Estranged from his first wife and family and with a drink problem, MacDiarmid, practically broken, had sought temporary relief in Shetland. At first, he seems to have fallen in love with the islands, but poor physical and mental health, exacerbated (if not caused) by chronic poverty, dogged him. Eventually, unwillingly conscripted to work in a Glasgow munitions factory, he left with his new wife and young son, never to return.

Although the majority of folk live in or around Symbister, the rest of Whalsay – which measures roughly two miles by eight – is quite evenly and fairly densely populated. Of the prehistoric remains, the most notable are the two **Bronze Age houses** on the northeastern coast of the island, half a mile south of Skaw, known respectively as the "Benie Hoose" and "Yoxie Biggins". The latter is also known as the "Standing Stones of Yoxie", due to the use of megaliths to form large sections of the walls, many of which still stand. The houses were clearly used over a very long period, as over 1800 tools were discovered in the Benie Hoose; the community also built the nearby chambered tomb.

Car ferries run regularly to Whalsay from Laxo on the Mainland (daily every 45min–1hr 15min; 30min); if you have a car, it's an idea to book ahead (ⓣ01806/566259). In bad weather, especially southeasterly gales, the service operates from Vidlin instead. There are also request-only **flights** from Tingwall (Mon, Wed & Thurs; ⓣ01595/840246); day-trips are only possible on Thursdays. For **B&B** enquire at the post office; otherwise you can stay at the **camping böd** of *Grieve House* in Sodom (ⓣ01595/694688, ⓦwww.camping-bods.com; April–Sept; no electricity). The house has lovely views overlooking Linga Sound, but is hidden from the main road, so ask for directions at the shop on the brow of the hill along the road to the Loch of Huxter. A little further along the road is the *Oot Ower Lounge*, an agreeable **pub** overlooking the loch, and pretty much the only place to eat and drink on the island, though you must book ahead if you want a full meal (ⓣ01806/566658). The island also has an eighteen-hole **golf course**, near the airstrip in Skaw, in the northeast, several shops, and a **leisure centre** with an excellent swimming pool close to the school in Symbister.

Out Skerries

Lying four miles out to sea, off the northeast tip of Whalsay, the **Out Skerries** ("Oot Skerries" or plain "Skerries" as the locals call them), consist of three tiny low-lying rocky islands, Housay, Bruray and Grunay, the first two linked by a bridge, with a population of around eighty. That people live here at all is remarkable, and that it is one of Shetland's most dynamic communities is astonishing, its affluence based on fishing from a superb, small natural harbour sheltered by all three islands, and on salmon farming in a nearby inlet. There are good, if short, walks, with a few prehistoric remains, but the majority of visitors are divers exploring the wreck-strewn coastline, and ornithologists who come here when the wind is in the east, in the hope of catching a glimpse of rare migrants.

The Skerries' jetty and airstrip are both on the middle island of **Bruray**, which also boasts the Skerries' highest point, Bruray Wart (173ft), an easy climb, and one which brings you up close to the islands' ingenious spiral channel collection system for rainwater, which can become scarce in summer. The easternmost island, **Grunay**, is now uninhabited, though you can clearly see the abandoned lighthouse keepers' cottages on the island's chief hill; despite appearances, the Stevenson-designed lighthouse itself sits on the outlying islet of Bound Skerry. The largest of the Skerries' trio, **Housay**, has the most indented and intriguing coastline, to which you should head if the weather's fine. En route, make sure you wander through the Battle Pund stone circle, a wide ring of boulders in the southeastern corner of the island.

Ferries to and from Skerries leave from Vidlin on the Mainland (Mon & Fri–Sun; 1hr 30min) and Lerwick (Tues & Thurs; 2hr 30min), but day-trips are only possible from Vidlin (Fri, Sat & Sun). Make sure you book your journey by 5pm the previous evening (Ⓣ01806/515226), or the ferry might not run. You can take your car over, but, with less than a mile of road to drive along, it's not worth it. There are also regular **flights** from Tingwall (Mon, Wed & Thurs), with day-trips possible on Thursdays. There is a shop, and a shower/toilet block by the pier, and **camping** is permitted, with permission. Alternatively, you can stay in *Rocklea* (Ⓣ01806/515228, Ⓦwww.rockleaok.co.uk; ❷), a friendly **B&B** on Bruray run by Mrs Johnson, who offers optional full board.

The North Isles

Many visitors never make it out to Shetland's trio of remote **North Isles**, which is a shame, as the ferry links are frequent and inexpensive, and the roads fast. Certainly, there is no dramatic shift in scenery: much of what awaits you is the familiar Shetland landscape of undulating peat moorland, dramatic coastal cliffs and silent glacial voes. However, with Lerwick that much further away, the spirit of independence and self-sufficiency in the North Isles is much more keenly felt. **Yell**, the largest of the three, is best known for its vast otter population, but is otherwise often overlooked. **Fetlar**, the smallest of the trio, is home to the rare red-necked phalarope, but **Unst** has probably the widest appeal, partly as the most northerly landmass in the British Isles, but also for its nesting seabird population.

Yell

Historically, **Yell** (Ⓦwww.yell-tourism.shetland.co.uk) hasn't had good write-ups. The writer Eric Linklater described it as "dull and dark", while the Scottish historian Buchanan claimed it was "so uncouth a place that no creature can live therein, except such as are born there". Certainly, if you keep to the fast main

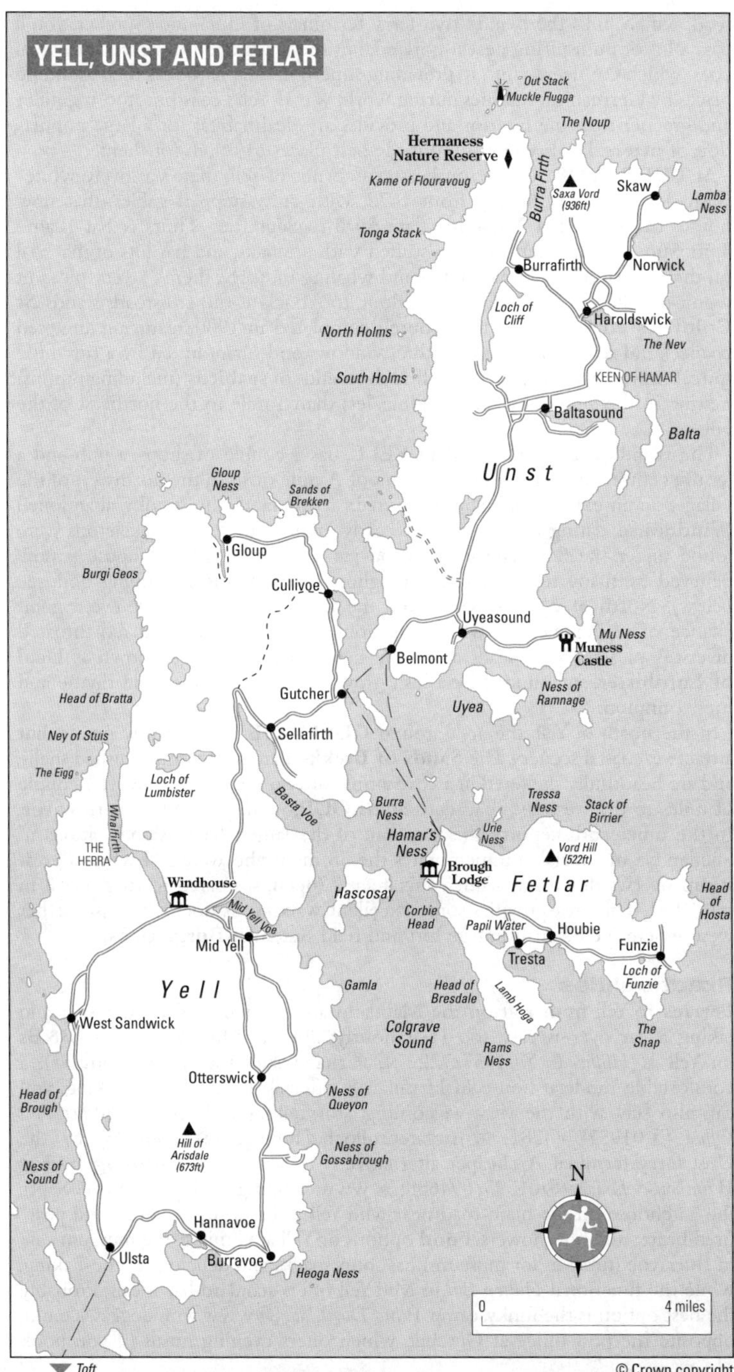
YELL, UNST AND FETLAR
Out Stack
Muckle Flugga
The Noup
Hermaness Nature Reserve
Burra Firth
Kame of Flouravoug
Saxa Vord (936ft)
Skaw
Lamba Ness
Tonga Stack
Burrafirth
Norwick
Loch of Cliff
Haroldswick
North Holms
The Nev
South Holms
KEEN OF HAMAR
Baltasound
Balta
Unst
Gloup Ness
Sands of Brekken
Gloup
Burgi Geos
Cullivoe
Uyeasound
Mu Ness
Muness Castle
Belmont
Gutcher
Head of Bratta
Ness of Ramnage
Uyea
Ney of Stuis
Sellafirth
The Eigg
Loch of Lumbister
Basta Voe
Burra Ness
Tressa Ness
Stack of Birrier
Whalfirth
Hamar's Ness
Urie Ness
Vord Hill (522ft)
THE HERRA
Brough Lodge
Windhouse
Hascosay
Fetlar
Head of Hosta
Mid Yell Voe
Corbie Head
Papil Water
Houbie
Mid Yell
Funzie
Tresta
Loch of Funzie
Gamla
Head of Bresdale
Yell
Lamb Hoga
West Sandwick
Colgrave Sound
The Snap
Rams Ness
Otterswick
Head of Brough
Ness of Queyon
Hill of Arisdale (673ft)
Ness of Gossabrough
Ness of Sound
N
Hannavoe
Ulsta
Burravoe
Heoga Ness
0
4 miles
Toft
© Crown copyright

road, which links the island's two ferry terminals of Ulsta and Gutcher, you'll pass a lot of uninspiring peat moorland, but the landscape is relieved by several voes, which cut deeply into it, providing superb natural harbours used as hiding places by German submarines during World War II. Yell's coastline, too, is gentler and greener than the interior and provides an ideal habitat for a large population of **otters**; locals will point out the best places to watch for them.

At **BURRAVOE**, in the southeastern corner of Yell, there's a lovely whitewashed laird's house dating from 1672, with crow-stepped gables, that now houses the **Old Haa Museum** (late April to Sept Tues–Thurs & Sat 10am–4pm, Sun 2–5pm; free), which is stuffed with artefacts, and has lots of material on the history of the local herring and whaling industry; there's a very pleasant wood-panelled café on the ground floor, too. Back at the crossroads stands **St Colman's Kirk**, a stylish little church completed in 1900, featuring an apsed chancel and several winsome Gothic windows and surmounted by a tiny little spire. From May to August, you'll find thousands of **seabirds** (including puffins) nesting in the cliffs above Ladies Hole, less than a mile to the northeast of the village.

The island's largest village, **MID YELL**, has a couple of shops, a pub and a leisure centre with a good swimming pool. A mile or so to the northwest of the village, on an exposed hill above the main road, stands the spooky, abandoned **Windhouse**, dating in part from the early eighteenth century; skeletons were found under the floor and in its wood-panelled walls, and the house is now believed by many to be haunted (its ghost-free lodge is a camping böd; see below). North of Windhouse, around the Loch of Lumbister, you've a good chance of seeing merlins, whimbrels, golden plovers, skuas and red-throated divers. A pleasant walk leads along the nearby narrow gorge known as **Daal of Lumbister**, surrounded by a lush growth of honeysuckle, wild thyme and moss campion.

In the north of Yell, the area around **CULLIVOE** has relatively gentle, but attractive, coastal scenery. The **Sands of Brekken** are made from crushed shells, and are beautifully sheltered in a cove a mile or two north of Cullivoe. A couple of miles to the west, the road ends at **GLOUP**, with its secretive, narrow voe. In the nineteenth century, this was one of the largest haaf-fishing stations in Shetland; a memorial commemorates the 58 men who were lost when a great storm overwhelmed six of their "sixareens" (open, six-oared rowing boats) in July 1881. This area provides some excellent walking, as does the coast further west, where there's an Iron Age fort and field system at **Burgi Geos**.

Practicalities

Ferries to Yell from Toft on the Mainland are frequent and inexpensive, and taking a car over is easy, too (1–2 hourly; 20min). One of the best **B&Bs** on Yell is *Hillhead* (ⓣ01957/722274, ⓔrita.leask@btopenworld.com; ❶), a comfortable modern house in Hamnavoe, offering great home cooking; you can also stay with the very welcoming, storytelling Tullochs at *Gutcher Post Office* (ⓣ01957/744201, ⓔmargaret.tulloch@btopenworld.com; ❷) by the Unst ferry terminal. A cheaper alternative is to stay in the **camping böd** at *Windhouse Lodge* (ⓣ01595/694688, ⓦwww.camping-bods.com; April–Sept), the gatehouse on the main road near Mid Yell; it has a small wood- and peat-fired heater and hot showers. **Food** options on Yell are limited: the museum café in Burravoe (times as for museum) has soup, snacks and delicious home-baking, while the functional *Hilltop Bar* in Mid Yell offers standard bar meals. Probably the best option is the funky, camp *Wind Dog Café* (ⓦwww.winddogcafe.co.uk), opposite the post office at Gutcher, which offers evening meals (if you book ahead), provides Internet access, as well as hosting storytelling from the inimitable Tullochs and other events.

Fetlar

Fetlar is the most fertile of the North Isles, much of it grassy moorland and lush green meadows with masses of summer flowers. It's known as "the garden of Shetland", though that's pushing it a bit, as it's still, relatively speaking, an unforgiving, treeless landscape. Around nine hundred people once lived here and there might well be more than a hundred now were it not for the activities of **Sir Arthur Nicolson**, who in the first half of the nineteenth century cleared many of the people at forty days' notice to make room for sheep. Nicolson's architectural tastes were rather more eccentric than some other local tyrants; his rotting but still astonishing **Brough Lodge**, a rambling castellated composition built in stone and brick in the 1820s, can be seen a mile or so south of the ferry terminal, and owes something – perhaps an apology – to Gothic, Classical and maybe even Tudor styles. Nicolson is also responsible for the nearby round-tower folly, which was built with stone taken from the abandoned crofthouses.

Today Fetlar's population lives on the southern and eastern sides of the island. At the main settlement, **HOUBIE**, in the centre of the island on the south coast, there's a rather less adventurously styled laird's house called Leagarth, with an impressive conservatory, built by Fetlar's most famous son, Sir William Watson Cheyne (1852–1932), who, with Lord Lister, pioneered antiseptic surgery. You can learn more about Cheyne's colourful life from the nearby **Fetlar Interpretive Centre** (May–Sept Mon–Fri 1–5pm, Sat & Sun 2–5pm; £2; Ⓦwww.fetlar.com), a welcoming museum with information on Fetlar's outstanding birdlife and the archeological excavations that took place near Houbie. Fetlar also shelters Britain's most northerly religious community, the Society of Our Lady of the Isles, which is based in the modern lodge on the edge of the cliffs at Aith Ness, to the southeast of Houbie.

Much of the northern half of the island around Fetlar's highest point, **Vord Hill** (522ft), is now an RSPB Reserve (mid-May to mid-July: phone for access Ⓣ01957/733246). As well as harbouring important colonies of arctic skuas and whimbrels, Fetlar is perhaps best known for having harboured Britain's only breeding pair of **snowy owls**, which bred on Stackaberg, to the southwest of Vord Hill, from 1967 to 1975. Fetlar is also one of very few places in Britain where you'll see the graceful **red-necked phalarope** (late May–early Aug): the birds are unusual in that the female does the courting and then leaves the male in charge of incubation. The island boasts ninety percent of Britain's phalarope population, and a hide has been provided overlooking the marshes (or mires) to the east of the **Loch of Funzie** (pronounced "Finny"); the loch itself is also a good place at which to spot the phalaropes, and is a regular haunt of red-throated divers.

If you're just looking for a nice sandy bay in which to relax, then head for **Tresta**, on the south coast, which boasts a beautiful, sheltered beach of golden sand, with the freshwater loch of Papil Water immediately behind it. Of the archeological remains on Fetlar, perhaps the most remarkable is the **Funzie Girt** or Finnigirt, an ancient stone boundary of uncertain date, which divides the island into two. Its southern end has been destroyed, but it is well preserved on the western and northern slopes of **Vord Hill** (see above). Fetlar also offers some great coastal walks along its jagged shores, which are punctuated by an enormous number of natural arches. The cliffs are particularly impressive on Lamb Hoga, the higher moorland peninsula to the southwest, where storm petrels return to their nests at night.

Practicalities

Ferries to Fetlar (5–6 daily; 25–40min) depart from both Gutcher on Yell and Belmont on Unst, though they are by no means as frequent as the ferries between the Mainland, Yell and Unst. The ferry docks at **Hamar's Ness**, three miles northwest of Houbie; the only public transport is an infrequent and small postcar (Mon, Wed & Fri 2 daily), so if you don't have a car you should try to negotiate a lift while on the ferry. If you do have a car, bear in mind that there's no petrol station on Fetlar, so fill up before you come across. **Accommodation** is in short supply, so book ahead either at *Gord* (Ⓣ01957/733227, Ⓔlynboxall@zetnet.co.uk; ❸), the comfortable modern house attached to the island shop in Houbie, which does dinner, bed and breakfast, or at the **camping böd** in Aithbank (Ⓣ01595/694688, Ⓦwww.camping-bods.com; April–Sept), a cosy wood-panelled cottage, a mile east of Houbie. The folk at *Gord* also run the *Garths* **campsite** (Ⓣ01957/733227; May–Sept), a simple field just to the west of Houbie, with toilets, showers and drying facilities. The post office, shop and **café** (closed Thurs & Sun) are all in one building in the middle of Houbie.

Unst

Much of **Unst** (Ⓦwww.unst.org) is rolling grassland – a blessed relief for some after the peaty moorland of Yell – but the coast is more dramatic: a fringe of cliffs relieved by some beautiful sandy beaches. As Britain's most northerly inhabited

△ Bobby's bus shelter

island, there is a surfeit of "most northerly" sights, which is fair enough, given that many visitors only come here in order to head straight for Hermaness, to see the seabirds and look out over Muckle Flugga and the northernmost tip of Britain, to the North Pole beyond. The island has been badly affected by the recent closure of the local RAF radar base at Saxa Vord, which used to employ a third of the island's population, which has now fallen to around six hundred (down from a peak of over 2250 in 1871).

On the south coast of the island, not far from the ferry terminal, is **UYEASOUND**, with Greenwell's Booth, an old Hanseatic merchants' warehouse by the pier, sadly now roofless. Further east lie the ruins of **Muness Castle**, a diminutive defensive structure, with matching bulging bastions and corbelled turrets at opposite corners. The castle was built in 1598 by the Scots incomer, Laurence Bruce, stepbrother and chief bullyboy of the infamous Earl Robert Stewart, and probably designed by Andrew Crawford, who shortly afterwards built Scalloway Castle for Robert's son, Patrick. The inscription above the entrance asks visitors "not to hurt this vark aluayis", but the castle was sacked by Danish pirates in 1627 and never really re-roofed. To gain entry, you must get the keys and a torch from the nearby cottage. A little to the north is a vast sandy beach, backed by the deserted crofting settlement of Sandwick.

Unst's main settlement is **BALTASOUND**, five miles north, whose herring industry used to boost the local population of around five hundred to as much as ten thousand during the fishing season. To learn more about the herring boom and other aspects of Unst's history, head for the excellent new **Unst Heritage Centre** (May–Sept daily 2–5pm; free), housed in the old school building by the main crossroads. Baltasound also boasts Britain's most northerly brewery, the **Valhalla Brewery**, source of the Shetland Ales you see around the islands, which welcomes visits by appointment (Ⓣ01957/711658, Ⓦwww.valhallabrewery.co.uk; Mon–Fri). As you leave Baltasound, heading north, be sure to take a look at **Bobby's bus shelter** (Ⓦwww.unstbusshelter.shetland.co.uk), an eccentric, fully furnished, award-winning Shetland bus shelter on the edge of the town.

From Baltasound, the main road crosses a giant boulder field of serpentine, a greyish-green, occasionally turquoise rock found widely on Unst, that weathers to a rusty orange. The **Keen of Hamar**, east of Baltasound, and clearly signposted from the main road, is one of the largest expanses of serpentine debris in Europe, and is home to an extraordinary array of plantlife. It's worth taking a walk on this barren, exposed, almost lunar landscape that's thought to resemble what most of northern Europe looked like at the end of the last Ice Age. With the help of one of the SNH leaflets (kept in a box by the stile), you can try and identify some of the area's numerous rare and minuscule plants, including Norwegian sandwort, frog orchid, moonwort, and the mouse-eared Edmondston's chickweed, which flowers in June and July and is found nowhere else in the world.

Beyond the Keen of Hamar, the road drops down into **HAROLDSWICK**, where near the shore you'll find the **Unst Boat Haven** (May–Sept daily 2–5pm; free), displaying a beautifully presented collection of historic boats with many tools of the trade and information on fishing. Less than a mile north of Haroldswick is **SAXA VORD**, the eyesore **RAF base** (also confusingly the name of the nearby hill), beyond which the road continues for another couple of miles before ending at Skaw, with a beautiful beach and the very last house in Britain.

The road that heads off northwest from Haroldswick leads to the head of **Burra Firth**, a north-facing inlet surrounded by cliffs and home to Britain's most northerly golf course. It is guarded to the east by the hills of **Saxa Vord** (936ft), Unst's highest point, topped by several Ministry of Defence installations. It was here that the country's unofficial wind-speed record of 194mph was recorded in 1992. To the west of Burra Firth lies the bleak headland of **Hermaness**, now a National Nature Reserve and home to more than 100,000 nesting seabirds. There's an excellent **visitor centre** in the former lighthouse keepers' shore station, where you can pick up a leaflet showing the marked routes across the heather, which allow you access into the reserve. Whatever you do, stick to the path so as to avoid annoying the vast numbers of nesting great skuas.

From Hermaness Hill, you can look down over the jagged rocks of the wonderfully named Vesta Skerry, Rumblings, Tipta Skerry and **Muckle Flugga**. There are few more dramatic settings for a lighthouse, and few sites could ever have presented as great a challenge to the builders, who erected it in 1858. Beyond the lighthouse is **Out Stack**, the most northerly bit of Britain, where Lady Franklin landed in 1849 in order to pray (in vain, as it turned out) for the safe return for her husband from his expedition to discover the Northwest Passage, undertaken four years previously. The views from here are inevitably marvellous, as is the birdlife; there's a huge gannetry on one of the stacks, and puffins burrow all along the clifftops. The walk down the west side of Unst towards Westing is one of the finest in Shetland: if the wind's blowing hard, the seascape is memorably dramatic.

Practicalities

Ferries shuttle regularly from Gutcher on Yell over to **BELMONT** on Unst (1–2 hourly; 10min); booking in advance is wise (ⓣ01957/722259). By far the best and most unusual **accommodation** is historic *Buness House* (ⓣ01957/711315, ⓦwww.users.zetnet.co.uk/buness-house; ⑥), a seventeenth-century haa in Baltasound still owned and run by the eccentric Edmondstons (of chickweed fame). Another very good bet is *Prestagaard* (ⓣ01957/755240, ⓦwww.prestegaard.shetland.co.uk; ②), a modest Victorian B&B with just a couple of rooms in Uyeasound, where there's also the very handy *Gardiesfauld Hostel* (ⓣ01957/755259, ⓦwww.gardiesfauld.shetland.co.uk; April–Sept), a clean and modern place near the pier which allows **camping**, and offers **bike rental**. Make sure you book yourself in for dinner, bed and breakfast or self cater, rather than resort to the bar food at the *Baltasound Hotel*. During the day, snacks and teas can be had at the **tearoom** in Nornova Knitwear just north of Muness Castle. The largest **shop** around is the NAAFI store within the old RAF base at Saxa Vord, which is now open to the public.

Travel details

Ferries to Shetland

Summer timetable only.

Aberdeen to: Lerwick (daily; 12hr).

Kirkwall (Orkney) to: Lerwick (3–4 weekly; 6hr).

Inter-island ferries

Summer timetable only.

To Bressay: Lerwick–Bressay (hourly; 7min).

To Fair Isle: Lerwick–Fair Isle (alternate Thurs; 4hr 30min); Grutness–Fair Isle (Tues, Sat & alternate Thurs; 3hr).

To Fetlar: Belmont (Unst) and Gutcher (Yell)–Hamar's Ness (5–6 daily; 25–40min).

To Foula: Scalloway–Foula (alternate Thurs; 3hr 30min); Walls–Foula (Tues, Sat & alternate Thurs; 2hr).

To Out Skerries: Lerwick–Skerries (Tues & Thurs; 2hr 30min); Vidlin–Skerries (1 on Mon, Fri–Sun 3 daily; 1hr 25min).

To Papa Stour: West Burrafirth–Papa Stour (Mon & Sun 1 daily, Wed, Fri & Sat 2 daily; 40min).
To Unst: Gutcher (Yell)–Belmont (1–2 hourly; 10min).
To Whalsay: Laxo–Symbister (every 45min; 30min).
To Yell: Toft–Ulsta (1–2 hourly; 20min).

Inter-island flights

Summer timetable only.
Sumburgh to: Fair Isle (Sat; 15min).
Tingwall to: Fair Isle (Mon, Wed & Fri 2 daily, 1 on Sat; 25min); Foula (Mon & Tues 1 daily, Wed & Fri 2 daily; 15min); Out Skerries, calling at Whalsay on request (Mon & Wed 1 daily, Thurs 2 daily; 20min); Papa Stour (Tues 2 daily; 10min).

Buses

Shetland Mainland

Lerwick to: Brae (Mon–Sat 4–6 daily, 1 on Sun in school term; 45min); Hamnavoe (Mon–Sat 2 daily; 30min); Hillswick (Mon–Sat 1 daily; 1hr 40min); Laxo (Mon–Sat 2 daily; 40min); Scalloway (Mon–Sat hourly; 15min); Sumburgh (Mon–Sat 5 daily, 3 on Sun; 45min); Toft (Mon–Sat 4–5 daily; 50min); Vidlin (Mon–Sat 2 daily; 45min); Voe (Mon–Sat 5–6 daily, 1 on Sun in school term; 30min); Walls (Mon–Sat 1–3 daily; 45min).

Unst

Baltasound to: Haroldswick (Mon–Sat 3–4 daily; 10min).
Belmont to: Baltasound (Mon–Sat 2–3 daily; 20min); Uyeasound (Mon–Sat 2–3 daily; 5min).

Yell

Mid Yell to: Gutcher (Mon–Sat 1–5 daily, 1 on Sun in school term; 20min).
Ulsta to: Burravoe (Mon–Sat 1 daily; 15min); Gutcher (Mon–Sat 1–3 daily, 1 on Sun in school term; 30min).

Contexts

Contexts

History

It's hard to look at a landscape in the Scottish Highlands and Islands and not have a sense of the stories from history swirling around, from the ancient Stone Age settlers whose dwellings and stone circles are still so well preserved around the Northern and Western Isles, to the empty villages and lonely glens depopulated during the Clearances. Unusually for Europe, the history of the region is dominated more by the wildness of the sea and harshness of the landscape than the politics of London or Paris, and even Edinburgh has often felt distant, another landscape, another language and another difficult journey away.

Prehistoric Scotland

Scotland's first inhabitants were Mesolithic **hunter-gatherers**, who arrived as the last Ice Age retreated around 8000 BC. They lived initially in the area south of Oban, where heaps of animal bones and shells have been excavated in the caves on the Mull of Kintyre and on the plains north of Crinan. From here there is evidence of their moving onto the islands of Arran, Jura, Rùm, Skye and Lewis, where the damp and relatively warm coastal climate would have been preferable to the harsher inland hills and glens. Around 4500 BC, **Neolithic farming peoples** from the European mainland began moving into Scotland. To provide themselves with land for their cereal crops and grazing for their livestock, they cleared large areas of upland forest, usually by fire, and in the process created the characteristic moorland landscapes of much of modern Scotland. These early farmers established permanent settlements, some of which, like the well-preserved village of **Skara Brae** on Orkney, were near the sea, enabling them to supplement their diet by fishing and to develop their skills as boatbuilders. The Neolithic settlements were not as isolated as was once imagined: geological evidence has, for instance, revealed that the stone used to make axeheads found in the Hebrides was quarried in Northern Ireland.

Settlement spurred the development of more complex forms of religious belief. The Neolithic peoples built large chambered burial mounds or **cairns**, such as Maes Howe in Orkney (see p.412) and the Clava Cairns near Inverness (see p.255). This reverence for human remains suggests a belief in some form of afterlife, a concept that the next wave of settlers, the **Beaker people**, certainly believed in. They placed pottery beakers filled with drink in the tombs of their dead to assist the passage of the deceased on their journey to, or their stay in, the next world. The Beaker people also built the mysterious **stone circles**, thirty of which have been discovered in Scotland. Such monuments were a massive commitment in terms of time and energy, with many of the stones carried from miles away, just as they were at Stonehenge in England, the most famous stone circle of all. One of the best-known Scottish circles is that of **Calanais** (Callanish) on the Isle of Lewis (see p.377), where a dramatic series of monoliths (single standing stones) form avenues leading towards a circle made up of thirteen standing stones. The exact function of the circles is still unknown, but many of the stones are aligned with the position of the sun at certain points in its annual cycle, suggesting that the monuments are related to the changing of the seasons.

The Beaker people also brought the **Bronze Age** to Scotland. Bronze, an alloy of copper and tin, was stronger and more flexible than its predecessor flint, which had long been used for axeheads and knives. New materials led directly to the development of more effective weapons, and the sword and the shield made their first appearance around 1000 BC. Agricultural needs plus new weaponry added up to a state of endemic warfare as villagers raided their neighbours to steal livestock and grain. The Bronze Age peoples responded to the danger by developing a range of defences, among them the spectacular **hillforts**, great earthwork defences, many of which are thought to have been occupied from around 1000 BC and remained in use throughout the Iron Age, sometimes far longer. Less spectacular but equally practical were the **crannogs**, smaller settlements built on artificial islands constructed of logs, earth, stones and brush, such as those found on Loch Tay (see p.181).

Conflict in Scotland intensified in the first millennium BC as successive waves of **Celtic** settlers, arriving from the south, increased competition for land. Around 400 BC, the Celts brought the technology of **iron** with them and, as Winston Churchill put it, "Men armed with iron entered Britain and killed the men of bronze." These fractious times witnessed the construction of hundreds of **brochs** or fortified towers. Concentrated along the Atlantic coast and in the Northern and Western Isles, the brochs were dry-stone fortifications (built without mortar or cement) often over 40ft in height. Some historians claim they provided protection for small coastal settlements from the attentions of Roman slave-traders. Much the best-preserved broch is on the Shetland island of **Mousa** (see p.465); its double walls rise to about 40ft, only a little short of their original height. The Celts continued to migrate north almost up until Julius Caesar's first incursion into Britain in 55 BC.

At the end of the prehistoric period, immediately prior to the arrival of the Romans, Scotland was divided among a number of warring Iron Age tribes, who, apart from the raiding, were preoccupied with wresting a living from the land, growing barley and oats, rearing sheep, hunting deer and fishing for salmon. The Romans were to write these people into history under the collective name Picti, or **Picts**, meaning "painted people", after their body tattoos.

The Romans

The **Roman conquest** of Britain began in 43 AD, almost a century after Caesar's first invasion. By 80 AD the Roman governor Agricola felt secure enough in the south of Britain to begin an invasion of the north, building a string of forts along the southern edge of the Highlands and defeating a large force of Scottish tribes at Mons Graupius. Precisely where this is remains a puzzle for historians, though most place it somewhere in the northeast, possibly on the slopes of Bennachie, near Inverurie in Aberdeenshire. The long-term effect of his campaign, however, was slight. Work on a major fort – to be the base for 5000 – at Inchtuthill, north of Perth on the Tay, was abandoned before it was finished, and the legions withdrew south. In 123 AD the **emperor Hadrian** decided to seal the frontier against the northern tribes and built **Hadrian's Wall**, which stretched from the Solway Firth to the Tyne and was the first formal division of the mainland of Britain. Twenty years later, the Romans again ventured north and built the **Antonine Wall** between the Clyde and the Forth, a clear statement of the hostility they perceived to the north. This was occupied for about forty years, but thereafter the Romans, frustrated by the inhospitable terrain of the Highlands, largely gave up their attempt to subjugate the north, and instead adopted a policy of containment.

It was the Romans who produced the first written accounts of the peoples of Scotland. In the second century AD, the Greco-Egyptian geographer Ptolemy drew up the first known map of Scotland, which identified seventeen tribal territories. Other descriptions were less scientific, compounding the mixture of fear and contempt with which the Romans regarded their Pictish neighbours. Dio Cassius, a Roman commentator writing in 197 AD, informed his readers that:

They live in huts, go naked and unshod. They mostly have a democratic government, and are much addicted to robbery. They can bear hunger and cold and all manner of hardship; they will retire into their marshes and hold out for days with only their heads above water, and in the forest they will subsist on barks and roots.

Another Roman account, by Tacitus, also identified the first inhabitant of Scotland whose name is known, a leader of the Pictish tribes called **Calgacus**, or "swordsman", who Tacitus claimed led 30,000 men. It is telling that, just as the uncomplimentary propaganda about primitive Highlanders had hardly changed by the time of Bonnie Prince Charlie's uprising in 1745, so too the number of fighting men he might have had at his disposal – had he been able to unite them – was largely the same.

The Dark Ages

In the years following the departure of the Romans, traditionally put at 450 AD, the population of Scotland changed considerably. By 500 AD there were four groups of people, or nations, dominant in different parts of the country. The **Picts** occupied the Northern Isles, the north and the east as far south as Fife. Today their settlements can be generally identified by place names with a "Pit" prefix, such as Pitlochry, and by the existence of carved symbol stones, like those found at Aberlemno in Angus. To the southwest, between Dumbarton and Carlisle, was a population of **Britons**. Many of the Briton leaders had Roman names, which suggests that they were a Romanized Celtic people, possibly a combination of tribes maintained by the Romans as a buffer between the Wall and the northern tribes, and peoples pushed west by the Anglo-Saxon invaders landing on the east coast. Both the Britons and the Picts spoke variations of P-Celtic, from which Welsh, Cornish and Breton developed.

On the west coast, to the north and west of the Britons (in what is now Argyll), lived the **Scotti**, Irish-Celtic invaders who would eventually give their name to the whole country. The first Scotti arrived in the Western Isles from Ireland in the fourth century AD, and about a century later their great king, Fergus Mor, moved his base from Antrim to Dunadd, near Lochgilphead, where he founded the kingdom of Dalriada. The Scotti spoke Q-Celtic, the precursor of modern Gaelic. On the east coast, the Germanic **Angles** had sailed north along the coast to carve out an enclave around Dunbar in East Lothian.

Within three centuries, another non-Celtic invader was making significant incursions. From around 795 AD, **Norse** raids began on the Scottish coast and Hebrides, soon followed by the arrival of settlers, mainly in the northern isles and along the Caithness and Sutherland coastline. In 872 AD, the King of Norway set up an earldom in **Orkney**, from which **Shetland** was also governed, and for the next six centuries the Northern Isles took a path distinct from the rest of Scotland, becoming a base for raiding and colonizing much of the rest of Britain and Ireland – and a link in the chain that connected Faroe, Iceland, Greenland and, more tenuously, North America.

The next few centuries saw almost constant warfare among the different groups. The main issue was land, but this was frequently complicated by the need of the warrior castes, who dominated all of these cultures, to exhibit martial prowess. Military conquests did play their part in bringing the peoples of Scotland together, but the most persuasive force was **Christianity**. Many of the Britons had been Christians since Roman times and it had been a Briton, St Ninian, who conducted the first missionary work among the Picts at the end of the fourth century. Attempts to convert the Picts were resumed in the sixth century by St Columba, who, as a Gaelic-speaking Scotti, demonstrated that Christianity could provide a bridge between the different tribes.

Christianity proved attractive to pagan kings because it seemed to offer them supernatural powers. As St Columba declared, when he inaugurated his cousin Aidan as king of Dalriada in 574, "Believe firmly, O Aidan, that none of your enemies will be able to resist you unless you first deal falsely against me and my successors." This combination of spiritual and political power, when taken with Columba's establishment of the island of **Iona** (see p.109) as a centre of Christian culture, opened the way for many peaceable contacts between the Picts and Scotti. Intermarriage became commonplace, and the Scotti king Kenneth MacAlpine, who united Dalriada and Pictland in 843, was the son of a Pictish princess – the Picts traced succession through the female line. Similarly, MacAlpine's creation of the united kingdom of **Alba**, later known as **Scotia**, was part of a process of integration rather than outright conquest, though it was the Scots' religion, Columba's Christianity and their language (Gaelic) that were to dominate the merger, allowing many aspects of Pictish life, including their language, to fall forgotten and untraceable into the depths of history. Kenneth and his successors gradually extended the frontiers of their kingdom by marriage and force of arms until, by 1034, almost all of what we now call Scotland – on the mainland, at least – was under their rule.

The Middle Ages

By the time of his death in 1034, **Malcolm II** was recognized as the king of Scotia. He was not, though, a national king in the sense that we understand the term, as under the Gaelic system kings were elected from the *derbfine*, a group made up of those whose great-grandfathers had been kings. The chosen successor, supposedly the fittest to rule, was known as the tanist. By the eleventh century, however, Scottish kings had become familiar with the principle of heredity, and were often tempted to bend the rules of tanistry. Thus, Malcolm secured the succession of his grandson **Duncan** by murdering a potential rival *tanist*. Duncan, in turn, was killed by **Macbeth** near Elgin in 1040. Macbeth was not, therefore, the villain of Shakespeare's imagination, but simply an ambitious Scot of royal blood acting in a relatively conventional way.

The victory of **Malcolm III**, known as Canmore (Bighead), over Macbeth in 1057 marked the beginning of a period of fundamental change in Scottish society. Having avenged his father Duncan, Malcolm III, who had spent the previous seventeen years at the English court, sought to apply to Scotland a range of ideas he had brought back with him. He and his heirs established a secure dynasty based on succession through the male line and introduced **feudalism** into Scotland, a system that was diametrically opposed to the Gaelic system, which rested on blood ties: the followers of a Gaelic king were his kindred, whereas the followers of a feudal king were vassals bought with land. The Canmores successfully feudalized much of southern and eastern Scotland by making grants to their Norman, Breton and Flemish followers; they preferred to make their capital in Edinburgh, and in these regions, Scots – a northern version of Anglo-Saxon – pushed out Gaelic as the lingua franca. They also began to reform the **Church**, a development started with the efforts of Margaret,

Malcolm III's English wife, who brought Scottish religious practices into line with those of the rest of Europe and was eventually canonized.

The policies of the Canmores laid the basis for a **cultural rift** in Scotland between the Highland and Lowland communities. Factionalism between various chiefs tended to distract the Highland tribes from their widening differences with the rulers to the south, while the ever-present Viking threat also served to keep many of the clans looking to the west and north rather than the south.

In 1098, a **treaty** between Edgar, King of Scots, and Magnus Bareleg, King of Norway, ceded sovereignty of all the islands to the Norwegians – Magnus even managed to include Kintyre in his swag by being hauled across the isthmus at Tarbet sitting in a boat, thus proving it an "island", as it could be circumnavigated. In practice, however, power in the western islands was in the control of local chiefs, lieutenants of a king on the Isle of Man who was himself subordinate to the King of Norway. By marrying the daughter of one of the Manx kings and skilful raiding of neighbouring islands, **Somerled**, King of Argyll, established himself and his successors as Lords of the Isles. Their natural ally was to the Scottish rather than the Norwegian king, and when **Alexander III** (1249–86), Scotland's strongest king in two centuries, sought to buy back the Hebrides from King Haakon of Norway in 1263, the offended Norwegian king sent a fleet to teach the Scots a lesson and drag the islands back into line. Initially the bullying tactics worked, but the fleet lingered too long, was battered by a series of autumnal storms, and retreated back to Orkney in disarray following a skirmish with Alexander's army at **Largs** on the Clyde coast. While in Orkney, King Haakon died, and three years later the **Treaty of Perth** of 1266 returned the Isle of Man and the Hebrides to Scotland in exchange for an annual rent.

In 1286 **Alexander III** died, and a hotly disputed succession gave Edward I, the king of England, an opportunity to subjugate Scotland. In 1291 Edward presided over a conference where the rival claimants to the Scottish throne presented their cases. Edward chose John Balliol in preference to Robert the Bruce, his main rival, and obliged John to pay him homage, thus turning Scotland into a vassal kingdom. Bruce refused to accept the decision, thereby continuing the conflict, and in 1295 Balliol renounced his allegiance to Edward and formed an alliance with France – the beginning of what is known as the "**Auld Alliance**". In the conflict that followed, the Bruce family sided with the English, Balliol was defeated and imprisoned, and Edward seized control of almost all of Scotland.

Edward had shown little mercy during his conquest of Scotland – he had, for example, had most of the population of Berwick massacred – and his cruelty seems to have provoked a truly national resistance. This focused on **William Wallace**, a man of relatively lowly origins from southwest Scotland who forged an army of peasants, lesser knights and townsmen that was fundamentally different to the armies raised by the nobility. Figures like Balliol, holding lands in England, France and Scotland, were part of an international aristocracy for whom warfare was merely the means by which they struggled for power. Wallace, by contrast, led proto-nationalist forces drawn from both Lowlands and Highlands determined to expel the English from their country. Probably for that very reason Wallace never received the support of the nobility and, after a bitter ten-year campaign, he was betrayed and executed in London in 1305.

With Wallace out of the way, feudal intrigue resumed. In 1306 **Robert the Bruce**, the erstwhile ally of the English, defied Edward and had himself crowned king of Scotland. Edward died the following year, but the unrest

△ Robert the Bruce

dragged on until 1314, when Bruce decisively defeated a huge English army under Edward II at the Battle of **Bannockburn**. At last Bruce was firmly in control of his kingdom, and in 1320 the Scots asserted their right to independence in a successful petition to the pope, now known as the **Declaration of Arbroath**.

In the years following Bruce's death in 1329, the Scottish monarchy gradually declined in influence. The last of the Bruce dynasty died in 1371, to be succeeded by the "Stewards", hence **Stewarts**, but thereafter a succession of Scottish rulers, culminating with James VI in 1567, came to the throne when still children. The power vacuum was filled by the nobility, whose key members exercised control as Scotland's regents while carving out territories where they ruled with the power, if not the title, of kings. The more vigorous monarchs of the period, notably **James I** (1406–37), did their best to curb the power of such dynasties, but their efforts were usually nullified at the next regency. **James IV** (1488–1513), the most talented of the early Stewarts, might have restored the authority of the Crown, but his invasion of England ended in a terrible defeat for the Scots – and his own death – at the Battle of **Flodden Field**.

Meanwhile, the shape of modern-day Scotland was completed when the Northern Isles were gradually wrested from Norway, which had united with Sweden under the Danish Crown in the fourteenth century. In 1469, a marriage was arranged between Margaret, daughter of the Danish king, Christian I, and the future **King James III** (1460–88) of Scotland. Short of cash for her dowry, Christian mortgaged Orkney to Scotland in 1468, followed by Shetland in 1469; neither pledge was ever successfully redeemed. The laws, religion and administration of the Northern Isles became Scottish, though their Norse heritage is still very evident in place names, dialect and culture. Meanwhile, the MacDonald Lords of the Isles had become too unruly for the more unified vision of James IV, and in 1493 the title reverted to the Crown. It still remains there: the current Lord of the Isles is Prince Charles.

The religious wars

In many respects the **Reformation** in Scotland was driven as much by the political intrigue of the reign of **Mary**, **Queen of Scots** (1542–67) as it was by religious conviction. Although in later years the hard-line Presbyterianism of the Highlands and Western Isles would triumph over political expediency, the revolutionary thinking of **John Knox** and his Protestant die-hards initially made little impact in the north. If some of the Lowland lords were still inclined to see religious affiliation as a negotiable tool in the quest for power and influence, the loyalty – if not, perhaps, the piety – of many of the Highland chiefs to both their monarch and the Catholic faith was much more solid.

James VI (1566–1625), who in 1603 also became James I of England, disliked Presbyterianism because its quasi-democratic structure – particularly the lack of royally appointed bishops – appeared to threaten his authority. In 1610 he restored the Scottish bishops, leaving a legacy that his son, **Charles I** (1625–49), who was raised in Episcopalian England, could not handle. He had little understanding of Scottish reformism and, by attempting to impose a new prayer book on the Kirk in 1637, laying down forms of worship in line with those favoured by the High Anglican Church, provoked the **National Covenant**, a religious pledge that committed the signatories to "Labour by all means lawful to recover the purity and liberty of the Gospel as it was established and professed".

Charles declared all the "**Covenanters**" to be rebels, a proclamation endorsed by his Scottish bishops. Consequently, when the king backed down from military action and called a General Assembly of the Kirk, the assembly promptly abolished the episcopacy. Charles pronounced the proceedings illegal, but lack of finance stopped him from mounting an effective military campaign – whereas the Covenanters, well financed by the Kirk, assembled a proficient army under Alexander Leslie. In desperation, Charles summoned the English Parliament, the first for eleven years, hoping it would pay for an army. But, like the calling of the General Assembly, the decision was a disaster and Parliament was much keener to criticize his policies than to raise taxes. In response Charles declared war on Parliament in 1642.

Until 1650, Scotland was ruled by the Covenanters and the power of the Presbyterian Kirk grew considerably. Laws were passed establishing schools in every parish and, less usefully, banning trade with Catholic countries. The only effective opposition to the theocratic state came from the **Marquis of Montrose**, who had initially supported the Covenant but lined up with the king when war broke out. Montrose was a gifted campaigner whose army was drawn from the Highlands and Islands, where the Kirk's influence was still weak, and included a frightening rabble of islanders and Irishmen under the inspiration of Colonsay chief Alasdair MacDonald, or **Colkitto**, whose appetite for the fray was fed by Montrose's willingness to send them charging into battle at the precise moment they could inflict most damage. For a golden year Montrose's army roamed the Highlands undefeated, scoring a number of brilliant tactical victories over the Covenanters, but the reluctance of his troops to stay south of the Highland Line made it impossible for him to capitalize on his successes and, as the clansmen dispersed with the spoils of victory back to their lands, Montrose was left weak and exposed. Unfailingly loyal to a king who was unwilling to take the same risks for his most gifted general, Montrose was eventually captured and executed in 1650.

Although the restoration of **Charles II** (1660–85) brought bishops back to the Kirk, they were integrated into an essentially presbyterian structure of Kirk sessions and presbyteries, though the General Assembly was not re-established. Over 300 clergymen, a third of the Scottish ministry, refused to accept the reinstatement of the bishops and were edged out of the Church, forced to hold open-air services, called **Conventicles**, which Charles did his best to suppress. Religious opposition inspired military resistance and the Lowlands witnessed scenes of brutal repression as the king's forces struggled to keep control in what was known as "The Killing Time". In the southwest, a particular stronghold of the Covenanters, the government imported Highlanders, the so-called "Highland Host", to root out the opposition, which they did with great barbarity.

Charles II was succeeded by his brother **James VII** (James II of England), whose ardent Catholicism caused a Protestant backlash in England. In 1689, he was forced into exile in France and the throne passed to **Mary**, his Protestant daughter, and her Dutch husband, **William of Orange**. In Scotland there was a brief flurry of opposition to William when **Graham of Claverhouse**, known as "Bonnie Dundee", united the Jacobite clans against the government army at the Pass of Killiekrankie, just north of Pitlochry. However, the inspirational Claverhouse was killed on the point of claiming a famous victory, and again the clans, leaderless and unwilling to press south, dissipated and the threat passed. William and Mary quickly consolidated their position, restoring the full presbyterian structure in Scotland and abolishing the bishops, though they chose not to restore the political and legal functions of the Kirk, which remained subject to parliamentary control. It was sufficient, however, to bring the religious wars to a close, essentially completing the Reformation in Scotland and establishing a platform on which political union would be built.

The Union

One thing that lingered, however, was Highland loyalty to the Stewart line, something both William and the political pragmatists saw as a significant threat. In 1691, William offered pardons to those Highland chiefs who had opposed his accession, on condition that they took an oath of allegiance by New Year's

Day 1692. Alasdair MacDonald of Glencoe had turned up at the last minute, but his efforts to take the oath were frustrated by the king's officials, who were determined to see his clan, well-known for their support of the Stewarts, destroyed. In February 1692, Captain Robert Campbell quartered his men in Glencoe and, two weeks later, in the middle of the night, his troops acted on their secret orders and carried out the infamous **massacre of Glencoe**. Thirty-eight MacDonalds died, and the slaughter caused a national scandal, especially among the clans, where "murder under trust" – killing those offering you shelter – was considered a particularly heinous crime.

The situation in Scotland was further complicated by the question of the succession. Mary died without leaving an heir and, on William's death in 1702, the crown passed to her sister **Anne**, James II's second daughter, who was also childless. In response, the English Parliament secured the Protestant succession by passing the **Act of Settlement**, which named the Electress Sophia of Hanover, a granddaughter of James VI (James I of England), as the next in line to the throne. The Act did not, however, apply in Scotland, and the English feared that the Scots would invite James Edward Stewart, the son of James II by his second wife, back from France to be their king. Consequently, Parliament appointed commissioners charged with the consideration of "proper methods towards attaining a union with Scotland". The project seemed doomed to failure when the Scottish Parliament passed the **Act of Security**, in 1703, stating that Scotland would not accept a Hanoverian monarch unless they had first received guarantees protecting their religion and their trade.

Nevertheless, despite the strength of anti-English feeling, the Scottish Parliament passed the **Act of Union** by 110 votes to 69 in January 1707. Some historians have explained the vote in terms of bribery and corruption. This certainly played a part (the Duke of Hamilton, for example, switched sides at a key moment and was subsequently rewarded with an English dukedom), but

The Highland clans

The term **"clan"**, as it is commonly used to refer to the quasi-tribal associations found in the Highlands of Scotland, only appears in its modern usage in the sixteenth century. In theory, the clan bound together blood relatives who shared a common ancestor, a concept clearly derived from the ancient Gaelic notion of kinship. But in practice many of the clans were of non-Gaelic origin – such as the Frasers, Sinclairs and Stewarts, all of Anglo-Norman descent – and it was the mythology of a common ancestor, rather than the actuality, that cemented the clans together. Furthermore, clans were often made up of people with a variety of surnames, and there are documented cases of individuals changing their names when they swapped allegiances. At the upper end of Highland society was the clan chief (who might have been a minor figure, like MacDonald of Glencoe, or a great lord, like the Duke of Argyll, head of the Campbells), who provided protection for his followers: they would, in turn, fight for him when called upon to do so. Below the clan chief were the chieftains of the septs, or sub-units of the clan, and then came the tacksmen, major tenants of the chief to whom they were frequently related. The tacksmen sublet their land to tenants, who were at the bottom of the social scale. The Highlanders wore a simple belted plaid wrapped around the body – rather than the kilt – and not until the late seventeenth century were certain tartans roughly associated with particular clans. The detailed codification of the tartan was produced by the Victorians, whose romantic vision of Highland life originated with George IV's visit to Scotland in 1822, when he appeared in an elaborate version of Highland dress, complete with flesh-coloured tights (for more on tartan, see p.250).

there were other factors. Scottish politicians were divided between the Cavaliers – Jacobites (supporters of the Stewarts) and Episcopalians – and the Country party, whose presbyterian members dreaded the return of the Stewarts more than they disliked the Hanoverians. To the Highlands and Islands, however, the shift of government four hundred miles further south from Edinburgh, itself distant enough for many, was to make relatively little difference to their lives for the best part of the rest of the century.

The country that was united with England in 1707 contained three distinct cultures: in south and east Scotland, they spoke Scots; in Shetland, Orkney and much of the northeast, the local dialect, though Scots-based, contained elements of Norn (Old Norse); in the rest of north and west Scotland, including the Western Isles, Gaelic was spoken. These linguistic differences were paralleled by different forms of social organization and customs. The people of north and west Scotland were mostly pastoralists, moving their sheep and cattle to Highland pastures in the summer, and returning to the glens in the winter. They lived in single-room dwellings, heated by a central peat fire and sometimes shared with livestock, and in hard times they would subsist on cakes made from the blood of their live cattle mixed with oatmeal. Highlanders supplemented their meagre income by raiding their clan neighbours and the prosperous Lowlands, whose inhabitants regarded their northern compatriots with a mixture of fear and contempt. In the early seventeenth century, Montgomerie, a Lowland poet, suggested that God had created the first Highlander out of horseshit. When God asked his creation what he would do, the reply was, "I will doun to the Lowland, Lord, and thair steill a kow." It was an attitude little improved from the days of the Roman chroniclers.

The Jacobite uprisings

When James VII/II was deposed, he had fled to France, where he planned the reconquest of his kingdom with the support of the French king. When James died in 1701, the hopes of the Stewarts passed to his only son, James Edward Stewart, the "Old Pretender" ("Pretender" in the sense of having pretensions to the throne; "Old" to distinguish him from his son Charles, the "Young Pretender"). After the accession to the British throne of the Hanoverian George I, son of Sophia, Electress of Hanover, the first major **Jacobite uprising** occurred in 1715: its timing appeared perfect. Scottish opinion was moving against the Union, which had failed to bring Scotland any tangible economic benefits. The English had also been accused of bad faith when, contrary to their pledges, they attempted to impose their legal practices on the Scots. Neither were Jacobite sentiments confined to Scotland. There were many in England who toasted the "King across the water" and showed no enthusiasm for the new German ruler. In September 1715, the fiercely Jacobite John Erskine, Earl of Mar, raised the Stewart standard at Braemar Castle. Just eight days later, he captured Perth, where he gathered an army of over 10,000 men, drawn mostly from the Episcopalians of northeast Scotland and from the Highlands. Mar's rebellion took the government by surprise. They had only 4000 soldiers in Scotland, under the command of the Duke of Argyll, but Mar dithered until he lost the military advantage. There was an indecisive battle at Sheriffmuir in November, but by the time the Old Pretender arrived the following month 6000 veteran Dutch troops had reinforced Argyll. The rebellion disintegrated rapidly and James slunk back to exile in France in February 1716.

Though better known, the **Jacobite uprising of 1745**, led by James's dashing son, Charles Edward Stewart (Bonnie Prince Charlie), had even less chance of success than the rising of 1715. In the intervening thirty years, the Hanoverians had consolidated their hold on the English throne, Lowland society had become uniformly loyalist, access into the Highlands for both trade and internal peacekeeping had been vastly improved by the military roads built by General Wade, and even among the clans regiments such as the Black Watch were recruited which drew on the Highlanders' military tradition but formed part of the government's standing army. The rebellion had a shaky start, with Charles landing on the west coast with only seven companions and no firm promises of clan support, and, however romantically inspired, it was a fated enterprise. He only attracted less than half of the potential 30,000 clansmen who could have marched with him, and promises of support from the French and English Jacobites failed to materialize. Nevertheless, after a decisive victory over government forces at Prestonpans, near Edinburgh, Charles made a spectacular advance into England, getting as far as Derby. London was in a state of panic: its shops were closed and the Bank of England, fearing a run on sterling, slowed withdrawals by paying out in sixpences. But Derby was as far as Charles got. On December 6, threatened by superior forces, the Jacobites decided to retreat to Scotland. The Duke of Cumberland was sent in pursuit and the two armies met on **Culloden Moor**, near Inverness, in April 1746. It was to be the last set-piece battle on British soil, the last time a claymore-wielding Highland charge would be set against organized ranks of musket-bearing troops, and the last time a Stewart would take up arms in pursuit of the throne. As with so many of the other critical points in the campaign, the Jacobite leadership at Culloden was divided and ill-prepared. When it came to the fight, the Highlanders were in the wrong place, exhausted after a forced overnight march, and seriously outnumbered and outgunned. They were swept from the field, losing over 1200 men compared to Cumberland's 300 plus. After the battle, many of the wounded Jacobites were slaughtered, an atrocity that earned Cumberland the nickname "Butcher". Charles took flight, living the next few months a fugitive as he dodged redcoat patrols across the Highlands and Islands, famously escaping from the outer isles to Skye in the company of Flora MacDonald (see p.349). Eventually a French ship came to his rescue and he returned to the Continent, where he lived out the rest of his life in drunken exile.

In the aftermath of the uprising, the wearing of tartan, the bearing of arms and the playing of bagpipes were all banned. Rebel chiefs lost their land and the Highlands were placed under military occupation. Most significantly, the government prohibited the private armies of the chiefs, thereby effectively destroying the clan system. Within a few years, more Highland regiments were recruited for the British army, and by the end of the century thousands of Scots were fighting and dying for their Hanoverian king against Napoleon.

The Highland Clearances

Once the clan chief was forbidden his own army, he had no need of the large tenantry that had previously been a vital military asset. Conversely, the second half of the eighteenth century saw the Highland population increase dramatically after the introduction of the easy-to-grow and nutritious potato. Between 1745 and 1811, the population of the Outer Hebrides, for example, rose from 13,000 to 24,500. The clan chiefs adopted different policies to deal with the new situation. Some encouraged emigration, and as many as 6000 Highlanders left for the Americas between 1800 and 1803 alone. Other landowners saw the economic advantages of developing alternative forms of employment for their tenantry, mainly fishing and kelping. **Kelp** (brown seaweed) was gathered and burnt to produce soda ash, which was used in the manufacture of soap, glass and explosives. There was a rising market for soda ash until the 1810s, with the price increasing from £2 a ton in 1760 to £20 in 1808, making a fortune for some landowners and providing thousands of Highlanders with temporary employment. Fishing for **herring** – the "silver darlings" – was also encouraged, and new harbours and coastal settlements were built all around the Highland coastline. Other landowners developed **sheep runs** on the Highland pastures, introducing hardy breeds like the black-faced Linton and the Cheviot. But extensive sheep farming proved incompatible with a high peasant population, and many landowners decided to clear their estates of tenants, some of whom were forcibly moved to tiny plots of marginal land, where they were to farm as **crofters**.

The pace of the **Highland Clearances** accelerated after the end of the Napoleonic wars in 1815, when the market price for kelp, fish and cattle declined, leaving sheep as the only profitable Highland product. The most notorious Clearances took place on the estates of the Countess of Sutherland, who owned a million acres in northern Scotland. Between 1807 and 1821, around 15,000 people were thrown off her land, evictions carried out by **Patrick Sellar**, the estate factor, with considerable brutality. Those who failed to leave by the appointed time had their homes burnt in front of them, and one elderly woman, who failed to get out of her home after it was torched, subsequently died from burns. The local sheriff charged Sellar with her murder, but a jury of landowners acquitted him – and the sheriff was sacked. Not all the Clearances were as brutal, but the consequences of overpopulation were again highlighted as a potato famine followed in 1846, forcing large-scale emigration to America and Canada and leaving the huge uninhabited areas found in the region today.

The crofters eked out a precarious existence, but they hung on throughout the nineteenth century, often by taking seasonal employment away from home. In the 1880s, however, a sharp downturn in agricultural prices made it difficult for many crofters to pay their rent. This time, inspired by the example of the Irish Land League, they resisted eviction, forming the **Highland Land Reform Association** and the **Crofters' Party**. In 1886, in response to the social unrest, Gladstone's Liberal government passed the **Crofters' Holdings Act**, which conceded three of the crofters' demands: security of tenure, fair rents to be decided independently, and the right to pass on crofts by inheritance. But Gladstone did not attempt to increase the amount of land available for crofting, and shortage of land remained a major problem until the **Land Settlement Act** of 1919 made provision for the creation of new crofts. Nevertheless, the population of the Highlands continued to fall into the twentieth century, with many of the region's young people finding city life more appealing.

For all the hardships of Highland life, however, the region was undergoing a re-evaluation particularly in the eyes of the well-educated and wealthier urban classes. In 1773 the famous London literary figure **Samuel Johnson** took a tour of the Highlands and Islands with his biographer, Edinburgh-born **James Boswell**; it was less than thirty years after Culloden – the pair even met Flora MacDonald in Skye – and travel was by no means easy, but the pair's descriptions of the noble wildness of the Highlands captured the imagination of British society (see p.529). The epic poems describing the exploits of the Celtic warrior Fingal, ostensibly penned by the third-century bard Ossian but in fact an elaborate and brilliant hoax by **James MacPherson**, further established the romantic idyll of the Highlands, a process taken to fruition by the novels of **Walter Scott**, who in 1822 orchestrated the state visit of George IV to Scotland, even dressing the monarch in a stylized version of the tartan plaid which had been worn by the pretender to his great-grandfather's throne. Meanwhile roads improved, railways and canals were built and, as access improved, so tourism grew. **Queen Victoria** fell in love with the Highlands, buying an estate at Balmoral, and the huge tracts of moorland owned by the Highland lairds became **sporting estates** for shooting grouse and deer, or fishing for salmon.

The World Wars

Depopulation of an all-too-familiar kind was present in the early decades of the twentieth century, with Highland regiments at the vanguard of the British Army's infantry offensives in both the Anglo-Boer wars at the start of the century and **World War I**. Few Highland communities were left untouched by the carnage of the trenches, with one particularly tragic episode taking place on New Year's Day 1919, when the steamer *Iolaire*, packed with returning servicemen, foundered on rocks at the entrance to Stornoway harbour, drowning over two hundred local men as their families looked on helpless from the pier (see p.372). The months after hostilities ended also saw one of the most remarkable spectacles in Orkney's long seafaring history, when seventy-four vessels from the German naval fleet, lying at anchor in Scapa Flow having surrendered to the British at the armistice, were scuttled by the skeleton German crews that remained aboard.

The same harbour was quickly involved in **World War II**, when a German U-boat breached the defences around Orkney in October 1939 and torpedoed HMS *Royal Oak*, with the loss of 833 men. Many more ships and lives were lost in the waters off the Hebrides during the hard-fought Battle of the Atlantic, when convoys carrying supplies and troops were constantly harried by German U-boats. Various bases were established in the west Highlands and Islands, including a flying-boat squadron at Kerrera, by Oban, with Air Force bases on Islay, Benbecula, Tiree and Lewis, and a Royal Naval anchorage at Tobermory; on the mainland, commandos were trained in survival skills and offensive landings in the area around lochs Lochy and Arkaig, near Fort William. Though men of fighting age again left the Highlands to serve in the forces, the war years were not altogether bleak, as the influx of servicemen ensured a certain prosperity to the places where they were based, and the need for the country to remain self-sufficient meant that farms and crofts – often worked by the women and children left behind – were encouraged to keep production levels high.

Even before the war, efforts had been made to recognize the greater social and economic needs of the Highlands and Islands with the establishment of the **Highlands and Islands Medical Service**, a precursor to the National Health Service introduced by the first postwar Labour government. Other agencies were set up in the 1940s, including the **North of Scotland Hydro Electric Board** and the **Forestry Commission**, both of which were tasked to improve the local infrastructure and create state-sponsored employment. In later decades the various **ferry** companies running to the Islands were coalesced into the State-subsidized Caledonian MacBrayne (or "CalMac", for short), and, partly benefiting from runways built in wartime, regular **airline** services to the islands started up.

The contemporary Highlands and Islands

After Britain joined the EEC in 1972, the Highlands and Islands were identified as an area in need of special assistance and, in harness with the **Highlands and Islands Development Board**, significant investment was made in the area's infrastructure, including roads, schools, medical facilities and harbours. European funding was also used to support the increased use and teaching of **Gaelic**, and the encouragement of Gaelic broadcasting, publishing and education, hand in hand with the embrace of Gaelic culture across Scotland as a whole, from the annual National Mod to the nationwide success of folk-rock bands such as Runrig and Capercaillie, means that the indigenous language and culture of the Highlands and Islands, while still vulnerable, is as healthy now as it has been for a century.

The strength of cultural identity – even in its more clichéd forms – has always been a vital aspect of the Highlands and Islands' attraction as a tourist destination. **Tourism** remains the dominant industry in the region, despite the furrowed brows of, on the one hand, businesses vulnerable to dips in numbers and spending, and on the other, conservationists concerned by the impact of increased numbers. The most recent attempt to address this dilemma has been the establishment of a system of **national parks** and, significantly, the first two to be declared in Scotland are both in the Highlands: the Loch Lomond and the Trossachs National Park, established in 2002, and the Cairngorms National Park, created in 2003. Meanwhile the main traditional industries, **farming** and **fishing**, continue with European support to struggle against European competition, while others, such as **whisky** and **tweed making**, remain prominent in certain pockets although they have never, in fact, been large-scale employers. New industries have arrived with the twentieth century, and while few have quite fulfilled the initial hopes raised of them, most remain to contribute to the economic diversity of the region. **Forestry**, for example, has seen large tracts of the Highlands planted, more sensitively now than in the past; North Sea **oil** has brought serious economic benefits not just to the northeast coast but also to Orkney and Shetland; **salmon farming** has become widespread, tainting many otherwise idyllic west coast scenes, but long accepted as a vital part of numerous coastal communities; and various set-piece industrial developments have made their mark, from the now-disused aluminium smelter at **Kinlochleven** to the **Dounreay** nuclear reactor and reprocessing plant near Thurso. Among the more recent arrivals on the economic map are various manifestations of **alternative energy**, most controversially large "wind farms" but also schemes to harness tidal and wave energy, and the phenomenon of "**cyber-crofting**" – essentially the operation of Internet-based businesses or services from remoter areas. The possibilities thrown up by the communications revolution have also led to the establishment of the **University of the Highlands**, with various colleges linked to each other and to outlying students by networked computers.

As remote living is made more viable, however, it is not just the indigenous population who benefit, and **immigration** into the Highlands now matches the long-term trend of emigration, with Inverness ranking as one of the fastest-growing urban areas in Britain. Traditionally regarded as the capital of the Highlands, Inverness was awarded city status in a millennium gesture by the government in 2000. The incomers – invariably called "white settlers" – are now an established aspect of Highland life, often providing economic impetus in the form of enthusiastically run small businesses, though their presence can still rankle in the intimate lives of small communities. Any prejudicial control from outside the region is looked on suspiciously, not least in the question of **land ownership**, which remains one of the keys to Highland development – some would say the most important of all. Some of the largest Highland estates continue to be owned and managed from afar, with little regard to local needs or priorities; two-thirds of the private land in Scotland is owned by a mere 1250 people, many of them aristocrats or foreign nationals. However, the success of groups of crofters in buying estates in Assynt and Knoydart, as well as the purchase of the islands of Eigg and Gigha by their inhabitants, hints at a broadening of land ownership, which many hope the land reforms brought in by the new Scottish Parliament will do more to promote.

With so many unique issues to tackle, it is perhaps not surprising that the Highlands and Islands have always maintained an independent and generally restrained voice in Scottish **politics**. Despite the unshakable Scottishness of the region, it has remained largely ambivalent to the surges of nationalism seen in other parts of the country. In local government, large numbers of independents are regularly returned, while in British (and more recently Scottish) elections, the tendency has always been towards strong, recognizable characters – mainly Liberals, with pockets of support for the SNP (Scottish National Party) in the east and for Labour in the Outer Isles.

The issue of **devolution** was long regarded with suspicion by Highlanders and Islanders for the likelihood of any Scottish Parliament being dominated by the politics of the Central Belt. Now that it has arrived, however, with the **Scottish Parliament** firmly established in Edinburgh, the demands for a more sensitive and understanding handling of the issues that matter to the Highlands and Islands have justifiably grown. After centuries of what has often seemed like ostracism from the rest of Scotland, the Highlands and Islands have good reason to believe that they are now partners in the dance.

Music

Scottish indigenous **music** has begun the twenty-first century in remarkably fine health. Outstanding young musicians and bands abound, either faithfully recreating the traditions of old or finding bold new ways to interpret and express them. After years of being stifled by the rigidly twee, cliché-ridden images of Scottishness as expressed by the likes of Andy Stewart and Jimmy Shand, the real spirit of Scots music enjoyed a significant rebirth towards the end of the twentieth century with a Celtic upsurge courtesy of bands like Silly Wizard, Tannahill Weavers and the Battlefield Band.

Scotland through the 1980s and 1990s saw an explosion of **roots** and **dance music** and, at the same time, a renewal and revisiting of traditions that had seemed perilously close to destruction. The influx of talent, energy and awareness in the national culture has been such that the scene is as vibrant now as it has been for years – from the thriving venues in Glasgow and the lively sessions in Edinburgh to the young musicians upholding their own tradition all over Shetland and the Orkneys. The revival has its own magazine *Living Tradition* and a selection of specialist record companies championing the music.

Things looked very different thirty years ago, when the stern disciplines and structures involved in effectively mastering Scottish **traditional music**, which allowed little scope for flair – particularly with bagpipe-playing, had seemed very outmoded alongside the poppier approach favoured south of the border. But taking their cue from the great Irish bands of the 1970s like Planxty and the Bothy Band, the young Scots musicians looked for new, more informal ways to express that tradition. Adopting non-traditional influences, they set about shaking the cobwebs off the old music. The virtuosos who've surfaced in their wake are themselves testament to the success of their musical revolution.

The Celtic folk band arrives

As in much of northern Europe, the story of Scotland's roots scene begins amid the **folk revival** of the 1960s, a time when folk song and traditional music engaged people who did not have strong family links with an ongoing tradition. For many in Scotland, traditional music had skipped a generation and they had to make a conscious effort to learn about it. At first, the main influences were largely American – skiffle music and artists like Pete Seeger – but soon people started to look to their own traditions, taking inspiration from the Gaelic songs of **Cathy-Ann McPhee**, then still current in rural outposts, or the old travelling singers like the **Stewarts of Blairgowrie**, **Isla Cameron**, **Lizzie Higgins** and, the greatest of them all, Lizzie's mother, **Jeannie Robertson**.

On the instrumental front, there were fewer obvious role models despite the continued presence of a great many people playing in **Scottish dance bands**, **pipe bands** and **Strathspey and Reel Societies** (fiddle orchestras). In the 1960s the action was coming out of Ireland and the recorded repertoire of bands like The Chieftains became the core of many a pub session in Scotland. Even in the early 1970s folk fiddle players were rare, although **Aly Bain** (see box opposite) made a huge impression when he arrived from Shetland and, soon after, Shetland reels started to creep into the general folk repertoire.

The art of the traditional musician was largely considered a purely solo affair, but in the 1960s a new phenomenon emerged to change these conceptions – the **Celtic folk band**. This soon created its own standard formula with a melody lead – usually fiddle or pipes – plus guitar, bouzouki and, more often than not, a singer, who became merely another element to the band rather than the focal point.

Instrumental in these developments was a Glasgow folk group, **The Clutha**, who in a folk scene dominated by singers and guitarists boasted not one but two fiddlers, along with a concertina and four strong singers – including the superb **Gordeanna McCulloch**.

The Clutha were hugely influential and became even more successful when **Jimmy Anderson** introduced a set of chamber pipes into the line-up. Jimmy was not only a great piper but was also a pipe-maker and he "invented" a set of pipes to be played in the key of D which sounded much quieter than the Highland pipes. This was essential at that time, as virtually all the venues were acoustic, and sound systems were not up to the job of balancing out the sounds of pipes, fiddle and voices.

Aly Bain and Shetland magic

Aly Bain has been a minor deity among Scottish musicians for well over three decades. A fiddle player of exquisite technique and individuality, he has been the driving force throughout that time of one of Scotland's all-time great bands, Boys of the Lough, while latterly teaming up with accordionist Phil Cunningham to act as roving ambassadors for Celtic music. In these guises, he has been instrumental in spreading the reach of Scottish music. First and foremost, though, Bain is a Shetlander, and his greatest legacy is the inspiration he has provided for a revival of Shetland's own characteristic tradition.

Aly was brought up in the capital of Shetland, Lerwick, and was inspired to play the fiddle by **Bob Duncan** – who endlessly played him records by the Strathspey king Scott Skinner – and later the old maestro, **Tom Anderson**. These two were the last of an apparently dying breed, and the youthful Aly was an odd sight dragging his fiddle along to join in with the old guys at the Shetland Fiddlers Society. Players like **Willie Hunter Jnr** and **Snr**, **Willie Pottinger** and **Alex Hughson** were legends locally, but they belonged to another age.

By the time the teenage Aly was persuaded to leave for the mainland, Shetland was changing by the minute, and the discovery of North Sea oil altered it beyond redemption, as the new industrial riches trampled its unique community spirit and sense of tradition. The old fiddlers gradually faded and died, and Shetland music, inflected with the eccentricity of the isolated environment and the influence of nearby Scandinavia, seemed destined to disappear too.

That it didn't is largely down to Aly. After a spell with Billy Connolly (then a folk artist) on the Scottish folk circuit, Aly found himself working with blues iconoclast Mike Whellans, and then the two of them tumbled into a link-up with two Irishmen, Robin Morton and Cathal McConnell, in a group they called **Boys of the Lough**. Aly's joyful artistry, unwavering integrity and unquenchable appetite and commitment to the music of his upbringing has kept Shetland music alive in a manner he could never have imagined. Even more importantly, it stung the imagination of the generation that followed.

These days, Aly spends as much time in Sweden as he does in Scotland, but Shetland music is buzzing again, with its own **annual festival** a treat of music-making and drinking. There are young musicians pouring out of the place, and a plethora of bands of all styles, including pop-oriented groups such as Rock, Salt & Nails and more recently Red Vans. The pick of the roots players, currently, is **Catriona MacDonald**, who was also taught by Tom Anderson in his last days. She is adept at classical music, and is fast becoming accomplished in Norwegian music; her mum went to school with Aly Bain – which in Shetland counts for an awful lot.

Key, too, to developments were the **Boys of the Lough**, a Scots-Irish group led by the Shetland fiddler **Aly Bain** (see box, p.511) and **The Whistlebinkies**. Developing in the Glasgow folk scene alongside The Clutha, both these groups took a strong instrumental line, rather than The Clutha's song-based approach. These two bands were in many ways Scotland's equivalent of Ireland's The Chieftains and through their musical ability and recognition outside the folk clubs, played an important part in breaking down musical barriers.

The Whistlebinkies were notable for employing only traditional instruments, including fine clarsach (Celtic harp) from **Judith Peacock**. However, the most important, and definingly Scottish, element of all three of these bands was the presence of **bagpipes**. Clutha had piper **Jimmy Anderson**, the Whistlebinkies featured **Rab Wallace**, who had a firm background in the Scots piping scene, while The Boys also had an experienced piper in **Robin Morton**. They were pioneers for what was to become a revolution in the late 1970s with bands like Battlefield Band, Tannahill Weavers, Silly Wizard, Alba and Ossian.

Pibroch: Scots pipes

Bagpipes are synonymous with Scotland yet they are not a specifically Scots instrument. The pipes were once to be found right across Europe, and pockets remain, across the English border in Northumbria, all over Ireland, in Spain and Italy, and in Eastern Europe, where bagpipe festivals are still held in rural areas. In Scotland, bagpipes seem to have made their appearance around the fifteenth century, and over the next hundred years or so they took on several forms, including quieter varieties (small pipes), both bellows and mouth blown, which allowed a diversity of playing styles.

The Highland bagpipe form known as **pibroch** (*piobaireachd* in Gaelic) evolved around this time, created by clan pipers for military, gathering, lamenting and marching purposes. Legendary among the clan pipers of this era were the MacCrimmons (they of the famous *MacCrimmon's Lament*, composed during the Jacobite rebellion), although they were but one of several important piping clans, among which were the MacArthurs, MacKays and MacDonalds. In the seventeenth and eighteenth centuries, through the influence of the British army, reels and strathspeys joined the repertoire and a tradition of military pipe bands emerged. After World War II they were joined by civilian bands, alongside whom developed a network of piping competitions.

The bagpipe tradition has continued uninterrupted, although for much of the last century under the domination of the military and the folklorist Piobaireachd Society. Recently, however, a number of Scottish musicians have revived the pipes in new and innovative forms. Following the lead of The Clutha, Boys of the Lough and Whistlebinkies, a new wave of young bands began to feature pipers, notably **Alba** with the then-teenage Alan McLeod, **Ossian** with Iain MacDonald and the **Battlefield Band** with Duncan McGillivray. Battlefield have subsequently used a selection of high-quality pipers, most recently the American Mike Katz. These players redefined the boundaries of pipe music using notes and finger movements outside the traditional range. They also showed the influence of Irish uillean pipe players (particularly Paddy Keenan of the **Bothy Band**) and Cape Breton style which many claim is the original, pre-military Scottish style.

In 1983 **Robin Morton** released *A Controversy of Pipers* on his Temple Records label, an album featuring six pipers from folk bands who were also top competitive players in the piping world. Up until this point, pipers in a folk band could be considered second-class by some in the piping establishment. This recording made a statement and soon the walls began to crumble.

Alongside all this came a revived interest in traditional piping, and in particular the strathspeys, slow airs and reels, which had tended to get submerged beneath the familiar military territory of marches and laments. The twentieth century's great bagpipe players, notably **John Burgess**, received a belated wider exposure. His legacy includes a masterful album and a renowned teaching career to ensure that the old piping tradition marches proudly into the twenty-first century.

Folk song and the club scene

While the folk bands were starting to catch up on the Irish and integrating bagpipes, **folk song** was also flourishing. The song tradition in Scotland is one of the strongest in Europe and in all areas of the country there are pockets of great singers and characters. In the 1960s the common ground was the folk club network and the various festivals dotted around the country.

The great modern pioneer of Scots folk song, and a man who perhaps rescued the whole British tradition, was the great singer and songwriter **Ewan MacColl**. Though born and raised in Salford in the north of England (about which he wrote one of his most famous songs, *Dirty Old Town*), he remained a fervently proud Scotsman all his life and saw folk song as a political tool of the working classes. He recorded the seminal *Scottish Popular Ballads* as early as 1956, and founded the first folk club in Britain. After MacColl, another of the building blocks of the 1960s folk revival was the Aberdeen group, **The Gaugers**. Song was the heart of this group – Tam Speirs, Arthur Watson and Peter Hall were all good singers – though they were also innovative in using instrumentation (fiddle, concertina and whistle) without a guitar or other rhythm instrument to tie the sound together.

Other significant Scots groups on the 1960s scene included the **Ian Campbell Folk Group**, Birmingham-based but largely Scots in character (and including future Fairport Daves, Swarbrick and Pegg, as well as Ian's sons, Ali and Robin, who went on to form UB40). They flirted with commercialism and pop sensibilities – as virtually every folk group of the era was compelled to do – and were too often unfairly bracketed with England's derided Spinners as a result. So too were **The Corries**, although they laced their blandness with enterprise, inventing their own instrumentation and writing the new unofficial national anthem, *Flower of Scotland*.

Other more adventurous experiments grew out of the folk and acoustic club scene in mid-1960s Glasgow and Edinburgh. It was at Clive's Incredible Folk Club in Glasgow that **The Incredible String Band** made their debut, led by **Mike Heron** and **Robin Williamson**. They took an unfashionable glance back into their own past on the one hand, while plunging headlong into psychedelia and other uncharted areas on the other. Their success broke down significant barriers, both in and out of Scotland, and in their wake came a succession of Scottish folk-rock crossover musicians. Glasgow-born **Bert Jansch** launched folk super-group Pentangle with Jacqui McShee, John Renbourn and Danny Thompson, and the flute-playing **Ian Anderson** found rock success with Jethro Tull. Meanwhile, a more traditional Scottish sound was promoted by the likes of **Archie**, **Ray** and **Cilla Fisher**, who sang new and traditional ballads, individually and together.

The great figure, however, along with MacColl, was the singer and guitarist **Dick Gaughan**, whose passionate artistry towers like a colossus above three decades. He started out in the Edinburgh folk club scene with an impenetrable accent, a deep belief in the socialist commitment of traditional song, and a guitar technique that had old masters of the art hanging on to the edge of their seats.

For a couple of years in the early 1970s, he played with Aly Bain in the Boys of the Lough, knocking out fiery versions of trad Celtic material. Gaughan became frustrated, however, by the limitations of a primarily instrumental (and fiddle-dominated) group and subsequently joined the innovative band **Five Hand Reed** as lead singer and also playing electric guitar. Again playing Scots-Irish traditional material, they might have been the greatest folk-rock band of them all if they hadn't just missed the Fairport/Steeleye Span boat.

Leaving to pursue an independent career, Gaughan became a fixture on the folk circuit and made a series of albums exploring Scots and Irish traditional music and reinterpreting the material for guitar. His *Handful of Earth* (1981) was perhaps the single best solo folk album of the decade, a record of stunning intensity with enough contemporary relevance and historical belief to grip all generations of music fans. And though sparing in his output, and modest about his value in the genre, he's also become one of the best songwriters of his generation.

Crucial contributions to folk song came, too, from two giants of the Scottish folk scene who were probably more appreciated throughout Europe than at home – the late **Hamish Imlach** and **Alex Campbell** – and from song collectors and academics such as **Norman Buchan**, with his hugely influential songbook *101 Scottish Songs*, and **Peter Hall** with *The Scottish Folksinger*. **Robin Hall** and **Jimmie McGregor**, too, while like The Corries often derided for their high profile and their occasional lapses into opportunist populism, were a formidable presence for many years. There has also been a massive contribution from **Hamish Henderson** both as folklorist and researcher, an immense conduit of songs and tunes. That Henderson also penned some of the most telling songs in modern currency adds to his legend.

Gaelic rocking and fusions

Scottish music took an unexpected twist in 1978 with the low-key release of an album called *Play Gaelic*. It was made by a little-known ceilidh group called **Runrig**, who took their name from the old Scottish field system of agriculture, and worked primarily in the backwaters of the Highlands and Islands. The thing, though, that stopped people in their tracks was the fact that they were writing original material in Gaelic. This was the first time any serious Scottish working band had achieved any sort of attention with Gaelic material, although Ossian were touching on it around a similar time, as were Nah-Oganaich.

Runrig marched on to unprecedented heights, appearing in front of rock audiences at concert halls around the world where only a part of the audience were Scots in exile. As their popularity grew the Gaelic content reduced, but they started a whole new ball rolling, chipping away at prejudices, adopting accordions and bagpipes, ever-sharper arrangements, electric instruments, full-blown rock styles, surviving the inevitable personnel changes and the continuous carping of critics accusing them of selling out with every new market conquered. They even made a concept album *Recovery*, which related the history of the Gael in one collection, provoking immense interest in the Gaelic language after years of it being regarded as moribund and defunct. They lost their main man **Donnie Munro** to politics during the 1990s but after an extended break made a solo comeback in 2000.

Capercaillie, too, rooted in the arrangements of **Manus Lunny** and the gorgeous singing of **Karen Matheson**, rose from Argyll pub sessions to flirt with mass commercial appeal, reworking Gaelic and traditional songs from the West Highlands and promoting Gaelic language and culture, primarily as a result of the songs learned by Matheson from her grandmother. They even got into the chart with one ancient Gaelic song, an ironic development considering the fact that Karen was actively discouraged from learning the language and her grandmother was made to feel ashamed of her Gaelic culture after moving to the Scottish mainland. Others have subsequently come to the fore, like **Margaret Bennett**, while the culture has remained defiantly intact courtesy of Scottish roots families in Cape Breton, Canada. **Mary Jane Lamond** is just one who's made the triumphant return journey back to Scotland with her repertoire of ancient Gaelic songs.

Of course, not everyone applauds. Critics point out that many singers using the language are not native Gaelic speakers and only learn the words phonetically, while further controversy has been caused by the "sampling" of archive recordings for use in backing tracks. For many people these songs are important and personal, and in the case of some of the religious singing, they felt very strongly that this use was in bad taste.

Nonetheless, the popularity of Gaelic roots bands undeniably paved the way for "purer" Scots musicians and singers: clarsach player **Alison Kinnaird**, for instance; singers **Savourna Stevenson**, **Christine Primrose**, **Flora McNeill**, **Cathy-Ann MacPhee**, **Heather Heywood** and **Jock Duncan**; and the **Wrigley sisters** from Orkney – who started out as teenagers playing traditional music with technical accomplishment and attitude, further demonstrating their vision in the fine band **Seelyhoo**.

And among the ranks of the roots or fusion bands, each with their own agendas and styles, have passed many – perhaps most – of Scotland's finest contemporary musicians. **Silly Wizard**, especially, featured a singer of cutting quality in **Andy M. Stewart** (and did he need that M.), while **Phil and Johnny Cunningham** went on to display pioneering zeal in their efforts on accordion and fiddle respectively to knit Scottish traditional material with other cultures. Phil Cunningham, in particular, has become an iconic figure in modern Scottish music, championing many up-and-coming musicians, composing modern symphonies for the accordion and even persuading ex-Fairground Attraction star **Eddi Reader** to turn her distinctive voice to a new interpretation of the songs of Robert Burns. The sudden death of Johnny Cunningham at the age of 46, shortly after completing an album with the Irish singer Susan McKeown in December 2003, robbed Scottish music of one of its very best and most influential instrumentalists. Apart from many years and numerous albums with Silly Wizard, he was also a key member of other leading bands – Relativity, Celtic Fiddle Festival and Nightnoise – and recorded with Bob Dylan, Bonnie Raitt and Hall & Oates as well as being an accomplished producer.

Mouth Music, too, were innovative: a Scots-origin (but recently Canadian) duo of **Martin Swan** and **Talitha MacKenzie**, who mixed Gaelic vocals (including the traditional "mouth music" techniques of sung rhythms) with African percussion and dance sounds. MacKenzie later went solo, radically transforming traditional Scottish songs, from which she clears the dust of folklore with wonderful multi-tracked vocals and the characteristic Mouth Music African rhythms. Swan's own subsequent work with various different incarnations of Mouth Music, often in partnership with Martin Furey, has wandered far from those "Gaelic-Afro-pop" beginnings but has been constantly challenging and often groundbreaking, if failing to capture public imagination.

Another development was the fusion of traditional music and **jazz** by bands such as **The Easy Club** and the duo of piper **Hamish Moore** and jazz saxophonist **Dick Lee**. Moore has since come full circle, now taking his inspiration

Ceilidhs, festivals and contacts

Scottish dances thrived for years under the auspices of the RSCDS, the Royal Scottish Country Dance Society. Their events tended to be fairly formal, with dancers who were largely skilled, but in the 1970s and 1980s more and more Scottish dances, or **ceilidhs** (pronounced "kay-lees"), adopted the English barn-dance practice of a "caller" to call out the moves. Nowadays there are two types of traditional dance events: ceilidh dances, usually with a caller and perhaps a more folky band, and **Scottish Country Dances**, usually with a more traditional Scottish dance band line-up and an expectation that the dancers will know the dance forms.

Scottish **music festivals** range from the Celtic Connections Festival (which takes place in Glasgow every January), where you can catch many of the top names in the Celtic music world in a comfortable concert setting, to lots of smaller festivals which offer a mix of concert, ceilidh and informal sessions. In recent years there has been an increase in the number of festivals where teaching takes a central role. Many of these are in the Highlands and Islands where the Feisean movement has introduced thousands of people to traditional music-making.

Scottish bands such as Capercaillie and Runrig feed the notion that folk music can be exciting, electric and diverse, without losing sight of its roots. However, the survival of traditional music depends on support from young players: they need to play it, listen to it and take it forward. In Scotland, change is coming from a grass-roots **Feisean Movement** (*feis* is Gaelic for festival). These festivals, held during summer months and school holidays, involve children receiving tuition in traditional music, drama, art, dance and Gaelic singing, with evening gigs in local venues. The teachers (and performers) are often leading musicians.

The idea began on the island of Barra, in the southern Hebrides, in 1981 and has spread to many parts of the Highlands and Islands. Its results have been remarkable. Beginners on the fiddle, clarsach, guitar, tin whistle or accordion have now begun to form bands and teach others. And the sheer numbers of young people coming through the Feis throughout the Highlands has resulted in more and more communities holding workshops and ceilidhs. In small communities there are great economic spin-offs for instrument-makers, music shops and teachers of traditional music.

Tuition projects have not been limited to the Highlands. In Edinburgh, Stan Reeves has made remarkable progress with the **Scots Music Group** within the Adult Learning Project (ALP), leading to several hundred people learning traditional instruments and an annual festival of fiddle music. In Glasgow, the **Glasgow Fiddle Workshop**, under the guidance of Ian Fraser, has made similar progress and is starting to widen its brief beyond fiddle tuition.

Contacts

ALP Scots Music Group ⓣ0131/347 9964, ⓦwww.alpscotsmusic.org.
Feisean nan Gaidheal ⓣ01478/613355, ⓦwww.feisean.org.
The Living Tradition ⓣ01563/571220, ⓦwww.folkmusic.net. A traditional music magazine covering music from Britain and Ireland, with a focus, obviously, on Scotland. They also run a mail-order service for traditional recordings.
The Piping Centre ⓣ0141/353 0220, ⓦwww.thepipingcentre.co.uk. The place to visit in Glasgow for anybody with an interest in piping. They have an exhibition, a teaching programme, concert space, café and even a hotel.
Royal Scottish Country Dance Society ⓣ0131/225 3854, ⓦwww.rscds.org.

from a parallel Scottish culture which has developed in Cape Breton. Scottish interest in Cape Breton music has also led to the more or less lost tradition of Scottish step dancing being reintroduced.

△ Ceilidh, Kirkwall

Contemporary Celts

Young Celtic music artists have been leading from the front in the touchy subject of **fusion** and **electronica**. The **Easy Club** pioneered Celtic swing years ago, their example propagated by drummer/composer and Scottish National Jazz Orchestra member John Rae and his band **Celtic Feet**, while **Salsa Celtica** have made a considerable mark lacing their Celtic background with a genuinely deep love and understanding of Latin music. At the other end of the spectrum **Jennifer** and **Hazel Wrigley** and **Catriona MacDonald** have done some stirring conceptual work, even incorporating an almost classical mentality to the complex instrumental pieces they have created. MacDonald's increasing influence is also underlined by her leading role in the band of massed fiddle players, **Blazing Fiddles**, currently one of the Highlands' most active exponents of "the living tradition". The likes of **Deaf Shepherd**, **Mad Pudding** and **Tartan Amoebas** have also provided an explosive new edge to old notions of Celtic folk rock, while Cape Breton's **Natalie McMaster** has produced a succession of brilliant fiddle albums involving daring variants on a Scottish traditional theme.

Perhaps most intriguing – and controversial – are those bending the music to its limits by taking it into the realms of a modern club and dance scene involving an alien world of samples, sequencers, loops, computers and drum machines. Even Capercaillie – and one of their offshoots **Big Sky** – experimented in this area with mixed results, while the likes of **Simon Thoumire** and **Paul Mounsey** have been at the forefront of these technological forays. Multi-talented Mounsey lived in Brazil for a decade and has made it count with a series of alluring electronic experiments. The idea of marrying the common ingredients of Scottish and Latino music has also been explored to good effect by **Mac Umba**, one of several Scots bands who've made their mark abroad.

Shooglenifty, who captured the imagination of a new audience with a style they wryly described as "acid croft", and who played at the 2000 Sydney Olympics, are among those who've embraced technology with the most conviction. While most have treated it with kid gloves, Shooglenifty have gone in with the brashness of youth to utilize all the sounds and equipment around them to enhance the music without any caution or the sense of guilt of older musicians. **Peatbog Faeries**, too – featuring excellent piper Peter Morrison and fiddle player/throat singer Ben Ivitsky – have pushed back the boundaries in stirring futuristic fashion without compromising the tradition in any way. Yet the man who's been most responsible for shifting the goalposts is **Martyn Bennett**. A thrilling fiddle and bagpipe player originally from Newfoundland, he drove the music, inspiringly, right to the edge with his albums *Bothy Culture* and *Hardland*. He made his mark as a dreadlocked busker in Edinburgh but proved his credentials with an extraordinary adaptation of Sorley McLean's equally extraordinary poem *Hallaig*, featuring McLean's own reading of it recorded shortly before his death. He also recorded his own mother, the Gaelic singer Margaret Bennett, surrounding her voice with an innovative collection of natural soundscapes of the Isle of Skye on the enlightening album *Glen Lyon*. And if any further evidence were needed that the old and the new and apparently alien cultures can clash to resounding effect, then Bennett provided it on his brilliant final album *Grit*. Perhaps his greatest achievement, it married the voices of some of the great travelling singers he'd known in his youth, like Jeannie Robertson and Lizzie Higgins, with his trademark techno beats and samples to brilliant effect. Sadly Bennett was by then too ill to play any instruments himself after a long valiant struggle with cancer and died at the age of 33 in 2005.

The new frontiers

As music generally has cross-fertilized, more Scots artists have crossed over from traditional roots into the mainstream without seemingly having any detrimental effect whatsoever on an ebullient traditional music scene. A browse round the music sessions frequently to be found in Edinburgh and Glasgow will tell you that.

Twin brothers Craig and Charlie Reid's incarnation as **The Proclaimers**, which shifted them from speccy geeks to unlikely pop stars (*Letter From America*, *I'm Gonna Be 500 Miles*) has now seen them acquire status as national treasures and part of Scottish heritage, guaranteed to send any festival home singing.

Almost equally unlikely is the rapid rise of ex-social worker **Karine Polwart**. She proved herself one of the most naturally gifted interpreters of traditional song in the band Malinky and showed glimpses of her songwriting talent in occasional duo MacAlias, before spending a year fronting Battlefield Band when Davy Steele was taken ill and subsequently died. Yet nobody was quite prepared for the outpouring of superb self-written songs when she finally launched her solo career with the *Faultlines* album, which was festooned in plaudits at the 2005 BBC Folk Awards and broke her into the mainstream. In the end her rise may have been slightly overshadowed by another rootsy female singer, **KT Tunstall** from St Andrews, who emerged from the band Oi Va Voi to entrance audiences with her sassy attitude and brilliant stage shows.

If Polwart and Tunstall spearhead the new Scots charge on the mainstream, plenty of others have emerged at a grass-roots level. The young sisters who make up **Give Way** won the BBC Young Folk Award in 2001 and have gone on to make three albums with their spirited take on traditional dance music, while the youthful **Julie Fowlis** from North Uist in the Outer Hebrides has even made Gaelic singing sound sexy and won much acclaim for her stirring album *Mar A Tha Mo Chridhe* (As My Heart Is).

Other new young artists determinedly making their mark include the wonderful young Black Isle fiddler **Lauren MacColl**, winner of the 2004 BBC Young Folk Award; and former Radio Scotland Young Traditional Musician of the Year and member of Unusual Suspects, **Emily Smith** from Dumfries, whose alluring voice and striking songs caused quite a stir on her album *A Different Life*.

Perhaps most startling of all of the new breed is **Alasdair Roberts**, a young singer discovered by Will Oldham and who initially started recording with a strange rock band Appendix Out. But with his hypnotic solo album *Farewell Sorrow*, he mixed his own songs with traditional themes in a fascinating manner and then followed it up in 2005 with a provocatively sparse series of murder ballads, *No Earthly Man*, which stripped the songs right back to their traditional roots in a way that divided opinion like no other.

Discography

In addition to the discs reviewed below, check out www.musicscotland.com – a wonderful site with links to many label and artist pages.

General compilations

The Caledonian Companion (Greentrax, Scotland). A 1975 live recording of four of Scotland's most respected northeast musicians – Alex Green, Willie Fraser, Charlie Bremner and John Grant – featuring solo fiddle, mouth organ, whistle and diddling.

The Nineties Collection (Greentrax, Scotland). Sixteen artists, including four pipers and well-known names such as Aly Bain and Phil Cunningham play all-new tunes in a traditional style. Also available is a companion book containing over 200 tunes, published by Canongate Books, Scotland.

The Rough Guide to Scottish Music (World Music Network, UK). An entirely new compilation, this collection has a youthful feel, a reflection of the rude health of contemporary Celtic music, with tracks from the likes of Deaf Shepherd, Capercaillie and Cliar alongside the haunting vocals of Alison McMorland and the unusual bagpipe calypso of Robert Mathieson.

Traditional singers

Jock Duncan is an authentic bothy ballad singer from Pitlochry who gets to the heart of any song. He made his recording debut aged 70, backed by musicians including his son, the piper Gordon Duncan, on *Ye Shine Whar Ye Stan'* (Springthyme, Scotland). Some of the traditional singing on this album is truly remarkable and the production from Battlefield Band founder Brian McNeill is impressive, too, creating an atmosphere that only falls a little short of the experience of a live performance.

Heather Heywood, from Ayrshire, is reckoned by many to be Scotland's foremost traditional singer of her generation. She performs largely core Scottish ballads and songs. *By Yon Castle Wa'* (Greentrax, Scotland) is a 1993 disc of epic ballads and contemporary songs, produced by Battlefield Band founder Brian McNeill. Heywood's forte is traditional song which she usually sings *a cappella*. McNeill makes the album accessible, without compromising the basic style, with the addition of accompaniment, including pipes – something which is difficult to do in live performance. This was a landmark recording in the traditional area.

Catherine-Ann MacPhee, from Barra, has a warm yet strong voice and her Gaelic has the soft pronunciation of the southern islands of the Outer Hebrides. *Canan Nan Gaidheal* (*The Language of the Gael*; Greentrax, Scotland) is a superb 1980s recording, re-released on CD, showing mature traditional singing from one of the best of the current generation of Gaelic singers.

Gordeanna McCulloch, the lead singer of seminal 1960s band, The Clutha, is another of the great voices of the Scottish folk revival. On *In Freenship's Name* (Greentrax, Scotland), her voice is a strong, sweet and flexible instrument, capable of a variety of tones. Here she is at home among some great Scots songs, all traditional bar one, and backed by some of Scotland's top musicians.

Eddi Reader is still best known as the flame-haired lead singer of Fairground Attraction, whose late-1980s number one *Perfect* remains a karaoke favourite. Reader's strong and distinctive voice took the Celtic Connections festival by storm in 2003 with her earthy interpretation of Burns' songs, captured on CD as *Eddi Reader Sings the Songs of Robert Burns* (Rough Trade, UK).

Jim Reid was, with Arbroath's Foundry Bar band, a well-known face at festivals and ceilidhs throughout Scotland for many years. One of the country's finest singers, whose *I Saw the Wild Geese Flee* (Springthyme, Scotland) is a selection of songs ranging from his own compositions to traditional ballads. Jim's version of *I Saw the Wild Geese Flee* alone makes this reissued album a classic.

Margaret Stewart and Allan MacDonald Lewis-born Stewart is a talented Gaelic singer; MacDonald is one of the famous piping families from Glenuig – his brother was the piper with Ossian and Battlefield Band. Their *Fhuair Mi Pog* (Greentrax, Scotland) is a fascinating CD of music and Gaelic song that works as terrific entertainment; lovely singing and great tunes, some of the best written by Allan himself.

Jane Turriff is a legendary song carrier. Born into the Aberdeenshire Stewart family in 1915, she grew up in a travelling family. *Singin is Ma Life* (Springthyme, Scotland) is a must for anyone interested in traditional song style. Content ranges from the "big" ballads such as *Dowie Dens of Yarrow* through to the classic C&W song *Empty Saddles*.

Sheena Wellington is a broadcaster and radio presenter, Fife Council's Traditional Arts development officer, and one of Scotland's leading traditional singers. *Strong Women* (Greentrax, Scotland) is a live recording showing off what Sheena does best: communicating traditional song to an audience.

Mick West, well known as a session singer, is now rated at home and abroad as one of the country's finest traditional singers. *Fine Flowers & Foolish Glances* (KRL, Scotland) is one of the most successful albums to use jazz musicians with a strong traditional singer. It may prove to be a classic.

Instrumentalists

Aly Bain, Shetland-born (see box on p.511), is one of the great movers in Scottish music's revival, through his band Boys of the Lough and a panoply of solo and collaborative ventures. *Aly Bain and Friends* (Greentrax, Scotland) is one of the best-selling Scottish albums of modern times, compiled from a TV series Bain produced on traditional Scottish music. The "friends" include Boys of the Lough, Capercaillie, Hamish Moore and Dick Lee, and zydeco star Queen Ida and her Bonne Temps band. *The Silver Bow: The Fiddle Music of Shetland* (Topic, UK) is a collection of Shetland fiddle tunes notable for bringing together Bain with his old teacher, Tom Anderson. They play both individually and together on the album and the effect is never less than enthralling. On *The Pearl* (Whirlie, Scotland), Bain teams up with Phil Cunningham, Scotland's finest accordion player, for some fabulous tunes from slow airs to Shetland reels, reflecting the incredible range of styles which this duo have mastered. Phil composed almost half of the tracks and he plays five of the six instruments featured.

John Burgess is arguably the twentieth century's greatest exponent of traditional bagpipes. On *King of the Highland Pipers* (Topic, UK), the maestro demonstrates his art to devastating effect through *piobaireachd*, strathspeys, hornpipes, reels and marches. Not for the faint-hearted!

Pete Clarke is a great fiddle-player whose skills with slow air playing also makes him in great demand as a song accompanist. *Fiddle Case* (Smiddymade, Scotland) comprises an hour of top-notch traditional music – not all Scottish fiddle though – with tunes from Europe and the US and even a couple of songs. There's a classical feel to some of the pieces which works well, with cello and flute parts.

Gordon Duncan, the son of bothy singer Jock, is one of Scotland's younger generation of pipers who is stretching the boundaries with some breathtaking solo piping. On *The Circular Breath* (Greentrax, Scotland), as well as performing on the Great Highland bagpipe, Gordon plays the practice chanter and low whistle. He is joined by banjo-player Gerry O'Connor, Ian Carr on guitar, Ronald MacArthur on bass guitar, Jim Sutherland playing clay pots and Andy Cook on Ugandan harp.

Alasdair Fraser is a master fiddler, renowned for his slow airs and now for his leading of The Skyedance Band, whose members provided music for the film *Braveheart*. *Dawn Dance* (Culburnie, Scotland) is an album of completely self-penned tunes in the traditional style which bounces along, defying you to sit still while you listen. Fraser has a rare clarity of playing, without sacrificing the feel and enthusiasm essential to traditional music.

Willie Hunter and Violet Tulloch Hunter was one of the all-time greats of the Shetland fiddle and Tulloch is one of Shetland's leading piano accompanists. *The Willie Hunter Sessions* (Greentrax, Scotland) is a set of recordings made over several years including Scots and Shetland strathspeys, reels and slow airs. "Traditional chamber music" of the highest order.

William Jackson is one of Scotland's best-known traditional composers. He wrote some – and arranged most – of the music for folk band Ossian, and now works solo. *Inchcolm* (Linn Records, Scotland) brings Billy's harp-playing to centre stage. It is a collection of largely unrelated tracks with some orchestral interludes and forays into early and Eastern musics.

Mac-Talla is a Gaelic supergroup, which in 1994 made a small number of concert appearances and one spectacular recording – *Mairidh Gaol is Ceol* (Temple, Scotland), featuring glorious harmony and solo singing, accordion and harp – before settling back into their own individual paths having "made the statement". Mac-Talla's members included singers Arthur Cormack, Christine Primrose and Eilidh MacKenzie plus Alison Kinnaird on clarsach, and ex-Runrig musician Blair Douglas.

Iain McLachlan is a well-known and respected accordion player who also plays fiddle and melodeon. From the writer of *The Dark Island*, *An Island Heritage* (Springthyme, Scotland) is real traditional music from the Western Isles played on accordion, fiddle, melodeon and pipes.

Hamish Moore is one of Scotland's finest contemporary pipers, playing Border pipes, Scottish small pipes and the great Highland bagpipe. Inspired by the Scottish culture he discovered in Cape Breton, on *Stepping on the Bridge* (Greentrax, Scotland) Moore plays Scottish pipes with Cape Breton accompanists to produce a lively glimpse of what piping may have been like before it became regimented.

Scott Skinner was a legendary Victorian-era fiddler, formidably kilted and moustachioed. *Music of Scott Skinner* (Topic, UK) is an essential roots album, featuring rare and authentic recordings by this elusive genius of the fiddle – and the weird strathspey style in particular – dating from 1908. Some of the quality is understandably distorted, though the collection is supplemented by modern interpretations by Bill Hardie.

"New Roots" groups

Battlefield Band has been perhaps the pre-eminent Scottish band of the last thirty years, despite numerous personnel changes. Some great musicians have come and gone – Brian McNeill has developed into one of Scotland's greatest modern songwriters – but Alan Reid remains a constant and the band even survived the death of its hugely popular singer Davy Steele and continues with one of the country's brightest young vocal talents Karine Polwart (also of Malinky and MacAlias). *Rain, Hail or Shine* (Temple, Scotland) features all the Battlefield Band trademarks in force – distinctive keyboard playing, well-chosen pipe tunes, guitar and bouzouki injecting excitement and tension, fine singing – and John McCusker's sharp fiddle-playing is a joy throughout.

Boys of the Lough have been a benchmark of taste for thirty years, with the virtuoso talents of Shetland fiddler Aly Bain and singer/flautist Cathal McConnell at the heart of the band. *The Boys of the Lough* (Shanachie, US) was the group's 1973 debut and remains one of their strongest sets, powered by contributions from Dick

Gaughan and piper Robin Morton. *The Day Dawn* (Lough Records, Scotland) is characterized by quality, taste, superb singing and the relaxed easy style that comes from skilled musicians with years of experience. Along with the concertina and mandola of Dave Richardson, Aly on fiddle and Cathal on flute, whistle and vocals, this album features singer and uillean piper Christy O'Leary.

Capercaillie is a hugely influential and successful group that has taken Gaelic music to a worldwide audience in a modern contemporary style from a traditional base. They have in Karen Mattheson one of the best singers around today. On *Beautiful Wasteland* (Survival Records, Scotland/Green Linnet, US), flute, whistle and uillean pipes pop up all over the place and a whole host of things are happening with fiddles, bouzoukis, keyboards and percussion.

Ceolbeg was not a full-time band but produced some of the finest albums of the genre, featuring some fabulous songs from their singer, Davy Steele. *An Unfair Dance* (Greentrax, Scotland) is an impressive collection of tunes played on a huge variety of instruments, with a great sense of light and shade.

Deaf Shepherd is a passionate contemporary band following in the footsteps of the Battlefield Band, rooted in the Scottish tradition and getting more skilled all the time. *Synergy* (Greentrax, Scotland) is a really varied album, including traditional and new material, and jumps from reels to jigs and back, involving vigorous fiddle-playing and powerful bouzouki. Poignant guitar, fiddle and whistle counter-melodies blend smoothly with the vocals.

The Easy Club, an admirably ambitious and sadly underrated group, took the baton from the more thoughtful Scots bands of the 1970s and ran with it at a pace, injecting traditional rhythms with a jazz sense. *Essential* (Eclectic, Scotland) is undoubtedly essential; MacColl's *First Time Ever I Saw Your Face* never sounded like this before.

Mouth Music – Talitha MacKenzie and Martin Swan – combined Gaelic nonsense songs (*puirt-a-beul*) with ambient dance, funk keyboards and African sampling. MacKenzie has gone on to a solo career but Mouth Music's first disc *Mouth Music* (Cooking Vinyl, UK) remains her finest hour, one of the best Celtic fusions committed to disc, featuring stunning rhythms, funk, Gaelic sea shanties and *puirt-a-beul*.

Ossian, a ground-breaking band formed in the 1970s, later reformed with a new line-up in 2004 featuring Iain MacInnes on pipes and Stuart Morrison on fiddle alongside founder members Billy Jackson on harp and Billy Ross on guitar and dulcimer. *The Carrying Stream* (Greentrax, Scotland) is a fine album, signalling the welcome return of Ossian's quintessentially Scottish sound. This is a collection of terrific tunes – first-rate jigs and reels, both traditional and contemporary, blended with songs in English, Scots and Gaelic.

Runrig, a band of Gaelic rock pioneers, was formed in North Uist in 1973 by brothers Rory (bass/vocals) and Calum MacDonald (drums/vocals), with singer Donnie Munro joining the following year. They worked their way up, over fifteen years, from ceilidhs to stadiums, going Top 10 in the UK charts in 1991. They are perhaps at their very best live, with memorable tunes and vocals and well-honed, subtle musicianship. *Alba* (Pinnacle, UK) is an excellent "best of" compilation from this most dynamic Gaelic band.

Seelyhoo, featuring the Wrigley sisters from Orkney, made their own statement with their own recordings.

On *Leetera* (Greentrax, Scotland), they're joined by several other musicians in a band which came out of the Edinburgh session scene and exemplifies a fresh approach to traditional tunes and Gaelic song using fiddle, guitar, bass guitar, accordion, whistle, keyboard and percussion. Vibrant music from some of Scotland's young rising stars.

Shooglenifty is a brilliant, innovative band which has had an impact well beyond the Scottish roots scene with its grafting of Scottish trad motifs and club-culture trance-dance. Live, they are unstoppable. *A Whisky Kiss* (Greentrax, Scotland) is the album that coined the term "acid croft", with elements of traditional music and house. A weird sound here, a strange tangent there, a sequence played in an odd way. There's nothing else like it.

Silly Wizard was a key roots band, featuring Andy M. Stewart (vocals, bouzouki, guitar), Phil (accordion, etc) and Johnny Cunningham (fiddle). Their albums are full of fresh, lively takes on the whole traditional repertoire and *Live Wizardry* (Green Linnet, US) features the band at its zenith in 1988, playing traditional and self-composed dance tunes and narrative ballads.

Andy M. Stewart, Phil Cunningham and Manus Lunny Two former members of Silly Wizard combine with an Irishman on *Fire In The Glen* (Shanachie, US), a formidable celebration of Scottish traditional music. Phil Cunningham's brilliance as an accordion player is demonstrated on any number of albums, but it's especially impressive placed against the wonderful singing of Andy M. Stewart.

The Whistlebinkies – often dubbed the "Scottish Chieftains" – are one of the founding folk groups in Scotland and are still playing music with a difference. *A Wanton Fling* (Greentrax, Scotland) has all the freshness of early Binkies recordings, a combination of Lowland pipes, clarsach, flute, concertina and fiddle.

Wolfstone plays folk rock from the Highlands – "stadium rock meets village-hall ceilidh" said one reviewer – full of passion and fire. *The Half Tail* (Green Linnet, Scotland) is a more subdued progressive sound than usual for Wolfstone, featuring amongst other tracks, a classic whaling song *Bonnie Ship the Diamond*, *The Last Leviathan* and catchy instrumental sets.

Folk singer-songwriters

Eric Bogle emigrated from Scotland to work in Australia as an accountant but when he returned home he was hailed for writing two of the great modern anti-war folk songs, *The Band Played Waltzing Matilda* and *Green Fields Of France* (or *No Man's Land* as he originally called it). Bogle's singing doesn't quite match his songwriting, but he has all-star support on *Something of Value* (Sonet, UK/Philo, US), which includes *Waltzing Matilda*.

Archie and Cilla Fisher The Fisher family – Archie, Ray and Cilla – were mainstays of the 1960s–70s Scottish folk club scene, reviving old ballads and creating new ones. *The Man With A Rhyme* (Folk Legacy, US) was Archie's finest hour, fourteen tracks from 1976 with the Fisher voice and guitar backed by concertina, banjo, dulcimers, cello, fiddle and flute. *Cilla and Artie* (Greentrax, Scotland), released in 1979 and featuring Cilla Fisher and Artie Trezise, still retains an ease and freshness; Cilla's imperious rendition of the late Stan Rogers' *The Jeannie C* is in itself worth the acquisition.

Dick Gaughan is one of the most charismatic of Scottish performers – a singer/guitarist/songwriter who can make you laugh, cry and explode with anger with every twist and nuance of delivery. His later material is still up there with his classic albums of the 1980s, and in 2001 he forged a hugely successful working partnership with another great Scottish music legend Brian McNeill. *Handful of Earth* (Sonet, UK/Philo, US) is the Gaughan classic: a majestic album of traditional and modern songs, still formidable a decade on. When *Folk Roots* magazine asked its readers to nominate the album of the 1980s, it won by a street – and deservedly so.

Robin Laing is one of the best songwriters and performers to emerge out of the Scottish folk scene in the 1990s. *Walking In Time* (Greentrax, Scotland) includes four reworkings of traditional songs – three by other writers and seven of Laing's own songs, accompanied by his own Spanish guitar. Producer Brian McNeill's multi-instrumental talents are also in evidence on most of the tracks.

Ewan MacColl was, simply, one of the all-time greats of British folk song. *In Black and White* (Cooking Vinyl, UK/Green Linnet, US) is a posthumous compilation, lovingly compiled by his family, showcasing MacColl's superb technique as a singer, his gift for choruses (*Dirty Old Town*), his colourful observation as a lyricist (*The Driver's Song*) and his raging sense of injustice (*Black And White*, written after the Sharpeville Massacre of 1963). A fitting epitaph.

Dougie MacLean, one-time member of Tannahill Weavers, has long carved out a successful solo career as an emotive singer-songwriter. *The Dougie MacLean Collection* (Putumayo, US) is a good selection from Dougie's extensive recorded output including perhaps his most famous song, the sentimental but moving confection of nostalgia and patriotism, *Caledonia*.

Adam McNaughtan has written many songs rich in Glasgow wit including one which has travelled the world, *Oor Hamlet*, a condensed version of Shakespeare's *Hamlet* to the tune of *The Mason's Apron*. He has a deep understanding of the tradition and is one of Scotland's national treasures. Adam's comic songs are masterpieces and on *Last Stand At Mount Florida* (Greentrax, Scotland) he is in excellent voice, accompanied by fellow Stramash members Finlay Allison, Bob Blair and John Eaglesham.

Brian McNeill is a man of amazing talents, the one-time fiddling founder of the Battlefield Band and a multi-instrumentalist and a songwriter of some substance. *No Gods* (Greentrax, Scotland) shows the broadening of McNeill's writing talent both in song and tunes. He is joined by ten backing musicians including masterful guitarist Tony MacManus.

by Pete Heywood and Colin Irwin

(Taken from the *Rough Guide to World Music* and updated by Colin Irwin)

Books

Out of print titles are indicated as o/p – these should be easy to track down in secondhand bookshops; ★ indicates titles that merit a special recommendation.

Art, architecture and historic sites

J. Gifford *Highlands and Islands*. Part of a series of definitive guides that are well illustrated, knowledgeable and readable.

Graham Ritchie & Mary Harman *Exploring Scotland's Heritage*. Detailed, beautifully illustrated series with the emphasis on historic buildings and archeological sites. Recently updated titles cover Orkney, Shetland, the Highlands, Aberdeen and North-east Scotland and Argyll and the Western Isles.

Andrew Gibbon Williams & Andrew Brown *The Bigger Picture: A History of Scottish Art*. Originally published to accompany a TV series, this is a richly illustrated survey of Scottish art from 1603 to the present day. Suitable for the lay reader.

History, politics and culture

Adamnan (trans. by John Marsden) *The Illustrated Life of Columba*. The original story of the life of St Columba, annotated and accompanied by beautiful photos of the places associated with him, in particular the Hebridean island of Iona.

Ian Adams & Meredith Somerville *Cargoes of Despair and Hope*. Riveting mixture of contemporary documents and letters telling the story of Scottish emigration to North America from 1603 to 1803.

★ **Neal Ascherson** *Stones Voices*. Intelligent, thought-provoking ponderings on the nature of Scotland and the road to devolution from Scots-born *Observer* journalist, interspersed with personal anecdotes.

★ **Joni Buchanan** *The Lewis Land Struggle*. A history of crucial encounters between the crofters of Lewis and their various landlords, written from the crofters' point of view using contemporary sources.

★ **Tom Devine** *The Scottish Nation 1700–2000*. Best post-Union history from the last Scottish Parliament to the new one.

Ian Donnachie *Collins Dictionary of Scottish History* A handy, inexpensive reference book for looking up people, places and events.

Diana Henderson *Highland Soldier: A Social History of the Highland Regiments 1820–1920*. Detailed history of the ten Highland regiments and the lives of their officers and men.

W.S. Hewison *Scapa Flow in War and Peace*. Very straightforward and readable quick rundown of Scapa Flow's wartime role, written by an ex-serviceman and *Orcadian* journalist.

Historic Scotland. A series of books covering many aspects of Scotland's history and prehistory, including the Picts, Vikings, Romans and Celts. All are colourful, accessible and well presented. Available at many Historic Scotland sites as well as bookshops.

★ **David Howarth** *The Shetland Bus*. Wonderfully detailed story of the espionage and resistance operations carried out from Shetland by British and Norwegian servicemen, written by someone who was directly involved.

Roger Hutchinson *The Soap Man*. The intriguing tale of Lord Leverhulme who bought Lewis and Harris and tried to impose his benevolent despotism on them.

Fitzroy Maclean *Bonnie Prince Charlie*. Very readable and more or less definitive biography of Scotland's most romantic historical figure written by the "real" James Bond.

John Marsden *Sea-road of the Saints: Celtic Holy Men in the Hebrides*. Famous early Christian saints, such as Columba and Brendan the Voyager, appear in the context of the remains that still exist in the islands.

Timothy Neat *The Summer Walkers*. The less-publicized wandering population of the northwest Highlands – tinkers, horse traders and pearl fishers – reveal something of their lives.

Orkneyinga Saga. Probably written about 1200 AD, this is a Norse saga which sheds light on the connection between Norway and the Northern Isles, still felt strongly today; contains history of the early earls of Orkney, and is, incidentally, a stirring, bloodthirsty thriller.

John Prebble *Glencoe*, *Culloden* and *The Highland Clearances*. Emotive and subjective accounts of key events in Highland history which are very readable.

John Purser *Scotland's Music*. Comprehensive overview of traditional and classical music in Scotland – thorough and scholarly, but readable.

Anna Ritchie *Prehistoric Orkney*. Orkney is an archipelago so rich in prehistoric sites that even the most casual visitor will feel the need for a book like this, which helps to paint a picture of the life of the early inhabitants.

Iain Crichton Smith *Towards the Human*. Selected essays, ranging widely over poetry and poets, language and community. He explores the writing of Hugh MacDiarmid, the vital role of Gaelic in Scottish culture and his own childhood in Lewis with perceptive intelligence.

Ronald Williams *The Lords of the Isles: The Clan Donald and the Early Kingdom of the Scots*. A book which covers the history of the early kingdom centred on Argyll and the islands from 500 AD to Robert the Bruce. It's a complicated period but the narrative carries you through.

Guides and picture books

Colin Baxter & Jim Crumley *Shetland – Land of the Ocean*. Best known for his ubiquitous postcards, Baxter's photographs succeed in capturing the grandeur of Scotland's moody landscapes.

George Mackay Brown *Portrait of Orkney*. A personal account by the famous Orcadian poet of the island, its history and way of life, illustrated with photographs and drawings.

Laurie Campbell & Roy Dennis *Golden Eagles*. Second only to the stag as a symbol of the Highlands of Scotland, the eagle is captured in this book in magnificent photographs.

Collins Gem Scots Dictionary Handy, pocket-sized guide to the mysteries of Scottish vocabulary and idiom.

Collins Guide *Scottish Wild Flowers*; *Scottish Birds*. Well-illustrated and informative small guides. Also in the guide series are *Clans and Tartans* and *Scottish Surnames*, which are a first step on the road to genealogy.

Derek Cooper *Skye*. A gazetteer and guide, and an indispensable mine of information; although first written in 1970, it has been revised where necessary.

Sheila Gear *Foula, Island West of the Sun*. An attempt to convey what it is like to live far out in the sea on an island of savage beauty.

James Shaw Grant *Discovering Lewis & Harris*. Anecdotal and informative book by former editor of the *Stornoway Gazette*.

Hamish Haswell-Smith *The Scottish Islands*. An exhaustive and impressive gazetteer with maps and absorbing information on all the Scottish islands. Filled with attractive sketches and paintings, the book is breathtaking in its thoroughness and lovingly gathered detail.

Mairi Hedderwick *Eye on the Hebrides*. The author of the Katie Morag children's books knows the Hebrides well, and with her enchanting watercolours takes you to meet all sorts of people in an affectionate look at the islands.

Charles Maclean *St Kilda*. Traces the social history of the island from its earliest beginnings to the seemingly inevitable end of the community with moving compassion.

Magnus Magnusson *Rùm: Nature's Island*. A detailed history of Rùm from earliest times up to its current position as a National Nature Reserve.

Gunnie Moberg & George Mackay Brown *Orkney – Pictures and Poems*. A book to treasure, with a wonderfully evocative combination of poetry and photographs.

Pevensey Island Guides. A surprisingly informative series with individual books on many of the islands, whose real strength lies in the colour photographs.

Colin Prior & Magnus Linklater *Highland Wilderness*. After looking at the magnificent photographs of the mountains, you'll be won over by the plea for their conservation.

Michael Russell *A Poem of Remote Lives: Images of Eriskay 1934*. An intriguing combination of photographs of the island taken in 1934 and the extraordinary story of the German photographer, Werner Kissling, who took them.

Mary Withall *The Islands that Roofed the World*. A history of Easdale, Luing and Seil, and particularly their industrial past, by the archivist of the Easdale Museum.

Folklore and legend

Alan J. Bruford & Donald Archie McDonald (eds) *Scottish Traditional Tales*. A huge collection of folk stories from all over Scotland, taken from tape archives.

Gordon Jarvie (ed) *The Penguin Book of Scottish Folk & Fairy Tales*. A collection of over a hundred folk tales from all over Scotland.

Alexander Mackenzie & Elizabeth Sutherland *The Prophecies of Brahan Seer*. These prophecies, which have received as much publicity as those of Nostradamus, were originally passed down orally in Gaelic from a mysterious figure who is said to have come from the Isle of Lewis. They were collected and written down in 1877. This edition tells you how far they've been fulfilled.

George W. Macpherson *Highland Myths and Legends.* Some of these colourful stories have never been published before.

Nigel Tranter *Tales and Traditions of Scottish Castles.* The myths and legends of some of Scotland's famous castles.

Memoirs and travelogues

Iain Banks *Raw Spirit.* A cross between a travel book and autobiography, but it's also a guide to whisky in its many distilleries.

George Mackay Brown *For the Islands I Sing: An Autobiography.* Published posthumously at his own request, this autobiography not only provides an insight into one of the most influential Scottish poets but also into his native Orkney.

Mike Cawthorne *Hell of a Journey.* If you want a harrowing armchair experience, trace this man's journey through the Highlands on foot in winter.

David Craig *On the Crofter's Trail.* Using anecdotes and interviews with descendants, Craig conveys the hardship and tragedy of the Highland Clearances without being mawkish.

Jim Crumley *Gulfs of Blue Air – A Highland Journey.* Recent travelogue mixed with nature notes and references to Scottish poets such as MacCaig and Mackay Brown. *Among Islands* is superbly illustrated, taking you to the outer fringes of islands from Shetland to St Kilda in poetic mood.

David Duff (ed) *Queen Victoria's Highland Journals.* The daily diary of the Scottish adventures of "Mrs Brown" – Victoria's writing is detailed and interesting without being twee, and she lovingly conveys her affection for Deeside and the Highlands.

Elizabeth Grant of Rothiemurchus *Memoirs of a Highland Lady.* Hugely readable recollections, written with wit and perception at the beginning of the eighteenth century, charting the social changes in Edinburgh, London and particularly Speyside.

Jim Hewitson *Clinging to the Edge.* Eight years of essays and jottings by the journalist author who came to live in Orkney on Papa Westray in the early 1980s.

Peter Hill *Stargazing.* Engaging account of being a tyro lighthouse keeper on three of Scotland's most famous lighthouses: Pladda, Ailsa Craig and Hyskeir.

Mike Hughes *The Hebrides at War.* This book demonstrates how crucial the Western Isles were to the defence of the Atlantic convoys against German U-boats. Excellent photographs from the period.

James Hunter *Scottish Highlanders.* Attempts to explain the strong sense of blood ties held by people of Scottish descent all over the world; lots of history and good photographs.

Kathleen Jamie *Findings.* Jamie brings her poetic eye to bear on travels round her native Scotland.

Samuel Johnson & James Boswell *A Journey to the Western Isles of Scotland* and *The Journal of a Tour to the Hebrides.* Lively accounts of a famous journey around the islands taken by the noted lexicographer Dr Samuel Johnson, and his biographer and friend.

Osgood MacKenzie *100 Years in the Highlands.* First published in 1921, this has become a classic social history of the Highlands in Victorian times.

Alasdair Maclean *Night Falls on Ardnamurchan*. First published in 1984 and recently reprinted, this is a classic story of the life and death of the Highland community in which the author grew up.

Iain Mitchell *Isles of the West, Isle of the North*. In the first book, Mitchell sails round the Inner Hebrides, talking to locals and incomers, siding with the former, caricaturing the latter, and, with a fair bit of justification, laying into the likes of the RSPB and SNH. *Isles of the North* gives Orkney and Shetland the same treatment, before heading off to Norway to find out how it can be done differently.

Edwin Muir *Scottish Journey*. A classic travelogue written in 1935 by the troubled Orcadian writer on his return to Scotland from London.

F.G. Rea *A School on South Uist*. As an Englishman who was headmaster of a South Uist school 1890 to 1913, Rea looks with a fresh eye at the life around him and notices details which native Hebridean writers often take for granted.

June Skinner Sawyers *The Road North*. An interesting collection of 300 years of Scottish travel writing, divided into regions.

Sir Walter Scott *The Voyage of the Pharos*. In 1814 Scott accompanied Stevenson senior on a tour of the northern lighthouses, visiting Shetland, Orkney, the Hebrides and even nipping across to Ireland; he wrote a lively diary of their adventures, which included dodging American privateers.

Mike Tomkies *A Last Wild Place*. Written by a journalist who lived in a derelict croft in northwest Scotland for twenty years, this is a perceptive and loving account of the natural world around him.

Food and drink

Annette Hope *A Caledonian Feast*. Authoritative and entertaining history of Scottish food and social life from the ninth to the twentieth centuries. Lots of recipes.

Michael Jackson *Malt Whisky Companion*. An attractively put-together tome, considered by many to be the bible of malt-whisky tasting.

Sue Lawrence *Scots Cooking*. This award-winning book offers traditional recipes from all over Scotland.

G.W. Lockhart *The Scots and Their Fish*. Tells the history of fish and fishing in Scotland, and ends with a selection of traditional recipes.

Claire Macdonald *Simply Seasonal*. Lady Claire Macdonald of Macdonald has become widely known and respected in Scottish cookery circles. She promotes the use of native food and runs a successful hotel on Skye (see p.334).

Charles McLean *Scotch Whisky* is a small, thorough, fact-filled book covering malt, grain and blended whiskies, plus whisky-based liqueurs.

Nick Nairn *Wild Harvest; Wild Harvest 2; Island Harvest; New Scottish Cookery*. Glossy TV tie-ins by an engaging talented Scottish chef, who took up the challenge of gathering and eating from the wild and is now promoting imaginative ways to serve Scottish traditional fare.

Fiction

George Mackay Brown *Beside the Ocean of Time*. A child's journey through the history of an Orkney island, and an adult's effort to make sense of the place's secrets in the late twentieth century. *Magnus* is his retelling of the death of St Magnus, with parallels for modern times.

George MacDonald Fraser *The General Danced at Dawn*; *The Sheikh and the Dustbin*. Touching and very funny collections of short stories detailing life in a Highland regiment after World War II.

Christine Marion Fraser *Kinvara*. Glasgow-born Fraser's family saga is centred on a lighthouse keeper on the west coast of Scotland. Her latest novels, *Children of Rhanna* and *Stranger on Rhanna*, trace the lives of four people who were brought up in a close-knit community on the island of Rhanna.

Lewis Grassic Gibbon *Sunset Song; Cloud Howe; Grey Granite*. This trilogy, known as *A Scots Quair* and set in northeast Scotland, has become a classic, telling the story of the conflict in one man's life between Scottish and English culture.

Neil M. Gunn *The Silver Darlings*. Probably Gunn's most representative and best-known book, evocatively set on the northeast coast and telling the story of the herring fishermen during the great years of the industry. Other examples of his romantic, symbolic works include *The Lost Glen, The Silver Bough* and *Wild Geese Overhead*.

Eric Linklater *The Dark of Summer*. Set on the Faroes, Shetland, Orkney (where the author was born) and in theatres of war, this novel exhibits the best of Linklater's compelling narrative style, although his comic *Private Angelo* is better known.

Compton MacKenzie *Whisky Galore*. Comic novel based on a true story of the wartime wreck of a cargo of whisky off Eriskay. Full of predictable stereotypes, but still funny.

Naomi Mitchison *The Bull Calves*. Written during World War II, but set in 1747, this comment on the after-effects of war is wrapped in a historical setting. *Lobster on the Agenda*. Written in 1952, this book closely mirrors contemporary life in Kyntyre where Mitchison lived, with its community trying to look forward while hampered by the prejudices of the past.

Nancy Brysson Morrison *The Gowk Storm*. Published in 1933, this novel vividly portrays the lives of three sisters trapped in a claustrophobic morally prejudiced society.

Anne Macleod *The Dark Ship*. A gripping love story set on the Isle of Lewis against the background of two world wars.

Neil Munro *The Complete Edition of the Para Handy Tales*. Engaging and witty stories relating the adventures of a Clyde puffer captain as he more or less legally steers his grubby ship up and down the west coast. Despite a fond – if slightly patronizing – view of the Gaelic mind, they are enormous fun.

M. Sinclair *Hebridean Odyssey: Songs, Poems, Prose and Images*. A useful anthology for getting the feel of the rich and varied culture of the Hebrides.

Iain Crichton Smith *Consider the Lilies*. Poetic lament about the Highland Clearances by Scotland's finest bilingual (English and Gaelic) writer.

Sir Walter Scott *The Pirate*. Inspired by stories of Viking raids and set in Orkney and Shetland, this novel was very popular in Victorian times.

Children's fiction

George Mackay Brown *Pictures in the Cave*. A collection of stories based on folk tales, told by a master poet. Suitable for 9-year-olds and over.

Rowena Farre *Seal Morning*. An absorbing account of a young girl growing up on a remote croft in the Highlands towards the beginning of the last century and the wild life she adopted. Eight-year-olds and upwards will love it and so will adults.

Kathleen Fidler *Desperate Journey*. Story of a family driven from Scotland in the Sutherland Clearances across the Atlantic to Canada. *The Droving Lad* is a thriller about a boy and his first experience of driving cattle from the Highlands to the Lowlands. Suitable for 9-year-olds and over.

Mairi Hedderwick *Katie Morag and the Two Grandmothers*. One of the many delightful stories of a little girl and the trouble she gets into on the West Coast island of Struay, beautifully illustrated by the author. Suitable for reading to under-5s.

Ted Hughes *Nessie the Mannerless Monster*. A verse story about the famous monster who goes to London to see the queen. Suitable for 5- to 8-year-olds.

Mollie Hunter *A Stranger Came Ashore*. Set in Shetland, this a tragic and gripping historical tale. Suitable for 10-year-olds and over.

Gavin Maxwell *Ring of Bright Water*. Heart-warming true tale of a relationship with three otters. Suitable for 7-year-olds upwards.

Stephen Potts *Hunting Gumnor*. A haunting story set on a Scottish island, both an adventure and a fantasy, which affirms the values of island life and the creatures that live there. For 10-year-olds upwards.

Robert Louis Stevenson *Kidnapped*. A thrilling historical adventure set in the eighteenth century, every bit as exciting as the better-known *Treasure Island*.

Poetry

George Mackay Brown *Selected Poems 1954–1992*. Brown's work is as haunting, beautiful and gritty as the Orkney islands which inspire it. The most recent collection, *Travellers* – compiled after his death – is work either previously unpublished or appearing only in newspapers and periodicals.

Robert Burns *Selected Poems*. Scotland's most famous bard. Immensely popular all over the world, his best-known works are his earlier ones, including *Auld Lang Syne* and *My Love is Like a Red, Red Rose*.

Crawford & Imlah *The New Penguin Book of Scottish Verse*. A historical survey of Scottish verse and its many languages, from St Columba to Don Paterson.

Norman MacCaig *Selected Poems*. This selection includes some of the best work from this important Scottish poet, whose deep love of nature and of the Highland landscape is always evident. *Norman MacCaig; A Celebration*, an anthology written for his 85th birthday, includes work by more than ninety writers, including Ted Hughes and Seamus Heaney.

Sorley Maclean (Somhairle Macgill-Eain) *From Wood to Ridge: Collected Poems*. Written in

Gaelic, his poems have been translated into bilingual editions all over the world, dealing as they do with the sorrows of poverty, war and love.

McMillan & Byrne (eds) *Modern Scottish Women Poets.* The work of over a hundred women writers of the twentieth century, some of whom had sunk into undeserved oblivion.

John McQueen & Tom Scott (eds) *The Oxford Book of Scottish Verse.* Claims to be the most comprehensive anthology of Scottish poetry ever published.

Edwin Morgan *New Selected Poems.* A love of words and their sounds is evident in Morgan's poems, which are refreshingly varied and often experimental. He comments on the Scottish scene with shrewdness and humour.

Edwin Muir *Collected Poems.* Muir's childhood on Orkney at the turn of the twentieth century remained with him as a dream of paradise from which he was banished to Glasgow. His poems are passionately concerned with Scotland.

Iain Crichton Smith *Collected Poems.* Born on the Isle of Lewis, Iain Crichton Smith wrote with feeling, and sometimes bitterness, in both Gaelic and English, of the life of the rural communities, the iniquities of the Free Church, the need to revive Gaelic culture and the glory of the Scottish landscape.

Outdoor pursuits and wildlife

Bartholomew Walks Series. The series covers different areas of Scotland, including Perthshire, Loch Lomond and the Trossachs, Oban, Mull and Lochaber, and Skye and Wester Ross. Each booklet has a range of walks of varying lengths, with clear maps and descriptions.

Donald Bennet *The Munros*; **Scott Johnstone et al** *The Corbetts.* Authoritative and attractively illustrated hill walkers' guides to the Scottish peaks. Also *Scottish Hill Tracks* – over 300 cross-country walks, suitable for a day or longer journeys linking routes.

Hamish Brown *Hamish's Mountain Walk and Climbing the Corbetts.* The best of the travel narratives about walking in the Scottish Highlands.

Anthony Burton *The Caledonian Canal.* A book for walkers, cyclists and boaters, with maps and details of boat rental, accommodation, etc. The author has also covered *The Southern Upland Way* and *The West Highland Way.*

Cunningham, Dix & Snow *Birdwatching in the Outer Hebrides.* Detailed maps of best locations, although the possible sightings are perhaps a tad optimistic.

Andrew Dempster *Classic Mountain Scrambles in Scotland.* Guide to hill walks in Scotland that combine straightforward walking with some rock climbing.

Richard Fitter, Alastair Fitter & Marjorie Blaney *Collins Pocket Guide to the Wild Flowers of Britain and Northern Europe.* An excellent, easy-to-use field guide.

David Hamilton *The Scottish Golf Guide.* An inexpensive paperback with descriptions of, and useful information about, 84 of Scotland's best courses from the remote to the Open Championship.

John Hancox *Collins Pocket Reference – Cycling in Scotland.* Spiral-bound edition with over fifty road routes of all grades up and down the country, each with a useful route map. For more off-road mountain-bike routes, try Harry Henniker *101 Bike Routes in Scotland*.

George Hendry *Midges in Scotland*. Everything you ever wanted to know about *Culicoides impunctatus* – a strangely satisfying read on warm, damp nights in the Highlands.

Philip Lusby & Jenny Wright *Scottish Wild Plants*. Beautifully produced book about the rarer plants of Scotland, their discovery and their conservation, produced in conjunction with the Royal Botanic Gardens of Edinburgh.

Michael Madders & Julia Welstead *Where to Watch Birds in Scotland*. Region-by-region guide with maps, details on access and habitat, and notes on what to see when.

Magnus Magnusson & Graham White (eds) *The Nature of Scotland – Landscape, Wildlife and People*. Glossy picture-based book on Scotland's natural heritage, from geology to farming and conservation. Good section on crofting.

Ian Mitchell *Mountain Days and Bothy Nights*. A slim but highly entertaining volume describing the characters and experiences of modern-day hill-climbing.

Hilary Parke *Ski & Snowboard: Scotland*. Informative book about where to go to get to the best slopes, with loads of useful advice.

Pastime Publications *Scotland for Game, Sea and Coarse Fishing*. General guide on what to fish, where to do it and for how much, along with notes on records, regulations and convenient accommodation.

Paul Ramsay *Lochs & Glens of Scotland*. Informative text and stunning photographs of the Highlands that make you want to book a holiday immediately.

Ralph Storer *100 Best Routes on Scottish Mountains*. A compilation of the best day-walks in Scotland, including some of the classics overlooked by the Munroing guides.

Recipes

Food in the Highlands and Islands has always been limited, dictated largely by natural conditions. Scotland's northerly situation means that the only cereal crops grown in any quantity have been **oats** and a very hardy form of **barley**, called "bere", still grown in Orkney. Yeasted bread was virtually unknown until the twentieth century, and today's **oatcakes**, one of Scotland's major exports, are the descendants of the unyeasted bread, cooked on a hot stone since prehistoric times. The **potato** has been a staple part of Highland diet since the late eighteenth century and, of course, **root vegetables** like the turnip/swede ("mashit tatties and neeps"), which were also used to feed the animals in winter. Shortage of pasture means that cattle have largely been kept for **milk**, **butter** and **cheese** in the Highlands rather than meat, but, of course, Scots beef (though from the Lowlands) is well-known for its excellence. Sheep, which ousted people during the Clearances, do appear on the menu now, but the oldest dishes are generally meatless. Consequently, many traditional dishes make good use of potatoes, oats and whisky, and are simple to cook. The recipes that follow are fairly simple; some of them you'll find on menus, but others have yet to be revived.

Soup

A good nourishing broth or soup has always been the foundation of a Scot's day in winter. **Scotch broth**, the best known, is made from meat stock, vegetables and any leftovers, but must include pearl barley, which is soaked overnight. In many households it was left on the stove for days and topped with water and titbits when the level fell.

Cullen Skink

More unusual than Scotch broth, this delicious soup is being found increasingly regularly on Scottish menus. It has its roots in Cullen, a small town on the Moray Firth coast, and is traditionally made from smoked fish – for the real thing, don't use the dyed variety. Serves four.

1 smoked haddock
1 onion, chopped
1 pint milk
1oz butter
Salt and pepper
A little mashed potato
Chopped parsley

Skin the haddock, place in a pan and cover with water. Bring to the boil, add the chopped onion, then simmer until the fish is cooked. Remove the fish, reserving the stock, and flake it, removing the bones. In another pan, bring the milk to the boil, then add the stock and the fish, with salt to taste (you probably won't need much). Add the butter, seasoning and enough mashed potato to thicken the soup, then stir well. Serve with chopped parsley.

Main courses

In hotels and restaurants, main courses generally include roast beef, salmon and chicken and imported dishes. The main-course recipes below are strictly traditional and based on the cheap fare of the peasant. They are, however, very tasty and can sometimes be found in good cafés where home cooking is offered.

Clapshot

This dish comes from Orkney, and can be served as a side vegetable or as a main course with the addition of cheese at the mashing stage. Serves four.

500g potatoes
500g swede or turnip
1 onion, finely chopped
1 tbsp chopped chives
Milk
Butter
Salt and pepper

Peel the potatoes and swede. Cut them into smallish pieces and put them in a large pan with the onion. Pour boiling water over them and simmer gently until just soft. Drain and mash thoroughly, adding the chives and enough milk and butter to make the mixture light and fluffy. Season with salt and pepper.

Rumbledthumps

The name for this dish means "mixed together" – rumbled – and "bashed together" – thumped. This is a meatless main course but can also be served as a vegetable dish along with meat. Serves four.

1lb potatoes
1lb white cabbage, spring cabbage or kale
3oz butter
1 medium onion or two trimmed leeks, finely chopped
1 small pot of single cream
Salt and black pepper
2oz mature Cheddar, grated
Chopped fresh chives

Slice the potatoes thickly and boil in a little salted water. Once cooked, drain and mash. Slice the cabbage and boil gently in salted water, being careful not to overcook. Melt the butter in a heavy-bottomed pan and sauté the onions or leeks until soft. Add the potatoes and cabbage, a little cream and seasoning to taste, then beat together with the chives. Place the mixture in an ovenproof dish, cover with grated Cheddar and brown under a hot grill or in a hot oven.

Stovies

Stovies are made from potatoes, onions and left-over cooked meat. They are a good example of a peasant dish; being mainly potato, it provided energy in the form of starch and bulk to fill empty stomachs. Despite the dish's "poor" origins, it is very tasty, filling and is often served with oatcakes at ceilidhs (country dances) and evening wedding receptions. Serves four.

2 medium onions, finely chopped
2oz beef dripping or 4 tbsp of sunflower oil
2lb potatoes, peeled and roughly sliced
4 tablespoons of gravy or stock
About 6oz cold roast beef, diced
Salt and pepper
Parsley, chopped

Cook the onions in the dripping until they are soft but not brown. Add the potatoes to the onions and mix well; cover and cook for about ten minutes, stirring occasionally to prevent sticking. Add the gravy, meat, salt and pepper and mix well. Cover again and cook over a low heat until the thinner potato slices are mushy and the thicker-cut ones are soft – an hour should be enough (this part of the cooking can be done in a large casserole dish in a medium oven, to give a crunchy topping). Garnish with parsley and serve with oatcakes and a glass of milk.

Puddings

Puddings were something of a luxury for the Highlander and a meal was more likely to be rounded off with a dram of whisky. There are one or two traditional recipes like the ones that follow.

Clootie dumpling

You'll find this spiced fruit pudding in many restaurants and even in tins, but, as you might expect, some are better than others. It's very filling and can be solid – a cross between a steamed pudding and a cake, it will serve either purpose. The following is just one of many variations on the recipe. Serves four.

750g self-raising flour
500g mixed dried fruit
1 1/2 tbsp mixed spice
1 heaped tsp baking powder
250g granulated sugar
250g suet or margarine
2 tbsp treacle or syrup
Milk

Mix the suet, flour, fruit, spice, baking powder and sugar together. Combine the treacle with a little milk and add to the mixture. Gradually stir in more milk until the mixture has a soft consistency, then place on a white square cloth that has been well floured (this is the *clout* or *cloot*). Gather the ends together, leaving room for the dumpling to expand, and tie them in a tight knot. Place it on a plate in a large pan of boiling water. Cover, and boil gently for two hours (make sure it doesn't boil dry). Turn it out of the cloth and allow it to dry out in a medium oven for ten to fifteen minutes.

Cranachan

Cranachan (also known as "Stapag on the Islands", where the raspberries are generally omitted) was traditionally served at harvest time, when all the ingredients were put upon the table and everyone filled their own dish and chose their own ratio of whisky to solids. It's now back on the menu and is delicious. Serves four.

50g medium oatmeal
10 fl oz fresh double cream
3 tbsp heather honey
3 tbsp whisky
350g fresh raspberries

Toast the oatmeal under a grill until it's golden, and let it cool. Whip the cream until it's stiff, then mix in the oatmeal, honey and whisky. In tall glasses, layer the raspberries with the cream mixture and chill in the fridge. Serve at room temperature, decorated with raspberries.

Carrageen jelly

This recipe comes from Lewis, and you're unlikely to find it on a menu. Its main interest is historical, as **carrageen** is a type of seaweed found in abundance in the Western Isles. Be careful to identify it correctly, as some seaweeds can have unfortunate results. Serves four.

250g carrageen, washed and soaked for two hours, then dried
Rind of 1 lemon, grated
500ml milk
Sugar to taste

Place the seaweed in a pan with the lemon rind and cover with milk. Bring it to the boil and simmer gently for thirty minutes. Stir in the sugar and then strain into a mould and allow to cool. It should set like a jelly and can then be turned out onto a plate.

Crowdie

A simple form of crofting cheese, anyone can make this at home. It's a very good way of using up milk that's gone sour, and goes well with oatcakes.

1 litre freshly sour or full cream milk
Salt
Cream

Pour the milk into a pan and place it on a slow heat until it curdles. Make sure it doesn't simmer or boil, or the curd will harden. Let the curds cool. Next, the liquid (or whey) needs to be drained off. Line a colander with muslin, put the curds in it and leave until the whey has drained away; squeeze the last bit out by hand or with the back of a spoon. You now have basic **crowdie**: it simply needs a little salt and cream and a rest in the fridge before consuming. It doesn't keep well, so eat it within three days.

Language

Language

Language

Language is a thorny, complex and often highly political issue in Scotland. If you're not from Scotland yourself, you're most likely to be addressed in a variety of **English**, spoken in a Scottish accent. Even then, you're likely to hear phrases and words that are part of what is known as Lowland Scottish or **Scots**, which is now officially recognized as a distinct language in its own right. To a lesser extent, **Gaelic**, too, remains a living language, particularly in the *Gàidhealtachd* or Gaelic-speaking areas of the Western Isles, parts of Skye and a few scattered Hebridean islands. In Orkney and Shetland, the local dialect of Scots contains many words carried over from **Norn**, the Old Norse language spoken in the Northern Isles from the time of the Vikings until the eighteenth century.

Scots

Lowland Scottish or **Scots** is spoken by thirty percent of the Scottish population, according to the latest survey. It began life as a northern branch of Anglo-Saxon, and emerged as a distinct language in the Middle Ages. From the 1370s until the Union in 1707, it was the country's main literary and documentary language. Since the eighteenth century, however, it has been systematically repressed in preference to English.

Robbie Burns is the most obvious literary exponent of the Scots language, but there was a revival in the last century led by poets such as Hugh MacDiarmid. (For examples of the works of both writers, see "Books", p.526.) Only very recently has Scots enjoyed something of a renaissance, getting itself on the Scottish school curriculum in 1996, and achieving official recognition as a distinct language in 1998. Despite these enormous political achievements, many people (rightly or wrongly) still regard Scots as a dialect of English.

HarperCollins in the UK publishes a handy, pocket-sized *Scots Dictionary* as a guide to the idioms of Scottish vocabulary.

Gaelic

Scottish **Gaelic** (*Gàidhlig*, pronounced "gallic") is one of only four Celtic languages to survive into the modern age (Welsh, Breton and Irish Gaelic are the other three). Manx, the old language of the Isle of Man, died out early last century, while Cornish was finished as a community language way back in the eighteenth century. Scottish Gaelic is most closely related to Irish Gaelic and Manx – hardly surprising, since Gaelic was introduced to Scotland from Ireland around the third century BC. Some folk still argue that Scottish Gaelic is merely a dialect of its parent language, Irish Gaelic, and indeed the two languages remain more or less mutually intelligible. From the fifth to the twelfth centuries, Gaelic enjoyed an expansionist phase, gradually becoming the national language, thanks partly to the backing of the Celtic Church in Iona.

At the end of this period, Gaelic was spoken throughout virtually all of what is now Scotland, the main exceptions being Orkney and Shetland.

From that high point onwards, Gaelic began a steady decline. Even before Union with England, power, religious ideology and wealth gradually passed into non-Gaelic hands. The royal court was transferred to Edinburgh and an Anglo-Norman legal system was put in place. The Celtic Church was Romanized by the introduction of foreign clergy and, most importantly of all, English and Flemish merchants colonized the new trading towns of the east coast. In addition, the pro-English attitudes held by the Covenanters led to strong anti-Gaelic feeling within the Church of Scotland from its inception.

The two abortive Jacobite rebellions of 1715 and 1745 furthered the language's decline, as did the Clearances that took place in the Gaelic-speaking Highlands from the 1770s to the 1850s, which forced thousands to migrate to central Scotland's new industrial belt or emigrate to North America. Although efforts were made to halt the decline in the first half of the nineteenth century, the 1872 Education Act gave no official recognition to Gaelic, and children were severely punished if they were caught speaking the language in school.

The 2001 census put the number of Gaelic speakers at under 60,000 (just over one percent of the population), the majority of whom live in the *Gàidhealtachd*, though there is thought to be an extended Gaelic community of perhaps 250,000 who have some understanding of the language. Since the 1980s, great efforts have been made to try to save the language, including the introduction of bilingual primary and nursery schools, and a huge increase in the amount of broadcasting time given to Gaelic-language and Gaelic music programmes, and the establishment of highly successful Gaelic colleges such as Sabhal Mòr Ostaig (Ⓦwww.smo.uhi.ac.uk).

Gaelic grammar and pronunciation

Gaelic is a highly complex tongue, with a fiendish, antiquated **grammar** and, with only eighteen letters, an intimidating system of spelling. **Pronunciation** is easier than it appears at first glance – one general rule to remember is that the **stress** always falls on the first syllable of a word. The general rule of syntax is that the verb starts the sentence whether it's a question or not, followed by the subject and then the object; adjectives generally follow the word they are describing.

Short and long vowels

Gaelic has both short and long vowels, the latter being denoted by an acute or grave accent.

a as in **cat**; before nn and ll, as in **cow**

à as in **bar**

e as in **pet**

é like **rain**

i as in **sight**

í like **free**

o as in **pot**

ò like **enthral**

ó like **cow**

u like **scoot**

ù like **loo**

Vowel combinations

Gaelic is littered with diphthongs, which, rather like in English, can be pronounced in several different ways depending on the individual word.

ai like **cat**, or **pet**; before dh or gh, like **street**

ao like the sound in the middle of **colonel**

ei like **mate**

ea like **pet**, or **cat**, and sometimes like **mate**; before *ll* or *nn*, like in **cow**

èa as in **hear**

eu like **train**, or **fear**

ia like **fear**

io like **fear**, or shorter than **street**

ua like **wooer**

L LANGUAGE | Gaelic

Consonants

The consonants listed below are those that differ substantially from the English.

b at the beginning of a word as in **b**ig; in the middle or at the end of a word, like the *p* in **p**air

bh at the beginning of a word like the *v* in **v**an; elsewhere it is silent

c as in **c**at; after a vowel it has aspiration *before* it

ch always as in lo**ch**, *never* as in **ch**urch

cn like the *cr* in **cr**owd

d like the *d* in **d**og, but with the tongue pressed against the back of the upper teeth; at the beginning of a word or before e or i, like the *j* in **j**am; in the middle or at the end of a word, like the *t* in ca**t**; after i, like the *ch* in **ch**urch

dh before and after a, o or u is an aspirated *g*, rather like a gargle; before e or i, like the *y* in **y**es; elsewhere silent

fh usually silent; sometimes like the *h* in **h**ouse

g at the beginning of a word, as in **g**et; before e, like the *y* in **y**es; in the middle or end of a word, like the *ck* in so**ck**; after i, like the *ch* in lo**ch**

gh at the beginning of a word as in **g**et; before or after a, o or u rather like a gargle; after i sometimes like the *y* in ga**y**, but often silent

l after i and sometimes before e like the *l* in **l**ot; elsewhere, a peculiarly Gaelic sound produced by flattening the front of the tongue against the palate

mh like the *v* in **v**an

p at the beginning of a word as in **p**et; elsewhere it has aspiration *before* it

rt pronounced as **sht**

s before e or i, like the *sh* in **sh**ip; otherwise as in English

sh before a, o or u, like the *h* in **h**ouse; before e, like the *ch* in lo**ch**

t before e or i, like the *ch* in **ch**urch; in the middle or at the end of a word it has aspiration *before* it; otherwise as in English

th at the beginning of a word, like the *h* in **h**ouse; elsewhere, and in the word *thu*, silent

Gaelic phrases and vocabulary

The choice is limited when it comes to **teach-yourself Gaelic** courses, but the BBC *Can Seo* cassette and book is perfect for starting you off. Drier and more academic is *Teach Yourself Gaelic*, which is aimed at bringing beginners to working competence. *Everyday Gaelic* by Morag MacNeill is the best phrasebook around. You can also get learning materials online from ⓦwww.smo.uhi.ac.uk.

Basic words and greetings

tha	yes
chan eil	no
hallo	hello
ciamar a tha thu?	how are you?
tha gu math	fine
tapadh leat	thank you
fàilte	welcome
thig a-staigh	come in
latha math	good day
mar sin leat	goodbye
oidhche mhath	goodnight
cò?	who?
càit a bheil...?	where is...?
cuine?	when?
dé tha ann?	what is it?
madainn	morning
feasgar	evening
là	day
oidhche	night
an seo	here
an sin	there
mar seo	this way
mar sin	that way
a-màireach	tomorrow
a-nochd	tonight
slàinte	cheers
an-dé	yesterday
an-diugh	today
maireach	tomorrow
a-nise	now
taigh-òsda	hotel

taigh	house
sgeul	story
òran	song
ceòl	music
leabhar	book
sgìth	tired
not/aichean	pound/s (sterling)
lòn	food
aran	bread
uisge	water
bainne	milk
leann	beer
fìon	wine
uisge beatha	whisky
post oifis	post office
Dun Eideann	Edinburgh
Glaschu	Glasgow
Ameireaga	America
Eire	Ireland
Sasainn	England
Lunnainn	London

Some useful phrases

Dè tha e 'cosg?	How much is that?
Dè 'n t-ainm a th'ort?	What's your name?
Gabh mo leisgeul	Excuse me
Dé am uair a tha e?	What time is it?
Tha am pathadh orm	I'm thirsty
'Se rùm dùbailte tha mi'giarraigh	I'd like a double room
A bheil Gàidhlig agad?	Do you speak Gaelic?
Dé a' Ghàidhlig a tha ... air?	What is the Gaelic for ...?
Chan eil mi 'tuigsinn	I don't understand
Chan eil fhios agam	I don't know
'S math sin	That's good
'S coma	It doesn't matter
Tha mi duilich	I'm sorry

Numbers and days

aon	1
dà/dhà	2
trì	3
ceithir	4
còig	5
sia	6
seachd	7
ochd	8
naoi	9
deich	10
aon deug	11
fichead	20
aon ar fhichead	21
deug ar fhichead	30
dà fhichead	40
lethcheud	50
trì fichead	60
ceud	100
mìle	1000
Diluain	Monday
Dimàirt	Tuesday
Diciadain	Wednesday
Diardaoin	Thursday
Dihaoine	Friday
Disathurna	Saturday
Didòmhnaich/ La na Sàbaid	Sunday

Gaelic geographical and place-name terms

The purpose of the list below is to help with place-name derivations from Gaelic and with more detailed map reading. For a list of place names derived from Norse, see p.546.

abhainn	river
ach or auch, from achadh	field
ail, aileach	rock
Alba	Scotland
aonach	ridge
ard, ardan or arden, from àird	a point of land or height
aros	dwelling
ault, from allt	stream
bad	brake or clump of trees
bagh	bay
bal or bally, from baile	town, village
balloch, from bealach	mountain pass
ban	white, fair

LANGUAGE | Gaelic

bàrr	summit
beg, from beag	small
ben, from beinn	mountain
blair, from blàr	field or battlefield
cairn, from càrn	pile of stones
camas	bay, harbour
cnoc	hill
coll or colly, from coille	wood or forest
corran	a spit or point jutting into the sea
corrie, from coire	round hollow in mountainside, whirlpool
craig, from creag	rock, crag
cruach	bold hill
drum, from druim	ridge
dubh	black
dun or dum, from dùn	fort
eilean	island
ess, from eas	waterfall
fin, from fionn	white
gair or gare, from geàrr	short
garv, from garbh	rough
geodha	cove
glen, from gleann	valley
gower or gour, from gabhar	goat
inch, from innis	meadow or island
inver, from inbhir	river mouth
ken or kin, from ceann	head
knock, from cnoc	hill
kyle, from caolas	narrow strait
lag	hollow
larach	site of an old ruin
liath	grey
loch	lake
meall	round hill
mon, from monadh	hill
more, from mór	large, great
ord	round mountain
rannoch, from raineach	bracken
ross, from ros	promontory
rubha	promontory
sgeir	sea rock
sgurr	sharp point
sron	nose, prow or promontory
strath, from srath	broad valley
tarbet, from tairbeart	isthmus
tigh	house
tir or tyre, from tìr	land
torr	hill, castle
tràigh	shore
uig	shelter
uisge	water

Norn (Orkney and Shetland)

Between the tenth and seventeenth centuries, the chief language of Orkney and Shetland was **Norn**, a Scandinavian tongue close to modern Faroese and Icelandic. After the end of Norse rule, and with the transformation of the church, the law, commerce and education, Norn gradually lost out to Scots and English, eventually petering out completely in the eighteenth century. Today, Orkney and Shetland have their own dialects, and individual islands and communities within each group have local variations. The **dialects** have a Scots base, with some Old Norse words; however, they don't sound strongly Scottish, with the Orkney accent – which has been likened to the Welsh one – especially distinctive. Listed below are some of the words you're most likely to hear, including some birds' names and common elements in place names.

Norn phrases and vocabulary

aak	guillemot
alan	storm petrel
ayre	beach
bister	farm
böd	fisherman's store
bonxie	great skua
bruck	rubbish
burra	heath rush
crö	sheepfold
eela	rod-fishing from small boats
ferrylouper	incomer (Orkney)
fourareen	four-oared boat
foy	party or festival
geo	coastal inlet
gloup	blowhole, behind a cliff face, where spray is blasted out from the cave below (from Old Norse *glup*, a throat)
haa	laird's house
haaf	deep-sea fishing. Lit. "heave" (Shetland)
hap	hand-knitted shawl
howe	mound
kame	ridge of hills
kishie	basket
maa	seagull
mool	headland
moorit	brown
mootie	tiny
muckle	large
noost	hollow place where a boat is drawn up
norie (or tammie-norie)	puffin
noup	steep headland
peerie/peedie	small
plantiecrub (or plantiecrö)	small drystone enclosure for growing cabbages
quoy	enclosed, cultivated common land
roost	tide race
scattald	common grazing land
scord	gap or pass in a ridge of hills
setter	farm
shaela	dark grey
simmer dim	summer twilight
sixern/sixareen	six-oared boat
solan	gannet
soothmoother	incomer (Shetland)
udal	Norse law designating land as a freehold without any charter or feudal type arrangement
voe	sea inlet

Glossary

Auld Old.

Aye Yes.

Bairn Baby.

Bannock Flat, unleavened bread traditionally made from oats or barley.

Baronial see "Scottish Baronial".

Ben Hill or mountain.

Blackhouse Thick-walled traditional dwelling.

Bonnie Pretty.

Bothy Primitive cottage or hut; farmworker's or shepherd's mountain shelter.

Brae Slope or hill.

Brig Bridge.

Broch Circular prehistoric stone fort.

Burn Small stream or brook.

Byre Shelter for cattle; cottage.

Cairn Mound of stones.

CalMac Caledonian MacBrayne ferry company.

Carse Riverside area of flat alluvium.

Ceilidh (pronounced "kay-lee") Social gathering involving dancing, drinking, singing and storytelling.

Central Belt The densely populated strip of central Scotland between the Forth and Clyde estuaries, incorporating the conurbations of Edinburgh, Glasgow and Stirling.

Clan Extended family.

Clearances Policy adopted by late eighteenth- and early nineteenth-century landowners to evict tenant crofters in order to create space for more profitable sheep grazing. Families cleared from the Highlands were often put on emigrant ships to North America or the colonies.

Clootie well A cloot is a cloth or rag; the well was festooned with these and folk would drink three sips and circle the well for good luck.

Corbett A mountain between 2500ft and 3000ft high.

Corbie-stepped Architectural term; any set of steps on a gable.

Covenanters Supporters of the Presbyterian Church in the seventeenth century.

Crannog Celtic lake or bog dwelling.

Croft Small plot of farmland with house, common in the Highlands.

Crow-stepped Same as corbie-stepped.

Dolmen Grave chamber.

Dram Literally, one-eighth of a fluid ounce. Usually refers to any small measure of whisky.

Dun Fortified mound.

First-foot The first person to enter a household after midnight on Hogmanay (see below).

Firth A wide sea inlet or estuary.

Gabbro Igneous basalt-like rock formed by molten lava and found in the Northwest Highlands of Scotland.

Gillie Personal guide used on hunting or fishing trips.

Glen Deep, narrow mountain valley.

Harling Limestone and gravel mix used to cover buildings.

Henge Circular ditch with a bank.

Hogmanay New Year's Eve.

Howe Valley.

Howff Meeting place; pub.

HS Historic Scotland, a government-funded heritage organization.

Ken Knowledge; understanding.

Kilt Knee-length tartan skirt worn by Highland men.

Kirk Church.

Laird Landowner; aristocrat.

Law Rounded hill.

Links Grassy coastal land; coastal golf course.

Loch Lake.

Lochan Little loch.

Mac/Mc These prefixes in Scottish surnames derive from the Gaelic, meaning "son of". In Scots "Mac" is used for both sexes. In Gaelic "Nic" is used for women: *Donnchadh Mac*

Aodh is Duncan MacKay, *Iseabail Nic Aodh* is Isabel MacKay.

Machair Sandy, grassy, lime-rich coastal land, generally used for grazing.

Manse Official home of a Presbyterian minister.

Munro A mountain over 3000ft high.

Munro-bagging The sport of trying to climb as many Munros as possible.

Neuk Corner.

NTS The National Trust for Scotland, a heritage organization.

Peel Fortified tower, built to withstand Border raids.

Pend Archway or vaulted passage.

Presbyterian The form of church government used in the official (Protestant) Church of Scotland, established by John Knox during the Reformation.

RIB Rigid Inflatable Boat.

RSPB Royal Society for the Protection of Birds.

Runrig A common form of land tenure in which separate ridges are cultivated by different occupiers under joint agreement.

Sassenach Literally "Saxon"; used by Highlanders to refer to Lowlanders, though commonly used to describe the English.

Scottish Baronial Style of architecture favoured by the Scottish landowning class featuring crow-stepped gables and round turrets.

Sept Branches of clans: often septs have a different surname to the clan name.

Shieling Simple huts or shelters used by shepherds during summer grazing.

Shinty Stick and ball game played in the Highlands, with similarities to hockey.

Smiddy Smithy.

SNH Scottish Natural Heritage, a government-funded conservation body.

SNP Scottish National Party.

Sporran Leather purse worn in front of, or at the side of, a kilt.

Tartan Check-patterned woollen cloth, particular patterns being associated with particular clans.

Tatties Potatoes.

Thane A landowner of high rank; the chief of a clan.

Tombolo A spit of sand connecting an island to the mainland.

Trews Tartan trousers.

Wee Small.

Wee Frees Followers of the Free Presbyterian or Free Church of Scotland.

Wynd Narrow lane.

Yett Gate or door.

Travel store

UK & Ireland
Britain
Devon & Cornwall
Dublin DIRECTIONS
Edinburgh DIRECTIONS
England
Ireland
The Lake District
London
London DIRECTIONS
London Mini Guide
Scotland
Scottish Highlands & Islands
Wales

Europe
Algarve DIRECTIONS
Amsterdam
Amsterdam DIRECTIONS
Andalucía
Athens DIRECTIONS
Austria
Baltic States
Barcelona
Barcelona DIRECTIONS
Belgium & Luxembourg
Berlin
Brittany & Normandy
Bruges DIRECTIONS
Brussels
Budapest
Bulgaria
Copenhagen
Corfu
Corsica
Costa Brava DIRECTIONS
Crete
Croatia
Cyprus
Czech & Slovak Republics
Dodecanese & East Aegean
Dordogne & The Lot
Europe
Florence & Siena
Florence DIRECTIONS
France
French Hotels & Restaurants
Germany
Greece
Greek Islands
Hungary
Ibiza & Formentera DIRECTIONS
Iceland
Ionian Islands
Italy
The Italian Lakes
Languedoc & Roussillon
Lisbon
Lisbon DIRECTIONS
The Loire
Madeira DIRECTIONS
Madrid DIRECTIONS
Mallorca DIRECTIONS
Mallorca & Menorca
Malta & Gozo DIRECTIONS
Menorca
Moscow
The Netherlands
Norway
Paris
Paris DIRECTIONS
Paris Mini Guide
Poland
Portugal
Prague
Prague DIRECTIONS
Provence & the Côte d'Azur
Pyrenees
Romania
Rome
Rome DIRECTIONS
Sardinia
Scandinavia
Sicily
Slovenia
Spain
St Petersburg
Sweden
Switzerland
Tenerife & La Gomera DIRECTIONS
Turkey
Tuscany & Umbria
Venice & The Veneto
Venice DIRECTIONS
Vienna

Asia
Bali & Lombok
Bangkok
Beijing
Cambodia
China
Goa
Hong Kong & Macau
India
Indonesia
Japan
Laos
Malaysia, Singapore & Brunei
Nepal
The Philippines
Singapore
South India
Southeast Asia
Sri Lanka
Taiwan
Thailand
Thailand's Beaches & Islands
Tokyo
Vietnam

Australasia
Australia
Melbourne
New Zealand
Sydney

North America
Alaska
Boston
California
Canada
Chicago
Florida
The Grand Canyon
Hawaii
Honolulu
Las Vegas DIRECTIONS
Los Angeles
Maui DIRECTIONS
Miami & South Florida
Montréal
New England
New Orleans DIRECTIONS
New York City
New York City DIRECTIONS
New York City Mini Guide
Orlando & Walt Disney World DIRECTIONS
Pacific Northwest
The Rocky Mountains
San Francisco
San Francisco DIRECTIONS
Seattle
Southwest USA
Toronto
USA
Vancouver
Washington DC
Washington DC DIRECTIONS
Yosemite

Caribbean & Latin America
Antigua & Barbuda DIRECTIONS
Argentina
Bahamas
Barbados DIRECTIONS
Belize
Bolivia
Brazil
Cancùn & Cozumel DIRECTIONS
Caribbean
Central America
Chile
Costa Rica
Cuba
Dominican Republic
Dominican Republic DIRECTIONS
Ecuador
Guatemala
Jamaica
Mexico
Peru
St Lucia
South America
Trinidad & Tobago
Yúcatan

TRAVEL

Africa & Middle East

Cape Town & the Garden Route
Egypt
The Gambia
Jordan
Kenya
Marrakesh DIRECTIONS
Morocco
South Africa, Lesotho & Swaziland
Syria
Tanzania
Tunisia
West Africa
Zanzibar

Travel Theme guides

First-Time Around the World
First-Time Asia
First-Time Europe
First-Time Latin America
Travel Online
Travel Health
Travel Survival
Walks in London & SE England
Women Travel

Maps

Algarve
Amsterdam
Andalucia & Costa del Sol
Argentina
Athens
Australia
Baja California
Barcelona
Berlin
Boston
Brittany
Brussels
California
Chicago
Corsica
Costa Rica & Panama
Crete
Croatia
Cuba
Cyprus
Czech Republic
Dominican Republic
Dubai & UAE
Dublin
Egypt
Florence & Siena
Florida
France
Frankfurt
Germany
Greece
Guatemala & Belize
Hong Kong
Iceland
Ireland
Kenya
Lisbon
London
Los Angeles
Madrid
Mallorca
Marrakesh
Mexico
Miami & Key West
Morocco
New England
New York City
New Zealand
Northern Spain
Paris
Peru
Portugal
Prague
Rome
San Francisco
Sicily
South Africa
South India
Spain & Portugal
Sri Lanka
Tenerife
Thailand
Toronto
Trinidad & Tobago
Tuscany
Venice
Washington DC
Yucatán Peninsula

Dictionary Phrasebooks

Croatian
Czech
Dutch
Egyptian Arabic
French
German
Greek
Hindi & Urdu
Italian
Japanese
Latin American Spanish
Mandarin Chinese
Mexican Spanish
Polish
Portuguese
Russian
Spanish
Swahili
Thai
Turkish
Vietnamese

Computers

Blogging
iPods, iTunes & Music Online
The Internet
Macs & OS X
Music Playlists
PCs and Windows
Website Directory

Film & TV

Comedy Movies
Cult Movies
Cult TV
Gangster Movies
Horror Movies
James Bond
Kids' Movies
Sci–Fi Movies

Lifestyle

Ethical Shopping
Babies
Pregnancy & Birth

Music Guides

The Beatles
Bob Dylan
Cult Pop
Classical Music
Elvis
Frank Sinatra
Heavy Metal
Hip-Hop
Jazz
Opera
Reggae
Rock
World Music (2 vols)

Popular Culture

Books for Teenagers
Children's Books, 0-5
Children's Books, 5-11
Conspiracy Theories
Cult Fiction
The Da Vinci Code
Lord of the Rings
Shakespeare
Superheroes
Unexplained Phenomena

Sport

Arsenal 11s
Celtic 11s
Chelsea 11s
Liverpool 11s
Man United 11s
Newcastle 11s
Rangers 11s
Tottenham 11s
Cult Football
Muhammad Ali
Poker

Science

The Universe
Weather

MAPS

NOTES

NOTES

NOTES

NOTES

NOTES

NOTES

NOTES

NOTES

Small print and

Index

A Rough Guide to Rough Guides

Published in 1982, the first Rough Guide – to Greece – was a student scheme that became a publishing phenomenon. Mark Ellingham, a recent graduate in English from Bristol University, had been travelling in Greece the previous summer and couldn't find the right guidebook. With a small group of friends he wrote his own guide, combining a highly contemporary, journalistic style with a thoroughly practical approach to travellers' needs.

The immediate success of the book spawned a series that rapidly covered dozens of destinations. And, in addition to impecunious backpackers, Rough Guides soon acquired a much broader and older readership that relished the guides' wit and inquisitiveness as much as their enthusiastic, critical approach and value-for-money ethos.

These days, Rough Guides include recommendations from shoestring to luxury and cover more than 200 destinations around the globe, including almost every country in the Americas and Europe, more than half of Africa and most of Asia and Australasia. Our ever-growing team of authors and photographers is spread all over the world, particularly in Europe, the USA and Australia.

In the early 1990s, Rough Guides branched out of travel, with the publication of Rough Guides to World Music, Classical Music and the Internet. All three have become benchmark titles in their fields, spearheading the publication of a wide range of books under the Rough Guide name.

Including the travel series, Rough Guides now number more than 350 titles, covering: phrasebooks, waterproof maps, music guides from Opera to Heavy Metal, reference works as diverse as Conspiracy Theories and Shakespeare, and popular culture books from iPods to Poker. Rough Guides also produce a series of more than 120 World Music CDs in partnership with World Music Network.

Visit www.roughguides.com to see our latest publications.

Rough Guide travel images are available for commercial licensing at www.roughguidespictures.com

Rough Guide credits

Text editor: Karoline Densley
Layout: Amit Verma
Cartography: Maxine Repath, Karobi Gogoi
Picture editor: Mark Thomas
Production: Aimee Hampson
Proofreader: Stewart Wild
Cover design: Chloë Roberts
Photographer: Helena Smith
Editorial: London Kate Berens, Claire Saunders, Geoff Howard, Ruth Blackmore, Polly Thomas, Richard Lim, Clifton Wilkinson, Alison Murchie, Andy Turner, Keith Drew, Edward Aves, Nikki Birrell, Helen Marsden, Alice Park, Sarah Eno, Joe Staines, Duncan Clark, Peter Buckley, Matthew Milton, Tracy Hopkins, David Paul, Lucy White, Ruth Tidball; **New York** Andrew Rosenberg, Richard Koss, Steven Horak, AnneLise Sorensen, Amy Hegarty, Hunter Slaton, April Isaacs, Sean Mahoney
Design & Pictures: London Simon Bracken, Dan May, Diana Jarvis, Jj Luck, Harriet Mills; **Delhi** Madhulita Mohapatra, Umesh Aggarwal, Ajay Verma, Jessica Subramanian, Ankur Guha, Pradeep Thapliyal
Production: Sophie Hewat, Katherine Owers
Cartography: London Ed Wright, Katie Lloyd-Jones; **Delhi** Manish Chandra, Rajesh Chhibber, Ashutosh Bharti, Rajesh Mishra, Animesh Pathak, Jasbir Sandhu, Amod Singh
Online: New York Jennifer Gold, Suzanne Welles, Kristin Mingrone; **Delhi** Manik Chauhan, Narender Kumar, Shekhar Jha, Lalit K. Sharma, Rakesh Kumar, Chhandita Chakravarty
Marketing & Publicity: London Richard Trillo, Niki Hanmer, David Wearn, Demelza Dallow, Louise Maher, Jess Carter; **New York** Geoff Colquitt, Megan Kennedy, Katy Ball; **Delhi** Reem Khokhar
Custom publishing and foreign rights: Philippa Hopkins
Manager India: Punita Singh
Series editor: Mark Ellingham
Reference Director: Andrew Lockett
PA to Managing and Publishing Directors: Megan McIntyre
Publishing Director: Martin Dunford
Managing Director: Kevin Fitzgerald

SMALL PRINT

Publishing information

This fourth edition published May 2006 by
Rough Guides Ltd,
80 Strand, London WC2R 0RL, UK
345 Hudson St, 4th Floor,
New York, NY 10014, USA
14 Local Shopping Centre, Panchsheel Park,
New Delhi 110017, India
Distributed by the Penguin Group
Penguin Books Ltd,
80 Strand, London WC2R 0RL, UK
Penguin Putnam, Inc.
375 Hudson Street, NY 10014, USA
Penguin Group (Australia)
250 Camberwell Road, Camberwell,
Victoria 3124, Australia
Penguin Books Canada Ltd,
10 Alcorn Avenue, Toronto, Ontario,
M4V 1E4, Canada
Penguin Group (New Zealand)
Cnr Rosedale and Airborne Roads
Albany, Auckland, New Zealand
Cover concept by Peter Dyer.

Typeset in Bembo and Helvetica to an original design by Henry Iles.
Printed and bound in China

584pp includes index
A catalogue record for this book is available from the British Library
ISBN 978-1-84353-690-1

3 5 7 9 8 6 4 2

Help us update

We've gone to a lot of effort to ensure that the fourth edition of **The Rough Guide to Scottish Highlands and Islands** is accurate and up to date. However, things change – places get "discovered", opening hours are notoriously fickle, restaurants and rooms raise prices or lower standards. If you feel we've got it wrong or left something out, we'd like to know, and if you can remember the address, the price, the time, the phone number, so much the better.

We'll credit all contributions, and send a copy of the next edition (or any other Rough Guide if you prefer) for the best letters. Everyone who writes to us and isn't already a subscriber will receive a copy of our full-colour thrice-yearly newsletter. Please mark letters: "**Rough Guide Scottish Highlands and Islands Update**" and send to: Rough Guides, 80 Strand, London WC2R 0RL, or Rough Guides, 4th Floor, 345 Hudson St, New York, NY 10014. Or send an email to **mail@roughguides.com**

Have your questions answered and tell others about your trip at **www.roughguides.atinfopop.com**

Acknowledgements

The authors would like to thank the National Trust for Scotland, Historic Scotland, VisitScotland (in various guises), Deborah Brown at CalMac and Karoline for trawling through Scotland twice.

Rob Humphreys would also like to thank Alasdair Enticknap for frontline dispatches, Val & Gordon for heading once more for the Borders and for sampling D&G, Val (again) for the Northern Isles, Kate, Stan & Josh for going to Skye out of season, and to Kate for lugging a rucksack around the Hebrides.

Donald Reid would also like to thank Rob, Karoline and Helena for staying the course and all they add to the book; also to Colin Hutchison for his enthusiasm, thoroughness and guidebook miles. Around the country there has been an abundance of useful insight, generous hospitality, timely assistance and friendly faces. Thanks to all. Granny R and Granny and Grandpa K had extra duties this time, but their support and encouragement was as valuable as ever. Most thanks and love to Riona, an island hopper before she could walk, and Mo, who keeps on taking me west.

Readers' letters

Thanks to all those readers of the third edition who took the trouble to write in with their amendments and additions. Apologies for any misspellings or omissions.

Gaele Amiot-Cadey, Helen Bennell, Anders Berglund, Ian and John Besch, Katy Broadhead, Adam Butler, Mary Byrne, Michaela Carlowe, Matt and Carrie, Guy and Varry Cocker, Jim Craig, Olga Crawford, Carolyn Datta, Linda Davis, Mike Dean, James Dress, Norinda Fennema, Chris Fort, Paul Gaskell, Andrew Godley, Colin Good, Phillip Greenstein, Matthew Hall, Alastair Hamilton, Andy Hamnett, Aybike Hatemi, Andrea Hemingway, Catherine Henderson, Ian and Mayumi Hepburn, Les and Faye Hinzman, Annelies van 't Hof, R Holland, Jerry Holmes, David Hopkinson, David Hoult, Linda Howe, Marian Hoyle, Margaret Hughes, David & Catriona Jones, Jody Joseph, Cindy Kasfikis, JC Kershaw, John F. King, Sheelagh Knapp, Reto Kromer, Mike and Cassandra Lawton, Andrea, Jochem, Bastian and Nils Liebermann, Jeff Lyons, Frank Maas, Doug MacDougall, Mrs Barbara MacGregor, Karin Mackinnon, Brent Marshall, Ben Mccallum, Karen McCaughtrie, Jim Murchison, Steve Murray, Steven & Judith Niechcial, Tom Paton, Alex Pattison-Appleton, Trevor Pollard, Hugh Raven, Grace Rose-Miller, Sheila Rowell, Mary Ellen Ryan, Ed Schlenk, Jackie Scott, Millicent Scott, Karen See, Alberto Saz Serraro, Annette Spencer, Rachel and Kerry Sutton-Spence, Sue Taylor, Stuart Todd, Mrs R. Thomas, Liz Wadsworth, David White, Adrian Wood, Helen Woods.

Photo credits

All photos © Rough Guides except the following:

Title page
Boat on land © Ken Kochey/Getty Images

Full page
Glencoe © Charles Bowman/Getty Images

Introduction
Stob Coire Easain © Ian Cumming/Axiom
Gannets nesting on cliff © Andy Rouse/Getty Images
Passing place sign © Donald Reid

Things not to miss
01 Mousa Broch, Shetland © Christina Knijff/Alamy
02 Walkers on Benn Alligan Ridge, Torridon © Ian Cumming/Axiom
04 Iona Abbey cloisters © Jerry Dennis
05 Glen Coe, Buachaille Mor © Jeremy Walker/Getty Images
07 Kinloch Castle © Michael Jenner/Alamy
08 Tobermory © Charles Bowman/Axiom
10 Shetland Folk Festival © Doug Houghton
11 Maes Howe, Orkney © Doug Houghton
13 South Harris beach © Rob Humphreys
16 Islay © Simon Grosset/Alamy
18 Skier, Cairngorms © StockShot/Alamy
19 Loch Houm, Knoydart © Peter Hayes/Alamy
21 Eigg © Rob Humphreys
22 Flying above Orkney © Rob Humphreys
23 Wester Ross © Gareth McCormack/Alamy
24 Loch Shiel © BL Images/Alamy
27 Speyside Way © David Kjaer/Stockscotland
28 Minke whale © Visual & Written SL/Alamy
30 Jarlshof, Shetland © Doug Houghton

Scottish food and drink colour insert
Roast beef © Chris Alack/Stockfood/Getty Images
Haggis © Gibson & Smith/Getty Images
Blender sampling from storage cask © Darren Robb/Getty Images

Wildlife colour insert
Scots pine © David Robertson/Alamy
Red deer stag © John Morgan/Alamy
Male otter © Niall Benvie/Corbis
Osprey © David Tipling/Alamy
Male capercaillie © Niall Benvle/Corbis
Sundew © Rob Humphreys

Black and whites
p.116 Windsurfing off the Hebridean Isles © TNT Magazine/Alamy
p.138 Brodick Castle © Graeme Wallace, Worldwide Picture Library/Alamy
p.146 Whisky barrels, Islay © Rob Humphreys
p.158 Mountaineers on Cairngorm Plateau © Roger Antrobus/Corbis
p.181 Scottish Crannog Centre © Doug Houghton
p.193 Mountain-biking, Glen Clova © Louisa Macdonell/Alamy
p.207 Skier on Coire na ciste © Stockshot/Alamy
p.224 Bottlenose dolphins, Moray Firth © Ronald Weir/Albaimages/Alamy
p.234 Commando Memorial © David Robertson/Alamy
p. 244 Inverness © nagelestock.com/Alamy
p.301 Sandwood Bay © Mark Thomas
p.342 Dunvegan Castle © nagelestock.com/Alamy
p.356 An Sgurr, Eigg © Rob Humphreys
p.370 Stornoway Harbour, Isle of Lewis © David Robertson/Alamy
p.378 Iron Age House at Bostadh © Powered by Light/Alan Spencer/Alamy
p.406 Orkney Folk Festival © Doug Houghton
p.420 Earl's Palace, Kirkwall © Rob Humphreys
p.429 Old Man of Hoy, Orkney © Navin Mistry/Alamy
p.440 Puffin © Rob Humphreys
p.450 Mousa Broch © Ronald Weir/Alamy
p.456 Lerwick Harbour © David Robertson/Alamy
p.462 Shetland pony © Doug Houghton/Alamy
p.488 Bobby's bus shelter © Rob Humphreys
p.500 Robert The Bruce © Mary Evans Picture Library/Alamy

Index

Map entries are in colour.

C

INDEX

E

F

G

H

I

J

K

L

M

N

O

P

Q

R

S

T

Map symbols

maps are listed in the full index using coloured text

International boundary
Chapter division boundary
Motorway
Pedestrianized street
Road
Track
Steps
Footpath
Wall
Railway
Cable car
Coastline/river
Ferry route
Point of interest
Peak
Viewpoint
Rocks
Lighthouse
Airport
Waterfall
Cave
Ruins/archeological site
Cairn(s)
Hill shading

Stately home
Castle
Museum
Gardens
Battlefield
Campsite
Accommodation
Parking
Tourist office
Post office
Whisky distillery
Skiing
Golf course
Swimming Pool
Bridge
Abbey
Monastery
Chapel
Building
Church
Cemetery
Park
Forest
Beach